GW00586798

LUGANDA DICTIONARY AND GRAMMAR

Luganda-English and English-Luganda dictionary
with notes on Luganda grammar

by

Alan Hamilton

with

Naomi Hamilton, Phoebe Mukasa and David Ssewanyana

General editor: Cephas Ssentoogo

Botanical editor: Christine Kabuye

Published by Alan Hamilton

Copyright © 2016 by Alan Hamilton

Alan Hamilton asserts his moral right to be identified as the author of this work. All rights reserved. No part of this publication may be reproduced, stored in a retrieval system or transmitted in any form or by any means, electronic, mechanical, photocopying, recording or otherwise, without the prior written permission of the copyright owner

Published 2016

ISBN

978-0-9541496-1-1

Suggested citation: Hamilton, A., Hamilton, N., Mukasa, P. Ssewanyana, D., Ssentoogo, C. and Kabuye, C. (2016). Luganda dictionary and grammar: Luganda-English and English-Luganda dictionary with notes on Luganda grammar. Published by Alan Hamilton. Godalming, UK

Published by

Alan Hamilton
128 Busbridge Lane
Godalming, Surrey GU7 1QJ, UK
Telephone: +44 (0)1483 414597
email: alancharleshamilton@gmail.com

Available from

www.amazon.com, www.amazon.co.uk and other retail outlets

Available in Uganda from

Gustro Limited
Plot No. 355, Kibuga Block 2
Sir Apollo Kagwa Road, P.O.Box 9997, Kampala
Telephone: +256 414 251467
www.gustro.com
email: info@gustro.com

Design and layout by Alan Hamilton

Printed by CreateSpace and (in Uganda) by Marianum Press Ltd.
marianumpress@yahoo.com
M.XII. 1500 JC 329/16

CONTENTS

LUGANDA GRAMMAR

OTHER NOTES

LIST OF FIGURES

LIST OF TABLES

OFFICE OF

THE KABAKA OF BUGANDA
P. O. Box 58,
KAMPALA - UGANDA

FOREWORD

One of the major challenges afflicting the development and extensive use of African languages in modern societies is the lack of written discourse to serve as a benchmark for our people especially the young generation. The Luganda language is no exception to this. The continuing effort of generating literature for our language by various writers is highly recognized and appreciated. For instance, some scientific and technological materials have been documented in Luganda and they are utilized in various social, educational and political settings.

It is with exceptional enthusiasm that, I welcome the undoubtedly important book in form of a dictionary titled Luganda Dictionary and Grammar. This book which was authored by Professor Alan Hamilton from the United Kingdom has come to us at an opportune time when so many people are showing interest in Luganda as a language of interaction in education, trade, politics, entertainment and much more. The dictionary will by all means benefit all Luganda users irrespective of their linguistic backgrounds. I also greatly believe that when we put this dictionary to its proper use, we will strengthen our understanding of the language as we cross check the meaning, grammatical and syntactical application of words depending on the context in which they   are   used.

Due to the multiplicity and multilingual environment in which we live, people, especially the youth tend to combine words from one language with other languages. While this may enrich our languages and perhaps make communication effective at a given moment, it may also affect the original usage and meanings of our words. Accordingly, the importance of this publication as a constant reference point cannot be over emphasized. For the native speakers of Luganda in particular, this dictionary is of uppermost importance because it immensely contributes our preservation of culture and language. Like one singer asserted in his timeless song "Olulimi Lwange", language is a forceful pillar in our culture; let us keep that in mind as we utilize this dictionary.

In addition, this dictionary is unique because the authors go an extra mile to include scientific names of plants plus their Luganda equivalents. Plants of any kind and the general environment have a special status in our lives as Baganda and definitely in all other African societies. The botanical, medicinal and nutritional value attached to plants by our people as illustrated in this work is highly acknowledged. Regular reminders on the significance of plants in our lives, through such descriptions as posted in this dictionary will attract serious attempt to safeguard their extinction.

I am extremely delighted with this work and I thank Prof. Alan Hamilton from the United Kingdom who heartily recognized the role language plays in a society's development and nurtured the concept of the Luganda-English and English-Luganda dictionary. I am confident that its style of presentation will offset more linguists to study and write about the Luganda language, the Baganda as a people and their culture.

I also appreciate the contribution of the technical team which has assisted with cultural, linguistic and scientific orientation of the words in the dictionary. I appeal to all Luganda language loving people to emulate Prof. Hamilton's efforts to write more books in the Luganda language and others describing the language. Such books will help us push the Luganda language to host more scientific expressions and knowledge of all kinds. For example, exploring how Emerging Technologies can be adopted in teaching of Luganda is another area of possible research.

Let us embrace and use this dictionary with unprecedented passion as we enjoy and preserve our language.

Ronald Muwenda Mutebi II
KABAKA

FOREWORD

by

Oweek. Nankindu Prosperous Kavuma Ph.D.

Minister of State for Education, Kingdom of Buganda

As Minister of State for Education, Kingdom of Buganda – the Kingdom that is the custodian of the Luganda Language – and also a researcher into language education, a Luganda teacher, a trainer of teachers at all levels, and an advocate for literacy and development, I thank you Professor Alan Hamilton with your team for giving me the opportunity to write a foreword to your *Luganda dictionary and grammar: Luganda-English and English-Luganda dictionary with notes on Luganda grammar.*

By writing this bilingual reference book with 10193 Luganda and 8098 English entries, Professor Hamilton has bridged a very big gap in the acquisition of both Luganda and English in Uganda, and of Luganda in the rest of the world. This dictionary comes at a time when we see large numbers of children, youth and others in Buganda who cannot read and write competently in either language, unfortunately including many of those teachers who have the responsibility of teaching these languages to children, or of teaching other subjects through the medium of these languages. The Luganda-English section of the dictionary will facilitate the learning of English by Luganda speakers, while the English-Luganda section will help English speakers who wish to express themselves in Luganda.

Although the aim of the author has been to provide an introductory dictionary of common words, a closer look at the text shows that this reference book goes far beyond that. It includes additional and very important material. Standard information expected to be found in a dictionary is included – entries and sub-entries (where applicable), meanings, synonyms, syntactical examples and etymologies – but also included are the scientific names of plants with their Luganda equivalents, lists of the kings of Buganda and of the counties (with the titles of their chiefs) and the names of the clans.

This reference book is simple to use, has a section explaining the equivalence of parts of speech in English and Luganda, and there are boxes provided for each letter of the alphabet in the Luganda-English section to help guide readers to find the correct entries. Both are helpful for the reader to locate and use Luganda words.

Luganda dictionary and grammar: Luganda-English and English-Luganda Dictionary with notes on Luganda grammar is thus a full reference book providing up-to-date information on Luganda and English for users at all levels.

Bulange House, Mengo
P.O.Box 7451
Kampala
Uganda

PREFACE AND ACKNOWLEDGEMENTS

Luganda is the most widely spoken of the 42 indigenous languages found in Uganda. It is the mother tongue of nearly all of the 5.6 million Baganda living in the country[1], used by many others as a lingua franca and spoken by a sizable number of Baganda who have settled abroad. English, on the other hand, is a global language and the required medium of instruction in schools in Uganda at all but the most elementary levels. The intention with the present work is to concentrate especially on commoner words in each of the two languages.

The changeable nature of the beginnings of words in Luganda presents challenges to both compilers and users of Luganda dictionaries. Words cannot simply be listed in alphabetic order according to how they are spelt, as can be done with English. For instance, the singulars of nouns can start quite differently from their plurals (*eg.* **omwezi** 'month', **emyezi** 'months') and the beginnings of verbs can vary according to the subject, object and tense (*eg.* **olaba** 'you see', **tunaabalaba** 'we shall see them')[2]. Steps taken in this dictionary to help the reader include sections explaining the equivalence of parts of speech in English and Luganda and advice on how to use the dictionary (Part 1), and notes on Luganda grammar (Part 4). Readers should pay attention to the boxes provided for each letter in the Luganda-English section (Part 2), since these contain important information on how to locate and use Luganda words.

I am most grateful to Fred Ssemugera and Phoebe Mukasa for each providing me with some elementary lessons in Luganda, from which the idea of writing this dictionary gradually developed. The main method used in its compilation has been the gathering of information during a series of face-to-face discussions held over several years variously with my wife Naomi, Phoebe Mukasa and David Ssewanyana. We have followed an iterative process involving the translation of concepts and words from one language into the other, then back to the first, and so on over several cycles. Drafts of the work were provided for editing to Dr. Keefa Ssentoogo, an expert on Luganda and familiar with compiling dictionaries. Dr Christine Kabuye edited and augmented the list of scientific names of plants with their Luganda equivalents (Note N31).

Dr Robert Kityo, Curator of the Zoology Museum of Makerere University, assisted with the names of animals and Proscovia Nanyombi with the names of birds. Dr Judith Nakayiza of the Department of African Languages at Makerere University in Kampala and Lutz Marten, Professor of General and African Linguistics at the School of Oriental and African Studies in London, gave advice on tonal marking in Luganda (but tonal markings are only given here to a very limited extent). Dr Eddie Kasirye discussed with me the meanings of many Luganda words. Anna Craven provided notes on vocabulary on the Ssese Islands. Those who have helped with the names of plants include Dennis Kamoga, Mpuuga Brian, Dr Paul Ssegawa, Sarah Pfannkuchen, Emamanuel Kibubuka and Dr Willy Kakuru. I am grateful for members of the committee of *Ekibiina ky'Olulimi Oluganda* (Luganda Language Society) for pointing out some errors in a draft of the notes on Luganda grammar (Part 4). Mike Lagan helped with computing and Patrick Hamilton with the design of the cover. Martin and Sarah Walters, and also Jiotty and Keshav Kaushal, gave advice on publication. Grace Nakaweesa kindly passed information to and from Keefa Ssentoogo during part of the editing process and encouraged me to continue with the work.

The inclusion of Note N31, giving the scientific names of plants with their Luganda equivalents, is in acknowledgement of the central roles of plants in the economy of Buganda and the wealth of knowledge about the types, uses and methods of management of plants traditionally held by the people. It is also in recognition of the importance of such knowledge as a key ingredient in finding improved ways to manage the environment. There are signs today that more attention needs to be given to such management, with reports of soil fertility and yields of crops declining, and of many patches of natural forest and woodland being destroyed. Some species of plants traditionally used for construction, crafts, food or healthcare are becoming scarce. Now is the time to recognise the treasury of knowledge and wisdom relating to plants embedded in Luganda.

---

[1] Uganda Bureau of Statistics (2016). The National Population and Housing Census 2014. Main Report. Kampala.
[2] The common element in these two Luganda words is the stem **-laba**, meaning 'see'.

This book could not have been written without reference to *A Luganda grammar* by E.O. Ashton, E.M.K. Mulira, E.G.M. Ndawula and A.N. Tucker (1954) and *Luganda-English dictionary* by John D. Murphy (1972). Both of these excellent works should be made more widely available. They provide many more details on Luganda grammar and the meanings of Luganda words than can be given here.

The dictionary started as a self-help two-way listing of common Luganda and English words, to which notes on Luganda grammar were added once it became clear that guidance on Luganda grammar was essential for English-language speakers trying to learn Luganda. The introductory *The essentials of Luganda* by Chesswas proved an excellent guide to the elements of Luganda grammar, as well as providing a basic vocabulary, so helping this linguistic journey to proceed further. Eventually the idea of preparing the dictionary in its present form emerged and the dictionary team was assembled to push the project through. Inevitably, the dictionary has been approached from the perspective of an English-language speaker trying to understand the linguistic concepts and culture of the Baganda.

Constructive comments are welcome and will be useful in making improvements.

Alan Hamilton

SELECTED BIBLIOGRAPHY

See also notes **N2** and **N30**.

Adia, M.M., Anywar, G., Byamukama, R., Kamatenesi-Mugisha, Sekagya, Y., Kakudidi, E.K. and Kiremire, B.T. (2014). Medicinal plants used in malaria treatment by Prometra herbalists in Uganda. *Journal of Ethnopharmacology* 155, 580-588.

Ashton, E.O., Mulira, E.M.K., Ndawula, E.G.M. and Tucker, A.N. (1954). *A Luganda grammar*. Longmans, Green and Co., London.

Bagunywa, A.M.K., Kyakulumbye, S.S.., Muwonge, S.W. and Ssentoogo, W. (2009). *A concise Luganda-English dictionary*. Fountain Publishers, Kampala.

Bagunywa, A.M.K., Kyakulumbye, S.S., Muwonge, S.W., Ssentoogo, W. and Tomusange, J.N. (2010). *Enkuluze y'Oluganda olw'ennono*. Wavah Books Ltd., Kampala.

Bukenya, A. and Kamoga, L. (2009). *Standard Luganda-English dictionary*. Fountain Publishers, Kampala.

Buganda Kingdom Website. www.buganda.or.ug

Chesswas, J.D. (1963) *The essentials of Luganda*. Third Edition. Oxford University Press, Nairobi.

Eggeling, W,J. and Dale, I.R. (1952). The *indigenous trees of the Uganda Protectorate*. Government Printer, Entebbe.

Galabuzi, C., Nabanoga, G.N., Ssegawa, P., Obua, J. and Eilu, G. (2015). Double jeopardy: bark harvest for malaria treatment and poor regeneration threaten tree population in a tropical forest of Uganda. *African Journal of Ecology* 53, 214-222.

Hamilton, A.C. (1991). *A field guide to Ugandan forest trees*. Makerere University Printery, Kampala.

Kamoga, D., Osinge, C. and Olwari F. (2008). *Medicinal plants for home health care use: knowledge and experience of local communities in Bunza Village, Mpigi District*. Joint Ethnobotanical Research and Advocacy, Kampala.

Katende, A.B., Birnie, A. and Tengnäs, B. (1995). *Useful trees and shrubs for Uganda*. Regional Soil Conservation Unit, RSCU/SIDA. Technical Handbook Series no. 10.

Katende, A.B., Ssegawa, P and Birnie, A. (1999). *Wild food plants and mushrooms of Uganda*. Regional Land Management Unit, Swedish International Development Corporation, Nairobi.

Kiingi, K.B. (2007). *Enkuluze y'Oluganda*. Fountain Publishers, Kampala.

Lind, E.M. and Tallantire, A.C. (1962). *Some common flowering plants of Uganda*. Oxford University Press, London.

Lye, K.A., Bukenya-Ziraba, R. Tabuti, J.R.S. and Waako, P.J. (2008). *Plant-medicinal dictionary for East Africa*. Makerere University Herbarium, Kampala.

Murphy, John D. (1972). *Luganda-English Dictionary*. The Catholic University of America Press, Washington, D.C.

Nurse, D. and Philippson, G. (2003). *The Bantu languages*. Routledge, London and New York.

Nuwagaba, T.F. (2014). *Totems of Uganda: Buganda edition*. Published by Naga Nuwagaba and Nathan Kiwere, Kampala.

Ssegawa, P. and Kasenene, J. (2007). Plants for malaria treatment in Southern Uganda: traditional use, preference and ecological viability. *Journal of Ethnobiology* 27, 110-131.

Richards, A. (1966). *The changing structure of a Ganda village*. East African Publishing House, Nairobi.

Wanyana-Maganyi, O. (1999). Some medicinal plants used by traditional birth attendants in the Buganda Region, Uganda. In Timberlake, J. and Kativu, S. (eds) *African Plants: Biodiversity, Taxonomy and Uses*, pp. 511-515. Royal Botanic Gardens, Kew.

PART 1

INTRODUCTION

References to notes (Part 4) are marked N1, N2, *etc*.

1.1. THREE BASIC ASPECTS OF LUGANDA GRAMMAR

An appreciation of three basic aspects of Luganda grammar will be helpful for users of this dictionary – agglutination, substitution and derivation.

Luganda is an **AGGLUTINATIVE** language, meaning that many words are compound, being composed of more fundamental parts (roots and stems) with components added to them (affixes) (**N2**). Roots and stems give the basic meanings of words – for example, the stem **-soma** means 'read' – while affixes provide further detail. The addition of the affix **n-** ('I') to **-soma** ('read') gives **nsoma** ('I read'), the addition of the affix **tu-** ('we') to **-soma** gives **tusoma** ('we read'), and so on. Stems are not necessarily totally unchangeable. For example, the stem **-soma** can be modified by substitution of the final **a** by **e** to give the subjunctive, *eg.* **Tusome.** ('Let us read.'). In contrast, the root is the final irreducible part of a word (**som** is the root in the case of the stem **-soma**).

With minor exceptions, Luganda entries provided with hyphens in this dictionary require other parts to be added to them to make complete words. Thus neither **n-** nor **tu-** are words in their own right. **soma** (without a hyphen) does exist, but only in the singular imperative **Soma!** ('Read!').

Affixes can be <u>additive</u>. Thus, starting from **tusoma** ('we read'), we can derive:

- **tubisoma** ('we read <u>them</u>'), referring to **ebitabo** ('books'), a noun in noun class *n8* (the concept of noun class is explained in **N4.1**).
- **tulibisoma** ('we <u>shall</u> read them'), **-li-** being the affix used for the far future tense (**N16**).
- **tulibisomako** ('we shall read <u>about</u> them'), the addition of the affix **-ko** further modifying the meaning (**N24.3**).

As may be seen from these examples, affixes can be placed <u>before</u> the stem (as with **tu-**, **-li-** and **bi-**) or <u>after</u> the stem (as with **-ko**). The former are termed prefixes and the latter suffixes. The additional term 'infix' is used for prefixes or suffixes that lie <u>within</u> words (rather than at their ends). **-li-** and **bi-** are infixes (as well as prefixes) in the above examples.

Affixes can be **SUBSTITUTIVE**. For example, taking the stem **-ntu** ('an existence'), a range of nouns can be formed by adding different prefixes, *eg.* <u>omu</u>ntu ('person'), <u>aba</u>ntu ('people'), <u>eki</u>ntu ('thing'), <u>ebi</u>ntu ('things'), <u>aka</u>ntu ('small thing'), <u>obu</u>ntu ('small things', also 'humanity'), <u>olu</u>ntu ('long thin thing'), <u>awa</u>ntu ('somewhere'), *etc.*

DERIVATION refers to the common practice in Luganda of deriving new stems and words from other stems and words. An example based on the verb **-manya** ('know') is shown in Figure 1. In this case, the derived stems and words include a number of verbs, nouns and adjectives.

1.2. PARTS OF SPEECH

English terms for parts of speech are used here for both English and Luganda. A common-sense approach has been used in classifying words into parts of speech, taking into consideration both grammatical use and ease of cross-reference between the languages.

Parts of speech in English or Luganda can be single words with one-to-one correspondence, *eg.* **ebitabo** ('books'). However, commonly, a word in one language is equivalent to more than one in the other or, alternatively, to just part of a single word. Thus, taking examples from Section 1.1 above, **akantu** is equivalent to two words in English ('small thing') and the **bi** in **tubisoma** means 'them', referring to books.

Parts of speech in either language can consist of more than a single word. On the whole, English is wordier than Luganda, as illustrated by the following English sentence and its Luganda translation:

(My aunt)[1] (is going to take)[2] (the food)[3] (that remains)[4] (to her home)[5].

Sseŋŋange[1] **anaatwala**[2] **emmere**[3] **esigadde**[4] **ewuwe**[5].

The English sentence contains examples of two nominal phrases (1, 3), an adjectival phrase (4), a verbal phrase (2) and an adverbial phrase (5), each translated by a single word in Luganda (numbered equivalently).

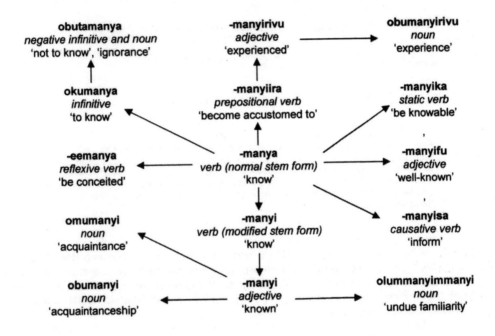

Figure 1. Examples of derivation: some words and stems derived from **-manya** ('know').

NOUNS

A noun in English is a word used for the name of a person (*eg.* 'John'), place (*eg.* 'Uganda'), thing (*eg.* 'table') or quality (*eg.* 'happiness'). In contrast, a noun in Luganda is a word (or phrase) that can induce **CONCORDANCE**, meaning that it carries the power to cause changes in sound and spelling to certain other neighbouring words (**N4**). The types of change so caused depend on the **NOUN CLASS** of the noun (**N4**). The twenty-one noun classes found in Luganda are listed on Figure 2. Luganda nouns fall into two categories, **ORDINARY NOUNS**, which are conceptually similar to English nouns and often have one-to-one equivalence (*eg.* **ekimuli** = 'flower') (**N6**), and **ADVERBIAL NOUNS**, which have no parallel in English (see under 'Adverbs' below).

ORDINARY NOUN CLASSES

Gender	Noun classes typically used for singulars		Noun classes typically used for plurals	
	Noun class number	Nominal concord	Noun class number	Nominal concord
mu/ba	1	**mu-**	2	**ba-**
mu/mi	3	**mu-**	4	**mi-**
li/ma	5	**li-**	6	**ma-**
ki/bi	7	**ki-**	8	**bi-**
n/n	9	**n-**	10	**n-**
lu/n	11	**lu-**	10	**n-**
ka/bu	12	**ka-**	14	**bu-**
ku/ma	15	**ku-**	6	**ma-**
gu/ga	20	**gu-**	22	**ga-**
tu/-	13	**tu-**	-	-

ADVERBIAL NOUN CLASSES USED FOR PLACE

Noun class number	Concord
16	**wa-**
23	**e-**
17	**ku-**
18	**mu-**

Figure 2. Luganda noun classes, showing how they are numbered and how ordinary nouns are grouped into genders. Some of the noun classes are also used for adverbial noun classes of time, manner, or cause and reason (**N4.1**). The nominal concord is the type of concord found on nouns and adjectives (**N6, N7**). The concords shown for the adverbial noun classes are pronominal concords, found with adverbs, *etc.*

CONCORDS are the parts of words through which concordance is expressed (**N4**). They are found on nouns (*eg.* **ki-** of **ekimuli**) and on words in concordance with them. An **INITIAL VOWEL** is often present before the concord (*eg.* **e-** of **ekimuli**) (**N3**). Each noun class has concords of three types – nominal, numeral and pronominal. The **NOMINAL CONCORD** is the type found on nouns and adjectives.

Most ordinary noun classes are grouped in pairs known as **GENDERS**, one typically used for the singulars of nouns and the other for the plurals (Figure 2). Gender exists in English, but in a much more restricted way than in Luganda. Most nouns in English are 'neutral', gender only being recognised in connection with a few words relating to the male/female dichotomy and a handful of inanimate objects (*eg.* a 'ship' is feminine). Gender in Luganda is not connected to the male/female dichotomy, which is less expressed grammatically than in English.

ADJECTIVES AND DETERMINERS

An **ADJECTIVE** is a word that adds a quality to a noun (*eg.* '<u>big</u> flower'). In Luganda, adjectives take the **NOMINAL CONCORD** and nearly always follow the noun, *eg.* **ekimuli ekinene** ('big flower') (**N7**). The adjectival stem in this case is **-nene** ('big'), used here with the nominal concord **ki-** (agreeing with the noun class of its noun **ekimuli**) and having an initial vowel (**e-**). Other ways of expressing adjectival concepts are through the use of subject relative clauses, *eg.* **ekimuli ekibuze** ('the lost flower', *lit.* 'the flower which is lost') or possessive phrases starting with the preposition **-a** ('of'), *eg.* **ekimuli kya bbululu** ('blue flower', *lit.* 'flower of blue').

4

Adjectives grade into **DETERMINERS**, which are words preceding nouns modifying their meaning. The main types of determiners in English are: (1) **ARTICLES**: 'a', 'an' and 'the'; (2) **DEMONSTRATIVE DETERMINERS**, indicating position (*eg.* 'this book'); (3) **POSSESSIVE DETERMINERS**, indicating ownership or affiliation (*eg.* 'my book'); (4) **NUMBERS**, both **CARDINAL** (*eg.* 'two books') and **ORDINAL** (*eg.* 'the second book'); and (5) **INDEFINITE DETERMINERS** (*eg.* 'some books'). There are no words in Luganda equivalent to the English articles, though the inclusion of an initial vowel can sometimes indicate greater precision and its absence greater indefinitiveness (**N3**). For demonstrative and possessive determiners, see under 'Pronouns' below. The concepts of cardinal and ordinal numbers exist in Luganda, as in English. The cardinal numbers 1-5 and the indefinite determiner 'some' are stems taking the **NUMERAL CONCORD** (**N4**, **N8**). Numbers above five are nouns (**N8**). Ordinal numbers are usually expressed by phrases starting with the preposition **-a** ('of') (**N7.1**).

PRONOUNS

A pronoun in English is a word that replaces a noun. The types include (relevant pronouns underlined): (1) **SUBJECT PRONOUNS** (*eg.* 'he hits you'); (2) **OBJECT PRONOUNS** (*eg.* 'he hits you'); (3) **REFLEXIVE PRONOUNS**, which are used when the same person or thing is both the doer and receiver of an action (*eg.* 'he hit himself') or to provide emphasis (*eg.* 'David himself is coming'); (4) **RELATIVE PRONOUNS**, which are either **SUBJECT RELATIVES** (*eg.* 'I know who is coming') or **OBJECT RELATIVES** (*eg.* 'I know who you are'); (5) **DEMONSTRATIVE PRONOUNS** (*eg.* 'these are mine'); (6) **POSSESSIVE PRONOUNS** (*eg.* 'these are mine'); (7) **INTERROGATIVE PRONOUNS** (*eg.* 'which are mine?'); and (8) **INDEFINITE PRONOUNS**, with less certain points of reference and which either include the word 'of' (*eg.* 'some of them') or are compound words beginning 'every-', 'some-' or 'any-' (*eg.* 'something').

Many pronouns in English are either **PERSONAL** or **IMPERSONAL**, the former being used when the noun of reference is a person or persons and the latter in other cases. The personal pronouns include words such as 'I', 'me', 'who' and 'mine' and the impersonal pronouns words such as 'it', 'which' and 'its'. The same distinction between personal and impersonal pronouns is found in Luganda, the personal pronouns being conveniently considered as variants of noun class 1 (for singulars) or noun class 2 (for plurals) (the **PERSONAL NOUN CLASSES**). There are three singular and three plural **CASES** of personal pronouns in both English and Luganda, the subject pronouns for the 1st, 2nd and 3rd cases in English being 'I', 'you' and '(s)he' in the singular and 'we', 'you' and 'they' in the plural.

Most types of pronoun in Luganda make use of the **PRONOMINAL CONCORD** (**N4**). This is attached as a prefix to a verb in the case of subject or object pronouns (**N15**) and to stems of other types in the case of demonstratives (**N9**), object relatives (**N10.1**), possessives (**N11.1**) and some interrogatives (**N13**). An initial vowel is sometimes present (**N3**). Subject relatives are formed by adding an initial vowel to the verb (**N7.1**). Reflexive pronouns associated with verbs are expressed by adding the prefix **-ee-** to the verb (**N18**).

There are two types of **FREE-STANDING PRONOUNS** in Luganda, based on the stems **-o** and **-e**. Both take the pronominal concord (**N10.1**). These stems are sometimes called the **PARTICLE OF REFERENCE** (**-o**) and the **PARTICLE OF EMPHASIS** (or prominence) (**-e**), terms which give some indication of their use. Pronouns based on the stem **-e** serve several roles in Luganda, including acting as object relatives (*eg.* 'who', 'which'), conjunctions (*eg.* 'where', 'when') (**N10.2**) and copulas. **COPULAS** are words (or phrases) linking subjects already mentioned (nouns or pronouns) to complements that follow. An example of a copula in English is the phrase 'it is' in the following exchange: 'What is that car?' "That car, it is a Ford.'

Demonstrative and possessive pronouns in Luganda share the same (or similar) stems to

5

those used for demonstrative and possessive determiners (see under 'Adjectives and determiners' above) and it is convenient to group them together as **DEMONSTRATIVES (N9)** and **POSSESSIVES (N11.4)**. There are three types of demonstratives in Luganda, rather than the two of English ('this', 'that'), the additional category being known as the **DEMONSTRATIVE OF REFERENCE** (having the stem **-o**).

VERBS

A verb in English is a word describing an action or state. Many are classifiable as **TRANSITIVE** or **INTRANSITIVE**, depending on whether they take or imply direct objects (transitive) or cannot do so (intransitive). A **DIRECT OBJECT** is a noun or pronoun to which an action is done (*eg.* 'I built a <u>house</u>'). Some English verbs can additionally have **INDIRECT OBJECTS**, that is nouns or pronouns indicating to or for whom an action is performed, *eg.* 'I built <u>him</u> a house'. Indirect objects can be distinguished from direct objects in that they can be alternatively rendered by phrases (known as **PREPOSITIONAL COMPLEMENTS**) starting with prepositions such as 'to', 'for' or 'without', *eg.* 'I build a house <u>for him</u>.'

Nearly all verbs in the present dictionary, both English and Luganda, are designated as transitive or intransitive (or both), since this will often be helpful to readers to understand how they are used and how the two languages interrelate. However, both languages have many verbs with intermediate properties. Designations of Luganda verbs as transitive or intransitive in the present dictionary largely follow Murphy in *Luganda-English Dictionary*.

AUXILIARY verbs are verbs closely associated with **PRIMARY** (or main) verbs, providing extra information on mood, tense, *etc.* (*eg.* 'we <u>must</u> go'). The verbs 'be' and 'have' are widely used as auxiliary verbs, giving a range of **COMPOUND TENSES** (*eg.* 'We <u>have been</u> cooking.'). Both auxiliary verbs and compound tenses are found in Luganda (**N19, N20.3**).

Verbs in Luganda differ fundamentally from those in English in being stems to which affixes must normally be added to make understandable words (**N14**). Almost all verbs have two forms of stem, a **NORMAL STEM FORM** and a **MODIFIED STEM FORM** (abbreviated *msf*). An example of a Luganda verb is **-kola** ('work'), the *msf* being **-koze**. The normal stem forms of nearly all Luganda verbs end with the vowel **a** (very rarely **i**), except in the case of the subjunctive (**N17**) or when terminated by one of the four enclitics (**-wo, -yo, -ko** and **-mu**) (see under 'Adverbs' below). There are several types of prefix found on verbs in Luganda, including subject and object pronouns (**N15.1**), prefixes denoting tense (**N16, N18**), the reflexive **-ee-** (**N18**) and the negative prefixes **si-, te-** and **-ta-** (**N21**).

A feature of Luganda is that many simpler verbs are associated with other more complex verbs, generally carrying related meanings. Such **DERIVED VERBS** also exist in English, for example the various verbs beginning with the prefix 'un-' carrying a reversive meaning, *eg.* '<u>undo</u>' (derived from 'do'), <u>un</u>cork (derived from 'cork'). Some of the commonest types of derived verbs in Luganda are the associative, causative, conversive, passive, prepositional and static, each formed by addition of a particular suffix (or suffixes) to the verb (**N22**). Examples of derived verbs based on the simple verb **-kola** ('work') are **-kolagana** (associative 'work together'), **-koza** (causative 'make work'), **-kolebwa** (passive 'be worked'), **-kolera** (prepositional 'work for/at') and **-koleka** (static 'be workable').

There are many verbs in English that, in effect, consist of more than a single word. They consist of normal (single word) verbs and following adverbs or prepositions. An example of a **PHRASAL VERB** (with an adverb) is 'get up', as in the sentence 'She got up from her bed.' An example of a **PREPOSITIONAL VERB** (with a preposition) is 'put on', as in the sentence 'She put on her clothes.' The existence of many derived verbs in Luganda, and phrasal and prepositional verbs in English, creates complexities in matching the two languages.

6

ADVERBS

An adverb in English is a word modifying a part of speech, answering such questions as 'how?', 'when?', 'why?', 'where?' or 'to what extent?', *eg.* 'it fed quickly', 'very quick', 'relatively quickly'. Whole phrases or clauses can be adverbial, *eg.* 'the cat ate, as I watched'). There are many ways of expressing adverbial concepts in Luganda. There are some words whose meanings are basically adverbial and many verbs that incorporate adverbial concepts into their meanings. Adverbial concepts can be expressed using certain verb tenses (**N18**), auxiliary verbs (**N19**), derived verbs (**N22**), suffixes on verbs or adjectives (**N24.2**), and in other ways.

ADVERBIAL NOUNS are a feature of Luganda lacking a parallel in English. These words (or combinations of words) are regarded as nouns because of their power to induce concordance (**N4**). Different types of adverbial concepts are associated with particular noun classes. There are four **ADVERBIAL NOUN CLASSES OF PLACE** (not used for ordinary nouns) (**N24**). These **wa**, **e**, **ku** and **mu** adverbial noun classes refer respectively to 'place' (in general), 'place over there', 'place on top' and 'place within'. There are a total of six **ADVERBIAL NOUN CLASSES OF TIME** (**N25**), all also used for other purposes – three otherwise used for ordinary nouns and three for adverbial nouns of place. There are also five **ADVERBIAL NOUN CLASSES OF MANNER** (**N26**) and four **ADVERBIAL NOUN CLASS OF CAUSE AND REASON** (**N27**), none exclusively used for these purposes.

One use of the four adverbial noun classes of place in Luganda is as **CLITICS**, that is words or affixes that cannot be used on their own, but rather 'lean on' other words clarifying their meanings. There are two types of clitics, proclitics and enclitics. The **PROCLITICS** are the words **we**, **gye**, **kwe** and **mwe**, associated respectively with the **wa**, **e**, **ku** and **mu** adverbial noun classes of place. These proclitics are found immediately preceding verbs, giving emphasis to place in answers to questions (**N10.2**). The four **ENCLITICS** are the suffixes **-wo**, **-yo**, **-ko** and **-mu**. They are most commonly encountered on verbs, in which role they can be thought of as **OBJECTS OF PLACE** (**N24.2**).

PREPOSITIONS

A preposition in English is a word that describes a relationship between words. An example of a preposition is 'of', which, in Luganda, is translated by **-a**, a stem taking the pronominal concord (**N11**). **-a** is described by Ashton and co-authors in *A Luganda Grammar* as the **PARTICLE OF POSSESSION**, a term signifying a somewhat wider role than that of the English 'of'.

The Luganda words **e** ('at/to'), **ku** ('on') and **mu** ('in'), associated with the **e**, **ku** and **mu** adverbial noun classes of place, are simple prepositions with straightforward English equivalents, *eg.* **e Kampala** ('to Kampala'), **ku mmeeza** ('on the table'), **mu nnyumba** ('in the house') (**N24.1**). These three words, plus the prefix **wa-** (associated with the **wa** adverbial noun class), can further be found as prefixes or words heading short phrases carrying prepositional meanings, *eg.* **wansi wa** ('below'), **emabega wa** ('behind'), **kumpi na** ('near'), **mu maaso ga** ('in front of').

Another way of expressing prepositional concepts in Luganda is through the use of certain types of derived verbs (see under 'Verbs' above). Prepositional verbs incorporate prepositions such as 'for' and 'to' into their inherent meanings. Passive verbs can incorporate the preposition 'by'.

CONJUNCTIONS

A conjunction in English is a coordinating word connecting words, phrases or clauses. The items so connected may be of equivalent strength and independent of one another (*eg.* 'Peter and Paul') or else one may be subordinate to the other (*eg.* 'we talked <u>while</u> we walked'). Some English conjunctions are more or less matched by corresponding Luganda words, *eg.* **na** or **ne** ('and'), **naye** ('but'), **oba** ('or'). However, many conjunctions lack precise equivalence between the two languages. Some subordinate conjunctions in English are translated in Luganda by words based on the stem **-e**, *eg.* **bwe** ('how'), **we** ('where'), **lwe** ('when') (**N10.2**). These **e**-stem conjunctions are grammatically identical in construction to object relative pronouns (**N10.1**), though concordant with adverbial rather than ordinary noun classes.

EXCLAMATIONS AND INTERJECTIONS

These related parts of speech occur in both English and Luganda. They are used to express a sudden emotion (an exclamation) or to interrupt one's own or another's speech (an interjection). While some exclamations and interjections are words, others are sounds, *eg.* 'um' in English (representing a pause in speech) and **mmm** in Luganda (used in greetings). Only a few such sounds have been included in the dictionary.

1.3. UNDERSTANDING THE ENTRIES IN PARTS 2 AND 3

WORDS AND STEMS. Luganda nouns are entered as words, *eg.* **ekintu** ('thing'). Luganda verbs and adjectives are entered as stems, *eg.* **-kola** ('work'), **-nene** ('big').

ALPHABETIC ORDER. Luganda headwords are ordered according to their first consonants, *eg.* **ekintu** ('thing') is entered under **K** (not **E**). A headword is the word (or words) at the beginning of each entry (in larger type in the present dictionary.)

INITIAL VOWELS (N3) are included for Luganda entries, except where rarely used. Readers should note that many words that usually have initial vowels sometimes lack them and, conversely, that initial vowels may sometimes be present on words from which they are normally absent.

FORMATION OF PLURALS AND SINGULARS of nouns in Luganda are indicated in boxes at the lower right of some pages. The plurals of nouns in noun classes *n5* and *n11* are included as headwords, since the spellings of their singular forms may not be obvious.

THE COMMON ENTRY -a refers to the preposition **-a** ('of') (**N11**). There are many adjectives in Luganda consisting of short phrases starting with the preposition **-a** ('of') followed by a noun, *eg.* **-a omuti** ('wooden', *lit.* 'of wood'). These adjectives require the addition of a concord to the **-a** to be used and there is also an option of adding an initial vowel. Whatever is decided – and this depends on the precise meaning intended (**N11.1**) – either the **a** of the 'of word' or the initial vowel of the following noun must be dropped. Thus, **ekintu w' omuti** and **ekintu wa muti** are acceptable, but **ekintu wa omuti** is not.

THE SUFFIXES -wo, -yo, -ko and -mu (enclitics) can be found at the end of many words in Luganda, especially verbs. They are indicators of place or diminution (**N24**). Verbs with these suffixes are included in Part 2 of the dictionary only when their use is particularly common.

SUBENTRIES IN LARGER TYPE are used to divide up the entries for clarity, especially to draw attention to the enclitic forms of Luganda verbs and to divide certain English verbs into transitive and intransitive uses.

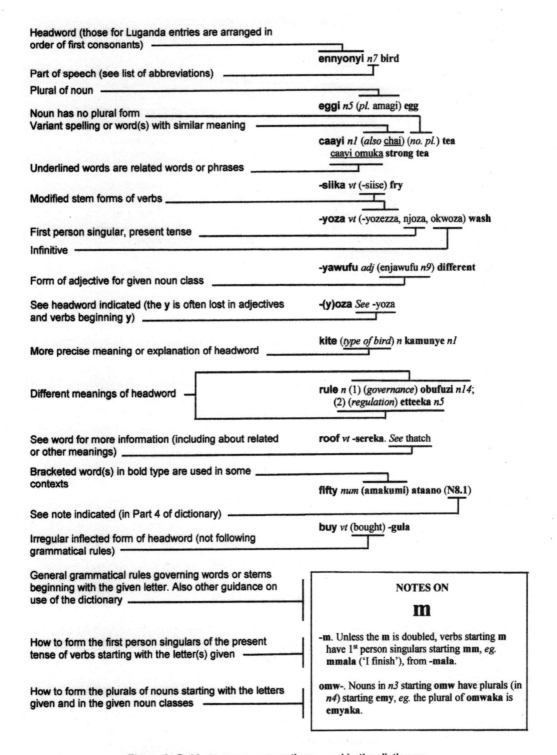

Headword (those for Luganda entries are arranged in order of first consonants)

ennyonyi *n7* bird

Part of speech (see list of abbreviations)

Plural of noun

Noun has no plural form

eggi *n5* (*pl.* amagi) egg

Variant spelling or word(s) with similar meaning

caayi *n1* (*also* <u>chai</u>) (*no. pl.*) tea
<u>caayi omuka</u> **strong tea**

Underlined words are related words or phrases

-siika *vt* (-siise) **fry**

Modified stem forms of verbs

-yoza *vt* (-yozezza, njoza, okwoza) **wash**

First person singular, present tense

Infinitive

-yawufu *adj* (enjawufu *n9*) **different**

Form of adjective for given noun class

See headword indicated (the y is often lost in adjectives and verbs beginning y)

-(y)oza *See* -yoza

kite (*type of bird*) *n* kamunye *n1*

More precise meaning or explanation of headword

Different meanings of headword

rule *n* (1) (*governance*) obufuzi *n14*;
(2) (*regulation*) etteeka *n5*

See word for more information (including about related or other meanings)

roof *vt* -sereka. *See* thatch

Bracketed word(s) in bold type are used in some contexts

fifty *num* (amakumi) ataano (N8.1)

See note indicated (in Part 4 of dictionary)

buy *vt* (bought) -gula

Irregular inflected form of headword (not following grammatical rules)

General grammatical rules governing words or stems beginning with the given letter. Also other guidance on use of the dictionary

How to form the first person singulars of the present tense of verbs starting with the letter(s) given

How to form the plurals of nouns starting with the letters given and in the given noun classes

---

NOTES ON

m

-m. Unless the m is doubled, verbs starting **m** have 1st person singulars starting **mm**, *eg.* **mmala** ('I finish'), from -mala.

omw-. Nouns in *n3* starting **omw** have plurals (in *n4*) starting **emy**, *eg.* the plural of **omwaka** is **emyaka**.

Figure 3. Guide to some conventions used in the dictionary.

1.4. ABBREVIATIONS

abbrev	abbreviation	*lit.*	literally
adj	adjective [1]	*msf*	modified stem form
adv	adverb	*n*	noun [2]
aux v	auxiliary verb	*neg*	negative
conj	conjunction	*num*	number
dem	demonstrative	*pl.*	plural
det	determiner	*pos*	possessive
eg.	for example	*pre*	preposition
etc.	etcetera	*pro*	pronoun
excl	exclamation	*Prot*	Protestant
ie.	that is to say	*RC*	Roman Catholic
inf	infinitive	*rel*	relative
interj	interjection	*si.*	singular
interr	interrogative	*syn.*	synonym
IV	initial vowel	*v*	verb [3]

1. A number following an adjective (*n1*, *n2*, *etc.*) indicates the form of the adjective used with that noun class.

2. The number following the **n** (*n1*, *n2*, *etc.*) indicates the noun class of the noun.

3. Verbs may be intransitive (*vi*), transitive (*vt*), both intransitive and transitive (*vit*), or reflexive (*vr*).

TONAL MARKS
(used to indicate pronunciation)

à indicates low tone

á indiates high tone

â indicates falling tone

a indicates mid tone

Tonal marks are only included in the dictionary for some pairs or triplets of Luganda headwords that are actually different words, but happen to be spelt in the same way. Infinitives have been used in the case of verbs.

PART 2

LUGANDA-ENGLISH

References to notes (Part 4) are marked N1, N2, *etc.*

A,a

-a *pre* **of** (N11.1). *Takes pronominal concord* (N4.2), *eg.* (1) *ekiso kya Musoke* ('knife of Musoke'); (2) *ente ya Musoke* ('cow of Musoke').
aaa *interj* **no**

B,b

(a)b' *abbrev of* (a)ba; be
¹oba *adv* **maybe**, *eg. Oba tugende tumulabe.* ('Maybe we will go and see her.'), **perhaps**
²oba *conj* **or, either, if, whether**, *eg. Simanyi oba njagala kino oba kiri.* ('I don't know whether I like this or that.') <u>oba si ekyo</u> **otherwise**
³(a)ba *pre* **of**, *eg. abaana ba Musoke* ('children of Musoke'). *Can be a prefix* **(a)ba-** (N11.4), *eg. bange* ('mine').
⁴-ba *vi* (-badde) **be**, *eg. Ajja kuba wano.* ('He will be here.'). *Commonly used as aux v* (N20.3), *eg. Mbadde nkola.* ('I have been working.'). *'ba' is one part of a verb* ('ba/-li') *having two roots, the choice of root depending on the tense and sense* (N20.1). <u>-ba na</u> **have** (N20.2), *eg. Nja kuba n'amagi.* ('I will have some eggs.'), **possess** **-baako** (-baddeko) **be on**, *eg. Ku mmeeza kujja kubaako emmere.* ('There will be food on the table.') **-baamu be in**, *eg. Mu nnyumba mujja kubaamu abantu bangi.* ('There will be many people in the house.'), **contain, consist of**, *eg. Omugoyo gubaamu lumonde n'ebijanjaalo.* ('Mash consists of potatoes and beans.') **-baawo be** (*at a place*), *eg. Tujja kubaawo ku mukolo.* ('We shall be at the function.'), **be present, exist, take place, happen.** *See obutabaawo* **-baayo be** (*over there*), *eg. Musoke ajja kubaayo mu lukuŋŋana.* ('Musoke will be at the meeting.')
baaba *n1* **please**, *eg. Baaba nnyamba.* ('Please help me.'). *Also a form of address to an elder brother or sister.*
baabali **there they are**
baabano **here they are**
baabo **there they are**
(a)baabwe *pos* **their(s)** (N11.4)
Abaadiventi *See* Omwadiventi
Abaafirika *See* Omwafirika
-baaga *vt* (-baaze) **slaughter, skin, butcher** <u>-baaga ensolo</u> **scrape an animal skin** (*eg. of goat or cow*)
abaagazi *See* omwagazi
baagi *n9* **badge**
baaki? *interr* **what for?**
baakisimba *n1* (1) **name of main drum in a set**; (2) **a certain drum beat and dance.** *Meaning:* 'They planted it.' <u>baakisimba song</u> **sung to accompany this dance** (*praising the people who*

first planted the 'embidde' banana and recognised its value for beer)
-baalaala *vi* (-baaladde) **be hot** (*of spicy food*)
-baalaavu *adj* **hot** (*of spicy food*), **spicy**
-baalabaala *vi* (-baddebadde) **walk in a leisurely way, stroll (about), ramble, prowl**
baalansi *n1* **balance** (*from payment*), **change**
-baama *vi* (-baamye) **become wild** (*in behaviour*)
abaamasaza *See* owessaza
Abaamerika *See* Omwamerika
abaami *n2* **gentlemen**; *pl. of* omwami
-baamuufu *adj* **wild** (*in behaviour*), **uncontrollable**
-baamuuka *vi* (-baamuuse) (1) **be(come) wild** (*in behaviour*); (2) **flare up** (*of anger or a fire*)
-baamuula *vt* (-baamudde) **make wild** (*a person*)
-baamya *vt* (-baamizza) **cause to go wild**
abaana *n2* **children**; *pl. of* omwana
baanabagalye *n1* **person with gonorrhoea.** *Meaning:* 'Let the children eat.' – *because I am too ill to get out of bed.*
baani? *interr* **who?, whom?**
abaanjuzi *See* omwanjuzi
-baatabaata *vi* (-baasebaase) **waddle**
abaatiikirivu *See* omwatiikirivu; -yatiikirivu
-baatira *vi* (-baatidde) **waddle**
abaavu *See* omwavu; -yavu
abaawufu *See* -yawufu
abaawule *See* omwawule
abaazi *See* omwazi
baba **they are** (*stem* -ba)
-babaalukana *vi* (-babaalukanye) **do recklessly**, *eg. Ababaalukana nnyo ng'avuga mmotoka.* ('He drives recklessly.')
ababe *pos* **hers, his**
Ababiito b'e Kkooki *n2* **princes of Kkooki** (*a Kiganda clan*). *Also known as Ababoobi and Ngabi Mbiito.*
-babika *vt* (-babise) **hit hard** (*a person*) <u>-babika kibooko</u> **hit with a stick** <u>-babika oluyi</u> **spank**
-babira *vt* (-babidde) **expose** (*something*) **briefly to fire** (*taking care not to burn it*) <u>-babira embugo</u> **expose barkcloth briefly to fire** <u>akasana ka -babira</u> **be too hot** (*of sunshine*), *eg. Akasaana katubabira.* ('The sun is too hot for us.')
babiri *num* **two**
-babirira *vi* (-babiridde) **be on the point of burning** (*of things*), *eg. Entebe eri kumpi n'omuliro ebabiridde.* ('The chair is too close to the fire and will get scorched.')
Babirye *n1 title* **female elder of twins**
ababo *pos* **yours**
Ababoobi *See* Ababiito
-babuka *vi* (-babuse) **be singed** (*eg. of a banana leaf*) <u>emimwa -babuka</u> **crack** (*of the lips*)
-babula *vt* (-babudde) **singe**, *eg. Ababula empombo.* ('She is singeing the banana leaves.') <u>omusana -babula</u> **scorch** (*of the sun*)
-babule *adj* **scorched, singed**

-babuukirira *vi* (-babuukiridde) **have a burning sensation, feel burning**

-badala *vi* (-badadde) **express indifference, be flippant**

-badde *See* -ba; -beera

(a)baffe *pos* **our(s)** (N11.4)

-eebafu *adj* (omwebafu *n1*) **sleepy, dull, retarded**

-baga *vt* (-baze) **do initial stages** (*of a task*), **do a temporary job**   -baga ekiwandiiko **draft a document**   -baga ennyumba **carry out initial stages of building a house, put up framework for a building**

-eebagajja *vt* (-eebagazze) **carry** (*something*) **on the chest** (*holding with the hands*)   -eebagajja olugendo **travel a long way**, *eg. Olugendo yalwebagajja bwomu. ('He travelled a long way alone.')*

-eebagala *vt* (-eebagadde) **ride/mount** (*an animal*)

-bagalira *vt* (-bagalidde) **carry** (*something*) **on the shoulders**

abaganda *n2* **people of Buganda**; *pl. of* omuganda   baganda **family of** (N12), *eg. baganda wange ('my family')*

bagandesezza *n1* **type of banana** (*used for making beer*)

-baguka *vi* (-baguse) **react suddenly** (*through surprise or shock*), **start up**

-baguliza *vt* (-bagulizza) **draw the attention of**

-bajja *vit* (-bazze) **do woodwork, make** (*of wood*), **carve**

-bajjagala (*also* -eebajjagala) *vi* (-bajjagadde) **belch**

-bajjirira *vi* (-bajjiridde) **do carpentry clumsily, do carpentry of all sorts**

-bajjuka *vi* (-bajjuse) **split (off), splinter**

-bajjula *vt* (-bajjudde) **split (off)**

[1]**-baka** *vt* (-base) **catch** (*in the hand*)

[2]**-eebaka** *vi* **sleep, fall asleep, lie down** (*eg. for a rest*)   -eebaka n'omuntu **have sexual intercourse**
   -eebakako (-eebaseeko) **take a nap**   -eebakako emisana **take a siesta**

baketi *n9* **bucket, pail**

-bakira *vt* (-bakidde) **catch for/at**, *etc., eg. Yabakira omupiira waggulu. ('He caught the ball high up.')*

-bakirira *vt* (-bakiridde) **manage to catch** (*something falling*), **stop from toppling**

-eebakiriza *vi* (-eebakirizza) **be half-asleep**   -eebakiriza omwana **put a child to sleep**

bakoddomi *n2* **in-laws of** (N12), *eg. bakoddomi bange ('my in-laws')*

bakuntumye *n1* **patrol car**. *Meaning: 'They have sent me to fetch you.'*

abakyala *n2* **ladies**; *pl. of* omukyala

[1]**-bala** *vi* (-baze) **yield** (*of crops*), **fruit**, *eg. Omuyembe gubaze. ('The mango is fruiting.')*. *Pronunciation*: okubálà

[2]**-bala** *vt* **count, calculate, compute**. *See* okubala. *Pronunciation*: okubálá

[3]**-eebala**. *Verb occurring only in these forms*:

beebaze **thank them**, gyebale **thank you** (*for your work*), mwebaze **thank her/him**, mwebale **thank you** *pl.*, weebale **thank you** *si.*

-eebalaamiriza *vt* (-eebalaamirizza) **make a detour around** (*to avoid being seen*), **go around**

-balaata *vi* (-balaase) **treat lightly, make light of matters**

-balagala *vit* (-balagadde) **sting** (*through contact with certain substances, eg, soap in the eyes*), **smart, hurt**, *eg. Amaaso gambalagala. ('My eyes hurt.')*   Gambalagala **Rwenzori Mountains**   omukka ogubalagala **tear gas**

-balagavu *adj* **stinging, smarting**

-balagaza *vt* (-balagazizza) **(cause to) sting**

-eebalama *vt* (-eebalamye) **pass by, avoid** (*by making a detour*)   -eebalama ekibuuzo **avoid a question**

[1]**-balankanya** *vt* (-balankanyizza) **mislead** (*by confusing*), *eg. Yambalankanya. ('He misled me.')*   -balankanya amazima **avoid telling the truth to**   -balankanya essente **not be straightforward with** (*financially*)

[2]**-eebalankanya** *vi* **avoid doing a task** (*by doing something else*), **act evasively**

[1]**bali** *dem* **those (people)**

[2]**bali** **they are** (*stem* -ba)

-baliga *vi* (-balize) **(1) be splayfooted; (2) go off the track** (*when travelling*), **be sexually unfaithful**

-balira *vt* (-balidde) **count for**   -baliramu (-baliddemu) **count in, include**, *eg. Mu bitabo baliramu na kino.' ('Include this book with the others.')*

-balirira *vt* (-baliridde) **(1) keep counting, add up, estimate** (*an amount needed*); **(2) take into consideration, make allowance for**, *eg. Omwana ojja kumubalirira omuwe kitono okwetikka. ('Have pity, give the child a small load.')*   -balirira ssente **do the accounts, add up money** (*in accounting*)

-eebaliza (-eebalizza) *vt* **thank for** (*on someone's behalf*), *eg. Banneebalize. ('Thank them on my behalf.')*

balo *n1* **your husband**

balubu *n9* **light bulb**

balugu *n1* **yam** (*type with prickly stem and long tuber with yellowish flesh*) *Dioscorea abyssinica-rotundata.* Saying: *'Ayuuga nga balugu atannakwata mutuba.' ('He is swaying about like a*

NOTES ON
a

a-. Words starting **a** containing consonants are entered under their first consonants, *eg.* **akambe** under **K**.

VERBS AND ADJECTIVES BEGINNING YA are listed under **Y**. Many have forms in which the **Y** is lost (N5).

yam not yet attached to a barkcloth tree.', meaning 'He is fickle.')

-baluka *vi* (-baluse) **make a crackling sound, crackle** <u>olutalo -baluka</u> **break out** (*of war*)

-balula *vt* (-baludde) **hit hard** (*a person*)

baluuni *n9* **balloon**

-bama *vi* (-bamye) **rush about wildly** (*as a thief being chased*) <u>-bama bubami</u> **rush about in a wild and careless way**

[1]**-bamba** *vt* (-bambye, mmamba) **stretch out** (*eg. skin to dry*), **peg out** (*a hide*)

[2]**-eebamba** <u>-tuula -eebamba</u> **sit with legs apart**, *eg. Atuula yeebambye. ('He is sitting with legs spread apart.')*

-bambaala *vi* (-bambadde) **be unrestrained in behaviour** (*in a socially unacceptable way, especially of the young*), **be uncontrolled**

-bambaavu *adj* **unrestrained** (*in behaviour*), **uncontrolled, wild**

bambi *excl* **poor thing** (*indicating sympathy*)

-bambika *vt* (-bambise, mmambika) **stick on** <u>-bambika oluyi</u> **-slap hard**

-bambira *vt* (-bambidde, mmambira) **meddle in other people's affairs**, *eg. Leka kubambira bitakukwatako. ('Don't meddle in affairs that don't concern you.')*

-bambuka *vi* (-bambuse) **peel off** (*eg. of scalded skin*), **flake off**

-bambula *vt* (-bambudde, mmambula) **peel off** (*something stuck down, eg. a label*), **unpeg** (*a hide*), **strip off, tear off** **-bambulako** (-bambuddeko) **peel/tear off from**

-bambulukuka *vi* (-bambulukuse) **be stripped off, peel off** (*eg. of paint*)

-bambulula *vt* (-bambuludde, mbambulula) **strip off carefully**

(a)bammwe *pos* **your(s)** pl. (N11.4)

bampaane. *Meaning: 'Let them praise me.'* (*stem* -waana). <u>ekikolwa ekya bampaane</u> **showing-off** <u>-kola bampaane</u> **show off** (*seeking praise*)

abamu *det/pro* **some (people)**

bana *num* **four**

-bandaala *vi* (-bandadde, mmandaala) **spend a long time at a place**

bandaali *n9* **bundle of paper money**

bandole *n9* **double-decker bus**. *See* kabandole

-banduka *vi* (-banduse) **break open forcefully and noisily, burst (open)** (*as a seed pod*), **crack** (*as glass*) <u>emmundu -banduka</u> **go off** (*of a gun*)

-bandula *vt* (-bandudde, mmandula) **break open forcefully and noisily**

-bandwa *vi* (-bandiddwa) **be possessed** (*by a spirit*)

[1]**obanga** *conj* **if**, *eg. Simanyi obanga anaagenda. ('I do not know if she will go.')*

[2]**-banga** *vt* (-banze) **begin**

[1]**abange** *interj* **Hey, you there!**

[2]**(a)bange** *pos* **my, mine**. (N11.4)

abangu *See* -yangu

-banja *vt* (-banze, mmanja) **ask for** (*or* **demand**) **repayment of debt from**, *eg. Yagenda ku kyalo kubanja Musoke amuwe essente ze. ('He went to the village to claim the money Musoke owed him.')*

-banjibwa *vi* (-banjiddwa) **be in debt**

-banjirira *vi* (-banjiridde, mmanjirira) **continually ask for repayment of debt**

banna- *n2* **people** (*or* **members**) **of, friends** (*or* **companions**) **of**. *See* munna-

bannaabwe *n2* **their companions/friends**

bannaffe *n2* **our companions/friends**

bannammwe *n2* **your** pl. **companions/friends**

bannange *n2* **my companions/friends** <u>Bannange!</u> **My goodness!**

banne *n2* **her/his companions/friends**

banno *n2* **your** si. **companions/friends**

bannyi- *n2* **brothers/sisters of**. *See* mwannyi-

bano *dem* **these (people)**

bantadde *n1* **type of drum beat** (*announces arrival or departure of Kabaka from palace; formerly also sounded at dawn and dusk; drumbeat of the princes*). *Meaning: 'They have released me.'*

banzi *n9* (*also* <u>ka banzi</u>) **bun**

-eebasa *vt* (-eebasizza) **put to sleep**

-eebasabasa *vt* (-eebasizzabasizza) **pretend to be asleep**

basatu *num* **three**

abasi *n1* **pepperbark tree** (*medicinal*) *Warburgia ugandensis*

basitoola *n9* **pistol, revolver**

bataano *num* **five**

batiisimu *n9* **baptism**

-batika *vt* (-batise) **hold in the mouth**

-batiza *vt* (-batizza) **baptise**. *See* okubatiza

-batizibwa *vi* (-batiziddwa) **be baptised**

batyanno? **how are they?**

Abawawa *n2* **name of the people who formerly occupied the land that is now Buganda**. *They are said to have kept moving from place to place, lacking permanent settlements. See* muwawa

abawuliriza *n2* **audience**

bayibuli *n9* **bible**

bayiro *n9* **biro**

-eebaza *vt* (-eebazizza) **thank**. *See* okwebaza

-bazaamu *vt* (-bazizzaamu) **multiply** (*in maths*). *See* okubazaamu

baze *n1* **my husband**

[1]**bba** *n1* **husband**, *eg. Oyo ye bba. ('That is her husband.')* <u>bba-</u> **husband of** (N12), *eg. bbaffe ('our husband')*

[2]**-bba** *vit* (-bbye) **steal, rob**. *See* okubba **-bbako** (-bbyeeko) **steal some** (*leaving some behind*)

[3]**-ebba** *vi* **escape stealthily, sneak off** **-ebbako** **run away** (*eg. of a wife or servant*)

ebbaafu *n5* (*pl.* amabaafu) **bath**

ebbaagiro *n5* (*pl.* amabaagiro) **place where animals are slaughtered**. *See* lufula

ebbaala *n5* (*pl.* amabaala) **bar** (*drinking place*)

ebbaasa *n9* envelope, bribe (*slang*). *From:* '*bahasha*' *(Swahili)*.

ebbaasi *n9* bus, coach

ebbaati *n5* (*pl.* amabaati) **iron sheet**

bbaatule *n9* **battery** (*larger type*)

ebbabe *n5* (*no pl.*) **burning smell from metal saucepan**

ebbago *n5* (*pl.* amabago) **draft, outline**

ebbajjiro *n5* (*pl.* amabajjiro) **carpentry workshop**

ebbakaasa *n9* **envelope**

ebbakuli *n9* **bowl, dish**

ebbala *n5* (*pl.* amabala) **mark, birthmark, stain** -ggya mu bbala **spoil the appearance of** -va mu bbala **become spoilt in appearance**

bbalaafu *n1* (*no pl.*) **ice**

Bbalaza *n9* **Monday**

ebbali *adv* **at/to the side, aside** ebbali wa **at/to the side of** -dda ebbali **go to the side, step aside** -kuba ebbali **miss the target** -leka ebbali **exclude** -zza ebbali **move** (*something*) **aside**

ebbalirirwe *adv* **not too often, occasionally, rarely**

ebbaluwa *n9* **letter, certificate, diploma, epistle;** *in pl.* **post, mail** ebbaluwa ebanja **demand note** (*requesting payment*)

ebbanda *n5* (*pl.* amabanda) **piece** (*or* stem) **of bamboo;** *in pl.* **bamboo**

bbandeegi *n9* **bandage**

bbandi *n9* (*also* bbanda) **band**

bbando *n1* **cassava flour/meal** (*sometimes mixed with maize flour*)

ebbanga *n5* (*pl.* amabanga) **space, room, time, duration, interval, opportunity** ebbanga eddene **big space, long time, ages** ebbanga erijja mu maaso **the future** ebbanga ery'edda **ancient times** Ebbanga liyise. **Time has passed.** -mala ebbanga **spend time** (*eg. at a place*) mu bbanga **in the air** mu bbanga ttono **in a little while** -teeka mu bbanga **expose** (*eg. a scandal*)

ebbango *n5* (*pl.* amabango) **hump** (*on back of person or animal*) ow'ebbango *n1* **hunchback**

ebbanja *n5* (*pl.* amabanja) **debt**

bbanjo *n9* **banjo**

bbanka *n9* **bank** bbanka enkulu **central bank**

ebbanyi *n5* (*no pl.*) **inflamed breast, mastitis**

ebbasi *n5* (*pl.* amabasi) **middle plank of canoe**

bbata *n1* (*no pl.*) **butter**

ebbatirizo *n5* (*pl.* amabatirizo) **baptistery, font**

ebbavu *n5* (*pl.* amabavu) **blister, callus**

-bbe *adj* (enzibe *n9*) **stolen**

bbeedi *n9* **seedbed**

ebbeere *n5* (*pl.* amabeere) **breast, udder.** *The pectoral fins of the lungfish ('emmamba') are known as 'amabeere'.* ebbeere ery'enkima **type of tree** *Tabernaemontana pachysiphon. Meaning: 'the breast of the monkey' – after the shape of the fruit.*

ebbeetu *n5* (*no pl.*) **freedom** (*to do what one likes*)

ebbeeyi *n9* (*no pl.*) **price(s), cost** -a ebbeeyi *adj* **expensive**

ebbega *n5* (*pl.* amabega) **back** (*of the body*). *The plural 'amabega' is usually used.* -kuba amabega **turn one's back on** -kuba ku mabega **carry** (*something*) **on one's back**

ebbenseni *n9* **basin**

bbenzi *n9* **Mercedez Benz**

[1]**ebbi** *adj. See* -bi

[2]**bbi** *n1* **excrement, faeces**

ebbibiro *n5* (*pl.* amabibiro) **large embankment, dam** ebbibiro ery'amasannyalaze **hydroelectric dam**

bbiiki *n9* **beach**

[1]**-bbika** *vi* (-bbise) **be stealable, be easy to steal**

[2]**-bbika** *vt* (-bbise) **dip, immerse, submerge**

[3]**-ebbika** *vr* **immerse oneself**

ebbina *n5* **large protroducing buttocks** (*of a woman*)

ebbinika *n9* **kettle**

ebbinu *n9* **enjoyable time, celebration**

[1]**-bbira** *vi* (-bbidde) **become submerged, dive, sink** -bbira mu mazzi **go under water**

[2]**-bbira** *vt* (-bbidde) **steal in/for,** *etc., eg. Ebintu byaffe baabibbira Nairobi. ('Our goods were stolen in Nairobi.')* -bbira mu bibuuzo **cheat in a test** -bbirako (-bbiddeko) **tell privately, inform** (*someone*) **of,** *eg. Yamubbirako ebibuuzo. ('He informed her of the exam questions.')*, **tip off**

bbiri *num* **two**

bbiriŋŋanya *n9* **aubergine** *Solanum melongena. From: 'brinjal' (Hindi)*

[1]**-bbirira** *vit* (-bbiridde) **do stealthily** -bbirira amaaso **glance at stealthily** -bbirira ensolo **poach animals**

[2]**-ebbirira** *vi* **escape stealthily, sneak off**

-bbisa *vt* (-bbisizza) **cause to steal**

bbiya *n9* **beer**

ebboggo *n5* (*no pl.*) **harsh/rude manner of speech** n'ebboggo **harshly, rudely** ow'ebboggo *n1* **person who speaks harshly**

bbogoya *n1* **type of large dessert banana.** *Known scientifically as 'Gros Michel' or 'Cavendish'.* bbogoya omumyufu **red bbogoya** (*a variety of bbogoya*)

ebbomba *n9* **pump** ebbomba y'eggaali **bicycle pump**

ebbombo *n5* (*no pl.*) **climbing plant with yellow fruits** (*medicinal; used as deodorant and in twin ceremonies*) *Momordica foetida*

bbomu *n9* **bomb**

bbongo *n1* (*no pl.*) **curdled milk, yoghurt**

bboodingi *n9* **traditional dress worn by Baganda women** (= busuuti). *From: 'boarding (school)' (English)*

bboofulo *n9* **loaf** (*of bread*)

bbookisi *n9* **box, metal container with tight lid** (*used for steaming food*)

ebbuba *n5* (*no pl.*) **sexual jealousy** (*as felt by a man*)

ebbugga *n5* (*no pl.*) **red spinach** *Amaranthus lividus*

bbugubugu *adv* **flaring up**. *Saying: 'Bbugubugu, si muliro.'* (*'Mere flaring up is not a fire.'*)

ebbugumu *n5* (*no pl.*) **heat, temperature**

bbugwe *n1* **fence of upright reeds** (*around palace*)

bbulawuzi *n9* **blouse**

bbuli *n9* **teapot**

bbulooka *n1* (*pl.* ba bbulooka) **broker** bbulooka w'amayumba **house broker** bbulooka w'ettaka **land broker**

bbulu *See* bbululu

-bbulukuka *vi* (-bbulukuse) **emerge from under water, surface, rise up** (*in a liquid*)

-bbulula *vt* (-bbuludde) **raise from under water**

bbululu (*also* bbulu) *n1* (*no pl.*) **blue**, (*formerly*) **blue tablet used when rinsing white clothes**

bbuluugi *n9* **bugle**

ebbumba *n5* (*no pl.*) **type of clay** (*used for pottery and making medicinal clay sticks 'emmumba'; also smoked and then chewed by some pregnant women*)

ebbumbiro *n5* (*pl.* amabumbiro) **pottery workshop**

bbumbuzzi *n1* **mason wasp** (*black and yellow, makes pot-like nest on ceilings*)

bbunwe *n1* (*no pl.*) **hipbone** (*of human*)

ebbuto *n5* **big tummy**

bbuukamugogo *n1* **African thrush** (*type of bird*)

bbuulwe *n9* **shoebill** (*type of bird*)

bbuutu *n9* **boot**

ebbwa *n5* (*pl.* amabwa) (1) **sore, ulcer, open wound**; (2) **big dog** amabwa mu ssebusa **stomach ulcers**

-bbye *See* -bba

[1]**be** *pos* **her/his** (**N11.4**), *eg. abaana be* (*'her children'*)

[2]**be** *pre* **of** (= b'e) (**N11.1**)

[3]**be** *pro* (*relative pronoun and pronoun of emphasis* **N10.1**) **they, who, whom, that.** *Can be equivalent to short phrases of emphasis, eg. Abakozi bano be basimye ekinnya.* (*'It is these workers that dug the hole.'*). *Can be a prefix* **be-** (**N11.6**), *eg. abaami bennyini* (*'the chiefs themselves'*).

[4]**be** be cce **absolutely silent** be ddu **with a thump, full to capacity**

-bebbera *vi* (-bebbedde) -tambula -bebbera **trudge along** (**N19**), *eg. Twatambula tubebbera.* (*'We trudged along.'*)

beebaze thank them

abeegendereza *See* omwegendereza

abeekalakaasa *See* eyeekalakaasa

abeekalakaasi *See* omwekalakaasi

abeekanasi *See* omwekanasi

abeekitiibwa *See* oweekitiibwa

abeemanyi *See* eyeemanyi

abeemiruka *See* owoomuluka

abeemuluganya *See* eyeemuluganya

Beene *n1 title* (1) **a name of the Kabaka**; (2) **someone in authority**

abeepansi *See* omwepansi

[1]**-beera** *vi* (-badde) **be in/at, live in/at**, *eg. Abeera Makindye.* (*'She lives at Makindye.'*), **stay, remain, attend** **-beeramu** (-baddemu) **be** (*within*), *eg. Nnabaddemu mu lukiiko.* (*'I was at the meeting.'*), **inhabit, occupy, consist of,** *eg. Enkokoto ebeeramu omusenyu, seminti n'amayinja.* (*'Concrete consists of sand, cement and stones.'*) -beeramu amabala **become stained** **-beerawo be present** (*at a place*), *eg. Yabaddewo.* (*'She was there.'*) **-beerayo be there**, *eg. Nnabaddeyo ku kuziika.* (*'I was there at the funeral.'*)

[2]**-beera** *vt* (-bedde) *vt* **help, assist**

[3]**-eebeera** *vr* **help oneself**

-beeragana *vi* (-beeraganye) **help one another**

abeereere *See* -yereere

-beerera *vi* (-beeredde) **be** (*as a condition of being, or relating to a person's qualities*), *eg. Kyamubeeredde kyangu okukola omulimu ogwo.* (*'He found it easy to do that job.'*) Abeerera awo. **He's just there.** (*left unattended, poor fellow*)

abeeru *adj. See* -yeru

abeeru *n. See* omweru

-beerwa *vi* (-beereddwa) **be helped**

-beesabeesa *vt* (-beesezzabeesezza) **provide company to**

abeesigwa *See* omwesigwa

abeesimbu *See* omwesimbu

abeesimbyewo *See* eyeesimbyewo

abeetegefu *See* omwetegefu

abeetissi *See* omwetissi

abeetoowaze *See* omwetoowaze

abeetoozitoozi *See* omwetoozitoozi

abeewozi *See* omwewozi

abeewulize *See* omwewulize

abeeyazika *See* eyeeyazika

abeeyimirizi *See* omweyimirizi

-beeza *vt* (-beezezza) **cause to be** **-beezaawo** (-beezezzaawo) **maintain**, *eg. Essente eziva ebweru ze zimubeezaawo.* (*'The money from abroad is maintaining her.'*), **sustain, rely on** -beezaawo obulamu **maintain health**

-eebeezaawo *vi* **sustain oneself, be self-reliant**

abeezi *See* omwezi

[1]**-bega** *vt* (-beze) **serve** (*food onto plates*). *Pronunciation: okubégà*

[2]**-bega** *vt* **spy (on)**. *Pronunciation: okubégà*

abeggombolola *pl. of* oweggombolola

-bejjagala (*also* -eebejjagala) *vi* (-bejjagadde) **belch**

-bejjuka *vi* (-bejjuse) **split (off), splinter**

-bejjula *vt* (-bejjudde) **split (off)**

Bemba Musota *n1* **snake-king** (*conquered by*

Kabaka Kintu according to Kiganda legend; estimated reign 1180-1200 AD)

-bembeera *vi* (-bembedde) **form a skin/crust** (*eg. on left-over matooke*)

-bembeka *vt* (-bembese, mmembeka) **place on carefully**

-bemberera *vi* (-bemberedde) **teem on, crowd over, swarm on/over**, *eg. Ensowera zibemberedde ku nnyama. ('Flies are swarming over the meat.')*

-bembula *vt* (-bembudde, mmembula) **remove** (*something stuck down*) -bembula emmembe ku matooke amavumbike **remove crust from left-over cooked matooke**

bendera *n9* **flag, banner**

bennyini *pro* **themselves** bo bennyini **they themselves**

abenzi *See* omwenzi

-bereberye *adj* **first**

-bereega *vi* (-bereeze) **speak in a joky way**

[1]**-bereka** *vt* (-berese) **superimpose**

[2]**-eebereka** *vit* **attach oneself uninvited, mount** (*of a male animal*), **be an imposter.** *Saying: 'Ofuuse kyebereka?') ('Have you imposed yourself?' - said to someone interferring)*

-berenguka *vi* (-berenguse) **be broken into pieces** (*as wood eaten away by termites*)

[1]**-berengula** *vt* (-berengudde) **break into pieces** (*eg. cake to give out*)

[2]**-eeberengula** *vi* **be very hot** (*of sunshine*), **cry a lot** (*of a child*), **be in a rage**

-betenta *vt* (-betense) **break into pieces** (*eg. a tablet*), **crumble, crush, squash**

-betenteka *vi* (-betentese) **be squashed**

-bi *adj* (ebbi *n5*, embi *n9*) **bad, evil, ugly** eby'embi **unlukily, unfortunately**

ebibalabala -a ebibalabala *adj* **spotted, stained**

ebibeere *n8* **testicles;** *pl. of* ekibeere

-bibinala *vi* (-bibinadde) **protrude, stick out**

-bibinaza *vt* (-bibinazizza) **(cause to) protrude**

-bibira *vt* (-bibidde) **dam (up)**

bibiri *num* **two, two hundred. (N8.1)**

ebibomboola -a ebibomboola *adj* **patterned** (*eg. of a material*)

ebibuuzo *n8* **examination;** *pl. of* ekibuuzo

ebibye *pos* **hers, his**

ebibyo *pos* **yours** *si.*

ebifa *n8* **news**

ebifaayo *n8* **news**

ebigalanga *n8* **illness associated with body pains and strange dreams** (*psychosomatic condition, especially of women; associated with witchcraft*)

ebigenge *n8* **leprosy** ow'ebigenge *n1* **leper**

ebigere *n8* **footsteps.** *See* ekigere

ebigezo *n8* **examination;** *pl. of* ekigezo

ebigimusa *n8* **fertiliser**

ebigomba *See* ekigomba

-biguka *vi* (-biguse) **be uprooted**

[1]**-bigula** *vt* (-bigudde) **uproot** -tambula -bigula

walk with a wiggle (N19)

[2]**-eebigula** *vr* **make oneself wiggle**

ebiguuna *n8* **ringworm** (*on the head*)

-biibiita *vt* (-biibiise) **pamper**

biibino **here they are**

biibiri **there they are**

biibyo **there they are**

-biika *vt* (-biise) **lay** (*an egg*)

Biikira Maliya *n1* **Virgin Mary**

biiru *n9* **bill** (*for payment*)

-bijja *vi* (-bizze) **be(come) ugly**

[1]**-bika** *vt* (-bise) **announce the death of**

[2]**-(y)abika** *See* -yabika

ebikakampa *n8* **dry flaky place on skin;** *in si.* **scab**

ebikamulo *n8* **residue/leavings** (*especially of squashed bananas and grass from beer making*) ebikamulo bya caayi **used tea leaves**

ebikanja *n8* (1) **residue/leavings** (*eg. from something squeezed or drained, especially from brewing 'amalwa'*), **dregs;** (2) **white fungus inside a termite mound**

biki? *interr* **what are they?**

-bikira *vt* (-bikidde) **announce a death to,** *eg. Baatubikira nga Musoke afudde. ('They announced to us the death of Musoke.')*

[1]**-bikka** *vt* (-bisse) **cover, close** (*eg. lid or book*), **mulch** -bikka kibooko **hit** (*someone*) **with a stick** -bikka ku **drape over** -bikkako ku (-bisseeko ku) **suppress** (*eg. an emotion*)

[2]**-eebikka** *vr* **cover oneself (with),** *eg. Nneebisse bulangiti. ('I have covered myself with a blanket.')*

-bikkibwa *vi* (-bikkiddwa) **be covered/mulched**

[1]**-bikkirira** *vt* (-bikkiridde) **shield** (*someone*) **from blame,** *eg. Yamanya omuntu yakikoze naye n'abikkirira. ('He knew what the person had done but didn't say.')*, **cover up for**

[2]**-eebikkirira** *vr* **cover oneself temporarily**

-bikkuka *vi* (-bikkuse) **be(come) uncovered, come open** (*eg. of a book*), **be revealed**

[1]**-bikkula** *vt* (-bikkudde) **take cover off, uncover** -bikkula ekitabo **open a book** -bikkula entimbe **part curtains** -bikkula olupapula **turn over a page**

[2]**-eebikkula** *vr* **uncover oneself**

-bikkulirwa *vi* (-bikkuliddwa) **have a revelation.** *See* okubikkulirwa

ebiko *n8* **female private parts**

ebikolobero *n8* **atrocities**

ebikonde *n8* **fists, boxing.** *See* ekikonde

ebikozesebwa *n8* **equipment**

ebikudumu *n8* **dregs, sediment** (*in a liquid*)

ebikukujju *n8* **wrong/reverse side** ku bikukujju **inside out**

ebikunta *n8* **bedding**

ebikya *n8* **neck tendons** -leega ebikya **be worked up emotionally**

-bimba *vi* (-bimbye) **boil/foam up** (*eg. of milk*)

ebimu *det/pro* **some**

bina

bina *num* **four, four hundred. (N8.1)**

-bindabinda *vi* (-binzebinze) **be imminent** enkuba
-bindabinda **be about to rain** omwana
-bindabinda **be about to cry** (*of a child*). *Saying:*
'*Omwana abindabinda ng'eneetonnya.*' (*'The child is about to cry – it's going to rain.'*)

-binduuka *vi* (-binduuse) **be in plenty** ensawo
-binduuka **bulge to bursting point** (*of a sack*)
olubuto -binduuka **be swollen** (*of a stomach*)

ebinege (*impolite*) *n8* **testicles**

-binika *vt* (-binise) **overload**

-binikibwa *vi* (-binikiddwa) **be burdened (with)**
-binikibwa ebizibu bingi **be burdered with many problems**

ebinkumu *n8* **fingerprints.** *See* ekinkumu

binnaabyo *n8* **their companions**

binnaakyo *n8* **its companions**

bino *dem* **these**

ebintu *n8* **possessions, goods;** *pl. of* ekintu

-binuka *vi* (-binuse) **be levered up, romp, make merry, enjoy oneself**

-binula *vt* (-binudde) **lever up, heave up**

ebinyeebwa *n8* **peanuts.** *See* ekinyeebwa

ebinzaali *n8* **curry powder**

ebirerya *n8* **things that are empty inside** (*eg. unfilled samosas, bean pods lacking seeds*), **chaff**

[1]**biri** *dem* **those**

[2]**-biri** *num* **two (N8.1).** *Takes numeral concord* (N4),
eg. (1) abantu babiri (*'two people'*); (2) emiti ebiri
(*'two trees'*). *See* okubiri -biri -biri **two-by-two**,
eg. Ente zazze bbiri bbiri. (*'The cows came two-by-two.'*) abiri **two, twenty. (N8.1)**

[3]**biri they are** (*stem* -li)

[1]**-biriga** *vt* (-birize) -biriga ekigwo **throw on the ground** (*someone in wrestling*) -biriga embirigo **play the game of embirigo**

[2]**-eebiriga** *vi* **roll on the ground** (*of person or animal*), **tumble about, play the game of embirigo**

ebirime *n8* **crops**

-(y)abirira *See* -yabirira

-biririra *vi* (-biriridde) **be watery** (*of matooke*)

-biririvu *adj* **watery** (*of matooke*)

ebiro *n8* **period, era, times.** *See* ekiro

ebirogologo *n8* **rash** (*caused by allergic reaction*), **urticaria, hives**

ebisa *n8* **labour pains, contractions**

ebisaaniiko *n8* **rubbish, litter**

ebisaanyizo *n8* **qualifications**

ebisale *n8* **fees, subscription;** *pl. of* ekisale

ebisanja *See* ekisanja

ebisasiro *n8* **rubbish**

bisatu *num* **three, three hundred. (N8.1)**

ebiseera *See* ekiseera

ebisenge *pl. of* ekisenge

ebisesemye *n8* **vomit**

-bisi *adj* (embisi *n9*) **in a natural state, raw, uncooked** (*of meat*), **unripe, wet, damp,**
unseasoned (*of wood*), **uninformed, naïve**

ebisibosibo *n8* **crumbly stone** (*used in pottery*), **sandstone**

ebisigadde (*also* ebisigaddewo) *n8* **remains**

bisikwiti (*also* busukuuti, *or* bisikuti) *n9* **biscuit(s)**

ebisiriiza (*also* ebisirinza) *n8* **charred wood, charcoal, cinders**

ebisirikko *n8* **ruts** (*on road*). *See* ekisirikko

-bisiwala *vi* (-bisiwadde) **become damp, be naïve**

-bisiwaza *vt* (-bisiwazizza) **make damp, moisten**

ebisoobooza *n8* **young bean leaves** (*eaten as vegetable*)

ebisooto *n8* **mud**

ebisukko *n8* **roughness and irritation of the skin** (*caused by shaving*)

ebisusunku *n8* **husks, shells** (*of coffee, beans, etc.*), **chaff**

ebitaala *n8* **traffic lights.** *See* ekitaala

bitaano *num* **five, five hundred. (N8.1)**

ebitaliimu -yogera ebitaliimu **talk nonsense**

bitanga *See* embuzi

ebitege *n8* **inward-pointing feet, bow legs**
ow'ebitege *n1* **person with inward-pointing feet**

ebiti *n8* **waistband** (*with beads, worn by very young girls; formerly made with sticks*); *pl. of* ekiti

ebitoomi *n8* **mud**

ebitosi *n8* **mud** -a ebitosi *adj* **muddy**

ebituulituuli *n8* **skin rash**

ebiwata *n8* **banana peelings** (*sometimes fed to livestock*)

ebiyengeyenge *n8* **tears in the eye** (*about to cry*)

ebiyiriro *n8* **cataract, rapids;** *pl. of* ekiyiriro

ebiyobyo *n8* **fungal infection of the skin.** *Said to indicate that a mother is pregnant again, if contracted by her child.*

[1]**ebiza** *n8* **pubic hair**

[2]**-(y)abiza** *See* -yabiza

ebizibu *n8* **hardship, trouble;** *pl. of* ekizibu

ebizigo *n8* **lotion, ointment**

bizineesi *n9* **business**

ebiziyiza *n8* **brakes** (*of a vehicle*)

ebizizi *n8* **framework of mud and wattle wall;** *pl. of* ekizizi

[1]**abo** *dem* **those (people)**

[2]**bo** *pos* **your** *si.*

[3]**bo** *pro* **they, them.** *Can be a suffix* **-bo** (N10-12),
eg. nabo (*'and them'*).

-bobba *vit* (-bobbye) **throb** (*of a headache*)

bodaboda *n9* **motorcycle taxi.** *From: 'border'*
(*English*) – because motocycle taxis were once used to ferry travellers across the border between Uganda and Kenya. owa bodaboda *n1*
motorcycle taxi driver

-boggoka (*also* -koboggoka) *vi* (-boggose) **speak harshly**

-boggola *vi* (-boggodde) **bark, speak harshly**

-boggolera *vt* (-boggoledde) **bark at, speak harshly to**

-boggoza *vt* (-boggozezza) **cause to bark, cause to speak harshly.** *See* Kaboggoza

-bojja *vt* (-bozze) **peck, bite** (*by snake*)

-bojjagana (*also* -bojjana) *vi* (-bojjaganye) **peck one another**

-bojjebwa *vi* (-bojjeddwa) **be bitten** (*by a snake*)

-bojjerera *vt* (-bojjeredde) **keep pecking at, nag** -bojjerera enswa **pick up and eat flying termites**

bokka *det/pro* **only (them), by themselves**

-bolerera *vi* (-boleredde) **become overripe**

-bolerevu *adj* **overripe**

-bomba *vi* (-bombye, mmomba) **escape from custody, flee, run away**

bombi (*also* bombiriri) *det/pro* **both (of them)**

-bonaabona *vi* (-bonyeebonye) **suffer hardship, experience misery**

-eebonanya *vt* (-eebonanyizza) **choose, select**

-boneka *vi* (-bonese) **appear** (*of the new moon*)

-bonerera *vi* (-boneredde) **repent, be penitent**

-bonereza *vt* (-bonerezza) **punish**

boneti *n9* **bonnet** (*of a car*)

¹-bonga *vt* (-bonze, mmonga) **spin**

²-eebonga *vi* **spin**

-bongofu *adj* **chipped**

-bongoka *vi* (-bongose) **be chipped, be notched**

-bongola *vt* (-bongodde, mmongola) **chip (off), make a notch in**

-bongoota *vi* (-bongoose, mmongoota) **be sleepy**

bonna *det/pro* **all (of them)**

-bonyaabonya *vt* (-bonyaabonyezza) **cause suffering to, torture, make life difficult for**

-boobera *vi* (-boobedde) **be cooked thoroughly** (*of matooke*)

-boobevu *adj* **thoroughly cooked** (*of matooke*)

-boobeza *vt* (-boobezza) **cook** (*matooke*) **thoroughly.** *This involves returning the matooke to the pot for further cooking after mashing. It improves the taste.*

-booga *vit* (-booze) **be full to the brim, regurgitate** (*of a baby*)

aboogezi *See* omwogezi

abookerezi *See* omwokerezi

-boola *vt* (-bodde) **ignore/disregard** (*a family member*), *eg. Musoke aboola ssengaawe.* (*'Musoke ignores his aunt.'*), **sideline**

abooluganda *n2* **blood relatives, family;** *pl. of* owooluganda

oboolyawo *adv* **maybe, possibly, probably**

aboonoonefu *See* omwonoonefu

aboonoonyi *See* omwonoonyi

-bootaboota *vi* (-booseboose) **be too soft** (*as an over-ripe fruit*)

-booteevu *adj* **too soft** (*as an over-ripe fruit*)

-bootonga *vi* (-bootonze) **contract syphilis** -bootonga akamwa **use obscene language**

-botofu *adj* **holed, perforated**

-botoka *vi* (-botose) **be(come) holed, develop holes,** *eg. Esseffuliya ebotose.* (*'The pan has developed*

holes.'), **be(come) perforated** (= -wummuka)

-botola *vt* (-botodde) **make hole(s) in, perforate** (= -wummula)

-bowa *vt* (-boye) **(1) seize goods** (*as payment for debt*), **confiscate, appropriate; (2) arrest on behalf of the Kabaka**

-boyaana *vi* (-boyaanye) **be restless** (*of a sick person*), **toss about restlessly**

obubaani (*also* obubaane) *n14* **incense, resin.** *Saying: 'Alemeddewo, kabaani ku ndongo.' ('It is difficult to remove resin stuck to a bow.', meaning 'It is hard to change the mind of a determined person.')*

obubaka *n14* **message**

obubalagaze *n14* **stinging pain**

obubambaavu *n14* **unrestrained behaviour, mischief**

bubami *See* -bama

obubba *adv* **stealthily, furtively**

obubbi *n14* **theft, burglary, robbery**

obubebenu *n14* **cartilage**

obubeererevu *n14* **virginity**

obubi *adv/n14* **badly, wickedness, faeces**

bubiri *num* **two**

Bubirigi *n9* **Belgium**

obubisi *n14* **wetness, naivity**

obubudamo *n14* **sanctuary, asylum.** *See* obuddukiro -saba obubudamo **ask for asylum** -wa obubudamo **grant asylum**

bubungeesi *See* -bungeesa

obubwe *pos* **hers, his** ku bubwe **on her/his initiative**

obubwo *pos* **yours** *si.* ku bubwo **on your** *si.* **initiative**

obucaafu *n14* **dirtiness** (= obukyafu)

¹-budaabuda *vt* (-buzeebuze) **comfort**

²-eebudaabuda *vr* **comfort oneself**

Budaaki *n9* **Holland,** (*formerly*) **Germany**

budalasiini *n1* **cinnamon**

-budama *vi* (-budamye) **take refuge/shelter,**

obudde *n14* **time of the day, part of the day,** *eg. Obudde bugenze.* (*'Time has gone by.'*), **weather,** *eg. Obudde bunnyogoga.* (*'It is cold.'*) Obudde bukyali. **It is early.** Obudde buyise. **It is late.** obudde -camuka **brighten up** (*of the weather*) obudde -fuukuuka **become stormy** obudde gye bujja **in the future** obudde -keera (*also* obudde -kya, *or* obudde -saasaana) **dawn** obudde -kwata **get dark** (*of the sky*) obudde obukkakkamu **settled weather** obudde obunnyogovu **cold weather** obudde obw'ekiddedde (*also* obudde obw'ekikome) **cloudy weather** obudde obw'ekimpoowooze **cool weather** obudde obw'enkuba **rainy weather** obudde obw'oku makya **morning-time** obudde -tabanguka **become unsettled** (*of the weather*) obudde -tangaala **become light** (*at dawn*) obudde -weweera **cool down** (*of the weather*) obudde -wungeera **become**

evening obudde -ziba **become dark/night** obudde -zijjagala **be threatening** (*of the weather*) -kwata obudde **be punctual** -mala obudde **spend** (*or* **waste**) **time** (*part of the day*)

obuddiro *n14* **recurrence, return**

[1]**obuddu** *n14* **slavery**

[2]**Buddu** *n1* **county of Buganda**

obuddugavu *n14* **black(ness), dark(ness)**

obuddukiro *n14* **place of safety, refuge.** *See* obubudamo

obudinda *adv/n14* **like a xylophone, corrugations** (*on a road*)

obudongo *n14* **mud** (*for building*)

obuduuze *n14* **scorn, mockery, sarcasm**

Bufalansa *n9* **France**

obufubi *n14* **effort, exertion**

obufuge *n14* **subjection**

[1]**obufumbo** *n14* **marriage** obufumbo obutukuvu **holy matrimony**

[2]**obufumbo** *pl. of* akafumbo (*type of plant*)

obufunze mu bufunze **in brief**

obufuzi *n14* **rule, governance** obufuzi bw'amatwale **colonialism** eby'obufuzi *n8* **politics**

-eebuga *vi* (-eebuze) **bustle about excitedly**

-bugaabugana *vi* (-bugaabuganye) **bustle about excitedly and happily** -bugaabugana n'ebbugumu **feel too hot**

-bugaana *vt* (-bugaanye) **be filled with,** *eg.* Musoke abugaanye essanyu okutulaba. (*'Musoke was filled with happiness to see us.'*)

obugabi *n14* **generosity**

obugagga *n14* **wealth, affluence** obugagga obw'ensibo **natural resources**

obugala *n14* **tufts of young papyrus**

obugalo *See* akagalo

Buganda *n9* **Buganda** Buganda *n1* **name of a king** (*who reigned ca. 1120-1140 AD, before the time of the Kintu dynasty). His reign is said to have been peaceful because he listened to other people's opinions.* Obuganda *n14* **the people of Buganda** *n14* (*word used in sayings*), *eg.* 'Obuganda bwonna buli wano.' (*'The whole of Buganda is here.'* – *referring, for instance, to a large gathering of people come to see the Kabaka*)

obuganga *n14* **gunpowder, dynamite**

Bugangazzi *n1* **former county of Buganda** (*one of the 'lost counties' N29*)

obuganzi *n14* **favouritism.** *See* Ssaabaganzi

obugayaavu *n14* **laziness**

obugazi *n14* **thickness, width, breadth** -gwa obugazi **fall flat on one's back**

obugeme *n14* **wine made from empirivuma fruits**

obugenderevu *n14* **intentionality** mu bugenderevu *adv* **intentionally, on purpose**

obugenyi *n14* **food/drink offered to a visitor** ku bugenyi **on a visit**

obugeregere *n14* **athlete's foot**

Bugerere *n1* **county of Buganda**

obugevvu *n14* **plumpness, fatness, obesity**

obugezi *n14* **cleverness, wisdom**

obuggalamatu *n14* **type of mall inedible termite**

obuggereggere *adv* **softly, stealthily** -tambuza buggereggere **walk quietly/stealthily**

[1]**obuggya** (*also* obupya) *n14* **newness**

[2]**obuggya** *n14* **envy, jealousy** (*in general*), **sexual jealousy** (*as felt by a woman*) ow'obuggya *n1* **envious person**

obugimu *n14* **fertility** (*of the soil*)

Obugirimaani (*also* Girimaani) *n9* **Germany**

-bugiriza *vt* (-bugirizza) **surround completely** Olubugo lubugiriza. **The barkcloth surrounds her/him.** (*implies providing protection*)

obugole *n14* **state of being newly wed**

obugolokofu *n14* **rightfulness, uprightness**

obugongobavu *n14* **deformity**

obugonvu *n14* **softness, pliability**

obugoogwa *n14* **sisal** (*fibre*)

-bugijja *vi* (-buguzze) **crackle** (*of a fire*), **have a fever.** *Saying: 'Bali mu kubugujja.'* (*'They are extremely busy.'*)

obugulumivu *n14* **elevation, height** (*of a building, hill, etc.*)

-buguma *vi* (-bugumye) **be(come) warm, become excited**

obugumiikiriza *n14* **patience**

obugumu (*also* obuvumu) *n14* **toughness, durability, courage, confidence**

-bugumya *vt* (-bugumizza) **warm, heat**

-bugumye *adj* **warmed, heated (up)**

obugunjufu *n14* **civilisation, culture**

-buguta *vt* (-buguse) **pester**

-buguumirira *vi* (-buguumiridde) **begin to warm up, cheer up, be(come) enthusiastic, be(come) excited**

-buguumiriza *vt* (-buguumirizizza) *vt* **excite**

-buguutana *vi* (-buguutanye) **have much to do,** *eg.* Tubadde tubuguutana okumaliriza emirimu olw'abagenyi abajja. (*'We have much to do before the visitors come.'*), **be frantic**

-buguutanya *vt* (-buguutanyizza) **hurry** (*someone*) **up, rush** (*someone*)

-buguyala *vi* (-buguyadde) **be lightly cooked** (*especially of matooke*), **be dense** (*mentally*), **be senile**

-buguyavu *adj* **lightly cooked, dense** (*mentally*), **senile**

-buguyaza *vt* (-buguyazza) **cook for a short time** (*eg. vegetables, to retain their food value*), **cause** (*someone*) **to look stupid**

obuguzi *n14* **buying**

obugwagwa (*also* obugwenyufu) *n14* **depravity, immorality, debauchery, decadence**

obugwanjuba *n23* **west** ebugwanjuba **to/at the west**

bugwi *See* -gwa

obujama *n14* **dirtiness, squalor**

obujeemu *n14* rebellion, insurgency, mutiny

bujja *gye bujja* when the time comes, in the future

Bujjabukula *n9* reception building at entrace to royal tombs at Kasubi

obujjanjabi *n14* nursing (*as an art or profession*) obujjanjabi obusookerwako first aid

obujjumbizi *n14* strong interest, eagerness

obujonjo *n14* secretion from the eye

obujoozi *n14* bullying

obujulizi *n14* evidence, testimony obujulizi obutamala insufficient evidence obujulizi obutamatiza unconvincing evidence

-(y)abuka *See* -yabuka

obukaafiiri *n14* paganism, atheism

obukaali *n14* harshness, ferocity, brutality, cruelty, severity

obukaayi *n14* bitterness, hatred

obukaba *n14* sexual immorality, promiscuity

¹obukadde *n14* old age

²obukadde *n14/num* millions

obukakafu *n14* proof, certainty, confirmation

obukakanyavu *n14* stiffness, obstinancy

obukalabakalaba *n14* shrewdness, quickness of mind, cleverness

obukalu *n14* dryness

obukalubo *n14* hardness, difficulty

obukambwe *n14* harshness, ferocity, severity

bukanusi *See* -kanuka

Obukatoliki *n14* Catholicism

obukazi *n14* femininity, female private parts, vagina

obukeedo *n14* dried strips cut from midrib of banana leaf (*used in basketry*)

obukessi *n14* spying, espionage

obukiika *adv/n14* at an angle, sideways, across, diagonally, side (*contrasted with ahead or behind*) obukiika bwa ddyo south obukiika bwa kkono north

Obukirisito *n14* Christianity (*standardised spelling*)

Obukirisitu *n14* Christianity (*RC*)

obukkakkamu *n14* calm(ness) mu bukkakkamu calmly

obukkufu *n14* satiety, repletion

obuko *n14* relationship through marriage. *See* obulwadde

obukodo *n14* miserliness, meanness

obukokkoliko *n14* dirt (*on poorly washed utensils*)

obukoowu *n14* tiredness

obukopa *n14* edible cormlets of 'ejjuuni erikaluba' (*tannia*)

obukovvu *n14* thinness (*after losing weight*)

Obukristaayo *n14* Christianity (*non-standard spelling*)

Obukristu *n14* Christianity (*non-standard spelling*)

obukubakuba *n14* intermitent light rain, drizzle

obukudumu *n14* dregs/sediment (*in a liquid*)

obukugu *n14* expertise, proficiency

obukuku *n14* mould, mildew, fungus

obukulembeze *n14* leadership

Obukulisitaayo *n14* Christianity (*Prot*)

obukulu *n14* adulthood, age, importance,

NOTES ON
b

-b. Unless the **b** is doubled, verbs starting **b** have 1st person singulars starting either **mb** (non-nasal verbs) or **mm** (nasal verbs) (**N5**), *eg.* (1) **mbaka** ('I catch'), from -**baka**; (2) **mmomba** ('I flee'), from -**bomba**. 1st person singulars are shown only for nasal verbs.

aba-. Many nouns in *n2* starting **aba** are entered only as their singulars (in *n1*) starting **omu**, *eg.* for **abantu** see **omuntu**. If the plural starts **abaa**, then the singular starts **omwa**.

banna-. Nouns in *n2* starting **banna** have singulars (in *n1*) starting **munna**, *eg.* the singular of **bannakyalo** is **munnakyalo**.

-bb. Verbs starting -**bb** have 1st person singulars starting **nzi**, *eg.* **nziba** ('I steal'), from -**bba**.

ebb-. Nouns in *n5* starting **ebb** have plurals (in *n6*) starting **amab**, *eg.* the plural of **ebbala** is **amabala**.

abee. Nouns in *n2* starting **abee** have singulars (in *n1*) starting either: (1) **omwe**, *eg.* the singular of **abeezi** is **omwezi**; or (2) **eyee**, *eg.* the singular of **abeesimbyewo** is **eyeesimbyewo** (grammatically, the latter are subject relative clauses **N7.1**)

ebi-. Many nouns in *n8* starting **ebi** are entered only as their singulars (in *n7*) starting **eki**, *eg.* for **ebintu** see **ekintu**.

obu-. Many nouns in *n14* starting **obu** are entered only as their singulars (in *n12*) starting **aka**, *eg.* for **obutale** see **akatale**. There are also many nouns starting **obu** lacking singular forms.

obuta-. This is the prefix of the negative infinitive (**N18**), *eg.* **obutasoma** ('not to read'), from -**soma** ('read'). Some negative infinitives also serve as nouns.

obwa-. If they have singulars, nouns in *n14* starting **obwa** have singulars (in *n12*) starting **akaa**, *eg.* for **obwana** see **akaana**.

eby-. (1) Many nouns in *n8* starting **eby** are entered only as their singulars (in *n7*) starting **eky**, *eg.* for **ebyanzi** see **ekyanzi**. (2) Some nouns in *n8* starting **eby** are compound, consisting of **ebya** ('of') and a following noun, *eg.* **ekyokulya**. If the initial vowels are dropped, then this is so for both parts of the noun, *eg.* **byakulya** (**N11.2**).

NOUNS IN *n9*. Most nouns in *n9* have identically spelt plurals (in *n10*).

greatness, seniority, high position, headship -lya obukulu assume an important position

obukuluppya *n14* fraud

[1]**bukumbu** *adv* in vain. *Saying: 'Yamuvuddeko bukumbu nkuyege ku ggi.' ('However much the termite tried to bite the egg, it got nowhere.')*

[2]**bukumbu** *n1* type of small plant *(medicinal)*, plantain *Plantago palmata*

obukunya *adv* naked, nude

obukusu *adv* like a parrot

obukuusa *n14* deceit *(through not revealing information)*, double-dealing -a obukuusa *adj* fraudulent mu bukuusa deceitfully

obukwafu *n14* darkness, gloom

bukya *conj* since

obukyafu *n14* dirtiness

bukyali *adv* while there is still time, early Obudde bukayli. It is early.

obukyamu *n14* crookedness, wrong

obukyayi *n14* hatred

[1]**-bula** *vi* (-buze) become lost (to), *eg. Endiga ebuze. ('The sheep is lost.')*, be missing, be lacking, disappear, vanish, stray, become scarce. *A person affected can be indicated by an object pronoun, eg. Endiga yange embuze. ('I have lost my sheep.'). 'bula' can indicate 'time to the hour'* (**N25.1**), *eg. Ebula eddakiika kkumi okuwera essaawa ttaano. ('The time is 10.50.'). 'bula' with combined adverbial affixes means* lack, be deficient in (**N24.2**), *eg. (1) Mu kisenge mubulamu entebe emu. ('One chair is lacking from the room.'); (2) Ebulayo entebe bbiri okuwera ze twetaaga. ('We need two more chairs to make up the number we need.')*

[2]**-(y)abula** *See* -yabula

obulaala *n14* staleness *(referring to cassava infected with black fungus)*, *eg. Muwogo alimu obulaala. ('The cassava is stale.')* -a obulaala *adj* stale

bulaasi *n9* brush bulaasi esiiga langi paintbrush bulaasi y'enviiri hairbrush

Bulaaya *n9* Europe

bulaaza *n1* (*pl.* ba bulaaza) brother *(religious)*

obulabe *n14* enmity, hostility

obulabirizi *n14* diocese

obulagajjavu *n14* carelessness, negligence

obulago *n14* throat, neck

obulaguzi *n14* fortune-telling, divination, prophecy

obulala *adv* in another way, differently

obulalu *n14* madness, unruly behaviour

obulambuzi *n14* tourism

obulamu *n14* life, health obulamu obutaggwaawo eternal life -lya obulamu enjoy life

Bulange *n9* parliamentary building of Buganda

bulangiti *n9* blanket

obulebevu *n14* looseness, slackness

obuleebo *n14* fragments and spray from bark of

barkcloth tree when beaten

buleeki *n9* brake (pedal)

buleezi *See* -leega

obulema *n14* state of being handicapped or crippled)

Bulemeezi *n1* county of Buganda

obulemu *n14* something that causes a person to fail, handicap, disability

obulenzi *n14* boyhood; *pl. of* akalenzi

[1]**buli** *dem* those

[2]**buli** *det/pro* each, every, whoever. (**N3**) buli kaseera constantly buli kimu everything buli kiseera always buli lunaku daily buli lwe whenever buli mwaka annually buli omu everyone buli wantu everywhere buli we wherever buli-wooli-nkufuna mobile phone -a buli mwaka *adj* annual -a buli wantu *adj* universal

[3]**obuli** small things which are obuli bw'enguzi *n14* bribery

obuligo *n14* dirtiness *(of the body)*, uncleanliness

bulijjo *adv* everyday, usually, normally, habitually, always -a bulijjo *adj* usual, ordinary, common engoye eza bulijjo everyday clothes omuntu owa bulijjo the common man si -a bulijjo *adj* rare, uncommon, unusual, abnormal

obulimba *n14* lying, falsehood, deception

[1]**-bulira** *vi* (-bulidde) be lost in/at, *etc., eg. Ekitabo kyabulira mu nnyumba. ('The book was lost in the house.')*

[2]**-(y)abulira** *See* -yabulira

obuliri *n14* (made-up) bed

obuliwo small things that are there -a obuliwo *adj* instant, immediate, on-the-spot, *eg. Omutango gw'abadde gwa buliwo. ('He had an on-the-spot fine.')* essente za buliwo cash

obulo *n14* finger millet *Eleusine coracana*

obulogo *n14* witchcraft, sorcery

obulokozi *n14* salvation

obulombolombo *n14* customs, traditions, folk beliefs

obulongoofu *n14* purity. *Saying: 'Amakubo si malongoofu.' ('The way is not straightforward.')*

bulubbanda *n1* (no pl.) margarine, butter. *From: 'Blue Band' (brand).*

-(y)abulukuka *See* -yabulukuka

-(y)abulula *See* -yabulula

obulumba *n9* stern *(of a canoe)* ebulumba at the stern

obulumi *n14* pain, ache

obulungi *adv/n14* well, properly, good, goodness, beauty

bulungibwansi *n14* communal labour. *Meaning: 'for the good of the country'.*

obulunzi *n14* animal husbandry

Buluuli *n1* county of Buganda

-(y)abuluza *See* -yabuluza

[1]**obulwa** *n14* trouble

²**-bulwa** vi (-buliddwa) **lack**, eg. Bwe nnali e London nnabulwa omulimu. ('I lacked work when I was in London.'), **be at a loss for** (eg. an answer). See okubulwa -bulwa otulo **be unable to sleep**

obulwadde n14 **illness, disease** obulwadde bw'obuko **shaking disease, Parkinson's disease** obulwadde bwa sukaali **diabetes** obulwadde obukwata **infectious disease** obulwadde obutawona (also obulwadde obw'olukonvuba) **incurable illness**

obulyake n14 **corruption, extortion**

obumalirivu n14 **determination, resolve, persistence**

obumanyi n14 **acquaintanceship**

obumanyirivu n14 **skill, experience** mu bumanyirivu **through experience**

obumativu n14 **satisfaction**

-bumba vt (-bumbye, mmumba) **make pottery, make** (with clay), eg. Mmumba ekikopo. ('I am making a cup.')

-bumbujja vi (-bumbuzze) **blaze** (with visible flames, of a fire), **speak hesitantingly**

obumenyi bw'amateeka n14 **criminality**

obummonde See akammonde

obumpi (also obumpimpi) n14 **shortness** mu bumpi **in brief**

obumpoowooko n14 **type of small inedible termite**

obumpwankipwaki n14 **snack(s)**

¹**obumu** adv/n14 **togetherness, oneness**

²**obumu** det/pro **some**

¹**buna** num **four**

²**-buna** vi (-bunye) **become widespread, spread everywhere, reach everywhere, go around** (of food being distributed), **be shared by all, be enough for all** (all get some), eg. Ebitabo bibunye. ('The books were enough for all.')

obunaanya n14 **indolence**

obunafu n14 **weakness, impotence**

obunaku n14 **distress, misery, poverty**

obunakuwavu n14 **sadness, distress, misery**

-bundabunda vi (-bunzebunze) **lack fixed abode**

-bunduggula vt (-bunduggudde, mmunduggula) **pour out** (a liquid in large quantity) -bunduggula omukisa **bestow blessings on** (biblical)

-bunduka vi (-bunduse) **hang down** (of fruit, breasts, hair, etc.), **overhang** (of part of busuuti over belt), **be tipped off** (of a liquid)

-bundula vt (-bundudde, mmundula) **hang over**, eg. Abakyala babundula bulungi busuuti zaabwe. ('The ladies dress well, hanging their dresses nicely over their belts), **tip off**, eg. Yabundula amazzi okuva mu kalobo. ('He tipped off some water from the bucket.')

obunene n14 **bigness, size, dimension(s), girth, obesity**

-bunga vi (-bunze) **move here and there**

-bungeesa vt (-bungeesezza, mmungeesa)

-bungeesa olugambo **spread gossip or a rumour**

-bungeesebwa vi (-bungeeseddwa) **be(come) spread about** (eg. of a rumour or a fire)

-bungeeta vi (-bungeese, mmungeeta) **wander about aimlessly, be homeless** -bungeeta bubungeesi **be a vagabond**

Bungereza n9 **England, Britain, United Kingdom**

obungi n14 **quantity, amount**

-eebungulula vt (-eebunguludde) **surround** (eg. an enemy), **encircle**

-eebungululwa vi (-eebunguluddwa) **be surrounded (by)** (eg. an enemy)

-eebunguluza vt (-eebunguluzza) **(cause to) surround** (militarily)

-bunira vi (-bunidde) **keep one's mouth shut**

-buniza vt (-bunizza) -buniza emimwa **(cause to) shut one's mouth**

obunkenke adv **on tiptoe** ku bunkenke **in a state of anticipation, on tenterhooks**

bunnaabwo n14 **their companions**

obunnabbi n14 **prophecy**

bunnambiro adv **quickly** (in running)

obunnanfuusi n14 **hypocricy**

obunnyogovu n14 **cold, coldness**

buno dem **these**

obuntu n14 **humanity, mankind**; pl. of akantu -a obuntu adj **humane**

obuntubulamu n14 **politeness, courtesy, decency, good manners**

-bunya vt (-bunyizza) **spread everywhere, distribute to all**

obunyazi n14 **looting**

obunyiikaavu n14 **misery,(mental) depression**

obunyiikivu n14 **diligence, perseverance**

obunyiivu n14 **annoyance**

obunyirivu n14 **attractive appearance, smartness, state of being polished, shininess**

obunyonyoogeze n14 **tickle**

obunyoomi n14 **contempt, disdain**

obunyuma n14 **buttocks**

obunyuunyuntuvu n14 **deliciousness** (especially of fruit)

obunywanywagavu n14 **tingling of the cheeks**

obunzaali n14 **curry powder**

obupya (also obuggya) n14/adv **newness, anew**

¹**obusa** adv **in vain, without benefit**

²**obusa** n14 **dung**

obusaakaavu n14 **hoarseness** (of the voice)

obusaamusaamu n14 **moderation**

obusaasizi n14 **sympathy, compassion, pity**

obusagwa n14 **venom, poison** -a obusagwa adj **venomous**

obusajja n14 **masculinity, male private parts**

obusammambiro n14 **extremity, outskirts**

obusannyalavu n14 **numbness**

obusanyufu n14 **(state of) happiness**

obusasamavu n14 **riotousness**

busatu num **three**

obusawo *n14* medicine (*as an art or profession*)
obuseegu *n14* sodomy
obuseekende *n14* bunch of dry stems (*inflammable*); *pl. of* akaseekende
obuseerezi *n14* slipperiness
obuseezi *n14* overcharging
obusembi *n14* recommendation
obusenze *n14* state of being a newcomer
obusera *n14* finger millet porridge. *'obushera' as widely advertised for sale in parts of Kampala is different. It is a Rukiga word referring to an alcoholic drink made from finger millet.*
obusezi *n14* night-dancing (*a black magic cult*)
obusibe *n14* imprisonment
obusika *n14* inheritance
obusikaawutu *n14* scouting
[1]**obusimba** *adv* vertically, upright -a obusimba *adj* vertical Genda busimba. Go straight on. -yimirira busimba stand upright
[2]**obusimba** *n14* genets (*pl. of* akasimba)
obusimbalaala *n14* uprightness -yimirira obusimbalaala stand at attention
obusimooni *n14* wealth
obusimu *n14* nerves
Obusiraamu *n14* Islam
obusirifu *n14* quietness, silence
obusirise *n14* quietness (*of a person*)
Busiro *n1* county of Buganda. *The central and most ancient part of Buganda. Meaning: 'the place of shrines' (many deceased kings are buried here).*
obusiru *n14* stupidity, folly, foolishness
obusirusiru *n14* stupidity, folly, foolishness
obusitaani *n14* type of shrub with yellow flowers, yellow oleander (*fruits used as rat poison*) *Thevetia peruviana*
obusiyazi *n14* homosexuality
obuso *n14* raffia fibre (*from ekibo palm*)
obusobozi *n14* ability, competence
obusomi *n14* spirituality
obusomyo *n14* marrow (*of a bone*)
obusongovu *n14* sharpness (*of a point*)
obusosoze (*also* obusosozi) *n14* discrimination
obussi *n14* killing
Busujju *n1* county of Buganda
obusukko *n14* cellulitis
obusumba *n14* parish (*ecclesiastical*)
obusungu *n14* anger, rage, hot temper -a obusungu *adj* enraged, furious, hot-tempered ow'obusungu *n1* hot-tempered person
obusuubuzi *n14* trade
obusuulu *n14* (land) rent. *Original meaning: labour obligation of a commoner to a chief. The Busuulu and Envujjo Law (1927) gave rights to men occupying land under customary tenure to pass it on to their heirs.* busuulu w'ennyumba *n1* house rent
obusuulubu *n14* moustache
busuuti *n9* traditional dress worn by Baganda women

obuswavu *n14* shame, humiliation -a obuswavu *adj* shameful
obuswiriri *n14* whiskers, pointed moustache
-butaabutana *vi* (-butaabutanye) be at one's wits' end, *eg. Yabutaabutana okuliisa abaana bange. ('She felt at her wits' end having so many of my children to feed.'),* be at a loss about what to do, be overwhelmed (*by tasks*) -butaabutana n'ebigambo have difficulties in expressing oneself
obutaamaavu *n14* uncontrolled behaviour, wildness (*of behaviour*)
butaano *num* five
obutaba *n14* not to be obutaba na kisobyo innocence (*without sin*) obutaba na musango innocence (*legal*)
obutabaawo *n14* absence
obutabalika *n14* infinity
obutafa *n14* immortality
obutafaayo *n14* indifference, complacency
obutafuluma *n14* state of not coming out, constipation
obutagali ow'obutagali *n1* knock-kneed person
obutaggwa *adv* continuously, endlessly
obutaggwaawo *n14* eternity
obutagumiikiriza *n14* impatience
obutaka *n14* clan land, ancestral home
obutakkirizaganya *n14* disagreement
obutakoma *n14* ceaselessly
obutakya *adv* incessantly
obutalagge *n14* rust
obutalekeraawo *adv* ceaselessly
obutalibwenkanya *n14* inequality
obutalowooza *n14* thoughtlessness
obutalwawo *adv* without delay
obutamala *adv* endlessly, continuously
obutamanya *n14* ignorance olw'obutamanya through ignorance
Butambala *n1* county of Buganda
obutambuze *n1* travel, promiscuity
obutamiivu *n14* drunkenness
obutangaavu *n14* light, brightness, transparency
obutasalawo *n14* indecision
obutasobola *n14* inability
obutategeera *n14* incomprehension, unconsciousness
obutategeeragana *n14* misunderstanding
obutatereera *n14* restlessness
obutawulira *n14* not hearing, disobedience, insubordination
obutayagala *n14* dislike
obutayinza *n14* inability
obuteebaka *n14* insomnia
obuteefu *n14* calm, tranquility mu buteefu calmly
obuteekakasa *n14* self-doubt
obuteekomako *n14* uncontrolled behaviour

(*lacking self-discipline*)
obuteeyabya *n14* constipation
obutegeevu *n14* discernment, understanding
obutemu *n14* murder
butengerera *adv* standing upright, balanced upright
obutengu *n14* disobedience˙
obutereevu *n14/adv* straight, directly, straightness -simba butereevu stand (*something*) upright -yimirira butereevu stand upright (*of oneself*)
obuti *n14* fearfulness, cowardice
butida *n9* catapult
obutiiti *n14* beads. *See* akatiiti
obutiitiizi *n14* timidity, cowardice
obutikkiro *n14* crown of the head Butikkiro *n9* residence of the Prime Minister of Buganda
obutiko *n14* mushrooms
obutiti *n14* cold
obuto *n14* childhood, infancy, youth
obutonde (*also* obutonzi) *n14* creation, nature
obutongole *n14* (1) land granted to a chief as a reward for services; (2) state of being official mu butongole officially
obutono *n14* smallness, thinness, leanness
obutta *n14* cassava meal
obutto *n14* vegetable oil
-butuka *vi* (-butuse) develop a skin rash
obutukuvu *n14* holiness
obutulututtu *n14* skin rash
obutume *n14* mission, delegation
obutunzi *n14* selling
obutuufu *n14* rightness, correctness mu butuufu actually
obutuukirivu *n14* righteousness
obutuuliro *n14* buttocks
obutuulituuli *n14* skin rash
obutuuze *n14* residence
obutwa *n14* poison, type of very poisonous tree *Spondianthus preusii*
buubuli there they are
buubuno here they are
-buubuuka *vi* (-buubuuse) burn fiercely
buubwo there they are
obuugi *n14* maize porridge
-buuka *vit* (-buuse) fly, jump (over) -buuka olunyiriri jump a queue -buuka omuguwa skip (*with a rope*) -buukawo (-buuseewo) jump over, skip (over), leave out, *eg. Gaba ebitabo nga obuukawo abantu babiri.* ('Distribute the books to every third person.')
-buukira *vit* (-buukidde) jump into/onto, fly up, *eg. Ennyonyi zibuukidde mu kibinja.* ('The birds flew up in a flock.')
-buulira *vt* (-buulidde) tell, inform, report, relate, preach. *See* okubuulira
-buulirira *vt* (-buuliridde) advise (*on how to behave*), counsel

-buuliriza *vit* (-buulirizza) survey (*by asking around*), investigate, interrogate
-buulirwa *vi* (-buuliddwa) be told/informed
-buusa *vt* (-buusizza) make fly, cause to jump -buusa amaaso look beyond
-buusabuusa *vit* (-buusizzabuusizza) be doubtful (about), doubt, waver. *See* okubuusabuusa -buusabuusa omwana toss up a child
-buutikira *vt* (-buutikidde) cover completely, cover up, *eg. Ekiswa bakibuutikidde.* ('They have covered up the termite mound.'), envelope completely
[1]**-buuza** *vt* (-buuzizza) ask (*a question*), question, enquire (about), greet -buuza ebbeeyi ask the price
[2]**-eebuuza** *vr* ask oneself. *See* okwebuuza -eebuuza ku (*also* -eebuuzaako) consult, *eg. Njagala kwebuuza ku bannange.* ('I want to consult my friends.'), confer with
-buuzabuuza *vt* (-buuzizzabuuzizza) ask repeatedly
-buuzibwa *vi* (-buuziddwa) be questioned, be examined, be interrogated. *See* okubuuzibwa
-eebuuzibwako *vi* (-eebuuziddwaako) be consulted
obuvanjuba *n23* east ebuvanjuba to/at the east
obuvubuka *n14* youth, puberty, adolescence
Buvuma *n1* county of Buganda
obuvumu (*also* obugumu) *n14* courage, boldness
obuvunaanyizibwa *n14* responsibility
obuvundu *n14* rot, decay
obuvune *n14* (1) fracture; (2) slight pain (*where there has previously been a break, fracture or dislocation of a bone*)
obuvvoozi *n14* blasphemy
obuwagizi *n14* support, backing
obuwale *See* akawale
obuwambe *n14* captivity
obuwandiike mu buwandiike in writing
obuwangaazi *n14* durability, longevity -a obuwangaazi *adj* durable, long-lasting
obuwanguzi *n14* victory, conquest, success, achievement
obuwangwa *n14* culture (*tribal/national*), traditions
Buwanika *n9* residence of the Royal Treasurer of Buganda
obuwanvu *n14* length, height, depth, stature
obuwaŋŋanguse *n14* exile
obuwaze *n14* force, compulsion olw'obuwaze by force, of necessity
Buweekula *n1* county of Buganda
obuweereza *n14* service (*eg. to the community*)
obuwemu *n14* disgrace -a obuwemu *adj* disgraceful
[1]**obuwere** *n14* infancy. *Pronunciation*: obuwére
[2]**obuwere** *n14* type of skin condition, itch. *Pronunciation*: obuwéré
obuweweevu *n14* coolness, smoothness

obuwombeefu *n14* gentleness, meekness, deference

obuwoomerevu *n14* sweetness

obuwoomi *n14* deliciousness, bliss

obuwooteevu *n14* dejection

obuwulize *n14* obedience

obuwunga See akawunga

obuwutta *n14* unpalatability (*of root crops*), senility

obuwuulu *n14* unmarried state (*for a man*), bachelorhood

obuya *n14* pitfall trap (*dug to catch animals*)

Buyaga *n1* former county of Uganda (*one of the 'lost counties' N29*)

obuyambi *n14* help, aid, assistance

obuyanja *n14* (1) type of grass (*grows in rocky places near lakes; used for making baskets*) *Eragrostis olivacea*; (2) small lakes

obuyeekera *n14* guerilla warfare

obuyigganyi *n14* persecution

obuyigirize *n14* education   obuyigirize obwa waggulu higher education

Buyindi *n9* India

obuyindiyindi *n14* type of bean (*with flattened seeds*) *Phaseolus lunatus*

obuyinike *n14* grief, sorrow, suffering

obuyinza *n14* authority, power

obuyitirivu *n14* excessiveness, extremeness

Buyonaani *n9* Greece

obuyongobevu *n14* lethargy, listlessness

obuyonjo *n14* cleanliness, neatness. *See* akayu

obuyungo *n14* ladder (*used for stripping bark from barkcloth trees*)   Buyongo *n1* first person to make barkcloth, chief barkcloth maker of the Kabaka (*also called Kaboggoza*)

obuyunzi *n14* bonesetting

-buza *vt* (-buzizza) lose, misplace, mislay
   -buzaako (-buzizzaako) lack (*on*), *eg. Tubuzaako ebikopo bibiri ku mmeeza.* ('*We lack two cups on the table.*')   **-buzaamu** lack (*within*), *eg. Tubuzaamu ebikopo bibiri mu kabada.* ('*We lack two cups in the cupboard.*')   **-buzaawo** lack, *eg. Tubuzaawo emiti ebiri.* ('*We lack two pieces of wood.*')   **-buzaayo** lack, *eg. Abuzaayo ssiringi kikumi okuweza za yeetaaga.* ('*She lacks a hundred shillings to make up the amount she needs.*')

[1]**-buzaabuza** *vt* (-buzizzaabuzizza) lose often, mislead, decoy

[2]**-eebuzaabuza** *vi* make oneself unavailable, be evasive

obuzaaliranwa *n14* culture (*associated with place of birth*), traditions

obuzaalisa *n14* midwifery

obuzadde *n14* parentage

buzannyi See -zannya

-buze See -bula

ebuziba *adv* in deep water, *eg. Abavubi bali buziba.* ('*The fishermen are in deep water.*')   mu buziba

bw'ennyanja in the middle of the lake

obuzibe *n14* blindness   obuzibe bw'amaaso blindness   obuzibe bw'amatu deafness

obuzibu *n14* difficulty

obuzigu *n14* terrorism

obuziina *n14* rags

obuzira *n14* bravery, heroism

obuzito *n14* weight

(o)bw' *abbrev of* (o)bwa; bwe

(o)bwa *pre of, eg. obuso bwa Musoke* ('*knives of Musoke*'). *Can be a prefix* **(o)bwa-** (N11.4), *eg. bwaffe* ('*our*'). *After* ku *and followed by a noun means* on the initiative of (N11.4), *eg. ku bwa Musoke* ('*on Musoke's initiative*').   obw'olumu very occasionally

(o)bwabwe *pos* their(s) (N11.4)   ku bwabwe on their initiative

(o)bwaffe *pos* our(s) (N11.4)   ku bwaffe on our initiative

obwagalwa *n14* liking, love

obwagazi *n14* liking, love, passion

obwakabaka *n14* kingdom, kingship

obwakatikkiro *n14* prime ministerial affairs

Obwakatonda *n14* divinity, God-head

bwaki? *interr* what for?

-eebwalabwala *vi* (-eebwaddebwadde) try to avoid being seen, *eg. Yatambula yeebwalabwala emabega w'ennyumba.* ('*He walked behind the house to avoid being seen.*')

-bwama *vi* (-bwamye) crouch

obwamalaaya *n14* prostitution

obwamemba *n14* membership

obwami *n14* chieftainship

obwaminisita *n14* ministerial affairs (*governmental*)

(o)bwammwe *pos* your(s) *pl.* (N11.4)   ku bwammwe on your initiative

obwana See akaana

obwanda *n14* low spreading weed (*used as vegetable*) *Portulaca quadrifida*

obwandu *n14* wind (*of babies*), colic

(o)bwange *pos* my, mine. (N11.4)   ku bwange on my initiative

obwangu *n14* speed, agility, easiness   mu bwangu quickly

obwannakyemalira *n14* dictatorship, tyranny

obwannakyewa *n14* voluntarism   ekibiina eky'obwannakyewa voluntary society

obwannamwandu *n14* widowhood

obwannannyini *n14* ownership

obwanyo *n14* inflorescence of spear grass

obwappaapa *n14* papacy

-bwatuka *vi* (-bwatuse) go bang, explode, clap (*of thunder*), *eg. Eggulu libwatuka.* ('*There's a thunderclap.*')

obwavu *n14* poverty, destitution

obwawule *n14* ministry (*Prot*)

[1]**bwe** *conj* when, while, after, if, whether, how

(N10.2, N25.3, N26, N27), *eg. (1) Bwe nnagenda okumulaba yali alima. ('When I went to see him he was digging.'); (2) Simanyi bwe kikola. ('I don't know how it works.'). 'bwe' with '-ti' or '-tyo' means* like this, like that, likewise *(N13), eg. (1) Afaanana bw'ati. ('He looks like this.'); (2) Afaanana bw'atyo. ('He looks like that.'). 'bwe' followed by negative infinitive means* therefore ... not *(N27), eg. Mulwadde bwe butakola. ('She is ill, therefore she is not working.'). See* nga ... bwe bwe -tyo bwe -tyo so-so *(N13)*

²**bwe** *pos* her/his *(N10.1), eg.* obuso bwe ('her knives'). *Can be a suffix* **-bwe** *meaning* their *(N10-12), eg. (1)* embwa yaabwe ('their dog'); *(2)* eryato lyabwe ('their boat').

³**bwe** *pre* of (= bw'e) *(N11.1)*

⁴**bwe** *pro (relative pronoun and pronoun of emphasis N10.1)* they, which, that. *Can be equivalent to short phrases of emphasis, eg.* Obwambe buno bwe bwa Musoke. *('It is these knives that are Musoke's.'). Can be a prefix* **bwe-** *(N11.6), eg.* obwana bwennyini *('the children themselves').*

-bwebwena *vt* (-bwebwenye) consume all, devour, *eg. Omuliro gwabwebwena essubi. ('The fire has devoured all the grass.')* -bwebwena ennyama eat up all the meat

obwedda *adv* all the while, all along

obwediimo *See* akeediimo

obwegassi *n14* cooperativeness ekibiina ky'obwegassi cooperative (society)

obwegendereza *n14* care, caution mu bwegendereza carefully, cautiously n'obwegendereza with care, carefully

obwegombi *n14* covetousness

obwejalabi *n14* lururiousness

obwekwekero *n14* hiding place

obwengula *n14* great open space obwengula bw'ebbanga deepest space obwengula bw'ennyanja the high seas

obwenkanya *n14* equality, fairness, justice mu bwenkanya equally, fairly, justly obutali bwenkanya inequality

obwenkulumu *n14* cud -zza obwenkulumu chew the cud

obwennyamivu *n14* regret

obwenzi *n14* adultery, fornication

obwepansi *n14* pomposity, self-centredness

obweraliikirivu *n5* worry, anxiety, concern

obwerazi *n14* boastfulness, showing-off. *See* -eeraga

obwereere *adv/n14* pointlessly, with nothing, without charge, without benefit, in vain, nudity, nakedness -a obwereere *adj* pointless, free, unpaid, fruitless

obwerende *n14* watchfulness. *Traditionally a nine day period of rest for the Kabaka after enthronement. He stayed in a special hut and was served only by men.* ekiseera kya bwerende

period of sexual abstinence *(for men)* ennaku z'obwerende period of watchfulness ku bwerende in a state of anticipation, on high alert, on tenterhooks olunaku olw'obwerende day of rest, day off, Saturday *(for Seventh-Day Adventists)*

¹**ebweru** *adv* out, outside, abroad ebweru w'eggwanga abroad ebweru wa *pre* outside -a ebweru *adj* outer, external

²**obweru** *n14* lightness *(of skin colour)*

obwesengeze *n14* land granted in perpetuity *(to someone by the Kabaka)*

obwesige *n14* trust

obwesigwa *n14* trustworthiness, faithfulness, reliability

obwesimbu *n14* uprightness, straightforwardness

obwetaavu *n14* need, necessity

obwetegefu *n14* preparedness, readiness

obwetikkiro *n14* crown of the head *(the part on which things are carried)*

obwetoowaze *n14* humility, deference

obwewulize *n14* arrogance, snobbery

obweyamo *n14* pledge, vow

bwino *n1 (no pl.)* ink

¹**obwo** *dem* those

²**bwo** *pos* your *si.*

³**bwo** *pro* they, them. *Can be a suffix* **-bwo** *(N10-12), eg.* nabwo *('and them').*

obwogi *n14* sharpness

obwoka *n14* wind *(of babies)*, colic

obwokerezi *n14* arson

obwomu *adv* alone *(of a person)*

obwongo *n14* brain

obwonoonefu *n14* spoilt behaviour

obwonoonyi *n14* sinfulness

obwosi *n14* nutritional deficiency *(of a child, caused by premature weaning)*

obwoya *n14* hair *(one* akooya*)*

(e)by' *abbrev of* (e)bya; bye

¹**(e)bya** *pre* of, *eg.* ebiso bya Musoke ('knives of Musoke'). *Can be a prefix* **(e)bya-** *(N11.4), eg.* byaffe *('our').*

²**-(y)abya** *See* -yabya

(e)byabwe *pos* their(s) *(N11.4)*

-byabyatala *vi* (-byabyatadde) get flattened (out), get squashed, *eg. Yatuula ku mugugu ne gubyabyatala. ('She sat on the bundle and it got squashed.')*

-byabyatavu *adj* (embyabyatuvu *n9*) flattened, wide

-byabyataza *vt* (-byabyatazizza) flatten, squash

ebyafaayo *n8* history

(e)byaffe *pos* our(s) *(N11.4)*

byaki? *interr* what for?

-byala *vt* (-byadde) plant *(sweet potatoes)*

ebyamateeka *n8* legislation

ebyambalo *n8* clothes, attire

ebyambyone *n8* deeds done deliberately to annoy

or harm, bad behaviour, improper acts

(e)byammwe *pos* your(s) *pl.* (N11.4)

-byangatana *vi* (-byangatanye) have too many things to do/hold, *eg. Omukyala abyangatana n'emirimu. ('The lady has too much to do.')*

(e)byange *pos* my, mine. (N11.4)

ebyawandiikibwa *n7* writing ebyawandiikibwa ekitukuvu scripture

¹bye *pos* her/ his (N11.4), *eg. ebiso bye ('her knives')*

²bye *pre* of (= by'e) (N11.1)

³bye *pro (relative pronoun and pronoun of emphasis N10.1)* they, which, that. *Can be equivalent to short phrases of emphasis, eg. Ebimuli bino bye njagala. ('It is these flowers that I like.'). Can be a prefix* **bye-** (N11.6), *eg. ebintu byennyini ('the things themselves').*

ebyebikkwa *n8* coverings, bedding

ebyeddiini *n8* divinity *(the subject)*

ebyekyama *n8* confidentiality

ebyembeera *n8* welfare

ebyembi *conj* but unfortunately, *eg. Yabadde agenda ebyembi emmotoka n'emuleka. ('He had prepared to go, but unfortunately the vehicle left him behind.')*

ebyemisana *n8* lunchhour

ebyemizannyo *n8* games

ebyempuliziganya *n8* telecommunications

ebyenda *n8* intestines ebyenda ebinene large intestine ebyenda ebitono small intestine guts, offal

ebyendiisa *n8* nutrition

ebyenfuna *n8* economics

ebyenjigiriza *n8* education

ebyensikano *n8* heritage

ebyensimbi *n8* finance omwaka gw'ebyensimbi financial year

¹ebyo *dem* those

²byo *pos* your *si.*

³byo *pro* they, them. *Can be a suffix* **-byo** (N10-12), *eg. nabyo ('and them').*

ebyobufuzi *n8* politics

ebyobugagga *n8* riches, treasure

ebyobugwemufu *n8* profanities, shameful language

ebyobulambuzi *n8* tourism affairs

ebyobulamu *n8* health matters

ebyobulimi *n8* agriculture, farming

ebyobulunzi *n8* animal husbandry

ebyobusiraamu *n8* Islamic affairs

ebyobusuubuzi *n8* business affairs, commerce

ebyobuto *n8* childish things

ebyobuwangwa *n14* traditions *(associated with tribe or country)*, traditional culture

ebyobuwemu *n8* profanities, shameful language

ebyobuyeekera *n8* guerilla activities

ebyobuyonjo *n8* hygiene, sanitation

ebyobuzaaliranwa *n8* traditions *(associated with place of birth)*

ebyokukozesa *n8* equipment

ebyokulwanyisa *n8* armaments

ebyokulya *n8* things to eat, food, eats

ebyokumanya *n8* information

ebyokumanyisa *n8* sources of information

ebyokunywa *n8* things to drink, drinks

ebyokuteesaako *n8* agenda

ebyokutunda *n8* merchandise, wares

ebyokuzaalisa *n8* obstetrics

ebyokwambala *n8* clothes

ebyokwerinda *n8* defence affairs, security

ebyokweyalira *n8* bedding

ebyolutalo *n8* warfare

ebyomuzannyo *n8* things relating to games or plays

byonna *det/pro* all (things)

ebyovu *n8* foam, suds, lather

ebyoya *See* ekyoya

C,c

-caafu *(also* -kyafu) *adj* dirty

-caafuwala *also* -kyafuwala) *vi* (-caafuwadde) be(come) dirty

-caafuwaza *also* -kyafuwaza) *vt* (-caafuwazizza) make dirty

-caakaala *vi* (-caakadde) become commonplace, become popular, *eg. Empale empanvu zicaakadde mu bakazi ennaku zino. ('Trousers are popular with women these days.')*

caanisi *n1 (no pl.)* playing cards

caayi *(also* chai) *n1 (no pl.)* tea, bribe *(slang)* caayi omuka strong tea

-cacanca *vi* (-cacancizza) be elated and merry

-cakala *vi* (-cakadde) have a good time, enjoy oneself

-camufu *(also* -kyamufu) *adj* cheerful

-camuka *(also* -kyamuka) *vi* (-camuse) cheer up, become more lively, brighten up *(of a person or the weather)* amazzi -camuka boil *(of water), eg. Amazzi gacamuse. ('The water is boiling.')*

-camula *(also* -kyamula) *vt* (-camudde) cheer up

¹-canga *vt* (-canze) deliberately mix things up -canga caanisi shuffle cards -canga omupiira show fancy footwork *(in football)*

²-eecanga *vi* become worked up *(emotionally)*, become agitated

-cangacanga *vt* (-canzecanze) -cangacanga ebigambo deliberately mix up words

cce be cce absolutely silent, *eg. Yali asirise be cce. ('She was absolutely silent.')*

ccumu *See* katunguluccumu

eccupa *n9* bottle

ccuucu *See* kyukyu

chai *See* caayi

chapati *n9* chapati

chaps *n9* mixture of minced beef, flour and egg

(fried and sold as a snack)
-**cokooza** (-cokoozezza) *See* -kyokooza
-**cuuma** *vi* (-cuumye) **omit an offensive smell, stink**
-**eecwacwana** *vi* (-eecwacwanye) **become enraged, fly into a rage**, *eg. Yeecwacwanye ebbaasi bwe yamulese. ('He flew into a rage when the bus left him behind.')*

D,d

-**daaga** *(also* -daagana*) vi* (-daaze) **experience hard times**
-**daaladaala** (-daaladadde) **walk in a leisurely way** (= -baalabaala)
-**dagada** *vi* (-dagaze) **walk gracefully and proudly** *(like a well-dressed Muganda woman)*
dakitaari *n1* (*pl.* ba dakitaari) **doctor**
-**daliza** *vt* (-dalizizza) **place an edge on** *(an article of clothing)* -**daliza omudalizo** **put decorative strip on busuuti**
Daudi *(also* Dawudi*) n1* **David**
dayirekita *n1* (*pl.* ba dayirekita) **director**
[1]**edda** *adv* **long ago, some time ago, in the past, formerly**; *(with verb in future tense)* **at a future time, later** -**a edda** *adj* **old, ancient** ab'edda *n2* **ancestors** **eddako a short time ago**; *(with verb in future tense)* **a little later**
[2]-**dda** *vi* (-zze) **return**, *eg. Yadda eka. ('She returned home.')*, **come back, go (in a certain direction)**, *eg. Baava wano ne badda wali. ('They went from here to there.')* -**dda awalala go somewhere else** -**dda ebbali go to the side, step aside** -**dda emabega go to the back, reverse, retreat, regress** -**dda engulu regain consciousness** -**dda ennyuma go backwards** -**dda ku adjust, alter** -**dda ku ddyo go to the right, turn right** -**dda ku kkono go to the left, turn left** -**dda ku mulimu go back to a job** *(that one was doing; resume work)* -**dda mu succeed** *(in a position)*, **retract into** -**dda mu kifo kya replace, supplant** -**dda mu maaso go to the front, go forward** -**ddako** (-zzeeko) **be next**, *eg. Y'eyaddako okufuna omulimu. ('He was the next to get a job.')*, **come next, be adjusted** *(of clothing, behaviour, etc.)*, **be altered** -**ddamu answer, reply, repeat, recur, do again, resume**. *See* okuddamu -**ddamu amaanyi** *(also* -ddamu endasi*)* **regain strength**, *(of person or animal after illness)* -**ddawo return** *(to a place)*, *eg. Awo tujja kuddawo olunaku olulala. ('We shall return to the place another day.')* -**ddayo return** *(there)*, **go back** *(there)*, *eg. Yaweta emmotoka n'addayo gye yali ava. ('He made a U-turn and went back to where he came from.')*
[2]-**edda** -**eddako** (-ezzeeko) **improve one's behaviour** -**eddamu reconsider**
-**ddaabiriza** *vt* (-ddaabirizza) **mend, repair**
ddaaki *adv* **eventually**

eddaala *n5* (*pl.* amadaala) **step, ladder, level** *(in an organisation)*, **rank** *(eg. in army)*, **stage** *(in a career)*, **grade** *(in an hierarchy)*; *in pl.* **staircase, scaffolding**
eddaame *n5* (*pl.* amalaame) **final testament of the Kabaka, will of the Kabaka**
eddagala *n5* **medicine, drug, chemical, dye**. *The plural* amalagala *means* **cuttings of sweet potatoes**. eddagala eritta ebiwuka **insecticide, pesticide** eddagala eritta obuwuka **antibiotic, antiseptic** eddagala ly'amannyo **toothpaste** eddagala ly'ebizigo **ointment** eddagala ly'ekinnansi **traditional medicine** eddagala ly'engatto **shoe polish** eddagala ly'okweyabya **purgative** eddagala ly'oluzaalo **medicine to induce pregnancy** ekimera ky'eddagala **medicinal plant**
eddakiika *n9* **minute**
[1]**eddala** *adj. See* -lala
[2]**ddala** *adv* **truly, really, indeed, completely, thoroughly, certainly** -a ddala *adj* **real, genuine, true, authentic** naddala **especially**
eddalu *n5* (*no pl.*) **madness, bad behaviour, mischief**
eddamba *See* -lamba
eddamu *See* -lamu
ddamula *n1* **sceptre of the Katikkiro**. *From:* -lamula *('arbitrate')*.
eddanga *n5* (*pl.* amalanga) **canna lily** *Canna bidentata*
eddebe *n5* (*pl.* amalebe) **four gallon tin**
eddembe *n5* (*no pl.*) **freedom, liberty, ease, leisure**
eddene *See* -nene
ddereeva *n1* (*pl.* ba ddereeva) **driver**
ddi? *interr* **when?** (N13)
eddiba *n5* (*pl.* amaliba) **skin, hide, leather**
eddibu *n5* (*pl.* amalibu) **gap, notch, chip, gap between teeth** *(caused by tooth loss)*, **breach** ow'eddibu *n1* **person with tooth missing**
-**ddibwamu** *vi* (-ddiddwaamu) **be answered, be repeated, be done again**
ddiifiri *n1* (*pl.* ba ddiifiri) **referee**
ddiikoni *n1* (*pl.* ba ddiikoni) **deacon**
eddiini *n9* **religion**. *From: 'dini' (Swahili).* eddiini ey'obuwangwa **traditional religion**
eddiirawamu *n9* **type of bird** *(eats birds)*. *Meaning: 'It eats in one place.', ie. stays there until it has finished its meal.*

NOTES ON
c
-**c**. Verbs starting **c** have 1st person singulars starting **nc**, *eg.* **ncamula** ('I cheer up'), from -**camula**.
NOUNS IN *n9*. Most nouns in *n9* have identically spelt plurals (in *n10*).

---

eddiiro *n5* (*pl.* amaliiro) **eating place, living room**
eddiiro ery'emiryango **front room of a house**
eddiiro ery'emmanju **back room of a house**   -sala
eddiiro **change one's political party**

eddinda *n5* (*pl.* amadinda) (1) **hem**; (2) **key of a xylophone**; *in pl.* **xylophone**

-ddiŋŋana *vt* (-ddiŋŋanye) **do repeatedly, play a return match**

[1]**-ddira** *vt* (-ddidde) **return to** (*a previous activity*), **resume**, *eg. Nnaddira omulimu nga mmaze okulya.* (*'I resumed work after eating.'*)   **-ddiramu** (-ddiddemu) (1) **repeat to**; (2) **let off** (*someone from further punishment*), **be lenient with, take pity on**

[2]**-eddira** *vit* **avoid eating** (*one's totem*), **honour** (*one's totem*), *eg. Yeddira ngabi.* (*'The bushbuck is his totem.'*)

-ddirira *vit* (-ddiridde) (1) **come next, come after, follow**, *eg. Enjiri ya Makko eddirira eya Matayo.* (*'The gospel of Mark follows that of Matthew.'*); (2) **deteriorate** (*in conduct, studies, etc.*), **regress**

eddirisa *n5* (*pl.* amadirisa) **window**

-ddiriza *vit* (-ddirizza) **relax** (*level of tightness, harshness, etc.*), **release** (*eg. clasp on belt*), **loosen**
-ddiriza ku kibonerezo **lessen a punishment**
-ddiriza ku muwendo **lower a price**

[1]**-ddiza** *vt* (-ddizza) **return to**, *eg. Nnamuddiza ekitabo kye.* (*'I returned her book to her.'*)   -ddiza emmere **give food on one's plate to**, *eg. Musoke yaddiza omwana emmere.* (*'Musoke gave food on his plate to the child.'*)   -ddiza ssente **refund money**

[2]**-eddiza** *vt* **regain**

ddobbi *n1* (*pl.* ba ddobbi) **washerman, laundryman**

eddobo *n5* (*pl.* amalobo) **hook, fishhook**

eddoboozi *n5* (*pl.* amaloboozi) **voice, sound**

eddogo *n5* (*pl.* amalogo) **evil spell**

eddogojjo *n5* (*no pl.*) **delirium**

ddole *n1* **doll**

ddolera   -kuba eddolera **trick, feint, fool**

eddonde *See* -londe

ddongo   ku ddongo **on the ground**

ddongobulaaya *n9* **big caste iron cooking pot**

eddookooli *n5* (*pl.* amalookooli) **Adam's apple, goitre**

ddoti *n9* **fart**   -kuba ddoti **pass wind**

ddu   be ddu **with a thump**, *eg. Yakubawo omugugu wansi be ddu.* (*'He placed the bundle down wth a thump.'*), **full to capacity**

eddubi *n5* (*no pl.*) **deep water**   -gwa mu ddubi **fall into deep water, get into serious trouble**

eddubu *n9* **bear** (*type of animal*)

-ddugala *vi* (-ddugadde) **be(come) dark/dirty**

-ddugavu *adj* (eriddugavu *n5*, enzirugavu *n9*) **black, dark**   -ddugavu zigizigi **jet black**

-ddugaza *vt* (-ddugazizza) **blacken, make dirty**

-dduka *vi* (-dduse) **run, flee**. *See* okudduka   -dduka embiro (*also* -dduka emisinde, *or* -dduka

kafubutuko) **run very fast, sprint**   -dduka muwawa **run away in panic**

-ddukana *vi* (-ddukanye) **have diarrhoea**

-ddukanya *vt* (-ddukanyizza) **manage, operate, run, cause diarrhoea**

-ddukira *vt* (-ddukidde) **come for** (*to get*), **run to/on, flee (in)to**

edduloowa *n9* **drawer**

ddumbi *n1* **rainy season** (*September-November*)

eddumi   enjoka z'eddumi **menstrual pains**

Ddunda *n1* **God** (*as the chief herdsman*)

eddundiro *n5* (*pl.* amalundiro) **farm** (*for livestock*), **ranch**

eddungi *See* -lungi

eddungu *n5* (*pl.* amalungu) **wilderness, desert**
Ddungu *n1* **Kiganda deity** (*lubaale*), **god of hunting**

edduuka *n5* (*pl.* amaduuka) **shop**   edduuka ery'oku lubalaza **shop on the pavement**   edduuka lya kolijja **wholesale shop**   edduuka lya lejjalejja **retail shop**   ow'edduuka *n1* **shopkeeper**

-dduukirira *vt* (-dduukiridde) **come/run to the help of**, *eg. Yadduukirira muliraanwa we.* (*'He went to help his neighbour.'*)   -dduukirira enduulu **ululate** (*requesting people to come and help*)

eddwaliro *n5* (*pl.* amalwaliro) **hospital, health centre, dispensary, clinic**. *Note: the 'a' is pronounced long.*

eddwaniro *n5* (*pl.* amalwaniro) **battlefield**. *Note: the 'a' is pronounced long.*

eddya *n5* (*pl.* amalya) **stage of married life** (*for a woman*)   Sirina ddya. **I am not married., My marriage is not working.**

ddyo *n1* (*no pl.*) **right** (*direction*)   -a ddyo *adj* **right**

Deesemba **December**

-diba *vi* (-dibye) **become obsolete, become redundant, go out of date, fail to get married or get a partner**, *eg. Maliya ediba.* (*'Mary has failed to get a partner.'*)   emmere -diba **be left over** (*of food*)

-dibaga *vt* (-dibaze) **treat as of no value, be dismissive, put down** (*a person*)   -dibaga omukazi **neglect** (*or disregard*) **a woman**

-dibira *vt* (-dibidde)   Omuwala yadibira ku luggya. **The girl failed to get a husband.**, *lit.* **The girl became unmarriageable in the courtyard.** (*referring to the courtyard of her parents*)

-dibya *vt* (-dibizza) **make obsolete, desert** (*of a husband*), *eg. Yadibya omukyala oyo.* (*'He has deserted that wife.'*)

-digida *vi* (-digize) **move to a rhythm, show rejoicing through rhythmic movement**

digiri *n9* **degree**   owa digiri *n1* **graduate**

-diibuula (*also* -diibuuda) *vt* (-diibuuze) **use wastefully**   -diibuula emmere **waste food**

-diibuuzi *adj* **wasteful**

-eediima *vi* (-eediimye) **(go on) strike** (*by workers*)

-diimuuka *vi* (-diimuuse) **speed along**

-diimuula *vt* (-diimudde) **move forward at great speed, hurl forward** -diimuula emmotoka **drive a car very fast** -diimuula omupiira **kick a ball hard**

dimansi *n9* **week**

disiko *n9* **disco**

disitulikiti *n9* **district**

adivansi *n9* **advance**

dividi *n9* **DVD**

dizero *n1* **diesel**

-dobonkana *vi* (-dobonkanye) **be bungled, be messed up**

-dobonkanya *vt* (-dobonkanyizza) **bungle, mess up**

-dooba *vi* (-doobye) **suffer greatly**

doodo *n1* **type of spinach** *Amaranthus dubius*. *Also the name of a variety of mango.* doodo w'amaggwa **spiny spinach** *Amaranthus spinosus*

-doodooma *vi* (-doodoomye) **speak in a deep low voice**

doola *n9* **dollar**

-duda *vi* (-duze) **become rotten** (*eg. of fish*)

-duduma *vi* (-dudumye) **make a deep heavy sound** eggulu -duduma **rumble** (*of thunder*) emmundu -duduma **fire** (*of guns*)

-duula *vi* (-dudde) **be sarcastic, be scornful**

-duulira *vt* (-duulidde) **be sarcastic to, be scornful towards, mock**

-duumira *vt* (-duumidde) **command, order**

-duumuuka *vi* (-duumuuse) **grow too much,** *eg. Omwana aduumuuse. ('The child is oversize for her age.')*

E,e

[1]**-e** *conj* **where, when** (N10.2). *Takes pronominal concord* (N4.2), *eg. (1) Simanyi gye kiri. ('I do not know where it is.'); (2) Simanyi lwe bajja. ('I do not know when they will come.').*

[2]**-e** *pos* **her, his** (N11.4). *Takes pronominal concord* (N4.2), *eg. (1) omwana we ('her child'); (2) ente ye ('her cow').*

[3]**e** *pre* **at, to.** *Followed by name of a place* (N24.1), *eg. Ŋŋenda e Kampala. ('I am going to Kampala.'). Can be a prefix* **e-** *on certain stems* (N24.1), *eg. (1) eka ('at home'); (2) emugga ('at the water source').*

[4]**-e** *pro (relative pronoun and pronoun of emphasis)* **he, her, it, them, who, which.** (N10.1). *Takes pronominal concord* (N4.2), *eg. Emiggo gye ndeese gibuze. ('The sticks which I brought are lost.'). Can be equivalent to short phrases of emphasis, eg. Ebitabo bino by'ebyange. ('It is these books that are mine.').*

F,f

[1]**-fa** *vi* (-fudde) -fa ku (*also* **-faako**) **care about,** *eg. Afa ku bintu bye. ('She cares about her things.')* **-faayo** (-fuddeyo) *See* obutafaayo; okufaayo -faayo ku **care about,** *eg. Musoke afaayo ku mulimu gwe. ('Musoke cares about his work.')* -faayo ennyo ku **care a lot about, be vigilant about** Tofaayo. (*pl.* Temufaayo.) **Don't worry.**

[2]**-fa** *vi* (-fudde) **die,** *eg. Yafa jjo. ('She died yesterday.'),* **break down** (*irretrievably, of machinery*), **go off** (*of milk*). *See* okufa -fa ekibwatukira (*also* -fa ekikutuko) **die unexpectedly** essente -fa **make a loss** (*financially*), *eg. Essente zaamufa ng'asuubula emmotoka. ('He made a loss trading in cars.')* **-faako** (-fuddeko) *Meaning similar to '-fa'. A grieving party can be indicated by an object pronoun, eg. Omwana waffe atufuddeko. ('Our child has died.')* -faako ennaku **be overwhelmed by grief** -faako enseko **laugh a lot**

[3]**-fa** *vi* (-fudde) **happen,** *eg. Ebifa e Kampala? ('What is happening in Kampala?')* **-faayo** (-fuddeyo) **happen,** *eg. Biki ebyafaayo jjo? ('What happened yesterday?'). The understood noun 'amawulire' ('news') is found in greetings such as* Agafaayo? ('What news?') (N28)

[4]**-eefa** *See* -eefaako

-faabiina *vi* (-faabiinye) **work hard** (*in a long-term committed way*), **toil away**

-faafaagana *vi* (-faafaaganye) **be badly damaged, be ruined, be wrecked**

-faafaaganya *vt* (-faafaaganyizza) **ruin, wreck**

-eefaako *vr* (-eefuddeko) **look after oneself** -eefaako -okka **be selfish,** *eg. Musoke yeefaako yekka. ('Musoke is a selfish person.')*

[1]**-faanaanyiriza** *vt* (-faanaanyirizza) **look like to** (*someone*), *eg. Mmufaanaanyiriza Musoke. ('He looks like Musoke to me.')*

[2]**-eefaanaanyiriza (ne)** *vt* **liken oneself (to)**

-faanagana *vi* (-faanaganye) **look alike.** *See* okufaanagana

-faanaganira *vi* (-faanaganidde) **look alike to,** *eg. Anfaanaganira Musoke. ('He looks like Musoke to*

NOTES ON d

-d. Unless the **d** is doubled, verbs starting **d** have 1st person singulars starting **nd**, *eg.* **nduumira** ('I command'), from **-duumira**.

-dd. Verbs starting **dd** have 1st person singulars starting **nzir**, *eg.* **nzira** ('I return'), from **-dda**.

edd-. Nouns in *n5* starting **edd** have plurals (in *n6*) starting either **amad** or **amal** (see individual entries).

NOUNS IN *n9*. Most nouns in *n9* have identically spelt plurals (in *n10*).

me.')

-faanaganya *vt* (-faanaganyizza) **make look alike**

-faanana *vi* (-faananye) **resemble, look like, seem,** *eg. Afaanana okuba omulungi. ('He seems to be good.')*

-faananya *vt* (-faananyizza) **make (look) like, find resemblance with**

falaawo *n1* **casuarina** (*tree*) *Casuarina equisitifolia*

-famba *vi* (-fambye) **be(come) weak at the knees**

famire *n9* **family**

fayinolo *n9* **final** (*eg. of a competition*)

fayiro *n9* **file**

Febwali **February**

federesoni *n9* **federation**

federo *n9* **federalism**

-feekeera *vi* (-feekedde) **be blocked up** (*of the nose*)

-feesa *vit* (-feesezza) **snort, snuffle**

ffaamu *n9* **farm**

ffalanga *n5* (*pl.* amafalanga) **franc**

ffampa (*also* ppamba) *n1* **cotton**

ffe *pro* **we, us.** *Can be a prefix* **ffe-** (N7.3) *or suffix* **-ffe** (N10-12), *eg.* (1) *ffekka ('only us')*; (2) *naffe ('and us')*.

ffeeza *n1* (*no pl.*) **silver**

ffekka *det/pro* **only (us), by ourselves**

ffembi *det/pro* **both (of us)**

ffene (*also* ekifenensi) *n1* **jackfruit** (*tree; fruit*) *Artocarpus heterophyllus*

ffenna *det/pro* **all (of us)**

ffennyini *pro* **ourselves**   ffe ffennyini **we ourselves**

effirimbi *n9* **whistle**

ffitina *n9* (*no pl.*) **ill feelings, rancour**   -siikuula ffitina **stir up bad feelings**

effujjo *n5* (*no pl.*) **rowdiness**   effujjo erisusse **anti-social behaviour disorder**   -kola bya ffujjo **make an utter mess**

ffukutu *n1* **climbing herb with large red to yellow flowers** *Gloriosa superba* (= emmere ya nnamunye)

effukuzi *n5* (*pl.* amafukuzi) **mole-rat**

effulaano *n9* **vest.** *From: 'flannel' (English).*

effulungu *n5* (*pl.* amafulungu) **turaco**

effumbe *n5* (*pl.* amafumbe) **civet**

effumbiko *n5* (*pl.* amafumbiko) **heap of rubbish** (*collected by flowing water*)

effumbiro *n5* (*pl.* amafumbiro) **kitchen**

effumu *n5* (*pl.* amafumu) **spear, spearhead**

ffundi *n1* (*pl.* ba ffundi) **skilled worker, mechanic, artisan**

-fiira *vt* (-fiiridde) **die at/in,** *etc., eg. Yafiira Mengo. ('She died at Mengo.')*   -fiira mu mazzi **drown**

-fiirira *vt* (-fiiridde) **die for,** *eg. Yafiirira ensi ye. ('She died for her country.')*

-fiirwa *vit* (-fiiriddwa) **be bereaved (of), lose** (*through death*), *eg. Afiiriddwa omukyala we. ('He has lost his wife.').* *See* okufiirwa   -fiirwa ssente **waste money**

[1]**ofiisa** *n1* (*pl.* ba ofiisa) **officer**

[2]**-eefiisa** *vi* (-eefiisizza) **pretend to be dead**

ofiisi *n9* **office**

fiizi *n10* **fees**

-fikka *vi* (-fisse) **be surplus, be left over, remain**   emmere efisse **left-over food**   **-fikkako** (-fisseeko) **be surplus**

firiigi *n9* **refrigerator**

Afirika *n9* **Africa**

firimu *n9* **film, DVD**

-fissa *vt* (-fissizza) **have left over, have to spare**

-footoka *vi* (-footose) **get squashed** (*of something very soft, eg. overripe pawpaw*), **become crushed, become mushy, become deflated** (*emotionally*)

-footola *vt* (-footodde) **squash** (*something very soft, eg. pawpaw*), **crush**

-footose *adj* **squashed**

-fu *adj* **dead, broken/faulty** (*of machinery*)

-fuba *vi* (-fubye) **exert oneself, try hard, work hard, strive.** *See* okufuba

-fubira *vi* (-fubidde) **exert oneself in/for,** *etc.*

-fubirira *vt* (-fubiridde) **try hard in/for,** *etc., eg. Yafubirira okusoma ayite ebibuuzo. ('She tried hard in her studies to pass the examination.')*

-eefubitika *vit* (-eefubitise) **dash/rush into**

-fubutuka *vi* (-fubutuse) **rush out, dash**

-fubutula *vt* (-fubutudde) **flush out at a run** (*eg. animal in a hunt*)

-fudde *See* -fa

-fudemba *vi* (-fudembye) **go on and on** (*of rain*)

-fufuggala (*also* -fufunyala) *vi* (-fufuggadde) **be badly damaged** (*of something solid*), **be crushed, be crumpled (up)**

-fufuggavu *adj* **damaged, crushed, crumpled (up)**

-fufuggaza (*also* -fufunyaza) *vt* (-fufuggazizza) **damage badly** (*something solid*), **crush, crumple (up), destroy**

[1]**-fuga** *vt* (-fuze) **rule, reign over, govern, control, regulate, tame.** *See* okufuga. *Saying: 'Omwami tafuga ttaka afuga bantu.' ('A chief does not rule land, he rules people.')*

[2]**-eefuga** *vr* **be self-controlled, be independent** (*of a country*). *See* okwefuga

-fuge *adj* **ruled, tame, domesticated**

-fugibwa *vi* (-fugiddwa) **be governed/tamed**

-fugika *vi* (-fugise) (1) **be governable**; (2) **cover a placenta with banana sheaths** (*part of a traditional rite*)

-fuguma *vi* (-fugumye) **grunt, snort**

-fujja *vi* (-fuzze) **spit**

-fuka *vt* (-fuse) **pour, urinate**   -fuka amazzi **poor water, urinate**   -fuka ku buliri **wet one's bed**

-fukaamirira *vt* (-fukaamiridde) **kneel before** (*as a mark of respect*), *eg. Olina okufukaamirira ssengaawo. ('You have to kneel before your aunt.')*

-fukamira *vi* (-fukamidde) **kneel** (*eg. in church*)

-fukira *vt* (-fukidde) **pour in/for,** *etc.*

-eefukira *vr* **urinate on oneself** (*of a man*)

-fukirira *vt* (-fukiridde) **keep pouring water for,** *eg.*

Afukirira abagenyi okunaaba mu ngalo. ('She is pouring water for the guests to wash their hands.') -fukirira ebimera **water plants**

-fukula *vt* (-fukudde) **throw up** (*earth, as by a burrowing animal*)   -fukula olubuto **dance vigourously** (*in the Kiganda way, moving the tummy*)

-fukumuka *vi* (-fukumuse) **pour out** (*of solids*), *eg. Ebijanjaalo bifukumuse okuva mu nsawo. ('The beans have poured out of the bag.')*

-fukumula *vt* (-fukumudde) **pour out** (*solids*)   -fukumula ebigambo **talk too much**   -fukumula ebintu **empty out things**

fulaawo *n1* casuarina (*type of tree*)

fulampeni *n9* **frying pan**

fulati *n9* **flat** (*apartment*)

Fulayide *n1* **Friday**

fulu *n1* (*no pl.*) **influenza, flu**

-fulufu *adj* **abandoned, deserted**

-fuluka *vi* (-fuluse) **become abandoned** (*eg. of a home*), **lose supernatural power, lose potency**, *eg. Obusawo bwe bwafuluka. ('His healing power has left him.')*   amagezi -fuluka **go** (*of the mind*), *eg. Amagezi ge gafuluse. ('His mind has gone.')*   enjuki -fuluka **desert a hive** (*of bees*)

-eefulukuta *vi* (-eefulukuse) **rummage through**

-fuluma *vit* (-fulumye) **go out, come out, exit, defecate**

-fulumira *vt* (-fulumidde) **go out through**. *See* okufulumira   w'ofulumira *n16* **exit**

-fulumya *vt* (-fulumizza) **cause to go out, take out from within**   -fulumya amawulire **disseminate information**

-eefuluusa *vi* (-eefuluusizza) **pretend to be asleep by faking snoring**

-fuluuta *vi* (-fuluuse) **snore**

[1]**-fuma** *vit* (-fumye) **tell** (*story, legend, etc.*). *See* okufuma

[2]**-fuma** *vi* **fade, lose colour**

-fumba *vt* (-fumbye) **cook, boil**. *See* okufumba   -fumba nnabugi **heat bark of barkcloth tree** (*wrapped in banana leaves; done before beating, to make the bark softer, also helps ensure a good colour*)   Ofumbye nnyo nnyabo. **Thank you for cooking madam.** (*complement given after a meal*)

-fumbe *adj* (enfumbe *n9*) **cooked, boiled**   emmwanyi enfumbe **roasted coffee beans**

-fumbeka (*also* -fumbika) *vi* (-fumbese) **be crowded to capacity, be stuffed up** (*eg. of the nose*), **be jammed in**

-fumbekera (*also* -fumbikira) *vi* (-fumbekedde) **be crowded with**, *eg. Ekisenge kyali kufumbekedde abantu. ('The room was crowded with people.')*, **be stuffed with, be jammed with**

-fumbira *vt* (-fumbidde) **cook for/at**, *etc.*, *eg. Nja kufumbira abagenyi emmere. ('I am going to cook food for the guests.')*

-fumbiriganwa *vi* (-fumbiriganiddwa) **marry one another**

-fumbirira *vt* (-fumbiridde)   -fumbirira omugole **prepare bride for marriage**

-fumbirwa *vt* (-fumbiddwa) **marry** (*a man by a woman*)

-fumbisa (*also* -fumbya) *vt* (-fumbisizza) **cook with**, *eg. Afumbisa nku. ('She cooks with firewood.')*

-fumiitiriza *vit* (-fumiitirizza) **think carefully (about), weigh up** (*one's course of action*)

-fumira *vt* (-fumidde) **tell a story to**, *eg. Yamufumira olugero. ('She told him a story.')*

-fumita *vt* (-fumise) **pierce, stab, prick**   -fumita effumu **spear**   -fumita ekiso **knife**

-funa *vt* (-funye) **get, obtain, procure**   -funa eggwako **become pregnant** (*of an animal*)   -funa emitawaana **experience trouble**   -funa ensisi **go into shock**   -funa entengero **shake with fright**   -funa olubuto **be(come) pregnant** (*of a woman*)   -funamu (-funyemu) **profit from, benefit from**   -funamu amagoba **make a profit**   -funamu ekitiibwa **earn respect**

[1]**-funda** *adj* **narrow, constricted**

[2]**-funda** *vi* (-funze) **be(come) narrow/confined**   -funda ne **prefer** (*of two poor choices*)

-fundikira *vt* (-fundikidde) **tuck in, bring to an end, conclude**   -fundikira essaati **tuck in a shirt**   -fundikira obuliri **tuck in bedding**   -fundikira okwogera **conclude a speech**   -fundikira olukuŋŋaana **close a meeting**

-fundikirwa *vi* (-fundikiddwa) **be tucked in**

-funduukulula *vt* (-funduukuludde) **undo** (*something wrapped*)

funduukululu *adv* **to the ultimate, in great abundance, too much**. *Saying: 'Azinye funduukululu ng'amazina g'ekisaanyi.' ('He has outdanced himself.').*   -nywa funduukululu **drink too much**

-fungalala *vi* (-fungaladde) **get out of shape**

-fungiza (*also* -eefungiza) *vt* (-fungizza) (1) **hold up, tuck in**; (2) **gird oneself** (*for action*)   -fungiza empale **hold up trousers**   -fungiza engoye **hold up clothing**   -fungiza essaati **tuck shirt into trousers**

[1]**-fungula** *vt* (-fungudde) (1) **pull/lift up** (*one's clothing*), *eg. Yafungula olugoye ng'atambula mu mazzi. ('She lifted up her dress when she walked through the water.')*; (2) **expose** (*another person*)

NOTES ON
e

e-. Words or stems starting **e** containing consonants are entered under their first consonants, *eg.* **ente** under N.

VERBS AND ADJECTIVES BEGINNING YE are listed under Y. Many have forms in which the Y is lost (**N7.3**).

indecently

[2]-eefungula *vr* expose oneself indecently (*eg. through lifting up one's clothing*)

-fungulira *vi* (-fungulidde) expose oneself before (*people*)

-funika *vi* (-funise) be obtainable

-funira *vt* (-funidde) get for/at, *etc., eg. Ajja kufunira Musoke omulimu.* ('*He will get a job for Musoke.*'), provide for

-funtula *vt* (-funtudde) hit with the fist, punch

[1]-funya *vt* (-funye) fold. *See* -zinga -funya ekikonde clench the fist -funya emikono fold up sleeves -funya empale fold up trousers -funya engalo bend the fingers

[2]-eefunya *vi* be(come) folded -eefunya amagulu draw up one's legs

[1]-funyafunya *vt* (-funyefunye) fold many times, crumple (up) (*something soft*)

[2]-eefunyafunya *vi* be(come) crumpled (up) (*of something soft*)

-eefunyirira *vi* (-eefunyiridde) apply oneself diligently, persist (*in a task*)

-funyisa *vt* (-funyisizza) cause to get -funyisa olubuto make pregnant

-funza *vt* (-funzizza) (make) narrow, make short, constrict, restrict, condense, summarise

-funzibwa *vi* (-funziddwa) become narrowed

-fuuka *vit* (-fuuse) become (*in state or looks*), *eg. Afuuse wa kisa.* ('*He has become kind.*'), change (*in nature*) -fuuka omuzibe become blind -fuuka omuzira become frozen

-fuukira *vi* (-fuukidde) change for, *etc., eg. Ekintu kyatufuukira eky'omutawaana.* ('*Something became problemtic for us.*') -fuukira omuteego become problematic (*of person or thing*), become impossible

-fuukuuka *vi* (-fuukuuse) become disturbed, be stirred up (*of a lake*), become rough (*of water*), become mucky (*of water*) emmeeme -fuukuuka feel sick, *eg. Emmeeme yamufuukuuka ekyavaamu n'asesema.* ('*She felt sick and eventually vomited.*) obudde -fuukuuka become stormy (*of the weather*)

-fuukuula *vt* (-fuukudde) disturb, stir up (*eg. sediment in liquid*), make rough (*water*), rummage through, *eg. Kaamuje yafuukuula ettaka ng'asimula ebinyeebwa.* ('*The squirrel rummaged through the earth and dug up the peanuts.*') -fuukuula ettaka throw up earth (*eg. by burrowing animal or big earthmover*)

[1]-fuula *vt* (-fudde) change (*in nature*) -fuula ku bikukujju turn inside out -fuula omusigire make deputy

[2]-eefuula *vr* pretend (to be), *eg. Yeefuula omulwadde.* ('*She pretended to be ill.*'), disguise oneself

-fuumuuka *vi* (-fuumuuse) be blown (away/about), *eg. Enfuufu efuumuuka.* ('*The dust is being blown about.*'), evaporate quickly (*eg. of petrol*)

-fuumuuka embiro run fast

-fuumuula *vt* (-fuumudde) blow away/about, *eg. Empewo efuumuula ebisaaniiko.* ('*The wind is blowing rubbish about.*')

[1]-fuusa *vt* (-fussizza) cause to become, change, convert (*in fundamental nature*), perform magic

[2]-eefuusa *vr* change oneself, pretend to be, disguise oneself as -eefuusa omulwadde feign illness

fuuti *n9* foot (*measure*), ruler (*for measuring*)

-fuutiika *vt* (-fuutiise) cram in carelessly, stuff in, *eg. Yafuutiise engoye mu ssanduuko.* ('*He crammed the clothes into the suitcase.*')

-fuutuuka *vi* (-fuutuuse) break out (*of a skin rash*), become worse (*of a sore*)

-fuuwa *vit* (-fuuye) blow, play (*a wind musical instrument*) -fuuwa effirimbi blow a whistle -fuuwa eŋŋombe blow a horn -fuuwa oluwa whistle (*through the lips*) -fuuwa omuliro blow out a flame (*eg. of a candle*) -fuuwa ssente give money in appreciation (to) (*eg. dancer or musician*), *eg. Yazinye bulungi ne mmufuuwa ssente.* ('*She danced well so I give her money.*') -fuuwa ssigala smoke a cigarette -fuuwa taaba smoke tobacco empewo -fuuwa feel cold (*with personal object*), *eg. Empewo enfuuwa.* ('*I feel cold.*') **-fuuwamu** (-fuuyeemu) blow into -fuuwamu omukka mu inflate

-fuuweeta *vt* (-fuuweese) blow out -fuuweeta emmindi smoke a pipe -fuuweeta olulimi speak a language fluently -fuuweeta ssigala smoke a cigarette -fuuweeta taaba smoke tobacco

-fuuyira *vt* (-fuuyidde) blow in/on, *etc.*, spray, fumigate

-fuuyirira *vt* (-fuuyiridde) blow on -fuuyirira akagalo (*also* -fuuyirira akanwe) make a wish (*lit. 'blow on one's little finger'*), *eg. Nfuuyirira akagalo Musoke ayite ebibuuzo.* ('*I hope that Musoke passes the exam.*') enkuba -fuuyirira drizzle

-fuuyisa *vi* (-fuuyisizza) urinate

-fuuza *vt* (-fuuyizza) search (*eg. a person or a property*)

-fuuzi *adj* orphaned

G,g

(a)g' *abbrev of* (a)ga; ge

(a)ga *pre* of, *eg. amanda ga Musoke* ('*charcoal of Musoke*'). *Can be a prefix* **(a)ga-** (N11.4), *eg. gange* ('*mine*').

(a)gaabwe *pos* their(s) (N11.4)

agaafaayo? *greeting* what news? (N28)

-(y)agaagala *See* -yagaagala

gaagali there they are

gaagano here they are

-(y)agaagaza *See* -yagaagaza

gaago there they are

gaaki? *interr* what for?

gaalubindi *n10* spectacles   gaalubindi eziraba ewala (*also* gaalubindi ezizimbukusa) binoculars   gaalubindi z'omusana sunglasses

[1]**-gaana** *vit* (-gaanyi, ŋŋaana) refuse, defy, forbid, protest, turn down. *See* okugaana

[2]**-eegaana** *vt* disavow, *eg. Omuwala yeegaana bakadde be olw'okubanga baali baavu. ('The girl disavowed her parents because they were poor.'),* disown, deny (*an accusation*)

[3]**-(y)oogaana** *See* -yoogaana

-gaanira *vit* (-gaanidde, ŋŋanira) refuse in/for, *etc.*, *eg. Ente yagaanirayo mu kiraalo. ('The cow refused to come out of the pen.')*

-gaaya *vt* (-gaaye) chew

-gaba *vt* (-gabye) give out/away, donate, distribute, issue, be generous   -gaba caanisi deal cards

-gabana *vit* (-gabanye) divide up among oneselves, *eg. Abaana bagabana amenvu. ('The children are dividing up the bananas among themselves.'),* share with one another

-gabangula *vt* (-gabangudde) give out generously, give out lavishly

-gabanya *vt* (-gabanyizza) divide up (*for distribution*), *eg. Abakozi yabagabanyizza ssente. ('He divided up the money between the workers.'),* share out, allot, apportion

-gabira *vt* (-gabidde) give to, *eg. Yangabira ekirabo. ('She gave me a present.'),* distribute to, *eg. Omusomesa yagabira abasomi ebitabo. ('The teacher distributed books to the pupils.'),* allocate, issue to   **-gabiramu** (*also* -gabira mu) (-gabiddemu) divided by (*in maths*), *eg. Nnya gabiramu bbiri ofuna bbiri. ('Four divided by two is two.')*

-gabirira *vt* (-gabiridde) give regularly   amabeere -gabirira give a lot of milk (*of breasts*)

-gabiza *vit* (-gabizza) divide (*in maths*)

-gabula *vt* (-gabudde) entertain (*at a social occasion*), provide food for   Ogabudde. Thank you. (*addressed to a host after eating*)

-gabulira *vt* (-gabulidde) entertain at

Gabunga *n1 title* chief of the Kabaka's navy, admiral, head of the Lungfish Clan

agafaayo? *greeting* what's news? (N28)

(a)gaffe *pos* our(s) (N11.4)

agafuddeyo? *greeting* what's news? (N28)

-gaga *vi* (-gaze) go bad (*eg. of cooked food*)

-gagambuka *vi* (-gagambuse) come off (*of something stuck down, eg. sole of a shoe*), become unstuck, peel off, *eg. Akapande kagagambuseeko. ('The label has peeled off.')*

[1]**-gagambula** *vt* (-gagambudde) take/strip off (*something stuck down*), unstick, peel off   -gagambula amagalagamba remove scales (*of a fish*)

[2]**-eegagambula** *vi* become unstuck

agage *pos* hers, his

-gagga *adj* rich

-gaggawala *vi* (-gaggawadde) be(come) rich

-gaggawaza *vt* (-gaggawazizza) make rich

agago *pos* yours *si.*

-(y)agala *See* -yagala

-galamira *vi* (-galamidde) lie down, recline   saagala agalamidde type of drum beat (*calls people to communal labour*)

-galamiza *vt* (-galamizza) cause to lie down, lay down

-(y)agalana *See* -yagalana

-eegalangajja *vi* (-eegalangazze) sprawl oneself out

-galangatana *vi* (-galangatanye) not do things properly, do incompletely, *eg. Mu kifo ky'okukola n'obwegendereza, yabadde agalangatana n'ebintu nga talina ky'amala. ('Instead of working carefully, he was doing this and that in an incomplete sort of way.').* Saying: *'Yabadde agalangatana ng'ebigaali by'abayiga.' ('He was not doing it properly, just like drivers of carts who are learning.')*

-galangatanya *vt* (-galangatanyizza) cause not to do as planned, cause disturbance, *eg. Enkuba yangalangatanyizza ne ntuuka nga buyise. ('The downpour caused me to arrive late.').* Saying: *'Agenze kugalangatanya kiwanga mu ngalo.' ('He has gone to sleep.')*   -galangatanya bintu clatter about, *eg. Temugalangatanya bintu, nze njagala kwebaka. ('Stop clattering about, I want to rest.')*

-galanjuka *vi* (-galanjuse) fall sprawling on the ground

gali *dem* those

-(y)agalibwa *See* -yagalibwa

[1]**-galika** *vt* (-galise) set down on the back, turn over on the back

[2]**-eegalika** *vi* lie on one's back, *eg. Agalamidde nga yeegalise. ('He is lying on his back.')*

galiki *n1* garlic

-(y)agaliza *See* -yagaliza

-galula *vt* (-galudde) raise (*a weapon to strike*), brandish (*a weapon*)   -galula effumu raise a spear (*to strike*)

-(y)agalwa *See* -yagalwa

**NOTES ON
f**

-f. Verbs starting **f** have 1st person singulars starting **nf**, *eg.* **nfumba** ('I cook'), from -**fumba**.

eff-. Nouns in *n5* starting **eff** have plurals (in *n6*) starting **amaf**, *eg.* the plural of **effumu** is **amafumu**.

NOUNS IN *n9*. Most nouns in *n9* have identically spelt plurals (in *n10*).

-gamba *vit* (-gambye, ŋŋamba) **say (to), tell** gamba nga nze **a person like me,** *eg. Gamba nga nze sisobola kusitula kintu kizitowa. ('A person like me can't lift something heavy.')* kwe kugamba nti **that is to say**

Gambalagala Rwenzori Mountains. *Meaning: 'My eyes hurt.' ('amaaso' 'eyes' understood – because the mountains are so far away)*

-gambibwa *vi* (-gambiddwa) **be said, be alleged**

(a)gammwe *pos* **your(s)** *pl.* **(N11.4)**

agamu *det/pro* **some**

-ganda *adj* (eŋŋanda *n9*) **Kiganda,** *eg. ennyumba eŋŋanda ('Kiganda house')* ensimbi eŋŋanda **cowries used as money** omwenge omuganda **(Kiganda) banana beer**

-gandaala *vi* (-gandadde, ŋŋandaala) **take a siesta, relax**

[1]**-ganga** *vt* (-ganze, ŋŋanga) **treat** (*a sickness*)

[2]**-eeganga** *vr* **treat oneself.** *Saying: 'Omuganga teyeeganga.' ('A doctor does not treat himself.')*

(a)gange *pos* **my, mine.** **(N11.4)**

-ganja *vi* (-ganze, ŋŋanja) **be a favourite**

gannaago *n6* **their companions**

gannaalyo *n6* **its companions**

gano *dem* **these**

-ganya *vt* (-ganyizza, ŋŋanya) **make possible for** (*someone to do something*), **permit, allow,** *eg. Ssentebe w'olukiiko teyamuganya kwogera. ('The chairman did not allow her to speak.')* A verb usually used in the negative.

-ganyula *vit* (-ganyudde) **be profitable (to)**

-ganyulwa *vi* (-ganyuddwa, ŋŋanyulwa) **profit (from),** *eg. Yagezaako okusuubula naye teyaganyulwa. ('He tried to trade but did not profit from it.')*, **benefit from** aganyuddwa (*pl.* abaganyudwa) **beneficiary of a will**

-ganza *vt* (-ganzizza, ŋŋanza) **make a favourite of**

-ganzi *adj* (eŋŋanzi *n9*) **favourite**

-ganzika *vt* (-ganzise, ŋŋanzika) **lay down carefully**

-gaŋŋalama *vi* (-gaŋŋalamye, ngaŋŋalama) **lie down anyhow** (*of person or animal, eg. when tired*), **flop down, sprawl oneself out**

-gasa *vit* (-gasizza) **be useful (to), be profitable, benefit**

-gasibwa *vi* (-gasiddwa) **be benefitted by**

Gatonnya January

[1]**-gatta** *vt* (-gasse) **add** (*two or more things together*), **combine, unite, unify, marry** (*through Christian rites*), **make up to** (*in a relationship*), **pay damages to, compensate.** *See* okugatta -gatta ku **put onto, annex, supplement** -gatta wamu **amalgamate, put together,** *eg. Ebintu bino bigatte wamu na biri. ('Add these things together with those.')* **-gattako** (-gasseeko) **put together, add to** -gattako na **add** (*items*)

[2]**-eegatta** *vi* **unite, join, becomed involved.** *See* okwegatta -eegatta ku **join with** (*a group*), **become involved with** -eegatta mu mukwano **have sexual intercourse**

-gatte *adj* **joined, united**

-gattibwa *vi* (-gattiddwa) **be joined in marriage** (*in church*)

-gattika *vt* (-gattise) **mix up** (*different types of things*), **bring together** (*incompatable things*), *eg. Bagattika okusoma n'okulaba ttivvi. ('They are studying while watching TV.')*

-gattiriza *vt* (-gattirizza) **mix up, jumble up**

-gattulula *vt* (-gattuludde) **take apart** (*things joined together*) -gattulula ekigambo mu nnyingo **break a word into syllables** -gattulula obufumbo **grant a divorce,** *eg. Musoke ne mukyala we baabagattulula mu bufumbo. ('Musoke and his wife were granted a divorce.')*, **annul the marriage of**

-gattululwa *vi* (-gattuluddwa) **be taken apart** (*eg. of a jigsaw puzzle*) -gattululwa mu bufumbo **be granted a divorce,** *eg. Musoke ne mukyala we baagattululwa mu bufumbo. ('Musoke and his wife were granted a divorce.')*

gavana *n1* (*pl.* ba gavana) **governor**

gavumenti *n9* **government**

[1]**-gaya** *vt* (-gaye) **consider incapable, underestimate**

[2]**-eegaya** *vr* **underestimate oneself**

-gayaala *vi* (-gayadde) **be lazy**

-gayaalira *vit* (-gayaalidde) **not do something one should,** *eg. Omulimu gwe yagugayaalira. ('He did not get on with his work.')*, **be lazy about** (*doing something*), **treat lightly**

-gayaavu *adj* **lazy**

[1]**-gayaaza** *vt* (-gayaazizza) **make lazy**

[2]**-eegayaaza** *vi* **work half-heartedly, laze about**

agayanja *n22* **oceans**; *pl. of* oguyanja

[1]**-gayirira** *vt* (-gayiridde) **greatly underestimate, put off** (*doing something*)

[2]**-eegayirira** *vt* **implore, beseech**

-gazi *adj* **wide, broad, thick**

-(y)agazisa *See* -yagazisa

-gaziwa *vi* (-gaziye) **become wide, expand**

-gaziya *vt* (-gaziyizza) **widen**

[1]**ge** *pos* **her/his** (**N11.4**), *eg. amanda ge ('her charcoal')*

[2]**ge** *pre* **of** (= g'e) (**N11.1**)

[3]**ge** *pro* (*relative pronoun and pronoun of emphasis* N10.1) **they, which, that.** *Can be equivalent to short phrases of emphasis, eg. Oleese ki? Amagi ge ndeese. ('What have you brought? It is eggs that I have brought.'). Can be a prefix* ge- (**N11.6**), *eg. amaato gennyini ('the boats themselves').*

-geegeenya *vt* (-geegeenyezza) **mimic**

geeti *n9* **gate**

-gejja *vi* (-gezze) **gain weight, grow fat, increase**

-gejjulukuka *vi* (-gejjulukuse) **grow obese**

[1]**-gema** *vt* (-gemye) **protect from misfortune, avert, forestall, ward off** -gema akafuba **vaccinate against TB** -gema endwadde **prevent illness, inoculate, vaccinate, immunise** -gema

enkuba **prevent rain**   -gema kabaka **prevent the king** (*from doing something foolish*)

[2]**-eegema** vr **protect oneself from** (*eg. disease*)
-eegema okuzaala **practice birth control**

-genda v (-genze, ŋŋenda) (1) vi **go**, *eg. Agenda eka.* (*'She is going home.'*), **leave**; (2) *aux v (followed by inf N19)* **be about to**, *eg. Abantu bagenda okulya.* (*'The people are about to eat.'*)

[1]**-gendera** vt (-gendedde, ŋŋendera) **go in/for**, *etc.*
-genderako (-gendeddeko) **go with** (*a person*)

[2]**-eegendera** vi (1) **go oneself** (*rather than someone else going*); (2) **soil oneself** (*through defecation*)

-genderera vit (-genderedde, ŋŋenderera) **do deliberately**, *eg. Sigenderedde.* (*'I did not do it on purpose.'*), **do/go with the intention of, intend, aim** (*at an objective*)

-eegendereza vit (-eegenderezza) **be careful (about), be cautious (about).** *As aux v, can be equivalent to adverb* **carefully** (N19). *See* okwegendereza

-geneka vi (-genese) **be strained** (*of salt solution from ashes*)

-genekera vt (-genekedde) **strain** (*ashes for salt*)

-gengewala vi (-gengewadde, ŋŋengewala) **contract leprosy**

agenti n1 **agent**

-genyi adj **visiting**

-genyiwala vi (-genyiwadde) **be/go on a visit**

-genyiwaza vt (-genyiwazizza) **receive on a visit**

[1]**-gera** vt (-geze) **measure, weigh, estimate, assess, judge** (*quantity needed*)   -gera akaseera **do after a while**, *eg. Ogera akaseera n'olaba emmere gye tufumba.* (*'After a while check the food which we are cooking.'*)

[2]**-gera** vt **tell** (*story, proverb, etc.*), **narrate**

[3]**-(y)ogera** *See* -yogera

-geraageranya vt (-geraageranyizza) **compare, estimate, evaluate, assess, weigh up**

-(y)ogeragana *See* -yogeragana

-(y)ogerayogera *See* -yogerayogera

-gere adj (eggere n5) **measured, definite, limited** ekiseere ekigere (*also* ebbanga ggere) **limited period of time**, *eg. Aluba ebbanga ggere okudda.* (*'He has a limited period of time to come back.'*)

-gereesa vi (-gereesezza) **speak in riddles, speak enigmatically**

-geregeza vi (-geregezezza) **dribble, slobber**

-gereka vt (gerese) **grade, assess, put into categories**

-gerekera vi (-gerekedde) **be overlapping** (*of teeth*)

-gerengetanya vit (-gerengetanyizza) **devise a means (for), try every device, be resourceful**

[1]**-gerera** vt (-geredde) **measure out**

[2]**-(y)ogerera** *See* -yogerera

-(y)ogereza *See* -yogereza

-gevvu adj **fat, corpulent, obese**

-geya vt (-geye) **backbite, talk behind the back of.** *Saying:* 'Ssebageya nnyonyi nga nnamunye ali ku nju. (*'You are backbiting while the wagtail is in the house.', meaning 'Backbiting is bad, he will get to know.'*)

[1]**-geza** vt (-gezezza) **try out, have a go.** *See* okugeza
-gezaako (-gezezzaako) **try (out), attempt**

[2]**-eegeza** vr **test/try oneself**   -eegezaamu **try on** (*eg. clothing*), **practice, rehearse**

[3]**-(y)ogeza** *See* -yogeza

-(y)ogezayogeza *See* -yogezayogeza

-gezesa vt (-gezesezza) **try out, test, experiment (with)**   -gezesaako (-gezesezzaako) **give a chance to** (*someone*), **give probation to**

-gezi adj **clever, wise**

-gezigezi adj **astute, shrewd, quick-witted, sly, cunning**

-geziwala vi (-geziwadde) **grow clever/wise**

[1]**-geziwaza** vt (-geziwazizza) **make clever**

[2]**-eegeziwaza** vi **pretend to be clever**

-gezza vt (-gezzezza) **fatten, expand**

eggaali n9 **bicycle**   eggaali y'omukka **train** ow'eggaali n1 **cyclist**

ggaamu n1 (*no pl.*) **glue, gum**

ggaasi n1 (*no pl.*) **gas**

eggabogabo *See* omwezi

[1]**eggala** n5 (*pl.* amagala) **basket trap** (*for fish; has hole at base*)

[2]**-ggala** vt (-ggadde) **shut, close.** *Usually in enclitic form* -ggalawo (-ggaddewo).

eggalagamba n5 (*pl.* amagalagamba) **scale** (*of animal or fish*)

eggalagi n9 **garage**

ggalani n9 **gallon**

-ggale adj (enzigale n9) **shut, closed**

[1]**-ggalira** vt (-ggalidde) **shut in**, *eg. Aggalidde enkoko mu kisibo.* (*'She has shut the chicken in the pen.'*)

[2]**-eggalira** vr **shut oneself in**

eggalwo n5 (*no pl.*) **inner fibre of dried banana stem** (*used for caulking canoes*)

-ggalwa vi (-ggaliddwa) **be closed**

[1]**eggama** n9 **mug**

[2]**-eggama** vit (-eggamye) **take shelter (from)** (*rain*), *eg. Yeggama enkuba wansi w'omuti.* (*'She sheltered from the rain under a tree.'*)

eggana n5 (*pl.* amagana) **herd, flock**

eggandaalo n5 (*no pl.*) **period of rest** (*lying down*), **siesta**

egganduula n5 (*pl.* amaganduula) **robe** (*type worn as sign of office*)

eggego n5 (*pl.* amagego) **molar tooth**

eggemo n5 (*pl.* amagemo) **ivory bracelet, hem** (*on dress*); *in pl.* **turn-ups** (*on trousers*), **cuffs**

eggendo n5 (*pl.* amagendo) **long journey**

[1]**eggere** adj. *See* -gere

[2]**eggere** n5 (*pl.* amagere) **big foot**

ggeyeena n9 **hell**

eggi n5 (*pl.* amagi) **egg**

eggigi n5 (*pl.* amagigi) **curtain** (*big thick type used*

as a divider, eg. in theatre or Jewish temple)
eggigi ly'embugo **barkcloth divider** (*for
partitioning a room*)

-ggiira *vi* (-ggiiridde) **be burned** (*in a house fire*),
eg. *Nnataasa abaana ne bataggiira mu nnyumba.*
(*'I saved the children from being burnt in the
house.'*)

eggimu *See* -gimu

eggiraasi *n9* **glass, tumbler**

eggirigimba *n5* (*pl.* amagirigimba) **fin** (*of a fish*)

eggirikiti (*also* ejjirikiti) *n5* **coral tree** (*used
medicinally to control nausea; floats for fishing net
made from bark; dead dogs are dumped under this
tree*) Erythrina abyssinica

eggirita *n9* **razor blade.** *From: 'Gillette' (brand).*

ggita *n9* **guitar**

ggiya *n9* **gear**

-ggiza *vt* (-ggizizza) **thin** (*seedlings*)

¹ggobe mu ggobe **on heat**, eg. *Embwa yange eri
mu ggobe.* (*'My dog is on heat.'*)

²eggobe *n5* (*no pl.*) **edible green powder** (*made
from crushed dried cooked leaves of empindi*)

eggoga *See* -eemala

ggoloofa *n9* **multi-storey building** ennyumba ya
ggoloofa **house of more than one storey** mu
ggoloofa **upstairs**, eg. *Asula mu ggoloofa.* (*'He
lives upstairs.'*)

eggombolola *n9* **sub-county** (N29). *See*
oweggombolola ggombolola *n1* **hearth with
perpetual fire** (*kept burning during the lifetime of
the Kabaka*)

ggomesi *n9* **traditional dress of Baganda women**
(= busuuti). *From the name of a Goanese tailor
who designed this garment for Gayaza High School
in 1905.*

eggomo *n5* (*pl.* amagomo) **stomach of non-
ruminant animal** (*eg. pig; inflated used as a
fishing float*)

eggongolo *n5* (*pl.* amagongolo) **millipede**

eggonjebwa *n5* (*no pl.*) **humility, meekness**
ow'eggonjebwa *n1* **humble person**

eggono *n5* (*no pl.*) **gentleness, mildness** n'eggono
clearly and pleasantly (*of talking or singing*)
-yimba n'eggono **sing in a traditional Kiganda
way** (*clearly and pleasantly*)

eggonvu *See* -gonvu

eggoolo *n9* **goal**

¹egguggwe *n5* (*pl.* amawuggwe) **lung**

¹eggugu *n5* **type of sedge** (*found in swamps; used
for making mats and extracting salt*) Pycreus
nitidus

²eggugu *n5* (*pl.* amagugu) **large load/bundle**

¹-gguka *vt* (-gguse) -gguka ku/mu **arrive at** (*after
passing through somewhere*), **get to eventually**, eg.
Yita awo ogguke mu luguudo. (*'Go that way and
eventually you will get to the road.'*)

²-gguka *vi* (-gguse) **come open** (*eg. of a door*)

-ggula *vt* (-ggudde) **open.** *Usually in enclitic form*

-ggulawo (-gguddewo).

ggulama *n9* **grammar**

-ggule *adj* (enzigule *n9*) **open**

eggulo *n5* (*no pl.*) **afternoon** olw'eggulo **in the
afternoon**, eg. *Ssande olw'eggulo* (*'Sunday
afternoon'*)

eggulu *n5* (*no pl.*) **sky, heaven, paradise** Ggulu *n1*
Kiganda deity (*lubaale*), **god of the sky** eggulu
-bwatuka **clap** (*of thunder*) eggulu -duduma
rumble (*of thunder*) eggulu -gwa **strike** (*of
lightning*) eggulu -myansa **flash** (*of lightning*)

eggulumu *n5* (*pl.* amagulumu) **big mound of earth**

eggumba *n5* (*pl.* amagumba) **bone**

eggume *n5* (*no pl.*) **gloominess, reserved in
character** (*of a person*) -a eggume *adj* **gloomy**
ow'eggume *n1* **gloomy person, person of sour
disposition, reserved person**

-ggumira *vi* (-ggumidde) **be packed tightly**

-ggumivu *adj* (enzigumivu *n9*) **tightly packed**

-ggumiza *vt* (-ggumizza) **pack tightly, emphasise.**
Saying: 'Emiti emito gye giggumiza ekibira. (*'It is
the young trees that determine the future of the
forest.', meaning 'It is the young that will keep
tradition alive.'*) -ggumiza ensonga **stress a point**
-ggumiza essubi **pack thatch tightly** (*during
thatching*) -ggumiza ettaka **compact soil**
omutuba -ggumiza **be ready** (*for harvesting, of a
barkcloth tree; shown by having a full flush of
young leaves*)

eggumu *See* -gumu

¹-ggunda *vt* (-ggunze) **hurl down** (*eg. heavy load*)

²-eggunda *vi* **have a heavy fall** (*of oneself*), **be
dashed down**

egguniya *n9* **sack, gunny bag**

eggunju *n9* **marsh mongoose, large grey
mongoose**

-ggwa *vi* (-wedde) **be(come) finished**, eg. *Omulimu
guwedde.* (*'The job is finished.'*), **be(come)
exhausted, be ended** -ggwaako (-weddeko)
be(come) finished (*on something*), eg. *Omuyembe
guweddeko ebibala.* (*'The mango tree has finished
fruiting.'*), **expire** (*of time*) essente -ggwaako **be
broke** (*lacking money*), eg. *Essente zimpweddeko.*
(*'I am broke.'*) enkuba -ggwaako **end** (*of rain*)
-ggwaamu **be(come) finished** (*within something*),
eg. *Amazzi gajja kuggwaamu mu ttanka.* (*'The
water will get finished in the tank.'*) -ggwaamu
amaanyi **feel deflated, loose heart** -ggwaamu
amaanyi ag'ekisajja **lose sexual potency** (*of a man*)
-ggwaamu endasi **lose strength** -ggwaamu
essuubi **lose hope, despair** -ggwaawo **be(come)
finished** (*at a place*), **be(come) used up**, eg.
Sukaali aweddewo. (*'The sugar is used up.'*). *See*
obutaggwaawo -ggwaawo enkaayana **resolve a
dispute** -ggwaayo **be(come) finished** (*over
there*), eg. *Sukaali aweddeyo mu sitoowa.* (*'The
sugar has become finished in the store.'*)

eggwaala *n5* (*pl.* amagwaala) **trombone, trumpet**

eggwaatiro *n5* (*pl.* amawaatiro) **peeling place for bananas**

eggwagi *n5* (*pl.* amawagi) **central post of round house**

eggwako *n5* (*no pl.*) **pregnancy** (*of an animal*)

¹**eggwanga** *n5* (*pl.* amawanga) **nation, tribe.** *Pronunciation*: eggwángà eggwanga erikuumibwa **protectorate** ggwanga mujje **type of drum beat** (*calls people to come and help*) -a eggwanga *adj* **national, tribal** Amawanga Amagatte **United Nations**

²**eggwanga** *n5* (*no pl.*) **vengeance.** *Pronunciation*: eggwángá obuko bw'eggwanga **shaking disease** -woolera eggwanga **take vengeance**

eggwanika *n5* (*pl.* amawanika) **store, cupboard, safe, treasury**

eggwanvu *See* -wanvu

ggwe *pro* **you** si.

-ggweera *vt* (-ggweeredde) **take all** (*referring to capacity*), *eg.* Amazzi gaggweera mu sseffuliya. (*'The pan took all the water.'*) **-ggweeramu** (-gweereddemu) **be contained within, fit in,** *eg.* Bonna bajja kuggweeramu mu takisi. (*'They will all fit into the taxi.'*)

-ggweerera *vi* (-ggweeredde) **become used up** (*eg. of a tablet of soap*), **become worn down** (*eg. of a pencil*), **become exhausted**

-ggweereza *vt* (-ggweerezza) **use up** (*pencil, tyre, etc.*), **wear out**

eggwiiso *n5* (*no. pl.*) **good luck, good fortune**

eggwolu *n5* (*pl.* amawolu) **lump of left-over cooked matooke;** *in pl.* **left-over food kept for eating later.** *See* -vumbika

eggwolezo *n5* (*pl.* amawolezo) **place of justice, courtroom, tribunal**

eggwoolezo *n5* (*pl.* amawoolezo) **place were dues are collected, customshouse**

eggwoowo *n5* (*no pl.*) **pleasant smell of food** (*especially of sauce 'enva'*)

¹**-ggya** *adj* (eppya *n5*, amapya *n6*, empya *n9*) **new** -ggyaamu **fairly new**

²**eggya** *n5* (*pl.* amagya) **adze**

³**-ggya** *vi* (-yidde) **be ready** (*of cooked food*), **be fermented** (*of beer*) -ggya (omuliro) **be burnt,** *eg.* Njidde. (*'I am burnt.'*) Emmere eyidde. **Food is ready.**

⁴**-ggya** *vt* (-ggye) **take away, take from,** *eg.* Yaggya ekikopo mu kabada. (*'She took a cup from the cupboard.'*), **remove** -ggya mu bufuzi **depose** **-ggyako** (-ggyeeko) **take off,** *eg.* Ggyako ebintu ku mmeeza. (*'Take the things off the table.'*), **deduct, detach, subtract**. *See* okuggyako -ggyako amagalagamba **remove scales** -ggyako amasannyalaze **switch off electricity** -ggyako eddogo **remove an evil spell** -ggyako ku mabeere **wean** -ggyako olububi **skim off scum/cream** **-ggyamu remove** (*from within*), *eg.* Nja kukiggyamu mu kabada. (*'I will remove it*

from the cupboard.'*), **take out/from, extract, empty out, unpack, evacuate** -ggyamu kopi **copy** -ggyamu olubuto **have an abortion** -ggyamu omukka mu mupiira **deflate a tyre** **-ggyawo remove,** *eg.* Ggyawo essowaani. (*'Take the plates away.'*), **clear away, revoke, repeal, abolish** -ggyawo enkaayana **resolve a dispute** -ggyawo etteeka **repeal a law** **-ggyayo take away** (*from over there*), **remove** (*from over there*), **withdraw,** *eg.* Ŋŋenda kuggyayo ssente mu bbanka. (*'I am going to withdraw money from the bank.'*), **retract**

⁵**-eeggyako** (*also* -eeggya ku) *vt* **distance oneself from, get rid of, give up** (*an addiction or bad habit*), *eg.* Yasalawo okweggya ku kunywa ssigala. (*'He decided to give up smoking.'*)

¹**eggye** *n5* (*pl.* amagye) **army** -a amagye *adj* **military**

²**-ggye** *v. See* -ggya

-gidde *See* -gira

egigye *pos* **hers, his**

egigyo *pos* **yours** si.

giigino here they are

giigiri there they are

giigyo there they are

-eegimba *vi* **try hard, become an epidemic** (*of a disease*)

¹**-gimu** *adj* (eggimu *n9*) **fertile** (*of land*), **flourishing** (*of plants*), **luxuriant** (*of vegetation*)

²**egimu** *det/pro* **some**

-gimuka *vi* (-gimuse) **be fertile** (*of land*), **flourish** (*of plants*)

-gimusa *vt* (-gimusizza) **make fertile** (*land*),

NOTES ON
g

-g. Unless the **g** is doubled, verbs starting **g** have 1st person singulars starting either **ng** (non-nasal verbs) or **ŋŋ** (nasal verbs) (**N5**), *eg.* (1) ngaba ('I give out'), from -gaba; (2) ŋŋamba ('I say'), from -gamba. 1st person singulars are not shown if they start **ng**.

aga-. This is the plural prefix (in *n22*) of nouns having singulars (in *n20*) starting **ogu**.

-gg. Verbs starting **gg** have 1st person singulars starting **nzig**, *eg.* nzigya ('I take away'), from -ggya.

egg-. Many (not all) nouns in *n5* starting **egg** have plurals (in *n6*) starting **amag**, *eg.* the plural of **eggi** is **amagi**.

ogu-. Nouns in *n20* starting **ogu** have plurals (in *n22*) starting **aga**, *eg.* the plural of **ogutaba** is **agataba**.

gy and **ggy** can be pronounced similarly to **j**. Check for unknown words under **j** as well as **g**.

NOUNS IN *n9*. Most nouns in *n9* have identically spelt plurals (in *n10*).

fertilise

ginale *n9* ginnery

gindi *interr pro* **what's-it-called?** (*referring to a place whose name is not remembered*)

[1]**-ginga** *vt* (-ginze, ŋŋinga) **make up** (*using one's imagination*), **fake**

[2]**-eeginga** *vi* **play the clown, make funny faces**

-gingirira (*also* -gingaginga) *vt* (-gingiridde, ŋŋingirira) **copy roughly, forge, counterfeit, fake** -gingirira omukono **forge a signature** -gingirira ssente **forge money**

-gingirire (*also* -gingeginge) *adj* **improvised, made up, forged, counterfeit, fake, false**

-eeginika *vi* (-eeginise) **be reluctant to work** (*holding the work demeaning*)

ginnaagwo *n4* **its companions**

ginnaagyo *n4* **their companions**

ginnaayo *n9* **its companion**

ginnaazo *n9* **its companions**

gino *dem* **these**

-ginya *vt* (-ginyizza, nginya) **give excessive freedom to** (*eg. a child*), **indulge**

[1]**-gira** *v* (-gidde) **do, act.** '-gira' *followed by the narrative tense means* **now and then** *or* **occasionally** (N16), *eg. Agira n'atufumbira emmere.*') ('*Now and then he cooks for us.*'). *The suffix* -nga *is added for past and future tenses* (N18), *eg. Yagiranga n'ajja okutulabako.* ('*He used to come and see us occasionally.*'). *The modified stem form* -gidde *is always followed by a verb in the subjunctive* (N17) *and means* **since** (*in the sense of enabling something to be done*) *or* **now that**, *eg. Omusawo agidde ajje, ajja kuwa Musoke eddagala.* ('*Now that the doctor has come, he will give Musoke medicine.*'). gira (*pl.* mugire) *followed by the subjunctive conveys the idea of needing to get on with something* (N17), *eg. Gira tugende.* ('*Come on, let's go.*'). -gira ekisa **show kindness** -gira ekyejo **spoil** (*eg. a child*)

[2]**-eegiragira** *vi* **pretend not to like something** (*that one actually like*) (= -eekozaakoza)

giri *dem* **those**

giriisi *n1* **grease**

Girimaani (*also* Bugirimaani) *n9* **Germany**

[1]**ago** *dem* **those**

[2]**go** *pos* **your** *si.*

[3]**go** *pro* **they, them.** *Can be a suffix* -go (N10-12), *eg. nago* ('*and them*').

-goba *v* (-gobye) (1) *vi* **arrive** (*of a means of transport*), *eg. Ebbaasi egobye.* ('*The bus has arrived.*'); (2) *vi* **win** (*in sports*), *eg. Bagobye eggoolo bbiri ku emu.* ('*They won two goals to one.*'); (3) *vt* **chase, drive away, divorce, steer** (*a vehicle*), **repel, dismiss, send away/back, oust, rout, sack** (*a worker*), **expel, bar, evict, beat** (*in sports*) -goba emmotoka **drive a car** -goba ensonga **argue logically** -goba ettale **land ashore** -goba ku mulimu **fire from a job** -goba omuzimu **exorcise a spirit**

-gobamu (-gobyemu) **drive out, depose**

-gobera *vt* (-gobedde) **chase/drive into,** *etc.*

-goberera *vt* (-goberedde) **follow, come after** -goberera empisa **conform** (*culturally*)

-gobolola *vi* (-gobolodde) **make a profit,** *eg. Mu kutunda obutunda okuva mu nnimiro ye yagobolola nnyo.* ('*He profited a lot from selling passion fruits from his garden.*')

-eegoga *vi* (-eegoze) **try to vomit, retch**

-gogola *vt* (-gogodde) **clear out** (*eg. a drain*), **dredge** -gogola omumiro (*also* -gogola obulago) **clear the throat**

gogolo *n1* **game** (*played especially by boys, involves sliding down a steep slope on a banana stem* '*omugogo*')

-gogombola *vt* (-gogombodde) **split and detach** (*layers of a banana trunk*) -gogombola omugogo **chop up banana trunk**

-golokofu *adj* **straight**

-golokoka *vi* (-golokose) **wake up and get up** (*of oneself*), **stand up** (*in church, to sing a hymn or say the creed*)

-golokosa *vt* (-golokosezza) **wake up** (*someone*), **rouse**

[1]**-golola** *vt* (-golodde) **stretch out, straighten** -golola ekisobyo **correct a mistake** -golola engoye **iron/press clothes** -golola ensonga **sort out affairs** -golola omufu **lay out a dead body** -golola omukono **raise one's hand**

[2]**-eegolola** *vr* **stretch oneself**

-golongotana *vi* (-golongotanye) **talk deliriously**

-goma *vi* (-gomye) **run about wildly, rampage**

[1]**Gomba** *n1* **county of Buganda**

[2]**-gomba** *vt* (-gombye, ŋŋomba) **intertwine, interweave,** *eg. Jjo nnali ŋŋomba mmuli.* ('*Yesterday I was interweaving reeds.*')

[3]**-eegomba** *vt* **want, desire, covet, crave, lust after**

-eegombebwa *vi* (-eegombeddwa) **be desired, be coveted, be admired,** *eg. Endabika ya Saala yeegombebwa buli omulaba.* ('*Everyone who sees Sarah admires her beauty.*')

-gombagana *vi* (-gombaganye, ŋŋombagana) **become intertwined**

-gombaganya *vt* (-gombaganyizza, ŋŋombaganya) **intertwine** -gombaganya emikono **fold one's arms**

-gombera *vt* (-gombedde, ŋŋombera) **weave for/in,** *etc.* -gombera emmuli **interweave reeds**

-eegombesa *vt* (-eegombesezza) **cause to want/desire**

-gombeza *vt* (-gombezza, ŋŋombeza) **(cause to) interweave,** *eg. Twagenda mu lubiri okugombeza emmuli.* ('*We went to the palace to interweave reeds.*'), **entangle** -gombeza amagulu **sit cross-legged on the ground, sit in yoga position** -gombeza emikono **fold one's arms** -gombeza emmuli **interweave reeds** -gombeza enga interweave cane -gombeza ensonga twist the truth

-gombolola vt (-gombolodde, ŋŋombolola) disentangle

-gonda vt (-gonze, ŋŋonda) be(come) soft, be(come) tender, be(come) pliable, be(come) submissive, become weak (of a sick person)

-gondera vt (-gondedde, ŋŋondera) be submissive towards, obey, eg. Yamugondera. ('He obeyed her.') (= -wulira)

-gongobala vi (-gongobadde, ŋŋongobala) lose shape (of something solid through damage), be(come) deformed, be(come) dented

-gongobavu adj (eŋŋongobavu n9) out-of-shape, deformed, dented

-gongobaza vt (-gongobazizza, ŋŋongobaza) cause deformity, deform, dent

gonja n1 type of banana (used for roasting and frying) (single fruit omugonja n3)

-gonjoola vt (-gonjodde, ŋŋonjoola) put in good order -gonjoola ensonga sort out affairs

-gonvu adj (eggonvu n5, eŋŋonvu n9) soft, tender (of meat), pliable, flexible, submissive, obedient, weak (from illness)

[1]-gonza vt (-gonzezza, ŋŋonza) soften, tenderise, make flexible, make weak, eg. Obulwadde bumugonzezza. ('The illness has weakened her.')

[2]-eegonza vr make oneself submissive

goofu n9 golf

-gooma vi (-goomye) lose shape, be deformed, be warped, be bent

-goomu adj (eŋŋoomu n9) out-of-shape, deformed, warped, bent

-goomya vt (-goomezza, ŋŋoomya) make out-of-shape, (cause to) deform, warp, bend

goonya n9 crocodile

-gootaana (also -gozoobana) vi (-gootaanye) be in bad condition (of affairs), be messed up, go badly

-gootaanya vt (-gootaanyizza) put in a bad condition, mess up (affairs)

-gotta vt (-gosse) pound (with small pestle)

-gotteka vt (-gottese) put together carelessly, eg. Engoye zonna yazigottese wamu, enjoze n'ezitali njoze. ('He carelessly put together the washed and unwashed clothes.')

-goya vt (-goye) mix/mash (something thick), stir together -goya akalo mash millet meal -goya akawunga mash maize meal

-gozoobana (also -gootana) vi (-gozoobanye) go badly (of affairs, eg. confused and bogged down), experience trouble (in affairs)

-guba vi (-gubye) be(come) permanently discoloured, be(come) stained

-gubaasira vi (-gubaasidde) be dirty/filthy (of parts of clothing, eg. cuffs), eg. Bwe yamala okulima empale ye yali egubaasidde. ('After digging, the bottoms of his trousers were dirty.'), be soiled

-gubu adj permanently discoloured/stained

-gubya vt (-gubizza) permanently discolour, stain

-gudde See -gwa

gudu n1 type of large edible mushroom (found in grassland and banana gardens, rare)

-gugumuka vi (-gugumuse) make off in a panic, stampede

-gugumula vt (-gugumudde) (cause to) panic, (make) stampede

-eegugunga vi (-eegugunze) engage in disturbances, riot

ogugwe pos hers, his

ogugwo pos yours si.

gujwa na guno gujwa up to now

[1]-gula vit (-guze) buy, shop (for), cost, be worth (financially). See okugula

[2]-(y)agula See -yagula

gulaamu n9 gram

gulamufooni n9 gramophone

guli dem that

-gulika vi (-gulise) be affordable

-gulira vt (-gulidde) buy for

-gulirira vt (-guliridde) bribe

-guluba vi (-gulubye) stamp/run heavily about

gulugulu adv very firmly, very tightly

-gulukira vi (-gulukidde) be top-heavy

-gulumba vi (-gulumbye) rumble (of the stomach)

-gulumira vi (-gulumidde) be very high (of a termite mound, hill, etc.), be lofty

-gulumivu adj very high (of a termite mound, hill, etc.), lofty

[1]-gulumiza vt (-gulumizza) make high (eg. a building), exact, glorify

[2]-eegulumiza vr exalt oneself, act important

-guma vi (-gumye) be strong, be durable -guma mu mwoyo be strong in spirit

[1]-gumba adj infertile/barren (of a woman)

[2]-gumba vi (-gumbye) gather in a group, congregate, assemble

-gumiikiriza vit (-gumiikirizza) be patient (with), be long-suffering, endure, tolerate, eg. Yagumiikiriza empisa zaabwe embi. ('He tolerated their bad manners.')

-gumira vt (-gumidde) put up with, endure -gumira ebizibu put up with difficulties -gumira enjala keep going despite hunger -gumira obulumi endure pain

-gumiza vt (-gumizza) strengthen in/for

[1]-gumu adj (eggumu n5, eŋŋumu n9) strong, solid, firm, durable, courageous, daring, steadfast

[2]gumu num one

[1]-gumya vt (-gumizza, ŋŋumya) make firm, strengthen -gumya omwoyo hearten

[2]-eegumya vr take courage

gundi pro (pl. ba gundi) what's-(s)he-called? (used when someone's name is not remembered), so-and-so

-gunjufu adj cultured, civilised, well-mannered

-gunjuka vi (-gunjuse, ŋŋunjuka) be(come)

cultured, be(come) civilised

-gunjula *vt* (-gunjudde, ŋŋunjula) **civilise, educate**

gunnaagwo *n3* its companion

gunnaagyo *n3* their companion

guno *dem* this

Agusito August

guuguli there it is

guuguno here it is

guugwo there it is

-guumaala *vi* (-guumadde) **be fooled, be deceived, be tricked**

-guumaaza *vt* (-guumaazizza) **fool, deceive, trick**

-guumaazibwa *vi* (-guumaaziddwa) **be deceived**

-eeguya *vit* (-eeguyizza) **ingratiate oneself (with), be obsequious (to)**, *eg. Maria yafumbirwa Musoke nga amweguyaako ssente. ('Maria married Musoke for his money.'). Saying: 'Teyeeguya bagagga.' ('He is not obsequious to the rich.')*

oguyanja *n20* (*pl.* agayanja) **ocean**

-guza *vt* (-guzizza) **sell to**

(o)gw' *abbrev of* (o)gwa; gwe

[1]**(o)gwa** *pre* of, *eg. omuti gwa Musoke ('tree of Musoke'). Can be a prefix* **(o)gwa-** (N11.4), *eg. gwange ('mine'). 'ogwa' appears in ordinal numerals (N7.1), eg. omuti ogw'okubiri ('second tree'). Elision is sometimes seen, eg.omuti ogwokubiri ('second tree').*

[2]**-gwa** *vi* (-gudde) **fall**, *eg. Yagwa ku madaala. ('She fell down the stairs.')*, **topple over, collapse.** *Pronunciation: The 'a' in the enclitic forms (-gwako, etc.) is pronounced long.* **-gwa bugazi** (*also* -gwako bugazi) **fall flat on one's back** -gwa bugwi **be unexpected, arrive unannounced**, *eg. Abagenyi baagudde bugwi. ('Visitors arrived unannounced.')* -gwa ebibuuzo **fail an examination** -gwa eddalu **go mad** -gwa emmeeme **have a prolapse of the rectum** -gwa ensimbu **have an epileptic fit** -gwa ku bbanja **fall into debt** -gwa ku leenya (*also* -gwako leenya) **fall into big trouble** -gwa ku mutawaana **get into trouble** -gwa maliri **fall together** (*as two interlocked wrestlers*), **tie** (*in sports*) -gwa mu bbugo **bribe to keep silent** -gwa mu bintu **have good fortune** -gwa mu buzibu **fall into difficulties** -gwa mu ddubi **fall into deep water, get into serious trouble** -gwa mu katego **fall into a trap** -gwa mu kifuba **embrace affectionately, hug** -gwa olubege **be biased** eggulu -gwa **strike** (*of lightning*) enjuba -gwa **set** (*of the sun*)

-gwako (-guddeko) **fall on**, *eg. Aguddeko omutawaana bamugobye ku mulimu. ('She has fallen on troubled times because she was fired from her job.')* **-gwamu fall into**, *eg. Omwana yagudde mu kidiba. ('The child fell into the pond.')* -gwamu ekidumusi **have diarrhoea** -gwamu ensisi **go into shock** **-gwawo fall** (*there*), *eg. Waagwawo omutawaana. ('There was a problem.')* **-gwayo fall** (*over there*)

(o)gwabwe *pos* their(s) (N11.4)

(o)gwaffe *pos* our(s) (N11.4)

-gwagwa (*also* -gwenyufu) *adj* **depraved, immoral, lewd**

-gwagwawala (*also* -gwenyuka) *vi* (-gwagwadde) **be(come) depraved, be(come) immoral/indecent**

-gwagwawaza (*also* -gwenyula) *vt* (-gwagwawazizza) **deprave, make immoral**

gwaki? *interr* **what for?**

(o)gwammwe *pos* your(s) *pl.* (N11.4)

-gwana (*also* -saana) *vi* (-gwanye) **be suitable**

(o)gwange *pos* my, mine. (N11.4)

-gwanira (*also* -saanira) *vt* (-gwanidde) **be suitable for**

-gwanyiza (*also* -saanyiza) *vt* (-gwanyizza) **judge worthy of, consider suitable for**

[1]**gwe** *pos* her/his (N11.4), *eg. omuti gwe ('her tree')*

[2]**gwe** *pre* of (= gw'e) (N11.1)

[3]**gwe** *pro* (*relative pronoun and pronoun of emphasis N10.1*) **it, who, whom, which, that.** *Can be equivalent to short phrases of emphasis, eg. Omuti guno gwe njagala okutema. ('It is this tree that I want to cut.'). Can be a prefix* **gwe-** (N11.6), *eg. omuti gwennyini ('the tree itself').*

-gwenyufu See -gwagwa

-gwenyuka (-gwenyuse) See -gwagwawala

-gwenyula (-gwenyudde) See -gwagwawaza

[1]**-gwira** *adj* **foreign, alien** emmere engwira **foreign food** empisa engwira **alien customs**

[2]**-gwira** *vt* (-gwiridde) **fall on/in**, *etc., eg. Omuti gwagwiridde ennyumba. ('A tree fell on the house.'). See engwira*

-gwirana *vi* (-gwiranye) **fall over oneself** -gwirana na/ne **contend with**

-gwisa *vt* (-gwisizza) **make fall**

[1]**ogwo** *dem* that

[2]**gwo** *pos* your *si.*

[3]**gwo** *pro* it. *Can be a suffix* **-gwo** (N10-12), *eg. nagwo ('with it').*

[4]**ogwo-** See ogwa ('of')

(e)gy' *abbrev of* (e)gya; gye

[1]**(e)gya** *pre* of, *eg. emiti gya Musoke ('trees of Musoke'). Can be prefix* **(e)gya-** (N11.4), *eg. gyange ('mine').*

[2]**-gya** *vi* (-gyidde) **fit** (*into a space*), *eg. Abantu abo bonna tebagya mu kisenge ekyo. ('All those people cannot fit into that room.')*, **accommodate.** *Pronunciation: The 'a' in the enclitic forms (-gyamu, etc.) is pronounced long.* **-gyamu** (-gyiddemu) **fit** (*within a space*), *eg. Engoye zigyamu mu ssanduuko. ('The clothes fit into the case.')* **-gyawo fit** (*in a space*), *eg. Emmeeza tegyawo wano. ('The table does not fit here.')* **-gyayo fit in** (*a space over there*), *eg. Ebintu bijja kugyayo mu kisenge ekyo. ('The things will fit into that room.')*

(e)gyabwe *pos* their(s) (N11.4)

(e)gyaffe *pos* our(s) (N11.4)

gyaki? *interr* **what for?** (N13)

(e)gyammwe *pos* **your(s)** *pl.* (N11.4)

(e)gyange *pos* **my, mine.** (N11.4)

[1]**gye** *equivalent to various parts of speech in English (conjunction, relative pronoun, etc.)* (N10.1, N10.2): (1) **which,that,** *eg. Emiti gino gye njagala okutema. ('It is these trees which I want to cut.');* (2) **(over there) where,** *eg. Ente eri eyo embuzi gy'eri. ('The cow is over there where the goat is.');* (3) *Can be equivalent to short adverbial phrases of emphasis, eg. Ekitabo gye kiri mu nnyumba? Yee, gye kiri. ('Is the book in the house? Yes, it is there.'). Can be a prefix* **gye-** (N11.6), *eg. emiti gyennyini ('the trees themselves')* gye bujja **when the time comes, in the future, later** Gye ndi. *(response to a greeting)* **I'm OK.** (N28) gy'oli **on your part, for you,** *eg. Ekyo kinaaba kirungi gy'oli? ('Will that be good for you?')* Gy'oli? **greeting How are you?**

[2]**gye** *pos* **her/his** (N10.1), *eg. emiti gye ('her trees')*

[3]**gye** *pre* **of** (= gy'e) (N11.1)

gyebale (emirimu) thank you *(for your work)*

-gyidde *See* -gya

-gyisaamu *vt* (-gyisizzaamu) **fit in,** *eg. Nnakigyisaamu mu kisenge. ('I fitted it in the room.')*

[1]**egyo** *dem* **those**

[2]**gyo** *pos* **your** *si.*

[3]**gyo** *pro* **they, them.** *Can be a suffix* **-gyo** (N10-12), *eg. nagyo ('and them').*

J,j

Jaaka *n1* **Jack** *(the name)*

-jabiriza *vi* (-jabirizza) **intrude into a conversation** *(in an uninformed way)*

-jabula *vi* (-jabudde) **do in a slapdash way,** *eg. Yajabula omuddo ne gumera mangu. ('He did not weed properly so the weeds have quickly grown again.'),* **beat about the bush**

-eejaga *vi* (-eejaze) **bustle about, busy oneself**

-jagalala *vi* (-jagaladde) **be in a state of unrest** *(of a crowd),* **be riotous.** *Saying: 'Ojagalala nga ebyoya by'ekivu.' ('You are unsettled like the wings of a tsetse fly.')*

-jaganya *vi* (-jaganyizza) **rejoice, make merry, be jubilant**

-jagujagu *adj* **quick to act, adroit**

-jaguza *vi* (-jaguzizza) **celebrate, rejoice**

-eejalabya *vr* (-eejalabizza) **give oneself a treat, enjoy oneself,** *eg. Musoke agenda ku bbiiki okwejalabyamu. ('Musoke goes to the beach to enjoy himself.')*

-jama *adj* **filthy, dirty**

-jamawala *vi* (-jamawadde) **become filthy/dirty**

-jamawaza *vt* (-jamawazizza) **make filthy/dirty**

jambula *n1* **java plum** *(tree; fruit) Syzygium cumini*

-janjaala *vi* (-janjadde) **spread all over, become commonplace**

Janwali January

-jeeja (-yeeze) *See* -yeeya

-jeema *vi* (-jeemye) **rebel, revolt**

-jeemera *vt* (-jeemedde) **rebel against**

-jeemu *adj* **rebellious**

-jeemulukuka *vi* (-jeemulukuse) **end a rebellion**

-jegeja *vi* (-jegeze) **creak**

-jegera *vi* (-jegedde) **talk incessantly, go on and on,** *eg. Omwana ajegera bujegezi – maama, maama, maama. ('The child goes on and on – mummy, mummy, mummy.').* *See* chatter

-jegeza *vt* (-jegezezza) **cause to creak**

jenero *n1* (*pl.* ba jenero) **general** *(in army)*

-jerega (-jereze) *vt* **despise, deride, ridicule, jeer at**

Jesika *n1* **Jessica**

jiija *n1* **type of grass with narrow leaves** *(planted in courtyards) Cynodon transvaalensis*

[1]**-jja** *v* (1) (-zze, nzija) *vi* **come,** *eg. Abantu bazze. ('The people have come.'),* **arrive, appear;** (2) *aux v (indicating future tense and followed by inf* N19*)* (-zze, nja) **will** (N19), *eg. Bajja kugenda mangu. ('They will go soon.').* **-jjako** (-zzeeko) **come (onto), form on** gye bujja **when the time comes, the future, later** -jjako olwatika **be(come) cracked** *(eg. of glass)* **-jjamu come** *(within)* -jjamu amabala **be(come) stained** **-jjawo come** *(to a place)*

[2]**-jja** *Misspelling of* -ggya *('remove')*

jjaaga *n9* **jug, jar**

jjaamu *n1* (*no pl.*) **jam** jjaamu w'emmotoka **traffic jam**

jjajja *n1* (*pl.* ba jjajja) **grandparent, ancestor** jjajja omukazi **grandmother** jjajja omusajja **grandfather** **jjajja-** **grandparent of** (N12), *eg. jjajjange ('my grandparent').* *See Table 10 for the various forms.*

ejjamba *n9* **assistance**

ejjambiya *n5* (*pl.* ejjambiya *n10, or* amajambiya *n6*) **machete, panga**

ejjanga *n5* (*no pl.*) **conjunctivitis**

jjangu *interj* **come** *(as a request or command).* *Derivation: 'Jja mangu.' ('Come quickly.').* Jjangu wano. **Come here.**

[1]**-jjanjaba** *vt* (-jjanjabye) **nurse, treat** *(a patient)*

[2]**-ejjanjaba** *vr* **nurse/treat oneself**

ejjanjabiro *n5* (*pl.* amajanjabiro) **treatment centre** *(where medical help is available)* ejjanjabiro ly'ebigenge **leprosarium**

ejjanzi *n5* (*pl.* amayanzi) **grasshopper**

ejjeeke *n9* **jack** *(for lifting)*

-ejjeerera *vi* (-ejjeeredde) **be exonerated** -ejjeerera omusango **be acquitted** *(of a charge)*

-ejjeereza *vt* (-ejjeerezza) **exonerate, acquit**

jjegejege *n10* **coins**

jjegeju *n1* **insect that bores into barkcloth trees**

jjejjerebu -kuba jjejjerebu **be elated and merry,**

eg. Yakuba jjejjerebu bwe yawulira nga ttiimu ye ewangudde. ('He was elated to hear his team had won.')

ejjembe *n5 (pl.* amayembe) **horn** *(of an animal)*, **fetish, spirit of a fetish**

ejjengo *n5 (pl.* amayengo) **wave;** *in pl.* **wavelength** *(eg. of a broadcast)*

ejjenje *n5 (pl.* amayenje) **type of large cricket** *(eaten by young boys, common in groundnut fields)*

jjenjeero -a jjenjeero *adj* **commonplace, plentiful,** *eg. Ekintu kya jjenjeero. ('There's a lot of it about.')*

ejjerengesa *n5* **type of plant** *(used for basket-making, eg. for making the fish trap 'omugomo')* Acalphya bipartita

ejjiba *n5 (pl.* amayiba) **dove**

-jjidde *See* -jjira

ejjiini *n5 (pl.* amajiini) **genie**

ejjimbi *n5 (pl.* amajimbi) **short stinging hair** *(eg. on grass or caterpillar),* **bristle, spicule**

ejjindu *n5 (pl.* amajindu) **spur, spike**

ejjinja *n5 (pl.* amayinja) **stone, slate** *(for writing on)* ejjinja lya bbalaafu **piece of ice** ejjinja lya gulamufooni **gramophone record**

-jjira *vi* (-jjidde) **come by/for,** *etc., eg. Yajjira mu mmotoka. ('He came by car.')*

ejjiribwa *n9* **(carpenter's) vice**

ejjirikiti *See* eggirikiti

jjo *adv* **yesterday,** *(occasional meaning)* **tomorrow** jjo ku makya **yesterday morning** jjo olweggulo **yesterday afternoon** okwosa jjo **day before yesterday**

ejjoba *n5 (pl.* amajoba) **crest** *(on bird's head),* **tuft of hair** *(on otherwise shaven head)*

ejjobyo *n5* **herb used as spinach** *(also medicinal)* Cleome gynandra katamiira jjobyo **person addicted to alcoholic drink**

ejjoogo *n5 (no pl.)* **disrespect**

ejjoola *n9* **roll/bolt of cloth**

ejjovu *n5 (no pl.)* **foam, suds**

-jjukanya *vi* (-jjukanyizza) **remind one another**

-jjukira *vit* (-jjukidde) **remember, recall.** *See* okujjukira

¹-jjukiza *vt* (-jjukizza) **remind**

²-ejjukiza *vr* **remind oneself**

¹-jjula *vi* (-jjudde) **be(come) full, be filled up, have the capacity of, take** *(a certain volume), eg. Ebbinika eyo ejjula liita bbiri. ('That kettle takes two litres.').* Pronunciation: okujjùlà

²-jjula -jjula emmere **dish up food** *(take food parcel out of pot and remove covering leaves).* Pronunciation: okujjúlá

-jjulukuka *vi* (-jjulukuse) **be(come) undone**

¹-jjulula *vt* (-jjuludde) **undo, change location, shift,** *eg. Ekitongole ky'obulamu kyejjulula n'ekiva ku Buganda Road n'ekidda ku Jinja Road. ('The department of health has shifted from Buganda Road to Jinja Road.')*

²-ejjulula *v* **change location**

-jjumbira *vt* (-jjumbidde) **be zealous about, be keen on**

-jjumbiza *vt* (-jjumbizza) **inspire, motivate**

-jjumbizi *adj* **zealous, keen, eager**

-ejjusa *vit* (-ejjusizza) **feel remorse, regret, go to confession** *(RC)*

ejjute *n5 (pl.* amayute) **boil**

ejjuuga *n5 (pl.* amayuuga) **big cheek;** *in pl.* **jowls**

-ejjuukiriza *vi* (-ejjuukirizza) **regret**

jjuule *n1* **dilute drink** -a jjuule *adj* **dilute,** *eg. emicungwa gya jjuule ('dilute orange juice'),* **watered-down**

-jjuuliriza *vt* (-jjuulirizza) **fill to capacity, top up**

¹Jjuuni **June**

²ejjuuni *n5 (pl.* amayuuni) **type of root vegetable** *(young leaves 'ettimpa' also eaten). Two species:* (1) ejjuuni erigonda *(leaf stalk attached away from edge of leaf; grows in wet places)* **cocoyam, taro** Colocasia esculenta; (2) ejjuuni erikaluba *(leaf stalk attached on edge of leaf; grows on dry land)* **tannia** Xanthosoma violaceum. *The edible cormlets of 'ejjuuni erikaluba' are known as 'obukopa'.*

jjuuzi *adv* **recently, the other day**

-jjuvu *adj* (enzijuvu *n9)* **full**

-jjuza *vt* (-jjuzizza) **fill (up)**

-jogoolikana *vi* (-jogoolikanye) **make a lot of noise,** *eg. Endegeya zijogoolikana. ('Weaver birds make a lot of noise.'),* **speak angrily exchanging words**

-jolonga *vt* (-jolonze) **belittle, put down** *(someone verbally),* **treat with contempt,** *eg. Byonna bye nnayogedde yabadde abijolonga. ('Everything I said he treated with contempt.')*

-jonjobala *vi* (-jonjobadde) **be(come) soaked**

-jooga *vt* (-jooze) **bully, domineer, disrespect**

-joogebwa *vi* (-joogeddwa) **be bullied**

-joonyesa *vt* (-joonyesezza) **torment, torture**

-jugumira *vi* (-jugumidde) **tremble, shake**

-jugumiza *vt* (-jugumizza) **(cause to) tremble, shake**

Julaayi **July**

-julira *vt* (-julidde) (1) **appeal to** *(higher authority);* (2) **be a witness for,** *eg. Ojulidde Musoke. ('He stood as a witness for Musoke.').* See okujulira

-juliza *vt* (-julizza) **refer to, cite, quote**

-junga *vt* (-junze) **order in an unpleasant way**

-jungulula *vt* (-junguludde) **dilute, water down**

-jweteka *vt* (-jwetese) **make up** *(false stories, lies, etc.), eg. Omusajja oyo ajweteka ebigambo. ('That man makes up false stories.')* **-jwetekako** (-jweteseeko) **make up false stories about,** *eg. Yanjwetekako ebigambo, omusango ne gunsinga. ('He made up false stories about me and I was convicted.')*

-jwetekwa *vi* (-jwetekeddwa) **be made up** *(of stories, lies, etc. against someone)*

K,k

(a)k' *abbrev of* (a)ka; ke

¹-ka *adj* **strong** (*eg. of drink*), **too much of** (*in food or drink*) caayi omuka **strong tea** omwenge omuka **strong drink** sukaali omuka **too much sugar** (*in tea*)

²eka *adv* **at home, homewards**

³ka *detached prefix* (*in noun class n12*). *Used with certain nouns, espcially those of English origin, eg. ka banzi ('bun'). The plural is 'bu', eg. bu banzi ('buns').*

⁴ka *invariable v* (*followed by subjunctive N17*) (1) *Encourages an action, eg. Ka tugende. ('Come on, let's go.');* (2) *Indicates the intention of doing something soon, eg. Ka nkubuulire amazima. ('Let me tell you the truth.')*

⁵(a)ka *pre* **of**, *eg. akaana ka Musoke ('child of Musoke'). Can be a prefix* **(a)ka-** *(N11.4), eg. kange ('mine'). 'aka' is found in ordinal numerals (N7.1), eg. akaana ak'okubiri ('second baby'). Elision is sometimes seen, eg. akaana akookubiri ('second baby')*

⁶-(y)aka *v. See* -yaka

-kaaba *vi* (-kaabye) **cry, weep, call** (*of animals or birds*), **bleat, mow** (*as a cow*), **neigh** -kaaba amaziga **weep**

-kaabakaaba *vi* (-kaabyekaabye) **cry habitually**

-kaabira *vt* (-kaabidde) **cry for**

-kaabirira *vit* (-kaabiridde) **keep on crying** (*of a baby*). *An object pronoun indicates the person with the baby, eg. Akaana kamukaabirira. ('Her baby is crying a lot.').*

-kaabuga *vi* (-kaabudde) **carry out initial stages of building a house** -kaabugawo ekikaabugo **make a temporary shelter**, *eg. Yaakaabugawo ekikaabugo mwe yasula. ('He built a temporary structure to spend the night.')*

kaabulakata *adv* **nearly, almost**. *Used with subjunctive (N17), eg. Enkuba yatonnye nnyo era kaabulakata omugga gubimbe. ('It rained so heavily that the river almost overflowed.')*

kaabuuyi *n1* **meat under the hide**

kaabuyonjo *n12* **pit latrine, lavatory** kaabuyonjo k'olukale **public toilet**

(a)kaabwe *pos* **their(s)** (N11.4)

-kaabya *vt* (-kaabizza) **make cry**

kaada *n9* **card**

akaagaanya *n12* **small gap**

kaakali **there it is**

¹kaakano *adv* **now**

²kaakano **here it is**

kaakati *adv* **now**

kaaki? *interr* **what for?**

kaako **there it is**

¹akaala *n12* (*pl.* obwala) **small nail/claw**

²akaala *n12* (*pl.* obwala) **small stream**

-kaalaama *vi* (-kaalaamye) **be(come) very hot** (*of sunshine*), **become very angry**

-kaalaamuka *vi* (-kaalaamuse) **speak loudly in anger**

-kaalaamya *vt* (-kaalaamizza) **make angry** -kaalaamya eddoboozi **raise one's voice in anger**

-kaalakaala *vi* (-kaddekadde) **walk in a showy way, strut about** (*showing one's importance*)

¹kaama *n1* **wild yam**. *Two species*: (1) (*in wooded grassland*) *Dioscorea abyssinica*; (2) (*in riverine forest*) *Dioscorea odoratissima*. *Possible origin of word: from 'kaama' ('whisper'), meaning that the place it is found should be kept secret. Saying: 'Omunaku kaama yeerandiza yekka.' ('A poor man must support himself.')*

²akaama *n12* (*pl.* obwama) **whisper**

kaamuje *n1* **ground squirrel**. *Saying: 'Okajjadde nga kaamuje ku malaalo.' ('You are putting on airs.' – like a squirrel standing on a grave)*

kaamukuukulu *n1* (1) **laughing dove**; (2) **type of sedge** (*with white flowers*)

kaamulali *n1* **chilli pepper** (*plant; fruit*). *Two species: Capsicum annuum, C. frutescens*

Kaamuswaga *n1* *title* **chief of Kkooki County**

kaamwaka *n1* **millipede-like animal** (*appears at a particular time of the year*)

akaana *n12* (*pl.* obwana) **small child, baby** obwana bw'enkoko **chicks**

-eekaanya *vi* (-eekaanyizza) **express reluctance** (*to do something*), **be grumpy**, *eg. Nnamugambye agende ayoze engoye ne yeekaanya. ('He was grumpy when I told him to wash the clothes.')*, **be surly**

kaasa *n1* **type of large stinging ant** (*forms columns*), **one thousand shillings** (*slang*)

kaasi *n9* **cash**

kaasuzekatya *n1* **gift from bridegroom to bride's parents** (*on morning of wedding*)

akaato *n12* (*pl.* obwato) **small boat, canoe**

NOTES ON j

j can be pronounced similarly to **gy** or **ggy** Check for unknown words under **g** as well as **j**.

-j. Unless the **j** is doubled, verbs starting **j** have 1ˢᵗ person singulars starting **nj**, *eg.* **njeema** ('I rebel'), from **-jeema**.

ejj-. Many (not all) nouns in *n5* starting **ejj** have plurals (in *n6*) starting **amay**, *eg.* the plural of **ejjinja** is **amayinja**.

-jj. Verbs starting **jj** have 1ˢᵗ person singulars starting **nzij**, *eg.* **nzija** ('I come'), from **-jja**. The only exception is **-jja** when used an axilliary (**nja**) (N19).

NOUNS IN *n9*. Most nouns in *n9* have identically spelt plurals (in *n10*).

-kaatuufu *adj* **sour**

-kaatuuka *vi* (-kaatuuse) **become sour**

¹kaawa *n1* (*no pl.*) **coffee** (*ground; the drink*)

²-kaawa *vi* (-kaaye) **be bitter, be sour**

akaawunta *n9* **account** (*financial*)

-kaaya *vt* (-kaayizza) **make bitter**

-(y)akaayakana *See* -yakaayakana

-kaayana *vi* (-kaayanye) **disagree, argue, protest, dispute**

-kaayanira *vt* (-kaayanidde) **disagree about, argue about,** *eg. Baali bakaayanira ettaka.* (*'They are arguing about the land.'*), **protest about, dispute over**

-kaayirira *vi* (-kaayiridde) **be bitter**

-kaazakaaza *vt* (-kaazizzakaazizza) **drag away** (*an unwilling person*) **by force, frogmarch**

¹akaba *n12* **jawbone** (*of dead person*) akaba ka Kabaka **royal jawbone**

²-kaba *adj* **sexually immoral/depraved**

³-eekaba (-eekabye) *vi* **look serious and emotionally cold, look stern**

akabaafu *12* **small bath**

akabaala *n12* **small brownish-white mushroom** (*found where embaala termites occur*) (= nnamulondo). *Often added to sauce; always added to sauce served at traditional functions.*

akabaani *n12* **incense.** *See* obubaani

akababba *n12* (*no pl.*) **a certain type of annoying behavior** (*self-assertive and conceited*), **bumptiousness** ow'akababba *n1* **loud-mouthed person**

kabada *n9* **cupboard**

akabaga *n12* **party**

akabajjo *n12* **small chip/shaving, splinter**

kabaka *n1* (*pl.* ba kabaka) **king** Kabaka *title* **King of Buganda**

kabakanjagala *n1* **type of tree** *Aleurites moluccana.* Meaning: *'The Kabaka likes me.'*

¹akabala *n12* **small mark/stain**

²-kabala *vt* (-kabadde) **dig/cultivate deeply**

akabalabe *n12* **small pimple**

kabalagala *n1* **pancake**

-kabale *adj* **deeply dug** (*of land*)

kabalira *n12* **type of medium-sized fig tree** (*fruit edible*) *Ficus sur*

akabaluwa *n12* **note** (*written*)

kabambamaliba *n1* **plant used to make pegs** (*for stretching skins*)

kabandole (*also* bandole) *n9* **double-decker bus.** *Meaning: 'Let them see me.'* (Lunyoro)

akabanga *n12* (*no pl.*) **brief period of time, momentary opportunity**

-kabassana *vi* (-kabassanye) **work hard, struggle**

-kabawala *vi* (-kabawadde) **be(come) sexually depraved**

-kabawaza *vt* (-kabawazizza) **deprave** (*sexually*)

akabazi *n12* **calculator**

akabazzi *n12* **small axe**

kabbira *n1* (*pl.* ba kabbira) **expert thief**

akabbiro *n12* **second totem of a clan**

akabbo *n12* **small basket**

akabe *n12* **small jackal**

akabebenu *n12* **cartilage, grissle**

akabega *n12* **small back** -teekerawo akabega **assist** (*someone*) **in a court case, vouch for**

kabegi *n9* **cabbage**

Kabejja *n1* *title* (*formerly*) **second wife of the Kabaka** (*or major chief*)

akabengo *n12* **small grindstone, enlarged spleen**

akabenje *n12* **accident**

akabezo *n12* **piece of banana leaf** (*or a plate*) **used to serve cooked matooke from an omuwumbo**

akabi *n12* **danger, harm, peril.** *See* obubi -a akabi *adj* **dangerous**

akabigo *n12* **fish trap** (*made from reeds*)

akabiina *n12* **small society, sect** (*eg. of a religion*)

kabiite *n1* (*pl.* ba kabiite) **favourite boyfriend, favourite girlfriend, darling, sweetheart**

akabina *n12* (*no pl.*) **buttocks** (*of a woman*), **rump** akabina akakikinavu **protruding bottom** akabina akamuserebende **flat bottom** ow'akabina *n1* **woman with a protruding bottom**

akabindo *adv* **to the absolute limit** -tikka akabindo **be overloaded.** *Saying: 'Atisse akabindo k'emmere.'* (*'He has overloaded his plate.'*, ie. *stuffed himself with food*)

akabinja *n12* **small group, small flock** (*of birds*), **small swarm**

akabira *n12* **small forest**

akabiriiti *n12* **match**

kabisikuti *n12* (*pl.* bisikuti *n9*) **biscuit**

Kaboggoza *n1* **name given to Buyungo** (*first person to make barkcloth*). *Abbreviated from: 'Aboggoza ensaamu.'* (*'He is making the mallets bark.'* – from the sound of his hammering*)

akabombo *n12* **herbaceous climber** (*with small fleshy leaves; used to wipe off banana sap*) *Cyphostemma adenocaule*

kabona *n1* (*pl.* ba kabona) **priest**

akabondo *n12* (1) **faction** (*of a political party*); (2) **place on foot where jigger grows** (*when small*)

akabonero *n12* **sign, symbol, punctuation mark, signal, logo, seal, badge, label** akabonero k'obusuubuzi **trade mark**

kabootongo *n1* (*no pl.*) **syphilis** owa kabootongo *n1* **person with syphilis**

akabowabowa *n12* **type of creeping herb** *Ipomoea tenuirostris*

akabu *n12* **fruit fly** *Drosophila*

akabubi *n12* **thin layer, membrane**

akadiba *n12* **small pool**

kabugu *n1* (1) **type of climbing woody shrub** (*used for making fish traps*) *Paullinia pinnata*; (2) **rope used to hang oneself.** *Saying: 'Yeeyimbyemu ogwa kabugu.'* (*'He has committed suicide.'*, ie. *hanged himself with kabugu*)

akabuguumiriro *n12* exciting event

kabula *n1* type of banana (*used for making beer*) Kabula county of Buganda

kabuladda *n1* (*pl.* ba kabuladda) beloved person not seen for a long time

kabulamuliro *n1* prison, jail. *Meaning: 'Where there is no light.'*

akabuno *n12* (1) palate; (2) eaves (*of house*)

kabuuti *n9* heavy overcoat

akabuuza *n12* question mark

akabuzi *n12* small goat, kid

[1]**akabwa** *n12* small dog, puppy

[2]**akabwa** *n12* small wound

akabyangatano *n12* (*no pl.*) state of having too much to do

akacupa *n12* small bottle

akacwano *n12* terrible event, disaster

akadaala *n12* small step, platform (*eg. from which a speech is delivered*)

kadaali *n1* (1) shrubby plant with fern-like foliage (*stems placed in ventilators to stop entry of bats*) *Asparagus africanus*; (2) bridal headdress

akaddannyuma *adv/n12* (*no pl.*) going backwards, retrogression, backstitch

[1]**-kadde** *adj* old, worn-out

[2]**akadde** *n12* time, *eg. Sirina kadde. ('I am busy.' lit. 'I have no time.'),* time of day, brief moment

-kaddiwa *vi* (-kaddiye) become old. *See* okukaddiwa

-kaddiya *vt* (-kaddiyizza) make old

Kaddulubaale *n1* title (*formerly*) principal wife of the Kabaka (*or* major chief)

kadduwannema *n1* (*pl.* ba kadduwannema) cripple, lame person

akade *n12* small bell   akade k'oluggi doorbell

akadeeya *n12* thick cloth (*used as apron, for wrapping up bundle of cotton, etc.*)

akadinda *n12* hem, xylophone (*big type, with 22 keys*); *in pl.* corrugations (*on road*)

akadingidi *n12* one-stringed fiddle, tube fiddle

kadoma *n1* stingless bee

akadomola *n12* small jerrycan (*5 litre*)

akadondi *n12* small spool

[1]**akadongo** (*also* akadongo k'abaluulu, *or* akadongo ka Maria) *n12* thumb piano

[2]**akadongo** *n12* mud (*for building*)

kadongokamu *n1* guitarist (*one who sings while playing*)

akaduuka *n12* small shop

akaduukulu *n12* prison cell

akafansonyi *n12* sensitive plant (*leaves or leaflets fold up when touched*). *Meaning: 'It dies of shame.'. Species with this property include: Aeschynomene sensitiva, Biophytum and Mimosa pudica.*

kafecce *n1* (*no pl.*) blood pudding

(a)kaffe *pos* our(s) (N11.4)

kafiifi *n1* spoilt cotton (*on boll attacked by insect*)

[1]**kafuba** *n1* type of banana (*used for making matooke*)

[2]**akafuba** *n12* small chest; *in si.* tuberculosis

akafubo *n12* (*no pl.*) work session   mu kafubo in a work session, *eg. Tuli mu kafubo ka kulongoosa ennyumba. ('We are in a work session to clean the house.'),* privately

akafubutuko *adv* rapidly   -a kafubutuko *adj* rapid   embiro z'akafubutuko sprint, dash

kafugankande *n1* type of woody herb *Microglossa pyrifolia*

akafuko *n12* crowded place

kafulu *n1* confidence trickster

kafumbe *n1* small herb. *Two species:* (1) kafumbe omukazi *Galinsoga parviflora*; (2) kafumbe omusajja *Conyza bonariensis.*

akafumbo *n12* type of herb (*cotton-like hairs on seeds, traditionally used for stuffing cushions, etc.*) *Gomphocarpus physocarpus*

kafumitabagenda *n1* type of herb with fruits having many small bristles *Oxygonum sinuatum*. *Meaning: 'It pierces walkers.'*

kafumitattaka *n1* type of plant *Afromomum mildbraedii. Meaning: 'It pierces the ground.'*

akafumu *n12* small spear, nib

akafuufu *n12* dust

Kafuumuulampawu April. *Meaning: 'Time of blowing termites away.' – emerging from their mounds*)

akagaali *n12* bicycle   akagaali k'abalema wheelchair

akagaati *n12* bun

akagabi *n12* antelope

akagala *n12* young tuft of papyrus

akagalo *n12* small finger   Alimu obugalo. He is a petty thief.

akaganda *n12* small bundle, small Muganda person   akaganda k'enku small bundle of firewood

akagere *n12* toe   akagere ka nnasswi (the) little toe   -kuba akagere go on foot

akagga *n12* stream

[1]**Kaggo** *n1* title chief of Kyaddondo County

[2]**akaggo** *n12* small stick

[1]**Kaggwa** *n1* title name given to a male child following a child following twins

[2]**akaggwa** *n12* small thorn

kaggwensonyi *n1* (*pl.* ba kaggwensonyi) shameless person

akagina *n12* egg of jigger

kagiri *n1* type of grass (*a weed, hard to uproot*) *Sporobulus africanus*. *Saying: 'Ennaku enkooza kagiri.' ('I am having a very hard time.')*

akagirita *n12* small razor blade

akagoba *n12* score, point in a game

akagoogwa *n12* piece of sisal fibre   kagoogwa *n1* variety of mango (*a type long in Buganda; unripe fruits craved by some pregnant women*)

akagugumuko

akagugumuko *n12* **stampede**

akagugumusi *n12* **small finch**. *Appears to include several types of small finch-like birds, including cordon-bleus and waxbills. Found in small flocks in grassland and on the ground. Flocks said to have even numbers of birds. Derivation: from '-gugumuka' ('make off in panic'), because of their behaviour when disturbed. See* finch (*in part 3 of the dictionary*)

akaguli *n12* **cage, dock** (*in courtroom*)

akagulumu *n12* **small mound of earth, small road hump**

akaguwa *n12* **small rope, string** akaguwa k'engatto **shoelace, bootlace**

akajagalalo *n12* **state of civic unease, state of being riotous**

akajanja *n12* (*no pl.*) **overfamiliarity, intrusiveness** ow'akajanja *n1* **busybody**

akajegere *n12* **small chain**

akajiiko *n12* **small spoon, teaspoon**

kajjampuni *n1* **type of weed, sorrel** (*used for polishing bracelets and treating sores*) *Oxalis corniculata*

akajoozi *n12* **small T-shirt**

akajugo *n12* **penholder**

akajumbi *n12* **worn-out garment** (*used when hunting, etc.*)

akajwenge *n12* **fringe** (*on clothing*)

[1]-kaka (-kase) *See* -kakaabiriza

[2]-eekaka *See* -eekakaba

-kakaabiriza (*also* -kaka) *vt* (-kakaabirizza) **force**

kakaaga *n12/num* **six thousand**

-kakaalukana *vi* (-kakaalukanye) **be burdened** (*with a difficult task*), *eg. Akakaalukana mu mirimu mingi n'akomawo ng'akooye nnyo.* ('She is burdened with many tasks and comes back very tired.')

-kakaalukanya *vt* (-kakaalukanyizza) **burden** (*someone with a difficult task*)

-kakaalukanyizibwa *vi* (-kakaalukanyiziddwa) **be burdened (with)**, *eg. Abaana abato bakakaalukanyizibwa mu mirimu egitatuukana na myaka gyabwe.* ('Young children are burdened with hard work unsuitable for their ages.')

-kakaatika *vt* (-kakaatise) **force in** (*something that does not easily fit*), **jam in**

akakaaya *n12* **veil**

-eekakaba (*also* -eekaba) (-eekakabye) *vi* **make an effort** (*eg. to do something when ill*), **force oneself, nerve oneself, steel oneself**

akakadde *n12/num* **million**

-kakafu *adj* **certain, proven, confirmed**

akakalu *n12* **bail, guarantee, surety, collateral** (= omusingo) -siba akalulu **draw lots**

akakakampa *n12* **dried particle in nose**

-eekakamula *vi* (-eekakamudde) **make an effort to get up** (*eg. when ill*), **struggle to one's feet**

akakansokanso *See* akakwansokwanso

-kakanyala *vi* (-kakanyadde) **be(come) hard** (*especially of cold cooked matooke*), **become stiff** (*of a hide*), **be obstinate, be unbending**

-kakanyavu *adj* **hard** (*especially of cold cooked matooke*), **stiff** (*of a hide*), **obstinate/difficult** (*of a person*) -a omutima omukakanyavu **hard-hearted**

-kakanyaza *vt* (-kakanyazizza) **harden, make stiff**

[1]-kakasa *vt* (-kakasizza) **prove, assure, confirm, authenticate**

[2]-eekakasa *vi* **be self-confident**

-kakasibwa *vi* (-kakasiddwa) **be proved, be assured**

-kakata *vi* (-kakase) **be certain, become official, be a must**

akake *pos* **hers, his**

akakebe *n12* **small tin/can**. *Saying: 'Omutwe gwe kakebe.' ('His head is empty.' – meaning mentally)*

akakeedo *n12* **thin strip** (*or* **fibre**) **cut from midrib of banana leaf** (*dried and used in basket-making*)

kakensa *n1* (*pl.* ba kakensa) **expert**

akakenyera *n12* (*no pl.*) **reluctance, misgiving**

akakere *n12* **small frog**

akakerenda *n12* **pill, tablet**

-kakibwa *vi* (-kakiddwa) **be forced**

akakiiko *n12* **committee**

akakindo *n12* **crease**

kakku *adv* **quickly**

akako *pos* **yours** *si.*

akakoba *n12* **small belt/strap**

kakobe -a kakobe *adj* **purple**

kakobogo *invariable adj* **genuine, pure, real** (*of people*), **very hard, very strong**

akakodyo *n12* **trick, ruse**

akakoko *n12* **chick**

akakoloboze *n12* **small line, small scratch**

akakolwa *n12* **banded mongoose**

akakomo *n12* **small bracelet**

akakondo *n12* **small post, peg, bolt** (*formerly one of wood*) engatto y'akakondo **high-heeled shoe**

akakongovvule *n12* **ankle**

akakookolo *n12* **frightening mythological creature with deformed face, mask, balaclava, scarecrow**

kakoolakoola -a kakoolakoola **partially cooked** (*of matooke*), *eg. Emmere ya kakoolakoola.* ('The food is partially cooked.')

akakopa *si.* of obukopa

kakovu *n1* **sow-thistle** (*type of plant*) *Sonchus oleraceus*

akakowekowe *n12* **eyelash**

kakubampanga *n1* **hawk**. *Meaning: 'It strikes the cock.' – because it preys on chickens.*

akakubansimu *n12* **type of herb** (*difficult to weed*)

kakubansiri *n1* **basil** (*medicinal, used for stomach upsets*) *Ocimum basilicum. Meaning: 'It strikes mosquitoes.'*

akakubo *n12* **narrow road, path** akakubo

k'ebigere **footpath**

akakule *n12* **burst of scornful laughter** -kuba (*or* -tema) akakule **burst into scornful laughter**

akakulula *n12* **scratcher** (*for hair*)

akakulungutanyi *n12* **type of mushroom**

akakulwe *n12* **tadpole**

akakumirizi *n12* **type of small bush** (*used for making brooms; medicinal*) *Sida tenuicarpa*

akakundi *n12* **faction** (*eg. of political party*)

akakunizo *n12* **small cramped enclosure in which movement is difficult, trap, puzzle, crossword puzzle**

akakunkumuka *n12* **crumb, scrap** (*of food*)

akakunkuna *n12* (*no pl.*) **doubt, lack of conviction** -sigalamu akakunkuna **be unconvinced**

akakunŋunta *n12* **small sieve**

akakuta *n12* **husk** (*of rice, coffee bean, etc.*), **shell**

akakuubagano *n12* **friction between people, feud**

akakuubo *n12* **thin stripe**

akakuufu *n12* **small chain, necklace**

akakuukuulu *n12* **small crowd**

akakwansokwanso (*also* akakansokanso) *n12* **type of small tree** (*fruit edible*). *Two species: Rhus natalensis, R. vulgaris.*

akakwe *n12* **deceitful act, dirty trick**

¹**akala** *n12* **small spot/stain**

²**-kala** *vi* (-kaze) **become dry/parched**

kalaadi *n9* **Muslim prayer beads**

kalabaalaba *n1* (*pl.* ba kalabaalaba) **master of ceremonies** kalabaalaba w'omugole **matron of honour** kalabaalaba w'omugole omusajja **best man** kalabaalaba w'omukolo **master of ceremonies**

-kalabakalaba *adj* **shrewd, quick-witted, sly, cunning** (= -gezigezi)

akalabba *n12* **gallows, scaffold**

akalagala *n12* **small banana leaf**

-eekalakaasa *vi* (-eekalakaasizza) **hold a demonstration** (*for a cause*). *See* okwekalakaasa

-kalakata *vt* (-kalakase) **scrape** -kalakata ekyennyanja **scrape scales off a fish** -kalakata muwogo **scrape cassava** (*done after the skin has been peeled off*)

kalalankoma *n12* **hornet**

akalende *n12* **young mudfish 'emmale'**

akalali *n12* **loud high-pitched laughter** -kuba (*or* -tema) akalali **burst into laughter**

-kalambala *vi* (-kalambadde) **become stiff/hard**

-kalambavu *adj* **stiff, hard, rigid**

-kalambaza *vt* (-kalambazizza) **make stiff**

kalandalugo *n1* **type of creeping grass.** *Cynodon* (*several species*). *Meaning: 'It spreads in cattle pens.'*

akalandira *n12* **rootlet**

¹**akalanga** *n12* **mouth organ, harmonica**

²**-kalanga** *vt* (-kalanze) **fry, roast** (*peanuts or maize*)

kalati *n9* **carrot**

akalazi *n12* **pointer** (*on computer screen*)

kale *interj* **OK, all right** kale nno **well then**

akalebule *n12* (*no pl.*) **untruth, slander, libel** -a akalebule *adj* **slanderous, libelous** ow'akalebule *n1* **slanderer**

akaleega *n12* **brassiere, bra**

akaleku *n12* **small gourd**

kalenda *n9* **calendar**

kalenge *n1* (*no pl.*) **fog, mist**

akalenzi *n12* **small boy;** *in pl.* **boyhood**

kalenziwe *n1* **type of grass** (*spread on floors of shrines*)

¹**akalere** *n12* **piece.** *Pronunciation:* akaléré akalere k'olugoye **piece of material, strip of cloth** akalere ka muwogo **slice of cassava**

²**akalere** *n12* **small flute/pipe.** *Pronunciation:* akalérè

akalevu *n12* **chin, goatee**

kali *dem* **that**

akaliba *n12* **small animal skin/hide** kaliba *n1* **umbrella tree** *Musanga cecropioides*

kalibu *interj* **come in** (*call permitting someone to enter*)

kalibujoozi *n1* (*pl.* ba kalibujoozi) **bully**

kalidaali *n1* (*no pl.*) **mustard**

kaliddalu *n1* (*pl.* ba kaliddalu) **unruly person**

kalifuwa *n1* **perfume**

¹**akaliga** *n12* **lamb**

²**-kaliga** *vt* (-kalize) **tie (up)** (*a person*), **imprison** (*for a period*), *eg. Omusango gwamusinze ne bamukaliga emyaka etaano.* (*'He lost the case and was imprisoned for five years.'*)

kaliisoliiso *n1* (*pl.* ba kaliisoliiso) **person who keeps an eye on things, one who sees all** kaliisoliiso wa gavumenti ku bulyake **anti-corruption chief** kaliisoliiso wa gavumenti ku poliisi **independent police commissioner**

akalikonda *n12* **remote dark corner** akalikonda k'ekyenda **appendix** (*of intestine*)

akalimaawa *n12* **lime** (*fruit*)

¹**kalimagezi** *n1* (*pl.* ba kalimagezi) **wise person**

²**kalimagezi** *n9* **computer**

kalimbira *n1* (*pl.* ba kalimbira) **habitual liar**

kalimbwe *n1* **bird droppings**

akalimi *n12* **small tongue, hand** (*of clock/watch*) -kuba akalimi **sweet-talk**

kalimpitawa *n12* **condom**

kalina *n9* **multi-storey building** kalinaabiri **two-storey building** kalinaasatu **three-storey building** -a kalina *adj* **multi-story** mu kalina **upstairs**

Kalindaluzzi (*also* Kalinda) *n1 title* **keeper of the royal well**

akalippagano k'emmotoka *n12* **traffic jam**

¹**akalira** *n12* **umbilical cord** (*dried*)

²**-kalira** *vi* (-kalidde) **dry up at/in**, *etc.*, *eg. Enva zijja kukalira nga tosaanikidde sseffuliya.* (*'The sauce will dry up if you do not cover the pan.'*), **evaporate** -kaliramu (-kaliddemu) **stand up to**

(*someone, eg. bully or person overcharging*), **face up to, confront**

-kalirira *vt* (-kaliridde) **cook/dry** (*over a fire*), **grill, smoke**   -kalirira ebyennyanja **dry fish**   -kalirira ennyama **preserve meat** (*by drying over heat*)   -kalirira taaba **cure tobacco**

-eekaliriza *vt* **look at closely, scrutinise**

kalittunsi *n1* (*no pl.*) **eucalyptus**

akalo *n12* **millet meal/flour;** *in pl.* **finger millet**

akalobo *n12* **bucket**

akalogojjo *n12* **temporary craziness, delirium**

akalombolombo *n12* **custom, tradition**

kalonda *n1* (*no pl.*) **large number of assorted things, miscellany** (= omuyoolerero)

¹Kalooli *n1* **Charles**

²kalooli *n9* **marabou stalk**

akaloolo *n12* **chicken mite**

akaloosa *n12* (*no pl.*) **pleasant smell, fragrance**

-kalu *adj* **dry**   ebintu ebikalu **concrete things, real property**   ensawo enkalu **empty purse**   essente (*or* ensumbi) enkalu **(hard) cash**   kaawa omukalu **coffee without milk**   -kuba ekikalu **tuck in one's shirt**   n'engalo enkalu *adj* **empty-handed**   omutwe mukalu *adj* **empty-headed,** *eg. Musoke mutwe mukalu.* ('*Musoke is empty-headed.*')   -siba enkalu **trip up** (*in wrestling*)

-kaluba *vi* (-kalubye) **be hard, be difficult, be tough** (*of meat*)

-kalubo *adj* **hard, difficult**

-kalubya *vt* (-kalubizza) **make hard/difficult**

akalulu *n12* **vote, ballot, lottery, lottery ticket**   -kuba akalulu **vote, play the lottery**

akalulwe *n12* **gall bladder**

kalumannyweera *n1* (*no pl.*) **unresolved problems between parties, matters of contention**   mu kalumannyweera **at loggerheads**

akalumba *n12* **rear seat in canoe** (*for the helmsman*)

akalunginsanvu *n12* **type of tree** (*medicinal*) *Syzygium guineense.* Meaning: '*It treats seven diseases.*'

kalusu *n1* **foot-and-mouth disease**

-kaluubirira *vt* (-kaluubiridde) **be difficult for,** *eg. Muliraanwa ankaluubirira.* ('*My neighbour is difficult for me.*')

-kaluubirirwa *vi* (-kaluubiriddwa) **have difficulties in affairs**

-kaluubiriza *vt* (-kaluubirizza) **make difficult for, hinder, impede, inconvenience**

-kama *vt* (-kamye) **milk**

akamagu *n12* (*no pl.*) **inability to concentrate, tendency to distraction**   ow'akamagu *n1* **person easily distracted**

-kamala *vi* (-kamaze) **act to excess, be extreme.** *See* okukamala   Ng'okamaze. **You have really botched things up.**

Kamalabyonna *n1 title* **Prime Minister of Buganda**

akamalirizo *n12* **last thing/event**   -a akamalirizo *adj* **final**   empaka ez'akamalirizo **final** (*of a competition*)   okubuuza okw'akamalirizo **final examinations**

akamasu *n12* **mouse/rat trap**

-kambagga *vi* (-kambazze) **have a tart taste** (*as unripe fruit*)

akambe *n12* (*pl.* obwambe) **knife** (*curved type used for peeling matooke*)   akambe ak'engera **knife without a handle**

akambugu *n12* **couch grass** *Digitaria abyssinica.* Saying: '*Abataka abaagalana be balima akambugu.*' ('*Neighbours who get on well weed together.*')

-kambuwala *vi* (-kambuwadde) **become fierce**

-kambwe *adj* **fierce, ruthless, savage, brutal, cruel, strict, strong** (*of alcoholic drink*)

akameeza *n12* **small table, desk**

kamenya *n1* (*no pl.*) **cramp, stitch**

kamiimo *invariable adj* **tight-fitting**   empale ya kamiimo (*also* empale kamiimo) **drain-pipe trousers**

-eekamirira *vi* (-eekamiridde) **drink too much alcohol**

akamiro *n12* **oesophagus**

-kamiza *vi* (-kamizza) **cease giving milk** (*of a cow*)

akammonde (akazungu) *n12* **Irish potato** *Solanum tuberosum*   obummonde obusiike **fried potatoes**

kammunguluze *n1* (*no pl.*) **dizziness, vertigo**

(a)kammwe *pos* **your(s)** *pl.* (N11.4)

akamogo *n12* (*no pl.*) **blemish, flaw, imperfection, defect.** Saying: '*Omulungi tabulako kamogo.* ('*A beautiful person does not lack a blemish.*', meaning '*Nobody is perfect.*')

akamooli *n12* **ventilator**

Kampala **Kampala.** *Possible meaning: 'small hill of the 'empala' ('akasozi' understood). The identity of the antelope 'empala' is uncertain. It is possible that the word comes from English, wrongly applied to an antelope resembling an impala.*

kampeyini *n9* **campaign**

kamu *num* **one**

-kamuka *vi* (-kamuse) **become drier**

-kamula *vt* (-kamudde) **squeeze** (*to extract fluid*)   -kamula emicungwa **squeeze oranges** (*to extract juice*)   -kamula engoye **wring out clothes** (*to remove water*)

akamuli *n12* **woody herb, rosy periwinkle** (*decorative; medicinal*) *Catharanthus roseus*

kamunye *n14* (1) **kite** (*type of bird*); (2) **shrub with small whitish flowers** (*used medicinally for cuts*) *Hoslundia opposita*; (3) **fourteen-seater communal taxi**

kamuseenene *n12* **shrub with yellow flowers** (*used for hedges; fruits used as rat poison*) (= obusitaani) *Thevetia peruviana*

akamuserebende   akabina akamuserebende **flat**

bottom (*of a person*)

akamwa *n12* **mouth** akamwa akabi **bad-mouthing** akamwa ebirevu **razor** ekisasi mu kamwa **palate**

kamwakoogera I myself (*as the person speaking*)

akamwanyimwanyi *n12* **small forest tree resembling coffee.** *Member of family Rubiaceae, but otherwise identity uncertain; possibly Psydrax parviflora and/or Oxyanthus speciosus.*

akamwenyumwenyu *n12* **grin, smile**

akamweso *n12* **razor**

[1]**kamyu** *n1* **type of climbing stinging herb** *Tragia benthami*

[2]**akamyu** *n12* **rabbit, hare**

akanaabiro *n12* **small bathroom**

kanaana *n12/num* **eight thousand** kanaana *n1* **variety of mango**

kanabba *n1* (1) **type of drum beat** (*announces a death in the royal family*); (2) **child of a prince** (*in the king's lineage*)

akanakanaka *n12* **small white edible mushroom** (*grows where ennaka termites occur*) *Termitomyces aurantiacus*

-eekanasa *vi* (-eekanasizza) **be very selective** (*especially regarding food*), **be fastidious, dislike dirty things**

-eekanasi *adj* **fastidious, finicky**

[1]**-kanda** *vi* **persist in** (*despite lack of success*), **keep on.** *Verb followed by the infinitive of another verb, eg. Nnakanda kulinda nga tajja. ('I kept on waiting but he did not come.').*

[2]**-kanda** *vt* (-kanze) **knead and make flat** (*eg. dough when making a chapati*), **force** (*a person*) -kanda ssente **extort money**

-eekandagga *vi* (-eekandazze) **leave in protest, storm out of a meeting**

-kanduka (*also* -kanyuka) *vi* (-kanduse) **begin to look old, look haggard, become worn-out**

-eekandula *vi* (-eekandudde) **leave in protest, go off in a rage**

kaneene *n12* **type of small carnivore** (*said to like eating 'emmale' catfish, possibly marsh mongoose*)

[1]**-kanga** *vt* (-kanze) **startle, shock**

[2]**-eekanga** *vit* **be startled/shocked (at/by)**

-eekangabiriza *vi* (-eekangabirizza) **deny something that one has done, be adamant about one's innocence, be unyielding**

-kangalala *vi* (-kangaladde) **stand on tiptoe**

-kangavvula *vt* (-kangavvudde) **discipline** (*usually implying physically*)

(a)kange *pos* **my, mine.** (N11.4)

-kangisa *vt* (-kangisizza) **intimidate, threaten**

[1]**-kanika** *vt* (-kanise) **repair/fix** (*something mechanical*). *From: 'mechanic' (English).*

[2]**-kanika** *vt* **exaggerate, raise, inflate**

-eekaniikiriza *vi* (-eekaniikiridde) **exert oneself to do something difficult**

-kankamuka *vi* (-kankamuse) **become drier,** *eg. Engoye zikankamuse. ('The clothes have become*

drier.') enkuba -kankamuka **ease up** (*of rain*)

-kankamukamu (-kankamuseemu) **become a bit drier** obulwadde -kankamukamu **get slightly better** (*from an illness*)

-kankana *vi* (-kankanye) **tremble, vibrate, quake, shake,** *eg. Omukono gwe gukankana. ('His hand is shaking.')*

-kankanya *vt* (-kankanyizza) **cause to tremble, shake,** *eg. Musisi akankanya ennyumba. ('The earthquake is shaking the house.')*

kannaabwo *n12* **their companion**

kannaako *n12* **its companion**

kannassogolero *n12* **type of mushroom**

[1]**akannyo** *n12* **small tooth**

[2]**akannyo** *n12* **stretcher** (*one used for carrying dead people*), **bier**

kano *dem* **this**

-eekansa *vi* (-eekansizza) **be expert and confident** (*in an accomplishment*), **be outstanding,** *eg. Yeekansa mu kukola entebbe. ('He is an outstanding chair maker.')*

kantoolooze *n1* (*no pl.*) **dizziness, vertigo**

akantu *n12* **something small**

kantuntunu *n1* **blindfold**

[1]**kanu** *n9* **clinker-built boat**

[2]**akanu** *n11* **small wooden mortar**

-kanuka *vi* (-kanuse) **be wide open** (*of the eyes, eg. due to rage or fright*), **protrude** (*of the eyes*), **be on the point of death**

-kanula *vt* (-kanudde) -kanula amaaso **open one's eyes wide** Akanula bukanuzi amaaso. **He has nothing to say.**

-kanulira *vt* (-kanulidde) **stare at**

akanuunansubi *n12* **sunbird.** *Meaning: 'It sucks grass.'*

akanuunu *n12* **withered flower at end of banana** (*persistent in some varieties*)

akanwe *n12* (1) **(the) little finger;** (2) **tiny banana, tiny cassava/potato tuber,** *eg. akanwe ka lumonde ('tiny potato')*

-kanyiza (*also* -kanya) *vi* (-kanyizza) **persevere at,** *eg. Akanyizza okulima. ('She has persevered at farming.')*, **be prolonged, be persistent** (*of rain or work*), *eg. Enkuba ekanyiza okutonnya. ('The rain is persistent.')*

akanyamberege *n12* (1) **fibre-producing plant** *Hibiscus diversifolius*; (2) **crisis, disaster**

kanyeebwa *n1* (1) **type of small weed, sorrel.** *Said to have been introduced by agricultural scientists to provide ground cover under coffee, today a serious weed. Oxalis latifolia;* (2) **type of red bean resembling a groundnut** *Phaseolus vulgaris*

akanyeenyenkule *n12* **cricket** (*type of insect; omen of death if heard sounding in the house at night*)

akanyego *n12* (*no pl.*) **response**

akanyere *n12* **bracelet**

akanyigo *n12* (*no pl.*) **squeeze, congestion, tight**

situation, difficult situation mu kanyigo crowded together

akanyolo *n12* small drum stick, door-handle, bolt (*originally one of metal*)

akanyonyi *n12* small bird

akanyonyoogano *n12* wrangle, scuffle

-kanyuga *vt* (-kanyuze) throw, hurl

-kanyuka *See* -kanduka

akanzironziro *n12* small tree (*medicinal, used to treat skin disease*) *Psorospermum febrifugum*

-kapa *adj* without fat (*of meat*), lean

akapale *n12* small trousers. *See* empale akapale k'omunda underpants, panties

akapande *n12* small sign, label

akapapajjo *n12* small piece, fragment, splinter (of wood) -tuula ku kapapajjo sit on the edge of a chair, sit on the edge of a carrier (*of a bike*)

akapapula *n12* small piece of paper, leaflet

kapere *n1* clown Kapere *n1* Captain Lugard -a kapere *adj* checked (*with squared pattern*)

akapiira *n12* small ball, condom

kapiso *n9* capsule

kapiteeni *n1* (*pl.* ba kapiteeni) captain

karibu *interj* come in. *From Swahili.*

akasaale *n12* arrow, dart

akasaamusaamu *n12* black-eyed Susan (*type of climbing or creeping herb*) *Thunbergia alata*

akasaana *n12* type of acacia (*leaves yield a red dye*) *Acacia hockii*

akasaanikira *n12* small lid/cover, bung akasaanikira eccupa bottle-top

akasaanyi *n12* small caterpillar, silkworm

akasaasi *n12* rattle (*of baby*)

akasaka *n12* (1) small thicket; (2) small earthenware cooking pot

akasambandege *n12* type of small shrub (*with inflated pods*). *Meaning:'It kicks the bells.'* – *referring to the seeds rattling about in the dry pods.* *Crotolaria* spp.

akasambattuko *n12* stampede, commotion

akasambo *n12* fine-meshed fishing net (*for catching enkejje*) (= ekiragala)

Kasambula July

akasana *n12* (*no pl.*) sunshine

kasandasanda *n1* small herb with white latex (*a weed*) *Euphorbia hirta*

akasanduuko *n12* small box akasanduuko k'ebbaluwa post box (*at post office*)

akasanjasanja *n12* mushroom (*grows on dry bananas leaves in gardens*)

akasanke *n12* small finch (*flies in flocks, various species – mannikin, etc.*). *See* finch (*in Part 3 of the dictionary*)

akasanso *n12* slender part of a tree, tip of branch

[1]**akasanvu** *n12* (*no pl.*) forced labour

[2]**kasanvu** *n12/num* seven thousand

[3]**akasanvu** *n12* broken-off twig

akasasamalo *n12* riotousness

akasasiro *n12* small piece of rubbish

akasattiro *n12* restlessness (*of a crowd moving about*), commotion

akasavu *n12* little piece of fat. *Saying: 'Kasavu ka nnyama.'* ('Little piece of fat, little piece of meat.' – used to indicate seating order alternating the sexes)

akasawo *n12* small bag

akaseekende *n12* flowering stem of etteete grass

akaseera *n12* short period (*of time*), moment

akaseerezi *n12* slippery place

akasejjeresejjere *n12* type of mushroom (*found where ensejjere termites occur*)

akasekere *n12* sty (*in eye*)

Kasenge *n1* head forester of the Kabaka

akasengejja *n12* filter, sieve, strainer, colander

kasennyanku *n1* (*no pl.*) insect that carries around a home resembling a tiny bundle of firewood (*larval stage of a moth*). *Meaning: 'Little gatherer of firewood.'*

akasenso *n12* fibre skirt (*worn by dancers*)

akasenya *n12* toothbrush

akaserengeto *n12* downward slope, decline

akasero *n12* little basket kasero Dutchman's pipe (*type of climbing plant*) *Aristolochia elegans.* *The name is derived from the shape of the fruit.*

akasiimo *n12* gift of appreciation, gratuity, tip

kasiisa *n1* type of tree *Trema orientalis*

akasiisira *n12* small thatched hut

kasiki *n12* party for bride or groom before wedding

kasikisa *n1* (*no pl.*) type of caterpillar (*reddish brown, with long hairs*)

akasiko *n12* small bushy area

kasikonda *n12* (*no pl.*) hiccup(s)

akasimba *n12* genet

akasimu *n12* nerve, mobile phone akasimu k'omu ngalo mobile phone

akasirabo *n12* oribi (*type of antelope*)

akasiriikiriro *n12* period of silence, quiet, lull akasiriikiriro mu kulwana truce

akasiriivu *n12/num* hundred thousand

akasirikitu *n12* something very small

akasirikko *n12* depression in road; *in pl.* corrugations, ruts

akasirisa *n12* full stop

kasirise *adv* quietly, silently

kasiru *n1* (*pl.* ba kasiru) dumb person (*unable to speak*)

kasita *conj* but fortunately, but at least, *eg.* *Amatooke gaweddewo kasita tulina omuceere.* ('The matoke is finished but at least we have rice.')

[1]**akaso** *n12* small knife. *Pronunciation:* akasô

[2]**akaso** *n12* piece of raffia fibre. *Pronunciation:* akasô

kasodde *n1* (*no pl.*) dried sliced sweet potatoes (*for storage*). *From: 'ekisodde' ('old potato field').*

akasolo *n12* little animal, penis

akasolya *n12* roof ow'akasolya *n1* head of a clan

akasonga *n12* pointer (*eg. used on blackboard*)

akasongezo *n12* tip (*of something pointed*)

[1]**kasonso** *interj* Serves you right!

[2]**akasonso** *n12* elephant shrew

akasonzi *n12* small eel-like catfish

akasoobo *adv* slowly (*in doing things*) -kola (*or -tambula*) kasoobo work slowly

kasooka (*also* kasookedde) *conj* up to the time when, *eg. Musoke kasooka akula kutuuka awo talabanga ku nnyanja.* ('*Up to the time when Musoke reached that age, he has never seen a lake.*'), **since** kasooka nga ever since

kasookolindo *n1* (*no pl.*) bird droppings

kasooli *n1* (*no pl.*) maize *Zea mais*

akasowaani *n12* small plate

akasozi *n12* small hill, (upward) slope, *eg. Waliwo akasozi okugenda ku kkanisa.* ('*There is a slope up to the church.*')

akasubi *n12* piece of dry grass Kasubi burial site for royalty in Buganda. *Two of its buildings are*: (1) Bujjabukula *n9* reception building at entrance; (2) Ndogoobukaba *n9* building housing drums).

Kasujju *n1* title chief of Busujju County (*guardian of the princes*), head of Ngeye Clan

-kasuka *vt* (-kasuse) throw, fling, hurl, toss

akasukusuku (*also* akassukussuku) *n12* type of mushroom (*grey with brown gills; found in banana gardens; stirred into matooke, not boiled like other mushrooms*)

akasukwasukwa *n12* very young shoot of beer banana plant

kasulubbana (*also* kasulu) *n1* elephant snout fish *Mormyrus kannume*

akasumagizi *n12* (*no pl.*) (1) illness (*marked by a tendency to sleepiness*); (2) blue kingfisher

akasumbi *n12* small water pot

akasunguyira *n12* quick temper, tendency to aggression

akaswanyu *n12* stick (*for administering punishment*)

akaswiriri *n12* whisker

kata *adv* almost, nearly. *Used with subjunctive* (N17), *eg. Kata ayite ebibuuzo.* ('*She almost passed the examination.*').

akataago *n12* spleen

akataala *n12* small lamp

akataasa *n12* small basin for washing hands

akataayi *n12* swallow/swift (*types of bird*)

akatabalika *n12* an enormous number, millions

akatabanguko *n12* disturbance ebiseera by'akatabanguko state of emergency

akatabi *n12* small branch, twig

akatabo *n12* small book, booklet -kuba akatabo tell a lie

katadooba *n12* small paraffin lamp

katakketakke -a katakketakke *adj* fairly light-skinned

akatakkuluze *n12* loose skin at base of nail

akatale *n12* market

akatambaala *n12* small cloth, handkerchief akatambaala ak'oku mutwe headscarf

Katambala *n1* title chief of Butambala County

akatanda *n12* small bed akatanda k'ebbaasi carrier (*on roof of bus*) akatanda k'omwana cot

akatandaalo *n12* rack/table (*for drying utensils*)

akatanga *n12* climbing plant with small hard inedible gourd-like fruits (*used as emulsifier when washing clothes*) *Lagenaria sphaerica*

katangambale *See* embuzi

katazzamiti *n1* small tree (*medicinal*) *Bridelia micrantha*

akatebe *n12* small chair, stool

akateebe *n12* bog, quagmire

akateeteeyi *n12* small/short dress

kateetera *adv* on the point of death, *eg. Aliko kateetera.* ('*She is on the point of death.*')

kateeyamba *n1* (*pl.* ba kateeyamba) person who requires help for everyday functions, disabled person

akatego *n12* trap, bait

katekiisimu *n9* catechism

katemba *n1* play (*as in the theatre*), drama, performance

akatengotengo *n12* herb with purplish flowers and yellow fruits (*fruit* entengo) *Solanum incanum. Identity needs confirmation.*

[1]**kati** *adv* now

[2]**akati** *n12* small tree, small piece of wood, small stick akati akapima stick used for measuring akati akasokoola amannyo toothpick akati k'ekibiriiti match(stick)

akatiba *n12* mould (*for brick-making*), bailing bowl

akatiiti *n12* small bead -yambala obutiiti mu kiwato wear beads around the waist (*a love charm worn by women*)

akatikitiki *n12* second (*unit of time*)

katikkiro *n1* (*pl.* ba katikkiro) chief minister of a clan Katikkiro title Prime Minister of Buganda

akatiko *n12* mushroom akatiko akazungu oyster mushroom

akatima *n12* small heart, valve (*of tyre*)

akatimba *n12* small net akatimba akabikka ku byokulya net covering food (*protection from flies*) akatimba akabikka ku kibaya net covering cot akatimba k'ensiri mosquito net

akatinko *n12* obsession, fad ow'akatinko *n1* someone obsessed

katinvuma *n12* type of small climbing plant (*second totem of Nvuma Clan*) *Rhynchosia hirta*

Kato *n1* title male younger of twins

akatofaali *n12* cell (*of the body*)

akatogo *n12* food (*made from different ingredients, cooked together unwrapped in banana leaves*). *Originally 'akatogo' was a mixture of beans with*

sweet potatoes or matooke. <u>mu katogo</u> **in a difficult messy situation**
-katoliki *adj* **Catholic**
akatolobojjo *n12* **tiny spot, speck**
Katonda *n1* **God** (*as Creator*)
akatonnyeze *n12* **dot, point, full stop**
akatono *adv* **a little, slightly, briefly;** (*with subjunctive N17*) **almost, nearly** <u>n'akatono</u> (*also* <u>wadde n'akatono</u>) (*after verb in negative*) **not at all, not even a little**
katoola *n1* (*no pl.*) **large amount** <u>taliimu katoola</u> **naïve person** (*person incapable of picking up ideas*)
kattaddogo *n1* **type of herb** (*medicinal*) *Chenopodium ambrosioides. Meaning: 'It kills evil spirits.'*
kattamukago *n1* **ceremony at which roasted coffee beans are offered to visitors**
kattannyenje *n1* **mothball(s)** (*insecticide*). *Meaning: 'It kills cockroaches.'*
akatugu *n12* **sand fly**
akatuli *n12* **small hole, puncture**
akatulume *n12* **banded mongoose**
akatulututtu *n12* **infected pimple, small sore, patch of skin rash**
Katumba *n1* **male name in Nkima Clan.** *A man of this name looked after Kimera when he was a baby in Bunyoyo (N29). See* enkyima
akatunda *n12* **passion fruit** (*plant; fruit*) *Passiflora edulis*
akatundatunda *n12* **type of mushroom** (*grows near entunda termite mounds*) *Termitomyces eurrhizus*
akatundwe *n12* **pumpkin flower** (*eaten*)
akatungulu *n12* **onion**
katunguluccumu *n1* **garlic**
akatunku *n12* **fruit of omutunku** (*edible*)
katunkuma *n1* **shrub bearing small bitter fruits, fruit of this plant** (*edible*) *Solanum anguivii*
akatuntunu akatono *n12* **herb** (*related to cape gooseberry*) *Physalis minima*
akatuubagiro *n12* **crisis**
akatuugo *n12* **fan palm** *Borassus aethiopum*
akatuulituuli *n12* **small swelling, blister;** *in pl.* **skin rash**
katuuso *n1* (*no pl.*) **food prepared for the Kabaka, especially prepared food**
katwalo *n1* **type of banana** (*used for making beer*)
akatyabaga *n12* **trouble**
akavamagombe *n12* **small climbing plant** (*used medicinally in childbirth and to treat gonorrhea*) *Cissampelos mucronata. Meaning: 'It comes from the underworld.'*
akaveera *n12* **plastic bag, polythene sheet**
akavuvunnano *n12* (*no pl.*) **confusion** (*involving more than one person*), **fracas, scuffle**
akavuyo *n12* **mess**
-kavvula *vt* (-kavvudde) **eat ravenously, devour**

kawaali *n1* (*no pl.*) **smallpox** <u>Kawaali</u> **Kiganda deity** (*lubaale*), **god of smallpox**
akawaatwa *n12* **small space/gap**
akawaayiro *n12* **something added on, supplement, annex**
akawago *n12* **bladder** (*of person*), **inner tube, rubber** (*of valve*)
akawakatirwa *n12* **side-shoot** (*of plant*), **extension to a word** (*in grammar*)
akawale *n12* **small trousers** <u>obuwale obw'omunda</u> **small underpants, knickers** (*for a child*)
Kawamigero *n1* **God** (*as the dispenser of fate*)
kawammansi *n1* (*no pl.*) **pains after childbirth**
akawanga *n12* **skull**
akawanika *n12* **brassiere, bra**
kawawa *n12* **horsefly, gadfly**
kaweefube *n1* **campaign**
akaweke *n12* **small seed, tablet, grain**
akawemba -a kawembawemba *adj* **reddish-brown** (*sorghum-coloured*)
akawembe *n12* **razor blade**
kawenkene *invariable adj* **very bad person,** *eg. Musoke yali kawenkene. ('Musoke was a very bad man.')*
akawere <u>akaana akawere</u> *n12* **newborn baby**
akawero *n12* **cloth, small rag**
akawewo *n12* **breeze**
kawo *n1* (*no pl.*) **pea(s)** *Pisum sativum*
akawompo *n12* **fontanel**
akawoowo *n12* (*no pl.*) **fragrance, scent, perfume**
akawugula *n12* **woody herb with yellow flowers** (*source of twine*) *Triumfetta rhomboidea*
akawujjo *n12* **spoon** (*made from banana leaf*), **scoop** (*for extracting paraffin, oil, etc.*)
akawuka *n12* **insect** <u>Kawuka</u> *n1 title* **chief goatherd of the Kabaka** <u>akawuka akatalabika</u> **germ**
kawule *n1* **type of thorny shrub/climber** (*medicinal*) *Toddalia asiatica*
akawulunguta *n12* **charm put inside a drum** (= ndikungulu)
akawumbi *n12* **ten million**
kawumpuli *n1* (*no pl.*) **bubonic plague** <u>Kawumpuli</u> **Kiganda deity** (*lubaale*), **god of the plague**
kawuna *n12* **game of tag**
akawunde *n12* **type of horn** (*musical instrument decorated with beads; played with royal drums*)
akawundo *n12* **bat** (*insectivorous*)
akawunga *n12* **maize meal.** *The plural* <u>obuwunga</u> *means flour (of any type).* <u>obuwunga bwa kasooli</u> **maize flour** <u>obuwunga bwa muwogo</u> **cassava flour** <u>edduuka y'obuwunga</u> **shop selling all types of flour**
akawungeezi *n12* **evening**
kawunta *n9* **counter**
kawuukuumi *n1* **type of beetle** (*eats dry beans*)
Kawuula *n1 title* **chief drummer of the Kabaka**

Kawuuta *n1 title* chief cook of the Kabaka

akawuuwo *n12* (1) small strip of banana leaf placed on top of food within food bundle; (2) tail of snake/lizard

kawuuzi *n1* beetle larva (*bores into sweet potatoes*)

akawuzi *n12* thin thread

kayaayaana *n1* type of shrub (*used for bathing newborn babies; brings good fortune*) *Vernonia cinerea*

akayaayu *n12* wild/feral cat

akayamba *n12* type of small fish

akayana *n12* calf

akayanja *n12* small lake. *See* obuyanja

akayigo *n12* outside bathroom

Kayima *n1* (1) *title* chief of Mawokota County; (2) name used by princes

akayindiyindi *n12* type of bean (*with flattened seeds; Lima bean*) *Phaseolus lunatus*

akayinja *n12* pebble

akayiringito *n12* downward slope, descent

akayisanyo *n12/adv* (*no pl.*) movement towards an exit, in the opposite direction -yisa kayisanyo pass one another (*moving in opposite directions*)

akayole (k'essubi) *n12* small bundle of grass (*for thatching*) Wabulaakayole *n1* chief thatcher of the Kabaka

kayombera *n1* quarrelsome person

kayondo *n12* (1) herb with long fleshy leaves *Kalanchoe*; (2) name used by princes and and other males in the Mpologoma and Ngo Clans

kayongo *n1* fern. *Also name of males in Kkobe Clan.*

akayovu *n12* small elephant kayovu *n1* banana weevil

akayozi *n12* gerbil

akayu *n12* toilet akayu k'olukale public toilet akayu ka buyonjo pit latrine

-kayuka (*also* -kanduka) *vi* (-kayuse) begin to look old, look haggard, become worn-out

akayumba *n12* small house akayumba k'enkoko chicken coop akayumba ka buyonjo outside toilet akayumba ka penitensia confessional

akayuuguumo *n12* state of civic unrest, turmoil, commotion

akayuukiyuuki *n12* shrub. *Two species:* (1) (*flowers pink and yellow; an invasive weed*) *Lantana camara*; (2) (*flowers pale purple or pink; used for toothsticks*) *Lantana trifolia*.

[1]**-kaza** *vt* (-kazizza) dry

[2]**-eekaza** *vr* dry oneself

-eekazaakaza *vi* (-eekazaakazizza) refuse to take the blame

kazambi *n1* filth, waste, sewage

-kazana *vi* (-kazanye) work hard (*in a long-term committed way*), try hard

kazannyirizi *n1* playful person, jester, clown

akazannyo *n12* game of short duration, trick

-kazi *adj* female

kazigizigi *n1* extreme darkness -a kazigizigi *adj* very dark kiseera kya kazigizigi very bad time

akazigo *n12* (small amount of) ghee

akaziina *n12* worn-out garment, rag

akazimu *n12* whirlwind, small spirit, pain (*eg. in the joints*)

akazindaalo *n12* small funnel, microphone akazindaalo ak'oku matu headphone

-kaziwala *vi* (-kaziwadde) become a woman

Kazooba Monday

akazoole *n12* (*no pl.*) mania, (fit of) madness

akazungirizi *n12* type of gnat (*annoying type that buzzes around the head*)

kazunzanjuki *n1* type of herb (*roots used medicinally to induce labour*) *Justicia exigua*. Meaning: 'It makes the bees move.'

[1]**ke** *pos* her/his (**N11.4**), *eg. akaana ke* ('*her child*')

[2]**ke** *pre* of (= k'e **N11.1**)

[3]**ke** *pro (relative pronoun and pronoun of emphasis* **N10.1**) it, which, that. *Can be equivalent to short phrases of emphasis, eg. Akambe kano ka Musoke.* ('*It is this knife that is Musoke's.*'). *Can be a prefix* **ke-** (**N11.6**). *eg. nze kennyini* ('*I myself*').

-eekebejja (-eekebezze) *See* -eekebera

[1]**-kebera** *vt* examine, inspect, check, mark -kebera ebibuuzo correct an examination

[2]**-eekebera** (*also* -eekebejja) *vr* examine oneself (*to check one's appearance*)

-kedde *See* -keera; -kya

akeediimo *n12* (*pl.* obwediimo) strike (*by workers*)

akeegugungo *n12* riot

keeke *n9* cake

-keera *vi* (-kedde) be early, rise early obudde -keera dawn, *eg. Obudde bukedde.* ('*The day has dawned.*')

-keerewa *vi* (-keereye) be late

-keereya *vt* (-keereyizza) make late

akeeru *See* -yeru

-keesa *vi* (-keesezza) -keesa obudde go through the night, *eg. Omulwadde yakeesezza obudde.* ('*The patient survived the night.*'), do until dawn

-keeta *vit* (-keese) cause heartburn (to), cause a sickening feeling (to), *eg. Kinkeese.* ('*I am fed up with it.*')

akeetalo *n12* (*no pl.*) bustling about, *eg. Abantu baabadde mu keetalo nga balindirira abagenyi.* ('*The people were bustling about waiting for the visitors.*')

keeyeeyo *n12* small shrub with yellow flowers (*used medicinally for muscle pain and in bone-setting; also for making brooms*) *Sida tenuicarpa*

-eekeja *vi* (-eekeze) be busy, *eg. Nnasiibye nneekeja nga nneetegekera omukolo.* ('*I was busy all day preparing for the function.*')

-eekeka *vt* (-eekese) mistrust

-kekejjana *vi* (-kekejjanye) struggle to do things (*especially when sick or old*), *eg. Omukadde ayimirira ng'akekejjana.* ('*The elderly person is* *struggling to stand up.'*)

-kekema *vi* (-kekemye) **cackle, cluck**

-kekera *vi* (-kekedde) **be continuing** (*of a sound, especially of fighting*), *eg. Emmundu zikekera.* (*'The shooting is continuing.'*)

-keketa *vt* (-kekese) **gnaw**

-kekkera *vi* (-kekkedde) **act helpless, pretend to be unable,** *eg. Omusajja akekkera yeefuula atasobola kusitula ssanduuko mbu ezitowa.* (*'The man says he cannot lift the case because it is too heavy.'*)

-kekkereza *vt* (-kekkerezza) **use sparingly, economise,** *eg. Akekkereza ssente kubanga alina ntono.* (*'She is economising because she has little money.'*)

-kema *vt* (-kemye) **tempt**

-kemba *vi* (-kembye)   -tambula -kemba **strut (about)**

-kemebwa *vi* (-kemeddwa) **be tempted**

-kemekkereza *vt* (-kemekkerezza) **tempt, dig out the truth from, persuade to reveal**

-kena *vt* (-kenye) **give too little (to),** *eg. Abakozi baabakena emisaala.* (*'They gave the workers very low wages.'*)

kenda *n12/num* **nine thousand**

-kendeera *vi* (-kendedde) **decrease, diminish, become reduced**   -kendeera okwaka **grow dim** (*of the light level*)

-kendeeza *vt* (-kendeezezza) **decrease, reduce**   -kendeeza ku ddoboozi **lower one's voice**   -kendeeza obuwanvu **shorten**   -kendeeza sipiidi **slow down** (*a vehicle*)

akendo *n12* **small gourd** (*used as cup or ladle*)

-kenduka *vi* (-kenduse) **be thin-waisted**

-kenena *vi* (-kenenye) **become extremely thin and unhealthy**   -kenena endusu **drool, dribble**

-kenenuka *vi* (-kenenuse) **flow** (*of a thick substance*), **ooze out, drip**

-kenenula *vt* (-kenenudde) **make** (*a liquid*) **free of impurities, decant, clarify,** *eg. Yakenenula omubisi ne gutukula be ttukutuku.* (*'She decanted the juice, so it became clear.'*)

-kenenya *vt* (-kenenyezza) **cause to become extremely thin and unhealthy**   -kenenya endusu **give** (*someone*) **a hard time**

-kenga *vt* (-kenze) **detect,** *eg. Yakenga mangu omubbi n'akuba enduulu.* (*'He soon detected the thief and raised the alarm.'*)

-eekengera *vt* (-eekengedde) **be suspicious of, suspect, be watchful of, keep an eye on,** *eg. Alabye omusajja n'amwekengera okuba omubbi.* (*'He watched the man carefully because he suspected he was a thief.'*)

-eekenneenya *vt* (-eekenneenyezza) **examine carefully, scrutinise**

kennyini *pro* **-self** (**N11.6**)   nze kennyini **I myself,** ggwe kennyini **you yourself,** ye kennyini **he himself, she herself**

-kenyera *vt* (-kenyedde) **be reluctant about, be**

unsure about, have misgivings about, *eg. Yabadde akenyera nga tayagala kugenda.* (*'He had misgivings about going.'*)

-(y)okerera *See* -yokerera

-kessi *adj* **relating to spying** (*or detective*) **work**

-ketta *vt* (-kesse) **spy (out/on), reconnoitre**

ki? *interr* **what?, which?;** (2) (*with prepositional verb N22*) **why?**   -aki? **what for?,** *eg. Ekiso kino kyaki?* (*'What is this knife for?'*)

ekibaala *n7* **mound made by 'embaala' termites**

ekibabu *n7* (*no pl.*) **horror, disaster, catastrophe**

ekibaddewo *n7* **event**

ekibajje *n7* **piece of carpentry, something made of wood, carving**

ekibajjo *n7* **piece of wood** (*deliberately removed from another, eg. for carpentry*)

¹**ekibala** *n7* **fruit;** *in pl.* **agricultural produce, crops.** *Pronunciation:* ekibàlà

²**ekibala** *n7* **spot, stain.** *Pronunciation:* ekibálá

ekibalangulo (*also* ekibangulo) *n7* **whetstone, strop**

ekibambulira *n7* **something very dangerous** (*like a rampaging fire*), **horror**

ekibambya *n7* **stain** (*eg. on clothes*), **patch of different coloured skin**

ekibangirizi *n7* **area** (*of definite size, eg. football field or house plot*), **open space/area, clearing** (*in the jungle*)

ekibanja *n7* **plot of land, building site.** *Traditionally, this is a subsistence holding of unspecified size, having a house, banana garden and outfields.*

ekibanyi *n7* **rack** (*suspended from roof in a kitchen, used for storage or smoking food*)

ekibatu *n7* **palm** (*of the hand*)

ekibaya *n7* **crib, Mose's basket**

ekibbe *n7* **something stolen**

ekibbiitu *n7* **celebration** (*with something provided in abundance, especially food*)

ekibbo *n7* **basket** (*bowl-shaped stiff type, usually made from akakeedo*)

ekibe *n7* **jackal**

ekibebenu *n7* **cartilage, grissle**

ekibeerawo *n7* **event**

ekibeere *n7* **udder, testicle**

kibeeredde   kye kibeeredde *conj* **the reason why**

ekibegabega *n7* **shoulder**

ekibejjagalo *n7* **belch**

ekibi *n7* **something bad, evil, sin**

ekibibi *n7* **mound of earth** (*especially one on which sweet potatoes are planted*)

ekibiina *n7* **group, association, organisation, society, club, sect class, form, level** (*in school*), *eg. ekibiina eky'okusatu* (*'Level 3'*)   Ekibiina Ekigatta Amawanga ga Bulaaya **European Union**   ekibiina ky'abakozi **trade union**   ekibiina ky'abasuubuzi **trade association**   ekibiina ky'obufuzi **political party**   ekibiina ky'obwegassi cooperative (society) Ekibiina ky'Olulimi Oluganda **Luganda Language Society** ekibiina kya ba nnakyewa **voluntary society, NGO**

ekibikka *n7* **cover**

ekibinja *n7* **group, crowd** ekibinja ky'abantu **crowd of people** ekibinja ky'ebinyonyi **flock of birds** ekibinja ky'enjuki **swarm of bees**

ekibinuko *n7* **social event** (*with excitement and merry-making*)

ekibira *n7* **forest**

ekibiriiti *n7* **matchbox**; *in pl.* **matches**

[1]ekibo *n7* **type of biting insect** (*resembles a bedbug*)

[2]ekibo *n7* **raffia palm** *Raphia farinifera*, **midrib of leaf of this palm**

ekibobe *n7* (*no pl.*) **bunged-up nose, rhinitis**

ekibogwe -a ekibogwe *adj* **half-done, partially ripe** (*of a fruit*), **semi-trained**

ekibombo *n7* **herb used to wash sap from hands** (*after peeling matooke*) *Cyphostemma* sp.

ekibondo *n7* **place on foot where jigger grows**

Kiboneka *n1* **name given to a male child born at the time of the new moon**

ekibonerezo *n7* **punishment, sentence**

ekibonoobono *n7* **suffering, ordeal**

kibonoomu *n1* **shooting star**. *Meaning: 'It is seen by one person.' ('-bona' is from Lunyoro)*

ekibonyoobonyo *n7* **torture**

ekiboobi *n7* **type of millipede** (*found in thatch*)

kibooko *n9* **whip, cane** -babika kibooko **beat with a cane**

ekibowabowa *n7* **climbing herb** *Glycine wightii*

ekibuga *n7* **town**. *Historic use: densely settled area around the Kabaka's palace* ekibuga ekikulu **capital (city)**

kibugga *n1* **stinging nettle** *Laportea ovalifolia*

ekibululu *n7* (*no pl.*) **semi-darkness**

ekibumba *n7* **liver**

ekibumbe *n7* **something made of clay, piece of pottery**

ekibumbiro *n7* **brick-making area**

ekibundubundu *n7* **pretend** (*or imitation*) **gun**

ekibungu -a ekibungu *adj* **toothless** ow'ekibungu *n1* **toothless person**

ekibuno *n7* **gum** (*in mouth*)

Kibuuka *n1* **Kiganda deity** (*lubaale*), **god of war**. *Son of Wannema.*

ekibuuzo *n7* **question, examination**

kibuyaga *n1* (*no pl.*) **strong wind, storm, gale**

kibuzi *n1* **type of banana** (*used for matooke*)

ekibwankulata *n7* **tall herbaceous plant with fleshy leaves** (*medicinal*) *Tetradenia urticifolia*

ekibwatuka *n7* **sudden noise, explosion, bang**

ekibwatukira *adv* **suddenly, unexpectedly** -fa ekibwatukira **die suddenly** (*or unexpectedly*)

ekibya *n7* **earthenware bowl**

ekicupa *n7* **big bottle**

ekidaala *n7* **temporary construction** (*eg. made for an event*), **temporary shelter, shed**

ekiddako *adv* **next, subsequently**

ekiddedde obudde obw'ekiddedde *n14* **cloudy weather, overcast weather**

ekiddibwamu *n7* **something repeated, chorus** (*in singing*)

ekiddirira *adv* **next, subsequently**

ekiddo *n7* (*no pl.*) (1) **fresh pasture** (*with rampant growth, eg. grassland after burning*); (2) **bad weed**; (3) **roadblock** (*one mounted by police – a use of the word that originated with taxi drivers*) ekiddo ku nnyanja **water hyacinth** *Eichhornia crassipes*

ekidduka *n7* **vehicle**

ekiddukano *n7* (*no pl.*) **diarrhoea** ekiddukano ky'omusaayi **dysentery**

ekiddukiro *n7* **refuge**

ekide *n7* **bell**

ekidiba *n7* **pool, pond** ekidiba ekiwugirwamu **swimming pool**

ekidigida *n7* **dance**

ekido (*slang*) *n7* **two hundred shilling coin** (= engege)

ekidoli *n7* **bed pan, potty**

ekidomola *n7* **jerry can**

ekidondi *n7* **spool**

ekidongo *n7* **guitar**

ekidumusi *n7* (*no pl.*) **diarrhoea**

ekiduula *n7* **crowd**

ekidyeri *n7* **ferry**

ekifa *n7* **a happening**; *in pl.* **news**

kifaalu *n9* **whip, lash** amayembe aga kifaalu **bad alien spirits**

ekifaananyi *n7* **image, picture, photograph, drawing, model** ekifaananyi ekisiige **painting** ekifaananyi eky'omu ndabirwamu **reflection** (*in a mirror*)

ekifaayo *n7* **event**; *in pl.* **news**

ekifabakazi *n7* **tulip tree** (*medicinal*) *Spathodea campanulata*. *Meaning: 'It dies because of women.'*

kifampa (*also* kifamba) *n1* **kapok tree** *Ceiba pentandra*

ekifenensi *n7* **jackfruit** (*tree; fruit*) *Artocarpus heterophyllus*

ekifi *n7* **piece of meat**

ekifisseewo *n7* **surplus**

ekifo *n7* **place, position, vacancy** -dda mu kifo kya **replace** -koonola ekifo **receive a high position unexpectedly** mu kifo kya **instead of**

ekifu *n7* (*no pl.*) **mist** ekifu ku maaso **blurred vision**

ekifuba *n7* **chest** (*of the body*), **cough, chest** (*or bust*) **measurement, span** (*ditance from fingertip to fingertip of outstretched arms*) ekifuba ekikalu **dry cough** ekifuba ekikutuka **wet cough** ekifuba ekiraakiira **whooping cough** -gwa mu kifuba **embrace, hug** omuntu w'ekifuba **forceful person**

ekifugi *n7* **verandah** (*on platform raised above*

ground level)

ekifuko *adv/n7* (*no pl.*) **crowded together, too close, crowdedness** -a ekifuko *adj* **crowded**

ekifulukwa *n7* **abandoned house**

ekifumu *n7* **digging spear** (*digging implement*)

ekifumufumu *n7* **tall herb with orange to yellow flowers** *Leonotis nepetifolia*

ekifundikwa *n7* **knot** (*tied in cloth*)

ekifunvu *n7* **mound** (*of earth*)

ekifuta -a ekifuta *adj* **oily** (*eg. of skin*)

ekigaaga *n7* **type of broad flat bean** (*butter bean*) *Phaseolus lanatus*

ekigaali *n7* **railway carriage, cart, wheelbarrow, old bicycle**

ekigagi *n7* **aloe** (*medicinal*)

ekigalagamba *n7* **scale** (*eg. of fish*), **scab** (*on wound*)

ekigalanga *See* ebigalanga

[1]ekigali *n7* **camel-foot tree** *Bauhinia* spp., *Piliostigma thonningii*

[2]ekigali *n7* **offering** (*to a lubaale*), **basket in which such an offering is placed**

ekigambo *n7* **word**; *in pl.* **remark, statement** ebigambo bya nkukutu **secret words** Kigambo ki? **What news?** -lemera ku kigambo **be insistent** -sala ebigambo **slander** Si kigambo. **It doesn't matter.** -tema ebigambo **slander** -yiwa ebigambo **come out with lots of words** (*eg. in abuse*)

ekiganda *n7* **large bundle** ekiganda entuumu **large pile of firewood** -a ekiganda *adj* **Kiganda**

ekigango *n7* **open-sided building used for meetings, attendance hall**

ekigenderere *adv* **purposefully**

ekigendererwa *n7* **purpose, motive, aim, intention**

ekigere *n7* **foot, paw, trotter, footstep, footprint, pedal** ekigere ekisajja **big toe** ekigere ky'eggaali **bicycle pedal** omwenge bigere **banana beer** ow'ebigere *n1* **walker, pedestrian**

ekigero *n7* **measure, measurement, dose** -a ekigero *adj* **average, medium**

ekigezesebwa *n7* **experiment**

ekigezo *n7* **test**; *in pl.* **examination**

kiggala *n1* (*pl.* ba kiggala) **dear person**

ekiggwa *n7* **shrine** (*of a lubaale*)

[1]ekiggya *n7* **family graveyard, (traditional) temple** (= essabo)

[2]ekiggya *n7* **something new, novelty**

ekigimusa *n7* **fertiliser**

ekigingirire *n7* **forgery**

ekigo *n7* **large enclosure** (*especially RC*), **fort**

ekigobero *n7* **landing site, terminus**

ekigodo *n7* **thick fatty skin** (*eg. of a pig*)

ekigogo *n7* **sheath of banana leaf.** *See* olugogo

ekigojja *n7* **basket trap for catching enkejje** (*type of small fish*)

ekigomba *n7* **dish prepared from dry powdered bananas mixed with sweet potatoes and sometimes beans** (*the bananas are usually beer bananas or gonja*)

ekigongo *n7* (*pl. rare*) **backbone** (*of an animal*) Kigongo *n1* *title* **name of child born before twins**

ekigoogwa *n7* **sisal** (*plant*) *Agave sisalana*

ekigotta *See* ekisotta

ekiguddewo *n7* **event**

ekiguli *n7* **cage**

ekigulumu *n7* **mound of earth, bump, speed hump** oluguudo olw'ebigulumu **bumpy road**

ekigunga *n7* **fruit of omugunga, giant yellow mulberry**

ekiguuna *n7* **patch of ringworm** (*on head*); *in pl.* **ringworm**

ekigwagwa *n7* **depraved person, imbecile**

ekigwawo *n7* **event**

ekigwengere *n7* **depraved person, imbecile**

ekigwo *n7* **fall, wrestling, throw** (*in wrestling*) -biriga ekigwo **throw** (*someone*) **on the ground** (*in wrestling*)

[1]-kiika *vi* (-kiise) **attend a meeting**

[2]-kiika *vt* **put sideways, place across**

[3]-eekiika *vr* **place oneself sideways, be across, block** -eekiika mu kkubo lya **stand in the way of**

kiikino **here it is**

kiikiri **there it is**

-kiikirira *vt* (-kiikiridde) **represent, deputise for**

-kiikiriza *vt* (-kiikirizizza) **interpose**

-kiikulukuka *vi* (-kiikulukuse) **be dismissed** (*of those at a meeting*)

-kiikulula *vt* (-kiikuludde) **dismiss** (*those at a meeting*)

kiikyo **there it is**

-kiina *vt* (-kiinye) **derive, sneer at, mock.** *See* -kiina. '*-kiina*' is more derisory or aggressive than '*-duula*'.

kiisi *det* **each, every**

kiizi *n9* **cheese**

ekijaguzo *n7* **celebration, jubilation, rejoicing**

ekijanjaalo *n7* **bean** (*in general*), **kidney bean** *Phaseolus vulgaris*

ekijiiko *n7* **spoon, spoonful** ekijiiko ekisena **ladle, scoop, serving spoon** -kuba ekijiiko **fry**

ekijjukizo *n7* **memorial, reminder, souvenir**

ekijjulo *n7* **meal for invited guests, banquet, feast**

ekijoozi *n7* **T-shirt**

ekijugo *n7* **penholder**

ekika *n7* **type, kind, make, category, clan** ekika ky'omusaayi **blood group** ow'ekika *n1* **member of a clan**

ekikaabugo *n7* **temporary shelter** (*eg. made to sleep in overnight when travelling*)

kikafuuwe *excl* **never again**

ekikajjo *n7* **sugar cane** *Saccharum officinarum*

ekikakala *n7* **woody herb** *Pseudarthria hookeri*

ekikakampa *n7* **scab** (*on wound*); *in pl.* **dry flaky place on skin**

ekikalappwa *n7* cocoon

ekikalu *n7* something dry   -kuba ekikalu tuck in (*shirt or blouse*)

ekikaluubiriza *n7* something that makes difficult, obstacle, hindrance

ekikamulo *si. of* ebikamulo. *See* ebikamulo

ekikande *n7* fallow/overgrown land

ekikangabwa *n7* terrifying/shocking event

ekikankano *n7* (*no pl.*) trembling

ekikapu *n7* shopping bag (*large woven type*)

ekikata *n7* mound of earth for planting sweet potatoes   ekikata kya lumonde earth mound planted with sweet potatoes

ekikeerezi *adv* late, belatedly

kikeesa *n7* nightclub

ekikeeto *n7* (*no pl.*) heartburn

ekikemo *n7* temptation

ekikennembi *n7* type of large sugar-loving ant

ekikere *n7* frog, toad

kiki? *interr* (*pl.* biki?) what is it? (N13)

-kikiitana *vi* (-kikiitanye) struggle with something difficult to do (*eg. try to insert something that does not quite fit*)

-kikinala (*also* -kukunala) *vi* (-kikinadde) stick out, protrude, be disrespectful

-kikinaza (*also* -kukunaza) *vt* (-kikinazizza) cause to stick out kikiri *n7* nightclub

kikirikisi *n7* type of mouse (*found in banana gardens, but only rarely; probably dormouse*)

ekikko *n7* depression in the landscape, valley

ekikkowe *n7* sigh

ekiko *n7* private parts (*especially of a woman*)

ekikokyo *n7* riddle, enigma, puzzle

ekikole *n7* product

ekikoleeza *n7* lighter

ekikoligo *n7* something that weighs on the mind (*restricting one's freedom*), burden

ekikolimo *n7* curse

ekikolo *n7* (1) lower part of tree or shrub (*above and below ground*); (2) stem (*of a word in grammar*)

ekikolobero *n7* atrocity, abomination, disgrace

ekikolokomba *n7* stalk of banana bunch (*where exposed above the leaf sheaths*). *See* omututumba

ekikololo *n7* cough

ekikolondolwa *n7* sputum, phlegm

ekikolwa *n7* act, action, deed, verb   ekikolwa eby'obukambwe violence   ekikolwa ekya bampaane showing-off   Ebikolwa by'Abatume Acts of the Apostles

kikomando *n7* chapati roll stuffed with beans

ekikome   obudde obw'ekikome *n14* cloudy weather, overcast weather

ekikomera *n7* boundary wall (*of plot*), brick wall

[1]**ekikomo** *n7* bracelet, copper   ekikomo eky'omu bulago necklace

[2]**ekikomo** *n7* end point

ekikompe *n7* communion cup, chalise

ekikonde *n7* fist   -kuba ebikonde box

ekikondo *n7* post

[1]**kikonge** *n1* type of shrub (*with white to pale blue flowers*) Clerodendron myricoides

[2]**ekikonge** *n7* big tree stump, high official

ekikongo *n7* type of yam (*takes a long time to cook, but then remains edible for several weeks*) Dioscorea minutiflora

ekikongoliro *n7* core of maize cob (*after removal of grains*)

ekikonko *n7* small depression in road, pothole

ekikookooma *n7* shrub (*leaves used as toilet paper*) Vernonia auriculifera, toilet paper

ekikoola *n7* leaf

ekikoomi *n7* smoky fire (*of grass, rubbish, etc.*)

ekikoonagana *n7* contradiction

ekikoosi *n7* a particular group of people, faction (*eg. of a political party*)

ekikooyi *n7* undergarment (*worn under busuuti*)

ekikopo *n7* cup, cupful

ekikowe *n7* eyelid

ekikozesebwa *n7* tool; *in pl.* equipment

ekiku *n7* (1) bedbug; (2) large piece of firewood

ekikubagizo *n7* consolation, comfort

ekikubiro *n7* overgarment, apron

ekikubo *n7* rough road, track

ekikuggu   -a ekikuggu *adj* docked, cropped   engalo ya kikuggu finger with part missing   omukira gwa kikuggu docked tail

ekikugunyu *n7* hip

ekikula *n7* structure

ekikulejje (*also* ekikulekule) *n7* something very abnormal, person (*or animal*) with physical deformity, children's game (*dressing up to scare*)

ekikulu *n7* something important/significant

kikumi *n7/num* hundred

ekikunta *n7* piece of bedding; *in pl.* bedding

[1]**kikuŋŋunta** *n1* gale, gust, squall

[2]**ekikuŋŋunta** *n7* sieve

ekikuta *n7* strip of barkcloth (*used as clothing by men*), outer covering, skin (*of fruit*), rind, shell, pod, peel(ing), bark   ebikuta by'ebinjanjaalo bean pods   ebikuta by'olubaawo wood shavings   ebikuta bya lumonde potato peelings   ebinyeebwa by'ebikuta peanuts in their shells

ekikutuko   -fa ekikutuko die suddenly or unexpectedly)

ekikuubo *n7* passage (*between buildings in a town*), alley, stripe   -a ebikuubo *adj* striped

ekikuufiira *n7* helmet, old hat, worn-out hat

ekikuukuulu *n7* cluster, group, gang, crowd

ekikuusi   -a ekikuusi (*also* -a ekikuusikuusi) *adj* red (*colour of subsoil*)

ekikwakwaya *n7* rustling sound

ekikwangala *n7* something counterfeit, fake, sham   -a ekikwangala *adj* counterfeit, fake, *eg.* omusawo w'ekikwangala ('fake doctor')

ekikwanso (*also* ekikwaso) *n7* safety pin

ekikwaso *n7* brooch
ekikwatako *n7* concern
ekikwatandiga *n7* type of grass (*with seeds that stick on clothes*) *Setaria verticillata. Meaning: 'It sticks on sheep.'*
ekikwate *n7* passage to be memorised
ekikwekweto *n7* secret scouting patrol, reconnaissance
ekikyamu *n7* something gone wrong, something crooked
ekikye *pos* hers, his
ekikyo *pos* yours *si.*
ekikyupa *n7* jar
-kima *vt* (-kimye) fetch, go for
ekimala *adv* enough, sufficiently
kimala empaka kikoowa Mexican sunflower *Tithonia diversifolia. Name needs confirmation.*
ekimbala *n7* goliath heron
Kimbugwe *n1 title* chief of Buluuli County (*traditional guardian of the 'omulongo' of the Kabaka*). *Also a royal name and a name used in the Mpologoma Clan.*
ekimenyoomenyo *n7* (*no pl.*) rheumatism, general body pain
ekimera *n7* plant ekimera ekiranda creeping (*or* climbing) plant ekimera ky'eddagala medicinal plant
ekimererezi *n7* self-sown plant
ekimmonde *n7* larva of bott fly
kimogo ensuwa ya kimogo *n9* pot with broken lip
kimote olubugo olwa kimote *n3* high quality barkcloth (*deep brown in colour and very soft*)
ekimpoowooze *adv* calmly, gently -a ekimpoowooze *adj* cool (*of the weather*), calming (*of music*)
kimu *num/adv* one, alike, in the same way kimu kimu one-by-one kimu kya kubiri half kimu kya kuna quarter kimu kya kusatu one-third kye kimu the same kye kimu na the same as, *eg. Ekikopo kino kye kimu na kiri.* ('*This cup is the same as that one.'*) -ssa kimu think alike
ekimuli *n7* flower
ekimyanso *n7* flash, gleam -kuba ekimyanso reflect
ekimyu *n7* band/cloth tied around waist (*a sign of mourning*)
ekimyula *n7* (1) tall herb with yellow flowers (*yields a reddish dye*) *Guizotia scabra*; (2) very beautiful woman
ekinaabaawo *n7* event (*in the future*)
ekinaabiro *n7* bathroom, washroom
ekinaabirwamu *n7* something used for washing one's body (*eg. basin*)
ekinaala *n7* large clinker-built boat
kinaana *n7/num* eighty
ekinazi *n7* fruit of a palm (*of various species*), coconut (*fruit*)
ekindaazi *n7* (*pl.* amandaazi *n6*) doughnut

ekinenyo *n7* blame, criticism
ekinkumu *n7* thumbprint, fingerprint
kinna...-mu *adv* one-by-one (N8.1). *Takes numeral concord* (N4.2), *eg.* (1) *Baabala ebiwuka kinnakimu.* ('*They counted the insects one-by-one.'*); (2) *Baabala obutungulu kinnakamu.* ('*They counted the onions one-by-one.'*)
kinnaabyo *n7* their companion
kinnaakyo *n7* its companion
ekinnansi *n7* something pertaining to a country or place -a ekinnansi *adj* indigenous, native, traditional eddagala ly'ekinnansi traditional medicine
kinnawadda *adv* very well, proficiently, *eg. Musoke oluganda alwogera kinnawadda.* ('*Musoke speaks Luganda very well.'*). *Meaning: 'It comes from long ago.'*)
kinneemu *adv* one-by-one (N8.1)
kinnoomu *adv* one-by-one (*of people*) (N8.1)
ekinnya *n7* pit, hole, ditch, burrow ekinnya kya buyonjo pit latrine ekinnya mu luguudo pothole
ekinnyi *n7* pubic region (*of a woman*)
kino *dem* this
ekinonko *n7* noise produced by cracking the knuckles
ekinoso *n7* leech
ekinsambwe *n7* type of shrub with yellow flowers *Triumfetta macrophylla*, strip of bark (*or* cord) from this plant (*used in stitching, eg. bundles of reeds in roof of round hut*)
kinsimbye *n1* (*no pl.*) sudden pain in the side or shoulder
ekintabuli *n7* mixture, jumble, hodgepodge, assortment ekintabuli ky'omuziki music of all sorts essomero ery'ekintabuli co-educational school
ekintu *n7* thing, substance; *in pl.* possessions, goods Kintu *n1* (1) first king of Buganda (*in present dynasty*). *His reign is estimated as 1200-1230 AD. He replaced King Bemba Musota of the Tonda line, who ruled both Buganda and Bunyoro*; (2) first person who came to Buganda from heaven; (3) male name used in the Ngo Clan
ekinu *n7* mortar (*for grinding*)
ekinunulo *n7* ransom
ekinusu *n7* coin (*mostly used for 100 shilling coin*)
ekinuubule *n7* bruise
ekinuulo *n7* hoof
ekinya *n7* gecko
ekinyaanya *n7* tree tomato (*fruit shaped like entula*) *Cyphomandra betacea*
ekinyeebwa *n7* peanut *Arachis hypogaea* ekinyeebwa ekizungu oysternut (*large climber with large flat seeds*) *Telfairia pedata. The seeds are roasted, pounded and cooked as a sauce 'enva', tasting much the same as peanut sauce (hence the name). The seeds are planted in pairs, a larger 'female' one ('ekikazi') with a smaller 'male' one*

('ekisajja'). *Said to have come from Busoga, where it is known as 'mulekula'.* ebinyeebwa ebisiike **roasted peanuts** ebinyeebwa eby'ebikuta **peanuts in their shells** enva z'ebinyeebwa **peanut sauce**

ekinyegenyege *n7* **excited state**

ekinyiigo *n7* **anger**

ekinyiiza *n7* **annoyance, irritation**

ekinyira *n7* **fruit bat**

ekinyirikisi *n7* **sponge made from beaten 'mututumba'** (*pith within stalk of inflorescence*)

ekinyomo *n7* **drop-tail ant** (*large black type*)

ekinyonyi *n7* **bird**

kinyoozi *n1* (*pl.* ba kinyoozi) **barber**

kinyulwa *n1* **type of mauve edible mushroom** (*found in mulched banana gardens or where empawu termites occur*)

ekinyumu *n7* **enjoyable social event, celebration, entertainment.** *From: '-nyuma' ('be enjoyable').*

ekinyusi *n7* **kernel, core of a boil, gist, substance,** *eg. By'oyogedde temuli kinyusi. ('There's no substance in what you have said.')*

[1]**ekinywa** *n7* **tendon, ligament.** *Pronunciation:* ekinywà

[2]**ekinywa** *n7* **bundle.** *Pronunciation:* ekinywà ekinywa ky'emmuli **bundle of reeds** ekinywa ky'enku **bundle of firewood**

ekinywabwino *n7* (*no pl.*) **blotting paper.** *Meaning: 'It drinks ink.'*

ekinywi *n7* (*no pl.*) **drinking party, friendship** (*through compatability*) -ba ab'ekinywi **make a common cause** wa kinywi (*pl.* ba kinywi) **close friend**

ekipaapi *n7* **patch**

ekipakiti *n7* **packet**

ekipande *n7* **sign, notice, chart, poster, placard, billboard** ekipande ky'oluguudo **road sign**

ekipapajjo *n7* **piece, fragment**

ekipapula *n7* **paper** ekipapula eky'okwerongoosesa **toilet paper**

ekipimo *n7* **measurement**

ekipooli *n7* **thick sauce made from pounded termites and peanuts** gavumenti y'ekipooli **coalition government**

-kira *vt* (-kize) **be more/better than** (*indicating personal preference or advantage*), *eg. Ekitabo kino kikira kiri. ('This book is better than that.'),* **be superior to.** *Proverb: Asuubira, akira aloota. ('He who hopes is superior to he who dreams.')*

ekiraalo *n7* **cattle pen, kraal, stockade**

ekiraamo *n7* **will** (*written*), **last testament**

ekiraato *n7* **sheath** (*for dagger or sword*), **shoe, boot**

[1]**ekirabo** *n7* **gift, donation, offering** (*in church*), **reward, present, prize.** *Pronunciation:* ekirábo -solooza ebirabo **take a collection**

[2]**ekirabo** *n7* **restaurant.** *From: 'club' (English). Pronunciation:* ekirábo ekirabo ky'omwenge **bar**

ekiragaano *n7* **agreement, contract, covenant**

[1]**ekiragala** -a kiragala *adj* **green**

[2]**ekiragala** *n7* **fishing net** (*for catching enkejje*) (= akasambo)

ekiragiro *n7* **order, command, decree**

ekirago *n7* **mat used by itinerant labourers** olumbe lw'ekirago **source of much trouble** (*referring to a person*)

ekiraka *n7* **patch**

ekiranda *n7* **creeping/climbing plant, runner** (*of a plant*)

ekirangiriro (*also* ekirango) *n7* **proclamation, announcement, advertisement, publicity, notice**

ekirawuli *n7* **glass chimney** (*of lamp*)

ekirayiro *n7* **oath, vow**

ekire *n7* **cloud**

kireereese *n1* (*pl.* ba kireereese) **wanderer, vagabond**

ekireka *n7* **banana leaf** (*when turning yellow*)

ekiremba *n7* **turban, headcloth**

ekiremesa *n7* **something that makes impossible,**

NOTES ON
k

-k. Unless the **k** is doubled, verbs starting **k** have 1st person singulars starting **nk**, *eg.* **nkola** ('I work'), from **-kola**.

aka-. Nouns in *n12* starting **aka** have plurals (in *n14*) starting **obu**, *eg.* the plural of **akatale** is **obutale**. However, if the noun starts **akaa**, then the plural starts **obwa**, *eg.* the plural of **akaana** is **obwana**.

eki-. Nouns in *n7* starting **eki** have plurals (in *n8*) starting **ebi**, *eg.* the plural of **ekintu** is **ebintu**.

-kk. Verbs starting **kk** have 1st person singulars starting **nzik**, *eg.* **nzika** ('I descend'), from **-kka**.

ekk. Nouns in *n5* starting **kk** have plurals (in *n6*) starting **amak**, *eg.* the plural of **ekkobe** is **amakobe**.

oku-. This is the infinitive prefix (**N18**), *eg.* **okusoma** ('to read'), from **-soma** ('read'). There is no plural. Otherwise, there are only two nouns (in *n15*) with this prefix, namely **okugulu** ('leg') and **okutu** ('ear'). Their plurals (in *n6*) are **amagulu** and **amatu**.

eky-. Nouns in *n7* starting **eky** have plurals (in *n8*) starting **eby**, *eg.* the plural of **ekyalo** is **ebyalo**. Some nouns in *n7* starting **eky** are compound, consisting of **ekya** ('of') and a following noun (**N11.2**), *eg.* **ekyemisana** ('lunch'). If the initial vowels are dropped, then this is so for both parts of the word, *ie.* **kyamisana**.

NOUNS IN *n9*. Most nouns in *n9* have identically spelt plurals (in *n10*).

---

obstacle

ekirenge *n7* cooked hoof of cow

ekirerya *n7* something empty inside (*eg. bean pod with no seeds*). See ebirerya

ekirevu *n7* beard   akamwa ekirevu **razor**

[1]kiri *dem* **that**

[2]kiri **it is** (*stem* -li)

ekiribaawo *n7* **(future) event**

ekiriisa *n7* **nourishment, nutrient, vitamin**

kirimaanyi *n1* (*pl.* ba kirimaanyi) **strong man**

ekirime (*also* ekirimbwa) *n7* **cultivated plant, crop**

kirimegga **-a kirimegga** *adj* **huge, gigantic**

ekirimi *n7* (*no pl.*) **lisp**   -lya ekirimi **interrupt a speaker,** *eg. Omwogezi yali aky'ayogera n'amulya ekirimi.* (*'The speaker was still speaking when she interrupted him.'*)   ow'ekirimi *n1* **person with a lisp**   -yogera n'ekirimi **talk with a lisp**

ekirimibwa (*also* ekirime) *n7* **cultivated plant, crop**

kirimululu *n1* **cuckoo**

kiriniki *n9* **clinic**

[1]ekirira *n7* **umbilical cord**

[2]-(y)akirira See -yakirira

Kirisitu *n1* **Christ** (*RC*)

ekiriwo *n7* **event**

[1]ekiro *adv/n7* **at night, night, night-time;** *in pl.* **period, era, times**   ekiro kya jjo **last night**   ekiro kya leero **tonight**   ebiro eby'edda **olden times**

[2]kiro *n9* **kilo**

ekirogologo *n7* **skin rash** (*caused by allergic reaction*)

ekirombe *n7* **mine, quarry**   ekirombe ky'amafuta **oilwell**   ekirombe ky'amayinja **stone quarry**   ekirombe ky'ekikomo **copper mine**

kiromita *n9* **kilometre**

ekirooto *n7* **dream**   ekirooto ekibi **nightmare**

ekiroowa *n7* **shrub or small tree** (*used in vetinerary medicine*) *Jatropha multifida*

ekirowoozo *n7* **thought, idea;** *in pl.* **mind**

ekiruke *n7* **something woven**

ekirumbirumbi *n7* **sugarcare** (*type with thin stem*)   lutalo lwa birumbirumbi **ritual battle fought with ebirumbirumbi during the coronation ceremony**

kirundu *n1* **type of tall tree** (*yields inferior barkcloth*) *Antiaris toxicaria*

ekirungo *n7* **substance, secretion, spice, seasoning, flavouring**   ekirungo ekiyongeza sukaali mu mubiri **insulin**   ekirungo eky'obutwa **poisonous substance**   ekirungo ky'enva **mixture of ingredients used to make a sauce** (*eg. onions, tomatoes, curry powder*)

ekiruyi *n7* (*no pl.*) **grudge, vendetta**

ekiryo *n7* (1) **pumpkin** (*plant*) *Cucurbita pepo*; (2) **gourd** (*plant*) *Lagenaria siceraria*

[1]ekisa *n7* (*no pl.*) **kindness, mercy**   -a ekisa *adj* **kind, merciful**   lwa kisa **through kindness**   ow'ekisa *n1* **kind person**

[2]ekisa *n7* **labour pain;** *in pl.* **contractions**

[3]-kisa *vit* (-kisizza) **conceal information (from).**

Saying: 'Kabaka akisizza omukono.' ('The Kabaka has hidden his hand.', meaning 'The Kabaka has passed away.')

ekisaaganda *n7* **bunch, bundle** (*of the size that can be held with one or both hands*), *eg. ekisaaganda ky'ebimuli ('bunch of flowers')*

ekisaakaate *n7* (1) **reed fence** (*with crossed reeds, around a chief's compoound*), **enclosure within a reed fence;** (2) **temporary construction or shelter**   mu kisaakaate **in a cultured environment**   -siiga mu kisaakaate **send** (*a person, usually a child*) **to the service of a chief**

ekisaalu *n7* **area of essaalu grass**

ekisaaniiko *n7* **piece of rubbish;** *in pl.* **rubbish**

ekisaanikira *n7* **lid, cover, stopper, large bung**

ekisaanyi (*also* ekisaanikizo) *n7* **caterpillar**

ekisaanyizo *n7* **suitability, qualification;** *in pl.* **competences**

ekisaawe *n7* **area of cut/slashed vegetation**   ekisaawe ky'emizannyo **playground, sportsground**   ekisaawe ky'ennyonyi **airfield, airport**   ekisaawe ky'omupiira **football pitch**

ekisagazi *n7* **elephant grass** *Pennisetum purpureum*

ekisago *n7* **injury**

ekisaka *n7* **thicket, bush**

ekisakiro *n7* **crop** (*of a bird*)

ekisala *n7* **knife**

ekisale *n7* **cut, something cut, set payment, fee, charge, subscription;** *in pl.* **fees**

ekisaliddwawo *n7* **decision**

ekisamba *n7* **island of floating vegetation** (*that has broken away from a swamp*)

ekisambandege *n7* **leguminous shrub with inflated pods** *Crolalaria*

ekisambi *n7* **thigh**

ekisambu *n7* **weedy plot** (*after the harvest*)

ekisandasanda *n7* **type of tree** (*with white latex*) *Mimusops bagshawei*

ekisanduuko *n7* **big** (*or old*) **case, trunk**

ekisanirizo *n7* **comb**

[1]ekisanja *n7* (1) **dry withered banana leaf** (*when tied in a bundle*); (2) **turn** (*in a polygamous marriage*). *The meanings are related. A man would leave very early in the morning, using tied together withered banana leaves to clear the path of dew. On reaching another of his homes to work, he would tie up the banana leaves on the verandah, serving as a signal. Saying: 'Ekisanja kyange.' ('It's time to prepare everything for my husband.'). A bundle of banana leaves ebisanja can be tied to the door of a night-dancer when he or she is absent. This is said to prevent him or her finding the way home).*   ebisanja by'oluggi **banana fibre hung as a screen in a doorway**

[1]kisansa *n1* **type of banana** (*used for making matooke*)

[2]ekisansa *n7* **palm leaf**

ekisanyusa *n7* **something that causes pleasure,**

amusement, fun

ekisasi *n7* porch (*of grass hut*), eaves, dripline (*of roof*) ekisasi mu kamwa **palate** amazzi g'ekisasi **water from the eaves/porch** (*the second totem 'akabbiro' of the Ababiito b'e Kkooki Clan*)

ekisasiro *n7* piece of rubbish; *in pl.* rubbish

ekisasulibwa *n7* payment

ekisawo *n7* bag (*large or in poor condition*)

ekisebe *n7* type of large soft pink yam *Dioscorea alata*

[1]**ekiseera** *n7* period of time, duration, time, season (*of the year*) ekiseera eky'omu maaso **the future** kiseera kya kazigizigi **very bad time** ekiseera kya bwerende **period of sexual abstinence** (*for a man*) kiseera kya malya (*also* kiseera kya kulya) **mealtime** ekiseera ky'enkuba **rainy season** ekiseera kyonna **all the time, always, constantly** ebiseera eby'akatabanguko **state of emergency** ebiseera eby'eddembe **leisure time** -a buli kiseera *adj* **constant** -a ekiseera *adj* **part-time, temporary, transient, provisional** buli kiseera **all the time, always** ku kiseera kye kimu ne **at the same time as** -mala ebiseera **waste time**

[2]**ekiseera** *n7* line on hand or neck

ekiseke *n7* wrist

ekisekeseke *n7* types of plant used for making straws *Clerodendrum capitatum, Peucadenum grantii*

Kisekwa *n1 title* name of a senior official ekkooti ya Kisekwa **court for settling land and other disputes**

ekisembayo *adv* finally, lastly

ekisenge *n7* wall, partition, room, bedroom. *See* omukka ebisenge by'enjuki **honeycomb**

ekisenso *n7* skirt of palm fibre (*worn by dancers*)

ekisenyi *n7* swamp

ekisero *n7* basket (*stiff type with handle*)

ekisiba *n7* something used for tying or fastening, fastener

ekisibe *n7* something tied, fastened or locked

ekisibo *n7* pen (*for animals*), herd, flock

ekisibye *n7* blockage

ekisigadde (*also* ekisigaddewo) *n7* remainder ekisigaddeyo **remainder** (*over there*)

ekisige *n7* eyebrow

ekisigule *n7* something uprooted

okisigyeni *n9* oxygen

ekisiibo *n7* fast Kisiibo **Lent**

ekisiikirize *n7* shade, shadow

ekisikattiza *n7* obstruction

ekisiki *n7* partially burnt piece of wood, log for firewood

ekisiko *n7* bushy area, scrub

ekisimbe *n7* plant (*one that has been planted*)

ekisime *n7* something dug up

ekisimule *n7* something uprooted

ekisinde *n7* trail (*where an animal has passed*)

ekisinja *n7* (small) barbel (*type of fish*)

ekisinziiro *n7* heel

ekisiraani *n7* bad luck, misfortune

ekisirikko *n7* hole (*in a road*), depression, rut; *in pl.* corrugations (*in a road*), ruts -a ebisirikko *adj* **bumpy** oluguudo lw'ebisirikko **rutted road**

ekisirinza (*also* ekisiriiza) *n7* piece of charred wood; *in pl.* charcoal, cinders

ekisisimuka *n7* period during the night, watch of the night

ekisitaferi *n7* custard apple (*fruit*)

ekiso *n7* knife ekiso eky'engera **knife without a handle**

ekisobu *n7* error, fault, flaw, blemish, defect, wrong

ekisobye *n7* something gone wrong

ekisobyo *n7* mistake, wrong-doing, transgression, guilt, foul (*in football*)

ekisodde *n7* (1) gorilla; (2) old potato field

ekisoko *n7* saying with a hidden meaning, idiom, metaphor, variation on a theme, improvisation

ekisokomi *n7* type of white larva (*of a beetle, lives in rotting vegetation*)

ekisolo *n7* animal

ekisoobooza *n7* bean leaf (*eaten as vegetable*)

ekisoolisooli *n7* maize stalk (*after removal of cobs*)

ekisooto *n7* piece of mud (*on foot, shoe, etc.*)

ekisosonkole *n7* shell ekisosonkole ky'eggi **egg shell** ekisosonkole ky'ekkovu **snail shell** ekisosonkole ky'essasi **bullet case**

ekisotta (*also* ekigotta) *n7* small pestle, masher ekisotta ky'eggaali **bicycle pedal**

ekissi *n7* something used for killing

[1]**ekisu** *n7* nest

[2]**ekisu** *n7* bad smell

[1]**kisubi** *n1* type of banana (*used for making beer*)

[2]**ekisubi** *n7* (1) piece of dry grass; (2) lemon grass *Cymbopogon citratus*

[1]**ekisula** omunnyo ogw'ekisula *n3* **rock salt**

[2]**ekisula** -lya ekisula **spend the night**

[1]**ekisulo** *n7* place of stay, dormitory. *Pronunciation*: ekisúlo ekisulo ky'abayizi **student hostel**

[2]**ekisulo** *n7* (*no pl.*) twitching of the eye. *Pronunciation*: ekisúlo

ekisulwamu *n7* bedroom

ekisumulula *n7* opener ekisumulula emikebe **tin opener**

ekisumuluzo *n7* key

ekisusunku *n7* (*usually pl.* ebisusunku) husk, shell (*of bean pod, coffee bean, etc.*)

ekisuubizo *n7* promise

ekisuyu *n7* cold sore

ekiswa *n7* termite mound, ant hill ekiswa ekifulufu **abandoned ant hill**

ekiswaza *n7* disgrace

[1]**kita-** *n1* (*pl.* ba kita-) father of (N12) kitange **my**

father, kitaawo your father, kitaawe her/his
father, kitaffe our father, kitammwe your father,
kitaabwe their father

²**ekita** *n7* large gourd *Lagenaria siceraria*

kitaabwe *n1* their father

ekitaala *n7* large light   ebitaala bya tulafiki traffic
lights

kitaawe *n1* her/his father

kitaawo *n1* your *si.* father

ekitaba *n7* puddle

ekitabo *n7* book. *From: 'kitabu' (Swahili).*   Ekitabo
Ekitukuvu Bible   ekitabo ky'olugero novel

ekitabule *n7* mixture

kitaffe *n1* our father

Kitaka *n1* Kiganda deity (*lubaale*), **god of the
earth, male name in Mmamba Clan.** *Saying:
Kataka yamulidde. ('He has died.', lit. 'Kitaka has
eaten him.')*   -a ekitaka *adj* **brown** (*earth
coloured*)

ekitakyusibwa *n7* something immutable

ekitala *n7* sword

ekitaliimu (nsa) *n7* nonsense

ekitaliri *n7* large strainer of sticks and grass used
in making beer

ekitalo *n7* (*no pl.*) something wonderful,
something outstanding, splendour, tragedy   -a
ekitalo *adj* amazing, magnificent, outstanding,
remarkable, splendid   eky'ekitalo amazingly
enough   Nga kitalo! How tragic!,
Commiserations!

ekitambaala *n7* cloth, belt of busuuti   ekitambaala
ky'emmeeza tablecloth

ekitambi *n7* undergarment (*worn under busuuti, a
type of ekikooyi*)

ekitambiro *n7* sacrifice   Ekiseera kino kyakuwaayo
ekitambiro ky'emmisa. It is time to say a mass for
the deceased. (*RC*)

ekitambo *n7* spirit possession (*associated with
night-dancing*)

ekitambulizo *n7* identity card

ekitamiiza *n7* intoxicant, intoxicating drink

kitammwe *n1* (*pl.* ba kitammwe) your *pl.* father

ekitanda *n7* bed

ekitangaala *n7* (*no pl.*) something transparent

kitange *n1* my father

ekitanyi *n7* afterbirth, placenta

ekitategeerekeka *n7* mystery

ekitawuliro *n7* torch (*of grass, wood, etc.*)

ekitawuluzi *n7* parish court

ekitebe *n7* (1) poorly made chair, worn-out chair;
(2) embassy   ekitebe ekikulu headquarters
ekitebe kya gavumenti seat of government
ekitebe kya Uganda Ugandan embassy

ekiteeso *n7* something discussed, bill (*in
parliament*), proposal

ekiteeteeyi *n7* dress, frock

ekitema   -a ekitema *adj* of medium stature
ow'ekitema *n1* person of medium stature

ekitembe *n7* wild banana plant (*seed* ettembe)
Ensete ventricosum

ekitengejja *n7* something floating, floating water
plant   kitengejja *n1* water lettuce *Pistia stratiotes*

ekitengi *n7* type of printed cloth

ekitengo *n7* trembling, shivering, chill

ekitengotengo *n7. Type of small shrub. Solanum
sp. Needs confirmation.*

ekitentegere *n7* barkcloth after first stage of
processing (*rough, worn by peasants*)

ekitereke *n7* parcel

ekitetaagisa *n7* something superfluous

kitezi *n1* hunter (*one who uses traps*)

ekiti *n7* piece of wood, chopping block (*of butcher*).
See ebiti

ekitigi *n7* (*no pl.*) naughtiness, cheek, bad manners

ekitiibwa *n7* (*no pl.*) honour, prestige, dignity,
respect   -a ekitiibwa *adj* honourable, eminent
ow'ekitiibwa *n1* dignatory   Ow'ekitiibwa *title* the
Honourable, *eg. Ow'ekitiibwa Mukyala Mpanga
('the Honourable Mrs Mpanga')*

ekitiisa *n7* something frightening

ekitiiyo *n7* spade, shovel

ekitikkiro *n7* something covering a summit or
roof, dome, spire

ekitimba *n7* long net used for hunting, internet.
*Saying: 'Omwana omulalu bamuteza bitimba.' ('A
wild child needs trapping with hunting nets.')*

Kitinda *n1* Kiganda deity (*lubaale*), **god of
crocodiles**

ekitindiro *n7* framework

-kitiza *vi* (-kitizizza) be infatuated (*especially in a
love affair*)

Okitobba October

ekitogi *n7* collar

ekitole *n7* portion, piece, *eg. ekitole kya ssabbuuni
('piece of soap')*   ekitole ky'ettooke lump of
matooke taken into the fingers to eat

ekitonde *n7* something created, creature

ekitone *n7* gift, natural ability, talent

ekitongole *n7* (1) department (*of an organisation*),
section; (2) office of omutongole (*an appointed
chief*)

kitonto *n1* herb (*medicinal, used to treat fresh
wounds*) *Crassocephalum vitellinum*

ekitoogo *n7* papyrus *Cyperus papyrus*

ekitooke *n7* banana plant   ekitooke ekikazi
'female' banana plant (*any type except beer
banana plants*)   ekitooke ekisajja 'male' banana
plant (*beer banana plants only*)

ekitoomi *n7* piece of mud; *in pl.* mud

ekittavvu *n7* place for depositing ashes (*in the
lusuku; where money was traditionally kept
because it was believed that it would not be
attacked by insects*)

ekitukuvu *n7* something holy

ekituli *n7* hole, aperture

ekitundu *n7* part, section, district, region,

component, portion, instalment, fraction, half, lesson (*Bible reading*) ekitundu ky'omuzannyo part in a play, role

ekitundutundu -sasula mu bitundutundu **pay in instalments**

ekitungulu *n7* **tall herb of wet places** (*with edible fruit 'ettungulu'*) *Afromomum mildbraedii*

kitunzi *n1* (*pl.* ba kitunzi) **sales representative** (**N12**), *eg. kitunzi wa Shell* ('*Shell sales rep*') Kitunzi *title* **chief of Ggomba County**

ekituttwa *n7* **knot**

ekituufu *n7* **the truth, fact** Kituufu. **That's right., Exactly.**

ekituulituuli *n7* **swelling on skin;** *in pl.* **skin rash**

ekituuseewo *n7* **event**

ekituuti *n7* **pulpit, pedestal**

ekivaako *n7* **cause** Ekivaako? **What is causing it?**

ekivaamu *n7* **result, consequence**

ekiviiri ekigule *n7* **wig**

ekivu *n7* **tsetse fly**

ekivuddeko *n7* **cause**

ekivuddemu *n7/conj* **result, consequently** ekivuddemu mu **as a result of**

ekivuga *n7* **something that makes a sound, musical instrument**

Kivumbuzi *n1* **legendery name of the man who discovered how to make barkcloth**

ekivumo *n7* **insult, abuse**

ekivundu *n7* **smell of rot or drain, stink**

ekivunze *n7* **something decayed/rotten**

kivuvvu *n1* **type of sweet banana with greyish tinge** (*often cooked in its skin*). *From: 'evvu'* ('*ashes*'). -a ekivuvvu *adj* **grey**

ekivvulu *n7* **show, festival**

ekiwaanyi (*also* ekiwaani) *n7* (*no pl.*) **fake** enviiri za kiwaanyi **wig** essente za kiwaanyi **counterfeit money**

ekiwaawaatiro *n7* **wing**

ekiwaawo *n7* **something shaped like an open bowl** (*eg. piece of broken gourd*) ekiwaawo ky'eggaali **hand grip** (*of bike*) ekiwaawo ky'enfudu **shell of tortoise** -a ekiwaawo *adj* **bowl-shaped**

ekiwaayiro *n7* **something added on, extension, annex, supplement, appendix**

ekiwabyo *n7* **sickle**

ekiwagala *n7* **sharpener**

ekiwagu *n7* **hand of bananas**

ekiwalaata *n7* (*no pl.*) **bald head, baldness** ow'ekiwalaata *n1* **bald person**

ekiwalakata *n7* **scraper**

ekiwalakate *n7* **scraped area of ground**

ekiwalazima *adv* **rushing off suddenly in panic,** *eg. Ababbi bwe baalaba abaserikale ne badduka kiwalazima.* ('*When the thieves saw the police, they rushed off in panic.*')

ekiwaluko *n7* (*no pl.*) **diarrhoea** ekiwaluko ky'omusaayi **dysentary**

ekiwandiike *n7* **something written**

ekiwandiiko *n7* **something written, document, text, statement, article, script, record**

ekiwanga *n7* **skull**

ekiwanirira *n7* **something used for holding up, support, prop**

Kiwanuka *n1* **Kiganda deity** (*lubaale*), **god of thunder and lightning**

ekiwata *n7* (*usually pl.* ebiwata) **plantain peeling**

ekiwato *n7* **waist**

ekiwayi *n7* **slice, portion, part, sect** ekiwayi kya muwogo **slice of cassava**

ekiweebwayo *n7* **something given, donation, contribution, offering**

Kiweewa *n1* *title* **eldest son of the Kabaka**

ekiwempe *n7* **mat, rug, carpet** edduuka y'ebiwempe **shop with mat roof and walls** ekkanisa y'ebiwempe **born-again church**

ekiwendo *n7* (*formerly*) **random sweep** (*of people, to execute on the order of the Kabaka, to sacrifice as prescribed by priests*) ekiwendo ky'abasuubuzo b'abaddu **expedition of slave traders**

ekiwere *n7* **type of plant yielding a red dye** (*totem of the Kiwere Clan*) *Rumex abyssinicus*

ekiwero *n7* **piece of cloth, rag, duster**

ekiwewa *n7* **something used for winnowing**

ekiweweeza *n7* **something calming/cooling** ekiweweeza omumiro **soft drink**

ekiwo *n7* **skin disease, septic dermatitis**

ekiwojjolo *n7* **butterfly, moth**

ekiwombo *n7* **basin made from banana leaves** (*placed at interception of two paths; used for bathing to get rid of an evil spirit*)

ekiwondowondo *n7* **type of small tree** *Maesa lanceolata*

ekiwonvu *n7* **valley**

ekiwonya *n7* **cure, remedy**

ekiwoobe *n7* **wail, lamentation**

ekiwoomerera *n7* **something sweet**

ekiwowongole *n7* **hollow**

ekiwu *n7* (1) **carpet of skins** (*for the Kabaka*); (2) **calf's sleeping place in kraal**

ekiwujjaalo *n7* **rest during the day, siesta**

ekiwujjo *n7* **fan, tennis racket, propeller**

ekiwuka *n7* **insect** ebiwuka by'omu lubuto **intestinal worms**

ekiwuliriza *n7* **stethoscope**

ekiwumi *n7* **lump, mass, piece** ekiwumi ky'essaami **cake made of lake flies** ekiwumi ky'ettooke **piece of left-over matooke**

ekiwummulo *n7* (**period of**) **rest, break, recess**

ekiwunde *n7* **carver**

ekiwundu *n7* **wound**

ekiwunya *n7* **smell**

ekiwutta *n7* **unpalatable food** (*referring to root crops left too long in the ground*) Kiwutta **name used in Mmamba Clan** -a ekiwutta *adj* **unpalatable,** *eg. muwogo wa biwutta* ('*unpalatable* *cassava')*

ekiwuubaalo *n7* (*no pl.*) **emptiness, loneliness**

ekiwuugulu *n7* **owl**

ekiwuuma *n7* **type of sound** (*hum, rumble, etc.*)

ekiyenje *n7* **cockroach**

ekiyigo *n7* **bathroom, urinal**

ekiyiiye *n7* **invention, composition**

Kiyimba *n1* (1) *title* **chief of Bugangazzi County;** (2) **name used in Balangira Clan;** (3) **name used for men in Mpologoma Clan**

ekiyindiru *n7* **type of small trailing or creeping plant with purple to whitish flowers** (*used medicinally for wounds; a wild relative of cowpea*) *Vigna unguiculata*

ekiyinda *n7* **prow** (*of canoe*)

ekiyingula *n7* **large piece of meat**

Kiyini *n1* *title* **chief tanner to the Kabaka**

Kiyira *n1* **River Nile**

ekiyiriitiro *n7* (*no pl.*) **wheeze, choking sound**

ekiyiriro *n7* **waterfall;** *in pl.* **rapids**

ekiyitirirwa *n7* **arch**

ekiyondo *n7* **type of succulent plant** (*medicinal*)
ekiyondo ekiddugavu *Kalanchoe lanceolata*
ekiyondo ekyeru *Kalanchoe densiflora*

¹ekiyonjo *n7* **something clean**

²ekiyonjo *n7* **nesting basket** (*for hens; suspended from above; made from three twigs connected by banana fibre*)

ekiyubwe *n7* **cast-off skin of a snake**

ekiyulu *n7* **type of plant** (*produces 'enjulu' fibre/cane*) *Marantochloa purpurea*

ekiyungu *n7* **outside kitchen**

ekiza *n7* **pubic hair**

ekizannyiro *n7* **playground, playing field, gymnasium**

ekizibaawo *n7* **coat**

ekizibikira *n7* **stopper, plug, obstruction**

ekizibiti *n7* **exhibit** (*in a trial*)

ekizibu *n7* **difficulty;** *in pl.* **hardship, trouble**

ekizibuwaza *n7* **something that makes difficult, obstacle, hindrance**

kizibwe *n1* (*pl.* ba kizibwe) **cousin of opposite sex on father's side**

ekizibye *n7* **something that blocks, obstruction, plug**

¹ekizigo *n7* (*usually pl.* ebizigo) **ointment**

²ekizigo *n7* **place where an animal is cornered in hunting**

ekiziina *n7* **worn-out clothing, rag**

ekizikiza *n7* (*no pl.*) **darkness**

ekizimba *n7* **swelling, tumour, cyst** ekizimba ky'amasira **abscess**

ekizimbe *n7* **building, construction** ekizimbe kya kalina **building of more than one storey**

ekizimbulukusa *n7* **baking powder, yeast** ekyuma ekizimbulukusa **microscope**

ekizimu *n7* **whirlwind**

ekizindo *n7* **raid**

ekizinga *n7* **island**

ekiziyiro *n7* (*no pl.*) **suffocation**

ekiziyiza *n7* **something that prevents, obstacle, restriction, blockage, brake** (*of vehicle*)

ekizizi *n7* (1) **band of reeds** (*in framework of mud and wattle wall*); *in pl.* **framework of mud and wattle wall;** (2) **layer of mud in mud and wattle wall;** (3) **bundle of reeds in roof of circular thatched house**

ekizizika *n7* **prop**

ekizizo -a ekizizo *adj* **taboo**

ekizoosi *n7* **exhaust pipe**

ekizungu *adj/adv* **European, in a white person's way**

Kizza *n1* *title* **name of first child born after twins** (*the child may be male or female*)

¹-okka *adj/adv* **only, alone.** (N7.3). *Takes pronominal concord (N4), eg. (1) emiti gyokka ('only the trees'); (2) amagi gokka ('only the eggs'). The personal forms are irregular (see Column 11 of Table 2).* ekyo kyokka **only that, merely**

²-kka *vi* (-sse) **descend,** *eg. Bakka ku madaala. ('They descended the steps.')*, **go/come down** -kka obusungu **be(come) abated,** *eg. Obusungu bwe bwakka. ('His anger abated.')* -kka wansi **step down** ebbeeyi -kka **decrease** (*of the price*) omutima -kka **be down-hearted,** *eg. Omutima gunzise. ('I am down-hearted.')* -kkako (-sseeko) **come down a little**

-kkaali *adj* **fierce**

¹-kkaanya *vit* (-kkaanyizza) **agree (on),** *eg. Twakkaanyizza ebbeeyi. ('We agreed on the price.')*, **come to an agreement (on)**

²-ekkaanya *vit* **examine/inspect closely, scrutinise**

-kkaatiriza *vt* (-kkaatirizza) **emphasise**

ekkabyo *n5* (*no pl.*) **sternness, dourness** -a ekkabyo *adj* **stern, dour, sullen**

ekkajjolyenjovu *n5* **small tree** (*with very long narrow leaves, medicinal*) *Dracaena steudneri. Meaning: 'The sugar cane of the elephant.'*

-kkakkamu *adj* (enkakkamu *n9*) **calm, settled** (*of the weather*)

-kkakkana *vi* (-kkakkanye) **calm (down), subside** (*of anger, pain, etc.*), *eg. Omusujja gukkakkanye. ('The fever has subsided.')*, **relax** (*of a muscle*)

-kkakkanya *vt* (-kkakkanyizza) **calm (down), ease, pacify, assuage, alleviate**

kkakki *n1* **khaki cloth**

ekkalaamu *n9* **pencil.** *From: 'kalamu' (Swahili).* ekkalaamu enkalu **pencil** ekkalaamu ya bwino **fountain pen** ekkalaamu ya langi **coloured pencil**

kkalaani *n1* (*pl.* ba kkalaani) **clerk**

kkalaayi *n9* **metal basin**

ekkalalume *n5* (*no pl.*) **musky smell** (*of python, male goat, etc.*)

kkalata *n9* **game of chance, gambling** -kuba kkalata **gamble**

-kkalira *vi* (-kkalidde) **take a seat, settle down** (*into one's seat*), eg. *Omugenyi omukulu bwe yayingidde bonna ne batuula era ne bakkalira.* ('On arrival of the guest of honour, they all sat down and settled into their seats.')

ekkaliya *n9* **passenger seat on bike, pillion, carrier**

kkamera *n9* **camera**

kkampuni *n9* **company**

Kkanada *n9* **Canada**

Kkangaawo *n1 title* **chief of Bulemeezi County**

ekkanisa *n9* **church** (*Prot*) **ekkanisa lutikko cathedral** (*Prot*) **ekkanisa y'abalokole born-again church** **ekkanisa y'abasoddookisi Orthodox church**

kkansa *n1* **cancer** **kkansa w'amawuggwe lung cancer** **kkansa w'ebbeere breast cancer** **kkansa w'omu musaayi cancer of the blood, leukemia**

kkantiini *n9* **canteen**

ekkanzu *n9* **gown** (*traditional dress of Baganda men*)

kkapa *n9* **cat**

ekkatala *n5* (*pl.* amakatala) **set manual task, assignment, chore**

-kkatira *vit* (-kkatidde) **apply force to, press down, pack tightly** (*eg. when filling a hole*), **push in** (*something compressible, eg. clothes into a sack*), **cram in**

ekkato *n5* (*pl.* amakato) **large needle, injection**

ekkeesi *n9* **case, suitcase, coffin**

ekkengere *n9* **bicycle bell**

ekkerenda *n5* (*pl.* amakerenda) **large pill/tablet.** *Saying:* '*Emboozi yagwa amakerenda.*' ('We had a long pleasant conversation.')

kkerere *n* **unwanted noise.** *From* '*kelele*' (*Swahili*). **-kuba kkerere be all talk and no action**

ekkereziya *n9* **church** (*RC*). *From:* '*ecclesia*' (*Latin*). **ekkereziya enkulu cathedral**

-kkibwako *vi* (-kkiddwako) **be descended on** **-kkibwako Omwoyo Omutukuvu be possessed by the Holy Spirit**

-kkirira *vi* (-kkiridde) **go downhill, descend** (*a slope*), eg. *Twakkirira ku lusozi.* ('We descended the hill.')

-kkiriza *vit* (-kkirizza) **agree, approve, permit, believe, allow, accept, defer (to), acknowledge.** *See okukkiriza* **-kkiriza ekisobyo admit guilt** **-kkiriza omusango confess a crime**

-kkirizaganya *vi* (-kkirizaganyizza) **agree with (one) another, come to an agreement,** eg. *Bakkirizaganyizza.* ('They came to an agreement.')

-kkirizibwa *vi* (-kkiriziddwa) **be allowed**

-kkirizisa *vt* (-kkirizisizza) **convince**

ekko *n5* (*no pl.*) **dirt**

ekkobe *n5* (*pl.* amakobe) **bud yam** (*produced by omukobe in leaf axil*), **air potato** *Dioscorea bulbifera* **Kkobe name of a clan**

kkolegi *n9* **college**

ekkolero *n5* (*pl.* amakolero) **factory, workshop**

ekkomagiro *n5* (*pl.* amakomagiro) **shelter for making barkcloth** (*should be well ventilated*)

ekkomera *n5* (*pl.* amakomera) **prison, jail**

ekkomo *n5* (*pl.* amakomo) **limit**

ekkondeere *n5* (*pl.* amakondeere) **horn** (*musical instrument; made from a type of endeku gourd*)

kkondo *n1* (*pl.* ba kkondo) **violent robber**

kkondomu *n9* **condom**

Kkongo *n9* **Congo**

kkongojjo *n1* (*no pl.*) **hopscotch**

ekkonkome *n5* (*pl.* amakonkome) **agama lizard** (*with blue head*). *Saying:* '*Alina amayuuga nga ag'ekkonkome.*' ('He has big jowls like those of a lizard.')

kkono *n1* (*no pl.*) **left** (*direction*) **-a kkono** *adj* **left** **ku kkono on the left**

kkonsati *n9* **concert**

kkoodi *greeting* **Hello, may I come in?** (*friendly call used outside house or room requesting entry*)

Kkooki *n1* **county of Buganda.** *Kkooki became a county of Buganda under an agreement signed in 1896 between the then Kamuswaga (traditional ruler) of the Kingdom of Kkooki and the then Kabaka of Buganda.*

kkooko *n1* **cocoa**

kkookolo *n1* (*no pl.*) **cancer**

ekkookootezi *n5* (*pl.* amakookootezi) **plantain-eater** (*type of bird*)

kkoolaasi *n1* **tarmac, macadam.** *From:* '*coal*' (*English*).

ekkoona *n5* (*pl.* amakoona) **corner** (*eg. on road*), **bend**

ekkoonofu *See* -koonofu

ekkooti *n9* (1) **court**; (2) **coat, jacket** **ekkooti ento magistrate's court** **ekkooti ey'oku ntikko supreme court** **ekkooti ya Kisekwa court for settling land and other disputes**

ekkovu *n5* (*pl.* amakovu) **snail, slug**

ekkubo *n5* (*pl.* amakubo) **road, path, route** **ekkubo eggolokofu the straight path to heaven**

-kkufu *adj* **satisfied** (*with food*), **full**

ekkufulu *n9* **padlock, lock** **ekkufulu y'oluggi doorlock**

ekkula *n5* (*pl.* amakula) **something very wonderful or precious;** *in pl.* **presents given to the Kabaka** **makula** *invariable adj* **wonderful, splendid,** eg. *Luno olugoye makula gennyini.* ('That cloth is really splendid.')

-kkulira *vi* (-kkulidde) **(begin to) sprout** (*of a recently planted banana plant*), eg. *Ekitooke kikkulidde.* ('The banana plant has started to produce shoots.')

kkulungabusa *n5* **dung beetle.** *Meaning:* '*It rolls dung.*'

kkumi *n5/num* (*pl.* amakumi) **ten** **-a ekkumi** *adj* **tenth**

ekkundi *n5* (*pl.* amakundi) **navel, belly button**

kkunguvvu *n1* **pin-tailed whydah** (*type of bird*).

Folk belief: A man fingering a feather of this bird in his pocket while chatting up a girl will increase the chances that she will accept his advances.

ekkuŋŋaaniro *n5* (*pl.* amakuŋŋaaniro) **meeting place**

-kkusa *vt* (-kkusizza) **satisfy** (*with food*), **feed** (*someone*) **to repletion**

-kkuta *vi* (-kkuse) **be satisfied with food, be full of food**

ekkutiya *n9* (hessian) **sack**

kkwale *n9* **quarry**

ekkwanzi *n5* (*pl.* amakwanzi) **fish eagle**

Kkweeba *n1 title* **chief of Ssese County**

kkwete *n1* **beer** (*made from maize*)

kkwini *n1* (*pl.* ba kkwini) **queen** (*eg. of England*)

[1]**ko** *adv/conj* **then, in addition**

[2]**ako** *dem* **that**

[3]**ko** *pos* **your** *si.*

[4]**ko** *pro* **it.** *Can be a suffix* **-ko** (**N10-12**), *eg. nako* (*'and it'*).

-eekobaana *vit* (-eekobaanye) **collude**

-koboggoka (-koboggose) *See* -boggoka

-eekoboggoza *vi* (-eekoboggozezza) **refuse to comply with, be defiant**

-kodo *adj* **miserly, mean**

-kodowala *vi* (-kodowadde) **be(come) miserly**

-kodowalira *vt* (-kodowalidde) **be miserly to**

kofini *n9* **coffin**

-kogga *vi* (-kozze) **grow thin** (*of person or animal*), **lose weight**

kojja *n1* (*pl.* ba kojja) **uncle** (*maternal*) **kojja-uncle of** (**N12**), *eg. kojjange* (*'my uncle'*). *The various forms are given on Table 12.*

-kokota *vt* (-kokose) **clear/clear out,** *eg. Bakokota omufulejje.* (*'They are cleaning out the drain.'*)

-kokya *vi* (-kokyezza) **speak in riddles**

-kola *v* (-koze) (1) *vi* **work, labour, process, function;** (2) *vt* **do, excecute** (*a task*), **make, produce, manufacture** -kola amagoba **make a profit** -kola bampaane **show off** -kola ebya vvulugu **do a messy job** -kola ekyejo **be naughty** (*of a child*) -kola endagaano **make a contract** -kola kopi **make a copy** -kola mu mpalo **work in turns/shifts** -kola nga **be acting** (*in a position*) -kola olukalala **make a list** -kola olukwe **scheme against** -kola pulakitisi **practice** -kola susu **urinate** (*especially of a child*) **-kolako** (-kozeeko) (*also* -kola ku) **attend to,** *eg. Abasawo bakoze ku balwadde bonna.* (*'The doctors have attended to all the patients.'*), **deal with, handle** (*issues*), **affect,** *eg. Ky'oyogedde kinkolako.* (*'What you have said affects me.'*) **-kolamu make into,** *eg. Amata bagakolamu omuzigo.* (*'They make ghee from milk.'*), **transform**

-kolagana *vi* (-kolaganye) **work together, cooperate, collaborate**

-kolebwa *vi* (-koleddwa) *vi* **be made, be done** **-kolebwamu** (-koleddwamu) **be made into**

-koleera *vi* (-koledde) **be ignited** omuliro -koleera **catch** (*of a fire*)

-koleeza *vt* (-koleezezza) **ignite, light** -koleeza ettala **switch on a light** -koleeza omuliro **light a fire**

-koleka *vi* (-kolese) **be doable**

[1]**-kolera** *vt* (-koledde) **work for/at,** *etc., eg. Akolera Musoke e Kampala.* (*'He works for Musoke in Kampala.'*), **make for/at,** *etc. See* okukolera -kolera ku mawanga **go abroad to work** -kolera ssente **earn money** w'okolera *n16* **workplace**

[2]**-eekolera** *vr* **work for oneself**

-kolerera *vt* (-koleredde) **work for** (*a purpose, eg. to earn money*)

kolijja -a kolijja *adj* **wholesale**

-kolima *vi* (-kolimye) **curse, uttter curses**

-kolimira *vt* (-kolimidde) **curse** (*someone*)

-kolobofu = -kulubufu

-koloboka (-kolobose) = -kulubuka

[1]**-kolobola** (-kolobodde) = -kulubula

[2]**-eekolobola** = -eekulubula

-koloboza (-kolobozezza) = -kulubuza

-kologa *vt* (-koloze) **mix, stir** -kologa obuugi **stir porridge**

kologeeti *n9* **toothpaste.** *From: 'Colgate' (brand).*

-kolokoota (*also* -koota) *vi* (-kolokoose) **itch** (*of the throat*)

-kolokota (*also* -kokota) *vt* (-kolokose) **scrape (off)** -kolokota gonja **scrape a plantain** -kolokota kasooli **scrape a burnt maize cob** -kolokota muwogo **scrape off inner skin of cassava**

-kolola *vi* (-koledde) **cough**

-kolondola *vi* (-kolondodde) **bring up phlegm**

-kolwa *vi* (-koleddwa) **be done/made**

-koma *vi* (-komye) **go as far as, stop (at),** *eg. Ettaka lyange likoma wano.* (*'My land stops here.'*), **terminate at** -koma awo **stop at a place,** *eg. Koma awo!* (*'Stop there!'*) **-komako** (-komyeko) **limit, restrict** (*what someone can do*), **restrain, caution** (*not to continue talking on a subject*) -komako awo **come close** (*but fail to reach*), *eg. Yankomako awo.* (*'She came close but did not visit me.'*) **-komawo come back, return** -komawo mu **rejoin** **-komayo recover from near-death experience**

-komaga *vt* (-komaze) **beat** (*barkcloth*)

-eekomako *vi* **restrain oneself, pause and reconsider** (*what one is saying*) omuntu ateekomako **person lacking self-discipline, person without boundaries** (*in behaviour*)

-komba *vt* (-kombye) **lick, lap** **-kombako** (-kombyeko) **taste**

-komeka *vit* (-komese) **put in compact form, pack neatly, stack**

-komekkereza *vit* (-komekkerezza) **come/bring to an end** -komekkereza okwogera **conclude a speech**

-komera *vt* (-komedde) **fence (in), barricade**

-komerera *vt* (-komeredde) **nail (down), ram down, hammer** -komerera ku musaalaba **crucify** -komerera omusomaali **hit a nail** **-komererayo** (-komereddeyo) **be last**

-kommonta *vt* (-kommonse) **blow** -kommonta effirimbi **blow a whistle** -kommonta eŋŋombe **blow a hunting horn** -kommonta oluwa **whistle** (*through the lips*) -kommonta ssigala **smoke a cigarette**

-komola *vt* (-komodde) **cut out carefully, trim, circumcise**

-eekomomma *vi* (-eekomommye) **avoid direct contact with people** (*because of shyness*), **huddle up** (*through shyness*)

kompyuta *n9* **computer**

-komya *vt* (-komezza) **cause to stop, put a stop to, end,** *eg. Nkomezza wano. ('I have ended here.'),* **cease** **-komyawo** (-komezzaawo) **bring back, return**

-kona *vi* (-konye) (1) **fail to cook properly;** (2) **fail to grow properly** (*of people, animals or plants*), **be stunted**

kondakita *n1* **conductor**

¹-konga *vt* (-konze) **sniff, get the scent of**

²-eekonga *vi* (-eekonze) **make funny faces**

¹-kongojja *vi* (-kongozze) **hop**

²-kongojja *vt* **carry** (*a person*) **on the shoulders.** *Sayings: (1) 'Akongozze omumbejja nnamaalwa.' ('She is drunk.'); (2) 'Akongozze omulangira ssegaamwenge.' ('He is drunk.')*

-kongoka *vi* (-kongose) **drop off** (*of ripe fruit*)

-kongola *v* (-kongodde) (1) *vi* **not do one's share of the work, kill time instead of working, loaf about,** *eg. Akongodde ku mulimu. ('He is loafing about.');* (2) *vt* **snap/pluck off** -kongola kasooli **remove grains from a maize cob**

-kongoola *vt* (-kongodde) **claw at** (*someone, as a gesture of contempt*)

-konjera (-konjedde) -konjera ebigambo **slander, malign**

-konkona *vt* (-konkonye) **knock** (*eg. on a door*), **rap, tap**

konteyina *n9* **container**

-kontola *vi* (-kontodde) **click the tongue** (*a gesture of disapproval or sorrow*)

-konvuba *vi* (-konvubye) **waste away through incurable illness**

-konziba (-konzibye) *See* -koozimba

-koobera *vi* (-koobedde) **lag behind, be bottom of the class, be last in line**

akoogi *See* -yogi

-kooka *vi* (-koose) **sing in a loud clear voice**

-kookera *vt* (-kookedde) **add to** -kookera ebigambo **put words into someone's mouth,** *eg. Tokookera ebigambo mu ebyo bye njogedde. ('Don't add extra words to those I said.')* **-kookerako** (-kookeddeko) **add onto, extend** (*a structure*) (= -waayirako) **-kookeramu insert**

-kookolima *vi* (-kookolimye) **crow**

-kookoonya *vt* (-kookoonyezza) **tease by pretending to offer, taunt, tantalise**

-koola *vt* (-kodde) **weed**

-eekooloobya *vit* (-eekooloobezza) **make a detour (around)** (*to avoid being seen*), **take a longer route**

-koomera *vt* (-koomedde) **smoke** -koomera embugo **smoke barkcloth** (*to refresh it*). *See* omugavu -koomera enjuki **smoke out bees**

-koomerwa *vi* (-koomeddwa) **be smoked**

¹-koona *vt* (-koonye) **knock,** *eg. Yakoona eggiraasi y'amazzi ne gayiika. ('She knocked the glass and spilt the water.'),* **hit** -koona ekigere **stamp one's foot** **-koonako** (-koonyeko) **knock onto** -koonako sitampu **put one's seal**

²-eekoona *vr* **knock/hit oneself** (*on something*)

-koonagana *vi* (-koonaganye) **knock against one another, come into conflict, clash** -koonagana ne **contradict**

-koonofu *adj* (ekkoonofu *n9*) **partially broken and hanging** (*eg. branch of a tree*)

-koonoka *vi* (-koonose) **partially break** (*eg. of a branch*), **droop, bend over, snap**

-koonola *vt* (-koonodde) **partially break** (*eg. a branch*), **snap, start fruiting** (*of a banana plant*), *eg. Ekitooke kitandise okukoonola. ('The banana plant has started fruiting.')* -koonola ekifo **receive a high position unexpectedly**

-koonyesa *vt* (-koonyesezza) **hit hard with,** *eg. Akoonyesa ennyondo okumenya ekisenge. ('He is hitting the wall with a hammer to break it.')*

-koota (-koose) *See* -kolokoota

-kootakoota *vi* (-koosekoose) **be bent over** (*of a person*), **be hunched over** (*as an old person*)

-koowa *vi* (-kooye) **become tired**

-koowoola *vt* (-koowodde) **call to from a distance**

-koowu *adj* **tired**

¹akooya *n12* (*pl.* obwoya) **small hair**

²-kooya (*also* -kooyesa) *vt* (-kooyezza) **tire, make tired**

-kooye *adj* **tired, worn-out**

-kooza *vt* (-koozezza) *vt* **tear off a piece of** -kooza olulagala **tear off a piece of banana leaf** (*eg. to make a spoon or funnel*)

-koozimba (*also* -konziba) *vi* (-koozimbye) **grow very poorly, grow thin, become atrophied**

¹-kopi *adj* **peasant-like, uncouth**

²kopi *n9* **copy**

-koppa *vt* (-koppye) **copy, imitate, mimic**

koppe *n1* **stiff skin** (*type that used to be worn by the common people*)

¹-kosa *vt* (-kosezza) **hurt/injure** (*through knocking or scratching a wound*)

²-eekosa *vr* **hurt oneself** (*through knocking a wound*), *eg. Nneekosa mu kiwundu. ('I knocked my wound.')*

-koteka *vt* (-kotose) -koteka omutwe **bow one's**

head (eg. in shame)

-kotoggera vt (-kotoggedde) sabotage, undermine, block, eg. Musoke yakotoggera Mukasa n'atafuna mulimu. ('Musoke blocked Mukasa from getting the job.')

-kovvu adj thin (after losing weight)

-koza vt (-kozezza) dip (food) in sauce

-eekozaakoza vi (-eekozezzakozezza) pretend not to like something (that one actually does) (= -eegiragira)

-koze See -kola

[1]-kozesa vt (-kozesezza) use, employ -kozesa ssente spend money

[2]-eekozesa vi work for oneself, be self-employed

-kozza vt (-kozzezza) make thin (person/animal)

kozzi adv incidentally, by the way. Used when recalling, but indicating doubt, eg. Kozzi twajjidde mu mmotoka? Nedda twajjidde mu bbaasi. ('Did we come by car? No, we came by bus.')

[1]ku det some, eg. Yalidde ku mmere. ('She has eaten some food.'). 'ku' (and/or enclitic -ko) is used in polite forms of address (N24.3), eg. Lyako ku binyeebwa. ('Please, do eat some groundnuts.')

[2]ku pre on, upon, onto, to, at, off, about, for, concerning, regarding. (N3) ku bwa (also ku bwa-) on the initiative of (N11.4), eg. (1) ku bwa Musoke ('on Musoke's initiative'); (2) ku bwange ('on my initiative') ku lwa (also ku lwa-) on behalf of, by reason of, for. (N11.4), eg. (1) ku lwa Musoke ('for Musoke'); (2) ku lwange ('for me') okuva ku from

[1]kuba (also olw'okuba) conj because; inf of -ba

[2]-kuba (-kubye) vt hit, strike, beat, spank, play (struck musical instrument, eg. drum or guitar) -kuba akaama whisper -kuba akagere go on foot -kuba akakindo put on a crease -kuba akakule burst into scornful laughter -kuba akalali burst into laughter -kuba akalimi sweet-talk -kuba akalulu vote, play the lottery -kuba amabega turn one's back on -kuba amatama be all talk and no action -kuba caanisi play cards -kuba ddoti fart -kuba ebbali miss the target -kuba ebikonde box -kuba ebinonko crack finger joints -kuba ebiwoobe wail -kuba eddolera fool, feint -kuba eggoolo score a goal -kuba ekibejjagalo belch -kuba ekide ring/toll a bell -kuba ekifaananyi draw a picture, photograph -kuba ekijiiko fry -kuba ekikalu tuck in (shirt or blouse) -kuba ekimyanso reflect -kuba ekiraka patch -kuba ekiwoobe wail -kuba ekyeyo work abroad (implying illegally) -kuba embeekuulo chatter loudly (as children at play) -kuba emibirigo play the game of embirigo -kuba emizinga give a gun salute -kuba emizira cheer -kuba emmundu fire a gun -kuba empiiyi belch -kuba empiso give an injection -kuba endiima give a good kick (in football) -kuba endobo tackle hard (in football) -kuba endongo play the guitar (or other struck

musical instrument) -kuba enduulu ululate, raise the alarm -kuba engalabi drum -kuba engalo clap (hands) -kuba engolo wrap on the head -kuba enkasi paddle -kuba ennanga play the harp/organ -kuba ennoga take lump of matooke, make depression in it, fill with sauce and eat -kuba ennyanda strike at goal (in football) -kuba entiisa frighten -kuba entoli snap the fingers -kuba enviiri brush hair -kuba eŋŋoma drum -kuba eŋŋombe blow a horn, hoot -kuba eppaasi iron (clothes) -kuba essimu telephone -kuba ettaka survey land -kuba jjejjerebu be elated and merry -kuba kampeyini campaign -kuba kibooko cane -kuba kifaalu whip, lash -kuba kkalata play cards, gamble -kuba kkoodi ask to enter a house or room by calling 'kkoodi' -kuba ku bukenke be on tenterhooks -kuba ku mabega carry on the back -kuba ku mbuutu drum -kuba ku ngatto eddagala polish shoes -kuba mailo survey land -kuba mu kyapa print -kuba mu ngalo clap hands -kuba olukato give an injection -kuba olukoloboze draw a line -kuba olukuŋŋaana hold a meeting -kuba oluwenda make a path through vegetation -kuba oluyi slap, smack -kuba omukono flag/wave down (eg. a taxi) -kuba omulanga cry out in distress -kuba omumiro click the throat -kuba omupiira play football -kuba polisi polish -kuba potolo raid (house-to-house by police) -kuba pulasita ku plaster -kuba saluti salute -kuba ssabbaawa shoot at a target -kuba tayipu type -kuba ttena play tennis -kuba ttooci shine a torch -kuba zzaala play cards, gamble

-kubako (-kubyeko) pat -kubako sitampu put on a stamp -kubamu -kubamu ekituli punch a hole

[3]-eekuba vr hit oneself -eekuba endobo contradict oneself -eekuba mpiso inject oneself

-kubagana vi (-kubaganye) hit one another, rattle, clatter

-kubaganya vt (-kubaganyizza) cause to hit one another -kubaganya ebirowoozo have a discussion, exchange ideas, debate

-kubagiza vt (-kubagizza) comfort (a bereaved person), console

okubala n15 arithmetic, mathematics; inf of -bala okubala abantu mu ggwanga census

kubanga (also olw'okubanga) conj because

okubatiza n15 baptism; inf of -batiza

okubazaamu n15 multiplication; inf of -bazaamu

okubba n15 stealing; inf of -bba

-kubibwa vi (-kubiddwa) be hit

[1]-kubiira vt (-kubidde) bend to one side -kubiira ensingo turn one's neck to one side (a gesture of disapproval or irritation)

[2]-eekubiira vi (1) lean to one side, be lop-sided, list (of a ship), be askew; (2) be biased, be prejudiced, side (with a faction)

okubikkulirwa *n15* revelation; *inf of* -bikkulirwa
Okubikkulirwa **(Book of) Revelations**

[1]-kubira *vt* (-kubidde) **hit for/at**, *etc.*, **telephone**, *eg.*
*Nnakubira Musoke jjo. ('I telephoned Musoke
yesterday.')* -kubira enduulu **sound the alarm
against**, *eg. Nja kukukubira enduulu. ('I shall
sound the alarm call against you.')* -kubira essimu
telephone -kubira oluwenda **facilitate an
introduction** (*to someone*) -kubira omulanga
appeal for help to

[2]-eekubira -eekubira enduulu **appeal for help on
one's own behalf**

okubiri -a okubiri *adj* **second (N7.1)**, *eg. omuti
ogw'okubiri ('second tree'). An elided form is
sometimes seen, eg. omuti ogwokubiri ('second
tree').*

-kubirira *vt* (-kubiridde) **beat/hit repeatedly**

-kubiriza *vt* (-kubirizza) **urge, exhort, stress
repeatedly, chair** (*a meeting*)

[1]-kubisa *vt* (-kubisizza) **hit with** -kubisa
ekifaananyi **take a photograph**

[2]-eekubisa -eekubisa ekifaananyi **have one's
photograph taken** (*by someone else*)

okubuguumirira *n15* excitement; *inf of*
-buguumirira

okubulwa *inf of* -bulwa okubulwa otulo **insomnia**

okubuulira *n15* sermon, preaching; *inf of* -buulira

okubuusabuusa *n15* doubt, scepticism; *inf of*
-buusabuusa

okubuuzibwa *n15* examination; *inf of* -buuzibwa

[1]kubwa = ku bwa **(N11.4).** *See* ku

[2]-kubwa *vi* (-kubiddwa) **be hit/beaten**

okubwatuka *n15* bang; *inf of* -bwatuka
okubwatuka kw'eggulu **clap of thunder**

-kubya *vt* (-kubizza) **hit with**

okuddamu *n15* reply, answer; *inf of* -ddamu

okudduka *n15* running; *inf of* -dduka

okufa *n15* death; *inf of* -fa. *'okufa' can act as an
intensifier of a previous verb, eg. Azina okufa.
('She dances very well.').* okufa ekibwatukira
sudden death

okufaanagana *n15* likeness, correspondence; *inf
of* -faanagana

okufaayo *n15* concern, care; *inf of* -faayo

okufiirwa *n15* bereavement; *inf of* -fiirwa

okufuba *n15* effort, excertion; *inf of* -fuba

okufuga *n15* reign; *inf of* -fuga

okufulumira *inf of* -fulumira aw'okufulumira *n16*
exit

okufuma *n15* story-telling; *inf of* -fuma

okufumba *n15* cooking; *inf of* -fumba

okugaana *n15* refusal; *inf of* -gaana

okugatta *n15* addition (*in maths*); *inf of* -gatta

okugeza *conj* for example; *inf of* -geza

okuggyako *pre* except (for), apart from; *inf of*
-ggyako

-kugira *vt* (-kugidde) **put an edge on, hem, tuck,
limit** -kugira abaana **restrict children** (*from*

wandering off) -kugira ennyumba **put fence
around house**

-kugu *adj* expert

-kuguka *vi* (-kuguse) **become expert/skilful, be
proficient**

okugula *n15* buying, shopping; *inf of* -gula

okugulu *n15* (*pl.* amagulu) **leg**

okujjukira *n15* memory; *inf of* -jjukira

okujulira *n15* appeal; *inf of* -julira

okukaddiwa *n15* ageing; *inf of* -kaddiwa

okukamala *adv* excessively, too much, extremely,
eg. Ayogera okukamala. ('She talks too much.'),
extremely well (*or* **very badly**); *inf of* -kamala
Mulungi okukamala **He is a very good person.**, **He
is very handsome.**

okukiina *n15* mockery; *inf of* -kiina

okukkiriza *n15* faith, acceptance; *inf of* -kkiriza

okukolera *inf of* -kolera aw'okukolera *n16*
workplace

-kukula *vi* (-kukudde) **become mouldy**

-kukulira *vt* (-kukulidde) **hide, conceal**

okukulugguka *inf of* -kulugguka okukulugguka
kw'ettaka *n15* **landslide**

okukulukuta *inf of* -kulukuta okukulukuta
kw'ettaka *n15* **soil erosion**

-eekukuma *vr* (-eekukumye) **hide oneself from
danger**

-kukumba *vt* (-kukumbye) **gather up
indiscriminently** (*eg. suspects*), **round up, scoop
up**

-kukunala (*also* -kulumbala) *vi* (-kukunadde) **jut
out** (*of something, caused by something inside*),
make bulge out, *eg. Ekikopo kikukunadde mu
nsawo. ('The cup is bulging out the bag.'),* **stick
out, protrude**

-kukunavu (*also* -kulumbavu) *adj* **jutting out,
bulging out**

-kukunaza (*also* -kulumbaza) *vt* (-kukunazizza)
(cause to) bulge out, *eg. Ebisumuluzo bikukunaza
ensawo y'empale ye. ('The keys are making the
pocket of his trousers bulge out.')*

okukungubaga *n15* mourning; *inf of* -kungubaga

-kukunuka *vi* (-kukunuse) **emerge from a hiding
place**

-kukunula *vt* (-kukunudde) **take out from a hiding
place**

-kukusa *vt* (-kukusizza) **hide** (*during transit*),
smuggle

-kukuta *vi* (-kukuse) **do secretly**

okukuusa *n15* falsification; *inf of* -kuusa

-kukuvu *adj* **mouldy**

-kukuza *vt* (-kukuzizza) **make mouldy**

okukwatagana *n15* similarity, correspondence;
inf of -kwatagana

okukwataganya *n15* cooperation; *inf of*
-kwataganya

[1]okukwe *adv* on her/his place (N11.5)

[2]okukwe *pos* her(s), his. (N11.4)

[1]**okukwo** *adv* on your *si.* place (N11.5)

[2]**okukwo** *pos* your(s) *si.* (N11.4)

kukyaliko there is/are still (*on top*)

okukyamira *inf of* -kyamira aw'okukyamira *n16* place where one turns off, turning place

okukyuka *n15* conversion; *inf of* -kyuka

okukyukira *inf of* -kyukira aw'okukyukira *n16* place for turning around, turning place

-kula *vi* (-kuze) grow (up), mature

kulaaki *n9* clutch (*of vehicle*)

-kulaakulana *vi* (-kulaakulanye) develop, progress (*eg. in a job*), advance (*of someone in an organisation*)

-kulaakulanya *vt* (-kulaakulanyizza) develop, progress

Kulaani *n9* Koran

okulaba *n15* sight, eyesight; *inf of* -laba ekintu kisaana kulabako something worth seeing

okulabikirwa *n15* miraculous sighting, vision; *inf of* -kulabikirwa

okulabira *inf of* -labira okulabira ku looking at

okulabirira *n15* supervision; *inf of* -labirira

okuleekaana *n15* shouting, din; *inf of* -leekaana

okulemala *n15* paralysis; *inf of* -lemala

-kulembera *vit* (-kulembedde) go first, lead, guide

[1]**kuli** *adv* on there

[2]**kuli** *dem* that

[3]**okuli** where there is/are (*on top*). *Can be equivalent to conjunction* where *or preposition* to (N7.2).

kulika *interj* (*pl.* mukulike) congratulations, bravo Kulika omwaka. Happy New Year. Kulikayo. Welcome back. (N28)

kuliko there is/are (*on top*)

[1]**-kulira** *vt* (-kulidde) be in charge of, head

[2]**-kulira** *vt* (-kulidde) grow up at/in, *etc.*, *eg.* Yakulira Ssese. ('She grew up in Ssese.')

[1]**-kulisa** *vt* (-kulisizza) congratulate

[2]**-eekulisa** *vr* congratulate oneself

Kulisito *n1* Christ (*Prot*)

okulonda *n15* election; *inf of* -londa okulonda okwa wamu (*also* okulonda okwa bonna) general election

okulongoosa *n15* surgery, operation (*surgical*); *inf of* -longoosa

okulowooza *n15* thinking, thoughtfulness; *inf of* -lowooza

-kulu *adj* mature, adult, important, chief

[1]**-kulubeesa** *vt* (-kulubeesezza) pull/drag along -kulubeesa ebbina have a big bottom/belly -kulubeesa ebbuto ingratiate oneself (*eg. with a potential donor*)

[2]**-eekulubeesa** *vi* walk in a proud heavy way

-kulubufu (*also* -kolobofu) *adj* scratched, scraped

-kulubuka (*also* -koloboka) *vi* (-kulubuse) be scratched, be scraped, *eg.* Emmotoka yange ekulubuse. ('My car has been scraped.')

[1]**-kulubula** (*also* -kolobola) *vt* (-kulubudde) scratch, mark with a point, scrape against

[2]**-eekulubula** (*also* -eekolobola) *vr* scrape oneself against

-kulubuza (*also* -koloboza) *vt* (cause to) scratch -kulubuza omusittale draw a margin

-kulugguka *vi* (-kulugguse) flow in large quantity (*eg. of soil*), flow by (*of time*), pass by in large numbers (*of people*). *See* okukulugguka

-kulukusa *vt* (-kulukusizza) cause to flow -kulukusa amaziga shed tears, weep -kulukusa ettaka erode soil, *eg.* Mukoka akulukusizza ettaka. ('The water is eroding the soil.')

-kulukuta *vi* (-kulukuse) flow. *See* okukulukuta

-kulukutira *vt* (-kulukutidde) flow into/along

[1]**-kulukuunya** *vt* (-kulukuunyizza) rub in dirt

[2]**-eekulukuunya** *vr* roll about on the ground, wallow -eekulukuunya mu ttaka roll about in dirt, take a dust bath -eekulukuunyaako (-eekulukuunyizzako) rub oneself against (*someone else*)

[1]**-kulula** *vt* (-kuludde) drag, pull along, persuade (*a reluctant person*) -kulula enviiri comb the hair (*with a scratcher*)

[2]**-eekulula** (*also* -eewalula) *vr* pull oneself along

-kulumbala *vi* (-kulumbadde) jut out, *eg.* Yatisse loole ensawo ne zikulumbala. ('He loaded the lorry and the sacks jutted out.'), stick out

-kulumbavu *adj* jutting out, sticking out

-kulumbaza *vt* (-kulumbazizza) cause to jut out, *eg.* Yatisse loole ensawo n'azikulumbaza. ('He loaded the lorry and caused the sacks to jut out.')

kulumbisi *See* enseenene

[1]**-kulunga** (*also* -kulungula) *vt* (-kulunze) make round, roll (along), *eg.* Akulunga ennyama mu buwunga. ('She is rolling the meat in flour.'). *See* -vulunga -kulunga ebbumba knead clay (*in pottery; second stage, after '-vulunga ebbumba'*) -kulunga ettooke roll lump of matooke into a ball

[2]**-eekulunga** (*also* -eekulungula) *vi* make a circle, roll on the ground

-eekulungirivu *adj* spherical

-eekulungiriza *vt* (-eekulungirizza) make round, make spherical

-kulungutana *vi* (-kulungutanye) have too much to do when unprepared, be preoccupied, do things behind someone's back -kulungutana n'ebigambo struggle to find the right words -kulungutana n'ebintu move things about (*having insufficient space*)

-kulungutanya *vt* (-kulungutanyizza) cause disruption for (*someone*), make demands on, push (*someone to act*), *eg.* Yankulungutanyizza ng'ayagala mmuyoleze engoye ze mu bwangu. ('He pushed me to wash his clothes quickly.') -kulungutanya emmere mu kamwa move about food in the mouth (*being too hot*)

kulunkalu *See* enseenene

-eekuluumulula *vi* (-eekuluumuludde) gather

together in great numbers, *eg. Beekuluumuludde okujja okulaba ppaapa. ('They gathered together in great numbers to see the pope.')*, **assemble in mass, heap up** *(of clouds)*

-kuluusana *vi* (-kuluusanye) **toil away**

kulwa = ku lwa (**N11.4**). *See* ku

okulwana *n15* **fight, fighting;** *inf of* -lwana

okulya *n15* **eating;** *inf of* -lya   okulya mu ndago **singing**

¹-kuma *vt* (-kumye) **heap (up), pile (together)**   -kuma omuliro **kindle/light a fire   -kumamu** (-kumyemu)   -kumamu omuliro **make a fire** *(within something)*, **incite**

²-eekuma *vi* **cluster together,** *eg. Obukoko bwekumye wamu enkuba bwe yatonnye. ('The chicks clustered together when it rained.')*, **become concentrated**

-kumaakuma *vt* (-kumyekumye) **keep on heaping up, mobilise**

-kumba *vi* (-kumbye) **march**

-kumpanya *vt* (-kumpanyizza) **be devious towards, cheat, embezzle, defraud**   -kumpanya ebigambo **engage in double talk**

okumpi *adv* **near, nearby, nearly, almost, soon**   kumpi na/ne **near, close to**   kumpi okuva wano **a short distance from here**

kumu *num/adv* **one, at the same time,** *eg. Bajjira kumu. ('They came at the same time.')*

kumukumu *adv* **close together, one after another**

okuna   -a okuna *adj* **fourth** (**N7.1**), *eg. omuti ogw'okuna ('fourth tree'). An elided form is sometimes seen, eg. omuti ogwokuna ('fourth tree').*

okunaabira *inf of* -naabira   omw'okunaabira *n18* **washing place** *(for people)*

-kunama *vi* (-kunamye) **expose oneself** *(referring to private parts)*

-kunamira *vt* (-kunamidde) **expose oneself towards**   -kunamira olusuku **expose oneself towards someone's plantation** *(shows disdain)*

-kundugga *vi* (-kunduzze) **be stunted in growth** *(of an animal)*

-kunga *vt* (-kunze) **(1) be amazed at** *(often in a negative sense)*; **(2)** *(modern usage, substituting for -kuŋŋaanya)* **gather** *(people)* **together, mobilise**

-kungiriza *vit* (-kungirizza) **make repeated exclamations of astonishment**

-kungubaga *vi* (-kungubaze) **mourn.** *See* okukungubaga

-kungubagira *vt* (-kungubagidde) **mourn for,** *eg. Akungubagira omwami we. ('She is mourning for her husband.')* **-kungubagirako** (-kungubagiddeko) **commiserate with**

-kungula *vt* (-kungudde) **harvest**

kungulu *adv* **on top, on the surface**   kungulu ku **on top of, on the surface of, on**

-kunkumuka *vi* (-kunkumuse) **be shaken off, fall in flakes, crumble** *(of bread)*   ebikoola -kunkumuka

fall off *(of leaves from a tree)*

¹-kunkumula *vt* (-kunkumudde) **shake off**   -kunkumula ebikoola **shed leaves** *(of a tree)*   -kunkumula omusulo **urinate** *(by a man)*

²-eekunkumula *vr* **shake oneself**   -eekunkumulako (-eekunkumuddeko) **shake off from oneself,** *eg. Embwa yeekunkumulako amazzi. ('The dog is shaking off water.')*

-eekunkumulira *vr* (-eekunkumulidde) **urinate on oneself** *(of a male)*

¹kuno *adv* **(on) here**

²kuno *dem* **this**

-kunta *vi* (-kunye) **blow** *(of the wind)*

-kununkiriza *(also* -kunuukiriza*) vit* (-kununkirizza) **reach (for),** *eg. Yakunuukiriza ssabbuuni. ('He reached for the soap.')*

-kunya *vt* (-kunye) **rub together** *(eg. clothes in washing)*

-kunye *adj* **soft** *(as a carefully scraped animal skin used for clothing)*

-kuŋŋaana *vi* (-kuŋŋaanye) **come together, gather, assemble**   abantu abakuŋŋaanye **congregation**

-kuŋŋaanya *vt* (-kuŋŋaanyizza) **bring together, gather, compile, assemble, collect, mobilise, round up** *(animals).* *See* -kunga

-kuŋŋunta *vt* (-kuŋŋunse) **sift, sieve**

okusa *n15* **digestion;** *inf of* -sa

okusaalirwa *n15* **regret;** *inf of* -saalirwa

okusaba *n15* **(church) service, praying, application;** *inf of* -saba   okusaba kw'akawungeezi **evening service**   okusaba kw'enkya **morning service**

okusalawo *n15* **decision;** *inf of* -salawo

okusatu   -a okusatu *adj* **third** (**N7.1**), *eg. omuti ogw'okusatu ('third tree'). An elided form is sometimes seen, eg. omuti ogwokusatu ('third tree')*

okuseera *n15* **overcharging;** *inf of* -seera

okusembera *n15* **holy communion;** *inf of* -sembera

-kusensa *vi* (-kusense) **contract measles**

okusiima *n15* **appreciation;** *inf of* -siima

okusinga *conj* **more than,** *eg. Njagala kino okusinga ekyo. ('I like this more than that.')*; *inf of* -singa. *Also used in other comparisons, eg. Omwezi mutono okusinga ensi. ('The moon is smaller than the earth.')*   okusinga awo **beyond there, further than there**

okusinza *n15* **(church) service;** *inf of* -sinza

okusinziira *n15* **starting point;** *inf of* -sinziira   okusinziira ku **according to,** *eg. okusinziira ku kye nnakugambye ('according to what I told you')*

okusoma *n15* **reading, studying;** *inf of* -soma

okusomesa *n15* **teaching;** *inf of* -somesa

okusomokera *inf of* -somokera   aw'okusomokera *n16* **place for crossing water, ford**

okusonyiwa *n15* **forgiveness;** *inf of* -sonyiwa

okusooka *adv* **first,** *eg. Okusooka fumba emmere. ('First cook the food.')*; *inf of* -sooka

okussa *n15* **breathing, respiration;** *inf of* -ssa

okussaako *inf of* -ssaako   okussaako emikono *n15* **confirmation** (*Christian rite*)

okusukkawo *adv* **further than there**; *inf. of* -sukkawo

okutaali **where there was/were not** (*on top*)

okutaano -a okutaano *adj* **fifth** (**N7.1**), *eg. omuti ogw'okutaano* ('*fifth tree*'). *An elided form is sometimes seen, eg. omuti ogwokutaano* ('*fifth tree*').

okutali **where there is/are not** (*on top*). *Can be equivalent to preposition* **without** (**N7.2**).

-kutama *vi* (-kutamye) **stoop, bend (over)**

okutambula *n15* **movement, travel(ling), journey, walk(ing)**; *inf of* -tambula

-kutamya *vt* (-kutamizza) **cause to bend over** -kutamya ku mutwe **bow one's head** (*in prayer, respect, etc.*)

okuteeba *n15* **game of guessing** (*of what's in the hand*); *inf of* -teeba

okuteekateeka *n15* **preparations**; *inf of* -teekateeka

okuteesa *n15* **discussion**; *inf of* -teesa

okutegeera *n15* **consciousness**; *inf of* -tegeera

okutta *n15* **killing**; *inf of* -tta

-kutte *See* -kwata

okutu *n15* (*pl.* amatu) **ear**

-kutufu *adj* **broken** (*often implying in two*)

-kutuka *vi* (-kutuse) **break** (*into two or more pieces*), *eg. Omuguwa gukutuse mu bitundu bisatu.* ('*The rope has broken into three.*'), **be broken, be split, snap, die** -kutuka ekiwalaata **become bald** -kutuka n'omuntu **struggle to deal with** (*someone*) ekifuba ekikutuka **wet cough** **-kutukako** (-kutuseeko) **break off**, *eg. Oluggi lukutuseeko omunyolo.* ('*The handle has broken off the door.*') **-kutukamu break into** (*two or more pieces*)

-kutula *vt* (-kutudde) (1) **break** (*into two or more pieces*), *eg. Yakutudde omuguwa mu bitundu bisatu.* ('*He has broken the rope into three pieces.*'); (2) **break free** (*from a tether*), *eg. Embuzi ekutudde.* ('*The goat has broken free.*') -kutula ekigambo **break a word into syllables** -kutula omutima **shock** **-kutulamu** (-kutuddemu) -kutulamu wakati **break into two, halve** **-kutulawo decide**

-kutulakutula *vt* (-kutusekutuse) **break into many pieces**

okutunda *n15* **selling**; *inf of* -tunda

okutundira *inf of* -tundira   okutundira ku lubalaza *n15* **selling from the pavement**

[1]**okutuuka** *n15* **arrival**; *inf of* -tuuka

[2]**okutuuka** *pre* **as far as, up to, to.** '*okutuuka*' *is followed by* e *for names of places, but otherwise* **ku**, *eg.* (1) *Yagenda okutuuka e Masaka.* ('*She went as far as Masaka.*'); (2) *Yagenda okutuuka ku ssomero.* ('*She went as far as the school.*'). okutuuka kati **up to now**   okutuuka wano **up to here, on arrival**

okutuukiriza *n15* **achievement**; *inf of* -tuukiriza

okutuula *n15. inf of* -tuula   okw'okutuula *n17* **seating area**

okutuusa *inf of* -tuusa   okutuusa lwe (*also* okutuusa bwe) *conj* **until**, *eg. Nnakola emirimu okutuusa lwe yajja.* ('*I worked until he came.*', *meaning* '*until the day he came*')   okutuusa kaakati **hitherto, until now**

okutwalira *inf of* -twalira   okutwalira awamu **altogether, in general, considering everything**

okutya *n15* **fear**; *inf of* -tya

-kuuba *vt* (-kuubye) **rub against, brush against**

-kuubagana *vi* (-kuubaganye) **be hostile to one another, rub one another up the wrong way**

-kuubuufu *adj* **rough** (*to the touch*)

-kuubuuka *vi* (-kuubuuse) **be rough** (*to the touch*)

-kuubuula *vt* (-kuubudde) **make rough**

-kuuka *vi* (-kuuse) **be extracted, come out from a socket** (*of a handle, tooth, etc.*), **be uprooted** **-kuukamu** (-kuuseemu) **come out from**, *eg. Oluggi lukuuseemu omunyolo.* ('*The handle has come out of the door.*')

-kuula *vt* (-kudde) **extract, pull out** (*eg. a plant*), **uproot, detach** -kuula erinnyo **extract a tooth** -kuula omuti **uproot a tree** **-kuulamu** (-kuddemu) **pull out of**, *eg. Yakuulamu omunyolo mu luggi.* ('*He pulled the handle out of the door.*')

[1]**akuuma** *n12* **small machine** akuuma akakwata amaloboozi **voice recorder** akuuma akasala omuddo **lawnmower**

[2]**-kuuma** *vt* (-kuumye) **protect, watch out for, look after, watch over, guard, safeguard** Akuume. **Let God guide you.** (*said when leaving someone who you will probably not see for a long time*)

[3]**-eekuuma** *vr* **protect oneself, be on one's guard, beware of** -eekuuma mu njogera **be guarded in speech** Weekuume embwa. **Beware of the dog.**

-kuumira *vt* (-kuumidde) **keep guard for/at**, *etc.*

-kuumuuka *vi* (-kuumuuse) **be crumbly** (*of sweet potatoes*)

-kuunyuuka *vi* (-kuunyuuse) **be torn off** (*of pieces from something*)

-kuunyuula *vt* (-kuunyudde) **tear/pull off pieces from**, *eg. Akuunyuula omugaati.* ('*She is pulling off pieces of bread.*')

[1]**-kuusa** *vit* (-kuusizza) **hide the truth (from), keep secret (from)**, *eg. Yankuusa ku ssente ze yafuna.* ('*He would not tell me about the money he received.*'), **deceive** (*by not revealing information*). *See* okukuusa

[2]**-eekuusa** *vi* (-eekuusizza) **rub oneself against** -eekuusa ku **border on** (*eg. criminality*)

-kuusiira *vi* (-kuusidde) **become discoloured with soil**

[1]**-kuuta** *vt* (-kuuse) **scrub, rub hard, scour** -kuuta endingidi **play the fiddle**

[2]**-eekuuta** *vr* **scrub/rub oneself**

-kuutira (-kuutidde) *vt* **be insistent with**, *eg.*

Yamukuutira obutaba n'akyayogera kyonna. ('He insisted that she should never say anything.')

okuva *pre* **from**, *eg. Pima okuva wano okutuuka wali. ('Measure from here to there.'); inf of* -va. *'okuva' referring to place is often followed by 'e', 'ku' or 'mu', eg. Yatambula okuva mu kibuga. ('She walked from the town.'). See* from; since *(both in Part 3 of the dictionary)* Okuva **Exodus** *(book in the Bible)* okuva ... bwe **since** *(referring to reason)* okuva kaakati **from now on** okuva ku **according to**, *eg. Okuva ku bye yayogera kyeraga lwatu nti yali mubbi. ('From what he said, it was obvious that he was a thief.'),* **depending on, since** *(referring to a particular time)* okuva lwe **(ever) since** *(referring to a particular day), eg. Okuva lwe yatuuse, akoze nnyo. ('Since he arrived here, he has worked hard.')* kumpi okuva wano **a short distance from here** wala okuva wano **far from here**

okuvuba *n15* **fishing**; *inf of* -vuba
okuvuga *n15* **driving**; *inf of* -vuga
okuwaayo *n15* **contribution**; *inf of* -waayo
okuwagulula *inf of* -wagulula okuwagulula kw'amazzi *n15* **flood**
okuwalirizibwa *n15* **coercion**; *inf of* -walirizibwa
okuwandiika *n15* **writing**; *inf of* -wandiika
okuwandiikiragana *n15* **correspondence**; *inf of* -wandiikiragana
okuwangaala *n15* **longevity**; *inf of* -wangaala
okuwanirira *n15* **support**; *inf of* -wanirira
okuwoggana *(also* okuwowoggana*) n15* **(a lot of) noise, shouting**; *inf of* -woggana
okuwulira *n15* **hearing, feeling**; *inf of* -wulira
okuwummula *n15* **retirement, rest, break**; *inf of* -wummula
okuwuuma *n15* **type of sound, hum, rumble**; *inf of* -wuuma
okuyiga *n15* **learning**; *inf of* -yiga okuyiga kw'obukulu **adult education**
okuyigiriza *n15* **teaching**; *inf of* -yigiriza
okuyimba *n15* **singing**; *inf of* -yimba
okuyingirira *inf of* -yingirira aw'okuyingirira *n16* **entrance**
okuyita *inf of* -yita okuyita ku *pre* **past** Okuyitako *n15* **Passover**
okuyitibwa *n15* **calling, vocation**; *inf of* -yitibwa
okuyongobera *n15* **drowsiness**; *inf of* -yongobera
[1]-kuza *vt* (-kuzizza) **(cause to) grow, rear** *(child or animal)*, **promote** *(person in rank)* -kuza olunaku **make a day special, celebrate a special day** -kuza omwana **raise a child**
[2]-eekuza *vr* **promote oneself**
okuzaala *n15* **birth**; *inf of* -zaala
okuzannyira *inf of* -zannyira aw'okuzannyira *n16* **playground**
okuziika *n15* **funeral, burial**; *inf of* -ziika
okuzimba *n15* **building**; *inf of* -zimba
okuzina *n15* **dancing**; *inf of* -zina

okuzirika *n15* **coma**; *inf of* -zirika
(o)kw' *abbrev of* ku; (o)kwa; kwe
(o)kwa *pre* (1) **of**, *eg. okugulu kwa Musoke ('leg of Musoke')*; (2) **on the place/home of**, *eg. Okwa Musoke teekako amagi abiri. ('Put two eggs on Musoke's.' – 'plate' understood). Can be a prefix* **(o)kwa-** **(N11.5)**, *eg. okwange ('on my place').*
[1]okwabwe *adv* **on their place/home (N11.5)**, *eg. Okwabwe kuliko ekipande. ('There is a poster on theirs.' – house understood)*
[2](o)kwabwe *pos* **their(s) (N11.4)**, *eg. Okwabwe kwabwe twabadde kulungi. ('Their talk was good.')*
[1]okwaffe *adv* **on our place/home (N11.5)**
[2](o)kwaffe *pos* **our(s) (N11.4)**
-kwafu *adj* **dense** *(in consistency),* **thick** *(of vegetation, sauce, etc.),* **dark**, *eg. ekisaka ekikwafu ('dark thicket')*
okwagala *n15* **liking, love, passion**; *inf of* -yagala
kwaki? *interr* **what for?**
-kwakkula *(also* -pakula*) vt* (-kwakkudde) **snatch, grab**
kwako *command* **Take it.**
-kwakwaya *vi* (-kwakwayizza) **rustle** *(make sound like dry leaves being blown about),* **make crackling sound** *(as static on radio)*
kwaliko **there was/were** *(on top)*
okwalula *inf of* -yalula okwalula abalongo *n15* **birth rites for twins**
[1]okwammwe *adv* **on your** *pl.* **place/home (N11.5)**
[2](o)kwammwe *pos* **your(s)** *pl.* **(N11.4)**
-kwana *vt* (-kwanye) **befriend, flirt with**
[1]okwange *adv* **on my place (N11.5)**
[2](o)kwange *pos* **my, mine. (N11.4)**
okwanjula *n15* **presentation of man to family of prospective wife**; *inf of* -yanjula
-kwasa *vt* (-kwasizza) **cause to hold, clasp, grasp, grip, net, hand (over), stick, glue, tack** -kwasa ensonyi **embarrass** -kwasa ku/mu **touch** -kwasa obuggya **make envious** **-kwasaako** (-kwasizzaako) **attach, stick on**
kwasakko *n1* **kwashiorkor**
[1]-kwata *v* (-kutte) (1) *vi* **be stuck down, adhere, go solid, coagulate, freeze, clot, be dense** *(of vegetation)*; (2) *vt* **hold, clasp, seize, rape, arrest, trap, catch, memorise.** *Proverb: 'Akwata empola atuuka wala.' ('He who goes slowly goes far.')* -kwata amateeka **conform** *(to rules or the law)* -kwata bbalaafu **freeze** -kwata bukusu **learn by heart** -kwata ekigwo **wrestle** -kwata empola **be gentle, handle carefully** -kwata ku/mu **touch, hold onto, concern** -kwata mu mbinabina **put hands on hips** -kwata mu ngalo **hold in the hand, shake hands** -kwata obudde *(also* -kwata essaawa*)* **be punctual** -kwata olububi **form a skin** *(eg. on gravy)* -kwata omuliro **catch fire** -kwata omuzira **freeze** ennaku -kwata **be distressed** obudde -kwata **become dark** *(of the sky)* obulwadde -kwata **catch** *(of an illness)*

-eekwata

omuliro -kwata **catch** (*of fire*) **-kwatako** (*also* -kwata ku) (-kutteko) **affect**, *eg. Jjangu owulire ensonga eno ekukwatako. ('Come and hear this matter, since it affects you.')*, **concern**

²-eekwata *vr* **take for oneself, book, reserve** (*eg. goods*) -eekwata ekisenge **reserve a room** -eekwata ku **hold onto**, *eg. Weekwate ku mpagi oleme kugwa. ('Hold onto the post so you don't fall.')* -eekwata ku kisenge **support oneself on a wall**

-kwatagana *vi* (-kwataganye) **hold/touch one another, have one's hands full, get on well, match**, *eg. Ebikopo bino tebikwatagana. ('These cups do not match.')*, **complement** (*eg. of items of clothing*), **coincide, be contiguous.** *See* okukwatagana -kwatagana emikono **hold hands** -kwatagana na/ne **relate to** (*of affairs*)

-kwataganya *vt* (-kwataganyizza) **unite, join together.** *See* okukwataganya

-kwatakwata *vt* (-kuttekutte) **handle, fondle, finger**

-kwatakwatana *vi* (-kwatakwatanye) **be very close to one another**

-kwatibwa *vi* (-kwatiddwa) (1) **be held (by), be seized (by), be arrested**; (2) **feel** (*an emotion*) -kwatibwa ebbuba **be jealous** (*sexual, as felt by a man*) -kwatibwa ekisa **feel merciful towards** -kwatibwa empewo **feel cold** -kwatibwa ensonyi **feel shame, feel shy** -kwatibwa obuggya **envy** -kwatibwa obulwadde **catch an illness** -kwatibwa omusujja **feel feverish**

-kwatika *vi* (-kwatise) **be holdable**

-kwatira *vit* (-kwatidde) **hold for/to**, *etc.*, **adhere to, stick to**, *eg. Erangi ekwatidde ku ngoye. ('The paint is stuck to the clothes.')*, **become stuck to, be sticky** (*eg. of a label*)

-kwatirira *vi* (-kwatiridde) **keep holding onto, hope for the best, keep one's fingers crossed** **-kwatiririrako** (-kwatiriddeko) **hold on for a while, be patient**, *eg. Kwatiriirako mmale okukola emirimu gino. ('Wait until I have finished these jobs.')*

-kwatiriza *vt* (-kwatirizza) **catch in the act**, *eg. Nnamukwatiriza ng'abba emmere. ('I caught him stealing food.')*

¹kwaya *n1* **choir**

²-kwaya *vi* (-kwaye) **make rustling sound** (*as dry leaves being blown about*), **rustle**

¹kwe *equivalent to various parts of speech in English (conjunction, relative pronoun, etc. N10.2)*: (1) **on which**, *eg. Eno ye mmeeza kwe watadde ekitabo. ('This is the table on which you put the book.')*, **where**; (2) *Can be equivalent to short adverbial phrases of emphasis*, *eg. Akambe kali ku mmeeza? Yee, kwe kali. ('Is the book on the table? Yes, it is on there.')*; (3) (*followed by inf*) **therefore** (N27), *eg. Nnawulidde amawulire kwe kujja. ('I heard the news, therefore I came.')*, **that's why** kwe kugamba nti **that is to say**

²kwe *pos* **her/his** (N11.4), *eg. okusoma kwe ('her studies')*

okwebaza *n15* **acknowledgements**; *inf of* -eebaza

okwebuuza *n15* **consultation**; *inf of* -eebuuza

okwefuga *n15* **independence, self-rule**; *inf of* -eefuga

okwegatta *n15* **unity, sexual intercourse**; *inf of* -eegatta

okwegendereza *n15* **carefulness, caution**; *inf of* -eegendereza

okwegezaamu *n15* **exercise, rehearsal, practicing**; *inf of* -eegezaamu

¹-kweka *vt* (-kwese) **hide**

²-eekweka *vit* **hide oneself (from)** **-eekwekamu** (-eekweseemu) **hid oneself within**

okwekalakaasa *n15* **protest, demonstration**; *inf of* -eekalakaasa

-kwekera *vt* (-kwekedde) **hide in/for**, *etc.*

¹-kwekula *vt* (-kwekudde) **bring out of hiding, reveal** (*something hidden*)

²-eekwekula *vi* **come out of hiding**

-kwekweta *vi* (-kwekwese) **move about secretively, scout out**

okwemanya *n15* **conceit**; *inf of* -eemanya

okwerongoosesa *inf of* -eerongoosesa ekipapula eky'okwerongoosesa **toilet paper**

okwesimbawo *n15* **candidacy**; *inf of* -eesimbawo

okwetaaga *n15* **need**; *inf of* -eetaaga

okwetala *n15* **bustling about**; *inf of* -eetala

okwetonda *n15* **apology**; *inf of* -eetonda

okwetta *n15* **suicide**; *pl. of* -eetta

okwewaayo *n15* **devotion**; *inf of* -eewaayo

okwewulira *n15* **arrogance**; *inf of* -eewulira

okweyisa *n15* **behaviour**; *inf of* -eeyisa

okweyisaawo *n15* **forwardness**; *inf of* -eeyisaawo

¹okwo *adv* **on there**

²okwo *dem* **that**

³kwo *pos* **your** *si.*

⁴kwo *pro* **it.** *Can be a suffix* **-kwo** (N10-12), *eg. nakwo ('and it')*.

okwogera *n15* **speech, talk, lecture**; *inf of* -yogera

okwoleza *inf of* -yoleza aw'okwoleza *n16* **place for washing** (*things*)

okwosa *inf of* -yosa okwosa enkya **day after tomorrow** okwosa jjo **day before yesterday**

(e)ky' *abbrev of* (e)kya; kye

¹(e)kya *pre* **of**, *eg. ekiso kya Musoke ('knife of Musoke').* *Can be a prefix* **(e)kya-** (N11.4), *eg. kyange ('mine'). 'ekya' is seen in ordinal numbers* (N7.1), *eg. ekintu eky'okubiri ('second thing'). Elision is sometimes seen, eg ekintu ekyokubiri ('second thing').*

²-kya *vi* (-kedde) **dawn, let up** enkuba -kya **stop** (*of rain*) obudde -kya **dawn**, *eg. Obudde bukedde. ('It has dawned.')*

³-(y)okya *See* -yokya

Kyabazinga *n1 title* **King of Busoga**

ekyabeerawo *n7* **event**

(e)kyabwe *pos* their(s) (N11.4)
Kyaddondo *n1* county of Buganda
ekyafaayo *n7* (past) event; *in pl.* history
(e)kyaffe *pos* our(s) (N11.4)
-kyafu *adj* dirty
-kyafuwala *vi* (-kyafuwadde) be(come) dirty
-kyafuwaza *vt* (-kyafuwazizza) make dirty
kyaggulo *n7* dinner, supper (= ekyeggulo)
Kyaggwe *n1* county of Buganda
ekyagi *n7* granary
-kyajinga *vt* (-kyajingisizza) charge (*a battery*)
¹kyaki? *interr* what for?
²kyaki *n1* mat made from whole palm leaflets
kyakiro *n7* dinner, supper (= ekyekiro)
kyakubiri *adv* secondly (= ekyokubiri)
kyakukola *n7* task (= ekyokukola)
kyakulabako *n7* something to look at
   (= ekyokulabako)
kyakulabirako *n7* example (= ekyokulabirako)
kyakulwanyisa *n7* weapon (= ekyokulwanyisa)
kyakulya *n7* something to eat (= ekyokulya)
kyakunywa *n7* something to drink
   (= ekyokunywa)
kyakwambala *n7* garment (= ekyokwambala)
kyakwebikka *n7* cover (= ekyokwebikka)
-kyala *vi* (-kyadde) visit (*a place*)
ekyalaani *n7* sewing machine
kyalakimpadde *n1* (*pl.* ba kyalakimpadde) thief
-kyali *See* -li ('*be*')
ekyaliiro *n7* something spread on the floor, floor
   covering
-kyalira *vt* (-kyalidde) visit (*a person*), call on
¹ekyaliwo *n7* (past) event
²ekyaliwo it is still there
ekyaliyo there still is/are (*over there*)
ekyalo *n7* village   ow'ekyalo *n1* villager
¹ekyama *n7* secret   -a ekyama *adj* secret, private,
   confidential   mu kyama secretly
²-kyama *vi* (-kyamye) turn (off), branch (off) (*from
   a road*), make a turn, be bent, be crooked, go
   wrong   -kyamako (-kyamyeko) deviate
ekyamagero *n7* miracle
ekyamazima *n7* the truth
Kyambalango *n1* title chief of Buyaga County
ekyambalo *n7* article of clothing, garment
ekyambyone *n7* something done deliberately to
   annoy or harm
-kyamira *vt* (-kyamidde) turn off (*at a place*), *eg.*
   Okyamira ku mayiro ttaano n'odda ku kkono.
   ('*Turn off left at mile five.*'). *See* okukyamira
   w'okyamira *n16* place where one turns off
kyamisana *n7* lunch (= ekyemisana)
(e)kyammwe *pos* your(s) *pl.* (N11.4)
-kyamu *adj* crooked, bent, perverted, wrong
-kyamufu *See* -camufu
-kyamuka *See* -camuka
-kyamula *See* -camula
-kyamya *vt* (-kyamizza) change, make crooked,

bend, distort, mislead, lead astray
ekyana *n7* (1) plump little child; (2) trailer
(e)kyange *pos* my, mine. (N11.4)
kyangu *adv* easily. *See* -yangu
ekyangwe *n7* loofah *Luffa cylindrica*, sponge
kyanisi *n1* (*no pl.*) playing cards (= caanisi)
kyankya *n7* breakfast (= ekyenkya)
kyannyanja *n7* fish (= ekyennyanja)
ekyanzi *n7* milk pot/vessel
ekyapa *n7* printing press, print, type(face), font,
   patch   ekyapa ky'ettaka land title   -kuba mu
   kyapa print   mu kyapa in print   -wandiika mu
   kyapa write in capital letters
kyapati *n9* chapati
ekyapulaasitiika *n7* plastic container
ekyasa *n7* one hundred, century
ekyasalibwawo *n7* decision
ekyasembebwa *n7* recommendation
ekyasi *n7* gunshot. *See* essasi
ekyateesebwa *n7* what was discussed
kyava *conj* therefore (= kye ava N10.2)
ekyavaako *n7* result
ekyavaamu *adv* eventually
ekyavuddemu *n7* result
-kyawa *vt* (-kyaye) hate
ekyawongo *n7* offering to a lubaale
ekyawula *n7* something that causes division,
   divide, partition
ekyawulamu *n7* divider, partition
ekyayi *n7* banana fibre (*piece of*)
Kyayina *n9* China
-kyayisa *vt* (-kyayisizza) cause to hate
ekyayongerwako *n7* extension
ekyayuuyo *n7* yawn
-kyaza *vt* (-kyazizza) receive (*someone, as a visitor
   or guest*)
ekyaziyazi *n7* rock outcrop
¹kye *pos* her/his (N11.4), *eg.* ekiso kye ('*her knife*')
²kye *pre* of (= ky'e N11.1)
³kye *pro* (*relative pronoun and pronoun of emphasis*
   N10.1) it, which, what, that, *eg. Mmanyi kye
   njagala.* ('*I know what I want.*'). *Can be equivalent
   to short phrases of emphasis, eg. Oyagala kitabo
   kino oba ekyo? Kino kye njagala.* ('*Do you want
   this book or that? It is this that I want.*'). *Can be a
   prefix* kye- (N11.6), *eg. ekintu kyennyini* ('*the
   thing itself*'). kye-...-va *declinable conjunction*
   that is why, that is the reason, therefore (N10.2),
   eg. Enjala emuluma kyava alya. ('*She is hungry,
   therefore she is eating.*') ky'ekimu the same, *eg.
   Ekitabo kino ky'ekimu n'ekyo.* ('*This book is the
   same as that one.*') Kye kyo. (*also* Kye kyo
   kyennyini.) That's it., Indeed.
kyebereka *n1* (*pl.* ba kyebereka) uninvited guest
ekyebikiro *n7* bad omen, evil portent
ekyebikkwa *n7* something for covering oneself
ekyebonere *n7* something very rare, marvel
ekyeggulo *n7* dinner, supper

77

ekyejo *n7* (*no pl.*) **impertinence, insolence, outrage** -a ekyejo *adj* **impertinent** -gira ekyejo **spoil** (*a child, through overindulgence*) ow'ekyejo *n1* **impertinent person**

ekyekango *n7* **fright** (*when startled*), **shock**

kyeke *n9* **cheque**

ekyekiro *n7* **dinner, supper**

kyekubiira *n7* **bias, prejudice**

ekyekwaso *n7* **excuse**

ekyembeewo *n7* **chisel** (*for woodwork*)

ekyemisana *n7* **lunch**

ekyemulugunyizibwako *n7* **complaint**

[1]**ekyenda** *n7* (*mostly used in pl.* ebyenda) **intestine**

[2]**kyenda** *n7/num* **ninety**

ekyengera *n7* (*no pl.*) **time of plenty** (*of food, especially matooke*)

kyengi *n1* **money in small denominations, change**

ekyenjawulo *n7* **exception**

kyenkana *adv* **equally** Kyenkana wa? (*pl.* Byenkana wa?) **What size is it?**

ekyenkanyi *n7* **equality, fairness**

ekyenkomerero *n7/adv* **something that comes at the end, finally, lastly**

ekyenkukunala *n7* **something obvious**

ekyenkya *n7* **breakfast**

ekyennyanja *n7* **fish**

kyennyini kyo kyennyini **it itself** Kye kyo kyennyini. **Yes indeed.**

ekyennyumannyuma *adv* **backwards**

ekyensuti *n7* **backside of a bird**

ekyentiisa *n7* **something frightening**

kyenva *conj* **therefore** (= kye nva **N10.2**)

ekyenvu *n7* (*no pl.*) **yellowness** -a ekyenvu *adj* **yellow**

kyenvudde *conj* **therefore** (= kye nvudde **N10.2**)

ekyenyi *n7* **forehead**

ekyenyinyalwa *n7* **something disgusting, something revolting**

ekyenyinyaza *n7* **something that causes disgust**

ekyeraliikiriza *n7* **worrying**

ekyesero *n7* **watering place** (*for livestock*)

kyesi *n9* **chess**

ekyesittazo *n7* **stumbling block**

ekyetaagisa *n7* **need, necessity**

ekyetaago *n7* **need, want**

kyetutumula *n1* **type of yam** *Dioscorea acuminata-rotundata*

kyewaggula *n1* (*pl.* ba kyewaggula) **someone who takes her/his own course in life, non-conformist, rebel**

kyewamala *n1* **type of shrub** (*medicinal, combats allergies*) *Tetradenia riparia*

ekyewuunyisa *n7* **wonder, marvel, surprise**

ekyeya *n7* **dry season, drought**

kyeyagalire *adv* **voluntarily**

ekyeyago *n7* (*no pl.*) **type of skin disease** (*causes severe scratching*)

kyeyitabya *n7* **echo**

ekyeyo *n7* **broom** (*a badly made or delapitated one*) -genda ku kyeyo **go abroad to work** (*implying illegally*)

kyipusi *n10* **(potato) chips**

[1]**ekyo** *dem* **that** olw'ekyo **therefore**

[2]**kyo** *pos* **your** si.

[3]**kyo** *pro* **it.** *Can be a suffix* -kyo (**N10-12**), *eg.* nakyo ('and it').

ekyobulamu *n7* **something relating to health**

ekyobulimba *n7* **lie**

ekyobuwangwa *n1* **custom/tradition** (*of tribe or nation*)

ekyobuzaaliranwa *n1* **custom/tradition** (*associated with place of birth*)

ekyogero *n7* **basin for bathing babies, herbal mixture for bathing babies.** *The plants used can include akabombo, ekiyondo, ekkajjolyenjovu, kamunye, kayaayaana, magejjo and nnabbugira.*

ekyogi *See* -yogi

ekyokero *n7* **furnace, kiln**

[1]**kyokka** *adj/adv* **only, alone** ekyo kyokka **merely, that only**

[2]**kyokka** *conj* **nevertheless, however, but** Kyokka bannange. **Good gracious.**

ekyokoola *n7* **evil spirit** (*controlled by a living person*)

-kyokooza (*also* -cokooza) *vt* (-kyokoozezza) **pick a quarrel with, provoke** (*to a fight*)

ekyokubiri *adv* **secondly**

ekyokukola *n7* **something to do, task, exercise**

ekyokukozesa *n7* **piece of equipment, resource**

ekyokulabako *n7* **something to look at**

ekyokulabirako *n7* **example, specimen**

ekyokulimisa *n7* **tool for cultivation**

ekyokulwanyisa *n7* **weapon;** *in pl.* **arms**

ekyokulya *n7* **something to eat**

ekyokuna *adv* **fourthly**

ekyokunywa *n7* **something to drink**

ekyokusatu *adv* **thirdly**

ekyokuteesa *n7* **something to discuss**

ekyokutimba *n7* **something to decorate, decoration**

ekyokutunda *n7* **ware** (*for sale*)

ekyokuzannyisa *n7* **something used to play a game, prop** ekyokuzannyisa ky'omwana **toy**

ekyokwambala *n7* **garment**

ekyokwebikka *n7* **cover** (*on oneself, eg. blanket*)

ekyokwerongoosesa *n7* **toilet paper**

ekyokweyalira *n7* **piece of bedding**

ekyokya *n7* **something that burns**

ekyolooni *n7* **toilet, latrine**

ekyombo *n7* **boat** (*types with sails*), **dhow**

ekyomubulago *n7* **necklace**

ekyomuliro *n7* **accelerator pedal**

ekyomuzizo *n7* **taboo**

ekyondo *n7* **bay, gulf**

kyonna *pro* **any(thing), whatever**

ekyonoono *n7* **sin**

ekyonziira *n7* animal to which an evil spirit is transferred, scapegoat

ekyoogo *n7* herbal mixture for bathing adults

ekyoto *n7* fireplace, hearth

kyova *conj* therefore (= kye ova **N10.2**)

ekyovu *n7* foam, suds, lather

ekyoya *n7* (*mostly used in pl.* ebyoya) feather, hair (*of an animal, or on the human body*), wing (*of termite*) ebyoya by'ekinyonyi plumage ebyoya by'enswa something worthless, empty promise (*lit. 'wings of termites'*). Saying: 'Yatuwadde byoya bya nswa.' ('There is nothing of worth in what he gave us.')

ekyoyo (*also* ekyoyooyo) *n7* yearning, craving

-kyuka *vi* (-kyuse) change, turn, be converted. *See* okukyuka   -kyuka mu ddiini change one's religion

-kyukakyuka *vi* (-kyusekyuse) keep changing, be fickle

-kyukira *vt* (-kyukidde) turn to, have a change of feelings towards (*a person*). *See* okukyukira w'okukyukira *n16* turning place (*where one can turn around*)

kyukyu (*also* ccuucu) *n1* type of tall spiky grass *Brachiaria decumbens*   Kyukyu **a title of the Kabaka**

ekyuma *n7* metal, iron, machine   ekyuma ekikuba mu kyapa **printer** (*for printing papers*)   ekyuma ekizimbulukusa **microscope**   ekyuma ki kalimagezi **computer**   kyuma kya mbwa **dog bell**

[1]-kyusa *vt* (-kyusizza) (cause to) change, alter, convert, move, shift (*eg. location*), transfer, switch, transform. *'kyusa' followed by verb in narrative* (**N16**) *in neg* (**N21**) *means* change one's mind, *eg.* Yakyusizza n'atagenda. ('He changed his mind and is not going.'). *See* okukyusa   -kyusa eddiini change one's religion   -kyusa mu lulimi translate   -kyusa okudda mu convert   -kyusa omulimu change one's job   -kyusa ssente change money (*between currencies*)   -kyusa -yita awalala divert   **-kyusaako** (-kyusizzaako) vary, amend   **-kyusaamu** modify, revise

[2]-eekyusa *vr* change one's position (*physically or mentally*), change one's outlook

-kyusakyusa *vt* (-kyusizzakyusizza) change many times

-kyusibwa *vi* (-kyusiddwa) be changed   -kyusibwa -yita awalala be diverted

-kyusiza *vt* (-kyusizza) change at/in, *eg.* Ŋŋenda kukyusiza engoye zange mu nnyumba. ('I am going to change my clothes in the house.')

L, l

-(y)ala *See* -yala

-laajana *vi* (-laajanye) make an outcry, cry out (*for pity or help*), beg pitifully. *See* plead

-laakiira *vi* (-laakidde) gasp   ekifuba ekiraakiira whooping cough

[1]-laala *vi* (-ladde) be calm (*of the lake*). *See* eradde

[2]-(y)alaala *See* -yalaala

-laalaasa *vt* (-laalaasizza) spread (*something confidential or untrue*)   -laalaasa ebigambo divulge confidential information   -laalaasa ekyama divulge a secret

-laalika *vt* (-laalise) designate (*someone to a task*), appoint, assign

-laalira *vi* (-laalidde) get stuck, *eg.* Emmeeza eraalidde mu mulyango. ('The table is stuck in the doorway.')

-laama *vi* (-laamye, nnaama) make a will

-laamira *vt* (-laamidde, nnaamira) bequeath to, *eg.* Yalaamira mutabani we ennyumba ye. ('He bequeathed his house to his son.')

laasi *n9* lace (*material*)

laatiri *See* eraatiri

-laawa *vt* (-laaye) castrate

-laawe *adj* (endaawe *n9*) castrated

-laaya *vi* (-laayizza, ndaaya) prostitute oneself

-laba *vit* (-labye) see, look at, find, watch, perceive, be conscious, be apparent to. *See* okulaba   -laba bulabi be obvious (*eg. of a motive*), be conspicuous   -laba ennaku suffer hardship   Ndaba ku ki? **Whom do I see?** (*expression of pleasure when meeting a long-absent friend; also used when seeing something rare*)   Ng'olabye! (*pl.* Nga mulabye!) **I'm so sorry for you!**   Nga ndabye! **Alas!**   **-labako** (-labyeeko) (*also* -laba ku) take a look, *eg.* Bikkula ekirabo njagala kulabako. ('Open the present, I want to take a look.')   Nzize kukulabako. **I have come to see you for a brief while.**   **-labayo** see (*over there*)

-labagana *vi* (-labaganye) see one another, meet up with

-labankana *vi* (-labankanye) look around in a distracted way, have one's mind elsewhere

-labankanya *vi* (-labankanyizza) distract

labba *n9* rubber (*eraser*)

-labika *vi* (-labise) be seen, be visible, turn up, be apparent, appear, seem, *eg.* Alabika mulwadde. ('He seems ill.'), be likely   -labika bulabisi be obvious, be conspicuous   -labika obulungi look attractive

-labikalabika *vi* (-labiserabise) be seen frequently, occur commonly

-labikira *vt* (-labikidde) appear before/at, *etc.*

-labikirwa *vi* (-labikiddwa) cause to be seen. *See* okulabikirwa

-labira *vt* (-labidde) see for/in, *etc.*, find (*a person*) for (*eg. worker for someone*), give regards to, *eg.* Omundabire. ('Give her my regards.'), greet for, look at the work of (*cheating in a test*). *See* okulabira   -labira awo be unaware, be unexpected, *eg.* Nnalabidde awo nga ssente azireese. ('He unexpectedly brought me the

money.') -labika bulabisi **be obvious** -labira ku
be inspired by, follow the example of, *eg. Labira
ku musomesa wo naawe oyambale bw'otyo.
('Follow the example of your teacher and dress like
her.'),* **emulate** Tunaalabira awo. **We shall see.**
(what will happen)

-labirira *vt* (-labiridde) **look after, take care of,
supervise, manage.** *See okulabirira*

-labiriza *vt* (-labirizza) **divert the attention of,
distract** *(with criminal or mischievous intention)*

-labisa *vt* (-labisizza) **cause to see**

-labuka *vi* (-labuse) **be forewarned, be(come)
aware**

-labula *vt* (-labudde) **warn, forewarn, alert, caution**

laddu *See* eraddu

-lafuubana *vi* (-lafuubanye) **work hard, toil away**

-laga *vit* (-laze) **show,** *eg. Nnamulaze ekitabo
kyange. ('I showed him my book.'),* **indicate (to),
give notice of visiting**

-lagaalaganya *vi* (-lagaalaganyizza) **procrastinate,
keep on postponing**

-lagaana *vi* (-lagaanye) **agree, make an agreement
or arrangement,** *eg. Baalagaanye okusisinkana
mu wooteeri. ('They agreed to meet at the
restaurant.')*

-lagaanya *vt* (-lagaanyizza) **make an agreement
arrangement with**

-lagajjala (-lagajjadde) *vi* **be careless, be negligent**

-lagajjalira *vt* (-lagajjalidde) **neglect**

-lagajjavu *adj* **careless, negligent**

-lagaya *vi* (-lagaye) **be loose, sag** *(eg. of a wire)*

-lagira *vt* (-lagidde) **order, command, decree**

-lagirira *vt* (-lagiridde) **instruct, direct,
demonstrate, show how**

-lagiriza *vt* (-lagirizza) **send for** *(someone),* **order**
(something) **from a distance, import** -lagiriza
ebigambo **speak to at a distance,** *eg. Yamulagiriza
ebigambo ng'ayita mu ddirisa ly'emmotoka. ('She
spoke to him through the window as she went off in
the car.')*

-lagirwa *vi* (-lagiddwa) **be ordered**

-lagula *vi* (lagudde) **tell a fortune, divine, foretell,
predict, prophesy**

-lagulwa *vi* (-lagulidwwa) **be prophesied**

-lakira *vt* (-lakidde) **choke,** *eg. Kindakidde. ('It is
choking me.')*

-lala *adj* (eddala *n5,* endala *n9*) **other, another,
different, alternative**

-lalama *vi* -lalamye) **look up** *(tilting the head back)*

-lalambala *vi* (-lalambadde) **be stiff**

-lalika *vt* (-lalise) **raise, lift up** -lalika omutwe **tilt
the head back** *(eg. to look upwards)*

-lalu *adj* (endalu *n9*) **mad, unruly, badly-behaved**

-laluka *vi* (-laluse) **go mad, become unruly, be
badly behaved, be infatuated,** *eg. Balaluse
n'omupiira.' ('They are infatuated by football.')*

-lalulalu *adj* **mischievous**

-lalusa *vt* (-lalusizza) **drive mad, cause to become**
wild *(in behaviour)*

-lama *vi* (-lamye, nnama) **survive** *(a calamity), eg.
Musoke yalama baasi bwe yatomera. ('Musoke
survived the bus crash.'),* **be spared**

-lamaga *vi* (-lamaze) **make a pilgrimage**

Alamanzaani *n9* **Ramadhan**

[1]**-lamba** *adj* (eddamba *n5,* ennamba *n9*) **entire, the
whole, undivided**

[2]**-lamba** *vt* (-lambye, nnamba) **label, mark**

-lambula *vt* (-lambudde, nnambula) **tour, inspect**
(on a tour) -lambula ennyiriri z'abaserikale
inspect soldiers on parade

-lamu *adj* (eddamu/eriramu *n5,* ennamu *n9*) **live,
healthy, in good condition, working** *(of
machinery),* **fresh** *(of milk)*

-lamuka *vi* (-lamuse, nnamuka) **regain good
condition, be(come) healthy, be(come) functional**
(of machinery), **be repaired**

-lamula *vt* (-lamudde, nnamula) **judge, arbitrate**
-lamula omuwendo **set a price**

-lamusa *vt* (-lamusizza, nnamusa) **bring back to
life, make functional, repair, greet**

-lamuuliriza *vi* (-lamuulirizza, nnamuuliriza)
bargain, haggle

-lamuza *vt* (-lamuzizza, nnamuza) **ask the price of**

[1]**landa** *See* eranda

[2]**-landa** *vi* (-lanze) **throw out shoots, climb, creep,**
eg. ekimera ekiranda ('creeping plant'), **spread** *(of
a plant or fire), eg Omuliro gulanze. ('The fire has
spread.')*

[3]**-landa** *vt* (-lanze, nnanda) **plane** *(wood)*

-landagga *vi* (-landazze, nnandagga) **ramble,
digress, be long-winded**

-landulula *vt* (-landuludde, nnandulula) **pull down**
(a climbing plant), **tear down**

[1]**-langa** *vt* (-lanze, nnanga) **announce, advertise,
promote** *(a product),* **publicise, give notice of,
broadcast, accuse, blame**

[2]**-langa** *vt* (-lanze, nnanga) **twist** *(to make a rope),*
twine, weave, plait

-langajja *vi* (-langazze, nnangajja) **be aware of
something but be unconcerned about it, stand
idly by**

langi *See* erangi

-langira *vt* (-langidde, nnangira) **dig up** *(something
unpleasant)* **about** *(a person being addressed)*

-langirira *vt* (-langiridde, nnangirira) **proclaim, give
public notice of** -langirira olutalo **proclaim war**

-langulukuka *vi* (-langulukuse) **become unplaited,
become untwisted, become unravelled**

-langulula *vt* (-languludde, nnangulula) **unplait,
untwist, unravel** -langulula ensonga **disentangle
problems**

-lannama (-lannamye, nnannama) -tuula -lannama
sit with legs extended

-lanya *vi* (-lanyizza, nnanya) **pay a formal call on
the Kabaka, recite one's lineage before the
Kabaka**

-lasa *vt* (-lasizza) **shoot, fire, flick away** -lasa akasaale **shoot an arrow** -lasa butida **sling** (*eg. stone*) **with a catapult** -lasa emmundu **fire a gun**

-lasana *vi* (-lasanye) **make a lot of noise** (*of many people talking, loudly and unpleasantly*)

-latta *vi* (-lasse) **pay no attention**

lattuliini *n9* **latrine**

-lawa *vi* (-laye) **sound** (*of drums*)

-lawuna *vi* (-lawunye) **make one's rounds** (*eg. of a doctor*), **patrol**, *eg. Poliisi erawuna ekibuga. ('The police are patrolling the town.')*

-laya *vt* (-layizza) -laya eŋŋoma **sound drums** (*as a warning*)

layini *n9* **line**

-layira *vit* (-layidde) **take an oath, vow, swear**, *eg. Yalayira nti ayogera mazima. ('He swore that he was telling the truth.')*

layisi *n1* **bargain, sale** -a layisi *adj* **cheap** ku layisi **cheaply**

layisinsi *n9* **licence** layisinsi y'okuvuga **driving licence**

-layiza *vt* (-layizza) **swear in** (*an office holder*)

-lebera *vi* (-lebedde) **be(come) loose, be(come) slack, lose stiffness** (*of materials*)

-lebevu *adj* **loose, slack**

-lebeza *vt* (-lebezezza) **loosen, slacken**

lebiizi *n1* **rabies**

-lebula *vt* (-lebudde) **libel, slander.** *See* -waayiriza

-leebeesa *vt* (-leebeesezza) **dangle**

-leebeeta *vi* (-leebeese) **hang down, dangle**

-leebuukana *vi* (-leebuukanye) **constantly return to the same task, move about constantly** (*eg. searching for something*), *eg. Ennaku zino abavubuka baleebuukana okunoonya emirimu wano ne wali. ('These days young people are constantly moving about all over the place looking for jobs.')*

-leebuukanya *vt* (-leebuukanyizza) **make** (*someone*) **move about constantly** (*to do tasks*), *eg. Emirimu gibaleebuukanya. ('The work is making them move about all over the place.')*

leediyo *n9* **radio**

-leega *vt* (-leeze) **draw taut, stretch, tune** (*stringed musical instrument*) leega buleezi **go straight on** (*instruction in giving directions*) -leega ebikya **be worked up emotionally** -leega eŋŋoma **stretch a drum** -leega okugulu **stretch one's leg** -leega olukoba lw'ennanga **tune a harp** -leegamu (-leezeemu) **aim at** (*something, eg. with a gun or knife*)

-leegulula (*also* -leegula) *vt* (-leeguludde) **make loose, slacken**

-leeguula *vt* (-leegudde) **widen, stretch apart**, *eg. Yatudde nga aleegudde amagulu.' ('He sat with legs stretched apart.')*, (*occasional meaning*) **slacken**

-leekaana *vi* (-leekaanye) **make a lot of noise, shout, yell, scream.** *See* okuleekaana -yogera

-leekaana **speak loudly**

-leekinga *vt* (-leekinze) **rake (up)**

[1]**leenya** *n1* (*no pl.*) **serious trouble** -gwako leenya **get into big trouble**

[2]**-leenya** *vi* (-leenye) **be septic** (*of a wound*)

-leereeta *vi* (-leereese) **wander about aimlessly, be a vagabond**

leero *adv* **today** -a leero *adj* **modern**, *eg. empisa za leero ('modern customs')* olwa leero **today**

leerwe *n9* **railway**

leesu *n9* **cloth worn by women** (*eg. as headscarf or shawl*), **shawl**

-leeta *vt* (-leese) **bring, produce, lead to, provide, cause** -leeta ekirowoozo **suggest** -leeta ekiteeso **propose** -leeta emitunsi **sprout** (*especially of sweet potatoes or beans*) -leeta omusaayi **bleed** (*of a wound*)

-leetebwa *vi* (-leeteddwa) **be brought**

-leetera *vt* (-leetedde) **bring for, cause for**, *eg. Kye yayogera kyamuleetera omutawaana. ('What he said caused him trouble.')*, **supply**

leeti *adv* **late**

[1]**leeya** engoye eza leeya *n10* **ordinary clothes** (*eg. as contrasted with a uniform*)

[2]**-leeya** *vi* (-leeye) **loaf about, loiter**

-leeze *See* -leega

-lega *vi* (-leze) **taste** (*usually referring to drink*). *Saying: 'Tugende tulege.' ('Let's have a drink.')*

-legama *vi* (-legamye) **get trapped** (*of a liquid*), **puddle/pool up**

-legejja (*also* -legesa, *or* -lejja) *vi* (-legezze) **talk incessantly, prattle on and on, chatter**

-legesa (-legesezza) *See* -legejja

lejjalejja *adv* **one at a time, at retail** edduuka lya lejjalejja **retail shop** omulimu gwa lejjalejja **casual work** omupakasi wa lejjalejja **casual worker**

[1]**-leka** *v* (-lese) (1) *vt* **leave**, *eg. Emmotoka nja kugireka mu ggalagi. ('I will leave the car in the garage.'),* **leave behind, abandon**; (2) *aux v* (*followed by subjunctive* N17) **let**, *eg. Leka asome. ('Let him read.'),* **permit, allow** -lekako (-leseeko) **leave** (*on*), *eg. Lekako essowaani ku mmeeza. ('Leave some plates on the table.')* **-lekamu leave some** (*inside*), *eg. Mu jjaagi yalekamu amata. ('She left some milk in the jug.')* **-lekawo leave** (*there*), *eg. Lekawo amazzi agokunywa. ('Leave some water for drinking.')* **-lekayo leave** (*over there*)

[2]**-(y)oleka** *See* -yoleka

[1]**-lekera** *vt* (-lekedde) **leave with/at**, *etc., eg. Lekera Musoke essente. ('Leave some money with Musoke.')* **-lekeraawo** (*also* -lekera awo) (*followed by inf*) **stop** (*doing something*), *eg. Lekera awo okukola, ojje olye. ('Stop working and come and eat.'),* **leave** (*what one is doing*) **right there, halt, cease, give up, discontinue.** *See* N21

[2]**-(y)olekera** *See* -yolekera

-lekeraawo *See* -lekera awo

-lekerera *vt* (-lekeredde) **give up, abandon**

-lekulira *vit* (-lekulidde) **resign, abdicate**

[1]-lema *adj* (ennema *n9*) **crippled, disabled, lame**

[2]-lema *vit* (-lemye, nnema) (1) **fail**, *eg. Emmere yamulema kulya. ('He failed to eat the food.')*; (2) **be too much for**, *eg. Omulimu gwamulema okukola. ('The job proved too much for her to do.')*, **be unable to, be left over** (*of food*), *eg. Emmere yalemye. ('There is food left over.')*. *As an auxiliary ver, '-lema' is used to form the negative subjunctive* (**N21**), *eg. Mugambe aleme kugenda. ('Tell him not to go.')*.

-lemagana *vi* (-lemaganye) **fail to come to an agreement, be deadlocked, be unresolved**

-lemala *vi* (-lemadde, nnemala) **be(come) lame, be(come) crippled, be(come) disabled.** *See* okulemala

-lemaza *vt* (-lemazizza, nnemaza) **make lame, cripple**

-lembalemba *vi* (-lenzelenze, nnembalemba) **walk in a leisurely way**

-lembegga *vi* (-lembezze, nnembegga) **talk very slowly, drawl**

-lembeggerera *vi* (-lembeggeredde, nnembeggerera) **talk very slowly, drawl**

-lembeka *vt* (-lembese, nnembeka) **catch** (*a liquid*) **in a vessel, place** (*something*) **to catch a liquid** -lembeka amazzi **catch water** (*in a container*) -lembeka engalo **cup the hands**

-lembereza *vt* (-lemberezza, nnembereza) **deal carefully with** (*a person through being considerate*), **do carefully**, *eg. Enkoko nnagiremberezza ne ngikwata. (' I approached the chicken carefully and caught it.')*

-lemera *vi* (-lemedde, nnemera) **refuse to move, adhere** (*eg. to a belief*) -lemera ku kigambo **be insistent** -lemera ku nsonga **stick to one's point** (*eg. in an argument*), *eg. Omukulu w'essomero baamuwakanya kyokka n'alemera ku nsonga. ('They disagreed with the headmaster but he stuck to his point.')* **-lemerako** (*also* -lemera ku) (-lemeddeko) **persist** alemeddeko kabaani ku ndongo **person who keeps to his/her decision** -lemerawo **adhere** (*at a place*)

-lemerera *vi* (-lemeredde, nnemerera) **be utterly impossible for, lose control**, *eg. Bwe yali aweta ekkoona emmotoka n'emulemerera n'egwa mu kinnya. ('As he was cornering, he lost control of the car and it fell into the ditch.')*

-lemererwa *vi* (-lemereddwa, nnemererwa) **fail completely**

-lemesa *vt* (-lemesezza, nnemesa) **make impossible for**

-lemwa *vit* (-lemeddwa, nnemwa) **fail**, *eg. Yalemwa okutuuka. ('He failed to arrive.')*, **be unable**, *eg. Yalemwa okuzuula ennyumba yange. ('He was unable to find my house.')*, **be defeated (by)**

-lemwa okusalawo **fail to come to a decision**

-lenga *vt* (-lenze, nnenga) **measure (out), arrange in groups** (*eg. for sale*)

-lengejja *vi* (-lengezze) **hang down, dangle**

-lengera *vit* (-lengedde, nnengera) **see at a distance**, *eg. Lekera Musoke azannya ttena. ('See over there, Musoke is playing tennis.')*

-lengerekeka *vi* (-lengerekese) **be visible from afar**, *eg. Ennyanja erengerekeka okuva wano. ('The lake is visible from here.')*

-lengeza *vt* (-lengezezza, nnengeza) **show from a distance**

-lengezza *vt* (-lengezzezza, nnengezza) (1) **hang down, dangle**; (2) **hold in contempt**, *eg. Yamulengezza. ('She held him in contempt.')*

-lera *vt* (-leze) **hold in the lap, nurse** (*a child*) -lera engalo **be idle** -lera omwana **raise a child**

aleruuya *interj* **alleluia**

[1]-lesa *vt* (-lesezza) **cause to leave** (*something behind*), **make leave**, *eg. Nnamulesa ekitabo kye. ('I made him leave his book.')*

[2]-(y)olesa *See* -yolesa

-lese *See* -leka

-(y)olesebwa *See* -yolesebwa

lesoni *n9* **lesson**

-(y)oleza *See* -yoleza

[1]-li *adv* **there** (**N9.2**). *Takes pronominal concord* (**N4**). *The four forms are:* wali **there**, eri **over there**, kuli **on there**, muli **in there**.

[2]-li *dem* **that, those.** (**N9.1**). *Takes pronominal concord* (**N4**), *eg (1)* akaana kali *('that baby')*; *(2)* obwana buli *('those babies')*.

[3]-li *vi* (no msf, ndi) **be**, *eg. Ali awo. ('He is there.')*, **exist.** *Commonly used as aux v* (**N20.3**), *eg. Yali akola mu nnimiro. ('She was working in the garden.')*. *'-li' is one part of a verb (-ba/-li) having two roots, the choice of root depending on the tense and sense* (**N20.1**). **-kyali be still**, *eg. Nkyali mulwadde. ('I am still ill.')*. *An enclitic may be present* (**N20.4**), *eg. Akyaliwo.' ('She is still there.')*. *Saying: 'Obudde buba bukyali.' ('There's still time.')*. **-liko be on**, *eg. Aliko kateetera. ('He is on the point of death.')* **-limu be in**, *eg. Taliimu mu nnyumba. ('She is not in the house.')*, **contain**, *eg. Caayi alimu sukaali. ('The tea contains sugar.')* -limu enkenyera **express reluctance, have misgivings** **-lina have** (**N20.2**), *eg. Alina embwa. ('She has a dog.')*. *'-lina' followed by inf means* **have to** *in the sense of necessity, eg. Alina okukola buli lunaku. ('He has to work everyday.')* -lina ennyiike **have a** (*personal*) **problem** -lina ettigi **be insolent** -lina olutwe **be serially unlucky**

-linga *aux v* (1) (*in present tense*) **be likely, appear**, *eg. Alinga eyazze wano. ('It appears that she came here.')*, **be like, be similar to.** *Can be equivalent to adverbs* **maybe, perhaps** (**N19**), *eg. Enkuba eringa eneetonnya. ('Maybe it will rain.')*; (2) (*in past tense*) *Indicates a habitual activity in*

the past (**N20.3**), *eg. Nnalinga ŋŋenda okumulaba buli lunaku. ('I used to go and see her every day.')*
-liwo **be** (*at a place*), *eg. Twaliwo ku mukolo. ('We were at the function.')*, **be present, take place, happen** **-liyo** **be** (*over there*), *eg. Musoke yaliyo mu lukuŋŋaana. ('Musoke was there at the meeting.')*
-libufu *adv* **chipped, notched**
-libuka *vi* (-libuse) **be chipped, be notched**
-libula *vt* (-libudde) **chip, notch**
-lidde *See* -lya
-ligga *vt* (-lizze) -ligga ekigwo **throw down heavily** (*someone in wrestling*), *eg. Amulizze ekigwo. ('He has thrown him on the ground.')*
-ligguula *vt* (-liggudde) **uproot**
liggwa *See* eriggwa
-ligita *vi* (-ligise) **romp, frolic**
-liibwa *vi* (-liiriddwa) **be eaten**
liigenti *n1* (*pl.* ba liigenti) **regent**
[1]**-liika** *vi* (-liise) **be edible**
[2]**-liika** *vt* (-liise) -liika essente **ask for too much money** -liika omusolo **overtax**
[1]**-liira** *vt* (-liiridde) **eat at/with**, *etc., eg. Nnaliira ekyemisana mu wooteeri. ('I ate lunch at the restaurant.')* enva ez'okuliira ku mmere (*also* enva endiirwa) **greens** (*eaten with the main dish 'emmere'*)
[2]**-(y)aliira** *See* -yaliira
liiri *n9* **silk**
liirino **here it is**
-(y)aliirira *See* -yaliirira
liiriri **there it is**
liiryo **there it is**
-liisa *vt* (-liisizza) **feed, eat with** -liisa omululu **eat greedily, be a glutton**
-liisibwa *vi* (-liisiddwa) **be fed**
liiso *See* eriiso **Liisoddene** **God** (*as the big eyed*)
liita *n9* **litre**
-liivula *vt* (-liivudde) **relieve** (*on rotation*)
-lijja *vt* (-lizze) **tie**
-(y)alika *See* -yalika
-liko *See* -li
likoda *n9* **record**
-lima *vit* (-limye, nnima) **cultivate, dig, garden, grow** (*plants*), **farm** -lima empindi ku mabega **talk behind someone's back** -lima n'enkumbi **hoe** -lima ne tulakita **plough** (*with a tractor*)
-limba *vit* (-limbye, nnimba) **lie (to), deceive**
limbo *n9* **(public) graveyard** (*mostly used for burying foreigners*)
-limisa *vt* (-limisizza, nnimisa) **cultivate with** (*eg. a hoe*), **make cultivate**, *eg. Baalimisa basibe. ('They made the prisoners cultivate.')* -limisa enkumbi **cultivate with a hoe**
[1]**limu** *num* **one**
[2]**-limu** *v. See* -li
-lina *See* -li
-linda *vit* (-linze, nninda) **wait (for)** -lindako

(-linzeewo) **wait a bit**
-lindigga (*also* -lindiggula) *vt* (-lindizze, nnindigga) **throw down** (*a load*)
-lindirira *vit* (-lindiridde, nnindirira) *vit* **keep waiting (for), await**
-linga *See* -li
-lingiriza *vit* (-lingirizza, nningiriza) **keep on peeping (at), spy on** (*by looking secretly*), **be nosy**
-lingiza *vit* (-lingizza, nningiza) **peep at**
linnaago *n5* **their companion**
linnaalyo *n5* **its companion**
[1]**linnya** *See* erinnya
[2]**-linnya** *vit* (-linnye, nninnya) **climb, ascend, mount, step on, tread on, board, embark on, increase** (*of prices*) -linnya eddaala **be promoted** (*in rank*) -linnya eggere mu **make impossible for** -linnya omuliro **rev an engine**
-linnyibwako *vi* (-linnyiddwako, nninnyibwako) **be stepped on** -linnyibwako empewo **be possessed by a spirit**
-linnyika *vt* (-linnyise) **be climbable, surmount**
-linnyira *vt* (-linnyidde, nninnyira) **board at/in, mount** (*by male animal*) tonninnyira mu kange **ready-to-eat food** (*sold from the pavement*). *Meaning: 'Don't step in mine.'*
-linnyirira *vt* (-linnyiridde, nninnyirira) **trample on, treat with contempt**
-linnyisa *vt* (-linnyisizza, nninnyisa) **cause to climb, assist** (*someone*) **to lift, raise, hoist, assist to board** (*a vehicle*) -linnyisa ebbeeyi **raise the price** -linnyisa eddoboozi **raise the voice** (*in volume*)
linnyo *See* erinnyo
lino *dem* **this**
linto *n9* **lintel**
lipoota *n9* **report**
-(y)alira *See* -yalira
-liraana *vi* (-liraanye) **be next to, adjoin, neighbour**
-liraanagana *vi* (-liraanaganye) **be neighbours**
-liraanya *vt* (-liraanyizza) **put next to**
liri *dem* **that**
lisiiti *n9* **receipt**
-liwa *vt* (-liye) **pay damages to**, *eg. Bwe yamutomera n'amuliwa. (He bumped into him and paid damages to him.')*, **compensate**
-liwo *See* -li
-liyira *vt* (-liyidde) **compensate** (*referring to a third party*), *eg. Nnamuliyira ente mu kifo ky'embuzi. ('I compensated him with a cow instead of a goat.')*
-liyirira *vt* (-liyiridde) **compensate with, pay as damages to** (*someone*) **for**, *eg. Omulamuzi yamulagira amuliyirire ente bbiri olw'emu gye yatomera. ('The magistrate ordered that he must reimburse him with two cows for the one he collided with.')*
-liyisa *vt* (-liyisizza) **make** (*someone*) **compensate**
-liyo *See* -li
-loba *vit* (-lobye) **hook, fish** (*with a hook*)

-lobolako *vt* (-loboddeko) **take off**, *eg. Yalobako ekita ky'omwenge okuwa omwami. ('He took off one gourd of beer to give to the chief.')*, **subtract**

-loga *vit* (-loze) **practice witchcraft, bewitch, cast an evil spell (on)**

-logojjana *vi* (-logojjanye) **be delirious**

-logootana *vi* (-logootanye) **have disturbing dreams**

-logwa *vi* (-logiddwa) **be bewitched**

-loka *vi* (-lose) **start growing** (*of a plant*), **sprout** (*of a shoot or cutting*), **take root** (*of a cutting*)

-lokoka *vi* (-lokose) **be saved** (*through religion*)

-lokola *vt* (-lokodde) **save** (*through religion*)

-lokole *adj* **saved** (*through religion*)

-lolobala *vi* (-lolobadde) **stare vacantly and idiotically**

-londa *vt* (-lonze, nnonda) **choose, pick (up), select, appoint** (*person to a position*), **elect**. *See okulonda* **-londamu** (-lonzeemu) **pick out**

-londalonda *vt* (-lonzelonze, nnondalonda) **pick up one-by-one, glean** -londalonda ebisaaniiko **pick up rubbish**

-londe *adj* (eddonde *n5*) **chosen, elected**

-londerera *vt* (-londeredde) **keep on picking up, pick up** (*several things*)

-londoola *vt* (-londodde, nnondoola) **go wherever** (*a person or animal*) **goes, trail after, track down, follow** -londoola ensonga **follow a line of reasoning**

-longo *adj* **twin**

-longoofu *adj* **in good order, tidied up, pure, clean, improved**

-longooka *vi* (-longoose) **be put in good order, be tidied (up), improve, become clean**

-longoosa *vt* (-longoosezza, nnongoosa) **put in good order, make better, tidy up, straighten out, improve, correct, reform, clean, purify, operate on** (*medically*). *See okulongoosa* -longoosa empisa **correct one's behaviour** -longoosa ensobi **correct a mistake**

-longoose *adj* **purified**

loodibulooka *n9* **roadblock**

-loola *vi* (-lodde) **look coy/shy** (*as a bride at her wedding*)

loole *n9* **lorry, truck**

-loopa *vt* (-loopye) **report a wrong-doing, denounce, expose.** *Saying: 'Guno nagwo musango muloope.' ('This is serious trouble.')*

-loota *vi* (-loose) **dream**

looti *n9* **shroud, unit of measure for burial cloth** (*about four metres*)

-lootolola *vt* (-lootolodde) **interpret** (*a dream*) **for,** *eg. Yanlootolodde ekirooto kyange. ('He interpreted my dream for me.')*

-lootololera *vt* (-lootololedde) **tell** (*one's dream*) **to,** *eg. Yandootololedde ekirooto kye yaloose. ('She told me the dream she had had.')*

looya *n1* (*pl.* ba looya) **lawyer**

-lowoolereza *vt* (-lowoolerezza) **keep on thinking about**

-lowooza *vit* (-lowoozezza) **think, consider, be of the opinion that, presume, suppose.** *See* okulowooza **-lowoozaako** (*also* -lowooza ku) (-lowoozezzaako) **reflect (on), think about, contemplate**

-lowoozebwa *vi* (-lowoozeddwa) **be suspected**

-lozaako *vt* (-lozezzaako) **taste**

-lozoolera *vi* (-lozooledde) **stare vacantly and idiotically**

oluba *n11* (*pl.* emba) **jaw** -luma emba **clench the teeth**

lubaale *n1* (*pl.* ba lubaale) **type of spirit, deity** (*in Kiganda traditional religion*). *See* god (*in Part 3 of the dictionary*)

olubaawo *n11* (*pl.* embaawo) **plank, bench, board, blackboard;** *in pl.* **timber** olubaawo olutuulwako **bench** embaawo embisi **unseasoned wood**

olubajjo *n11* (*pl.* embajjo) **piece of wood that has been removed, chip** (*of wood*), **shaving**

olubalaato *n11* (*pl.* embalaato) **joke, jest**

olubalama *n11* (*pl.* embalama) **shore, bank, beach** olubalama lw'ennyanja **coast**

olubalaza *n11* (*pl.* embalaza) **verandah.** *From: 'baraza' (Swahili).*

olubale *n11* (*pl.* embale) **cut on head** (*from fighting*), **gash**

olubambo *n11* (*pl.* emmambo) **peg** (*for stretching skins*)

olubanga *n11* (*pl.* emmanga) **seat in a canoe** **Lubanga** *n1* **Kiganda deity** (*lubaale*)

olubatu *n11* (*pl.* embatu) **handful**

lubbira *n9* **submarine**

lubeere *n1* **variety of mango**

olubeerera -a olubeerera *adj* **permanent, lasting**

olubega *n11* (*pl.* embega) **helping/serving** (*of food*) olubega olw'okubiri **second helping**

olubengo *n11* (*pl.* emmengo) **(lower) grindstone**

olubereberye *adv* **at first, in the beginning** **Olubereberye (Book of) Genesis** -a olubereberye *adj* **first** ku lubereberye **in the beginning** **Omwezi ogw'olubereberye January**

olubibiro *n11* (*pl.* embibiro) **dam, embankment**

olubimbi *n11* (*pl.* emmimbi) **a day's digging**

olubirango *n11* (*pl.* embirango) **type of long poisonous snake** (*possibly mamba*)

olubiri *n11* (*pl.* embiri) **palace, palace compound** **Lubiri lw'e Mengo Mengo Palace** -siiga mu lubiri **send** (*a person, usually child*) **to the service of the Kabaka**

olubiriizi *n11* (*pl.* embiriizi) **rib, side** (*of a person's body*) mu mbiriizi **to/at the side**

oluboozi *n11* **long conversation**

olubu *n11* (*pl.* embu) **lineage, row** (*eg. of beads*) olubu lw'amannya **noun class** (*in grammar*) olubu lw'amannyo **row of teeth** olubu lw'ebigambo **part of speech** olubu lwa ssapule prayers of the rosary ow'olubu *n1* member of the same lineage

olububi *n11* (*no pl.*) **skin** (*on gravy or heated milk*), **scum, cream**

lubuga *n1* (*pl.* ba lubuga) **consort of an heir, co-heir**

olubugo *n11* (*pl.* embugo) **piece of barkcloth**; *in pl.* **barkcloth**

olubugumu *n11* (*no pl.*) **warmth**

olubumbiro *n11* (*pl.* emmumbiro) **potter's wheel**

olubuto *n11* (*pl.* embuto) **stomach, tummy, abdomen, pregnancy** olubuto -eesiba **be constipated** olubuto -gulumba **rumble** (*of the stomach*) olubuto -vaamu **have a miscarriage** -eesiba olubuto **be constipated** -fukula olubuto **dance vigorously** (*in the Kiganda way, moving one's tummy*) -funa olubuto **get pregnant** -funyisa (*or* kola) olubuto **make pregnant** -ggyamu olubuto **have an abortion** -li olubuto **be pregnant** ow'olubuto *n1* **pregnant woman**

lubyamira *n1* (*no pl.*) **pneumonia, bronchitis**

oludda *n11* (*no pl.*) **direction**, *eg.* Bagenda ku ludda lw'omugga. (*'They are going in the direction of the river.'*), **side, faction, political party.** *See* erudda; -yolekera oludda olulala **reverse side** oludda oluvuganya gavumenti **(political) opposition** ludda wa? **where?** (N13) ku ludda olulala **on the other hand** ku ludda lwa **in the direction of** ku ludda olulala lwa **after, beyond**

oluddako *adv* **next day**

-ludde *See* -lwa

-luddeddaaki = -ludde ddaaki. *See* -lwa

lufaaya *adv* **all together, indiscriminately, without exception.** *From:* '*All fire.*' (*English*) – *a military command.*

Olufalansa *n11* **French** (*language*)

olufu *n11* (*no pl.*) **mist, fog, haze**

olufuba *n11* (*no pl.*) **asthma**

lufula *n1* **abattoir.** *See* ebbaagiro

olufumo *n11* (*pl.* enfumo) **folk story, legend, fable, myth**

olufunyiro *n11* (*pl.* enfunyiro) **fold, seam**

olufuufu *n11* **mud** (*when used as plaster*)

oluga *n11* (*pl.* enga) **cane, rattan** *Calamus deeratus*

olugaayu -lyamu (*or* -yisaamu) olugaayu **pass one's leg over** (*a person, a gesture of disrespect, formerly done by children*)

Lugaba *n1* **God** (*as the giver*). *From Lunyoro.*

olugali *n11* (*pl.* engali) **winnowing tray**

olugalo *n11* (*pl.* engalo) **finger**; *in pl.* **fingers, hands** -lina engalo (*also* -limu engalo empanvu) **be a thief** engalo ensajja *n9* **thumb** -kuba engalo (*also* -kuba mu ngalo) **clap** n'engalo enjereere (*also* n'engalo enkalu) **empty-handed** ow'engalo *n1* **light-fingered person, petty thief** -wumba engalo **do nothing**

olugambo *n11* (*pl.* eŋŋambo) **rumour, gossip, idle**

talk -beera mu lugambo gossip -bungeesa olugambo **spread a rumour** ow'olugambo *n1* **gossip** (*person*)

oluganda *n11* (*pl.* eŋŋanda) **kinship, relationship** (*by blood*), **brotherhood** Oluganda **Luganda** (*language*) ow'oluganda *n1* **family member, relative** ab'oluganda *n2* **family, kin**

olugave *n11* (*pl.* engave) **pangolin**

olugendo *n11* (*pl.* eŋŋendo) **long journey, voyage, trip**

¹**olugero** *n11* (*pl.* engero) **measure(ment).** *Pronunciation*: olugéró

²**olugero** *n11* (*pl.* engero) **story, saying, proverb, parable.** *Pronunciation*: olugéró

oluggi *n11* (*pl.* enzigi) **door** oluggi lw'emiryango **front door** oluggi lw'emmanju **back door**

Luggo name of a forest on Ssese Islands (*from which materials for 'ddamula' 'Katikkiro's staff' originate*)

oluggya *n11* (*pl.* empya) **(court)yard, compound** oluggya lw'emiryango **front yard** oluggya lw'emmanju **back yard**

oluggyo *n11* (*pl.* enzigyo) **curved fragment of pottery** (*used eg. for mixing pigments*), **shard**

Olugirimaani *n11* **German** (*language*)

olugo *n11* (*pl.* engo) **cattle pen, fence of cattle pen**

olugogo *n11* (*pl.* engogo) **gutter.** *See* ekigogo

olugongogongo *n11* **backbone**

olugono *n11* (*no pl.*) **aggressiveness, pugnacity** -a olugono *adj* **aggressive** ow'olugono *n1* **person**

NOTES ON
l

l. The letter **l** replaces **r** after all letters except **e** and **i**. Compare: (1) **Omuntu alaba.** ('The person sees.') with **Enjovu eraba.** ('The elephant sees.'); (2) **-limba** ('deceive') with **-eerimba** ('deceive oneself').

-l. Verbs starting **l** have 1st person singulars starting either **nd** (non-nasal verbs) or **nn** (nasal verbs) (N5), *eg.* (1) **ndaba** ('I see'), from **-laba**; (2) **nnonda** ('I choose'), from **-londa**. 1st person singulars are not shown if they start with **nd**.

olu-. Nouns in *n11* starting **olu** typically have plurals (in *n10*) starting **en**, *eg.* the plural of **olugalo** is **engalo** ('fingers'). However, sound and spelling change often occurs (N5).

olw-. Some words in *n11* starting **olw** are compound, consisting of **olwa** ('of') and a following noun (N11.2), *eg.* **Olwokuna** ('Thursday'). If the initial vowels are dropped, then this is so for both parts of the word, *ie.* **Lwakuna.**

NOUNS IN *n9*. Most nouns in *n9* have identically spelt plurals (in *n10*).

who readily picks a fight

olugoye *n11* (*pl.* engoye) **dress, cloth, fabric, material**; *in pl.* **clothes, clothing** olugoye lwa bikuubo **striped material** olugoye olumyamyansa **shiny material** engoye enkadde **second-hand clothes** engoye entunge **ready-made clothes** engoye ez'okwoza **laundry** engoye eza bulijjo **everyday clothes** engoye eza leeya **civilian clothes, ordinary clothes** (*eg. as compared to a uniform*)

oluguudo *n11* (*pl.* enguudo) **road, highway, street**

oluguwa *n11* (*pl.* enguwa) **narrow string** nga luguwa **like a stick** (*of someone very thin*)

olugwanyu *n11* (*pl.* eŋŋwanyu) **pole supporting a hunting net** -yita ku lugwanyu **have a narrow escape**

olujegere *n11* (*pl.* enjegere) **chain** olujegere lw'embwa **dog chain/lead**

lujjudde mu lujjudde *adv* **in public** -vaayo mu lujjudde **become public knowledge**

lujjula *n1* (*no pl.*) **climbing plant with yellow fruits** (*medicinal*) *Momordica foetida*

olujjuliro *n11* (*pl.* enzijuliro) **serving place** (*for food*)

lujjulungu -a lujjulungu *adj* **dilute, watered down**, *eg. Caayi wa lujjulungu.* (*'The tea is watered-down.'*) obujulizi obw'olujjulungu **unconvincing evidence**

-luka *vt* (-luse, nduka) **weave** (*mat or basket*), **knit, splice**

lukaaga *n11/num* **six hundred**

olukalabule *n11* (*no pl.*) **too much**, *eg. olukalabule lwa sukaali* (*'too much sugar'*) olukalabule lw'omukazi **aggressiveness** (*of a woman*)

olukalala *n11* (*pl.* enkalala) **list, line, queue** olukalala lw'ensimbi **strand of cowrie shells** (*formerly used as currency*)

olukale *n11* (*no pl.*) **something public, something communal** -a olukale *adj* **public, communal** akayu k'olukale **public toilet** mu lukale **in public**

olukalu *n11* (*no pl.*) **land** (*contrasted with water*) ebisolo by'oku lukalu **terrestrial animals** ku lukalu **ashore**

olukampa *See* enkampa

olukandwa *n11* **type of small tree** (*with white berries*) *Flueggea virosa*

olukanyanya *n11* (*pl.* enkanyanya) **wrinkle** (*on the skin from ageing*)

olukato *n11* (*pl.* enkato) **needle** (*used in basket-making*), **awl**

-luke *adj* **woven**

lukeemiya *n9* **leukemia**

olukende *n11* (*pl.* enkende) **thin waist**

olukiiko *n11* (*pl.* enkiiko) **council, assembly, parliament, congress, meeting** olukiiko lw'abamawulire **press conference** olukiiko lw'eggwanga **national parliament** olukiiko lwa Buganda olukulu **Buganda parliament** olukiiko

olw'amangu **emergency meeting**

olukindo *n11* (*pl.* enkindo) **crease, scar** (*from surgery*)

olukindukindu (*also* olukindu) *n11* (*pl.* enkindukindu) **wild date palm** *Phoenix reclinata*

olukira *n11* (*pl.* enkira) **long tail**

-lukisa *vt* (-lukisizza, ndukisa) **weave/knit with**

Lukka *n1* **Luke**

olukko *n11* (*pl.* enziko) **long valley**

olukoba *n11* (*pl.* enkoba) **belt, strap, string of a musical instrument** olukoba lw'embwa **dog collar** olukoba lwa ggita **guitar string** olukoba olupima **tape measure**

olukobo *n11/adv* **slowness** (*in doing things*), **slowly** ow'olukobo *n1* **person slow at doing things** -yogera olukobo **speak for too long**

olukokobe *n11* (*pl.* enkokobe) **person or animal that won't go away, hanger-on, sponger, (human) pest**

olukokola *n11* (*pl.* enkokola) **elbow**

olukoloboze *n11* (*pl.* enkoloboze) **scratch, drawn** (*straight*) **line**

olukoloddoli *n11* (*pl.* enkoloddoli) **something very long**, *eg. olukoloddoli lwa bbaasi* (*'very long bus'*). *Impolite if applied to a person.*

olukolokolo *n7* **thorny climber** (*used as twine; used to make baskets to carry fish*) *Smilax anceps*

olukoma *n11* (*pl.* enkoma) **pole of wild date palm**

olukomera *n11* (*pl.* enkomera) **fence, hedge, barricade, palisade**

olukonko *n11* (*pl.* enkonko) **ravine, crevasse, gully, chasm, erosion channel**

olukono *n11* (*pl.* enkono) **long arm** -simba olukono **recline on one arm**

olukonvuba *n11* (*no pl.*) **incurability** -a olukonvuba *adj* **incurable**

olukoola *n11* (*pl.* enkoola) **dry area of land, savannah**

lukoota *n12* **type of mushroom** (*delicious, but leaves an itchy throat*). *From: '-koota' ('itch' – of the throat).*

oluku *n11* (*pl.* enku) **piece of firewood**; *in pl.* **firewood**

olukugiro *n11* (*pl.* enkugiro) **hem, tuck**

olukuku *n11* (*no pl.*) **itchy patches on skin** (*of people and dogs*), **mange**

olukulukuse *n11* (*pl.* enkulukuse) **stream of flowing liquid**; *in pl.* **traces left by flowing liquid**

lukululana *n9* **long truck**

lukulwe *invariable adj* **famous, renowned**, *eg. Bawagizi lukulwe ba mupiira.* (*'They are renowned football supporters.'*)

lukumi *n11/num* (*pl.* enkumi) **thousand**

olukuŋŋaana *n11* (*pl.* enkuŋŋaana) **meeting, gathering, conference** -kuba olukuŋŋaana **hold a meeting**

olukusa *n11* (*no pl.*) **permission, permit, authorisation**

olukusense *n11* (*no pl.*) **measles**

olukuta *n11* (*pl.* enkuta) **peel(ing), skin, rind**

olukuubo *n11* (*pl.* enkuubo) **corridor, passage, aisle**

olukuusi *n11* (*no pl.*) **(red) subsoil, grave,** *eg. Baamutaddeyo ku lukuusi.* ('*He was lowered into the grave.*')

olukwagulo *n11* (enkwagulo) **scratch** (*made by claws or nails*)

Lukwata *n1* **name of a huge crocodile** (= Lutembe)

olukwe *n11* (enkwe) **conspiracy, treachery, treason, betrayal, plot, guile, intrigue** -a enkwe *adj* **treacherous** -lyamu olukwe **plot against, betray** ow'enkwe *n1* **traitor**

olukya *n11* (*no pl.*) **stiff neck**

olukyala *n11* (*pl.* enkyala) **visit**

[1]**-lula** *vi* (-luze) **have a lucky escape**

[2]**-(y)alula** *See* -yalula

olulagala *n11* (*pl.* endagala) **banana leaf** endagala ezisaaniika **banana leaves placed on food bundle** (*in preparation for cooking food*)

olulago *n11* (*pl.* endago) **long neck** -lya mu ndago sing -yogera olulago **talk incessantly**

olulala *adv* **another day**

Olulattini *n11* **Latin**

olulembe *n11/adv* (*no pl.*) **slowness** (*in doing things*), *eg. Akola na lulembe.* ('*He does things slowly.*'), **in a slow way** ow'olulembe *n1* **person slow at doing things**

olulenga *n11* (*pl.* ennenga) **tree frog**

olulere *n11* (*pl.* endere) **slice** (*eg. of a root crop*), **thin strip** endere za lumonde **dried sliced potatoes** endere za mbidde **dried sliced beer bananas** endere za muwogo **dried sliced cassava**

[1]**luli** *adv* **the other day**

[2]**luli** *dem* **that**

olulimi *n11* (*pl.* ennimi) **tongue, language** olulimi lw'omuliro **flame**

olulondakambe *adv* **endlessly** (*of talking*)

-luluma *vi* (-lulumye, nduluma) **come back among the living** (*as a spirit or ghost*)

-lulumira *vt* (-lulumidde, ndulumira) **haunt**

olulundulirunduli *n11* (*pl.* ennundulirunduli) **tibia**

-lulunkana *vi* (-lulunkanye, ndulunkana) **be greedy**

-lulunkanira *vt* (-lulunkanidde) **be greedy for**

olulwe *pos* **hers/his** ku lulwe **on her/his behalf, for her/him**

olulwo *pos* **yours** *si.* ku lulwo **on your behalf, for you**

olulyo *n11* (*pl.* endyo) **lineage, pedigree, breed** olulyo olulangira **royal family** ow'olulyo *n1* **family member**

-luma *vt* (-lumye, nnuma) **hurt,** *eg. Omukono guluma.* ('*The arm hurts.*'), **ache, bite, sting.** *The person concerned can be indicated by an object pronoun, eg. Omukono gunnuma.* ('*My arm hurts.*') -luma amannyo **grind the teeth** -luma emba **clench the teeth** enjala -luma **be hungry**

ennyonta -luma **be thirsty** erinnya -luma **have toothache** omutwe -luma **have a headache** omwoyo -luma **be broken-hearted**

Lumaama *n1* *title* **chief of Kabula County** (*head of the princes*)

olumaggamagga *adv* **sporadically** -a olumaggamagga *adj* **scattered**

olumala *conj* **as soon as**

-lumba *vt* (-lumbye, nnumba) **attack, assault**

-lumbagana *vi* (-lumbaganye) **attack one another**

olumbe *n11* (*pl.* ennyimbe) **serious illness, death rites** -yabya olumbe **carry out ceremony to install an heir**

-lumbibwa *vi* (-lumbiddwa, nnumbibwa) **be attacked**

olumbugu *n11* **couch grass** *Digitaria scalarum*

-lumbwa *vi* (-lumbiddwa, nnumbwa) **be attacked**

-lume *adj* (ennume *n9*) **male** (*of certain animals*)

-lumika *vt* (-lumise, nnumika) **bleed** (*eg. by cupping*) -lumika ebigambo **eavesdrop on**

-lumira *v* (-lumidde) (1) *vi* **be gritty** (*of food*); (2) *vt* **bite at/in,** *eg. Embwa yamulumira mu luggya.* ('*The dog bit him in the courtyard.*')

-lumirirwa *vit* (-lumiriddwa, nnumirirwa) **be greatly concerned (about)** (*feeling someone's pain*)

-lumiriza *vt* (-lumirizza, nnumiriza) **accuse repeatedly** (*of something denied*), **instruct repeatedly** (*to ensure something is done*)

-lumizibwa *vi* (-lumiziddwa, nnumizibwa) **be hurt, be injured**

olummanyimmanyi *n11* (*no pl.*) **overfamiliarity.** *Saying: 'Olummanyimmanyi olukwasa embwa mu mannyo.' ('Overfamiliarity may cause you to touch the inside of a dog's mouth.', meaning 'It is dangerous.').*

lumonde *n1* (*no pl.*) **sweet potato(es)** *Ipomoea batatas* lumonde omuganda **sweet potato(es)** lumonde muwuttaavu (*also* lumonde wa biwutta) **unpalatable old potato(es)** (*kept too long in the ground*) lumonde omumyufu **red sweet potato(es)** lumonde omweru **white sweet potato(es)** lumonde omwokye **roast(ed) potato(es)** mutere wa lumonde **dried sliced potatoes** (*for storage*)

olumuunyere *adv* **incessantly** -yogera olumuunyere **talk for too long** (*with nothing much to say*). *Saying: 'Ayogera lumuunyere ng'omulere gwa Ssuuna.' ('He talks non-stop.'). The reference is to Kabaka Ssuuna who enjoyed playing the flute all the time.*

lumu *num/adv* **one, one day, once** olumu n'olumu **occasionally** lwali lumu **once upon a time**

olumuli *n11* (*pl.* emmuli) **stem of elephant grass, cane, reed** emmuli ennombeze **interwoven reeds**

-lumwa *vi* (-lumiddwa, nnumwa) **be hurt** (*physically or mentally*), **be injured, be in pain, be bitten, be stung** -lumwa enjala **be hungry** -lumwa ennyonta **be thirsty** -lumwa okuzaala (*also*

-lumya

-lumwa omwana) **be in labour** -lumwa omugongo
have back pain

-lumya *vt* (-lumizza, nnumya) **cause pain to, hurt,**
*eg. Yamukuba n'amulumya omukono. ('He hit her
and hurt her arm.')*, **injure, molest**

olunaamala *conj* **as soon as**

lunaana *n11/num* **eight hundred**

olunaanu *n11* (*pl.* ennaanu) **string of saliva** (*in
mouth*); *in pl.* **slime**

olunaba *n11* **type of tree, African false nutmeg**
Pycnanthus angolensis

olunaku *n11* (*pl.* ennaku) **day, date** Olunaku
lw'Amatabi (*also* Olunaku lw'Ensansa) **Palm
Sunday** olunaku lw'emizannyo **sports day**
olunaku lw'omwezi **day of the month** olunaku
lwa kukola **working day** Olunaku
Olw'Obwerende **Saturday** (*for a Seventh-Day
Adventist*) olunaku olw'okuwummula **day of rest,
day off** ennaku ez'edda **in olden days** ennaku
zino **nowadays**

-lunda *vt* (-lunze, nnunda) **look after** (*animals*),
keep (*livestock*), **herd**

-lunde *adj* (ennunde *n9*) **domesticated**

olunderebu *n11* (*no pl.*) **overfamiliarity**
ow'olunderebu *n1* **busybody**

-lundugga *vi* (-lunduzze) **be in heat, rut**

-lunga *vt* (-lunze, nnunga) **flavour, season** (*food*),
dissolve -lunga eddagala **add plant extract to
water** -lunga omunnyo **season food with salt**
-lunga sukaali **add sugar** (*eg. to tea*)

Olungereza *n11* **English** (*language*)

-lungi *adj* (eddungi *n5*; ennungi *n9*) **good, beautiful,
handsome, desirable** -lungiko (*also* -lungirungi)
fairly good, fairly beautiful

-lungiwa *vi* (-lungiye, nnungiwa) **be(come)
beautiful, be(come) handsome, improve** (*in
behaviour*)

-lungiya *vt* (-lungiyizza, nnungiya) **make beautiful,
make handsome, beautify**

Lungujja **suburb of Kampala.** *From: 'long journey'
– overheard from soldiers who set up camp here
after journeying on foot up from the coast with
Captain Lugard.*

olunkulu *n11* (*no pl.*) **snobbery** ow'olunkulu *n1*
snob

lunkupe *n1* (*pl.* ba lunkupe) **very poor person**

lunnaalwo *n11* **its companion**

lunnaazo *n11* **their companion**

olunnya *n11* (*pl.* ennyinya) **trench**

¹**olunnyo** *n11* (*pl.* ennyinyo) **stretcher** (*one used for
carrying sick people*). **Pronunciation:** olunnyò

²**olunnyo** (*also* olunnyu) *n11* (*no pl.*) **infertile land.**
Pronunciation: olúnnyò -a olunnyo *adj* **infertile**
(*of land*) ettaka ly'olunnyo **infertile land**

luno *dem* **this**

olunwe *n11* (*pl.* ennwe) **index finger;** *in pl.* **fingers**
(*excluding thumb*)

olunyago *n11* (*pl.* ennyago) **shaft of spear**

Olunyankole *n11* **language of Ankole**

Olunyarwanda *n11* **Language of Rwanda,
Kinyarwanda**

olunyata *n11* (*no pl.*) **smouldering embers**

olunye *adv* **constantly, from time to time**

olunyereketo *n11* **types of small herbaceous
climber.** *Two species: Cardiospermum
grandiflorum, C. halicacabum.*

olunyiriri *n11* (*pl.* ennyiriri) **line, row, queue, verse**
(*of the Bible*), **division of a clan** olunyiriri
lw'abaserikale **column/rank of soldiers**

Olunyoro *n11* **language of Bunyoro**

olunywa *n11* (*pl.* ennywa) **Achilles tendon**

lunywamunte *n11* **white-tailed mongoose.**
Meaning: 'It drinks from cows.'

olunywankoko *n11* (*no pl.*) **drizzle.** *Meaning: 'The
chicken can drink.'*

olupande *n11* (empande) **piece of material** (*cut
from roll*)

olupanka *n11* (*pl.* empanka) **rim** (*of a wheel*)

olupapula *n11* (*pl.* empapula) **paper, page, sheet**
(*of paper*) olupapula lw'amawulire **newspaper**
olupapula lw'ensimbi **bank note** olupapula
olusabika **wrapping paper**

olupiira *n11* (*pl.* empiira) **hose**

lupiiya *n10* **money.** *From: 'lupaiya' (Hindi).*

olusaago *n11* **joke**

olusaalu *n11* **marshy area with essaalu grass**

olusalosalo *n11* (*pl.* ensalosalo) **ditch dug as
boundary between properties;** *in pl.* **lines on a
drooping face**

olusamba *n11* **kick**

olusambaggere *n11* **kick** (*in fighting*)

olusambya *n11* (*pl.* ensambya) **type of tree** (*valued
for construction; the wood is termite resistant*)
Markhamia lutea. See omusambya

olusansa *n11* (*pl.* ensansa) **palm leaf** (*especially
that of olukindukindu*)

lusanvu *n11/num* **seven hundred**

olusebenju *n11* (*no pl.*) **outer edge of a house**

olusegere *n11* (*no pl.*) **place at the side** ku
kusegere **alongside, (close) beside,** *eg. Abamuli ku
lusegere tebaamubuulira. ('Those close to him did
not tell him.')*

lusejjera *n1* **swarm of young locusts** engatto za
lusejjera **canvas shoes**

oluseke *n11* (*pl.* enseke) **tube, straw** (*for drinking*),
stem (*of smoker's pipe*) -simbako oluseke **extort**

olusekese *n11* (*pl.* ensekese) **long bundle** (*of
firewood, sticks or reeds*)

olusenke *n11* **area of essenke grass**

olusenyi *n11* **sandy area of land**

oluseregende *n11* (*no pl.*) **large number**
oluseregende lw'abantu **long line of people**
oluseregende lw'ebidduka **long line of vehicles**

Olusese *n11* **language of Ssese Islands** (*closer to
Lunyoro than Luganda; no longer spoken*)

olusiisira *n11* (*pl.* ensiisira) **thatched hut, group of**

huts, encampment

olusiiti *n11* type of bush or small climber (*medicinal; the red and black seeds 'ensiiti' are used in games*) *Abrus precatorius*

olusinda *n11* (*pl.* ensinda) type of blue bead

olusinga *n11* (*pl.* ensinga) (1) bracelet made from tail hair of giraffe or elephant (*worn by some to ward off evil spirits*); (2) fibre used to seal seams of canoe

olusirika *n11* (*no pl.*) period of quietness, (religious) retreat   mu lusirika in private contemplation

olusiriŋŋanyi *n11* (*pl.* ensiriŋŋanyi) earthworm

oluso *n11* (*pl.* enso) long knife   oluso olusaawa slasher (*for cutting grass*)

Olusoga *n11* language of Busoga

olusoggo *n11* funnel-like structure (*of folded leaf or paper, used to catch termites*), cone (*eg. for holding peanuts*)   empale ya lusoggo drain-pipe trousers

olusolo *n11* (*no pl.*) patch of rough skin

olusolobyo *n11* (*pl.* ensolobyo) pruning pole, billhook

olusoma *n11* (*pl.* ensoma) (school) term, semester

olusoobo *n11* (*no pl.*) slowness (*in doing things*)   n'olusoobo slowly

olusoove *n11* cormorant

olusozi *n11* (*pl.* ensozi) hill, mountain   Olusozi Gambalagala Rwenzori Mountains   Olusozi Masaaba Mount Elgon   olusozi oluwandula omuliro volcano   -a ensozi *adj* hilly

olusu *n11* (*pl.* ensu) bad body smell

olusubi *n11* (*pl.* ensubi) long piece of grass

olusuku *n11* (*pl.* ensuku) banana garden

lusumba *n1* type of banana (*used for matooke*)

olususu *n11* (*pl.* ensusu) skin

olusuubo *n11* (*pl.* ensuubo) swing-like structure used for storage, swing   mu lusuubo in suspense

Oluswayiri *n11* Swahili (*language*)

oluswiriri *n11* (*pl.* enswiriri) whisker

oluta *n11* (*pl.* enta) span (*distance from end of thumb to end of middle finger, stretched apart*)

olutaggwa *adv* endlessly, incessantly

olutakoma *adv* endlessly, without stopping

olutalo (*also* olutabaalo) *n11* (*pl.* entalo) battle, war

olutambi *n11* (*pl.* entambi) tape   olutambi lw'ettaala wick   olutambi lwa vidiyo video

olutata *adv* endlessly, incessantly

oluteega *n11* (*pl.* enteega) Achilles tendon

olutegetege *n11* (*pl.* entegetege) tendon at back of knee

¹Lutembe *n1* name of a huge crocodile (*former inhabitant of Lutembe Beach*) (= Lukwata)

²olutembe *n11* (*pl.* entembe) necklace made from ettembe seeds

olutente *n11* (*pl.* entente) basket for catching lake flies

olutentezi   -a olutentezi *adj* chronic (*usually*

referring to an illness), recurrent

oluti *n11* (*pl.* enti) long stick, skewer

olutiba *n11* (entiba) wooden bowl, mould (*for making bricks*), bailing bowl

lutikko *n9* cathedral

olutiko *n11* (*no pl.*) goose pimples

olutimba *n11* (*pl.* entimba) long net

olutimbe *n11* (*pl.* entimbe) curtain, screen

olutindo *n11* (*pl.* entindo) bridge

olutinkizo *n11* (*no pl.*) infatuation

oluto. *Saying: 'Lukyali luto.' ('There is a lot left to do.')*

olutobazzi *n11* (*pl.* entobazzi) wetland, marsh

olutubatuba *n11* (*pl.* entubatuba) strip of bark from barkcloth tree. *See* enkuyo

olutungotungo *n11* wild simsim *Sesamum angustifolia* (= (*also* ebitungotungo)

olutuuka *adv* on arrival

¹olutuula *n11* sitting, session

²olutuula *n11* (*pl.* entuula) long hunting net (*used for catching small animals, eg. cane rats*)

olutwe *n11* (*no pl.*) continued misfortune   -lina olutwe be serially unfortunate   ow'olutwe *n1* (1) someone serially unfortunate; (2) scapegoat

olutyatya *n11* (*pl.* entyatya) beer basket (*in which beer is brewed; the basket is made from 'enjulu'*)

-luubirira *vt* (-luubiridde) strive towards (*academically or professionally*), aspire (*to be*)

luula *n9* ruler (*for measuring*)

luululi there it is

luuluno here it is

luulwo there it is

oluuma *n11* (*no pl.*) wire   oluuma olubaka aerial

¹-luusi *adj* (enduusi *n9*) female

²oluusi *adv* sometimes   oluusi n'oluusi occasionally

³Luusi *n1* Lucy, Ruth

oluuyi *n11* (*pl.* enjuuyi) side. *See* eruuyi

oluvannyuma *adv* afterwards, later, eventually, finally   oluvannyuma ennyo in the long run   oluvannyuma lwa *conj* after   -a oluvannyuma *adj* final, last   eky'oluvannyuma subsequently

oluvi *n11* (*pl.* envi) grey hair (*one*)

oluviiri *n11* (*pl.* enviiri) hair (*one*)   enviiri za kiwaanyi wig   enviiri z'oluwe stubble

oluvunyu *n11* long maggot

oluvuuvuumo *n11* murmur, murmuring, buzz

¹-luwa? *interr v* where is? (N13), *eg. Aluwa? ('Where is he?'). '-luwa' preceded by the letters 'e' or 'i' becomes '-ruwa' (N5), eg. Ekiso kiruwa? ('Where is the knife?'). Derivation: from '-li wa?' ('be where?')*

²oluwa *n11* (empa) whistle (*made through lips*)

oluwaanyi (*also* omulamula) *n11* (*pl.* empaanyi) small tree with long thin leaves (*used for marking boundaries between plots*) *Dracaena fragrans*

oluwago *n11* (*pl.* empago) bladder, inner tube

Oluwalabu *n11* Arabic (*language*)

oluwalo *n11* (*pl.* empalo) **turn, shift** -kola mu mpalo **work in turns/shifts**

oluwandaggirize *n11* (*pl.* empandaggirize) **drizzle**

luwandulamasasi *n9* **machine gun**

oluwanga *n11* (*pl.* empanga) **skull** (*of dead person*)

Luwangula *n1* title (*of the Kabaka*) **Conqueror**

oluwawu *n11* (*no pl.*) **leaf of omuwawu tree** (*used as sandpaper*), **sandpaper**

oluwayi *n11* (empayi) **slice, piece, portion**

oluwe *n11* (*pl.* empe) **hen roost** enviiri z'oluwe **short hair, stubble**

Luweekula *n1* title **chief of Buweekula County**

oluwenda *n11* (*pl.* empenda) **path made through vegetation** -kuba oluwenda (1) **make path through vegetation, make a way**; (2) **facilitate** (*eg. introduction to someone influential*) -tema oluwenda (1) **cut path through vegetation**; (2) **draw up a plan**

oluwewere -a oluwewere *adj* **thin**

oluwoko *n11* **type of shrub or scrambling plant** (*medicinal, used as an arborticide and molluscicide; snakes are said to avoid this plant*) *Phytolacca dodecandra*

oluwokyo *See* enjokyo

oluwombo *n11* (*pl.* empombo) (1) **young untorn banana leaf used to wrap food for cooking** (*especially liquid or moist food*); (2) **parcel of food so wrapped** oluwombo lw'ebinyeebwa **parcel of groundnut sauce** oluwombo lw'ennyama **parcel of meat**

oluwonvu *n11* (*pl.* ebiwonvu *n8*) **long valley**

oluwonzi *n11* (*pl.* emponzi) **comb** (*on chicken's head*)

oluwoomerambuzi *n11* **type of herbaceous plant** (*a weed*) *Lactuca capensis. Meaning: 'Goats like eating it.'*

oluwugge *n11* (*no pl.*) **metallic smell**

oluwummula *n11* (*pl.* empummula) **period of rest, holiday**

oluwumu *n11* (*no pl.*) **ringworm** (*on the body, contagious*)

oluyange *n11* (*no pl.*) **styles of maize flower** (*medicinal*)

oluyi *n11* (*pl.* empi) **slap**

oluyiira *n11* (*pl.* empiira) **grass/forest fire, area of burnt vegetation**

oluyimba *n11* (*pl.* ennyimba) **song, tune**; *in pl.* **music** oluyimba lw'eddiini (*also* oluyimba lw'ekkanisa) **hymn** oluyimba lw'eggwanga **national anthem**

oluyina *n11* (*pl.* empina) **strand of banana leaf folded along the midrib** (*tied around food bundle, worn around waist of dancer or tied around calabash of beer*)

Oluyindi *n11* **Indian language**

oluyingo *n11* (*pl.* ennyingo) **joint** (*of the body*). *See* ennyingo

oluyokyo *n11* (*pl.* enjokyo) **tribal mark** (*on body, made by burning*)

oluyombo *n11* (*pl.* ennyombo) **quarrel, row**

Oluyonaani *n11* **Greek** (*language*)

oluyoogaano *n11* (*no pl.*) **din** (*made by people*), **uproar**

oluyulu *si.* of enjulu

oluzaala *n11* (*pl.* enzaala) **occasion of giving birth, birth, confinement** ow'oluzaala olumu *n1* **woman who has given birth once** ow'enzaala ebbiri *n1* **woman who has given birth twice**

oluzaalo eddagala ly'oluzaalo *n5* **medicine to induce pregnancy**

oluzibaziba *n11* **type of small tree** (*medicinal, yields a brown dye*) *Alchornea cordifolia*

oluziina *n11* (*pl.* enziina) **worn-out garment, rag**

oluzizi *n11* (*pl.* enzizi) **course of reeds in mud and wattle wall**; *in pl.* **framework of mud and wattle wall**

Oluzungu *n11* **white person's language**

oluzzi *n11* (*pl.* enzizi) **well**

(o)lw' abbrev of (o)lwa; lwe

[1]**olwa** *conj* **because of, due to, through**

[2]**(o)lwa** *pre* of. Can be a prefix **(o)lwa-** (N11.4), *eg.* lwange ('my'). 'olwa' is seen in ordinal numbers (N7.1), *eg.* oluguudo olw'okubiri ('second road'). Elision is sometimes seen, *eg.* oluguudo olwokubiri ('second road'). lwa nsonga ki? **why?** olw'eggulo **in the afternoon** olw'ekisa **through kindness** olw'ekyo **because of that, therefore** olw'empaka **by force** olw'ensonga eno **because of this, therefore** olw'obutamanya **through ignorance** olw'obuwaze **by force** olw'okuba (*also* olw'okubanga) **because** olwa leero **today** ku lwange **for me,** ku lwaffe **for us, etc.** (N11.4)

[3]**-lwa** *vi* (-ludde) **delay, take a long time,** *eg.* Aludde okujja wano. ('He has not been here for a long time.') -lwa ddaaki (*also* -lwaddaaki) **do eventually,** *eg.* Yalwa ddaaki n'agenda. ('He left eventually.') **-lwawo** (-luddewo) **delay** (*at a place*), *eg.* Aluddewo wano. ('He has been here for some time.'), **spend a long time** (*at a place*), **take time -lwayo** **delay** (*over there*)

(o)lwabwe *pos* **their(s)** (N11.4) ku lwabwe **on their behalf, for them**

-lwaddaaki *See* -lwa ddaaki

-lwadde *adj* **ill, sick**

(o)lwaffe *pos* **our(s)** (N11.4) ku lwaffe **on our behalf, for us**

lwaggulo *adv* **in the afternoon** (= olweggulo)

[1]**lwaki** *conj* **why**

[2]**lwaki?** *interr* **why?, what for?** (N13)

Lwakubiri *n11* **Tuesday** (= Olwokubiri)

Lwakuna *n11* **Thursday** (= Olwokuna)

Lwakusatu *n11* **Wednesday** (= Olwokusatu)

Lwakusooka *n11* **Monday** (= Olwokusooka)

Lwakutaano *n11* **Friday** (= Olwokutaano)

[1]**olwala** *n11* (*pl.* enjala) **nail, claw, talon**

[2]**-lwala** *vi* (-lwadde) **be(come) ill/sick** -lwala

embiro **have diarrhoea** -lwala enjovu **have elephantiasis** -lwala kkookolo **contract cancer** -lwala omwezi **menstruate**

-lwalalwala *vi* (-lwaddelwadde) **be sickly**

olwaleero *adv* **today**

lwali lumu *adv* **one day, once upon a time**

olwali olwo *adv* **at one time**

olwaliiro *n11* (*pl.* enjaliiro) **lining, banana leaf used as a lining** (*eg. in basket, or placed to lead juice from trampling bananas into pot*); *in pl.* **lining of banana leaves** olwaliiro lw'akasolya **crossbeam** (*horizontal timber in roof*), **joist** enjaliiro z'enku **long logs placed at base of pile of firewood** (*to keep them dry and away from termites*)

olwamala *conj* **as soon as, after, when**

olwambalizo *n11* (*pl.* ennyambalizo) **sling** (*for carrying a bundle, usually on the shoulder*)

(o)lwammwe *pos* **your(s)** *pl.* (**N11.4**) ku lwammwe **on your behalf, for you**

Lwamukaaga *n11* **Saturday** (= Olwomukaaga)

-lwana *vi* (-lwanye, nnwana) **fight**. *See* okulwana

(o)lwange *pos* **my, mine.** (**N11.4**) ku lwange **on my behalf**

olwaniko *n11* (*pl.* ennyaniko) **place for drying** (*clothes, coffee, etc.*)

-lwanira *vt* (-lwanidde) **fight over/for**

-lwanirira *vt* (-lwaniridde, nnwanirira) **fight for a long time**

-lwanyisa *vt* (-lwanyisizza, nnwanyisa) **fight with,** *eg. Balwanyisa mmundu.* ('*They are fighting with guns.*'), **fight against**

olwasa (*slang*) *n11* (*pl.* enjasa) **one thousand shillings**

olwatika *n11* (*pl.* enjatika) **crack, fissure, split**

lwatu mu lwatu **openly, publicly**

olwatuuka awo olwatuuka **once upon a time**

olwayi *n11* **long strand of banana fibre**

-lwaza *vt* (-lwazizza) **make ill,** *eg. Emmere yandwaza.* ('*The food made me ill.*')

olwazi *n11* (*pl.* enjazi) **rock outcrop, boulder**

olwaziyazi *n11* (*pl.* enjaziyazi) **rock outcrop**

¹lwe *conj* **when** (**N10.2**), **then,** *eg. Soma nnyo lw'onoofuna omulimu.* ('*Study hard then you will get work.*') buli lwe **every time, whenever** okutuusa lwe **until**

²lwe *pos* **her/his** (**N11.4**), *eg. olutimbe lwe* ('*her curtain*')

³lwe *pre* **of** (= lw'e **N11.1**)

⁴lwe *pro* (*relative pronoun and pronoun of emphasis* **N10.1**) **it, which, that.** *Can be equivalent to short phrases of emphasis, eg. Olukoma luno lwe lulungi okusimba wano.* ('*It is this palm pole that should be put here.*'). *Can be a prefix* **lwe-** (**N11.6**), *eg. olugalo lwennyini* ('*the finger itself*').

olweggulo *adv* **in the afternoon**

olwekyo *conj* **because of that** olwekyo kye **about the matter that,** *eg. Nnazze okukulaba olwekyo kye wampitidde.* ('*I have come to see you about the*

matter you called me for.')

lwenda *n11/num* **nine hundred**

olwendo *n11* (*pl.* ennyendo) **long-necked gourd** (*cut for use as cup or scoop*), **ladle** (*made from a gourd*). *Saying: 'Nywamu olwendo lw'amazzi.'* ('*Have a drink.*' – *expression of welcome for a visitor*)

olweyo *n11* (*pl.* enjeyo) **broom, brush**

-lwira *vt* (-lwiridde) **delay for/at,** *etc., eg. Yalwira awo mu kibuga.* ('*He delayed in the town.*')

-lwisa *vt* (-lwisizza) **delay,** *eg. Enkuba yandwisa ng'etonnya nnyo.* ('*The downpour delayed me.*')

-lwisibwa *vi* (-lwisiddwa) **be delayed, be held up**

¹olwo *adv* **that's the day that, then,** *eg. Olwo ne ŋŋenda mmulaba.* ('*Then, I went to see him.*')

²olwo *dem* **that**

³lwo *pos* **your** *si.*

⁴lwo *pro* **it.** *Can be a suffix* **-lwo** (**N10-12**), *eg. nalwo* ('*and it*').

olwobutamanya *adv* **through ignorance**

olwoka *n11* (*usually pl.* enjoka) **tummy pain.** *See* enjoka

Olwokubiri *n11* **Tuesday**

Olwokuna *n11* **Thursday**

Olwokusatu *n11* **Wednesday**

Olwokusooka *n11* **Monday**

Olwokutaano *n11* **Friday**

Olwomukaaga *n11* **Saturday**

olwoya *n11* (enjoya) **long hair**

ly' *abbrev of* (o)lya; lye

¹(o)lya *pre* **of,** *eg. eddirisa lya Musoke* ('*window of Musoke*'). *Can be a prefix* **(o)lya-** (**N11.4**), *eg. lyange* ('*my*').

²-lya *vt* (-lidde, ndya) (1) **eat,** *eg. Alidde ekyemisana.* ('*She has eaten lunch.*'); (2) **assume** (*an office*), *eg. Alidde obwami.* ('*He has assumed the chiefainship.*'). *See* okulya -lya ebbanja **incur debt** -lya ebigambo **mumble** -lya ekinywi **make a common cause** -lya ekirimi **interrupt** (*a speaker*) -lya ekisula **spend the night** -lya enguzi **take a bribe** -lya ensimbi **steal money** -lya mu ndago **sing** -lya obugenyi **take food** (*or* **drink**) **as a visitor** -lya obukulu **assume an office** -lya obulamu **enjoy life** -lya obwakabaka **inherit the kingdom** -lya olukwe **betray** -lya ssente **steal money** **-lyako** (-liddeko) -lyako katono **eat a little, nibble** **-lyamu** -lyamu enkizo **do/be better than** (*someone else*), *eg. Bombi balusi balungi naye muto we yamulyamu enkizo.* ('*Both are good weavers, but her younger sister is better than she is.*') -lyamu olugaayu *See* olugaayu -lyamu olukwe **plot (against),** *eg. Ba minisita baalyamu pulezidenti olukwe.* ('*The ministers plotted against the president.*'), **betray**

lyabwe *pos* **their**

lyaffe *pos* **our**

lyaki? *interr* **what for?**

lyammwe *pos* **your** *pl.*

Iyanda *See* eryanda

Iyange *pos* my

Iyangu *See* -yangu

Iyato *See* eryato

-Iyazaamaanya *vit* (-lyazaamaanye) **deliberately fail to repay a debt to, defraud, cheat**

[1]**Iye** *pos* **her/his (N11.4)**, *eg. eddirisa lye ('her window')*

[2]**Iye** *pre* **of** (= ly'e **N11.1**)

[3]**Iye** *pro* (*relative pronoun and pronoun of emphasis* **N10.1**) **it, which, that.** *Can be equivalent to short phrases of emphasis, eg. Linnyo ki erikuluma? Lino lye linnuma. ('Which tooth is hurting you? It is this one that hurts.'). Can be a prefix* **Iye-** (**N11.6**), *eg. eryato lyennyini ('the boat itself').*

-Iyebuka *vi* (-lyebuse) **split open**

-Iyebula *vt* (-lyebudde) **split open**

Iyenvu *See* eryenvu

Iyereere *See* -yereere

Iyeru *See* -yeru (= eryeru)

[1]**Iyo** *pos* **your** *si.*

[2]**Iyo** *pro* **it.** *Can be a suffix* (**N10-12**), *eg. nalyo ('and it').*

-Iyoka *aux v* (-lyose) (*followed by narrative tense* **N16**) **be advantageous that, be good that,** *eg. Yalyoka n'agenda. ('It's good that he went.'). Can be equivalent to conjunctions: (1) (in narrative tense and preceded by 'ne')* **and then** (**N16**), *eg. Yalya n'anywa n'alyoka yeebaka. ('He ate, drank and then slept.');* (2) (*in subjunctive tense, followed by subjunctive*) **so that** (**N17**), *eg. Nnajja ndyoke nkulabe. ('I came so that I could see you.'),* **in order to, then**

Iyokka *adj* **only**

M, m

Maaci March

Maaka *n7* **Mecca**

-maala *vt* (-madde) -maala obusa **smear cow dung on earth floor** (*to trap dust and give a smooth finish*)

amaalo *n6* **unrefined behaviour.** *Derivation: from 'ekyalo' ('village'), because a person fresh from the village may not have learnt the sophisticated ways of the town.* wa maalo *n1* **country bumpkin**

maama *n1* (*pl.* ba maama) **my mother, mummy, mother,** *eg. maama wo ('your mother'); in pl.* **mothers** (*female elders on mother's side*) maama omuto **(maternal) aunt**

-maamira *vt* (-maamidde) **incubate** (*eggs*)

maamu *response to greeting* **all's well** (**N28**). *Abbreviation of 'abantu abaamu' ('the people of the place').*

-maanya *vt* (-maanyizza) **pluck (out)** (*feathers*) -maanya enkoko **pluck a chicken**

amaanyi *n6* **strength, power, potency, energy,**

force amaanyi g'ekisajja **virility** (*of a man*) -a amaanyi *adj* **strong, powerful, virile** -ddamu amaanyi **regain one's strength** -ggwaamu amaanyi **lose heart** n'amaanyi **forcefully** -ssaamu amaanyi **put effort into** (*what one is doing*) -wa (*or* -zaamu) amaanyi **encourage, inspire**

-maanyuuka *vi* (-maanyuuse) **come out/off** (*of hair or feathers*)

-maanyuula *vt* (-maanyudde) **pluck (out)**

maapu *n9* **map**

amaaso *n6* **face;** *pl. of* eriiso. *See* eriiso

amaato *pl. of* eryato

Maayi May

amabaafu *See* ebbaafu

amabaagiro *See* ebbaagiro

amabaala *See* ebbaala

amabaati *See* ebbaati

amabaga *n6* **early stages of a task.** *Motto of Gayaza School: 'Gakyali mabaga.' ('Never give up.' lit. 'Much remains to be done.')*

amabago *See* ebbago

amabajjiro *See* ebbajjiro

amabala *See* ebbala

amabaluwa *incorrectly used for plural of 'ebbaluwa' ('letters', 'post')*

amabanda *n6* **bamboo;** *pl. of* ebbanda

amabanga *See* ebbanga

amabango *See* ebbango

amabanja *See* ebbanja

amabasi *See* ebbasi

amabatirizo *See* ebbatirizo

amabavu *See* ebbavu

emabbali *adv* **at/to the side** ku mabbali **aside** ku mabbali ga **on/at the side(s) of, beside**

amabeere *See* ebbeere

[1]**emabega** *adv* **behind, back, at the back, backwards, in arrears** emabega wa **at the back of, behind** -dda emabega **go backwards, reverse** emabegako **in the near past, earlier**

[2]**amabega** *n6* **back** (*of the body*). *See* ebbega

amabibiro *See* ebbibiro

amabidde *See* embidde

amabugo *n6* **contribution to family of the deceased** (*before the burial*). *Derivation: from 'embugo' ('barkcloth'), because barkcloth was traditionally given for use as a shroud.*

amabujje *See* ebbujje

amabumbiro *See* ebbumbiro

amabwa *See* ebbwa

amadaala *n6* **staircase;** *pl. of* eddaala

amadda *n6* **return journey**

-madde *See* -maala

amaddu *n6* **strong desire** (*especially for food*), **craving**

amadinda *n6* **xylophone.** *pl. of* eddinda (= entaala)

amadirisa *See* eddirisa

amaduudu *n6* **herb or shrub with large trumpet-**

shaped flowers. *Two species*: (1) **thorn-apple** *Datura stramonium*; *also* **poison and intoxicant from this plant**; (2) **angel's trumpet** *Brugmansia suaveolens*. -nywesa amaduudu **administer trial by ordeal**

amaduuka *See* edduuka

amafalanga *See* effalanga

amafukuzi *See* effukuzi

amafulungu *See* effulungu

amafumbe *See* effumbe

amafumbiro *See* effumbiro

amafumu *See* effumu

amafuta *n6* (*liquid*) **fuel, petrol, oil** amafuta g'emmotoka **petrol** amafuta g'entungo **sesame oil** amafuta g'ettaala **kerosene**

amafuukuule -yogerera mafuukuule **upbraid, rave against**

amagala *See* eggala

amagalagamba *See* eggalagamba

-magalala *vi* (-magaladde) **be startled**

magalo *n9* **pliers, pincers, tongs**

-magamaga *vi* (-mazemaze) **look from side to side**

amagambo *n6* **news**

amagana *See* eggana

amaganduula *See* egganduula

amagego *See* eggego

magejjo *n6* **type of plant** (*used in 'ekyogero', a herbal mixture for bathing babies*)

amagemo *n6* **cuffs** (*on shirt*), **turn-ups** (*on trousers*). *See* eggemo

amagenda *n6* **outward journey**

amagero *n6* **wonders, marvels** -a amagero *adj* **wonderful, marvellous**

magetisi *n9* **wellington boot**

amagezi *n6* **wisdom, knowledge, intelligence, cleverness, advice** amagezi amangi **ingenuity** amagezi g'omusawuzi **supernatural power** -sala amagezi **find a way** -salira amagezi **find a way to/for** -wa amagezi **advise**

magga *n1* **bird that hovers, pied kingfisher, kestrel**

amaggwa *See* eriggwa

amagi *See* eggi

amagigi *See* eggigi

amagirigimba *See* eggirigimba

magirini *n1* **margarine**

amagoba *n6* **profit** (*financial*), **interest** -a amagoba *adj* **profitable** (*financially*)

[1]**emagombe** *adv* **deep in the grave, in the underworld**

[2]**amagombe** *n6* **place of the dead, the underworld**

amagongolo *See* eggongolo

amagugu *See* eggugu

-maguka *vi* (-maguse) **turn the head suddenly** (*eg. when startled*)

amagulu *See* okugulu

amagulumu *See* eggulumu

amagumba *See* eggumba

amaguzi eby'amaguzi *n8* **merchandise**

amagya *See* eggya

amagye *See* eggye

mailo (*also* mayiro) *n9* (1) **mile**; (2) **type of landed property in Buganda** -kuba mailo **survey land**

amajaani *n6* **tea leaves**

amajambiya *See* ejjambiya

amajanjabiro *See* ejjanjabiro

majegere *n6* **bulldozer**

amajiini *See* ejjiini

amajimbi *See* ejjimbi

amajindu *See* ejjindu

amajoba *See* ejjoba

amaka *n6* **homestead** (*consisting of house, courtyard, garden, etc.*), **home, household** amaka ga ba mulekwa **orphanage**

makaayi *n1* **yellow-flowered herb** (*medicinal*) *Aspilia africana*

makanika *n1* (*pl.* ba makanika) **mechanic**

makansi *n9* **scissors**

amakatala *See* ekkatala

amakato *See* ekkato

amakazi *adv* **in a womanly way**

amakebe *n6* **East Coast fever** (*cattle disease*)

amakerenda *See* ekkerenda

makinoda *n9* **pack** (*carried on the back*). *From: 'march in order' (English, a military command).*

amakiro *n6* **mental illness of a young woman after giving birth** (*from breaking a taboo*)

amakkati (*also* amasekkati) *n6* **middle, centre** amasekkati g'Afirika **the centre of Africa** Afirika ey'amasekkati **Central Africa** mu makkati **in the middle** mu makkati ga **in the middle of**

Makko *n1* **Mark**

amakobe *See* ekkobe

amakolero *See* ekkolero

amakomagiro *See* ekkomagiro

amakomera *See* ekkomera

amakomo *See* ekkomo

amakondeere *See* ekkondeere

amakonkome *See* ekkonkome

amakookootezi *See* ekkookootezi

amakoola *n6* **time for weeding**

amakoona *See* ekkoona

amakovu *See* ekkovu

amakubo *See* ekkubo

[1]**amakula** *See* ekkula

[2]**-eemakula** *vi* (-eemakudde) **have the habit of picking up things, fidget** (*handling things*)

amakulu *n6* **meaning, sense, significance**

amakumi *See* ekkumi

amakundi *See* ekkundi

amakungula *n6* **harvest, harvest time**

amakuŋŋaaniro *See* ekkuŋŋaaniro

amakwanzi *See* ekkwanzi

amakya *n6* **early morning**

[1]**-mala** *v* (-maze) (1) *vi* **be enough (for)**, *eg. (1) Sukaali amaze. ('The sugar is enough'); (2) Sukaali*

abamala. *('The sugar is enough for them.')*; (2) *vt* **finish**, *eg. Mmaze okubibala.* *('I have finished counting them.').* *Followed by the infinitive, can be equivalent to adverbs* **first**, **already** **(N19)**, *eg.* *(1) Mala okulya emmere.* *('First eat the food.');* *(2) We nnatuukirayo yali amaze okutuuka.* *('He had already arrived when I got there.').* *Followed by the inf and preceded by* **nga**, *can be equivalent to conjunction* **after** **(N25.3)**, *eg. Tujja kugenda e Kampala nga tumaze okulya.* *('After eating we will go to Kampala.').* *Followed by narrative* **(N16)**, *can be equivalent to adverb* **eventually**, *eg. Yamala n'ambulira ekituufu.* *('She eventually told me the truth.').* *Followed by negative narrative* **(N16)**, *can mean* **change one's mind**, *eg. Mmaze ne sigenda.* *('In the end I decided not to go.').* *Saying:* *'Kimala empaka, kusirika.'* *('What settles disputes is to keep quiet.').* *Followed by verb with subject prefix* **ga**-*can be equivalent to adverb* **anyhow**. -mala ebbanga **spend time** *(at a place), eg. Yamala ebbanga ng'ali London.* *('She spent some time in London.')* -mala ebiseera **waste time** -mala ekiseera **be for some time** *(in a certain state), eg. Musoke amaze ekiseera ng'akola.* *('Musoke has been working for some time.'),* **spend time** -mala omulimu **finish a job**, **retire** *(from work)*
-malako (-mazeeko) **get to the end of**, *eg. Twamazeeko omwaka.* *('We got to the end of the year.')* -malamu **finish** *(all within), eg. Malamu caayi wo tugende.* *('Finish your tea and let's go.')* -malamu omweso **win at omweso** -malawo **finish off completely**, *eg. Amazeewo omunnyo.* *('She has finished off the salt.'),* **use up, eliminate, exterminate** -malawo ebbanga **spend time** *(there)* -malawo obwetaavu **meet a need**
-malayo finish completely *(over there)* -malayo ebbanga **spend time** *(at a place over there), eg. London nnamalayo ebbanga lya myaka ebiri.* *('I spent two years in London.')*
[2]**-eemala** *vi* **be self-sufficient, be independent** -eemala eggoga **do to one's heart's desire**
amalaalo *n6* **grave, tomb**
amalaame *See* eddaame
malaaya *n1 (pl.* ba malaaya) **prostitute**
amalagala *n6* **cuttings of sweet potato.** *See* eddagala
amalala *n6* **pride** -a amalala *adj* **proud**
amalanga *See* eddanga
malayika *n1 (pl.* ba malayika) **angel.** *From:* *'malaika' (Swahili).*
amalebe *See* eddebe
amaleere *n6* **type of whitish-yellow bracket fungus** *(grows on dead wood) Letinus prolifer*
maleeriya *n9* **malaria**
maleeto *n1 (pl.* ba maleeto) **person of mixed race**
amaliba *See* eddiba
amalibu *See* eddibu
amaliiro *See* eddiiro

-malira *vt* (-malidde) **finish in/at** *(indicating the point reached),* **stop** *(because the amount done is enough)* -malira awo **stop there**, *eg. Malira awo w'otuuse.* *('Stop there where you have got to.')* Malira ku kino? **Shall I stop with this?** *(asking if this is where to finish doing a certain task)* Omalidde wa? **How far have you gone?** *(with a job)*
amaliri -gwa maliri **fall together** *(as two interlocked wrestlers),* **tie** *(with equal scores in sports)*
[1]**-malirira** *vi* (-maliridde) **be determined, be resolute, be devoted**
[2]**-eemalirira** *vi* **be self-reliant, be independent, stand on one's own two feet**
-malirivu *adj* **determined, resolute, devoted**
-maliriza *vt* (-malirizza) **finish completely, bring to an end, complete, conclude**
Maliya *n1* **Maria** Biikira Maliya **Virgin Mary**
Maliyamu *n1* **Mariam**
amalobo *See* eddobo
amaloboozi *See* eddoboozi
amalogo *See* eddogo
amalookooli *See* eddookooli
amaluma *n6* **food without sauce**, *eg. Alya amaluma.* *('He is eating food without sauce.')*
amalundiro *See* eddundiro
amalungu *See* eddungu
amalusu *n6* **saliva, spit**
amalwa *n6* **beer** *(made from finger millet)*
amalwaliro *See* eddwaliro
amalwaniro *See* eddwaniro
[1]**amalya** *n6* **stages of married life** *(for a woman).* *See* edya. *Pronunciation:* amalyá
[2]**malya** *n6* **mealtime.** *Pronunciation:* amalyâ
Malyamu *n1* **Mary**
[1]**emambuka** *adv* **uphill, in/at the north**
[2]**amambuka** *n6* **uphill journey, north**
amambulugga *n6* **mumps**
-mamirira *vt* (-mamiridde) **sprinkle** *(a solid, eg. salt)*
amampaati *n6* **showing-off, cockiness** ow'amampaati *n1* **show-off** *(person)*
amanda *n6* **charcoal** *(one piece* eryanda)
amandaazi *n6* **doughnuts** *(one* ekindaazi *n7)*
amanege *(impolite) n6* **testicles**
maneja *n1 (pl.* ba maneja) **manager**
mangada *n1* **tangerine** *Citrus reticulata*
amangu *adv* **soon, quickly, at once, early** olukiiko olw'amangu **emergency meeting**
amangwago *(also* amangu ago) *adv* **immediately, at once**
amankwetu *n6* **secretiveness** -a amankwetu *adj* **secretive, clandestine** mu mankwetu **in secret** ow'amankwetu *n1* **secretive person**
amannya *pl. of* erinnya
amannyo *pl. of* erinnyo
-mansa *vt* (-mansizza) **sprinkle** *(a liquid)*

-mansira *vt* (-mansidde) **sprinkle on**, *eg. Mansira amazzi ku engoye. ('Sprinkle water on the clothes.')*

-mansula *vt* (-mansudde) **shake off**

-eemansulako *vt* (-eemansuddeko) **distance oneself from** (*a person or group*), **shun**, *eg. Baganda be yabeemansulako. ('He has shunned his relatives.')*

-mantaala *vi* (-mantadde) **be inattentive**

-mantaavu *adj* **inattentive**

manti *interj* (*of sympathy, mainly used for children*) **I'm sorry.**

manvuuli *n9* **umbrella**

[1]**-manya** *vt* (-manyi) **know** -manya ekivaako **diagnose**

[2]**-eemanya** *vr* **be vain, be conceited.** *See* okwemanya

-manyi *adj* **known** (*to a person*)

-manyibwa *vi* (-manyiddwa) **be(come) known**

-manyifu *adj* **known** (*to many people*), **widely known**

-manyigana *vi* (-manyiganye) **know one another, be(come) acquainted with one another**

-manyiira *vt* (-manyidde) **become accustomed to, become used to** (*eg. hard work*) -manyiira nnyo **be overfamiliar (with)**

-eemanyiiza *vit* (-eemanyiizizza) (1) **familiarise oneself (with)**; (2) **make a habit (of)**, *eg. Yeemanyiizizza okunywa omwenge. ('He has become a habitual drinker.')* -eemanyiiza nnyo **be overfamiliar (with)**, *eg. Musoke aneemanyiizizza nnyo. ('Musoke has become overfamiliar with me.')*

-manyika *n1* (-manyise) **be(come) known, be knowable**

-manyirivu *adj* **knowledgeable, experienced, skilful**

-manyisa *vt* (-manyisizza) **(cause to) make known, make aware, inform**

amapaapaali *See* eppaapaali

amapeera *See* eppeera Mapeera **Father Pierre Lourdel** (*first Catholic missionary in Buganda*)

amapeesa *See* eppeesa

amapipa *See* eppipa

amasa *See* essa

Masaaba Mount Elgon

amasaabiro *See* essaabiro

amasaakalamentu *See* essaakalamentu

amasabo *See* essabo

amasajja *adv* **in a manly way, manfully**

amasalambwa *See* essalambwa

-masamasa *vi* (-masamasizza) **shine, glitter, sparkle**

amasamba *See* essamba

amasambo *See* essambo

amasanda *n6* **gum, latex, sap** amasanda ga matooke **sap from cooking bananas**

amasanga *See* essanga

amasannyalaze *n6* **tingling in the limbs, pins and needles, numbness, electricity**

amasaŋŋanzira *n6* **crossroads, junction**

amasasa *See* essasa

amasasi *See* essasi

amasavu *n6* **fat** (*of an animal*) (*one piece* essavu)

amasaza *See* essaza

amasekkati *See* amakkati

amasengejjero *See* essengejjero

amasengere *n6* **iron ore** Masengere (1) (*traditional use*) **audience hall of the Kabaka**; (2) (*modern use*) **office building at the Bulange** Kabaka ali mu Masengere. **The Kabaka is in audience.**

amaserengeta *adv/n6* **downhill, downward journey, south**

[1]**amasiga** *n6* **time for sowing**

[2]**amasiga** *n6* **cooking area**; *pl. of* essiga ('sub-clan'; 'cooking stone')

masiikiini *n1* (*pl.* ba masiikiini) **very poor person, beggar**

masiini *n9* **machine**

amasiinya *See* essiinya

amasiira *n6* **embroidered red design** (*at base of 'kkanzu'*)

amasimba *n6* **time for planting**

amasinzizo *See* essinzizo

amasira *n6* **pus**

amasiro *n6* **royal cemetery**

Masiya *n1* **Messiah**

amasoggola *n6* **time for digging up sweet potatoes**

amasogola *n6* **time for crushing bananas** (*to extract juice*)

amasogolero *See* essogolero

amasomero *See* essomero

amasomo *See* essomo

amasongezo *See* essongezo

amasonko *See* essonko

-masuka *vi* (-masuse) **go off** (*of trap or spring*), **be released, be sprung**

-masula *vt* (-masudde) **set off** (*trap/spring*), **release, spring** (*a trap*)

amasundiro *See* essundiro

amasuulemu *See* amatooke

amasuulubu *n6* **moustache**

amata *n6* **milk** amata amafumbe **boiled milk** amata ga bbongo **curdled milk**

amataaba *n6* **contribution to family of the deceased** (*presented after the burial*). *From: 'taaba' ('tobacco') – which was traditionally presented.*

amataba *n6* **flood**

amatabaaliro *See* ettabaaliro

amatabi *See* ettabi

amatako (*impolite*) *n6* **buttocks**

amatalaga *adv/n6* **at intervals, intervals, spaces, gaps**, *eg. olukomera lw'amatalaga ('fence with gaps')*

amatale *n6* **slag** (*waste from smelting iron ore*)

matalisi *n1* (*pl.* ba matalisi) **herald**
amatama *See* ettama
amatambiro *See* ettambiro
amatanga *See* ettanga
matankane *invariable adj* **striking** (*in appearance, especially referring to clothes*), *eg. Abayimbi bambala matankane.* (*'The singers have striking costumes.'*)
matatu *n9* **minibus taxi.** *From Swahili.*
Matayo *n1* **Matthew**
amateeka *See* etteeka
amategula *See* ettegula
amatembe *See* ettembe
amatendekero *See* ettendekero
mateniti *n9* **maternity, maternity home/ward**
amaterekero *See* etterekero
amatikkira *n6* **coronation, degree ceremony**
-matira *vi* (-matidde) **be satisfied**
-mativu *adj* **satisfied**
[1]**-matiza** *vt* (-matizza) **satisfy**
[2]**-eematiza** *vr* **satisy oneself, masterbate**
amatofaali *See* ettofaali
amatogero *See* ettogero
amatondo *See* ettondo
amatongo *n6* **deserted village/area**
amatooke *n6* **cooking bananas, cooked bananas;** *pl. of* ettooke. *See* ettooke
amatovu *See* ettovu
[1]**amatu** *See* okutu
[2]**amatu** *See* ettu
amatugunda *See* ettugunda
amatuluba *See* ettuluba
amatulutulu *n6* **dawn** mu matulutulu **at dawn**
amatundiro *See* ettundiro
amatundubaali *See* ettundubaali
amatungulu *See* ettungulu
amatutuma *See* ettutuma
amatuulituuli *n6* **skin rash** (*with large swellings*)
amatwale *See* ettwale
amaviivi *See* evviivi
amavuunya *See* evvuunya
amavuuvuumira *See* evvuuvuumira
awawaala *See* eggwaala
amawaatiro *See* eggwaatiro
amawagi *See* eggwagi
amawanga *See* eggwanga
amawanika *See* eggwanika
Mawogola *n1* **county of Buganda**
Mawokota *n1* **county of Buganda**
amawolu *See* eggwolu
amawoolezo *See* eggwoolezo
amawuggwe *See* egguggwe
amawulire *n6* **news, newspaper** ow'amawulire *n1* **journalist**
amawulugungu *n6* **tall ginger-like herb of damp forest** (*cane used in basketry*) *Marantochloa leucantha*
amyangi *n6* **big sea** Mayanja *n1* **name of a river**

in Buganda emitala w'amayanja **overseas, abroad**
amayanzi *See* ejjanzi
amayembe *See* ejjembe
amayengo *n6* **waves, wavelength** (*of a broadcast*). *See* ejjengo
amayiba *See* ejjiba
amayinja *See* ejjinja
mayiro *n9* (1) **mile;** (2) **type of landed property in Buganda.** *Usually spelt 'mailo'.*
mayiti *n9* **corpse of a Muslim**
amayu *See* enju
amayute *See* ejjute
amayuuga *See* ejjuuga
amayuuni *See* ejjuuni
amazaalibwa *n6* **birthday**
amazaaliro *See* ezzaaliro
amazi (*impolite*) *n6* **shit** (*impolite*)
amaziga *See* ezziga
amaziina *n6* **worn-out clothing, rags**
amazike *See* ezzike
amazima *n6* **truth, honesty** -a amazima *adj* **honest** eky'amazima *n7* **the truth** mu mazima **truthfully, frankly** n'amazima **honestly** ow'amazima *n1* **honest person**
amazina *n6* **dance, dancing**
-eemazisa *vi* (-eemazisizza) **masterbate**
amazooba *See* ezzooba
amazuukira *n6* **resurrection** Amazuukira **Easter**
amazzi *n6* **water** amazzi agabuguma **warm water** amazzi agannyogoga **cold water** amazzi ageesera **boiling water** amazzi agookya **hot water** amazzi amafumbe **boiled water** amazzi g'ekisasi **water from the porch/roof** amazzi g'enkuba **rain water** amazzi g'omukisa **holy water** ow'amazzi *n1* **plumber**
[1]**mba I am** (*stem* -ba)
[2]**emba** *See* oluba
embaala *n9* **type of edible termite** *Termitomyces microcarpus. Makes 'ebibaala' termite mounds.*
embaale *n9* **very hard substance** (*stone, metal, etc.*)
embaalebaale *n10* **hard stone** (*used in pottery*)
embaata *n9* **duck** embaata kabuzi **spur-winged goose.** *Meaning: 'a duck almost as big as a small goat'.*
embaawo *n10* **timber.** *See* olubaawo
embaga *n9* **wedding, party, feast** embaga y'obugole **wedding party/feast**
embagirawo *adv* **suddenly, hurredly, abuptly, with immediate effect.** *Saying: 'Ebintu eby'embagirawo tebinyuma.' ('Things that are done hurredly are not done properly.')* -a embagirawo *adj* **sudden**
embajjo *See* olubajjo
[1]**embala** *n9* **way of counting**
[2]**-(y)ambala** *See* -yambala
embalaasi *n9* **horse**

embalaato *See* olubalaato

embalabe *n9* **pimple**; *in pl.* **acne, eczema**

embalama *See* olubalama

embalasaasa *n9* **skink** (*red and black type*)

embalaza *See* olubalaza

embale *See* olubale

embaliga *n9* **splayfootedness** ow'**embaliga** *n1* **splayfooted person**

embalirira *n9* **way of counting** embalirira y'ensimbi **budget**

embaluka *n9* **syphilitic chancre**

embatu *See* olubatu

-(y)ambaza *See* -yambaza

embazi *n9* **calculator**

embazzi *n9* **axe**

embeekuulo -kuba embeekuulo **chatter loudly** (*as children at play*)

embeera *n9* **being, state, situation, mood, condition** embeera enkakkamu **settled situation** embeera y'ebyenfuna **the economy** embeera y'ensi **natural environment** embeera y'obudde **weather, climate** embeera y'obulamu **well-being** eby'embeera y'abantu *n8* **public welfare**

embeerera *n9* **virgin** (*girl*)

¹mbega *n1* (*pl.* ba mbega) **spy, detective**

²embega *See* olubega

emberege *n9* **small reddish-coloured pig**

emberenge *n9* (1) **dry maize cob/grain**; *in pl.* **popcorn**; (2) **concentrated banana juice**; (3) **sorghum added to banana juice** (*in beer making*)

¹embi *See* -bi

²-ombi (*also* -ombiriri) *det* **both** (**N7.3**). *Takes pronominal concord* (**N4**), *eg.* (1) amagi gombi (*'both eggs'*); (2) ente zombi (*'both cows'*). *The personal forms are irregular, declining in a similar way to '-okka' (see Column 11 of Table 2).*

embibiro *See* olubibiro

embidde *n9* (*pl.* amabidde *n6*) **type of banana** (*used for extracting juice and making beer; has symbolic role in birth rites*). *The plural* amabidde *usually refers to bunches of bananas for making beer. There are many varieties. See under 'banana' in Part 3 of the dictionary.* mutere wa mbidde **dried sliced beer bananas**

-(y)ambika *See* -yambika

embikko *n9* **covering, cover**

mbinabina -kwata mu mbinabina **put hands on hips**

embira *n9* **bead**

embirango *See* olubirango

embiri *See* olubiri

embirigo *n9* **game played by boys with short sticks** (*involves tumbling about*), **stick used in this game**

embiriizi *See* olubiriizi

-ombiriri (*also* -ombi) *det* **both** (**N7.3**). *Takes pronominal concord* (**N4**), *eg.* amagi gombiriri (*'both eggs'*).

embiro *n10/adv* **speed** (*in running*), *eg. Adduka embiro. ('He runs fast.')* embiro akafubatuko **sprint, dash** embiro z'empaka **running race** -lwala embiro **have diarrhoea**

embisi *See* -bisi

embizzi *n9* **pig** embizzi ey'omu nsiko **wild pig**

embo *n9* **fruit of raffia palm**

embobya *n9* **type of small edible termite**

emboga *n9* **cabbage**

embogo *n9* **buffalo**. *Also name of a variety of barkcloth (with largish leaves and little sap).*

embojjanyi *n9* **rubbing one another up the wrong way, disagreement**

embolo *n9* **penis**

emboobo *n9* (1) **end of tail** (*of cow, elephant, etc., the part used by the animal as a fly whisk*); (2) (**fly**) **whisk**

embooge *n9* **type of spinach** (*with small leaves; rarely eaten nowadays; cooks very quickly*) *Amaranthus lividus* subsp. *polygonoides. Saying: 'Yatudde katono nnyo n'embooge teyabugumye n'agenda.' ('He came for a very short time.')* embooge entono **type of spinach** *Amaranthus graecizans* subsp. *sylvestris*

embooko *n10* **whips, canes** (*pl. of* kibooko)

emboozi *n9* **conversation, talk**. *See* oluboozi

¹mbu *conj* **that** (*introducing reported speech and implying uncertainty*), *eg. Mbu yazze wano. ('I heard that he came here.')*. *Can be equivalent to adverbs* **supposedly, apparently**, *eg. Mbu enkuba yatonnye e Kampala. ('Apparently it rained in Kampala.')*. -a mbu *adj* **disputable, uncertain**

²embu *pl. of* olubu

embuga *n9* **chief's enclosure/court** embuga y'omwezi **halo around the moon**

embugo *See* olubugo

embugubugu *n9* **hollow/drawn cheeks** (*eg. through old age or loss of teeth*)

-(y)ambuka *See* -yambuka

-(y)ambula *See* -yambula

-(y)ambulula *See* -yambulula

embutamu *n9* **small creeping herb** (*medicinal*) *Centella asiatica*

embuto *See* olubuto

Mbuubi *n1* **chief of Buvuma County**

embuukuuli *n9* **club** (*large-headed stick*)

embuulira *n9* (*no pl.*) **preaching**

embuutu *n9* **drumming**

embuyaga *n9* **strong wind**

mbuzeekogga *n1* **prison, jail**. *Meaning: 'The goat gets thin.'*

embuzi *n9* **goat** embuzi eya bitanga **goat with two-coloured coat** embuzi eya katangambale **goat with three-coloured coat**

embwa *n9* (1) **dog**; (2) **type of biting fly** *Simulium* embwa etaayaaya **stray dog**

mbwazirume (nga nneriira ku ttooke) *n1* **type of banana** (*used for making matooke*). *Meaning:*

*'Let the flies bite.' – while I am eating matooke).
Originally called 'mwanaakufe', but this was
changed to 'mbwazirume' during the reign of
Ssekabaka Mwanga II.*

embyabyatavu *See* -byabyatavu

embyala *n9 (no pl.)* **way of planting sweet potatoes**

embyone -a embyone *adj* **improper**, *eg. Byonna
by'akola bya mbyone. ('Everything he does is
improper.')*

ambyulensi *n9* **ambulance**

ameereere *See* -yereere

ameeru *See* -yeru

meeya *n1* **mayor**

-megga *vt (-mezze)* -megga ekigwo **throw to the
ground** (*someone, in wrestling*)

-meggana *vi (-megganye)* **wrestle**

-megufu (*also* -mogofu) *adj* **broken off**

-meguka (*also* -mogoka) *vi (-meguse)* **break off**
(*eg. of a piece of a wall*), **fall off**

-megula (*also* -megula) *vt (-megudde)* **break off a
piece of** (*in a disorganised way*), *eg. Yamegula
ekisenge. ('She broke off a piece of the wall.')*

-meka? *interr* **how many/much? (N8.1).** *Takes
numeral concord* (**N4**), *eg. (1) ebisenge bimeka?
('how many rooms?'; (2) amata ebikopo bimeka?
('how many cups of milk?')* emirundi emeka? **how
often?** Essaawa mmeka? **'What time is it?'**
Essente mmeka? **How much money?**

-meketa *vt (-mekese)* **chew** (*something hard*),
crunch (on) -meketa amannyo **grind teeth**

memba *n1 (pl.* ba memba) **member**

memeta *n9* **thermometer**

amenvu *See* eryenvu

[1]**-menya** *vt (-menye)* **break, break through** (*eg. a
door by forced entry*), **itemise** -menya etteeka **be
illegal** -menya omutima **break** (*someone's*) **heart**
-menyako (-menyeko) **break off** **-menyamu**
break into (*parts*), *eg. Menyamu ebitundu bibiri.
('Break it in two.')* **-menyawo destroy,
demolish, retract**, *eg. Yamenyawo bye yali
ayogedde. ('He retracted what he had said.')*

[2]**-eemenya** *vi* **admit being wrong**, *eg. Bwe
yeerowooza ne yeemenya. ('After thinking about it,
she admitted she was wrong.')*

-menyamenya *vt (-menyemenye)* **break into many
pieces** -menyamenya omugaati **break bread** (*in
communion*)

-menyefu *adj* (emmenyefu *n9*) **broken, fractured**

-menyeka *vi (-menyese)* **be broken/fractured**

-mera *vi (-meze)* **germinate, grow** (*of plants*),
become established (*of plants*), **sprout** (*of shoots*)
-mera envi **become grey-haired** -mera olutiko
develop goose pimples

-meremeenya *vi (-meremeenye)* **shine, glisten**

-merenguka *vi (-merenguse)* **fall to pieces,
crumble away, be(come) crushed, be pulverised**

-merengula *vt (-merengudde)* **crumble** (*eg. a
tablet*), **crush, pulverise**

-merengule *adj* **crushed, pulverised**

-mererera *vi (-mereredde)* **be self-sown**

Amerika *n9* **America**

-meruka *vi (-meruse)* **sprout, germinate**

[1]**-metta** *vt (-messe)* **put on too much** (*eg. ointment*)

[2]**-eemetta** *vr* **put too much on oneself** (*eg.
ointment*)

emicungwa *See* omucungwa

emigugu *n4* **luggage;** *pl. of* omugugu

[1]**-miima** *vit (-miimye)* **be tight for/on**, *eg. Empale
emumiima. ('The trousers are tight on him.')*

[2]**-eemiima** *vi* **contract** (*of a muscle*)

amiina *interj* **amen**

miita *n9* **metre**

emikululo *See* omukululo

minisita *n1 (pl.* ba minisita) **minister** (*of
government*)

minisitule *n9* **ministry** (*of government*)

-eemiisa (*also* -miisa) *vi (-eemiisizza)* **eat slowly**
(*enjoying the food*), *eg. Yalidde emmere nga
yeemiisa. ('He ate slowly enjoying the food.')*

minsani *n9* **mission**

eminyira *n4* **mucus** (*from nose*), **snot**

minzaani *n9* **scales** (*for weighing*)

[1]**-mira** *vt (-mize)* **swallow**

[2]**-(y)amira** *See* -yamira

emirannamiro *adv/n23* **(at the) foot of the bed**

emirembe *n4* **peace, era, times**, *eg. mu mirembe
gya Kintu ('in Kintu's times')*; *pl. of* omulembe. *See*
omulembe.

emirerembe *n4* **problems**

emirimu *n4* **work;** *pl. of* omulimu

miriyoni *n9* **million**

emirundi *n4* **times** (*referring to quantity*),
multiplication table; *pl. of* omulundi. *See*
omulundi

-mirungusa *vt (-mirungusizza)* **eat with zest,
devour, gobble up**

emiryango *See* omulyango

emisana *n4* **daytime, daylight.** *See* omusana

emisinde *adv* **speedily** (*in running*)

Misiri *n9* **Egypt**

emisomo *n4* **studies;** *pl. of* omusomo

emitaafu *See* omutaafu

emitala *adv* **on the other side** (*eg. of a river of
swamp*). *See* omutala emitala w'amayanja
oberseas, abroad

emitwetwe *n23/adv* **(at the) the head of the bed**

emivubo *n4* **bellows.** *See* omuvubo

emiwogo *n4* **pieces of cassava.** *See* muwogo

emiyirikiti *n4* **coral trees** *Erythrina abyssinica.* *See*
eggirikiti

emizannyo *n4* **athletics;** *pl. of* omuzannyo

emizira *See* omuzira

-mma *vt (-mmye, nnyima)* **refuse to give**, *eg.
Nnamusabye ssente n'azinnyima. ('I asked him for
money but he refused to give me any.')*, **withhold
(from), deprive**

emmaali *n9* (*no pl.*) **money, wealth**

mmaanu *n1* (*no pl.*) **manna**

mmaaya *n9* **ostrich**

emmale *n9* **mudfish, catfish** *Clarias*

emmamba *n9* **lungfish** *Protopterus aethiopicus.* Saying: *'Omulya mmamba aba omu, n'avumaganya ekika.'* (*'He who eats the lungfish [being his totem] brings the whole clan into disrepute.', ie. 'The wrong-doing of one brings disgrace to all.').* See ebbeere. *'mmamba'* is also used as slang for **armoured personnel carrier**

emmambo See olubambo

emmambya *n9* (*no pl.*) **dawn**

emmana (*vulgar*) *n9* **vagina**

Mmande *n1* **Monday**

emmanduso *n9* **switch, trigger, shutter release** (*of camera*), **starter, starting button**

[1]**mmandwa** *n1* **person possessed by a nature spirit, medium**

[2]**emmandwa** *n9* **nature spirit** (*associated with certain trees, rocks, etc.*)

[1]**emmanga** *adv* **downhill, down, below** (*on a slope*), **lower**

[2]**emmanga** See olubanga

emmangala *n9* **lesser cane rat**

mmange *n1* **my mother**

emmanju *adv/n23* (**at/to the) back of the house** emmanju wa **behind the house of** -a emmanju *adj* **back** -kubira emmanju **be uncultured** oluggya lw'emmanju **back yard**

emmanvu *n9* **dugout canoe, beer canoe, manger**

emmeeme *n9* (*no pl.*) **seat of the emotions, soul, heart** emmeeme -fuukuuka (*also* emmeeme -sinduukirira) **feel sick** (*nauseous*) -gwa emmeeme **have a prolapse** (*of the rectum*) emmeeme -tyemuka **suffer from shock** (*with the heart racing*) -sinduukiriza (*or* zza) emmeeme **nauseate** -tabanguka emmeeme **feel nausea** -tyemula emmeeme **shock**

Mmeere *n1* **Mary**

emmeeri *n9* **ship, steamer, ferry.** *From: 'mail' (English), because mail was formerly carried on ships.*

emmeeza *n9* **table**

mmeka? *interr* **how many?** Ssente mmeka? **How much?**

emmembe *n9* (*no pl.*) **crust on left-over cooked matooke.** See -vumbika

emmengo See olubengo

emmenyefu See -menyefu

emmere *n9* (*no pl.*) **food** (*especially matooke*) emmere efisse **left-over food** emmere empolu **cold cooked food** emmere engwira **foreign food** emmere ennuma **food without sauce** emmere ensuulemu **food cooked unwrapped in banana leaves** emmere ey'omu ttaka **root crop** emmere y'amawolu **left-over food kept for eating later** emmere ya nnamunye **climbing herb with large**

yellow to red flowers *Gloriosa superba.* *Meaning: 'food of the pied wagtail'.*

emmese *n9* **mouse, rat**

-mmibwa *vi* (-mmiddwa) **be refused, be deprived (of)**

emmimbi See olubimbi

emmimbiri *n9* **type of tree** (*very poisonous*) *Spondianthus preussii*

emmindi *n9* **pipe** (*for smoking tobacco*) emmindi y'omukadde **Dutchman's-pipe** (*type of climbing plant*) *Aristolochia elegans.* *Meaning: 'the old man's pipe'*

emmisa *n9* **mass** (*RC*)

emmizi -a emmizi *adj* **discreet** ow'emmizi *n1* **discrete person, confidant**

mmoggo *n9* **larva which eats entula fruits**

emmondo *n9* **serval cat**

mmongoota *n1* (*no pl.*) **sleeping sickness**

emmotoka *n9* **car** emmotoka eya muserebende **saloon car** emmotoka kamunye **communal taxi**

-mmuka *vi* (-mmuse) **produce suds,** *eg. Ssabbuuni ammuse.* (*'The water is soapy enough.'*), **lather, come out of oneself** (*emotionally*), **become bubbly, become sharper** (*mentally*)

emmuli See olumuli

mmumba **I am making pottery** (*stem* -bumba)

emmumbiro See olubumbiro

emmumbwa *n9* **medicinal clay stick**

emmundu *n9* **gun, rifle, gun shot.** *From: 'bunduki' (Swahili).* emmundu emmenye **someone who can sort out problems** emmundu ewandula amasasi **machine gun**

emmunye *n9* **pupil** (*of eye*)

emmunyeenye *n9* **star, firefly**

emmwanyi *n9* **coffee** (*berry; bean; plantation*). See omulamwa emmwanyi enfumbe *n10* **roasted coffee beans**

mmwe *pro* **you** *pl. Can be a prefix* **mwe-** (*N7.3*) *or suffix* **-mmwe** (*N10-12*), *eg.* (1) mwekka (*'only you'*); (2) nammwe (*'and you'*).

omo *n9* **washing powder**

-mogofu (*also* -megufu) *adj* **broken off**

-mogoka (*also* -meguka) *vi* (-mogose) **break off**

-mogola (*also* -megula) *vt* (-mogodde) **break off**

molinga *n1* **type of tree** *Moringa oleifera* (= omulinga)

-eemonkoola *vi* (-eemonkodde) **play the clown, make funny faces**

amookye See -yokye

[1]**-moola** *vi* (-modde) -moola amaaso **look coy, look in a seductive way**

[2]**-eemoola** *vi* **make funny faces, play the clown, look down in shyness**

-moolera *vt* (-mooledde) -moolera amaaso **roll one's eyes at** (*someone*) **in contempt**

[1]**empa** See oluwa

[2]**mpa** **I give, give me** (*stem* -wa)

empaaba *n9* **way of presenting a court case**

mpaabaana *n1* hadada ibis. *Meaning: 'Give me the children.' – after the sound of its call (onomatopoeic).*

empaabi *n9* **court fee**

empaanyi *See* oluwaanyi

empaawo *n9* **bowl/cup made from gourd**

empabiro *n9* **point from which one can get lost**

empafu *n9* **fruit of omuwafu tree** *(edible)*

empagama *n9* **something stuck in the throat**

empagi *n9* **pillar, post, pole**

empago *See* oluwago

empaka *n10* **competition, contest, race, dispute, strife, match**. *Saying: 'Ekimala empaka kusirika.' ('What settles disputes is to keep quiet.')* empaka z'akafubutuko **short-distance race** empaka z'akamalirizo **final** *(of a competition)* empaka z'ebikonde **boxing match** empaka z'obulungi **beauty contest** empaka z'okuyimba **singing competition** empaka z'omupiira **football match** -a empaka *adj* **argumentative** olw'empaka **by force** ow'empaka *n1* **argumentative person**

empala *n9* **Uganda kob**

empaladdume *n9* **big and tall person**, *eg. empaladdume y'omusajja ('giant of a man')*

empalana *n9* **hostility, harassment** empalana y'eddiini **religious intolerance**

empale *n9* **trousers, pants**. *See* akapale empale empanvu **long trousers** empale ennyimpi **shorts** empale ya lusoggo **drainpipe trousers**

empalo *See* oluwalo

empami *n9* **piercing in lower lip** *(for stud)*

empandaggirize *See* oluwandaggirize

[1]empande *n9* **bambara groundnut** *Vigna subterranea*

[2]empande *See* olupande *(piece of material)*

empandiika *n9 (no pl.)* **way of writing, writing, spelling, handwriting, orthography**

[1]empanga *See* oluwanga

[2]empanga *See* enkoko

empangaazi *See* -wangaazi

empango *n9* **pole, post** empango y'ekikajjo **stick of sugar cane**

empanka *See* olupanka

empano *n9* **wedge**

empanvu *See* -wanvu

empapula *See* olupapula

empataanya *n9* **small gap** empataanya z'engalo **spaces between the fingers**

empawu *n9* **type of edible termite**

empayi *See* oluwayi

empe *See* oluwe

empeefu *n9* **type of very large greyish mushroom** *(found in grassland; harvested cautiously by first banging with a stick – because snakes are often found beneath)*

empeera *n9 (no pl.)* **way of rewarding, recompense, pay, wage, salary, reward, benefit**

empeereza *n9 (no pl.)* **service**

empeerezi *(also* ennyukuta empeerezi*) n9* **vowel**

empeewo *n9* **bush duiker**

empeke *n9* **grain**, *eg. empeke za kasooli ('grains of maize')* empeke y'eddagala **pill, tablet** essente ez'empeke **cash**

empenda *See* oluwenda

emperekeze *n9* **accompanying person, bridesmaid, companion, escort**

empero *See* oluwero

empeta *n9* **ring** *(jewellery)*, **nut** *(for bolt)* empeta nkusibiddaawo **engagement ring** omukyala w'empeta **official wife** *(ie. the one with the ring)*

empewere *n9* **type of tall forest tree**. *Two similar-looking species: Newtonia buchananii, Piptadeniastrum africana. Wood used for making canoes.*

empewo *n9 (no pl.)* **wind, air, draught, cold** empewo -fuuwa **feel cold** *(of a person)*, **blow** *(of the wind)* empewo -kunta **become windy and stormy** -a empewo *adj* **cold** -linnyibwako empewo **be possessed by a spirit**

empewufu *See* -wewufu

[1]-mpi *adj* (ennyimpi *n9*) **short, brief**

[2]empi *See* oluyi

empiiga *n10* **pushiness**

empiima *n9* **dagger**

empiira *See* olupiira; oluyiira *(the plurals of these two words are spelt the same way, but are pronounced differently)*

empiiyi *n9* **smelly wind** *(brought up through the mouth)* -kuba empiiyi **belch**

empiki *n9* **seed used as counter in game of omweso**. *Today, these come from 'omuyiki' (Sapindus saponaria). However, S. saponaria is an American plant unlikely to have been in Uganda before 1900 AD. The most probable candidate for seeds used as counters in omweso in earlier times is 'ekitembe' ('wild banana plant'), the seed of which is known as 'ettembe'. Replacement of Ensete seeds by Sapindus seeds could have been because the latter are smaller and rounder, so easier to handle.*

empima *n9 (no pl.)* **way of measuring**

empina *pl. of* oluyina

empindi *n9* **cowpea** *Vigna unguiculata* -lima mpindi ku mabega **backbite**

[1]empingu *n9* **fleet** *(of canoes)*, **navy**

[2]empingu *n10* **handcuffs**

empiri *n9* **type of small poisonous snake**

empirivuma *n9* **fruit of wild date palm** *(medicinal; used for making wine 'obugeme')*

empisa *n9* **habit, custom**, *eg. empisa z'ekiganda ('Kiganda customs'); in pl.* **conduct, behaviour** *(way of behaving)*, **character, morality, morals, manners** empisa embi **vulgarity** empisa engwira **alien customs** -a empisa embi *adj* **badly-behaved** -a empisa nnungi *adj* **well-mannered** ow'empisa *n1* **well-mannered person**

empisi *n9* hyena

empiso *n9* needle, syringe, injection

mpita I call/pass, call me (*stem* -yita)

empitambi *n9* (*no pl.*) faeces, excrement

empitirivu See -yitirivu

empogola *n9* something cooked whole. *Saying:* *'Amagezi gakuweebwa munno, empogola egawa mususi.'* (*'Advice given by a friend is easy to take.'* – *a banana cooked in its skin splits along one side, so is easy to peel*) amatooke ag'empogola plantains cooked in their skins eggi ery'empogola boiled egg

mpokya *n1* (*no pl.*) green gram, mung bean *Phaseolus aureus*

empola *adv* slowly, calmly, carefully. *Saying:* *'Akwata empola atuuka wala.'* (*'He who goes slowly goes far.'*)

empolampola *adv* slowly and carefully, quietly, softly

mpolembuzi *n1* variety of barkcloth tree (*yields the best barkcloth*). *The name in full (and derivation) is 'Mpola embuzi ndikuwa ente. ('Lend me a goat and I will give you a cow.')*

empologoma *n9* lion

empolu See -wolu

empombo See oluwombo

empompogoma *n9* deep hole, hollow, cavity empompogoma y'ekiswa cavity under a termite mound empompogoma y'olusozi cave on a hill empompogoma y'omuti hollow in a tree

emponge See -wonge

emponzi See oluwonzi

empooza *n9* (*no pl.*) way of taxing, tax, duty, customs duty

empovu See -wovu

empoza *n9* (*no pl.*) way of arguing, plea, defence (*in court*), prosecution

mpozzi *adv* maybe, perhaps

mpuga I swim (*stem* -wuga)

empuku *n9* cave

empuliziganya *n9* communication

mpulubujju -a mpulubujju *adj* disputable

empulukanya *n9* (*formerly*) type of severe punishment (*resulting in facial deformity*)

mpulukutu *n10* (*formerly*) type of severe punishment (*resulting in facial deformity* place on the face immediately in front of the ear (*where slaps are administered*). *Saying: 'Mpulukutu za musota zigenda na muggo.' ('A dangerous snake that comes to a homestead should leave at the slightest scare. If it does not it should be killed with a stick.'). This refers to the traditional Baganda custom of not killing snakes that are harmless because killing them may bring bad luck.*

empulunguse *n10* siftings (*larger pieces of groundnuts, etc. remaining after pounding or sieving*), remnants, remains

empumbu *n9* (*no pl.*) dust (*produced by boring insect*), bloom (*on stems of some plants*)

empumi *n9* projecting forehead ow'empumi *n1* person with projecting forehead

empummula See oluwummula

empummumpu *n9* male inflorescence of banana plant

empungu *n9* eagle

empunya *n9* smell

empunzi *n9* person lacking fixed abode

emputtu *n10* obstinacy, stubbornness -a emputtu *adj* obstinate, stubborn ow'emputtu *n1* obstinate person

empuunyi *n9* type of drum (*keeps the beat*)

empuuta *n9* Nile perch *Lates albertianus*

empuuzo *n9* mallet used in the second stage of making barkcloth

¹empya *adj* new. See -ggya; -pya

²empya See oluggya

¹mu *conj* and. *Used to connect numerals above twenty* (N8.1), *eg. ana mu nnya ('forty-four').*

²-mu *num* one (N8.1). *Takes numeral concord (N4), eg. (1) omuntu omu ('one person'); (2) ente emu ('one cow'). The plural (with initial vowel N3) means some (N8.1), eg. (1) abantu abamu ('some people'); (2) ente ezimu ('some cows'). 'mu' is preceded by the pronoun of emphasis -e (N10.1) in the following: (1)* -e -mu the same, *eg. Ebimuli bino bye bimu. ('These flowers are the same.'); (2)* -e -mu ne the same as, *eg. Ebimuli bino bye bimu n'ebyo? ('Are these flowers the same as those?').* -mu -mu one-by-one, *eg. Abantu bazze omu omu. ('The people came one-by-one.').* muntu n'omu (*after neg N21*) no-one, *eg. Simanyi muntu n'omu. ('I know no-one.')* obw'omu (*also* obwomu) alone (*of a person*)

³mu *pre* in, into, among, through, during. (N3)

muba you *pl.* are (*stem* -ba)

omubaazi *n1* person who slaughters and skins animals, butcher, flayer

omubadazi *n1* person who is easy-going, one who enjoys a good time (*eg. habitual nightclub goer*)

omubajja *n3* type of medicinal plant (*used for fever*)

omubajjangabo *n3* type of forest tree *Erythrina excelsa. Meaning: 'It makes shields.'*

omubajjangalabi *n3* type of tall forest tree *Alstonia boonei. Meaning: 'It makes drums.'*

omubaka *n1* messenger, representative, emissary, envoy, delegate omubaka w'ensi ambassador, diplomat

omubala *n3* drumbeat of a clan

omubalirizi w'ebitabo *n1* accountant

omubambaavu *n1* unruly person

omubambamaliba *n1* person who pegs out hides

omubazi *n1* one who counts, counter omubazi w'ebitabo accountant

omubazzi *n1* carpenter, woodcarver

omubbi *n1* thief, burglar, robber

101

omubbirizi *n1* cheat

omubeezi *n1* helper, assistant, second-in-charge
omubeezi wa ssettendekero **vice-chancellor** (*of a university*)

omubezi *n1* server (*of food, especially matooke*)

omubi *n1* bad person, ugly person

omubiikira *n1* nun, (religious) sister

omubinikiro *n3* funnel (= omuzindaalo)

omubiri *n3* human body, lap

Omubirigi *n1* Belgian (*person*)

omubisi *n3* juice (*especially banana*) omubisi
gw'enjuki **honey** omubisi gwa kadoma **honey**
from stingless bees omuntu omubisi **naïve**
person

omubombi *n1* escaped prisoner, run-away,
fugitive

Omuboobi *See* Ababoobi

omuboole *n1* ignored family member (*eg. one not
invited to social occasions*)

omubudami *n1* refugee

omubuguyavu *n1* stupid/ignorant person

omubulooka *n1* broker omubulooka w'ennyumba
house broker omubulooka w'ettaka **land broker**

omubumbi *n1* potter

omubungeesi *n1* vagabond

omubuulizi *n1* preacher omubuulizi w'enjiri
evangalist

omubuuza *n1* questioner

omubuyabuya *n1* simpleton

omuceere *n3* (*no pl.*) rice. *From: 'mchele'*
(*Swahili*).

omucungwa *n3* orange (*tree; fruit*) *Citrus sinensis*;
in pl. orange juice emicungwa emika
concentrated orange juice

omucuuzi *n3* (*no pl.*) gravy, soup

omuda *n3* (*slang*) ten thousand shillings. *Abbrev of
'omudikisi'. Possibly originally from 'dix' ('ten' in
French*).

Omudaaki *n1* Dutch (*person*), (*formerly*) German
(*person*). *Originally from: 'deutsche' ('German
person – in German language*).

omudaala *n3* market stall

omudaali *n3* medal, medallion, pendant

omudalasiini *n3* cinnamon (*tree*)

omudalizo *n3* decorative strip on busuuti

omuddiikoni *n1* deacon

omuddo *n3* (*no pl.*) grass, herb(s), weed(s)

omuddu *n1* slave

omuddukanya *n1* manager

omuddusi *n1* runner

omudduukirize *n1* one who comes to help or
rescue

omudibazi *n1* bungler

omudigido *n3* rhythmic movement, dance

omudingidi *n1* fiddle player

omudokolo (*slang; may be considered impolite*) *n1*
person from northern Uganda

omudongo *n1* musician, lyre player, guitarist

omudumu *n3* pipe, nozzle, jug, drainpipe
omudumu gw'amazzi **water pipe** omudumu
gw'emmundu **gun barrel** omudumu gw'okussa
windpipe omudumu gw'omukka **chimney**
omudumu ogw'omu ttaka **underground pipe**

omuduumizi *n1* commander

omuduuze *n1* person who scorns, sarcastic
person, mocker

omuduuzi *n1* person who is habitually sarcastic

Omufalansa *n1* French person

Omufalisaayo *n1* Pharisee

omufaliso *n3* mattress

omufamba *n3* silk cotton tree *Ceiba pentandra*

omufere (*also* omufezi) *n1* confidence trickster

omufu *n1* dead/deceased person

omufuge *n1* one who is ruled, subject

omufuko *n3* bag, purse, quiver. *From: 'mfuko'*
(*Swahili*).

omufulejje *n3* drain. *From: 'mfereji' (Swahili*).
omufulejje gwa kazambi **waste pipe, sewer**

[1]**omufumbi** *n1* cook, chef

[2]**omufumbi** *n3* biceps (*when contracted*)

omufumbo *n1* married person

omufumisi *n1* spearsman

omufumite *n1* person wounded by knife or spear

omufumu *n1* doctor-diviner. *From Lunyoro.*

omufundi *n1* skilled worker, mechanic, artisan

omufuusa *n1* magician

omufuuyi *n1* blower, musician (*one who plays a
blown instrument*) omufuuyi w'endere **flute
player** omufuuyi wa ssente **person who tips a
performer** omufuuyi wa ssigala **smoker** (*of
cigarettes*) omufuuyi wa tulampeti **trumpeter**

omufuuzi *n1* person who searches

omufuzi *n1* ruler

omuga *n3* musky smell (*of earthenware pot 'enswa'
that has been prepared for holding water; also,
palatable smell of sauce, especially one containing
mushrooms*)

omugaati *n3* bread, loaf omugaati omwokye **toast**

Omugabe *n1* title King of Ankole

[1]**omugabi** *n1* giver, generous person, donor

[2]**omugabi** *n3* divisor (*in maths*)

omugabo *n3* share, allocation, portion; *in pl.*
shares (*in a company*)

omugabuzi *n1* host/server at a feast

omugagga *n1* rich person

omugala *n3* framework of sticks built over a
termite mound (*made when catching termites*)

omugalabi *n3* long slender drum (*beaten with both
hands*)

omugalagala *n1* person who serves in the palace

[1]**omuganda** *n1* person of Buganda muganda
brother (*or cousin*) of (**N12**), eg. muganda wange
('my brother'). The plural (baganda) means **family**,
eg. baganda we ('her family'). See -ganda

[2]**omuganda** *n3* bundle, bunch. *Saying: 'Kamu
kamu gwe muganda.' ('Many small things make a*

bundle.' – 'akati' 'small stick' understood)
omuganda entuumu **large heap of firewood**
omuganga *n1* **doctor, healer**
omugano *n3* **swarming** (*of termites, grasshoppers, etc.*)
omuganyulo *n3* **profit, benefit, advantage**
omuganzi *n1* **favourite (person), boyfriend, girlfriend, love** muganzi wange **my love**, muganzi wo **your love,** *etc.* (**N12**)
omugaso *n3* **benefit, use, profit, value** -a omugaso *adj* **beneficial, useful, advantageous, profitable, valuable**
¹**omugatte** *n1* **married person** (*one who married in church*)
²**omugatte** *n3* **total** (*of summed figures*)
omugavu *n3* **type of tree** (*timber, medicinal; has the wood used for smoking barkcloth*) *Albizia coriaria* -nyookeza n'omugavu **smoke barkcloth using omugavu wood** (*adds a pleasant smell*), *eg. Embugo nnazikoomera n'omugavu.* ('I have smoked the barkcloth with omugavu wood.')
omugayaavu *n1* **lazy person**
omuge *n3* **headband, wreath, halo** (*around a saint's head*)
omugejjo *n3* **corpulence, fatness, obesity**
Mugema *n1 title* **one of the principal chiefs, head of the Nkima Clan.** *Traditionally, plays a leading role in the instalation of kings; ritual father of the Kabaka.* ettu lya Mugema **pregnancy** (*of the Queen*)
omugendo *n3* **trail** omugendo gw'ensanafu **column of safari ants**
omugenge *n1* **leper**
omugenyi *n1* **guest, visitor** omugenyi omukulu **guest of honour**
omugenzi *n1* **deceased person.** *As invariable adj* **the late,** *eg. omugenzi Mukasa* ('*the late Mukasa'*). *See* nguli
omugereko *n3* **measured amount, share**
omugerengetanya *n1* **person who finds a way** (*to do something*), **resourceful person**
Mugerere *n1 title* **chief of Bugerere County**
omugeresi *n1* **person who allots, assessor** omugeresi w'omusolo **tax assessor** Kawamegero *n1* **God** (*as the dispenser of fate*)
omugeto *n3* **string of fish** (*offered for sale*)
omugevvu *n1* **person who has gained weight**
omugezi *n1* **clever/wise person**
omugezigezi *n1* **cleaver person** (*can imply devious*)
¹**emugga** *adv* **at the water source** (*spring, well or river*)
²**omugga** *n3* **river** Omugga Kiyira **River Nile**
omuggalanda *n1* **last-born child.** *Meaning:* '*The one who closes the womb.'*
omuggazi *n1* **doorkeeper, gatekeeper**
omuggo *n3* **stick, walking stick** omuggo gw'abalema **crutch** omuggo ogusima lumonde

stick for digging up sweet potatoes
omuggulanda *n1* **first-born child.** *Meaning:* '*The*

NOTES ON
m

-m. Unless the **m** is doubled, verbs starting **m** have 1st person singulars starting **mm**, *eg.* **mmala** ('I finish'), from -**mala**.

ama-. Many nouns in *n6* starting **ama** have singulars (in *n5*) formed from the initial vowel (**e**) plus the first consonant after **ama** doubled, *eg.* the singular of **amagi** is **eggi**.

emi-. Most nouns in *n4* starting **emi** are entered here only under their singulars (in *n3*) starting **omu**, *eg.* for **emiggo** see **omuggo**. If the next letter is **r**, then the singular starts **l**, *eg.* for **emirimu** see **omulimu**.

mb are the initial letters of the 1st person singulars of verbs starting **b** (non-nasal verbs), *eg.* **mbala** ('I count'), from -**bala**.

mm are the initial letters of the 1st person singulars of verbs starting **b** (nasal verbs only), **m** and **p** (**N5**), *eg.* **mmala** ('I finish'), from -**mala**.

-mm. Verbs starting **mm** have 1st person singulars starting **nnyim**, *eg.* **nnyima** ('I refuse to give'), from -**mma**.

mp- are the initial letters of the 1st person singulars of verbs starting **p** or **w**, *eg.* **mpulira** ('I hear'), from -**wulira**.

omu-. (1) Nouns in *n1* starting **omu** have plurals (in *n2*) starting **aba**, *eg.* the plural of **omuntu** is **abantu**; (2) nouns in *n3* starting **omu** have plurals (in *n4*) starting **emi**, *eg.* the plural of **omuti** is **emiti**. However, if an *n3* noun starts **omul**, then the plural starts **emir**, *eg.* the plural of **omulembe** is **emirembe**.

munna-. Nouns in *n1* starting **munna** have plurals (in *n2*) starting **banna**, *eg.* the plural of **munnakyalo** is **bannakyalo**.

omwa-. (1) Nouns in *n1* starting **omwa** have plurals (in *n2*) starting **abaa**, *eg.* the plural of **omwana** is **abaana**; (2) nouns in *n3* starting **omwa** have plurals (in *n4*) starting **emya**, *eg.* the plural of **omwaka** is **emyaka**.

omwe-. Nouns in *n1* starting **omwe** have plurals (in *n2*) starting **abee**, *eg.* the plural of **omwetissi** is **abeetissi**.

omwo-. Nouns in *n1* starting **omwo** have plurals (in *n2*) starting **aboo**, *eg.* the plural of **omwogezi** is **aboogezi**.

emy-. Nouns in *n4* starting **emy** are entered here only under their singulars (in *n3*) starting **omw**, *eg.* for **emyezi** see **omwezi**.

NOUNS IN *n9*. Most nouns in *n9* have identically spelt plurals (in *n10*).

one who opens the womb.'

omuggya *n1* newcomer   mukazi muggya fellow wife

omugigi *n3* stage of advancement in Catholicism

omugiini *n3* inn, rest house

Omugirimani *n1* German (*person*)

omugo *n3* rim   omugo gw'ekibbo rim of a basket   omugo gw'entamu rim of a cooking pot

omugoba *n1* helmsman, steersman   omugoba w'emmotoka car driver   omugoba w'ennyonyi pilot (*of an aeroplane*)   omugoba wa loole lorry driver

omugoberezi *n1* follower, adherent   omugoberezi w'ensolo beater (*in a hunt*)

omugogo *n3* (1) pseudostem ('*trunk'*) of a banana plant; (2) pair, *eg. omugogo gw'engatto ('pair of shoes')*

omugole *n1* (*pl.* abagole) (1) bride; (2) newly appointed (*or* qualified) person (*graduate, minister, etc.*); *in pl.* newly weds, bride and bridegroom   omogole omusajja bridegroom

omugoma *n1* drummer

omugomo *n3* type of fish trap (*made from sticks of ejjerengesa*)

omugondoli *n3* string of banana fibre (*used to lift off leaves covering food bundle after cooking*)

omugongo *n3* back (*of the body*), keel, ridge   omugongo gw'ente head of cattle   -fukula omugongo dance vigorously

omugongobavu *n1* deformed person

omugonja *n3* single fruit of gonja (*type of banana*)

omugonjo *n3* fishing line (*with hooks at intervals*)

omugonvu *n1* submissive person, person weak from illness

omugoŋŋoonyo *n3* midrib of banana leaf (= omuziŋŋoonyo)

omugoyo *n3* (*no pl.*) mash of sweet potatoes and beans

omugozoobano *n3* trouble (*in affairs*)

omugugu *n3* load, piece of luggage, bundle wrapped in cloth (*for transport*), burden, heavy responsibility; *in pl.* luggage, baggage

Mugulansigo March

omugumu *n1* courageous/intrepid person

omugunga *n3* giant yellow mulberry (*tree, has edible fruit* ekigunga) *Myrianthus holstii*

omugunjufu *n1* civilised/cultured person

omugunjuzi *n1* educator

omuguwa *n3* rope

omuguya *n3* young lungfish

omuguzi *n1* buyer, customer

omugwagwa (*also* omugwenyufu) *n1* depraved person, imbecile

mugwanya *n1* latrine, toilet. *Derivation: From the name of a Katikkiro who enforced the digging of pit latrines during the reign of Kabaka Mwanga II.*

omugwi *n3* type of forest tree *Trilepsium madagascariense*

omugwira *n1* foreigner, stranger

omujaaja *n3* type of shrub (*used to flavour tea; medicinal*) *Ocimum gratissimum*   omujaaja ogw'oku ttale wild type of omujaaja (*preferred in tea*)

omujaasi *n1* soldier, (*formerly*) commander-in-chief

mujaguzo *n1* (*no pl.*) (1) set of royal drums; (2) type of drumbeat (*announces a function attended by the Kabaka*)   abaana ba mujaguzo royal family

omujama *n1* dirty person (*habitually*)

omujeemu *n1* rebel, insurgent, mutineer

omujjanjabi *n1* nurse

omujjonkezi *n3* mouse bird

omujjumbizi *n1* zealot

omujjwa *n1* son of a man's sister, nephew, niece

omujoona *n1* potter in the service of the Kabaka

[1]**omujoozi** *n1* bully

[2]**omujoozi** *n3* T-shirt

omujulirwa *n1* witness, godparent, martyr, referee (*for a job*)   omujulirwa w'omugole omukazi matron of honour   omujulirwa w'omugole omusajja best man

omujulizi *n1* witness, martyr

omujunga *n3* tassel

[1]**omuka** *invariable adj* (1) strong, *eg. omwenge omuka ('strong drink')*; (2) too much, *eg. omunnyo omuka ('too much salt')*

[2]**muka** *n1* (*pl.* baka) wife of (**N12**), *eg. muka Musoke ('Musoke's wife')*

omukaabiransiko *n3* type of tree (*yields an orange dye*) *Harungana madagascariensis. Meaning: 'It cries for the jungle.' – because it emits copious orange sap when cut.*

Mukaabya *n1* name given to Kabaka Muteesa I. *Meaning: 'He causes weeping.' – because of his cruelty.*

omukaafiiri *n1* infidel, pagan, aetheist

mukaaga *n3/num* six   -a omukaaga *adj* sixth

mukaamwana *n1* daughter-in-law of (**N12**), *eg. mukaamwana wange ('my daughter-in-law.')*

omukaba *n1* sexy person, promiscuous person

omukadde *n1* old person   mukadde parent of (**N12**), *eg. mukadde wange ('my parent')*

omukago *n3* (*no pl.*) blood brotherhood, alliance   ow'omukago *n1* blood brother, ally   -tta omukago make blood pact

omukakaalukanyi *n1* person who keeps striving to achieve, intrepid person

omukakanyavu *n1* unyielding/difficult person

omukalabakalaba *n1* clever and witty person

omukalabanda *n3* type of wooden shoe, clog

omukalo *n3* dried meat, biltong

omukalubo *n3* hardness, toughness, hard-heartedness

omukalukalu *n1* canny person

[1]**Omukama** *n1 title* King of Bunyoro, King of Toro

²**mukama** *n1* boss of (N12), *eg. mukama wange ('my boss')* Mukama Katonda **Lord God** mukamaawo **your** *si.* **boss** mukamaawe **her/his boss**

omukambwe *n1* fierce person, cruel person

Omukanada *n1* Canadian (*person*)

omukandala *n3* belt of cloth (*used by women to keep money*), girdle

omukanzi *n1* person who terrifies, terrorist omukanzi w'ensolo **beater** (*in a hunt*)

Mukasa *n1* Kiganda deity (*lubaale*) (*the life-giver, bringer of children and crops; spirit of Lake Victoria*). *Son of Wannema.*

Omukatoliki *n1* Catholic (*person*)

omukazi *n1* woman mukazi muggya **fellow wife**

omukebe *n3* can, tin

omukebezi *n1* inspector, examiner, marker omukebezi w'amawulire **newspaper editor** omukebezi w'ebitabo **auditor**

omukebu *n3* type of tree *Cordia africana*

omukeeka *n3* mat (*well-made; woven from split palm leaflets*)

omukekkereza *n1* thrifty person

omukemi *n1* tempter

mukene *n1* (*no pl.*) type of small silvery fish *Rastrineobola argentea*

mukenenya *n1* (*no pl.*) AIDS

omukessi *n1* spy, scout

Omukiga *n1* member of the Bakiga people

omukiikiro *n3* crossbeam (*horizontal timber in roof above ceiling*)

omukiinyi *n1* mocker

omukiise *n1* formal representative, delegate; *in pl.* delegation, deputation

omukinga *n3* type of tree *Acacia mildbraedii*

omukinjaaje *n1* butcher

omukira *n3* tail omukira gwa nkuggu **docked tail**

Omukirisito *n1* Christian (*person*) (*standardised spelling*)

Omukirisitu *n1* Christian (*person*) (*RC*)

omukisa *n3* luck, good luck, chance, fortune, opportunity, blessing omukisa omubi **bad luck** -a omukisa *adj* lucky, fortunate, blessed eky'omukisa **luckily, fortunately** eky'omukisa omubi **unluckily, unfortunately** ow'omukisa *n1* **lucky person** -wa omukisa **bless**

omukka *n3* (*no pl.*) breath, air, gas, vapour, smoke, steam, fumes omukka ogubalagala **tear gas** omukka ogw'obulamu **oxygen** ekisenge mu ffumbiro kikutte omukka **wall in kitchen coated with soot** -ggyamu omukka **inflate** -ssa omukka **breathe**

omukkufu *n1* satisfied person (*through eating*)

omukkuto *n3* satiety, repletion

¹**omuko** *n1* male in-law, brother-in-law, father-in-law; *in pl.* in-laws

²**omuko** *n3* layer (*in a pile of things*), page omuko gw'amalagala **slip of a sweet potato plant** (*for planting*) omuko gw'ekizimbe **floor** (*of a multistorey building*) omuko gw'olulagala **small part of a banana leaf** (*used for small tasks, eg. cupped to hold water*) omuko gw'olupapula **page** (*of book*) omuko ogusooka **front page** (*eg. of newspaper*)

omukobe *n3* bud yam (*plant*) *Dioscorea bulbifera*

mukoddomi *n1* male in-law of (N12), *eg. mukoddomi wange ('my brother-in-law'). The plural bakoddomi means* in-laws of (*incudes both genders*).

omukodo *n1* miser, mean person

mukoka *n1* (*no pl.*) water flowing on the ground (*during or after rain*)

mukokota *n1* (1) charm used by hunters (*lures animals into traps*); (2) undersized fishing net (*illegal*)

omukolo *n3* function, social event, ceremony

omukomago *n3* log on which barkcloth is beaten. *Made from strong long-lasting wood, as from omusambya, kabalira or muzzanvuma.*

omukomakoma *n3* small tree (*yields twine*) *Grewia mollis*

omukomamawanga *n3* pomegranate (*plant*) *Punica granatum*

omukomazi *n1* barkcloth maker/beater

omukomba *n3* rafter, sloping pole of round house (*from roof top to ground*)

omukomole *n1* circumcised person

omukomozi *n1* cutter (*eg. of cloth*), tailor

omukonda *n3* handle (*eg. of cup*)

omukondeere *n1* horn player

Omukongo *n1* Congolese (*person*)

omukongozzi *n1* bearer of person on the shoulders omukongozzi w'emmandwa **bearer of a spirit** (*of someone possessed*), **principal medium of a spirit**

omukonjezi *n1* slanderer

omukono *n3* arm, hand, trunk (*of elephant*), sleeve; *in si.* handwriting omukono ogwa ddyo **the right (side)** omukono ogwa kkono **the left (side)** -kuba omukono **wave down** (*eg. a taxi*) -lina omukono **have the touch** (*eg. of a skilled craftsman*) -ssaako emikono **confirm** (*in Christian faith*) -ssaako (*or* teekako) omukono **sign**

mukonzikonzi *n1* guinea grass (*used for making brooms*) *Panicum maximum* mukonzikonzi *n9* **aerial**

omukooge *n3* tamarind *Tamarindus indica*

Omukooki *n1* person of Kkooki

omukookolo *n1* person with cancer

omukookoowe *n3* type of fig tree (*yields barkcloth; used for making beer canoes and for building poles*) *Ficus ovata*

omukoowu *n1* tired person

omukopi *n1* peasant, commoner (*ie. not royalty*), uncultured person. *Sometimes used in a derogatory way. From: 'koppe' ('stiff skin'),* *referring to the less processed animal hides formerly worn as clothing by ordinary people.*

omukovvu *n1* person who has lost weight

omukozi *n1* worker, employee, servant, subject (*of a sentence in grammar*) omukozi w'awaka house servant, maid omukozi wa gavumenti civil servant omukozi wa lejjalejja temporary worker

Omukristaayo *n1* Christian (= Omukulisitaayo)

Omukristu *n1* Christian (= Omukirisitu)

omukubi *n1* person who strikes, musician (*one who plays a struck musical instrument*) omukubi w'ebifaananyi photographer omukubi w'ebikonde boxer omukubi w'ekyapa printer omukubi w'endongo (*also* omukubi wa ggita) guitar player omukubi w'engatto shoeshiner omukubi w'ennanga harpist, organist omukubi w'eŋŋoma drummer omukubi wa kkalata gambler omukubi wa pulaani architect omukubi wa ssabbaawa marksman omukubi wa zzaala gambler

omukubiriza *n1* chair(person) (*of a meeting*)

omukubirizi *n1* beater (*in a hunt*)

omukubyabyayi *n1* soft-hearted person, lenient person. *Literally: 'person who hits with banana fibre'.*

omukugu *n1* expert, specialist

omukulembeze *n1* leader, guide omukulembeze w'eggwanga president (*of a country*)

mukulike *interj* congratulations (*pl. of* kulika) mukulikeeyo *greeting* welcome back (N28)

Omukulisitaayo *n1* Christian (*person*) (*Prot*)

omukulu *n1* adult, elder, head, boss, superintendant mukulu boss of (N12), *eg. mukulu wange ('my boss')* omukulu w'ekibuga town clerk omukulu w'ekika head of a clan omukulu w'essaba head of a shrine omukulu w'essomero headteacher omukulu w'olubiri head of palace administration omukulu w'oluggya head of a family line

Mukulukusabitungotungo October

omukululo *n3* track emikululo gy'emmotoka tyre tracks

omukuluppya *n1* con man

omukumpanya *n1* fraudster, cheat

omukungu *n1* high-ranking chief (*in the service of the Kabaka*)

omukungubazi *n1* mourner

omukunguzi *n1* harvester

omukunyu *n3* type of large fig tree (*fruit edible*). *Two species: Ficus mucuso, F. sycomorus.*

omukuŋŋaanya *n1* person who assembles, collector, gatherer omukuŋŋaanya w'amawulire reporter

omukusu *n3* freshwater mangrove (*type of tree with stilt roots, common in Ssese Islands*) *Uapaca guineensis. Meaning: 'tree of the parrots' (because parrots eat its fruits).*

omukutu *n3* channel, canal, portal, frequency, wavelength omukutu gwa interneti internet provider

Mukutulansanja February

omukuufu *n3* chain omukuufu gw'ebisumuluzo key chain omukuufu gw'essaawa watch chain

omukuumi *n1* protector, guard, security guard, sentry, warden, custodian omukuumi w'ekiro night watchman omukuumi w'ekkomera prison officer

omukuusa *n1* person who hides the truth

omukuza *n1* guardian (*of a minor*) omukuza wa Kabaka regent

omukuzannume *n3* pepperbark tree *Warburgia ugandensis. Meaning: 'It treats impotence.'*

omukuzannyana *n3* type of tree *Blighia unijugata. Meaning: 'It nurtures calves.'*

omukwano *n3* friendship, (romantic) love, love affair; *in pl.* friends, *eg. emikwano gyaffe ('our friends')* mukwano (*without an initial vowel* N3) friend of (N12). *'mukwano' (in the singular, meaning 'friend of') causes concordance in more than one noun class* (N6), *eg. Mukwano gwange omu yekka azze. ('My one and only friend has arrived.').* ow'omukwano *n1* friend

omukwate *n1* someone arrested

Mukwenda *n1* title chief of Ssingo County

omukyala *n1* lady, *eg. Abakyala bali wano. ('The ladies are here.'),* wife, *eg. omukyala wa Musoke ('wife of Musoke')* Mukyala title (*abbrev* Muky.) Mrs., *eg. Muky. Musoke ('Mrs. Musoke')* omukyala w'empeta official wife (*married in church*)

mukyalimu there still is/are

omukyawe *n1* someone hated

omukyayi *n1* hater

omukyula *n3* small tree with yellow flowers (*medicinal*) *Senna didymobotrya*

omukyuzi (*also* omucuuzi) *n3* gravy, soup

omulaalo *n1* herdsman

omulaamire *n1* inheritor, beneficiary of a will, legatee

omulaasi *n1* dropout, rastafarian

omulaawe *n1* eunuch

omulabba *n3* ridgepole (*uppermost horizontal timber in roof*)

omulabe *n1* enemy

omulabi *n1* spectator, viewer, watcher; *in pl.* audience

omulabirizi *n1* bishop

omulagirizi *n1* instructor, demonstrator

omulaguzi *n1* fortune-teller, diviner, oracle

omulala *n1* another person, someone else

omulalu *n1* mad person, unruly person

omulalulalu *n1* lout

mulalama *n1* meningitis

omulamazi *n1* pilgrim

omulambo *n3* corpse

omulambuzi *n1* inspector (*one who tours*), tourist

omulamu *n1* healthy/living person mulamu (*with pos* **N12**) (1) (*for a man*) **sister of one's wife**, *eg. mulamu wange* ('my sister-in-law'); (2) (*for a woman*) **brother of one's husband**, *eg. mulamu wange* ('my brother-in-law')

omulamula *n3* **small tree with long thin leaves** (*used for marking boundaries of plots*) *Dracaena fragrans. From:* '-lamula' ('judge'), *because this tree shows where the corners of a plot should be, even when ditches dug as boundaries between plots* ('ensalosalo') *have become infilled.* (= oluwaanyi)

omulamuzi *n1* **judge, magistrate, arbitrator** omulamuzi omukulu **chief justice**

omulamwa *n3* **core, essence, subject** (*for discussion*), **theme.** *Saying:* 'Emmwanyi gye weesiga tebaamu mulamwa.' ('The coffee berry that you trust may not have a bean in it.', ie. 'Appearances can be deceptive.'). A coffee berry with one bean inside is known as 'omulamwa' and one with two beans as 'emilamwa'. They are considered 'male' and 'female' respectively.*

omulanda *n3* **trailing shoot of a plant** (*especially of sweet potatoes*)

omulandira *n3* **root**

¹omulanga *n1* **harpist, organist**

²omulanga *n3* **cry of distress, wail** -kubira omulanga **appeal to** -tema omulanga **cry out in distress**

omulangaatira *n3* **tall strong person**

omulangira *n1* **prince** mulangira *n1* **measles**

¹omulanzi *n1* **announcer**

²omulanzi *n1* **person who planes** (*wood*)

Omulasengeye *n1* **legendary name of former inhabitant of the land that is now Buganda** (*before the arrival of the Baganda*). *Meaning:* 'He shoots colobus monkeys.'

omulasi *n1* **archer, shooter**

omulawo *n3* **large wooden cooking spoon**

omuleera *n3* **embroidered red design** (*on neck of* 'kkanzu')

omuleezi *n1* **person who stretches** (*eg. hides or drums*)

mulekula (*Lusoga*) *See* ekinyeebwa ekizungu

mulekwa *n1* (*pl.* ba mulekwa) **orphan** (*one who has lost one parent*) amaka ga ba mulekwa **orphanage**

omulema *n1* **lame person, disabled person**

omulembe *n3* **period, era, generation**, *eg. omulembe gw'abakadde baffe* ('our parents' generation'); *in pl.* **peace** omulembe gw'ennaku zino **modernity** -a omulembe *adj* **fashionable, stylish, modern** emirembe n'emirembe **for ever and ever** -a emirembe *adj* **peaceful** -tuukira ku mulembe **be fashionable, be modern**

omulende *n3* **young 'emmale'** (*mudfish*)

omulenganjuba *n3* **timepiece, watch, clock.** *Derivation: from* '-lenga' ('measure out') *with* 'enjuba' ('sun').

omulengo *n3* **pile** (*eg. of fruit for sale*)

omulenzi *n1* **boy** mulenzi **boyfriend of** (**N12**), *eg. mulenzi wange* ('my boyfriend')

¹omulere *n1* **flute player.** *Pronunciation:* omulére

²omulere *n3* **flute, pipe, trumpet, saxophone.** *Pronunciation:* omulére. *Saying:* 'Bafuuyira ndiga mulere.' ('They are playing a pipe hoping that the sheep will come.', meaning 'It is hopeless.')

omulerembe *n3* **something bothersome, vexation**; *in pl.* **problems**

¹omulezi *n1* **nurse** (*of a child*). *Pronunciation:* omulézi

²omulezi *n1* **taster** (*of beer*). *Pronunciation:* omulézì

¹muli *adv* **in there, within**

²omuli *n1* **eater** omuli w'enguzi **taker of a bribe**

³omuli **where there is/are** (*within*). Can be equivalent to conjunction **where** *or preposition* **to** (**N7.2**).

⁴muli *you pl.* **are** (*stem* -li)

omuligo *n1* **dirty/untidy person** (*by nature*), **clumsy uncultured person**

omuliika *n1* **person who asks for compensation or a bribe**

omuliimu *3* **lemon** (*tree*) *Citrus limon*

omulimaawa *n3* **lime** (*tree*) *Citrus aurantifolia*

omulimba *n1* **liar**

omulimi *n1* **cultivator, farmer, gardener**

¹omulimu *n3* **work, employment, job.** *The plural* emirimu *can also mean* 'work'. omulimu gw'ekiseera **temporary work** omulimu gw'enkalakkalira **permanent job** omulimu gwa lejjalejja **casual work**

²mulimu **there is/are** (*within*).

omulindi *n3* **ambatch tree** (*small tree of wet places, with very light wood*) *Aeschynomene elaphroxylon*

omulinga (*also* molinga) *n1* **type of tree** *Moringa oleifera*

omuliraano *n3* **neighbourhood, vicinity** ow'omuliraano *n1* **neighbour**

muliraanwa *n1* (*pl.* ba muliraanwa) **neighbour of** (**N12**), *eg. muliraanwa wange* ('my neighbour')

omulirina *n3* **beer made from mixture of maize and other ingredients**

omulirira *n3* **type of tree** (*yields an orange dye*) *Harungana madagascariensis. An extract from the bark was traditionally used for bathing brides before marriage.*

omuliro *n3* (*no pl.*) **fire** -yongeza omuliro **increase the heat, accelerate** (*a vehicle*)

-mulisa *v* (-mulisizza) (1) *vi* **flower**; (2) *vt* **shine a light on, illuminate**

omulobi *n1* **fisherman** (*one who uses hooks*), **angler**

omuloge *n1* **bewitched person**

omulogo *n1* **bewitcher, wizard, witch, sorcerer** omulogo w'omupiira **expert footballer**

omulokole *n1* **saved person** (*through religion*)

omulokole omuzuukufu **born-again person** (*strict type*) omulokole omwebafu **born-again person** (*more liberal type*)

omulokozi *n1* **saviour** (*religious*)

omulombe *n1* **miner**

omulondo *n3* **climbing shrub** (*roots used as an aphrodisiac by men*) *Mondia wightii*

omulongo *n1* (1) **twin**; (2) **umbilical cord of the Kabaka**

omulongooti *n3* **mast** omulongooti gw'essimu **telephone mast** omulongooti gwa bendera **flagpole** omulongooti gwa leediyo **radio mast**

omulonzi *n1* **elector, voter**

omuloope *n1* **person who is reported on**

omuloopi *n1* **reporter of a wrong-doing, denouncer, informer**

omulubaale *n1* **person possessed by a spirit, medium of a lubaale**

-eemulugunya *vi* (-eemulugunyizza) **complain, grumble**

-eemulugunyiza *vt* (-eemulugunyizizza) **complain about**

omulugwa *n3* **hollowed-out log** (*for carving into a drum*)

omuluka *n3* **parish, a traditional unit of government (N29).** *See* owoomuluka

muluku omutono *n1* **herb with pink to purple flowers** (*used as fish poison*) *Tephrosia nana*

-eemulula *vi* (-eemuludde) **slip/glide away** (*as a snake*), **sneak away steathily**

¹**omululu** *n3* (*no pl.*) **greed** -a omululu *adj* **greedy** -liisa omululu **eat greedily, be a glutton** ow'omululu *n1* **greedy person**

²**omululu** *n3* **type of large tree** (*with edible fruits*) *Chrysophyllum albidum*

omululuuza *n3* **shrub** (*anti-malarial*) *Vernonia amygdalina*

omulumba *n1* **rear paddler** (*in canoe*)

omulumbaganyi (*also* omulumbi) *n1* **attacker, assailant**

omulumyo *n3* **boring tool** (*used red hot to pierce holes in wood*)

omulundi *n3* (1) **time**, *eg. emirundi ebiri* ('*two times*'), **occasion, occurrence**; (2) *in pl.* **multiplication table** omulundi gumu **once** emirundi egimu **sometimes** emirundi emeka? **how often?** emirundi mingi **often, frequently**

omulungi *n1* **beautiful/handsome person, good/virtuous person**

-mulunguka *vi* (-mulunguse) **be pulverised, be crushed, crumble**

-mulungula *vt* (-mulungudde) **pulverise, crush, crumble** -mulungula amaaso **roll one's eyes** -mulungula ensonga **make clear**

-mulungule *adj* **pulverised, crushed**

omulunnyanja *n1* **sailor, seaman**

omulunzi *n1* **person who looks after animals, livestock keeper, herdsman**

omulusi *n1* **weaver**

Omuluulu *n1* **member of the Luo people**

omulwadde *n1* **ill person, patient**

omulwanyi *n1* **fighter**

omulwanyisa w'obulyake *n1* **fighter against corruption**

omulyake *n1* **cunning and deceitful person, extortionist**

omulyango *n3* **doorway** emiryango *adv/n23* (**at the**) **front of the home** oluggya lw'emiryango **front yard**

omulyanguzi *n1* **person who takes a bribe**

omulyazaamaanyi *n1* **person who deliberately fails to repay a debt**

omumagufu *n1* **person easily distracted**

¹**omumanyi** *n1* **someone known, acquaintance**

²**omumanyi** *n1* **knowledgeable person, expert.** *Pronounciation differs from above.*

omumanyibwa *n1* (1) **acquaintance**; (2) **well-known person**

omumanyifu *n1* **well-known person**

omumanyirivu *n1* **knowledgeable person**

Omumasaaba *n1* **person of Mount Elgon** (= Mugisu)

omumbejja *n1* **princess**

omumbowa *n1* **palace guard**

omumbuti *n1* **dwarf, pygmy**

omumegganyi *n1* **wrestler**

omuminsani *n1* **missionary**

omumiro *n3* **oesophagus, gullet, throat, trachea** -kuba omumiro **click the throat**

Omumisiri *n1* **Egyptian**

omumonaaki *n1* **monk**

omumuli *n3* **torch** (*made of reeds*)

omumuzika (*also* omuziki) *n3* **music**

omumwa *n3* **lip, mouth, spout, rim** (*of a cup*) omumwa gw'ennyonyi **beak, bill** -songoza omumwa **pout**

omumwanyi *n3* **coffee** (*tree*)

omumwe *adv* **inside her/his place/home (N11.5)**

omumwo *adv* **inside your** *si.* **place/home (N11.5)**

omumyuka *n1* **second-in-command**

omunaala *n3* **mast, tower** omunaala gw'ekkanisa **steeple** omunaala gw'essimu **telephone mast** omunaala gw'omuzigiti **minuret**

munaana *n3/num* **eight** -a omunaana *adj* **eighth**

omunaanaagize *n1* **stutterer, stammerer**

omunaanansi *n3* **pineapple beer/juice**

omunaanya *n1* **indolent person**

omunaba *n3* **African false nutmeg** (*type of tree*) *Pycnanthus angolensis*

omunafu *n1* **weak person**

omunagiro *n3* **cloak, wraparound**

omunaku *n1* (1) **poor person**; (2) **person on his/her own** Munakweyeegulira **name of a market at Kisubi.**

omunakuwavu *n1* **sad person, distressed person, miserable person**

omunazi *n3* (1) **palm tree** (*general term*); (2) **coconut tree** *Cocos nucifera*

munda *adv* **inside, within** <u>munda mu</u> *pre* **within, inside** <u>-a munda</u> *adj* **inner, internal**

mundabire **give her/him my regards** (*verb* -labira)

omunene *n1* (1) **fat person**; (2) **rich person**

Omungereza *n1* **English/British person**

¹Mungu *n1* **God** (*used by Muslims*)

²omungu *n3* (*pl.* emyungu) **variety of gourd** (*with edible rounded fruits; little grown, being watery and of little food value*) *Lagenaria siceraria*. Saying: *'Kulya, mungu buteesokoola.' ('Eating mungu leaves nothing between the teeth.', meaning 'The task is easily done.')*

munna- *n1* (*pl.* banna-) (1) (*used with place name, occupation, etc.*) **person** (*or* **member**) **of** (**N12**), *eg. Munnabuddu ('person of Buddu')*; (2) (*used with possessive pronoun*) **friend** (*or* **companion**) **of** (**N12**) <u>munnange</u> **my friend**, <u>munno</u> **your friend**, <u>munne</u> **her/his friend**, <u>munnaffe</u> **our friend**, <u>munnammwe</u> **your friend**, <u>mannaabwe</u> **their friend**. *See* -nna-

munnabbanka *n1* **banker**

Munnabulaaya *n1* **European** (*person*)

munnabyabufuzi *n1* **politician**

munnaddiini *n1* (1) **member of a religious order**; (2) **kind-hearted person**

munnaggwanga *n1* **foreigner**

munnakatemba *n1* <u>munnakatemba omukazi</u> **actress** <u>munnakatemba omusajja</u> **actor**

Munnakenya *n1* **Kenyan** (*person*)

munnakibiina *n1* **member of a society/group**

munnakibuga *n1* **town dweller**

munnakyalo *n1* **villager**

munnamateeka *n1* **lawyer**

munnamawulire *n1* **reporter, journalist**

munnanfuusi *n1* **hypocrite**

munnange *n1* **my companion/friend** <u>munnange</u> *affectionate form of address* **my dear**

munnansi *n1* **citizen, native** (*of a country*)

munnasangwawo *n1* **person already present at a place, original inhabitant, first-comer**

munnassaayansi *n1* **scientist**

Munnayuganda *n1* **Ugandan** (*person*)

munne *n1* **her/his companion/friend**

munno *n1* **your** *si.* **companion/friend**

omunnyo *n3* (*no pl.*) **salt** <u>omunnyo ogw'ekisula</u> **rock salt**

muno *adv* **(in) here**

omunoonyerezi *n1* **researcher, investigator, explorer**

omunoonyi *n1* **seeker** <u>omunoonyi w'obubudamo</u> **asylum seeker, refugee**

omuntu *n1* **person, human** <u>muntu n'omu</u> (*with verb in neg N21*) **no-one** <u>omuntu omubisi</u> **ignorant/naïve person** <u>omuntu wa bulijjo</u> **the common man** <u>omuntu wa mmizi</u> **confidant** <u>omuntu yenna</u> **anyone**

omuntumulamu *n1* **well-mannered person, decent person**

muntunsolo *n1* **commando**

omununule *n1* **freed person**

omununuzi *n1* **rescuer, saviour, redeemer**

munuunansubi *n3* **sunbird**

omunuunyi *n1* **drinker** (*using a straw*) <u>omunuunyi w'oluseke</u> **drunkard**

omunwe *n3* **unit, a single**, *eg. omunwe gwa lumonde ('a single potato')*

omunya *n3* **lizard**

omunyaanya *n3* **tomato** (*plant*) *Lycopersicon esculentum*

omunyage *n1* **victim of robbery/plunder**

omunyago *n3* **booty, loot, plunder**

omunyakuzi *n1* **snatcher** (*type of thief*)

Omunyani *n1* **member of a certain Hindu merchant caste**

Omunyankole *n1* **person of Ankole**

Omunyarwanda *n1* **person of Rwanda**

omunyazi *n1* **looter, robber, plunderer, pirate** <u>Munyazi bunyazi.</u> **He is just a thief.**

-munyeenya *vi* (-munyeenye) **shine on and off** (*eg. of star or firefly*), **twinkle, glimmer**

munyeera *n1* **type of very small ant**

omunyenye *n3* **type of tree** (*medicinal*). *Two types*: <u>omunyenye omusajja</u>, <u>omunyenye omukazi</u>. *One is probably Zanthoxylum gilletii and the other Z. rubescens.*

omunyiikaavu *n1* **person who is dejected, person suffering from depression**

omunyiikivu *n1* **hard-working person**

omunyinya *n3* **small tree of drier areas** *Acacia gerrardii*

omunyolo *n3* **doorhandle, doorhandle and bolt** (*in combination*), **bolt** <u>omunyolo gw'eŋŋoma</u> **drumstick**

omunyoomi *n1* **person who shows contempt, scoffer**

Omunyoro *n1* **person of Bunyoro**. *'omunyoro' in Lunyoro is equivalent to 'omwami' in Luganda.*

-munyunguza *vi* (-munyunguzizza) **rinse, gargle**

omunyunyunsi *n1* **extortionist**

munywanyi *n1* **(close) friend of** (*with pos N12*), *eg. munywanyi wange ('my friend')*

omunywi *n1* **drinker** <u>omunywi wa taaba</u> **smoker**

omupaapaali *n3* **pawpaw** (*tree*) *Carica papaya*. *Crushed leaves used for cleaning hands after peeling matooke.*

omupakasi *n1* **hired worker, labourer** <u>omupakasi wa lejjalejja</u> **casual labourer**

omupangisa *n1* **person who rents, tenant**

omupeera *n3* **guava** (*tree; leaves medicinal*) *Psidium guajava* <u>Mupeera</u> **nickname of Father Pierre Lourdel** (*first Catholic missionary in Uganda*)

omupiira *n3* **something made of rubber, ball, football, tyre** <u>omupiira gw'eccupa</u> **cork**

omupiira gw'enkuba **raincoat**   omupiira
gw'omunda **inner tube** (*of tyre*)   omupiira -yabika
have a blowout (*of a tyre*)   -sala omupiira **referee
a football match**

omupoliisi *n1* **police man/woman**

Omupolotesitante (*also* Omupoto) *n1* **Protestant**

omupunga *n3* **rice**. *The plural* emipunga *means
'types of rice'. Derivation: 'mpunga' (Swahili) and
earlier probably an Indonesian language.*

omupunta *n1* **surveyor** (*of land*)

¹**Musa** *n1* **Moses**

²**omusa** *n3* **blade** (*eg. of knife*), **appendage at end
of banana leaf**

omusaabaze *n1* **passenger**

omusaala *n3* **pay, wage, salary**; *in pl.* **wages**

omusaalaba *n3* **cross, crucifix**   -ba/-li ku
musaalaba **be on a cross, have a lot of problems**

omusaali *n3* **two types of tree** (*with edible fruits*).
The types: omusaali omuganda *Garcinia
buchananii,* omusaali omuzungu **loquot** *Eriobotrya
japonica.*

omusaalo *n3* **prayer mat** (*of Muslims*)

omusaasaanyi *n1* **person who spreads** (*things,
ideas, etc.*)   omusaasaanyi w'olugambo **rumour-
monger**

omusaasizi *n1* **compassionate person,
sympathetic person**

omusaayi *n3* **blood**   musaayi *n1* **type of red-leafed
hibiscus, roselle** (*swollen calyxes used to make a
health drink which is used to treat anaemia*)
Hibiscus subdariffa

omusaazi *n1* **joker, jester**

omusabi *n1* **person who asks**

omusabirizi *n1* **beggar**

musaggi *See* omutima

omusajja *n1* **man**

omusala *n3* **(1) barkcloth tree that has been
stripped of its bark once; (2) first class barkcloth**
(*very soft, from any stripping of a barkcloth tree
except the first*). *Saying:* 'Omugenyi ow'omukwano
omwaliirira omusala. ('You bring out your best
barkcloth for your best friend to sit on.').*

omusale *n3* **cut** (*on the body*)

omusambi *n1* **kicker**   omusambi w'omupiira
footballer

omusambwa *n3* **manifestation of a nature spirit**
(*appearing in the form of a woman*), **ghost**

omusambya *n3* **type of tree** (*valued for
construction*) *Markhamia lutea.* 'olusambya' *is
used for smaller trees.*

omusamize *n1* **person who participates in a spirit
possession ritual**

omusana *n3* (*no pl.*) **sunshine, sunlight**. *See*
emisana

omusandasanda *n3* **type of tree** *Mimusops
bagshawei*

musangi *n1* **husband of sister's wife (N12)**, *eg.
musangi wange* ('*my brother-in-law*')

omusango *n3* **accusation, offence, charge, (court)
case, trial, crime**   omusango -singa **lose a case**
-ejjeerera omusango **be acquitted of a charge**
-kkiriza omusango **confess a crime**   -sala
omusango **pass sentence**   -saliriza omusango **be
biased** (*of a judge*)   Si musango. **There is no
case.**, **It's not a problem.**   -singa omusango **win a
case**   -zza omusango **commit a crime**

¹**omusanvu** *n3* **broken-off branch** (*placed on road
or path to block entry*). *Saying:* 'Ekkubo
nnalisuulamu omusanvu.' ('I no longer go there.'),
meaning 'The relationship is finished.')   omusanvu
mu kkubo **road barrier** (*eg. mounted by police*)

²**musanvu** *n3/num* **seven**   -a omusanvu *adj* **seventh**

omusanyufu *n1* **happy person**

omusasa *n3* **type of tree** (*name used in traditional
medicine to push people apart*) *Shirakiopsis
elliptica. From:* '-sasa' ('scatter'). *Used for
construction of 'ebiggwa' (traditional shrines);
should not be used for construction of ordinary
houses – the owners will become hated or go mad.*
See omuzzannanda

omusaseredooti *n1* **Priest** (*RC*) (= omusossodooti)

omusasi *n1* **forager**   omusasi w'amawulire
reporter

omusawo *n1* **doctor**   omusawo omuganda
traditional doctor   omusawo omuzungu **western
doctor** (*doctor trained in western medicine*)
omusawo w'amannyo **dentist**   omusawo w'ebisolo
veterinarian   omusawo w'obwongo **psychiatrist**

omusawuzi *n1* **healer** (*one who communicates with
a spirit*), **doctor**

omusazi *n1* **person who cuts**   omusazi w'ebigambo
false accuser   omusazi w'emisango **judge,
magistrate**   omusazi w'ensawo **pickpocket**
omusazi w'enviiri **hairdresser**   omusazi
w'omupiira **referee**

omuseegu *n1* **dissolute/shameless person**

omuseenene *n3* **type of tree** (*timber; ornamental*).
Two genera: Afrocarpus, Podocarpus.   Museenene
November (*month of 'enseenene' grasshoppers*)

omuseetwe *n3* **level area of land, plain, plateau**
-a omuseetwe *adj* **level/flat** (*of land*)

omuseezi *n1* **one who overcharges, swindler**

omusege *n3* **wolf**

omusekese *n3* **long bundle**, *eg.* omusekese
gw'enku ('long bundle of firewood')   omusekese
gw'ennyumba **long badly built house**

omusekuzo *n3* **big wooden pestle**

omusenyu *n3* **sand**   omusenyu gw'ennyanja **lake
sand** (*used in cement made for brick-laying*)
omusenyu gw'omugga **fine-grained sand** (*from
river valleys; used in making plaster*)

omusenze *n1* **newly settled person** (*in a place*),
newcomer, immigrant. *Traditionally a client to a
chief.*

omusera *n3/adv* **full serving**, *eg. Mpa ekikopo
ky'omwenge musera.* ('Give me a full cup of

beer.'), **to the brim**

omuserebende *n3 (no pl.)* **flat bottom** (*of a person*) emmotoka eya muserebende **saloon car** owa muserebende *n1* **person with a flat bottom**

omuseresi *n1* **roofer, thatcher**

omuserikale *n1* **uniformed state official, soldier** omuserikale w'amagye **soldier** omuserikale w'ekkomera **prison warder** omuserikale w'ennyota **officer** (*in army or police*) omuserikale wa poliisi **police officer**

Omusese *n1* **person of the Ssese Islands**

Omuseveniside *n1* **Seventh-Day Adventist**

omusezi *n1* **night-dancer** (*member of a black magic cult*)

omusheshe (*slang; may be considered impolite*) *n1* **person from western Uganda**

omusibe *n1* **prisoner, detainee, convict**

omusibi *n1* **person who ties** omusibi w'abagole **dresser of brides** omusibi w'enviiri **braider of hair**

omusigire *n1* **deputy, assistant.** *Saying: 'Omusigere amala bitono.' ('An assistant cannot make a final decision.')*

omusiguze *n1* **person who leads astray, corrupter, seducer**

musiibye mutyano? *greeting* **How have you** *pl.* **spent the day?, good afternoon, good evening.** (N28)

omusiige *n1* **page in service of the Kabaka**

omusiizi *n1* **painter** omusiizi w'ebifaananyi **artist** omusiizi w'enjala **painter of nails** omusiizi w'ennyumba **house painter**

omusika *n1* **heir, inheritor, successor**

omusikaawutu *n1* **scout**

omusimbi w'oluseke *n1* **extortionist**

omusimbu *n1* **epileptic**

omusinde *n3* **(sound of) trampling** omusinde gw'emmundu **gunfire**

Omusingasinga *n1* **Sikh**

omusingi *n3* **foundation**

omusingo *n3* **collateral, surety, bail, guarantee, down payment** (= akakalu)

omusipi *n3* **belt** omusipi ogw'oku ntebe **seat belt**

Omusiraamu *n1* **Muslim**

omusiri *n3* **patch of crops,** *eg. omusiri gwa lumonde ('patch of potatoes'),* **(cultivated) plot**

omusirise *n1* **quiet person** (*by nature*)

omusiru *n1* **stupid person, fool**

omusirusiru *n1* **idiot**

musisi *n1 (no pl.)* **earthquake** Musisi **Kiganda deity** (*lubaale*)**, god of earthquakes**

omusitaferi *n3* **custard apple** (*plant*) *Annona reticulata*

omusito *n3* **wooden skewer**

omusittale *n3* **ruled line** (*drawn as margin*)

omusiyazi *n1* **homosexual**

[1]**omusizi** *n1* **sower.** *Pronunciation:* omusízi

[2]**omusizi** *n3* **type of tree** (*yields timber*) *Maesopsis*

eminii. Pronunciation: omusízi

omusobya *n1* **person at fault, wrong-doer, transgressor**

omusoddookisi *n1* **member of the Eastern Orthodox church**

Omusoga *n1* **person of Busoga**

omusogasoga *n3* **castor-oil** (*plant*) *Ricinus communis*

omusogozi *n1* **brewer**

musoke *n1 (no pl.)* **rainbow** Musoke **Kiganda deity** (*lubaale*)**, god of the rainbow** (*remover of problems*)**.** *Also a name used for males.*

omusolo *n3* **tax, duty** wangaala nga musolo **graduated tax** (*type of tax deducted at source*)**.** *Literal meaning: 'long-lived tax' – because there is no way to avoid paying).*

omusolooza *n1* **collector** (*of fees, fares, etc.*) Musolooza *title* **caretaker of the royal hearth**

Omusomali *n1* **Somali** (*person*)

omusomesa *n1* **teacher**

omusomi *n1* **reader, scholar** omusomi w'amawulire **newsreader** omusomi w'eddiini **religious believer**

omusomo *n3* **course** (*of studies*)**; in** *pl.* **studies** omosomo gw'okweyatulira **confirmation course**

omusono *n3* **fashion, style**

omusonso *n3* **elephant shrew**

omusontwa *n3* **type of slender insect resembling a grasshopper**

omusoobolokofu *n1* **tall handsome person**

musoolesoole *adv* **few at a time,** *eg. Abantu bajja musoolesoole. ('They are coming a few at a time.')*

omusossodooti *n1* **priest** (*RC*)

omusota *n3* **snake** omusota gw'obutwa **poisonous snake**

musotataluma *n1* **prostrate/twining herb with white flowers.** *Meaning: 'The snake does not bite.'*

omussa *n3* **sausage tree** *Kigelia africana*

omussi *n1* **killer**

omusu *n3* **(savannah) cane rat** omusu omwene **marsh cane rat**

omusubbaawa *n3* **candle**

omusubi *n3* **large amount of grass, grassy area**

Omusudaani *n1* **Sudanese** (*person*)

omusuga *n3* **type of small tree** *Ehretia cymosa*

omusugga *n3* **Elgon olive** (*type of large tree*) *Olea capensis* subsp. *welwitschii*

omusujja *n3* **fever** omusujja gw'ensiri **malaria**

omusulo *n3 (no pl.)* **dew, urine**

omusumaali *n3* **nail** omusumaali gw'enjola **screw**

omusumaami *n1* **waiter, servant, houseboy.** *From: 'msumari' (Swahili).*

omusumba *n1* **shepherd, vicar, pastor, bishop**

omusumeeno *n3* **saw**

omusunyi *n1* **person who plucks** omusunyi w'endongo **lyre player, guitar player**

omususa *n3* **type of shrub** (*medicinal; very bitter*)

omususi *n1* **peeler**

omusuubuzi *n1* **trader, businessman, dealer**
omusuubuzi omunene **wholesaler** omusuubuzi
ow'edduuka **retailer** omusuubuzi w'oku lubalaza
trader selling from the pavement

omusuwa *n3* **blood vessel, artery, vein**

omuswaki *n3* **tooth-cleaning stick, toothbrush**

omutaafu *n3* **frown line on forehead** -siba
emitaafu **frown**

omutabaazi *n1* **warrior**

omutabaganya *n1* **mediator**

mutabani *n1* **son** (*with pos* **N12**), *eg. mutabani
wange* (*'my son'*), **nephew of** (*blood related*)

omutaka *n1* **head of a clan or subdivision of a
clan, long term resident of the land**

omutakansi *n1* **long-term resident of the land**
(*closely connected to the ancestral spirits of a
place; less closely connected to the Kabaka than
omutaka*)

omutala *n3* **traditional village area, distance
between two swamps/valleys** (*a traditional unit of
measurement*) emitala w'amayanja **overseas**
emitala wa *adj* **across**, *eg. emitala w'omugga*
(*'across the river'*), **on the other side of, beyond**

omutali **where there is/are not** (*within*). *Can be
equivalent to preposition* **to** (**N7.2**).

omutambizi *n1* **person who sacrifices, executioner**
omutambizi w'emmisa **celebrant** (*of mass; RC*)

omutambuze *n1* **traveller, promiscuous person**

omutamiivu *n1* **drunkard**

omutanda *n3* **strip of barkcloth** (*used as clothing
by women*)

omutandisi *n1* **someone who starts, founder,
originator**

omutango *n3* **fine, indemnity** omutango ogwa
buliwo **on-the-spot fine**

Omutanzaniya *n1* **Tanzanian** (*person*)

omutaputa *n1* **interpreter**

omutasalanjala *n3* **lily trotter** (*type of bird*).
Meaning: 'the one that does not cut its nails'.

mutasukkakkubo *n1* **creeping plant growing on
edges of paths** *Desmodium ascendens. Meaning:
'It does not cross the path.'*

omutawaana *n3* **problem, trouble, difficulty**

omutayimbwa *n3* **security bar** (*eg. on window*),
crowbar

omutayirire *n1* **circumcised person**

omutayirizi *n1* **person who circumcises, pesterer,
nagger**

omute *n1* **freed person**

omuteebi *n1* **person who takes aim, marksman,
shooter, striker** (*in football*)

omuteego *n3* **evil spell** (*affecting a whole family or
neighbourhood*) -fuukira omuteego **become
problematic** (*of a person or situation*), **become
impossible**

omuteeko *n3* **heap/pile** (*of an organised sort, eg. of
counters in a game, or of items to divide between
people*)

Muteesa *n1 title* (1) **chief of Mawokota County;**
(2) **name of two former kings of Buganda** (**N29**)

omuteezi *n1* **ambusher, player offside in football**
omutwe omuteezi **migraine**

omutegeevu *n1* **discerning person**

omutegesi *n1* **arranger, organiser** omutegesi
w'amawulire **newspaper editor**

omutego *n3* **trap, snare**

omutembeeyi *n1* **itinerant trader, peddler**

omutemu *n1* **murderer, assassin**

omutemule *n1* **someone murdered**

omutemwa *n3* **share, allocation, portion**

omutendera *n3* **stage** (*in a process*), *eg. Ennyumba
gye bazimba etuuse omutendera ogusemba.* (*'The
house they are building has reached the last
stage.'*), **phase**

omutendesi *n1* **trainer, coach**

mutenzaggulu *n1* **earthquake.** *Meaning: 'It shakes
the sky.'*

mutere *n1* (*no pl.*) **dried sliced food** (*stored for
future use; pounded into flour before use*) mutere
wa lumonde **dried sliced potatoes** mutere wa
mbidde **dried sliced beer bananas** mutere wa
muwogo **dried sliced cassava**

omutete *n1* **sub-chief of village**

omuteteme *n3* **chopped up banana pseudostem**
(*'trunk'*) (*lying on the ground*)

omutetere *n3* **exposed layer of trunk of barkcloth
tree** (*after removal of bark*). *Must be wrapped
immediately in banana leaves for the bark to
regrow.*

omuti *n3* **tree, piece of wood, wood** (*as material*),
log, pole omuti gw'amasannyalaze **electricity
pole** omuti gw'essimu **telephone pole** omuti
gw'ettaala **lamppost** omuti gw'olweyo
broomstick omuti omubisi omuti gwa ppamba
Kapok tree *Ceiba pentandra* omuti gwa
ssabbuuni **bar of soap** **unseasoned wood** -a
omuti *adj* **wooden**

¹omutiini *n1* **teenager**

²omutiini *n3* **fig tree** (*as in the Bible*) *Ficus carica*

omutiitiizi *n1* **timid person, coward**

omutima *n3* **heart, spirit, mind** omutima
-eewuuba **have palputations** (*of the heart*)
omutima gw'eŋŋoma **charm put in a drum**
(*rattles about inside*) omutima gw'ettaka
stinkhorn fungus. *The Luganda meaning is 'heart
of the soil.'. It has been suggested that 'omutima
gw'ettaka' is actually the parasitic plant Hydnora
(possibly it is both stinkhorn and Hydnora).*
omutima -tujja **beat rapidly** (*of the heart*) -a
omutima omubi *adj* **bad-hearted** -a omutima
omukakanyavu *adj* **hard-hearted** -gwaamu
mutima **lose heart** Kika kya Mutima **Heart Clan.**
There are two heart clans: Mutima Muyanja *and*
Mutima Omusaggi; *they have different totems and
secondary totems* (Table 19). -nyolwa mu mutima
be broken-hearted -ssa omutima **feel down-**

hearted

omutimbagano *n3* internet

omutindo *n3* standard (*eg. of education*), grade (*of product*), level of competency or attainment, quality, rank omutindo gwa waggulu high quality ku mutindo in fashion

omuto *n1* young person

omutonde *n1* person (*as a created being*)

omutongole *n1* official (*person*), (*traditionally*) office-holder appointed directly by the Kabaka. *Traditionally, some abatongole were responsible for the collection of military levies for the Kabaka, and others for liturgical or other functions.*

omutonyi *n1* decorator

omutonzi *n1* creator

omuttanjoka *n3* types of shrubs (*with yellow flowers, medicinal*). *Three species: Senna hirsuta, C. occidentalis, S. ramosissimum. Meaning: 'It kills stomach pain.'*

omuttankuyege *n3* neem tree (*insecticidal*) *Azadirachta indica. Meaning: 'It kills termites.'*

Muttanzige *n1* Lake Albert. *Meaning: 'It kills locusts.'*

omutte *n1* someone killed

omutto *n3* pillow, cushion

omuttunta *n3* (*no pl.*) soft hair (*eg. on forehead*), down

omutuba *n3* (1) barkcloth tree *Ficus natalensis*; (2) sub-division of a clan (N29). *Traditionally, 'omutuba' was planted on the founding of an estate or a unit of government.* Omutubagiza ensonga legendary name of the first barkcloth tree (*so called because problems that had become disentangled remained with it*) ow'omutuba *n1* chief of a subdivision of a clan

omutugunda *n3* small tree (*fruit 'ettugunda' edible*) *Vangueria apiculata*

omutujju *n1* gunman, thug, terrorist, suicide bomber

omutula *n3* small shrub (*fruit 'entula' edible*) *Solanum gilo*

mutulika *n1* type of bush or small tree (*medicinal, treats measles*) *Phyllanthus ovalifolius*

Omutuluuki *n1* Turk

omutume *n1* someone sent, apostle

Mutunda September

omutunku *n3* type of tree (*fruit. edible*) *Dovyalis macrocalyx*

omutunsi *n3* growing point, bud, young shoot (*especially of sweet potatoes or beans*)

[1]**omutunzi** *n1* seller, salesperson. *Pronunciation*: omutúnzí omutunzi w'oku lubalaza trader selling from the pavement

[2]**omutunzi** *n1* sewer, seamstress, tailor. *Pronunciation*: omutûnzi omutunzi w'engatto shoe repairer

omututumba *n3* pith in stalk of inflorescence of banana plant (*inside the leaf sheaths*). *Beaten to*

make a sponge ('ekinyirikisi'). Cut into wedges and used to help strip bark from barkcloth trees – helps to prevent them tearing. See ekikolokomba

omutuukirivu *n1* saint Omutuukirivu Ppaapa His Holiness the Pope

Mutuuza *n1* title person responsible for the seating of the Kabaka

omutuuze *n1* inhabitant, resident

omutwalo *n3/num* (1) bundle, load; (2) ten thousand; (3) brideprice (*payment by groom to family of bride*). *The following terms were previously used in connection with brideprice*: omutwalo gw'embugo bundle of barkcloth, omutwalo gw'enswa package of termites.

omutwe *n3* head (*of the body*) omutwe gw'ebikulu caption omutwe gw'ekiwandiiko heading omutwe oguluma headache omutwe omukulu headline omutwe omuteezi migraine omutwe omwereere empty-headed person omutwe -wunga lose one's mind -koteka omutwe bend the head, be submissive

omutyabi w'enku *n1* firewood collector

mutyanno? *greeting* how are you? (N28)

-muumuunya *vi* (-muumuunyizza) make 'um' sound (*eg. when pausing in speech*) -muumuunya oluyimba hum a tune

omuvubi *n1* fisherman

omuvubuka *n1* youth

omuvuganyi (*also* omuvvunkanyi) *n1* participant in a competition, competitor, opponent, rival, contestant

omuvule *n3* type of tree (*yields timber*) *Milicia excelsa*

omuvumbuzi *n1* discoverer, explorer

omuvumirizi *n1* person who talks badly (*about someone or something*)

omuvumu *n1* courageous person, determined person (= omugumu)

omuvuyo *n3* mess, chaos, muddle

omuvuzi *n1* driver omuvuzi w'ennyonyi pilot omuvuzi w'eryato paddler (*of canoe*)

omuvvoozi *n1* blasphemer

omuvvunkanyi *See* omuvuganyi

omuvvuunuzi *n1* translator, interpreter

omuwaabi *n1* accuser, plaintiff, prosecutor omuwaabi wa gavumenti state prosecutor

omuwaanyiwaanyi *n1* flatterer

omuwaatwa *n3* gap, opening, (mountain) pass

omuwaawa *n3* medium-sized tree of drier areas *Acacia sieberiana*

omuwaayirizi *n1* person who makes false allegations, slanderer

omuwafu *n3* incense tree *Canarium schweinfurthii*

omuwagaleko *n1* educated person

omuwagguufu *n1* tall well-built person

omuwagizi *n1* supporter, fan, backer

Muwakanya August

omuwakanyi *n1* disputant, contender, protestor,

opponent

omuwala *n1* girl   muwala **daughter of** (N12), *eg. muwala wange ('my daughter')*

Omuwalabu *n1* **Arab**

omuwalanyi *n1* **persecutor, harasser, tormenter**

omuwalimu *n1* **Muslim teacher, imam**

Muwamadi *n1* **Mohammed**

omuwambe *n1* **captive, prisoner-of-war, hostage**

omuwambi *n1* **captor**

omuwambiro *n3* **handle of shield**

omuwambo *n3* **tree planted near house to ward off evil spirits**

omuwandiisi *n1* **writer, scribe, author, clerk, secretary**   omuwandiisi w'amawulire **journalist**

Muwanga *n1* **Kiganda deity** (*lubaale*)

omuwanguzi *n1* **winner, conquerer**

[1]**omuwanika** *n1* **treasurer**

[2]**omuwanika** *n3* **thorny shrub or small tree** *Dichrostachys cinerea*

omuwanula *n3* **small deciduous savannah tree** *Steganotaenia araliacea*

omuwaŋŋanguse *n1* **exile**

[1]**muwawa** *adv* **aimlessly, without paying attention**   -dduka muwawa **run away in panic**   -yogera muwawa **talk without thinking**

[2]**Omuwawa** *n. See* abawawa

omuwawaabirwa *n1* **person charged with an offence, defendant**

omuwawu *n3* **type of tree** (*leaves used as sandpaper*) *Ficus exasperata*

omuwazi *n1* **person who scrapes, tanner, person who planes wood** (*being a carpenter*)

omuweereza *n1* **person who serves, attendant, church warden, waiter, waitress**

omuweesi *n1* **metal worker, blacksmith**

omuwemba *n3* (*no pl.*) **sorghum**

omuwendo *n3* **number, price, value, cost**   -a omuwendo *adj* **expensive, valuable**   -sala ku muwendo **reduce the price** (*through bargaining*)   -sala omuwendo **set the price**

omuwere *n1* **newborn child**

omuwi *n1* **giver**   omuwi w'amagezi **adviser**   omuwi w'omusolo **taxpayer**

omuwo *n3* **type of fig tree** (*medicinal, used to treat 'ekiwo'*) *Ficus saussureana*

muwogo *n1* **cassava** *Manihot esculenta. See* emiwogo. *From: 'muhogo' (Swahili) and earlier 'mandioca' (Tupi-Guarani, an indigenous American language).*   muwogo omuwutta **unpalatable old cassava** (*having been too long in the ground*)   muwogo wa bulaala **stale cassava** (*with black streaks*)   mutere wa muwogo **dried sliced cassava** (*for storage*)

omuwolereza *n1* **advocate, intercessor**

omuwombeefu *n1* **unassertive/meek person**

omuwooza *n1* **tax collector**

omuwozi *n1* **lender** (*of money*)

omuwula *n3* **piece of something divisible, segment**

omuwula gw'ennyama **piece of boneless meat** omuwula gwa ffene **piece of jackfruit** (*containing a seed*)   omuwula gwa katunguluccumu **clove of garlic**   omuwula gwa mucungwa **segment of orange**

omuwuliriza *See* abawuliriza

omuwulize *n1* **obedient person**

omuwumbo *n3* **parcel of food wrapped in banana leaves for cooking**   omuwumbo gw'amatooke **parcel of cooking matooke** (*cooking bananas*)   omuwumbo gwa muwogo **parcel of cassava**

omuwunda *n3* **metal spike** (*at end of pole or spear*)

omuwunzi *n1* **carver** (*of wood*)

omuwutta *n3* **unpalatable root crop** (*left too long in the ground*), **demented person, senile person**   lumonde omuwutta **unpalatable old potato**   muwogo omuwutta **unpalatable old cassava**

omuwuttaavu *n1* **demented person, senile person**

omuwuukuufu *n1* **person with an endless appetite**

omuwuulu *n1* **unmarried man, bachelor**

omuwuzi *n1* **swimmer**

omuya *n3* **fishing basket** (*used for catching enkejje*)

omuyaaye *n1* **drop-out, lout, hooligan, drug adict**

omuyaayu *n3* **wild/feral cat**

omuyaga *n1* **smoker of cannabis, drug addict**

omuyala *n1* **hungry/starving person**

omuyambi *n1* **helper, assistant**

omuyanja *n3* **tree with red flowers** (*latex used as gum*) *Symphonia globulifera*   Omuyanja *n1* **member of the Mutima Muyanja Clan**

omuyatiikirivu *n1* **well-known person, distinguished person**

omuyeekera *n1* **guerrilla**

omuyembe *n3* **mango** (*tree; fruit*) *Mangifera indica*

omuyezi *n1* **sweeper**

omuyi *n1* **very ill person**

omuyigganyi *n1* **persecutor**

omuyiggo *n3* **hunt, prey**

omuyigiriza *n1* **teacher**

omuyigirize *n1* **educated person**

omuyigirizwa *n1* **disciple**

omuyiikiriza *n1* **person who takes advantage of another person, bully**

omuyiiya *n1* **inventor, composer**

omuyiki *n3* **small tree** (*seed 'empiki' used as counter in game of 'omweso'*) *Sapindus saponaria*

omuyiko (*also* omwiko) *n3* **trowel**

[1]**omuyima** *n1* **herdsman**   Omuyima **Muhima** (*member of the Bahima people*)

[2]**omuyima** *n1* **person who backs another, godparent, guarantor, patron, sponsor**

omuyimbi *n1* **singer, musician**

omuyimbisa *n1* **conductor** (*of a choir*)

Omuyindi *n1* **Indian** (*person*)

omuyini *n3* **handle** (*of a tool, especially hoe*)

omuyirikiti *n3* **coral tree** *Erythrina abyssinica* (= eggirikiti)

omuyise *n1* **passer-by**

Omuyitale *n1* Italian (*person*)
omuyizi *n1* learner, student, pupil
omuyizzi *n1* hunter
muyizzitasubwa *n1* mason wasp (*black wasp, makes pot-like nest on ceiling; used as a charm by hunters and fishermen*). Meaning: *'The hunter does not miss.'*
omuyombi *n1* quarrelsome person
Omuyonaani *n1* Greek (*person*)
omuyongobevu *n1* weak/sickly person, listless person
[1]**omuyonjo** *n1* clean and neat person (*by nature*)
[2]**omuyonjo** *n3* chicken basket. Saying: *'Omuyonjo omutono gukyamya enkoko ekyensuti.'* (*'A small basket makes the chicken's tail crooked.', meaning 'A lack of space makes one feel uncomfortable.'*)
omuyoolerero *n3* (*no pl.*) large number of assorted things, miscellany (= kalonda) -a omuyoolerero *adj* miscellaneous, eg. engoye ez'omuyoolerero (*'a miscellaneous collection of clothes'*), indiscriminate
omuyovu *n3* mahogany *Entandrophragma* (*several species*) Omuyovu name used in Njovu Clan
Omuyudaaya *n1* Jew
omuyunzi *n1* bonesetter
omuyuuganyi *n1* unstable/fickle person
omuzaale *n1* person (*as a born being*)
omuzaaliranwa *n1* locally born person
omuzaalisa *n1* birth attendant, midwife omuzaalisa w'ekinnansi traditional birth attendant
omuzaana *n1* wife of a prince, lady who serves the Kabaka with a child
omuzabbibu *n3* grape (*plant; fruit*) *Vitis vinifera*
omuzadde *n1* parent
omuzannyi *n1* player, performer, actor, actress omuzannyi mu bifaananyi movie star
omuzannyo *n3* game, sport, play, performance; in pl. athletics. Saying: *'Si bya muzannyo.'* (*'It is not a joke.', meaning 'This is a serious matter.'*) omuzannyo gwa ssemufu children's game (*pretending to be dead*)
omuze *n3* bad habit
omuzeeyi *n1* old person
omuzeyituuni *n3* olive tree (*as in the Bible*) *Olea europea*
omuzibe *n1* blind person omuzibe w'amaaso blind person omuzibe w'amatu deaf person -fuuka muzibe become blind
muzibiro blood clotted in the heart (*secondary totem of Mutima Musaggi Clan*)
omuzigiti *n3* mosque
[1]**omuzigo** *n3* (*no pl.*) ghee. Pronunciation: omuzígò eddagala ly'omuzigo ointment
[2]**omuzigo** *n3* small apartment (*in block*), doorway (*in block of apartments*), gap between incisor teeth. Pronunciation: omuzígó
[3]**Muzigo** May. Pronunciation: Muzígò

omuzigu *n1* murderous thief
omuziisa *n3* tendon of the back
omuziki (*also* omumuziki) *n1* music
[1]**omuziku** *n1* person with gonorrhoea
omuzimbandegeya *n3* type of plant (*used for hedges and making ropes*) *Sesbania sesban*. Meaning: *'The weaver bird builds nests from it.'*
omuzimbi *n1* builder
omuzimu *n3* spirit of departed person, ghost, apparition
muzimya-mwoto *n1* (*pl.* bazimya-mwoto) fireman
omuzinda *n3* African breadfruit tree *Treculia africana*
omuzindaalo *n3* funnel, loudspeaker, megaphone (= omubinikiro)
omuzindo *n3* raid, invasion
omuzinga *n3* something cylindrical, artillery piece, cannon omuzinga (gw'enjuki) beehive
muzinge *n1* peacock
omuzingo *n3* roll omuzingo gw'endagala pile of folded banana leaves
omuzingu *n3* type of tree (*anti-malarial*) *Hallea*
omuzinyi *n1* dancer
omuzinzi *n1* raider, invader
omuziŋŋamu *n1* paralysed person
omuziŋŋoonyo *n3* midrib of banana leaf (= omugoŋŋoonyo)
[1]**omuzira** *n1* brave person, hero. Pronunciation: omuzírá
[2]**omuzira** *n3* (*no pl.*) hail, snow, ice, frost. Pronunciation: omuzírá
[3]**omuzira** *n3* shout of approval; in pl. cheers. Pronunciation: omuzírà -kuba emizira cheer
omuziro *n3* totem
omuziru *n3* type of tree (*with edible fruit 'enziru'*) *Pseudospondias microcarpa*
omuziziko *n3* something placed to prevent movement, barrier (*eg. log or banana trunk placed to prevent movement of beans drying on mat*), prop (*eg. placed under a patient's head*)
omuzizo *n3* taboo -a omuzizo *adj* taboo, forbidden
omuzoole *n1* person having a fit of madness, crazy person, deranged person
Omuzungu *n1* white person. From: *'-zunga'* (*'be here and there', a reference to the restlessness of the early European explorers*).
muzuukizi *n1* type of plant (*medicinal; yields a dark purple dye*) *Hypoestes aristata*
omuzuukufu *n1* someone saved. See omulokole
omuzzaŋŋanda (*also* omuzzanvuma) *n3* type of tree *Shirakiopsis elliptica*. Name used in traditional medicinal to reconcile people. From: *'-zza oluganda'* (*'restore brotherhood'*). See omusasa
omuzzi w'emisango *n1* criminal, offender
omuzzukulu *n1* grandchild, descendant omuzzukulu nakabirye great-great grandchild

omuzzukulu omulenzi **grandson** omuzzukulu omuwala **granddaughter** omuzzukulu omwana **great grandchild** muzzukulu **grandchild of** (N12), *eg. muzzukulu wange ('my grandchild')*

[1] **(o)mw'** *abbrev of* (o)mwa; mwe

[2] **Mw.** *abbrev of* Omwami *('Mr.')*

[1] **omwa** *pre* **at the home/place of**, *eg. omwa Musoke ('at Musoke's home'). Saying: 'Omwa kanyumiza temwala nkoko.' ('In the home of a good host chickens never get finished.'). Can be used before an infinitive to describe the place within which an activity is performed (the resulting nouns are in noun class n18). Examples:* omw'okunaabira **washing place** *(for people)*, omw'okuzannyira **place for playing within**, omw'okwoleza **washing place** *(for things).*

[2] **-mwa** *vt* (-mwedde) **shave**

[3] **-eemwa** *vr* **shave oneself**

omwabwe *adv* **inside their place/home** (N11.5), *eg. Omwabwe mulimu ettaala. ('There is a light in their home.')*

Omwadiventi *n1* (*pl.* Abaadiventi) **Seventh-Day Adventist**

omwaffe *adv* **inside our place/home** (N11.5)

Omwafirika *n1* (*pl.* Abaafirika) **African** *(person)*

omwagaagavu *See* -yagaagavu

omwagaanya *n3* **gap, opening**

omwagalwa *n1* (*pl.* baagalwa) **boyfriend** *(or girlfriend) of (with pos N12), eg. omwagalwa wange ('my boyfriend'),* **loved one, beloved** omwagalwa omulenzi **boyfriend** omwagalwa omuwala **girlfriend**

omwagazi *n1* (*pl.* abaagazi) **lover** omwagazi w'omupiira **football lover**

omwaka *n3* **year** omwaka gw'ebyensimbi **financial year** omwaka ogujja **next year** omwaka oguyise **last year** -a buli omwaka *adj* **annual**

omwala *n3* **stream, water channel** *(eg. through a swamp)*

omwali **in which there was/were**. *Can be equivalent to conjunction* **where** (N7.2).

omwaliiro *n3* (*pl.* emyaliiro) **something spread out for a purpose, lining, covering, layer** omwaliiro gw'ekizimbe **storey** *(of a multistorey building)* omwaliiro gw'essenke **layer of grass** *(placed within a cover over a termite mound, the termites then sliding down into a hole prepared to receive them)* omwaliiro gw'olupapula **page** *(eg. of a book)*

mwalimu **there was/were** *(within)*

omwalo *n3* **harbour, port, landing** (place) *(general area where boats are landed)*

mwamba *n9* **file** *(the tool)* ennyumba eya mwamba **rectangular house with corrugated iron roof**

Omwamerika *n1* (*pl.* Abaamerika) **American** *(person)*

omwami *n1* (*pl.* abaami) **master, chief**, *eg. omwami*

w'ekyalo *('village chief')*, **husband**, *eg. omwami wa Maria ('Mary's husband'); in pl.* **gents** *(toilet)* Mwami *title (abbrev* Mw.) **Mister**, *eg. Mw. Musoke ('Mr. Musoke')* omwami w'ekyalo **village chief**

omwammwe *adv* **inside your place/home** (N11.5)

omwana *n1* (*pl.* abaana) **child** mwana **child of** (N12), *eg. omwana wange ('my child')* omwana omuwala **daughter** omwana w'emabega *(also* omwana w'okubiri*)* **placenta** mwana wattu *form of address* **My friend., My mate.** abaana b'eŋŋoma *(also* abaana ba mujaguzo*)* **royal family**

mwanaakufe *n1* **type of banana** *(used for making matooke). See* mbwazirume

omwange *adv* **in my place/home** (N11.5)

omwango *n3* **frame** omwango gw'eddirisa **window frame** omwango gw'oluggi **door frame**

omwangu *See* -yangu

omwanjuzi *n1* (*pl.* abaanjuzi) **announcer** omwanjuzi w'omukolo **master of ceremonies**

mwannyi- *n1* (*pl.* bannyi-) **brother/sister of** *(of the other gender)* (N12). *The singular forms are:* mwannyinaze **my brother/sister**, mwannyoko **your brother/sister**, mwannyina **her brother, his sister**, mwannyinaffe **our brother/sister**, mwannyinammwe **your brother/sister**, mwannyinaabwe **their brother/sister**.

omwasa *n3* **type of tree** *(used for making paddles) Beilschmiedia ugandensis*

omwasi *n3* **sneeze**

mwasuze mutyanno? *greeting* **How did you** *pl.* **spend the night?, Good morning.** (N28)

omwatiikirivu *n1* (*pl.* abaatiikirivu) **distinguished person**

mwattu *abbrev of* mwana wattu

omwavu *n1* (*pl.* abaavu) **poor person** omwavu lunkupe **destitute person** omwavu w'empisa **bad-mannered person**

omwawufu *See* -yawufu

omwawule *n1* (*pl.* abaawule) **ordained person, reverend, minister, priest**

omwazi w'obuliri *n1* (*pl.* abaazi w'obuliri) **bed-maker**

[1] **mwe** *equivalent to various parts of speech in English (conjunction, relative pronoun, etc.)* (N10.2): (1) **in which, where**, *eg. Eyo kabada mwe muli ebitabo. ('That is the cupboard in which the books are.')*; (2) *Can be equivalent to short adverbial phrases of emphasis, eg. Akambe kali mu kabada? Yee, mwe kali. ('Is the knife in the cupboard? Yes, it is in there.').*

[2] **mwe-** *pro* **you** *pl.* (N7.3), *eg, mwenna ('all of you').* *See* mmwe

omwebafu *See* -eebafu; omulokole

mwebale **thank you** *pl.*

mwebaze **thank her/him**

-mwedde *See* -mwa

omweganza *n3* **type of small tree with large**

leaves (*in swamps*) *Macaranga schweinfurthii*
omwegendereza *n1* (*pl.* abeegendereza)
careful/cautious person
omwejalabi *n1* person enjoying luxury
omwekalakaasi *n1* (*pl.* abeekalakaasi)
demonstrator (*for a cause*)
omwekanasi *n1* (*pl.* abeekanasi) **finicky/fastidious person**
mwekka *det/pro* **only you, by yourselves**
mwembi *det/pro* **both (of you** *pl.*)
-mwemwetuka (*also* -mwetuka) *vi* (-mwemwetuse)
burst into laughter
mwenda *n3/num* **nine** -a omwenda *adj* **ninth**
omwene *n3* **marsh cane rat**
omwenge *n3* **alcoholic drink, beer, spirit**
omwenge omuganda (*also* omwenge bigere)
(Kiganda) banana beer   omwenge omuka **strong drink** (*alcoholic*)
omwenkanonkano *n3* **equality**
mwenna *det/pro* **all (of you** *pl.*)
omwennyango *n3* **stinging nettle** *Urtica massaica*
mwennyini *pro* **yourselves**   mmwe mwennyini **you yourselves**
-mwenya *vi* (-mwenye) **smile**
-mwenyamwenya *vi* (-mwenyemwenye) **smile often**
-mwenyereketa *vi* (-mwenyerekese) **overdo laughing or smiling**
omwenzi *n1* (*pl.* abenzi) **adulterer, fornicator**
omwepansi *n1* (*pl.* abeepansi) **pompous person, self-important person**
omwera *n3* (*pl.* emyera) **something unattached** -a omwera *adj* **loose**, *eg. amatooke ag'omwera ('loose plantains' – not attached to a hand)*, **unstrung** (*of coins, referring to the coins with holes that were formerly used*)
mweraba *goodbye pl.*
mweramannyo *n1* type of tree *Acacia sieberiana*
omwereere *See* -yereere
[1]omweru *adj. See* -yeru
[2]omweru *n1* (*pl.* abeeru) **light-skinned person**
omwesigwa *n1* (*pl.* abeesigwa) **reliable person, trustworthy person, faithful person**
omwesimbu *n1* (*pl.* abeesimbu) **upright** (*or straightforward*) **person**
omweso *n3* **type of board game** (*played with seeds 'empiki' or stones; a compartment on an omweso board is 'essa'*), **chess**. *Traditionally, a ritual game of omweso forms part of the installation ceremony of kings (who win). See* empiki
omwetango *n3* **type of plant** (*used to clean hands after peeling plantains*) *Chenopodium opulifolium*
omwetegefu *n1* (*pl.* abeetegefu) **someone ready or prepared**
omwetissi *n1* (*pl.* abeetissi) **person who carries, porter**
omwetoowaze *n1* (*pl.* abeetoowaze) **humble person**

omwetoozitoozi *n1* (*pl.* abeetoozitoozi) **petty thief, pilferer**
-mwetuka *vi* (-mwetuse) **burst into laughter**
omwewozi *n1* (*pl.* abeewozi) **borrower** (*of money*)
omwewulize *n1* (*pl.* abeewulize) **arrogant person, snob**
omweyimirizi *n1* (*pl.* abeeyimirizi) **guarantor**
[1]omwezi *n1* (*pl.* abeezi) **sweeper**. *Pronunciation*: omwézí
[2]omwezi *n3* (*pl.* emyezi) **moon, month**. *Pronunciation*: omwêzi   omwezi gw'eggabogabo **full moon**   omwezi ogubonese **new moon**   -lwala omwezi **menstruate**
omwiko (*also* omuyiko) *n3* **trowel** (*for brick-laying*)
[1]omwo *adv* **in there**
[2]omwo *pro* **where there is/are** (*within*). *Can be equivalent to conjunction* **where** (*N7.2*).
omwogererwa *n3* **microphone**
omwogezi *n1* (*pl.* aboogezi) **speaker, spokesperson**
omwokerezi *n1* (*pl.* abookerezi) **arsonist, incendiary**
omwoko *n3* **pole for punting a canoe**
omwokye *See* -yokye
omwoleso *n3* **exhibit, exhibition, display, demonstration, fair**
omwoloola *n3. Two species of tree:* (1) **flame tree** *Delonix regia;* (2) **type of small savannah tree** *Entada abyssinica. The name for the indigenous 'Entada' is likely original, becoming attached to the introduced 'Delonix' because of certain similarities in appearance (eg. leaves, pod).*
omwonoonefu *n1* (*pl.* aboonoonefu) **spoilt person**
omwonoonyi *n1* (*pl.* aboonoonyi) **sinner, evildoer**
omwoyo *n3* (1) **life force** (*of the living body*), **spirit** (*of a person*), **soul;** (2) **spirit** (*in general*)   omwoyo -luma **be broken-hearted**   omwoyo omubi **demon**   Omwoyo Omutukuvu **Holy Spirit**   -ggwaamu omwoyo **lose hope**   -gumya omwoyo **comfort**   -ssaako (*or* -teekako) omwoyo **concentrate**   -ssaayo omwoyo **concentrate**   -suulira omwoyo **think about** (*especially a person*)
emyaliiro *pl. of* omwaliiro
-myamyansa *vi* (-myamyansizza) **flash on and off, gleam, flicker**
-myansa *vi* (-myansizza) **flash, shoot** (*of pain*)
emyera *See* omwera
-myufu *adj* **red**   bbogoya omumyufu **red bbogoya** (*type of desert banana*)
-myufumyufu *adj* **reddish**
[1]-myuka *vi* (-myuse) **be(come) red, blush**. *Pronunciation*: okumyúká
[2]-myuka *vit* (-myuse) **be deputy (to)**. *Pronunciation*: okumyúká
-myukirivu *adj* **reddish**
-myumyula *vt* (-myumyudde) **tighten**
emyungu *See* omungu
-myusa *vt* (-myusizza) **make red**

N,n

n' *abbrev of* na; ne

¹**na** *conj/pre* **and, with, including.** (**N5**). *Can be equivalent to adverbs* **as well, also, too.** *Can be a prefix* **na-** (**N10.1**), *eg. (1)* nange *('with me'); (2)* nakyo *('and it').* n'akatono *(also* wadde n'akatono*)* **not even a little**

²**-na** *num* **four** (**N8.1**). *Takes numeral concord* (**N4**), *eg. (1)* abantu bana *('four people'); (2)* emiti ena *('four trees'). See* okuna ana **four, forty.** (**N8.1**)

-naaba *vi* (-naabye) **wash** (*oneself*), **take a dust bath** (*of a chicken*) -naaba eddagala **take a herbal bath**

-naabira *vt* (-naabidde) **wash oneself in/at,** *eg.* Anaabira bweru. (*'She is washing outside.'*). *See* okunaabira

-naabisa *vt* (-naabisizza) **wash with,** *eg.* Anaabisa ssabbuuni. (*'She is washing with soap.'*)

-naaliza *vt* (-naalizza) **wash** (*someone*) **in/at,** *eg.* Ajja kunaaliza omwana mu bbenseni. (*'She will wash the baby in the basin.'*)

-naanaagira *vi* (-naanaagidde) **stutter, stammer**

-naanika *vt* (-naanise) **put on** (*something tight in dressing, eg. shoe, bracelet*), **slip on(to),** *eg.* Yamunaanika empeta eya zaabu ku ngalo. (*'He slipped a gold ring onto her finger.'*)

-naanuuka *vi* (-naanuuse) **be stretched, be elastic, be slimy**

-naanuula *vt* (-naanudde) **stretch** (*something elastic or sticky*)

-naanya *vi* (-naanyizza) **be indolent, not put one's mind on what one is doing**

naaawe and/with you *si.*

-naaza *vt* (naazizza) **wash** (*someone*) **-naazaako** (-naazizzaako) **cleanse spiritually**

nabo and/with them

nabusa *n1* **type of banana** (*used for making matooke*)

nabwo and/with them

babyo and/with them

naddala *adv* **especially, particularly**

naffe and/with us

-nafu *adj* **weak, feeble, impotent**

-nafuwa *vi* (-nafuye) **become weak**

-nafuya *vt* (-nafuyizza) **weaken, enfeeble**

nago and/with them

nagunogujwa *adv* **up to now**

nagwo and/with them

nagyo and/with them

nakabirye *See* omuzzukulu

Nakaggwa *n1 title* **name given to female child following a child following twins**

nako and/with it

-naku *adj* **poor, distressed**

-nakuwala *vi* (-nakuwadde) **be(come) miserable, be(come) distressed, be(come) depressed** (*mentally*)

-nakuwavu *adj* **miserable, distressed, depressed** (*mentally*)

-nakuwaza *vt* (-nakuwazza) **cause distress to**

nakwo and/with it

nakyo and/with it

nalwo and/with it

nalwo and/with it

nambaale *n1* **type of bean**

nammwe and/with you *pl.*

-nana *vi* (-nanye) **be/look pleasing, be well done**

nange and/with me

nate *adv/conj* **again, and also**

natwo and/with it

Nawume *n1* **Naomi**

¹**naye** *conj* **but, however**

²**naye and her/him, with her/him**

nayikonto *n9* **hand pump** (*for drawing water*), **borehole** (*for water*)

nayo and/with it

nazo and/with them

¹**enda** *n9* **womb** ow'enda emu *n1* **child of the same mother**

²**-(y)enda** *See* -yenda

endaawe *adj* **castrated** (*stem* -laawe)

¹**endaba** *n9* (*no pl.*) **way of seeing**

²**ndaba I see** (*stem* -laba)

endabika *n9* (*no pl.*) **appearance, impression**

endabirira *n9* (*no pl.*) **way of looking after, superintendence**

endabirwamu *n9* **mirror** endabirwamu y'emmotoka **windscreen**

ndabye I have seen (*stem* -laba)

ndaga I show (*stem* -laga)

endagaano *n9* **agreement, contract, covenant, treaty** Endagaano Empya **New Testament** Endagaano Enkadde **Old Testament**

endagala *See* olulagala

endaggu *n9* **type of yam** (*fist-sized, bristly*) Dioscorea abyssinica-rotundata

endagi *n9* **small savannah tree** Combretum molle

endagiriro *n9* **instruction, guideline, directory, direction(s), indication, index, address**

endago *See* olulago

endala *See* -lala

endali *n9* **squint** ow'endali *n1* **person with a squint**

endalu *See* -lalu

endasi *n9* **strength** (*of person or animal*) -ddamu endasi **regain strength** (*after illness*)

endeerwe *n9* **type of white mushroom** (*grows on dung*)

endege *n9* **small bell** (*tied on dancer, baby, medium, etc.*)

endegeya *n9* **weaver bird**

endeku *n9* **small gourd with a neck.** *There are many varieties used for various purposes, eg. drinking vessel, bowl, container for storing* *grasshoppers, etc.).*

¹endere *n9* **flute, pipe.** *Pronunciation*: endérè

²endere *n10* **slices of dried food** (*for storage*); *pl.* of olulere. *See* olulere. *Pronunciation*: endéré

enderema *n9* **creeping/twining herb** (*with edible leaves*) *Basella alba*

¹-ndi *pro.* **Indicates uncertainty in naming.** *See* gindi; gundi

²ndi I am (*stem* -li)

endibota *n9* **bale** (*eg. of cotton or clothing*)

endiga *n9* **sheep** endiga enkazi **ewe**

endigida *n9* **way of moving to a rhythm, dancing**

endiima *n9* **extreme speed,** *eg. Yali adduka endiima emmotoka n'emulemerera.* (*'He was overspeeding and lost control of the car.'*) -kuba endiima **give a good kick** (*in football*)

endiirwa enva endiirwa *n10* **greens** (*served with the main food 'emmere'*)

endiisa *n9* (*no pl.*) **way of feeding.** *See* ennyonyi

ndiizi *n1* (*pl.* bu ndiizi) **type of small desert banana**

ndikungulu *n12* **charm put in a drum.** *Meaning: 'I am on top.'* − *onomatopeic, from the sound made by a charm when a drum is shaken.* (= akawaulunguta)

endingidi *n9* **one-stringed fiddle, tube fiddle**

ndiwulira *n1* (1) **maggot found in maize grains;** (2) **obstinate person who will not listen to advice.** *Meaning: 'I will hear later.'*

endobo *n9* **bucket** -kuba endobo **tackle hard** (*in football*), **trip up** (*in wrestling*) -eekuba endobo **contradict oneself**

endobolo *n9* **share for a chief** (*of produce, or income from produce*) endobolo ekimu eky'ekkumi **tythe** (*for the church, tenth of income*)

endoddo *n9* **log** (*for timber*)

Ndogoobukaba *n9* **building at Kasubi in which drums are housed**

endogoyi *n9* **donkey**

endokwa *n9* **seedling, cutting, sprout, shoot**

endongo *n9* **lyre** (*two-barred stringed musical instrument with crossbar*), **guitar** (= entongooli)

endowooza *n9* (*no pl.*) **way of thinking, theory, assumption, concept, view, opinion, attitude**

endu *n9* **bud on stump of banana plant**

ndudde I was delayed, I have taken long (*stem* -lwa)

nduka I weave (*stem* -luka)

endukusa (*also* ensukusa) *n9* **young shoot of banana plant** (*originally Buddu dialect*)

enduli *n9* **stem** (*of a plant*), **trunk**

endusu *See* -kenena

enduulu *n10* **ululation, alarm call** -dduukirira enduulu **ululate** (*requesting people to help*) -eekubira enduulu **appeal on one's own behalf** -kuba enduulu **ululate, raise the alarm** -kubira enduulu **raise the alarm against** (*someone*)

enduusi *See* -luusi

ndwa (*also* ndwawo) **I delay, I take time** (*stems* -lwa; -lwawo)

endwadde *n9* **disease** endwadde y'enjovu **elephantiasis** endwadde y'obukaba **venereal disease** endwadde y'olukonvuba **incurable disease**

ndwala I become ill (*stem* -lwala)

¹endya *n9* **way of eating, diet**

²ndya I eat (*stem* -lya)

endyo *See* olulyo

ne *conj/pre* **and, with, also.** (**N5**). *Introduces the narrative tense* (**N16**). ne bwe **even if,** *eg. Ne bw'anajja, sijja kumulaba.* (*'Even if she comes, I will not see her.'*)

nedda *interj* **no**

neemu (= n'emu **N8.1**) *num* **and one,** *eg. kkumi neemu* (*'eleven'*)

-neguka *vi* (-neguse) (1) **slip over** (*to the side when walking*), **give way** (*of the foot*), *eg. Nnali ntambula ne nneguka.* (*'I was walking and my foot gave way.'*); (2) **become partially broken,** *eg. Ettabi lineguse.* (*'The branch is broken.'* - *and left dangling*) omutwe -neguka **fall over** (*of the head, when dozing off when seated*)

-nekaaneka (*also* -nekaanekana) *vi* (-neseenese) **be resplendent, be dressed to perfection**

-nene *adj* (eddene *n5*) **big, large, long** (*of time*), **fat** (*of a person*)

-nenenŋana *vi* (-nenenŋanye) **quarrel**

¹-nenya *vt* (-nenyezza) **blame, reproach, scold**

²-eenenya *vi* **say sorry,** *eg. Musoke yeenenyezza.* (*'Musoke has said sorry.'*), **blame oneself, repent, confess**

-eenenyereza *vt* (-eenenyerezza) **apologise to,** *eg. Musoke yeenenyereza Mukasa.* (*'Musoke apologised to Mukasa.'*)

-eenenyeza *vr* (-eenenyezza) **say sorry,** *eg. Musoke yeenenyezza.* (*'Musoke has said sorry.'*)

-nenyezebwa *vi* (-nenyezeddwa) **be blamed**

newankubadde (*also* newaakubadde, wadde) *conj* **although, even though, despite**

enfaana *n9* **round worm** (*found in gut; Ascaris*)

enfaanana *n1* (*no pl.*) **resemblance, likeness, looks**

enfikkira *n9* **remainder, balance** (*from payment*)

enfissi *n9* **balance** (*from payment*), **change, remainder, surplus** -a enfissi *adj* **surplus, left-over**

enfudu *n9* **tortoise, turtle**

enfuga *n9* **way of ruling/governing** enfuga eya nnakyemalira **dictatorship, tyranny**

enfumba *n9* **way of cooking, recipe**

enfumbe *See* -fumbe

enfumo *See* olufumo

enfuna *n9* **income**

enfunyiro *See* olufunyiro

enfuufu *n1* (*no pl.*) **dust**

¹enfuuzi *n9* (*pl.* abaana enfuuzi) **orphan** (*one who has lost both parents*). *Pronunciation*: enfúùzi

²enfuuzi *n9* **barkcloth torch/taper** (*made from 2 or*

ng'

3 *pieces of interwoven barkcloth*). *Pronunciation*: enfúúzí

ng' *abbrev of* nga

¹nga *adv* (1) **about**, *eg. Abantu nga bataano bakola.* (*'About five people are working.'*); (2) (*in exclamations*) **how** (**N26**), *eg. Nga mulungi nnyo!* (*'How beautiful she is!'*). As *suffix* **-nga**: (1) (*on many verbs*) indicates repetitive or habitual action (**N18**), *eg. Nnafumbanga buli lunaku.* (*'I used to cook every day.'*); (2) (*on verb '-li'* **-linga**) *means* **be likely** *or is equivalent to adverb* **probably** (**N20.1**), *eg. Alinga akola.* (*'She is probably working'*). Nga kitalo. **I am very sorry.** Ng'olabye. (*pl.* Nga mulabye.) **How tragic.**

²nga *conj* **when, while, if, whether, like.** (**N25.3, N26**), *eg.* (1) *Yambala bulungi ng'ogenda mu ssomero.* (*'Dress properly when you go to school.'*); (2) *Simanyi nga waali.* (*'I do not know if he is here.'*); (3) *Ayogera ng'Omungereza.* (*'She speaks like a Britain.'*). *'nga'* can be equivalent to the English present participle, *eg. Nnabasanga nga bagula mu katale.* (*'I found them shopping in the market.'*). *'nga'* with the *'not yet' tense* (**N18**) is equivalent to conjunctions **before, until** (**25.3**), *eg. Nga tonnagenda Kampala, sooka oyoze engoye.* (*'Before you go to Kampala, wash the clothes.'*) nga ... bwe **as, while, since.** (**N27**), *eg. Nga bwe bamanyiganye, baleke bakolere wamu.* (*'Since they know one another, let them work together.'*)

³enga *n. See* oluga

⁴nga *pre* **on** (*with date*), *eg. Jjangu wano mu Maaci nga bbiri.* (*'Come here on the second of March.'*)

engaba *n9* (*no pl.*) **distribution**

engabanya *n9* (*no pl.*) **way of distributing**

engabi *n9* **bushbuck** Kika kya Ngabi **Bushbuck Clan.** *There are two sections in the clan* Ngabi Ennyunga *and* Ngabi Nsamba. *'Ennyunga' is from '-yunga'* (*'set a bone'*), *because the people are renouned for bonesetting. A common plant used for this purpose is 'keeyeeyo'.*

engabo *n9* **shield.** *Saying:* '*Kabaka aggye omukono ku ngabo.* (*'The Kabaka has removed his hand from the shield.', meaning 'The Kabaka has passed away.'*). *See* Ababiito engabo ya Kabaka **type of cactus** *Opuntia ficus-indica*

engajaba *n9* **lazy person, person who won't work** -a engajaba *adj* **lazy, useless**

engalabi *n9* **type of long drum**

engali *See* olugali

engalo *See* olugalo

engassi *n9* (*no pl.*) **compensation, damages, fine** -wa engassi **pay damages**

engatto *n9* **shoe, sandal** engatto z'akakondo **high-heeled shoes** engatto za lusejjera **canvas shoes**

engave *See* olugave

-nge *See* nze

engege *n9* (1) **tilapia**; (2) **two hundred shilling coin** (*slang; from the fish shown on the coin*)

¹engera -a engera *adj* **without a handle** (*eg. ekiso eky'engera* (*'knife without a handle'*). *Saying:* '*Tusigadde ngera.'* (*'What a loss.'* – *referring to a death*)

²engera *n9* **way of measuring**

³-(y)engera *See* -yengera

⁴-(y)ongera *See* -yongera

engeraageranya *n9* **estimate**

engeregeze *n10* **dribble** (*of saliva*)

engereka *n9* (*no pl.*) **grading, estimate** engereka y'ensimbi **budget** amannyo ag'engereka **unevenly spaced teeth, overlapping teeth**

-(y)engerera *See* -yengerera

-ngereza *adj* **English, British**

engeri *n9* **way, manner, kind, variety** engeri y'okuzimba **architecture** engeri y'okwogera **accent** mu ngeri y'emu **in the same way, likewise**

engero *See* olugero

-(y)engevu *See* -yengevu

engeye *n9* **black and white colobus monkey**

-(y)ongeza *See* -yongeza

engezi *n9* **current** (*in water*)

-ngi *adj* (nnyingi *n10*) **many, much, a lot of.** (**N3**)

engiri *n9* **warthog**

¹engo *n9* **leopard**

²engo *See* olugo

engogo *See* olugogo

engolo *n9* **monstrous imaginery figure** (*used to frighten children*) -kuba engolo **wrap on the head**

engoye olugoye

engozi *n9* **cloth for carrying babies on the back**

engozoobana *n9* (*no pl.*) **trouble** (*in affairs*), **difficulties, complications**

-(y)angu *See* -yangu

engugu *n9* (a lot of) **luggage**

engule *n9* **crown** engule y'amaggwa **crown of thorns**

nguli *invariable adj* **the late** (*referring to someone who has been dead for some time*), *eg. Nguli Musoke* (*'the late Musoke'*). *See* omugenzi

engulu *adv* **uphill** engulu ku lusozi **up the hill** -dda engulu **regain consciousness**

enguudo *See* oluguudo

enguuli *n9* (*no pl.*) **Ugandan gin, waragi**

¹enguwa *See* oluguwa

²-(y)anguwa *See* -yanguwa

-(y)anguya *See* -yanguya

-yanguyira *See* -yanguyira

-(y)anguyiriza *See* -yanguyiriza

-(y)anguyisa *See* -yanguyisa

-(y)anguyiza *See* -yanguyiza

enguzi *n9* (*no pl.*) **bribe, bribery** -fuuka omuli w'enguzi **start to take bribes** -lya enguzi **take a bribe** omuli w'enguzi *n1* **person who takes bribes**

engwira *See* -gwira ettooke ery'engwira **bunch of bananas** (*one that has come down without human* *agency*)

ani? *interr* (*pl.* baani?) **who?, whom?** (N13)   -a ani
whose?, *eg. Engatto zino z'ani? ('Whose shoes are
these?')*

-(y)aniikiriza *See* -yaniikiriza

-(y)anika *See* -yanika

-(y)aniriza *See* -yaniriza

-(y)anjaala *See* -yanjaala

enjaba *n9* **crab**   enjaba y'obusagwa **scorpion**

enjabifu *See* -yabifu

enjabirivu *See* -yabirivu

enjaga (*also* enjaaye) *n9* (*no pl.*) **cannabis**

enjagaagavu *See* -yagaagavu

enjagi *n9* **fruit of omutula** (= entula)

[1]**enjala** *n9* (*no pl.*) **hunger, famine, starvation.**
Pronunciation: enjálá   enjala -luma **be hungry**

[2]**enjala** *See* olwala ('nail'). *Pronunciation*: enjálà

[3]**-(y)anjala** *See* -yanjala

enjaliire *See* -yaliire

enjaliiro *See* olwaliiro

enjasa *See* olwasa

enjatifu *See* -yatifu

enjatika *See* olwatika

enjatula *n9* **way of pronouncing words**   Enjatula
Prayer Book (*of Anglicans*)

enjatuza *n9* **vowel**

enjawufu *See* -yawufu

enjawukana *n9* **separation**

enjawulo *n9* **difference**   -a enjawulo *adj* **different,
special**   kya njawulo **differently**

enjawuza *n9* **separation**

enjaza *n9* **reedbuck**

enjazi *See* olwazi

enjazike *See* -yazike

enjaziyazi *See* olwaziyazi

enje *n9* **seed of omuwafu** (*used as spinning top*)

-(y)enjeera *See* -yenjeera

-(y)enjeerera *See* -yenjeerera

enjegere *See* olujegere

njera I **sweep** (*stem* -yera)

enjereere *See* -yereere

enjeru *See* -yeru

njeruka *n1* **special type of light coloured barkcloth**
(*sown together with dark coloured thread; worn by
royals*)

enjeyo *See* olweyo

njigaayigana I **am restless** (*stem* -yigaayigana)

njigga I **hunt** (*stem* -yigga)

njigganya I **harass** (*stem* -yigganya)

njigiikiriza I **am propping up** (*stem* -yiigikiriza)

[1]**enjigiriza** *n9* (*no pl.*) **way of teaching,
interpretation**

[2]**njigiriza** I **teach** (*stem* -yigiriza)

enjiibwa *n9* **pigeon**

[1]**enjiiya** *n9* **way of inventing or composing**

[2]**njiiya** I **invent** (*stem* -yiiya)

enjiri *n9* **gospel**

enjobe *n9* **sitatunga**

enjoga *n9* **hyrax**

enjogera *n9* **way of speaking, saying, proverb,
speech, pronunciation, accent**

enjoka *n10* **internal/tummy pain, cramps,
intestinal worms**   enjoka ensaanuusi **recurring
internal pain**   enjoka ensajja **gonorrhoea**   enjoka
ez'eddumi **menstrual pains**   enjoka zi nnamumwa
tapeworm

enjokye *See* -yokye

enjokyo *n10* **tribal marks on body** (*made by
burning; one* oluyokyo)

enjola *n9* **groove, cut on waist** (*decoration formerly
used by women*); *in pl.* **thread** (*of a screw*), **tread**
(*of a tyre*)

enjole *n9* **corpse of the Kabaka**   enjole y'essubi
bundle of grass (*for thatching*)

enjovu *n9* **elephant**

enjoya *See* olwoya

enju *n9* (*pl.* enju *n10, or* amayu *n6*) **house**

enjuba *n9* **sun**   enjuba y'eggi **egg yolk**

enjuki *n9* **bee.** *Saying: 'Enjuki yeetala.' ('The bee is
buzzing.' – a sign that visitors will come).*   -eesiba
enjuki ku kugulu **tie bee on leg** (*done by the chief
brewer; it is said to prevent other bees from
coming; the bee is subsequently released*)

-(y)anjula *See* -yanjula

enjulu *n9* **fibre/cane from ekiyulu plant** (*used for
making baskets and shields*)

-(y)anjulukuka *See* -yanjulukuka

-(y)anjulula *See* -yanjulula

-(y)anjuluza *See* -yanjuluza

enjuyi *See* oluuyi

enjwanjwa   ebya njwanjwa *n8* **unfounded
assertions**

nkaaga *n9/num* **sixty**

enkaayana *n9* **argument, controversy**

enkabala *n9* (*no pl.*) **deep digging**

enkago *n9* (1) **African rubber tree** (*name used
when the tree is used for timber*) Funtumia
africana; (2) **'female' type of banana.** *See* banana
(*types of*) (*in Part 3 of the dictionary*)

enkaka *n9* (*no pl.*) **jaundice**

enkakasa *n9* (*no pl.*) **way of proving**

enkakkamu *See* -kkakkamu

enkalakkalira *n9* (*no pl.*) **permanence**   -a
enkalakkalira *adj* **permanent,** *eg. omukozi
ow'enkalakkalira ('permanent employee')*

enkalala *See* olukalala

enkalamata *n9* **extreme thirst**

enkali *n9* (*no pl.*) (*rather impolite*) **urine**

enkaliriza (*also* enkalirira) *n9/adv* **stare, with a
fixed stare**   -tunula enkaliriza **glare**   -tunuulira
enkaliriza **examine very carefully, scrutinise,
glare at**

enkalu *See* -kalu

enkambi *n9* **military encampment**

enkambo *n9* **type of bird**

enkampa *n10* **stockings** (*for a man*) (*one* olukampa)

-(y)enkana *See* -yenkana

enkandaggo *n9* self-standing ladder (*in form of a tripod*)

enkanga *n9* basket (*used for carrying fish, storage of grasshoppers or beans, etc.; woven from obuyanja*)

enkanja *n10* scum (*from making banana beer or amalwa*), **(unwanted) froth, dregs, sediment**

-(y)enkanya *See* -yenkanya

-(y)enkanyankanya *See* -yenkanyankanya

enkanyanya *See* olukanyanya

enkasi *n9* paddle, oar

enkata *n9* pad (*on head for load*)

enkato *See* olukato

enkazaluggya *n9* sparrow. *Meaning: 'It dries up the courtyard.'*

enkebera *n9* way of examining

enkebuka *n9* human excrement

enkeera *adv* morning next day

enkejje *n9* type of small fish *Haplochromis*

enkende *See* olukende

enkenene *n9* (1) wild raspberry (*plant; fruit*) *Rubus*; (2) mulberry (*food of silkworms*) *Morus alba*

enkenyera *n9* (*no pl.*) something unsatisfactory failure to be convinced -limu enkenyera have misgivings, be in poor health, *eg. Alimu enkenyera. ('He is in poor health.')* -sigalamu enkenyera be unconvinced -wulira enkenyera feel unwell

enkerebwe *n9* tree squirrel

enkessi *n9* way of spying -suuliza enkessi look for on behalf of

enkiiko *See* olukiiko

enkima *n9* monkey (*any type*), vervet monkey enkima nnakabugo red-tailed monkey Kika ky'Enkima Monkey Clan. *Members of this clan do not prostrate themselves before the Kabaka. This is because they are ritual grandfathers of the royal line, starting with Kabaka Kimera. Kimera was looked after by Katumba, a member of this clan, when he was a baby in Bunyoro (N29). See* Katumba

enkindo *See* olukindo

enkindukindu *See* olukindukindu

enkinga *n9* fly whisk (*made from a tail*)

enkiringi *n9* droppings (*of goats, rabbits, etc.*)

enkiso *n9* (*no pl.*) secrecy -a enkiso *adj* secret mu nkiso secretly

enkizi *n9* spinal cord

enkizo *n9* advantage (*over another person*) -lya enkizo do/be better than (*someone else*)

¹enkoba *n9* type of tree *Lovoa brownii*

²enkoba *See* olukoba

enkobe *n9* baboon

enkobogo *n9* bow legs ow'enkobogo *n1* person with bow legs

enkodomali *n9* stupid person. *Saying:*

'Enkodomali eyita enkoko ennyama?' ('He serves chicken as cow meat?')

enkofu *n9* guinea fowl

enkoko *n9* chicken enkoko empanga cockerel (*male chicken*), cock enkoko enkulu (1) adult chicken; (2) gizzard (*traditionally only eaten by the head of the household*) enkoko ennyolo Bunyoro-type chicken enkoko enseera young hen (*before laying*) enkoko enzungu broiler, layer enkoko eŋŋanda free-range chicken

enkokobe *See* olukokobe

enkokola *See* olukokola

enkokoto *n9* (*no pl.*) concrete

enkola *n9* (*no pl.*) way of doing/working, method, design, nature (*of something inanimate*), model, form, shape, brand, technique, procedure, process, policy, practice, system

enkolagana *n9* (*no pl.*) way of working together, cooperation enkolagana y'ekyama secret dealings

enkoligo *n7* something that removes freedom when fitted, yoke, muzzle

enkolo *n9* stump of a banana plant

enkoloboze *See* olukoloboze

enkoloddoli *See* olukoloddoli

enkolokooto -wera enkolokooto pledge revenge

enkolongo *n9* squeaker catfish (*resembles 'emmale', but has tiny bones*) *Synodontis victoriae*

¹enkoma *n9* on-shore wind from Lake Victoria

²enkoma *n10* palm posts (*one olukoma*). *Pronunciation:* enkómà

enkomakoma *n9* type of shrub or small tree (*yields twine*) *Grewia mollis*

enkomamawanga *n9* pomegranate (*fruit*)

enkomera *See* olukomera

enkomerero *n9* end, finish -a enkomerero *adj* final, last

enkomyo *n9* detention, imprisonment

enkondo *n9* post, stake, peg enkondo y'ekitanda bed post

enkonge *n9* (1) tree stump; (2) moss, alga, (slimy) water weed

enkongolamabeere *n1* praying mantis. *Meaning: 'It claws at breasts.'*

enkoni *n9* pipe euphorbia (*type of succulent shrub used for fencing*) *Euphorbia tirucalli*

enkonko *See* olukonko

enkonkonamuti *n9* woodpecker. *Meaning: 'It knocks the tree.'*

enkono *See* olukono

enkonokono ow'enkonokono *n1* left-handed person

enkonyo *n9* wooden hammer (*used for beating cores of banana stem in making sponges; not common nowadays*)

enkonyogo *n9* throwing stick

enkooge *n9* fruit of omukooge

enkoola *See* olukoola*

enkoolimbo *n9* pigeon pea *Cajanus cajan*
enkoomi *n9* bonfire (*smoky slow-burning type*)
enkoona *n9* back of the head
enkoonamasonko *n9* open-billed stork. *Meaning:* '*It knocks shells.*'
enkota *n9* bunch of bananas
enkoto *n9* back of the neck, area at back of fireplace
enkovu *n9* scar
enkozesa *n9* way of using
enku *n10* firewood (*one piece* oluku)
enkuba *n9* (*no pl.*) rain   enkuba -bindabinda be about to rain   enkuba -fudemba go on and on (*of rain*)   enkuba -kankamuka (*also* enkuba -sammuka) ease up (*of rain*)   enkuba -kanyiza kutonnya rain persistently (*for days to months*)   enkuba -kya stop raining   enkuba -tokomoka rain heavily   enkuba -tonnya rain. *Saying:* '*Enkuba ejja kutonnya.*' ('*It is going to rain.*', *meaning* '*I am happy to see you.*').   enkuba -wandaggirira drizzle
enkubi *n7* mallet used in first stage of beating bark to make barkcloth (= ensaasi)
enkuggu   -a enkuggu *adj* cropped, docked (*eg. of a tail*)   akateteeyi ak'enkuggu mini-skirt
enkugiro *See* olukugiro
enkukunala *n9* (*no pl.*) way of protruding   -a enkukunala *adj* protroding, obvious, *eg. ekyokulabirako eky'enkukunala* ('*an obvious example*')   kya nkukunala obviously   obujulizi obw'enkukunala straightforward evidence   obulimba obw'enkukunala flagrant lie
enkukunyi *n9* flea   -siikuula enkukunyi create hard feelings   -eesiikuulira enkukunyi stir up trouble for oneself
enkukutu *n9* secrecy   mu nkukutu secretly
¹enkula *n9* rhinoceros. *Pronunciation:* enkúlá
²enkula *n9* (*no pl.*) way of growing, way of developing, shape, form, nature (*of something living*), character, make-up, temperament. *Pronunciation:* enkúlà
enkulaakulana *n9* (*no pl.*) development, progress
enkulukuku *n9* type of termite mound (*small, dark-coloured and very hard*)
enkulukuse *n10* traces left by a flowing liquid. *See* olukulukuse
enkulungo *n9* circle, roundabout
enkulungutanyi *n9* type of mushroom (*traditionally harvested in handfulls of nine and not eaten by women*)
enkuluze *n9* royal treasury of Buganda   enkuluze y'ebigambo dictionary   enkuluze y'ebitabo library
enkumbi *n9* hoe. *Also* small towel used by women.
enkumi *See* olukumi
enkumuliitu (*also* enkumu) *n9* (*no pl.*) great quantity, a lot, *eg. enkumuliitu y'abantu* ('*lots of people*'), multitude
enkunga *n9* type of tall spinach *Amaranthus*

enkunya *n9* (*no pl.*) way of rubbing clothes together (*when washing them*)
enkuŋŋaana *See* olukuŋŋaana
nkusibiddaawo *n9* call used in akawuna ('*tag*'). *Meaning:* '*I have tied you there.*'   empeta nkusibiddaawo engagement ring
enkusu *n9* parrot
enkuta *See* olukuta
enkuubo *See* olukuubo
enkuufiira *n9* hat, cap   enkuufiira y'omujunga fez
enkuuka *n9* massive gathering of people, big celebration, festivity
enkuukuulu *n9* candelabra tree *Euphorbia candelabrum*
enkuunokuuno *n9* pubic region (*of a man*)
enkuyanja *n9* (*no pl.*) a lot, a multitude, *eg. Enkuyanja y'abantu baali ku mbaga ya Kabaka.* ('*Lots of people attended the Kabaka's wedding.*')
enkuyege *n9* termite, white ant
enkuyo *n9* spinning top; *in pl.* game played with spinning tops by boys. *The tops are spun using* '*olutubatuba*'.
enkuyu *n9* barbel (*type of fish*)
enkwa *n9* tick
enkwagulo *See* olukwagulo
enkwakwa *n9* shoulder blade (*usually of cow*)
enkwale *n9* francolin, partridge
enkwaso *n9* bait, pincers
enkwawa *n9* armpit
enkwe *See* olukwe
enkwenge *n9* glossy starling
enkya *n9/adv* (*no pl.*) morning, tomorrow, in the morning   enkya ku makya tomorrow morning   enkya ya leero this morning
enkyakya *n10* cracked skin on foot (*especially heel*). *Believed to be caused by contact of bare feet with dew.*
enkyala *See* olukyala
enkyuka *n9* change, alteration
enkyukakyuka *n9* many changes, developments, revolution (*social or political*)   enkyukakyuka mu gavumenti changes in government   enkyukakyuka y'obudde changeable weather
enkyusa *n9* something that causes change
¹-onna *det/pro* all, any. (**N7.3**). *Takes pronominal concord* (**N4**), *eg.* (1) abantu bonna ('*all the people*'); (2) ebintu byonna ('*all the things*'). *The personal forms are irregular, declining in a similar way to* '*-okka*' (*See Column 11 of Table 2*).
²-nna- *pos n* friend/companion of (**N12**), *eg. Ente eri ne zinnaayo mu ttale.* ('*The cow is with its companions in the pasture.*'). *The singular personal forms are:* munnange my friend, munno your *si.* friend, munne her/his friend, munnaffe our friend, munnammwe your *pl.* friend, munnaabwe their friend.
Nnaabagereka *n1* title Queen of Buganda. *Also a name used in the Butiko Clan.*

Nnaabakyala *n1 title* First Lady of Buganda, the Queen

nnaakalyakaani *n1* socialism

Nnaalinnya *n1 title* Queen-sister (*co-heir of the Kabaka*)

nnaalongo *n1* type of herb (*anti-malarial*) *Justicia betonica* Nnaalongo *title* mother of twins

ennaanansi *n9* pineapple *Ananas comosus*

ennaanu *n10* slime; *pl. of* olunaanu

nnaasi (*also* nnansi) *n1* nurse

nnaava *n1* daughter of a princess

nnabaana *n1* uterus, womb

nnabaliwo *n1* morning star, Venus

nnabangogoma *n1* stick grasshopper (*resembles a praying mantis; lives in stems of banana plants*) *Pseudorhynchus lanceolatus*

nnabansasaana *n1* (*no pl.*) double banana fruit

nnabbi *n1* prophet. *From: 'nabii' (Swahili).*

nnabbubi *n1* spider, cobweb

nnabbugira *n1* mint (*herb used to flavour food*)

nnabeefunye *n1* (*no pl.*) looper caterpillar. *From: '-eefunya' ('become folded').*

nnabisaaniiko *n1* Jupiter (*the planet*)

nnabugi *n1* (*no pl.*) first strip of bark taken from barkcloth tree. *Saying: 'Baamututte nga nnabugi si mufungize. ('They took him before he could fold the bark.' – said of someone taken away by slavers)*

nnabusa *n1* type of cooking banana

nnaddibanga *n1* hammerkop (*type of bird*). *From: '-diba' ('fail to get married'). Folk belief: The use of a stick from the nest of a hammerkop as fuel when cooking for 'okwanjula' ('marriage ceremony') will result in the girl never being able to marry. The bird and its nest are traditionally protected.*

nnaggagga *n1* very rich person

Nnaggomola *n1. Name of a former chief guilty of horrible deeds.* omusango ogwa Nnaggomola horrible deed

ennagisi *n9* faeces

nnajjolo *n9* sickle

ennaka *n9* type of small edible termite

nnakabugo *n1* red-tailed monkey

nnakabululu *n1* type of banana (*used for making matooke*)

nnakalanga *n1* mythological inhabitant of Mabira forest (*dwarf with a big head*)

nnakalazi *n1* preposition (*part of speech*)

nnakanyama *n1* (*no pl.*) muscle ache

nnakasigirwa *n1* pronoun (*part of speech*)

nnakasugga (*also* nnakati) *n1* type of spinach *Solanum aethiopicum*

Nnakato *n1 title* female younger of twins

nnakavundira *n1* manure

nnakawere *n1* mother of newborn child

nnakayunga *n1* conjunction (*part of speech*)

nnakazadde *n1* mother (*in an honorific sense*)

nnakiboneka *n1* name given to a girl child born at the time of the new moon

nnakigwanyizi *n1* person who readily associates with anyone (*indiscriminate in relationships*)

nnakimu *n1* person with a harelip

nnakinsige *n1* firefinch (*type of small red bird*). *See* finch (*in Part 3 of the dictionary*)

nnakitembe *n1* type of banana (*used for making matooke; plays a symbolic role in birth rites*)

nnakongezakikolwa *n1* adverb

nnakongezalinnya *n1* adjective

¹ennaku *n9* sadness, misery, grief, sorrow ennaku -kwata be distressed ennaku -yitirira be overwhelmed with grief Ennaku zinsanze! Woe is me! -laba ennaku suffer hardship

²ennaku *n10* days (*one* olunaku)

nnakyemalira *n1* dictator, tyrant

nnakyewa *n1* volunteer, charity worker -a nnakyewa *adj* voluntary

nnakyeyombekedde *n1* woman living alone (*lacking a husband*), spinster

Nnalubaale *n9* Lake Victoria

nnalugooti *n1* tall thin woman

nnalukalala *n1* outspoken and aggressive person

nnalulungi *n1* very pretty woman/girl

nnalwenaanya *n1* indolent person, someone who avoids work

nnamagoye *n1* albino

Nnamalere *n1* name of a traditional deity (*lubaale*)

Nnamasole *n1 title* Queen-mother

nnamatimbo *n1* larva inside a cocoon (*at the stage when it starts shaking*)

¹ennamba *adj. See* -lamba

²ennamba *n9* number ennamba y'emmotoka number plate

Nnambi *n1* (1) wife of Kintu. *See* Kintu; (2) name used in the Ndiga Clan nnambi type of banana (*used for making beer*)

nnamirembe *n1* hairy herb with small purple to white flowers *Aegeratum conyzoides* Nnamirembe name of a hill in Kampala. *Also a name used for females who lack clans.*

nnampala *n1* task master, foreman, headman, supervisor

nnampawengwa *n1* neutral person, non-committed person

ennamu *See* -lamu

nnamugala *n1* blue starling (*type of bird*)

Nnamugereka *n1* God (*as the alloter of destiny*)

nnamugoya *n1* blind snake

nnamukago *n1* rubber tree (*name when used medicinally*) *Funtumia africana*

ennamula *n9* judgement, arbitration

nnamulimi *n1* ant bear, aardvark

¹nnamulondo *n1* type of small mushroom (= akabaala)

²nnamulondo *n9* throne

nnamumwa enjoka zi nnamumwa *n10* tapeworm.

So-called because it can fix itself to the body with a mouth.

nnamunene *n1* **fat person**

nnamungi *n1* **large number** (*usually referring to people*), *eg. nnamungi w'abantu* ('*large number of people*')

nnamunigina *n1/adv* **(a person) alone** (*as a general condition in life, or temporarily separated from others*) bwa nnamunigina **alone**, *eg. Atudde yekka bwa nnamunigina.* ('*He is sitting alone*')

nnamunjoloba *n1* **smallest drum in a set** (= nnankasa)

nnamunkanga *n1/9* (*pl.* bi nnamunkanga *n8*) **dragonfly.** *See* ennyonyi

nnamunnungu *n1* **porcupine**

nnamunswa *n1* (*pl.* bi nnamunswa *n8*) **queen termite.** *Saying: 'Nnamunswa alya ku nswa ze.'* ('*The queen termite feeds on her own ants.*')

nnamunye *n1* **pied wagtail** ekinjanjaalo ekya nnamunye **type of bean** (*having white seeds with black lines*)

nnamunyeenye *n1* **mole cricket** (*type of insect, omen of death*)

nnamuŋŋoona *n1* **crow**

ennamusa *n9* **greeting**

nnamusuna *n1* (*no pl.*) **chicken pox**

nnamuziga *n1* **wheel, hoop**

nnamwandu *n1* **widow**

ennanda *n9* **creeping herb with blue flowers** *Commelina benghalensis*

nnandibadde I would have been (*stem* -beera)

nnandigoya *n1* **type of large soft pink yam** *Dioscorea alata*

nnandiki *conj* **or rather, preferably**

ennanga *n9* (1) **harp, bow-harp, organ;** (2) **anchor**

ennangaazi *n9* **hartebeest**

nnankani *pro* **what's-it-called?** (*referring to something whose name is not remembered*)

nnankasa *n9* (1) **type of drumbeat and dance;** (2) **smallest drum in a set** (= nnamunjoloba)

nnannyini *n1* (*pl.* ba nnannyini) **owner of** (*followed by item owned*) (**N16**), *eg. nnannyini nnyumba* ('*house owner*'). *Also a stem* **nnannyini-** (*with pronoun suffix* **N11.6**), *eg. nnannyinizo* ('*their owner*', *eg. referring to houses*): nnannyinimu **house owner**

nnansangwawo *n1* **person found at a place, original inhabitant, indigenous person**

nnansi (*also* nnaasi) *n1* **nurse**

nnantayitwakomusota *n1* **type of hairy herb** *Hibiscus surattensis. Meaning: 'The snake cannot pass over it.'*

nnantooke *n1* **woody herb** (*fruits eaten*) *Tristemma mauritianum*

nnappi *n9* **nappy**

Nnassaza *n1 title* (*formerly*) **third wife of the Kabaka or major chief**

Nnassolo *n1 title* **eldest daughter of the Kabaka**

nnassubula *n1* **barkcloth tree** (*when stripped of bark*)

nnasswi *n9* **little finger** akagere ka nnasswi **little toe**

nnatti *n9* **nut** (*for bolt*)

nnawandagala *n1* **small green snake**

nnawolovu *n1* **chameleon**

ennazi *n9* **coconut oil**

nnazikuno *adv* **in olden days/times**

enneeyisa *n9* (*no pl.*) **behaviour**

ennema *See* -lema (*lame*)

ennembeko *n9* **receptacle for catching rain water**

Nnende *n1* **Kiganda deity** (*lubaale*)

ennenga *See* olulenga

Nneyanzizza Thank you. (*stem* -eeyanza)

enniimu *n9* **lemon** (*fruit*)

[1]**ennima** *n9* **way of cultivating/farming**

NOTES ON n

-n. Unless the **n** is doubled, verbs starting **n** have 1st person singulars starting **nn**, *eg.* **nnaaba** ('I wash'), from **-naaba**.

en-. Nouns in *n9* usually have identically spelt plurals (in *n10*), *eg.* **ente** (*n9* 'cow'), **ente** (*n10* 'cows'). **en-** (*n10*) is also the plural prefix of nouns (in *n11*) starting **olu**, *eg.* the plural of **olunaku** (*n11* 'day') is **ennaku** (*n10* 'days').

nd are the initial letters of the 1st person singulars of non-nasal verbs starting **l**, *eg.* (1) **ndeeta** ('I bring'), from **-leeta**.

nj are the initial letters of the 1st person singulars of many verbs starting **y**, *eg.* **njiga** ('I learn'), from **-yiga**.

[1]**nn.** **nn** are the initial letters of the 1st person singulars of nasal verbs starting **l** or **y** (**N5**), *eg.* **nninda** ('I wait'), from **-linda**; (2) **nnyamba** ('I help'), from **-yamba**.

[2]**-nn.** Verbs starting **nn** have 1st person singulars starting **nnyin**, *eg.* **nnyinyika** ('I soak'), from **-nnyika**.

nna-. The plurals of nouns in *n1* referring to people and starting **nna** (without an initial vowel) typically follow the following pattern: **nnaasi** (nurse *si.*), **ba nnaasi** (nurses).

nnyi are the initial letters of the 1st person singular of verbs starting **mm** or **nn**, *eg.* **nnyima** ('I refuse to give'), from **-mma**.

nzi- is the 1st person singular prefix of verbs starting with double **b,d,g,j,k,s,t,v** or **z** *eg.* **nzija** ('I come'), from **-jja**. If the verb starts with double **d**, then **dd** is replaced by **nzir**, *eg.* **nziruka** ('I run'), from **-dduka**.

NOUNS IN *n9*. Most nouns in *n9* have identically spelt plurals (in *n10*).

---

²**nnima** I am digging, I cultivate (*stem* -lima)

ennimaawa *n9* lime (*fruit*)

ennimi See olulimi

ennimiro *n9* garden, farm, field

nnina I have (*stem* -lina)

nninda I wait (*stem* -linda)

enningu *n9* type of fish (*much favoured as food; no longer found in Lake Victoria, eradicated by the Nile perch*) *Labeo victorianus*

nno *emphasises the preceding word* kale nno **well then** so nno **but actually**

ennoga *n9* (*no pl.*) depression made in lump of matooke (*when held in fingers to eat*). See -kuba ennoga

ennongo *n9* type of medium-sized/tall tree. *Several species: Albizia glaberrima, A. grandibracteata, A. zygia. From: 'Nnongoosa.' ('I make better.').*

ennoni *n9* (*no pl.*) chalk

ennono *n9* fundamentals, fundamental nature, essence

ennukuta (*also* ennyukuta) *n9* letter (*of the alphabet*

ennuma emmere ennuma *n9* food without sauce

¹**ennumba** *n9* wasp (*black to brownish*)

²**nnumba** I attack (*stem* -lumba)

ennumbu *n9* Livingstone potato *Plectranthus punctatus. Otherwise known as 'Plectranthus yam'.*

ennume *adj* male (*stem* -lume) ennume y'ekyalo type of thorny plant *Solanum macrocarpon*

nnumiriza I accuse repeatedly (*stem* -lumiriza)

¹**ennunda** *n9* method of animal husbandry

²**nnunda** I look after (*animals*) (*stem* -lunda)

ennunde See -lunde

ennundulirunduli See olulundulirunduli

nnunga I flavour/dissolve (*stem* -lunga)

ennungi See -lungi

nnungiwa I become good/beautiful (*stem* -lungiwa)

ennusu *n9* coin; (*formerly*) one hundred shilling coin

ennuuni *n9* pancreas

nnwana I fight (*stem* -lwana)

ennwe *n10* fingers (*excluding thumb*); *pl. of* olunwe

¹**nnya** *num* four

²**nnya-** *n1* (*pl.* ba nnya-) mother of (N12), *eg. nnyaffe ('our mother')* nnyina **her/his mother,** nnyaffe **our mother,** nnyammwe **your** *pl.* **mother,** nnyaabwe **their mother**

-**nnyaala** (*impolite*) *vi* (-nnyadde, nnyinyaala) urinate

ennyaanya *n9* tomato (*fruit*)

ennyaanyaagize *n9* cicada

nnyabo *n1* madam

ennyago See olunyago

ennyama *n9* (*no pl.*) meat, flesh, muscle

ennyambalizo See olwambalizo

-**eennyamira** *vi* (-eennyamidde) be upset, regret, be distraught with grief

-**eennyamivu** *adj* unhappy, regretful, distraught

-**nnyampa** (*impolite*) *vi* (-nnyampye, nnyinyampa) fart (*impolite*)

ennyana *n9* calf, heifer

ennyanda -kuba ennyanda strike at goal

ennyanga *n9* bottomless pit, abyss ennyanga za Walumbe place where Walumbe disappeared (*in Kiganda mythology*)

ennyange *n9* cattle egret

ennyangu See -yangu

ennyaniko See olwaniko

ennyanja *n9* lake, sea ennyanja ya Kabaka royal lake (*near Mengo Palace*)

ennyanjula *n9* introduction

nnyazaala *n1* mother-in-law

ennyendo See olwendo

ennyenje *n9* cockroach

ennyiike *n9* (*no pl.*) sadness, sorrow, problem ennyiike y'amaanyi mu bulamu (mental) depression

-**nnyika** *vt* (-nyise, nnyinyika) soak -nnyika mu ddagala (*or* langi) dye

-**nnyike** *adj* (ennyinyike *n9*) soaked

-**nnyikira** *vi* (-nnyikidde) become soaked

nnyima I refuse to give (*stem* -mma)

ennyimba *n10* music; *pl. of* oluyimba

ennyimbe See olumbe

ennyimpi See -mpi

nnyina *n1* her/his mother

ennyindo *n9* nose

nnyingi See -ngi

ennyingiza *n9* importation, income

ennyingo *n9* joint, segment; *pl of* oluyingo ennyingo y'ekikajjo segment of sugar cane ennyingo y'ekigambo syllable

nnyini *n1* (*pl.* ba nnyini) owner of (*followed by item owned N11.6*), *eg. nnyini nnyumba ('house owner'). Can be a prefix* nnyini- *to an ordinary pronoun (N10.1), eg. myiniyo ('its owner', eg. referring to a house). Can be a suffix* -nnyini *to a pronoun of emphasis (N10.1) meaning* self, actually *or* exactly, *eg. (1) ennyumba yo yennyini ('the house itself'); (2) Omwami ye yennyini ye yazze wano. ('The actual chief came here.'); (3) Leeta ebikopo kikumi kyennyini. ('Bring exactly one hundred cups.'). The personal forms are given in Column 10 of Table 2, eg. nze kennyini ('I myself').* nnyinimu **house owner** (N11.6)

ennyinya See olunnya

ennyinyike See -nnyike

ennyinyo See olunnyo

ennyinyogovu *adj* cold (*stem* -nnyogovu)

ennyinyonnyola *n9* (*no pl.*) explanation

ennyiriri See olunyiriri

ennyo *adv* very, a lot, much nnyo nnyini very much, *eg. Nsanyuse nnyo nnyini. ('Thank you very much.', lit. 'I am very happy.')*

-nnyogoga *vi* (-nnyogoze, nnyinyogoga) **be cold**

-nnyogovu *adj* (ennyinyogovu *n9*) **cold, chilly**

nnyoko *n1* (*impolite*) **your** *si.* **mother**

ennyombo *See* oluyombo

ennyondo *n9* **hammer**

ennyongeza *n9* **way of increasing, increment, bonus**

ennyonjo *See* -yonjo

-nnyonnyoka *vi* (-nnyonnyose) **be explained, become clear, be(come) understood**

-nnyonnyola *vt* (-nnyonnyodde, nnyinyonnyola) **explain, clarify, elucidate, describe**

ennyonoonefu *See* -yonoonefu

ennyonta *n9* (*no pl.*) **thirst**

ennyonyi *n9* **aeroplane, bird**   ennyonyi ndiisa **yellow-thoated longclaw** (*type of bird*). *Meaning: 'I make graze.' – because the bird moves with cattle and is believed to make them eat.*   ennyonyi nnamunkanga **helicopter**

ennyonza *n9* **robin chat** (*type of bird*)

nnyooge *Saying: 'Ennamusa etuuse ku nnyooge.' ('Things have reached a crisis.' – like an extended greeting).*

ennyota *n9* **pip** (*on shoulder pad*)   omuserikale ow'ennyota **army/police officer**

-nnyuka *vi* (-nnyuse, nnyinyuka) (1) **finish work** (*at one's regular time*); (2) **retire** (*from work*)

ennyukuta (*also* ennukuta) *n9* **letter** (*of the alphabet*); *in pl.* **alphabet**   ennyukuta empeerezi (*also* ennyukuta enjatuza) **vowel**   ennyukuta ennene **capital letter**   ennyukuta ensirifu **consonant**   ennyingo y'ennyukuta **syllable**

¹-nnyula *vt* (-nnyudde, nnyinyula) **(cause to) stop work**, *eg. Omukulu yatunnyula n'atugamba tugende eka. ('The boss told us to stop work and go home.')*, **relieve** (*someone on duty*)

²-ennyula *vi* (-enyudde) **stop work** (*of one's own accord*). *Saying: 'Yalidde ne yennyula.' ('He ate to bursting point.')*

-nnyulukusa *vt* (-nnyulukusizza, nnyinyulukusa) **draw out of water**

-nnyulula *vt* (-nnyuludde, nnyinyulula) **take out of water** (*eg. cloth being dyed*)

ennyuma *n9/adv* **buttocks, behind, bottom**   ennyuma wa *pre* **behind**

ennyumanju *adv* **behind the house**

ennyumba *n9* **house**   ennyumba y'abalalu **mental asylum**   ennyumba y'essanja **house thatched with banana fibre**   ennyumba y'essubi **thatched house** (*thatched with grass*)   ennyumba ya ggoloofa **multistorey house**   ennyumba ya mwamba **rectangular house with corrugated iron roof**

ennyumbu *n9* **mule**

ennyunga *See* engabi

ennyunguli *n9* **type of fish** (*which replaced 'enningu' in Lake Victoria after the Nile perch was introduced, but which itself has now become rare*)

-nnyuukirira *vi* (-nnyuukiridde) **become damp** (*of something that absorbs moisture, eg. salt*)

ennywa *See* olunywa

ennywanto *n9* **nipple, teat**

¹-no *adv* **here** (**N9.2**). *Takes pronominal concord* (**N4**). *The four forms are:* wano **here**, eno **over here**, kuno **on here**, muno **in here**.   ab'eno *n2* **people of over here**

²-no *dem* **this, these** (**N9.1**). *Takes pronominal concord* (**N4**), *eg. (1) omuntu ono ('this person'); (2) ente eno ('this cow').*

-noba *vi* (-nobye) **leave one's husband**

¹-noga *vi* (-noze) **be enough** (*of salt, sugar, flavouring, dye, etc.*), *eg. Oyo sukaali ajja kunoga mu caayi. ('That amount of sugar will be enough in the tea.'). Pronunciation:* okunógà

²-noga *vt* (-noze) **pick** (*eg. fruit or vegetable*), **pluck**. *Pronunciation:* okunógá

-nogebwa *vi* (-nogeddwa) **be picked/plucked**

-nogoka *vi* (-nogose) **drop off** (*of a ripe fruit*), **be partially broken off** (*of a branch*)

-nogola *vt* (-nogodde) **detach from a stem, pluck**

-nokola *vt* (-nokodde) **bring out** (*reasons*), *eg. Yanokola ensonga ssatu ezimutwaza Bulaaya. ('He brought out three reasons for going to Europe.')*
   -nokolayo (-nokoddeyo) **choose from among, pick out as an example**, *eg. Yanokoddeyo Musoke ng'omu ku bakoze obulungi. ('He picked out Musoke as an example of one who did well.')*

-nona *vt* (-nonye) **fetch, go for**

-nonkola *vi* (-nonkodde)   -nonkola ebinonko **crack one's finger joints**

-nononkola *vt* (-nononkodde) **provoke, irritate**

-nonoogana *vi* (-nonooganye) **provoke one another** (*exchanging angry words*)

noomu *num* **and one** (= n'omu **N8.1**), *eg. kkumi noomu ('eleven')*

-(y)onoona *See* -yonoona

-(y)onooneka *See* -yonooneka

-noonya *vt* (-noonyezza) **look for, search for, seek**   -noonya obubudamo **seek asylum**

-noonyanoonya *vt* (-noonyezzanoonyezza) **look for everywhere**

-noonyereza *vt* (-noonyerezza) **investigate, explore, research, survey, prospect for**

-noonyeza *vt* (-noonyezzza) **look for on behalf of**, *eg. Nja kumunoonyeza omukozi. ('I will look for a worker for her.')*

nooti *n9* **nought**

Noovemba **November**

-noza *vt* (-nozezza) **put/have enough of** (*seasoning, flavouring, dye, etc.*), *eg. Nnozezza sukaali mu caayi. ('I have enough sugar in my tea.')*

ensa *n9* (*no pl.*) **pleasant smell/taste** (*of food*), *eg. Emmere ebaddemu ensa. ('The food was flavoursome.')*, **good-looking** (*of a person*), **sense, significance**   ekitaliimu nsa **nonsense**   ow'ensa *n1* **good-looking person**

ensaali *n9* **fruit of omusaali**

ensaalwa *n9* envy ensaalwa embi jealousy

ensaamu *n9* mallet *(for making barkcloth). See* mallet *(in Part 3 of the dictionary)*

ensaanuusi enjoka ensaanuusi *n10* sudden recurring abdominal pain

ensaasi *n9* shaker *(musical instrument, a gourd containing seeds or stones)*; (2) coarsely-grooved mallet *(used in the first stage of beating bark to make barkcloth). This is also known as 'enkubi'.*

ensaata *invariable adj* barren *(of certain animals), eg. ente ensaata ('barren cow')*

ensaka *n9* earthenware cooking pot

ensala *n9* way of cutting, decision ensala y'olugoye cut of cloth ensala y'omusango judgement, verdict, ruling

ensalawo *n9* way of deciding

ensalika *n9* painful cut *(especially between fingers or toes)*

ensalo *n9* limit, boundary, border, frontier

ensalosalo *See* olusalosalo

ensama *n9* waterbuck

ensamba *See* engabi

ensambya *See* olusambya

ensanafu *n9* safari ant

ensanda *n9* flag *(or other decoration)* on prow of board *(shows its identity)*

ensandaggo *n9* border strip of mat

ensanjabavu *n9* swollen lymph gland

ensansa *See* olusansa

nsanvu *n9/num* seventy

ensasi *n9* spark

-onsatule *det* all three (N7.3). *Takes pronominal concord* (N4), *eg. (1) amagi gonsatule ('all three eggs'); (2) ebintu byonsatule ('all three things'). The personal forms are irregular, declining in a similar way to '-okka' (Column 11 of Table 2).*

ensawo *n9* bag, sack, satchel, purse, pocket ensawo ey'omu ngalo handbag ensawo y'enkima type of small climbing plant, Dutchman's-pipe *Aristolochia elegans. Meaning: 'the bag of the monkey'.*

enseege *n9* rattle *(reedbox type)*

enseenene *n9* type of edible grasshopper *Ruspolia differens. The colour variants include:* enseenene kulumbisi *(green)*, enseenene kulunkalu *(brown)*, enseenene mwebe *(purplish with black face).* Ekika ky'Enseenene Grasshopper Clan

enseera *n9* overcharging enkoko enseera young hen *(before laying)*

ensega *n9* vulture

ensejjere *n9* type of edible termite

enseke *See* oluseke

ensekere *n9* louse

ensekese *See* olusekese

enseko *n10* laugh, laughter

ensenke *n9 (no pl.)* cataract *(on eye)*

ensi *n9* world, earth, land, country Ensi Entukuvu Holy Land -a ensi *adj* belonging to the land (or earth), national

¹ensibo *n9 (no pl.)* ground-up pieces of broken pots *(added to clay in pottery making)*, grog. *Pronunciation:* ensíbó

²ensibo *n9* reserve *(of food, etc.). Pronunciation:* ensíbó obugagga obw'ensibo natural resources

ensibuka *n9* seedling, cutting, sprout, shoot

ensibuko *n9* source, origin

ensigo *n9* seed, kidney

ensiisira *See* olusiisira

ensiitaano *n9* struggle, big effort

ensiiti *n9* seed of olusiiti *(red and black)*

ensikirano *n9* heredity -a ensikirano *adj* hereditary

ensiko *n9* wild area, uncultivated land, jungle, bush -a omu nsiko *adj* wild, *eg. ensolo z'omu nsiko ('wild animals')*

ensikya *n9* back of the neck

ensimba *n9* way of planting, planting, parking

ensimbi *n9* cowry shell; *in pl.* money, currency ensimbi ennanda cowries used as money

ensimbu *n9 (no pl.)* epilepsy, epileptic fit

ensimu *n9* worn-out hoe

ensinda *See* olusinda

ensinga *See* olusinga

ensingo *n9* neck

ensinjo *n9* chisel *(type used in metal work)*

ensinza *n9 (no pl.)* worship

ensiri *n9* mosquito

ensiriba *n9* charm, amulet. *For good luck, worn around waist or upper arm.*

ensirifu ennyukuta ensirifu *n9* consonant

ensiriŋŋanyi *See* olusiriŋŋanyi

ensisi *n9* shock

ensisinkano *n9* meeting, encounter, appointment

¹enso *n9* grindstone *(upper). Pronunciation:* ensó enso y'evviivi kneecap

²enso *n10* long knives *(pl. of* oluso*). Pronunciation:* ensô

ensobi *n9* error, mistake mu nsobi wrongly

ensobyo *n9* stick for digging out sweet potatoes

ensoga *n9* Victoria robber *(type of fish in Lake Victoria)*

ensogasoga *n9* castor-oil berry

ensokolosokolo *n9* isolated area, remote place *(difficult to access), eg. Ateeka ssente ze mu nsokolokosokolo. ('He puts his money in a remote place.')*

ensolo *n9* animal

ensolobyo *See* olusolobyo

ensolosozi *n9* small black stinging ant

ensoma *See* olusoma

ensombabyuma *n9* giant pouched rat. *Meaning: 'It collects metal things.'*

ensomesa *n9* way of teaching

ensonda *n9* corner, angle

ensonga *n9 (usually pl.)* reason, logic, argument, cause, matter, issue, affair ensonga lwaki

justification ensonga z'ebweru **foreign affairs**
ensonga z'omunda **internal affairs** awatali
nsonga **without reason** eky'ensonga n7
something that matters -gonjoola ensonga **sort
out affairs** -langulula ensonga **disentangle
problems** -lemera ku nsonga **stick to one's point**
-londoola ensonga **follow a line of reasoning** lwa
nsonga ki? **for what reason?, why?** nga tewali
nsonga **without reason** olw'ensonga eno **because
of this** Si ensonga. **Never mind.** -tereeza
ensonga **sort out affairs** y'ensonga lwaki **that's
the reason why**
ensonyi n10 **shyness, modesty, (feeling of) shame,
embarrassment** -a ensonyi adj **shy, modest**
-kwasa ensonyi **shame** (someone), **embarrass**
-kwatibwa (or -wulira) ensonyi **feel shame, feel
shy**
ensonzi n9 **catfish** (small eel-like type, found in
rivers) Clarias carsoni
nsotoka n1 (no pl.) (1) **cattle plague, rinderpest;**
(2) **type of chicken disease**
ensowera n9 **fly**
ensozi See olusozi
ensu See olusu
ensubi See olusubi
ensugga n9 **type of spinach** Solanum nigrum
ensujju n9 **pumpkin** (fruit)
[1]ensuku n9 **red duiker**
[2]ensuku n10 **banana gardens;** pl. of olusuku.
Pronunciation: ensúkù.
ensukusa (also endukusa) n9 **young shoot of
banana plant** (Kyaggwe dialect)
ensulo n9 **water source, spring, gland**
ensuma n9 **type of fish** (resembling an elephant-
snout fish in having a protruding mouth, but is a bit
larger)
ensumbi n9 **long-necked water pot, pitcher**
ensumbi y'emimwa ebiri **water pot with two
spouts** (called 'Wasswa' and 'Kato')
ensumika n9 **way of dressing**
ensundo n9 **wart**
ensungwe (also ensundwe) n9 **foetal membranes,
amniotic sac**
ensunu n9 **antelope**
ensusso n9 **extremeness** -a ensusso adj **extreme**
ensusu See olususu
ensusuuti n9 **cucurbitaceous climber** (with edible
fruits) Sechium edule
ensuubo See olusuubo
ensuulemu See emmere
ensuuluulu n9 **pickaxe**
ensuwa n9 **water pot/jar, pitcher.** See -nyookezi
ensuwa y'omutwe **obstinate person**
enswa n9 (no pl.) **termite(s)** (flying stage), **flying
ant(s)**
enswagiro n10 **light noise of footsteps** (of unknown
origin)
enswaswa n9 **monitor lizard**

enswera n9 **cobra**
enswiriri n10 **whiskers;** pl. of oluswiriri
enta See oluta
entaala n9 **xylophone** (= amadinda)
entaana n9 **hole dug for human burial**
entabaalo See olutabaalo (under olutalo)
entabagana n9 **cooperation**
entabiro n9 **joint, seam, centre, central** (or pivital)
point, junction
entalabuusi n9 **round cap** (worn by Muslims)
entalaga adv **at intervals** -a entalaga adj **spaced-
out** amannyo ag'entalaga **spaced-out teeth**
entalaganya n9 **blue duiker**
entale n9 **lion.** From Lunyoro.
entaleyaddungu n9 **type of tree** (anti-malarial)
Zanthoxylum chalybeum. Meaning: 'lion of the
wilderness'.
entalo See olutalo
entambi See olutambi
entambula n9 (no pl.) **way of travelling, way of
walking, transport** engeri y'entambula **gait**
entambula y'omusaayi **circulation of the blood**
entamu n9 **earthenware cooking pot** entamu
enjaliire n'emizinnoonyo **pot lined with pieces of
midrib of banana leaf** (on which to place an
'omuwumbo' for steaming)
entanda n9 (no pl.) **food for a journey.**
Traditionally prepared for a long journey and
typically including cooked 'ekikongo' yam,
'lumonde omwokye' ('roasted potatoes') and 'amagi
ag'empogola' ('boiled eggs').
entandikwa n9 (no pl.) **beginning, start** ku
ntandikwa **in the beginning, at first** ku
ntandikwa ya **in/at the beginning of**
entangawuuzi n9 (no pl.) **ginger**
entaputa n9 **interpretation, translation**
entaseesa n9 **type of tree** (medicinal) Prunus
africana
entawunzi n9 **green pigeon**
ente n9 **cow** ente endaawo **bullock, ox** ente
ennyana **calf** ente enduusi **female cow** (before
breeding) ente enkazi **female cow** (one that has
given birth) ente ennume **male cow, bull**
entebe n9 **chair** mu ntebe ya **in the position of**
enteebereza n9 **forecast, guess, estimate**
enteebereza y'obudde **weather forecast**
enteega See oluteega
enteeka invariable adj **virgin,** eg. omuwala enteeka
('virgin girl')
nteesa n1 **variety of barkcloth** (good looking,
brownish)
enteesaganya n10 **dialogue, negotiation**
entegeeragana n9 **mutual understanding**
entegeeza n9 **definition**
entegeka (also enteekateeka) n9 **preparation,
arrangement, programme, plan**
entegetege n10 **tendons at back of knee;** pl. of
olutegetege. Yayimirira nga entegetege

gimufamba. **He stood trembling.**

entembe *See* olutembe

entengero *n9* **fright, trembling** (*through fear*)

entengo *n9* **fruit of akatengotengo** (*medicinal, used as an antidote to puff adder bite*). *Identification needs confirmation.*

entengotengo *n9* **spiny shrub with purple flowers** *Solanum campylacanthus. Identification needs confirmation.*

entente *See* olutente

entenvu *n9* **beetle larva found in stems of banana plants** Ntenvu **December**

interneti *n9* **internet**

[1]**nti** *conj* **that** (*introducing reported speech*)

[2]**anti** *interj* **surely**

[3]**enti** *See* oluti

entiba *See* olutiba

entiisa *n9* (*no pl.*) **fright, scare** eky'entiisa *n7* **something frightening**

entikko *n9* **top, summit, peak, crest, climax**

[1]**entimba** *n9* **way of decorating, way of hanging curtains**

[2]**entimba** *See* olutimba

entimbe *See* olutimbe

entindo *See* olutindo

entinnamuti *n9* **pigeon pea** *Cajanus cajan*

entobazzi *See* olutobazzi

entobo *n9* **bottom** (*of container*), **base**

entoko *n9* **large number**

entoli -kuba entoli **snap the fingers**

entondo *n10* **touchiness** ow'entondo *n1* **person easily offended**

entongooli *n9* **lyre** (= endongo)

entonnyeze *n9* **insect that secrets fluid** (*spittle bug, froghopper, etc.*)

entubatuba *See* olutubatuba

entubiro *n9* **muddy place** (*where one might get stuck*), **bog, quagmire**

ntuddebuleku *n1* **black-eyed Susan** (*type of climbing or creeping herb*) *Thunbergia alata*

entugga *n9* **giraffe**

entujjo *n9* **celebration, merry-making.** *Derivation: '-tujja' ('be beaten, of drums').*

entula *n9* **fruit of omutula** (*edible*)

entulege *n9* **zebra**

entumba *n9* **stoop** ow'entumba *n1* **stooped-over person**

entumbi *n9* (*no pl.*) **swollen stomach disease**

entumbwe *n9* **calf** (*of the leg*)

[1]**entunda** *n9* **type of edible termite.** *Pronunciation:* entúndà

[2]**entunda** *n9* **way of selling, marketing.** *Pronunciation:* entúndá

entunge *See* -tunge

entungo *n9* **simsim** *Sesame indicum*

entunku *n9* **fan palm** *Borassus aethiopum*

entunnunsi *n9* **pulse**

entuntunu *n9* **cape gooseberry** (*plant; fruit*)

Physalis peruviana

entunuka *n9* **inflamation of finger or toe**

entuuko *n10* **destined time,** eg. Newankubadde baamugambye aleme kugenda kyokka yeewalirizza n'agenda era bw'atyo n'afiira mu kabenje. Entuuko ze zaabadde zituuse. (*'Although they advised him not to go, he was determined and went anyway and died in an accident. It was his destined time.'*)

entuula *See* olutuula

entuumu *n9* **pile, heap**

entuuyo *n10* **sweat, perspiration**

entyatya *See* olutyatya

-(y)anukula *See* -yanukula

-(y)anula *See* -yanula

-nunula *vt* (-nunudde) **save, rescue, ransom, liberate, redeem**

-nunulwa *vi* (-nunuddwa) **be saved**

-nuubuka *vi* (-nuubuse) **be grazed** (*of the skin*), **be bruised**

-nuubula *vt* (-nuubudde) **scrape** (*the skin*), **graze, bruise**

-nuuka *vi* (-nuuse) **come out of a socket, be dislocated.** *The person concerned can be indicated by an object pronoun, eg. Omukono gunnuuse. ('My arm is dislocated.').*

-nuula *vt* (-nudde) **take out of a socket, dislocate, pull out** -nuula ensingo **stretch the neck** -nuula kasooli **pluck a maize cob**

-nuuna *vt* (-nuunye) **suck (on)**

Nuwa *n1* **Noah**

enva *n10* **sauce, vegetable(s), relish, side dish** enva endiirwa **green vegetables** (*eaten with the main food 'emmere'*) enva ez'okuliira ku mmere **sauce** (*served with the main dish*) enva z'ebinyeebwa **groundnut sauce** ekirungo ky'enva **mixture of ingredients used to make sauce** (*onions, tomatoes, curry powder, etc.*)

envi *n10* **grey hair.** *See* oluvi

enviiri *n10* **hair.** *See* oluviiri

envinnyo *n9* **wine**

invoyisi *n9* **invoice**

envubo *n9* **hole dug on sun-facing side of termite mound**

envubu *n9* **hippopotamus**

envuga *n9* **way of sounding, way of driving**

envujjo *n9* **land tax, tribute.** *Traditionally, tribute in kind given to a chief (of beer, barkcloth, etc.). See* busuulu

envuma *n9* **fruit of a water plant** (*contains a large edible seed*) *Trapa natans* Ekika kya Nvuma **Nvuma Clan**

envumbi *n9* **pile of rubbish, pile of dung**

envumbo *n9* **wax, wax seal**

envunyu *n9* **maggot**

envunza *n9* **jigger**

envuumuulo *n9* **sling** (*for slinging stones*)

-nya (*impolite*) *vi* (-nyedde) **shit** (*impolite*)

-nyaala (*rather impolite*) *vi* (-nyadde) **urinate**

-nyaaluka *vi* (-nyaaluse) **be(come) sickly and thin, be(come) emaciated**

-nyaanyaagira *vi* (-nyaanyaagidde) **make a din, blare** (*as a trumpet*)

-nyaanyaagiza *vt* (-nyaanyaagizizza) **make a din, chirp** (*as cicadas*), **blare** (*as a trumpet*)

[1]-nyaga *vt* (-nyaze) **seize by force, plunder, loot, pillage**

[2]-eenyaga *vi* **have loose bowels, be incontinent**

-nyage *adj* **plundered, looted**

-nyakula *vt* (-nyakudde) **snatch**

-nyeenya *v* (-nyeenyezza) (1) *vi* **not be fixed properly, move to and fro, be shaky, be wobbly**, *eg. Emmeeza enyeenya.* (*'The table is wobbly.'*); (2) *vt* **shake** -nyeenya amatabi **shake palm leaves** (*on Palm Sunday*) -nyeenya omutwe **nod**, *eg. Yanyeenya omutwe nga akkiriza.* (*'He nodded in agreement.'*)

-nyega *vit* (-nyeze) **give a response, respond (to)** (*with sound or comment; a verb often used in the negative*), *eg. Nnamuyita naye teyanyega.* (*'I called him, but he did not respond to me.'*)

-nyegenya *vi* (-nyegenyezza) **be wobbly/shaky**

-nyereketa (*also* -nyerettuka) *vi* (-nyerekese) **be shiny/oily, be glossy** (*of the skin*)

-nyerettufu *adj* **oily/glossy** (*of the skin*)

-nyiga *vt* (-nyize) **squeeze, press** -nyiga emmere **squash cooked matooke** (*inside food bundle, to mash it*)

-nyiganyiga (*also* -nyigootola *or* -nyogootola) *vt* (-nyizenyize) **handle and squeeze** (*something soft*), **knead** (*dough*)

-nyigibwa *vi* (-nyigiddwa) **be squeezed, get squashed**

-eenyigira *vi* (-nyigidde) **participate, take part**

-nyigiriza *vt* (-nyigirizizza) **squeeze, press, repress, oppress, suppress, compress, pressurise**

-nyigootola (-nyigootodde) *See* -nyiganyiga

-nyiiga *vi* (-nyiize) **be annoyed/upset, become inflated**

-nyiigira *vt* (-nyiigidde) **be(come) annoyed with**

-nyiigulukuka *vi* (nyiigulukuse) **calm down** (*from anger or being annoyed*)

-nyiigulula *vt* (-nyiiguludde) **calm** (*an angry or annoyed person*), **appease the anger of**

-nyiikaala *vi* (-nyiikadde) **be miserable** (*eg. when faced with a lot of problems*), **feel dejected, be depressed**

-nyiikaavu *adj* **dejected, depressed**

-nyiikira *vi* (-nyiikidde) **be hard-working**, *eg. Yanyiikira okusoma.* (*'She worked hard at her studies*), **persevere**

-nyiikirira *vi* (-nyiikiridde) **be hard-working in, persevere at**

-nyiikivu *adj* **hard-working, diligent, persistent, ernest**

-nyiinyiitira *vi* (-nyiinyiitidde) **persist, intensify**,

eg. Enkuba yanyiinyiitidde n'etonnyera ddala olunaku lwonna. (*'The rain intensified and fell throughout the day.'*), **drag on**

-nyiinyiitivu *adj* **persistent** (*eg. of rain*)

-nyiivu *adj* **annoyed, irritated**

-nyiiza *vt* (-nyiizizza) **annoy, irritate, offend**

-eenyiizanyiiza *vi* (-eenyiizizzanyiizizza) **sulk**

-nyiizibwa *vi* (-nyiiziddwa) **be irritated**

-eenyinyala *vi* (-eenyinyadde) **be repulsed (by)** (*eg. someone's behaviour*)

[1]-nyinyimbwa *vi* (-nyinimbiddwa) **be disgusted (by)**

[2]-eenyinyimbwa *vi* **be repulsed (by)** (*eg. someone's behaviour*), *eg. Bwe yawulira ebigambo eby'obuwemu ne yeenyinyimbwa.* (*'When she heard obscene words she showed her disgust.'*), **grimace in disgust**

-nyinyimbya *vt* (-nyinyimbizza) **cause to view with disgust**

-nyirira *vi* (-nyiridde) **have an attractive appearance, look smart, look elegant, be shiny, be glossy, look healthy, be polished**

-nyirivu *adj* **attractive** (*in appearance*), **smart, elegant, well-groomed, shiny, polished**

[1]-nyiriza *vt* (-nyirizza) **make smart, polish, shine** -nyiriza engatto **shine shoes**

[2]-eenyiriza *vr* **smarten oneself up**

-nyiwa *vit* (-nyiye) **be(come) fed up with**. *Reversed subject and object compared with English, eg. Amagi gannyiwa.* (*'I am fed up with eating eggs.'*)

-nyiza *vi* (-nyizizza) **blow one's nose**

-nyogootola (-nyogootodde) *See* -nyiganyiga

-nyolwa *vi* (-nyoleddwa) **be pained** (*emotionally*) -nyolwa mu mutima **be broken-hearted, be in anguish**

-nyonyoogera *vt* (-nyonyoogedde) **tickle**

-nyonyoogana *vi* (-nyonyooganye) **wrangle, bicker**

-nyooka *vi* (-nyoose) **smoke** (*of a fire*)

-nyookeza *vt* (-nyookezezza) **cause to smoke, fumigate** -nyookeza akayu **smoke a pit latrine** (*done with grass*) -nyookeza embugo **smoke barkcloth** -nyookeza enjuki **smoke out bees** -nyookeza ensuwa **prepare water pot for use** (*by burning mixture of banana peelings and charcoal*

NOTES ON
ŋ

ŋŋ are the initial letters of the 1st person singulars of verbs starting **g** (nasal verbs) or **ŋ** (N5), *eg.* **ŋŋenda** ('I go'), from **-genda**.

eŋŋ are the initial letters of nasal nouns (in *n10*) havings singulars (in *n11*) starting **olug**, *eg.* the plural of **olugendo** is **eŋŋendo**.

NOUNS IN *n9*. Most nouns in *n9* have identically spelt plurals (in *n10*).

inside) -nyookeza obubaane burn incense

-nyoola vt (-nyodde) twist, wind up, screw -nyoola omunyolo turn a door handle

-nyoolwa vi (-nyooleddwa) be twisted

-nyooma (also -nyoomoola) vt (-nyoomye) despise, look down on (someone), show contempt for, snear at, eg. Musoke yannyooma. ('Musoke sneered at me.')

-nyoomebwa vi (-nyoomeddwa) be despised

-nyuma vi (-nyumye) look good, be pleasing, be enjoyable, be interesting

-nyumiikiriza vit (-nyumiikirizza) keep on chatting (to), eg. Ogira onyumiikiriza abagenyi nga nange bwe nzija. ('Please keep on chatting to the visitors until I come.'), keep conversing (with)

-nyumira vt (-nyumidde) be pleasing to, look good on, eg. Olugoye olwo lumunyumidde. ('That dress looks good on her.')

-eenyumiriza vr (-eenyumirizza) be proud of achievements

-nyumirwa vit (-nyumiddwa) be satisfied with, enjoy, eg. Anyumirwa olugero. ('He is enjoying the story.'), have fun, be interested in. See okunyumirwa

-nyumisa vt (-nyumisizza) cause satisfaction for, make pleasing to

-nyumiza vt (-nyumizza) inform, narrate -nyumiza olugero tell a story to

-nyumunguza vt (-nyumunguzizza) rinse, gargle -nyumunguza engoye rinse clothes

-nyumya vi (-nyumizza) converse, chat

-nyuunyunta vt (-nyuunyunse) suck through a straw

-nyuunyuntula vi (-nyuunyuntudde) be delicious (especially of fruit)

-nyuunyuntuvu adj delicious (especially of fruit)

-nywa vt (-nywedde) drink -nywa funduukululu drink too much (alcohol) -nywa ssigala smoke a cigarette -nywa taaba smoke tobacco ggoolo -nywa be scored (of a goal)

-nywanywagala vt (-nywanyagadde) have a tart taste (causing tingling in the cheeks), tingle (of the cheeks)

-nywedde See -nywa

-nywegera vt (-nywegedde) kiss, embrace

-nyweka vi (-nywese) be drinkable

[1]-nywera vi (-nywedde) be firm, hold firm, be secure, stand steady

[2]-nywera vt (-nywedde) drink for/at, etc.

-nywerera vi (-nyweredde) hold firmly -nywerera ku hold firmly to (a point of view), insist on

-nywereza vt (-nywerezezza) cling (to something physically)

-nywesa vt (-nywesezza) give a drink to (eg. a baby or sick person) -nywesa amaduudu administer trial by ordeal -nywesa ggoolo score a goal

-nywevu adj firm, fixed, steady

-nyweza vt (-nywezezza) make firm/secure, eg.

Yaggalawo n'anyweza oluggi. ('He closed the door firmly.'), tighten -nyweza ekifundikwa tighten a knot (eg. in barkcloth, on installation of an heir) -nyweza gulugulu secure very firmly

enzaala See oluzaala

enzaalwa n9 native, son/daughter (of), eg. Mwana nzaalwa y'e Kenya. ('He is a son of Kenya.')

enzannya n9 way of playing

nze pro I, me. Can be a prefix nze- (N7.3), eg. nzekka ('I alone'). The equivalent suffix is -nge (N10-12), eg. nange ('and I').

enzeere n9 butterfish (type of catfish)

nzekka det/pro only me, by myself

nzenna pro all of me

enzeyituuni n9 olive (fruit)

enzibe See -bbe

enzigale See -ggale

enzige n9 locust

enzigi See oluggi

enzigule See -ggule

enzigumivu See -ggumivu

enzigyo See oluggyo

enziina See oluziina

enzijuliro See olujjuliro

enzijuvu See -jjuvu

enzikiriza n9 (no pl.) way of agreeing, belief, faith, doctrine, creed

enzikirizaganya n9 (no pl.) agreement

enzikiza n9 (no pl.) darkness

enziko See olukko

enziku n9 (no pl.) gonorrhoea

enzimba n9 (no pl.) way of building

enzingu n9 type of tree (anti-malarial) Hallea

enziro n9 (no pl.) soot -siiga enziro defame

enziru n9 fruit of omuziru tree (edible)

enzirugavu See -ddugavu

enzirugaze n9 mistletoe (types with orange to reddish flowers) Loranthaceae

enzirukanya n9 (no pl.) management

enzituzi n9 mallet (finely-grooved, used in final stage of beating bark to make barkcloth)

enzivuunuko n9 far side of a hill

enzivuunula n9 translation

enzizi n10 framework of mud and wattle wall; pl. of oluzizi; oluzzi

enzizizza See -zza

enzo n9 type of tree (used for making walking sticks and mallets) Teclea nobilis -babika enzo beat (someone) hard with a stick

nzuuno here I am

ɲ, ŋ

ŋŋaali n1 crested crane

eŋŋaano n9 (no pl.) wheat, wheat flour

eŋŋaaŋa n9 hornbill

eŋŋambo See olugambo

eŋŋamira *n9* camel

eŋŋanda *See* -ganda; oluganda

eŋŋango *n9* **space** (*within something*) eŋŋango y'ekikopo **space within a cup handle** eŋŋango y'empiso **eye of a needle**

eŋŋanzikiro *n9* **slat** (*piece of wood for hanging tiles or sheets on roof*)

eŋŋendo *See* olugendo

eŋŋoma *n9* **drum** abaana b'eŋŋoma **royal family** -laya eŋŋoma **sound a drum**

eŋŋombe *n9* **horn** (*of vehicle or for hunting*)

eŋŋombeze *adj* **interwoven**

eŋŋombo *n9* **habit of speech, common utterance, expression, slogan**

eŋŋonge *n9* **otter** Kika kya Ŋonge **Otter Clan** (*traditional makers of barkcloth*)

eŋŋonvu *See* -gonvu

eŋŋoomu *See* -goomu

eŋŋumbagumba *n9* **skeleton**

eŋŋumu *See* -gumu

eŋŋwanyu *See* olugwanyu

-ŋoola *vt* (-ŋodde, ŋŋoola) **express contempt** (*through making a certain sound*)

O, o

¹-o *adv* **there** (N9.2). *Takes pronominal concord* (N4). *The four forms are:* awo **there**, eyo **over there**, okwo **on there**, omwo **in there**.

²-o *dem* **that, those.** (N9.1). *Takes pronominal concord* (N4), *eg.* (1) omuntu oyo ('that person'); (2) ente eyo ('that cow').

³-o *pos* **your** *si.* (N11.4) . *Takes pronominal concord* (N4), *eg.* (1) omwana wo ('your child'); (2) ente yo ('your cow').

⁴-o *pro* **it, them.** (N10.1). *Takes pronominal concord* (N4), *eg.* (1) Ekitabo, kyo kituuse? ('The book, has it arrived?'); (2) Ebitabo, byo bituuse? ('The books, have they arrived?').

P, p

-paala *vi* (-padde) **rush about wildly** (*as a chicken being chased*), **get away** (*as an escaped animal*)

-paaluuka *vi* (-paaluuse) **rush about wildly**

-paapira *vt* (-paapidde) **patch**

Paasika *n9* **Easter**

paasipalamu *n1* **type of lawn grass** *Paspalum*

paasipooti *n9* **passport**

¹-paatiika *vt* (-paatiise) **attribute** **-paatiikako** (-paatiiseeko) **attribute falsely** -paatiikako ebigambo **attribute words falsely**, *eg.* Yampaatikako ebigambo. ('He falsely attributed words to me.') -paatiikako erinnya **nickname**

²-eepaatiika intrude oneself -eepaatiika erinnya **take an alias** -eepaatiika ku **attach oneself uninvited to** (*a person or group*), **impose oneself on**, *eg.* Yeepaatiika ku kibiina ky'abakyala. ('She imposed herself on the women's group.') erinnya eppaatiike *n5* **nickname** (*as a noun*)

-paaza *vt* (-paazizza) **cause to rush about wildly** -paaza omuwala **steal someone's girlfriend** -paaza omuwendo **put up the price**

pajama *n9* **underpants** (*boxer type*)

-pakasa *vit* (-pakasizza) **work for money, employ, hire** (*a person*)

-pakira *vt* (-pakidde) **pack, load**

pakiti *n9* **packet**

-pakuka *vi* (-pakuse) **rush about** omutima -pakuka **palpitate** (*of the heart*)

-pakula *vt* (-pakudde) **snatch, grab** (= -kwakkula) -pakula empisa **adopt a custom/habit**

-pakulula *vt* (-pakuludde) **unload** (*item by item, eg. boxes from a lorry*), **unpack**

pakupaku *adv* **in a rush, hurredly**

pala *n1* **rubber tree** *Hevea brasiliensis*

palafiini *n9* (*no pl.*) **paraffin**

palamenti *n9* **parliament**

-palappalanya *vi* (-palappalanyizza) **make false excuses, stall for time.** *Saying:* 'Apalappalanya ng'atatte mukago. ('He is beating about the bush as if unwilling to become a blood brother.')

paleedi *n9* **parade**

-pama (*impolite*) *vi* (-pamye) **defecate**

pamiti *n9* **permit**

pampu *n9* **pump** pampu y'amafuta **petrol pump**

-panga *vt* (-panze) **put in order, pile (up)** (*bricks, firewood, etc.*), **heap neatly**

-pangibwa *vi* (-pangiddwa) **be heaped up**

-pangisa *vt* (-pangisizza) **rent, hire, lease**

-pangulukuka *vi* (-pangulukuse) **be put into disorder**

-pangulula *vt* (-panguludde) **take apart** (*eg. machinery*), **disassemble**

-eepanka *vi* (-eepanse) **be pompous, be egotistical, be arrogant**

-papa *vi* (-papye) **rush (about)**, *eg.* Nnabadde mpapa. ('I was in a rush.'). Can be used as aux v to mean **hurriedly** (N19).

-papala *vi* (-papadde) **flap/flutter about**

-papiriza (*also* -papya) *vt* (-papirizza) **hurry** (*someone*)

-pasuka *vi* (-pasuse) **snap open** (*of something under*

NOTES ON

o. Words starting **o** are entered under their first consonants, *eg.* omuntu under **M**.

VERBS AND ADJECTIVES BEGINNING YO are listed under **Y**. Many have forms in which the **Y** is lost (N5).

tension), **burst open** (*eg. of parcel or seed pod*) -pasuka emisinde **run fast**

-patana *vit* (-patanye) **agree on a work relationship**, *eg. Yapatana okukola omulimu ogwo.* (*'He took on the contract for that job.'*)

Paulo *n1* **Paul**

pawuda *n1* **powder**

pawunda *n9* **pound** (*currency*)

payini *n1* **pine** (*type of tree*)

payinti *n9* **pint**

-peeka *vt* (-peese) **pester** (*making demands*), **importune**

peeni *n9* **pen**

-pekuka *vi* (-pekuse) **rush about** (*of a person*)

peneti *n9* **penalty**

Pentekoti *n9* **Pentecost**

-pepeya *vi* (-pepeye) **enjoy life** -pepeya n'omuntu **move about with someone enyoying one another's company**

Petero *n1* **Peter**

petulooli *n1* **petrol**

peya *n9* **pear**

Epifaniya *n9* **Epiphany**

[1]**-piika** *vt* (-piise) **overload** -piika emmere **overfeed** -piika ssente **give too much money**

[2]**-eepiika** **have too much, stuff oneself with** (*food or drink*) -eepiika emmere **gorge**

-pika *vt* (-pise) **press in** (*air*), **pump up** -pika ebigambo **pressurise** (*someone verbally*) -pika omukka mu **inflate** (*using a pump*)

-pikiriza *vt* (-pikirizza) **push** (*someone*) **to do something, egg on, urge**

-pikisa *vt* (-pikisizza) **(cause to) press in**

-pima *vt* (-pimye) **weigh, measure**

-pinduuka *vi* (-pinduuse) **be overstretched** (*to bursting point*) olubuto -pinduuka **be bloated** (*of the stomach*)

-pipira *vi* (-pipidde) **splutter along, run poorly** (*of an engine*), *eg. Emmotoka epipira.* (*'The engine is running poorly.'*)

pirokesi *n9* **pillowcase**

piyano *n9* **piano**

apo *n9* **apple**

pokopoko *n1* **propaganda**

poliisi *n9* (*pl.* ba poliisi) **police, police station** owa poliisi *n1* **police man/woman**

polisi *n9* **polish**

ponyoka *n1* **cast net** (*for fishing*)

Pookino *n1 title* **chief of Buddu County**

pooliyo *n9* **polio**

potolo *n9* **patrol** -kuba potolo **raid house-to-house** (*by police*)

ppaaka *n9* **park** ppaaka ya takisi **taxi park**

ppaapa *n1* (*pl.* ba ppaapa) **pope**

eppaapaali *n5* (*pl.* amapaapaali) **pawpaw** (*fruit*). *Unripe fruits are used to soften meat.* eppaapaali essajja **male pawpaw fruit** (*small and inedible, medicinal*)

eppaasi *n9* **iron** (*for pressing clothes*)

ppamba (*also* ffampa) *n1* (*no pl.*) **cotton** (*from cotton plant, kapok tree or akafumbo*)

eppata *n9* **hinge**

eppeera *n5* (*pl.* amapeera) **guava** (*fruit*). *The unripe fruits can be craved by pregnant women.*

eppeesa *n5* (*pl.* amapeesa) **button**

ppereketya *n1* **hot dry weather**, *eg. Omusana gwaka ppereketya.* (*'It is really hot.'*)

ppikipiki *n9* **motorbike** owa ppikipiki *n1* **motorcyclist**

eppini *n9* **pin**

eppipa *n5* (*pl.* amapipa) **barrel, drum, keg, tub**

ppiripiri *n1* **chilli pepper**. *Two species: Capsicum annuum, C. frutescens (with very small fruits).*

eppitirivu *See* -yitirivu

ppoosita *n9* **post office**

ppoti *n9* **potty**

ppusi *n9* **cat**

eppya *See* -ggya; -pya.

pulaaga *n9* **plug**

pulaani *n9* **plan**

pulaasitiika *n9* **plastic**

pulakitisi *n9* **practice**

pulasita *n1* **plaster**

pulayimale *n9* **primary** (*school*)

puleesa *n1* **pressure, high blood pressure**

pulezidenti *n1* (*pl.* ba pulezidenti) **president**

Apuli **April**

puliida *n1* (*pl.* ba puliida) **lawyer, pleader**

pulogulaamu *n9* **programme** (*on TV/radio*)

pulojekiti *n9* **project**

puloti *n9* **plot**

-puluka *vi* (-puluse) **escape from, fly away** (*of a bird from the nest, or hat in the wind*) **-pulukako** (-puluseeko) **lose supernatural power**, *eg. Amagezi g'omusawuzi gaamupuluseeko.* (*'The healer has lost his power.'*)

-pya *adj* (eppya *n5*, amapya *n6*, empya *n9*) **new**

R,r

[1]**era** *conj* **and, besides** era ne **and also**

[2]**-(y)era** *See* -yera

eraatiri (*also* laatiri) *n9* **pound** (*weight*)

-eeraba *vr* (-eerabye) **see oneself, look at oneself** weeraba (*pl.* mweraba) **goodbye**

-eerabira *vt* (-eerabidde) **forget**

-eerabirira *vr* (-eerabiridde) **look after oneself**

-eerabiriza *vi* (-eerabirizza) **delay on purpose** (*to avoid doing something that one should*)

-eerabiza *vt* (-eerabizza) **cause to forget**

eradde *greeting* **Is all peaceful?** (N28). *From: '-laala' ('be calm, of the lake').*

eraddu (*also* laddu) *n9* (*no pl.*) **lightning, thunderbolt**

-eeraga *vi* (-eeraze) **show off**, *eg. Yabadde yeeraga* bw'alina olugoye olulungi. ('She showed off her beautiful dress.') -eeraga bwerazi be proud of oneself -eeraga -okka be obvious (of a motive), eg. Kyeraga kyokka nti ayagala ssente. ('It is obvious he's after money.'), be conspicuous, eg. Emmotoka ye yeeraga. ('His car is conspicuous.')

-eeraguza vi (-eeraguzizza) **consult a fortune-teller**

-eeraliikirira vi (-eeraliikiridde) **worry** (of oneself), **be anxious (about)**

-eeraliikirivu adj **worried, anxious**

-eeraliikiriza vt (-eeraliikirizza) **worry** (someone), **cause anxiety to**

-eeralusa vi (-eeralusizza) **pretend to be mad, become unruly**

eranda (also landu) n9 **plane** (tool for carpentry)

-eerandiza vi (-eerandizza) **support oneself** (of a plant or person)

erangi (also langi) n9 **colour, pigment, paint, dye** erangi y'emimwa **lipstick** -a erangi adj **coloured, painted**

erawuna See -lawuna

-eerayirira vi (-eerayiridde) **swear** (that one will do something)

-eereega vi (-eereeze) **become tightened, become taut, protest angrily, make a fuss, rant** ebbeeyi -eereega **be exorbitant** (of a price)

-(y)ereere See -yereere

-eereeta vi (-eereese) **do on one's own initiative** -eereeta -okka **come uninvited**, eg. Yeereeta yekka okundaba. ('She came uninvited to see me.')

-eereetera vt (-eereetedde) **bring on/for oneself** -eereetera emitawaana **bring problems on oneself**

-eerekereza vr (-eerekerezza) **deny oneself, give up**, eg. Yeerekereza omwenge mu Kisiibo. ('He gave up drinking for Lent.'), **forgo**

-eerema vi (-eeremye) **flatly refuse**

-eerembereza vit (-eerembezza) **do carefully and slowly, be deliberate and slow in one's actions** (towards)

eremeti n9 (erementi) also **helmet**

-eeresa vt (-eeresezza) **forgo, forsake**

[1]**eri** adv **(over) there** (stem -li)

[2]**eri where there is/are**. Can be equivalent to conjunction **where** or preposition **to** (N7.2).

[3]**-ri** See -li (demonstrative); -li (verb) . '-ri' is used instead of '-li' when the preceding letter is **e** or **i** (N5).

eriddugavu See -ddugavu

-eeriga vi (-eerize) **wrestle** (with one another)

eriggwa (also liggwa) n5 (pl. amaggwa) **thorn, spine, prickle** (= liggwa)

-eeriira vt (-eeridde) **eat** (for oneself)

eriiso (also liiso) n5 (pl. amaaso) **eye**; in pl. **face** (= liiso) -dda mu maaso **go forwards** mu maaso **in front, forward, in the future** mu maaso ga **in front of, before, facing, opposite** -yisaamu amaaso **show disrespect for**

-eerima vr (-eerimye) **scratch oneself excessively**

-eerimba vr (-eerimbye) **deceive oneself**

-eerimbika vi (-eerimbise) **attach oneself, be an imposter**

-rina See -lina (under -li). '-rina' is used instead of '-lina' when the preceding letter is **e** or **i** (N5).

-eerinda vi (-eerinze) **be on one's guard, be prepared, be ready for action**. Saying: 'Okwerinda si buti.' ('Being prepared is not cowardice.')

-eerindiggula vi (-eerindiggudde) **be thrown down heavily, fall heavily**, eg. Nneerindiggudde ennume y'ekigwo. ('I had a heavy fall.')

erinnya (also linnya) n5 (pl. amannya) **name, noun** (= linnya) erinnya eppaatiike **nickname** (noun) -paatiika erinnya **nickname** (verb)

erinnyo (also linnyo) n5 (pl. amannyo) **tooth** (= linnyo) amannyo ag'engereka **overlapping teeth** amannyo ag'entalaga **spaced-out teeth** amannyo g'ensaamu **teeth of barkcloth mallet**

-eerippa vi (-eerippye) **cling (to)**

erirye pos **hers, his**

eriryo pos **yours** si.

[1]**eriyo** n9 **aerial**

[2]**eriyo there is/are** (over there)

-eeroboza vt (-eerobozezza) **choose for oneself, pick out for oneself**

Roma n7 **Rome**

-eeronda vi (-eeronze) **be choosy, be fussy**

-eerondera vr (-eerondedde) **choose for oneself, pick out for oneself**

-eerongoosa vr (-eerungoosezza) **put oneself in good order, clean oneself**. See okwereongoosesa

-eerooterera vi (-eerooteredde) **have a wet dream**

-eerowooza vi (-eerowoozezza) **think about, reflect on** -eerowoozaako (-eerowoozezzaako) **think about oneself** -eerowoozaako -okka **be selfish**

-(y)eru See -yeru

erudda adv **on the side**. See oludda erudda n'erudda **on both sides**

-(y)eruka See -yeruka

Rukiga n11 **language of the Bakiga**

-(y)erula See -yerula

-eerumika vi (-eerumise) **have a nosebleed**

-rungi See -lungi

-eerungiya vr (-eerungiyisizza) **make oneself beautiful**

NOTES ON
p

-p. Verbs starting -p have first person singulars starting **mp**, eg. **mpima** ('I weigh'), from -pima.

epp-. Nouns in n5 starting **epp** have plurals (in n6) starting **amap**, eg. the plural of **eppipa** is **amapipa**.

-(y)erusa *See* -yerusa

eruuyi n'eruuyi *adv* on both sides

-ruwa? where is? (N13). *'-ruwa' is used instead of '-luwa' when the preceding letter is* e *or* i (N5).

-eerwanako *vr* (-eerwanyeko) fight for oneself, defend oneself

-eerwaza *vi* (-eerwazizza) pretend to be ill

-eerwisa *vi* (-eerwisizza) linger, *eg. Yeerwisizza ku kkanisa oluvannyuma lw'okusaba. ('She lingered at the church after the service.')*

ery' *abbrev of* erya

erya *pre* of, *eg. eddirisa erya Musoke ('window of Musoke'). Can be a prefix* erya- (N11.4), *eg. eryange ('mine'). 'erya' appears in ordinal numerals* (N7.1), *eg. eryato ery'okubiri ('second boat'). Elision is sometimes seen, eg. eryato eryokubiri ('second boat').*

eryabwe *pos* theirs

eryaffe *pos* ours

eryammwe *pos* yours *pl.*

eryanda (*also* landa) *n5* (*pl.* amanda) piece of charcoal, battery; *in pl.* charcoal

eryange *pos* mine

eryangu *See* -yangu

eryato (*also* lyato) *n5* (*pl.* amaato) canoe, boat, trough eryato ery'omwenge beer boat (*hollowed-out tree trunk used for brewing*), vat

eryenvu (*also* lyenvu) *n5* (*pl.* amenvu) ripe banana, dessert banana

eryereere *See* -yereere

eryeru *See* -yeru

eryo *dem* that

eryokye *See* -yokye

S,s

[1] -sa *adj* empty, *eg. Ennyumba nsa. ('The house is empty.')*

[2] -sa *vt* (-sedde) grind (*between stones*), mill. *See* okusa

[3] -(y)asa *See* -yasa

[4] -(y)osa *See* -yosa

-saaba *vt* (-saabye) smear (on), *eg. Yasaaba omuzigo ku mubiri. ('She smeared ointment on her body.')*

-saabaana *vi* (-saabaanye) become covered with (*eg. dirt*), *eg. Omusajja abadde asitula ensawo z'amanda n'asaabaana enziro. ('The man was carrying sacks of charcoal and got covered with soot.')*

-saabala *vi* (-saabadde) travel by (*a means of transport*), *eg. Yasaabala mu nnyonyi. ('She travelled by plane.')*

-saabaza *vt* (-saabazizza) cause to travel by, help board, *eg. Nnasaabaza omwana ku bbaasi. ('I helped the child board the bus.')*

-saabulukuka *vi* (-saabulukuse) be diluted, be watered down

-saabulula *vt* (-saabuludde) dilute, water down

-saaga *vi* (-saaze) joke, jest

-saaka *vt* (-saase) beat bark (*in first stage of barkcloth making*)

-saakaala *vi* (-saakadde) become hoarse (*of the voice*)

-saakaanya *vit* (-saakaanyizza) join in (*denouncing, congratulating, etc.*), add one's voice (to)

-saakaatira *vi* (-saakaatidde) be bushy/leafy

-saakaativu *adj* bushy, leafy

-saakaavu *adj* hoarse (*of the voice*), husky

-saakiriza *vt* (-saakirizza) overpraise

[1] Saala *n1* Sarah

[2] -saala *vi* (-sadde) hiss, *eg. Ebbinika esaala. ('The kettle is hissing.')*, sizzle. *Pronunciation:* okusáálá

[3] -saala *vi* (-sadde) pray (*of Muslims*). *Pronunciation:* okusáàlà

-saalimba *vi* (-saalimbye) trespass

-saalimbira *vt* (-saalimbidde) go where not wanted or allowed, *eg. Ente zaasaalimbira mu nnimiro ne zoonoona ebirime. ('The cows wandered all over the farm spoiling the crops.')*

-saalirwa *vi* (-saaliddwa) be disappointed, regret. *See* okusaalirwa

-saaliza *vt* (-saalizizza) cause (*someone*) to wish to have

-saamaavu *adj* wild (*in behaviour*), unrestrained

-saamira *vt* (-saamidde) beat heavily -saamira omubbi beat up a thief -saamira eŋŋoma beat a drum

-(y)asaamirira *See* -yasaamirira

-saamusaamu *adj* moderate, fair, mild, good enough

-saana *aux v* (-saanye) be suitable, should, be good. (N17), *eg. Kisaana okyogereko ne mukama wo. ('It would be good if you talked about it to your boss.')* -saanawo (-saanyewo) be destroyed without trace

-saaniika *vt* (-saanise) cover, wrap up (*food bundle before cooking*) -saaniika emmere (*also* -saaniika omuwumbo) cover food bundle with banana leaves (*before cooking*) endagala ezisaaniika *n10* banana leaves placed on food bundle (*in preparation for cooking*)

-saanikira *vt* (-saanikidde) put cover/lid on, *eg. Yasaanikira ebbakuli. ('She put a cover on the bowl.')*

-saanira *vt* (-saanidde) be suitable for, be good if, deserve, ought (N17), *eg. Kisaanidde Musoke agende alabe ssengaawe. ('Musoke ought to go and see his aunt.')*

-saanukuka *vi* (-saanukuse) become uncovered (*through removal of a lid*)

-saanukula *vt* (-saanukudde) uncover (*a container*), take cover/lid off

-saanuuka *vi* (-saanuuse) become stirred up (*of ants, bees, etc.*), become agitated, melt, become

molten (*of metal*)

-saanuula *vt* (-saanudde) **stir up** (*people, ants, etc.*), eg. *Musoke yasaanudde abakozi ne beediima.* (*'Musoke stirred up the workers and they went on strike.'*)

-saanuusa *vt* (-saanuusizza) **melt, liquify, smelt**

-saanyaawo *vt* (-saanyizzaawo) **destroy**

-saanyiza *vt* (-saanyizza) **consider suitable for**, eg. *Emmotoka eyo ngikusaanyiza.* (*'I consider that car suitable for you.'*)

-saasaana *vi* (-saasaanye) **become scattered, scatter disperse, spread** obudde -saasaana **dawn**

-saasaanya *vt* (-saasaanyizza) **(cause to) scatter, disperse, spread** -saasaanya amawulire **spread news, divulge information**, eg. *Yasaasaanya amawulire g'okufa kw'omukuumi mu makya nnyo.* (*'He divulged that the watchman had died very early in the morning.'*) -saasaanya obulwadde **spread a disease** -saasaanya olugambo **spread a rumour** -saasaanya ssente **spend money wastefully**

[1]**-saasira** *vt* (-saasidde) **feel sorry for, sympathise with, pity**

[2]**-eesaasira** *vi* **feel sorry for oneself**

-saatawala *vi* (-saatawadde) **become fat and barren** (*of an animal*)

-saatuuka *vi* (-saatuuse) **be stirred up** (*eg. of bees*)

-saatuula *vt* (-saatudde) **stir up**

-saawa *vt* (-saaye) **cut** (*grass, weeds, etc.*), **slash** (*vegetation*), eg. *Asaawa omuddo.* (*'He is slashing the grass.'*)

-saawula *vt* (-saawudde) **beat, thrash**

-(y)asaayasa *See* -yasaayasa

-saayira *vt* (-saayidde) **cut for**

-saba *vit* (-sabye) **ask, ask for, apply for, request, pray**. *See* okusaba -saba omulimu **apply for a job**

[1]**-sabika** *vt* (-sabise) **wrap** (*eg. a parcel*)

[2]**-eesabika** *vr* **wrap oneself (up)**

-sabikibwa *vi* (-sabikiddwa) **be wrapped (up)**

-sabikira *vt* (-sabikidde) **wrap for** (*someone*)

-sabira *vt* (-sabidde) **pray for/at**, *etc.*, eg. *Tusabira omulwadde awone.* (*'We are praying for the patient to get better.'*)

-sabirira *vt* (-sabiridde) **pray ardently**, eg. *Nsabirira omwana ayite ebibuuzo.* (*'I pray that the child passes the examination.'*)

-sabiriza *vt* (-sabirizza) **beg** (*as a beggar*)

-sabuka *vi* (-sabuse) **become chafed** (*of the skin*)

-sabuliza *vi* (-sabulizza) **talk rapidly and unclearly, gabble, jabber**

-sabuukulukuka *vi* (-sabuukulukuse) **be(come) unwrapped**

-sabuukulula *vt* (-sabuukuludde) **unwrap**

-saddaaka *vt* (-saddaase) **sacrifice** (*an animal, to a god or spirit*)

-sagaasagana *vi* (-sagaasaganye) **move about** (*of something not securely fastened*), eg. *Omugugu gusagaasagana mu mmotoka.* (*'The luggage is*

moving about in the car.'*), **be unsettled** (*of a person*), **fidget, waver**

-sagala *vi* (-sagadde) **be(come) loose** (*eg. of a belt*), **be loose-fitting (on)** (*of clothes*)

-sagambiza *vi* (-sagambizza) **be elated and merry, be in high spirits**

-sagaza *vt* (-sagazizza) **loosen** (*eg. a belt*)

-saggula *vt* (-saggudde) **drive out of hiding by beating bushes, flush out** -saggula abawagizi **recruit supporters**

-sajja *adj* **male**

-sajjakula *vi* (-sajjakudde) **mature** (*of a boy*), **become a man**

-sajjuka *vi* (-sajjuse) **get worse** ebwa -sajjuka **get worse** (*of a sore*) embeera -sajjuka **become unbearable** (*of a situation*) emboozi -sajjuka **be spoilt** (*of a conversation*) lumonde -sajjuka **become unpalatable** (*of potatoes*)

-saka *vit* (-sase) **gather** (*wild food*), **forage** -saka amawulire **gather news/information** -saka emmere **be given food** (*in exchange for a job*)

-sakaatira (*also* -saakaatira) *vi* (-sakaatidde) **be leafy**

-sakata *vt* (-sakase) **beat mercilessly** -sakata emiggo **beat mercilessly with sticks**

[1]**-sala** *vt* (-saze) **cut, slit** -sala amagezi **make a plan, find a way**, eg. *Yasala amagezi okufuna emmere y'abaana.* (*'She found a way to feed the children.'*) -sala ebigambo **tell untruths** -sala eddiiro **change one's political party** -sala ekkubo **cross a road** -sala endagala **cut off banana leaves** -sala ensawo **pickpocket** -sala ku muwendo **reduce the price** (*through bargaining*) -sala ku sipiidi **slow down** (*a vehicle*) -sala omuddo **mow grass** -sala omuntu (1) **cut a person**; (2) **dodge a player** (*in football*) -sala omupiira **referee a football match** -sala omusango **pass sentence** emmambya -sala **dawn** (*first signs of light*) -salako (-sazeeko) **cut off/short, reduce, amputate, dock** (*a tail*), **interrupt** (*a speaker*) -salako ku musaala **dock pay** -tuula -salako **sit with legs crossed** (*above the knees*) -salamu (1) **cut in(to)**, eg. *Salamu bibiri.* (*'Cut it in two.'*); (2) **abort** (*eg. a journey*), **give up on** -salamu bisatu **cut into three** -salawo **decide**. *See* okusalawo

[2]**-eesala** *vr* **cut oneself**

-salaasala *vt* (-sazeesaze) **cut up**, eg. *Asalaasala ebiwero mu lugoye.* (*'She is cutting up the cloth into pieces.'*), **slice**

-salibwa *vi* (-saliddwa) **be cut** -salibwa omusango

NOTES ON
r

r.. The letter **l** replaces **r** after all letters except **e** and **i**. Compare **ebintu ebirungi** ('good things' with **amagi amalungi** ('good eggs').

be condemned (*of a crime*) **-salibwako**
(-saliddwako) **be decided**
-salika *vi* (-salise) **be cutable**
-salinkiriza *vt* (-salinkirizza) **make a diversion to**
avoid being seen, *eg. Yagenda asalinkiriza mu*
lusuku. (*'He went through the banana garden to*
avoid being seen.')
-salira *vt* (-salidde) **cut for/at**, *etc.*, **condemn**
(*legally*) -salira amagezi **find a way for/to**, *eg.*
Nja kukisalira amagezi. (*'I shall find out how to do*
it.') -salira ekitooke **prune a banana plant**
(*remove old leaves*) -salira omusango **pass**
sentence on, convict Saliraawo. (*also* Salira
awo.) **Cut it right there.**
-saliriza *vt* (-salirizza) **judge unfairly** -saliriza
omupiira **be biased** (*of a football referee*) -saliriza
omusango **pass sentence unfairly on**
-(y)asama *See* -yasama
-samaalirira *vi* (-samaaliridde) **be transfixed, be**
dumbstruck
[1]**-samba** *vt* (-sambye) **kick** -samba akalobo **knock**
over a bucket -samba eggaali **peddle a bicycle**
-samba obudongo **trample on mud** (*to use in*
building) -samba omupiira **play football**
[2]**-eesamba** *vi* **keep to oneself, distance oneself**
(from)
-sambagala *vi* (-sambagadde) **kick legs about**
uncontrollably (*eg. in response to pain*)
-sambula *vt* (-sambudde) **clear** (*vegetation in*
preparation for planting), *eg. Twasambula ensiko.*
(We cleared the land.')
-samira *vit* (-samidde) **communicate with** (*a spirit*
by a group of people, accompanied by drumming,
etc.), **communicate with a spirit**
-sammuka *vi* (-sammuse) **splash** enkuba
-sammuka **ease up** (*of rain*)
[1]**-sammula** *vt* **splash, shake off** (*a liquid, sand, etc.*)
[2]**-eesammula** *vr* **flick off from oneself** (*eg. a*
caterpillar), **shake off from oneself, dissociate**
oneself, *eg. Yeesammula eŋŋambo zonna ezaali*
zibungeesebwa. (*'She dissociated herself from all*
the rumours.'), **repudiate** -eesammula amazzi mu
ngalo **shake water off one's hands**
-sammulira (*also* -sammuliza) *vt* (-sammulidde)
splash on/at, *etc.*, *eg. Emmotoka yasammulidde*
Musoke amazzi. (*'The car splashed water on*
Musoke.')
sampulo *n9* **sample**
-(y)asamya *See* -yasamya
-sandagga *vt* (-sandazze) **put border on** (*mat*)
[1]**osanga** *adv* **maybe**
[2]**-sanga** *vt* (-sanze) **meet, come upon, find,**
encounter (Ennaku) Zinsanze! **Woe is me!**
[3]**-eesanga** *vr* **find oneself** (*eg. doing something one*
did not intend)
-sangagana *vi* (-sanganye) **meet one another**
-sangibwa *vi* (-sangiddwa) **be found**
-sangiriza *vt* (-sangirizza) **come across**

unexpectedly, catch in the act
-sanguka *vi* (-sanguse) **be wiped off, be erased**
[1]**-sangula** *vt* (-sangudde) **wipe off, erase, efface**
[2]**-eesangula** *vr* **wipe oneself**
[1]**-sanguza** *vt* (-sanguzza) **erase with**
[2]**-(y)asanguza** *See* -yasanguza
[1]**-sanirira** *vt* (-saniridde) **comb**
[2]**-eesanirira** -eesanirira enviiri **comb one's hair**
-sanjaga *vt* (-sanjaze) **kill** (*by slashing deeply with a*
machete)
-sannyalala *vi* (-sannyaladde) **be(come) numb,**
be(come) paralysed, have pins and needles
-sansagala *vi* (-sansagadde) **thrash about** (*eg. as a*
response to pain)
-sansuka (*also* -sattulukuka) *vi* (-sansuse) **come**
apart
-sansulukuka (*also* -sattulukuka) *vi* (-sansulukuse)
come apart
-sansulula (*also* -sattulula) *vt* (-sansuludde) **take**
apart
-sanyufu *adj* **happy, pleased, cheerful**
-sanyuka *vi* (-sanyuse) **be happy, be glad**
-sanyukira *vt* (-sanyukidde) **be happy for/about**,
eg. Twasanyukira abagenyi. (*'We were happy to*
get visitors.')
-sanyusa *vt* (-sanyusizza) **make happy, please,**
amuse
-sasamala *vi* (-sasamadde) **be riotous** (*of a crowd*),
eg. Abantu basasamadde nga bawulidde emmundu.
(*'The people become riotous when they heard*
shooting.')
-sasamavu *adj* **riotous** (*of a crowd*)
-sasamaza *vt* (-sasamazizza) **incite** (*to riot*)
-sasambuka *vi* (-sasambuse) **peel off**
-sasambula *vt* (-sasambudde) **peel off.** *Saying:*
'Yamuvumye n'amusasambula.' (*'He abused her*
very bitterly.')
-(y)asamya *See* -yasamya
-sasira *vt* (-sasidde) **scatter** (*grass on floor*), **strew**
-sasula *vt* (-sasudde) **pay, repay** -sasula mu
bitundutundu **pay in instalments** -sasula
omutango **pay a fine** **-sasulako** (-sasuddeko)
pay part -sasulako ssente **repay part of money**
owed
-sasulira *vt* (-sasulidde) **pay for/at**, *etc, eg. Nsobola*
okusasulira ebyokunywa. (*'I can pay for the*
drinks.')
[1]**-sasuza** *vt* (-sasuzizza) **make pay**
[2]**-eesasuza** *vr* **retaliate, avenge oneself**
satifikeeti *n9* **certificate**
-sattira *vi* (-sattidde) **move from place to place** (*of a*
person), **move about restlessly.** *Saying:*
'Basattira.' (*'They are restless.', used, for example,*
when an outcome is uncertain).
-sattiza *vt* (-sattizizza) **cause to move about**
-sattulukuka (*also* -sattuka) *vi* (-sattulukuse) **come**
apart (*of something sewn or woven*), **become**
unravelled, become unstitched, become

unplaited (*of a mat*), **become undone**

-sattulula (*also* -sattula) *vt* (-sattuludde) **take apart** (*something sewn or woven*), **unravel, unstitch, unpick, unplait, undo**

-satu *num* **three (N8.1)**. *Takes numeral concord* (**N4**), *eg. (1) emiti esatu ('three trees'); (2) ebiso bisatu ('three knives'). See okusatu* -satu -satu **three-by-three** asatu **three, thirty. (N8.1)**

-sava *adj* **fatty** (*of meat*)

-savu *adj* **fat** (*of an animal*)

-savuwala *vi* (-savuwadde) **be(come) fat** (*of an animal*)

-savuwaza *vt* (-savuwazza) **fatten, exaggerate**

-saza *vt* (-sazizza) **make cut** -saza akabiriiti **strike a match** -saza omusittale **draw/rule a margin**

-sazaamu (-sazizzaamu) **cross out, cancel, nullify**

-sazibwamu *vi* (-saziddwaamu) **be cancelled**

-sazisa *vt* (-sazisizza) **cut with**, *eg. Nkisazisa kaso. ('I am cutting it with a knife.')*

-sebbuka *vi* (-sebbuse) **disintegrate, be eroded** (*of soil*)

-sebbula *vt* (-sebudde) **(cause to) disintegrate, erode**

-sedde *See* -sa

-eeseebulula *vi* (-eeseebuludde) **move away stealthily, steal away**

-seebwa *vi* (-seereddwa) **be ground/milled**

eseemwesi *n9* **text message, SMS**

[1]**-seera** *vt* (-seeredde) **mill for/at**, *etc., eg. Obulo yabuseera ku jjinja eryo. ('He ground the millet on that stone.'). Pronunciation: okuséérá*

[2]**-seera** *vt* (-sedde) **charge** (*someone*) **too much (for), overcharge (for)**, *eg. Baaseera Musoke bwe yagula emmotoka empya. ('They overcharged Musoke when he bought his new car.'). Pronunciation: okuséérá. See okuseera*

-seerera *vi* (-seeredde) **be slippery, slip, slide**

-seerevu *adj* **slippery**

-seereza *vt* (-seerezezza) **cause to be slippery**

seero *n9* **petrol station.** *From: 'Shell' (company name).*

-seesa *vt* (-seesezza) **push forward** -seesa ebigere **drag one's feet** -seesa omuliro **stoke a fire** (*by pushing in firewood*)

-seeseetuka *vi* (-seeseetuse) **slip/shift from position**

-seeseetula *vt* (-seeseetudde) **(cause to) shift from position**

-seeteera *vi* (-seetedde) **be level/flat** (*of land*)

-seeteevu *adj* **level** (*of land*), **flat**

-seeteeza *vt* (-seeteezezza) **make level** (*land*), **flatten**

-seetuka *vi* (-seetuse) **make room for someone to sit, move aside** (*of oneself*), **shift along**

-seetula *vt* (-seetudde) **move along/aside** (*person or object to make room*), **move** (*something*) **forward bit by bit, slide along**

-seeyeeya *vi* (-seeyeeye) **travel in a leisurely way, drift, float about, sail** -seeyeeya mu bbanga **glide**

-eesega *vit* (-eeseze) **move out of harm's way, move away from**

-seguka (*also* -eesegula) *vi* (-seguse) **move about a little** (*of oneself*), **go from one place to another** (*within a limited range*)

-segula *vt* (-segudde) **move** (*something*) **about a bit**

-segulira *vt* (-segulidde) **make room for, give up one's seat for**, *eg. Asegulidde omukyala atuule. ('He gave up his place so that the lady could sit.')*

-sejjera *vi* (-sejjedde) **totter along**, *eg. Musajja mukulu yasejjedde mpolampola n'atuuka. ('The old man tottered along and eventually arrived.'), **hobble along**

-seka *vi* (-sese) **laugh**

-sekaaseka *vi* (-seseesese) **keep laughing, giggle**

-sekebbuka *vi* (-sekebbuse) **be pounded** (*of a drum*), *eg. Engalabi zaasekebbuse ng'omugole atuuse. ('The drums were pounded when the bride arrived.')*

-sekebbula *vt* (-sekebbudde) **pound** (*a drum*), *eg. Yalabye omugole n'abalagira basekebbule eŋŋoma. ('When he saw the bride, he told them to pound the drums.')*

sekendule *n9* **secondary (school)**

-sekerera *vt* (-sekeredde) **laugh at**

-sekula *vt* (-sekudde) **pound** (*something in a mortar*)

-sekule *adj* **pounded, crushed**

sekulitale *n1* **secretary**

[1]**-semba** *vi* (-sembye) **be last** (*in line, order, etc.*), **be bottom** (*eg. of a class*), **be at the rear, lag behind** emmere -semba **disgust** (*of food*), *eg. Emmere ensembye. ('The food disgusts me.')* **-sembayo** (-sembyeyo) **be last**, *eg. Ye yasembayo okwogera. ('She was the last to speak.')*

[2]**-semba** *vt* **support** (*a person*), **be in favour of** (*a proposal*), **recommend, second, endorse**

-sembera *vi* (-sembedde) **come close, receive Holy Communion.** *See okusembera*

-semberera *vt* (-semberedde) **approach**, *eg. Emmotoka etusemberedde. ('The car is approaching us.'), **come near to**

-sembeza *vt* (-sembezza) **bring near, entertain** (*guests*), **host** (*people at a function*), **administer (Holy) Communion to**, *eg. Omwawule asembeza abantu. ('The minister is administering communion to the people.')*

-sembya *vt* (-sembezza) **put/make last.** *Often with enclitic* **-yo**, *ie.* **-sembyayo** (-sembezzaayo).

seminti *n1* **cement**

-sena *vt* (-senye) **laddle (out), bail (out)** (*a boat*) -sena amazzi **draw water**

-senda *vt* (-senze) **push back** (*eg. earth, to level it*) -senda ebisaaniiko **shove rubbish**

-sendasenda *vt* (-senzesenza) **persuade, entice**

-senga *vi* (-senze) **be a newcomer** (*to a place*),

settle in a new place, *eg. Yakasenga e Kampala.* *('He has just settled in Kampala.')*, immigrate. Traditional meaning: become a client to a chief (request land and enter into service).

-sengejja *vt* (-sengezze) strain, filter

-sengejjebwa *vi* (-sengejjeddwa) be filtered

-sengeka *vt* (-sengese) arrange in order, *eg. Sengeka ebitabo bulungi mu masa gaabyo.* *('Arrange the books properly on their shelves.')*, categorise, stack

-senguka *vi* (-senguse) move home, leave home permanently, emigrate

-sengukira *vt* (-sengukidde) move home to, *eg. Yasengukidde Kampala. ('He has moved to Kampala.')*

-sennya *vt* (-sennye) -sennya enku gather firewood

-sensebuka *vi* (-sensebuse) be completely destroyed

-sensera *vi* (-sensedde) slip/creep into (*eg. animal into the bush*)

-sensufu (*also* -sensuse) *adj* ragged, frayed, shredded

-sensuka *vi* (-sensuse) be(come) ragged, be(come) frayed, be(come) shredded

-sensula *vt* (-sensudde) fray, tear to shreds

sentensi *n9* sentence

-senvula *vi* (-senvudde) move along slowly, plod along, make a little progress

-senya *vt* (-senyezza) -senya amannyo brush teeth

-senza *vt* (-senzezza) receive (*a newcomer to a place*)

[1]-sera *vi* (-seze) take part in night-dancing (*associated with a black magic cult*)

[2]-eesera *vi* boil (*of a liquid*)

-sereba *vi* (-serebye) diminish in strength (*of a person*) amaanyi -sereba lose strength, *eg. Amaanyi gange gaserebye. ('My strength is declining.')*

-serebera *vi* (-serebedde) be too watery (*of food*), *eg. Omuceere guserebedde. ('The rice is too watery.')*, be sodden

-serebevu *adj* too watery (*of food*), sodden

-serebeza *vt* (-serebezza) make too watery (*food*)

-sereekulula *vt* (-sereekuludde) remove roof/thatch from

-sereka *vt* (-serese) roof, thatch -sereka n'essubi thatch

-serengeta *vi* (-serengese) descend a slope

-seresa *vt* (-seresezza) thatch with, roof with *eg. Ennyumba yagiseresa mategula. ('He has roofed the house with tiles.')*

-seruza *vt* (-seruzizza) -seruza enva add greens to a food parcel (*when cooking*)

-sesa *vt* (-sesezza) make laugh

-sesebbufu *adj* smashed

-sesebbuka *vi* (-sesebbuse) be broken into many pieces, be smashed, crumble away (*eg. of a wall*)

-sesebbula *vt* (-sesebbudde) break into pieces, smash -sesebbula emiggo beat (*a person*) severely with sticks

-sesema *vi* (-sesemye) vomit

-sesemya *vt* (-sesemezza) cause to vomit

si *adv* not (N21), *eg. Musoke looya, si musawo.* *('Musoke is a lawyer, not a doctor.')*. Can be a prefix si- (*negative of first person singular N21*), *eg. Sikola. ('I am not working.')*. si kulwa nga *conj* lest, in case, *eg. Sigala wano si kulwa ng'ajja. ('Stay here in case she comes.')*

[1]-siba *vt* (-sibye) tie (up), lock, knot, braid, tether, fasten, bind, seal, pack, imprison, detain -siba amazzi turn off water -siba bbandeegi bandage -siba eggaali apply the breaks (*of a vehicle*) -siba ekifundikwa tie a knot (*in barkcloth, on investment*) -siba ekitereke tie up a parcel -siba ekituttwa tie a knot -siba ekiwaanyi fool, dupe -siba ekiwundu dress a wound -siba ekkufulu padlock -siba emigugu pack luggage -siba emitaafu frown -siba emmere (*also* -siba omuwumbo) tie up a food parcel (*for cooking*) -siba emmotoka break a car (*to slow down*) -siba engatto tie shoelaces -siba enkalu trip up (*in wrestling*) -siba entanda pack food for a journey -siba enviiri plait hair -siba kantuntunu blindfold -siba mu kkomera imprison -siba n'eppini pin -siba yingini overhaul an engine **-sibako** (-sibyeko) tie on -sibako ebigambo make a false accusation -sibako ssente make a down payment

[2]-eesiba *vit* fasten oneself, attach oneself (to) -eesiba busuuti dress oneself in a busuuti -eesiba ku persist in one's demands on (*someone*) -eesiba olubugo dress in barkcloth (*of a woman*) olubuto -eesiba (*also* -eesiba olubuto) be constipated, *eg. Yeesibye olubuto. ('He is constipated.')*

-sibagana *vi* (-sibaganye) become entangled with one another, tie (*in sports*)

-sibe *adj* tied, teathered, locked, plaited

-sibibwa (*also* -sibwa) *vi* (-sibiddwa) be tied (up), be locked (up), be imprisoned

-sibira *vt* (-sibidde) tie at, lock in, *eg. Yasibidde ssente mu ssanduuko. ('He locked the money in the case.')*, confine -sibira mu nnyumba put under house arrest

-sibirira *vt* (-sibiridde) tie hastily -sibirira entanda (1) pack (*food*) for a journey for, *eg. Yabasibirira emmere ey'okutwala. ('He packed some food for them to take.')*; (2) give items to a bride who is starting a home

-sibisa (*also* -sibya) *vt* (-sibisizza) tie with, *eg. Yakisibisa akaguwa. ('He tied it with string.')*

-sibuka *vi* (-sibuse) originate, rise (*of a river*), sucker (*of a plant*)

siddi *n9* CD

asidi *n1* (*no pl.*) acid

[1]-siga *vt* (-size) sow

2-eesiga *vt* **trust, rely on**

-sigala *vi* (-sigadde) **remain, stay (behind)**, *eg. Abalala bwe baagenda ye n'asalawo asigale. ('When the others left, he decided to stay behind.'),* **be left (over/with).** *Used with time to denote 'minutes to', eg. Esigadde eddakiika kkumi okuwera essaawa ssatu. ('8.50', lit. 'There reamins ten minutes to reach nine o'clock.').* Often used with combined affixes of place (N24.2). -sigala emabega **lag (or straggle) behind** **-sigalako** (-sigaddeko) (1) **remain** (*on top*), *eg. Ku mmeeza kusigaddeko essowaani bbiri. ('Two plates remain on the table.')*; (2) **make up to**, *eg. Kusigaddeko essowaani bbiri okuwera ze twetaaga. ('Two more plates are needed to make up the number we need.')* **-sigalamu remain** (*within*), *eg. Mu sitoowa musigaddemu emmere entono. ('Only a little food remains in the store.')* -sigalamu enkenyera (*also* -sigalamu akakunkuna) **be unconvinced** **-sigalawo remain** (*at a place*)*, eg. Waasigalawo emmere ku mmeeza. ('There remained some food on the table.'),* **be left with** **-sigalayo remain** (*over there*)*, eg. Nnasigalayo emabega. ('I remained behind.')*

-sigalira *vt* (-sigalidde) **be left with** (*something to do*)*, eg. Nsigalidde okukusasula ensimbi. ('All that remains for me to do is to pay you.')*

-eesigama *vi* (-eesigamye) **lean on/against**, *eg. Eddaala lyesigamye ekisenge. ('The ladder is leaning on the wall.')*

-eesigamya *vt* (-eesigamizza) **lean on, rest against**

-sigaza *vit* (-sigazza) **cause to remain, retain, be left with**, *eg. Essente nnazikozesezza ne nsigaza ensawo nkalu. ('I have used up the money and am left with an empty purse.')* **-sigazaamu** (-sigazzaamu) **retain** (*within*) **-sigazaawo retain**, *eg. Lyako katono osigazeewo bye tunaalya oluvannyuma. ('Eat a little and retain some for us to eat later.')*

-sigira *vt* (-sigidde) **make deputy, delegate to**

-siguka *vi* (-siguse) **be uprooted**

-sigula *vt* (-sigudde) **uproot, seduce, lead astray** -sigula ensukusa **remove banana shoot** (*for transplanting*)

-siguukulula *vt* (-siguukuludde) **uproot**

-eesigwa *adj* **trustworthy, reliable, faithful**

-siiba *vi* (-siibye) **pass the day, fast** -siiba enjala **go the day without food** Osiibye otyanno? *greeting* (*pl.* Musiibye mutyano?) **How have you spent the day?, Good afternoon., Good evening.** (N28)

-siibula *vt* (-siibudde) **say goodbye to, discharge**

-siibulwa *vi* (-siibuddwa) **be discharged**

-siibya *vt* (-siibizza) **cause to spend the day**, *eg. Yasiibya omwana enjala. ('She made the child go through the day without food.')*

1-siiga *vt* (-siize) **apply** (*cream, paint, etc.*)*,* **smear, annoint, contaminate** -siiga bbata **spread butter** -siiga eddagala **smear ointment, impregnate with**

preservative -siiga enziro **defame** -siiga erangi **paint** -siiga obulwadde **infect** -siiga olufuufu **plaster** (*with mud*)

2-siiga send (*boy or girl*) **to the service of king or major chief** -siiga mu kisaakaate **send** (*someone*) **to the service of a major chief** -siiga mu lubiri **send** (*someone*) **to the service of the Kabaka**

3-eesiiga *vit* **smear oneself** -eesiiga langi ku mimwa **put on lipstick**

-siigibwa *vi* (-siigiddwa) **be(come) smeared, be(come) infected**

-siika *vt* (-siise) **fry, roast**

-siike *adj* (essiike *n5*) **fried, roast** (*of peanuts or grains of maize*)

-siikiriza *vt* (-siikirizza) **shade** -siikiriza okulaba **block the view of**

siiko-seero *n9* **sickle cell disease**

-siikuufu *adj* **mucky** (*of water*)

-siikuuka *vi* (-siikuuse) **be stirred up, become agitated** (*of a lake*)*,* **become mucky** (*of water*)*,* **be disturbed, become turbulent, become rough** (*of water*) emmeeme -siikuuka **feel sick**, *eg. Emmeeme ensiikuuse. ('I feel sick.')*

-siikuula *vt* (-siikudde) **stir up, agitate, disturb, make turbulent, make rough** (*water*) -siikuula ffitina **stir up hard feelings**

-eesiikuulira *vt* (-eesiikuulidde) **stir up for oneself** -eesiikuulira enjuki **stir up bees** -eesiikuulira enkukunyi **stir up trouble for oneself**

1-siima *vit* (-siimye) **appreciate, be grateful for, be pleased with**. *See* okusiima

2-eesiima *vi* **be fortunate/lucky/pleased**

-siimagana *vi* (-siimaganye) **appreciate one another**

-eesiimira *vi* (-eesiimidde) **do through one's own choose**

-siimuula *vt* (-siimudde) **wipe, mop, rub, massage** -siimuula eddagala **rub in ointment** -siimuula enfuufu **dust** -siimuula olubaawo **clean the blackboard**

-siimuuza *vt* (-siimuuzizza) **wipe with**

siiniya *n9* **senior (school), secondary school**

-siira *vi* (-sidde) -tambula -siira **walk slowly, dawdle**

siiringi *n9* **ceiling**

-siisiitira *vt* (-siisiitidde) **rock** (*a baby to sleep*)*, eg. Asiisiitira omwana yeebake. ('She is rocking the baby to sleep.'),* **lull**

-siisira *vi* (-siisidde) **set up camp, build a thatched hut or temporary shelter** -siisira mu kifo **stay settled in a place for a long time**

1-siisiriza *vt* (-siisirizza) **spread** (*ointment*) **on with the hand, soothe** (*with the hand, eg. an insect bite*)

2-eesiisiriza *vr* **soothe oneself with the hand** -eesiisiriza ebizigo **put lotion on oneself**

-siitaana *vi* (-siitaanye) **work hard, toil away**

-siiwa *vit* (-siiye) **itch**, *eg. Omubiri gunsiiwa. ('My body itches.')*

-siiwuufu *adj* **faded, dry** (*of the skin*)

-siiwuuka *vi* (-siiwuuse) **fade, lose colour, become dry** (*of the skin*)

-siiwuusa *vt* (-siiwuusizza) **(cause to) fade**

-siiya *vit* (-siiyizza) **shoo away**

[1]-sika *vi* (-sise) **be an heir, inherit.** *Pronunciation:* okusíká

[2]-sika *vt* **pull, heave on, tow, haul.** *Pronunciation:* okusíká   -sika amazzi **flush a toilet**   -sika omuguwa **have a tug of war**   -sika omukka **breathe in, inhale**   **-sikamu** (-siseemu) **pull out** (*eg. a nail*)

-eesika *vr* **have convulsions**

sikaala *n9* **scholarship** (*grant for studying*)

-sikaasikanya *vt* (-sikaasikanyizza) **pull against one another**   -sikaasikanya ennyama **eat undercooked meat**

sikaati *n9* **skirt**

[1]-sikambula *vt* (-sikambudde) **snatch away**

[2]-eesikambula *vi* **pull oneself away** (*from being held*)

-sikattira *vi* (-sikattidde) **be obstructed in movement, be temporarily delayed, be held up, hesitate, come unwillingly, be reluctant to move,** *eg. Omwana nnamutwala nga asikattira.* (*'I took the child, but she was reluctant to go.'*)

-sikattiza *vt* (-sikattizza) **(cause to) hold up**

-sikira *vt* (-sikidde) **be heir to**

-sikiriza *vt* (-sikirizza) **persuade, entice**

-sikondoka *vi* (-sikondose) **hiccup**

sikulwa nga *See* si kulwa nga

-sima *vt* (-simye) **dig, burrow, excavate, mine**   -sima lumonde **dig out potatoes** (*with a stick*). *See* -soggola   -sima nayikonto **make a borehole**

-simattuka (-simattuse) *See* -sumattuka

-simattula (-simattudde) *See* -sumattula

[1]-simba *vt* (-simbye) **plant** (*a plant, post, etc.*), **place upright, erect.** *The following refer to sitting positions when seated on the ground:* -simba olukokola **recline on one elbow,** -simba olukono **recline on one arm.**   -simba emmotoka **park a car**   -simba eweema **pitch a tent**   -simba olunyiriri **line up, queue**   -simba oluseke **extort**   **-simbako** (-simbyeko) **plant on/in**   -simbako essira **emphasise**   -simbako oluseke **extort**

[2]-eesimba *vi* **plant oneself, take up position, be upright** (*eg. of a post*)   -yimirira -eesimba **stand upright**   **-eesimbawo** (-eesimbyewo) **stand in an election, be a candidate.** *See* eyeesimbyewo; okwesimbawo

-eesimbu *adj* **upright** (*in character*), **straightforward, forthright**

-simbuka *vi* (-simbuse) **set off from** (*on a journey*), *eg. Yasimbuka Kampala.* (*'She set off from Kampala.'*)

-simbula *vi* (-simbudde) **dig up, uproot, depart** (*on a journey*), *eg. Eryato lisimbula mangu.* (*'The boat departs soon.'*), **set off on a journey,** *eg.*

Twasimbula ku makya. (*'We set off early in the morning.'*)   -simbula ekirowoozo **originate an idea**   -simbula emboozi **launch a conversation**

-simbulawo (-simbuddewo)   -simbulawo eweema **strike a tent**

-simbuliza *vt* (-simbulizza) **transplant, move from one place to another,** *eg. Yasimbuliza embuzi.* (*'She has moved the goat.'*, *eg. to a new post*)

[1]-simula *vt* (-simudde) **dig up**   -simula omufu **dig up a dead body, exhume**   -simula omupiira **kick a ball a long way**

[2]-(y)asimula *See* -yasimula

-sina *vt* (-sinye) **offend**

-sinda *vi* (-sinze) **moan, groan**   -sinda mukwano **make love**   -sinda obulwadde **groan in pain**

-sindiikiriza *vt* (-sindiikirizza) **push back** (*in a continuing way*), **encourage** (*someone unwilling*)

-sindika *vt* (-sindise) **push, thrust, send** (*a person*)   -sindika akasaale **shoot an arrow**   -sindika mu maaso **push forward**   -sindika omwana **push hard in labour**

-sindikagana *vi* (-sindikaganye) **push one another, jostle**

-sindikira *vt* (-sindikidde) **push in/at,** *etc.*, **send to** (*a person*)   -sindikira embwa **set a dog on,** *eg. Nja kukusindikira embwa.* (*'I will set a dog on you.'*)   -sindikira omuntu **send a person to,** *eg. Nja kukusindikira omuntu akuyambe.* (*'I will send a person to help you.'*)

-sindogoma *vi* (-sindogomye) **groan in distress, cry in anguish**

-sinduka *vi* (-sinduse) **be uprooted, topple (over),** *eg. Ekisenge kyasinduse ne kigwa.* (*'The wall toppled over.'*)

-sindula *vt* (-sindudde) **uproot, topple,** *eg. Kibuyaga yabadde mungi n'asindula ebitooke.* (*'The storm toppled the banana plants.'*)

-sinduukirira *vi* (-sinduukiridde)   emmeeme -sinduukirira **feel nausea** (*with personal object*), *eg. Emmeeme ensinduukirira.* (*'I feel sick.'*)

-sinduukiriza *vt* (-sinduukirizza)   -sinduukiriza emmeeme **nauseate, make feel sick**

sineema *n9* **cinema, movie**

[1]singa (*also* ssinga) *conj* **if.** *'ssinga' is used instead of 'singa' when stress is required, mostly at the beginning of sentences.*

[2]-singa *vit* (-sinze) **be more (than), surpass (in), exceed,** *eg. Obulungi bwabwe bwasinze kye nnabadde nsuubira.* (*'Their beauty exceeded my expectations.'*), **be best,** *eg. Yasinga mu kibiina.* (*'She was best in class.'*), **win,** *eg. Musoke yasinze abalala okudduka.* (*'Musoke won the running race.'*). *Can be equivalent to* **most of, mostly,** *eg. Abantu abasinga bambadde enkuufiira.* (*'Most of the people are wearing hats.'*). *'-singa' can be used in superlatives and comparisons, the quality considered being given as a noun after the verb, eg. (1) Omuti guno gwe gusinga obuwanvu mu kibira.*

('This is the tallest tree in the forest.'); (2) Omuti guno gusinga ogwo obuwanvu. ('This tree is taller than that one.'). See okusinga **-singa obubi be worse (than)** **-singa obulungi be better (than)** **-singa obunene be most** (*eg. in size or extent*) **-singa obungi be more (than)** **-singa omusango win a (court) case,** *eg. Omusango yagusinga. ('He won the court case.')* **-singa -onna be better than all, dominate** *omusango -singa* **lose a (court) case** (*with personal object*), *eg. Omusango gwamusinga. ('He lost the court case.')* **-singako** (-sinzeeko) **be slightly better than,** *eg. Asingako munne okusoma. ('He is slightly better at reading than his friend.'),* **be slightly more than** **-singawo** (1) **exceed, be more than;** (2) **put up as a guarantee,** *eg. Yasingawo nnyumba ye. ('He put up his house as a guarantee.'),* **bet** **-singayo put up as a guarantee**

-singira *vt* (-singidde) (1) **be preferable for;** (2) **put as collateral for** (*someone*), *eg. Yansingira ekibanja kye ne mmuwola ensimbi akakadde kamu. ('He put up his plot as collateral to borrow one million from me.')*

-sinika *vt* (-sinse) **-sinika amannyo bare one's teeth**

-(y)asinkana *See* **-yasinkana**

sinki *n9* **sink, basin**

sinnakindi *conj* **or else, otherwise**

-sinsimula *vt* (-sinsimudde) **shake vigourously** **-sinsimula emmere divide up hot lumps of food** (*eg. to cool for a child to eat*) **-sinsimula emiggo beat** (*someone*) **with sticks** **-sinsimula engoye shake out wet clothes** (*when hanging them out to dry*)

-sinsimulira *vt* (-sinsimulidde) **shake vigorously (for),** *eg. Ekitambaala kisinsimulire ebweru. ('Shake the tablecloth outside.')*

-sinwa *vi* (-siniddwa) **be nauseated** (= *-tamwa*)

[1]**-sinza** *vt* (-sinzizza) **(cause to) surpass,** *eg. Musoke asinza Mukasa amaanyi. ('Musoke is stronger than Mukasa.'). Saying: 'Oli takusinga nsumika, nti ebijja bituutidde. ('Don't be envious of someone who dresses better than you.', meaning 'He is probably after something.')* **-sinza amaanyi overpower** **-sinza amagezi outwit**

[2]**-sinza** *vt* **worship.** *See okusinza*

-sinziira *vi* (-sinzidde) **start or act from a given place or point.** *Can be equivalent to preposition* **from,** *eg. Yasinziira mu nnyumba n'ayita omwana. ('He called the child from within the house.'). See okusinziira*

-siŋŋaana *vt* (-siŋŋaanye) **meet, encounter**

sipeeya *n1* **spare (part)**

sipesulo *n9* **taxi** (*individually hired*). *From: 'special (hire)' (English).*

sipiidi *n9* (*no pl.*) **speed**

sipiika *n1* (*pl.* ba sipiika) **speaker** (*of parliament*)

sipongi *n1* **sponge, foam** (*eg. in mattress*)

-sira *vt* (-size) **rub off and dissolve, grate** (*to make powder*) **-sira emmumbwa rub and dissolve medicinal clay stick**

-siraamu *adj* **Islamic**

-siramuka *vi* (-siramuse) **become a Muslim**

-sirifu *adj* **silent, quiet**

siriimu *n1* (*no pl.*) **AIDS**

-siriira *vi* (-siridde) **be burnt** (*eg. of food in a pot*), **be scorched, be charred**

-siriiza *vt* (-siriizizza) **burn** (*accidentally*), **scorch, char**

-sirika *vi* (-sirise) **be quiet, be(come) silent, stop crying**

-sirikira *vit* (-sirikidde) **keep quiet about,** *eg. Amawulire yagasirikira. ('He kept quiet about the news.')*

-sirikitu *adj* **very small, tiny**

-sirikka *vi* (-sirisse) **be destroyed without trace.** *Mostly used in connection with fire, eg. Ennyumba yayidde n'esirikka. ('The house was burnt and completely destroyed.')*

-sirikkira *vi* (-sirikkidde) **be completely destroyed in/by,** *etc., eg. Ennyumba esirikkidde mu muliro. ('The house has been destroyed by fire.')*

-sirisa *vt* (-sirisizza) **silence, hush, quieten, stop** (*someone*) **crying.** *Saying: 'Kisirisa afumba ajja okulya takimanya. ('He who comes to eat cannot know why the cook keeps quiet.'* *akasirisa n12* **full stop**

-sirise *adj* **quiet** (*of a person, by nature*)

-sirissa *vt* (-sirissizza) **destroy without trace** (*in a fire*)

-siru *adj* **foolish, silly**

-sirusiru *adj* **idiotic**

-siruwala *vi* (-siruwadde) **be(come) stupid**

-siruwaza *vt* (-siruwazizza) **make stupid, make a fool of, deprave**

-eesisiggiriza *vi* (-eesisiggirizza) **remain**

NOTES ON
s

-s. Unless the s is doubled, verbs starting s have 1st person singulars starting **ns,** *eg.* **nsa** ('I grind'), from **-sa.**

ess-. Nouns in *n5* starting **ess** have plurals (in *n6*) starting **amas,** *eg.* the plural of **essanga** is **amasanga.**

-ss. Verbs starting **ss** have 1st person singulars starting **nzis,** *eg.* **nzisa** ('I put down'), from **-ssa.**

ssa- and **sse-.** The plurals of nouns in *n1* referring to people and starting **ssa** or **sse** (without initial vowels) typically follow these patterns: (1) **ssalongo** (*pl.* **ba ssalongo**); (2) **ssenga** (*pl.* **ba ssenga**)

NOUNS IN *n9*. Most nouns in *n9* have identically spelt plurals (in *n10*).

unresponsive, be unforthcoming

-sisimuka *vi* (-sisimuse) **wake up suddenly from deep sleep** (*of oneself*)

-sisimula *vt* (-sisimudde) **wake** (*someone*) **up suddenly from deep sleep**

-sisinkana *vit* (-sisinkanye) **meet**

-eesisiwala *vi* (-eesisiwadde) **be shocked, shudder with shock, be taken aback, wince, cringe**

-eesisiwaza *vt* (-eesisiwazizza) **shock**

Sitaani *n1* **Satan**

sitakange *n1* **conservative person** (*socially or politically*)

-sitama *vi* (-sitamye) **squat**

sitampu *n9* **stamp**

siteegi *n9* **stage/stop** (*for bus/taxi*) siteegi ya bbaasi **bus stop**

siteeringi *n9* **steering, steering wheel**

sitenseni *n9* **station, petrol station, crossroads**

sitoovu *n9* **stove**

sitoowa *n9* **store, warehouse**

-eesittala *vi* (-eesittadde) **stumble, trip up**

-eesittaza *vt* (-eesittazizza) **(cause to) stumble, trip** (*someone*) **up**

situdiyo *n9* **studio**

[1]**situka** *n9* **dandruff**

[2]**-situka** *vi* (-situse) **stand up** (*from a sitting position*)

-situla *vit* (-situdde) **lift, start a journey, depart, take off** (*of an aeroplane*)

-situlira *vt* (-situlidde) **lift for**, *eg. Yamusitulirako ensawo.* (*'He lifted the bag for her.'*), **carry for** (*eg. shopping bag in a market*)

situlooka *n9* **stroke** (*illness*)

-situnkana *vi* (-situnkanye) **keep standing up to do things**

-siwa *vt* (-siye) **add** (*an ingredient*) **to** (*food or drink*), **flavour with, season** -siwako (-siyeeko) **add** (*an ingredient*) **to**, *eg. Omubisi yagusiyeeko omwenge.* (*'He added sorghum to banana juice to make beer.'*)

siyaagi *n1* (*no pl.*) **butter.** *From Swahili.*

-siyagguka *vi* (-siyagguse) **travel far** -siyagguka olugendo **take a long trip**

so *conj* **whereas, while, but, yet.** *Word used to keep a conversation going, eg. ... so Daudi agambye ... ('... yet David said ...').* so nga **but actually,** *eg. Nze saamulabye mu kkanisa so nga yabaddeyo.* (*'I did not see him in church but actually he was there.'*), **whereas** so nno **actually,** *eg. So nno twagenda okumulaba.* (*'We actually went to see him.'*) so si **and not,** *eg. Ye ggwe, so si nze.* (*'It is you and not me.'*)

-soba *vi* (-sobye) **be/go wrong,** *eg. Nnatunze olugoye ne lisoba.* (*'I sewed the dress but it went wrong.'*), **err.** *Can mean* **be more than,** *eg. Yazaala abaana abasoba mu kkumi.* (*'She produced more than ten children.'*) **-sobako** (-sobyeko) **go wrong for,** *eg. Ebintu bimusobyeko.*

(*'Things have gone wrong for him.'*), **be mistaken**

-sobamu **go slightly wrong, be not quite right,** *eg. Ebintu bisobyemu.* (*'Things are not quite right.'*)

-sobera *vt* (-sobedde) **confuse** (*with personal object*), *eg. Eky'okukola kimusobedde.* (*'He is confused about what to do.'*), **perplex, baffle**

-soberwa *vi* (-sobeddwa) **be confused, be perplexed, be baffled**

-sobeza *vt* (-sobezza) **cause to be confused, exasperate**

-soboka *vi* (-sobose) **be possible, be controllable, be manageable** kisoboka okuba nga **maybe,** *eg. Kisoboka okuba nga yadduse mu Uganda.* (*'It maybe true that he fled from Uganda.'*)

[1]**-sobola** *aux v* (-sobodde) **be able, manage**

[2]**-eesobola** *vi* **be capable of managing one's own affairs**

-sobozesa *vt* (-sobozesezza) **make possible, enable, facilitate**

-sobu *adj* **wrong**

-sobya *vit* (-sobezza) **make a mistake, err, violate, do wrong (to)** -sobya ku muwala **rape a girl** **-sobyako** (-sobezzaako) **do wrong to**

-soggola (-soggodde) *vt* **dig up** (*potatoes, using a hoe*). *See* -sima

-sogola *vt* (-sogodde) **crush bananas to extract juice, tread on bananas** (*in beer making*) -sogola n'ebigere **extract** (*juice*) **by trampling** -sogola n'engalo **extract** (*juice*) **by crushing with the hands** -sogola omubisi **extract juice from bananas** (*by crushing them*) -sogola omwenge **make beer** (*from bananas*)

-sogonyoka *vt* (-sogonyose) **be spoilt** (*by being crushed or mashed*), *eg. Yawanudde eppaapaali ne ligwa ne lisogonyoka.* (*'He dropped the pawpaw and it got squashed.'*)

-sogonyola *vi* (-sogonyodde) **spoil through being crushed or squashed,** *eg. Weegendereze ojja kusogonyola amenvu ago.* (*'Be careful or you will squash those bananas.'*)

-sogoza *vt* (-sogozza) **make beer using,** *eg. Baasala essubi basogoze omwenge.* (*'They cut spear grass for beer making.'*) -sogoza bigere **tread on bananas** (*in beer making*), *eg. Omwenge bagusogoza bigere.* (*'They make beer by trampling bananas.'*)

-sojja *vt* (-sozze) **peck, nag, make jibes at**

-sojjagana *vi* (-sojjaganye) **bicker**

-sojjolimba *vi* (-soggolimbye) **walk cautiously**

-soka *vt* (-sose) **stuff in** (*eg. reeds into thatched roof*)

soketi *n9* **(electric) socket**

[1]**-sokoola** *vt* (-sokodde) **pick out, dig out** **-sokoolamu** (-sokoddemu) **pick out from within,** *eg. Yasokoolamu obusomyo mu ggumba.* (*'She picked out the marrow from the bone.'*) akati akasokoola amannyo **toothpick**

[2]-eesokoola *vr* **pick out from oneself** -eesokoola mu mannyo **pick one's teeth** -eesokoola mu nnyindo **pick one's nose**

-sokotta *vt* (-sokosse) **prod, probe, poke**

-solobeza *vit* (-solobezza) **suck noisily (on)** (*in eating or drinking*), **slurp, drool** -solobeza ekikajjo **chew sugarcane**

-solobya *vt* (-solobye) **prune** (*with a pruning pole*)

-solooza *vt* (-soloozezza) **collect** (*money*) -solooza ebirabo **take a collection** (*eg. in church*) -solooza ebisale **collect fees**

-sooloozebwa *vi* (-sooloozeddwa) **be collected** (*of fees, contributions, etc.*) ssente ezisoloozebwa **collection** (*in church*)

-soma *vit* (-somye) **read, study, study for.** *See* okusoma -soma eddiini **practice religion** -soma mu kkanisa **attend church** -soma mu ssomero **attend school**

somatulye *n1* **elephant snouth fish.** *Meaning: 'Pray and let's eat.' – said by the elder among the fishermen, so that the fish can be eaten straight away (this fish is considered especially tasty).*

-somba *vt* (-sombye) (1) **bring together** (*over several trips*), **collect together**; (2) **regularly repeat a journey**, *eg. Nsomba abaana bange buli lunaku okuva ku ssomero. ('Every day I take my children to school.')*

-somera *vt* (-somedde) **read for/to, study at/in**, *eg. Asomera Gayaza. ('She is studying at Gayaza.')*

-somerera *vt* (-someredde) **study for** (*eg. a degree*)

-somesa *vt* (-somesezza) **teach.** *See* okusomesa

-somoka *vit* (-somose) **travel across water, cross** (*water*), **ford** (*a river*)

-somokera (-somokedde) *vt* **cross water at.** *See* okusomokera w'osomokera *n16* **place for crossing water, ford**

-somola *vt* (-somodde) **take away gradually**, *eg. Abaana baasomodde omugaati. ('The children took off pieces from the loaf.')*, **steal one-by-one** -somola amawulire **ferret out information**

-sona *vt* (-sonye) **stitch together** (*a mat from woven strips*)

[1]-sonda *vt* (-sonze) **gather** (*little by little*) -sonda ssente **collect money in contributions**

[2]-eesonda *vr* **contribute** (*voluntarily*) **towards a cause**

-sondowala *vi* (-sondowadde) **taper**

-sondowaza *vt* (-sondowazizza) **taper**

[1]songa = so nga. *See* so

[2]-songa *vi* (-sonze) **point (to/at)**, *eg. Asonga ku nnyumba. ('He is pointing at the house.')* -songa engalo ku **point a finger at** -songa olunwe **point with the finger** -songako (-sonzeeko) **point at, point out** -songamu **point with** -songamu emmundu **point a gun at** -songamu omumwa **point with the lips**

-songola *vt* (-songodde) **point, sharpen**

-songovu *adj* **pointed, sharp**

-songoza *vt* (-songozezza) **make pointed** -songoza omumwa **point with the lips** (*in annoyance*), **pout**

[1]-sonseka *vt* (-sonsese) **insert** (*eg. stick into bundle*), **slip in, push in** (*eg. piece of paper between pages of a book*)

[2]-eesonseka *vr* **insert oneself in, slip into, enter**, *eg. Omusota gwesonsese mu kituli. ('The snake entered the hole.')*

-sonsomola *vit* (-sonsomodde) **sting**

-sonyiwa *vt* (-sonyiye) **forgive, excuse, pardon, let off.** *See* okusonyiwa **Nsonyiwa. I'm sorry.**

-sonyiwala *vi* (-sonyiwadde) **feel ashamed, look shy**

-sonyiyibwa *vi* (-sonyiyiddwa) **be forgiven**

-sooba *vi* (-soobye) **move slowly** (*like a snail*), **be sluggish.** *Used as aux v* (**N19**), *eg. (1) Atambula asooba. ('She walks slowly.'); (2) Akola asooba. ('He works sluggishly.')*

-sooberera *vt* (-sooberedde) **stalk**

[1]-sooka *vit* (-soose) **be/do first** (**N17, N19**), *eg. Sooka ofumbe emmere. ('First cook the food.'). 'sooka' can be used in relative phrases to mean first* (**N7.1**), *eg. (1) omuti ogusooka ('the first tree'); (2) akaana akasooka ('the first baby'). See* okusooka -sookayo (-sooseeyo) **precede**

[2]-eesooka *vit* **point out one's preference, want** (*something, pre-empting others*), *eg. Ku nnyumba zonna nneesoose okugula ennyumba eriraanye omuyembe. ('Out of all the houses, I want to buy the one near the mango tree.'). Saying: 'Okubwesooka si kubulya. ('You don't necessarily get what you want.')*

-sookera *vi* (-sookedde) **be/do first in, start with**, *eg. Sookera ku kulongoosa mu kisenge. ('Start with cleaning the bedroom.')* obujjanjabi obusookerwako **first aid**

soole *n9* **sole** (*of a shoe*)

-soolooba *vi* (-sooloobye) **be out of line**, *eg. Ettofaali erimu lisooloobye mu lunyiriri. ('One brick is out of line.')*, **project beyond, stick out, extend beyond** -sooloobako (-sooloobyeko) **go a little beyond, stick out a little**, *eg. Ekizimbe kino kisooloobyeko ku birala ('This building sticks out above the others.')* **-sooloobamu** **stick out** (*from within*), **project** (*from*)

-sooloobya *vt* (-sooloobezza) **cause to exceed, cause to extend beyond, put out of alignment**

-soomooza *vt* (-soomoozezza) **challenge**

-soomoozebwa *vi* (-soomoozeddwa) **be challenged**

-soona *vt* (-soonye) **(narrowly) beat** (*a person*) **to** (*an opportunity*), **pre-empt**, *eg. Yansoonye okugula ettaka. ('He beat me to buying the land.')*, **pre-empt** -soona omuwala **get a girl** (*before someone else*)

-soonooka *vi* (-soonoose) **move very slowly** -soonooka ng'ekkovu **move at snail pace**

-soonookereza *vt* (-soonookerezza) **move up to and take by surprise, stalk**

-soosootoka *vi* (-soosootose) **lose shape** (*eg. of a* bundle through loss of contents or from being squashed), **come apart gradually** (through losing contents)

-soosootola vt (-soosootodde) -soosootola emmere **unwrap a bundle of cooked food to serve**

-sooza vit (-soozezza) **make sucking noise with the lips** (a gesture of contempt), **hiss (at)**

-sosola vt (-sosodde) **pick out** (unwanted things), **discriminate against** (a person) -sosola endaggu **peel yams after cooking** **-sosolamu** (-sosoddemu) **pick out from within** -sosolamu amagumba **pick out bones** (from a fish)

-sosolwa vi (-sosoleddwa) **be discriminated against**

-sosonkereza vt (-sosonkerezza) **pick a quarrel with, challenge aggressively, provoke**

-sotta vt (-sosse) **pound** (with a small pestle), **crush, mash** -sotta eggaali **pedal a bicycle**

-sowoka vi (-sowose) **come out of place, slip out** (of an item from a bundle) omukono -sowoka **dislocate an arm** **-sowokamu** (-sowoseemu) eggwako -sowokamu **abort** (of an animal)

-sowola vt (-sowodde) **pull out** (eg. a stick from a bundle), **extract, abort** (by an animal), eg. Ente esowodde. ('The cow has aborted.') asowodde **passenger occupying front window seat of communal taxi** (with part of arm extending out of window) **-sowolamu** (-sowoddemu) **pull out from within, extract**

-sowottoka vi (-sowottose) **become loose** (of something through losing contents, eg. of a poorly tied bundle), **lose weight**, eg. Ensawo ya muwogo yasowottose. ('The sack of cassava has lost weight.')

[1]**essa** n5 (pl. amasa) **shelf, compartment of omweso board** amasa g'ebitabo **bookcase** -teeka mu ssa lya wansi **be demoted**

[2]**-ssa** vit (-ssizza, nzisa) (1) **move to a lower level, place down, decrease** (price, tax, etc.), **lower**; (2) **fruit** (of a banana plant), eg. Kissizza. ('The banana plant is fruiting.'); (3) **breathe**. See okussa -ssa amaaso **lower one's gaze** -ssa ebbeeyi **decrease the price** -ssa eddaala **demote** -ssa ekikkowe **sigh** -ssa ekimu **think alike** -ssa ekitiibwa **respect** -ssa ennyonyi ku ttaka **land an aeroplane** -ssa essira **stress, emphasise** -ssa mu bumpi **summarise** -ssa omukka **breathe out** -ssa omuwendo **decrease the price** -ssa wabbali **put to/on the side** -ssa wansi **set/put down**, eg. Yassa kye yali akutte wansi. ('He put down what he was holding.') **-ssaako** (-ssizzaako) **put on**, eg. Ku mmeeza njagala kussaako ebimuli. ('I want to put some flowers on the table.'), **switch on** (electricity), **add on**, eg. Nja kussaako n'ebintu bino. ('I shall add on these as well.'). See okussaako -ssaako ekinkumu **put one's thumbprint** -ssaako emikono **confirm** (in Christian faith) -ssaako essira **emphasise**

-ssaako omukono **sign** (eg. a document) -ssaako omusika **install an heir** -ssaako omwoyo **concentrate** -ssaako sitampu **put one's mark/seal** **-ssaamu put in/on.** Saying: 'Ssaamu engatto tugende.' ('Let's go.', lit. 'Put on your shoes, let's go.'). -ssaamu amaanyi **put effort into** (what one is doing) -ssaamu ekitiibwa **honour, respect, venerate** **-ssaawo put down** (there), **establish** **-ssaayo put down** (over there) -ssaayo omwoyo **concentrate**

ssaabaddu n1 **second chief in importance**, eg. ssaabaddu w'oweggombolola ('deputy sub-county chief')

Ssaabaganzi n1 title **senior uncle** ('kojja') of the Kabaka (eldest brother of the Kabaka's mother)

ssaabakaaki n1 **head of servants living in the compound of a king/chief**

ssaabalabirizi n1 **archbishop**

Ssaabalangira n1 title **head of the princes**

ssaabaminisita n1 **prime minister** (of a country)

Ssaabasajja n1 title **first among men** (a title of the Kabaka)

ssaabasumba n1 **archbishop** (RC)

Ssaabataka n1 **overlord of the land** (a title of the Kabaka)

essaabiro n5 **collar bone**

essaala n9 **prayer**

ssaali n9 **sari** (type of dress worn by Indian women)

Ssaalongo n1 title **father of twins**

essaalu n9 **area of a certain type of grass** (found in wet or swampy places)

essaaniiko n5 (no pl.) **used up banana leaves** (after cooking a food bundle), **rubbish**

essaati n9 **shirt**

ssaava n1 **son of a princess**

essaawa n9 **watch, clock, hour, time** (of the day) essaawa y'ekide **alarm clock** Essaawa mmeka? **What is the time?** essaawa y'oku mukono **wristwatch**

ssaayansi n1 **science**

ssabbaawa n9 **target**

essabbiiti n9 **week, Sunday, Sabbath** Olunaku lwa Ssabbiiti **Saturday** (for Jews and Seventh Day Adventists)

ssabbuuni n1 (no pl.) **soap**

essabo n5 (pl. amasabo) **shrine** (of a lubaale) (= ekiggwa) essabo lya ssekinnoomu **personal shrine**

ssaddaaka n9 (no pl.) **animal sacrifice**

ssafaali n9 **long journey, safari**

essaakalamentu n5 (pl. amasaakalamentu) **sacrament** amasaakalamentu amavannyuma **last rites**

essalambwa n5 **puff adder, Gabon viper**

essamba n5 (pl. amasamba) **farm**

essambo n5 (pl. amasambo) **fishing net** (used for trawling)

essami n5 (no pl.) **lake flies**

Ssande *n9* Sunday

essanduuko *n9* box, suitcase, chest, trunk
essanduuko y'ebyuma **metal box**   essanduuko
y'omufu **coffin**

essanga *n5* (*pl.* amasanga) **tusk, ivory**

essanja *n5* (*no pl.*) **dry banana leaves**

essanyu *n5* (*no pl.*) **happiness, joy**

ssapatu *n9* **flip-flop, slipper**

ssapule *n9* **rosary** (*RC*)

essasa *n5* (*pl.* amasasa) **metal workshop, forge**

essasi *n5* (*pl.* amasasi) **bullet, lead** (*the metal*),
solder. *See* ekyasi

Ssatade *n1* Saturday

ssatu *num* **three**

essavu *n5* (*pl.* amasavu) **piece of animal fat**; *in pl.*
fat

essaza *n5* (*pl.* amasaza) **county** (**N29**), **diocese**
(*RC*). *See* owessaza

-sse *See* -kka; -tta.

Ssebaaseka June

Ssebalijja *n1 title* **chief herdsman** (*cattle keeper*) **of**
the Kabaka

ssebo *n1* **sir, mister**. *A form of address to a man;*
also to a queen or princess.

ssebusa *n1* (*no pl.*) **stomach**

Ssebutemba September

Ssebwana *n1 title* **chief of Busiro County**

sseccungwa *n1* **grapefruit**

sseddume *n1* (*no pl.*) **male of certain ruminants**,
eg. sseddume w'endiga ('ram'), **bull**

sseefu *n9* **safe** (*secure place for valuables*)

sseffuliya *n9* **metal cooking pot, saucepan**

sseggereeti *n1* (*no pl.*) **cigarette**

sseggwanga *n1* **cockerel, cock**   Sseggwanga **a**
title of the Kabaka. *Meaning: 'head of the tribe'.*

ssekabaka *n1* **deceased king of Buganda**

ssekanyolya *n1* (*pl.* bi ssekanyolya *n8*) **heron**

ssekavubira *n1* **pied kingfisher** (*type of bird*)

Ssekiboobo *n1 title* **chief of Kyaggwe County**

ssekinnoomu *n1* **person who does things on**
her/his own, person living alone. *See* essabo

ssekitulege *n1* **ground-bow** (*one-stringed musical*
instrument played by boys)

ssekkesa *n1* (*no pl.*) **type of hairy caterpillar**
(*camouflaged flat hairy type, sometimes with red*
bristles at ends)

ssekkokko *n9* **turkey**

Ssekukkulu *n9* **Christmas**. *From: 'siku kuu' ('big*
day') (Swahili).

ssemaka *n1* **big man** (*having more than one major*
asset, eg. homes, money, wives, children)

ssematalo *n1* **major/world war**

ssemateeka *n1* **constitution** (*of a country*)

ssemazinga *n1* **continent**

sseminaariyo *n9* **seminary**

ssemufu *n1* **effigy**   omuzannyo gwa ssemufu
children's game in which someone pretends to
be dead

ssemulindi *n1* **type of bird** (*found in Ssese Islands*)

ssemutundu *n9* **type of medium-sized catfish**
Bagrus docmax

ssenga *n1* (*pl.* ba ssenga) **(paternal) aunt,** *eg.*
ssenga wa Musoke ('Musoke's aunt')   **ssenga-**
aunt of (**N12**)   ssennange **my aunt**, ssengaawo
your aunt, ssengaawe **her/his aunt**, ssengaffe **our**
aunt, ssengammwe **your aunt**, sengaabwe **their**
aunt

essengejjero *n5* (*pl.* amasengejjero) **place of**
straining and filtering juice (*when making beer*)

essenke *n9* **spear grass** (*used for thatching and in*
beer making) *Imperata cylindrica*

ssenkulu *n1* **head of an organisation**

ssennyiga *n1* (*no pl.*) **cold** (*illness*)

ssentala *n1* **market supervisor**

essente *n9* **cent**; *in pl.* **money, currency**   ssente
mmeka? **how much?**   ssente enkalu **(hard) cash**
ssente entereke **savings**   ssente ezisoloozebwa
collection (*eg. in church*)   ssente -ggwaako **be**
broke   ssente z'ennyumba **house/room rent**
ssente z'olugendo **fare**   ssente za buliwo **on-the-**
spot payment   ssente za jjegejjege **coins**   ssente za
kiwaani **counterfeit money**   eby'essente *n8*
finance

ssentebe *n1* **chairman**

ssennange *n1* **my aunt**

ssennenge *n1* **barbed wire**

sseppeewo *n9* **hat** (*type with wide brim*)

sseppiki *n9* **saucepan, cooking pot**

ssere *n1* **type of herb, black jack** (*common weed;*
used to treat burns) *Bidens pilosa*

sserugooti *n1* **tall thin man**

sserumbeete *n9* **brass band**

Sseruti *n1 title* **chief brewer to the Kabaka**

Ssese *n1* **group of islands in Lake Victoria,**
county of Buganda

ssetaaba *n1* **stout herb, false tobacco** (*used as a*
substitute for tobacco) *Laggera alata*

ssettaala *n1* **type of tree** (*with soft wood, used for*
carving) *Polyscias fulva*

ssettendekero *n1* **training institute** (*of higher*
level), **university**

ssewagaba *n1* **grey-cheeked mangabey** (*monkey*)

Ssewannaku *n1* **God** (*as the one with no*
beginning)

ssewava *n1* **son of a princess**

ssezaala *n1* **father-in-law**

Ssezzibwa *n3* **river and waterfall in Kyaggwe**

ssezzira *n1* **low spreading herb** (*used as a*
vegetable) *Portulaca oleracea*

-ssibwa *vi* (-ssiddwa) **be placed**   **-ssibwako**
(-ssiddwako) **be placed on**   -ssibwako emikono **be**
confirmed (*in Christian faith*)

essiga *n5* (*pl.* amasiga) (1) **cooking stone**; (2)
sub-clan (**N29**). *The plural can mean* **cooking area**
(*of a traditional hearth, also of a modern stove or*
oven).   ow'essiga *n1* **head of a sub-clan**

ssigala *n1* **cigarette**
ssigga *n1* **centipede**
essigiri *n9* **charcoal stove**
essiike *See* -siike
essiinya *n5* (*pl.* amasiinya) **beetle larva** (*found in 'ekibo' palm stems on Ssese Islands*)
essimbo *n5/adv* (*no pl.*) **dignity, in a dignified way** -tambuza ssimbo **walk in a dignified way** -yogeza ssimbo **speak in a dignified way**
essimu *n9* **telephone, telephone call** essimu ey'omu ngalo **mobile phone** essimu y'olukale **public telephone** -kubira essimu **telephone**
ssinga *See* singa
Ssingo *n1* **county of Buganda**
ssinziggu *invariable adj* **huge, important, main,** *eg.* ensonga ssinziggu ('the main point')
essinzizo *n5* (*pl.* amasinzizo) **place of worship**
essira *n5* (*no pl.*) **emphasis, stress,** *eg. Bwe yayogera essira yaliteeka ku bwesigwa. ('When he spoke he stressed the importance of being trustworthy.')*
essiringi *n9* **shilling**
-ssizza *See* -ssa
essogolero *n5* (*pl.* amasogolero) **place for crushing bananas** (*to extract juice*)**, brewery**
essokisi *n9* **sock(s)**
essomero *n5* (*pl.* amasomero) **school** essomero ly'ekisulo **boarding school** essomero lya sekendule (*also* essomero lya siiniya) **secondary school**
essomo *n5* (*pl.* amasomo) **lesson** (*in school*)
ssonga = so nga. *See* so
essongezo *n5* (*pl.* amasongezo) **canine tooth**
essonko *n5* (*pl.* amasonko) **snail shell**
essoosi *n9* **saucer**
ssossolye *n1* **bulbul** (*type of bird*). *Saying: 'Ssossolye bw'atafa atuuka ku lyengedde.' ('If the bulbul does not die, it eventually comes across a ripe banana.', meaning 'Patience is a virtue.').*
essowaani *n9* **plate**
ssoya *n1* (*no pl.*) **soya**
essubi *n9* (*no pl.*) **grass** (*suitable for thatch, fodder, brewing or strewing on floor*) essubi essenke **spear grass** (*used for thatching and in beer making*) Imperata cylindrica essubi etteete **lemon-scented grass** (*spread on floors*) Cymbopogon nardus -a essubi *adj* **thatched** enjole y'essubi **bunch of grass** (*for thatching*)
ssumbuusa *n9* **samosa**
essundiro *n5* (*pl.* amasundiro) **pumping place** essundiro ly'amafuta **petrol station** essundiro ly'amazzi **hand pump** (*for drawing water*)
essunsa *n5* (*no pl.*) **young pumpkin leaves** (*eaten as vegetable*)
ssupu *n1* (*no pl.*) **gravy, sauce, soup**
essuubi *n5* (*no pl.*) **hope, expectation, anticipation**
[1]**essuuka** *n9* **(bed)sheet, cloth** (*worn as garment*)**, apron**

[2]**-ssuuka** *vi* (-ssuuse) **improve in health, get better** (*from illness*)
essuula *n9* **chapter**
essuuti *n9* **suit**
sswakaba ebintu bya sswakaba **nonsense**
-su *adj* **fresh/recent** (*of news, newly-brewed beer, etc.*)
-suba *vt* (-subye) **miss (out on).** *The subject and object are reversed compared to English, eg. Ekirabo kinsubye. ('I missed out on a present.').*
-subula *vt* (-subudde) **strip off** -subula omutuba **strip off bark from a barkcloth tree**
-subwa *vt* (-subiddwa) **miss (out on)** (*an opportunity*)*, eg. Nsubiddwa ekirabo. ('I missed getting a present.')*
Sudaani *n9* **Sudan**
-suffu *adj* **excessive,** *eg. Ebbeeyi nsuffu. ('The price is excessive.')***, extreme**
sukaali *n1* (*no pl.*) **sugar, diabetes**
-sukka *vi* (-susse) **be more than.** *Often followed by* ku *or* mu*, eg. Omuwendo gususse ku gwe mbadde nsuubira. ('The price is more than I had hoped.')***, exceed.** *Often with enclitic* (**N24.2**)*, eg. Essente zino zisusseemu ku ze nneetaaga. ('This is more money than I need.'). See* okusukkawo
-sukkirira *vi* (-sukkiridde) **be superfluous**
sukuluduleeva *n9* **screwdriver**
[1]**sukuma** *n9* **Kikuyu cabbage**
[2]**-sukuma** *vt* (-sukumye) **push**
-sula *vi* (-suze) **pass the night,** *eg. Poliisi yasuze erawuna okukakasa nga mu kitundu mulimu emirembe. ('The police passed the night patrolling.')***, dwell, stay,** *eg. Asula wano. ('She stays here.')* -sula enjala **spend the night without food** -sula waka **pass the night at home** Wasuze otyanno? **greeting** (*pl.* Mwasuze mutyanno?) **Good morning. (N28)**
[1]**-sulika** *vt* (-sulise) **put/hold at an angle, incline, slant, tilt**
[2]**-eesulika** *vi* **be at an angle, be tilted**
-sulirira *vt* (-suliridde) **spend the night in preparation, expect to do next day,** *eg. Nnasuliridde kugenda Masaka. ('I expected to go to Masaka next day.')* -sulirira okufa **be on the point of death** -sulirira okutambula **travel tomorrow** (*after sleeping*)
-sumagira *vi* (-sumagidde) **doze/nod off**
-sumattuka (*also* -simattuka) *vi* (-sumattuse) **slip off,** *eg. Embwa esumattuse. ('The dog has slipped off.')***, slip from** (*one's grasp*)**, escape** (*from a leash*). *An object pronoun can indicate a possessive, eg. Ekikopo kinsumattuse ne kigwa. ('The cup slipped from my hand.').*
[1]**-sumattula** (*also* -simattula) *vt* (-sumattudde) **let loose** (*eg. a teathered animal*)**, allow to escape** -sumattula amazima **blurt out the truth** -sumattula ebigambo **speak without thinking**
[2]**-eesumattula** *vr* **free oneself (from), escape**

(from), *eg. Embwa yeesumattudde ku lujegere.* *('The dog escaped from its leash.')*, **break free**

-sumba *vt* (-sumbye) **look after** (*sheep or goats*)

-sumika *vt* (-sumise) **tie a knot** (*in barkcloth*) -sumika olubugo **knot on barkcloth** (*of a man*), **dress in barkcloth** -sumika omusika **invest an heir**

-sumulukufu *adj* **untied, unlocked**

-sumulukuka *vi* (-sumulukuse) **become undone, come open** (*of something tied or wrapped*), **become untied, become unfastened, become unlocked** Asumulukuse. **She has given birth.**

-sumulula *vt* (-sumuludde) **undo, open, untie, unfasten, unclasp, unlock, uncork, unscrew**

¹-suna *vt* (-sunye) **pinch, pluck, play** (*plucked musical instrument*) -suna endongo **play the guitar**

²-suna *vi* **begin to grow** (*of breasts*)

¹-sunda *vt* (sunze) **churn, shake, agitate** -sunda amata **churn milk** -sunda amazzi **pump water** (*with a hand pump*)

²-eesunda *vi* **be thrown about** (*as in a vehicle on a rough road*), **be tossed about**

-sunde *adj* **shaken, churned**

-eesunga *vt* (-eesunze) **anticipate with pleasure, look forward to**, *eg. Beesunga abagenyi. ('They are looking forward to receiving the visitors.')*

-eesunguusula *vi* (-eesunguusudde) **show annoyance** (*or* **displeasure** *or* **irritation**) (*for a short period of time*), **show that one is upset**

-sunguwala *vi* (-sunguwadde) **be(come) angry** -sunguwala mangu **be easily upset**

-sunguwalira *vt* (-sunguwalidde) **be(come) angry with**

-sunguwavu *adj* **angry**

-sunguwaza *vt* (-sunguwazizza) **anger**

-sunirako *vt* (-suniddeko) (1) **tell a secret to**, *eg. Yabasunirako nti abapoliisi bajja. ('He told them that the police were coming.')*, **divulge to** (*private or secret information*); (2) **share a little with** (*food, especially given to children*), *eg. Omwana yamusunirako ku mugaati. ('She took off a small piece of bread for the child.')*

-sunsula *vt* (-sunsudde) **remove** (*wanted from unwanted*). *eg. Baanoga ppamba ne bamusunsula. ('They picked the cotton and separated the fibres from the seeds.')*, **sort out** -sunsula emmwanyi **remove coffee beans from husks** -sunsula enviiri **comb hair** -sunsula essunsa **remove wanted parts of pumpkin leaves** (*before cooking as vegetable*) -sunsula ppamba **gin cotton**

-sunsumala *vi* (-sunsumadde) **stand/stick up** (*of hair*), **be dishevelled**

-sunya *vt* (-sunyizza) **cause to pinch, pinch with** -sunyako (-sunyizzaako) **touch someone** (*as a signal*), **caution**

-susa *vt* (-susizza) **remove outer covering of** (*vegetable or fruit*), **peel** (*by hand*), **shell, husk**

¹-sussa *vt* (-sussizza) **exceed, be more than**, *eg. Nja kubeera mu kibuga okusussa ennaku ttaano. ('I will be in town for more than five days.')*, **(cause to) go beyond**

²-eesussa *vi* **make time** (*to do something*)

susu *n1* (*no pl.*) **urine**

-susumbuka *vi* (-susumbudde) **peel off** (*of bark*), *eg. Emiti gya kalittunsi gisusumbuka nnyo. ('Eucalyptus bark readily peels off.')*

-susumbula *vi* (-susumbudde) **debark**

¹-suuba *vt* (-suubye) **swing** (*back and forth*), **rock**

²-eesuuba *vr* **swing/rock oneself**

-suubira *vit* (-suubidde) **hope, expect, anticipate**

-suubiriza *vt* (-suubirizza) **suspect**

-suubirwa *vi* (-suubiddwa) **be hoped, be expected**

-suubiza *vt* (-suubizizza) **promise**

-suubula *vit* (-suubudde) **trade (in), deal in**, *eg. Asuubula engoye. ('She deals in clothes.')*

-suubulasuubula *vit* (-suubuddesuubudde) **trade in all sorts of things**

-suubulira *vt* (-suubulidde) **trade at**, *eg. Asuubulira Mengo. ('She trades at Mengo.')*

-suubuza *vt* (-suubuzizza) **cause to trade, trade with/using**

¹-suukunda *vt* (-suukunze) **churn, shake, agitate**

²-eesuukunda *vi* **be shaken about, shake** (*up and down*), *eg. Ekkubo lyabadde bbi. Emmotoka yatusuukunze nnyo ne tukoowa. ('The road was rough. The vehicle shook us about, so we became tired.')*

-suukunde *adj* **shaken, churned**

¹-suula *vt* (-sudde) **throw down/away, discard.** Often used with enclitic (**N24.2**), *eg. Awo abantu basuulawo ebisaaniko. ('People are throwing rubbish there.')* -suula ebikoola **shed leaves** -suula eddalu **drive crazy** (*make infatuated*), *eg. Ansudde eddalu. ('She is driving me crazy.')* -suula ennanga **anchor** -suula ettale (1) **end a relationship**; (2) **fail to achieve re-election** -suula gavumenti **overthrow a government** -suula omuntu **end a relationship** -suula wansi **drop** -suulayo (-suddeyo) **drop off** (*eg. children at school*)

²-eesuula *vr* **throw oneself down, keep at a distance** (*from*), **keep aloof** (*from people*)

-suulasuula *vt* (-suddesudde) **throw away anywhere, throw anyhow**

-suulemu *adj* **cooked unwrapped** (*in banana leaves*) amatooke amasuulemu **bananas cooked unwrapped** muwogo omusuulemu **cassava cooked unwrapped**

¹-suulira *vt* (-suulidde) **throw for/at**, *eg. Yasuulira embwa akati ekanone. ('She threw a stick for the dog to fetch.')* -suulira omwoyo **think about** (*a person*), *eg. Musoke twamusuulira omwoyo ne tugenda okumulaba. ('We thought about Musoke and went to see him.')*

²-eesuulira *vr* **throw over the shoulder** (*eg. a*

149

garment)

-suulirira *vt* (-suuliridde) **neglect** (*a personal relationship, or matter in hand*)

-suuliza *vt* (-suulizizza) **cause to throw at/for,** *etc.* -suuliza enkessi **look around for, scout out for,** *eg. Onoonsuuliza enkessi olabe kkampuni ya bbaasi ennungi egenda Mbarara? ('Can you scout around for me for a good bus company that goes to Mbarara?')* -suuliza eriiso **cast a glance (at)**

-suumuka *vi* (-suumuse) **start to mature**

-suuta (*also* -suusuuta) *vt* (-suuse) **praise**

suuti *n9* **suit**

-suuza *vt* (-suuzizza) **make drop**

-suza *vt* (-suzizza) **put up for the night, accommodate, keep company during the night,** *eg. Ebbugumu lyatusuza tetwebase. ('It was hot so we could not sleep.')*

-swaga *vt* (-swaze) **harpoon**

-swakira *vi* (-swakidde) *vi* **be(come) furious,** *eg. Yaswakidde nga mukazi we amubbyeeko ebintu bye mu maka. ('He became furious when his wife ran away with some of his things.')*

-swala *vi* (-swadde) **feel ashamed,** *eg. Nswadde olw'ekintu ky'enkoze. ('I feel ashamed for what I have done.'),* **feel embarrassed**

-swalira *vi* (-swalidde) **feel ashamed before,** *eg. Omwana bwe yabba emmere, yaswalira maama we. ('The child felt ashamed before his mother for stealing food.'),* **feel embarrassed before**

-swankula *vit* (-swankudde) **eat/chew noisily**

-swanyuula *vt* (-swanyudde) **whip, flog**

-swavu *adj* **shameful**

-swaza *vt* (-swazizza) **put to shame, disgrace, humiliate,** *eg. Omusomesa yamuswazizza mu kibiina. ('The teacher humiliated her in front of the class.')*

swiki *n9* **switch**

switi (*also* ka switi) *n1* **sweet(s)**

T,t

[1]**-ta** *vt* (-tadde) **free, release, let go of**

[2]**-(y)ota** *See* -yota

taaba *n1* (*no pl.*) **tobacco.** *From: 'tabako' (indigenous Caribbean language).*

-taabuukana *vi* (-taabuukanye) **have a hard time** (*mentally*), **be distressed** -taabuukana n'emirimu **be troubled by work** -taabuukana n'omwana **be troubled by a child**

-taabuukanya *vt* (-taabuukanyizza) **reduce to distress,** *eg. Omwana yalwadde n'ataabuukanya emirimu gyange ne sikola bulungi kyabadde kinsuubirwamu. ('The baby fell ill and caused me great distress, so I was unable to work as I was expected to do.')*

-eetaaga *vt* (-eetaaze) **need, require, want.** *See* okwetaaga

-eetaagibwa *vi* (-eetaagiddwa) **be needed**

-eetaagisa *vit* (-eetaagisizza) **be required,** *eg. Essente zeetaagisa okugula ebintu. ('Money is required to buy things.'),* **necessitate**

-taagufu *adj* **scratched** (*by claws/nails*), **ripped, torn**

-taaguka *vt* (-taaguse) **be scratched/ripped** (*by claws or nails*), **get torn**

-taagula *vt* (-taagudde) **tear** (*with nails or claws*), **claw, lacerate, scratch, rip, mangle**

-taakiriza *vt* (-taakirizza) **rescue, salvage**

-taaluuka *vi* (-taaluuse) **become wild in behaviour**

-taaluula *vt* (-taaludde) **drive wild**

-taaluusa *vi* (-taaluusizza) **(cause to) drive wild**

-taamaavu (*also* -tamaavu) *adj* **wild and angry, deranged, uncontrollable** (*in behaviour*)

-taamuuka (*also* -taama) *vi* (-taamuuse) **grow wild and angry** (*of person or animal*), **become deranged**

-taamuula *vt* (-taamudde) **make wild,** *eg. Omulalu abantu abangi baamutaaludde n'atandika okukuba amayinja. ('The crowd perturbed the madman and he started to throw stones.')*

-taamya *vt* (-taamizza) **(cause to) make wild**

-taano *num* **five (N8.1).** *Takes numeral concord* (**N4**), *eg. abantu bataano ('five people'); (2) emiti etaano ('five trees'). See* okutaano ataano **five, fifty. (N8.1)**

taapu *n9* **tap** (*eg. on pipe*)

[1]**-taasa** *vt* (-taasizza) **save from danger, rescue, go to the rescue of, separate** (*people or animals fighting*)

[2]**-eetaasa** *vr* **protect oneself, defend oneself**

taata *n1* (*pl.* ba taata) **father** taata omuto **(paternal) uncle**

-taataagana *vi* (-taataaganye), **be distressed, be disorganised** (*of affairs*), **be destablised**

-taataaganya *vt* (-taataaganyizza) **cause distress to, disorganise, destabilise,** *eg. Okuwagulula kw'amazzi kutaataaganyizza olutindo. ('The flood has destabilised the bridge.')*

-taawa *vi* (-taaye) **be on the point of death**

-taayaaya *vi* (-taayaaye) **roam about without restrictions** embwa etaayaaya **stray dog**

-taayiza *vt* (-taayizza) **cut off** (*an escape route*), **intercept**

[1]**-taba** *vt* (-tabye) **join (together),** *eg. Omubazzi yatabye ebitundutundu by'entebe. ('The carpenter joined together the pieces of the chair.'),* **sew/stitch together,** *eg. Omutunzi yatabye ebiwero ng'atunga essaati. ('The sewer sewed together the pieces of the shirt.')* -taba engalo **interdigitate one's fingers** omuliro -taba **spread** (*of a fire*)

[2]**-eetaba** *vi* **participate,** *eg. Essomero lyange lyetabye mu mpaka z'okuyimba. ('My school is participating in the singing competition.'),* **take part**

-tabaala *vit* (-tabadde) **wage war (on)**

-tabagana *vi* (-tabaganye) **be reconciled**

-tabaganya *vt* (-tabaganyizza) **make peace between, reconcile, mediate between**

-tabanguka *vi* (-tabanguse) **be(come) stirred up** (*of sediment*), **become turbulent** emmeeme -tabanguka **feel nausea** obudde -tabanguka **be unsettled** (*of the weather*)

-tabangula *vt* (-tabangudde) **stir up** (*sediment or people*), **make turbulent** -tabangula emirembe **disturb the peace**

[1]-tabika *vt* (-tabise) **mix (up)**

[2]-eetabika *vr* **get mixed up** (*of things*)

-tabikatabika *vt* (-tabisetabise) **mix up**, *eg. Ebigambo yabitabisetabise tetwamutegedde.* (*'He mixed up what he said so we did not understand him.'*)

-tabike *adj* **mixed**

-tabuka *vi* (-tabuse) **be mixed, go wrong** -tabuka omutwe **be mentally disturbed, become worked up** (*emotionally*)

-tabukatabuka *vi* (-tabusetabuse) **be thrown into confusion**. *The name* kutabukatabuka *was given to the period of turmoil in Buganda in the 1890s when many villagers resettled after it had became known that the British authorities intended to divide the country into separate areas for Protestants, Catholics and Muslims.*

[1]-tabula *vt* (-tabudde) **mix (up), stir, blend, perturb, disturb, muddle (up), jumble (up)** -tabula eddembe **disturb the peace** -tabula omutwe **disturb** (*someone mentally*), **upset, confuse**

[2]-eetabula *vr* (1) **be mixed up, work oneself up** (*emotionally*); (2) **involve oneself**, *eg. Yeetabula mu bintu ebitamukwatako.* (*'He involves himself in things that do not concern him.'*)

-tabulatabula *vt* (-tabuddetabudde) **throw into confusion, muddle up**

-tabule *adj* **mixed**

tabuliki *n1* **Muslim fundamentalist**

-tabulwa *vi* (-tabuddwa) **be confused**

-tabulwatabulwa *vi* (-tabuddwatabuddwa) **be thrown into confusion**

-tadde *See* -ta; -teeka

tadooba *n9* (*pl.* bu tadooba *n14*) **small paraffin lamp** (*with naked flame*)

-taga *vi* (-taze) **seek a place to lay eggs** (*of a hen*)

-tagala *vi* (-tagadde) **stagger about**, *eg. Atambula atagala.* (*'She is staggering.'*), **reel about**

-taganjuka *vi* (-taganjuse) **be(come) disorganised, be ransacked**

-taganjula *vt* (-taganjudde) **rummage through, ransack, search thoroughly**

-taganjulwa *vi* (-taganjuddwa) **be ransacked**

-taggulukuka (*also* -tandulukuka) *vi* (-taggulukuse) **be(come) disentangled**

-taggulula (*also* -tandulula) *vt* (-tagguludde) **disentangle**

takisi *n9* **taxi**   owa takisi *n1* **taxi driver**

[1]-takkuluza *vt* (-takkuluzizza) **release the hold on, loosen** (*eg. a belt*), **unclasp, separate** (*people locked together in a fight*)

[2]-eetakkuluza *vit* **free oneself (from)**, *eg. Nneetakkuluza ku mulalu.* (*'I freed myself from the madman's grip.'*), **get loose (from)**

[1]-takula *vt* (-takudde) **scratch**

[2]-eetakula *vr* **scratch oneself**

[1]-tala *vi* (-taze) **move here and there** (*of a person*), **range oneself for combat**

[2]-eetala *vi* (-eetaze) **move about busily, bustle about**. *See* okwetala

-talaaga *vi* (-talaaze) **travel all over** -talaaga wonna **go everywhere**, *eg. Abaserikale baatalaaga wonna.* (*'The soldiers were everywhere.'*)

-talagga *vi* (-talazze) **rust** -talagga obwongo **go senile**

-talavvu *adj* **rusty**

-tali *neg of* -li (*'be'*) (N21)

taliiwo **he/she is not here**

-eetalira (*also* -talira) *vi* (-talidde) **move about** (*within a limited area*), *eg. Omusajja oyo yeetalira wano.* (*'That man is moving about around here.'*)

-taliza *vt* (-talizza) **spare** (*from death or destruction*), *eg. Yataliza doodo nga alima.* (*'She spared the spinach while weeding.'*), **preserve**

-tama *vt* (-tamye) **be(come) fed up with** (*with reversed subject and object compared to English*), *eg. Obulamu buntamye.* (*'I am fed up with life.'*), **disgust, sicken, offend**

-tamattama *vi* (-tamyettamye) **be uncertain (about), be hesitant (about)**, *eg. Omwana ennyukuta akyazitamattama.* (*'The child is still hesitant about the letters of the alphabet.'*), **be inconsistent (about)**

-tamba *vt* (-tambye) **sacrifice**

-tambaala *vt* (-tambidde) **stand up to** (*eg. a bully*), **face up to, confront**

-tambira *vt* (-tambidde) **sacrifice for/in**, *etc.* Tugenda okutambira. **We are going to mass.** (*RC*)

-tambula *vi* (-tambudde) **travel, walk, move**. *Can be followed by aux v in present tense modifying its meaning* (N19), *eg.*: -tambula -bebbera **trudge along**, -tambula -bigula **walk with a wiggle**, -tambula kasoobo **walk slowly**, -tambula -kemba **strut (about)**, -tambula -senvula **plod along**, -tambula -sooba **walk slowly**, -tambula -tagala **stagger about** (*especially when drunk*), -tambula -yanguwa **walk fast**, -tambula -yuuga **walk swaying from side to side**, -tambula -zunga **stagger**. *See* okutambula **-tambulako** (-tambuddeko) **take a walk, stroll**

-tambulatambula *vi* (-tambuddetambudde) **walk from place to place continuously** -tambulatambulako **stroll, ramble**

-tambulira *vt* (-tambulidde) **travel by**, *eg. Atambulidde ku ggaali.* (*'He travelled by bike.'*)

-tambuza *vt* (-tambuzizza) **cause to travel, walk with, take for a walk, transport, ship** (*goods*), **take** (*items*) **here and there** (*in the hope of selling them*), **hawk** (*goods for sale*). *Can be followed by aux v in present tense modifying its meaning* (**N19**), *eg.*: -tambuza bigere **travel by foot,** -tambuza bitege **walk with inward-pointing feet,** -tambuza buggereggere **walk quietly, walk stealthily,** -tambuza bunkenke **walk on tiptoe,** -tambuza ebigambo **spread a rumour,** -tambuza emmere **carry around food to sell,** -tambuza mbaliga **walk with outward-pointing feet,** -tambuza ssimbo **walk with dignity.**

-tamiira *vi* (-tamidde) **get drunk, be intoxicated** -tamiira enjaga **be high** (*on drugs*) -tamiira omupiira **be obsessed with football** -tamiira omuwala **be obsessed with a girl**

-tamiirukuka *vi* (-tamiirukuse) **sober up**

-tamiivu *adj* **drunk, intoxicated**

-tamiiza *vt* (-tamiizizza) **make drunk**

tamusiya *n9* **umbrella**

[1]**-tamwa** *vit* (-tamiddwa) **be(come) fed up with/by,** *eg. Nnatamwa amagi.* (*'I am fed up with eating eggs.'*), **be offended by**

[2]**-eetamwa** *vt* **be(come) fed up with/by,** *eg. Yeetamiddwa okulya amatooke buli lunaku.* (*'She is fed up with eating matooke every day.'*), **be disgusted with/by, feel revolted by**

-tana *vi* (-tanye) **be(come) infected** (*of a wound*), **grow septic**

-tandika *vt* (-tandise) **begin, start** **-tandikawo** (-tandiseewo) **establish**

-tandikira *vt* (-tandikidde) **start with/at,** *eg. Tandikira ku mulimu guno.* (*'Start with this job.'*)

-tandulukuka (*also* -taggulukuka) *vi* (-tandulukuse) **be(come) disentangled**

-tandulula (*also* -taggulula) *vt* (-tanduludde) **disentangle**

-tanga *vi* (-tanze) **give proprietary gifts, pay a fine**

-tangaala *vi* (-tangadde) **be light, be bright, be transparent** obudde -tangaala **become light** (*at the start of the day*), **become clear** (*of the weather or sky*)

-tangaalirira *vi* (-tangaaliridde) **be transfixed, be stupified, be in a daze** (= -wuniikirira)

-tangaavu *adj* **bright, light, clear, transparent**

-tangaaza *vt* (-tangaazizza) **make light, make bright, clarify, elucidate, enlighten, magnify**

-tangalijja *vi* (-tangalizze) **shine, glitter**

-tangira *vt* (-tangidde) **restrain** (*animals from wandering or eating crops*), **hold back** (*animals going the wrong way*)

-tankuufu (*also* -tinkufu) *adj* **disorganised** (*of things*)

-tankuuka (*also* -tinkuuka) *vi* (-tankuuse) **be disorganised, be ransacked** (*of things*)

-tankuula (*also* -tinkuula) *vt* (-tankudde) **disorganise** (*things*), **ransack** -tankuula

entawaana **stir up trouble**

-tanula *vi* (-tanudde) **begin**

-tanza *vt* (-tanzizza) **fine**

Tanzaniya *n9* **Tanzania**

-taŋŋana *vi* (-taŋŋanye) **let go of one another**

-taputa *vit* (-tapuse) **interpret**

-tattana *vt* (-tattanye) **damage, ruin**

-tawaana *vi* (-tawaanye) **be preoccupied, take trouble,** *eg. Yatawaana nnyo okukola obulungi.* (*'He took trouble to do the job properly.'*), **struggle** (*with many things to do*)

-tawaanira *vt* (-tawaanidde) **take trouble for, make an effort with** -tawaanira bwereere **make an effort in vain**

[1]**-tawaanya** *vt* (-tawaanyizza) **cause problems for, give trouble to, bother,** *eg. Omwana yamutawaanya.* (*'The child was bothering him.'*)

[2]**-eetawaanya** *vr* **make trouble for oneself**

-tawuka *vi* (-tawuse) **move about here and there doing things, be busy**

-eetawula *vi* (-eetawudde) **move about in anticipation of trouble,** *eg. Poliisi yabadde yeetawula ng'esuubira omutawaana.* (*'The police were moving about expecting trouble.'*)

tayifooyidi *n9* **typhoid**

tayipu *n9* **typewriter, type, typeface**

-tayira (-tayidde) *vi* **dart to and fro.** *From: 'akataayi'* (*'swallow'*).

[1]**-tayirira** *vt* (-tayiridde) **pester, circumcise**

[2]**-eetayirira** *vt* **pester, whirl around annoyingly**

tayiro *n9* **tile** (*on floor or wall*)

ate *conj* **and so, and then**

-tebenkera *vi* (-tebenkedde) **be(come) settled and peaceful** (*of a situation*), *eg. Yatebenkera ku mulimu kati akola bulungi.* (*'He has settled into the work and doing well.'*)

-tebenkevu *adj* **settled and peaceful** (*of a person*), *eg. Kaakati mutebenkevu.* (*'Nowadays he is a settled person.'*)

-tebuka *vi* (-tebuse) **trick**

-teeba *vit* (-teebye) **guess, shoot.** *See* okuteeba -teeba eggoolo **shoot at goal** -teeba emmundu **shoot** (*with a gun*)

-teebeeka *vt* (-teebeese) -teebeeka ebigambo **make up a (false) story**

-teebereza *vt* (-teeberezza) **estimate, imagine, speculate, forecast**

-teebwa *vi* (-teereddwa) **be set free**

-teefu *adj* **calm, quiet, serene**

-teega *vit* (-teeze) **lie in wait (for), ambush, be offside** (*in football*)

[1]**teeka** *vi* (-teese) **be(come) serene, be(come) calm** (*of a body of water, situation, etc.*), **be(come) clear** (*of water containing sediment*)

[2]**-teeka** *vt* (-teese, *or* -tadde) **put, place.** '-teeka' *is unusual in having two forms of modified stem form* (*used interchangeably*) (**N14**). -teeka amateeka **legislate** -teeka awamu **put together** -teeka

ebbala stain -teeka ekkomo **set a limit** -teeka essira stress -teeka ku ddaala lya wansi **demote** -teeka mu bbanga **put in the open, expose** (*eg. a scandal*) -teeka mu kifo kya **substitute for** **-teekako** (-teeseeko) **put on**, *eg. Ku mmeeza teekako ekitambaala. ('Put the cloth on the table.')*, **apply on, install** (*eg. a new bishop*), **switch on** (*electricity*) -teekako eddinda **put hem on dress** -teekako ekinkumu **put one's thumbprint** -teekako ekiraka **put on a patch** -teekako emikono **confirm** (*in Christian faith*) -teekako ettaala **put on an electric light** -teekako leediyo **turn on a radio** -teekako olukoloboze **draw a line** -teekako omudalizo **put decorative strip on busuuti** -teekako omukono **sign** (*eg. a document*) -teekako omwoyo **pay attention, concentrate** **-teekamu put in**, *eg. Mu ssefuliya teekamu amazzi. ('Put water in the pan.')*, **install** (*eg. a new sink*), **include** -teekamu akakindo **put on a crease** -teekamu essente **invest money** -teekamu giriisi **grease** -teekamu obubonero **punctuate** -teekamu omuliro mu mmotoka **switch on a car engine** -teekamu oyiro **lubricate** **-teekawo put there**, *eg. Yateekawo olukomera okuziyiza ente okufuluma. ('He put a fence to stop the cows straying.')*, **establish, impose** -teekawo engalo **cup the hands** -teekawo omukono **open one's hand** (*to receive something*) **-teekayo put** (*over there*), *eg. Mu kisenge teekayo ettaala. ('Put a lamp in the room.')* -teekayo omwoyo **pay attention, concentrate** -teekayo ssente mu bbanka **deposit money in bank** [1]**-teekateeka** *vt* (-teeseteese) **prepare, get ready, plan, arrange.** *See okuteekateeka* [2]**-eeteekateeka** *vr* **prepare oneself, get** (*oneself*) **ready** **-teekebwa** *vi* (-teekeddwa) **be put/placed** **-teekera** *vt* (-teekedde) **put for** **-teekerako** (-teekeddeko) **put for** (*on top*), *eg. Musoke muteekereko emmere ('Put on more food for Musoke.')* **-teekeramu put for** (*within*), *eg. Teekeramu Nawume caayi mu kikopo. ('Put tea in the cup for Naomi.')* **-teekerawo put for** (*there*) -teekerawo akabega **assist** (*someone*) **in a court case** **-teekerayo put for** (*over there*) **-teekulula** *vt* (-teekuludde) **unstack** **-teekwa** *aux v* (-teekeddwa) **must, should, ought, be obliged**, *eg. Musoke ateekwa okusasula ebisale. ('Musoke is obliged to pay the fees.')* **-teera** *vt* (-teeredde) **free for/at**, *etc.* [1]**-teesa** *vit* (-teesezza) (*often followed by* **ku**) **discuss**, *eg. Twateesa ku bye tugenda okusomesa. ('We discussed what we would teach.')*, **negotiate**, *eg. Tutuule tuteese. ('Let us sit down and negotiate.')*, **confer.** *See okuteesa* Oteesezza. **You have planned well.** (*complement paid to the host about food served at a function*) **-teesaako** (-teessezzaako) **discuss** (*about something*)

[2]**-eeteesa** *vi* **make up one's mind, come to an agreement** **-teesaganya** *vi* (-teesaganyizza) **discuss with one another** **-teese** *See* -teeka **-teesebwako** (*vi* -teeseddwako) **be discussed** **-teetera** *vi* (-teetedde) **breathe with extreme difficulty** (*on the point of death*), **idle** (*of an engine*), **beat faintly** (*eg. as a heartbeat, or as visible on a fontanel*) **-teewulukuka** (*also* -toowolokoka) *vi* (-teewulukuse) **(be)come reduced** (*of pressure*), **be(come) relieved, grow slack, be(come) relaxed, be(come) deflated, go down** (*of a swelling*), **subside** [1]**-teewuluza** (*also* -teewulula) *vt* (-teewuluzizza) **reduce the pressure, slacken, loosen, relieve**, *eg. Musoke bwe yagudde olwa kantoolooze baamwanguyidde ne bamuteewulula amapeesa g'essaati. ('When Musoke collapsed they quickly went to relieve him by unbuttoning his shirt.')*, **deflate** [2]**-eeteewuluza** (*also* -toowolokosa) *vi* (-eetteewuluzizza) **relieve oneself, go to the toilet** **-tega** *vt* (-teze) **set** (*a trap*), **trip (up)**, *eg. Yamutega ng'atambula. ('He tripped her up while he was walking.')* -tega amatu **listen carefully** -tega obusukko **develop skin sores through witchcraft** -tega omukono **open one's hand** (*to catch something*) -tega omutego **set a trap** **-tegana** *vi* (-teganye) **take trouble**, *eg. Yategana okutuyamba. ('He took trouble to help us.')*, **make an effort** -tegana n'emirimu **struggle with many things to do** **-teganira** *vt* (-teganidde) **take trouble with**, *eg. Ateganira abaana be. ('She took trouble to look after her children.')*, **take pains over** **-teganya** *vt* (-teganyizza) **make demands on, bother, be a nuisance to** **-tegeera** *vt* (-tegedde) **understand, be conscious, discern, recognise, comprehend, realise, know.** *See okutegeera* **-tegeeragana** *vi* (-tegeeraganye) **understand one another, come to an understanding, communicate** (*in the sense of understanding one another*) **-tegeerekeka** *vi* (-tegeerekese) **be understandable, be comprehensible, become clear** **-tegeevu** *adj* **understanding, discerning, cultured** **-tegeeza** *vt* (-tegeezezza) **inform, mean, signify, define** **-eetegefu** *adj* (omwetegefu *n1*) **prepared, ready** [1]**-tegeka** *vt* (-tegese) **put in order, prepare, arrange, plan, organise, sort (out), make ready** -tegeka emmeeza **lay the table** [2]**-eetegeka** *vr* **prepare oneself, get ready**, *eg. Yeetegese okugenda. ('She is preparing to go.')* **-tegeke** *adj* **prepared**

-tegekebwa *vi* (-tegekeddwa) **be prepared, be arranged**

[1]**-tegekera** *vt* (-tegekedde) **prepare for**

[2]**-eetegekera** *vr* **prepare oneself for**

[1]**-tegereza** *vit* (-tegerezza) **listen carefully (to), pay attention (to), note**

[2]**-eetegereza** *vt* **scrutinise, look carefully, examine**

-teguka *vit* (-teguse) **be cleared out of the way, get out of the way**

[2]**-tegula** *vt* (-tegudde) (1) **put/clear away** (*things that have been arranged*); (2) **release** (*by removing something preventing movement*), **untrap** -tegula ekisenge **clear a room** -tegula emmeeza **clear the table** -tegula emmotoka **jump start a car**

[2]**-eetegula** *vi* **move of its own accord**, *eg. Emmotoka yeetegudde n'egenda wansi. ('The car started moving downhill of its own accord'.)*

-tegulira *vt* (-tegulidde) **clear away for**

-tegulula *vt* (-tegududde) **set free from a trap**

tekinologiya *n9* **technology**

tekuli (*also* tekuliiko) **there is/are not** (*on top*)

tekwali (*also* tekwaliko) **there was/were not** (*on top*)

[1]**-tema** *vt* (-temye) **chop, cut down, fell** -tema akakule **burst into scornful laughter** -tema akalali **burst into laughter** -tema ebikata **make earth mounds for planting sweet potatoes** -tema oluwenda **cut path through vegetation, make a way** -tema omulanga **cry out in distress**

-temako (-temyeko) **chop a little, lop**

[2]**-eetema** *vr* **undertake**, *eg. Mukasa yeetemye okuwa embuzi. ('Mukasa undertook to give a goat.'),* **pledge** (*a particular item or amount*)

-temaatema *vt* (-temyetemye) **chop into pieces, mutilate**

-temagana *vi* (-temaganye) **sparkle**

-tembeeya *vi* (-tembeeye) **walk about.** *From: '-tembea' (Swahili).* -tembeeya okutunda **hawk** (*goods*)

-temera *vt* (-temedde) (1) **chop/cut for,** *eg. Atemera ente omuddo. ('She is cutting grass for the cows.');* (2) **earth up** (*plants*), *eg. Tutemera lumonde. ('We are earthing up the potatoes.')* Temeraawo! (*also* Temera awo!) **Chop it there!**

-temereza *vi* (-temerezza) **blink continually, flicker** (*of a paraffin lamp*)

-temula *vt* (-temudde) **murder, assassinate**

temuli (*also* temuliimu) **there is/are not** (*within*)

temwali (*also* temwalimu) **there was/were not** (*within*)

-temya *vi* (-temezza) **blink** -temyako (-temezzaako) **wink at** (*as a signal*), **hint to** (*through the eyes*)

-tenda *vt* (-tenze) **praise** (= -waana)

-tendeka *vt* (-tendese) **train, coach** -tendeka ebibuuzo **set an examination** -tendeka lubaale **train a spirit how to deal with people, induct a spririt** (*for spirit possession*)

-tendeke *adj* **trained**

-tendekebwa *vi* (-tendekeddwa) **be trained**

-tendereza *vt* (-tenderezza) **praise highly**

-tenga *vt* (-tenze) (1) **wag** (*a tail*); (2) **beat** (*bark, in second stage of barkcloth making*) -tenga olubuto **massage tummy with herbal ointment** (*of a pregnant woman*)

-tengejja *vi* (-tengezze) **float**

[1]**-tengerera** *vi* (-tengeredde) **stand without support.** *Song: 'Tengerere, tengerere, tengerere, omwana ayimiridde.' ('The child is standing on her/his own.')*

[2]**-eetengerera** *vr* (1) **balance oneself, stand without support** (*as a child learning to walk*); (2) **stand on one's own two feet** (*able to sustain oneself*)

-eetengereza *vt* (-eetengerezza) **assist** (*a child*) **to walk by itself**

-tenguwa *vit* (-tenguye) **disobey**

-tera *aux v* (-teze). *Followed by inf* (N19): (1) (*in present tense* N16) **be/do habitually, be/do usually,** *eg. Ntera okuvuga. ('I usually drive.');* (2) (*in near future tense* N16) **be about to,** *eg. Nnaatera okuyimba. ('I am about to sing.').* 'tera' *can be equivalent to adverbs* **usually, occasionally, almost, soon** (N19), *eg. (1) Tutera okugenda mu kkanisa ku Ssande. ('We usually go to church on Sunday.'); (2) Tunaatera okugenda. ('We are going soon.').*

-terebuka *vi* (-terebuse) **despair, lose one's nerve**

-terebula *vt* (-terebudde) **cause to despair**

-tereekereza *vt* (-tereekerezza) **save, spare** (*eg. a small amount of a soda to drink later*)

-tereera *vi* (-teredde) **be straight, be level, be in equilibrium, be stabilised, settle down** (*eg. in a chair to one's work*) Tuula otereere. **Sit properly., Make yourself comfortable.**

-tereevu *adj* **straight**

-tereeza *vt* (-tereezezza) **straighten (out), put right, make level, correct** -tereeza ensonga **sort out affairs**

-tereka *vt* (-terese) **store, put away/aside**

-terekera *vt* (-terekedde) **store for/at,** *etc. Saying: 'Katonda ky'aterekera omulamu tekivunda.' ('What God puts aside for someone does not rot.')*

-teresa *vt* (-teresezza) **cause to store (for),** *eg. Yamuteresa ebitabo. ('He gave her the books to store for him.')*

[1]**teri** (*also* teriiyo) **there is/are not** (*over there*)

[2]**eteri** **where there is/are not** (*over there*). *Can be equivalent to preposition* **without** (N7.2).

-teta *vi* (-tese) **burn** (*eg. of a house*) Omuliro guteta. **The cooking is going well.** (*lit. 'The fire is burning.'*)

tetanaasi *n1* **tetanus**

-tetenkanya *vt* (-tetenkanyizza) **use all sorts of means** (*to do something*), *eg. Yatetenkanya okulaba ng'abaana basoma. ('He used all sorts of*

means to make sure his children get educated.'),
concoct (*a plan*), improvise

tewaabadde (*also* <u>tewaabaddewo</u>) **there has/have
not been**

tewaabe (*also* <u>tewaabeewo</u>) **there will not be**

tewaali (*also* <u>tewaaliwo</u>) **there was/were not**

tewabadde (*also* <u>tewabaddeewo</u>) **there has/have
not been**

tewali (*also* <u>tewaliiwo</u>) **there is/are not**

tewaliba (*also* <u>tewalibaawo</u>) **there will not be**

teyali (*also* <u>teyaliiyo</u>) **there was/were not** (*over
there*)

¹-teza *vt* (-tezezza) **trap with**

²-(y)oteza *See* -yoteza

¹-ti *adj* **fearful**

²-ti *verb* (*used only in present tense N13.1*) **like this,**
eg. Asoma bw'ati. ('He reads like this.')

-tibula *vi* (-tubudde) <u>-tibula ekyejo</u> **be insolent**

-tidde *See* -tya

-(y)atifu *See* -yatifu

-tigiinya *vt* (-tigiinyizza) **tamper with**

-tigoma *vi* (-tigomye) **run about all over the place,**
*eg. Emmese zitigoma wonna mu nnyumba. ('Rats
are running about all over the house.')*

-tigomya *vt* (-tigomezza) **cause to run about all
over the place**

-eetigoonyola (*also* <u>-tigoonyola</u>) *vi*
(-eetigoonyodde) **wriggle, writhe**

-tiguka *vi* (-tiguse) **romp, frolic**

-tigula *vi* (-tigudde) **keep on being mischievous**

-tiibwa *vi* (-tiiriddwa) **be feared**

-(y)atiikirira *See* -yatiikirira

-(y)atiikiriza *See* -yatiikiriza

-tiiriika *vi* (-tiiriise) **squirt (out), spurt out, leak**

-tiiriisa *vt* (-tiirisizza) **squirt (out)** <u>-tiiriisa ekitigi</u>
be insolent, be naughty, be out of control (*of a
child*) <u>-tiiriisa amazzi</u> **gush out water** <u>-tiiriisa
ekyejo</u> **be very naughty**

-tiisa *vt* (-tiisizza) **frighten, scare, terrify**

-tiisatiisa *vt* (-tiisizzatiisizza) **threaten, intimidate**

-tiitiira *vi* (-tiitidde) **shake with fear, be scared, be
timid, be cowardly**

-tiitiizi *adj* **fearful, timid, cowardly, intimidated**

-tijja *vi* (-tizze) **be overjoyed,** *eg. Yatizze nga mukazi
we azadde. ('He was overjoyed when his wife gave
birth.')*, **be infatuated** (*with*) <u>-tijja n'omupira</u> **be
obsessed with football** <u>-tijja n'omuwala</u> **be
obsessed with a girl**

-(y)atika *See* -yatika

-(y)atikayatika *See* -yatikayatika

¹-tikka *vt* (-tisse) **put on the head of, load** (*onto
someone's head*) <u>-tikka ennyo</u> (*also* <u>-tikka
akabindo</u>) **overload**

²-eetikka *vt* **carry, load** (*onto one's own head*)
<u>-eetikka butengerera</u> **balance on the head**
<u>-eetikka ebizibo bingi</u> **be burdened with many
problems** <u>-eetikka ku mabega</u> **carry on the back**
<u>-eetikka ku mutwe</u> **carry on the head**

¹-tikkira *vt* (-tikkidde) **put on the head of** <u>-tikkira
engule</u> **crown**

²-eetikkira *vr* **put on one's own head,** *eg. Yeetikkira
enkuufiira. ('He put on a hat.')*

-tikkirwa *vi* (-tikkiddwa) **be crowned, be ordained**

-tikkuka *vi* (-tikkuse) **come off** (*of something
carried, eg. load from one's head*), **fall off**

¹-tikkula *vt* (-tikkudde) **unload** <u>-tikkula omuntu</u>
unload from someone's head

²-eetikkula *vr* **unload oneself**

-timba *vt* (-timbye) **decorate, hang (up)** (*picture,
curtain, etc.*)

-timbula *vt* (-timbudde) **take down** (*eg. picture*)

-tinda *vt* (-tinze) **put a bridge across, bridge,** *eg.
Baatinda omugga. ('They bridged the river.')*

-tindigga *vi* (-tindizze) **walk/go quickly** <u>-tindigga
eggendo</u> **make a very long journey**

-tindikira *vt* (-tindikidde) **pile high**

-tindira *vt* (-tindidde) **bridge over** <u>-tindira entamu</u>
put a framework in a pot (*to support a food
bundle during steaming*)

-tini *adj* **tiny**

-tinka *vi* (-tinse) **become a fad**

-tinkiza *vi* (-tinkizza) **be obsessed,** *eg. Atinkiza
n'omuwala oyo. ('He is obsessed with that girl.')*,
be infatuated

-tinkuufu *adj. See* -tankuufu

-tinkuuka (-tinkuuse) *See* -tankuula

-tinkuula (-tinkudde) *See* -tankuula

-tintima *vi* (-tintimye) **shiver** (*uncontrollably, eg.
from cold or illness*), **tremble**

-tiribira *vi* (-tiribidde) **shiver** (*in a way that is
potentially controlable*), **tremble**

-tiribiza *vt* (-tiribizza) **make tremble** <u>-tiribiza
akabino</u> **make one's bottom wiggle** (*while
walking*) <u>-tiribiza eddoboozi</u> **make one's voice
tremble**

-(y)atisa *See* -yatisa

-tisse *See* -tikka

-to *adj* **not fully grown, young**

-toba *vi* (-tobye) **get wet, get soaked**

-tobeka *vt* (-tobese) **make variegated** (*of various
shapes, textures, colours, etc.*), *eg. Yakola
omukeeka n'atobeka ensansa emyufu n'enjeru.*

**NOTES ON
t**

-t. Unless the **t** is doubled, verbs starting **t** have
1st person singulars starting **nt**, *eg.* **nteeka** ('I
put'), from **-teeka**.

-tt. Verbs starting **tt** have 1st person singulars
starting **nzit**, *eg.* **nzita** ('I kill'), from **-tta**.

ett-. Nouns in *n5* starting **ett** have plurals (in *n6*)
starting **amat**, *eg.* the plural of **ettu** is **amatu**.

otu-. Nouns in *n13* starting **otu** lack plurals.

NOUNS IN *n9*. Most nouns in *n9* have
identically spelt plurals (in *n10*).

-tobeke

('She made a red and white palm leaf mat.')

-tobeke *adj* **variegated**

-toberera *vi* (-toberedde) **get slightly wet**

-tobya *vt* (-tobezza) **make wet, drench**

-togoonyoka *vi* (-togoonyose) **be squeezed, be squashed** *(of something soft, eg. of bananas when juice is being extracted)*

-togoonyola *vt* (-togoonyodde) **squeeze** *(something soft)*, **squash**

-tokomoka *vi* (-tokomose) **perish,** *eg. Ebintu bitokomoka singa omuliro gukwata ennyumba. ('Things perish if fire takes hold of a house.')*

-tokomokera *vi* (-tokomokedde) **be utterly destroyed (in),** *eg. Ebintu bye byatokomokedde mu muliro. ('His possessions were utterly destroyed in the fire.')*

-tokosa *vt* (-tokosezza) **boil**

-tokota *vi* (-tokose) **make a sound as a kettle heating, make a rasping noise** olubuto -tokota **rumble** *(of the stomach)* yingini -tokota **be running** *(of an engine)*

-toloka *vi* (-tolose) **escape,** *eg. Embuzi zatolose okuva mu kisibo. ('The goats escaped from the pen.')*, **run away**

-tolotooma *vi* (-tolotoomye) **mumble in dissatisfaction, grumble**

-toma *vi* (-tomye) **express dissatisfaction** *(with what one has been given)*, **be unappreciative**

-tomera *vt* (-tomedde) **bump/run into, collide with, crash into, knock (into), ram (into)**

-tomeragana *vi* (-tomereganye) **bump into one another, collide**

-tomeza *vt* (-tomezza) **(cause to) crash**

[1]**-tona** *vt* (-tonye) **decorate, make a pattern on** *(eg. by painting)*, **adorn.** *Pronunciation:* okútónà

[2]**-tona** *vt* **give** *(a present)*. *Pronunciation:* okútónà

-tonatona *vt* (-tonyetonye) **put decorative marks on** *(eg. a pot)*

[1]**-tonda** *vt* (-tonze) **create**

[2]**-eetonda** *vi* **apologise.** *See* okwetonda

-eetondera *vt* (-eetondedde) **apologise to**

[1]**-tone** *adj* **adorned, decorated**

[2]**-tone** *adj* **presented** *(of a gift or prize)*

-tonera *vt* (-tonedde) **give a gift to,** *eg. Yamutonera ekirabo. ('She gave him a gift.')*

-tongola *vi* (-tongodde) **become an official, receive official recognition**

-tongole *adj* **official**

-tongoza *vt* (-tongozezza) **make official, appoint** *(to an official position)*, *eg. Yatongoza Musoke okubeera omwami. ('He appointed Musoke a chief.')*, **recognise officially**

-toniwa *vi* (-toniye) **become small, grow thin, become fewer**

-toniya *vt* (-tonyizza) **make smaller, make thinner, make fewer**

tonninnyira *See* -linnyira

-tonnya *vi* (-tonnye) **fall** *(of rain)*, **drip, leak**

-yambala -tonnya **be very smartly dressed**

-tonnyatonnya *vi* (-tonnyetonnye) **keep dripping** *(eg. liquid through a hole in a container)*

-tonnyerera *vi* (-tonyeredde) **keep dripping** enkuba -tonnyerera **keep drizzling on and off**

-tonnyeza *vt* (-tonnyezza) **mark, dot, drip in** -tonnyeza eddagala mu maaso **put drops of medicine in the eyes**

tonninnyira-mu-kange **ready-to-eat food** *(served from the pavement)*

-tonnyolokoka *vi* (-tonnyolokose) (1) **get soaked,** (2) **be dressed very smartly**

-tono *adj* **small, thin, few**

-tonotono *adj* **fairly small/thin/few**

-toola *vt* (-todde) **take some,** *eg. Toola ssente ogule omugaati. ('Take some money and buy bread.')*

  -toolako (-toddeko) **take off some,** *eg. Toolako empapula bbiri. ('Take off two pieces of paper.', eg. from a pile)*, **subtract, deduct** **-toolamu take some** *(from within)*, *eg. Mu nsawo toolamu emicungwa ebiri. ('Take two oranges from the bag.')* **-toolawo take some** *(from a place)*, *eg. Yatoolawo amatofaali ataano. ('He took five bricks.')* **-toolayo take some** *(from over there)*, *eg. Yatoolayo amatofaali ataano okuva ku ntuumu eyo. ('He took five bricks from that pile.')*

-eetoolatoola *vi* (-eetoddetodde) **pilfer**

-eetooloola *vit* (-eetooloodde) **go around,** *eg. Yatambula ne yeetooloola ennyumba. ('He walked around the house.')*, **surround, encircle, revolve around, rotate, take a detour around** -yogera -eetooloola **talk in circles, beat about the bush**

-eetooloolera *vt* (-eetoolooledde) **revolve in, circle around,** *eg. Ennyonyi yeetooloolera mu bbanga. ('The plane is circling around in the sky.')*

-eetooloolwa *vi* (-eetoolooddwa) **be surrounded (by)**

-eetooloovu *adj* (enneetooloovu *n9*) **round, circular**

-eetoolooza *vt* (-eetooloozezza) **cause to go around, put around, revolve, surround with, enclose in, rotate** -eetoolooza amaaso **gaze in all directions**

-eetoowaliza *vt* (-eetoowalizza) **humble oneself before, be deferential towards**

[1]**-toowaza** *vt* (-toowazizza) **humiliate**

[2]**-eetoowaza** *vr* **humble oneself, be deferential**

-toowolokoka *(also* -teewulukuka*) vi* (-toowolokose) **grow slack, be(come) deflated**

-toowolokosa *(also* -teewulula*) vt* (-toowolokosezza) **cause to become slack**

-totobala (-totobadde) *vi* **be wet through**

toyireeti *n9* **(flush) toilet**

[1]**-tta** *vt* (-sse, nzita) **kill, excecute.** *See* okutta -tta ennyonta **quench one's thirst** -tta ku liiso **overlook a fault** -tta omukago **make a blood pact** -tta omukwano **kill off a friendship** ennaku -tta **be grief-stricken**

²-etta *vr* **kill oneself**. *See* okwetta

ettaabu *n9* (*no pl.*) **trouble**

ettaala *n9* **lamp, lantern, light** ettaala y'amafuta **paraffin lamp** ettaala y'amasannyalaze **electric light** ettaala y'omukono **hand-held light**

ttaano *num* **five**

-ttaanya *vt* (-ttaanyizza) **level down** (*eg. earth*), **smooth down, spread evenly** (*eg. dung on a garden*)

ettaayi *n9* **tie**

ettaba *n5* (*pl.* amataba) **big pool**; *in pl.* **flood**

ettabaaliro *n5* (*pl.* amatabaaliro) **battlefield**

ettabaaza *n9* **lamp, light**

ettabi *n5* (*pl.* amatabi) **branch** ettabi ly'ekibiina **branch of an organisation** -eenyeenya amatabi **shake palm leaves** (*on Palm Sunday*) Olunaku lwa Matabi **Palm Sunday**

ettafaali *See* ettofaali

ettaka *n5* (*no pl.*) **soil, ground, land** ettaka eriddugavu **black soil** ettaka erimyufu **red soil** ettaka ly'olunnyo **infertile land**

ettale *n5* (*no pl.*) **grazing area, pasture** -goba ettale **land ashore** -suula ettale **finish a job, end a relationship**

ettalo *n5* (*no pl.*) **hex, spell**

ettama *n5* (*pl.* amatama) **cheek** (*of the face*) -kuba amatama **be all talk and no action**

ettambiro *n5* (*pl.* amatambiro) **place of sacrifice or execution**

ettamiiro *n5* (*no pl.*) **alcoholism**

ettanda *n9* (*no pl.*) **place of the dead** (*where Walumbe descended*)

ettanga *n5* (*pl.* amatanga) **sail**

ttani *n9* **ton**

ttanibboyi *n1* (*pl.* ba ttanibboyi) **person who helps load and unload trucks, turnboy**

ttanka *n9* **tank** ttanka y'amazzi **water tank**

ttanuulu *n9* **blacksmith's furnace** ttanuulu y'amatofaali **brick kiln** -yita mu ttanuulu **pass through a hard time**

-ttattana *vi* (-ttattanye) **be damaged badly, be wrecked**

-ttattanya *vt* (-ttattanyizza, nzitattanya) **damage badly, wreck**

ettawaaza *n9* **lamp**

ettawulo *n9* **towel**

etteeka *n5* (*pl.* amateeka) **law, regulation, commandment** Ekintu ky'etteeka. (*also* Kya tteeka.) **It is compulsory.**

etteete *n6* **type of grass** (*lemon-scented, spread on floors*) Cymbopogon nardus

ettegula *n5* (*pl.* amategula) **roof tile**. *From: 'tegula' (Latin).*

ettembe *n5* (*pl.* amatembe) **seed of ekitembe**. *Used for making necklaces and RC rosaries; likely used as a counter in omweso prior to the introduction of 'omuyiki'. See* empiki

ettemu *n5* (*no pl.*) **murder, assassination**

ttena *n9* **tennis, tennis ball**

ettendekero *n5* (*pl.* amatendekero) **training institute, college**

ettendo *n5* (*no pl.*) **praise, glory** -a ettendo *adj* **praiseworthy**

ettengo *n5* **small spiny shrub with large yellow fruits, fruit of this plant** (*fruit used for washing and as an antidote to puff adder bites*) Solanum aculeastrum.

etterekero *n5* (*pl.* amaterekero) **storage place, cupboard** etterekero ly'amata **dairy** etterekero ly'ebitabo **library** etterekero ly'essente (*or* ensimbi) **place for storing keeping money, bank** etterekero ly'omusaayi **blood bank**

ttibbi *n1* **tuberculosis**

-ttibwa *vi* (-ttiddwa) **be killed**

ettigi (*also* ekigi, ttigimbuli *or* ettiyuuko) *n5* (*no pl.*) **mischief, insolence, cheek, bad manners**. *'ettigi' describes a worse type of behaviour than 'ekyejo'. See* ekitigi -li wa ettigi **be mischievous**

ttiimu *n9* **team**

ettiini *n9* **fig** (*fruit of omutiini*)

ttikiti *n9* **ticket**

ettima *n5* (*no pl.*) **spite, malice, ill will** -a ettima *adj* **spiteful, malicious** n'ettima **spitefully** ow'ettima *n1* **bad-hearted person, spiteful person**

ttimba *n1* **python**

ettimpa *n5* (*no pl.*) **leaf of ejjuuni, edible powder made from this leaf**

ttingatinga *n9* **bulldozer** (*type with tracks*)

ettipoota *n9* **teapot**

-ttira *vt* (-ttidde, nzitira) **kill at/for**, *etc.*

ttivvi *n9* **TV**

ettofaali (*also* ettafaali) *n5* (*pl.* amatofaali) **brick** ettofaali eritali lyokye **sun-dried brick** ettofaali eryokye **furnace-baked brick**

ettogero *n5* (*pl.* amatogero) **large earthenware pot** (*used, eg. for collecting juice from the crushing of bananas*)

ttoggo *n1* (*no pl.*) **long rainy season** (*March-May*)

ettondo *n5* (*pl.* amatondo) **drop**

ettooke *n5* (*pl.* amatooke) **cooking banana(s)** (*single fruit or bunch*); *in pl.* **cooked bananas** ettooke evumbike **matooke that has been placed in ashes** (*for keeping warm*) amatooke ag'akatogo **bananas cooked in sauce** (*not wrapped in banana leaves*) amatooke amasuulemu **bananas cooked in water** (*not wrapped in banana leaves*) amatooke ag'empogola **bananas cooked in their skins** ekitole ky'ettooke **lump of matooke** (*as taken into the fingers to eat*)

ttooki *n9* **torch**

ettoomi *n5* (*no pl.*) **mud**

ettosi *n5* (*no pl.*) **wet mud** (*as in valleys*), **wet clay**

-ttottola *vt* (-ttottodde, nzitottola) **relate in detail**

ettovu *n5* (*pl.* amatovu) **spiny shrub with purple-pink flowers** Acanthus pubescens

ettu *n5* (*pl.* amatu) **packet made from banana fibre,**

157

eg. *ettu ly'emmwanyi ('packet of coffee beans')* ettu ly'enswa **packet of flying ants** ettu lya Mugema **pregnancy** (*of the Queen*), eg. *Alina ettu lya Magema. ('The Queen is pregnant.')*

ettugunda *n5* (*pl. amatugunda*) **fruit of omutugunda** (*edible*)

-ttuka *vi* (-ttuse) **recur**

-ttula *vt* (-ttudde, nzitula) **beat** (*bark, in final stage of barkcloth making*)

ettule *n9* **tray**

ettulu ow'ettulu *n1* **person blind in one eye**

ettuluba *n5* (*pl. amatuluba*) **category, class, group,** eg. *Yamuvunaanidde mu ttuluba lya buli bwa nguzi. ('She was accused under the bribery act.')*

-ttulukuka *vi* (-ttulukuse) **trickle** -ttulukuka entuuyo **drip sweat**

-ttulula *vt* (-ttuludde, nzitulula) **pour out, strain, decant** -ttulula amazzi mu **drain out water from** (*eg. cooked vegetables*)

ettumbi *n5* (*no pl.*) **depth of the night**

ettundiro *n5* (*pl. amatundiro*) **place of selling**

ettundubaali *n5* (*pl. amatundubaali*) **tarpaulin, canopy, awning**

ettungulu *n5* (*pl. amatungulu*) **fruit of ekitungulu** (*red, edible*)

-ttunka *vi* (-ttunse) **burn fiercely, contest fiercely** -ttunka ne **make a huge effort against,** eg. *Arsenal ejja kuttunka ne ManU. ('Arsenal will make a huge effort to beat ManU.')*

ettuntu *n5* (*no pl.*) **hottest part of the day** (*about midday to 3 pm*)

ettunzi *n5* (*no pl.*) **sale** si kya ttunzi **something that failed to sell**

ettutuma *n5* (*pl. amatutuma*) **coucal** (*type of bird*)

ettutumu *n5* (*no pl.*) **fame, renown** -a ettutumu *adj* **renowned, popular** ow'ettutumu *n1* **famous person**

ettwale *n5* (*pl. amatwale*) **colony, deanery**

ettwatwa *n5* **woody herb with pink to purple flowers** (*medicinal, assists with childbirth*) *Bothriocline longipes*

tuba **we are** (*stem* -ba)

[1]**-tubika** (-tubise) *See* -tutubika

[2]**-eetubika** *See* -eetutubika

-tubira *vi* (-tubidde) **get stuck in mud**

-tubiza *vt* (-tubizizza) **cause to get stuck in mud**

-tudde *See* -tuula

[1]**-tuga** *vt* (-tuze) **strangle, throttle**

[2]**-eetuga** *vr* **hang oneself**

[1]**-tugga** *vt* (-tuzze) **knot, tangle (up)**

[2]**-eetugga** *vi* **get knotted, be(come) entangled, shrink** (*of materials*)

-tugumbula *vt* (-tugumbudde) **strangle**

-tujja *vi* (-tuzze) **be beaten** (*of a drum*), **throb,** eg. *Omutima guntujja. ('My heart is throbbing.')*, **pulsate**

-(y)atuka *See* -yatuka

-tukula *vi* (-tukudde) **be(come) clean, be holy**

-tukuulirira *vi* (-tukuuliridde) **grow pale**

-tukuvu *adj* **holy, sacred, consecrated, clean** Ekitabo Ekitukuvu **Holy Bible**

-tukuza *vt* (-tukuzizza) *vt* **make clean, make holy, sanctify, consecrate**

-(y)atula *See* -yatula

tulafiki *n9* **traffic**

tulakita *n9* **tractor**

tulampeti *n9* **trumpet**

[1]**tuli** *dem* **that**

[2]**tuli** **we are** (*stem* -li)

-tulika *vi* (-tulise) **burst** (*making a sound*), eg. *Yatulika n'eseka. ('He burst out laughing.')*, **explode, go off** (*of a gun*), **pop**

-eetulinkiriza *vit* (-eetulinkirizza) **be presumptuous, usurp, appropriate**

-(y)atulira *See* -yatulira

-tulisa *vt* (-tulisizza) **burst** (*making a sound*), **explode**

otulo *n13* (*no pl.*) **sleep**

-tulugunya *vt* (-tulugunyizza) **torment**

[1]**-tuma** *vt* (-tumye) **send** (*a person*), eg. *Ntuma omwana agule sukaali. ('I am sending a child to buy sugar.')*

[2]**-eetuma** *vit* **do/go on one's own initiative**

-tumbiira *vi* (-tumbidde) **rise to a great height** (*eg. of a mountain or aeroplane*), eg. *Ennyonyi etumbidde. ('The plane is flying very high.')*, **swell up**

-tumbiivu *adj* **extremely high, swollen**

-tumbuka *vi* (-tumbuse) **be raised to a higher level** (*of flame, sound, etc.*), **be turned up, expand, well up** (*of an emotion*) -tumbuka ne **burst into** (*laughter or tears*), eg. *Yatumbuka n'aseka. ('He burst into laughter.')* olubuto -tumbuka **bulge out** (*of the stomach*)

-tumbula *vt* (-tumbudde) **raise the level of** (*flame, sound, etc.*), **boost** -tumbula leediyo **turn up the radio** -tumbula omuliro **turn up the heat** -tumbula omutindo **uplift the standard**

-tumibwa *vi* (-timiddwa) **be sent** (*of a person*)

-tumira *vt* (-tumidde) **send** (*someone*) **to,** eg. *Mbatumidde Musoke. ('I have sent Musoke to them.')*, **send greetings to,** eg. *Mbatumidde. ('I am sending greeings to them.')*

-tumiriza *vt* (-tumirizza) **keep sending** (*someone*) **unnecessarily**

-tumya *vt* (-tumizza) **send for,** eg. *Ntumizza amagi. ('I have sent for eggs.')*

-tunda *vt* (-tunze) **sell.** *See* okutunda -tunda buliwo **sell for cash** -tunda omuwendo ogwa wansi **sell cheaply**

-tundira *vt* (-tundidde) **sell for/at,** etc. *See* okutundira

-tundula *vt* (-tundudde) **extract with an implement** (*eg. thorn from skin with a needle*), **dig out** (*from within*) -tundula ebimuli bya vanira **pollinate vanilla** -tundula envunza **remove a jigger**

-tunga *vt* (-tunze) **sew, darn, embroider** -tunga kaddannyuma **sew backstitch**

[1]**tungatunga** *adv* **at close grips, close together**

[2]**-tungatunga** *vt* (-tunzetunze) **sew roughly**

-tunge *adj* **sewn**

-tungira *vt* (-tungidde) **sew for** (*someone*) engoye entungire ddala **ready-made clothes**

-tungulukuka *vi* (-tungulukuse) **become unstitched**

-tungulula *vt* (-tunguludde) **unstitch, unpick**

otunnyo *n13* (*no pl.*) **pinch of salt**

tuno *demo* **this**

-tuntumuka *vi* (-tuntumuse) **rage** (*of a fire*), *eg. Omuliro gutuntumuse. ('The fire is raging.')*, **flare up**

-tuntuza *vt* (-tuntuzizza) **overwork, mistreat**

-tunula *vi* (-tunudde) **look, stare, be awake** -tunula enkaliriza **stare, glare** -tunula ku **face (towards)**, *eg. Ennyumba zitunula ku nnyanja. ('The houses face the lake.')* obudde -tunula **be(come) daylight**

-tunulagana *vi* (-tunulaganye) **look at one another, face one another**, *eg. Ennyumba zitunulaganye. ('The houses face one another')*

-tunuulira *vt* (-tunuulidde) **overlook, stare at** -tunuulira enkaliriza **look closely at with a purpose, scrutinise, glare at**

-tunuza *vt* (-tunuzizza) **look** (*in a certain manner*) -tunuza ekkabyo **look stern** -tunuza ettima **look unsmiling** -tunuza obukambwe **look fierce**

-tuŋŋununa *vi* (-tuŋŋununye) **have a tart taste** (*as an unripe raspberry*)

otuta *n13* (*no pl.*) **drop of milk**

-tutte *See* -twala

-tutubika (*also* -tubika) *vt* (-tutubise) **dip in** (*eg. a ladle, to extract some liquid*), **immerse.** *Derivation: onomatopoeic (based on the sound of a gourd 'ekita' being filled).*

-eetutubika (*also* -eetutubika) *vr* **immerse oneself**

-tutumufu *adj* **famous, popular**

-tutumuka *vi* (-tutumuse) **become famous**

-tutumula *vt* (-tutumudde) **make famous**

otutwe *pos* **hers, his**

otutwo *pos* **yours** *si.*

-tuubatuuba *vi* (-tuubyetuubye) **be about to cry** (*of a baby*)

-tuufu *adj* **right, correct, true, pure, suitable**

-tuuka *vi* (-tuuse) **arrive (at), reach, get up to, fit** (*eg. of clothing*), **suit.** *See* okutuuka -tuuka ku lukalu **land ashore** -tuukawo (-tuuseewo) **arrive** (*at a place*), **happen**, *eg. Ekituuseewo? ('What has happened?)*, **arise** (*of matters*) -tuukayo **arrive there, get there**

-tuukana (*also* -tuukagana) *vi* (-tuukanye) (1) **suit one another, harmonise**, *eg. Omwana ne nnyina baatuukagana mu mpisa. ('The baby and her mother harmonised their behaviour.')*; (2) **come together** (*as of two tables touching*)

-tuukanya *vt* (-tuukanyizza) (1) **make equal** (*eg. in length*), **equalise, make conform, make**

harmonise; (2) **put together** (*eg. two tables to touch one another*)

[1]**-tuukira** *vi* (-tuukidde) **arrive at** tuukira ku/mu *Can be equivalent to adverbial phrase* **on arrival**, *eg. Twatuukira ku kunywa caayi. ('We had tea on arrival.')* -tuukira ku mulembe **be fashionable, be modern** -tuukira ku nsonga **get straight to the point**

[2]**-eetuukira** *vi* (-eetuukidde) **go oneself** (*rather than someone else going*)

-tuukirira *vi* (-tuukiridde) **approach, go personally** (*to a person*), **happen** (*of a prophecy*)

-tuukirivu *adj* **righteous, holy, perfect**

-tuukiriza *vt* (-tuukirizza) **carry out successfully, achieve, accomplish, attain, fulfil, conform to, follow**, *eg. Abaana batuukiriza amateeka g'essomero. ('The children are following the school rules.')*, **succeed at.** *See* okutuukiriza

-tuula *vi* (-tudde) **sit.** *Can be followed by aux v in present tense modifying its meaning N19), eg.* (1) -tuula -eebamba **sit with legs spread apart**; (2) -tuula -lannama **sit with legs extended**, *eg. Atuula alannamye. ('He is sitting with legs extended.')*; (3) -tuula -salako **sit with legs crossed.** -tuula ku kapapajjo **sit on the edge of a chair** (*or of a carrier of a bike*)

-tuulibwa (*also* -tuulwa) *vi* (-tuuliddwa) **be seated**

-tuulwako *vi* (-tuuluddwako) **be sat on**, *eg. Leeta omukeeka ogutuulwako. ('Bring a mat for sitting on.')*

[1]**-tuuma** *vt* (-tuumye) **give a name to** (*a person*), **name**

[2]**-tuuma** *vt* **collect in a heap, pile/heap (up)**

-tuumibwa *vi* (-tuumiddwa) **be named**

-tuumuuka *vi* (-tuumuuse) **be emitted with force** (*of a strong smell, smoke, fire, etc.*), *eg. Ennyumba yonna yabadde etuumuuka ng'ewunya ekisu ekibi. ('The whole house was suddenly filled with a bad smell.')* ekiwunya -tuumuuka **suddenly stench** (*eg. of a drain*) omukka -tuumuuka **be too much** (*of smoke*)

[1]**-tuusa** *vt* (-tuusizza) **cause to arrive, take, bring, deliver, import.** *See* okutuusa

[2]**-eetuusa** *vr* **advance oneself** (*through self-help*)

-tuuse *See* -tuuka

tuutuli **there it is**

tuutuno **here it is, here we are**

tuutwo **there it is**

-tuuyana *vi* (-tuuyanye) **sweat, perspire** -tuuyana n'ebizibu (*also* -tuuyana n'omulimu) **do a difficult job**

-tuuza *vt* (-tuuzizza) **seat** (*someone*)

-tuyira *vi* (-tuyidde) **hold one's breath** -tuyira olw'obusungu **burst with rage**

-(y)atuza *See* -yatuza

otuzigo *n13* **very small amount of ghee or ointment**

-tuzza *vt* (-tuzzizza) **beat** (*a drum*), **(cause to) throb**

otuzzi *n13* (*no pl.*) **drop of water, very little water**

(o)tw- *abbrev of* (o)twa; twe

otwa *pre* **of**. *Can be a prefix* **(o)twa-** (N11.4), *eg. twange* (*'my'*).

(o)twabwe *pos* **their(s)** (N11.4)

(o)twaffe *pos* **our(s)** (N11.4)

-twakaala *vi* (-twakadde) **be(come) brightly coloured** amaaso -twakaala **be(come) bloodshot** (*of the eyes*) enjuba -twakaala **be(come) red** (*of the rising or setting sun*), *eg. Enjuba etwakadde.* (*'The sun has turned red.'*)

-twakaavu *adj* **strikingly/brightly coloured**

[1]-twala *vt* (-tutte) **take, affect** (*emotionally*), *eg. Anaakitwala atya?* (*'How will it affect her?'*) -twala ekiseera (*or* ebbanga) **take time** (*eg. to decide what to do*) -twala olw'empaka **take by force, abduct** **-twalako** (-tutteko) **take some, give a lift to** (*someone in a vehicle*)

[2]-eetwala *vi* **take oneself** (*somewhere*), **go of one's own accord, go without being invited, become independent** (*of a country*)

twalatugende *n1* **disorganised assortment of things, miscellany**

-twalibwa *vi* (-twaliddwa) **be taken**

-twalira *vt* (-twalidde) **take to**, *eg. Mutwalire ekkeesi ye.* (*'Take his case for him.'*). *See okutwalira* -twalira ebbanga **take a long time** (*to do something*), *eg. Kyantwalira ebbanga okumala omulimu.* (*'It took me a long time to finish the work.'*)

-twaliriza *vi* (-twalirizza) **persist** (*in the face of difficulties*) Otulo tumutwaliriza. **He is falling asleep.**

(o)twammwe *pos* **your(s)** *pl.* (N11.4)

(o)twange *pos* **my, mine.** (N11.4)

-twaza *vt* (-twazizza) **cause to take**

[1]twe *pos* **her/his** (N11.4)

-twekobaana *vi* (-twekobaanye) **hold a private** (*or secret*) **meeting**

Twekobe *n9* **official residence of the Kabaka**

otwenge *n13* (*no pl.*) **a few drops of beer**

[1]otwo *dem* **that**

[2]two *pos* **your** *si.*

[3]two *pro* **it**. *Can be a suffix* **-two** (N11.4), *eg. natwo* (*'and it'*). Otwo twenge twange. **Please don't touch my little drink.**

[1]-tya *vit* (-tidde) **be afraid (of), fear, respect.** *See okutya*

[2]-tya? *interr v* (*used only in present tense* N13) **how?**, *eg. Wakikola otya?* (*'How did you do it?'*), **what ... like?**, *eg. Ennyumba efaanana etya?* (*'What does the house look like?'*)

-tyaba *vt* (-tyabye) -tyaba enku **gather firewood**

-tyanno? *interr v* (*used in greetings* N28), *eg. Wasuze otyanno?* (*'Good morning.'*)

-tyemuka *vi* (-tyemuse) emmeeme -tyemuka **suffer from shock** (*with the heart racing*), *eg. Emmeeme yamutyemuse.* (*'She was shocked.'*) omutima

-tyemuka **be startled and frightened** (*with the heart racing*), **be shocked**, *eg. Bwe nnalabye engo omutima ne guntyemuka.* (*'I was shocked when I saw the leopard.'*)

-tyemula *vt* (-tyemudde) **cut open** -tyemula emmeeme **shock** (*someone*) -tyemula omutima **startle and shock**, *eg. Embwa yatyemula omwana omutima.* (*'The dog startled the child.'*)

-tyetyemuka *vi* (-tyetyemuse) **burst into laughter**

[1]otyo! *interj* **That's right!, There you are!**, *etc.*

[2]-tyo *v* (*used only in present tense* N13) **like that**, *eg. Asoma bw'atyo.* (*'He reads like that.'*) bwe -tyo bwe -tyo **so-so, fifty-fifty.** (N13), *eg. Oli bulungi? Bwe ntyo bwe ntyo.* (*'How are you? So-so.'*)

-tyoboola *vt* (-tyobodde) **discredit**

V, v

[1]ova *n1* (*pl.* bi ova *n8*) **avocado** *Persea americana*

[2]-va *vi* (-vudde) **come from**, *eg. Yava mu kyalo.* (*'He came from the village.'*), **arise from, get out of, go from, alight, vacate.** *As aux v can be equivalent to adverb* **just** (N19), *eg. Tuva kulya.* (*'We have just eaten.'*). *See okuva* -va ku **give up** (*with a person or plan*), *eg. Yava ku kumuyamba.* (*'He gave up trying to help her.'*), **abandon, relinquish, turn off/away from, stray, deviate** -va ku bwakabaka **abdicate the kingship** -va ku kirowoozo **give up with an idea** -va ku mabeere **be weaned** -va mu **leave** (*from within*), **vacate** (*eg. a room*), **disembark** -va mu buliri **get up** (*from being in bed*) -va mu kifo **step down from a position** kye-...-va *declinable conjunction* **that is why, therefore.** (N10.2) **-vaako** (-vuddeko) **come off, get off**, *eg. Ppusi yavaako ku mmeeza.* (*'The cat got off the table.'*), **get away from, quit, become detached, leave alone**, *eg. Yali muzibu ne bamuvaako.* (*'He was difficult so they left him alone.'*), **cause**, *eg. Kiki ekivaako omwana okulwala?* (*'What has caused the child's illness?'*)

-vaamu **come out** (*from within*), *eg. Mu nnyumba baavuddemu.* (*'They came out of the house.'*), **get from**, *eg. Ensawo ya kasooli yavaamu ssiringi kikumi.* (*'He got 100 shillings [from selling] the bag of maize.'*), **evacuate, vaccate, withdraw from, leave, get out** (*of a vehicle*), **result in, produce, emit** -vaamu erangi **lose colour** (*eg. of cloth*) -vaamu olubuto (*also* olubuto -vaamu) **have a miscarriage** **-vaawo move, come from, leave** (*a place*), **depart** Vaawo! **Go away!** **-vaayo move from** (*over there*), *eg. Yavaayo mu kyalo.* (*'He moved from the village.'*), **leave** (*from over there*), *eg. E Kampala yavuddeyo ku ssaawa bbiri.* (*'He left Kampala at 8 o'clock.'*) enjuba -vaayo **rise** (*of the sun*), **dawn**

-eevaamu *vi* (-eevuddemu) **nerve oneself** (*to do something*), **resolve, dare**

ovakkedo (*also* <u>ova</u>, *or* <u>vvakkedo</u>) *n1* **avocado**
Persea americana

vanira *n1* **vanilla**

-vannyuma *adj* **last, final**

vasiriini *n9* **vaseline**

oveni *n1* **oven**

vesiti *n9* **vest**

vidiyo *n9* **video**

-viira *vit* (-viiridde) **move away from, get out of the way of,** *eg. Ggwe omwana, viira emmotoka.* (*'Hey you child, get out of the way of the car.'*)
　-viiramu **get out** (*of a vehicle*), *eg. Yayogera nti aviiramu awo.* (*'He said he was getting out there.'*)

vitamiini *n9* **vitamin**

-(y)avu *See* -yavu

-vuba *vit* (-vubye) **fish (for).** *See* okuvuba

-vubiikiriza *vt* (-vubiikirizza) **suppress** (*information*), **cover up, hush up**

-vubiriza *vt* (-vubirizza) **soften** (*with water or saliva*), **suppress pain** (*with water or saliva*), **douse** (*a fire with water*)

-vubuka *vi* (-vubuse) **reach adolescence, be(come) a youth**

-vudde *See* -va

[1]-vuga *vi* (-vuze) **make a sound, sound, ring** (*of a bell or telephone*) 　<u>ekintu ekivuga</u> **a sound** 　<u>emmundu -vuga</u> **go off** (*of a gun*), **fire**

[2]-vuga *vt* **drive, steer, navigate** 　<u>-vuga eggaali</u> **ride a bicycle** 　<u>-vuga endiima</u> **drive very fast** 　<u>-vuga ennyonyi</u> **fly an aeroplane**

-vuganya *vt* (-vuganyizza) **compete (against),** *eg. Musoke avuganya ne Mukasa mu kuzannya omweso.* (*'Musoke is competing with Mukasa in chess.'*), **contest (with)**

-vujjirira *vt* (-vujjiridde) **compensate for a bad situation** 　<u>-vujjirira envujjo</u> **deliver tribute**

-(y)avula *See* -yavula

-vulubana *vi* (-vulubanye) **be(come) covered with, be(come) smeared with,** *eg. Omwana avulubanye emmere.* (*'The baby is smeared with food.'*)

-eevulubanya *vr* (-eevulubanyizza) **get oneself covered with** (*food, dirt, etc.*), *eg. Omwana yeevulubanyizza emmere.* (*'The baby has smeared itself with food.'*)

-vuluga *vt* (-vuluze) **mess up, muddle up, bungle, throw into confusion**

-vulula *vit* (-vuludde) **bubble, blow (bubbles)** (*of saliva*), *eg. Omwana avulula amalusu.* (*'The baby is blowing bubbles.'*)

[1]-vulunga *vt* (-vulunze) **roll around** (*eg. meat in flour*), **mix up by rolling around.** *See* -kulunga
　<u>-vulunga ebbumba</u> **initial stage in rolling clay** (*in preparation for making pottery*) 　<u>-vulunga ettooke</u> **roll around a ball of matooke in sauce**

[2]-eevulunga *vr* **roll** (*in the dirt, eg. of a pig*)

[1]-vuma *vt* (-vumye) *vt* **insult, revile, be abusive towards**

[2]-eevuma *vr* **revile oneself**

-vumagana *vi* (-vumaganye) **insult one another**

-vumaganya *vt* (-vumaganyizza) **cause to be reviled, disgrace.** *See* emmamba

-vumbagira *vt* (-vumbagidde) **put hands around**
　<u>-vumbagira enkoko</u> **creep up and catch a chicken**
　<u>-vumbagira omubbi</u> **arrest a thief**

-vumbeera *vi* (-vumbedde) **be blocked up** (*of the nose*)

-vumbika *vt* (-vumbise) **put under hot ashes**
　<u>-vumbika eggwolu</u> **bury left-over matooke in hot ashes** (*wrapped in banana leaves, to eat next day*). *See* -bembula

-vumbuka *vi* (-vumbuse) **be discovered, turn up** (*of something lost*)

-vumbula *vt* (-vumbudde) **discover**

-vumirira *vt* (-vumiridde) **insult** (*someone*) **repeatedly, speak badly about, condemn**

-vumu *adj* **courageous, daring** (= -gumu)

-vumula *vt* (-vumudde) **be/give an antidote (to), cure,** *eg. Musoke alina eddagala erivumula abojjeddwa omusota.* (*'Musoke has a medicine for curing snake bite.'*) 　<u>-vumula akajanja</u> **stop** (*someone*) **fussing about** 　<u>-vumula eddogo</u> **remove an evil spell** 　<u>-vumula obulwadde</u> **cure an illness**

-vumulula *vt* (-vumuludde) **remove a curse from** (*on the part of the original curser*), *eg. Omulogo baamukubye emiggo n'akkiriza okuvumulula omwana.* (*'The witchdoctor was beaten up and forced to remove the spell on the child.'*)

-vunaana *vt* (-vunaanye) **accuse, hold responsible**

-vunaanibwa (*also* <u>-vunaanwa</u>) *vi* (-vunaaniddwa) **be accused** (*of an offence*)

-vunaanyizibwa *vi* (-vunaanyiziddwa) **be held responsible**

-vunda *vi* (-vunze) **rot, decay**

-vundu *adj* **rotten, putrid**

[1]-vungavunga *vt* (-vunzevunze) **crumple (up), crease**

[2]-eevungavunga *vi* **be crumpled/creased**

-vungisa *vt* (-vungisizza) 　<u>-vungisa ssente</u> **break money into smaller denominations**

-vunnama *vi* (-vunnamye) **bow in respect**

NOTES FOR
v

-v. Unless the **v** is doubled, verbs starting **v** have 1st person singulars starting **nv**, *eg.* **nva** ('I come from'), from **-va**.

-vv. Verbs starting **vv** have 1st person singulars starting **nziv**, *eg.* **nzivuunula** ('I translate'), from **-vvuunula**.

evv-. Nouns in *n5* starting **evv** have plurals (in *n6*) starting **amav**, *eg.* the plural of **evviivi** is **amaviivi**.

NOUNS IN *n9*. Most nouns in *n9* have identically spelt plurals (in *n10*).

-vunza *vt* (-vunzizza) **rot, cause to decay**

-vuubiika *vt* (-vuubiise) **cram/stuff in**, *eg. Olya ng'ovuubiika. ('You are cramming food into your mouth.')* -vuubiika emmere **stuff food into one's mouth**, *eg. Yalya avuubiika emmere. ('He stuffed food into his mouth.')*

-vuuma *vi* (-vuumye) **voom** (*make noise like a revving car*), **growl**

-vuumira *vt* (-vuumidde) **growl at**

-vuumuula *vt* (-vuumudde) **hurl forward** -vuumuula ejjinja **sling a stone** -vuumuula emmotoka **drive a car very fast**

¹**-vuunika** *vt* (-vuunise) **turn upside down, overturn**

²**-eevuunika** *vi* **be turned upside down**, *eg. Agalamidde nga yeevuunise. ('He is lying face down.')*, **capsise**

-vuunula *vt* (-vuunudde) **turn right way up**

-vuuvuuma *vi* (-vuuvuumye) **hum** (*as a bumble bee*), **buzz, mutter, murmur**

-vuvuŋŋana *vi* (-vuvuŋŋanye) **be in a state of confusion** (*of a number of people*), **mill about in confusion**

-(y)avuwala *See* -yavuwala

-(y)avuwaza *See* -yavuwaza

-vuya *vi* (-vuye) **be in a confused state** (*of a person*), **be muddled up**

vvakkedo *See* ovakkedo

evviini *n9* **wine**

evviivi *n5* (*pl.* amaviivi) **knee**

-vvoola *vt* (-vvodde) **blaspheme**

evvu *n5* (*no pl.*) **ash(es)**

vvulugu **mess, muddle** -kola ebya vvulugu **do a messy job, mess things up** -wandiika vvulugu **scribble** -yogera vvulugu **talk nonsense**

evvumbe *n5* (*no pl.*) **smell of burning flesh or fur**

-vvunkana *vi* (-vvunkanye) **take part in a competition**

-vvuunuka *vi* (-vvuunuse) **go over a hill**, *eg. Bavvuunuka olusozi Lubaga okutuuka ku dduuka. ('They are going over Rubaga hill to get to the shop.')*, **overcome** (*an obstacle or difficulty*), **surmount**

-vvuunula *vt* (-vvuunudde) **interpret, translate**

evvuunya *n5* (*pl.* amavuunya) **fold, pleat**

evvuuvuumira *n5* (*pl.* amavuuvuumira) **bumble bee**

W,w

(o)w' *abbrev of* (o)wa; **we**

¹**wa?** *interr* **where?** (N13)

²**(a)wa** **place/home of**, *eg. awa Musoke ('Musoke's place')*. *Can be a prefix* **awa-**: (1) (*in possessives* N11.5), *eg. awange ('my place')*; (2) (*in nouns of*

noun class *n16*), *eg. awalime ('dug-over land')*. *The following are nouns (in noun class n16) referring to places where certain activities are performed*: (1) aw'okufulumira (*also* w'ofulumira) **exit**; (2) aw'okukolera (*also* w'okolera) **workplace**; (3) aw'okukyamira (*also* w'okyamira) **turning place** (*for turning off*); (4) aw'okukyukira (*also* w'okyukira) **turning place** (*for turning around*); (5) aw'okusomokera (*also* w'osomokera) **place where water is crossed, ford**; (6) aw'okuyingirira (*also* w'oyingirira) **entrance**; (7) aw'okuzannyira (*also* w'ozannyira) **playground**; (8) w'otuula **seating area**.

³**ewa** **at/to the place/home of, to**, *eg. Tugenda ewa Musoke. ('We are going to Musoke's home.')*. *Can be a prefix* **ewa-** (**N11.5**), *eg. ewange ('at my place')*. ewa ddobbi *n23* **laundry**

⁴**(o)wa** *pre* **of** (**N11.1**), *eg. omwana wa Musoke ('child of Musoke')*. *Can be a prefix* (**o**)**wa-** (**N11**), *eg.* (1) wange ('mine'); (2) owaakasolya ('head of a clan'); (3) owooluganda ('blood relative of'). *'owa' appears in ordinal numbers* (**7.1**), *eg. omuntu ow'okubiri ('second person')*. *Elision is sometimes seen, eg. omuntu owookubiri ('second person')*.

⁵**-wa** *vt* (-wadde) **give** -wa amaanyi **encourage** -wa amagezi **advise** -wa ekifo **give a place to** (*eg. in a school*), *eg. Yawa Musoke ekifo mu ssomero. ('He gave a place to Musoke in school.')* -wa ekitanda mu ddwaliro **admit to hospital** -wa ekitiibwa **honour, pay homage to** -wa engassi **pay compensation** -wa enguzi **bribe** -wa erinnya **name** -wa obubudamo **give refuge** -wa obujulizi **testify** -wa obutwa **poison** -wa olukusa **authorise** -wa omukisa **bless** **-waako** (-waddeko) **give some**, *eg. Ku sukaali ajja kukuwaako kiro emu. ('She will give you one kilo of the sugar.')* **-waawo give** **-waayo give** (*over there*), **offer, hand in, commit, submit, surrender**. *See* okuwaayo -waayo ekirabo **make an offering**, *eg. Bwe tugenda okusaba ku kkanisa tuwaayo ebirabo. ('When we go to church we make offerings.')* -waayo ekirowoozo **submit a proposal** -waayo engalo **cup the hands** (*to receive something politely*)

⁶**-eewa** *See* -eewaayo

-waaba *vi* (-waabye) **make a complaint, report a wrong-doing** -waaba omusango **file a charge** -waaba omusango mu kkooti **bring a case to court**

awaabadde **where there was/were**

waabaddewo **there was/were**

-waabira (*also* -wawaabira) *vt* (-waabidde) **make a complaint against, inform on** -waabira mu kkooti **take** (*someone*) **to court** -waabira omusango **charge** (*legally*), *eg. Abapoliisi baabawaabira omusango. ('The police charged them with the crime.')*

-waabirwa (*also* -wawaabirwa) *vi* (-waabiddwa) **make a charge against**, *eg. Yeegaana byonna* *ebyamuwawaabirwa.* *('She denied all the charges made against her.')*

[1]awaabwe *adv* **their place/home (N11.5)**

[2]ewaabwe *adv* **at their place/home (N11.5)**

[3](o)waabwe *pos* **their(s) (N11.4)**

waada *n9* **ward** waada y'olukale **public ward**

owaakasolya *n1* (*pl.* abaakasolya) **head of a clan**

waaki? *interr* **what for?**

waakiri *adv* **preferably, rather**

[1]awaali **where there was/were**

[2]waali **he/she is there/here** waali waliwo **there was/were**

waaliwo **there was/were**

[1]-waana *vt* (-waanye) **praise, complement** (= -tenda)

[2]-eewaana *vr* **boast, brag**

-waanawaana *vt* (-waanyewaanye) **flatter**

-waaniriza *vt* (-waanirizizza) **flatter continuously**

-waanyisa *vt* (-waanyisizza) **exchange, barter** -waanyisa ssente **change money** (*between currencies*) **-waanyisaamu** (-waanyisizzaamu) -waanyisaamu ssente **change money into smaller denominations**

-waanyisaganya *vi* (-waanyisaganyizza) -waanyisaganya ebirowoozo **exchange ideas**

-waata *vt* (-waase) **peel** (*with a knife*)

-waawaala *vi* (-waawadde) **resonate, echo, reverberate**

waawali **there is the place**

waawano **here is the place**

waawo **there is the place**

waaya *n9* **wire, cable, line** waaya y'amasannyalaze **electricity cable**

waayaleesi *n9* **wireless**

-waayira *vt* (-waayidde) **add onto** **-waayirako** (-waayiddeko) **add on,** *eg. Yawaayirako ekiwero ku kitambaala.* *('She added a piece of material to the tablecloth.')* (= -kookerako) **-waayiramu add within, insert,** *eg. Yawaayiramu ekiwero okugaziya olugoye.* *('She inserted some material to widen the dress.'),* **supplement**

-waayiriza *vt* (-waayirizza) **accuse falsely**

-eewaayo *vit* (-eewaddeyo) **give oneself (to), dedicate oneself, volunteer, yield, surrender.** *See* okwewaayo

-waba *vit* (-wabye) **go astray** (*physically or in behaviour*), **go out of control,** *eg. Emmotoka ewabye.* *('The car went out of control.', ie. off the road).* *Saying: 'Okubuuza si kuwaba.'* *('There is no harm in asking.')*

awabadde **where there has/have been**

wabaddewo **there has/have been**

wabbali *adv* **at/to the side, aside** wabbali wa **at/on the side of, beside**

-wabisa (*also* -wabya) *vt* (-wabisizza) **lead astray, subvert**

[1]wabula *conj* **unless, nevertheless**

[2]-wabula *vt* (-wabudde) **show** (*someone*) **the right**

way to do things, set (*a person*) **straight**

Wabulaakayole *n1* *title* **chief thatcher of the Kabaka** (*a member of the Ngeye Clan*)

wabweru *adv* **outside** wabweru wa *pre* **outside**

-wabya *vt* (-wabizza) **lead astray**

[1]wadde (*also* yadde, *or* newankubadde) *conj* **although,** *eg. Wadde siri mulwadde, sijja kugenda.* *('Although I am not sick, I am not going.'),* **not even, nor.** *See* akatono

[2]-wadde *v. See* -wa (*'give'*)

waddewaddeko (*also* waddeko) *adv* **slightly better, not too bad,** *eg. Lino ettooke waddewaddeko. (This bunch of bananas is slightly better.').* *Saying: Waddewaddeko ng'omubi omweru.' ('Although she is ugly, she is at least light-skinned.', meaning 'There's some good in every ill.')*

[1]awaffe *adv* **our place/home (N11.5)**

[2]ewaffe *adv* **at our place/home (N11.5)**

[3](o)waffe *pos* **our(s) (N11.4)**

awafulumirwa *n16* **exit**

[1]-wagaanya *vit* (-wagaanyizza) **force one's way, squeeze through,** *eg. Yawagaanya mu bantu n'ayitawo. ('He squeezed through the people.'),* **push through** (*a narrow space*), **force into**

[2]-eewagaanya *vr* **force oneself through**

wagaba *n1* **grey-cheeked mangabey** (*monkey*)

-wagala *vt* (-wagadde) **sharpen, grind** (*a blade*) si muwagaleko **uneducated person**

-wagama *vi* (-wagamye) **get stuck, get lodged**

-wagamira *vt* (-wagamidde) **get stuck in/at,** *etc., eg. Emmeeza ewagamidde mu mulyango. ('The table got stuck in the doorway.')*

-eewaggula *vi* (-wagguse) **rebel** (*against social norms*)

waggulu *adv* **above, up, high (up), loudly** waggulu ku **on top of** waggulu mu kalina **upstairs** waggulu wa **above,** *eg. Ofiisi ye eri waggulu w'edduuka. ('His office is above the shop.')* -a waggulu *adj* **upper, high,** *eg. omutindo ogwa waggulu ('high quality')* owa waggulu *n1* **person of high social status** wagguluko **higher up**

-wagguufu *adj* **big-bodied and tall** (*of a person*)

-wagguuka *vi* (-wagguuse) **be(come) big-bodied and tall** (*of a person*)

-wagika *vt* (-wagise) **wedge in,** *eg. Yawagika ejjinja ku mupiira gw'emmotoka. ('He wedged a stone under the tyre.', eg. to stop the car from moving),* **prop up**

awagimu *n16* **fertile place**

-wagira *vt* (-wagidde) **support** (*person/opinion, eg. in an election*), **back**

-wagirwa *vi* (-wagiddwa) **be supported**

awagongobavu *n16* **dent**

-waguka *vi* (-waguse) **come off** (*of bananas from a hand*), **be detached, be broken** (*but not detached*), *eg. Ettabi liwaguse. ('The branch is broken and* *hanging down.')*

-wagula *vi* (-wagudde) **come out from a normal place, break out** (*of livestock from a pen*) -wagula ekiwagu **detach a hand of bananas** omugga -wagula **overflow** (*of a river*)

-wagulawagula *vt* (-waguddewagudde) **detach** (*individual bananas*)

-wagulira *vt* (-wagulidde) **break off for/in**, *etc.*, **force one's way for/in** -wagulira amatooke **detach individual bananas** (*from a hand or bunch*), *eg. Awagulira amatooke. ('She is detaching the bananas.')* **-wagulirako** (-waguliddeko) **detach** (*individual bananas*) **for** (*someone*)

-wagulula *vi* (-waguludde) **overflow** (*of water from a normal course*), *eg. Omugga gwaguludde. ('The river has overflowed.')*

-waguluza *vt* (-waguluzizza) **cause to overflow**

-waguza *vit* (-waguzizza) **force one's way through** (*of a person*), *eg. Yawaguza n'ayita mu nsiko n'atuuka eka. ('He forced his way through the bush and arrived at home.')* -waguza mu bantu **force one's way through a crowd**

awajjanjabirwa *n16* **medical treatment centre**

[1]**awaka** *adv* **home, at home, homestead** -a awaka *adj* **domestic**

[2]**-waka** *vi* (-wase) **be(come) pregnant** (*of an animal*)

awakabale *n16* **deeply dug land**

awakalakate *n16* **scraped area of ground**

-wakana *vi* (-wakanye) **dispute, have objections, argue, compete** (*in sports*)

-wakanira *vt* (-wakanidde) **object to, argue about, protest about, compete for** (*eg. a trophy*)

-wakanya *vt* (-wakanyizza) **dispute with**, *eg. Twamuwakanya. ('We were disputing with him.')*, **argue with, object to**

-wakanyizibwa *vi* (-wakanyiziddwa) **be contested**

wakati *adv* **in the middle** wakati mu **in the middle of** (*referring to a space*) wakati mu bantu **in the presence of people** wakati wa **in the middle of, between**, *eg. Ayimiridde wakati w'abaserikale babiri. ('He is standing between two policemen.')* -a wakati *adj* **middle, central**

-wakatira *vi* (-wakatidde) **be laden** (*eg. through holding many things under one's arms*)

Wakayima *n1* **Mr Hare**

-wakula *vt* (-wakudde) **snatch, acquire** -wakula empisa **adopt alien customs** -wakula enjuki **take honey from bees** -wakula obulwadde **contract a disease** -wakula olutalo **pick a fight**

wakyaliwo **there is/are still**

[1]**ewala** *adv* **far, far away, distant** wala okuva **far from** -a wala *adj* **remote** walako **rather far**

[2]**-wala** *vt* (-waze) **drag along, scrape with a hoe** -wala omuddo **weed** (*with a hoe*)

[3]**-eewala** *vt* **keep away from, avoid, refrain from, dodge, be repelled by** (*eg. someone's behaviour*) -eewala okufa **escape death**

-walaawala *vt* (-wazeewaze) **drag along** (*an unwilling person*) **by force**

-walabana *vi* (-walabanye) **strive, struggle**

-walabanya *vt* (-walabanyizza) **drag along**, *eg. Embwa yazze ewalabanya enkoko gye yasse. ('The dog came dragging along the hen which it had killed.')*

-walabuka *vi* (-walabuse) **move at speed**

-walaggana *vi* (-walagganye) **be hostile to one another**

-walagganya *vt* (-walagganyizza) **harass**

walagi *n1* (*no pl.*) **Ugandan gin**. *From: 'war gin' (English) – because soldiers used to carry gin when they were fighting.*

-walakata *vt* (-walakase) **scrape (off)** (*eg. with a hoe*), *eg. Awalakata omuddo mu lusuku. She is scraping off weeds in the banana garden.')* -walakata omuti **shave wood** -walakata omutwe **shave the head**

awalala *adv* **elsewhere**

-walampa *vt* (-walampye) **climb**

-walana *vt* (-walanye) **give** (*someone*) **a hard time, vex, harass**

-walattuka *vi* (-walattuse) **fall down, topple over, tumble down**

[1]**wali** *adv* **there**

[2]**awali** (*also* awaliwo) **where there is/are**. *Can be equivalent to conjunction* **where** *or preposition* **to** (N7.2).

awaliba **where there will be**

walibaawo **there will be**

walifu *n9* **alphabet**

-eewalika *vi* (-eewalise) **be avoidable**

awalime *n16* **dug-over land**

-walira *vi* (-walidde) **resist being moved**, *eg. Embuzi ewalira. ('The goat is resisting being moved.')*, **come unwillingly, move reluctantly, hang back, drag one's feet**

[1]**-waliriza** *vt* (-walirizza) **force, compel**

[2]**-eewaliriza** *vr* **force oneself**

-walirizibwa *vi* (-waliriziddwa) **be forced**. *See* okuwalirizibwa

waliwo **there is/are** awaliwo *See* awali

-waluka *vi* (-waluse) **have diarrhoea**

[1]**-walula** *vt* (-waludde) **drag, pull (along), haul**

[2]**-eewalula** *vr* **pull oneself along** (*as a cripple*), **creep (along)** (*as a soldier inching forward*), **slither along** (*as a snake or lizard*)

Walumbe *n1* **Kiganda deity** (*lubaale*), **god of death and disease**

awalungi *n16* **beautiful place**

Wamala *n1* **Kiganda deity** (*lubaale*), **god of Lake Wamala** (*inventor of barkcloth making*). *Also a name used for Baganda males.*

-wamatuka *vi* (-wamatuse) **rush out** (*eg. of an animal in a hunt*), **burst out**

-wamatula *vt* (-wamatudde) **cause to rush out** (*eg. an animal in a hunt*), **drive out of hiding**

-wamatula ebigambo **speak without thinking**

-wamba *vt* (-wambye) **capture, commandeer**

-wambaatira *vt* (-wambaatidde) **hug, clutch, embrace**

wamberi *adv* **in front of the hearth**

Wambuzi *n1* **Mr Goat**

wamma! *excl (expresses emphasis, approval or surprise)* **Oh my!, My dear!**

-wammanta *vit* (-wammanse) **grope (for)** *(in the dark)*, **feel about (for)**

Wammunyeenye *n1* **Saturday.** *From: 'emmunyeenye' ('stars') − related to traditional religious beliefs.*

[1]**awammwe** *adv* **your pl. place/home (N11.5)**

[2]**ewammwe** *adv* **at your place/home (N11.5)**

[3]**(o)wammwe** *pos* **your(s) pl. (N11.4)**

-wampanya *vi* (-wampanyizza) **be devious, be fraudulent**

awampi *n16* **short distance**

Wampisi *n1* **Mr Hyena**

Wampologoma *n1* **Mr Lion**

awamu *adv* **in one place, together** wamu ne **together with,** *(before a pronoun N10.1)* **na-,** *eg. wamu nange ('together with me')* byonna awamu **altogether, in general** okutwalira *(or* okugatta*)* awamu **generally**

awanaaba **where there will be**

wanaabaawo **there will be**

-wanda *vt* (-wanze) **spit (out)** -wanda amalusu **spit** *(saliva)* -wanda emmere **spit out food**

-wandaggirira *vi* (-wandaggiridde) enkuba -wandaggirira **drizzle**

-wandiika *vt* (-wandiise) **write, inscribe, record, register, list, spell.** *See* okuwandiika -wandiika mu kyapa **write in capital letters**

-wandiikira *vt* (-wandiikidde) **write to/for,** *eg. Yamuwandiikira ebbaluwa y'omusomesa. ('He wrote a letter to the teacher for her.'),* **correspond with**

-wandiikiragana *vi* (-wandiikiraganye) *vi* **write to one another, correspond.** *See* okuwandiikiragana

[1]**-wandiisa** *vt* (-wandiisizza) **write with, recruit, enrol** -wandiisa abakozi **engage workers**

[2]**-eewandiisa** *vr* **enrol/register oneself**

-wandula *vit* (-wandudde) **spit (out)**

-wanduukulula *vt* (-wanduukuludde) **cross out** *(eg. item on list),* **strike off** *(person from an official list, eg. errant doctor)*

[1]**Wanga** *n1* **Sunday.** *From: '-wanga' ('fit in') − related to traditional religious beliefs.*

[2]**-wanga** *vt* (-wanze) **fit in/on** *(eg. handle on door),* **insert** *(pole in ground, bullet in gun, etc.)* awanga obugaali **bicycle repairer**

-wangaala *vi* (-wangadde) **live/last long,** *eg. Ennyumba eno ewangadde. ('This house has stood here a long time.'). See* okuwangaala

-wangaazi *adj* (empangaazi *n9*) **long-lived, long-lasting, enduring, durable**

[1]**awange** *adv* **my place/home (N11.5)**

[2]**ewange** *adv* **at my place/home (N11.5)**

[3]**(o)wange** *pos* **my, mine. (N11.4)** Owange. **Hey, you there.**

awangi *adv* **in many places** Wangi. **Here I am.** *(response to being called)*

Wango *n1* **Mr Leopard**

-wanguka (-wanguse) *vi* **come out** *(of something inserted, eg. handle of hoe),* **become detached**

[1]**-wangula** *vt* (-wangudde) **take out** *(something inserted, eg. handle of hoe),* **detach**

[2]**-wangula** *vt* (-wangudde) **win, defeat, conquer, overcome, subdue**

-wangulwa *vi* (-wanguddwa) **be defeated**

[1]**-wanika** *vt* (-wanise) **put at a higher level, raise, hang (up), suspend** -wanika ebbeeyi **raise the price** -wanika ebibegabega **shrug the shoulders** -wanika emikono **raise one's hands** *(in surrender)* -wanika ku kalabba **hang someone** *(execute)* -wanika omukono **raise one's hand** -wanika omuwendo **raise the price**

[2]**-eewanika** *vr* **elevate oneself, be conceited**

-wanikibwa *vi* (-wanikiddwa) **be raised up, be hung up, be suspended**

-wanirira *vt* (-waniridde) **prevent from falling** *(in a temporary sort of way),* **hold up, prop up** *(eg. drooping branch with a stick),* **support** *(person, mentally, physically or financially),* **sustain.** *See* okuwanirira

-wanjaga *vi* (-wanjaze) **appeal for help**

-wanjagira *vt* (-wanjagidde) **appeal for help to,** *eg. Yawanjagira abantu bazimbe essomero. ('She appealed to people to help build the school.')*

Wanjovu *n1* **Mr Elephant**

wankaaki *n1* **main gate, front entrance**

Wankoko *n1* **Mr Chicken**

Wannema *n1* **name of father of the lubaale Mukasa and Kibuuka.** *Said to have been a powerful wizard who once lived on the Ssese Islands.*

wano *adv* **here** wano na wali **here and there** -a wano *adj* **local** owa wano *n1* **local person**

wansi *adv/n16* **down, below, lower, under, downwards, on the ground, downstairs, ground floor, bottom, floor** wansi mu *pre* **below** *(within), eg. eggaali y'omukka eyita wansi mu ttaka ('underground train', lit. 'train which passes under within the earth')* wansi wa *pre* **below, under** -a wansi *adj* **low** owa wansi *n1* **lower class person, backward person**

wansiko *(also* wansinsi*) adv* **a little lower**

awantu *n16/adv* **some place, somewhere,** *eg. awantu awali ettosi ('muddy place')* awantu awamu **in one place** buli wantu **everywhere**

-wanuka *vi* (-wanuse) **come down** *(through the force of gravity),* **fall down/off**

-wanula *vt* (-wanudde) **move from a higher to lower position, lower, drop, take down**

(*something hanging*), *eg. Yawanula omuyembe n'aguteeka mu kisero. ('She picked the mango and put it in the basket.')*

-wanvu *adj* (eriwanvu *or* eggwanvu *n5*, empanvu *n9*) **long, high, tall, deep, steep**

-wanvuwa *vi* (-wanvuye) **be(come) long/high**

-wanvuya *vt* (-wanvuyizza) **lengthen, heighten, deepen**

-waŋŋanguka *vi* (-waŋŋanguse) **be exiled**

-waŋŋangusa (*also* -waŋŋangula) *vt* (-waŋŋangusizza) **(cause to) exile**

-wasa *vt* (-wasizza) **marry** (*a woman by a man*)

awasaawe *n16* **area with cut vegetation**

awasomokerwa *n16* **place for crossing water, ford**

Wasswa *n1 title* **male elder of twins**

wasuze otyanno? *greeting* **How did you** *si.* **spend the night?, Good morning.** (N28)

awataabe **where there will not be**

awataali **where there was/were not**

awatabadde **where there has/have not been**

awatali *pre* **where there is/are not.** *Can be equivalent to preposition* **without** (N7.2). awatali ensonga **without reason**

awataliba **where there will not be**

wattu Mwana wattu. *interj* **My dear.**

awatuulwa (*also* awatuulibwa) *n16* **seating area**

-wawaabira (-wawaabidde) *See* -waabira

-wawaabirwa (-wawaabidwa) *See* -waabirwa

-wawamuka *vi* (-wawamuse) -wawamuka mu tulo **start up from sleep**

awawe *adv* **her/his place, her/his home** (N11.5)

awawo *adv* **your** *si.* **place/home** (N11.5)

awawowongofu *n16* **dent**

-wawula *vt* (-wawudde) **rub smooth, sand**

awayiibwa ebisaaniiko *n16* **rubbish dump**

awayingirirwa *n16* **entrance**

-wayira *vi* (-wayidde) **marry**

wayirindi *n1* (*no pl.*) **scabies**

awayulifu *n16* **tear** (*eg. in cloth*)

wazira *conj* **unless, except**

[1]**we** *can be equivalent to various parts of speech in English (conjunctions, relative pronouns, etc. N10.2):* (1) **where, when;** (2) *Can be equivalent to short adverbial phrases of emphasis, eg. Akambe we kali? Yee, we kali. ('Is the knife there? Yes, it is there.')*

[2]**we** *pos* **her/his** (N10.2), *eg. omwana we ('her child')*

[3]**we** *pre* **of** (= w'e N11.1)

[4]**we** *pro* **you** *si. Can be a prefix* **we-** (N7.3) *or suffix* **-we** (N10-12), *eg.* (1) *wekka ('only you')*; (2) *naawe ('and you').*

-wedde *See* -ggwa; -weera.

weebale **Thank you.** *si.* Weebalege. **Thank you.** (*intensive form*)

-weebuuka *vi* (-weebuuse) **be discredited, be dishonoured**

-weebuula *vt* (-weebudde) **discredit, dishonour**

-weebwa *vi* (-weereddwa) **be given**

-weeka *vt* (-weese) **carry behind** (*eg. passenger or load on bike*), **carry on the back** (*eg. child*)

-weekeera *vi* (-weekedde) **be out of breath**

oweekitiibwa *n1* (*pl.* abeekitiibwa) **honourable person** (*abbrev* Oweek.)

eweema *n9* **tent**

[1]**-weera** *vi* (-wedde) **become relieved** (*of worries*), **become settled** (*of a dispute*), **calm down.** *Pronunciation:* okuwéérá

[2]**-weera** *vt* (-weeredde) **give for, give on behalf of.** *Pronunciation:* okuwéèrà **-weerayo** (-weereddeyo) **give for,** *eg. Yaweerayo Musoke ssente. ('He gave money on Musoke's behalf.')*

weeraba **goodbye** *si.*

weereere *adv* **place where there is nothing** (*stem* -yereere)

-weerera *vt* (-weeredde) **pay fees for** (*eg. pupil at school*) -weerera ebisa **push hard** (*in childbirth*) -weerera embwa **set a dog on** -weerera ennyukuta **complete a syllable with a vowel**

-weereza *vt* (-weerezza) **send to,** *eg. Yaweereza Musoke amagi. ('He sent eggs to Musoke.'),* **serve, wait upon, hand to, pass, transmit** -weereza eseemwesi **send a text message**

-weerezi ennyukuta empeerezi *n9* **vowel**

-weesa *vit* (-weesezza) **do metalwork, manufacture** (*metal items*), **forge** (*from metal*)

weewaawo *interj* **indeed**

-weeweeta *vt* (-weeweese) **stroke, rub, fondle**

weewumbeko muko wuuyo ajja *n1* **sensitive plant.** *Meaning: 'Sit properly, the brother-in-law is coming.'*). Sensitive plants include: *Aeschnomene sensitiva, Biophytum* spp. *and Mimosa pudica.*

-weeza *vt* (-wedde) **give a break to,** *eg. Yamusaba ssente nga tamuweeza. ('He was continually pestering him for money without giving him a break.')*

oweggombolola (*also* ow'eggombolola) *n1* (*pl.* abeggombolola) **sub-county chief**

-wejjawejja *vi* (-wezzewezze) **be out of breath, pant**

wekka *det/pro* **only you** *si.,* **by yourself**

-wema *vt* (-wemye) **eat from the palm**

wembe *n9* **razor blade**

-wembejja *vt* (-webezze) **give special attention to** (*someone special, eg. child or loved one*)

-wemmenta *vt* (-wemmense) **exhaust, finish off,** *eg. Siriimu awemmense abantu bangi. ('AIDS has finished off a lot of people.')* -wemmenta emmere **eat up supplies of food** -wemmenta ssente **use up money wastefully, squander money**

-wemuka *vi* (-wemuse) **feel ashamed**

-wemukira *vt* (-wemukidde) **disgrace** -wemukira abantu **be disgraced before people**

-wemula *v* (-wemudde) (1) *vi* **behave shamelessly, use obscene language, curse;** (2) *vt* **disgrace**

-wemuukiriza *vt* (-wemuukirizza) **put to shame,**

disgrace, catch in the act

-wenja vt (-wenze) **search for** (*in cluttered, bushy or crowded places*)

-wenjuka vi (-wenjuse) **come partially open**, eg. *Olutimbe luwenjuse.* (*'The curtain has come slightly open.'*), **come apart** (*of an article of clothing*), **fall open**

-wenjula vt (-wenjudde) **open partially**, eg. *Empewo ewenjudde olutimbe.* (*'The wind has caused the curtain to come open.'*), **uncover partially**, eg. *Yawenjula olutimbe alingize abagenyi.* (*'He pulled back the curtain to peep at the guests.'*)

wennyini ggwe wennyini **you** si. **yourself** wo wennyini **the actual place**

-wenya vt (-wenyezza) **beckon/motion (to)**

-wenyera vi (-wenyedde) **limp** (*in walking*)

-wenyuka vi (-wenyuse) -wenyuka emisinde **run very fast, dash**

[1]**-wera** vit (-weze) **be quite a lot**, eg. *Abantu baaweze mu kkanisa.* (*'There were quite a lot of people in church.'*), **have enough** (*for a purpose*), **amount to** (*in total*), **reach, accumulate**. *Pronunciation*: okuwérà **-werako** (-wezeeko) **be quite a few**

[2]**-wera** vi **pledge loyalty**, eg. *Yawera mu maaso ga kkwini.* (*'She pledged loyalty to the queen.'*), **brandish weapons**. *Pronunciation*: okuwérá -wera enkolokooto **pledge revenge**

[3]**-wera** vt **ban, forbid, prohibit**. *Pronunciation*: okuwérá

-were adj **banned, forbidden, prohibited**

-wereekereza vt (-wereekerezza) **drive** (*someone*) **away** -wereekereza amasasi **shoot at** (*someone running away*) -wereekereza ebigambo **insult** (*someone*) **as (s)he is going away**

-werekera vt (-werekedde) **accompany** (*on a visit, journey, etc.*), **escort, see off** -werekera omugenyi **escort a visitor a short distance on the way**

[1]**-werera** vt (-weredde) **pledge allegiance to**, eg. *Baamuwerera.* (*'They pledged allegiance to her.'*)

[2]**-eewerera** vi **set one's mind on doing harm** (*to someone*)

owessaza (*also* ow'essaza) n1 (*pl.* abaamasaza) **county chief**

[1]**-weta** vit (-wese) **bend, veer, swerve, turn (off)**, eg. *Yaweta emmotoka n'addayo gye yali ava.* (*'He turned the car and returned the way he came.'*)

[2]**-eeweta** vi **be bent (over)**

-wetera vi (-wetedde) **turn off at**, eg. *Twawetera ku kkanisa.* (*'We turned off at the church.'*)

-wewa vt (-weye) **winnow**

-weweenyula vt (-weweenyudde) **flog, whip, beat** -weweenyula emiggo **beat mercilessly with sticks**

-weweera vi (-wewedde) (1) **be smooth/soft** (*to the touch*); (2) **become cool** (*of the weather*)

-weweevu adj (1) **smooth/soft** (*to the touch*); (2) **cool** (*of the weather*)

-weweeza vt (-weweezezza) **make smooth/cool, make soft** (*to the touch*) -weweeza obulago (*also* -weweeza omumiro) **soothe the throat, take a drink** -weweeza obulumi **reduce pain**

-wewufu adj (eriwewufu n5, empewufu n9) **light** (*in weight*)

-wewuka vi (-wewuse) **be light** (*in weight*), **be easy** (*of a job*)

-wewusa (*also* -wewula) vt (-wewusizza) **make light** (*in weight*), **make easier** (*eg. a job*), **facilitate**

-weza (-wezezza) vit (1) **make up to** (*a required amount*), **reach** (*a number or amount*), **complete** (*a sum*); (2) **accummulate, amass**

wiigi n9 **wig**

wiiki n9 **week** wiiki ejja **next week** wiiki eyise **last week**

wiikendi n9 **weekend**

[1]**awo** adv **there** wo wennyini **the actual place**

[2]**awo** conj **then** awo olwatuuka **once upon a time**

[3]**wo** pos **your** si., eg. *mukyala wo* (*'your wife'*)

-woggana (*also* -wowoggana) vi (-wogganye) **make a lot of noise, shout.** *See* okuwoggana -yogerera -woggana **speak loudly**

-wogoka vi (-wogose) **be broken off** (*eg. of a branch from a tree*), **snap off**

-wogola vt (-wogodde) **break/snap off** (*eg. a branch*)

-eewogoma vit (-wogomye) **shelter (from)** (*sun or rain*)

wokka adv **at one place only**, eg. *wano wokka* (*'here only'*)

[1]**-wola** vi (-woze) **cool (down), become cold.** *Pronunciation*: okuwólà

[2]**-wola** vt **lend** (*money*). *Pronunciation*: okuwólá

[3]**-eewola** vit **borrow** (*money*)

[1]**-wolereza** vt (-wolerezza) **plead for, represent, defend**

[2]**-eewolereza** vr **plead for oneself, defend oneself**

-wologoma (*also* -wuluguma) vi (-wologomye) **roar**

-woloma vi (-wolomye) **howl, roar, bellow**

-wolottala vi (-wolottadde) **be overcooked** (*of sweet potatoes*)

-wolu adj (empolu n9) **cold**

-eewoma vit (-eewomye) vt **avoid** (*something thrown*), **take cover, dodge**

-womba -womba amaaso **lower one's gaze, look down**

**NOTES FOR
w**

w sometimes replaces **u** or **uy** before a vowel, eg. (1) **twakola** ('we worked'), from **tu-** ('we') + **-a-** (past tense) + **-kola** ('work') (**N5**).

-w. Verbs starting **w** have 1st person singulars starting **mp**, eg. **mpa** ('I give'), from **-wa**.

-wombeefu *adj* gentle, meek, unassertive, subservient

[1]-wombeeka *vt* (-wombeese) <u>-wombeeka amaaso</u> compose one's face

[2]-eewombeeka *vi* (-eewombeese) be gentle, be meek, be unassertive, be subservient

-womoggoka *vi* develop holes, become eroded (*of a road, wall, etc.*), eg. *Oluguudo lwonna luwomoggose.* ('*The whole road has become eroded.*')

-womoggola *vt* (-womoggodde) make hole(s) through, eg. *Ababbi baawomoggola ekisenge ne bayingira.* ('*The thieves broke through the wall and entered.*')

-wona *vi* (-wonye) be cured (of), eg. *Awonye obulwadde.* ('*She has been cured of the illness.*'), be saved, escape from misfortune, get rid of <u>-wona akabenje</u> survive an accident <u>-wona okufa</u> escape death <u>Awonye.</u> She has given birth.

-wonawo (-wonyewo) be spared (*a misfortune, eg. accident*)

-wondera *vt* (-wondedde) follow (shortly after), pursue

[1]-wonga *vit* (-wonze) make an offering (*traditionall, to a lubaale or spirit*), dedicate, eg. *Nnatutte enkoko mu kkanisa okugiwonga eri Mukama.* ('*I took a hen to church to dedicate to God.*'), pray. Saying: '*Weebale kuwonga.*' (*Thank you for praying for a good outcome.*'). <u>-wonga embuzi</u> dedicate a goat to a god

[2]-eewonga *vr* consecrate (*or dedicate*) oneself (*spiritually*), eg. *Twewonga eri Mukama mu masinzizo.* ('*We go to worship God in places of worship.*')

-wonge *adj* (emponge *n9*) dedicated (*to a lubaale or spirit*), consecrated, sacrificial

-wongera *vt* (-wongedde) sacrifice/offer to (*traditionally, a lubaale or spirit*), dedicate to, pray for/on (*to have a good outcome*) <u>-lina okuwongera ennyanja</u> pray for a good outcome on the lake (*eg. on a fishing trip*)

wonna *adv* everywhere

wonnawonna *adv* absolutely everywhere

-wonya *vt* (-wonyezza) cure, heal, save

-wonyezebwa *vi* (-wonyezeddwa) be saved

wonzi *n1* comb (*on chicken's head*)

owoo- *See* owa ('*of*')

-wooba *vi* (-woobye) wail, lament

-woola *vt* (-wodde) scoop out (*eg. log to make drum or canoe*), hollow out, engrave

-woolera *vt* (-wooledde) avenge <u>-woolera eggwanga</u> take vengeance (on), eg. *Eyatta omwana we, naye yawoolera eggwanga n'amutta.* ('*When his child was killed, he took revenge by killing the killer.*')

owooluganda *n1* (*pl.* abooluganda) (blood) relative

owoolulyo *n1* (*pl.* aboolulyo) member of a lineage

woolutaali *n1* altar

-wooma *vi* (-woomye) be pleasing (*in taste or appearance*), look smart, be tasty, eg. *Emmere ewooma?* ('*Is the food tasty?*'), be interesting

-woomera *vt* (-woomedde) be pleasing to, look good on, be tasty to, like (*the food*), eg. *Emmere etuwoomera.* ('*We like the taste of the food.*')

-woomerera *vit* (-woomeredde) taste sweet (to)

-woomerevu *adj* sweet

-woomerwa *vi* (-woomeddwa) enjoy, eg. *Nnawoomerwa emmere.* ('*I enjoyed the food.*')

-woomesa (*also* <u>-woomya</u>) *vt* (-woomesezza) make pleasing, make tasty

-woomu *adj* pleasing, interesting

owoomuluka (*also* <u>ow'omuluka</u>) *n1* (*pl.* abeemiruka) parish chief

-wooteera *vi* (-wootedde) feel dejected, be downcast

wooteeri *n9* hotel, restaurant

-wooteevu *adj* dejected, downcast

woowe *interj* alas, oh dear

-woowoola *vi* (-woowodde) howl

-wooyawooya *vt* (-wooyewooye) soothe, speak softly to. *See* appease

-wooza *vt* (-woozezza) charge (*eg. a fee*), tax

-wotofu *adj* withered, wilted

-wotoka *vi* (-wotose) wither, wilt, shrivel

-wotookerera *vi* (-wotookeredde) begin to wither

-wovu *adj* (empovu *n9*) cold, cool

-wowoggana *See* -woggana

-wowogganira *vt* (-wowogganidde) shout at, rant at

[1]-woza *vit* (-wozezza) argue a case, plead <u>-woza ensonga</u> argue logically <u>-woza omusango</u> argue a case in court

[2]-woza *vt* cool (down) (*eg. food*) <u>-woza obusungu</u> cool one's anger <u>-woza oluyombo</u> cool a quarrel

-eewozaako *vr* (-eewozezzaako) explain oneself

-wozesa *vt* (-wozesezza) cross-examine (*in a court case*)

-wubako (*also* <u>-wuba</u>) *vt* (-wubyeko) slip from the mind, overlook (*with personal object*), eg. *Kyamuwubyeko.* ('*He overlooked it.*')

-wubwa *vi* (-wubiddwa) be mistaken

-wuga *vi* (-wuze) swim

-eewugguusa *vit* (-eewugguusizza) feign ignorance, pretend not to know

-wuguka *vi* (-wuguse) turn off/away, deviate

-wugula *vt* (-wugudde) distract, eg. *Eddoboozi ly'ennyonyi lyampugudde ne linzigya ku bigambo bya leediyo.* ('*The sound of the aircraft distracted me from the radio.*'), divert

-wugulala *vi* (-wuguladde) be absent-minded, be distracted

-wugulavu *adj* absent-minded

-wugulaza *vt* (-wagulazizza) distract

-wujja *vt* (-wuzze) fan

-wujjaala *vi* (-wujjadde) take a rest during the day,

take a nap, take a siesta

wujju *n1* giant granadilla (*large-fruited relative of the passion fruit*) *Passiflora quadrangularis*

-(y)awuka *See* -yawuka

-(y)awukana *See* -yawukana

-(y)awukanya *See* -yawukanya

-(y)awula *See* -yawula

-(y)awulayawula *See* -yawulayawula

-wulikika *vi* (-wulikise) **be heard/audible**

[1]**-wulira** *vt* (-wulidde) **sense, perceive** (*through any sense except sight*), **detect, experience, hear, listen (to), feel** (*mentally*), **obey**, *eg. Yamuwulira.* (*'He obeyed her.'*). *See* okuwulira -wulira bubi **feel bad, feel unwell, feel uncomfortable** -wulira bulungi **feel well** -wulira empewo **feel cold** -wulira ensonyi **feel shame** -wulira obuzibu **experience difficulty** -wulira otulo **be sleepy** ndiwulira **maggot found in maize grains** Otuwulire. **Let us know.**

[2]**-eewulira** *vr* **be arrogant, be snobbish.** *See* okwewulira -eewulira bulungi **feel well**

-wuliriza *vt* (-wulirizza) **listen to**

-wuliza *vt* (-wulizizza) **hear from**

[1]**-wulize** *adj* **obedient**

[2]**-eewulize** *adj* **arrogant**

-wulizigana *vi* (-wuliziganye) **listen to one another**

-wuliziganya *vi* (-wuliziganyizza) **communicate** (*at a distance*)

-wuluguma (*also* -wologoma) *vi* (-wulugumye) **roar**

-wulula *vt* (-wuludde) **strip off** (*eg. leaves from a branch*), **unstring** (*eg. beads from a string*)

-wulunga *vt* (-wulunze) **roll** (*eg. clay or dough*)

-wulunguta *vi* (-wulunguse) **roll about** (*as an object in a container*), **rattle (about)** (*in a container*)

-(y)awulwa *See* -yawulwa

[1]**-wumba** *vi* (-wumbye) **be(come) worm-eaten.** *Pronunciation*: okuwúmbá **-wumbako** (-wumbeko) -wumbako emmere **wrap up food** (*make an omuwumbo*)

[2]**-wumba** *vt* **wrap up.** *Pronunciation*: okuwûmbá -wumba emimwa **keep one's lips sealed, keep mum** -wumba engalo **do nothing** (*ie. sit on one's hands*)

[3]**-eewumba** *vi* **close up** (*eg. of a flower*)

-wumbawumba *vt* (-wumbyewumbye) **gather up all of** -wumbawumba ebbumba **gather together clay** (*in pottery making*) -wumbawumba emboozi **wind up a conversation** -wumbawumba okwogera **wind up a speech** -wumbawumba omuntu **comfort a person**

-wumbulula *vt* (-wumbuludde) **unwrap** (*bundle of cooked food to serve*)

-wummuka *vi* (-wummuse) **be holed, be pierced, be bored** (= -botoka)

[1]**-wummula** *vt* (-wummudde) **make** (*a hole*), *eg. Yawummula ekituli mu luggi.* (*'He made a hole in the door.'*), **pierce, bore, drill.** *Pronunciation*: okuwúmmùlà (= -botola) -wummula obutuli **perforate**

[2]**-wummula** *vi* (-wummudde) **rest, relax, have a holiday, take a break, have a recess, retire** (*from work*). *Pronunciation*: okuwúmmùlà

-wummuza *vt* (-wummuzizza) **suspend** (*eg. someone from school*) -wummuza ku mulimu **retire** (*someone from a job*)

-wunda *vt* (-wunze) **finish off well** (*carving, basket, etc.*) **decorate, adorn, ornament, embellish**

[1]**-wunga** *vt* (-wunze) **be out of one's mind, become senile.** *Pronunciation*: okuwúngá

[2]**-wunga** *vt* **catch** (*lake flies with a basket*). *Pronunciation*: okuwûngá

-wungeera *vi* (-wungedde) **become evening**, *eg. Obudde buwungedde.* (*'The evening has come.'*)

-wunguka *vi* (-wunguse) **be ferried across** (*water*)

[1]**-wungula** *vt* (-wungudde) **ferry** (*across water*)

[2]**-eewungula** *vr* **go away for a while**, *eg. Omwana yeewungudde emmanju.* (*'The child went round to the back of the house.'*)

-wunguutufu *adj* **mentally deranged, senile, stupid**

-wunguutuka *vi* (-wunguutuse) **be(come) deranged, grow senile**

-wuniikirira *vit* (-wuniikiridde) **be dumbfounded (by), be taken aback (by)** (= -tangaalirira)

-wuniikiriza *vt* (-wuniikirizza) **dumbfound**

-wunjuka *vi* (-wunjuse) **change one's course**

-wunjula *vt* (-wunjudde) **turn aside**

-wunya *vi* (-wunye) **smell, produce a smell**, *eg. Ewunya.* (*'It smells.'*) -wunya obubi **stink** -wunya obulaala **smell stale**

-wunyira *vt* (-wunyidde) **smell to**, *eg. Kimpunyira bubi.* (*'It smells bad to me.'*)

-wunyiriza *vit* (-wunyirizza) **sniff at/about**, *eg. Embwa egenda ewunyiriza.* (*'The dog is sniffing about.'*)

-wunyirwa *vt* (-wunyiddwa) **smell**, *eg. Ngiwunyirwa.* (*'I smell it.'*), **scent**

awunzi *n9* **ounce**

[1]**-wunzika** *vt* (-wunzise) **put/hold at an angle, slant, tilt, incline** -wunzika emboozi **wind up a conversation** -wunzika ensonga **conclude one's arguments**

[2]**-eewunzika** *vi* **be slanting**, *eg. Ekikondo kyewunzise.* (*'The post is slanting.'*), **be tilted, be at an angle, lean over** -eewunzika ddala **be turned upside down**

[1]**-wunzikira** *vi* (-wunzikidde) **lean on/towards**, *eg. Ekidomola akiwunzikira ku ludda lw'omuliro.* (*'He is leaning the jerry can towards the fire.'*)

[2]**-eewunzikira** *vi* **be slanting towards, be leaning on/towards, be askew, be biased**

-wutta *vi* (-wusse) **spoil** (*of root crops left too long in the ground*), **become senile, become demented**

-wuttaavu *adj* (1) **spoilt** (*of root crops, through* being left too long in the ground), eg. lumonde omuwuttaavu ('old unpalatable potatoes'); (2) **demented**, eg. omuntu omuwuttaavu ('demented person'), **senile**

-wuttuka vi (-wuttuse) **become demented, become senile**

-wuttula vi (-wuttudde) **hit with the fist, punch, thump** -wuttula ekigwo **throw to the ground** (someone in wrestling)

¹-wuuba vt (-wuubye) **swing, wave** -wuuba emikono **swing one's arms** -wuuba omukira **wag the tail**

²-eewuuba vr **swing oneself, go to and fro, visit** (a place) **frequently** omutima -eewuuba **palpitate** (of the heart)

-wuubaala vi (-wuubadde) **feel lonely, feel empty** (emotionally)

-wuubaavu adj **lonely**

-wuubira vt (-wuubidde) **wave to, conduct** (eg. singers)

-wuukuufu adj **insatiable** (for food)

-wuukuuka vi (-wuukuuse) **have an endless appetite, be insatiable** -wuukuuka n'okulya enguzi **become totally corrupt** (through bribe taking)

-wuukuula vt (-wuukudde) **scoop out, excavate**

-wuula vt (-wudde) **beat hard**

wuuli there he/she is

wuulu n9 **wool**

¹ewuuma n9 **fork**

²-wuuma vi (-wuumye) **whistle** (of the wind), **hum** (as an engine), **buzz** (of the ear). See okuwuuma

-wuuna (also -wuunuuna) vit (-wuunye) **respond (to)** (with a sound rather than words), eg. Nnamubuuza naye teyampuuna. ('I greeted him but he did not respond.')

wuuno here he/she is

-eewuunuunya vi (-eewuunuunyizza) **mumble to oneself, soliloquise**

-eewuunya vit (-eewuunyizza) **be amazed (at), wonder (at), be surprised (at)**

-eewuunyisa vt (-eewuunyisizza) **amaze, astonish, surprise, dismay**

-wuuta vt (-wusse) **sip** -wuuta ssupu **eat soup**

wuuyo there he/she is

¹ewuwe adv **at her/his place or home** (N11.5)

²owuwe pos **hers, his** (N11.4)

¹ewuwo adv **at your** si **place or home** (N11.5)

²owuwo pos **yours** si. (N11.4)

ewuzi n9 **thread** ewuzi ya nnabbubi **spiderweb**

Y,y

y' abbrev of (e)ya; ye

(e)ya pre **of**, eg. ente ya Musoke ('cow of Musoke'). Can be a prefix **(e)ya-** (N11.4), eg. yange ('my'). 'eya' appears in ordinal numbers (N7.1), eg. ente

ey'okubiri ('second cow'). Elision is sometimes seen, eg. ente eyookubiri ('second cow').

²-(y)oya See -yoya

(e)yaabwe pos **their(s)** (N11.4)

yaadi n9 **yard** (unit of length)

yaaki? interr **what for?**

yaaya n1 (pl. ba yaaya) **children's nurse, nanny, ayah**. From: 'aya' (Hindi), earlier from 'avia' ('grandmother' – Latin).

-yaayaana vi (-yaayaanye, njaayaana, okuyaayaana) **have a craving**

-yaayaanira vt (-yaayaanidde, njaayaanira, okuyaayaanira) **crave**

-yabifu adj (enjabifu n9) **burst, split**

-yabika vi (-yabise, okwabika) **burst, split** omupiira -yabika **have a puncture**

-yabirira vi (-yabiridde, okwabirira) **be worn thin** (of cloth or garment)

-yabirivu adj (enjabirivu n9) **worn thin** (of cloth or garment)

-yabise adj **burst, split**

¹-yabiza vt (-yabizza, njabiza, okwabiza) **burst, split**

²-eeyabiza vt **be open with** (someone mentally)

-yabuka vi (-yabuse, okwabuka) **disperse** (of people after a gathering), **be disbanded** (of a meeting), **be adjorned**

-yabula vt (-yabudde, njabula, okwabula) **disband** (a meeting), **adjourn**

-yabulira vt (-yabulidde, njabulira, okwabulira) **abandon, desert**

-yabulukuka vi (-yabulukuse, okwabulukuka) **be disbanded**

-yabulula vt (-yabuludde, njabulula, okwabulula) **disband** (an organisation)

-yabuluza vt (-yabuluzza, njabuluza, okwabuluza) **tear open** (something sealed)

¹-yabya vt (-yabizza, njabya, okwabya) **burst, split** -yabya olumbe **conclude funeral rites** (when an heir is installed)

²-eeyabya vr **relieve oneself, go to the toilet** eddagala ery'okweyabya n5 **purgative**

yadde (also wadde, or newankubadde) conj **not even**, eg. Sirina ssente yadde ssiringi ekikumi. ('I do not have money, not even one hundred shillings.') yaddeko **slightly better**

yaddeyaddeko adv **slightly better** (in health or in how one feels)

(e)yaffe pos **our(s)** (N11.4)

-yagaagala vi (-yagaagadde, okwagaagala) **be spread out, be flattened, be wide**

-yagaagavu adj (omwagaagavu n3, enjagaagavu n9) **spread out, broad, wide**, eg. omugugu omwagaagavu ('wide bundle') Alina omutwe omwagaagaavu. **He has a large head.**

-yagaagaza vt (-yagaagazizza, njagaagaza, okwagaagaza) **cause to spread out, flatten**

¹-yagala v (-yagadde, njagala, okwagala) (1) vt **like, love, want**; (2) aux v **be about (to)**, eg. Enkuba *eyagala kutonnya. ('It is about to rain.'),* **be likely (to)**. *Can be equivalent to adverb* **willingly**. *See* okwagala

[2]-eeyagala *vr* **enjoy oneself**

-yagalana *vi* (-yagalanye, okwagalana) **love one another, be in love**

-yagalibwa (*also* -yagalwa) *vi* (-yagaliddwa, njagalibwa, okwagalibwa) **be liked, be loved, be popular**

-yagaliza *vt* (-yagalizza, njagaliza, okwagaliza) **wish for** (*on someone else's behalf*), *eg. Nkwagaliza birungi. ('I wish you the best.')*

-yagazisa *vt* (-yagazisizza, njagazisa, okwagazisa) **cause to like, interest**

[1]-yagula *vt* (-yagudde, njagula, okwagula) **scratch**

[2]-eeyagula *vr* **scratch oneself**

-yaka *vi* (-yase, okwaka) **burn, shine, start** (*of an engine*)

-yakaayakana *vi* (-yakaayakanye, okwakaayakana) **shine, glitter**

-yakirira *vi* (-yakiridde, okwakirira) **burn poorly** (*eg. of a lamp*)

Yakobo *n1* **Jacob**

[1]-yala *vi* **increase** (*in number or amount*), **multiply**, *eg. Enkoko ziyaze. ('The chickens have multiplied.')*, **be(come) plentiful**, *eg. Emmere eyaze mu katale. ('Food has become plentiful in the market.')*, **become common**. *Pronunciation:* okwâlà

[2]-yala *v* (-yaze, njala, okwala) (1) *vi* **be made** (*of a bed*), *eg. Obuliri bwale. ('The bed is made.')*; (2) *vt* **spread out** (*mat, cloth, skin, etc.*), *eg. Yayala omukeeka. ('He spread out a mat.')*, **lay out**. *Pronunciation:* okwálá -yala obuliri **make a bed**, *eg. Ayaze obuliri. ('She has made the bed.')*

[3]-eeyala *vr* **prostrate oneself** (*eg. before the Kabaka*)

-yalaala *vi* (-yaladde, okwalaala) **spread all over** (*of water*), **flood**

-yaliira *vt* (-yalidde, njaliira, okwaliira) **spread out, put a lining** -yaliira endagala **spread out banana leaves, put lining of banana leaves** (*eg. in basket*) -yaliira essubi **spread out grass** -yaliira omukeeka **spread out a mat**

-yaliire *adj* (enjaliire *n9*) **spread out**

-yaliirira *vt* (-yaliiridde, njaliirira, okwaliirira) **spread out for**, *eg. Yayaliirira ekiwempe okuteekako essowaani. ('She spread out a mat to put the plates on.')*

-yalika *vi* (-yalise, njalika, okwalika) **arrive at an empty space, finish one's turn** (*in the game of omweso*), **go broke** (*financially*), **lose one's last born**

[1]-yalira *vt* (-yalidde, njalira, okwalira) **make a bed for**, *eg. Nnakwalidde. ('I have made a bed for you.')*

[2]-eeyalira *vr* **make a bed for oneself**

yaliyo **there was/were** (*over there*)

-yalula *vt* (-yaludde, okwalula) **hatch (eggs)**. *See* okwalula -yalula abalongo **perform birth rites for twins** -yalula obuliri **take off bedding**

-eeyama *vi* (-eeyamye) **vow, pledge**

[1]-yamba *vt* (-yambye, nnyamba, okuyamba) **help**

[2]-eeyamba *vr* **help oneself, go to the toilet**

-yambagana *vi* (-yambaganye) **help one another**

-yambala *vit* (-yambadde, nnyambala, okwambala) **dress** (*oneself*), **wear** -yambala obutiiti **wear beads** -yambala -tonnya **be very smartly dressed**

[1]-yambaza *vt* (-yambazizza, nnyambaza, okwambaza) **dress** (*another person*), **clothe**

[2]-eeyambaza *vr* **dress (oneself)**

-yambi *adj* **helpful**

[1]-yambika *vt* (-yambise, nnyambika, okwambika) **put around the neck** (*of person or animal*), *eg. Embuzi eyo gyambike omuguwa. ('Put a rope around that goat's neck.')*, **dress** (*someone*)

[2]-eeyambika *vt* **put around one's neck, dress oneself**

-eeyambisa *vt* (-eeyambisizza) **make use of, use**

-yambuka *vi* (-yambuse, nnyambuka, okwambuka) **go uphill, climb**, *eg. Yayambuka n'atuuka ku kkanisa. ('She climbed the hill and arrived at the church.')*

[1]-yambula *vt* (-yambudde, nnyambula, okwambula) **undress** (*someone*)

[2]-eeyambula *vr* **undress (oneself)**

-yambulula *vt* (-yambuludde, nnyambulula, okwambulula) **remove** (*an evil spirit*), **cleanse spiritually**

-yamira *vt* (-yamidde, nnyamira, okwamira) **urge on with shouting** -yamira embwa **urge on dogs** (*in hunting*)

(e)yammwe *pos* **your(s)** *pl.* **(N11.4)**

(e)yange *pos* **my, mine. (N11.4)**

-yangu *adj* (omwangu *n1*, abangu *n2*, eryangu *n5*, ekyangu *n7*, ennyangu *n9*) **fast, quick, agile, simple, easy**

-yanguwa *vi* (-yanguye, nnyanguwa, okwanguwa) **be quick**, *eg. Yanguwa ogende ogule omugaati. ('Go quickly and buy bread.')*, **hurry (up)**

-yanguya *vt* (-yanguyizza, nnyanguya, okwanguya) **do quickly**, *eg. Kola emirimu ng'oyanguya. ('Do the work quickly.')*

-yanguyira *vt* (-yanguyidde, nnyan…, okwan…) **rush to/for, hurry to**

-yanguyiriza *vt* (-yanguyirizza, nnyan…, okwan…) **do/go quickly**

-yanguyiza *vt* (-yanguyizza, nnyanguyiza, okwanguyiza) **make easy for**

-yaniikiriza *vt* (-yaniikirizza, nnyaniikiriza, okwaniikiriza) **put out to dry repeatedly**

-yanika *vt* (-yanise, nnyanika, okwanika) **put out to dry, expose** -yanika ku kaguwa **put on a line to dry** -yanika ku ttaka **put on the ground to dry** -yanika taaba **cure tobacco** (*in the sun*)

-yaniriza *vt* (-yanirizza, nnyaniriza, okwaniriza)

welcome

-yanja *vt* (-yanze, nnyanja, okwanja) **present,
submit** -yanja emboozi **launch a conversation**
-yanja omupiira **kick off** (*in football*)

-yanjaala *vi* (-yanjadde, okwanjaala) **flood**

-yanjala *vt* (-yanjadde, nnyanjala, okwanjala) **spread
(out)**, *eg. Tuyanjala ebijanjaalo bikale. ('We are
spreading out the beans to dry.')* -yanjala engalo
be empty-handed -yanjala omuddo **spread out
weeds while digging**

[1]**-yanjula** *vt* (-yanjudde, nnyanjula, okwanjula)
introduce (*person or proposal*), **announce**. *See*
okwanjula -yanjula ensonga **bring up a matter**
(*eg. at a meeting*), **submit a proposal**

[2]**-eeyanjula** *vr* **introduce oneself**

-yanjulukufu *adj* **opened (up)**

-yanjulukuka *vi* (-yanjulukuse, okwanjulukuka)
be(come) unfolded, be(come) unrolled

-yanjulula *vt* (-yanjudde, nnyanjulula, okwanjulula)
unfold, unroll

-yanjuluza *vt* (-yanjuluzza, nnyanjuluza) **(cause to)
open up** (*or unfold, or unroll*)

-yanukula *vt* (-yanukudde, nnyanukula,
okwanukula) **answer (back), reply** (*when called*)

-yanula *vt* (-yanudde, nnyanula, okwanula) **take out
of the sun** (*something drying*)

-eeyanza *vit* (-eeyanzizza) **thank** Nneeyanzizza.
Thank you. Nneeyanzizza nneeyanzeege. **Thank
you very much.**

[1]**-yasa** *vt* (-yasizza, njasa, okwasa) **split, chop up,
crack, shatter**. *Pronunciation*: okwâsa -yasa enku
chop up firewood

[2]**-yasa** *vt* **(cause to) burn**. *Pronunciation*: okwása

-yasaamirira *vi* (-yasaamiridde, njasaamirira,
okwasaamirira) **be open-mouthed, gape**

-yasaayasa *vt* (-yasizzayasizza, njasaayasa,
okwasaayasa) **split into many pieces, shatter**

-yasama *vi* (-yasamye, njasama, okwasama) **open
one's mouth**

-yasamya *vt* (-yasamizza, njasamya, okwasamya)
-yasamya omumwa **open the mouth** (*of someone*),
*eg. Yayasamya omumwa gw'omwana. ('She opened
the baby's mouth.')*

-yasanguza *vt* (-yasanguzizza, njas…, okwas…)
announce publicly (*something previously private*),
*eg. Yayasanguza nti afuuse Omusiraamu. ('He
announced that he had become a Muslim.')*, **expose**
-yasanguza ebigambo **announce something that
should be private**

-yasiikana (*also* -yasinkana) *vi* (-yasiikanye) **bicker,
wrangle, shout at one another** (*without listening
to the other person*)

-yasimula *vi* (-yasimudde, njasimula, okwasimula)
sneeze

-yasisa *vt* (-yasisizza, njasisa) **split with**, *eg.
Yakyasisa mbazzi. ('He split it with an axe.')*

eyatayimu *n9* **airtime**

-yatifu *adj* (enjatifu *n9*) **broken, cracked**

-yatiikirira *vi* (-yatiikiridde, njatiikirira,
okwatiikirira) **be(come) well known, be
distinguished, be outstanding**

-yatiikirivu *adj* (omwatiikirivu *n1*, abaatiikirivu *n2*)
well-known, distinguished

-yatiikiriza *vt* (-yatiikirizza, njatiikiriza,
okwatiikiriza) **make well known, make
distinguished**

-yatika *vi* (-yatise, okwatika) **be broken, be cracked**

-yatikayatika *vi* (-yatiseyatise, okwatikayatika) **be
broken** (*or cracked*) **in many places, be
shattered**

-yatisa *vt* (-yatisizza, njatisa, okwatisa) **cause to
break, break with, shatter with**

-yatuka *vi* (-yatuse) **come out** (*into the public
domain*), **be revealed** (*eg. of a secret*), **become
audible**

-yatula *vt* (-yatudde, njatula, okwatula) **speak out
what is not publicly known, make public, reveal,
declare openly**, *eg. Njatula nti ndokose. ('I am
declaring that I am saved.')* -yatula ebigambo **be
able to read whole words**

[1]**-yatulira** *vt* (-yatulidde, njatulira, okwatulira)
disclose to (*someone what one knows about
her/him*), **reveal to, inform**, *eg. Yamuyatulira nti
amanyi nga y'eyabba ssente. ('He informed her
that he knew that it was she that had stolen the
money.')*, **inform**

[2]**-eeyatulira** *vi* **express oneself** omusomo
gw'okweyatulira *n3* **confirmation course**

-yatuza *vt* (-yatuzizza, njatuza, okwatuza) **cause to
express** ennyukuta enjatuza *n9* **vowel**

-yavu *adj* (omwavu *n1*, abaavu *n2*) **poor**

-yavula *vi* (-yavudde, njavula, okwavula) **crawl**

-yavuwala *vi* (-yavuwadde, njavuwala, okwavuwala)
be(come) poor, be(come) impoverished

-yavuwaza *vt* (-yavuwazizza, njavuwaza,
okwavuwaza) **impoverish**

-yawufu *adj* (omwawufu *n1*, abaawufu *n2*, enjawufu
n9) **different**

-yawuka *vi* (-yawuse, njawuka, okwawuka) **be
separate, separate**, *eg. Nga bamaze okwogera,
omukyala yayawuka ku banne. ('When they
finished talking, the lady separated from her
friends.')* **-yawukako** (-yawuseeko) **be different,**
*eg. Ekitabo ekyo kyawuseeko ku ebyo ebirala.
('That book is different from those others.')*

-yawukana *vi* (-yawukanye, okwawukana) **diverge,
differ, part company, terminate** -yawukana mu
bufumbo **separate** (*in marriage*)

-yawukanya *vt* (-yawukanyizza, njawukanya,
okwawukanya) **(cause to) separate**

[1]**-yawula** *vt* (-yawudde, njawula, okwawula)
separate, *eg. Yayawula ebikopo ebinene ne bitono.
('She separated the big cups from the small ones.')*,
distinguish, differentiate, ordain Yazina
n'okwawula n'ayawula. **She danced kicking her
leg in the air.** **-yawulako** (-yawuddeko)

separate (*some items*) **from others**, *eg. Yayawulako ebibala ebimu. ('She separated some fruits from the others.')*, **subtract** **-yawulamu** **divide into** (*lots/parts*)

²-eeyawula *vr* **separate oneself** (*from a person or group*), *eg. Musoke yeeyawula ku baganda be n'asula yekka. ('Musoke separated himself from his brothers and lived alone.')*, **dissociate oneself**

-yawulayawula *vt* (-yawuddeyawudde, njawul..., okwawul...) **separate into different lots/parts**

-yawulwa *vi* (-yawuddwa, njawulwa, okwawulwa) **be separated, be ordained**

-yayuuya *vi* (-yayuuye, njayuuya, okwayuuya) **yawn**

¹-yaza *vt* (-yazizza, njaza, okwaza) **search (for)** (*illicit goods*), **frisk**. *Pronunciation*: okwázá

²-yaza *vt* (**cause to**) **increase** (*in number or amount*), *eg. Ayazizza ente ze. ('He has increased the number of his cows.')*, **produce in abundance** (*farm produce*), **multiply**. *Pronunciation*: okwâzà

-yaziina *vi* (-yaziinye, njaziina, okwaziina) **call to prayers** (*of Muslims*), *eg. Ayaziina. ('He is calling the people to prayers.')*

-yaziirana *vi* (-yaziiranye, njaziirana, okwaziirana) **wail in grief**

¹-yazika *vt* (-yazise, njazika, okwazika) **lend** (*things*)

²-eeyazika *vt* **borrow** (*things*)

-yazike *adj* (ekyazike *n7*, enjazike *n9*) **lent** (*of things*)

¹ye *pos* **her/his** (**N11.4**), *eg. emmere ye ('her food')*

²ye *pre* **of** (= y'e **N11.1**)

³ye *pro* **he, she, him, her**. *Can be equivalent to short phrases of emphasis* (**N10.1**)*, eg. Omusajja ali mu ssaati emyufu y'oyo gwe njagala. ('The man in the red shirt is the man I want.'). Can be a prefix* **ye-** (**N7.3**) *or suffix* **-ye** (**N10-12**)*, eg. (1) yekka ('only him'); (2) ye yennyini ('he himself', 'she herself'); (3) naye ('and he/she').*

yee *interj* **yes**

yeekaalu *n9* **Jewish temple, church**

eyeekalakaasa *n1* (*pl.* abeek...) **demonstrator** (*for a cause*)

-yeekera *vi* (-yeekedde, njeekera, okuyeekera) **wage guerrlla warfare**

eyeemanyi *n1* (*pl.* abeemanyi) **pompous person**

eyeemulugunya *n1* (*pl.* abeem...) **complainant**

eyeesimbyewo *n1* (*pl.* abeesimbyewo) **candidate**

-yeeya (*also* -jeeja) *vt* (-yeeyezza, njeeya, okuyeeya) **repeat again and again annoyingly, harp on about, mock** (*through annoying repetition*)

eyeeyazika *n1* (*pl.* abeeyazika) **borrower** (*of things*)

-yeeyereza *vt* (-yeeyerezza, njeeyereza) **constantly harp on about**

yegeyege *invariable adj* **wobbly, loose, shaky**, *eg. Oluggi lufuuse yegeyege. ('The door has become shaky.')*

yegu *n1* **flu**. *From: 'ague' (English).*

yekka *det/pro* **only her/him, by herself/himself**

-yenda *vi* (-yenze, nnyenda, okwenda) **commit adultery, fornicate**

-yenga *vt* (-yenze, nnyenga, okuyenga) **squeeze and dissolve** (*eg. herbs in water*)

-yengera *vi* (-yengedde, okwengera) **become ripe, ripen**

-yengerera *vi* (-yengeredde, okwengerera) **start to ripen** (*of fruit*), **become red hot** (*of metal*) ejjute -yengerera **become inflamed** (*of a boil*)

-yengevu *adj* **ripe**

-yenja *vi* (-yenze, okuyenja) **float about**

-yenjeera *vi* (-yenjedde, nnyen..., okwenj...) (1) **wander about aimlessly**; (2) **continually float about**; (3) **go around many places** (*eg. looking for something*), *eg. Nnayenjedde mu kibuga nga nnoonya ebintu bya Jane ne nkoowa. ('I went everywhere in town looking for things for Jane and got tired.')*

-yenjeerera *vi* (-yenjeeredde, nnyenjeerera, okwenjeerera) **roam about aimlessly in**, *eg. Ayenjeerera mu kibuga. ('She is wandering about aimlessly in town.')*

-yenkana *vi* (-yenkanye, nnenkana, okwenkana) **be equal (in/to)** (*a quantity, eg. size, age*), **be similar, be the same (in)**. *Can be followed by an abstract noun, eg. Byombi byenkana obuzito. ('Both things are the same weight.')*. -yenkana na/ne **be equal to**, *eg. Kino kyenkana n'ekyo. ('This is equal to that.')*, **be the same as** -yenkana wa? **be equal to what?, reach where?, what amount?** *Can be equivalent to how?, what?, eg. Omwana yenkana wa obukulu? ('What age has the child reached?')* Kyenkana wa? **How big is it?**

-yenkanankana *vi* (-yenkanyenkanye, nnenk..., okwenk...) **be equal**, *eg. Emigugu gyenkanyenkanye obuzito ('The bags are equal in weight.')*, **be the same**

-yenkanya *vt* (-yenkanyizza, nnenkanya, okwenkanya) **make equal to, make the same, equalise**

-yenkanyankanya *vt* (-yenkanyizzankanyizza, nnenk..., okwenk...) **make equal**, *eg. Njagala okwenkanyankanya sukaali gwe mpa ewa Musoke ne Mukasa. ('I want to give Musoke and Mukasa equal amounts of sugar.')*, **make the same**

yenna *det/pro* **all of her/him, any (person)**, *eg. Twala yenna gw'oyagala. ('Take any person you want.')*

yennyini *pro* **herself, himself** ye yennyini **he himself, she herself**

-yera *vt* (-yeze, njera, okwera) **sweep, brush**

-yereere *adj* (omwereere *n1*, abeereere *n2*, eryereere or lyereere *n5*, ameereere *n6*, enjereere *n9*, obwereere *n14*, weereere *n16*) **empty, bare, naked, nude, mere, ordinary**

-yeru *adj* (omweru *n1*, abeeru *n2*, eryeru *n5*, ameeru *n6*, enjeru *n9*, akeeru *n12*, obweru *n14*) **white,**

light-skinned

-yeruka *vi* (-yeruse, okweruka, njeruka) **be(come) lighter in colour**

-yerula *vt* (-yerudde, njerula, okwerula) **remove** (*untidy or unwanted things*), **clear/clean** (*up/out*), *eg. Yerula oluzzi. ('Clean out the well.')* -yerula empenda **clear path through vegetation**

[1]**-yerusa** *vt* (-yerusizza, njerusa, okwerusa) **make white, make lighter in colour**

[2]**-eeyerusa** *vr* **make oneself lighter in colour**

-yesa *vi* (njesa, -yesezza, njesa, okwesa) **play omweso**

Yesu *n1* **Jesus** (*Prot*)

Yezu *n1* **Jesus** (*RC*)

ayi *interj (used in entreaties)* **oh**, *eg. Ayi Katonda! ('Oh God [hear us]!')*

-yidde *See* -ggya ('be ready')

Yidi *n9* **Id**

-yiga *vt* (-yize, njiga) **learn.** *See* okuyiga

-eeyigaanya (*also* -yigaanya) *vr* (-eeyigaanyizza) **push/squeeze through**, *eg. Yeeyigaanyizza n'ayitawo. ('He pushed his way through the narrow space.')*, **elbow one's way**

-yigaayigana *vi* (-yigaayiganye, njigaayigana) **be restless**

-yigga *vt* (-yizze, njigga) **hunt**

-yigganya *vt* (-yigganyizza, njigganya) **persecute**

-yigika (*also* -yigiikiriza) *vt* (-yigise, njigika) **prevent from falling** (*in a temporary sort of way*), **hold up, prop up**

-yigira *vt* (-yigidde, njigira) **learn at/for**, *etc.*

[1]**-yigiriza** *vt* (-yigirizza, njigiriza) **teach, educate.** *See* okuyigiriza -yigiriza empisa **teach how to behave**

[2]**-eeyigiriza** *vr* **teach oneself**

-yigirize *adj* **learned, educated**

-yiguka *vi* (-yiguse) **be(come) moved from a firm position, give way, fall, collapse**, *eg. Omutwe gwe gwayiguka. ('His head fell over.', eg. when falling asleep in a chair)*

-yigula *vt* (-yigudde, njigula) **move from a firm position** (*physically or mentally*)

-yiguliza *vi* (-yigulizza, njiguliza) **stand with one hip higher than the other** (*can be used to indicate disrespect*)

-yigulukuka *vi* (-yigulukuse) **collapse** (*of a wall or the ground*), **give way**, *eg. Enkuba yatonnya nnyingi n'ettaka ne liyigulukuka. ('It rained a lot and the ground gave way.')*

-yiibwa *vi* (-yiiddwa) **be spilt, be dumped**

[1]**yiika** *n9* **acre**

[2]**-yiika** *vi* (-yiise, njiira) **pour out, be poured out, be spilt**, *eg. Amata gayiise. ('The milk is spilt.')*, **overflow**

-yiikiriza *vt* (-yiikirizza, njiikiriza) **take advantage of** (*a person, in an exploitative way*), *eg. Abaana abakulu mu ssomero baayiikiriza abato. ('The older pupils took advantage of the younger ones.')*,

impose one's will on, exploit, bully

-yiikuula *vt* (-yiikudde, njiikuula) **scoop out, excavate**

yiino **here it is**

-yiira *vt* (-yidde) **spill on**, *eg. Omwana ajja kukuyiira amata. ('The child will spill milk on you.')*

yiiri **there it is**

[1]**-yiisa** *vt* (-yiisizza, njiisa) **have cooked and ready to eat** (*food*), *eg. Amaze okuyiisa emmere. ('She has finished cooking the food.')*, **brew** (*beer*). *Pronunciation:* okuyîisà

[2]**-yiisa** *vt* **(cause to) spill.** *Pronunciation:* okuyíisá

-yiiya *vt* (-yiiye, njiiya) **invent, devise, design, create, originate, compose** -yiiya olugero **make up a story**

-yiiye *adj* **invented, composed**

yiiyo **there it is**

-yima *vi* (-yimye, nnyima) (1) **do from elsewhere.** *Can be equivalent to preposition* **from**, *eg. Nnyima wano ne mbayita. ('I am calling them from here.');* (2) **stand.** *With neg* (**N21**) *can mean* **be impotent** (*of a man*), *eg. Tayinza kuyima. (He is impotent.').*

[1]**-yimba** *vit* (-yimbye, nnyimba) **sing.** *See* okuyimba -yimba n'eddoboozi eritiribira obulungi **sing vibrato**

[2]**-eeyimba** *vr* **tie oneself** -eeyimbamu (-eeyimbyemu) **put a rope around one's neck** -eeyimbamu muguwa **hang onself** (*commit suicide*)

-yimbaala *vi* (-yimbadde) **grow dim** (*of sight*), *eg. Amaaso gange gayimbadde. ('My eyes have grown dim.')*, **be blinded** (*by a flash of light*)

-yimbagatanya *vi* (-yimbagatanyizza, nnyimb...) **do two or more tasks at once, multitask**

-yimbisa *vt* (-yimbisizza, nyimbisa) **cause to sing**

-yimbula *vt* (-yimbudde, nnyimbula) **set free** (*tethered or penned animal*), **release** -yimbula omutuba **strip bark from a barkcloth tree**

[1]**-yimirira** *vi* (-yimiridde, nnyimirira) **stop** (*of person or thing moving*), **stand** -yimirira busimba **stand upright** -yimirira busimbalaala **stand at attention** -yimirira butengerera **stand still** Yimirira ku magulu go! **Stand on your own two feet!** (*exhortation – 'Don't be intimidated.'*)

-yimirirawo (-yimiriddewo) **stay at a place, stand still** -yimirirawo ku lwa **depend on**

[2]**-eeyimirira** *vt* **stand up for, sponsor, put up security for, guarantee, be a referee for, serve as godparent to**

-yimiriza *vt* (-yimirizza, nnyimiriza) **cause to stand, stop** (*something moving*), **halt, suspend** (*an operation, someone from employment, etc.*) -yimiriza takisi **wave down a taxi** -yimirizaamu (-yimirizaamu) **pause**

-eeyimirizaawo *vr* (-eeyimirizaawo) **be independent, be able to sustain oneself**, *eg. Eggwanga okweyimirizaawo lyetaaga ssente nnyingi. ('A nation needs a lot of money to maintain itself.')*

-yimirizibwa *vi* (-yimiriziddwa) **be suspended** (*of an activity*)

-yimpawala *vi* (-yimpawadde) **be(come) short**

-yimpawaza (*also* -yimpaya) *vt* (-yimpawazizza, nnyimpawaza) **shorten**

-yimuka *vi* (-yimuse, nnyimuka) **get up** (*from being seated or lying down*), **stand up**

-yimusa *vt* (-yimusizza, nnyimusa) **raise** -yimusa amaaso **raise one's eyes** -yimusa eddoboozi **raise one's voice** -yimusa omukono **raise one's hand** -yimusa omutindo **raise the standard**

yingini *n9* **engine**

yinginiya *n1* (*pl.* ba yinginiya) **engineer**

-yingira *vit* (-yingidde, nnyingira) **enter, go into, penetrate, join** (*an organisation*) Yingira. **Come in.** **-yingiramu** (-yingiddemu) **allow in**, *eg. Bikka ku sukaali aleme kuyingiramu buwuka.* ('*Cover the sugar so the insects don't get in.*')

-yingirira *vt* (-yingiridde, nnyingirira) **force entry into, break into a house.** *The affected party can be indicated by an object pronoun, eg. Ababbi baatuyingirira.* ('*Thieves broke into our house.*'). *Saying: 'Toyingirira mulimu gw'otosobola.'* ('*Don't try something you cannot do.*'). See okuyingirira w'oyingirira *n16* **entrance**

-yingiriza *vt* (-yingirizza, nnyingiriza) **let in unintentionally**, *eg. Olese oluggi luggule ojja kutuyingiriza ensiri.* ('*You left the door open so mosquitoes will come into our house.*')

[1]**-yingiza** *vt* (-yingizizza, nnyingiza) **(cause to) enter** -yingiza mu **insert, allow in, bring in, admit, import, involve**

[2]**-eeyingiza** *vi* **insert oneself, let oneself in, meddle** (*in other people's affairs*), **interfere** -eeyingiza mu mboozi etemukwatako **enter a conversation** (*that does not concern one*) -eeyingiza mu nnyumba **enter a house** (*without advance notice or invitation*) **-eeyingizaamu** (-eeyingizizzaamu) **insert oneself into**

yinki *n9* **inch**

yinsuwa *n9* **insurance**

-eeyinula *vt* (-eeyinudde) **go along with** (*a bad crowd*), **behave badly** (*eg. through having too much money*), **go off the rails**

-yinza *aux v* (-yinzizza, nnyinza) **be able, can, might, be likely.** *Can be equivalent to adverbs* **maybe, perhaps**, *eg. Enkuba eyinza okutonnya gye bujja.* ('*Maybe it will rain.*').

-yinzika *vi* (-yinzise) **be possible/manageable**

-yira *vi* (-yize) **roar** (*of waterfall, rapids or rain*)

-yiriitira *vi* (-yiriitidde, njiriitira) **breath noisily, wheeze**

-yiringisa (*also* -yiringula) *vt* (-yiringisizza, njiringisa) **roll along** (*eg. a tyre*)

-yiringita *vi* (-yiringise, njiringita) **roll** (*of own accord*), **roll downslope**

yiriyiri *adv* **very fast, with great speed**

eyirizi *n9* **charm** (*worn by Muslims*)

oyiro *n1* **oil**

[1]**-yisa** *vt* (-yisizza, mpisa) **behave towards, treat** (*someone*) -yisa bubi **mistreat** **-yisaamu** (-yisizzaamu) -yisaamu amaaso **show disrespect** (*or* **contempt**) **towards/for**

[2]**-yisa** *vt* **(cause to) pass**, *eg. Ayisa ewuzi mu mpiso.* ('*She is passing a thread through a needle.*'), **go past, overtake, surpass** -yisa ekiteeso **pass a proposal** -yisa okugulu mu nju (*also* -yisaamu olugaayu) **pass one's leg over** (*a seated person, a gesture of disrespect, formerly done by children*) **-yisaamu pass** (*something*) **through, stick** (*something*) **through, protrude** (*something*) **through, extend through**

[3]**-eeyisa** *vi* **behave, conduct oneself.** *See* okweyisa -eeyisa bubi **behave badly** **-eeyisaawo show off, push oneself forward seeking advantage.** *See* okweyisaawo

-yisinnanya *vi* (-yisinnanyizza) **pass one another** (*moving in opposite directions*), *eg. Twayisinnanya ne famire ya Musoke.* ('*We passed Musoke's family.*' – *moving in the opposite direction*)

Yisirayiri *n9* **Israel**

[1]**-yita** *vi* (-yise, mpita) **pass.** *See* okuyita -yita ebibuuzo **pass an examination** -yita ku **go past**, *eg. Twayise ku ssomero.* ('*We went past the school.*') -yita ku lugwanyu **have a narrow escape** -yita ku muntu **pass someone without greeting** -yita mu **pass/go through** -yita mu tanuulu **pass through a very bad time** (*lit.* '*pass through a furnace*') Ebbanga liyise. **Time has**

NOTES FOR y

CONTRACTION OF VERBS AND ADJECTIVES. Many verbs and adjectives beginning **ya**, **ye** or **yo** contract on the addition of certain prefixes, the **y** being lost. Some verbs have alternative contracted and non-contracted forms, *eg.* **twagala** and **tuyagala** (both meaning 'we love'), from **-yagala** ('love').

FIRST PERSON SINGULARS of verbs beginning **y** take various forms. Most commonly, non-nasal verbs start **nj**, *eg.* **njoza** ('I wash'), from **-yoza**, and nasal verbs start **nny**, *eg.* **nnyamba** ('I help'), from **-yamba** (**n5**). 1st person singulars are given here for many verbs. **-yita** and related verbs begin **mp**, *eg.* **mpitaba** ('I respond'), from **-yitaba**.

INFINITIVES are shown for some verbs beginning **ya**, **ye** or **yo** to show whether contraction occurs. Some verbs are found in both contracted and non-contracted forms, *eg.* both **okwagala** *and* **okuyagala** mean 'to love'.

NOUNS IN *n9*. Most nouns in *n9* have identically spelt plurals (in *n10*).

-yita

passed. <u>Obudde buyise.</u> It is late. **-yitako**
(-yiseemu) **pass** (*by a small amount*), **pass at/on**,
*eg. ku ssaawa emu kuyiseeko eddakiika emu ('one
minute past seven o'clock', lit. 'at seven o'clock
has passed one minute'),* **pass briefly.** *See*
okuyitako **-yitamu protrude, stick out, be out-
of-line, be ahead** (*eg. in an election*), **extend
through -yitawo pass by,** *eg. Wayiseewo
ebbanga okuva taata we lwe yafa. ('Time has
passed since his father died.'),* **go past -yitayo
pass** (*over there*) <u>Oyitayo?</u> **Do you drink?** (*polite
way of asking if someone drinks alcohol*)
[2]**-yita** *vt* (-yise, mpita) **call, nickname, invite,
summon** <u>-yita olukuŋŋaana</u> **convene a meeting**
-yitaayita *vi* (-yiseeyise, mpitaayita) **call repeatedly**
-yitaba *vit* (-yitabye, mpitaba) **respond with 'wangi'**
(*when called*)
Yitale *n9* **Italy**
-yitibwa *vi* (-yitiddwa, mpitibwa) **be called, be
invite.** *See* okuyitibwa
-yitirira *vit* (-yitiridde) **be excessive, be extreme, be
too much.** *Can be equivalent to adverb* **extremely,**
eg. Kiyitirira obuwanvu. ('It is extremely long.').
<u>ennaku -yitirira</u> **be distraught with grief**
-yitirirako (-yitiriddeko) **overwhelm,** *eg. Ebizibu
byamuyitirirako obungi. ('She was overwhelmed by
difficulties.'),* **be too much (for)**
-yitirivu *adj* (eriyitirivu *or* eppitirivu *n5*, empitirivu
n9) **excessive, extreme** <u>-yitirivu obungi</u> **lots of**
-yitiriza *vt* (-yitirizizza, njitiriza) **make excessive**
-yiwa *vt* (-yiye, njiwa) **pour out, spill, disappoint,
jilt, develop a skin rash** (*through having measles*),
eg. Ayiye. ('She has measles.') <u>-yiwa amaziga</u>
shed tears <u>-yiwa ebigambo</u> **come out with lots of
words** (*eg. in abuse*) <u>-yiwa ebisaaniiko</u> **dump
rubbish** <u>-yiwa obutulututtu</u> **develop a skin rash**
eyiye *pos* **hers, his**
eyiyo *pos* **yours** *si.*
[1]**eyo** *adv* **there** (*not far away*)
[2]**eyo** *dem* **that**
[3]**oyo** *dem* **that (person)**
[4]**yo** *pos* **your** *si.*
[5]**yo** *pro* **it.** *Can be a suffix* **-yo** (N10.3), *eg. nayo
('and it').*
yogaayoga *excl* **congratulations, well done**
yogati *n1* **yoghurt**
-yogera *vit* (-yogedde, njogera, okwogera) **speak,
talk, comment, pronounce.** *See* okwogera
<u>-yogera bitaliimu</u> **talk nonsense** <u>-yogera bubi</u>
speak badly, speak rudely <u>-yogera butamala</u> **talk
for too long** <u>-yogera by'akalebule</u> **slander**
<u>-yogera -eetooloola</u> **talk in circles, beat about the
bush** <u>-yogera ku</u> **talk with** <u>-yogera mu kaama</u>
whisper <u>-yogera n'ebboggo</u> (*also* <u>-yogera
-boggoka</u>) **speak harshly** <u>-yogera n'eggono</u> **talk
in a clear pleasant way** <u>-yogera n'ekirimi</u> **talk
with a lisp** <u>-yogera olukobo</u> (<u>-yogera
olumuunyere</u>) **speak for too long** (*with nothing

much to say*) <u>-yogera olulondakambe</u> **talk on-
and-on** <u>-yogera vvolongoto</u> **talk nonsense**
-yogerako (*also* <u>-yogera ku</u>) (-yogeddeko) **talk
about,** *eg. Tujja kwogera ku bintu ebyetaaga
okukola. ('We will talk about the things that need to
be done.'),* **mention to, comment on, utter**
-yogeragana *vi* (-yogeraganye, okwogeragana) **talk
with one another**
-yogerayogera *vi* (-yogeddeyogedde, njoger...,
okwoger...) **talk too much** (*about things that
should not be said*)
-yogerera *vt* (-yogeredde, njogerera, okwogerera)
speak for/at, *etc., eg. Musoke y'eyayogerera
mukyala we. ('Musoke spoke on behalf of his wife.')*
<u>-yogerera amafuukuule</u> **upbraid, rave against**
<u>-yogerera waggulu</u> **speak loudly**
-yogereza *vt* (-yogerezza, njogereza, okwogereza)
chat up, date, court, woo
-yogeza *vt* (-yogezza, njogeza, okwogeza) **speak
in/with** (*a particular manner*) <u>-yogeza kisa</u> **speak
kindly** <u>-yogeza ssimbo</u> **speak in a dignified way**
-yogezayogeza *vt* (-yogezzayogezza, njogez...,
okwogez...) **chat away** (*eg. to keep a visitor
entertained*)
-yogi *adj* (ekyogi *n7*, akoogi *n12*) **sharp**
Yokana *n1* **John**
-yokerera *v* (-yokeredde, njokerera, okwokerera) (1)
vi **be(come) warm, be lukewarm, have a slight
fever;** (2) *vt* **burn down (a house)** (*as an act of
arson*)*. The victim can be given as an object
pronoun, eg. Yatuyokeredde. ('He burnt down our
house.')*
[1]**-yokya** *v* (-yokezza, njokya, okwokya) (1) *vi* **be hot,
be burning, burn, blister;** (2) *vt* **burn, roast,
scald, scorch, sting** (*by caterpillar or plant*)
<u>-yokya amatofaali</u> **fire bricks** <u>-yokya ebibumbe</u>
fire pottery <u>-yokya ekyuma</u> **heat iron** (*in metal
work*) <u>-yokya ennyumba</u> **set fire to a house**
<u>-yokya omusubi</u> **run away very fast** (*lit. 'burn the
grass'*) <u>-yokya siddi</u> **burn a CD**
[2]**-eeyokya** *vr* **burn oneself**
-yokye *adj* (omwokye *n1*, eryokye *or* eriyokye *n5*,
amookye *or* amayokye *n6*, enjokye *n9*) **burnt,
roast(ed)**
-yola *vt* (-yoze, njola, okuyola) **carve a pattern on**
(*wood or pottery*) <u>-yola omwana</u> **raise a child**
-yoleka *vi* (-yolese, okwoleka) **be displayed, be
exhibited**
-yolekera *vt* (-yolekedde, njolekera, okwolekera)
aim for, head for. *Can be equivalent to
preposition* **towards,** *eg. Yatunula okwolekera
ennyanja. ('He looked towards the lake.')*
-yolekeza *vt* (-yolekezza, njolekeza) **point
towards/at,** *eg. Yatwolekeza emmundu ne
tugalamira. ('He pointed the gun at us and we lay
down.'),* **aim at** (*eg. a person*) **with** (*eg. a gun*)
-yolesa *vt* (-yolesezza, njolesa, okwolesa) **show,
display, exhibit**

-yolesebwa *vi* (-yoleseddwa, njolesebwa, okwolesebwa) **be shown, be displayed, have a vision**

-yoleza *vt* (-yolezza, njoleza, okwoleza) **wash for/at,** *etc. See* okwoleza

-yomba *vi* (-yombye, nnyomba, okuyomba) **quarrel**

-yombagana *vi* (-yombaganye, okuyombagana) **quarrel with one another, squabble**

-eeyombekera *vi* (-eeyombekedde) **live alone** (*of a woman*). *See* nnakyeyombekedde

-yombera *vt* (-yombedde, nnyombera, okuyombera) **quarrel at/in**

-yombesa *vt* (-yombesezza, nnyombesa, okuyombesa) **quarrel with**

-yombi *adj* **quarrelsome**

[1]**-yongera** *vt* (-yongedde, nnyongera, okwongera) **increase, add/put more** -yongera obulungi **become better** (*eg. in an activity*) -yongera obunene **enlarge** **-yongerako** (-yongeddeko) (*also* -yongera ku) **add/put more** (*on*), **increase a little,** *eg. Ekisenge yakyongerako obuwanvu.* ('*He made the wall a bit higher.*'), **put a little more, extend** -yongerako wansi **lower** **-yongeramu** **add/put more** (*inside something*) -yongeramu ebigambo **put words into someone's mouth** **-yongerayo go further, advance, add more**

[2]**-eeyongera** *vit* **increase, intensify, improve** (*of oneself*), **have more,** *eg. Yeeyongera emmere.* ('*She had some more food.*'), **continue,** *eg. Tweyongere okwogera.* ('*Let us continue to talk.*', *eg. about a matter*), **advance** -eeyongera obubi **get worse** -eeyongera mu maaso **go forward** -eeyongera obulungi **get better, continue to improve** -eeyongera obungi **accumulate,** *eg. Essente zeeyongedde obungi.* ('*The money has accumulated.*') -eeyongera okwonooneka **deteriorate,** *eg. Embeera yeeyongedde okwonooneka.* ('*The situation has deteriorated.*') **-eeyongerako increase a little** (*of something*), *eg. Emiti gyeyongerako obuwanvu.* ('*The trees have grown taller.*') **-eeyongeramu increase** (*internally*), **have more** (*within something*), *eg. Nja kweyongeramu ekikopo kya caayi.* ('*I will have another cup of tea.*') **-eeyongerawo increase** (*in a place*), *eg. Weeyongeddewo abantu babiri abatuuse.* ('*Two more people have arrived.*') **-eeyongerayo increase** (*over there*), **proceed, advance, continue, extend, go further,** *eg. Bw'otuuka ku nnyumba ye, weeyongerayo mayiro bbiri.* ('*After arriving at his house, go two miles further.*') -eeyongerayo mu maaso **defer**

-yongeza *vt* (-yongezezza, nnyongeza, okwongeza) **(cause to) increase, have/put more, continue, augment** -yongeza ebbeeyi **raise the price** -yongeza eddoboozi **raise one's voice** (*in volume*) -yongeza obungi **accumulate** -yongeza omuliro **accelerate, raise the heat** -yongeza sipiidi **accelerate** **-yongezaako** (-yongezezzaako)

increase a little -yongezaako wansi **lower a little** -yongezaako waggulu **raise a little** **-yongezaamu add more, increase a little,** *eg. Weetaaga okwongezaamu omuwendo ssiringi ataano.* ('*We need to increase the price by fifty shillings.*') **-yongezaayo move** (*something*) **further away, postpone, defer**

-yongobera *vi* (-yongobedde, nnyongobera, okuyongobera) **be lethargic.** *See* okuyongobera

-yongobevu *adj* **lethargic**

-yonja *vt* (-yonze, nnyonja, okuyonja) **clean, make neat, smarten up**

-yonjo *adj* (ennyonjo *n9*) **clean, tidy, neat, smart**

-yonka *vit* (-yonse, nnyonka, okuyonka) **be breast-fed,** *eg. Omwana ayonka.* ('*The baby is breast-feeding.*'), **suckle** (*of a baby*)

-yonoona *v* (-yonoonye, nnyonoona, okwonoona) (1) *vi* **do wrong, sin, commit evil;** (2) *vt* **spoil, waste, squander, destroy, corrupt, damage** -yonoona ebiseera (*or* obudde) **waste time** -yonoona erinnya **lose one's reputation**

-yonoonefu *adj* (ennyonoonefu *n9*) **spoilt, badly behaved, ruined, faulty, broken, damaged**

-yonooneka *vi* (-yonoonese, nnyonooneka, okwonooneka) **be(come) spoilt, go wrong, deteriorate, be(come) badly behaved, be(come) ruined, be(come) faulty, be(come) damaged, break down** (*of machinery*)

-yonsa *vt* (-yonsezza, nnyonsa, okuyonsa) **breast-feed,** *eg. Ayonsa omwana.* ('*She is breast-feeding the baby.*'), **suckle** (*a baby*)

-yoogaana *vi* (-yoogaanye, njoog… okuyoog…) **make a din**

-yoola *vt* (-yodde, njoola, okuyoola) **scoop up, shovel up** (*eg. rubbish with a spade*), **pick up indiscriminately**

-yooyoota *vt* (-yooyoose, njooy…, okuyooy…) **finish off very well, make perfect, give the final touches to**

-yosa *vt* (-yosezza, njosa, okwosa) **miss a regular activity, miss/skip a day.** *See* okwosa **-yosaawo** (-yosezzaawo) **miss a regular activity** (= -yosa), *eg. Jjangu enkya, oyoseewo olwokusatu.* ('*Come tomorrow, skip Wednesday.*')

Yosefu *n1* **Joseph**

-yosera *vt* (-yosedde, njosera, okwosera) **wean too soon** (*a child, prematurely*)

-yota *vit* (-yose, njota, okwota) **warm oneself** (by) -yota omuliro **warm oneself by a fire** -yota omusana **bask in the sun**

[1]**-yoteza** *vt* (-yotezza, njoteza, okwoteza) **give a vapour bath to**

[2]**-eeyoteza** *vr* **take a vapour bath**

-yoya *vt* (-yoyezza, njoya, okwoya) **crave, yearn for**

-yoza *vt* (-yozezza, njoza, okwoza) **wash** (*things*) -yoza ebifaananyi **develop a film**

-yozaayoza *vt* (-yozezzayozezza, njoz..., okwoz...) **wash too frequently, wash inadequately,**

177

congratulate

-yozebwa *vi* (-yozeddwa, njozebwa, okwozebwa) **be washed**

-yozesa *vt* (-yozesezza, njozesa, okwozesa) **wash with**

-yubuka *vi* (-yubuse, njubuka) **peel off** (*of the skin, eg. through an allergic reaction*), *eg. Njubuse.* (*'My skin is peeling.'*), **flake off** (*eg. of paint*)

-eeyubula *vi* (-eeyubuse) **slough the skin** (*of a snake*)

-yubuluza *vt* (-yubuluzizza, njubuluza) -yubuluza olulagala **remove midrib of banana leaf**

Yuganda *n9* **Uganda**

-yulifu *adj* **torn**

-yulika *vi* (-yulise) **be torn**

-yulikayulika *vi* (-yuliseyulise) **be shredded**

-yulisa *vt* (-yulizza, njulisa) **(cause to) tear**

-yunga *vt* (-yunze, nnyunga) **join** (*end-to-end*), **set** (*a bone*), **connect, link** -yunga omukono **set a broken arm**

-yunguka (-yunguse, nnyunguka) *vi* **become disconnected, well up** (*of tears*), *eg. Ayunguse amaziga.* (*'Tears are welling up in her eyes.'*)

-yungula *vt* (-yungudde, nnyungula) **draft in** (*eg. reinforcements to quell trouble*), *eg. Bayungula abaserikale.* (*'They are drafting in soldiers.'*) -yungula abawanvu n'abampi **draft in all available resources**

yunivasite *n9* **university**

-yunja *vt* (-yunze, nnyunja) **harvest** (*bananas – a process that includes chopping down the plant*)

-yuuga *vi* (-yuuze) **move about, sway (about)**, *eg. Emiti giyuuga.* (*'The trees are swaying about.'*), **shake from side to side** -tambula -yuuga **walk swaying from side to side**

-yuugana *vi* (-yuuganye) **be unstable, shake, sway**

-yuuganya *vt* (-yuuganyizza, njuuganya) **make unstable, make sway, destabilise**

-yuuganyi *adj* **unstable, shaky, fickle**

-yuugayuuga *vi* (-yuuzeyuuze, njuugayuuga) **be unstable** (*of a person*), **repeatedly change one's mind**, *eg. Yali ayuugayuuga ku ky'okukola.* (*'He could not make up his mind what to do.'*), **waver, vacillate**

-yuuguuma *vi* (-yuuguumye) **move irregularly to and fro, shake, become agitated** (*of a crowd*)

-yuuguumya *vt* (-yuuguumizza, njuuguumya) **shake forcefully** (*to and fro*), *eg. Musisi ayuuguumizza ekifo.* (*'There's an earthquake.'*), **cause excitement** (*among people*)

-(y)ayuuya See -yayuuya

-yuuza *vt* (-yuuzizza, njuuza) **(make) sway**, *eg. Kibuyaga yayuuzizza emiti.* (*'The wind is making the trees sway.'*)

-yuuzayuuza *vt* (-yuuzizzayuuzizza, njuuza…) **keep swaying**

-yuza (-yuzizza, njuza) *vt* **tear, rip, rend** -yuzaamu (-yuzizzaamu) **tear into pieces**, *eg.*

Olugoye olwo luyuzeemu. (*'Tear that cloth into pieces.'*)

-yuzaayuza *vt* (-yuzizzayuzizza, njuz…) **shred**

-yuze *adj* **torn**

Z,z

(e)z' *abbrev of* (e)za; ze

[1] **(e)za** *pre* **of**, *eg. ente za Musoke* (*'cows of Musoke'*). *Can be a prefix* **(e)za-** (**N11.4**), *eg. zange* (*'my'*).

[2] **-(y)aza** See -yaza

[3] **-(y)oza** See -yoza

zaabu *n1* (*no pl.*) **gold**. *From: 'dhahabu' (Swahili).*

(e)zaabwe *pos* **their(s)** (**N11.4**)

zaaki? *interr* **what for?**

-zaala *vit* (-zadde) **give birth (to), reproduce, breed** (*of animals*), **produce shoots** (*of a banana plant*). *See okuzaala* -zaala ensukusa **bear a shoot** (*of a banana plant*) -zaala omwana **bear a child** (*of a woman*)

-zaalazaala *vt* (-zaddezadde) **have children by different men, have unplanned children**

-zaalibwa *vi* (-zaaliddwa) **be born**

-zaalira (-zaalidde) *vt* **give birth at/for**, *eg. Yazaalira waka.* (*'She gave birth at home.'*) -zaalira ku luggya **have a child before leaving one's parents' home**

-zaaliranwa *adj* **indigenous, native**

-zaalisa *vt* (-zaalisizza) **assist in/at childbirth, deliver** (*a baby*)

-zaawa *vi* (-zaaye) **be away for a long time** (*eg. of a person who has gone abroad*), *eg. Musoke yazaawa.* (*'Musoke has been away for a long time.'*)

-zaawuka *vi* (-zaawuse) **return, reappear, be found** (*of a long-absent person*)

-zaawula *vt* (-zaawudde) **(cause to) reappear** (*a long-absent person*), **find again**

-zaaya *vt* (-zaayizza) **cause** (*someone*) **to be away for a long time**

-zaaza *vt* (-zaazizza) **cause to give birth**

zabbuli *n9* **psalm** Zabbuli **Book of Psalms**

(e)zaffe *pos* **our(s)** (**N11.4**)

(e)zammwe *pos* **your(s)** *pl.* (**N11.4**)

(e)zange *pos* **my, mine.** (**N11.4**)

-zannya *vit* (-zannye) **play, perform** -zannya buzannyi **play games** (*not being serious*) -zannya caanisi **play cards** -zannya mu muzannyo **act in a play** -zannya omupiira **play football** -zannya tenna **play tennis**

-zannyiikiriza *vt* (-zannyiikirizza) **play around with** (*in a jokey way*), **tease, triffle with, toy with**

-zannyira *vt* (-zannyidde) **play in/at**, *etc., eg. Abaana bazannyira ebweru.* (*'The children are playing outside.'*). See okuzannyira w'ozannyira *n16* **playground**

-zannyirira *vi* (-zannyiridde) **be playful**

-zannyisa *vt* (-zannyisizza) **play/toy with, not take** (*someone*) **seriously**

-zazika *vt* (-zazise) **lay down** (*a child to sleep*)

[1]ze *pos* **her/his** (N11.4), *eg. ente ze* (*'her cows'*)

[2]ze *pre* **of** (= z'e) (N11.1)

[3]ze *pro* (*relative pronoun and pronoun of emphasis N10.1*) **they, which, that.** *Can be equivalent to short phrases of emphasis, eg. Ente ezo ze njagala.* (*'It is those cows that I like.'*). *Can be a prefix* **ze-** (*N11.6*), *eg. ente zennyini* (*'the cows themselves'*).

-zeeyuka *vi* (-zeeyuse) **be(come) elderly**

-ziba *v* (-zibye) (1) *vi* **become blocked, become obstructed;** (2) *vt* **block (up), obstruct** -ziba amaaso **become** (*or* **make**) **blind** -ziba amatu **become** (*or* **make**) **deaf** -ziba emimwa **become dumb** obudde -ziba **become dark/night**

-zibe *adj* **blocked**

-zibibwa *vi* (-zibiddwa) **be blocked (by)**

-zibiikiriza (-zibiikirizza) *vt* **conceal** (*information or an emotion*), **suppress** -zibiikiriza essanyu **conceal one's happiness**

-zibikira *vt* (-zibikidde) **block (up), fill in/up, cork (up)**

-zibira *vt* (-zibidde) **hinder the passage of** (*someone*), **withhold information (from)**, *eg. Yamuzibira ku bintu ebyatuukawo.* (*'He withheld the information from her about what happened.'*), **cover up for** (*shield from blame*)

-zibirira *vi* (-zibiridde) **close one's eyes** obudde -zibirira **close in** (*of darkness*)

-zibiriza *vt* (-zibirizza) -zibiriza amaaso **close one's eyes**

-zibu *adj* **difficult**

-zibuka *vi* (-zibuse) **be(come) unblocked** -zibuka amaaso **regain one's sight, become enlightened** -zibuka amatu **regain one's hearing**

-zibukuka *vi* (-zibukuse) **be(come) unblocked, be(come) unclogged**

-zibukula (-zibukudde) **open up, unblock, unclog**

-zibula *vt* (-zibudde) -zibula amaaso **open one's eyes, restore eyesight, enlighten** -zibula amatu **restore hearing**

-zibuwala *vi* (-zibuwadde) **be(come) difficult**

-zibuwalira *vi* (-zibuwalidde) **be(come) difficult for**, *eg. Kinzibuwalidde okutegeera.* (*'It has been difficult for me to understand.'*)

-zibuwaliza *vt* (-zibuwalizza) **make difficult for**, *eg. Omwana amuzibuwaliza okukola emirimu.* (*'The child makes it difficult for her to work.'*)

-zibuwalizibwa *vi* (-zibuwaliziddwa) **have difficulties** (*in affairs*)

-zibuwaza *vt* (-zibuwazizza) **make difficult**, *eg. Omwana azibuwaza okukola emirimu.* (*'The child makes it difficult to work.'*)

-zibya *vt* (-zibizza) **make blind** -zibya obudde **do all day, do until nightfall**, *eg. Enkuba yatonnye okuzibya obudde.* (*'It rained until nightfall.'*)

-ziga *vt* (-zize) **track down** (*eg. an animal in a hunt*), **scout out, reconnoitre** -ziga emmotoka **look for a car** (*to buy*) -ziga ennyumba **look for a house** (*to live in*)

-zigama *vi* (-zigamye) **become tarnished** (*loose shine, of metal*)

zigizigi extremely dark, *eg. Kiddugavu zigizigi.* (*'It is extremely dark.'*)

-zigula *vt* (-zigudde) **polish** (*metal*), **shine** (*eg. silver*)

-ziika *vt* (-ziise) **bury, inter.** *See* okuziika

-ziikula *vt* (-ziikudde) **dig up** (*something buried*) -ziikula omufu **exhume a dead body** (*as an act of theft or for infringement of a taboo*)

-ziimuula *vt* (-ziimudde) **roll one's eyes at** (*someone*) **in contempt**

-(y)aziina *See* -yaziina

-(y)aziirana *See* -yaziirana

ziizino here they are

ziiziri there they are

ziizo there they are

-zijjagala *vi* (-zijjagadde) **be huge, take up too much room**, *eg. Emigugu gizijjagadde mu kisenge.* (*'The bundles are taking up too much space in the room.'*), **be overgrown** (*of plants, a beard, etc.*) obudde -zijjagala **be threatening** (*of the weather*), *eg. Obudde buzijjagadde, enkuba eyagala kutonnya.* (*'The weather is threatening, it is going to rain.'*)

-zijjagavu *adj* **occupying too much space, overgrown** (*of plants*), *eg. Ekibera kizijjavavu.* (*'The forest is impassable.'* − *the tracks being overgrown*)

[1]-zika *vi* (-zise) **be(come) weedy/overgrown, run wild** (*of plants*)

[2]-(y)azika *See* -yazika

-zikira *vi* (-zikidde) **go out** (*of a fire or light*), **be extinguished**

NOTES FOR
z

-z. Unless the **z** is doubled, verbs starting **z** have 1st person singulars starting **nz**, *eg.* **nzina** ('I dance'), from **-zina**.

zi or **zi-** (*n10*). This word (or prefix) is used for the plurals (in *n10*) of certain nouns in *n9* (often of English origin), *eg.* **zi takisi** or alternatively **zitakisi** ('taxis'), from **takisi** *n9* ('taxi').

-zz. Verbs starting **-zz** have 1st person singulars starting **nziz**, *eg.* **nziza** ('I return), from **-zza**.

ezz. Nouns in *n9* starting **ezz** have plurals (in *n6*) starting **amaz**, *eg.* the plural of **ezziga** is **amaziga**.

NOUNS IN *n9*. Most nouns in *n9* have identically spelt plurals (in *n10*).

179

-zikirira *vi* (-zikiridde) **be completely destroyed, die out, perish**

-zikiriza *vt* (-zikirizza) **destroy, obliterate, annihilate**

-zikiza *vt* (-zikizza) **put out** (*fire/light*), **extinguish** -zikiza emmotoka **turn off a car engine** -zikiza ettaala **turn off a light** -zikiza omuliro **quench a fire** -zikiza omusubbaawa **blow out a candle**

[1]**-zimba** *vi* (-zimbye) **swell up, be swollen, bulge (out)**. *Pronunciation:* okuzîmbà. *See* -kukunala -zimba omutwe **become annoyed**

[2]**-zimba** *vt* (-zimbye) **build, construct.** *Pronunciation:* okuzímbá. *See* okuzimba

-zimbagala *vi* (-zimbagadde) **occupy too much space** (*of a person, items in a store, etc.*), *eg. Ensawo zaali zizimbagadde mu sitoowa.* ('*The sacks were taking up too much space in the store.*'), **be bulky, become annoyed** Ssekkokko azimbagadde. ('The turkey is annoyed.' – *indicating that it has ruffed up its feathers on seeing a rival*)

-zimbagalira *vi* (-zimbagalidde) **occupy too much space in, block**, *eg. Tozimbagalira mu mulyango. Viira abantu bayingire.* ('*Don't block the doorway. Let the people enter.*')

-zimbagatana *vi* (-zimbagatanye) **be bulky, become swollen** (*eg. of the face after being beaten up*), **puff up**

-zimbagavu *adj* **swollen, inflated**

[1]**-zimbira** *vt* (-zimbidde) **build for/at**, *etc.*, *eg. Taata we yamuzimbira ennyumba.* ('*His father built a house for him.*')

[2]**-eezimbira** *vt* **build for oneself** (*eg. a house*)

-zimbirira *vt* (-zimbiridde) **stay close to** (*a person against her/his will*), **be a burden to, encumber**

-zimbisa *vt* (-zimbisizza) **cause to build, build with**

-zimbulukuka *vi* (-zimbulukuse) **swell up, rise** (*of dough*), *eg. Omugaati guzimbulukuse.* ('*The dough has risen.*'), **expand, be magnified, be leavened**

-zimbulukusa *vt* (-zimbulukusizza) **(cause to) swell up, expand, magnify, leaven** -zimbulukusa ebigambo **exaggerate** ekyuma ekizimbulukusa **microscope**

-zimbulula *vt* (-zimbuludde) **demolish** (*a building or construction*), **dismantle**

-zimbya *vt* (-zimbizza) **cause to build, build with**

ezimu *det/pro* **some**

-zina *vi* (-zinye) **dance.** *See* okuzina -zina abalongo **perform birth rites for twins**

-zinda *vt* (-zinze) **invade, raid**

-zinduukiriza *vt* (-zinduukirizza) **come upon by surprise, make a surprise attack on, catch in the act, ambush**

-zinga *vt* (-zinze) **wind, fold (up), coil, roll up, wrap up.** *See* -funya -zinga ebendera **furl a flag** -zinga engoye okuziteeka mu ssanduuko **fold up clothes to put in a suitcase** -zinga omukeeka **roll up a mat** -zinga omulambo **wrap up a corpse**

-zingazinga *vt* (-zinzezinze) **wrap/fold badly**

-zingazinga ensonga **rubbish an argument**

-zingibwa *vi* (-zingiddwa) **be wrapped (up)**

[1]**-zingirira** *vt* (-zingiridde) **wrap/coil around**

[2]**-eezingirira** *vr* **wrap around oneself**

-zingiriza *vt* (-zingirizza) **confine, encircle, invest, besiege**

-zingiza *vt* (-zingizizza) **besiege**

-zingulukuka *vi* (-zingulukuse) **become unrolled, become unwound, become uncoiled**

-zingulula *vt* (-zinguludde) **unroll, unwind, uncoil**

zinnaayo *n10* **its companions**

zinnaazo *n10* **their companions**

zino *dem* **these**

zinsanze *See* ennaku

-zinyisa *vt* (-zinyisizza) **make dance**, *eg. Oluyimba lwatuzinyisizza.* ('*The tune made us dance.*') -zinyisa amaaso **roll one's eyes**

-ziŋŋama *vi* (-ziŋŋamye) **be stunted** (*of a child*), **fail to develop, not make progress** (*of a project*), *eg. Emirimu giziŋŋamye.* ('*The work is not progressing.*')

[1]**-zira** *adj* **brave, heroic**

[2]**-zira** *v* (-zize) (1) *vi* **be forbidden** (*on ritual grounds*), *eg. Okulya enseneene kizira.* ('*It is forbidden to eat grasshoppers.*' – *for a member of the Nseneene Clan*), **be taboo;** (2) *vt* **reject**, *eg. Yazira emmere gye baamuwa ku bugenyi.* ('*He rejected the food which they offered to him on his visit.*') -zira amabeere **reject feeding at the breast** (*of a child*)

ziri *dem* **those**

-zirika *vi* (-zirise) **lose consciousness, faint, pass out, go into a coma.** *See* okuzirika

-ziringitana *vi* (-ziringitanye) **have problems** (*in affairs*), **work ineffectively**

-zirira *vt* (-ziridde) **refuse to take** (*something offered*), *eg. Emmere yagizirira ku bugenyi.* ('*He refused the food offered to him during his visit.*')

-ziririra *vt* (-ziriridde) **refuse to take** (*in a deliberately insulting way*)

-zisa *vt* (-zisizza) **allow** (*land*) **to become overgrown**

-zito *adj* **heavy**

-zitoowerera *vt* (-zitooweredde) **be heavy for** (*of a load or problems*), **overburden, encumber**

-zitoowererwa *vi* (-zitoowereddwa) **be overburdened (by)**

-zitowa *vi* (-zitoye) **be heavy**

-zitoya *vt* (-zitoyezza) **make heavy**

-ziyira *vi* (-ziyidde) **be impeded in breathing, suffocate**

-ziyiza *vt* (-ziyizza) **prevent, deter, block** -ziyiza omusaayi **staunch flow of blood**

-ziza *vt* (-zizizza) **make taboo for oneself**

[1]**ezize** *pos* **hers, his**

[2]**-zize** *v. See* -ziga

[1]**-zizika** *vt* (-zizise) **place beneath to prevent movement, prop up** -zizika ekitooke **prop up a**

fruiting banana plant -zizika emmotoka n'ejjinja
put a stone to prevent movement of a car
-zizika ettaka put earth (*to prevent soil erosion*)
-zizika oluggi jam a door (*eg. in the open position*)
-zizika omutto place a pillow (*as support under
someone's head*)

²-eezizika *vit* prop oneself up (with), *eg. Njagala
omutto okwezizika. ('I want to have a pillow under
my head.')*

ezizo *pos* yours *si.*

¹ezo *dem* those

²zo *pos* your *si.*

³zo *pro* they, them. *Can be a suffix* -zo (*N10.3*), *eg.
nazo ('and them').*

-zoola *vi* (-zodde) have a fit of madness -zoola
amaaso roll one's eyes (*when mentally ill*)

-zunga *vi* (-zunze) be here and there, whirl about
(*as flies or bees*), swarm, stagger (about), *eg.
Atambula azunga. ('She is staggering.'),* reel
about

-zungirira *vi* (-zungiridde) swarm (*in the air, as
flies around meat*)

-zungu *adj* European, white person's

-zunza *vt* (-zunzizza) cause to move here and there
-zunza olugambo spread a rumour

-zuŋŋana *vi* (-zuŋŋanye) be here and there

-zuuka *vi* (-zuuse) be found, be discovered

-zuukira *vi* (-zuukidde) rise from the dead, be
resurrected

-zuukufu *adj* awakened

-zuukuka *vi* (-zuukuse) wake up (*of oneself*)

-zuukusa *vt* (-zuukusizza) wake up (*someone*)

-zuula *vt* (-zudde) find (*after searching*), locate

-zza *vt* (-zzizza, nziza) bring back, return
(*something*) -zza ebbali put aside -zza emabega
retrogress -zza emmeeme nauseate, *eg. Emmere
eno enzizizza emmeeme. ('This food nauseates
me.')* -zza obuggya/obupya) make like new,
revive, renovate, restore -zza obwenkulumu
chew the cud -zza omusango commit a crime

-zzaako (-zzizzaako) return (*onto*), *eg.
Essowaani gizzeeko ku mmeeza. ('Return the plate
to the table.'),* put back (*on*), have next (*a child
after an earlier one*), *eg. Yazzaako omuwala. ('She
had a girl next.')* -zzaako ku have another (*child*)
after, *eg. Yazzaako ku mulenzi. ('She had another
child after the boy.')* -zzaamu put back within,
return into -zzaamu amaanyi encourage
-zzaamu endasi give strength to -zzaawo return
(*to a place*), replace, restore -zzaayo return (*to
a place over there*), *eg. Yazzaayo ente mu kiraalo.
('He returned the cows to the pen.'),* take back,
send back

zzaala -kuba zzaala gamble

ezzaaliro *n5* (*pl.* amazaaliro) place for giving birth,
maternity home, maternity ward

ezzadde *n5* (*no pl.*) descendants, offspring,
progeny

-zze *See* -dda; -jja.

-zzeeko *See* -ddako; -jjako.

-zzeemu *See* -ddamu

zzeero *n9* zero

-zzeewo *See* -ddawo

-zzeeyo *See* -ddayo

ezziga *n5* (*pl.* amaziga) tear (*from the eye*)

ezzike *n5* (*pl.* amazike) chimpanzee

ezzirakumwa *n1* land of the dead. *Meaning:
'where people do not shave'.*

ezzooba *n5* (*pl.* amazooba) month, (*traditional
meaning*) lunar month. *From: 'izooba' (Lunyoro).*

-zzukuza *vi* (-zzukuzizza, nzizukuza) have a
grandchild

PART 3

ENGLISH-LUGANDA

References to notes (Part 4) are marked N1, N2, *etc*.

A,a

a *det* (an) *Not directly translated in Luganda.*

aardvark *n* nnamulimi *n1*

abandon *vt* -va ku, *eg. Gavumenti yavudde ku ntegeka. ('The government has abandoned the plan.'). See* desert; leave; reject; stop <u>become abandoned</u> -fuluka

abandoned *adj* -fulufu, *eg. ekiswa ekifulufu ('abandoned anthill')* <u>abandoned house</u> ekifulukwa *n7*

abate *vi* -kendeera, *eg. Obusungu bwe bukendedde. ('His anger has abated.'). See* calm

abattoir *n* lufula *n1. See* slaughtering place

abbreviate *vt* -funza

abdicate *vt* -lekulira, *eg. Yalekulira obuvunaanyizibwa bwe. ('He has abdicated his responsibilities.')* <u>abdicate the kingship</u> -va ku bwakabaka

abdomen *n* olubuto *n11* <u>abdominal pain</u> enjoka *n10. See* pain

abduct *vt* -twala olw'empaka

ability *n* obusobozi *n14*

able, be *aux v* -sobola, *eg. Ajja kusobola okujja enkya. ('She will be able to come tomorrow.'),* -yinza

abnormal *adj* si -a bulijjo, *eg. Kino kintu si kya bulijjo. ('This is something abnormal.')* <u>something very abnormal</u> ekikulejje *n7*

abode *n* amaka *n6*, awaka *n16* <u>person lacking fixed abode</u> empunzi *n9*

abolish *vt* -ggyawo, *eg. Gavumenti eggyeewo etteeka. ('The government has abolished the law.')*

abomination *n* ebikolobero *n8*

abort *v* (1) (*of an animal*) *vi* -sowola, *eg. Ente esowodde. ('The cow has aborted.')*; (2) (*give up on*) *vt* -salamu, *eg. Olugendo baalusazeemu nga bafunye akabenje. ('They aborted their journey after the accident.'). See* miscarry <u>have an abortion</u> -ggyamu olubuto, *eg. Aggyeemu olubuto. ('She has had an abortion.')*

¹**about** (*approximately*) *adv* nga, *eg. mayiro nga bbiri ('about two miles')*

²**about** (*of*) *pre* (1) ku (*or enclitic* -ko **N24.2**), *eg. Nkulowoozaako. ('I am thinking about you.')*; (2) (*relating to news*) *Use* -fa ku (*'happen'*) *in rel* (**N7.1**), *eg. amawulire agafa ku kyalo ('news about the village')*

about to, be *aux v* (1) *Use* -tera *in near future tense* (**N16**) *followed by inf* (**N19**), *eg. Nnaatera okugenda. ('I am about to go.')*; (2) (*more immediately*) *Use adv* kumpi (*'nearly'*), *eg. Ndi kumpi okugenda. ('I am about to go.')*

¹**above** *adv* waggulu

²**above** *pre* waggulu wa

abridge *vt* -funza

abroad *adv* ebweru w'eggwanga, emitala

w'amayanja. *See* outside <u>go abroad to work</u> -kolera ku muwanga, (*implying illegally*) -genda ku kyeyo

abruptly *adv* embagirawo

abscess *n* ekizimba ekirimu amasira *n7*, (*on finger or toe*) entunuka *n9. See* boil

absence *n* obutabaawo *n14* <u>be absent</u> *Use* -beerawo *or* -liwo (*'be present'*) *according to tense* (**N20.1**) *in neg* (**N21**), *eg. (1) Tajja kubeerawo mu kibiina enkya. ('He will be absent from class tomorrow.')*; (2) *Taliiwo. ('He is absent.'). See* away (be)

absent-minded *adj* -wugulavu <u>be absent-minded</u> -wugulala

absolutely *adv* ddala (*with prepositional verb* **N22**), *eg. Kibulidde ddala. ('It is absolutely lost.')*

absolve *vt* -sonyiwa, *eg. Omwawule yamusonyiwa ebibi bye. ('The priest absolved him of his sins.')*

absorb (*a fluid slowly*) *vi* -nnyuukirira, *eg. Omunnyo gunnyuukiridde. ('The salt has absorbed water.'). See* soaked (become)

abstain (from) *Use* -salawo (*'decide'*) *with neg* (**N21**), *eg. Yasalawo obutanywa mwenge. ('She decided to abstain from alcohol.')*

abundant *adj* -ngi, *eg. enkuba nnyingi ('abundant rain'). See* plentiful <u>become abundant</u> -yala, *eg. Lumonde kati ayaze mu katale. ('Potatoes have become abundant in the market.')*

¹**abuse** (*verbal*) *n* ekivumo *n7*

²**abuse** (*verbally*) *vt* -vuma, *eg. Yamuvuma. ('He was abusive towards her.')* <u>abuse one another</u> -vumagana

abyss *n* ennyanga *n9*

acacia (*tree*) *See* **N31** *for names of species.*

accede (to) *vt* -lya, *eg. Yalya obwakabaka. ('He acceded to the throne.')*

accelerate *vt* -yongeza omuliro/sipiidi

accelerator (*pedal*) *n* ekyomuliro *n7*

accent (*in speech*) *n* enjogera *n9*

accept *vt* -kkiriza

¹**access** *n. See* entrance; permission

²**access** (*obtain*) *vt* -funa

accident *n* akabenje *n12*

accommodate *vt* (1) (*put up for the night*) -suza, *eg. Oyinza okunsuza ekiro kino? ('Can you accommodate me tonight?')*; (2) (*fit in*) -gyamu, *eg. Ekisenge kino kigyamu abantu ataano. ('This room accommodates fifty people.'). See* patient with (be); take all

accompany (*escort*) *vt* -werekera. *See* company to (provide) <u>accompany a visitor</u> (*a short distance on the way*) -werekera omugenyi <u>accompanying person</u> emperekeze *n9*

accomplish (*achieve*) *vt* -tuukiriza

accomplished (*knowledgeable*) *adj* -manyirivu. *See* expert <u>accomplished person</u> omumanyirivu *n1*

according to *conj* okusinziira ku, *eg. Okusinziira*

ku mwami kyagamba, twandigenze kaakati.
('According to what the boss says, we should go
now.'), **okuva ku**

account n (1) financial) **akaawunta** n9; (2)
(explanation) **ennyinnyonnyola** n9 do the
accounts (financial) **-balirira essente** give an
account to (tell) **-buulira** on account of (because
of) **olwa**

accountant n **omubazi w'ebitabo** n1

accumulate v (1) vi **-wera**, eg. Essente ziweze.
('The money has accumulated.'), **-eeyongera
obungi**; (2) vt **-weza**, eg. Awezza ssente nnyingi.
('He has accumulated a lot of money.). See acquire;
gather; get

accurate adj **-tuufu**

accusation n **omusango** n3 make false accusations
-sibako ebigambo

accuse (hold responsible) vt **-vunaana**, eg.
Yamuvunaana obulimba. ('He accused him of
lying.'). See blame; charge; inform on accuse
falsely **-waayiriza** accuse repeatedly (of
something denied) **-lumiriza** accused person
omuwawaabirwa n1

accuser n **omuwaabi** n1 false accuser **omusazi
w'ebigambo** n1, **omuwaayirizi** n1. See slanderer

accustomed (to), be(come) vi **-manyiira**, eg.
Mmanyidde okuzuukuka nga obudde bugenze. ('I
am accustomed to getting up late.')

¹**ache** n **obulumi** n14 muscle ache **nnakanyama** n1

²**ache** vi **-luma** (the person concerned can be
indicated by an object pronoun), eg. Erinnyo
limuluma. ('Her tooth aches.')

achieve vt **-tuukiriza**. See complete; get

achievement n **obuwanguzi** n14

Achilles tendon n **oluteega** n11

acid n **asidi** n1

acidic (sour) adj **-kaatuufu** be(come) acidic
-kaatuuka

acknowledge vt **-kkiriza**, eg. Yakkiriza nti tamanyi
kuzannya bulungi. ('He acknowledged his
weakness at sports.'). See thank acknowledge
receipt Use **-buulira** ('inform'), eg. Yambuulira nti
yafunye ebbaluwa yange. ('He acknowledged
receipt of my letter.')

acknowledgements n **okwebaza** n15

acne n **embalabe** n10

acquaintance n **omumanyi** n1, **omumanyibwa** n1
be acquainted with (know) **-manya**, eg. Amumanyi.
('She is acquainted with him.') be(come)
acquainted with **-genda -manyiira**, eg. Agenda
amanyiira omulimu gwe omupya. ('He is becoming
acquainted with his new job.') be(come)
acquainted with one another **-manyigana**

acquire vt **-funa**

acquit vt **-singa omusango**, eg. Omulamuzi yasala
omusango Musoke n'agusinga. ('The judge
acquitted Musoke of the charge.') be acquitted (of
a charge) **-ejjeerera omusango**

acre n **yiika** n9

across pre (1) (in) **mu**, eg. Yateekawo ekiti mu
kakubo. ('He put a piece of wood across the
path.'); (2) (on the other side of) **emitala wa**, eg.
Abeera emitala w'omugga. ('He lives across the
river.') place (something) across **-kiika** place
oneself across **-eekiika**

¹**act** n (1) (deed) **ekikolwa** n7; (2) (law) **etteeka** n5
Acts of the Apostles **Ebikolwa by'Abatume**

²**act** (in a play) vi **-zannya mu muzaanyo** be acting
(in a position) **-kola nga**, eg. Akola ng'omukulu
w'essomero. ('He is the acting headmaster.')

action n **ekikolwa** n7

actor n **omuzannyi** n1, (emphasising male)
munnakatemba omusajja n1

actress n **munnakatemba omukazi** n1

actually adv **so nno**, eg. So nno twandisigadde
wano. ('Actually we should stay here.') but
actually **naye**, eg. Yagamba nti yazze jjo, naye
teyazze. ('He said he came yesterday, but actually
he didn't.'), **so nga** the actual **-nnyini** (**N11.6**), eg.
omwami ye yennyini ('the actual chief')

Adam's apple n **eddookooli** n5

add (two or more items together) vt **-gatta**, eg.
Omusomesa yabagamba okugatta bbiri ne ssatu.
('The teacher asked them to add two and three.')
add more **-yongera** (often with enclitic N24.2), eg.
(1) Ayongeddeko emicungwa ku mulengo. ('She has
added more oranges to the pile.'); (2)
Ayongeddemu amazzi mu sseffuliya. ('She has
added more water to the pan.') add to (1) (items)
-gattako, eg. Ebitabo bino gattako n'ebyo. ('Add
these books to those ones.') add onto **-waayirako**,
eg. Ku kitambaala ky'emmeeza waayirako ekiwero
kino. ('Add on this piece of material to the
tablecloth.'), **-kookerako**. See extend add roasted
sorghum to banana juice (in beer making) **-siwa
omuwemba** add together **-gatta wamu**, eg.
Yagatta wamu emirengo gy'emicungwa ebiri. ('She
added the two piles of oranges together.') add up
(eg. money needed for a task) **-balirira** add within
(insert) **-waayiramu** something added on
ekiwaayiro n7

adder, puff n **essalambwa** n5

addict, drug n **omuyaga** n1

addition (in maths) n **okugatta** n15

¹**address** n (1) (talk; speech) **okwogera** n15; (2)
(location) **endagiriro** n9

²**address** vt (1) (talk to) **-yogera**, eg. Omukulu
w'essomero yayogedde eri abazadde. ('The head of
the school addressed the parents.'); (2) (write
location) **-wandiika endagiriro**, eg. Owandiise
endagiriro ku bbaasa? ('Have you addressed the
envelope?')

adequate adj. Use **-mala** ('be enough'), eg.
Obuyigirize bwe bumala okukola omulimu guno.
('His qualifications are adequate for this job.')

adhere v (1) vi **-kwatira**, eg. Pulasita yakwatira ku

kisenge. ('The plaster adhered to the wall.'); (2) vt -lemera, eg. Yalemera ku nzikiriza ze mu bizibu byonna. ('She adhered to her beliefs through all the difficulties.')

adjective n nnakongezalinnya n1

adjoin (also be adjacent to) vi -liraana, eg. Ennyumba ye eriraanye eyaffe. ('His house is adjacent to ours.')

adjourn vt -yabula   be adjourned -yabuka

adjust vt -dda ku, eg. Adda ku mpale yange. ('She is adjusting my trousers.')   adjust one's behaviour (for the better) -eddako   be adjusted -ddako, eg. Eddinda lyetaaga okuddako. ('The hem needs adjusting.')

administrate (look after) vt labirira

admiral (chief of the Kabaka's navy) n **Gabunga** n1 title

admire (like) vt -yagala

admit (allow in) vt -yingiza, eg. Yannyingiza mu kisenge kye. ('He admitted me into his room.')   admit being wrong (eg. in an argument) -eemenya   admit guilt -kkiriza ekisobyo   admit to hospital (give a bed to) -wa ekitanda mu ddwaliro   admit to school (give a place to) -wa ekifo mu ssomero

admonish vt -nenya

adolescence n obuvubuka n14

adolescent n omuvubuka n1   be(come) an adolescent -vubuka

adopt (accept; agree) vt -kkiriza   adopt alien customs -wakula empisa

adore vt -yagala

adorn vt (1) (decorate, paint, etc.) -tona; (2) (embellish; ornament) -wunda

adorned adj -tone

adroit adj -jagujagu

[1]**adult** adj -kulu

[2]**adult** (person) n omukulu n1

adulterer n omwenzi n1

adultery n obwenzi n14   commit adultery -yenda

adulthood n obukulu n14

[1]**advance** (eg. of wages) n adivansi n9

[2]**advance** v (1) vi -eeyongera, eg. Yeeyongedde okusoma obulungi. ('She is advancing in her studies.'), -genda mu maaso, eg. Ebyenjigiriza bigenze mu maaso. ('Education has advanced.'); (2) (move forward) vt -yongerayo mu maaso, eg. Jenero eggye alyongeddeyo mu maaso. ('The general advanced the army.')   advance in position (eg. in work) -kulaakulana, eg. Akulaakulanye mu kkampuni. ('She is advancing in the company.')   advance oneself (through one's own efforts) -eetuusa

advantage n (1) (benefit) omugaso n3; (2) (over another person) enkizo n9   be advantageous that -lyoka followed by verb in narrative tense (N16), eg. Yalyoka n'ajja. ('It was advantageous that he came.')   take advantage of -yiikiriza, eg. Yayiikiriza Musoke. ('She took advantage of

Musoke.')   have an advantage (over another person; bully; exploit) -kira

advantageous (beneficial) adj -a omugaso

adverb n nnakongezakikolwa n1

adversary n (1) (enemy) omulabe n1: (2) (competitor) omuvuganyi n1

adversity (difficulties) n obuzibu n14

advertise vt -langa, -langirira

advertisement n ekirango n7, ekirangiriro n7

advice n amagezi n6

advise vt -wa amagezi, eg. Nnamuwa amagezi agende. ('I advised him to go.'), (on how to behave; counsel) -buulirira. See set straight

adviser n omuwi w'amagezi n1

advocate n omuwolereza n1. See lawyer; pleader   be an advocate for -wolereza

adze n eggya n5

aerial n mukonzikonzi n9, eriyo n9

aerodrome n ekisaawe ky'ennyonyi n7

aeroplane (also plane) n ennyonyi n9

aetheism n obukaafiiri n14

aetheist n omukaafiiri n1

afar   see from afar -lengera, eg. Yalengera ennyanja. ('He saw the lake from afar.')

affair n (1) (issue; matter) ensonga n9; (2) (secret sexual liaison) enkolagana y'ekyama n9   foreign affairs ensonga z'ebweru   have an affair (outside marriage) -baliga   internal affairs ensonga z'omunda   sort out affairs -gonjoola ensonga

affect vt -kwatako, eg. Kino kikukwatako ('This issue affects you.'), -kolako, eg. Okufa kw'omwana we kwamukolako. ('The death of his child affected him greatly.')

affection (liking) n okwagala n15

affirm vt -kakasa

affliction (suffering) n ekibonoobono n7. See illness

affluence n obugagga n14

affluent adj -gagga   be(come) affluent -gaggawala   make affluent -gaggawaza

afford (financially) vt -sobola okusasula   be affordable -gulika

afraid   be afraid (of) -tya

Africa n Afirika n9

African (person) n Omwafirika n1

[1]**after** conj (1) oluvannyuma lwa, eg. Oluvannyuma lw'okujja wano, yagenze eka. ('After coming here, he went home.'); (2) nga followed by -mala ('finish') and a verb in inf (N19), eg. Nga mmaze okugula ebintu, nja kugenda eka. ('After I have finished shopping, I will go home.'). See as soon as; when

[2]**after** pre. Use -yita ku ('go past'), eg. Oyita ku lutindo okutuuka ku nnyumba ye. ('His house is after the bridge.')

afterbirth n ekitanyi n7, omwana w'emabega n1

afternoon n eggulo n5, (hottest part of the day) ettuntu n5   Good afternoon. greeting Osiibye otyanno? (pl. Musiibye mutyanno?). (N28)   in the afternoon **olweggulo**   this afternoon **leero olw'eggulo**

afterwards *adv* **oluvannyuma**

again *adv* **nate**, *eg. Baagenze okumulaba nate? ('Did they go and see him again?')*   do again *(repeat)* **-ddamu**

against *pre* (1) *(with)* **ne/na**, *eg. Ab'e Kampala baazannya omupiira n'ab'e Masaka. ('Kampala played football against Masaka.')*; (2) *(onto)* **ku**, *eg. Yansindise ku kisenge. ('He pushed me against the wall.')*   be against *(disagree)* Use **-kkirizaganya** *('agree with one another')* in neg **(N21)**, *eg. Sikkirizaganya naawe. ('I am against your view.')*. *See* dispute; oppose

age *n* **obukulu** *n14*, *eg. Yenkana wa obukulu? ('What is his age?')*. *To give a person's age, refer to* **emyaka** *('years')* or **emyezi** *('months')*, *eg. Nnina emyaka ataano. ('My age is fifty.')*. *See* era   ages *(a long time)* Use **ebbanga eddene** *('a long time')* or **-lwawo** *('delay there')*, *eg.* (1) *Ebbanga ddene nga sibalaba. ('I have not seen them for ages.')*; (2) *Nduddewo okubalaba. ('I have not seen them for ages.')*   old age **obukadde** *n14*

aged *adj* **-kadde**

agenda *(things to discuss)* *n* **ebyokuteesaako** *n8*

agent *n* **agenti** *n1*

aggressive *adj* **-a olugono**. *See* fierce   aggressive person **ow'olugono** *n1*, *(and outspoken)* **nnalukalala** *n1*

aggressiveness *n* **olugono** *n11*. *See* ferocity

aggrevate *vt*. Use **-yongera** *('increase')*, *eg. Ebigambo bya Musoke byayongera mukyala we obusungu. ('Musoke's words aggrevated his wife's anger.')*

agile *adj* **-yangu**

agitate *vt* **-siikuula**, *eg. Kibuyaga yasiikuula ennyanja. ('The wind agitated the lake.')*. *See* anxious (make); incite to riot; stir up   become agitated **-siikuuka**, *eg. Amazzi gasiikuuse. ('The water has become agitated.')*. *See* worked up (become)   grow excited and agitated *(of a crowd; riotous)* **-eegugunga**. *See* riotous (be)

ago *adv*. Use **-yita** *('pass')* in rel **(N7.1)**, *eg. Nnamulaba ennaku ssatu eziyise. ('I saw her three days ago.')*   long ago **edda**   short time ago **eddako**

agony *n* **obulumi obungi** *n14*   be in agony **-lumwa ennyo**

agree *vi* **-kkiriza**, *eg. Bakkiriza ekyateesebwa okukola. ('They agreed on what to do.')*   agree on a work relationship **-patana**, *eg. Yapatana omulimu. ('She agreed to take on the job.')*   way of agreeing **enzikiriza** *n9*

agreement *n* **enzikirizaganya** *n9*, **endagaano** *n9*. *See* arrangement; understanding   come to an agreement (on) **-kkirizaganya**, *eg. Bakkirizaganyizza. ('They came to an agreement.')*, **-kkaanya**   fail to come to an agreement

-lemagana   make an agreement **-lagaana**, *eg. Twalagaana naye okunguza emmotoka. ('We agreed that he would sell the car to me.')*

agriculture *n* **ebyobulimi** *n8*

ahead *adv* **mu maaso**, *eg. Ali mu maaso. ('She is ahead.')*. *See* forward   ahead of **mu maaso ga**, *eg. Atambulira mu maaso ga ffe. ('She is walking ahead of us.')*   be ahead *(eg. in an election)* **-yitamu**

aid *n* **obuyambi** *n14*   first aid **obujjanjabi obusookerwako** *n14*

AIDS *n* **siriimu** *n1*, **mukenenya** *n1*

ail *(be sickly)* *vi* **-lwalalwala**. *See* ill (be)

ailment *(illness)* *n* **obulwadde** *n14*

[1]**aim** *(purpose)* *n* **ekigendererwa** *n7*

[2]**aim** *(have a purpose)* *vt* **genderera**, *eg. Agenderera kufuna digiri. ('She is aiming to get a degree.')*   aim at **-yolekeza**, *eg. Omuserikale yatwolekeza omudumu gw'emmundu. ('The soldier aimed a gun at us.')*   aim for *(head towards)* **-yolekera**, *eg. Yava mu dduuka n'ayolekera eka. ('She left the shop and aimed for home.')*. *See* aspire; strive   person who takes aim *(eg. with a gun)* **omuteebi** *n1*

aimlessly *adv* **muwawa**

air *n* (1) *(as evidenced by wind)* **empewo** *n9*; (2) *(for breathing)* **omukka** *n3*   in the air **mu bbanga**

aircraft *n* **ennyonyi** *n9*

airfield/airport *n* **ekisaawe ky'ennyonyi** *n7*

airtime *n* **eyatayimu** *n9*

aisle *n* **olukuubo** *n11*

[1]**alarm** *n*   alarm call **enduulu** *n9*   alarm clock **essaawa ey'ekide** *n9*   sound alarm call **-kuba enduulu**   sound alarm call against **-kubira enduulu**

[2]**alarm** *(make anxious)* *vt* **-eeraliikiriza**, *eg. Amawulire gatweraliikiriza. ('The news alarmed us.')*   be alarmed **-eeraliikirira**

albino *n* **nnamagoye** *n1*

alcohol *(drink)* *n* **omwenge** *n3*

alcoholic *(drunkard)* *n* **omutamiivu** *n1*

alert *vt* **-labula**, *eg. Yatulabula nti waliwo akabi. ('He alerted us to the peril.')*   be alerted **-labuka**   on high alert **ku bwerende**

alga *(slimy water weed)* *n* **enkonge** *n9*

alias, take an **-eepaatiika erinnya**

alien *adj* **-gwira**, *eg. empisa engwira ('alien customs')*

alight *(get out)* *vi* **-va** *(or* **-vaamu***)*, *eg. Yava mu bbaasi. ('She alighted from the bus.')*   be alight *(burn)* **-yaka**

align *vt* **-teeka mu lunyiriri**

alike   be/look alike **-faanagana**, *eg. Ennyumba ezo zifaanagana. ('Those houses look alike.')*   look alike to **-faanaganira**, *eg. Abalongo banfaanaganira. ('The twins look alike to me.')*   make look alike **-faanaganya**   think alike **-ssa ekimu**

alive *adj* **-lamu**   be alive **-li omulamu**, *eg. Akyali* mulamu. *('She is still alive.')*

all *det/pro* **-onna** **(N7.3)** *Takes pronominal concord* **(N4.2)**, *eg. (1)* ebintu byonna *('all things'); (2)* amata gonna *('all the milk').* all along **obwedda**, *eg.* Obwedda nnabadde ndowooza nti ajja. *('All along I was thinking he was coming.')* all of us **ffenna**, all of you **mwenna**, all of them **bonna**. **(N7.3)** All right. *(OK)* **Kale.** all together **lufaaya**

allege *(say)* *vt* **-gamba** be alleged **-gambibwa**, *eg.* Kigambibwa nti yali mufumbo. *('It is alleged that she was married.')*

allegiance, pledge **-wera**, *eg.* Baawera mu maaso ga kkwini. *('They pledged allegiance to the queen.')*

alleluia *interj* **aleruuya**

allergic reaction *(of the skin)* *n* **ebirogologo** *n8*

alleviate *vt* **-kkakkanya**. *See* reduce; soothe

alley *n* **ekikuubo** *n7*

alliance *n* **omukago** *n3*

allocate *vt* **-gabira**, *eg.* Baagabira abantu emmere mu bwenkanya. *('They allocated an equal amount of food to all.')* person who allocates **omugabi** *n1*, *(by measuring)* **omugeresi** *n1*

allocation *n* **omugabo** *n3*, **omutemwa** *n3*, *(measured amount)* **omugereko** *n3*

allot *vt* **-gabanya**

allow *vt (1) (agree; permit)* **-kkiriza**, *eg.* Yamukkiriza okuyingira. *('He allowed him to enter.'); (2) (make possible for)* **-ganya** *(verb often used in neg)*, *eg.* Omwana teyamuganya kukola mirimu. *('The child did not allow her to work.')*. *See* let allow in *(admit)* **-yingiza**, *(unintentionally)* **-yingiriza** be allowed **-kkirizibwa** go where not allowed **-saalimbira**, *eg.* Abasajja baasaalimbira mu nsi endala nga tebalina lukusa. *('The men entered the country without permission.')*

allowance for, make *vt* **-balirira**, *eg.* Omusomesa yamubalirira obuto bwe. *('The teacher made allowance for his youth.')*

allure *vt* **-sendasenda**

alluvium *(wet clay in valley)* *n* **ettosi** *n5*

ally *n* **ow'omukago** *n1*

almost *adv (1)* **kata** *(followed by subjunctive* **N17**), *eg.* Kata agwe. *('He almost fell.'); (2)* **kumpi**, *eg.* Ali kumpi okuweza emyaka ataano. *('She is almost fifty years old.'); (3)* Use **-tera** in near future tense **(N16)** *followed by inf* **(N19)**, *eg.* Emmere eneetera okuggya. *('The food is almost ready.')*

aloe *n* **ekigagi** *n7*

alone *adv* **-okka** **(N7.3)** *Takes pronominal concord* **(N4.2)**, *eg. (1)* Ente eri yokka mu ttale. *('The cow is alone in the pasture.'); (2) (of a person)* **obwomu**, *eg.* Ali bwomu. *('He is alone.')* live alone *(of a woman)* **-eeyombekera**

along *pre (1) (on)* **ku**, *eg.* Nnatambula ku kkubo. *('I walked along the path.'); (2) (at the side of)* **ku mabbali ga**, *eg.* Waliwo emiti ku mabbali g'omugga. *('There are trees along the river.')*

along with *(together with)* **awamu na/ne**, *eg.* Twala bino wamu n'ebyo. *('Take these along with those.')*

alongside *adv* **ku lusegere**, *eg.* Omwana amutambulira ku lusegere. *('The child is walking alongside her.')*. *See* beside; close

aloof, keep *vi* **-eesuula**, *eg.* Yeesuula ku bantu. *('He keeps aloof from people.')*

alphabet *n* **ennyukuta** *n10*, **walifu** *n9*

already *adv.* Use **-mala** *('end')* *followed by inf* **(N19)**, *eg.* Mmaze okulya. *('I have already eaten.')*

also *adv (1) (with noun)* **ne**, Njagala ne lumonde. *('I also like potatoes.'); (2) (with pronoun)* **na** *or* **na-** **(N10.1)**, *eg.* Nange njagala okujja. *('I also want to come.')* also me **nange**, also her/him **naawe**

altar *n* **woolutaali** *n1*

alter *vt* **-dda ku**, *eg.* Yadda ku mpale yange. *('She altered my trousers.')*. *See* change be altered **-ddako**, *eg.* Empale yeetaaga kuddako. *('The trousers need altering.')*

alteration *n* **enkyuka** *n9*

alternative *adj* **-lala**, *eg.* Wa olunaku olulala. *('Give an alternative date.')*

although *conj* **newankubadde**, **wadde**

altogether *(considering everything)* *adv* **okutwalira awamu**, *eg.* Okutwalira awamu yakola bulungi mu bibuuzo. *('Altogether she did well in the exams.')*

always *adv* **bulijjo**. *Sometimes expressed by adding the suffix* **-nga** **(N18)**, *eg.* Yagendanga okumulaba ku Bbalaza. *('He always went to see her on Mondays.')*.

am *See* be

amalgamate *vt* **-gatta awamu**

amass *vt* **-weza**, *eg.* Awezezza ettaka lingi. *('He has amassed a lot of land.')*

amaze *(also* astonish*)* *vt* **-eewuunyisa** be amazed *(at)* **-eewuunya**, *eg.* Omusomesa yeewuunya okusoma kw'omwana. *('The teacher was amazed by the child's good reading.')* make repeated expressions of amazement **-kungiriza** something amazing **ekyewuunyisa** *n7*

ambassador *n* **omubaka w'ensi** *n1*

ambatch tree *n* **omulindi** *n3*

ambulance *n* **ambyulensi** *n9*

ambush *vt* **-zinduukiriza** person who waits in ambush **omuteezi** *n1* wait in ambush *(for)* **-teega**

amen *interj* **amiina** *n9*

amend *vt* **-kyusaako**

America *n* **Amerika** *n9*

American *(person)* *n* **Omwamerika** *n1*

amniotic sac *n* **ensungwe** *n9*, **ensundwe** *n9*

among *pre (1) (within)* **mu**, *eg.* Yeekwese mu miti. *('She is hiding among the trees.'); (2) (of)* **ku**, *eg.* Ani ku mmwe ayagala okukola? *('Who among you wants to work?')*

[1]**amount** *(quantity)* *n* **obungi** *n14*. *For questions use* **-yenkana wa** *('be equal to what?')*, *eg.* Oyagala sukaali yenkana wa? *('What amount of sugar do*

you want?')

²**amount (to)** *vi* -**wera**, *eg. Essente ziwera mmeka?*
('What does the money amount to?')

amulet *(worn around upper arm)* *n* **ensiriba** *n9*
(gives good luck or protection)

amputate *vt* -**salako**

amuse *vt* -**sanyusa**

amusement *n* **ekisanyusa** *n7*

an *See* **a**

anaemic *adj. Refer to* **omusaayi** *('blood')* with neg
(**N21**), *eg. Talina musaayi. ('She is anaemic.')*

analysis *n. Use* -**laba** *('see')*, *eg. Okiraba otya?*
('What is your analysis?')

ancestor *n* **jjajja** *n1*   ancestors **ab'edda** *n2*
ancestral home *(clan land)* **obutaka** *n14*

¹**anchor** *n* **ennanga** *n9*

²**anchor** *vi* -**suula ennanga**

ancient *adj* -**a edda**, *eg. ebbanga ery'edda ('ancient*
times')

and *conj* (1) *(with noun)* **ne**, *eg. Ndaba Musoke ne*
Mukasa. ('I see Musoke and Mukasa.'); (2) *(with*
pronoun) **na-** (**N10.1**), *eg. nakyo ('and it', eg.*
referring to 'ekitabo' 'book').   and also **era ne**   and
I **nange**, and you *si.* **naawe**, and her/him **naye**   and
not **so si**   and so **ate**

anew *adv* **obupya**

angel *n* **malayika** *n1*   angel's trumpet *(type of plant)*
amaduudu *n6*

¹**anger** *n* **obusungu**

²**anger** *vt* -**sunguwaza**

angle *n* **ensonda** *n9*   at an angle **obukiika**, *eg.*
Emmeeza baagiteekawo bukiika mu kisenge. ('They
placed the table at an angle in the room.')   be at an
angle *(tilted)* -**eesulika**, *eg. Emmotoka yeesulise.*
('The car is at an angle.'), -**eewunzika**   put at an
angle *(tilt)* -**sulika**, -**wunzika**, *eg. Yawunzika*
ekikopo kya caayi n'ayiika. ('He held the cup at an
angle and the tea spilt.')

angler *(type of fisherman)* *n* **omulobi** *n1*

angry *adj* -**sunguwavu**   be(come) angry
-**sunguwala**, *eg. Nsunguwadde. ('I am angry.')*
be(come) angry with -**sunguwalira**, *eg.*
Mbasunguwalidde. ('I am angry with them.'). See
enraged (become)

anguish *n* **ennaku nnyingi** *n10*   be in anguish
(broken-hearted) -**nyolwa mu mutima**

animal *n* **ensolo** *n9*   animal husbandry **obulunzi** *n14*

animosity *n* **obukyayi** *n14*

ankle *n* **akakongovvule** *n12*

Ankole *n* **Ankole** *n9*   language of Ankole
Olunyankole *n11*   person of Ankole
Omunyankole *n1*

¹**annex** *(of document)* *n* **akawaayiro** *n12*

²**annex** *vt* (1) *(take)* -**twala**, *eg. Omulabe atutte ensi*
yaffe. ('The enemy has annexed our country.'); (2)
(add on) -**gatta ku**, *eg. Lipoota yagigatta ku*
kiwandiiko. ('He annexed the report to the
document.')

annihilate *vt* -**zikiriza**, -**malawo**

annoint *vt* -**siiga**

announce *vt* -**langa**, *eg. Yalanga olunaku*
lw'olukuŋŋaana. ('He announced the date of the
meeting.'), -**langirira**. *See* introduce   announce a
death to -**bikira**   announce openly *(something that*
should be private) -**yasanguza ebigambo**
announce the death of -**bika**, *eg. Yabika mukyala*
we. ('He has announced the death of his wife.')

announcement *n* **ekirango** *n7*, **ekirangiriro** *n7*

announcer *n* **omulanzi** *n1. See* presenter

annoy *vt* -**nyiiza**, *eg. Kye yagamba kyannyiizizza.*
('What he said annoyed me.'). See upset   be(come)
annoyed -**nyiiga**, *eg. Nnyiize. ('I am annoyed.')*
be(come) annoyed with -**nyiigira**, *eg.*
Mmunyiigidde. ('I am annoyed with her.')   deeds
done deliberately to annoy **ebyambyone** *n8*

annoyance *n* **obunyiivu** *n14*   something that
annoys **ekinyiiza** *n7*

annoyed *adj* -**nyiivu**

annual *adj* -**a buli mwaka**

annually *adv* **buli mwaka**

annul the marriage (of) *vt* -**gattulula mu**
bufumbo, *eg. Ppaapa yabagattulula mu bufumbo.*
('The pope has annulled their marriage.')

another *adj* -**lala**   another day **olulala**   in another
way **obulala**

¹**answer** *n* **okuddamu** *n15*

²**answer** *vt* -**ddamu**, *eg. Yanziramu. ('She answered*
me.'). See respond   be answered -**ddibwamu**, *eg.*
Ebbaluwa yaddibwamu. ('The letter was
answered.')

ant *n* *(general term for insect)* **ekiwuka** *n7*, *(safari*
ant) **ensanafu** *n9*, *(large stinging type, forms*
columns) **kaasa** *n1*, *(large black type, drop-tail*
ant) **ekinyomo** *n7*, *(large, sugar-loving)*
ekikennembi *n7*, *(very small)* **munyeera** *n1*,
(small black stinging type) **ensolosozi** *n9. See*
termite   ant bear *(aardvark)* **nnamulimi** *n1*   ant
hill **ekiswa** *n7. See* termite mound

antagonise *(annoy)* *vt* -**nyiiza**

antelope *n* **akagabi** *n12. See individual types, eg.*
bushbuck; duiker; kob

anthem, national *n* **oluyimba lw'eggwanga** *n11*

antibiotic *n* **eddagala eritta obuwuka** *n5*

anticipate *vt* -**suubira**

anticipation *n* **essuubi** *n5*   in a state of anticipation
(on tenterhooks) **ku bunkenke**

antidote to, give an *(also* be an antidote to*)* *vt*
-**vumula**, *eg. Omusota gwamubozze ne*
bamuvumula. ('The snake bit him and they gave
him an antidote.')

antiseptic *n* **eddagala eritta obuwuka** *n5*

anxiety *n* **obweraliikirivu** *n14. See* regret

anxious *adj* -**eeraliikirivu**   be anxious about
-**eeraliikirira**, *eg. Yeeraliikirira ebibuuzo. ('He*
was anxious about the exam.')   make anxious
-**eeraliikiriza**, *eg. Obulwadde bwe*

bwatweeraliikiriza. ('Her illness made us anxious.')

any *det/pro* **-onna** (**N7.3**). *Takes pronominal concord* (**N4.2**), *eg. Londako kyonna ky'oyagala. ('Choose any you like.').*

anybody/anyone *pro* **omuntu yenna**

anyhow *adv. Use* **-mala** (*'finish'*) *as aux v, followed by main verb with subject prefix* **ga-** (**N6**), *eg. Yamaze gasuulasuula engoye ye. ('He threw down his clothes anyhow.')*

anything *pro* **kyonna**

anyway *adv* **naye** *followed by narrative tense* (**N16**), *eg. Yaŋŋambye obutagenda naye ne ŋŋenda. ('He told me not to go, but I went anyway.')*

apart *See* come apart; stand apart; take apart apart from (*except*) **okuggyako**, *eg. Twala ente zonna okuggyako zino. ('Take all the cows apart from these.')*

apartment (*small unit in block*) *n* **omuzigo** *n3. See* flat; house

apathy *n* **obutafaayo** *n14*

aperture *n* **ekituli** *n7*

apologise *vi* **-eetonda**, *eg. Nneetonze. ('I have apologised.')* apologise to **-eetondera**, *eg. Nnamwetondera. ('I have apologised to her.')*

apostle *n* **omutume** *n1*

appal *vt* **-nyiiza nnyo**, *eg. Empisa zaabwe zaatunyiiza nnyo. ('Their behaviour appalled us.')*

apparent be apparent **-labika**, *eg. Ekintu ekituufu kirabika. ('The truth is apparent.'). See* obvious be apparent to **-laba**, *eg. Ekintu ekituufu nkiraba. ('The truth is apparent to me.')*

apparently (*indicating uncertainty*) *adv* **mbu**, *eg. Mbu yagenda Kampala. ('Apparently he went to Kampala.')*

apparition *n* **omuzimu** *n3*

[1]**appeal** (*in court case*) *n* **okujulira** *n15. See* request

[2]**appeal** (*in a court case*) *vi* **-julira**, *eg. Yajulidde mu kkooti enkulu. ('He appealed to the higher court.'). See* ask appeal for help **-wanjaga** appeal for help to **-wanjagira**, *eg. Twawanjagira Musoke. ('We appealed to Musoke for help.'),* **-kubira omulanga** appeal for help on one's own behalf **-eekubira omulanga**, *eg. Yeekubira omulanga abantu bamuyambe okuddaabiriza ennyumba ye. ('He appealed to the people to help repair his house.')*

appear *vi* **-labika**, *eg. Yalabikako mu kkanisa Ssabbiiti eyise. ('He appeared at church last Sunday.'),* (*of the new moon*) **-boneka**. *See* seem appear before **-labikira**, *eg. Yesu yalabikira abayigirizwa be. ('Jesus appeared before his disciples.')*

appearance *n* **endabika** *n9*

appease *vt* **-nyiigulula**, *eg. Yamunyiigulula. ('She appeased his anger.'). See* calm; soothe be(come) appeased (*after a burst of anger*) **-nyiigulukuka**

appendix *n* (1) (*supplement*) **ekiwaayiro** *n7*; (2) (*of the intestines*) **akalikonda k'ekyenda** *n12*

appetite have an endless appetite **-wuukuuka** person with an endless appetite **omuwuukuufu** *n1*

applaud (*with clapping*) *vt* **-kubira engalo**, *eg. Abantu baamukubira engalo. ('The audience applauded her.'). See* appreciate; cheer; praise

apple *n* **apo** *n9*

applicant *n. Use* **-saba** (*'ask for'*) *in rel* (**N7.1**), *eg. Abasaba emirimu baabano. ('The applicants for the jobs are here.')*

application (*request*) *n* **okusaba** *n15. See* diligence

apply (*paint, etc.*) *vt* **-siiga**, *eg. Yasiiga omuzigo ku mubiri gw'omwana. ('She applied cream to the child's body.')* apply for **-saba**, *eg. Nja kusaba omulimu. ('I shall apply for the job.')* apply on oneself (*eg. cream*) **-eesiiga** apply one's mind **-ssaako** (*or* **-teekako**) **omwoyo**, *eg. Yassaako omwoyo ku mulimu. ('She applied her mind to the job.')* apply oneself (*try hard*) **-fuba**, *eg. Yafuba mu kusoma. ('She applied herself to her studies.'). See* persevere

appoint (*to an official position*) *vt* **-tongoza**, *eg. Omulabirizi yamutongoza mu kifo. ('The bishop appointed her to the position.'). See* designate appointed person (*official*) **omutongole** *n1*

appointment (*to meet*) *n* **ensisinkano** *n9*

apportion *vt* **-gabanya**

appreciate *vt* **-siima**, *eg. Nsiima emmere gy'ofumba. ('I appreciate your cooking.'). See* pleased (be); understand

appreciation (*gratitude*) *n* **okusiima** *n15*

apprehend (*arrest*) *vt* **-kwata**. *See* round up

April *n* **Omwezi ogwokuna** *n3*, **Kafuumuulampawu, Apuli**

approach (*come closer*) *v* (1) *vi* **-sembera**, *eg. Kibuyaga asembedde. ('The storm is approaching.')*; (2) *vt* **-semberera**, *eg. Atusemberedde. ('She is approaching us.')*

[1]**appropriate** (*suitable*) *adj* **-tuufu**, *eg. Kino kiseera kituufu. ('This is an appropriate moment.')* be appropriate **-saana**, *eg. Yakoze ekintu ekitasaana. ('She did something that was not appropriate.'),* **-gwana** be appropriate for **-saanira**, *eg. Olugoye olwo lusaanira omukolo. ('That dress is appropriate for the occasion.'),* **-gwanira**

[2]**appropriate** (*seize goods*) *vt* **-bowa**

approve *vt* **-kkiriza**, *eg. Nzikiriza ky'asazeewo. ('I approve of his decision.')*

approximately *adv* **nga**

apron *n* **ekikubiro** *n7*

Arab *n* **Omuwalabu** *n1*

Arabic (*language*) *n* **Oluwalabu** *n11*

arbitrate *vt* **-lamula**

arbitration *n* **ennamula** *n9*

arbitrator *n* **omulamuzi** *n1*

arch *n* **ekiyitirirwa** *n7*

archbishop *n* **ssaabalabirizi** *n1*, (*RC*) **ssaabasumba** *n1*

archer *n* **omulasi (w'obusaale)** *n1*

architect *n* **omukubi wa pulaani** *n1*

architecture *n* **engeri y'okuzimba** *n9*

are *See* be

area (*of definite size, eg. house plot or football field*) *n* **ekibangirizi** *n7*. *See* building site; land; part; place. *For questions, use* **-yenkana wa?** (*'be equal where?'*), *eg. Ekibanja kyo kyenkana wa? ('What is the area of your plot?').*

argue *vi* **-kaayana**, *eg. Yali akaayana ne muliraanwa we. ('He was arguing with his neighbour.')* argue a case in court **-woza omusango** argue about (*dispute over*) **-kaayanira**, *eg. Tukaayanira olusalosalo. ('We are arguing about the boundary.')* argue with **-wakanya**, *eg. Nnabadde mmuwakanya. ('I was arguing with him.')*

argument *n* (1) (*controversy*) **enkaayana** *n9*; (2) (*reason*) **ensonga** *n9*. *See* dispute argumentative *adj* **-a empaka**. *See* stubborn argumentative person **omuwakanyi** *n1*, **ow'empaka** *n1*

arid *adj* **-kalu**

arise *vi* (1) (*get up, eg. from bed*) **-golokoka**; (2) (*of matters*) **-tuukawo**, *eg. Bino ebintu bipya ebituuseewo. ('These are new matters that have arisen.')*; (3) (*of a river*) **-sibuka**. *See* stand up

arithmetic *n* **okubala** *n15*

arm (*of a person*) *n* **omukono** *n3* arms (*or* armaments; *weapons*) **ebyokulwanyisa** *n8*

armoured personnel carrier *n* **mmamba** *n9*

armpit *n* **enkwawa** *n9*

army *n* **eggye** *n5*

aroma (*pleasant smell*) *n* **akawoowo** *n12*

around, go *vi* (1) (*encircle*) **-eetooloola**, *eg. Oluguudo lwetooloola olubiri. ('The road goes around the palace.')*; (2) (*all get some*) **-buna**, *eg. Emmere yabuna. ('The food went around.')*. *See* detour (make a); encircle; pass by; tour

arrange *vt* **-tegeka**, *eg. Ategeka olukuŋŋaana. ('He is arranging a meeting.')*, **-teekateeka** arrange for **-tegekera**, *eg. Abagenyi abategekera entebe. ('She is arranging the chairs for the guests.')*, (*find a person for*) **-labira**, *eg. Yandabira omubazzi. ('She arranged a carpenter for me.')* arrange in groups for sale **-lenga** arrange in order **-sengeka**, *eg. Ebitabo yabisengese mu buwanvu bwabyo. ('She arranged the books in order of their height.')* be arranged **-tegekebwa**

arrangement (*preparation*) *n* **entegeka** *n9*, **enteekateeka** *n9*. *See* appointment make an arrangement **-lagaana**, *eg. Nnalagaana ne Musoke okugenda na ye e Kampala. ('I made an arrangement with Musoke to go to Kampala with him.')* make an arrangement with **-lagaanya**

arranger *n* **omutegesi** *n1*

arrears in arrears **emabega**, *eg. Ali mabega mu kusasula ssente. ('He is in arrears with his payments.')*

arrest *vt* **-kwata**, (*on behalf of the Kabaka*) **-bowa**

be arrested **-kwatibwa** put under house arrest **-sibira mu nnyumba** someone arrested **omukwate** *n1*

arrival *n* **okutuuka** *n15* on arrival (*as soon as*) **olutuuka wano**, *eg. Olutuuka ku kyalo, genda olabe omwami. ('On arrival at the village, go and see the chief.')*. *See* as soon as

arrive (at) *vi* **-tuuka**, *eg. Tujja kutuuka e Masaka ku ssaawa kkumi. ('We will arrive at Masaka at 4 o'clock.')*, (*of a means of transport*) **-goba**, *eg. Ebbaasi egobye. ('The bus has arrived.')*. *See* come arrive at (*a place after a passage*) **-gguka**, *eg. Bwe twamala okuyita mu kibira ne tugguka ku ssomero. ('We arrived at the school after passing through the forest.')* arrive on time (*be punctual*) **-kwata obudde**, **-kwata essaawa** arrive unannounced **-gwa bugwi** cause to arrive **-tuusa**

arrogance *n* **obwewulize** *n15*. *See* pomposity

arrogant *adj* **-eewulize** arrogant person **omwewulize** *n1* be arrogant **-eewulira**

arrow *n* **akasaale** *n12*

arson *n* **obwokerezi** *n14* commit arson **-yokerera**. *The victim can be indicated by an object pronoun, eg. Banjokeredde. ('They have burnt down my house.').*

arsonist *n* **omwokerezi** *n1*

artery (*blood vesel*) *n* **omusuwa** *n3*

artful (*shrewd*) *adj* **-kalabakalaba**

artfulness *n* **obukalabakalaba** *n14*

article (*something written*) *n* **ekiwandiiko** *n7*

artillery piece *n* **omuzinga** *n3*

artisan *n* **omufundi** *n1*, **ffundi** *n1*

artist (*painter*) *n* **omusiizi w'ebifaananyi** *n1*

as *conj* (1) (*since*) **nga bwe** (**N27**), *eg. Enkuba nga bw'etonnya, sijja kugenda Kampala. ('As it is raining, I will not go to Kampala.')*; (2) (*like*) **nga** (**N26**), *eg. Ndi muwanvu nga ye. ('I am as tall as she.')* as far as **okutuuka ku**, *eg. Genda okutuuka ku ssomero. ('Go as far as the school.')*, (*with place names*) **okutuuka e**, *eg. Genda okutuuka e Masaka. ('Go as far as Masaka.')* as soon as (1) *Use tense prefix* **-aka-** (**N18**), *eg. Yagenda nga nze nnakatuuka. ('She left as soon as I arrived.')*; (2) *Use subject prefix* **lu-** *in rel* (**N7.2**), *eg. Olumala okukola, genda eka. ('As soon as you finish work, go home.')* as though **newankubadde**, **wadde** as well (1) (*with noun*) **ne**, *eg. Ne Musoke mutwale. ('Take Musoke as well.')*; (2) (*with pronoun*) **na-** (**N10.1**), *eg. Musoke naye mutwale. ('Take Musoke as well.')*

ascend (*climb*) *vt* **-linnya**, *eg. Twalinnya olusozi. ('We ascended the hill.')*. *See* uphill (go)

ashamed feel ashamed **-swala**, *eg. Nnaswadde. ('I feel ashamed.')*, **-sonyiwala**, **-wulira ensonyi** feel ashamed before **-swalira**, *eg. Nnamuswalira. ('I felt ashamed before her.')* make ashamed **-swaza**, *eg. Nnamuswazizza ('I made him feel ashamed.')*. *See* disgrace; shame

ash(es) *n* evvu *n5*   place for depositing ashes
ekittavvu *n7*   put under hot ashes -**vumbika**

ashore *adv* ku lukalu

aside *adv* ebbali, *eg. Yayimirira ebbali. ('He stood
aside.'),* **wabbali**   put aside *(store)* -**tereka**

ask *vt* (1) *(request)* -**saba**, *eg. Yansaba okujja. ('He
asked me to come.');* (2) *(question)* -**buuza**, *eg.
Yabuuza omuwendo gw'amenvu. ('She asked the
price of the bananas.')*   ask around *(for
information)* -**buuliriza**, *eg. Abaserikale bazze nga
babuuliriza ekibaddewo. ('The police came asking
around for what had happened.')*   ask for
repayment of debt -**banja**   ask oneself -**eebuuza**
ask the price of -**lamuza**   ask to enter *(house or
room, by calling 'kkoodi')* -**kuba kkoodi**   person
who asks *(requests)* **omusabi** *n1*. *See* questioner

askew, be *vi* -**eekubiira**, -**eewunzikira**, *eg.
Yabadde tasobola kuvuga ggaali ng'ensawo ya
kasooli yeewunzikidde ku ludda lumu. ('He could
not ride his bike properly while the sack of maize
was askew.')*

asleep, be/fall *vi* -**eebaka**   pretend to be asleep *(by
snoring)* -**eefuluusa**   tendency to fall asleep
akasumagizi *n12*

asparagus *(wild)* *n* kadaali *n1*

aspire *vi* -**luubirira**, *eg. Aluubirira kufuuka
musawo. ('He aspires to be a doctor.')*

ass *(animal)* *n* endogoyi *n9*

assail *vt* -**lumba**

assailant *n* omulumbaganyi *n1*, omulumbi *n1*

assassin *n* omutemu *n1*

assassinate *vt* -**temula**

assassination *n* ettemu *n5*

assault *(attack)* *vt* -**lumba**

assemble *v* (1) *vi* -**kuŋŋaana**, *eg. Abantu
baakuŋŋaana. ('The people assembled.');* (2) *vt*
-**kuŋŋaanya**, *eg. Baakuŋŋaanya abantu. ('They
assembled the people.')*. *See* collect; gather; join
assemble a food parcel -**siba emmere**   assemble in
great numbers *(of people)* -**eekuluumulula**, *eg.
Abantu beekuluumuludde okulaba omupiira. ('The
people assembled in great numbers to watch the
football game.')*

assembly *n* (1) *(gathering)* olukuŋŋaana *n11*; (2)
(council) olukiiko *n11*

assent *vi* -**kkiriza**

assertions *(unfounded)* *n* ebya njwanjwa *n8*

assess *vt* -**geraaganya**

assessment *n* engereka *n9*

assessor *n* omugeresi *n1*   tax assessor omugeresi
w'omusolo

assign *(give)* *vt* -**wa**, *eg. Yatuwa omulimu gwaffe.
('She assigned us our work.')*. *See* designate

assignment *n* (1) *(work)* omulimu *n3*; (2) *(chore)*
ekkatala *n5*

assist *(help)* *vt* -**yamba**, -**beera**. *See* facilitate;
vouch for   assist *(someone)* in court -**teekerawo
akabega**   assist to board *(a vehicle)* *(or* assist to

lift) -**linnyisa**

assistance *n* obuyambi *n14*, omubeezi *n1*. *See*
help

[1]**assistant** *adj. Use* -**ddirira** *('come next')* in rel
(N7.1), *eg. addirira omukulu w'essomero
('assistant school head')*

[2]**assistant** *n* (1) *(helper)* omuyambi *n1*, omubeezi
n1; (2) *(deputy)* omusigire *n1*

association *(society)* *n* ekibiina *n7*

assortment *n* (1) *(organised mixture)* ekintabuli
n7; (2) *(disorganised collection of things)*
twalatugende *n1*   assorted things *(large number
of; miscellany)* kalonda *n1*, *eg. Mu kisero mulimu
kalonda w'ebintu. ('In the basket were a large
number of assorted items.'),* omuyoolerero *n3*. *See*
mixture

assuage *vt* -**kkakkanya**, *eg. Yakkakkanya okutya
kwange. ('She assuaged my fear.')*

assume *(think)* *vi* -**lowooza**   assume an office -**lya**,
*eg. Yalya obwami. ('He assumed the
chieftainship.')*

assumption *(supposition)* *n* endowooza *n9*

assurance *n* akakalu *n12*, omusingo *n3*

assure *vt* -**kakasa**   be assured -**kakasibwa**

astern *adv* emabega

asthma *n* olufuba *n11*

astonish *vt* -**eewuunyisa**. *See* amaze   be astonished
(at) -**eewuunya**

astray   go astray *(physically or morally)* -**waba**
lead astray -**wabya**. *See* seduce

astute *adj* -**gezigezi**

asylum *n* (1) *(refuge)* obubudamo *n14*; (2) *(for the
insane)* ennyumba y'abalalu *n9*. *See* refuge
asylum seeker omunoonyi w'obubudamo *n1*   ask
for asylum -**saba obubudamo**   grant asylum -**wa
obubudamo**   seek asylum -**noonya obubudamo**

at *pre* (1) *(referring to place or time)* ku, *eg. Nja
kubeera ku ofiisi ku ssaawa emu. ('I will be at the
office at 7 o'clock.');* (2) *(in)* mu, *eg. Akola mu
ssomero. ('She works at the school.');* (3) *(before
name of place)* e, *eg. Yalaba maama we e Mmengo.
('He saw his mother at Mengo.');* (4) *(on certain
nouns and pronouns)* e-, *eg. ewange ('at my
home');* (5) *Use prepositional verb* **(N22)***, eg.
Akolera Mengo ('She works at Mengo.')*   at last
(eventually) *Use* -**mala** *followed by verb in
narrative tense* **(N16)***, eg. Nnamala ne nfuna
omulimu. ('At last I got a job.')*   at once
(immediately) **kaakati**

ate *See* eat

athlete's foot *n* obugeregere *n14*

athletics *n* emizannyo *n4*

atrocities *n* ebikolobero *n8*

atrophied, become *vi* -**konziba**, -**koozimba**. *See*
stunted (be)

attach *vt* -**kwasaako**. *See* tie on   attach oneself
-**eesiba**, *eg. Yeesiba ku kibiina. ('She attached
herself to the society.')*. *See* cling   attach oneself

uninivited **-eepaatiika ku**, **-eebereka**

attack *vt* **-lumba**   attack one another **-lumbagana**   be attacked **-lumbwa**

attacker *n* **omulumbaganyi** *n1*, **omulumbi** *n1*

attain (*accomplish*) *vt* **-tuukiriza**. *See* conquer; get

attempt *vt* **-gezaako**

attend *vi* **-beera** (*often used with enclitic* N24.2), *eg. Yabeerayo mu lukuŋŋaana.* ('*She attended the meeting.*')   attend a meeting (*or* council) **-kiika**   attend church **-soma mu kkanisa**   attend court (*pay a formal call on the Kabaka*) **-lanya**   attend on (1) (*serve*) **-weereza**; (2) (*look after*) **-labirira**   attend school **-soma mu ssomero**   attend to **-kolako**, *eg. Abasawo bamaze okunkolako.* ('*The doctors have attended to me.*')

attendant *n* **omuweereza** *n1*. *See* waiter

attention   draw the attention of **-baguliza**. *eg. Yatubagulizaako ku kizibu.* ('*She drew our attention to the problem.*')   give special attention to (*eg. a child or loved one*) **-wembejja**   pay attention (1) (*through care*) **-faayo ku**, *eg. Afaayo ku mulimu gwe nkola.* ('*He pays attention to what I do.*'); (2) (*put one's mind on*) **-teekayo** (*or* **-ssaayo**) **omwoyo**, *eg. Ateekayo omwoyo ku bintu bye mmusomesa.* ('*He pays attention to the things I teach him.*')   pay attention carefully to **-tegereza**, *eg. Tegereza ebintu by'agamba.* ('*Pay attention to what he is saying.*'). *See* unconcerned (be)   pay no attention **-latta**   stand at attention **-yimirira busimbalaala**

attire (*clothes*) *n* **ebyambalo** *n8*

attitude *n* **endowooza** *n9*. *See* behaviour

attorney *See* lawyer

attractive (*beautiful*) *adj* **-lungi**. *See* smart   look attractive **-labika obulungi**. *See* good (look); pleasing (be); well-dressed (be)   make oneself look attractive **-eerungiya**

attribute *vt*. Use **-gamba** ('*say*') with **kye-...-va** ('*come as a result of*' N10.2), *eg. Yagamba nti ebinjanjaalo bye okubala obulungi kyava ku kubisimba mangu.* ('*She attributed her good crop of beans to planting early.*')   attribute falsely **-paatiikako**, *eg. Yampaatiikako ebigambo.* ('*He attributed words to me that I did not say.*')

aubergine *n* **bbiriŋŋanya** *n1*

audacious *adj* **-zira**

audible, be *vi* **-wulikika**

audience (*listeners*) *n* **abawuliriza** *n2*   audience hall of the Kabaka **Masengere**

auditor *n* **omukebezi w'ebitabo** *n1*

augment *vt* **-yongeza**

August *n* **Omwezi ogw'omunaana** *n3*, **Muwakanya**, **Agusito**

aunt *n* (1) (*paternal*) **ssenga** *n1* (*with pos* N12), *eg. ssenga wo* ('*your aunt*'); (2) (*maternal*) **maama omuto** *n1*, *eg. maama wo omuto* ('*your aunt*')   my aunt (*paternal*) **sseŋŋange**, your aunt **ssengaawo**, *etc.* (*stem* **ssenga-** N12). *See Table 10.*

austere person *n* **ow'eggume** *n1*

authentic *adj* **-a ddala**

authenticate *vt* **-kakasa**

author *n* **omuwandiisi** *n1*

authorise *vt* **-wa olukusa**

authorisation *n* **olukusa** *n11*

authority *n* **obuyinza** *n14*

automobile (*car*) *n* **emmotoka** *n5*. *See* vehicle

available, be *vi* **-li** *or* **-ba** ('*be*') *according to tense* (N20.1) *and often with enclitic* (N24.2), *eg.* (1) *We kiri.* ('*It is available.*'); (2) *Kijja kubaawo.* ('*It will be available.*'). *Use* **-beerawo** *to emphasise* '*place*', *eg. Kijja kubeerawo.* ('*It will be available there.*').

avarice *n* **omululu** *n3*

avaricious *adj* **-a omululu**

avenge oneself *vr* **-eesasuza**. *See* vengeance

average *adj* **-a ekigero**

avert *vt* **-ziyiza**, (*disease, bad weather, etc.*) **-gema**

avocado *n* **ovakkedo** *n1*, **vvakkedo** *n1*, **ova** *n1*

avoid *vt* (1) **-eewala**, *eg. Yagezaako okwewala okwogera ne muliraanwa we.* ('*He tried to avoid speaking to his neighbour.*'); (2) (*dodge something thrown*) **-eewoma**, *eg. Yeewoma effumu.* ('*He avoided the spear.*'); (3) (*by taking a detour*) **-eebalama**, *eg. Lodibulooka yazeebalamye ng'ayita mu nsiko.* ('*He avoided the roadblocks by passing through the bush.*'). *See* distance oneself; move away; take cover   avoid direct contact with people (*through shyness*) **-eekomomma**   avoid doing a task (*by doing something else*) **-eebalankanya**   avoid telling the truth to **-balankanya**   be avoidable **-eewalika**

await *vt* **-lindirira**

awake, be *vi* **-tunula**, *eg. Musoke akyatunula.* ('*Musoke is still awake.*'). *See* conscious (be); wake up

awaken *v* (1) *vi* **-zuukuka**; (2) *vt* **-zuukusa**

¹award *n* **ekirabo** *n7*

²award *vt* **-wa ekirabo**

aware   be aware (*know*) **-manya**, *eg. Mmanyi nti ajja.* ('*I am aware she is coming.*')   make aware (*make known*) **-manyisa**, (*by winking*) **-temyako**, (*by touching lightly*) **-sunyako**. *See* forewarn

away *adv. Meaning can be incorporated in verb, eg. Yakitwala.* ('*She took it away.*').   be away for a long time (*eg. of a person who has gone abroad*) **-zaawa**, (*not knowing where the person has gone*) **-bula**   Go away! **Vaawo!**

awful (*bad*) *adj* **-bi ennyo**

awl *n* **olukato** *n11*

awning *n* **ettundubaali** *n5*

ayah *n* **yaaya** *n1*

axe *n* **embazzi** *n9*, (*small*) **akabazzi** *n12*

B,b

baboon *n* enkobe *n9*

baby *n* omwana *n1*, (*small*) akaana *n12*, (*newborn*) omuwere *n1*. *See* child; toddler have a baby -zaala omwana, (*before leaving one's parents' home*) -zaalira ku luggya

bachelor *n* omuwuulu *n1*

bachelorhood *n* obuwuulu *n1*

[1]**back** (*referring to a house*) *adj* -a emmanju, *eg. oluggi lw'emmanju ('back door')* back room (*of a house*) eddiiro ery'emmanju *n5* back yard oluggya lw'emmanju *n11*

[2]**back** *adv* bring back -zza, -komyawo come back -dda, -komawo go back (*to over there*) -ddayo

[3]**back** (*of the body*) *n* omugongo *n3*. *See* backside; bottom; buttocks; stern at the back emabega at the back of emabega wa, *eg. Sukaali ali mabega wa kabada. ('The sugar is at the back of cupboard.')* at the back of the house emmanju, *eg. Abaana bali mmanju. ('The children are at the back of the house.')* lie on one's back -eegalika, *eg. Embwa yeegalise. ('The dog is lying on its back.')* set down on the back -galika, *eg. Emmeeza bagigalise. ('They set the table down on its back.')*

[4]**back** (*support*) *vt* -wagira, *eg. Mpagira ekirowoozo ekyo. ('I am backing that idea.')*. *See* second

backbite *vt* -geya

backbone *n* (1) (*of a person*) olugongogongo *n11*; (2) (*of an animal*) ekigongo *n7*

backer (*supporter*) *n* omuwagizi *n1*. *See* sponsor

backing (*support*) *n* obuwagizi *n14*

backside *n* (1) (*bottom, of a person*) ennyuma *n9*; (2) (*of a bird*) ekyensuti *n7*. *See* back

backstitch *n* kaddannyuma *n12*, *eg. Atunga kaddannyuma. ('She is sewing backstitch.')*

backwards *adv* emabega, *eg. Emmotoka yadda emabega. ('The car went backwards.')* walk backwards -tambula kaddannyuma

bad *adj* -bi. *See* rotten bad attitude endowooza embi *n10* bad behaviour (*things done deliberately to annoy or harm*) ebyambyone *n8* bad feelings (*rancour*) ffitina *n9* bad habit omuze *n3* bad-hearted *adj* -a omutima omubi bad-hearted person ow'ettima *n1* bad language (*profanities*) ebyobugwemufu *n8* bad-mannered person omwavu w'empisa *n1* bad-mouthing akamwa akabi *n12* bad-tempered person ow'obusungu *n1* go bad -yonooneka, (*of cooked food*) -gaga, (*of milk*) -fa not too bad waddewaddeko something bad ekibi *n7* put in a bad condition (*mess up*) -gootaanya very bad person kawenkene *n1*

bade *See* bid

badge *n* akabonero *n12*, baagi *n9*

badly *adv* obubi badly behaved -lalu be badly behaved -laluka go badly (*of life or affairs*) -gootaana, *eg. Obulamu bwe bugootaanye. ('His life is going badly.')*, -gozoobana. *See* bungled (be); difficult

badness *n* obubi *n14*

baffle *vt* -sobera, *eg. Kinsobedde. ('It has baffled me.')* be baffled -soberwa, *eg. Nsobeddwa eky'okukola. ('I am baffled about what to do.')*

bag *n* ensawo *n9*, omufuko *n3*, (*large or in poor condition*) ekisawo, (*large matted type used for shopping*) ekikapu *n7*, (*polythene*) akaveera *n12*. *See* handbag; sack

baggage *n* emigugu *n4* (*one piece* omugugu *n3*), (*a lot*) engugu *n9*

[1]**bail** (*surety*) *n* akakalu *n12*, omusingo *n3* put up bail for -eeyimirira

[2]**bail (out)** (*a boat*) *vt* -sena bailing bowl olutiba *n11*, (*small*) akatiba *n12*

bait *n* akatego *n12*

bake (*cook*) *vt* -fumba

baking powder *n* ekizimbulukusa *n7*

balaclava *n* akakookolo *n12*

[1]**balance** *n* (1) (*from payment*) enfissi *n9*, baalansi *n1*; (2) (*for weighing*) minzaani *n9*

[2]**balance** *vt* -eetengereza, *eg. Yeetengereza omugugu ku mutwe. ('She is balancing the load on her head.')* balance oneself (*as a child learning to walk*) -eetengerera, *eg. Omwana yeetengerera bulungi. ('The child is balancing herself well.')*

baldness *n* ekiwalaata *n7* bald person ow'ekiwalaata *n1* be(come) bald -kutuka ekiwalaata

bale (*eg. of clothing or cotton*) *n* endibota *n9*

ball *n* omupiira *n3* roll a ball of -kulunga, *eg. Kkulungabusa likulunga obusa. ('The dung beetle is rolling a dung ball.')* tennis ball ttena *n9*

balloon *n* oluwago *n11*, baluuni *n9*

ballot *n* akalulu *n12*

bambara groundnut *n* empande *n9*

bamboo *n* amabanda *n6* (*one stem/piece* ebbanda *n5*)

ban *vt* -wera, *eg. Abaana baabawera okufuluma ebweru. ('The children have been banned from going outside.')*. *See* forbid

banana *See below* banana garden olusuku *n11*

ACTIVITIES INVOLVING BANANA PLANTS, FRUITS OR LEAVES

See also other sections.

chop up felled pseudostem (*'trunk' – involves splitting and detaching the leaf sheaths*) -gogombola omugogo

cover a placenta with banana sheaths (*part of traditional birth rites*) -fugika

crush bananas to extract juice -sogola omubisi

cut leaves (*to use*) -sala endagala

detach (1) (*hand of bananas*) -wagula; (2) (*individual bananas*) -wagulawagula; (3) (*individual bananas, for another person*) -wagulirako

harvest (*bananas*) -yunja, *eg. Yayunja amatooke.*
(*'She has harvested the plantains.'*)

make beer from bananas -sogola omwenge

peel plantains -waata amatooke

plant banana shoot -simba ensukusa

prop up fruiting banana plant -zizika ekitooke

prune banana plant (*cut off dead leaves and
sheaths*) -salira ekitooke, (*with a billhook*)
-solobya endagala

put lining of banana leaves in basket -yaliira
endagala mu kibbo

remove midrib of banana leaf -yubuluza
olulagala

remove shoot for planting -sigula ensukusa

tear off piece of banana leaf (*to make a spoon,
funnel, etc.*) -kooza olulagala

COOKING, SERVING AND EATING MATOOKE

Stages in preparing and cooking food in a parcel.

1. **wrap up food in banana leaves for cooking**
   -wumba omuwumbo, -siba emmere
2. **put food parcel in pan and cover with
   banana leaves** -saaniika emmere
3. **squeeze cooked bananas in food parcel** (*to
   mash them*) -nyiga emmere
4. **return mashed matooke to cook further**
   -boobeza emmere
5. **add small parcel of uncooked greens to
   omuwumbo** -seruza enva

Stages in dishing up food from a food parcel.

1. **take parcel out of pot and remove covering
   leaves** -jjula emmere, -jjula omuwumbo
2. **unwrap parcel in the dining room**
   -soosootola emmere
3. **serve food onto individual plates** -bega
   emmere.

Eating and keeping matooke.

lump of matooke (*as taken into the fingers to eat*)
ekitole ky'ettooke *n7* take lump of matooke,
make depression, fill with sauce and eat -kuba
ennoga roll lump of matooke into a ball -kulunga
ettooke dip ball of matooke in sauce -koza
ettooke roll around lump of matooke in sauce
-vulunga ettooke

left-over (cooked) matooke (1) amawolu *n6*,
(*one lump*) eggwolu *n5*, (*piece of*) ekiwumi
ky'ettooke *n7*; (2) (*that has been stored in hot
ashes*) ettooke evvumbike *n5* bury left-over
matooke in ashes (*wrapped in banana leaves, to
keep for eating next day*) -vumbika eggwolu
remove crust from left-over matooke (*that has been
stored in hot ashes*) -bembula emmembe ku

matooke

PRODUCTS OF THE BANANA PLANT

For more on fruits and leaves, see other sections.

basin/bath (*made from untorn banana leaves*)
ekiwombo *n7*

beer (*Kiganda type*) omwenge omuganda *n3*,
omwenge bigere

cooked bananas amatooke *n6* (*one fruit* omunwe
gw'ettooke *n3*), (*cooked in their skins*) amatooke
ag'empogola, (*cooked whole in sauce*) amatooke
ag'akatogo, (*cooked whole in water*) amatooke
amasuulemu. *A dish prepared from dry powdered
bananas (especially beer bananas or plantains)
mixed with sweet potatoes and sometimes beans is
ekigomba n7.*

dried sliced bananas (*stored for future use*)
mutere *n1*, *eg. mutere wa mbidde* ('*dried sliced
beer bananas*')

fibre ebyayi *n8* (*one piece* ekyayi *n7*), (*long thin
piece*) olwayi *n11*, (*string of banana fibre used to
lift leaves off a food bundle after cooking*)
omugondoli *n3*

food parcel (*food wrapped in banana leaves for
steaming*) (1) (*with solid food*) omuwumbo *n3*, *eg.
omuwumbo gwa muwogo* ('*parcel of cassava*'); (2)
(*with liquid or moist food*) oluwombo *n11*, *eg.
oluwombo lw'ennyama* ('*parcel of meat*')

gutter (*made from leaf sheath*) olugogo *n11*

juice (*from crushed bananas*) omubisi *n3*,
(*concentrated*) emberenge *n9*

lining of banana leaves (*eg. in basket*) enjaliiro
n10 (*one such leaf* olwaliiro *n11*)

scoop/spoon (*made from leaf*) (1) (*for drinking
soup*) akawujjo *n12*; (2) (*for serving matooke*)
akabezo *n12*

screen in doorway (*made from dry withered
banana leaves*) ebisanja by'oluggi *n8*

sponge (*made by beating pith from inflorescence
stalk*) ekinyirikisi *n7*

strip cut from midrib (*used in basketry*) akakeedo
n12

THE BANANA PLANT AND ITS PARTS

bloom (*powdery layer on stem*) empumbu *n9*

bud, young (*on stump*) endu *n9*

bunch of bananas enkota *n9*, *eg. enkota ya ndiizi*
('*bunch of small dessert bananas*'), (*of plantains*)
ettooke *n5*, (*one that has come down without
human agency*) ettooke ery'engwira

double banana fruit nnabansasaana *n1*

hand of fruits ekiwagu *n7*

inflorescene stalk (1) (*soft, inside leaf sheaths;
pith*) omututumba *n3*; (2) (*hard, where exposed
above the leaf sheaths; stalk of the fruit bunch*)

ekikolokomba *n7*
latex amasanda g'amatooke *n6*
leaf olulagala *n11*, (*turning yellow*) ekireka *n7*, (*dry; withered*) essanja *n9*, (*dry and withered, when tied into a bundle*) ekisanja *n7*. *The following refer to banana leaves used for different purposes*: (1) (*young and untorn, used for wrapping food parcels, especially of liquid food*) oluwombo *n11*; (2) (*small strip of leaf placed on top of food within food bundle*) akawuuwo *n12*; (3) (*leaves used to cover food bundle ready for cooking*) endagala ezisaaniika *n10*; (4) (*used-up leaves on top of food bundle, after cooking*) essaaniiko *n5*; (5) (*untorn leaf used for lining, eg. a food basket or to lead juice into a pot from bananas that are being crushed*) olwaliiro *n11*; (6) (*strand of leaf folded along the midrib and tied around a food bundle, calabash of beer, waist of dancer, etc.*) oluyina *n11*; (7) (*small part of a leaf used for a task, eg. cupped to hold water to drink*) omuko gw'olulagala *n3*. appendage at end of banana leaf omusa *n3* pile of folded banana leaves omuzingo gw'endagala *n3*
leaf sheath (*gutter-shaped, embraces the trunk*) ekigogo *n7*, (*when used as a gutter*) olugogo *n11*
male inflorescence empummumpu *n9*
midrib of leaf omugoŋŋoonyo *n3*, omuziŋŋoonyo *n3*
pith *See* inflorescence stalk
plant ekitooke *n7*, *eg.* ebitooke by'embidde ('*beer banana plants*')
pseudostem ('*trunk*') omugogo *n3*, (*chopped up trunk on the ground*) omuteteme *n3*
sap (*from cooking bananas*) amasanda g'amatooke *n6*
shoot ensukusa *n9*, endukusa *n9*, (*of a very young beer banana plant*) akasukwasukwa *n12* produce shoots -zaala, (*of a recently planted banana plant*) -kkulira
stump (*rhizome*) ekikolo *n7*
withered flower (*at end of banana*) akanuunu *n12*

TYPES OF BANANA PLANTS/FRUITS

Bananas are classified into two major categories, 'male' (**embidde** *n9*) *and 'female'* (**enkago** *n9*). *A 'male' banana plant is* **ekitooke ekisajja** *and a 'female' banana plant is* **ekitooke ekikazi**. *This classification has no connection with biological gender. 'Male' banana plants are types used to make beer. 'Female' banana plants are all other types. See 'Musa' in note* **N31** *for scientific classification.*

beer/juice bananas embidde *n9*. *Types include* bagandesezza, embidde, kabula, katwalo, kisubi, nnambi, *etc.* (*all in noun class n1*).
cooking bananas (*types steamed or boiled*)
amatooke *n6* (*one fruit* omunwe gw'ettooke *n3*). *Types include* kafuba, kibuzi, kisansa, lusumba, mbwazirume, nabusa, nnakabululu, nnakitembe, *etc.* (*all in noun class n1*). *A grey type often cooked whole in its skin is* kivuvvu *n1*.
dessert bananas (*includes sweet types and ripe cooking bananas*) amenvu *n6* (*one fruit* eryenvu *n5*). *Types include:* (*large*) bbogoya *n1*, (*small*) ndiizi *n1*. '*eryenvu*' *can apply to any ripe banana, not just of a dessert variety.*
plantains (*usually baked or roasted*) gonja *n1* (*one fruit* omugonja *n3*)
wild banana (*Ensete*) (1) (*plant*) ekitembe *n7*; (2) (*seed* ettembe *n5*) necklace made from ettembe seeds olutembe *n11*

band (*musical*) *n* bbandi *n9*, (*brass band*) sserumbeete *n9*. *See* headband; waistband band of reeds (*in mud and wattle wall*) ekizizi *n7* band member (*musician*) owa bbanda *n1*
[1]**bandage** *n* bbandeegi *n9*
[2]**bandage** *vt* -siba bbandeegi
bang (*sudden sound*) *n* ekibwatuka *n7* go off with a bang -bwatuka
banish (*exile*) *vt* -waŋŋangusa. *See* drive away be banished -waŋŋanguka
banishment (*exile*) *n* obuwaŋŋanguse *n14*
banjo *n* bbanjo *n9*
bank *n* (1) (*edge of lake or river*) olubalama *n11*; (2) (*embankment, to hold back water*) olubibiro *n11*; (3) (*financial*) bbanka *n9*, etterekero ly'essente *n5* bank note (*paper money*) olupapula lw'essente/ensimbi *n11* central bank (*financial*) bbanka enkulu
banker *n* munnabbanka *n1*
banned (*forbidden*) *adj* -were. *See* taboo
banner *n* bendera *n9*
banquet *n* ekijjulo *n7*
baptise *vt* -batiza
baptism *n* (1) (*Prot*) okubatiza *n15*; (2) (*RC*) batiisimu *n9*
baptistry *n* ebbatirizo *n5*
bar *n* (1) (*drinking place*) ebbaala *n5*; (2) (*security bar, eg. on window*) omutayimbwa *n3* bar of soap omuti gwa ssabbuuni *n3*
barbed wire *n* ssennenge *n1*
barber *n* kinyoozi *n1*. *See* hairdresser
bare (*empty*) *adj* -yereere
bare one's teeth -sinika amannyo
bargain *vi* -lamuuliriza
[1]**bark** (*of a tree*) *n* ekikuta (ky'omuti) *n7*, (*of a barkcloth tree after removal from tree*) nnabugi *n1* strip bark from (*a tree*) -susumbula strip bark from a barkcloth tree -subula (*or* -yimbula) omutuba heat bark of barkcloth tree (*wrapped in banana leaves, to soften and to assist the colour*) -fumba nnabugi strip of bark (1) (*from barkcloth tree*) olutubatuba *n11*; (2) (*from shrub Triumfetta;*

used as cord) **ekinsambwe** *n7*

²**bark** (*of a dog*) *vi* **-boggola**   bark at **-boggolera**

barkcloth *n* **embugo** *n10* (*one piece* **olubugo** *n11*). *Varieties of barkcloth include*: (1) (*light coloured, used by royals*) **njeruka** *n1*; (2) (*top quality type*) **mpolembuzi** *n1*; (3) (*whitish and strong*) **nnabugi** *n1*; (4) (*good looking, brownish*) **nteesa** *n1*. *Qualities of barkcloth include*: (1) (*top quality, from any stripping of a barkcloth tree except the first*) **omusala** *n3*; (2) (*second grade, but still good quality, deep brown and very soft*) **olubugo olwa kimote**; (3) (*third grade, coarse*) **ekitentegere** *n7*. barkcloth maker **omukomazi** *n1*, (*chief of the Kabaka*) **Buyungo** *n1*   barkcloth taper/torch **enfuuzi** *n9*   barkcloth tree **omutuba** *n3*, (*one stripped of bark*) **nnassubula** *n1*. *A barkcloth tree is ready for harvesting when it is in full flush of young leaves* ('**Omutuba guggumizza.**').   beat barkcloth **-komaga embugo**, (*first stage*) **-saaka**, (*second stage*) **-tenga**, (*third stage*) **-ttula**. *The final stage of beating barkcloth is said to be the most enjoyable, especially if two people are engaged, one beating at twice the speed of the other to make a good rhythm. Song sung during this beating*: '*Kankukube nkuttule, kankukube nkuttule, omukazi ky'atalya ky'ekiwunya olwendo lwe.*' ('*Let me beat you to the right size (x2), what a woman does not eat makes her ladle smell bad.*') exposed layer of trunk (*after removel of bark*) **omutetere** *n3* (*must be wrapped immediately in banana leaves for the bark to regrow*)   fragments and spray that come off bark when beaten **obuleebo** *n14*   knot barkcloth on (*heir*) **-sumika**, *eg. Yansumika.* ('*He knotted the barkcloth on me.*'), (*tying the knot*) **-siba ekifundikwa**   shelter in which barkcloth is made **ekkomagiro** *n5*   smoke barkcloth **-nyookeza embugo**. *See* smoke   strip of barkcloth (*used as clothing*) (1) (*by men*) **ekikunta** *n7*; (2) (*by women*) **omutanda** *n3*

barrel (*drum*) *n* **eppipa** *n5*   barrel of a gun **omudumu gw'emmundu** *n3*

barren *adj* (1) (*of a woman*) **-gumba**; (2) (*of certain animals*) **ensaata**, *eg. ente ensaata* ('*barren cow*') barren land **olunnyo** *n11*

¹**barricade** *n* **olukomera** *n11*

²**barricade** *vt* **-komera**

barrier (*something placed to prevent movement, eg. banana trunk on mat to prevent movement of drying beans*) *n* **omuziziko** *n3*. *See* barricade; roadblock

barter *vt* **-waanyisa**

base (*eg. of container*) *n* **entobo** *n9*, *eg. entobo y'akalobo* ('*base of the bucket*'). *See* headquarters

bash (into) (*knock*) *vt* **-tomera**

basil (*herb*) *n* **kakubansiri** *n1*

basin *n* **ebbenseni** *n9*, (*of metal*) **kkalaayi** *n9*, (*small, for washing hands*) **akataasa** *n12*, (*for bathing babies*) **ekyogero** *n7*, (*made from banana leaves*) **ekiwombo** *n7*

bask (in) *vi* **-yota**, *eg. Njota omusana.* ('*I am basking in the sun.*')

basket *n* (1) (*stiff type shaped like an open bowl, usually made from obukeedo*) **ekibbo** *n7*; (2) (*stiff type with handle*) **ekisero** *n7*; (3) (*used for carrying hens or dead fish*) **olusero** *n11*; (4) (*crib; Mose's basket*) **ekibaya** *n7*; (5) (*for carrying chickens*) **omuyonjo** *n3*; (6) (*nesting basket for chickens*) **ekiyonjo** *n7*; (7) (*for carrying fish, storage of beans, etc.*) **enkanga** *n9*; (8) (*for placing an offering to a spirit*) **ekigali** *n7*; (9) (*in which to brew beer*) **olutyatya** *n11*. *See* bag; trap (*for basket traps for fish or lake flies*); winnowing tray

bat *n* (1) (*insectivorous*) **akawundo** *n12*; (2) (*fruit*) **ekinyira** *n7*

bath *n* **ebbaafu** *n5*, (*made from banana leaves*) **ekiwombo** *n7*   give a vapour bath to **-yoteza**   take a dust bath (*of a chicken*) **-naaba**   take a vapour bath **-eeyoteza**

bathe *v* (1) (*oneself*) *vi* **-naaba**; (2) (*another person*) *vt* **-naaza**

bathroom *n* (1) **ekinaabiro** *n7*, **ekiyigo** *n7*; (2) (*small*) **akanaabiro** *n12*; (3) (*outside the house*) **akayigo** *n12*   go to the bathroom (*toilet*) **-eeyamba**

battery *n* (1) (*larger, eg. for car*) **bbaatule** *n9*; (2) (*smaller, eg. for torch*) **eryanda** *n5*

battle *n* **olutalo** *n11*, **olutabaalo** *n11*

battlefield *n* **ettabaaliro** *n5*, **eddwaniro** *n5*

bay (*of a lake*) *n* **ekyondo** *n7*

be *v* (am, are, was, were) **-ba**, **-li**. *These two roots belong to the same verb* (**-ba/-li**), *the choice of root depending on the tense and sense* (**N20.1**), *eg.* (*1*) *Aliba awo.* ('*She will be there.*'); (2) *Ali awo* ('*She is there.*'). *Both are commonly used with enclitics* (**N20.4**). *The verb* **-beera** *also means 'be', in the sense of 'be at', or to refer to something habitual, eg.* (*1*) *Tujja kubeerayo ku mukolo.* ('*We shall be at the event.*'); (2) *Mu kkanisa mubeeramu entebe nnyingi.* ('*There are many chairs in the church.*').

beach *n* **olubalama** *n11*, **bbiiki** *n9*

bead *n* **embira** *n9*, (*small*) **akatiiti** *n12*, (*seed of wild banana plant, used as bead*) **ettembe** *n5*. *See* charm; necklace; waistband   prayer beads (1) (*RC rosary*) **ssapule** *n9*; (2) (*of Muslims*) **kalaadi** *n9* string of beads (*worn by very young girls*) **ebiti** *n8*

beak *n* **omumwa** (**gw'ekinyonyi**) *n3*

beam (*horizontal timber in roof, above ceiling*) *n* **olwaliiro lw'akasolya** *n11*, **omukiikiro** *n3*

bean *n* (1) (*general name for bean; also kidney bean*) **ekijanjaalo** *n7*; (2) (*cowpea*) **empindi** *n9*; (3) (*Lima bean or butter bean, with flattened seeds*) **akayindiyindi** *n12*, (*with larger seeds*) **ekigaaga** *n7*; (4) (*mung bean*) **mpokya** *n1*. *See* coffee bean; groundnut. *Types of kidney bean include*: (1) (*with white seeds with black lines*) **nnamunye** *n1*; (2) (*with red seeds resembling peanuts*) **kanyeebwa** *n1*; (3) (*type with small seeds*) **nambaale** *n1*   bean and potato mash **omugoyo** *n3*   bean leaves (*young, eaten as vegetable*) **ebisoobooza** *n8*   coffee bean **emmwanyi** *n9*   edible powder (*made from leaves of empindi*) **eggobe** *n5*

¹bear (*type of animal*) *n* **eddubu** *n9*

²bear *vt* (bore; born) (1) (*carry*) **-eetikka**; (2) (*hold up*) **-wanirira**, *eg. Empagi eno ewaniridde akasolya.* (*'This post is bearing [the weight of] the roof.'*)   bear a child (*of a woman*) **-zaala omwana**   bear a grudge **-beera n'ekiruyi**   bear a shoot (*of a banana plant*) **-zaala ensukusa**   bear fruit *See* fruit   bear up well (*despite problems; endure*) **-gumira**, *eg. Yagumira ekizibu ky'okufiirwa.* (*'She bore up well despite the bereavement.'*)   be born (*of a child*) **-zaalibwa**

beard *n* **ekirevu** *n7*

bearer *n* (1) (*someone who carries*) **omwetissi** *n1*; (2) (*of person on shoulders*) **omukongozzi** *n1*; (3) (*of a spirit, by a person possessed; chief medium of a spirit*) **omukongozzi w'emmandwa**

beast *n* **ensolo** *n9*

beat *vt* (1) (*hit*) **-kuba**, (*someone hard*) **-babika**; (2) (*in sports*) **-goba**, *eg. ManU yagobye nga azannye ne Arsenal.* (*'ManU beat Arsenal.'*). *See* defeat   beat a drum **-tuzza** (*or* **-kuba**) **eŋŋoma**, (*hard; pound*) **-sekebbula eŋŋoma**   beat barkcloth *See* barkcloth   beat hard with a stick (*a person*) **-babika kibooko**   beat mercilessly with sticks (*a person*) **-weweenyula emiggo**, **-sakata emiggo**   beat up a thief **-saamira omubbi**   be beaten (*hit*) **-kubwa**, (*of a drum*) **-tujja**   narrowly beat (*a person*) **to** (*an opportunity*) **-soona**, *eg. Yansoonye okufuna omulimu.* (*'He beat me to the job.'*)

beater *n1* (1) (*of barkcloth*) **omukomazi** *n1*; (2) (*in a hunt*) **omukubirizi** *n1*, **omugoberezi** (*or* **omukanzi**) **w'ensolo** *n1*

beautiful *adj* **-lungi**, (*fairly*) **-lungirungi**   beautiful person **omulungi** *n1*   beautiful place **awalungi** *n16*   be(come) beautiful **-lungiwa**

beautify *vt* **-lungiya**   beautify oneself **-eerungiya**

beauty *n* **obulungi** *n14*   beauty contest **empaka z'obulungi** *n10*

because *conj* **kubanga**, *eg. Ndya kubanga enjala ennuma.* (*'I am eating because I am hungry.'*), **kuba**, **olw'okubanga**, **olw'okuba**   because of **olwa**, *eg. Olw'obwavu, tebaayinza kugula mmere.* (*'Because of poverty, they could not buy food.'*)   because of that **olwekyo**

beckon *vt* **-wenya**, *eg. Atuwenya tujje.* (*'He is beckoning us to come.'*)

become (*change in state or looks*) *vt* **-fuuka**, *eg. Afuuse omusawo.* (*'He has become a doctor.'*)

bed *n* (1) (*piece of furniture*) **ekitanda** *n7*; (2) (*made-up, for sleeping*) **obuliri** *n14*; (3) (*for seedlings*) **bbeedi** *n9*   bed post **enkondo y'ekitanda** *n9*   (at the) foot of the bed **emirannamiro**, *eg. Teeka awo emirannamiro.* (*'Put it at the foot of the bed.'*)   (at the) head of the

bed **emitwetwe**   make a bed **-yala obuliri**, *eg. Ayaze obuliri.* (*'She has made the bed.'*)   make a bed for **-yalira**, *eg. Yamwalidde.* (*'She has made a bed for him.'*)   make a bed for oneself **-eeyalira**

bedbug *n* **ekiku** *n7*, (*type of biting insect resembling a bedbug*) **ekibo** *n7*

bedding *n* **ebikunta** *n8* (*one piece* **ekikunta** *n7*), **ebyokweyalira** *n8* (*one piece* **ekyokweyalira** *n7*). *See* cover   remove bedding **-yalula obuliri**   -tuck in bedding **-fundikira obuliri**

bed-maker *n* **omwazi w'obuliri** *n1*

bedpan *n* **ekidoli** *n7*

bedroom *n* **ekisenge** *n7*, **ekisulwamu** *n7*

bedsheet *n* **essuuka** *n9*

bedsit (*small apartment in block*) *n* **omuzigo** *n3*

bee *n* (1) (*honey bee*) **enjuki** *n9*; (2) (*bumble bee*) **evvuuvuumira** *n5*; (3) (*stingless bee; small*) **kadoma** *n1*

beef *n* **ennyama y'ente** *n9*   mixture of minced beef, flour and egg (*fried; sold as snack*) **chaps** *n9*

beehive *n* **omuzinga gw'enjuki** *n3*

beer *n* (1) (*bottled*) **bbiya** *n9*; (2) (*made from bananas, Kiganda local brew*) **omwenge omuganda** *n3*, **omwenge bigere**; (3) (*made from pineapples*) **omunaanansi** *n3*; (4) (*made from maize*) **kkwete** *n1*; (5) (*made from a mixture of maize and other ingredients*) **omulirina** *n3*; (6) (*made from finger millet*) **amalwa** *n6*   beer basket (*basket in which beer is brewed*) **olutyatya** *n11*   beer boat (*hollowed-out log used for brewing*) **emmanvu** *n5*, (*bigger*) **eryato ery'omwenge** *n5*   make beer (*from bananas*) **-sogola omwenge**, *eg. Ali mu lyato asogola mwenge.* (*'He is in the trough making beer.'*)   make beer using **-sogoza**, *eg. Basogoza ebigere.* (*'They are making beer using their feet.'* − *trampling bananas to extract juice*)

beetle *n* (1) (*general word for insect*) **ekiwuka** *n7*; (2) (*eats dry beans*) **kawuukuumi** *n1*; (3) (*rolls along balls of dung*) **kkulungabusa** *n1*. *See* larva

¹before *conj* Use **nga** with verb in 'not yet' tense (**N18**), *eg. Nga tannajja, longoosa ennyumba.* (*'Before she comes, clean the house.'*)

²before *pre* (1) (*in front of*) **mu maaso ga**, *eg. mu maaso g'ennyumba* (*'before the house'*); (2) (*with time*) Use **nga** with 'not yet' tense (**N18**), *eg.* (1) **nga essaawa bbiri tezinnawera** (*'before 8 o'clock'*); (2) **Kyaliwo okuva nga tetunnazaalibwa.** (*'It existed before we were born.'*)

befriend *vt* **-kwana**

beg (*as a beggar*) *vi* **-sabiriza**. *See* ask   beg pitifully (*pleading for help*) **-laajana**

beggar *n* **omusabirizi** *n1*

begin *vt* **-tandika**. *See* first   begin a journey **-situla**, *eg. Asitudde ku ssaawa bbiri.* (*'He began the journey at 8 o'clock.'*)   begin at/with **-tandikira**, *eg. Njagala otandikire wano okulima.* (*'I want you to start digging here.'*). *See* first (do)

beginning *n* **entandikwa** *n9*. *See* early stages;

source at the beginning of **ku ntankikwa ya** in the beginning **ku ntandikwa**

behalf of, on *pre* **ku lwa**, *eg. ku lwa Musoke ('on behalf of Musoke'),* (*with pronoun*) **ku lwa-** (**N11.4**), *eg. ku lwaffe ('on our behalf')*

behave *vi* **-eeyisa**, *eg. Yeeyisa bubi. ('He behaved badly.')* be badly behaved **-laluka** behave towards **-yisa**, *eg. Amuyisa bulungi. ('He behaved well towards her.')*

behaviour *n* **enneeyisa** *n9,* (*way of behaving*) **empisa** *n10* bad behaviour **eddalu** *n5,* (*done deliberately to annoy or harm*) **ebyambyone** *n8.* *See* wrong-doing improve one's behaviour **-eddako** unrefined behaviour (*as a country bumpkin*) **amaalo** *n6*

[1]behind *adv* **emabega, ennyuma** behind a home **emmanju**

[2]behind (*buttocks*) *n* **ennyuma** *n9*

[3]behind *pre* **emabega wa, ennyuma wa** behind the home **ennyumanju** behind the home of **emmanju wa**, *eg. emmanju wa Musoke ('behind Musoke's home')*

being (*existence*) *n* **embeera** *n9*

belatedly *adv* **ekikeerezi**

[1]belch (*also* burp) *n* **ekibejjagalo** *n7*

[2]belch (*also* burp) *vi* **-bejjagala**

Belgian (*person*) *n* **Omubirigi** *n1*

Belgium *n* **Bubirigi** *n9*

belief *n* **enzikiriza** *n7*

believe *vit* **-kkiriza**

believer *n. Use* **-kkiriza** (*'believe'*) *in rel* (**N7.1**), *eg. abakkiriza ('believers')*

belittle *vt* **-jerega**

bell *n* **ekide** *n7,* (*small*) **akade** *n12,* (*small, tied on baby, dancer, etc.*) **endege** *n9* bicycle bell **ekkengere** *n9* doorbell **akade k'oluggi**

bellow (*as a cow*) *vi* **-woloma**

bellows (*used in iron-smelting*) *n* **emivubo** *n4*

belly *n* **olubuto** *n11* belly button **ekkundi** *n5*

belong (to) *vt. Use* **-a** (*'of'*) *without an initial vowel* (**N11.1**) , *eg. Embwa eno ya Musoke. ('This dog belongs to Musoke.')*

belongings *n* **ebintu** *n8*

beloved (person) *n* **omwagalwa** *n1. See* favourite beloved of **muganzi** (*with pos* **N12**) *eg. muganzi wange ('my beloved')*

[1]below *adv* **wansi**, (*on a slope*) **emmanga**

[2]below *pre* **wansi wa**, (*on a slope*) **emmanga wa**, *eg. Ennyumba ye eri mmanga w'ekkanisa. ('His house is below the church.')*

belt *n* **olukoba** *n11,* **omusipi** *n3* belt of cloth (*girdle used by women for keeping money*) **omukandala** *n3*

bench *n* **olubaawo (olutuulwako)** *n11*

[1]bend (*eg. on road*) *n* **ekkoona** *n5*

[2]bend *vt* (bent) (1) **-goomya**, *eg. Agoomezza akambwe. ('She has bent the knife.');* (2) (*something flexible*) **-weta**, *eg. Yaweta ettabi*

okudda wansi. ('She bent the branch down.'). See deform bend over (*of a person*) **-kutama**, *eg. Yakutama okusiba engatto ze. ('She bent over to tie her shoes.'). See* bow bend the fingers **-funya engalo** bend to one side **-kubiira** be(come) bent (1) **-gooma**, *eg. Ekijiiko kigoomye. ('The spoon is bent.');* (2) (*of something flexible*) **-eeweta**, *eg. Omuti gwewese. ('The tree has become bent.')* be bent over (*of a person*) **-kootakoota**, *eg. Omukadde akootakoota. ('The old person is bent over.'). See* bow

[1]beneath *adv* **wansi**, (*on a slope*) **emmanga**

[2]beneath *pre* **wansi wa**, (*on a slope*) **emmanga wa**

beneficial *adj* **-a omugaso**

beneficiary (*of a will*) *n* (1) **omulaamire** *n1;* (2) *Use* **-ganyulwa** (*'benefit from'*) *in rel* (**N7.1**), *eg. aganyuddwa ('beneficiary')*

[1]benefit *n* **omugaso** *n3* without benefit **obwereere** (*with prepositional verb* **N22**), *eg. Yakolera bwereere. ('He worked without benefit.')*

[2]benefit *vt* **-gasa**, *eg. Ekitabo kino kimugasa mu kusoma kwe. ('This book is benefitting him in his studies.')* benefit from (*financially, in status, etc.*) **-funamu**, *eg. Mu kulima yafunamu ssente. ('He has benefitted financially from farming.'),* **-ganyulwa** be benefitted by **-gasibwa**, *eg. Yagasibwa okusoma mu ssomero eddungi. ('He has benefitted by going to a good school.')*

[1]bent *adj* **-goomu**, *eg. ewuuma eŋŋoomu ('bent fork'),* (*and partially broken, eg. of branch of tree*) **-koonofu**

[2]bent *v. See* bend

bequeath (to) *vt* **-laamira**, *eg. Ennyumba ye yagiraamira Musoke. ('He bequeathed his house to Musoke.')*

bereaved bereaved person **omuntu eyafiirwa** *n1* be bereaved (of) **-fiirwa**, *eg. Yafiirwa omwana we. ('He has been bereaved of his child.')*

bereavement *n* **okufiirwa** *n15*

berry *n* (1) (*castor oil*) **ensogasoga** *n9;* (2) (*coffee*) **emmwanyi** *n9. See* fruit

beseech *vt* **-eegayirira**

beside *pre* **ku mabbali ga**, *eg. Oluguudo luli ku mabbali g'omugga. ('The road is beside the river.'). See* alongside

besiege *vt* **-zingiriza**

best best man (*at a wedding*) **kalabaalaba w'omugole omusajja** *n1* be best **-singa obulungi**, *eg. Be basinga okuyimba obulungi. ('They are the best at singing.')*

bestow blessings on *vt* **-bunduggula omukisa**

bet *vit* **-singawo**, *eg. Asinzeewo essiringi omutwalo gumu. ('He has bet ten thousand shillings.')*

betray *vt* **-lyamu olukwe**, *eg. Baalyamu ensi yaabwe olukwe. ('They have betrayed their country.')*

betrayal *n* **olukwe** *n11*

better (*in health, or in how one feels*) *adv* **bulungiko**, *eg. Mpulira nga ndi bulungiko. ('I feel* a bit better.') be better than -singa (obulungi), eg. Omuwala y'asinga omulenzi okubala. ('The girl is better than the boy at maths.'), (indicating personal preference or advantage) -kira, eg. Oyambadde n'okira bwe wayambala jjo. ('You have dressed better than yesterday.') become better -yongera obulungi, eg. Ayongedde okuwuga obulungi. ('He has become better at swimming.'), (in health) -ssuuka get better (cured) -wona make better -longoosa, eg. Alongoosezza empisa z'omulenzi. ('She has made the boy's behaviour better.'). See cure slightly better waddewaddeko

¹**between** adv wakati

²**between** (in the middle of) pre wakati wa

beverage n ekyokunywa n7

beware (of) vt -eekuuma, eg. Weekuume embwa. ('Beware of the dog.')

bewitch vt -loga be bewitched -logwa bewitched person omuloge n1

bewitcher n omulogo n1

beyond pre emitala wa, eg. Abeera emitala w'omugga. ('She lives beyond the river.') beyond there okutuuka awo

bhang n enjaga n9, enjaaye n9

bias n kyekubiira n7 be biased -saliriza, eg. Ddiifiri yasaliriza omupiira. ('The referee was biased.'), -eekubiira, -lina kyekubiira

bible n bayibuli n9, Ekitabo Ekitukuvu n7

biceps (when contracted) n omufumbi n3

bicker vi -sojjagana, -nyonyoogana, (with shouting, not listening to one another) -yasiikana

¹**bicycle** n eggaali n9, akagaali n12 bicycle bell ekkengere n5 bicycle pump ebbomba y'eggaali n9 bicycle repairer omuntu addaabiriza eggaali n1

²**bicycle** vi -vuga eggaali, -tambulira ku ggaali

bicyclist n ow'eggaali n1

bid (bade) bid farewell to -siibula

bier n akannyo n12

big adj -nene big man (having more than one major asset, eg. children, wives, houses, money) ssemaka n1 big tall person omuwagguufu n1 be(come) big-bodied and tall -wagguuka

bigness n obunene n14

bike See bicycle; motorcycle

bill n (1) (beak) omumwa (gw'ekinyonyi) n3; (2) (for payment) biiru n9, eg. biiru y'amazzi ('water bill'); (3) (in parliament) ekiteeso n7

billboard n ekipande n7

billhook (for pruning banana plants) n olusolobyo n11

binoculars n gaalubindi eziraba ewala n10, gaalubindi ezizimbulukusa

biltong (dried meat) n omukalo n3

bind vt (bound) -siba

bird n ekinyonyi n7

biro n bayiro n9

birth n okuzaala n15, (occasion of giving birth)

oluzaala n11. See child birth attendant omuzaalisa n1, (traditional) omuzaalisa w'ekinnansi birth rites for twins okwalula abalongo n15 give birth (to) -zaala, eg. Yazadde jjo. ('She gave birth yesterday.') give birth for/at -zaalira, eg. Yamuzaalira omwana omulenzi. ('She had a son for him.') have a child before leaving one's parents' home -zaalira omwana ku luggya have another child after -zzaako ku, eg. Yazzaako ku balongo. ('She had another child after the twins.') have children by different men (or unplanned) -zaalazaala have next (a child) -zzaako, eg. Yazzaako abalongo. ('She had twins next.') perform birth rites for twins -yalula (or -zina) abalongo practice birth control -eegema okuzaala She has given birth. Asumulukuse., Awonye okuzaala.

birthday n amazaalibwa n6

birthmark n ebbala n5

biscuit(s) n bisikwiti n9

bishop n omulabirizi n1

bishopric n obulabirizi n14

bit n ekitundu n7

bite vt -luma, (by snake) -bojja be bitten -lumwa, (by snake) -bojjebwa

bitterness n obukaayi n14 be bitter (1) (eg. as a lemon) -kaawa; (2) (as an unripe fruit; tart) -kambagga make bitter -kaaya

¹**black** adj -ddugavu, eg. engoye enzirugavu ('black clothes') black jack (type of herb) ssere n1 black pudding kafecce n1

²**black(ness)** n obuddugavu n14

blackboard n olubaawo n11

blacken vt -ddugaza

black-eyed Susan (type of climbing or creeping herb) n akasaamusaamu n12, ntuddebuleku n1

blacksmith n omuweesi n1 blacksmith's furnace ttanuulu n9 blacksmith's workshop essasa n9

bladder n akawago n12

¹**blame** n ekinenyo n7

²**blame** vt -nenya. See accuse; prosecute; responsible (hold) blame oneself -eenenya be blamed -nenyezebwa

blanket n bulangiti n9

blare (as a trumpet) vi -nyaanyaagiza

blaspheme (against) vit -vvoola, eg. Yavvodde Katonda. ('He blasphemed against God.')

blasphemer n omuvvoozi n1

blasphemy n obuvvoozi n14

¹**blaze** (fire) n omuliro n3

²**blaze** vi (1) -yaka ennyo, eg. Omusana gwaka nnyo. ('The sun is blazing.'); (2) (very hotly, of the sun) -eeberengula; (3) (of a fire) -tuntumuka, (burning with visible flames) -bumbujja

bleat vi -kaaba

bleed v (1) vi -leeta omusaayi, eg. Ekiwundu kireeta omusaayi. ('The wound is bleeding.'); (2) vt -lumika, eg. Omusawo yalumika omulwadde ku mutwe. *('The doctor bled the patient.',* eg. *by using suction on cuts on the scalp)* have a nose bleed -eerumika

blemish *n* akamogo *n12*

blend *vt* -tabula

bless *vt* -wa omukisa

blessed *adj* -a omukisa

blessing *n* omukisa *n3*

blew *See* blow

blind *vt* -ziba amaaso, eg. *Omusana omungi gwanziba amaaso. ('The strong sunshine blinded me.')* blind person omuzibe *n1, (in one eye)* ow'ettulu *n1* blind snake nnamugoya *n1* be(come) blind -ziba amaaso, -fuuka omuzibe make blind -zibya

¹blindfold *n* kantuntunu *n1*

²blindfold *vt* -siba kantuntunu

blindness *n* obuzibe *n14*

blink *vi* -temya, *(continually)* -temereza

blister *n* ebbavu *n5. See* skin condition

bloated, be *vi* -pinduuka, eg. *Alidde emmere nnyingi, olubuto lwe lupinduuse. ('She has eaten a lot and her stomach is swollen.')* be(come) less bloated -teewulukuka, eg. *Olubuto luteewulukuse. ('I feel less bloated.')*

block *vt* (1) *(block up; obstruct)* -ziba, eg. *Azibye ekituli. ('He has blocked the hole.'),* -zibikira; (2) *(obstruct someone)* -zibira, eg. *Yatuzibira ekkubo tuleme kuyita mu lusuku lwe. ('He blocked the path to stop us passing through his garden.');* (3) *(by being across)* -eekiika, eg. *Baateekawo omuti nga gwekiise mu luguudo. ('They put a log to block the road.');* (4) *(sabotage)* -kotoggera, eg. *Mukama wange yankotoggera ne sifuna mulimu. ('My boss blocked me from getting the job.'). See* place across; prevent block the view of -siikiriza okulaba, eg. *Omuti guno gutusiikiriza okulaba e Kampala. ('This tree blocks our view of Kampala.')* be blocked (by) *(deliberately)* -zibibwa, eg. *Oluguudo lwazibiddwa abapoliisi. ('The road was blocked by the police.')* be blocked up *(of the nose) See* nose become blocked *(obstructed)* -ziba, eg. *Ekituli kizibye. ('The hole is blocked.'),* -zibikira

blockade *vt* -zingiza

blockage *n* ekiziyiza *n7*

blocked *adj* -zibe

blood *n* omusaayi *n3* blood bank etterekero ly'omusaayi *n5* blood brotherhood omukago *n3* blood cell akatofaali k'omusaayi *n12* blood clotted in the heart *(secondary totem of Mutima Musaggi Clan)* blood group ekika ky'omusaayi *n7* blood pressure *(especially if high)* puleesa *n1* blood pudding kafecce *n1* blood vessel omusuwa *n3* make blood pact -tta omukago

bloodshot, be(come) *(of the eyes) vi* -twakaala

¹bloom *n* (1) *(flower)* ekimuli *n7;* (2) *(powdery layer found on stems of some plants, eg. bananas)* empumbu *n9*

²bloom/blossom *vi* -mulisa

blotting paper *n* ekinywabwino *n7*

blouse *n* bbulawuzi *n9*

blow *v* (blew; blown) TRANSITIVE USES -fuuwa, eg. *Empewo efuuwa tadooba. ('The wind is blowing the lamp.')* blow about/away -fuumuula, eg. *Empewo efuumudde enfuufu. ('The wind blew dust about.')* blow bubbles -vulula ebyovu, *(of saliva, by a baby)* -vulula amalusu blow on *(eg. food, to cool it)* -fuuyirira blow one's nose -nyiza blow out a flame *(eg. candle)* -fuuwa omuliro blow up a tyre *(inflate)* -fuuwamu omukka mu mupiira, *(using a pump)* -pika omukka mu mupiira INTRANSITIVE USES -kunta, eg. *Empewo ekunta. ('The wind is blowing.')* blow out *(burst, of a tyre)* -yabika, eg. *Omupiira gwabise. ('The tyre has blown out.')* be blown about/away -fuumuuka, eg. *Enfuufu efuumuuse. ('The dust is being blown about.')*

blower *(person, eg. of a wind musical instrument) n* omufuuyi *n1*

blue *n* bbululu *n1,* eg. *ekimuli ekya bbululu ('blue flower')*

blunt *adj. Use* obwogi *('sharpness')* with neg **(N21)**, eg. *Akaso tekaliiko bwogi. ('The knife is blunt.')*

blurred vision *n* ekifu ku maaso *n7*

blurt out *vt* -simattula, eg. *Yasimattula amazima bwe yali anyiize. ('He blurted out the truth when he got angry.')*

blush *vi* -myuka

¹board *(wooden) n* olubaawo *n11. See* canoe *(for boards of a canoe)* chopping board *(of butcher)* ekiti *n7*

²board *vt* -linnya, eg. *Yalinnya ebbaasi. ('She boarded the bus.')* board at/in -linnyira, eg. *Nnalinnyira takisi mu ppaaka. ('I boarded a taxi in the park.')*

boarding school *n* essomero ly'ekisulo *n5*

boast *vi* -eewaana

boastfulness *n* obwerazi *n14*

boat *n* (1) *(general word; also canoe)* eryato *n5;* (2) *(ship)* emmeeri *n9;* (3) *(clinker-built)* kanu *n9, (bigger, for cargo)* ekinaala *n7;* (4) *(type with sails; dhow)* ekyombo *n7. See* beer boat; canoe

body *(of a person) n* (1) *(living)* omubiri *n3;* (2) *(dead; corpse)* omulambo *n3, (of the Kabaka)* enjole *n9*

bodyguard *n* omukuumi *n1*

bog *n* entubiro *n9,* akateebe *n12* become bogged down *(stuck)* -tubira, eg. *Emmotoka etubidde. ('The car is bogged down.')*

¹boil *(on the body) n* ejjute *n5* core of a boil ekinyusi *n7*

²boil *vi* -eesera, eg. *Amazzi geeseze. ('The water is boiling.')* boil up *(rise up, eg. of boiling milk)* -bimba boil water -fumba amazzi

boiled *adj* -fumbe, eg. *amazzi amafumbe ('boiled*

water') boiled egg **eggi ly'empogola** *n5*

boiling *adj.* Use **-eesera** (*'boil'*) *in rel* (**N7.1**), *eg. amazzi ageesera* (*'boiling water'*)

bold *adj* **-gumu** bold person **omugumu** *n1*

boldness *n* **obugumu** *n14*

bolt (*for fastening*) *n* **akakondo** *n12*, **akanyolo** *n12*. *Originally 'akakondo' was a bolt of wood and 'akanyolo' a bolt of metal.* bolt of cloth (*roll*) **ejjoola** *n9*

bomb *n* **bbomu** *n9*

¹bond *n* (1) (*guarantee*) **omusingo** *n3*; (2) (*between individuals, based on compatability*) **ekinywi** *n7*

²bond (*stick together*) *vt* **-kwasa**

bone *n* **eggumba** *n5* set a bone **-yunga eggumba**

bonesetter *n* **omuyunzi** *n1*

bonesetting *n* **obuyunzi** *n14*

bonfire (*smoky slow-burning type*) *n* **ekikoomi** *n7*

bonnet (*of car*) *n* **boneti** *n9*

¹book *n* **ekitabo** *n7*

²book (*reserve, eg. a room*) *vt* **-eekwata**

bookcase *n* **amasa g'ebitabo** *n6*

bookkeeper *n* **omubazi w'ebitabo** *n1*

booklet *n* **akatabo** *n12*

boost (*turn up*) *vt* **-tumbula**

boot *n* **bbuutu** *n9* boot lace **akaguwa ka bbuutu** *n12* Wellington boot **magetisi** *n9*

booty *n* **omunyago** *n3*

¹border *n* (1) (*eg. between countries*) **ensalo** *n9*; (2) (*eg. between properties*) **olusalolo** *n11*; (3) (*of a mat*) **ensandaggo** *n9* put border on (*mat*) **-sandagga**

²border (*neighbour; adjoin*) *vi* **-liraana** border on **-eekuusa ku**, *eg. Enneeyisa ye yeekuusa ku bumenyi bw'amateeka.* (*'His behaviour borders on criminality.'*)

¹bore (*a hole*) *vt* **-wummula**, **-botola** boring tool (1) (*awl*) **olukato** *n11*; (2) (*used red hot to make a hole in wood*) **omulumyo** *n3* be bored **-wummuka**, **-botoka**. *See* worm-easten (be)

²bore (*meaning 'carried'*) *See* bear

borehole (*for water*) *n* **nayikonto** *n9* make a borehole **-sima nayikonto**

born *See* bear

born-again (*saved in a religious sense*) *adj* **-lokole** born-again person **omulokole** *n1*, (*strict type*) **omulokole omuzuukufu**, (*more liberal*) **omulokole omwebafu**

borrow *vt* (1) (*things*) **-eeyazika**; (2) (*money*) **-eewola**

borrower *n* (1) (*of things*) **omuntu eyeeyazika** *n1*; (2) (*of money*) **omuntu eyewola ssente**

bosom (*breasts*) *n* **amabeere** *n6*. *See* chest

boss *n* **omukulu** *n1* boss of **mukama** (*with pos* **N12**), *eg. mukama wange* (*'my boss'*) her/his boss **mukamaawe**, your *si.* boss **mukamaawo**

botch (up) (*an affair*) *vt* **-dobonkanya** be botched (up) **-dobonkana**

both (of) *det* **-ombi**, **-ombiriri**. (**N7.3**) *with* pronominal concord (**N4.2**), *eg. ebintu byombi* (*'both things'*). both of us **ffembi**, both of you **mwembi**, both of them **bombi**

bother (*be a nuisance to*) *vt* **-teganya**. *See* effort

bott fly (*larva of*) *n* **ekimmonde** *n7*

bottle *n* **eccupa** *n9*, (*big*) **ekicupa** *n7*, (*small*) **akacupa** *n12* bottle-top **akasaanikira eccupa** *n12*

bottom *n* (1) (*person's behind*) **ennyuma** *n9*, (*of a woman*) **akabina** *n12*; (2) (*of a container*) **entobo** *n9*, *eg. entobo y'endobo* (*'bottom of the bucket'*). *Types of bottom (buttocks) of women include:* (*protruding*) **akabina akakikinavu**, (*large and protruding*) **ebbina** *n5*, (*flat*) **akabina akamuserebende**. be bottom (*last*) **-semba**, *eg. Y'eyasemba mu kibiina.* (*'She was bottom of the class.'*) woman with a conspicuous bottom **ow'akabina** *n1*

bough (*branch*) *n* **ettabi** *n5*

bought *See* buy

boulder *n* **olwazi** *n11*

¹bound (*tied*) *adj* **-sibe**

²bound *v. See* bind

boundary *n* **ensalo** *n9* boundary wall (*of a property*) **ekikomera** *n7* ditch dug as boundary between properties **olusalolo** *n11* person lacking boundaries (*in behaviour*) **omuntu ateekomako** *n1*

¹bow (*for shooting arrows*) *n* **omutego** *n3*

²bow (*in respect or prayer*) *vi* **-kutamya ku mutwe**, (*more deeply*) **-vummama**. *See* prostrate oneself

bow legs (*spreading outwards from the knees*) *n* **enkobogo** *n9* bow-legged person **ow'enkobogo** *n1*

bowels *n* **ebyenda** *n8*

bow-harp (*musical instrument*) *n* **ennanga** *n9* bow-harp player **omukubi w'ennanga** *n1* ground bow (*one-stringed musical instrument played by boys*) **ssekitulege** *n9*

bowl *n* **ebbakuli** *n9*, (*made from gourd*) **empaawo** *n9*, (*earthenware*) **ekibya** *n7*, (*wooden*) **olutiba** *n11* bowl-shaped (*eg. as a piece of broken gourd*) *adj* **-a ekiwaawo** bailing bowl **olutiba** *n11*

¹box (*container*) *n* **bbookisi** *n9*, **essanduuko** *n9*, (*small*) **akasanduuko** *n12*, (*of metal*) **essanduuko y'ebyuma**. *See* letter box

²box (*fight with fists*) *vi* **-kuba ebikonde**

boxer *n* **omukubi w'ebikonde** *n1* boxer-type underpants **pajama** *n9*

boxing *n* **ebikonde** *n8* boxing match **empaka z'ebikonde** *n10*

boy *n* **omulenzi** *n1*

boyfriend *n* **mulenzi** *n1* (*with pos* **N12**), *eg. mulenzi wange* (*'my boyfriend'*), **omwagalwa (mulenzi)** *n1*, *eg. omwagalwa wange* (*'my boyfriend'*) favourite boyfriend **kabiite** *n1*

boyhood *n* **obulenzi** *n14*

bra *n* **akaleega** *n12*

bracelet *n* (1) (*general term*) **ekikomo** *n7*; (2)

(*small*) **akakomo** *n12*, **akanyere** *n12*; (3) (*of ivory*) **eggemo** *n5*; (4) (*made from tail hair of giraffe or elephant*) **olusinga** *n11*; (5) (*of beads, worn by very young girls*) **ebiti** *n8*

brag *vi* **-eewaana**

braid (*hair*) *vt* **-siba**

braider of hair *n* **omusibi w'enviiri** *n1*

brain *n* **obwongo** *n14* brains (*intelligence*) **amagezi** *n6*

¹**brake** (*eg. of vehicle*) *n* **ekiziyiza** *n7* brake pedal **buleeki** *n9* brakes (*of vehicle*) **ebiziyiza** *n8*

²**brake** (*a vehicle*) *vt* **-siba**

¹**branch** *n* **ettabi** *n5*, (*tip of*) **akasanso** *n12* branch of an organisation **ettabi ly'ekibiina** broken-off branch (*placed on road to block passage*) **omusanvu** *n3*

²**branch (off)** *vi* **-kyama**, *eg.* Yakyama okuva ku luguudo olunene. (*'She branched off from the main road.'*)

brand (*model*) *n* **enkola** *n7*

brandish (*a weapon*) *vt* **-galula** brandish weapons (*to display loyalty*) **-wera**

brass band *n* **sserumbeete** *n9*

brassiere *n* **akaleega** *n12*

brave *adj* **-zira** brave person **omuzira** *n1*

bravery *n* **obuzira** *n14*

bravo *interj* **kulika** (*pl.* **mukulike**)

bread *n* **omugaati** *n3*

breadfruit, African (*type of tree*) *n* **omuzinda** *n3*

breadth (*width*) *n* **obugazi** *n14*

¹**break** (*period of rest*) *n* **ekiwummulo** *n7* have a break (*rest*) **-wummula**

²**break** *v* (broken) **TRANSITIVE USES** (1) (*general word*) **-menya**, *eg.* Yamenya etteeka. (*'He broke the law.'*); (2) (*shatter, eg. pottery*) **-yasa**, *eg.* Njasizza ekikopo. (*'I have broken the cup.'*); (3) (*into two or more pieces*) **-kutula**, *eg.* Embuzi ekutudde omuguwa. (*'The goat has broken the tether.'*); (4) (*snap*) **-wogola**, *eg.* Kibuyaga yawogodde emiti mingi. (*'The gale broke many trees.'*). See smash break a car (*to slow down*) **-siba emmotoka** break a word into syllables **-gattulula ekigambo mu nnyingo** break (*someone's*) heart **-menya omutima** break into (*force entry*) **-yingirira**, *eg.* Ababbi bannyingirira. (*'The thieves broke into my house.'*) break into parts (1) (*general word*) **-menyamu**, *eg.* Muwogo nnamumenyamu ebitundu bibiri. (*'I broke the cassava into two parts.'*), (*many pieces*) **-menyamenya**; (2) (*shattered*) **-yasaayasa**; (3) (*into many pieces*) **-kutulakutula**; (4) (*smashed*) **-sesebbula** break money into smaller denominations **-waanyisaamu** (*or* **-vungisa**) essente break off (1) **-menyako**, *eg.* Ku keeke yamenyako ekitundu okuwa omwana. (*'She broke off a piece from the cake for the child.'*); (2) (*referring to lumps*) **-megula**, *eg.* Emmotoka yatomedde ekisenge n'ekimegula. (*'The car hit the*

wall and broke off a lump.'*); (3) (*from a stem*) **-nogola**, *eg.* Ku kiwagu ky'amenvu nogolako omunwe. (*'Break off one banana from the hand.'*). See detach break off a maize cob **-nuula kasooli** break open forcefully and noisily **-bandula**, *eg.* Ababbi baabandudde oluggi ne bayingira. (*'The thieves broke down the door and entered.'*) break with **-yasisa**, *eg.* Ensuwa nnagyasisa jjinja. (*'I broke the pot with a stone.'*) **INTRANSITIVE USES** break down (*of machinery*) **-yonooneka**, *eg.* Firiigi eyonoonese. (*'The fridge has broken down.'*), (*completely; cease working*) **-fa** break free (*escape*) **-eesumattula**, *eg.* Embuzi yeesumattudde ku muguwa. (*'The goat has broken free from its tether.'*), (*from a tether*) **-kutula** break off (*fall off*) (1) (*of a piece*) **-meguka**, *eg.* Ekisenge kimeguse. (*'A piece of the wall has broken off.'*); (2) (*of a fruit, or partially of a branch*) **-nogoka** break open forcefully and noisily **-banduka** break out (1) (*escape, eg. from prison*) **-toloka**; (2) (*of a skin rash*) **-butuka**; (3) (*of war*) **-baluka** break through a barrier (1) (*eg. of goats from a pen*) **-waguza**; (2) (*of a river*) **-wagulula** be broken (1) (*general word*) **-menyeka**; (2) (*of pottery, glass, etc.*) **-yatika**, *eg.* Ekikopo kyatise. (*'The cup is broken.'*); (3) (*into two or a few pieces*) **-kutuka**, *eg.* Omuguwa gukutuse. (*'The rope has broken.'*); (4) (*snapped*) **-wogoka**, *eg.* Ettabi liwogose. (*'A branch has broken.'*); (5) (*partially broken and hanging, of a branch*) **-koonoka**; (6) (*into many pieces; smashed*) **-sesebbuka**

breakfast *n* **ekyenkya** *n7*

breast (*woman's*) *n* **ebbeere** *n5*. See chest begin growing breasts **-suna amabeere** inflamed breast **ebbanyi** *n5*

breast-feed *vt* **-yonsa**, *eg.* Maama ayonsa omwana. (*'The mother is breast-feeding the baby.'*) be breast-fed **-yonka**, *eg.* Akaana kayonka. (*'The baby is breast-feeding.'*) reject feeding at the breast (*of a baby*) **-zira amabeere**

breath *n* **omukka** *n3* be out of breath **-wejjawejja** hold one's breath **-tuyira**

breathe *vi* **-ssa**, *eg.* Assa. (*'She is breathing.'*), (*with extreme difficulty, on the point of death*) **-teetera** breathe in **-sika omukka** breathe out **-ssa omukka**

breathing *n* **okussa** *n15* be impeded in breathing **-ziyira**, *eg.* Nziyira. (*'I can't breathe properly.'*)

¹**breed** *n* **olulyo** *n11*, *eg.* Embwa ya lulyo lulungi. (*'The dog is of a good breed.'*)

²**breed** *vi* **-zaala**, *eg.* Ebiwuka bizadde. (*'The insects have bred.'*)

breeze *n* **akawewo** *n12*

brew *vt* **-yiisa** brew banana beer **-sogola omwenge**

brewer *n* **omusogozi** *n1*, (*chief, of the Kabaka*) **Sseruti** *n1* title

brewery *n* **essogolero** *n5*

bribe

¹**bribe** *n* **enguzi** *n9. Slang words include* **caayi** (*'tea'*) *and* **ebbaasa** (*'envelope' – equivalent to 'brown envelope' in English*) start taking bribes -**fuuka omuli w'enguzi** take a bribe -**lya enguzi**, (*become totally corrupt through bribe-taking*) -**wuukuuka n'okulya enguzi** taker of a bribe **omuli w'enguzi** *n1*

²**bribe** *vt* -**wa enguzi**, -**gulirira**

bribery *n* **enguzi** *n9*, **obuli bw'enguzi** *n14*

brick *n* **ettaali** *n5*, (*baked in a furnace*) **ettofaali eryokye**, (*sun-dried*) **ettofaali eritali lyokye** brick kiln **ttanuulu y'amatofaali** *n9* brick-making area **ekibumbiro** *n7*

bride *n* **omugole** *n1* bride and bridegroom **abagole** *n2* bridal headdress **kadaali** *n1* prepare bride for marriage -**fumbirira omugole**

bridegroom *n* **omugole omusajja** *n1*

brideprice *n* **omutwalo** *n3*

bridesmaid *n* **emperekeze** *n9*

¹**bridge** *n* **olutindo** *n11*

²**bridge** *vt* -**tinda**, *eg. Baatinda omugga. ('They bridged the river.')* bridge over -**tindira**, *eg. Ekinnya baakitindidde n'amabanda. ('They bridged over the hole with bamboo.')*

briefly *adv* **katono** in brief **mu bufunze**, **mu bumpimpi** make brief (*eg. a talk*) -**funza**

bright *adj* (1) (*clear*) -**tangaavu**; (2) (*clever*) -**gezi** be(come) bright (1) (*of light*) -**tangaala**; (2) (*clever*) -**geziwala** brighten up (*of a person or the weather*) -**camuka** make bright (1) (*increase the light level*) -**tangaaza**; (2) (*cleverer*) -**geziwaza**

brightness *n* (1) (*of light*) **obutangaavu** *n14*; (2) (*cleverness*) **amagezi** *n6*

brim, to the *adv* **musera**, *eg. ekikopo musera ('cup full to the brim')*

bring *vt* (brought) -**leeta**, (*cause to arrive*) -**tuusa** bring back (*return*) -**zza**, -**komyawo** bring for -**leetera**, *eg. Yamuleetera ebimuli. ('He brought flowers for her.')* bring in -**yingiza** bring near -**sembeza** bring on oneself -**eereetera**, *eg. Yeereetera emitawaana. ('He brought problems on himself.')* bring out of hiding -**kwekula** bring out reasons -**nokola ensonga** bring to an end -**maliriza**, *eg. Omubuulizi yamaliriza okubuulira. ('The preacher brought his sermon to an end.')* bring together (*assemble*) -**kuŋŋaanya**, (*making several trips*) -**somba** bring up a child -**kuza omwana** bring up a matter (*at a meeting*) -**yanjula ensonga** bring up earth (*eg. by a burrowing animal*) -**fukula ettaka** bring up from under water -**bbulula** bring up milk (*of a child*) -**booga**, *eg. Akaana kabooga. ('The baby is bringing up milk.')* be brought -**leetebwa**

bristle *n* **ejjimbi** *n5*

Britain *n* (1) (*the country*) **Bungereza** *n9*; (2) (*person*) **Omungereza** *n1*

British *adj* -**ngereza**

broad *adj* -**gazi**. *See* spread out

broadcast *vt* -**langa**

broaden *vt* -**gaziya**. *See* flatten

brochure (*booklet*) *n* **akatabo** *n12*

broke, be (*lacking money*) *vi* **ssente** -**ggwaako** (*with personal object*), *eg. Essente zimuweddeko. ('He is broke.')*

¹**broken** *adj* -**menyefu**, *eg. entebe emenyefu ('broken chair'),* (*cracked or shattered*) -**yatifu**, *eg. ensuwa enjatifu ('broken pot'),* (*of machinery*) -**fu** broken-off (*eg. of part of a wall*) -**megufu** be broken-hearted **omwoyo** -**luma** (*with personal object*), *eg. Omwoyo gunnuma. ('I am broken-hearted.'),* -**nyolwa mu mutima**, *eg. Nnanyoleddwa mu mutima. ('I am broken-hearted.')*

²**broken** *v. See* break

broker *n* **bbulooka** *n1*, **omubulooka** *n1* house broker **bbulooka w'amayumba** land broker **bbulooka w'ettaka**

bronchitis *n* **lubyamira** *n1*

brood (*eggs*) *vt* -**maamira**. *See* ponder

brook *n* **akagga** *n12*

broom *n* **olweyo** *n11*, (*of Panicum grass*) **olweyo lwa mukonzikonzi** *n1*

broomstick *n* **omuti gw'olweyo** *n3*

brother *n* (*male blood relative in general*) **ow'oluganda** *n1*, (*of the same mother*) **ow'enda emu** *n1*, (*eldest, of the Queen Mother*) **Ssaabaganzi** *n1* title. *Brothers of males are* **muganda** (*with pos N12*), *eg. muganda wange ('my brother'). Brothers of females (having the same mother) are:* my brother **mwannyinaze,** your brother **mwannyoko,** her brother **mwannyina,** *etc.* (*stem* **mwannyi-** *N12*). *A brother as a member of a religious order is* **bulaaza** *n1*.

brotherhood *n* **oluganda** *n11* blood brotherhood **omukago** *n3*

brother-in-law (*of a man*) *n* **omuko** *n1*, **mukoddomi** (*with pos N12*), *eg. mukoddomi wo ('your brother-in-law'). A brother-in-law of a female is* **mulamu** *n1* (*with pos N12*), *eg. mulamu wange ('my brother-in-law').* wife's sister's husband **musangi** *n1* (*with pos N12*), *eg. musangi wange ('my brother-in-law')*

brought *See* bring

brow *n* **ekyenyi** *n7*

brown *adj* (1) (*colour of soil*) -**a ekitaka**; (2) (*colour of subsoil*) -**a ekikuusi**

¹**bruise** *n* **ekinuubule** *n7*

²**bruise** *vt* -**nuubula** be bruised -**nuubuka**

¹**brush** *n* **bulaasi** *n9*, (*broom*) **olweyo** *n11. See* scratcher hairbrush **bulaasi y'enviiri** paintbrush **bulaasi esiiga langi** shoe brush **bulaasi y'engatto** toothbrush **akasenya** *n12*

²**brush** (*sweep*) *vt* -**yera** brush against (*rub against*) -**kuuba** brush hair -**kuba enviiri** brush teeth -**senya amannyo**

brutal *adj* -**kambwe** brutal person **omukambwe** *n1*

brutality *n* obukambwe *14*

bubble (up) *vi* -vulula become bubbly (*of a person; active and responsive*) -mmuka

bubbles *n* ebyovu *n8*

bubonic plague *n* kawumpuli *n1*

bucket *n*) akalobo *n12* (*large* endobo *n9*), baketi *n9*

bud *n* omutunsi *n3*, (*on stump of banana plant*) endu *n9*

budge, refuse to *vi* -lemera, *eg. Ente yalemera mu kiraalo. ('The cow refused to budge from the pen.')*

budget *n* embalirira y'ensimbi *n9*

buffalo *n* embogo *n9*

bug (*general name for insect*) *n* ekiwuka *n7* bedbug ekiku *n7*

Buganda *n* Buganda *n9* language of Buganda Oluganda *n11* person of Buganda Omuganda *n1*

bugle *n* bbuluugi *n9*

build *vt* -zimba, (*thatched hut or temporary shelter*) -siisira build for -zimbira build for oneself -eezimbira

builder *n* omuzimbi *n1*

building *n* ekizimbe *n7*, (*open-sided, used for meetings*) ekigango *n7* building site ekibanja *n7*. *See* area multi-storey building ekizimbe kya kalina, kalina *n9*, ggoloofa *n9* three-storey building kalinaasatu *n9* two-storey building kalinaabiri *n9* way of building enzimba *n9*

bulb (*for lighting*) *n* balubu *n9*

bulbul (*type of bird*) *n* ssossolye *n1*

bulge (out) *vi* (1) (*become swollen*) -zimba, *eg. Nnapakidde ebintu byonna mu nsawo n'ezimba. ('I packed everything in the sack and it bulged out.')*; (2) (*cause to bulge out in one place*) -kukunala, *eg. Manvuuli ejja kukukunala mu nsawo. ('The umbrella will make the bag bulge out.'). See* occupy too much space

bulky, be (*occupy too much space*) *vi* (1) (*of a person, items in a store, etc.*) -zimbagala; (2) (*of a plant*) -zijjagala

bull *n* ente ennume *n9*, sseddume *n1*

bulldozer *n* ttingatinga *n9*, majegere *n9*

bullet *n* essasi *n5* bullet case ekisosonkole ky'essasi *n7*

bullock *n* ente endaawo *n9*

¹bully *n* omujoozi *n1*

²bully *vt* -jooga, (*take advantage of a person*) -yiikiriza

bullying *n* obujoozi *n14*

bum *n* (1) (*person's bottom*) ennyuma *n9*; (2) (*lout*) omuyaaye *n1*

bumble bee *n* evvuuvuumira *n5*

¹bump (*on road*) *n* ekigulumu *n7*. *See* swelling

²bump (into) *vt* (1) (*hit*) -tomera, *eg. Emmotoka yatutomedde. ('The car bumped into us.')*; (2) (*encounter by chance*) -sanga bump into one another -tomeragana

bumptiousness *n* akababba *n12*

bumpy *adj* -a ebisirikko, *eg. oluguudo olw'ebisirikko ('bumpy road')*, -a ebigulumu

bun *n* akagaati *n12*, banzi *n9*. *See* doughnut

bunch (*as can be held in the hand or hands*) *n* ekisaaganda *n7*, *eg. ekisaaganda ky'essubi ('bunch of grass'). See* bundle bunch of bananas enkota *n9*, *eg. enkota ya ndiizi ('bunch of small dessert bananas')*, (*of cooking bananas*) ettooke *n5*, (*one that has come down without human agency*) ettooke ery'engwira *n5*

bundle *n* omuganda *n3*, *eg. omuganda gw'emmuli ('bundle of reeds')*, (*small*) akaganda *n12*, (*wrapped in cloth for transporting*) omugugu *n3*, (*of firewood, sticks or reeds*) omusekese *n3*, *eg. omusekese gw'enku ('bundle of firewood'). See* banana (*for information on food parcels*); bunch bundle of barkcloth (*formerly part of brideprice*) omutwalo gw'embugo *n3* bundle of firewood ekinywa ky'enku *n7* bundle of grass (*for thatching*) enjole y'essubi *n9*, (*small*) akayole k'essubi *n12* bundle of paper money bandaali *n9* long bundle (*of sticks or reeds*) olusekese *n11*, *eg. olusekese lw'enku ('long bundle of firewood')*

bung *n* akasaanikira *n12*, (*large*) ekisaanikira *n7* be bunged up (*of the nose*) See nose bunged-up nose (*rhinitis*) ekibobe *n7*

bungle *vt* -dobonkanya, *eg. Omulimu gw'okulunda enkoko yagudobonkanya. ('He bungled the chicken project.'). See* mess up; spoil be bungled -dobonkana, *eg. Omulimu gudobonkanye. ('The job was bungled.')*

bungler *n* omudibazi *n1*

Bunyoro *n* Bunyoro *n9* language of Bunyoro Olunyoro *n11* person of Bunyoro Omunyoro *n1*

¹burden (*load; responsibility*) *n* omugugu *n3*, (*something weighing on the mind*) ekikoligo *n7* be a burden to -zimbirira, *eg. Anzimbiridde. ('He has become a burden to me.')*

²burden (*someone with a difficult task*) *vt* -kakaalukanya. *See* overburden; overload be burdened (*with a difficult task*) -kakaalukana

burglar *n* omubbi *n1*`

burglary *n* obubbi *n14*

burial *n* okuziika *n15* burial ground ekiggya *n7*, (*royal*) amasiro *n6*

¹burn (*tribal mark made on body*) *n* oluyokyo *n11* (*usually pl.* enjokyo *n10*)

²burn *v* (burnt) TRANSITIVE AND REFLEXIVE USES -yokya, *eg. Bayokya ebisaaniko. ('They are burning the rubbish.')*, (*accidentally*) -siriiza, *eg. Yasiriizizza emmere. ('She has burnt the food.'). See* fumigate; hot (be) burn a CD -yokya siddi burn down a house (*arson*) -yokerera. *The house owner can be indicated by an object pronoun, eg. Baanjokerera. ('They burnt down my house.).* burn incense -nyookeza obubaane burn oneself -eeyokya omuliro INTRANSITIVE USES -yaka, *eg. Omuliro gwaka. ('The fire is burning.')*, (*with visible flames*) -**bumbujja** be burning to the mouth (*of spicy food*) -**baalaala** be burnt (1) (*eg. of food in a pot*) -**siriira**; (2) (*of a house*) -**ggya omuliro**, *eg. Ennyumba eyidde omuliro.* ('*The house has been burnt.*') be burnt within -**ggiira mu**, *eg. Entebe yaggiira mu nnyumba.* ('*The chair was burnt in the house.*') be on the point of burning (*eg. of something too close to fire*) -**babirira** have a burning sensation -**babuukirira**

burnt *adj* -**yokye** area of burnt vegetation **oluyiira** *n11* burning smell (1) (*from metal saucepan*) **ebbabe** *n5*; (2) (*of burning flesh or fur*) **evvumbe** *n5*

burp *See* belch

¹**burrow** (*hole*) *n* **ekinnya** *n7*

²**burrow** (*dig*) *vi* -**sima**

¹**burst** *adj* -**yabifu**

²**burst** *v* TRANSITIVE USES -**yabya**, *eg. Njabizza ensawo.* ('*I have burst the bag.*'), (*making a sound*) -**tulisa**. *See* break burst banks (*of a river*) -**wagulula**, *eg. Omugga guwaguludde.* ('*The river has burst its banks.*') INTRANSITIVE USES -**yabika**, *eg. Ensawo eyabise.* ('*The bag has burst.*'), (*making a sound*) -**tulika**, *eg. Yatulika n'aseka.* ('*He burst out laughing.*') burst into (*laughter or tears*) -**tumbuka**, *eg. Yatumbuka n'akaaba.* ('*She burst into tears.*') burst out (*from a hiding place*) -**wamatuka**, (*and run away*) -**fubutuka** burst with rage -**tuyira olw'obusungu**

bury *vt* -**ziika** bury within ashes -**vumbika** (**mu vvu**), *eg. Yavumbika lumonde mu vvu.* ('*She buried the potatoes in the ashes.*')

bus *n* **ebbaasi** *n9*, (*double-decker*) **kabandole** *n9* bus park **ppaaka ya bbaasi** *n9* bus stop **siteegi ya bbaasi** *n9*

bush (*thicket*) *n* **ekisaka** *n7*. *See* bushland; jungle; tree bush duiker **empeewo** *n9* bush fire **oluyiira** *n11*

bushbuck *n* **engabi** *n9*

bushland *n* **ensiko** *n9*. *See* thicket

bushy (*thickly vegetated*) *adj* -**saakaativu** be bushy -**saakaatira**

business *n* **bizineesi** *n9* business affairs **ebyobusuubuzi** *n8* do business (*trade*) -**suubula**

businessman *n* **omusuubuzi** *n1*

Busoga *n* **Busoga** *n9* language of Busoga **Olusoga** *n11* person of Busoga **Omusoga** *n1*

bustle about *vi* -**eetala**, *eg. Yali yeetala nga yeetegekera abagenyi.* ('*She was bustling about preparing for the visitors.*'), (*excitedly*) -**eebuga**

bustling about *n* **akeetalo** *n12*

busy, be *vi* (1) (*go here and there doing things*) -**tawuka**, *eg. Nnabadde ntawuka mu kibuga leero.* ('*I was busy in town today.*'); (2) (*in preparation*) -**eekeja**. *See* preoccupied

busybody *n* **ow'olunderebu** *n1*

but *conj* **naye** but at least **kasita** but unfortunately **ebyembi**

¹**butcher** *n* (1) (*slaughterer and flayer*) **omubaazi** *n1*; (2) (*meat retailer*) **omukinjaaji** *n1*

²**butcher** *vt* (1) (*slaughter and skin*) -**baaga**; (2) (*chop/cut up carcasses*) -**temaatema**

butter *n* **siyaagi** *n1*, **bbata** *n1*, **bulubbanda** *n1*. *See* margarine butter bean **ekigaaga** *n7*

butterfly **ekiwojjolo** *n7*

buttocks *n* **obutuuliro** *n14*, **ennyuma** *n9*, **obunyuma** *n14*, **amatako** *n6* (*impolite*). *See* bottom

button *n* **eppeesa** *n5*, (*trigger, eg. on camera*) **emmanduso** *n9*

buy *vt* (bought) -**gula** buy for -**gulira**, *eg. Yakimugulira.* ('*He bought it for her.*')

buyer *n* **omuguzi** *n1*

¹**buzz** (*sound*) *n* **oluvuuvuumo** *n11*

²**buzz** *vi* (1) (*as a bumble bee*) -**vuuvuuma**; (2) (*of the ear*) -**wuuma**, *eg. Okutu kumpuuma.* ('*My ear is buzzing.*')

by (*near*) *pre* **kumpi na/ne**, *eg. Ente eri kumpi n'omugga.* ('*The cow is by the river.*'). There is no separate word for 'by' after a passive verb (**N22**). by the way (*indicating doubt*) **kozzi**

C,c

cabbage *n* **emboga** *n9*, **kabeji** *n9* Kikuyu cabbage **sukuma** *n9*

cable *n* **waaya** *n9* electricity cable **waaya y'amasannyalaze**

cackle *vi* -**kekema**

cactus (*Opuntia*) *n* **engabo ya Kabaka** *n9*

cafeteria *n* **wooteri** *n9*

¹**cage** *n* **ekiguli** *n7*, (*small*) **akaguli** *n12* chicken cage (*as seen in markets*) **ekiguli ky'enkoko** *n3*

²**cage** *vt* -**siba**

cajole *vt* -**sendasenda**

cake *n* **keeke** *n9*, (*made from lake flies*) **ekiwumi ky'essami** *n7*. *See* doughnut; pancake

calabash *See* gourd

calculate *vt* -**bala**

calculator *n* **akabazi** *n12*

calendar *n* **kalenda** *n9*

calf *n* (*pl.* calves) (1) (*of the leg*) **entumbwe** *n9*; (2) (*young cow*) **ennyana** *n9*

¹**call** (*telephone call*) *n* **essimu** *n9* alarm call **enduulu** *n9* make a telephone call -**kubira essimu** make an alarm call -**kuba enduulu**

²**call** *v* (1) (*of animals/birds*) *vi* -**kaaba**; (2) *vt* -**yita**, *eg. Yampita okujja.* ('*She called me to come.*'), (*repeatedly*) -**yitaayita**. *See* name; nickname; telephone; ululate call from a distance -**koowoola**, *eg. Yakoowodde omwana okujja.* ('*She called the child to come.*') call on (*visit*) -**kyalira** call to prayers (*of Muslims*) -**yaziina**

calling (*vocation*) *n* **okuyitibwa** *n15*

callus *n* **ebbavu** *n5*

¹**calm** *adj* -kkakkamu, -teefu
²**calm(ness)** *n* obukkakkamu *n14*, obuteefu *n14*
³**calm (down)** *v* TRANSITIVE USES
-kkakkanya, *eg. Yamukkakkanya. ('She calmed him down.')*, *(someone annoyed)* -nyiigulula. *See* lull; quieten; soothe INTRANSITIVE USES (1) *(of oneself, a situation, inflammation, anger, etc.)* -kkakkana, *eg. Yali anyiize naye kati akkakkanye. ('He was angry but has now calmed down.')*; (2) *(of oneself, from being annoyed)* -nyiigulukuka; (3) *(of a body of water)* -teeka, *eg. Ennyanja eteese. ('The lake is calm.')*; (4) *(through being relieved of worries)* -weera. *See* abate; relax; settled (become)
calmly *adv* mu bukkakkamu
came *See* come
camel *n* eŋŋamira *n9* camel-foot tree *(Bauhinia; Piliostigma)* ekigali *n7*
camera *n* kkamera *n9*
camp *(encampment)* *n* olusiisira *n11*, *(military)* enkambi *n9* set up camp -siisira. *See* pitch
¹**campaign** *n* (1) *(political)* kampeyini *n9*; (2) *(concerted effort)* kaweefube *n1*. *See* war
²**campaign** *(politically)* *vi* -kuba kampeyini
¹**can** *(tin)* *n* omukebe *n3*. *See* jerry can
²**can** *(be able)* *aux v* (could) -sobola, -yinza
Canada *n* Kkanada *n9*
Canadian *n* Omukanada *n1*
canal *n* omukutu *n3*
cancel *vt* -sazaamu, *eg. Nnasazizzaamu olugendo. ('I cancelled the trip.')* be cancelled -sazibwaamu, *eg. Olugendo lwasazibwaamu. ('The trip was cancelled.')*
cancer *n* kkookolo *n1*, kkansa *n1* breast cancer kkansa w'ebbeere contract cancer -lwala kkookolo lung cancer kkansa w'amawuggwe person with cancer omukookolo *n1*
candelabra tree *(euphorbia)* *n* enkuukuulu *n9*
candidacy *n* okwesimbawo *n15*
candidate *(in election)* *n*. Use -eesimbawo *('be a candidate')* in *rel* (N7.1), *eg. abantu abeesimbyewo ('candidates')* be a candidate -eesimbawo, *eg. Yeesimbyewo okumulonda okukiikirira ekitundu kino. ('She is standing for election to represent this area.')*
candle *n* omusubbaawa *n3*
¹**cane** *(for construction or crafts)* *n* (1) *(rattan)* oluga *n11*, *eg. entebe y'oluga ('cane chair')*; (2) *(of elephant grass)* olumuli *n11*; (3) *(of Marantochloa leucantha, giving a coarser type of cane)* amawulugungu *n6*; (4) *(of Marantochloa purpurea, giving a finer type of cane used in basketry)* enjulu *n9*. *See* sugar cane cane rat (1) *(savannah)* omusu *n3*; (2) *(marsh)* omusu omwene; (3) *(lesser)* emmangala *n9*
²**cane** *(for administering punishment)* *n* kibooko *n9*. *See* whip
³**cane** *(as a punishment)* *vt* -kuba kibooko,

(mercilessly with sticks) -weweenyula emiggo
canine tooth *n* essongezo *n5*
canna lily *n* eddanga *n5*
cannabis *n* enjaga *n9*, enjaaye *n9* smoker of cannabis omuyaga *n1*, omuyaaye *n1*
cannon *n* omuzinga *n3*
cannot *aux v* (1) Use -yinza *or* -sobola *('be able')* in neg (N21), *eg. Tasobola kutambula. ('He cannot walk.')*; (2) -bulwa, *eg. Nnabulwa otulo. ('I could not sleep.')*
canny person *n* omukalukalu *n1*
canoe *n* emmanvu *n5*, *(bigger)* eryato *n5*. *See* beer canoe; flag; seat *(for seats in canoe)*. The boards in a canoe are: (1) *(top)* oluwero *n11*; (2) *(middle)* ebbasi *n5*; (3) *(keel)* omugongo *n3*. The prow is ekiyinda *n7*.
canopy *n* ettundubaali *n5*
canteen *n* kkantiini *n9*
canvas *(tarpaulin)* *n* ettundubaali *n5* canvas shoes engatto za lusejjera *n10*
cap *n* (1) *(hat)* enkuufiira *n9*, *(round type, worn by Muslims)* entalabuusi *n9*; (2) *(of a bottle)* akasaanikira eccupa *n12*. *See* fez; hat
capability *n* obusobozi *n14*
capable *adj*. Use -sobola *('be able')* in rel (N7.1), *eg. abantu abasobola ('capable people')* be capable -sobola, *(of managing one's own affairs)* -eesobola
capacity have the capacity of -jjula, *eg. Endobo eno ejjula ggalani bbiri. ('This bucket has a capacity of two gallons.')*
cape gooseberry *n* entuntunu *n9*
capital (city) *n* ekibuga ekikulu *n7* capital letter ennyukuta ennene *n9* write in capital letters -wandiika mu kyapa
capsise *vi* -eevuunika
capsule *(of medicine)* *n* kapiso *n9*. *See* pill
captain *n* kapiteeni *n1*
caption *n* omutwe gw'ebikulu *n3*
captive *n* omuwambe *n1*
captivity *n* obuwambe *n14*
captor *n* omuwambi *n1*
capture *vt* -wamba
car *n* emmotoka *n9* saloon car emmotoka eya muserebende
card *n* kaada *n9*, *eg. kaada ya bbanka ('bank card')* identity card ekitambulizo *n7* playing cards caanisi *n1*
¹**care** *n* (1) *(concern)* okufaayo *n15*; (2) *(carefulness)* obwegenndereza *n14* take care of -labirira. *See* nurse; protect take care of oneself -eerabirira with care mu bwegenndereza
²**care (about/for)** *vi* -faayo *(or* -faako) ku, *eg. Olina okufaayo ku bintu byo. ('You should care for your things.')*
careful careful person omwegenndereza *n1* be careful (about) -eegenndereza
carefully *adv* n'obwegenndereza approach carefully

-lembereza do carefully and slowly
-eerembereza deal carefully with (*a person, being considerate*) -lembereza handle carefully (*eg. something delicate*) -kwata empola
careless *adj* -lagajjavu be careless -lagajjala
carelessness *n* obulagajjavu *n14*
caress *vt* -weeweeta
caretaker *n* omukuumi *n1*, (*of the royal hearth*) Musolooza *n1* title
carpenter *n* omubazzi *n1*
carpentry carpentry workshop ebbajjiro *n5* do carpentry -bajja, (*clumsily, or carpentry of all sorts*) -bajjirira piece of carpentry ekibajje *n7*
carpet *n* ekiwempe *n7*, (*of skins, for the Kababa*) ekiwu *n7*. See covering
[1]carrier (*on vehicle*)*n* (1) (*on bike*) ekkaliya *n9*; (2) (*on car or bus*) akatanda *n12*
[2]carrier (*person who carries*) *n* (1) (*porter*) omwetissi *n1*; (2) (*another person on the shoulders*) omukongozzi *n1*
carrot *n* kalati *n9*
carry *vt* -eetikka, *eg. Yeetisse emigugu. ('He is carrying the luggage.')* carry around food to sell -tambuza emmere carry behind (*eg. baby on back, or passenger or load on bike*) -weeka carry for -situlira, *eg. Nnaamusitulira ensawo. ('I carried the bag for her.')* carry (*load*) on the back -eetikka ku mabega carry on the chest (*holding with both hands*) -eebagajja carry (*load*) on the head -eetikka ku mutwe carry on the shoulders (1) (*something*) -bagalira; (2) (*person*) -kongojja carry out successfully (*a task; accomplish*) -tuukiriza
cartilage *n* akabebenu *n12*
cartridge *n* ekyasi *n7*
carve (*wood*) *vt* -bajja. See scoop out carve pattern on -yola, *eg. Ayola ensuwa. ('He is carving a pattern on the pot.')*
carver (*of wood*) *n* omubazzi *n1*
carving *n* ekibajje *n7*
case *n* (1) (*in court*) omusango *n3*; (2) (*matter; affair*) ensonga *n9*; (3) (*suitcase*) essanduuko *n9* in case *conj* si kulwa nga
cash *n* essente enkalu *n10*, essente za buliwo, kaasi *n9*
cassava (*also* manioc) *n* muwogo *n1*, (*pieces of*) emiwogo *n4*, (*stale and black-stained*) muwogo wa bulaala, (*old and unpalatable, can be very hard*) muwogo omuwutta, (*sliced and dried for storage*) mutere wa muwogo *n1* cassava meal obutta *n14*, bbando *n1*
cast (*throw, eg. spear*) *vt* kasuka cast a glance (at) -suuliza eriiso cast a shadow on -siikiriza cast a vote -kuba akalulu cast an evil spell (on) -loga
cast net (*for fishing*) *n* ponyoka *n1*
castor-oil *n* (1) (*plant*) omusogasoga *n3*; (2) (*berry*) ensogasoga *n9*
castrate *vt* -laawa

castrated *adj* -laawe castrated person omulaawe *n1*
casual casual labourer omupakasi wa lejjalejja *n1* casual work omulimu gwa lejjalejja *n3*
casuarina (*tree*) *n* falaawo *n1*
cat (*also* puss, pussy) *n* kkapa *n9*, ppusi *n9*. See civet wild (*or* feral) cat omuyaayu *n3*
catapult *n* butida *n9*
cataract *n* (1) (*on eye*) ensenke *n9*; (2) (*on river*) ebiyiriro *n8*
catastrophy *n* ekibabu *n7*
catch *v* (caught) (1) (*of a fire*) *vi* -koleera, *eg. Omuliro gukoledde. ('The fire has caught.')*; (2) (*in the hand, eg. ball*) *vt* -baka; (3) (*prisoner, animal, etc.*) *vt* -kwata, *eg. Omutego gukutte akasolo. ('The trap has caught a small animal.')* catch an illness obulwadde -kwata (*with personal object*), *eg. Obulwadde bumukutte. ('She has caught an illness.')* catch fire kwata omuliro, *eg. Ennyumba yakwata omuliro. ('The house caught fire.')* catch (*a liquid*) in a vessel -lembeka, *eg. Alembeka amazzi mu ppipa. ('She is catching water in a tub.')* catch in the act -kwatiriza. See surprise catch lake flies (*in a basket*) -wunga essami manage to catch (*something falling*) -bakirira, *eg. Yabakirira essowaani ng'egwa. ('She caught the plate as it was falling.')*
catechism *n* katekiisimu *n9*
category *n* ettuluba. See class; type put into categories (*grade*) -gereka
caterpillar *n* (1) (*general term*) ekisaanyi *n7*, (*small; also silkworm*) akasaanyi *n12*; (2) (*camouflaged flattish hairy type*) ssekkesa *n1*; (3) (*type with long hairs, reddish-brown*) kasikisa *n1*; (4) (*looper*) nnabeefunye *n1*
catfish See fish
cathedral *n* (1) (*Prot*) lutikko *n9*; (2) (*RC*) ekkereziya enkulu *n9*
Catholic *adj* -katoliki Catholic (*person*) Omukatoliki *n1*
Catholicism *n* Obukatoliki *n14*
cattle *n* ente *n10* cattle pen olugo *n11*, ekiraalo *n7* cattle plaque nsotoka *n1* head of cattle omugongo gw'ente *n3*
caught See catch
[1]cause (*reason*) *n* ensonga *n9*, ekivaako *n7* (*declinable according to the timing of the cause N6*) have a common cause -ba ab'ekinywi without cause obwereere
[2]cause (*bring*) *vt* -leeta, *eg. Kiki ekireese omutawaana guno? ('What has caused this problem?')*; (2) -vaako, *eg. Kiki ekivuddeko omutawaana guno? ('What has caused this problem?')*. Many simple verbs have causative forms, formed by making modifications to their final letters (**N22**), *eg.*: (1) cause to become (*change in fundamental nature; perform magic*) -fuusa (*from '-fuula' 'change'*); (2) cause to make

known (*ie. inform*) **-manyisa** (*from '-manya'* '*know'*), etc.   cause for Use **-leetera** (*'bring for'*) in rel (**N7.1**), eg. *Kiki ekimuleetedde omutawaana guno? ('What has caused this problem for her?')*

[1]**caution** *n* **obwegenderereza** *n14*   with caution **n'obwegenderereza**

[2]**caution** *vt* **-komako**, eg. *Yali ayogera ku mwami we nze ne mmukomako. ('She was talking about her husband and I cautioned her to stop.')*, (*by touching lightly*) **-sunyako**, eg. *Yamusunyako obutayogera. ('He cautioned her not to say anything.')*, (*by winking*) **-temyako**. *See* warn

cautious   cautious person **omwegenderereza** *n1*   be cautious (about) **-eegenderereza**, eg. *Beegenderereza nga basala ekkubo. ('They were cautious when crossing the road.')*

cautiously *adv* **mu bwegenderereza**

cave *n* **empuku** *n9*

cavity *n* **empompogoma** *n9*. *See* hollow   cavity under a termite mound **empompogoma y'ekiswa**

cavort *vi* **-ligita, -tiguka, -binuka**

CD *n* **siddi** *n9*

cease (*an activity*) *vt* **-lekera awo**, eg. *Alekedde awo okukola. ('He has ceased working.')*. *See* abandon; end; stop; suspend

ceaselessly *adv* **obutamala**

ceiling *n* **siiringi** *n9*

celebrant (*of mass*) *n* **omutambizi w'emmisa** *n1*

celebrate *vt* (1) (*eg. an anniversary*) **-jaguza**, eg. *Baakajaguza okuweza emyaka kkumi mu bufumbo. ('They have just celebrated their tenth wedding anniversary.')*; (2) (*a special day*) **-kuza**, eg. *Twawummudde okukuza Ssekukkulu. ('We had a holiday to celebrate Christmas.')*   celebrate Holy Communion (*by the celebrant*) **-sembeza mu kkanisa**

celebrated (*distinguished*) *adj* **-yatiikirivu**   be(come) celebrated **-yatiikirira**

celebration *n* **ekijaguzo** *n7*

celebrity *n* **omwatiikirivu** *n1*

cell *n* (1) (*in prison*) **akaduukulu** *n12*; (2) (*of a honeycomb*) **ekisenge ky'enjuki** *n7*; (3) (*of a plant or animal*) **akatofaali** *n12*. *See* prison

cellulitis *n* **obusukko** *n14*

cement *n* **seminti** *n1*

cemetery *n* **ekiggya** *n7*, (*royal*) **amasiro** *n6*

census *n* **okubala abantu mu ggwanga** *n15*

cent *n* **essente** *n9*

centipede *n* **ssigga** *n1*

central *adj* **-a wakati**, eg. *gavumenti ya wakati ('central government')*

centre *n* **amakkati** *n6*   in the centre **mu makkati, wakati**   in the centre of **mu makkati ga, wakati wa**   the very centre **amasekkati** *n6*, eg. *amasekkati g'Afirika ('centre of Africa')*

century *n* **ekyasa** *n7*, eg. *ekyasa eky'amakumi abiri ('20th century')*

ceremony *n* **omukolo** *n3*, (*one at which roasted*

coffee beans are offered to visitors) **kattamukago** *n1*   degree ceremony **amatikkira** *n6*

[1]**certain** (*sure*) *adj* **-kakafu**   be(come) certain **-kakata**   make certain **-kakasa**

[2]**certain** (*some*) *det* **-mu** (**N8.1**). *Takes numeral concord (**N4.2**), eg. Yasaba abantu abamu okujja. ('He asked certain people to come.')*

certainly (*indeed*) *adv* **ddala**

certainty *n* **obukakafu** *n14*

certificate *n* **ebbaluwa** *n9*, **satifikeeti** *n9*

chafed (*of the skin*) *adj* **-kuubuufu**   be(come) chafed **-kuubuuka**

chaff *n* **ebisusunku** *n8*

chain *n* (1) **olujegere** *n11*, (*small*) **akajegere** *n12*; (2) (*ornamental, or for keys or watch*) **omukuufu** *n3*, (*small*) **akakuufu** *n12*   dog chain **olujegere lw'embwa**

[1]**chair** *n* (1) (*for sitting on*) **entebe** *n9*, (*poorly made, or worn-out*) **ekitebe** *n7*; (2) (*presiding officer at meeting; chairperson*) **omukubiriza** *n1*, (*male*) **ssentebe** *n1*

[2]**chair** (*a meeting*) *vt* **-kubiriza**

chalise *n* **ekikompe** *n7*

chalk *n* **ennoni** *n9*

challenge *vt* **-soomooza**, eg. *Yansoomoozezza mu mbiro. ('He challenged me to a running race.')*, (*aggressively; provoke*) **-sosonkereza**, eg. *Yamusosonkereza alwane. ('He challenged him to a fight.')*. *See* contradict; dispute with   be challenged **-soomoozebwa**

chameleon *n* **nnawolovu** *n1*

chance (*luck*) *n* **omukisa** *n3*

chancellor (*of university*) *n* **omukulu wa ssettendekero** *n1*

[1]**change** *n* (1) (*alteration*) **enkyuka** *n9*, eg. *Wabaddewo enkyuka mu mulimu gwe. ('There has been a change in his work.')*; (2) (*from payment*) **enfissi** *n9*, **baalansi** *n1*; (3) (*money in small denominations*) **kyengi** *n1*   many changes (*alterations; developments*) **enkyukakyuka** *n10*, eg. *Wabaddewo enkyukakyuka mu ssomero. ('There have been many changes at school.')*   way of changing **enkyuka** *n9*

[2]**change** *v* TRANSITIVE USES (1) **-kyusa**, eg. *Yakyusa omupiira ku mmotoka. ('He has changed the car tyre.')*; (2) (*in nature*) **-fuula**, eg. *Eggalagi yafuula dduuka. ('He has changed the garage into a shop.')*. *See* adjust; alter; convert; divert; magic (perform)   change money (1) (*between denominations*) **-kyusa ssente**; (2) (*into smaller denominations*) **-vungisa ssente**   change one's political party **-sala eddiiro**   change one's position (*physically or mentally*) **-eekyusa**   change one's religion **-kyuka mu ddiini, -kyusa eddiini**   repeatedly change one's mind **-yuugayuuga**   INTRANSITIVE USES **-kyuka**, eg. *Obudde bukyuse. ('The weather has changed.')*, (*in nature*) **-fuuka** eg. *Yafuuka omuntu omulungi. ('She has*

changed into a good person.')

channel *n* (1) *(for water, also of a broadcast)* **omukutu** *n3*; (2) *(of water, eg. in a swamp)* **omwala** *n3*. See ditch; drain erosion channel *(made in earth by flowing water)* **olukonko** *n11*

chaos *n* **omuvuyo** *n3*. See confusion

chapati *n* **chapati** *n9*, *(stuffed with beans)* **kikomando** *n7*

chapter *n* **essuula** *n9*

char *vt* **-siriiza** be charred **-siriira**

character *n* (1) *(of a person; behaviour)* **empisa** *n10*; (2) *(make-up; nature)* **enkula** *n9*; (3) *(letter of the alphabet)* **ennyukuta** *n9*

charcoal *n* **amanda** *n6* (one piece **eryanda** *n5*), **ebisirinza** *n8* (one piece **ekisirinza** *n7*) charcoal stove **essigiri** *n9*

¹charge *n* (1) *(fee)* **ekisale** *n7* *(normally pl.* **ebisale** *n8)* (2) *(accusation)* **omusango** *n3*. See responsibility; tax be in charge of *(eg. an organisation)* **-kulira** file a charge against **-wawaabira** person in charge *(boss)* **omukulu** *n1* put in charge *(as deputy)* **-sigira** without charge **obwereere**

²charge *vt* (1) *(make responsible)* **-sigira**, *eg. Yansigira okulabirira edduuka. ('She charged me to look after the shop.')*; (2) *(hold responsible; accuse)* **-vunaana**, *eg. Baamuvunaana okuvuga emmotoka nga talina layisinsi. ('They charged him for driving without a licence.')*; (3) *(legally)* **-waabira omusango**, *eg. Yamuwaabira omusango mu kkooti. ('They charged him in court.')* charge a battery **-kyajinga bbaatule** charge a fee **-wooza ssente**, *eg. Bawooza ssente okuyingira wano. ('They charge to enter here.')* charge duty **-wooza omusolo** charge *(someone)* too much (for) **-seera**, *eg. Baseera ekintu kino. ('They are charging too much for this.')* be charged *(held responsible)* **-vunaanibwa** person charged *(legally)* **omuwawaabirwa** *n1*

charity *(voluntary organisation)* *n* **ekibiina kya ba nnakyewa** *n7*. See kindness; love charity worker **nnakyewa** *n1*

Charles *n* **Kalooli** *n1*

¹charm *(for good luck or protection)* *n* (1) **ensiriba** *n9*, *(used by Muslims)* **eyirizi** *n9*; (2) *(put in a drum)* **omutima gw'eŋŋoma** *n3*, **ndikungulu** *n12*, **akawulunguta** *n12*; (3) *(to lure animals in hunting)* **mukokota** *n1*; (4) *(love charm worn by women; waistband of beads)* **obutiiti** *n14*. See fetish

²charm *(please)* *vt* **-sanyusa**

chart *n* **ekipande** *n7*

charter *(hire)* *vt* **-pangisa**

chase (away) *vt* **-goba**, *eg. Yagoba embwa. ('She chased away the dog.')*

chasm *n* **olukonko** *n11*

chastise *vt* **-nenya**. See discipline

chat *vi* **-nyumya**, *eg. Mbadde nnyumya ne*

muliraanwa wange. ('I was chatting with my neighbour.'). See talk chat away *(eg. to keep a visitor entertained)* **-yogezayogeza** chat up *(woo)* **-yogereza** keep on chatting (to) **-nyumiikiriza**

chatter *vi* **-legesa**, **-legejja**, *(loudly, as children at play)* **-kuba embeekuulo**

cheap *adj* **-a layisi**, **-a essente entono**

cheaply *adv* **layisi** sell cheaply **-tunda omuwendo ogwa wansi**

¹cheat *n* (1) *(fraudster)* **omukumpanya** *n1*; (2) *(one who deliberately fails to repay a debt)* **omulyazaamaanyi** *n1*. See liar

²cheat *vt* (1) *(defraud)* **-kumpanya**; (2) *(deliberately fail to repay a debt to)* **-lyazaamaanya**. See deceive cheat in a test **-bbira mu bibuuzo**, *(by looking at someone's work)* **-labira mu bibuuzo**, *eg. Yalabira Musoke mu bibuuzo. ('He cheated by looking at what Musoke had written.')*

check *(inspect)* *vt* **-kebera**, *eg. Owa poliisi yakebedde empapula zange. ('The policeman checked my documents.')*. See impede; scrutinise check oneself *(pause and reconsider when talking on a subject)* **-eekomako**

checked *(with squared pattern)* *adj* **-a kapere**, *eg. essaati ya kapere ('checked shirt')*

cheek *n* (1) *(of face)* **ettama** *n5*; (2) *(nautiness)* **ekitigi** *n7*; (3) *(impertinence)* **ekyejo** *n7*. See naughtiness drawn or hollow cheeks *(due to old age or loss of teeth)* **embugubugu** *n10* place on face immediately in front of ear **mpulukutu** *n10*

¹cheer *(shout of approval)* *n* **omuzira** *n3* cheers **emizira** *n4*

²cheer *(cheer on)* *vt* **-kuba emizira**. See applaud cheer on dogs *(in hunting)* **-yamira embwa** cheer up *(a person)* **-camula**, *eg. Emboozi yamucamula. ('The conversation cheered him up.')*. See happy (make) be(come) cheered up *(of oneself)* **-camuka**, *eg. Nnamuwadde ekirabo n'acamuka. ('I gave her a present and she cheered up.')*

cheerful *adj* **-camufu**. See happy

cheese *n* **kiizi** *n9*

chef *n* **omufumbi** *n1*, *(chief, of the Kabaka)* **Kawuuta** *n1 title*

chemical *n* **eddagala** *n5*

cheque *(for payment)* *n* **kyeke** *n9*

chess *n* **kyesi** *n9*, **omweso** *n3*

chest *n* (1) *(of the body)* **ekifuba** *n7*: (2) *(container; box)* **essanduuko** *n9*

chew *vt* **-gaaya**, *(noisily)* **-swankula**, *(something hard; crunch on)* **-meketa**. See slurp chew sugarcane **-solobeza ekikajjo** chew the cud **-zza obwenkulumu**

chick *n* **akakoko** *n12* chicks **obwana bw'enkoko** *n14*

chicken *n* **enkoko** *n9*, *(young hen, before laying)* **enkoko enseera**, *(free-range)* **enkoko eŋŋanda**, *(broiler; layer)* **enkoko enzungu**, *(Bunyoro-type)* **enkoko ennyolo**. See cock chicken basket

omuyonjo *n3*   chicken cage **ekiguli ky'enkoko** *n7*
chicken coop **akayumba k'enkoko** *n12*   chicken
disease (*type of*) **nsotoka** *n1*
chickenpox *n* **nnamusuna** *n1*
¹**chief** *adj* **-kulu**
²**chief** *n* **omwami** *n1*, (*high-ranking, in the service of
the Kabaka*) **omukungu** *n1*, (*lesser ranking,
traditionally appointed directly by the Kabaka*)
omutongole *n1*. See boss; head. *The traditional
administrative hierarchy is:* (*county chief*)
owessaza *n1*, (*sub-county chief*) **oweggombolola**
n1, (*parish chief*) **owoomuluka** *n1*. *The second
chief in importance is* **ssaabaddu** *n1*, *eg.
ssaabaddu w'owessaza* (*'deputy county chief'*).
(**N29**) chief's enclosure (*or* court) **embuga** *n9*
chieftainship *n* **obwami** *n14*   assume chieftainship
-lya obwami
child *n* (*pl.* children) **omwana** *n1*, (*newborn*)
omuwere *n1*, (*first-born*) **omuggulanda** *n1*, (*last-
born*) **omuggalanda** *n1*, (*small*) **akaana** *n12*,
(*plump*) **ekyana** *n7*, (*of the same mother*) **ow'enda
emu** *n1*   have a child (*after another*) **-zzaako
mwana**, *eg. Ku balongo yazzaako mwana muwala.
('She had a baby girl after the twins.')* have
children frequently *Use* **-yosera** (*'wean too soon'*),
*eg. Mukyala wange abaana aboosera. ('My wife
has closely spaced children.', lit. 'My wife weans
children prematurely.')* have unplanned children
(*or* children by different men) **-zaalazaala**
childbirth *n* **okuzaala** *n15*   assist at/in childbirth
-zaalisa, *eg. Yamuzaalisa. ('She assisted her in
childbirth.')*
childhood *n* **obuto** *n14*   childish things **ebyobuto**
n8
childminder *n* **yaaya** *n1*
children *See* child
chilli (*pepper*) *n* **kaamulali** *n1*, **ppiripiri** *n1*
chilly (*cold*) *adj* **-nnyogovu**, *eg. obudde
obunnyogovu ('chilly weather')*
chimney *n* **omudumu gw'omukka** *n3*   chimney
glass (*of lamp*) **ekirawuli** *n7*
chimpanzee *n* **ezzike** *n5*
chin *n* **akalevu** *n12*
China *n* **Kyayina** *n9*
¹**chip** *n* (1) (*eg. on rim of cup*) **eddibu** *n5*; (2) (*of
wood, etc.*) **olubajjo** *n11* (*small* **akabajjo** *n12*)
(*potato*) chips **kyipusi** *n10*
²**chip** *vt* **-libula**, (*enamel*) **-bongola**   be chipped
-libuka, (*of enamel*) **-bongoka**
chipped *adj* **-libufu**, (*of enamel*) **-bongofu**
chirp (*as cicadas*) *vi* **-nyaanyaagiza**
chisel *n* (1) (*used in woodwork*) **ekyembeewo** *n7*;
(2) (*used in metalwork*) **ensinjo** *n9*
choir *n* **kwaya** *n1*
choke *vt* **-lakira**, *eg. Amazzi gamulakidde. ('The
water is choking him.'). See* strangle
choose *vt* (chose) **-londa**. *See* pick out   choose for
oneself **-eerondera**, (*pointing out one's preference,*

to pre-empt others) **-eesooka**   do through one's
own choice **-eesiimira**
choosy, be (*fussy*) *vi* **-eeronda**. *eg. Musoke si
mwangu kusanyusa kubanga yeeronda. ('Musoke is
not easy to please because he's so choosy.')*
chop *vt* **-tema**, (*into many pieces*) **-temaatema**
chop down a tree **-tema omuti**   chop for **-temera**,
*eg. Yamutemera omuti. ('She chopped down the
tree for her.')*   Chop it right there! **Temeraawo!**
chop up **-yasa**, (*into many pieces*) **-yasaayasa**
chop up banana pseudostem (*'trunk', after felling*)
-gogombola omugogo   chop up firewood **-yasa
enku**   chop up with **-yasisa**   chopped up banana
pseudostem (*'trunk'*) **omuteteme** *n3*   chopping
board (*used by butchers*) **ekiti** *n7*
chore *n* **ekkatala** *n5*
chorus (*in singing*) *n* **ekiddibwamu** *n7*
chose *See* choose
chosen *adj* **-londe**
Christ *n* (1) (*Prot*) **Kulisito** *n1*; (2) (*RC*) **Kirisitu** *n1*;
(3) (*standardised spelling*) **Kirisito** *n1*
christen *vt* **-batiza**
Christian (*person*) *n* (1) (*Prot*) **Omukulisitaayo** *n1*;
(2) (*RC*) **Omukirisitu** *n1*; (3) (*standardised
spelling*) **Omukirisito** *n1*
Christianity *n* (1) (*Prot*) **Obukulisitaayo** *n14*; (2)
(*RC*) **Obukirisitu** *n14*; (3) (*standardised spelling*)
Obukirisito *n14*
Christmas *n* **Ssekukkulu** *n9*
chronic (*of an illness*) *adj* **-a olutentezi**
church *n* (1) (*Prot*) **ekkanisa** *n9*; (2) (*RC*)
ekkereziya *n9*; (3) (*Eastern Orthodox*) **ekkanisa
y'Abasodookisi**; (4) (*born-again*) **ekkanisa
y'abalokole**; (5) (*emphasising church as a
building*) **ennyumba ya Katonda** *n9*   church
service **okusaba** *n15*. *See* service
churchwarden *n* **omuweereza** *n1*
churn *vt* **-sunda**
churned *adj* **-sunde**
cicada *n* **ennyaanyaagize** *n9*
cigarette *n* **ssigala** *n1*, **sseggereeti** *n1*
cinders *n* **ebisirinza** *n8*
cinema *n* **sineema** *n9*
cinnamon *n* (1) (*tree*) **omudalasiini** *n3*; (2) (*spice*)
budalasiini *n1*
circle *n* **enkulungo** *n9*
circular *adj* **-eetooloovu**
circulation *n* **entambula** *n9*   circulation of the
blood **entambula y'omusaayi**
circumcise *vt* **-tayirira**, **-komola**   circumcised
person **omutayirire** *n1*, **omukomole** *n1*   person
who circumcises **omutayirizi** *n1*
cite *vt* (1) (*quote*) **-juliza**; (2) (*pick out as an
example*) **-nokolayo**
citizen *n* **munnansi** *n1*
city *n* **ekibuga** (**ekinene**) *n7*
civet *n* **effumbe** *n5*
civic strife (*disturbance*) *n* **akatabanguko** *n12*. *See*

riot

civil servant *n* omukozi wa gavumenti *n1*

civilise *vt* -gunjula   be(come) civilized -gunjuka

civilised *adj* -gunjufu   civilized person omugunjufu *n1*

civilisation *n* obugunjufu *n14*

claim a debt from *vt* -banja

clamour (*shouting; din*) *n* oluyoogaano *n11*

clan (*division of a tribe*) *n* ekika *n7*. *The subdivisons of a clan are:* (*sub-clan*) essiga *n5*, omutuba *n3*, (*line*) olunyiriri *n11*, (*courtyard*) oluggya *n11*, (*house*) enju *n9*   clan land obutaka *n14*   chief minister of a clan katikkiro *n1*   head of a clan owaakasolya *n1*, (*of any subdivision of a clan*) omutaka *n1*   member of a clan ow'ekika *n1*

clandestine *adj* -a amankwetu. *See* secret

clap (hands) -kuba mu ngalo, -kuba engalo

clap of thunder *n* okubwatuka kw'eggulu *n15*

clarify (*elucidate*) *vt* -tangaaza. *See* decant; explain

clasp *vt* -kwata

class *n* (1) (*in school*) ekibiina *n7*; (2) (*quality of product*) omutindo *n3*, *eg. omutindo gwa waggulu* (*'first class'*); (3) (*category; type*) ekika *n7*, engeri *n9*. *See* level   noun class (*in grammar*) olubu lw'amannya *n11*

¹claw *n* olwala *n11*

²claw (*scratch or lacerate, as a cat*) *vt* -taagula   claw at (*as a gesture of contempt*) -kongoola

clay *n* (1) (*for pottery and making 'emmumbwa'*) ebbumba *n5*; (2) (*wet, in valley*) ettosi *n5*. *See* mud   clay stick (*medicinal*) emmumbwa *n9*   gather together clay (*in pottery making*) -wumbawumba ebbumba   something made of clay ekibumbe *n7*   work with clay -bumba

¹clean *adj* (1) -yonjo, *eg. ennyumba ennyonjo* (*'clean house'*); (2) (*of particular items*) *Use* -tukula (*'be clean'*) *in rel* (**N7.1**), *eg. engoye ezitukula* (*'clean clothes'*)   clean and neat person (*by nature*) omuyonjo *n1*

²clean *vt* -yonja, *eg. Ayonja ennyumba.* (*'She is cleaning the house.'*)   clean a blackboard (*by wiping*) -siimuula olubaawo   clean out -gogola, *eg. Yagogola omufulejje.* (*'He has cleaned out the drain.'*), (*remove all, eg. sediment in a well*) -kokota   clean teeth -senya ammanyo   be(come) clean (*of an item or a liquid*) -tukula, *eg. Yoza engoye zino zitukule.* (*'Wash these clothes until they are clean.'*)   make clean -tukuza, *eg. Atukuzizza engoye.* (*'He has cleaned the clothes.'*)

cleanliness *n* obuyonjo *n14*

cleanse (*spiritually*) *vt* -yambululako, *eg. Baamwambuluddeko emizimu emibi.* (*'They have cleansed her of evil spirits.'*)

¹clear (*transparent*) *adj* -tangaavu. *See* obvious

²clear *vt* (1) (*remove untidy or unwanted things; clear up/out*) -yerula, *eg. Yayerula oluwenda.* (*'He has cleared a path.'*); (2) (*remove things; clear away*) -ggyawo, *eg. Ggyawo ebintu ku mmeeza.*

(*'Clear the things from the table.'*); (3) (*put away*) -tegula, *eg. Ategudde ebintu ku mmeeza.* (*'She has cleared away the things from the table.'*)   clear away for -tegulira, *eg. Yamutegulira ebintu atuule.* (*'He cleared away the things so she could sit.'*)   clear out (*eg. a drain*) -gogola   clear path through vegetation -yerula oluwenda   clear the throat -gogola omumiro, (*by clicking*) -kuba omumiro, (*with spitting out phlegm*) -kolondola   clear up rubbish (*scoop up*) -yoola ebisaaniko, *eg. Abakozi bayoola ebisaaniko ku luguudo.* (*'The workers are clearing up the rubbish in the street.'*)   clear vegetation (*in preparation for planting*) -sambula ensiko   be(come) clear (1) (*of the weather or sky*) -tangaala; (2) (*of water containing sediment*) -teeka; (3) (*understood*) -tegeerekeka; (4) (*obvious, of a motive*) -eeraga   be cleared out of the way -teguka

clearing (*in the jungle*) *n* ekibangirizi *n7*

cleave *vt* -yasa

clench (*hold*) *vt* -kwata   clench the fist -funya ekikonde   clench the teeth -luma emba

clergyman *n* omwawule *n1*

clerk *n* omuwandiisi *n1*, kkalaani *n1*   town clerk omukulu w'ekibuga *n1*

clever *adj* -gezi. *See* shrewd   clever person omugezi *n1*   be(come) clever -geziwala   pretend to be clever -eegeziwaza

cleverness *n* (1) (*intelligence*) amagezi *n6*; (2) (*wisdom*) obugezi *n14*; (3) (*quickness of mind*) obukalabakalaba *n14*

click   click the throat -kuba omumiro   click the tongue -kontola

client (*to a chief*) *n* omusenze *n1*   become a client (*to a chief*) -senga

climate *n* embeera y'obudde *n9*

climax *n* entikko *n9*

climb *v* (1) (*of a plant*) *vi* -landa, *eg. Akatunda kalanze ku muti.* (*'The passion fruit is climbing on the tree.'*); (2) *vt* -linnya, *eg. Abaana balinnya omuti.* (*'The children are climbing the tree.'*), (*using all four limbs*) -walampa. *See* uphill (go)   climbing plant ekiranda *n7*

cling *vi* (clung) -eerippa, *eg. Omwana yeerippa ku maama.* (*'The child clung to her mother.'*). *See* hold onto   cling firmly to a point of view -nywerera ku ndowooza

clinic *n* kiriniki *n9*, (*larger*) eddwaliro *n5*. *See* treatment centre

clock *n* essaawa *n9*   alarm clock essaawa y'ekide

¹clog (*wooden shoe*) *n* omukalabanda *n3*

²clog (*block*) *vt* -zibikira, *eg. Ebisaaniko bizibikidde omudumu.* (*'The rubbish is clogging the drain.'*). *See* block   something that clogs ekizibikira *n7*

¹close (*near*) *adv* kumpi. *See* alongside   close to okumpi na   close together (*one after another*) kumukumu   come close -sembera, *eg. Yasembera.* (*'He came close.'*)   come close to

-semberera, *eg. Yansemberera. ('He came close to me.')* too close **kifuko**, *eg. Kasooli amusimbye kifuko. ('She has planted the maize too close together.')*

²**close** *(shut) vt* **-ggala** *(usually used with enclitic '-wo'* **N24.2**)*, eg. Ggalawo oluggi. ('Close the door.')* close a book **-bikka ekitabo** close one's eyes **-zibiriza amaaso, -zibirira** close up *(eg. of some flowers at night)* **-eewumba**

closed *(shut) adj* **-ggale**

closet *See* lavatory

clot *(of blood) vi* **-kwata**

cloth *n* **olugoye** *n11. Types of cloth or garment include:* (1) *(used for cleaning, etc.; duster)* **ekiwero** *n7 (small* **akawero** *n12);* (2) *(more formal, eg. used as a tablecloth)* **ekitambaala** *n7;* (3) *(undergarment worn under busuuti)* **ekikooyi** *n7;* (4) *(type of printed cloth)* **ekitengi** *n7;* (5) *(thin and coloured, worn by women eg. on head or shoulders; head scarf; shawl)* **leesu** *n9;* (6) *(large and sheet-like, worn by women under armpits)* **essuuka** *n9;* (7) *(for carrying baby on back)* **engozi** *n9;* (8) *(made of barkcloth)* **embugo** *n10 (one piece* **olubugo** *n11);* (9) *(tied around waist as sign of mourning)* **ekimyu** *n7;* (9) *(thick cloth used eg. to wrap bundles of clothes or cotton)* **akadeeya** *n12;* (10) *(khaki)* **kkakki** *n1;* (11) *(shroud)* **looti** *n9* strip of cloth *(or* barkcloth) *(used as clothing)* (1) *(by men)* **ekikunta** *n7;* (2) *(by women)* **omutanda** *n3*

clothe *(dress someone) vt* **-yambaza**

clothes/clothing *n* **engoye** *n10 (one article of clothing* **olugoye** *n11),* **ebyambalo** *n8 (one article of clothing* **ekyambalo** *n7)* everyday clothes *(eg. compared to Sunday best)* **engoye eza bulijjo** ordinary *(or* civilian) clothes *(eg. contrasted with a uniform)* **engoye eza leeya** ready-made clothes **engoye entunge** second-hand clothes **engoye enkadde**

cloud *n* **ekire** *n7*

cloudy *adj* **-a ekikome**, *eg. obudde bw'ekikome ('cloudy weather')* become cloudy *(with sediment)* **-fuukuuka**, *eg. Amazzi gafuukuuse. ('The water has become cloudy.')*

clove of garlic *n* **omuwula gwa katunguluccumu** *n3*

clown *n* **kapere** *n1*, **kazannyirizi** *n1* play the clown **-eemonkoola, -eemoola, -eeginga**

club *n* (1) *(social)* **ekibiina** *n7;* (2) *(large-headed stick for hitting)* **embuukuuli** *n9. See* mallet; stick

cluck *vi* **-kekema**

clung *See* cling

cluster together *vi* **-eekuma**

¹**clutch** *(of vehicle) n* **kulaaki** *n9*

²**clutch** *(hold) vt* **-kwata**. *See* embrace

¹**coach** *n* (1) *(trainer)* **omutendesi** *n1;* (2) *(bus)* **ebbaasi** *n9*

²**coach** *(train) vt* **-tendeka**

coagulate *vi* **-kwata**

coalition *n* **omukago** *n3* coalition government **gavumenti y'ekipooli** *n9*

coast *n* **olubalama lw'ennyanja** *n11*

coat *n* **ekkooti** *n9*, *(heavy overcoat)* **kabuuti** *n9*

coax *vt* **-sendasenda**

cob *(of maize) n* **omunwe gwa kasooli** *n3* core of maize cob **ekikongoliro** *n7*

cobbler *n* **omukozi w'engatto** *n1*, *(one who sews)* **omutunzi w'engatto** *n1*

cobra *n* **enswera** *n9*

cobweb *n* **nnabbubi** *n1*

cock(erel) *(male chicken) n* **enkoko empanga** *n9*, **sseggwanga** *n9*

cockiness *n* **amampaati** *n6*

cockroach *n* **ekiyenje** *n9*, *(small)* **ennyenje** *n9*

cocoa *n* **kkooko** *n1*

coconut *n* (1) *(tree)* **omunazi** *n3;* (2) *(fruit)* **ekinazi** *n7* coconut oil **ennazi** *n9*

cocoon *n* **ekikalappwa** *n7. See* larva

cocoyam *n* **ejjuuni (erigonda)** *n5*

coerce *vt* **-waliriza**

coercion *n* **okuwalirizibwa** *n15*

coffee *n* (1) *(ground; also the drink)* **kaawa** *n1;* (2) *(berry; bean; plantation)* **emmwanyi** *n9;* (3) *(tree)* **omumwanyi** *n3. See* ceremony; omulamwa *(in Part 2 of the dictionary)* coffee without milk **kaawa omukalu** roasted coffee beans **emmwanyi enfumbe** *(culturally significant)*

coffin *n* **essanduuko (y'omufu)** *n9*, **kofini** *n9*

co-heir *n* **lubuga** *n1*, *(of the Kabaka; Queen-sister)* **Nnaalinnya** *n1 title* (**N29**)

coil *vt* **-zinga** coil around **-zingirira**

coin *n* **ekinusu** *n7*, *(former usage)* **ennusu** *n9. See* shilling coins **(ssente za) jjegejege** *n10*

coincide *vi* **-kwatagana**

colander *n* **akasengejja** *n12*

¹**cold** *adj* (1) **-nnyogovu**, *eg. obudde obunnyogovu ('cold weather');* (2) *(of cooked food)* **-wolu**, *eg. emmere empolu ('cold food'). See* cool cold sore *(on lips)* **ekisuyu** *n7* be(come) cold (1) *(of things)* **-nnyogoga**, *eg. Amazzi gannyogoga. ('The water is cold.'),* *(after cooling)* **-wola**, *eg. Caayi awoze. ('The tea has gone cold.');* (2) *(of the weather)* **obudde** *(or* **empewo**) **-nnyogoga**, *eg. Empewo ennyogoga. ('It is cold.')* feel cold *(of a person)* **empewo -fuuwa**. *The person concerned can be indicated by an object pronoun, eg. Empewo enfuuwa. ('I feel cold.'),* **-wulira empewo**

²**cold** *n* (1) *(low temperature)* **obunnyogovu** *n14*, **empewo** *n9*, *(extreme)* **obutiti** *n14;* (2) *(illness)* **ssennyiga** *n1*, *(serious)* **yegu** *n1*

colic *(of babies) n* **obwoka** *n14*, **obwandu** *n14*

collaborate *vi* **-kolagana**

collapse *vi* **-gwa**, *(of a wall or the ground)* **-yigulukuka**

collar *n* **ekitogi** *n7* collar bone **essaabiro** *n5* dog collar *(on dog, not vicar)* **olukoba lw'embwa** *n7*

collateral *n* **omusingo** *n3*, **akakalu** *n12*   put up as collateral **-singayo** (*or* **-singawo**), *eg. Nsingayo emmotoka yange.* (*'I am putting up my car as collateral.'*)   put up as collateral for (*someone*) **-singira**

colleague *See* companion; friend

collect *vt* (1) (*fetch*) **-kima**, *eg. Yagenda okukima engoye.* (*'He went to collect the clothes.'*); (2) (*money; tax*) **-solooza**, *eg. Kondakita asolooza ssente z'olugendo.* (*The conductor is collecting the fares.'*); (3) (*assemble*) **-kuŋŋaanya**, *eg. Yakuŋŋaanya abantu bakole omulimu.* (*'He collected some people to do the job.'*). *See* assemble; gather   collect firewood **-sennya** (*or* **-tyaba**) **enku**   collect money in contributions **-sonda ssente**, *eg. Tusonda ssente z'embaga.* (*'We are collecting money for the wedding.'*)   collect rainwater in a vessel **-lembeka amazzi**   collect together (*assemble over several trips*) **-somba**, *eg. Asomba amatofaali ag'okuzimba.* (*'He is collecting bricks for building.'*)

collection (*in church*) *n* **ssente ezisoloozebwa** *n10*   take a collection (*eg. in church*) **-solooza ebirabo**

collector *n* **omukuŋŋaanya** *n1*, (*of money/tax*) **omusolooza** *n1*   firewood collector **omutyabi w'enku** *n1*   tax collector **omuwooza** *n1*

college *n* **ettendekero** *n5*, **kkolegi** *n9*

collide *vi* **-tomeragana**, *eg. Emmotoka zitomeraganye.* (*'The cars have collided.'*)   collide with **-tomera**, *eg. Ntomedde emmotoka ye.* (*'I collided with his car.'*). *See* knock

collude (with one another) *vi* **-eekobaana**, *eg. Beekobaana ne banteega ne bankuba.* (*'They colluded with one another, ambushed me and beat me up.'*). *See* conspire

colobus monkey (*black and white*) *n* **engeye** *n9*

colonialism *n* **obufuzi bw'amatwale** *n14*

colony *n* **ettwale** *n5*

colour *n* **erangi** *n9*   lose colour (*fade*) **-siiwuuka**   make of various colours **-tobeka**   make one's skin lighter in colour **-eeyerusa**

coloured *adj* **-a erangi**, (*strikingly*) **-twakaavu**   coloured pencil **ekkalaamu ya langi** *n9*   be(come) brightly coloured **-twakaala**

column (*row*) *n* **olunyiriri** *n11*. *See* post   column of safari ants **omugendo gw'ensanafu** *n3*

coma (*state of unconsciousness*) *n* **okuzirika** *n15*   go into a coma **-zirika**

[1]comb *n* (1) (*for hair*) **ekisanirizo** *n11*; (2) (*of a chicken*) **oluwonzi** *n1*. *See* scratcher

[2]comb *vt* **-sanirira**   comb hair **-sunsula enviiri**, (*with a scratcher*) **-kulula enviiri**   comb one's hair **-eesanirira enviiri**

combine *vt* **-gatta**, *eg. Bagatta obumanyirivu bwabwe.* (*'They are combining their skills.'*). *See* mix; put together

come *vi* (came) **-jja**, *eg. Ajja mu kaseera katono.* (*'She is coming soon.'*), (*by a means of transport*) **-jjira**, *eg. Nzijidde ku ggaali.* (*'I came by bicycle.'*)   come across/upon (*meet by chance*) **-sanga**   come apart (*of something sewn or woven*) **-jjulukuka**   come back (*return*) **-komawo**, **-dda**   come closer **-sembera**   come closer to **-semberera**   come down (*descend*) **-kka**, *eg. Ebinyonyi byakka okuva ku miti.* (*'The birds came down from the trees.'*), (*by the force of gravity*) **-wanuka**, *eg. Ekifaananyi kyawanuse ku kisenge.* (*'The picture came down from the wall.'*)   come for (*to get*) **-ddukira**, *eg. Yaddukidde nze.* (*'She came for me.'*)   come from **-va**, *eg. Yava Mengo.* (*'He came from Mengo.'*)   Come here. **Jjangu wano.**   Come in. **Yingira.**   come last **-semba**   come near to (*but fail to reach*) **-komako awo**   come next **-ddako**, *eg. Bbaasi y'e Masaka y'eyaddako.* (*'The bus from Masaka came next.'*), **-ddirira**   come off (1) (*detached*) **-vaako**, *eg. Amapeesa gavuddeko ku ssaati yange.* (*'The buttons have come off my shirt.'*); (2) (*of a fruit from a tree*) **-nogoka**. *See* unstuck (become)   come open (1) (*of something tied or wrapped*) **-sumulukuka**; (2) (*of something folded*) **-yanjulukuka**; (3) (*partially, eg. of an article of clothing*) **-wenjuka**   come out (1) (*exit, of a person or animal*) **-fuluma**, *eg. Yafuluma ennyumba.* (*'He came out of the house.'*), **-vaamu**; (2) (*from a socket*) **-kuuka**, *eg. Amannyo gange gakuuka.* (*'My teeth are coming out.'*); (3) (*of something inserted*) **-wanguka**, *eg. Enkumbi ewanguse.* (*'The hoe has come out.' – of its handle*); (4) (*slip out of place*) **-sowoka**, *eg. Olumuli lusowose.* (*'A reed has come out.', eg. from a bundle*); (5) (*of something into the public domain*) **-yatuka**   come out from under water **-bbulukuka**   come out of hiding **-eekwekula**   come out of oneself (*emotionally*) **-mmuka**   come to the help of **-dduukirira**   come together **-tuukagana**, *eg. Yateeka emmeeza bbiri nga zituukagana.* (*'She put the two tables so that they came together.', ie. touched*)   come unwillingly (1) (*resist being moved*) **-walira**; (2) (*of a person; reluctantly*) **-sikattira**   come with a purpose **-jjirira**, *eg. Ajjiridde kulaba mwana.* (*'She came to see the child.'*)   come without warning **-gwa bugwi**, *eg. Abagenyi baagwa bugwi.* (*'The visitors came without warning.'*)

[1]comfort (*consolation*) *n* **ekikubagizo** *n7*

[2]comfort (*a person*) *vt* **-budaabuda**, (*someone bereaved*) **-kubagiza**. *See* company to (provide)

[1]command *n* **ekiragiro** *n7*

[2]command *vt* **-lagira**, (*in army or police*) **-duumira**

commandeer *vt* **-wamba**

commander *n* **omuduumizi** *n1*   commander-in-chief **omujaasi** *n1* (*archaic*)

commandment *n* **etteeka** *n5*

commando *n* **muntunsolo** *n1*

commemorate *vt* **-jjukira**

commence *vt* **-tandika**

commencement *n* **entandikwa** *n9*

comment *vi* **-yogera** <u>comment on</u> **-yogera ku**, *eg. Yayogera ku bulungi bwa Maliya. ('He commented on Mary's beauty.')*

commerce *n* **ebyobusuubuzi** *n8*

commiserate with *vt* **-kungubagirako**, *eg. Nnagenda okumukungubagirako. ('I went to commiserate with her.')* <u>My commiserations!</u> **Nga kitalo!**

commissioner *n* **omukulu** *n1* <u>independent police commissioner</u> **kaliisoliiso wa gavumenti ku poliisi** *n1*

commit (*push; send*) *vt* **-sindika**, *eg. Omugabe yasindika abaserikale bonna mu lutalo. ('The general committed all his troops to the battle.')* <u>commit a crime</u> **-zza omusango** <u>commit a sin</u> **-yonoona** <u>commit oneself</u> **-eetema**, *eg. Beetemye okuzimba ekkanisa. ('They committed themselves to build the church.')*. *See* volunteer <u>commit suicide</u> **-etta**

committee *n* **akakiiko** *n12*

common *adj*. *Use* **-ngi** ('*many*'), *eg. Wano waliwo emiti gy'engeri eno mingi. ('These types of trees are common here.')* <u>become common</u> **-yala**, *eg. Emmotoka za Toyota kati zaaze. ('Toyotas have become common.')* <u>the common man</u> **omuntu wa bulijjo** *n1*

commoner (*peasant*) *n* **omukopi** *n1*

commonplace *adj* **-a jjenjeero**, *eg. Emmundu mu Amerika za jjenjeero. '(Guns are commonplace in America.')* <u>become commonplace</u> **-caakaala**

commotion (*involving more than one person*) *n* (1) (*fracas; scuffle*) **akavuvuŋŋano** *n12*; (2) (*with people moving about restlessly; turmoil*) **akayuuguumo** *n12*. *See* mess

communal *adj* **-a olukale** <u>communal labour</u> **bulungibwansi** *n14*

communicate (with one another) *vi* (1) (*at a distance*) **-wuliziganya**, *eg. Tuwuliziganyizza mu kuwandiikiragana mu bbaluwa. ('We are communicating through letters.')*; (2) (*understand one another*) **-tegeeragana**, *eg. Musoke ne mukyala we kati bategeeragana bulungi. ('Musoke and his wife are communicating well with one another.')* <u>communicate with a spirit</u> (*of a group of people, involving singing, drumming, etc.*) **-samira**. *See* possessed (be)

communication *n* **empuliziganya** *n9*

communion, (holy) *n* **okusembera** *n15* <u>communion cup</u> **ekikompe** *n7*

compact (*eg. soil*) *vt* **-ggumiza**

companion (*accompanying person*) *n* **emperekeze** *n9*. *See* friend <u>my companion</u> (*friend, mate; partner*) **munnange**, <u>your companion</u> **munno**, <u>her/his companion</u> **munne**, <u>our companion</u> **munnaffe**, <u>your companion</u> **munnammwe**, <u>their companion</u> **bannaabwe** (*stem* -nna- **N12**)

company (*business*) *n* **kkampuni** *n9* <u>part company</u> **-yawukana**, *eg. Tujja kwawukana nga tumaze okwogera. ('We will part company after we have finished talking.')* <u>provide company to</u> **-beesabeesa**, *eg. Nnagenda okubeesabeesa maama wange ng'afiiriddwa. ('I'm going to provide company to my mother after her loss.')*

compare *vt* **-geraageranya**

compassion *n* **obusaasizi** *n14* <u>compassionate person</u> **omusaasizi** *n1* <u>show compassion for</u> **-saasira**

compel *vt* **-waliriza, -kakaabiriza** <u>compel oneself</u> **-eewaliriza, -eekakaba** <u>be compelled</u> **-walirizibwa, -kakibwa**

compensate *vt* **-liwa**, *eg. Nja kukuliwa olw'ebyo bye nnyonoonye. ('I will compensate you for the damage I caused.')*, **-gatta**, *eg. Ente zange zaalya kasooli we nze ne mmugatta. ('My cows ate his maize and I compensated him for it.')*, (*addressing a third party*) **-liyira**, *eg. Nnamuliyira. ('I compensated her.')* <u>compensate for a bad situation</u> **-vujjirira** <u>give as compensation</u> **-liwa**, *eg. Yasasula ssente okuliwa emmotoka gye yayonoona. ('He paid money to compensate for the damage to the car.')* <u>make (someone) compensate</u> **-liyisa**, *eg. Yamuliyisa ekitabo. ('She made him compensate for losing the book.')*

compensation *n* **engassi** *n9* <u>give compensation</u> **-wa engassi** <u>person who asks for compensation</u> **omuliika** *n1*

compete *vi* **-li mu mpaka**, *eg. Ali mu mpaka z'okudduka. ('He is competing in the running race.')* <u>compete for</u> **-wakanira**, *eg. Awakanira ekirabo. ('She is competing for the prize.')* <u>compete with</u> **-vuganya ne**, *eg. Arsenal evuganya ne ManU. ('Arsenal is competing with ManU.')*

competence (*ability*) *n* **obusobozi** *n14*

competent *adj*. *Use* **-sobola** ('*be able*') *in rel* (**N7.1**), *eg. abantu abasobola ('competent people')*

competition *n* **empaka** *n10*, *eg. empaka z'okudduka ('running competition')* <u>participant in a competition</u> **omuvvunkanyi** *n1* <u>take part in a competition</u> **-vvunkana**

competitor *n* **omuvuganyi** *n1*. *See* disputant

compile *vt* **-kuŋŋaanya**

complacency *n* **obutafaayo** *n14*

complacent *adj*. *Use* **-faayo** ('*care*') *in rel* (**N7.1**) *in neg* (**N21**), *eg. abantu abatafaayo ('complacent people')*

complain *vi* **-eemulugunya**. *See* grumble; grumpy (be) <u>complain about</u> **-eemulugunyiza**

complainant *n* **eyeemulugunya** *n1*. *See* plaintiff

complaint *n* **ekyemulugunyizibwako** *n7* <u>make a complaint</u> **-waaba** <u>make a complaint against</u> **-waabira**

complement *vt* (1) (*match*) **-kwatagana ne**, *eg. Sikaati yo ekwatagana ne bbulawuzi. ('Your skirt complements your blouse.')*; (2) (*praise*) **-waana**, *eg. Yatuwaana. ('She complemented us.')*. *See* praise

complete

[1]complete *adj* (1) (*whole*) **-lamba**; (2) (*all*) **-onna** (N7.3)

[2]complete *vt* (1) (*finish completely*) **-maliriza**; (2) (*make up to a required amount*) **-weza**

completely *adv* **ddala**

complications (*in affairs*) *n* **engozoobano** *n9*

comply *v. Refer to* **etteeka** ('*regulation*'), *eg. Yakola nga amateeka bwe gagamba.* ('*He complied with all the regulations.*'). *See* **obey**

component *n* **ekitundu** *n7*

compose *vt* **-yiiya**   compose one's face **-wombeeka amaaso**

composed *adj* **-yiiye**

composer *n* **omuyiiya** *n1*

composition *n* **ekiyiiye** *n7*   method of composition **enjiiya** *n9*

compound (*courtyard*) *n* **oluggya** *n11*, (*large, especially RC*) **ekigo** *n7*. *See* **enclosure**; **plot** chief's compound **ekisaakaate** *n7*   palace compound **olubiri** *n11*

comprehend *vt* **-tegeera**   be comprehensible **-tegeerekeka**

compress *vt* **-nyigiriza**

compulsion *n* **obuwaze** *n14*   it is compulsory **kya tteeka** (*or* **ky'etteeka**) *followed by inf, eg. Kya tteeka okwambala ettaayi.* ('*It is compulsory to wear a tie.*')   under compulsion **olw'obuwaze**

compute *vt* **-bala**

computer *n* **kompyuta** *n9*, **ekyuma ki kalimagezi** *n7*, **kalimagezi** *n9*,

con man *n* **omukuluppya** *n1*, **omufere** *n1*, **omufezi** *n1*

conceal *vt* **-kweka**, *eg. Yakweka essente wansi w'ekitanda.* ('*She concealed the money under the bed.*'), (*an emotion*) **-bikkako**, *eg. Yabikkako obunakuwavu bwe.* ('*He concealed his sadness.*') conceal information (from) **-kisa**, *eg. Yalina amabanja n'agankisa.* ('*He had debts and concealed them from me.*'). *See* **hush up**   conceal oneself (from) **-eekweka**

conceited, be *vi* **-eemanya**

conceive (*get*) *vt* **-funa**   conceive a baby **-funa olubuto**   conceive an idea **-funa ekirowoozo**

concentrate (*mentally*) *vi* **-ssaako** (*or* **-teekako**) **omwoyo**, *eg. Assaako omwoyo ku musomesa ky'agamba.* ('*She is concentrating on what the teacher is saying.*')

concentrated *adj* **-ka**, *eg. emicungwa emika* ('*concentrated orange juice*')   become concentrated (*clustered together*) **-eekuma**

concentration (*cluster; group*) *n* **ekikuukuulu** *n7*

concept *n* **ekirowoozo** *n7*

[1]concern (*worry*) *n* **obweraliikirivu** *n14*   cause concern to **-eeraliikiriza**

[2]concern (*affect*) *vt* **-kwata ku** (*or* **-kwatako**), *eg. Kino kikwata ku kyalo kyonna.* ('*This matter concerns the whole village.*'). *See* **care**

concerned (*worried*) *adj* **-eeraliikirivu**   be concerned (about) **-eeraliikirira**, *eg. Nneeraliikirira obulamu bw'omwana we.* ('*I am concerned about the health of her child.*'). *See* **care**; **sympathise**

concerning (*about*) *pre* **ku**

concert *n* **kkonsati** *n9*

conclude *vt* **-maliriza**, *eg. Okusaba baakumaliriza n'essaala.* ('*They concluded the service with a prayer.*'). *See* **decide**   conclude a speech **-komekkereza okwogera**   conclude one's arguments **-wunzika ensonga**

conclusion *n* **ekyenkomerero** *n7*

concoct (*a plan*) *vt* **-tetenkanya**

concord *n* (1) (*peace*) **emirembe** *n4*; (2) (*agreement*) **endagaano** *n9*. *See* **cooperation**

concrete *n* **enkokoto** *n9*

concur *vi* **-kkiriza**

condemn *vt* **-vumirira**, *eg. Baamuvumirira olw'enneeyisa ye.* ('*They condemned him for his behaviour.*'). *See* **denounce**   condemn to/for **-salira**, *eg. Baamusalira omwaka gumu mu kkomera.* ('*They condemned him to one year in jail.*')   be condemned (*of a crime*) **-salibwa omusango**

condense *vt* (1) (*shorten*) **-funza**; (2) (*make smaller*) **-toniya**

condition (*state of being*) *n* **embeera** *n9*   regain good condition **-lamuka**

condolences to, express (*a bereaved person*) *vt* **-kubagiza**

condom *n* **akapiira** *n12*, **kkondomu** *n9*, **kalimpitawa** *n12*

[1]conduct (*way of behaving*) *n* **empisa** *n10*

[2]conduct (*eg. singers*) *vt* **-wuubira**   conduct oneself (*behave*) **-eeyisa**, *eg. Yeeyisizza bulungi.* ('*She conducted herself well.*')

conductor *n* (1) (*of singers*) **omuyimbisa** *n1*; (2) (*in taxi or bus*) **kondakita** *n1*

cone *n* **olusoggo** *n11*

confer (*discuss*) *vi* **-teesa**   confer with **-eebuuza ku** (*or* **-eebuuzaako ku**), *eg. Kabaka yeebuuzaako ku bantu abamuwa amagezi.* ('*The king conferred with his advisers.*')

conference *n* **olukuŋŋana** *n11*

confess *vt* **-eenenya**   confess a crime **-kkiriza omusango**   go to confession (*RC*) **-ejjusa**

confidant *n* **ow'emmizi** *n1*

confidence *n* **obugumu** *n14*   confidence trickster **omukuluppya** *n1*, **omufere** *n1*   be self-confident **-eekakasa**   have confidence in (*trust*) **-eesiga**

confidential *adj* **-a ekyama**

confine *vt* **-sibira**, *eg. Yasibira embuzi mu kisibo.* ('*She confined the goat in the pen.*')

confinement *n* (1) (*detention*) **enkomyo** *n9*; (2) (*occasion of giving birth*) **oluzaala** *n11*

confirm *vt* (1) (*prove*) **-kakasa**; (2) (*in Christian faith*) **-ssaako** (*or* **-teekako**) **emikono**, *eg. Omulabirizi yamussaako emikono.* ('*The bishop* *confirmed him.')*

confirmation *n* (1) (*proof*) **obukakafu** *n14*; (2) (*Christian rite*) **okussaako emikono** *n15* confirmation course **omusomo gw'okweyatulira** *n3*

confirmed (*proven*) *adj* **-kakafu** be confirmed (1) (*proven*) **-kakata**; (2) (*in Christian faith*) **-ssibwako emikono**, *eg. Yassibwako emikono ku Ssande.* ('He was confirmed on Sunday.')

confiscate *vt* **-bowa**

¹conflict (*war*) *n* **olutalo** *n11*. See disagreement; misunderstanding

²conflict *vi.* Use **-kwatagana** ('coincide') in neg (**N21**), *eg. Endowooza zaabwe tezikwatagana.* ('Their opinions conflict with one another.') rub one another up the wrong way **-kuubagana**

conform *vi* (1) (*follow rules or laws*) **-kwata amateeka**; (2) (*follow customs*) **-goberera empisa** conform to (*eg. rules*) **-tuukiriza** make conform **-tuukanya**, *eg. Omusomesa yasomesa abaana batuukanye amateeka.* ('The teacher taught the children to conform to the rules.')

confront (*stand up to someone*) *vt* **-kaliramu**, (*more aggressively*) **-tambaala**

confuse *vt* **-sobera**, *eg. Ebintu binsobedde.* ('Things have confused me.'), **-tabula omutwe**. See mess up; mislead be confused **-soberwa**, *eg. Nsobeddwa eky'okukola.* ('I am confused about what to do.')

confusion (*involving more than one person; fracas*) *n* **akavuvuŋŋano** *n12*. See mess be in a confused state (1) (*of a person*) **-vuya**; (2) (*of a number of people; mill about in confusion*) **-vuvuŋŋana** throw into confusion (*muddle up*) **-tabulatabula** be thrown into confusion **-tabulwatabulwa**

congestion *n* **akanyigo** *n12*

Congo *n* **Kkongo** *n9*

Congolese (*person*) *n* **Omukongo** *n1*

congratulate *vt* **-kulisa** Congratulations. **Kulika.** (*pl.* **Mukulike.**)

congregate *vi* (1) (*eg. of animals or discontented people*) **-gumba**; (2) (*assemble, eg. for a meeting or celebration*) **-kuŋŋaana**

congregation (*of people*) *n* **abantu abakuŋŋaanye** *n2*

congress (*assembly*) *n* **olukiiko** *n11*

conjunction (*part of speech*) *n* **nnakayunga** *n1*

conjunctivitis *n* **ejjanga** *n5*

conjurer *n* **omufuusa** *n1*

connect *vt* **-yunga**

conquer *vt* **-wangula**

conqueror *n* **omuwanguzi** *n1*

conquest *n* **obuwanguzi** *n14*

consciousness *n* **okutegeera** *n15* be conscious **-tegeera** lose consciousness **-zirika** regain consciousness **-dda engulu**

consecrate *vt* **-tukuza**. See dedicate consecrate oneself **-eewonga**

consecrated *adj* **-tukuvu**, (*to a lubaale or spirit*) **-wonge**, *eg. embuzi emponge* ('consecrated goat'). See dedicated

consent *vi* **-kkiriza**

consequence *n* **ekivaamu** *n7* as a consequence of (*because of*) **olwa**, *eg. Yafa olw'ebiwundu bye yafuna.* ('He died as a consequence of the wounds he had sustained.')

consequently *conj* **ekivuddemu**

conservative person (*politically or socially*) *n* **sitakange** *n1*

consider *vt* **-lowooza**, *eg. Nkyalowooza eky'okukola.* ('I am still considering what to do.'), (*carefully*) **-fumiitiriza**, *eg. Mbadde nfumiitiriza ekirabo eky'okumuwa.* ('I am considering what present to give her.') consider suitable for **-saanyiza** take into consideration **-balirira**, *eg. Bw'obalirira eky'etaagisa, olaba nga kizibu.* ('When you take into consideration what's required, you can see it will be difficult.')

considerate, be *vt* **-faayo**, *eg. Afaayo ku mukyala we.* ('He is considerate to his wife.')

considering *conj.* Use **bwe** ('if') with **-lowooza ku** ('think about'), *eg. Bw'olowooza ku bulema bwe, yakoze bulungi.* ('Considering her disability, she did well.') considering everything **okutwalira awamu**, *eg. Okutwalira awamu, ndowooza y'eyasobezza.* ('Considering everything, I think he did wrong.')

consist of (1) **-limu** *or* **-baamu** ('be in') according to tense (**N20.1**), *eg. Ettaka lino lirimu omusenyu.* ('This soil consists of sand.'); (2) **-beeramu**, *eg. Keeke mubeeramu obuwunga n'amagi ne sukaali.* ('Cakes consist of flour, eggs and sugar.')

consolation *n* **ekikubagizo** *n7*

console (*someone bereaved*) *vt* **-kubagiza**

consonant *n* **ennyukuta ensirifu** *n9*

consort (*of an heir*) *n* **lubuga** *n1*, (*of the Kabaka; Queen-sister*) **Nnaalinnya** *n1 title*

conspicuous *adj* **-a enkukunala**. See striking be conspicuous Use **-eeraga** ('show off') with **-okka** ('alone' **N7.3**), *eg. Ennyumba ye yeeraga yokka.* ('Her house is conspicuous.'), **-laba bulabi**, **-labika bulabiisi**

conspiracy *n* **olukwe** *n11*

conspire (against) *vt* **-lyamu olukwe**, *eg. Bandyamu olukwe ne bansibisa mu kkomera.* ('They conspired against me and caused me to go to prison.'). See collude

constantly *adv* **buli kaseera**

constipation *n* **obutafuluma** *n14*, **obuteeyabya** *n14* be constipated **olubuto -eesiba** (*or* **-eesiba olubuto**), *eg. Olubuto lwe lwesibye.* ('She is constipated.')

constrain *vt* **-gezaako okuziyiza**

constrict (*make narrow*) *vt* **-funza**. See squeeze be constricted **-funda**

constricted (*narrowed*) *adj* **-funda**

construct

construct vt (1) (*build*) **-zimba**; (2) (*make*) **-kola**

construction (*building*) n **ekizimbe** n7, (*temporary*) **ekisaakaate** n7, (*made for an event*) **ekidaala** n7. See shelter

consult vt **-eebuuzaako ku** (*or* **-eebuuza ku**), eg. *Twebuuzaako ku musajja ow'amagezi.* ('*We consulted the wise man.*') be consulted **-eebuuzibwako**

consume (*burn up*) vt **-yokya**, eg. *Omuliro gwayokezza ennyumba yonna.* ('*The fire consumed the whole house.*'). See drink; eat

contain vi (1) (*have within*) **-baamu** or **-limu** ('*be in*') according to tense (**N20.1**), eg. *Eccupa erimu liita bbiri.* ('*The bottle contains two litres.*'); (2) (*have the capacity of*) **-jjula**, eg. *Eccupa ejjula liita bbiri.* ('*The bottle contains two litres.*')

container (*large, of metal, for transporting goods by sea, etc.*) n **konteyina** n9

contaminate vt **-siiga**

contemplate (*think about*) vt **-lowoozako** (*or* **lowooza ku**), eg. *Alowooza ku bulamu bwe.* ('*He is contemplating his life.*') in private contemplation **mu lusirika**

contempt n **obunyoomi** n14. See disrespect person who shows contempt **omunyoomi** n1 roll one's eyes in contempt **-ziimuula**, eg. *Yanziimuula.* ('*She rolled her eyes at me in contempt.*'), **-moolera amaaso** show contempt for **-nyooma**, eg. eg. *Abaana banyooma omusomesa waabwe.* ('*The children show contempt for their teacher.*'), (*through making a sucking sound with the lips*) **-sooza**, (*though making a certain sound*) **-ŋoola** (*through clicking the tongue*) **-kontola**, (*through clawing at*) **-kongoola**, (*through using the eyes*) **-yisa amaaso** treat with contempt **-linnyirira**, **-jolonga**

contend (with) (*struggle against*) vt **-gwirana**, eg. *Yagwirana n'ebizibu bingi.* ('*She contended with many problems.*'). See dispute

contender (*competitor*) n **omuvuganyi** n1

contented (*satisfied*) adj **-mativu**, (*well fed*) **-kkufu** be contented **-matira**, (*with food*) **-kkuta**. See appreciative (be); happy (be) make contented **-matiza**, (*with food*) **-kkusa**

contention, matters of n **kalumannywera** n1, eg. *Kalumannywera avudde ku tteeka eppya.* ('*Matters of contention have arisen from the new law.*')

contentment (*satisfaction*) n **obumativu** n14, (*from eating*) **obukkufu** n14

¹**contest** (*competition*) n **empaka** n10

²**contest** vt **-wakanya**, eg. *Yasalawo okuwakanya ebyasalibwawo.* ('*She decided to contest the decision.*') contest with (*conpete with*) **-vuganya ne** be contested **-wakanyizibwa**

contestant (*competitor*) n **omuvuganyi** n1

contiguous, be vi **-kwatagana**

continent n **ssemazinga** n1

continually. Use **-onna** ('*all*') (**N7.3**), eg. *Enkuba yatonnya mu mwezi gwa Maayi gwonna.* ('*It rained continually during the month of May.*')

continue vi **-eeyongera**, eg. *Yeeyongerdde okusoma obulungi.* ('*She is continuing to study well.*')

continuously adv **obutamala**, **obutaggwa**

¹**contract** (*legal*) n **endagaano** n9. See agreement contractions (*in labour*) **ebisa** n8 make a contract (*legal*) **-kola endagaano**

²**contract** (*of a muscle*) vi **-eemiima**

contradict vt **-koonagana ne**, eg. *Yakoonaganye ne Musoke bye yayogedde.* ('*She contradicted what Musoke had said.*') contradict one another Use **-kwatagana** ('*match*') in neg (**N21**), eg. *Abajulizi bye baayogera tebikwatagana.* ('*The witnesses contradicted one another.*') contradict oneself **-eekuba endobo**

contradiction n **ekikoonagana** n7

contribute vt **-eesonda**, eg. *Beesonda ssente ez'okuzimba essomero.* ('*They contributed money to build the school.*'). See give

contribution (*to family of deceased*) n (1) (*before the burial*) **amabugo** n6; (2) (*after the burial*) **amataaba** n6. See gift

¹**control** n go out of control **-waba** lose control (*eg. of a vehicle*) **-lemerera**

²**control** vt **-fuga** be controlled **-fugibwa**

controversy n **empaka** n9, **enkaayana** n9

convene (*a meeting; call*) vt **-yita**

conversation n **emboozi** n9, (*long*) **oluboozi** n11. See talk

converse vi **-nyumya**, eg. *Nnanyumya nabo.* ('*I conversed with them.*') keep on conversing with **-nyumiikiriza**, eg. *Abadde anyumiikiriza abagenyi.* ('*She went on conversing with the visitors.*')

¹**convert** n. Use **-kyuka** ('*change*') in rel (**N7.1**), eg. *abakyuse* ('*converts*')

²**convert** vt **-kyusa okudda mu**, eg. *Yakyusa abantu bangi okudda mu ddiini ye.* ('*He converted many people to his religion.*'), (*in nature*) **-fuula**, eg. *Ggalagi yagifuula sitoowa.* ('*He converted the garage into a store.*'), (*in fundamental nature*) **-fuusa**, eg. *Yesu yafuusa amazzi omwenge.* ('*Jesus changed the water into wine.*') be converted **-kyuka**

convey (*take*) vt **-twala** convey greetings to **-labira**, eg. *Bandabire.* ('*Convey my greetings to them.*')

¹**convict** (*person convicted*) n **omusibe** n1

²**convict** vt **-salira omusango**, eg. *Omulamuzi yamusalira omusango.* ('*The judge convicted him.*')

convince vt **-kkirizisa**

convulsions, have (*as in epilepsy*) **-eesika**. See thrash about

¹**cook** n **omufumbi** n1, (*chief, of the Kabaka*) **Kawuuta** n1 title

²**cook** vt **-fumba**, (*over an open fire*) **-kalirira**, (*under ashes*) **-vumbika**, (*bananas thoroughly*) **-boobeza**, (*lightly, eg. vegetables to retain their*

food value) -**buguyaza**. See banana (*for more words relating to cooking and bananas*); overcooked (be) cook for/at -**fumbira**, eg. *Afumbira abaana ekyekiro*. ('She is cooking supper for the children.') cook with -**fumbisa**, eg. *Afumbisa masannyalaze*. ('She cooks with electricity.') be cooked (1) -**ggya**, eg. *Emmere eyidde*. ('The food is cooked.', ie. ready to serve); (2) (*of matooke*) (*thoroughly*) -**boobera**, eg. *Amatooke gaboobedde*. ('The plantains are thoroughly cooked.'), (*lightly*) -**buguyala** fail to cook properly -**kona**, eg. *Emmere ekonye*. ('The food has failed to cook properly.') have cooked and ready to eat -**yiisa**, eg. *Ayiisizza emmere*. ('She has cooked the food and it is ready to eat.')

cooked adj -**fumbe**, (*of matooke*) (*thoroughly*) -**boobevu**, (*lightly*) -**buguyavu**, (*partially*) -**a kakoolakoola** something cooked whole **empogola** n9, eg. *eggi ery'empogola* ('boiled egg')

cooking n okufumba n15 cooking area (*of a traditional hearth; also of a modern stove or oven*) **amasiga** n6. See hearth cooking oil **obutto** n14 cooking pot See pot cooking stone **essiga** n5 way of cooking **enfumba** n9

[1]**cool** (*of the weather*) adj -**weeevu**, eg. *obudde obuweweevu* ('cool weather'). See cold

[2]**cool(ness)** n obunnyogovu n14

[3]**cool (down)** v (1) vi -**wola**, eg. *Amazzi gawoze*. ('The water has cooled down.'), (*of the weather*) -**weweera**, eg. *Obudde buwewedde*. ('The weather has become cool.'); (2) vt -**woza**, eg. *Awoza emmere y'omwana*. ('She is cooling the child's food.')

coop, chicken n akayumba k'enkoko n12. See basket; cage

cooperate vi -**kolagana**

cooperation n enkolagana n9

cooperative (society) n ekibiina ky'obwegassi n7

cooperativeness n obwegassi n14

coordination n okukwataganya n15

copper n ekikomo n7 copper mine ekirombe ky'ekikomo n7

[1]**copy** n kopi n9

[2]**copy** vt -**ggyamu kopi**, -**koppa** make a copy -**kola kopi**

coral tree (*Erythrina abyssinica*) n eggirikiti n5

cord n akaguwa n12, (*made from strips of bark of shrub Triumfetta*) ekinsambwe n7

cordon-bleu (*type of bird*) n akagugumusi n12

core (*kernel*) n omulamwa n3 core of a boil ekinyusi n7 core of a maize cob ekikongoliro n7

[1]**cork** n omupiira gw'eccupa n3

[2]**cork (up)** vt -**zibikira**

cormorant n olusoove n11

corn (*maize*) n kasooli n1

corner n (1) (*angled, eg. of a rectangular room*) ensonda n9; (2) (*bend, eg. on road*) ekkoona n5 remote dark corner akalikonda n12

coronation n amatikkira n6. *The traditional nine-day period of rest for the Kabaka after enthronement is known as* **obwerende** n14.

corpse n (1) (*anonymous dead human body*) **omulambo** n3, (2) (*of someone known to the people concerned*) **omufu** n1, **omugenzi** n1; (3) (*of the Kabaka*) **enjole** n9; (4) (*of a Muslim*) **mayiti** n9

corpulence n obugevvu n14

corpulent adj -**gevvu** become corpulent -**gejja**

[1]**correct** adj -**tuufu**

[2]**correct** vt -**longoosa**, eg. *Yalongoosa ensobi*. ('She corrected the mistakes.'). See discipline; mark; straighten out correct a mistake -**golola ekisobyo** correct an examination -**kebera ebibuuzo** correct one's behaviour -**longoosa empisa** be correct (*right*) -**ba** or -**li** (*depending on the tense* N20.1) *followed by* -**tuufu** ('right'), eg. *Yali mutuufu ku by'embeera y'obudde*. ('She was correct about the weather.')

correctness (*rightness*) n obutuufu n14

correspond vi (1) (*match*) -**kwatagana**, eg. *Ennyinnyonnyola zombi ez'ebintu ebyatuuseewo zikwatagana*. ('Both accounts of what happened correspond.'); (2) (*write to one another*) -**wandiikiragana** correspond with (*write to*) -**wandiikira**, eg. *Yawandiikira mutabani we ali e Bungereza*. ('She corresponded with her son in England.')

correspondence n (1) (*ressemblance*) enfaanana n9; (2) (*exchanges of letters*) okuwandiikiragana n15

corridor n olukuubo n11

corrode (*rust*) vi -**talagga**. See spoilt (become)

corroded (*rusty*) adj -**talavvu**. See spoilt

corrosion (*rust*) n obutalagge n14

corrugated iron sheet n ebbaati n5

corrugations (*on road*) n ebisirikko n8

corrupt (*spoil*) vt -**yonoona**. See bribe; lead astray; seduce corrupt person (*taker of bribes*) **omuli w'enguzi** n1

corrupted adj -**yonoonefu** be(come) corrupted -**yonooneka**. See bribe (take a)

corrupter (*leads astray*) n omusiguze n1

corruption n obulyake n14, obuli bw'enguzi n14. See extortion anti-corruption chief **kaliisoliiso wa gavumenti ku bulyake** n1 fighter against corruption **omulwanyisa w'obulyake** n1

[1]**cost** (*price*) n omuwendo n3, ebbeeyi n9. See charge; fee

[2]**cost** vi -**gula**, eg. *Lumonde ono agula mmeka?* ('How much do these potatoes cost?')

costly (*expensive*) adj -**a omuwendo**, -**a ebbeeyi**

costume (*garment*) n ekyambalo n7

cot n akatanda k'omwana n12. See crib

cotton n (1) (*the plant*) ppamba n1; (2) (*the fibre, whether from cotton plant, kapok tree or akafumbo*) **ppamba**, **ffampa** n1. See thread spoilt cotton (*on boll attacked by insect*) **kafiifi** n1 coucal (*type of bird*) *n* ettutuma *n5*

couch grass *n* olumbugu *n11*

[1]cough *n* ekifuba *n7*, (*dry*) ekifuba ekikalu, (*persistent*) ekikololo *n7*, (*wet*) ekifuba ekikutuka whooping cough ekifuba ekiraakiira

[2]cough *vi* -kolola

could *See* can

council (*assembly; meeting*) *n* olukiiko *n11* attend council -kiika

counsel *vt* -buulirira. *See* advice (give)

count *vt* -bala count for -balira, *eg. Balira Musoke ssente ze ozimuwe.* (*'Count the money for Musoke and give it to him.'*) count in (*include*) -baliramu count up (*estimate an amount needed*) -balirira

counter *n* (1) (*person who counts*) omubazi *n1*; (2) (*in a shop*) kawunta *n9*; (3) (*seed used to play the game of omweso*) empiki *n9*

[1]counterfeit *adj* -gingirire, -a ekikwangala conterfeit money ssente za kiwaanyi *n10* something counterfeit ekigingirire *n7*, ekikwangala *n7*

[2]counterfeit *vt* -gingirira

country *n* (1) (*state*) ensi *n9*; (2) (*nation*) eggwanga *n5* country bumpkin wa maalo *n1*

county *n* essaza *n5*, *eg. Essaza ly'e Buddu* (*'County of Buddu'*) county chief owessaza *n1* sub-county eggombolola *n9* sub-county chief oweggombolola *n1*

courage *n* obugumu *n14*, obuzira *n14* give courage to -gumya take courage -eegumya

courageous *adj* -gumu, -zira courageous person omugumu *n1*, omuzira *n1*

course course of studies omusomo *n3* course of reeds (*in mud and wattle wall*) ekizizi *n7*, oluzizi *n11* Of course. Kale.

[1]court *n* ekkooti *n9*, (*of a chief*) embuga *n9*, (*of a parish*) ekitawuluzi *n7*, (*for settling clan disputes*) ekkooti ya Kisekwa. *See* courtyard court case omusango *n3* court fee empaabi *n9* attend court -kiika bring a case to court -waaba omusango mu kkooti magistrate's court ekkooti ento supreme court ekkooti y'oku ntikko take to court -waabira mu kkooti, *eg. Yawaabira muliraanwa we mu kkooti.* (*'He took his neighbour to court.'*)

[2]court (*woo*) *vt* -yogereza

courtesy (*good manners*) *n* obuntubulamu *n14*

courtroom *n* eggwolezo *n5*

courtyard *n* oluggya *n11*, (*of a chief*) embuga *n9* back (court)yard oluggya lw'emmanju front (court)yard oluggya lw'emiryango

cousin cousin of (1) (*general term*) muganda (*with pos* N12), *eg. muganda wange* (*'my cousin'*); (2) (*of opposite sex on father's side*) kizibwe *n1* (*with pos* N12), *eg. kizibwe wange* (*'my cousin'*)

covenant *n* endagaano *n9*

[1]cover *n* ekibikka *n7*, embikko *n9*, (*lid*) ekisaanikira *n7*, (*lining; covering*) omwaliiro *n3*. *See* shelter put cover on -saanikira take cover

(*eg. to avoid a thrown spear*) -eewoma take cover off -bikkula, *eg. Mbikkula obuliri.* (*'I am taking the cover off the bed.'*), (*partially*) -wenjula, (*lid*) -saanukula, *eg. Yasaanukula sseffuliya.* (*'She took the cover off the saucepan.'*)

[2]cover *vt* -bikka, *eg. Emmere ngibisse.* (*'I have covered the food.'*), (*completely; envelope*) -buutikira cover food bundle with banana leaves (*before cooking*) -saaniika emmere cover oneself (*with*) -eebikka, *eg. Yeebikka bulangiti.* (*'She covered herself with a blanket.'*) cover up (1) (*physically*) -bikkako, *eg. Bikkako ku mmere ereme kuwola.* (*'Cover up the food so it does not cool.'*); (2) (*conceal information*) -zibiikiriza cover up for -zibira, *eg. Musoke amanyi omuntu eyatutte ensawo naye yamuzibidde.* (*'Musoke knows who took the bag but covered up for him.'*) be(come) covered with -vulubana, *eg. Omwana avulubanye ettaka.* (*'The child is covered with mud.'*), -saabaana get oneself covered with (*food, dirt, etc.*) -eevulubanya, *eg. Omukyala yeevulubanyizza enziro nga ayoola amanda.* (*'The lady covered herself with soot when she scooped up the charcoal.'*)

covet *vt* -eegomba

covetousness *n* obwegombi *n14*

cow *n* ente *n9*, (*male*) ente ennume, (*female*) ente enkazi, (*female before breeding*) ente enduusi, (*without coloured patches on skin*) ente enjeru, (*young; calf*) ennyana *n9*. *See* bull; cattle

coward *n* omutiitiizi *n1*

cowardice *n* obutiitiizi *n14*

cowardly *adj* -tiitiizi be cowardly -tiitiira

cowpea *n* empindi *n9* wild relative of cowpea ekiyindiru *n7*

cowrie (shell) *n* ensimbi *n7* ensimbi eŋŋanda cowries (*as currency*) olukalala lw'ensimbi *n11* strand of cowrie shells

coy, look *vi* -moola, -loola

crab *n* enjaba *n9*

[1]crack *n* olwatika *n11* develop a crack -jjako olwatika, *eg. Eggiraasi ezzeeko olwatika.* (*'The glass has become cracked.'*)

[2]crack *v* (1) (*eg. of glass*) *vi* -yatika, *eg. Eddirisa lyatise.* (*'The window is cracked.'*), (*making a noise*) -banduka, *eg. Eccupa yabanduse nga ntaddemu amazzi agookya.* (*'The bottle cracked when I put hot water in it.'*); (2) *vt* -yasa, *eg. Omupiira guyasizza eddirisa.* (*'The ball cracked the window.'*) crack one's knuckles -nonkola ebinonko

cracked *adj* -yatifu

crackle (*making crackling sound*) *vi* -baluka, (*of a fire*) -bugujja, (*as static on radio*) -kwakwaya

cram (into) *vt* -fuutiika, *eg. Ebintu yabifuutiise mu kabada.* (*'He crammed the things into the cupboard.'*). *See* force into; press down; push into cram food in mouth -vuubiika emmere

cramp (*muscle pain*) *n* **kamenya** *n1*   cramps (*severe abdominal pain*) **enjoka** *n10*

crane, crested (*type of bird*) *n* **ŋŋaali** *n1*

crash *vt* **-tomeza**, *eg. Yatomezezza emmotoka.* (*'He has crashed the car.'*)   crash into **-tomera**, *eg. Emmotoka yatomera ekisenge.* (*'The car crashed into the wall.'*)

crave *vt* **-yoya, -yaayaanira.** *See* covet; want

craving *n* **ekyooyo** *n7*, **ekyoyooyo** *n7*, (*for food*) **amaddu** *n6*   have a craving **-yaayaana**

crawl *vi* **-yavula**

craziness *n* **eddalu** *n5*. *See* delirium; madness

crazy (*mad*) *adj* **-lalu**   crazy person **omulalu** *n1*   be crazy about (*infatuated*) **-suula eddalu** (*subject and object reversed compared to English*), *eg. Ansudde eddalu.* (*'I am crazy about her.'*)   go crazy (1) (*mad*) **-laluka**; (2) (*mentally disturbed*) **-tabuka omutwe**. *See* delirious (become); wild (go)   make crazy **-lalusa**, (*mentally disturbed*) **-tabula omutwe**

creak *vi* **-jegeja**   make creak **-jegeza**

cream *n* (1) (*on milk*) **olububi** *n11*; (2) (*ointment*) **ebizigo** *n8*

[1]**crease** (*eg. on trousers*) *n* **akakindo** *n12*   put on a crease **-kuba** (*or* **-teekamu**) **akakindo**, *eg. Akubye akakindo ku mpale.* (*'He has put a crease on the trousers.'*)

[2]**crease** (*crumple up*) *vt* **-vungavunga**, *eg. Yavungavunga essuuka.* (*'He creased the sheets.'*)   be creased (*eg. of sheets*) **-eevungavunga**

create *vt* **-tonda**. *See* invent

created   person (*as created being*) **omutonde** *n1*   something created **ekitonde** *n7*

creation *n* **obutonde** *n14*, **obutonzi** *n14*

creator *n* **omutonzi** *n1*. *See* inventor   The Creator (*God*) **Katonda** *n1*

creature (*animal*) *n* **ensolo** *n9*, (*as created being*) **ekitonde** *n7*

creed *n* **enzikiriza** *n9*

creep *vi* (1) (*of a plant*) **-landa**, *eg. Ennanda eranda.* (*'The commelina is creeping.'*); (2) (*as lizard or soldier inching forward*) **-eewalula**   creep away (*slip away stealthily*) **-eemulula**   creep into (*eg. animal into bush*) **-sensera**   creeping plant **ekiranda** *n7*

crest *n* (1) (*of a hill*) **entikko** *n9*; (2) (*on bird's head*) **ejjoba** *n5*   crested crane **ŋŋaali** *n1*

crevasse *n* **olukonko** *n11*

crib (*Mose's basket*) *n* **ekibaya** *n7*. *See* cot

cricket (*insect*) *n* (1) (*large type which is eaten by boys*) **ejjenge** *n5*; (2) (*not eaten*) **akanyeenyenkule** *n12*. *See* grasshopper   mole cricket (*type of insect*) **nnamunyeenye** *n1*

cried *See* cry

crime *n* **omusango** *n3*   commit a crime **-zza omusango**

criminal *n* **omuzzi w'emisango** *n1*

criminality *n* **obumenyi bw'amateeka** *n14*

cringe *vi* **-eesisiwala**

[1]**cripple** *n* **omulema** *n1*, (*one who requires help*) **kateeyamba** *n1*

[2]**cripple** *vt* **-lemaza**   be(come) crippled **-lemala**

crippled *adj* **-lema**   state of being crippled **obulema** *n14*

crisis *n* **akanyamberege** *n12*, **akatuubagiro** *n12*

criticise *vt* **-nenya**   be criticised **-nenyezebwa**

criticism *n* **ekinenyo** *n7*

crocodile *n* **goonya** *n9*

crook (*thief*) *n* **omubbi** *n1*

crooked *adj* **-kyamu**. *See* deformed   be(come) crooked **-kyama**   make crooked **-kyamya**   something crooked **ekikyamu** *n7*

crookedness *n* **obukyamu** *n14*

crop *n* (1) (*agricultural*) **ekirime** *n7*; (2) (*of a bird*) **ekisakiro** *n7*

cropped (*cut-off*) *adj* **-a enkuggu**   cropped tail **omukira gwa nkuggu**

[1]**cross** (*on which Jesus died*) *n* **omusaalaba** *n3*

[2]**cross** *vt* (1) (*a road*) **-sala**; (2) (*over water*) **-somoka**   cross out (*something written*) **-sazaamu**   be(come) cross (*annoyed*) **-nyiiga**   be(come) cross with **-nyiigira**   place for crossing water **w'osomokera** *n16*, **aw'okusomokera** *n16*, **awasomokerwa** *n16*

crossbeam (*horizontal timber in roof*) *n* **omukiikiro** *n3*, **olwaliiro lw'akasolya** *n11*

cross-examine (*in court case*) *vt* **-wozesa**

cross-eyes *n* **endali** *n9*   cross-eyed person **ow'endali** *n1*

crossroads *n* **amasaŋŋanzira** *n6*, **sitensensi** *n9*

crossways/crosswise *adv* **obukiika**, *eg. Yeebaka bukiika.* (*'He slept lying across the bed.'*)   place crosswise **-kiika**, *eg. Baakiika emmeeza mu kisenge.* (*'They placed a table crosswise in the room.'*)   put crosswise (*reeds or sticks when making a fence*) **-gomba**

crossword puzzle *n* **akakunizo** *n12*

crouch *vi* **-bwama**

[1]**crow** (*type of bird*) *n* **nnamuŋŋoona** *n1*

[2]**crow** (*as a cock*) *vi* **-kookolima**

crowbar *n* **omutayimbwa** *n3*

crowd *n* **ekikuukuulu** *n7*, **ekibinja ky'abantu** *n7*   small crowd **akakuukuulu** *n12*

crowded (together) *adv* **mu kanyigo**, *eg. Twabadde mu kanyigo mu kkanisa.* (*'We were crowded in church.'*)   crowd on (*as flies on meat*) **-bemberera**   be crowded to capacity **-fumbeka**   be crowded with **-fumbekera**, *eg. Ekkanisa yabadde efumbekedde abantu.* (*'The church was crowded with people.'*)

[1]**crown** (*on monarch's head*) *n* **engule** *n9*   crown of the head **obutikkiro** *n14*, (*on which things are carried*) **obwetikkiro** *n14*   crown of thorns **engule y'amaggwa**

[2]**crown** (*a monarch*) *vt* **-tikkira engule**   be crowned **-tikkirwa**

crucifix *n* omusaalaba *n3*

crucify *vt* -komerera ku musaalaba

cruel *adj* -kambwe

cruelty *n* obukambwe *n14*

crumb *n* akakunkumuka *n12*

crumble *vt* -merengula, *eg. Amerengula akakerenda. ('She is crumbling the tablet.')* crumble away *(eg. of a tablet)* -merenguka, *eg. Akakerenda kamerenguse. ('The tablet has crumbled away.'). See* break; disintegrate; erode be crumbly -kunkumuka, *eg. Omugaati gukunkumuka. ('The bread is crumbly.')*

crumple (up) *vt* (1) *(something soft)* -vungavunga, *eg. Yavungavunga essuuka ('She crumpled up the sheets.')*; (2) *(something solid, eg. car in accident)* -fufuggaza be crumpled (up) (1) *(of something soft)* -eevungavunga; (2) *(of something solid)* -fufuggala, *eg. Emmotoka yafufuggala mu kabenje. ('The car was crumpled up in the accident.')*

crumpled (up) *(of something solid, eg. car damaged in accident) adj* -fufuggavu

crunch (on) *(when eating) vt* -meketa, *eg. Ameketa emberenge. ('He is crunching on the popcorn.)*

crush *vt* (1) *(something soft, eg. pawpaw)* -footola; (2) *(something solid, eg. biscuit or tablet)* -merengula, -betenta; (3) *(bananas to extract juice)* -sogola, *eg. Asogodde embidde. ('She has crushed the bananas for juice.')*; (4) *(groundnuts, by pounding)* -sekula. *See* damage; destroy; spoil; squash; squeeze crush bananas by trampling *(in beer making)* -sogoza bigere be(come) crushed (1) *(of something soft)* -footoka, *eg. Yatuula ku ppaapaali ne lifootoka. ('He sat on the pawpaw and it got crushed.')*; (2) *(eg. of a tablet; pulverised)* -merenguka

crushed *adj* (1) *(of tablet, biscuit, etc.)* -merengule; (2) *(of something pounded, eg. groundnuts)* -sekule. *See* crumpled up; damaged

crushing place for crushing bananas *(in beer making)* essogolero *n5* time for crushing bananas amasogola *n6*

crust *(eg. on left-over cooked matooke) n* emmembe *n9* form a crust *(eg. on left-over matooke)* -bembeera remove crust from left-over matooke -bembula emmembe ku matooke amavumbike

crutch *(as used by cripples) n* omuggo *n3*

[1]**cry** *(of distress) n* omulanga *n3. See* wail

[2]**cry** *vi* (cried) -kaaba, *(a lot)* -kaabakaaba. *See* moan; wail cry for -kaabira, *eg. Yakaabira omwana we. ('She cried for her child.')* cry out (1) *(for pity or help)* -laajana; (2) *(in distress)* -tema omulanga be about to cry *(of a baby)* omwana -tuubatuuba keep on crying -kaabirira. *The person with the child can be indicated by an object pronoun, eg. Omwana amukaabirira. ('Her child is crying a lot.')* cause to stop crying *(someone)* -sirisa make cry -kaabya, *eg. Akaabya omwana. ('She made the child cry.')* stop crying

(of oneself) -sirika

cuckoo *n* kirimululu *n1* cuckoo-spit insect *(secretes fluid)* entonnyeze *n9*

cud *n* obwenkulumu *n14* chew the cud -zza obwenkulumu

cuffs *(on shirt) n* amagemo *n6*

cultivate *vit* -lima, *(with deep digging)* -kabala cultivate with -limisa, *eg. Alimisa enkumbi. ('She is cultivating with a hoe.')* cultivated land (1) *(newly dug)* awalime *n16*; (2) *(deeply dug)* awakabale *n16* cultivated plant ekirime *n7* cultivated plot omusiri *n3*

cultivation *n* ebyobulimi *n8* a day's cultivation olubimbi *n11* way of cultivating ennima *n9*

cultivator *(person) n* omulimi *n1*

culture *n* (1) *(associated with nation or tribe)* obuwangwa *n14*; (2) *(associated with place of birth)* obuzaaliranwa *n14*; (3) *(acquired through good breeding or refinement)* obugunjufu *n14* traditional culture ebyobuwangwa *n8*

cultured *adj* (1) *(civilised)* -gunjufu; (2) *(discerning)* -tegeevu cultured person (1) *(cilivised)* omugunjufu *n1*; (2) *(discerning)* omutegeevu *n1* be(come) cultured *(civilised)* -gunjuka

cunning *adj* -kalabakalaba, -gezigezi

cup *n* ekikopo *n7. See* gourd communion cup ekikompe *n7*

cup the hand(s) (1) *(to catch a liquid)* -lembeka engalo; (2) *(to receive something politely)* -waayo engalo

cupboard *n* eggwanika *n5*, kabada *n9*

cupful *n* ekikopo *n7*

curb *vt* -ziyiza

curdled milk *n* bbongo *n1*

[1]**cure** *(remedy) n* ekiwonya *n7*

[2]**cure** *vt* -wonya, *eg. Omusawo yamuwonya obulwadde bwe. ('The doctor cured her disease.')*, *(be an antidote to)* -vumula, *eg. Eddagala lino livumula endwadde eyo. ('This medicine cures that disease.')* cure tobacco -kaza taaba, *(in the sun)* -yanika taaba, *(over a source of heat)* -kalirira taaba be cured of an illness -wona obulwadde

currency *n* ensimbi *n10*, ssente *n10*

current *(in water) n* engezi *n9*

currently *(now) adv* kaakati

curry favour (with) -eeguya

curry powder *n* ebinzaali *n8*, obunzaali *n14*

[1]**curse** *n* ekikolimo *n7. See* spell (evil)

[2]**curse** *v* (1) *(utter curses) vi* -kolima, *eg. Bwe yanyiiga n'atandika okukolima. ('When he got annoyed he started to curse.')*; (2) *(use obscene language) vi* -wemula; (3) *(curse someone) vt* -kolimira, *eg. Yamukolimidde ku kye yakoze. ('He cursed him for what he had done.'). See* blaspheme; spell (cast a)

curtain *n* olutimbe *n11*, *(big thick type, used as divider in room, cinema, etc.)* eggigi *n5*

cushion *n* omutto *n3*. *See* pad

custard apple *n* (1) (*plant*) omusitaferi *n3*; (2) (*fruit*) ekisitaferi *n7*

custodian *n* omukuumi *n1*

custom *n* (1) (*tradition*) akalombolombo *n12*, (*associated with tribe or nation*) ekyobuwangwa *n7*, (*associated with place of birth*) ekyobuzaaliranwa *n7*; (2) (*habit*) empisa *n9*

customer (*buyer*) *n* omuguzi *n1*

customs duty (*tax*) *n* empooza *n9*, omusolo *n3*

customshouse *n* eggwoolezo *n5*

¹**cut** *n* ekisale *n7*, (*on the body*) omusale *n3*, (*on head from fighting*) olubale *n11*, (*on front of waist, a decoration formerly used by women*) enjola *n9*, (*between fingers or toes, painful*) ensalika *n9*. *See* tribal mark   cut area of vegetation awasaawe *n16*

²**cut** *vt* -sala, *eg*. Asaze omuguwa. (*'She has cut the rope.'*), (*carefully, eg. using a pattern*) -komola, (*with an axe*) -tema. *See* chop; clear; prune; slash   cut down tree -tema omuti   cut for -salira, (*with an axe*) -temera, *eg*. Baamutemera omuti. (*'They cut the tree for her.'*)   cut into parts -salamu ebitundu, *eg*. Keeke yagisalamu ebitundu bisatu. (*'He cut the cake into three parts.'*)   Cut it right there! Saliraawo!   cut off -salako, *eg*. Salako ettabi lino. (*'Cut off this branch.'*), (*intercept*) -taayiza, *eg*. Poliisi yataayiza ababbi. (*'The police cut off the thieve's escape route.'*)   cut off banana leaves -sala endagala, (*with a pruning pole*) -solobya endagala. *See* prune   cut oneself -eesala   cut path through vegetation -tema oluwenda   cut up (*into pieces*) -salaasala   cut with -saziza, *eg*. Nsazisizza makansi. (*'I am cutting with scissors.'*)   be cutable -salika

cutter (*person who cuts*) *n* omusazi *n1*, (*of cloth; tailor*) omukomozi *n1*

cutting (*of plant to grow*) *n* endokwa *n9*, ensibuka *n9*   cuttings of sweet potatoes amalagala *n6* (*one omuko gw'amalagala n3*)

cycle *See* bicycle; motorcycle

cyst *n* ekizimba *n7*

D,d

daddy *n* taata *n1*

dagger *n* empiima *n9*

daily *adv* buli lunaku

dairy *n* etterekero ly'amata *n5*

¹**dam** *n* ebbibiro *n5*   hydroelectric dam ebbibiro ery'amasannyalaze

²**dam (up)** *vt* -bibira

damage *vt* -yonoona, (*badly, of something solid*) -fufuggaza, *eg*. Yafufuggaza emmotoka. (*'He has badly damaged the car.'*)   be(come) damaged -yonooneka, *eg*. Engoye zange zaayonooneka mu muliro. (*'My clothes were damaged in the fire.'*), (*of something solid*) -fufuggala

damaged *adj* -yonoonefu, (*badly, of something solid*) -fufuggavu

damages (*compensation*) *n* engassi *n9*   pay damages to (*compensate*) -liwa

damp *adj* -bisi   get damp -bisiwala, *eg*. Nnatudde mu muddo, empale yange n'ebisiwala. (*'I sat down on the grass and my trousers got damp.'*), (*of something that absorbs moisture*) -nnyuukirira, *eg*. Omunnyo gunnyuukiridde. (*'The salt is damp.'*)   make damp -bisiwaza

¹**dance** *n* amazina *n6*, omudigido *n3*

²**dance** *vi* -zina, (*vigourously, in the Kiganda way, moving one's tummy*) -fukula olubuto, (*show rejoicing through rhythmic movement*) -digida. *See* night-dancing; rhythm

dancer *n* omuzinyi *n1*

dancing *n* okuzina *n15*, endigida *n9*

dandruff *n* situka (*mu mutwe*) *n9*

danger *n* akabi *n12*

dangerous *adj* -a akabi   something very dangerous ekibambulira *n7*

dangle *v* (1) *vi* -lengejja, -leebeeta; (2) *vt* -lengezza, -leebeesa

¹**daring** *adj* -gumu   daring person omugumu *n1*

²**daring** *n* obugumu *n14*

¹**dark** *adj* -ddugavu, (*very*) -ddugavu zigizigi, (*as within a dense forest*) -kwafu   be(come) dark -ddugala, *eg*. Addugadde omusana. (*'He has been in the sun and got darker,'*), (*of the sky*) obudde -kwata, *eg*. Obudde bukutte. (*'It is getting dark.'*)

²**dark(ness)** *n* enzikiza *n9*, (*extreme*) kazigizigi *n1*. *See* gloom   do until dark -zibya, *eg*. Nnakola ne nzibya. (*'I worked until it got dark.'*)   semi-darkness ekibululu *n7*

darling *n* kabiite *n1*

darn *vt* -tunga

dart *n* akasaale *n12*

dart to and fro (*like a swallow*) *vi* -tayira

¹**dash** (*sprint*) *n* embiro z'akafubatuko *n10*

²**dash** (*run*) *vi* -dduka   dash down (*hurl down, eg. heavy load*) -ggunda   dash into -eefubitika, *eg*. Engabi yeefubitise mu nsiko. (*'The bushbuck dashed into the bush.'*)   dash out -fubutuka, *eg*. Engabi efubutuse mu nsiko. (*'The bushbuck dashed out of the bush.'*)   be dashed down (*as in a vehicle on a rough road*) -eggunda

¹**date** (*day*) *n* olunaku *n11*. *Examples of date formation: (1)* kkumi na lumu Maaci (*'11ᵗʰ March'*); *(2)* Maaci kkumi na lumu (*'11ᵗʰ March'*)   go out of date -diba

²**date** *vt* -yogereza, *eg*. Yokana ayogereza Maliya. (*'John is dating Mary.'*)

daughter *n* omwana omuwala *n1*, (*of a princess*) nnaava *n1*, (*eldest, of the Kabaka*) Nnassolo *n1* title   daughter of muwala (*with pos* N12), *eg*. muwala wange (*'my daughter'*)

daughter-in-law *n* mukaamwana *n1* (*with pos* N12), *eg*. mukaamwana wange (*'my daughter-in-*

law')

David *n* Daudi *n1*, Dawudi *n1*

dawdle *(walk slowly)* *vi* -tambula -siira. *See* delay

¹dawn *n* emmambya *n9*. *See* morning

²dawn *vi* enjuba -vaayo, *eg. Enjuba evuddeyo.* *('It is dawning.')*, *(first signs, orange glow)* **emmambya -sala**, *eg. Emmambya esaze. ('It is dawning.')* do until dawn -keesa obudde, *eg. Akabaga kakeesezza obudde. ('The party went on until dawn.')*

day *n* olunaku *n11* day after tomorrow okwosa enkya day before yesterday okwosa jjo day off *(day of rest)* olunaku olw'okuwummula a working day olunaku lwa kukola another day olulala do all day *(until dark)* -zibya obudde, *eg. Twalima ne tuzibya obudde. ('We dug all day.')* hottest part of the day ettuntu *n5* in olden days ennaku ez'edda next day oluddako spend the day -siiba, *eg. Yasiibye waffe. ('She spent the day at our home.')* the other day luli, jjuuzi

daylight/daytime *n* emisana *n4*

daze, be in a *vi* -tangaalirira

deacon *n* omuddiikoni *n1*, ddiikoni *n1*

dead *adj* -fu. *See* deceased dead person *(one known to those concerned)* omufu *n1*, omugenzi *n1*. *See* corpse person risen from the dead *Use* -zuukira *('rise from the dead')* in rel (**N7.1**), *eg. abantu abazuukidde ('people risen from the dead')* place of the dead amagombe *n6*, *(where Walumbe disappeared)* ettanda *n9* pretend to be dead -eefiisa the rest *(holiday)* of the dead ekiwummulo *n7*

deadlocked, be *vi* -lemagana

deadly *adj* kawenkene *(invariable adjective)*, *eg. kawenkene Musoke ('the deadly Musoke')*

deaf deaf person kiggala *n1*, omuzibe w'amatu *n1* be(come) deaf -ziba amatu

deafen *vt* -ziba amatu, *eg. okuwoggana kwa bbandi kwanziba amatu. ('The noice of the band deafened me.')*

deafness *n* obuzibe bw'amatu *n14*, *(not wanting to hear)* obutawulira *n14*

deal *v* deal cards -gaba caanisi deal carefully with *(a person, handling with consideration)* -lembereza deal in *(trade in)* -suubula deal with *(attend to)* -kolako, *eg. Abalwadde bonna abasawo bamaze okubakolako. ('The doctors have dealt with all the patients.')*

dealer *(trader)* *n* omusuubuzi *n1*

deanery *n* ettwaale *n5*

dear *(expensive)* *adj* -a omuwendo, -a ebbeeyi my dear *affectionate form of address* munnange

death *n* okufa *n15* death rites olumbe *n11* announce a death to -bika be on the point of death -taawa conclude death rites *(when an heir is installed)* -yabya olumbe on the point of death kateetera, *eg. Asigaddemu kateetera. ('He remains on the point of death.')*

debark *vt* -susumbula debark barkcloth tree

-subula omutuba

debate *vi* -kubaganya ebirowoozo

debt *n* ebbanja *n5* ask for repayment of debt -banja, *eg. Musoke yabanja Mukasa. ('Musoke asked Mukasa to repay the debt.')*, *(frequently)* -banjirira be in debt -banjibwa. *See* arrears (in) deliberately fail to repay a debt (to) -lyazaamaanya fall into debt -gwa ku bbanja incur debt -lya ebbanja

debtor *n*. *Use* -banjibwa *('be in debt')* in rel (**N7.1**), *eg. abantu ababanjibwa ('debtors')* person who deliberately fails to repay a debt omulyazaamaanyi *n1*

decant *vt* -kenenula. *See* pour

¹decay *n* obuvundu *n14* cause to decay -vunza something decayed ekivunze *n7*

²decay *vi* -vunda

deceased *(dead)* *adj* -fu deceased person omufu *n1*, omugenzi *n1*. *See* late (the)

deceit *n* obukuusa *n14* deceitful act olukwe *n11* deceitful person omukuusa *n1*

deceitfully *adv* mu bukuusa

deceive *vt* (1) *(by not revealing information)* -kuusa; (2) *(trick)* -guumaaza. *See* evasive (be); lie deceive oneself -eerimba

December *n* Omwezi ogw'ekkumi n'ebiri *n3*, Ntenvu, Deesemba

decency *n* obuntubulamu *n14* decent person omuntumulamu *n1*

decide *vi* -salawo decide a court case -sala omusango

decision *n* ensala *n9*

declare *vt* -langirira, *eg. Yalangirira okwesimbawo kwe. ('He declared his candidacy.')*. *See* inform; public (make) declare openly -yatula declare openly to *(a person, what one knows about her or him)* -yatulira declare war -langirira olutalo

¹decline *(downward slope)* *n* akaserengeto *n12*

²decline *v* (1) *vi* *(decrease)* -kendeera, *eg.Abantu abajja wano bakendedde. ('The number of people who come here has declined.')* -sereba; (2) *(refuse)* *vt* -gaana, *eg. Yagaana okujja nga mmuyise. ('He declined to accept my invitation.')*. *See* decrease; diminish

decompose *vi* -vunda cause to decompose vunza

decomposed *adj* -vundu

decomposition *n* obuvundu *n14*

decorate *vt* (1) *(eg. a room)* -timba; (2) *(eg. pot by colouring)* -tona; (3) *(eg. pot or wood, by carving)* -yola; (4) *(with finishing touches; embellish)* -wunda way of decorating entimba *n9*

decorated *(eg. of pot)* *adj* -tone

decoration *n* ekyokutimba *n7*. *See* flag decorative strip on busuuti omudalizo *n3* put decorative strip on busuuti -teekako omudalizo, -daliza

decoy *vt* -buzaabuza

decrease *v* (1) *(be reduced)* *vi* -kendeera, *eg. Kasooli akendedde mu ggwanika. ('The maize has* decreased in quantity in the store.'); (2) (come down) vi **-kka**, eg. Ebbeeyi esse. ('The price has decreased.'); (3) (reduce) vt **-kendeeza**, eg. Yakendeezezza ebbeeyi. ('He has decreased the price.'); (4) (put down) vt **-ssa**, eg. Bassizza omusolo. ('They have decreased the rate of tax.'). See diminish

¹decree n **ekiragiro** n7

²decree vt **-lagira**

decrepit, become vi **-kanduka**, **-kayuka**

dedicate vt (1) (an offering to a lubaale or spirit) **-wonga**; (2) (a child to the service of the Kabaka or major chief) **-siiga**. See sacrifice   dedicate oneself **-eewaayo**, eg. Yeewaayo eri Katonda. ('He dedicated himself to the service of God.'), **-eewonga**   dedicate to **-wongera**, eg. Nnatutte enkoko mu kkanisa ne ngiwongera Mukama. ('I took a hen to church to dedicate to God.')   be dedicated (diligent) **-nyiikira**

dedicated adj (1) (diligent) **-nyiikivu**; (2) (to a lubaale or spirit) **-wonge**

dedication (diligence) n **obunyiikivu** n14

deduct (a part) vt **-toolako**, **-ggyako**, (to present to a chief) **-lobolako**

deed n **ekikolwa** n7

deep adj **-wanvu**   deep water **eddubi** n5   in deep water **ebuziba**

deepen vt **-wanvuya**

defame vt **-siiga enziro**, **-swaza**. See libel

defeat vt **-wangula**, eg. Eggye lyawangula abalabe. ('The army defeated the enemy.')   be defeated (by) (1) (conquered) **-wangulwa**; (2) (by a task) **-lema** (with personal object), eg. Omulimu gwamulemye. ('The job defeated him.'), **-lemwa** (with personal subject), eg. Yalemwa omulimu. ('She was defeated by the job.')

defecate vi **-fuluma**, **-pama** (impolite)

defect n (1) (flaw) **ekisobu** n7; (2) (eg. due to damage) **akamogo** n12

defective adj **-yonoonefu**

defend vt (1) (guard) **-kuuma**, eg. Eggye lyakuuma ekibuga. ('The army defended the city.'); (2) (in court) **-wolereza**. See protect   defend oneself (1) (in a fight) **-eerwanako**, eg. Twerwanako nga abalabe batulumbye. ('We defended ourselves when the enemy attacked us.'); (2) (in court) **-eewolereza**

defendant (in court) n **omuwawaabirwa** n1

defer v (1) (comply with another person's wishes or judgement) vi **-kkiriza**, eg. Yakkiriza Musoke kyagamba. ('He deferred to Musoke's opinion.'); (2) (postpone) vt **-yongezaayo mu maaso**, eg. Olugendo alwongezzaayo mu maaso. ('He has deferred the journey.');

deference n **obwetoowaze** n15   be deferential **-eetoowaza**   be deferential towards **-eetoowaliza**, eg. Yanneetoowaliza. ('He was deferential towards me.')

defiant, be vi **-eekoboggoza**, eg. Yaddamu ebibuuzo nga yeekoboggoza. ('He answered the questions defiantly.')

deficient   be deficient in **-buza** (often with enclitic N24.2), eg. Tubuzaayo amagi abiri. ('We are deficient in two eggs.')

defile a girl **-sobya ku muwala**

define vt **-tegeeza**, eg. Ekigambo kino kitegeeza ki? ('How do you define this word?')

definite adj (1) (certain) **-kakafu**; (2) (limited period, of time) **-gere**   make definite **-kakasa**

definition (meaning) n **amakulu** n6

deflate (release pressure) vt **-teewulula**   deflate a tyre **-ggyamu omukka mu mupiira**   be(come) deflated **-teewulukuka**, (with pressure reduced) **-footoka**   feel deflated (mentally) **-ggwaamu amaanyi**

deform vt **-goomya**, (permanently; cause deformity) **-gongobaza**   be deformed **-gooma**, (permanently) **-gongobala**

deformed adj **-goomu**, (permanently) **-gongobavu**

defraud vt **-kumpanya**, (through not repaying a debt) **-lyazaamaanya**

defy vt (1) (overcome; surmount) **-vvuunuka**; (2) (refuse to obey) **-gaana**

degrade vt **-yonoona**   become degraded **-yonooneka**

degree (university qualification) n **digiri** n9   degree ceremony **amatikkira** n6

deity See god; spirit

dejected adj (1) (downcast) **-nyiikaavu**; (2) (lethargic and miserable) **-yongobevu**. See sad   feel dejected (1) (downcast) **-nyiikaala**; (2) (lethargic and miserable) **-yongobera**

¹delay n   without delay **obutalwawo**

²delay v (1) vi **-lwa**, eg. Ndudde awaka. ('I delayed at home.'); (2) vt **-lwisa**, eg. Yandwisa. ('He delayed me.'). See late (be); postpone; procrastinate   delay on purpose (to avoid doing something that one should) **-eerabiriza**   be delayed **-lwisibwa**, eg. Nnalwisibwa we bakola oluguudo. ('I was delayed by the roadworks.'), (temporarily) **-sikattira**, eg. Twasikattidde mu kkubo olwa jjaamu. ('We were delayed on the road because of a traffic jam.')

¹delegate n **omukiise** n1

²delegate vt **-sigira**, eg. Baamusigira omulimu. ('They delegated him to do the work.')

delegation n **abakiise** n2

deliberate (on) (think about) vt **-fumiitiriza**

deliberately, do vi **-genderera**, eg. Yakigenderera. ('He did it deliberately.')   deliberately mix up **-canga**   deliberately mix up words **-cangacanga ebigambo**   be deliberate and slow in one's actions **-eerembereza**

delicious adj **-woomu**, (of fruit) **-nyuunyuntuvu**   be delicious **-wooma**, (of fruit) **-nyuunyuntula**

deliciousness (of food) n **obuwoomi** n14, (of fruit) **obunyuunyuntuvu** n14

¹**delight** *n* essanyu *n5*
²**delight** *vt* -sanyusa
delirium *n* akalogojjo *n12* be delirious -logojjana
deliver *vt* -tuusa, *eg. Obubaka mbutuusizza. ('I have delivered the message')* deliver a baby *(assist at childbirth)* -zaalisa
¹**demand** *(order) n* ekiragiro *n7* demand note *(requesting payment)* ebbaluwa ebanja *n9* make demands on *(harass someone to do things)* -kulungutanya
²**demand** *(order) vt* -lagira, *eg. Yabalagira okujja amangu. ('He demanded them to come quickly.')*. See ask demand repayment of debt from -banja, *eg. Yammanja mmusasule ssente ze. ('He demanded repayment of my debit to him.')* be demanding (1) *(giving trouble to)* -tawaanya; (2) *(make demands on)* -teganya, *eg. Abaana bateganya. ('The children are demanding.')*
demeanour *n* empisa *n10*
demented demented person omuwutta *n1*, omuwuttaavu *n1* be(come) demented -wutta, -wuttuka
demolish *vt* -menyawo. See dismantle
demon *n* omuzimu *n3*
demonstrate *v* (1) *(for a cause) vi* -eekalakaasa; (2) *(show how) vt* -laga, -lagirira
demonstration *n* (1) *(in pursuit of a cause)* okwekalakaasa *n15*; (2) *(display)* omwoleso *n3*
demonstrator *n* (1) *(for a cause)* omwekalakaasi *n1*; (2) *(to show how)* omulagirizi *n1*
demote *vt* -ssa eddaala
denigrate *vt* -jerega
denounce *vt* -loopa. See condemn
denouncer *n* omuloopi *n1*
dense *adj* (1) *(in consistency, eg. of porridge or vegetation)* -kwafu; (2) *(mentally)* -buguyavu be dense (1) *(of vegetation)* -kwata, *eg. Ekibira kino kikutte. ('This forest is dense.')*; (2) *(mentally)* -buguyala
¹**dent** *n* awawowongofu *n16*
²**dent** *vt* -gongobaza
dented *adj* -gongobavu be(come) dented -gongobala
dentist *n* omusawo w'amannyo *n1*
deny *(an accusation) vt* -eegaana, *eg. Yeegaana nti teyabba nkoko. ('He denied stealing the chickens.')* deny something one has done -eekangabiriza
depart *vi* -vaawo, *eg. Baavuddewo ku ssaawa bbiri. ('They departed at 8 o'clock.')*, *(on a journey)* -situla, *eg. Tujja kusitula ku ssaawa bbiri. ('We will depart at 8 o'clock.')*, *(on a journey, of a means of transport)* -simbula, *eg. Ebbaasi esimbula ku ssaawa bbiri. ('The bus departs at 8 o'clock.')*. See leave
department *n* ekitongole *n7*, *eg. ekitongole ky'obulamu ('department of health')*
depend on *vt* -yimirirawo ku lwa, *eg. Ayimiriddewo ku lwa muganda we. ('She is depending on her brother.')*. See trust depend on oneself *(be self-sufficient)* -eeyimirizaawo, -eebeezaawo
depending *conj* okuva ku, *eg. Okuva ku budde bwe bunaaba, nja kulima enkya. ('Depending on the weather, I will cultivate tomorrow.')*
depose *vt* -ggya ku bufuzi
¹**deposit** *n* make a deposit -sibako ssente, *eg. Yasibako ssente ku nnyumba. ('She put down a deposit on the house.')*
²**deposit** *(put down) vt* -teeka *(or* -ssa*)* wansi, *eg. Yateeka essanduuko wansi. ('She deposited the case on the floor.')* deposit money in a bank -teekayo ssente mu bbanka
deprave *vt* -gwagwawaza, *(sexually)* -kabawaza. See lead astray be(come) depraved -gwagwawala, *(sexually)* -kabawala
depraved *adj* -gwagwa, *(sexually)* -kaba depraved person ekigwagwa *n7*, *(sexually)* omukaba *n1*
depravity *n* obugwagwa *n14*, *(sexual)* obukaba *n14*
depressed *(mentally) adj* -nyiikaavu, -nakuwavu feel depressed -nyiikaala, -nakuwala. See dejected (be) person who is mentally depressed omunyiikavu *n1*
depression *n* (1) *(in a road)* ekisirikko *n7*; (2) *(in the landscape)* ekikko *n7*; (3) *(made in a lump of mattoke before dipping into sauce)* ennoga *n9*; (4) *(mental)* obunyiikaavu *n14*, ennyiike y'amaanyi mu bulamu *n9*. See ruts
deprive *vt* -mma, *eg. Yamumma emmere. ('He deprived her of food.')* be deprived (of) -mmibwa, *eg. Yammibwa emmere. ('He was deprived of food.')*
depth *n* obuwanvu *n14*
deputation *n* abakiise *n2*
deputise (for) *vt* -kiikirira, *eg. Yakiikirira ssentebe. ('She is deputising for the chairman.')*
deputy *(representing someone) n* omusigire *n1*. See helper make deputy -sigira
deranged *(insane and wild) adj* -taamuufu deranged person (1) *(mad)* omulalu *n1*; (2) *(suffering from a fit of madness)* omuzoole *n1* be(come) deranged -taamuuka. See mad (go)
deride *vt* -jerega
descend *vi* -kka, *eg. Twakka ku madaala. ('We descended the stairs.')*. See come down descend a slope -serengeta, *eg. Twaserengeta ku lusozi. ('We descended the hill.')*, -kkirira
descendant *n* omuzzukulu *n1* descendants *(progeny)* ezzadde *n5*
descent *(downward slope) n* akaserengeto *n12*
describe *vt* -nnyonnyola
¹**desert** *(wilderness) n* eddungu *n5*
²**desert** *(abandon) vt* -yabulira, *eg. Omuserikale yayabulidde banne. ('The soldier deserted his companions.')* desert a hive *(of bees)* enjuki -fuluka, *eg. Enjuki zifuluse. ('The bees have deserted the hive.')* desert one's husband -noba

desert one's wife -**dibya mukyala**
deserted *adj* -**fulufu**, *eg. ekiswa ekifulufu ('deserted ant hill')* deserted house **ekifulukwa** *n7*
deserve *vt* -**saanira**, -**gwanira**
[1]**design** *(make)* *n* **enkola** *n9*
[2]**design** *(invent)* *vt* -**yiiya**
designate *vt* -**laalika**, *eg. Yalaalika Musoke okutema emiti. ('He designated Musoke to cut the trees.'). See* appoint
designer *n* **omuyiiya** *n1*
desirable *adj* -**lungi**
desire *(covet; lust after)* *vt* -**eegomba**. *See* want be desired -**eegombebwa** cause to desire -**eegombesa**
desk *n* **akameeza** *n12*
despair *vi* -**ggwaamu essuubi**
despise *vt* -**nyooma**, -**jerega**. *See* contempt be despised -**nyoomebwa** person who despises **omunyoomi** *n1*
despite *conj* **newankubadde**, *eg. Newankubadde yali mulwadde, yajja okukola. ('Despite his illness he came to work.')*
destabilise *vt* -**taataaganya** be(come) destabilised -**taataagana**
destiny *(fate)* *n. Use* -**kakatako** *('be certain for'), eg. Kimukakatako. ('It was his destiny.')* destined time **entuuko** *n10*
destitute *adj* -**yavu ennyo** destitute person **lunkupe** *n1*
destitution *n* **obwavu** *n14*
destroy *vt* -**zikiriza**, -**saanyawo**, *(with fire)* -**sirissa**. *See* crush be destroyed -**zikirira**, -**saanawo**, *(by fire)* -**sirikka**, *eg. Ennyumba esirisse. ('The house has been destroyed by fire.')*
detach *vt* (1) *(take off)* -**ggyako**, *eg. Yaggyako omunyolo ku luggi. ('He detached the handle from the door.')*; (2) *(something inserted)* -**wangula**, *eg. Yawangula enkumbi. ('She detached the hoe.')*; (3) *(hand of bananas)* -**wagula**; (4) *(individual bananas)* -**wagulawagula**; (5) *(individual bananas, for someone else)* -**wagulira** detach from a stem -**nogola**, *eg. Yanogola ettabi ku muti. ('She detached a branch from the tree.')* be(come) detached (1) *(come off)* -**vaako**, *eg. Omunyolo gwavaako ku luggi. ('The handle became detached from the door.')*; (2) *(of something inserted)* -**wanguka**, *eg. Enkumbi ewanguse. ('The hoe has become detached.')*. *See* come off; drop off
detain *(delay)* *vt* -**lwisa**, *eg. Yandwisa nga ayogera obutamala. ('He detained me by talking for too long.'). See* imprison
detainee *(prisoner)* *n* **omusibe** *n1*
detect *(recognise)* -**tegeera**, *eg. Nnategera eddoboozi lye bwe yayogedde. ('I detected his voice when he spoke.')*
detective *n* **mbega** *n1*
detention *(imprisonment)* *n* **enkomyo** *n9*
deter *vt* -**ziyiza**

deteriorate *vi* -**yonooneka**, *eg. Embeera eyonoonese. ('The situation has deteriorated.')*, -**eeyongera okwonooneka**
determination *n* **obumalirivu** *n14*, **obunyiikivu** *n14*
determined *(resolute)* *adj* -**malirivu**, -**nyiikivu** be determined -**malirira**, -**nyiikira**
detest *vt* -**kyawa**
detour (around), make a -**eebalama**, *(to avoid being seen)*, -**eekooloobya**, -**eebalaamiriza**
devastate *vt* -**yonoona ennyo**
develop *(progress)* *v* (1) *vi* -**kulaakulana**; (2) *vt* -**kulaakulanya**, *eg. Akulaakulanya bizineesi ye. ('He is developing his business.')* develop a film -**yoza ebifaananyi** develop into *(become)* -**fuusa**, *eg. Afuuse omusajja ow'amaanyi. ('He has developed into a strong man.')*
development *n* **enkulaakulana** *n9*
deviate *vi* -**va ku**, *eg. Ddereeva yava ku luguudo bulijjo mw'ayita. ('The driver deviated from his normal route.')*, *(go off the track)* -**baliga**
Devil *(the Devil)* *n* **Sitaani** *n1*
devious devious person **omukumpanya** *n1* be devious towards -**kumpanya**. *See* excuses (make false)
devise *vt* -**yiiya** devise a way *(to do something)* -**sala amagezi**
devote *(offering to lubaale or spirit)* *vt* -**wonga** devote oneself (to) -**eewaayo**
devoted *(determined; resolute)* *adj* -**malirivu** be devoted *(determined)* -**malirira**
devour *vt* (1) *(eat with zest, enjoying the food)* -**miringusa**; (2) *(eat ravenously)* -**kavvula**
devout *adj. Use* -**faayo ennyo** *('care a lot') in rel* **(N7.1)**, *eg. Abakulisitaayo abafaayo ennyo ku diini yaabwe ('devout Christians')*
dew *n* **omusulo** *n3*
dhou *n* **ekyombo** *n7*
diabetes *n* **obulwadde bwa sukaali** *n14*, **sukaali** *n1*
diagnose *vt* -**manya ekivaako**
diagonally *adv* **obukiika**
diagram *n* **ekifaananyi** *n7*
dialogue *n* **enteesaganya** *n9*
diarrhoea *n* **ekiddukano** *n7* cause diarrhoea -**ddukanya** have diarrhoea -**ddukana**, -**lwala embiro**, -**waluka**
dictator *n* **nnaakyemalira** *n1*
dictatorship *n* **obwannaakyemalira** *n14*
dictionary *n* **enkuluze y'ebigambo** *n9*
did *See* do
die *vi* -**fa** die for -**fiirira**, *eg. Yesu yafiirira abantu bonna. ('Jesus died for all people.')* die out *(perish)* -**zikirira** die suddenly *(or unexpectedly)* -**fa ekikutuko**, *eg. Muganda wange yafudde kikutuko. ('My brother died suddenly.')*, -**fa ekibwatukira** die at/in -**fiira**, *eg. Yafiira mu ddwaliro. ('He died in hospital.')*
diesel *n* **dizero** *n1*

diet *n* endya *n9*

differ *vi* -yawukana, eg. *Kino kyawukanye ku kiri.* (*'This differs from that.'*), (*emphasising the difference*) -yawula, eg. *Abalongo bafaanana naye ekibaawula bwe buwanvu.* (*'The twins look alike but differ in height.'*)

difference *n* enjawulo *n9*

different *adj* -a enjawulo, eg. *mu ngeri ey'enjawulo* (*'in a different way'*), (*emphasising the difference*) -yawufu, eg. *Guno omuti mwawufu okuva ku miti emirala.* (*'This tree is different from the others.'*). See another   be different -yawukako, eg. *Ekiwandiiko kino kyawuseeko ku kye nnasooka okusoma.* (*'This document is a bit different from the one which I read first.'*)

differentiate *vt* -yawula

differently *adv* kya njawulo, obulala

difficult *adj* -zibu, -kalubo   difficult (*tight*) situation akanyigo *n12*   be(come) difficult -zibuwala, eg. *Omwana azibuwadde.* (*'The child has become difficult.'*), (*hard to do*) -kaluba, eg. *Kino kikalubye.* (*'This is difficult.'*)   be(come) difficult for -zibuwalira, -kaluubirira, eg. *Emirimu ginkaluubiridde.* (*'The work is difficult for me.'*)   fall into difficulties -gwa mu buzibu   have difficulties (*in affairs*) -kaluubirirwa   make difficulties -zibuwaza, -kalubya   make difficult for -zibuwaliza, -kaluubiriza

difficulty *n* obuzibu *n14*, obukalubo *n14*. See trouble   difficulties ebizibu *n8*, (*in affairs*) engozoobana *n9*

dig *vit* (dug) (1) (*cultivate*) -lima, (*deeply*) -kabala; (2) (*a hole*) -sima   dig out/up (1) (*tree stump, post, etc.*) -simula, eg. *Yasimudde enkonge.* (*'He dug out the tree stump.'*); (2) (*using an implement such as a needle*) -tundula, eg. *Yatundula eriggwa mu ngalo.* (*'He dug out the thorn from his hand.'*); (3) (*take out from within*) -sowola, eg. *Yasowola kasooli mu nsawo.* (*'She dug out a maize cob from the sack.'*); (4) (*something buried*) -ziikula, eg. *Yaziikula essanduuko mu ttaka.* (*'She dug up the box from the ground.'*). See excavate; exhume; scoop out; uproot   dig out/up potatoes (1) (*with a digging stick*) -sima lumonde; (2) (*with a hoe*) -soggola lumonde   dig out the truth from (*persuade to reveal*) -kemekkereza   dig up (*something unpleasant*) about the person being addressed -langira

digger (*person; cultivator*) *n* omulimi *n1*

digging   digging spear (*type of tool*) ekifumu *n7*   digging stick for sweet potatoes omuggo ogusima lumonde *n3*   a day's digging (*cultivating*) olubimbi *n11*   time for digging up sweet potatoes amasoggola *n6*   way of digging (*a plot*) ennima *n9*, (*deeply*) enkabala *n9*

dignitory *n* ow'ekitiibwa *n1*

dignity *n* ekitiibwa *n7*   walk with dignity -tambuza ssimbo

digress *vi* -landagga

dilemma, be in a *vi* -soberwa

diligence *n* obunyiikivu *n14*

diligent *adj* -nyiikivu   be diligent -nyiikira

¹dilute *adj* -a jjuule, eg. *omubisi gwa jjuule* (*'dilute banana juice'*), -a lujjulungu, eg. *Omwenge gwa lujjulungu.* (*'The beer is diluted.'*)

²dilute *vt* -jungulula, eg. *Omwenge yagwongeramu amazzi n'agujungulula.* (*'He added water to the beer and diluted it.'*), -saabulula

dim (*stupid*) *adj* -siru   dim person omusiru *n1*   dimness of sight ekifu ku maaso *n7*   become dim (1) (*stupid*) -siruwala; (2) (*of the light level*) -kendeera okwaka, eg. *Ettaala ekendedde okwaka.* (*'The lamp has become dim.'*)   grow dim with age (*of sight*) amaaso -yimbaala, eg. *Amaaso gange gayimbadde.* (*'My sight has grown dim.'*)

dimension(s) *n* obunene *n14*, eg. *obunene bw'emmeeza* (*'dimensions of the table'*)

diminish *v* (1) *vi* (*general word*) -kendeera, eg. *Kasooli akendedde mu ggwanika.* (*'The maize is diminishing in amount in the store.'*), (*of strength, of person or animal*) -sereba; (2) *vt* -kendeeza, eg. *Akendeeza kasooli mu ggwanika.* (*'He is diminishing the quantity of maize in the store.'*). See fewer (become); lose; smaller (become); thin (become); worn down (become)

din (*made by people*) *n* oluyoogaano *n11*. See shouting   make a din (1) (*of people*) -yoogaana; (2) (*of cicadas*) -nyaanyaagira

dine *vi* -lya   dining room eddiiro *n5*

diner *n* omuli *n1*

dinner (*evening meal*) *n* ekyeggulo *n7*, ekyekiro *n7*

diocese *n* (1) (*Prot*) obulabirizi *n14*; (2) (*RC*) essaza *n5*

dip (*immerse*) *vt* -bbika   dip in (eg. *ladle, to extract some liquid*) -tutubika   dip (*food*) in sauce -koza, eg. *Akoza amatooke.* (*'She is dipping the matooke in sauce.'*)

diploma *n* ebbaluwa *n9*

diplomat *n* omubaka w'ensi *n1*

direct (*show how*) *vt* -lagirira, eg. *Yandagirira bwe ntuuka ku kyalo.* (*'She directed me to the village.'*). See order

direction *n* oludda *n11*, eg. *Ŋŋende ku ludda luno oba olwo?* (*'Shall I go in this directon or that?'*), (*in relation to compass direction*) enjuuyi *n10*   directions (*as guidance*) endagiriro *n9*   in the direction of ku ludda lwa

directly *adv* obutereevu, eg. *Ekkubo lino ligenda butereevu e Masaka.* (*'This road goes directly to Masaka.'*). See as soon as

director *n* omukulu *n1*, dayirekita *n1*

directory *n* endagiriro *n9*

dirt *n* ekko *n5*, (*on poorly washed utensils*) obukokkoliko *n14*. See soil

dirtiness *n* obujama *n14*, obukyafu *n14*, obuligo *n14*

dirty *adj* -jama, -kyafu, (*permanently soiled*) -gubu

dirty person (*by nature*) **omujama** *n1* dirty trick (*deceitful act*) **akakwe** *n12* be(come) dirty (1) -**jamawala**, -**kyafuwala**, -**ddugala**, *eg. Omwana addugadde. ('The child is dirty.')*; (2) (*permanently soiled, of parts of clothing, eg. collar*) -**gubaasira**; (3) (*of the skin through not washing for some days*) -**kwata ekko** make dirty -**jamawaza**, -**kyafuwaza**, -**ddugaza**, (*permanently*) -**gubya** rub in dirt -**kulukuunya**

disability *n* **obulemu** *n14*

disabled *adj* -**lema** disabled person **omulema** *n1*, (*one who requires help*) **kateeyamba** *n1* be(come) disabled -**lemala**

disagree *vi*. Use -**kkiriza** ('*agree*') in neg (**N21**), *eg. Teyakkiriza. ('He disagreed.')* disagree with (*someone*) Use -**kkirizaganya ne** ('*agree with one another*') in neg (**N21**), *eg. Sakkirizaganya ne Musoke. ('I disagreed with Musoke.')*, (*of food or drink*) -**semba**, *eg. Emmere eno ensemba. ('This food disagrees with me.')*

disagreement *n* **obutakkirizaganya** *n14*. *See* misunderstanding rubbing one another up the wrong way **embojjanyi** *n9*

disappear *vi* -**bula**. *See* away (be)

disappoint (*let someone down*) *vt* -**yiwa** be disappointed -**saalirwa**, *eg. Nnasaaliddwa obutamulaba. ('I was disappointed not to see her.')*

disassemble *vt* -**pangulula**

disaster *n* **ekibabu** *n7*, **akacwano** *n12*,

disavow *vt* -**eegaana**

disband *vt* (1) (*a meeting*) -**yabula**, *eg. Ssentebe yayabudde olukiiko. ('The chair disbanded the meeting.')*; (2) (*an organisation*) -**yabulula** be disbanded -**yabuka**, *eg. Olukiiko lwabuse. ('The meeting was disbanded.')*

discard *vt* -**suula**

discern *vt* (1) (*understand*) -**tegeera**; (2) (*see*) -**laba**

discerning (*understanding*) *adj* -**tegeevu** discerning person **omutegeevu** *n1*

discernment *n* **obutegeevu** *n14*

discharge *vt* -**siibula**, *eg. Bamusiibudde mu ddwaliro. ('They discharged him from hospital.')* discharge a gun -**kuba emmundu** be discharged -**siibulwa**, *eg. Yasiibuddwa okuva mu ddwaliro. ('He was discharged from hospital.')*

disciple *n* **omuyigirizwa** *n1*

discipline *vt* -**kangavvula**. *See* punish; reprimand

disclose (*make known*) *vt* -**yogera**, *eg. Yayogera ebisumuluzo we biri. ('She disclosed where the keys are.')*. *See* inform; public (make); reveal disclose to (*someone one's knowledge of her/him*) -**yatulira**, *eg. Mukasa yayatulira Musoke nga bw'amanyi nti mubbi. ('He disclosed to Musoke that he knew he was a thief.')*. *See* reveal; tell

disco *n* **disiko** *n9*

discolour (*permanently*) *vt* -**gubya**. *See* dirty (make)

discoloured (*permanently*) *adj* -**gubu**, (*of collar, cuffs, etc.*) -**gubaasiivu** be(come) discoloured

-**guba**, (*of collar etc.*) -**gubaasira** become discoloured with soil -**kuusiira**

discontinue *vt* -**lekera awo** *followed by inf* (**N19**), *eg. Yalekera awo okusoma. ('He discontinued his studies.')*

discord (*strife*) *n* **empaka** *n10*

[1]**discourse** (*conversation*) *n* **emboozi** *n9*

[2]**discourse** (*hold a discussion*) *vi* -**nyumya**

discover *vt* -**vumbula**. *See* find be discovered -**vumbuka**

discoverer *n* **omuvumbuzi** *n1*

discredit *vt* -**weebuula** be discredited -**weebuuka**

discreet *adj* -**a emmizi** discreet person **ow'emmizi** *n1*

discrimination *n* **obusosoze** *n14* discriminate against -**sosola**, *eg. Basosola abakadde. ('They discriminate against the old.')*. *See* ignore be discriminated against -**sosolwa** be discriminating (*choosy*) -**eeronda**

discuss *vt* -**teesa (ku)** (*or* -**teesaako**), *eg. Twateesa ku by'embaga jjo. ('We discussed the wedding yesterday.')*. *See* talk about discuss with -**yogera ne**, *eg. Njogedde ne Musoke ku mawulire. ('I have discussed the news with Musoke.')* discuss with one another -**teesaganya**

discussion *n* **okuteesa** *n15* have a discussion -**kubaganya ebirowoozo** something for discussion **ekyokuteesa** *n7* something discussed **ekyateesebwa** *n7*

[1]**disdain** *n* **obunyoomi** *n14*

[2]**disdain** *vt* -**nyooma**

disease *n* **obulwadde** *n14*, (*infectious*) **obulwadde obukwata**, (*incurable*) **obulwadde obutawona**. *See* illness; madness; skin disease shaking disease (*Parkinson's disease*) **obulwadde bw'obuko** pyschosomatic disease of women **ebigalanga** *n8* spread a disease -**saasaanya obulwadde** swollen stomach disease **entumbi** *n9*

disembark *vi* -**va mu** (*or* -**vaamu**), *eg. Baava mu nnyonyi. ('They disembarked from the plane.')*

disentangle *vt* -**taggulula** disentangle problems -**langulula ensonga** be(come) disentangled -**taggulukuka**

disfigure *vt* -**goomya**, (*permanently*) -**gongobaza**

disfigured *adj* -**goomye**, (*permanently*) -**gongobavu** be(come) disfigured -**gooma**, (*permanently*) -**gongobala**

[1]**disgrace** *n* **obuwemu** *n14*. *See* atrocities

[2]**disgrace** *vt* -**wemula**. *See* shame be disgraced -**wemuka** be disgraced before -**wemukira**

disgraceful *adj* -**a obuwemu**

disguise oneself *vr* -**eefuula**, *eg. Yeefuula nga owa poliisi. ('He disguised himself as a policeman.')*

disgust (*make fed up*) *vt* -**tama**, *eg. Empisa ze zantama. ('His behaviour disgusts me.')*. *See* repel be disgusted -**eetamwa**, *eg. Yawulira okwetamwa we yamanya Musoke bye yali akoze. ('She felt disgusted when she heard what Musoke had done.')*

dish

show disgust **-eenyinyimbwa** something disgusting (*repugnant*) **ekyenyinyalwa** *n7*

dish (*bowl*) *n* **ebbakuli** *n9*, (*of earthenware*) **ekibya** *n7*. See plate

dish up *v*. See banana (*for words relating to dishing up food from a food parcel*)

disheartened, be *vi* **-ggwaamu omutima**

dishevelled, be *vi* **-sunsumala**

dishonour *vt* **-weebuula** be dishonoured **-weebuuka**

disintegrate *vi* **-sebbuka** cause to disintegrate **-sebbula**

disinter See exhume

¹dislike *n* **obutayagala** *n14*

²dislike *vt*. Use **-yagala** ('*like*') in neg (**N21**), *eg. Sikyagala.* ('*I dislike it.*')

dislocate *vt* **-nuula**, *eg. Musoke yanudde omukono gwange.* ('*Musoke has dislocated my arm.*') be dislocated **-nuuka**, *eg. Omukono gwe gunuuse.* ('*His arm is dislocated.*')

dismantle *vt* **-zimbulula**, *eg. Abazimbi baazimbulula ennyumba.* ('*The builders dismantled the house.*'). See demolish; disassemble; take apart

dismay *vt* **-eewuunyisa**, *eg. Amawulire gatwewuunyisa.* ('*The news dismayed us.*')

dismiss *vt* **-goba**, *eg. Omukulu yagoba omukozi.* ('*The boss dismissed the worker.*'), (*those attending a meeting*) **-yabula** be dismissed (*of those attending a meeting*) **-yabuka** be dismissive (*about a person*) **-dibaga**

disobedience *n* **obutengu** *n14*

disobey *vt* **-tenguwa**

disorganise *vt* (1) (*affairs*) **-taataaganya**, *eg. Yazze kikeerezi n'ataataaganya entegeka yaffe.* ('*He came late and disorganised our arrangements.*'); (2) (*items*) **-tankuula**, *eg. Yatankudde ebintu mu kabada.* ('*He has disorganised the things in the cupboard.*'). See mess up; ransack; rummage through be disorganised (1) (*of affairs*) **-taataagana**, *eg. Ebintu byonna bitaataaganye.* ('*All is disorganised.*'); (2) (*of things*) **-tankuuka**

disorganised (*of things*) *adj* **-tankuufu**

disown *vt* **-eegaana**

disparage *vt* **-jerega**. See underestimate

dispatch *vt* (1) (*a person*) **-tuma**; (2) (*something*) **-weereza** be dispatched (*of a person*) **-tumibwa**

dispensary *n* **eddwaliro** *n5*

disperse *v* (1) *vi* **-saasaana**, *eg. Abantu basaasaanye.* ('*The people dispersed.*'), (*of people after a meeting*) **-yabuka**, *eg. Abantu bayabuse nga olukiiko luwedde.* ('*The people dispersed when the meeting ended.*'); (2) *vt* **-saasaanya**, *eg. Empewo yasaasaanya ebisaaniiko.* ('*The wind dispersed the rubbish.*')

¹display *n* **omwoleso** *n3*

²display (*exhibit*) *vt* **-yolesa** be displayed **-yolesebwa**

displeased, be *vi*. Use **-sanyusa** ('*please*') in neg (**N21**), *eg. Engeri mutabani we gye yeeyisa teyamusanyusa.* ('*He was displeased by his son's behaviour.*'). See upset

disputable *adj* **-a mbu**, *eg. Bye baayogedde bya mbu.* ('*What they said was disputable.*)

disputant *n* **omuwakanyi** *n1*

¹dispute *n* **empaka** *n9*

²dispute *vi* **-wakana**, *eg. Twawakana ku ani asinga.* ('*We were disputing as to who is best.*') dispute about (*argue about*) **-kaayanira**, *eg. Twali tukaayanira ettaka.* ('*We were disputing [ownership of] the land.*') dispute with (*someone*) **-wakanya**, *eg. Yawakanya ekirowoozo kyange.* ('*He disputed my argument.*') be disputed **-wakanyizibwa**

disregard (*a family member*) *vt* **-boola**

¹disrespect *n* **ejjoogo** *n5* be held in disrespect **-joogebwa** show disrespect **-yisa amaaso**

²disrespect *vt* **-jooga**

disrupt (*cause disruption for someone*) *vt* **-kulungutanya**

dissatisfied, be *vi*. Use **-matira** ('*be satisfied*') in neg (**N21**), *eg. Simatidde na mulimu gwo.* ('*I am dissatisfied with your work.*'). See unsatisfactory (*something*) express dissatisfaction (*at what has been given*) **-toma**. See grumble

disseminate *vt* **-saasaanya**, *eg. Baasaasaanya mangu amawulire.* ('*They quickly disseminated the news.*'). See distribute disseminate information **-fulumya amawulire** be(come) disseminated **-saasaana**, *eg. Amawulire gaasaasaana wonna.* ('*The news was disseminated everywhere.*')

dissociate oneself *vr* **-eeyawula**, *eg. Nneeyawudde ku Musoke.* ('*I have dissociated myself from Musoke.*'), **-eesammula**. See distance oneself

dissolute *adj* **-gwenyufu**, (*sexually*) **-kaba** be(come) dissolute **-gwenyuka**, (*sexually*) **-kabawala**

dissolve *vt* **-lunga**. See stir rub and dissolve medicinal clay stick **-sira emmumbwa** squeeze and dissolve (*herbs in water*) **-yenga**

distance. For measures of distance use constructions such as '*Okuva wano okutuuka eyo waliwo mayiro emu.*' ('*The distance from here to there is one mile.*'). See measure(ment) a long distance from **wala okuva**, *eg. Kampala wala okuva wano.* ('*Kampala is a long distance from here.*') a short distance from **kumpi okuva**, *eg. Kampala kumpi okuva wano.* ('*Kampala is a short distance from here.*') be at a distance from (1) (*long way*) **-li wala**, *eg. Eddwaliro liri wala n'ennyumba ye.* ('*The clinic is at a distance from his house.*') keep a distance from (*other people*) **-eesuula**

distance oneself (from) (*a person*) *vt* **-eesamba**, **-eesuula**, **-eggyako**, *eg. Banne yabeggyako.* ('*He distanced himself from his friends.*'). See dissociate oneself

distant (*far*) *adv* **ewala**

distinguish (*separate*) *vt* **-yawula**, *eg. Tasobola kwawula ekirungi n'ekibi. ('He cannot distinguish good from evil.')*

distinguished (*outstanding*) *adj* **-yatiikirivu** be distinguished **-yatiikirira**

distort *vt* **-kyamya**

distract *vt* **-labiriza**, *eg. Yandabiriza n'abba ensawo yange. ('He distracted me and stole my bag.')* distract from **-ggya ku**, *eg. Amawulire ga ttivi gamuggye ku bye yabadde akola. ('The news on TV distracted him from what he was doing.')* look around in a distracted way **-labankana** person easily distracted **ow'akamagu** *n1*, **omumagufu** *n1* tendency to distraction **akamagu** *n12*

distraught, be (*with grief*) *vi* **-yitirira**, *eg. Ennaku emuyitiridde. ('She was distraught with grief.')*

distress *n* **ennaku** *n9* be distressed (1) (*distraught; troubled*) **-taabuukana**; (2) (*with grief*) **ennaku -kwata** (*with personal object*), *eg. Ennaku yankwata okumulaba nga mulwadde bw'atyo. ('I was distressed to see how ill she was.')* cause distress (*to/at*) **-taabuukanya**, *eg. Omwana we omuwala amutaabuukanya. ('Her daughter is causing her distress.')* cry of distress **omulanga** *n3* cry out loudly in distress **-tema omulanga**

distribute *vt* **-gaba**, *eg. Omwami agabye enkumbi. ('The boss distributed the hoes.')* distribute to **gabira**, *eg. Omwami yagabira abalimi enkumbi. ('The boss distributed hoes to the workers.')*. See divide up; give way of distributing **engabanya** *n9*

distributor *n* **omugabi** *n1*. See spreader

district *n* **disitulikiti** *n9*

distrust *vt*. Use **-eesiga** ('*trust*') in neg (**N21**), *eg. Simwesiga. ('I distrust him.')*

disturb *vt* **-tabula**, *eg. Ababbi batabudde emirembe mu kyalo. ('The thieves have disturbed the peace of the village.')*. See agitate; bother; confuse; harass; rough (make); stir up; worry disturb mentally **-tabula omutwe** be(come) disturbed (1) (*of bees, ants, etc.*) **-saanuuka**, *eg. Enjuki zisaanuuse. ('The bees have become disturbed.')*; (2) (*of water*) **-siikuuka**, *eg. Ennyanja esiikuuse. ('The lake has become disturbed.')*, **-fuukuuka**. See anxious (be); turbulent (be); worked up (be); worried (be) be in a disturbed and anxious state (*of a crowd*) **-sasamala**, **-jagalala** be mentally disturbed **-tabuka omutwe**, *eg. Atabuse omutwe. ('She is mentally disturbed.')*

disturbance (*civic*) *n* **akatabanguko** *n12* cause disturbance (*to a plan*) **-galangatanya** engage in disturbances (*of a crowd*) **-eegugunga**

ditch *n* **ekinnya** *n7*, (*dug as boundary between properties*) **olusalosalo** *n11*. See drain

dive *vi* **-bbira**

diverge *vi* **-yawukana**

divert *vt* (*change route*) Use **-kyusa** ('*change*') with

-yita awalala ('*pass elsewhere*'), *eg. Poliisi yakyusa emmotoka ziyite awalala. ('The police diverted the traffic.')*. See distract be diverted **-kyusibwa -yita awalala**, *eg. Emmotoka zaakyusibwa ne ziyita awalala. ('The cars were diverted.')* make a diversion (1) (*deviate*) **-kyamako**, *eg. Tukyameko ewa Musoke. ('Let's make a diversion to Musoke's.')*; (2) (*to avoid being seen*) **-salinkiriza**

divide (into) *vt* **-yawulamu**, *eg. Ebijanjaalo yabyawulamu ebitundu bisatu. ('He divided the beans into three parts.')* divide up (*for distribution*) **-gabanya**, *eg. Omukulu yagabanya ssente mu bakozi bonna. ('The boss divided up the money between all the workers.')*. See cut up divide up among oneselves **-gabana**, *eg. Twagabana ssente ze yatuwa. ('We divided up the money which he gave us.')* be divided by (*in maths*) **-gabiramu**, *eg. Kkumi gabiramu ttaano ziba bbiri. ('Ten divided by five is two.')*

divider *n* (1) (*partition*) **ekyawula** *n7*; (2) (*as a curtain*) **eggigi** *n5* divider of barkcloth (*in a room*) **eggigi ly'embugo** something that causes division between people **ekyawula** *n7*

divination *n* **obulaguzi** *n14* practice divination **-lagula**

diviner *n* **omulaguzi** *n1*

divinity (*the subject*) *n* **ebyeddini** *n8*

divisor (*in maths*) *n* **omugabi** *n3*

divorce (*grant a divorce*) *vt* **-gattulula obufumbo**. See separate; split up be granted a divorce **-gattululwa mu bufumbo**

divulge *vt* (1) (*something confidential or not true, divulged to many people*) **-laalaasa**; (2) (*private or secret information, divulged to one or a few people*) **-sunirako**

dizziness *n* **kammunguluze** *n1*, **kantoolooze** *n1*

[1]do (*function*) *n* **omukolo** *n3*

[2]do *v* (did) (1) (*behave*) *vi* **-eeyisa**, *eg. Weeyisa bulungi. ('You did well.')*; (2) (*perform a task*) *vt* **-kola**, *eg. Makanika yakola omulimu bulungi. ('The mechanic did a good job.')* do again (*repeat*) **-ddamu**, *eg. Njagala oddemu omulimu guno. ('I want you to do this job again.')*, (*repeatedly*) **-ddiŋŋana** Do as I do. **Kola nga nze bwe nkola.** do occasionally (*now and then*) **-gira** be doable **-koleka**

docile *adj* **-wombeefu** be docile **-eewombeeka**

docility *n* **obuwombeefu**

[1]dock (*in courtroom*) *n* **akaguli** *n12*. See harbour

[2]dock (*eg. tail of dog*) *vt* **-salako** dock pay **-salako ku musaala**

docked *adj* **-a enkuggu**, *eg. omukira gwa nkuggu ('docked tail')*

doctor *n* (1) **omusawo** *n1*, **dakitaali** *n1*; (2) (*trained in western medicine*) **omusawo omuzungu**; (2) (*traditional doctor*) **omusawo omuganda**, (*one who consults spirits*) **omusawuzi** *n1*. See healer

doctrine *n* enzikiriza *n9*

¹document *n* ekiwandiiko *n7*

²document *vt* -wandiika

dodge *vt* (1) (*keep away from*) -eewala, *eg.* Yasobola okwewala emmotoka zonna ng'asala oluguudo. (*'He managed to dodge all the cars when he crossed the road.'*); (2) (*something thrown*) -eewoma, *eg.* Yeewoma effumu. (*'He dodged the spear.'*). See avoid dodge a player (*in football*) -sala omuntu, (*displaying fancy footwork*) -canga omupiira

dog *n* embwa *n9*, (*stray*) embwa etaayaaya dog bell ekyuma ky'embwa *n7* dog chain/lead olujegere lw'embwa *n11* dog collar (*on dog, not vicar*) olukoba lw'embwa *n11*

doll *n* ddole *n1* be dolled up (*dressed to perfection*) -nekaanekana

dollar *n* doola *n9*

dome (*of a building*) *n* ekitikkiro *n7*

domestic *adj* -a awaka, *eg.* omukozi w'awaka (*'domestic servant'*)

domesticated *adj* -lunde. See tame

dominate *vt* -singa -onna, *eg.* Ttiimu yaabwe ye yasinga zonna mu mpaka. (*'Their team dominated the competition.'*). See rule

domineer *vt* -jooga

donate *vt* -gaba donate to -gabira, *eg.* Baagabira ekkanisa essente nnyingi. (*'They donated a lot of money to the church.'*)

donation *n* ekirabo *n7*

donkey *n* endogoyi *n9*

donor *n* omugabi *n1*

door *n* oluggi *n11*, (*back*) oluggi lw'emmanju, (*front*) oluggi lw'emiryango, (*main*) wankaaki *n1*

doorbell *n* akade k'oluggi *n12*

doorframe *n* omwango gw'oluggi *n3*

doorhandle *n* omunyolo *n3*

doorkeeper *n* omuggazi *n1*

doorlock *n* ekkufulu y'oluggi *n9*

doorway *n* omulyango *n3*, (*of unit in block*) omuzigo *n3*

dormitory *n* ekisulo *n7*

dormouse *n* ekikirikisi *n7* (*probably*)

dose *n* ekigero *n7*

¹dot *n* akatonnyeze *n12*

²dot *vt* -tonnyeza

double See two double-dealing obukuusa *n14* engage in double talk -kumpanya ebigambo

¹doubt *n* akakunkuna *n12*, *eg.* Sirina kakunkuna. (*'I have no doubt.'*)

²doubt *vit* -buusabuusa, *eg.* Mbuusabuusa ky'agamba nti kituufu. (*'I doubt what he says is true.'*). See hesitate; waver

doughnut *n* ekindaazi *n7* (*usually pl.* amandaazi *n6*)

dourness *n* ekkabyo *n5* look dour -eekaba, -tunuza ekkabyo

douse (*a fire*) -zikiza, (*with water*) -vubiriza

dour *adj* -a ekkabo

dove *n* ejjiba *n5* laughing dove kaamukuukulu *n1*

¹down (*below*) *adv* wansi down below (*on a hill*) emmanga down payment (*deposit*) omusingo *n3*, akakalu *n12*

²down (*soft short hair on body*) *n* ebyoya *n8*, (*on forehead*) omuttunta *n3*

³down (*below*) *pre* wansi wa

downcast, be (*miserable*) *vi* -nakuwala

downhearted, be *vi* -kka omutima

downhill *adv* amaserengeta go downhill -serengeta

downstairs/downwards *adv* wansi

downward downward journey amaserengeta *n6* downward slope akaserengeto *n12*

doze (off) *vi* -sumagira. See sleepy (be)

¹draft (*of a document*) *n* ebbago *n5*

²draft (*a document*) *vt* -baga draft in (*eg. reinforcements to quell trouble*) -yungula, (*all available resources*) -yungula abawanvu n'abampi

drag *vt* -walula, -kulula, *eg.* Baakulula bbookisi ku ttaka. (*'They dragged the box along the ground.'*) drag along -walabanya, (*unwilling person by force*) -walaawala, -kaazakaaza drag on (*persist, eg. of rain*) -nyiinyiitira drag one's feet (1) (*come unwillingly, of a person physically resisting*) -walira; (2) (*along the ground, not lifting them when walking*) -seesa ebigere drag oneself along (*as a cripple along the ground*) -eewalula, -eekulula

dragonfly *n* nnamunkanga *n1*

¹drain *n* omufulejje *n3*

²drain (*eg. a swamp*) *vt* -kaza drain out water from -ttulula amazzi mu, *eg.* Attulula amazzi mu mboga. (*'She is draining out the cabbage.'*)

drama (*play*) *n* katemba *n1*

drank See drink

drape (over) *vt* -bikka (ku), *eg.* Yabikka ekitambaala ku mmeeza. (*'She draped the cloth over the table.'*)

draught *n* empewo *n9*

draw (*have equal scores in a game*) *vi* -sibagana draw a line -kuba (*or* -teekako) olukoloboze, (*as a margin*) -saza omusittale draw a picture -kuba ekifaananyi draw near (*approach*) -sembera, *eg.* Enkuba esembedde. (*'The rain is drawing near.'*) draw near to -semberera draw out (*item from within, eg. stick from bundle*) sowolamu draw out of water (*eg. clothes being washed*) -nnyulula draw taut -leega draw up a plan -tema oluwenda draw up one's legs -eefunya amagulu draw water -sena amazzi

drawer *n* edduloowa *n9*

drawing *n* ekifaananyi *n7*

drawl *vi* -lembeggerera

¹dread (*fear*) *n* okutya *n15*

²dread (*fear*) *vt* -tya

dreadful (*awful*) *adj* -bi ennyo
[1]**dream** *n* ekirooto *n7* have a wet dream
-eerooterera have disturbing dreams -logootana
interpret a dream for -lootolola ekirooto tell one's
dream to -lootololera ekirooto
[2]**dream** *vi* -loota
dredge *vt* -gogola
dregs *n* (1) (*sediment in a liquid*) ebikudumu *n8*,
obukudumu *n14*; (2) (*from brewing 'amalwa'*)
enkanja *n10*. *See* residue; scum
drench *vt* -tobya. *See* soak
[1]**dress** *n* (1) ekiteeteeyi *n7*, olugoye *n11*; (2)
(*traditional kiganda dress*) busuuti *n9*, ggomesi
n9, bboodingi *n9*. *The undergarment worn with a
busuuti is* ekikooyi *n7*.
[2]**dress** *v* (1) (*oneself*) *vr* -yambala, (*with a busuuti*)
-eesiba, *eg. Yeesibye busuuti.* (*'She is getting
dressed in a busuuti.'*); (2) (*someone else*) *vt*
-yambaza dress a wound -siba ekiwundu dress
in barkcloth (1) (*of a man*) -sumika olubugo; (2)
(*of a woman*) -eesiba olubugo be dressed to
perfection (*dolled up*) -nekaanekana, -yambala
-tonnya, *eg. Yayambala n'atonnya.* (*'He is dressed
to perfection.'*) way of dressing ensumika *n9*
dresser of brides *n* omusibi w'abagole *n1*
[1]**dribble** (*of saliva*) *n* engeregeze *n10*
[2]**dribble** (*from the mouth*) *vi* -geregeza
dried/drier *See* dry
drift *vi* -seeyeeya drift about aimlessly (*of a person*)
-yenjeera
drill (*a hole*) *vt* -wummula, -botola be drilled
-wummuka, -botoka
[1]**drink** *n* ekyokunywa *n7*, (*alcoholic*) omwenge *n3*,
(*dilute*) jjuule *n1*, (*offered to a guest*) obugenyi
n14 give a drink to -wa ekyokunywa, *eg. Yawa
abagenyi ebyokunywa.* (*'He gave drinks to the
guests.'*), (*cause to drink directly*) -nywesa, *eg.
Anywesa omwana.* (*'He is giving a drink to the
child.'*) soft drink ekiweweeza omumiro *n7*
strong drink (*alcoholic*) omwenge omuka
[2]**drink** *vt* (drank) -nywa, (*using a spoon, or sipping
directly from the plate*) -wuuta, (*noisily; slurp*)
-solobeza drink in -nywera, *eg. Banywera mu
bbaala.* (*'They are drinking in the bar.'*) drink too
much -eekamirira, *eg. Yeekamirira omwenge
mungi n'azirika.* (*'He drank too much beer and fell
into a coma.'*) be drinkable -nyweka drinking
party ekinywi *n7*
drinker *n* omunywi *n1*
drip *vi* -tonnya, *eg. Amazzi gatonnya okuva ku
kasolya.* (*'Water is dripping off the roof.'*) drip in
-tonnyeza, *eg. Nnansi atonnyeza eddagala mu liiso
lye.* (*'The nurse is dripping medicine in his eye.'*)
drip sweat -ttulukuka entuuyo keep dripping
-tonnyerera
dripline (*of roof*) *n* ekisasi *n7*
drive (*a vehicle*) *vt* (drove) -vuga drive a car very
fast -vuga sipiidi, -diimuula (*or* -vuumuula)

emmotoka drive away (1) (*chase away*) -goba,
eg. Yagoba ente ku ttaka lye. (*'He drove the cows
off his land.'*); (2) (*using bullets, insults, etc.*)
-wereekereza drive crazy (1) (*mad*) -lalusa; (2)
(*cause infatuation*) -suula eddalu drive into
-gobera, *eg. Yagobera embuzi mu kisibo.* (*'She
drove the goats into the pen.'*) drive out of hiding
(*eg. animal in a hunt*) -wamatula, (*at a run*)
-fubutula, (*with beating of bushes*) -saggula, *eg.
Abayizzi baasaggula engabi mu kisaka.* (*'The
hunters drove the bushbuck out of the thicket.'*) be
driven out (*eg. of an animal in a hunt*) -wamatuka,
(*at a run*) -fubutuka
driver (*of vehicle*) *n* omuvuzi *n1*, omugoba *n1*,
ddereeva *n1* car driver omugoba w'emmotoka
n1 lorry driver omugoba wa loole
driving licence *n* layisinsi y'okuvuga *n9*
[1]**drizzle** *n* oluwandaggirize *n11*, (*intermittent light
rain*) obukubakuba *n14*, (*sufficient to allow a
chicken to drink*) olunywankoko *n11*
[2]**drizzle** *vi* enkuba -wandaggirira/-fuuyirira keep
drizzling on and off enkuba -tonnyerera
drool *vi* -solobeza
droop *vi* -koonoka
[1]**drop** (*of liquid*) *n* ettondo *n5* drop of milk otuta
n13 drop of water otuzzi *n13* put drops in the
eye (*of medicine*) -tonnyeza eddagala mu maaso
[2]**drop** *vt* -suula wansi, *eg. Nsudde ensawo yange
wansi.* (*'I have dropped my bag.'*). *See* lower drop
off (1) (*of a ripe fruit*) *vi* -nogoka, *eg. Eryenvu
linogose ku kiwagu.* (*'A banana has dropped off the
hand.'*); (2) *vt* -suulayo, *eg. Abaana nnabasuddeyo
ku ssomero.* (*'I have dropped the children off at
school.'*). *See* fall
droppings *n* (1) *of birds* kalimbwe *n1*,
kasookolindo *n1*; (2) (*of goats, rabbits, etc.*)
enkiringi *n9*. *See* dung
drosophila (*fruit fly*) *n* akabu *n12*
drought *n* ekyeya *n7*
drove *See* drive
drown *vi* -fiira mu mazzi
drowsy, be *vi* -bongoota tendency to drowsiness
akasumagizi *n12*
drug *n* eddagala *n5* drug addict omuyaga *n1*,
omuyaaye *n1*
[1]**drum** (*musical instrument*) *n* (1) (*types beaten with
hands or sticks*) eŋŋoma *n9*, embuutu *n9*; (2)
(*long slender type beaten with hands*) omugalabi
n3, engalabi *n9*; (3) (*smallest drum in a set*)
nnankasa *n9*, nnamunjoloba *n1*; (4) (*main drum
in a set*) baakisimba *n9*; (5) (*drum in a set that
keeps the beat*) empuunyi *n9* drum beat (*of a
clan*) omubala *n3*, *eg. omubala gw'Ekika
ky'Enseenene* (*'drumbeat of the Grasshopper Clan*)
drum stick omunyolo gw'eŋŋoma *n3* set of royal
drums mujaguzo *n1*
[2]**drum** (*barrel; tub*) *n* eppipa *n5*
[3]**drum** *vi* -kuba eŋŋoma, (*continuously*) -kuba ku

mbuutu. *See* pound; sound   be beaten (*of drums*) **-tujja**

drummer *n* **omugoma** *n1*, **omukubi w'eŋŋoma** *n1*, (*chief, of the Kabaka*) **Kawuula** *n1 title*

drumming (*sound of*) *n* **embuutu** *n9*, (*from omugalabi drum*) **engalabi** *n9*. *The following are types of* drumbeat: (1) (*associated with particular dances*) **baakisimba** *n1*, **nnankasa** *n9*; (2) (*signifies arrival or departure of the Kabaka from a palace; formerly sounded at dawn and dusk*) **bantadde** *n1*; (3) (*announces death of a member of the royal family*) **kanabba** *n1*; (4) (*announces a function attended by the Kabaka*) **mujaguzo** *n1*; (5) (*calls people to come and help*) **ggwanga mujje**; (6) (*calls people to communal labour*) **saagala agalamidde**.

drunk (*also* inebriated) *adj* **-tamiivu**   get drunk **-tamiira**   make drunk **-tamiiza**

drunkard *n* **omutamiivu** *n1*

drunkenness *n* **obutamiivu** *n14*

¹**dry** *adj* **-kalu**   dry season **ekyeya** *n7*   dry skin **olususu olusiiwuufu** *n11*   something dry **ekikalu** *n7*

²**dry** *vt* (dried) **-kaza**, (*over a fire, eg. meat or fish*) **-kalirira**. *See* cure; put out to dry; take in from drying   dry up **-kala**, *eg. Omugga gwakala.* ('*The river has dried up.*'), (*cease giving milk, of a cow*) **-kamiza**, *eg. Ente ekamizza.* ('*The cow has dried up.*')   dry up at/in **-kalira**, *eg. Amazzi gakalidde mu ntamu.* ('*The water has dried up in the pot.*')   become drier **-kamuka**, *eg. Engoye zikamuse.* ('*The clothes have become drier.*'), **-kankamuka** become dry (*of the skin*) **-siiwuuka**

dryness *n* **obukalu** *n14*

duck *n* **embaata** *n9*   walk like a duck (*waddle*) **-baatabaata**, **-baatira**. *See* splayfooted

due to (*because of*) *conj* **olwa**, *eg. Olw'obukoowu, yatomeza emmotoka.* ('*Due to tiredness, he crashed the car.*')

dues (*fees*) *n* **ebisale** *n8*. *See* tax

dug *See* dig   dug-over land **awalime** *n16*, (*deeply*) **awakabale** *n16*   deeply dug (*of land*) *adj* **-kabale**, *eg. omusiri omukabale* ('*deeply dug plot*')   something dug up **ekisime** *n7*

dugout (canoe) *n* **emmanvu** *n5*, (*bigger*) **eryato** *n5*

duiker *n* (1) (*bush*) **empeewo** *n9*; (2) (*red*) **ensuku** *n9*; (3) (*blue*) **entalaganya** *n9*

dumb person (*unable to speak*) *n* **kasiru** *n1*. *See* fool   be(come) dumb **-ziba emimwa**

dumbfound *vt* **-wuniikiriza**   be dumbfounded **-wuniikirira**

dump (*eg. rubbish*) *vt* **-yiwa**. *See* rubbish

dung *n* **obusa** *n14*. *See* droppings   dung beetle **kkulungabusa** *n1*   pile of dung **envumbi** *n9*

dungeon *n* **ekkomera** *n5*

durability *n* **obuwangaazi** *n14*

durable (*long-lasting*) *adj* **-wangaazi**   be durable **-wangaala**

duration *n* **ekiseera** *n7*

during *pre* **mu**

¹**dust** *n* **enfuufu** *n9*, (*produced by boring insect*) **empumbu** *n9*   take a dust bath (*of a chicken*) **-naaba**

²**dust** *vt* **-siimuula enfuufu**

duster *n* **ekiwero** *n7*, (*small*) **akawero** *n12*

Dutch person *n* **Omudaaki** *n1*   Dutchman's pipe (*type of plant*) **emmindi y'omukadde** *n9*, **ensawo y'enkima** *n9*, **kasero** *n12*

duty *n* (1) (*tax*) **omusolo** *n3*, **empooza** *n9*; (2) (*responsibility*) **obuvunaanyizibwa** *n14*   charge duty (*tax*) **-wooza omusolo**

DVD *n* **dividi** *n9*. *See* film

dwarf *n* **omumbuti** *n1*, (*with a big head, mythological inhabitant of Mabira forest*) **nnakalanga** *n1*   be dwarfed (*stunted*) (1) (*of a person*) **-kona**; (2) (*of an animal*) **-kundugga**

dwell *vi* (1) (*live at*) **-beera**; (2) (*stay the night at*) **-sula**

dwelling (*house*) *n* **ennyumba** *n9*, **enju** *n9*

dwindle (*eg. of bar of soap*) *vi* **-ggweerera**

¹**dye** *n* **eddagala** *n5*, **erangi** *n9*

²**dye** *vt* **-nnyika mu ddagala/langi**

dynamite *n* **obuganga** *n14*

dysentery *n* **ekiddukano ky'omusaayi** *n7*

E,e

each *det* **buli** (N3), *eg. buli lunaku* ('*each day*')

eager *adj* **-jjumbizi**   be eager about **-jjumbira**

eagerness *n* **obujjumbize** *n14*

eagle *n* **empungu** *n9*   fish eagle **ekkwanzi** *n5*

ear *n* **okutu** *n15*

earlier *adv* **emabegako**

early *adv* (1) (*quickly*) **mangu**, *eg. Yatuukayo mangu.* ('*She got there early.*'); (2) (*while there is still time; in time*) **bukyali**, *eg. Obudde bukyali.* ('*It is still early.*')   early stages (*of a task*) **amabaga** *n6*   be early **-keera**, *eg. Yakedde.* ('*He is early.*')

earn *vt* **-funamu**, *eg. Mu kuzannya omupiira yafunamu ekitiibwa.* ('*He earned respect for his skill at football.*')   earn money **-kolera essente**

earnest *adj* **-nyiikivu**   be earnest **-nyiikira**

earnestness *n* **obunyiikivu** *n14*

earth *n* (1) (*soil*) **ettaka** *n5*, (*red*) **olukuusi** *n11*; (2) (*world*) **ensi** *n9*. *See* soil

earth up (*plants*) *vt* **-temera ettaka**

earthquake *n* **musisi** *n1*

earthworm *n* **olusiriŋŋanyi** *n11*

¹**ease** (*leisure*) *n* **eddembe** *n5*

²**ease** *v* (1) *vi* **-kkakkana**, *eg. Obulumi bukkakkanye.* ('*The pain has eased.*'); (2) *vt* **-kkakkanya**, *eg. Eddagala likkakkanyizza obulumi.* ('*The medicine has eased the pain.*')   ease up (*of rain*) **enkuba -kankamuka**, *eg. Enkuba ekankamuse.* ('*The rain has eased up.*')

easier become easier **-wewuka**, *eg. Omulimu guwewuka nga waliwo abantu babiri abagukola. ('The job is easier when there are two people doing it.')* make easier **-wewusa, -wewula**

easily *adv* **kyangu**

east *n* **obuvanjuba** *n23* East Coast fever *(cattle disease)* **amakebe** *n6* at/to the east **ebuvanjuba**

Easter *n* (1) *(Prot)* **Amazuukira** *n6*; (2) *(RC)* **Paasika** *n9*

easy *adj* **-yangu**, *eg. Omulimu yagusanga nga mwangu. ('She found the work easy.')* be easy to do **-koleka** make easy for **-yanguyiza**

eat *vt* (ate) **-lya**, *(enough)* **-kkuta**, *(noisily)* **-swankula**, *(using a spoon, eg. for soup)* **-wuuta**, *(from the palm)* **-wema**, *(ravenously)* **-kavvula**, *(with zest, enjoying the food)* **-miringusa**, *(slowly, enjoying the food)* **-miisa**, *(greedily, be a glutton)* **-liisa omululu**. See slurp; suck eat at **-liira**, *eg. Yaliira ku mmeeza. ('He ate at the table.')* eat food as a guest **-lya obugenyi** eat too much **-eepiika emmere** eat with **-liisa**, *eg. Aliisa wuuma. ('She's eating with a fork.')* be eaten **-liibwa** things to eat **ebyokulya** *n8*

eater *(person) n* **omuli** *n1*

eating *n* **okulya** *n15* eating place **eddiiro** *n5*

eaves *n* **ekisasi** *n7* water from the eaves **amazzi g'ekisasi**

eavesdrop (on) *vit* **-lumika ebigambo**, *eg. Omuntu omubi alumika ebigambo bya banne. ('A bad person eavesdrops on others.')*

[1]echo *n* **kyeyitabya** *n7*

[2]echo *vi* **-waawaala**

economics *n* **ebyenfuna** *n8* the economy **embeera y'ebyenfuna** *n9*

economise (on) *vt* **-kekkereza**, *eg. Yakekkereza omunnyo. ('She economised on salt.')* person who is economical **omukekkereza** *n1*

edge *n* (1) *(of cloth or garment; seam; hem)* **olukugiro** *n11*; (2) *(border of a mat)* **ensandaggo** *n9*. See outskirts edge of roof **ekisasi** *n7* outer edge of house **olusebenju** *n11* put edge on (1) *(cloth or garment)* **-kugira**; (2) *(mat)* **-sandagga**; (3) *(decorative edge on busuuti)* **-daliza**

edible, be *vi* **-liika**

edict *n* **ekiragiro** *n7*

editor, newspaper *n* **omutegesi w'amawulire** *n1*

educate *vt* **-yigiriza**

educated *adj* **-yigirize** educated person **omuyigirize** *n1*

education *n* (1) *(as a subject)* **ebyenjigiriza** *n8*; (2) *(as an attainment)* **obuyigirize** *n14*, *eg. Obuyigirize bwe si bwa waggulu. ('He did not go far in his education.')*. See learning adult education **okuyiga kw'obukulu** *n15* higher education **obuyigirize obwa waggulu**

efface *vt* (1) *(erase)* **-sangula**; (2) *(spoil)* **-yonoona** efface with **-sanguza** be effaced **-sanguka**

effigy *n* **ssemufu** *n1*

effort (concerted) *n* **kaweefube** *n1* make an effort *(try hard)* **-fuba**, *(with someone)* **-tawaanira** make an effort to get up *(eg. when ill)* **-eekakamula** put effort into *(what one is doing)* **-ssaamu amaanyi**

effrontery *n* **ekyejo** *n7*

egg *n* **eggi** *n5* egg plant *(aubergine)* **bbiriŋŋanya** *n1* egg shell **ekisosonkole ky'eggi** *n7* egg yolk **enjuba y'eggi** *n9* boiled egg **eggi ly'empogola** fried egg **eggi essiike**

egg on *(urge) vt* **-pikiriza**

egret *n* **ennyange** *n9*

Egypt *n* **Misiri** *n9*

Egyptian *n* **Omumisiri** *n1*

eight *num* **munaana** eight hundred **lunaana** eight thousand **kanaana**

eighteen *num* **kkumi na munaana**

eighth *adj/num* **-a omunaana** (N7.1)

eighty *num* **kinaana** *n7*

either *conj* **oba**

eject *vt* **-goba**, *eg. Baamugaba mu kibiina. ('He was ejected from the club.')*

elastic, be *vi* **-naanuuka**

elated, be *(and merry) vi* **-cacanca, -sagambiza, -kuba jjejjerebu**. See happy (be); rejoice

elbow *n* **olukokola** *n11* elbow one's way **-eeyigaanya**, *eg. Yeeyigaanyizza okusobola okutuuka mu maaso. ('He elbowed his way to the front.')*

[1]elder *(older; chief) adj* **-kulu**

[2]elder *(person) n* **omukulu** *n1*

elderly *adj* **-kadde** elderly person **omukadde** *n1* be(come) elderly **-kaddiwa**

elect *vt* **-londa**

elected *adj* **-londe**

election *n* **okulonda** *n15* general election **okulonda okwa wamu, okulonda okwa bonna** stand in an election **-eesimbawo**

elector *n* **omulonzi** *n1*

electricity *n* **amasannyalaze** *n6* electric light **ettaala y'amasannyalaze** *n9*. See bulb

elegant *adj* **-nyirivu** look elegant **-nyirira**

elephant *n* **enjovu** *n9* elephant grass **ekisagazi** *n7*. See cane elephant shrew **omusonso** *n3* elephant snout fish See fish

elephantiasis *n* **endwadde y'enjovu** *n9* have elephantiasis **-lwala enjovu**

elevate *vt* **-wanika**. See promote elevate oneself *(be conceited)* **-eewanika**

elevation *n* **obugulumivu** *n14*. See height

eleven *num* **kkumi n'emu, kkumi na -mu** *(with numeral concord N4.2) (N8.1)*, *eg. ente kkumi n'emu ('eleven cows'). Elision is sometimes seen, eg. ente kkumi neemu ('eleven cows').*

Elgon *(mountain) n* **Masaaba** person of Mt Elgon *(living high on the slopes)* **Omumasaaba** *n1*

eliminate *vt* **-malawo**

elongate *vt* **-wanvuya**

elsewhere *adv* **awalala**

elucidate (*clarify*) *vt* **-tangaaza**

emaciated *adj* **-kovvu ennyo**   be(come) emaciated **-nyaaluka**. *See* weight (lose)

embankment *n* **olubibiro** *n11*. *See* mound

embark on (*eg. a ship*) *vi* **-linnya**

embarrass *vt* **-kwasa ensonyi**   feel embarrassed **-kwatibwa ensonyi**, **-swala**, *eg. Musoke yaswala.* (*'Musoke felt embarrassed.'*)   feel embarrassed before **-swalira**, *eg. Musoke yaswalira omusomesa.* (*'Musoke felt embarrassed before the teacher.'*)

embarrassment *n* **ensonyi** *n9*

embassy *n* **ekitebe** *n7*, *eg. ekitebe kya Bungereza* (*'British embassy'*)

embellish (*ornament; adorn*) *vi* **-wunda**

embers (*smouldering*) *n* **olunyata** *n11*

embezzle *vt* **-kumpanya**. *See* steal

embezzler *n* **omukumpanya** *n1*. *See* thief

emblem *n* **akabonero** *n12*

embrace (*hug*) *vt* **-wambaatira**, (*a person affectionately*) **-gwa mu kifuba**

embroider *vt* **-tunga**

embroidery (*red design on kkanzu*) *n* (1) (*around neck*) **omuleera** *n3*; (2) (*at base*) **amasiira** *n6*

emerge (from) *vi* **-va**, *eg. Ensolo zaava mu kibira ng'obudde buzibye.* (*'The animals emerged from the forest at dusk.'*)   emerge from a hiding place **-kukunuka**   emerge from under water **-bbulukuka**

emergency   emergency meeting **olukiiko olw'amangu** *n11*   state of emergency **ebiseera by'akatabanguko** *n8*

emigrate *vi* **-senguka**

eminent (*of a person*) *adj* **-a ekitiibwa**

emissary *n* **omubaka** *n1*

emit *vt* **-vaamu**, *eg. Yingini evaamu omukka.* (*'The engine is emitting smoke.'*)   be emitted with force (*of a strong smell, smoke, etc.*) **-tuumuuka**

emotion   become emotionally worked up **-eecanga**, *eg. Amawulire gaamuleetera okwecanga.* (*'The news caused him to get worked up.'*)   emotional core (*of a person*) **emmeeme** *n9*. *See* heart; soul

emphasis *n* **essira** *n9*   put emphasis **-teeka essira**

emphasise *vt* **-ggumiza**, **-kkaatiriza**

employ *vt* **-kozesa**

employee *n* **omukozi** *n1*

employer *n* **omuntu akozesa** *n1*. *See* boss

employment *n* **omulimu** *n3*

[1]**empty** *adj* **-yereere**, *eg. ennyumba enjereere* (*'empty house'*)   empty-handed **n'engalo enkalu**   be empty-handed **-yanjala engalo**   feel empty (*emotionally*) **-wuubaala**, *eg. Yawuubaala ng'abaana bagenze.* (*'She felt empty when her children left.'*)   things that are empty inside (*eg. empty bean pods*) **ebirerya** *n8*

[2]**empty (out)** *v* (1) *vi* **-vaamu**, *eg. Ensawo yayulika amanda ne gavaamu.* (*'The bag burst and the charcoal emptied out.'*); (2) *vt* **-ggyamu**, *eg.*

Yaggyamu ebintu byonna mu nsawo ye. (*'She emptied out everything from her bag.'*). *See* pour out

emulate *vt* **-labira ku**

enable *vt* **-sobozesa**

encampment *n* **enkambi** *n9*

encircle *vt* **-eetooloola**, *eg. Ekisenge kyetooloola olubiri.* (*'A wall encircles the palace.'*), (*in a military sense*) **-eebungulula**. *See* besiege

enclose (with) *vt* **-eetoolooza**, *eg. Ennyumba baagyetoolooza ekisenge.* (*'They enclosed the house with a wall.'*)

enclosure *n* (1) (*of a chief*) **embuga** *n9*; (2) (*for cattle*) **olugo** *n11*, **ekiraalo** *n7*. *See* compound   small cramped enclosure (*in which movement is difficult*) **akakunizo** *n12*

[1]**encounter** *n* **ensisinkano** *n9*

[2]**encounter** *vt* **sanga**, *eg. Nnamusanze mu katale.* (*'I encountered her in the market.'*)

encourage *vt* **-zzaamu amaanyi**, (*someone unwilling*) **-sindiikiriza**. *See* support

encumber *vt* (1) **-zimbirira** (*subject and object reversed compared with English*), *eg. Musoke emitawaana gimuzimbiridde.* (*'Musoke was encumbered with problems.'*); (2) *Use* **-yitirirako** (*'overwhelm'*), *eg. Musoke emitawaana gimuyitiriddeko.* (*'Musoke was encumbered with problems.'*). *See* burden; overburden

[1]**end** *n* **enkomerero** *n9*   end point **ekikomo** *n7*

[2]**end** *v* (1) *vi* (*of an activity*) **-koma**, *eg. Olugendo lukoma wano.* (*'The journey ends here.'*); (2) (*of rain*) *vi* **-ggwaako**, *eg. Ekiseera ky'enkuba kigenda kuggwaako.* (*'The rainy season is ending.'*); (3) (*bring to an end*) *vt* **-komya**, *eg. Poliisi egezaako okukomya obwamalaaya.* (*'The police are trying to end prostitution.'*). *See* finish; last (be)   be ended **-ggwa**, *eg. Omulimu tegunnaba kuggwa.* (*'The job is not yet ended.'*)

endeavour (*try*) *vi* **-gezaako**

endlessly *adv* **obutamala**, **obutakya**, **obutaggwa**, (*of talking*) **olulondakambe**. *See* incessantly

endorse *vt* **-semba**

endure (*difficulties*) *vt* **-gumira**, **-gumiikiriza**. *See* tolerate

enduring (*long-lasting*) *adj* **-wangaazi**   be enduring **-wangaala**

enemy *n* **omulabe** *n1*

energetic *adj* **-a amaanyi**

energy *n* **amaanyi** *n6*

enfeeble *vt* **-nafuya**

engage (*employ*) *vt* **-wandiisa**, *eg. Musoke awandiisizza abakozi.* (*'Musoke has engaged workers.'*). *See* employ; hire   engage the enemy (*militarily*) **-lumbagana abalabe**

engagement (*military*) *n* **olutalo** *n11*   engagement ring **empeta nkusibiddaawo** *n9*

engine *n* **yingini** *n9*

engineer *n* **yinginiya** *n1*

England *n* **Bungereza** *n9*
¹English *adj* **-ngereza**
²English *n* (1) (*person*) **Omungereza** *n1*; (2) (*language*) **Olungereza** *n11*
engrave (*carve pattern on*) *vt* **-woola**. *See* decorate; write
enigma *n* **ekikokyo** *n7*   speak enigmatically **-gereesa**
enjoy *vt* **-nyumirwa**, *eg. Ajja kunyumirwa omuzannyo*. (*'He will enjoy the game.'*), **-nyumira** (*subject and object reversed compared to English*), *eg. Omuzannyo gujja kumunyumira*. (*'He will enjoy the game.'*), (*food*) **-woomerwa**   enjoy oneself **-cakala**, *eg. Bagenze kucakala*. (*'They have gone to enjoy themselves.'*), **-eeyagala**   be enjoyable **-nyuma**   enjoyable social gathering **ekinyumu** *n7*   something enjoyable **ekintu ekinyuma** *n7*
enlarge *vt* **-yongera obunene**, *eg. Ffaamu agyongeddeko obunene*. (*'He has enlarged the farm.'*). *See* extend
enlighten *vt* **-tangaaza**   become enlightened **-zibuka amaaso**
enmity *n* **obulabe** *n14*
enormous *adj* **-nene nnyo**
enough   be enough (1) (*to complete a task*) **-mala**, *eg. Olina amafuta agamala okufumba emmere?* (*'Have you enough paraffin to cook the food?'*) (2) (*to be distributed everywhere; all get some*) **-buna**, *eg. Emmere ebunye*. (*'There was enough food for all.'*); (3) (*of spice, dye, etc.*) **-noga**, *eg. Omunnyo gunoze*. (*'There is enough salt in the food.'*); (4) (*for a purpose*) **-wera**, *eg. Abantu kaakati baweze tusobola okutandika olukiiko*. (*'There are enough people now for us to start the meeting.'*)   have enough (*for a purpose*) **-weza**, *eg. Mpezezza essente okuzimba ennyumba*. (*'I have enough money to build a house.'*)   have enough to eat **-kkuta**, *eg. Okkuse? Okkuse?* (*'Have you had enough to eat?'*)   put enough of (*spice, dye, etc.*) **-noza**, *eg. Nnanozezza sukaali mu caayi*. (*'I have put enough sugar in the tea.'*)
enquire (about) (*ask*) *vt* **-buuza**
enraged, become *vi* **-eecwacwana**, (*very*) **-swakira**. *See* angry
enrich *vt* **-gaggawaza**
enrol *v* (1) (*oneself*) *vr* **-eewandiisa**; (2) (*someone else*) *vt* **-wandiisa**
entangled, become *vi* **-eetugga**
enter *v* (1) *vi* **-yingira**, (*slip into, eg. snake into a hole*) **-eesonseka**; (2) *vt* **-yingiza**. *See* insert   enter a house (*without notice or invitation*) **-eeyingiza mu nnyumba**
entertain (*socially*) *vt* **-sembeza**, (*including providing food*) **-gabula**   entertain at **-gabulira**, *eg. Abantu yabagabulira ewuwe* (*'He entertained the people at his home.'*)
entertainment *n* **ekinyumu** *n7*
enthusiastic, be(come) *vi* **-buguumirira**

entice *vt* **-sendasenda**
entire *adj* (1) (*all*) **-onna** (**N7.3**); (2) (*whole; undivided*) **-lamba**
entirely *adv* **ddala**
entrails *n* **ebyenda** *n8*
entrance *n* **aw'okuyingirira** *n16*, **w'oyingirira** *n16*   main entrance (*eg. to a chief's court*) **wankaaki** *n1*
entreat *vt* **-eegayirira**
entrust (to) *vt* **-sigira**, *eg. Maria gwe basigidde okulabirira abaana*. (*'They entrusted the care of the children to Maria.'*)
enumerate *vt* **-bala**
¹envelope *n* **ebbaasa** *n9*
²envelope (*cover completely*) *vt* **-buutikira**. *See* cover
environment (*natural*) *n* **embeera y'ensi** *n9*
envoy *n* **omubaka** *n1*
¹envy *n* (1) (*jealousy*) **obuggya** *n14*; (2) (*through not having something that someone else has*) **ensaalwa** *n9*. *See* jealousy   cause envy **-kwasa obuggya**, *eg. Emmotoka gye yagula ekwasa obuggya*. (*'The car he bought is making people envious.'*)
²envy *vi* **-kwatibwa obuggya**, *eg. Yakwatibwa obuggya olw'omulimu gwa Musoke*. (*'He envied Musoke his job.'*)
epilepsy (*also* epileptic fit) *n* **ensimbu** *n9*   have an epileptic fit **-gwa ensimbu**   person with epilepsy **omusimbu** *n1*
Epiphany *n* **Epifaniya** *n9*
epistle *n* **ebbaluwa** *n9*
epoch (*era*) *n* **omulembe** *n3*, **ebiro** *n8*
equal   be equal (to) **-yenkana**, *eg. (1) Abalongo benkana obuwanvu*. (*'The twins are equal in height.'*); (2) *Ebitooke byo byenkana n'ebyange obunene*. (*'Your banana plants are equal in size to mine.'*)   make equal **-yenkanya**, **-yenkanyankanya**, *eg. Omukulu yenkanyankanya emisaala gyaffe*. (*'The boss made our pay equal.'*)
equalise *vt* **-yenkanya**
equality *n* **obwenkanya** *n14*
equally *adv* **mu bwenkanya**
equipment *n* **ebyokukozesa** *n8*
equity (*share in a company*) *n* **omugabo** *n3*
era (*epoch*) *n* **omulembe** *n3*, **ebiro** *n8*
eradicate *vt* **-malawo**
erase *vt* **-sangula**   erase with **-sanguza**, *eg. Yakisanguza labba*. (*'He erased it with a rubber.'*)
eraser (*rubber*) *n* **labba** *n9*
erect (*eg. a post*) *vt* **-simba**
ernest *adj* **-nyiikivu**   be ernest **-nyiikira**
erode (*soil*) *vt* (1) **-sebbula**; (2) *Use* **-twala** (*'take'*) *or* **-kulukusa** (*'make flow'*) *with* **ettaka** (*'soil'*), *eg. Mukoka yatwala ettaka ku mabbali g'oluguudo*. (*'Water has eroded the soil on the sides of the road.*)   be eroded (*of soil*) **-sebbuka**. *See* give way   soil erosion **okukulukuta kw'ettaka** *n15*
err *vi* **-sobya**
error (*mistake*) *n* **ekisobyo** *n7*. *See* defect

escape *vi* -**toloka**, (*from custody*) -**bomba**, *eg. Abasibe babombye okuva mu kkomera. ('The prisoners have escaped from the jail.')* escape from (*misfortune*) -**wona**, *eg. Yawonye akabenje. ('She escaped from the accident.')* escape from a leash (*eg. of a dog*) -**sumattuka** escape stealthily -**ebba**, -**eemulula** escape to -**ddukira**, *eg. Abantu b'e Rwanda baddukira Kkongo. ('The people of Rwanda escaped to Congo.')* have a narrow escape -**lula**

escapee *n* **omubombi** *n1*

[1]**escort** *n* **emperekeze** *n9*

[2]**escort** *vt* -**werekera** escort a visitor -**werekera omugenyi**

especially *adv* **naddala**, *eg. Njagala ebibala naddala emicungwa. ('I like fruit especially oranges.')*

espionage *n* **obukessi** *n14*

essence (*fundamental nature*) *n* **ennono** *n9*

establish *vt* -**teekawo**, *eg. Yateekawo ekibiina ky'abakyala. ('She established a women's group.')*. *See* prove become established (*of a plant*) -**mera**

esteem *n* **ekitiibwa** *n7* hold in high esteem -**ssaamu ekitiibwa**

[1]**estimate** *n* **enteebereza** *n9*

[2]**estimate** *vt* -**gera**, *eg. Ogera amazzi ag'okufumba. ('Estimate how much water is needed for cooking.')*, -**teebereza**, -**geraageranya**, (*involving counting*) -**balirira**, *eg. Balirira ssente ze weetaaga. ('Estimate how much money you need.')*

eternal *adj* -**a olubeerera**

eternity *n* **obutaggwaawo** *n14*

eucalyptus *n* **kalittunsi** *n1*

eunuch *n* **omulaawe** *n1*

euphorbia *n* (1) (*candelabra tree*) **enkuukuulu** *n9*; (2) (*pipe euphorbia, used for fencing*) **enkoni** *n9*

Europe *n* **Bulaaya** *n9*

[1]**European** *adj* -**zungu** European Union **Ekibiina Ekigatta Amawanga ga Bulaaya** *n7*

[2]**European** (*person*) *n* **Omuzungu** *n1*

evacuate *vt* -**ggyamu**, *eg. Abantu bonna baabaggyamu. ('They evacuated all the people.')*

evaluate *vt* -**geraageranya**

evangelist *n* **omubuulizi w'enjiri** *n1*

evaporate *vi* -**kalira**, *eg. Amazzi gakalidde. ('The water has evaporated.')*, (*quickly, eg. of petrol*) -**fuumuuka**, *eg. Petulooli afuumuuse. ('The petrol has evaporated.')*

evasive, be *vi* -**eebuzaabuza**. *See* devious (be); mislead; secretely (do) act evasively (*avoid doing something by doing something else*) -**eebalankanya** be evasive with -**balankanya**

even though *conj* **newankubadde**, *eg. Newankubadde yabaddewo, teyayambye. ('Even though she was there, she did not help.')*. *See* though not even **wadde**

evening *n* **akawungeezi** *n12* Good evening. *greeting* **Osiibye otyanno?** (*pl.* **Musiibye mutyanno?**) become evening -**wungeera**, *eg. Obudde buwungedde. ('The evening is drawing in.')*

event *n* (1) (*formal occasion*) **omukolo** *n3*; (2) (*exciting event with merry-making*) **ekibinuko** *n7*, **ebbinu** *n9*; (3) (*enjoyable social event*) **ekinyumu** *n7*; (4) (*as a celebration*) **envujjo** *n9*; (5) (*incident; happening*) **ekiriwo** *n7. The noun 'event' meaning 'happening' or 'incident' can vary in tense according to the timing* (**N6**), *eg. (1) (in the past)* **ekyaliwo**; (2) (*in the near future*) **ekinaabaawo**; (3) (*in the far future*) **ekiribaawo** *n7.*

eventually *adv* **ddaaki**. *See* afterwards do eventually *Use* -**lwa ddaaki** (*or* -**mala**) *followed by narrative tense* (**N16**), *eg. (1) Baalwa ddaaki ne bagenda. ('Eventually they went.'); (2) Baamala ne bagenda. ('Eventually they went.')* get to eventually (*a place*) -**gguka**, *eg. Ekkubo lino ligguka e Masaka. ('This road eventually gets to Masaka.')*

ever ever since **okuva lwe**, *eg. Okuva lwe yajja abadde mulwadde. ('Ever since she came here she has been ill.')*, **kasooka nga** for ever and ever **emirembe n'emirembe**

everlasting *adj* -**a olubeerera**, *eg. Okwagala kwa Katonda tekuggwaawo, kwa lubeerera. ('The love of God does not end; it is everlasting.')*

every *det* **buli** (**N3**), *eg. buli muntu ('every person')*

everyday *adv* **bulijjo** everyday clothes **engoye eza bulijjo** *n10*

everyone *pro* **buli omu**

everything *pro* **buli kimu**

everywhere *adv* **wonna**, *eg. Omwana agenda wonna we ŋŋenda. ('The child goes everywhere I go.')* absolutely everywhere **wonnawonna** go everywhere (in) -**talaaga**, *eg. Tujja kutalaaga Kampala nga tugema abaana. ('We are going everywhere in Kampala with the vaccination campaign.')*

evict *vt* -**goba**

evidence *n* **obujulizi** *n14*

[1]**evil** *adj* -**bi** evil portent (*premonition of death*) **ekyebikiro** *n7* evil spell **eddogo** *n5* evil spirit *See* spirit

[2]**evil** *n* **ekibi** *n7* commit evil -**yonoona**

evildoer *n* **omwonoonyi** *n1*

ewe *n* **endiga enkazi** *n9*

exact (*also* precise) *adj. Use* -**nnyini** (*with pronoun of emphasis as prefix* **N10.1**) (**N11.6**), *eg. Ekyo kye kibuuzo kyennyini kye yabuuza. ('That was the exact question he asked.')*

exactly (*also* precisely) *adv. Use* -**nnyini** (*with pronoun of emphasis as prefix* **N10.1**) (**N11.6**), *eg. essaawa bbiri zennyini ('exactly 8 o'clock')* That's exactly right. **Kye kyo kyennyini.**

exaggerate *vt* -**savuwaza**

exalt *vt* -**gulumiza**. *See* praise exalt oneself -**eegulumiza**

examination *n* ebibuuzo *n8*, ebigezo *n8* <u>final</u> <u>examination</u> **okubuuzibwa okw'akamalirizo** *n15* <u>sit an examination</u> **-tuula ekibuuzo**

examine *vt* (1) (*physically*) **-kebera**, *eg. Omusawo akebera omulwadde. ('The doctor is examining the patient.')*; (2) (*mentally*) **-wa ebibuuzo**, *eg. Omusomesa awa abayizi ebibuuzo. ('The teacher is examining the pupils.').* *See* scrutinise <u>examine</u> <u>oneself</u> (*physically*) **-eekebera**, (*to check one's appearance*) **-eekebejja** <u>be examined</u> (*questioned*) **-buuzibwa** <u>way of examining</u> **enkebera** *n9*

examiner *n* **omukebezi** *n1*

example *n* **ekyokulabirako** *n7. See* illustration <u>follow the example of</u> **-labira ku** <u>for example</u> **okugeza** <u>give as an example</u> (*choose from among*) **-nokolayo**

exasperate *vt* **-sobeza**

excavate (*dig deeply; dig out*) *vt* **-wuukuula, -yiikuula.** *See* dig

exceed *vt* **-singawo**, *eg. Yasinzeewo ku kye twabadde tusuubira. ('He exceeded our expectations.')*, (*beyond a certain measure, used mainly for numbers or money*) **-sukka**, *eg. Waliwo ebbanga erisukka mayiro ttaano okutuuka ku kyalo. ('The distance to the village exceeds five miles.')*

exceedingly *adv* (1) *Use* **-yitirivu** (*'excessive'*), *eg. Muyitirivu obulungi. ('She is exceedingly beautiful.')*; (2) **-suffu**, *eg. Kino kisuffu obulungi. ('This is exceedingly good.')*

excel *vi. Use* **bulungi ennyo** (*'very well'*), *eg. Asoma bulungi nnyo. ('He excels at his studies.')* <u>excel in</u> **-singa obulungi**, *eg. Musoke y'asinga okuzannya omupiira obulungi. ('Musoke excels at football.')*

excellent *adj* **-lungi ennyo**

except (for) *pre* **okuggyako**, *eg. Mwenna mujje wano okuggyako ggwe. ('All come here except you.')*

exception *n* **ekyenjawulo** *n7*

excessive *adj* **-yitirivu** <u>be excessive</u> **-yitirira**, *eg. Ebbugumu liyitiridde. ('The heat is excessive.')* <u>be</u> <u>excess to requirements</u> **-fikka**. *See* superfluous (be) <u>eat to excess</u> **-eepiika emmere** <u>to excess</u> **ennyo**, *eg. Anywa nnyo. ('He drinks to excess.')*

excessively *adv* **okukamala**

exchange *vt* **-waanyisa**, *eg. Baawaanyisa engoye. ('They exchanged clothes.')* <u>exchange currency</u> **-kyusa ssente** <u>exchange ideas</u> **-kubaganya** (*or* **-waanyisiganya**) **ebirowoozo**

excite *vt* **-buguumiriza** <u>be(come) excited</u> **-buguumirira**, *eg. Abantu babuguumirira nga Kabaka alabise. ('The people become excited when the king appears.')*

excitement *n* **okubuguumirira** *n15* <u>cause</u> <u>excitement</u> **-leeta akabuguumiriro**, *eg. Okujja kwa ppaapa kuleese akabuguumiriro. ('The visit of the pope has caused excitement.')*, (*involving moving about*) **-yuuguumya**, *eg. Ekinyumu*

kyayuuguumizza ekyalo. ('The celebration caused excitement in the village.') <u>exciting event</u> **akabuguumiriro** *n12*

exclude *vt. Use* **-londa** (*'choose'*) *in neg* (**N21**), *eg. Omutendesi teyalonda Daudi kuba mu ttiimu. ('The coach excluded David from the team.')* <u>exclude a</u> <u>family member</u> (*against cultural norms*) **-boola**, *eg. Baabodde ssenga waabwe ku mukolo. ('They excluded their aunt from the cultural event.')*

excrement *n* **bbi** *n1*, **obubi** *n14*

¹excuse *n* **ekyekwaso** *n7* <u>make false excuses</u> **-palappalanya**

²excuse *vt* **-kkiriza**

execute *vt* (1) (*do*) **-kola**; (2) (*kill*) **-tta** <u>place of</u> <u>execution</u> (*killing*) **ettambiro** *n5*

executioner (*person who kills*) *n* **omutambizi** *n1*

exercise *n* (1) (*something to do*) **ekyokukola** *n7*; (2) (*practice; rehearsal*) **okwegezaamu** *n15. See* work

exert oneself *vr* **-fuba**, (*to do something difficult*) **-eekaniikiriza**

exertion *n* **obufubi** *n14*

¹exhaust (pipe) *n* **ekizoosi** *n7*

²exhaust *vt* (1) (*tire*) **-kooya**, *eg. Abaana baakooya jjajja waabwe. ('The children exhausted their grandparent.')*; (2) (*use up*) **-malawo**, *eg. Baamazeewo emmere yonna mu sitoowa. ('They have exhausted all the food in the store.')* <u>be(come) exhausted</u> (1) (*tired*) **-koowa**, *eg. Akooye. ('She is exhausted.')*; (2) (*used up*) **-ggwa**. *Often used with enclitic* (**N24.2**), *eg. Sukaali aweddeyo mu sitoowa. ('The sugar is exhausted in the store.')*; (3) (*of something that becomes worn down, eg. tablet of soap*) **-ggweerera**

exhausted (*tired*) *adj* **-koowu**

exhaustion (*tiredness*) *n* **obukoowu** *n14*

¹exhibit *n* (1) (*display*) **omwoleso** *n3*; (2) (*in court case*) **ekizibiti** *n7*

²exhibit *vt* **-yolesa** <u>be exhibited</u> **-yolesebwa**

exhibition *n* **omwoleso** *n3*

exhort (*stress repeatedly*) *vt* **-kubiriza**

exhume (*a dead person*) (*also* <u>disinter</u>) *vt* **-simula**, (*as an act of theft or for infringement of a taboo*) **-ziikula**

¹exile *n* (1) (*person exiled*) **omuwaŋŋanguse** *n1*; (2) (*state of being exiled*) **obuwaŋŋanguse** *n14*

²exile *vt* **-waŋŋangusa** <u>be exiled</u> **-waŋŋanguka**

exist *vi* **-li**, *eg. Engo gye ziri mu Uganda. ('Leopards exist in Uganda.')*

¹exit *n* **awafulumirwa** *n16*, **w'ofulumira** *n16*

²exit *vi* **-fuluma**

Exodus (*book of*) *n* **Okuva** *n15*

exonerate *vt* **-ejjeereza** <u>be exonerated</u> **-ejjeerera**

exorbitant, be *vi* **-eereega**, *eg. Ebbeeyi eno yeereeze. ('This price is exhorbitant.')*

exorcise a spirit **-goba omuzimu**

expand *vt* (1) (*increase*) **-gaziya**, *eg. Yagaziya ffaamu. ('She has expanded the farm.')*; (2) (*something elastic*) **-leeguula**. *See* extend; increase;

weight (gain)

expect *vt* -suubira   expect to do next day -sulirira be expected -suubirwa

expectation *n* essuubi *n5*   have no expectations -labira awo, *eg. Tunaalabira awo. ('We shall see.' – what will happen)*

expel *vt* -goba. *See* strike off

expensive *adj* -a omuwendo, -a ebbeeyi

[1]**experience** *n* obumanyirivu *n14*   through experience **mu bumanyirivu**

[2]**experience** *vt* -wulira, *eg. Nnawulira obuzibu. ('I experienced difficulty.')*   experience misery -laba ennaku

experienced *adj* -manyirivu

[1]**experiment** *n* ekigezesebwa *n7*

[2]**experiment (with)** *vt* -gezesa

[1]**expert** *adj* -kugu

[2]**expert** *(person) n* omukugu *n1*, omumanyi *n1* become an expert -kuguka, *(and self-confident)* -eekansa

expertise *n* obukugu *n14*

expire *(of time) vi* -ggwaako, *eg. Ebbanga lye baamuwa lyaggwaako. ('The time given to you has expired.')*. *See* die

explain *vt* -nnyonnyola   explain oneself -eewozaako   be explained -nnyonnyoka

explanation *n* ennyinyonnyola *n9*

explode *v* (1) *vi* -tulika; (2) *vt* -tulisa. *See* bang

exploit *(a person, taking advantage of) vt* -yiikiriza

explore *vt* -noonyereza

explorer *n* omunoonyerezi *n1*

explosion *n* ekibwatuka *n7*

expose *vt* -yasanguza, *eg. Olupapula lw'amawulire lwayasanguzza obuli bw'enguzi. ('The newspaper exposed the corruption.'), (someone in an indecent way)* -fungula. *See* denounce; reveal; show; uncover   expose oneself indecently (1) *(through lifting up one's clothing)* -eefungula; (2) *(showing one's private parts)* -kunama   be(come) exposed *(public knowledge)* -manyika mu lujjudde, *eg. Amabanja ge gaamanyika mu lujjudde ng'afudde. ('His debts become exposed when he died.')*

express *(say) vt* -yogera, *eg. Yayogera bw'atasanyuse bwe yawulira amawulire. ('He expressed displeasure when he heard the news.')*   express amazement (at) -kungiriza   express indifference -badala   express reluctance *(in response to a request)* -eekaanya

expression *(common utterance) n* eŋŋombo *n9*

extend *vt* (1) *(add physically)* -yongerako, *eg. Yayongerako ku ttaka lye. ('He has extended his land.')*; (2) *(go further)* -eeyongerayo, *eg. Yeeyongerayo n'atuuka e Masaka. ('He extended his journey up to Masaka.')*; (3) *(enlarge a structure)* -kookerako, *eg. Ennyumba yagikookerako. ('He has extended the house.')*, -waayirako. *See* add; enlarge; expand; increase   extend beyond *(out of line)* (1) *vi* -soolooba,

-yitamu; (2) *vt* -sooloobya, -yisaamu

extension *n* ekyayongerwako *n7*, *(to a word in grammar)* akawakatirwa *n12. See* appendix; supplement

exterminate *vt* -malawo

external *adj* -a ebweru

extinguish *(light/fire) vt* -zikiza   be extinguished -zikira

extort money *(from)* -kanda, *eg. Yankanda ssente. ('He extorted money from me.')*

extortion *n* obulyake *n14*

extortionist *n* omulyake *n1*, omunyunyunsi *n1*

extract *vt* (1) *(pull out from within)* -sowolamu, *eg. Yasowolamu akati kamu mu muganda. ('She extracted one stick from the bundle.')*; (2) *(with an implement, eg. needle)* -tundula, *eg. Yatundula envunza mu kigere kye. ('She extracted a jigger from his foot.')*; (3) *(take out of a socket)* -kuula. *See* take   extract a tooth -kuula erinnyo   extract juice from bananas *(by crushing them)* -sogola omubisi   be extracted *(eg. of a handle)* -kuuka

extraordinary, something *n* ekitali kya bulijjo *n7*, ekikulejje *n7*

extravagant *(wasteful) adj* -diibuuzi   use extravagantly -diibuula, *eg. Essente yazidiibuula. ('He was extravagant with his money.')*

extreme *adj* -yitirivu, *eg. ebbugumu eriyitirivu ('extreme heat')*

extremely *adv* (1) *Use* -yitirira *('be extreme'), eg. Kiyitirira obuwanvu. ('It is extremely long.')*; (2) okukamala, *eg. Yalungiwa okukamala. ('She is extremely beautiful.')*

extremity *(outskirts) n* obusammambiro *n14*

exudate *n* (1) *(latex from plant)* amasanda *n6*; (2) *(from eye)* obujonjo *n14*

eye *n* eriiso *n5. See* roll   eye of a needle eŋŋango y'empiso   be wide open *(of the eyes, eg. due to fright)* -kanuka   close one's eyes -zibiriza amaaso, -zibirira   keep an eye on *(being suspicious)* -eekengera   open one's eyes -zibula, *(wide)* -kanula amaaso   person who keeps an eye on things kaliisoliiso *n1*   watery eyes *(about to cry)* ebiyengeyenge *n8*

eyebrow *n* ekisige *n7*

eyelash *n* akakowekowe *n12*

eyelid *n* ekikowe *n7*

eyesight *n* okulaba *n15. See* sight

F,f

fable *n* olugero *n11*

fabric *n* olugoye *n11*

fabricate *vt* (1) *(make)* -kola; (2) *(build)* -zimba. *See* lie

fabulous *adj* -lungi ennyo

[1]**face** *n* amaaso *n6. See* cheek   compose one's face -wombeeka amaaso   make faces -eeginga,

-eemoola

²face vt **-tunula ku**, eg. Ennyumba yange etunudde ku nnyanja. ('My house faces the lake.') face one another **-tunulagana**, eg. Ennyumba zitunulaganye. ('The houses face one another.') face up to (eg. a bully or someone overcharging) **-kaliramu**, (more aggressively) **-tambaala**

facemask n **akakookolo** n12

facilitate (make easier) vt **-wewula**. See enable; help facilitiate an introduction **-kubira oluwenda**, eg. Yakubira Musoke oluwenda okulaba omukulu w'essomero. ('She facilitated an introduction to the head of the school.')

facing pre **mu maaso ga**

fact n **ekituufu** n7

faction (eg. of a political party) n **akakundi** n12, **akabondo** n12, **ekikoosi** n7. See group

factory n **ekkolero** n5

fad n **akatinko** n12 become a fad **-tinka**, eg. Okwambala enkuufiira kutinse. ('Wearing a hat has become a fad.')

fade vi **-siiwuuka**, eg. Twayoza olugoye ne lusiiwuuka. ('We washed the dress and it faded.') make fade **siiwuusa**, eg. Omusana gusiiwuusizza olutimbe. ('The sun caused the curtain to fade.')

faded adj **-siiwuufu**

faeces n **bbi** n1, **obubi** n14

fail (in) vt **-lemwa**, eg. Yalemwa omulimu. ('He failed in the job.'), **-lema** (subject and object reversed compared to English), eg. Omulimu gwamulema. ('He failed in the job.'). See break down fail an examination **-gwa ebibuuzo** fail to come to a decision **-lemwa okusalawo** fail to come to an agreement **-lemagana** fail to cook properly (also fail to grow properly) **-kona** fail to progress (of a project) **-ziŋŋama**, eg. Emirimu giziŋŋamye. ('The work is failing to progress.')

faint vi **-zirika**

¹fair (moderate) adj **-saamusaamu**

²fair (event; show) n **omwoleso** n3

fairly (quite) adv. Use enclitic **-ko** or **-mu** (N24.3), eg. Mulungiko. ('He is fairly good.')

fairness n **obwenkanya** n14

faith n **enzikiriza** n9, **okukkiriza** n15

faithful adj **-eesigwa** faithful person **omwesigwa** n1 be faithful **-li** or **-ba** ('be') according to tense (N20.1) followed by **omwesigwa**, eg. Yali mwesigwa eri mukyala we. ('He was faithful to his wife.')

faithfulness n **obwesigwa** n14

¹fake adj (1) **-gingeginge**; (2) **-a ekikwangala**, eg. omusawo w'ekikwangala ('fake doctor'); (3) Use **-a ddala** ('genuine') with neg (N21), eg. Si musawo wa ddala. ('He is a fake doctor.')

²fake n (1) (item) **ekikwangala** n7, **ekiwaanyi** n7, eg. Eno Sony oba kiwaanyi? ('Is this a Sony or a fake?'); (2) (person) **omuntu eyeefuula ky'atali** n1

³fake (counterfeit) vt **-gingirira**. See pretend

¹fall n **ekigwo** n7

²fall vi (fell) **-gwa**, eg. (1) Yagwayo mu kinnya. ('She fell into the hole.'); (2) Yagwa ku madaala. ('She fell down the stairs.'), (of rain) **-tonnya**, eg. Enkuba etonnya. ('The rain is falling.'). See come down; drop off; fall asleep fall flat on one's back **-gwa bugazi** fall from a tree (of leaves) **-kunkumuka**, eg. Ebikoola bikunkumuse. ('The leaves have fallen off.') fall into difficulties **-gwa mu buzibu** fall off (of a ripe fruit) **-nogoka**. See break off fall open (eg. of an article of clothing) **-wenjuka** fall over (of the body or head when falling asleep in a chair) **-neguka**, eg. Yasumagidde n'aneguka. ('She dozed off and fell over.') fall to pieces (eg. of a wall) **-meguka**. See crumble fall together (as two interlocked wrestlers) **-gwa maliri**

fallow (land) n (1) (weedy, after the harvest) **ekisambu** n7; (2) (more overgrown) **ekikande** n7; (3) (uncultivated land) **ensiko** n9

false adj **si -tuufu**, eg. Ky'agamba si kituufu. ('What he says is false.'). See fake false accuser **omusazi w'ebigambo** n1 false statement(s) Refer to **akalebule** ('libel'), eg. Yamuyogerako ebintu eby'akalebule. ('He made false statements about her.') make false accusations **-sibako ebigambo** make false excuses **-palappalanya**

falsehood n **obulimba** n14

fame n **ettutumu** n5

familiar be(come) familiar with **-manyiira**, eg. Amanyidde omulimu. ('He has become familiar with the job.') be overfamiliar with **-eemanyiiza nnyo** undue familiarity **olummanyimmanyi** n11

familiarise oneself (with) vi **-eemanyiiza**, eg. Yeemanyiiza okukola buli lunaku. ('He is familiarising himself with working every day.')

family n **famire** n9, (blood relatives) **ab'oluganda** n2 family member (blood relative) **ow'oluganda** n1, (of the same lineage) **ow'olulyo** n1 family of baganda (with pos N12), eg. baganda bange ('my family') royal family **olulyo olulangira** n11, **abaana b'eŋŋoma** n2, **abaana ba mujaguzo**

famine n **enjala** n9 be famished **-lumwa ennyo enjala**

famous adj **-tutumufu**. See distinguished; renouned; well-known famous person **ow'ettutumu** n1 be(come) famous **-tutumuka** make famous **-tutumula**

¹fan n (1) (eg. for cooling) **ekiwujjo** n7; (2) (supporter) **omuwagizi** n1

²fan vt **-wujja**

fancy (like) vt **-yagala**

far adv **wala** far from **wala okuva**, eg. Ennyumba ye eri wala okuva wano. ('His house is far from here.') far side of a hill **enzivuunuko** n9 go as far as **-koma**, eg. Yakoma Masaka. ('He went as far as Masaka.') rather far **walako**

fare *n* ssente z'olugendo *n10*

farewell to, bid *vt* -siibula

[1]**farm** *n* ffaamu *n9*, (*of crops; garden*) **ennimiro** *n9*. See banana garden; plot; ranch

[2]**farm** *vt* -lima <u>keep animals</u> -lunda

farmer *n* omulimi *n1*, (*keeping animals*) **omulunzi** *n1*

farming *n* (1) (*growing crops*) ebyobulimi *n8*; (2) (*keeping livestock*) ebyobulunzi *n8* <u>way of farming</u> **ennima** *n9*

[1]**fart** (*impolite*) *n* ddoti *n9*

[2]**fart** (*impolite*) *vi* -kuba ddoti, -nnyampa (*impolite*)

[1]**fashion** *n* omusono *n3* <u>go out of fashion</u> -diba <u>in fashion</u> **ku mulembe**, *eg. Empale ennyimpi ziri ku mulembe. ('Short trousers are in fashion.')*

[2]**fashion** (*make*) *vt* -kola

fashionable *adj* -a omulembe, *eg. engoye z'omulembe ('fashionable clothes')* <u>be fashionable</u> (*of a person*) **-tuukira ku mulembe**

[1]**fast** (*quick*) *adj* -yangu

[2]**fast** (*quickly*) *adv* (1) mangu, *eg. Yakola mangu omulimu. ('She did the job fast.')*; (2) Use -yanguwa ('be quick') as aux v (**N19**), *eg. Yatambula ng'ayanguwa. ('She walked fast.')* <u>drive a car very fast</u> -vuumuula emmotoka <u>run fast</u> -dduka emisinde, -dduka embiro

[3]**fast** (*period without food*) *n* ekisiibo *n7*

[4]**fast** (*go without food*) *vi* -siiba

fasten *vt* -siba, (*securely*) -nyweza <u>be fastened</u> -sibwa, (*securely*) -nywera

fastened *adj* -sibe <u>something fastened</u> **ekisibe** *n7*

fastener *n* ekisiba *n7*

fastidious *adj* -eekanasi <u>fastidious person</u> **omwekanasi** *n1* <u>be fastidious</u> -eekanasa

[1]**fat** *adj* (1) (*of a person*) -nene; (2) (*of an animal*) -sava; (3) (*of a person or animal that has gained weight*) -gevvu. See fatty <u>fat person</u> **omunene** *n1*, **nnamunene** *n1*, (*one who has gained weight*) **omugevvu** *n1* <u>be(come) fat</u> (*of an animal*) -savuwala. See weight (gain) <u>become fat and barren</u> (*of an animal*) -saatawala

[2]**fat** (*of an animal*) *n* amasavu *n6* (*one piece* essavu *n5*). See butter; ghee; margarine

fate See destiny

father *n* taata *n1*, (*of twins*) **Ssaalongo** *n1* title <u>my father</u> **kitange**, <u>your father</u> **kitaawo**, *etc.* (*stem* **kita- N12**)

father-in-law *n* ssezaala *n1*. See in-law

fatigue *n* obukoowu *n14*

fatigued *adj* -koowu <u>fatigued person</u> **omukoowu** *n1* <u>be(come) fatigued</u> -koowa

fatness *n* obugevvu *n14*

fatten (*an animal*) *vt* -savuwaza

fatty (*of meat*) *adj* -sava, *eg. ennyama ensava ('fatty meat')* <u>thick fatty skin</u> (*eg. of pig*) **ekigodo** *n7*

fault *n* ekisobu *n7* <u>person at fault</u> **omusobya** *n1*

faulty *adj* -yonoonefu, (*of machinery*) Use -lamu ('in good condition') in neg (**N21**), *eg. Ekyuma si*

kiramu. *('The machine is faulty.')*, (*not working, of machinery*) **-fu** <u>be faulty</u> -yonooneka, (*not functioning properly*) Use -kola obulungi ('work well') in neg (**N21**), *eg. Yingini eno tekola bulungi. ('This engine is faulty.')*

favour <u>be in favour of</u> (*a proposal*) -semba, *eg. Nsemba eky'obutagenda. ('I am in favour of not going.')*. See prefer <u>curry favour (with)</u> -eeguya, *eg. Musoke tumweguyaako ssente ze. ('We are currying favour with Musoke to get his money.')*

favourite *adj* -ganzi, *eg. Ettiimu yange eŋŋanzi ye Liverpool. ('My favourite team is Liverpool.')* <u>favourite (person)</u> **omuganzi** *n1* <u>be a favourite</u> -ganja <u>make a favourite of</u> -ganza

favouritism *n* obuganzi *n14*

[1]**fear** *n* okutya *n15* <u>shake with fear</u> -tiitiira <u>something that causes fear</u> **ekitiisa** *n7*

[2]**fear** *vt* -tya <u>be feared</u> -tiibwa

fearful *adj* -tiitiizi

fearfulness *n* obutiitiizi *n14*

fearless *adj.* Use -tya ('fear') in rel (**N7.1**) in neg (**N21**), *eg. abaserikale abatatya ('fearless soldiers')*

feasible, be *vi* (1) (*doable*) -koleka; (2) (*possible*) -soboka

feast *n* ekijjulo *n7*. See party <u>giver of a feast</u> **omugabuzi** *n1*

feather *n* ekyoya *n7*

February *n* Omwezi ogw'okubiri *n3*, **Mukutulansanja, Febwali**

fed See feed <u>be(come) fed up with</u> -tamwa, *eg. Nnatamiddwa Musoke. ('I am fed up with Musoke.')*, -tama (*with personal object*), *eg. Lumonde antamye okulya. ('I am fed up with eating potatoes.')*, -nyiwa (*with personal object*), *eg. Lumonde annyiye okulya. ('I am fed up with eating potatoes.')*

federalism *n* federo

federation *n* federesoni *n9*

fee *n* ekisale *n7* <u>fees</u> **ebisale** *n8*, **fiizi** *n10* <u>court fee</u> **empaabi** *n9* <u>school fees</u> **ebisale by'essomero** *n8*

feeble *adj* -nafu <u>be(come) feeble</u> -nafuwa <u>make feeble</u> -nafuya

feed *vt* (fed) (1) (*with food*) -liisa, *eg. Aliisa mulwadde. ('She is feeding the patient.')*; (2) (*with a liquid*) -nywesa, *eg. Anywesa omwana. ('She is feeding the baby.')*; (3) (*people at a social occasion*) -gabula <u>feed at the breast</u> (1) *vi* -yonka; (2) *vt* -yonsa <u>feed to repletion</u> (1) *vi* -kkuta; (2) *vt* -kkusa <u>give food from one's plate to</u> -ddiza emmere <u>be fed</u> (*given food*) -liisibwa

feel (*mentally*) *vi* (felt) -wulira, *eg. Mpulira ndi mulwadde. ('I feel ill')*, -kwatibwa. See touch <u>feel about (for)</u> (*eg. to find something in the dark*) -wammanta <u>feel cold</u> -wulira (*or* -kwatibwa) **empewo, empewo** -fuuwa <u>feel fear</u> **wulira okutya** <u>feel feverish</u> -kwatibwa omusujja <u>feel shy</u> -kwatibwa ensonyi <u>feel unwell</u> -wulira bubi feel well **-wulira** (*or* **-eewulira**) **bulungi**

feeling (*mental*) *n* **okuwulira** *n15*   ill feelings (*rancour*) **ffitina** *n9*

fees *See* fee

feet *See* foot

feign *vt* **-eefuusa**, *eg. Yeefuusa omulwadde.* (*'She is feigning illness.'*)   feign ignorance **-eewugguusa**

feint *vi* **-kuba eddolera**

fell *vt* **-tema**

fellow *See* companion; friend   fellow wife **muggya** (*with pos* **N12**), *eg. muggya wo* (*'your fellow wife'*)

felt *See* feel

female *adj* **-kazi**, *eg. jjajja omukazi* (*'female grandparent', ie. 'grandmother'*), (*of ruminants*) **-luusi**, *eg. embuzi enduusi* (*'nanny goat'*)

femininity *n* **obukazi** *n14*

[1]**fence** *n* **olukomera** *n11*, (*of crossed reeds around a chief's compound*) **ekisaakaate** *n7*, (*of upright reeds around a palace*) **bbugwe** *n1*, (*around a cattle pen*) **olugo** *n11*

[2]**fence (in)** *vt* **-komera**

fermented, be (*of beer*) *vi* **-ggya**, *eg. Omwenge guyidde.* (*'The beer is ready.'*)

fern *n* **kayongo** *n1*

ferocious *adj* **-kambwe** (*or* **-kaali**) **ennyo**

ferocity *n* **obukambwe** *n14*, **obukaali** *n14*

[1]**ferry** *n* **ekidyeri** *n7*

[2]**ferry (across)** (*over water*) *vt* **-wungula**   be ferried across **-wunguka**

fertile (*of land*) *adj* **-gimu**, *eg. awantu awagimu* (*'fertile place'*)   be fertile **-gimuka**   make fertile **-gimusa**

fertilise (*soil*) *vt* **-gimusa**

fertiliser *n* **ebigimusa** *n8*

fertility (*of land*) *n* **obugimu** *n14*

fester (*of a wound*) *vi* **-tana**

festival *n* **ekivvulu** *n7*

fetch *vt* **-kima**, **-nona**. *See* collect   come to fetch **-ddukira**

fetish *n* **ejjembe** *n5*. *See* charm

[1]**feud** *n* **akakuubagano** *n12*. *See* quarrel

[2]**feud** *vi* **-kuubagana**. *See* quarrel

fever *n* **omusujja** *n3*   East Coast fever (*cattle disease*) **amakebe** *n6*   have a fever **-bugujja**

few *det* **-tono**   few at a time **musoolesoole**, *eg. Abantu bazze musoolesoole.* (*'The people came a few at a time.'*)   become fewer **-toniwa**   make fewer **-toniya**

fez *n* **enkuufiira y'omujunga** *n9*

fibre (*piece of*) *n* (1) (*from banana plant*) **ekyayi** *n7*, (*long and thin*) **olwayi** *n11*, (*inside fibre of stem, used for caulking canoes*) **eggwale** *n5*; (2) (*from raffia palm*) **akaso** *n12*; (3) (*from sisal*) **akagoogwa** *n14*; (4) (*from ekiyulu plant*) **enjulu** *n9*; (5) (*cotton, including fibre from kapok tree and akafumbo*) **ppamba** *n1*; (6) (*thin strip cut from midrib of banana leaf*) **akakeedo** *n12*. *See* string   fibre used to seal seams in canoes **ensinga** *n10*

fickle *adj* **-yuuganyi**   fickle person **omuyuuganyi** *n1*   be fickle **-kyukakyuka**

[1]**fiddle** (*one-stringed musical instrument; tube fiddle*) *n* **endingidi** *n9*. *See* ground-bow   fiddle player **omudingidi** *n1*   play the fiddle **-kuba endingidi**

[2]**fiddle** (*cheat; defraud*) *vt* **-kumpanya**

fidelity *n* **obwesigwa** *n14*

fidget *vi* (1) *Use* **-tereera** (*'be stable'*) *with* **mu kifo** (*'in position'*) *in neg* (**N21**), *eg. Omwana tatereera mu kifo.* (*'The child is fidgeting'*); (2) (*involving fingering things*) **-eemakula**

field *n* (1) (*grazing area*) **ettale** *n5*; (2) (*cut area of grass, eg. for games*) **ekisaawe** *n7*; (3) (*patch of crops*) **omusiri** *n3*. *See* garden; pasture; plot   old potato field **ekisodde** *n7*

fierce *adj* **-kambwe**, **-kkaali**. *See* aggressive; wild   fierce person **omukambwe** *n1*   be(come) fierce **-kambuwala**, (*of person or domesticated animal losing self-control*) **-taama**

fierceness *n* **obukambwe** *n14*, **obukaali** *n14*

fifteen *num* **kkumi na ttaano**, **kkumi na -taano** (*with numeral concord* **N4.2**) (**N8.1**), *eg. ebintu kkumi na bitaano* (*'fifteen things'*)

fifth *adj/num* **-a okutaano** (**N7.1**), *eg. ekintu eky'okutaano* (*'fifth thing'*). *Elision is sometimes seen, eg. ekintu ekyokutaano* (*'fifth thing'*).

fifty *num* (**amakumi**) **ataano** (**N8.1**)   fifty-fifty (*so-so*) **bwe -tyo bwe -tyo**. (**N13**)

fig (tree) *See* (1) barkcloth tree; (2) *Under 'Ficus' in* **N31** *for names of types*

[1]**fight** *n* **okulwana** *n15*. *See* battle; war

[2]**fight** *vi* **-lwana**. *See* wage war   fight for/over **-lwanira**, *eg. Balwanira ensalosalo.* (*'They are fighting over the boundary.'*)   fight for a cause **-lwanirira**, *eg. Mandela yalwanirira eddembe okumala emyaka mingi.* (*'Mandela fought for freedom for many years.'*)   fight with/against **-lwanyisa**, *eg. Batulwanyisa.* (*'They are fighting us.'*)

fighter *n* **omulwanyi** *n1*   person who readily picks a fight **ow'olugono** *n1*. *See* pugnacious

figure (*eg. drawing*) *n* **ekifaananyi** *n7*. *See* number

file (*for papers*) *n* **fayiro** *n9*

file a charge **-waaba omusango**   file a charge against **-waabira omusango**, *eg. Abapoliisi baawaabira Musoke.* (*'The police filed a charge against Musoke.'*)

fill *vt* **-jjuza**, *eg. Ekikopo akijjuzizza amazzi.* (*'She has filled the cup with water.'*). *See* block (up); full   fill to capacity **-jjuuliriza**   be filled up **-jjula**   be filled with (*heat, happiness, etc.*) **-bugaana**, *eg. Entamu ebugaanye omuliro.* (*'The cooking pot is hot inside.'*)

film *n* **firimu** *n9*   film star **omuzannyi mu bifaananyi** *n1*

[1]**filter** *n* **akasengejja** *n12*. *See* strainer

[2]**filter** *vt* **-sengejja**   place for filtering (*eg. when making beer*) **essengejjero** *n5*

filth *n* **kazambi** *n1*. See dirt
filthiness *n* **obujama** *n14*. See dirt
filthy *adj* **-jama, -ddugavu**. *See* dirty be filthy
 -jamawala, -ddugala make filthy **-jamawaza,
 -ddugaza**
fin (*of a fish*) *n* **eggirigimba** *n5*
[1]**final** *adj* (1) **-a enkomerero**, *eg. ebigezo
 eby'enkomerero* (*'final exams'*); (2) *Use* **-sembayo**
 (*'be final'*) *in rel* (**N7.1**), *eg. ebigezo ebisembayo*
 (*'final exams'*) final exams **okubuuzibwa
 okw'akamalirizo** *n15* be final (*last*)
 -komererayo, -sembayo
[2]**final** (*of a competition*) *n* **empaka z'akamalirizo**
 n10, **empaka ezisembayo, fayinolo** *n9*
finally *adv* **oluvannyuma, ekyenkomerero,
 ekisembayo**
finance *n* **ebyensimbi** *n8* financial year **omwaka
 gw'ebyensimbi** *n3*
finch (*bird*) *n* **akasanke** *n12*, **akagugumusi** *n12*,
 nnakinsige *n1*. *These three names are all applied
 to small finch-like birds found in flocks in
 grassland and on the ground. 'akasanke' appears to
 include mannikins, 'akagugumusi' waxbills and
 cordon-bleu, and 'nnakinsige' firefinch. Their
 assignment to English equivalents needs
 confirmation. See* sparrow
find *vt* (*found*) **-sanga**, *eg. Nnasanze engatto zange
 wansi w'ekitanda.* (*'I found my shoes under the
 bed.'*), (*after searching*) **-zuula, -laba**, *eg. Ekitabo
 nkirabye.* (*'I have found the book.'*). *See* discover
 find a new course (*of a river*) **-wagulula** find a
 way (*to do something*) **-sala amagezi**. *See* concoct;
 resourceful (*be*) find for **-labira**, *eg. Nnamulabira
 omuvuzi.* (*'I found a driver for him.'*) be found (1)
 (*of something lost*) **-zuuka**, *eg. Empeta yange
 yazuuse.* (*'My ring has been found.'*); (2) (*be at;
 live at*) **-beera**, *eg. Envubu zibeera wano.* (*'Hippos
 are found here.'*). *See* reappear
[1]**fine** (*good*) *adj* **-lungi**
[2]**fine** (*penalty*) *n* **omutango** *n3*. *See* damages on-
 the-spot fine **omutango ogwa buliwo**
[3]**fine** (*make pay a penalty*) *vt* **-tanza**, *eg.
 Bantanzizza.* (*'They have fined me.'*)
[1]**finger** *n* (1) (*general term*) **olugalo** *n11*; (2) (*index*)
 olunwe *n11*; (3) (*little*) **nnasswi** *n9*, **akanwe** *n12*.
 See thumb finger millet (1) (*plant*) **obulo** *n14*; (2)
 (*meal/flour*) **akalo** *n12*; (3) (*porridge*) **obusera**
 n14; (4) (*beer*) **amalwa** *n6*
[2]**finger** (*feel around something*) *vt* **-kwatakwata**
fingerprint *n* **ekinkumu** *n7*
finicky *adj* **-eekanasi** finicky person **omwekanasi**
 n1 be finicky **-eekanasa**
[1]**finish** *n* **enkomerero** give a good finish
 -yooyoota, *eg. Emmotoka bajoozezza ne
 bagiyooyoota.* (*'They washed the car and finished
 off the job very well.'*)
[2]**finish** *vt* **-mala**, *eg. Njagala okumala omulimu
 guno.* (*'I want to finish this job.'*). *Often with*

enclitic (**N24.2**), *eg. Amazeemu caayi.* (*'She has
 finished her tea.'*). *See* conclude; end; stop finish
 completely (1) (*a task*) **-maliriza**, *eg. Bamalirizza
 okusereka.* (*'They have finished roofing.'*); (2) (*use
 up*) **-malawo**, *eg. Yalya emmere n'agimalawo.* (*'He
 ate the food and finished it off completely.'*) finish
 in/at **-malira** finish off well (*a basket, carving,
 etc.; embellish*) **-wunda** finish one's turn (*in the
 game of omweso*) **-yalika** Finish with this one.
 (*indicating where to stop work*) **Malira ku kino.**
 finish work (*at one's regular time*) **-nnyula**
 be(come) finished **-ggwa**, *eg. Omulimu gujja
 kuggwa mangu.* (*'The job will be finished soon.'*)
[1]**fire** *n* **omuliro** *n3*, (*grass/forest*) **oluyiira** *n11*. *See*
 bonfire expose briefly to fire **-babira**. *See* singe
 kindle a fire **-kuma omuliro** set fire to a house
 -yokya ennyumba, -yokerera
[2]**fire** (*of guns*) *vi* **-duduma**, *eg. Emmundu ziduduma.*
 (*'The guns are firing*), **-vuga** fire a gun **-lasa** (*or
 -kuba*) **emmundu** fire bricks **-yokya amatofaali**
 fire from a job **-goba ku mulimu** fire pottery
 -yokya ebibumbe
firefinch (*small red bird*) *n* **nnakinsige** *n1*
firefly *n* **emmunyeenye** *n9*
fireman *n* **muzimya-mwoto** *n1*
fireplace *n* **ekyoto** *n7*. *See* hearth
firewood *n* **enku** *n10* (*one piece* **oluku** *n11*, *large
 piece* **ekiku** *n7*). *See* log firewood collector
 omutyabi w'enku *n1* chop firewood **-yasa enku**
 collect firewood **-tyaba** (*or -sennya*) **enku** large
 heap of firewood **omuganda entuumu** *n3*,
 ekiganda entuumu *n7*
[1]**firm** *adj* (1) (*well fixed*) **-nywevu**; (2) (*steadfast*)
 -gumu be firm (1) (*well fixed*) **-nywera**; (2)
 (*solid*) **-guma** make firm (1) (*well fixed*) **-nyweza**,
 eg. Yasimba ekikondo n'akinyweza. (*'He planted
 the post and made it firm.'*); (2) (*strengthen*)
 -gumya
[2]**firm** (*company*) *n* **kkampuni** *n9*
[1]**first** *adj/num* (1) *Use* **-sooka** (*'be first'*) *in rel*
 (**N7.1**), *eg. omuntu asooka* (*'first person'*); (2) **-a
 olubereberye**, *eg. omuntu w'olubereberye* (*'first
 person'*) first aid **obujjanjabi obusookerwako**
 n14 first-born child **omuggulanda** *n1* first stages
 (*of a task*) **amabaga** *n6* point out one's first
 choice **-eesooka** want to be first (*pre-empting
 others*) **-sookera**
[2]**first** *adv* **okusooka**, *eg. Okusooka yagenda mu
 katale.* (*'First he went to the market.'*), (*indicating
 the first task to be done*) *Use* **-sooka** (*'be first'*)
 with subjunctive (**N17**), *eg. Sooka ofumbe.* (*'First
 do the cooking.'*) be/do first **-sooka**, *eg. Ye
 yasooka okutuuka.* (*'He was the first to arrive.'*)
 go first (*lead*) **-kulembera**
first-comer (*to a place*) *n* **munnasangwawo** *n1*
[1]**fish** *n* **ekyennyanja** *n7*. *Types include:* (1) (*catfish;
 also known as mudfish*) **emmale** *n9* (*young
 akalende *n12*, **omulende** *n3*), (*medium-sized type*)

ssemutundu *n9*, (*small, eel-like, found in rivers*)
ensonzi *n9*; (2) (*elephant snout fish*) **kasulubbana**
n1, **kasulu** *n1*, **somatulye** *n1*; (3) (*resembles
elephant snout fish, but can be a bit larger*)
ensuma *n9*; (4) (*lungfish*) **emmamba** *n9* (*young
omuguya n3*); (5) (*tilapia*) **engege** *n9*; (6) (*Nile
perch*) **empuuta** *n9*; (7) (*sprat; Haplocromis*)
enkejje *n9*; (8) (*sprat, silvery; smaller than
enkejje*) **mukene** *n1*; (9) (*another small type*)
akayamba *n12*; (10) (*resembles emmale but has
tiny bones; squeaker catfish*) **enkolongo** *n9*; (11)
(*type of fish that was common in Lake Victoria
before introduction of Nile perch; Labeo
victorianus*) **enningu** *n9*; (12) (*Victoria robber*)
ensoga *n9*; (13) (*barbel*) **enkuyu** *n9* (*small
ekisinja n9*); (14) (*butterfish*) **enzeere** *n9*; (15)
(*another type of fish*) **ennyunguli** *n9*.   fish eagle
ekkwanzi *n5*   fish hook **eddobo** *n5*   fish trap *See*
trap   string of fish (*offered for sale*) **omugeto** *n3*
²**fish (for)** *vit* **-vuba**, *eg. Avuba engege.* ('*He is
fishing for tilapia.*'), (*with a hook*) **-loba**
fisherman *n* **omuvubi** *n1*, (*using hooks*) **omulobi** *n1*
fishing *n* **okuvuba** *n15*   fishing basket *See* trap
fishing line (*type with hooks fastened at intervals*)
omugonjo *n3*   fishing net *See* net
fissure *n* **olwatika** *n11*
fist *n* **ekikonde** *n7*
¹**fit** (*of madness*) *n* **akazoole** *n12*   epileptic fit
ensimbu *n9*   have an epileptic fit **-gwa ensimbu**
²**fit** *v* TRANSITIVE USES **-gyisaamu**, *eg.
Nnakigyisizzaamu mu ddiiro.* ('*I fitted it into the
room.*')   fit on **-wanga**, *eg. Nnawanga enkumbi.* ('*I
fitted the handle on the hoe.*')   INTRANSITIVE
USES (1) (*within a space*) **-gyamu**, *eg. Emmeeza
egyamu mu ddiiro.* ('*The table fits in the room.*');
(2) (*into a container*) **-ggweeramu**, *eg. Ebintu
biggweereddemu mu nsawo yange.* ('*The things
fitted into my bag.*'); (3) (*be right size for; suit*)
-tuuka, *eg. Olugoye lukutuuka.* ('*The dress fits
you.*')
fitting   be fitting (*suitable*) **-saana**, *eg. Ekirabo
kisaana.* ('*The present is fitting.*'), **-gwana**   be
fitting for **-saanira**, *eg. Ekirabo kimusaanira.* ('*The
present is fitting for him.*'), **-gwanira**
five *num* **ttaano**. *The stem is* **-taano** (*with numeral
concord* **N4.2**) (**N8.1**), *eg. abantu bataano* ('*five
people*').   five hundred **bikumi bitaano** (**N8.1**)
five thousand **enkumi ttaano**
fix (*secure firmly*) *vt* **-nyweza**. *See* mend   fix up with
-labira, *eg. Yamulabira omuwala.* ('*She fixed him
up with a girl.*')   not be fixed properly (*eg. of a
post*) **-nyeenya**
fixed (*firm*) *adj* **-nywevu**   be fixed **-nywera**
flag *n* **bendera** *n9*   flag (*or other decoration*) at
front of canoe (*to show its identity*) **ensanda** *n9*
flag down (*eg. taxi*) *vt* **-kuba omukono, -yimiriza**
flagpole *n* **omulongooti gwa bendera** *n3*
flagrant *adj* **-a enkukunala**, *eg. obulimba*

obw'enkukunala ('*flagrant lying*')
flake (off) *vi* **-bambuka**, *eg. Erangi ebambuse.*
('*The paint is flaking.*'), (*of the skin*) **-yubuka**, *eg.
Ayubuse.* ('*Her skin is flaking.*')
flame *n* **olulimi lw'omuliro** *n11*   flame tree
(*Delonix regia*) **omwoloola** *n3*
flap about (*as a harassed chicken*) *vi* **-papala**
flare (up) (*of a fire*) *vi* **-tuntumuka**
¹**flash** *n* **ekimyanso** *n7*
²**flash** *vi* **-myansa**, *eg. Eggulu limyansa.* ('*The
lightning is flashing.*'), (*continuously*)
-myamyansa
flashlight (*torch*) *n* **ttooki** *n9*
¹**flat** (*of land*) *adj* **-a omuseetwe**, *eg. oluguudo lwa
museetwe* ('*flat road*'), **-seeteevu**   flat area of land
(*level*) **omuseetwe** *n3*   be flat (*of land*) **-seeteera**
make flat (*land*) **-seeteeza**
²**flat** (*apartment*) *n* **fulati** *n9*
flatten *vt* **-yagaagaza, -byabyataza**. *See* level;
squash   be flattened **-yagaagala, -byabyatala**
flattened *adj* **-yagaagavu, -byabyatavu**. *See*
levelled; squashed
flatter (*praise insincerely*) *vt* **-waanawaana**, *eg.
Yamuwaanawaana.* ('*She flattered him.*')
flatterer *n* **omuwaanyiwaanyi** *n1*
¹**flavour** (*pleasant smell of food*) *n* **eggwoowo** *n5*
²**flavour** *vt* **-lunga**   flavour correctly (*food*) **-noza**,
eg. Nnozezza omunnyo. ('*I have added enough
salt.*')   flavour (*food or drink*) with **-siwa**   be
flavoured correctly (*of food*) **-noga**, *eg. Oyo sukaali
ajja kunoga mu caayi.* ('*That amount of sugar will
be the right amount in the tea.*')
flavouring *n* **ekirungo** *n7*
flaw (*defect*) *n* **akamogo** *n12*
flay (*remove skin*) *vt* **-baaga**
flayer *n* **omubaazi** *n1*
flea *n* **enkukunyi** *n9*. *See* jigger
flee (*run away*) *vi* **-dduka**. *See* escape   flee to
-ddukira, *eg. Baddukira ku kkanisa.* ('*They fled to
the church.*')
fleet (*of canoes*) *n* **empingu** *n9*
flesh *n* **ennyama** *n9*
flew *See* fly
flexible *adj* **-gonvu**. *See* loose   be flexible **-gonda**
make flexible **-gonza**
flick (away) (*with the finger*) *vt* **-lasa**   flick off (*eg.
water or caterpillar*) **-eesammula**
flicker *vi* (1) (*as a star or electric light*)
-myamyansa; (2) (*as a paraffin lamp*) **-temereza**
fling *vt* (flung) **-kasuka**
flip-flop (*type of slipper*) *n* **ssapatu** *n9*
flippant, be *vi* **-badala**
¹**float** (*used when fishing, made from inflated
stomach*) *n* **eggomo** *n5*
²**float** *vi* **-tengejja**   float about (*drift*) **-yenja**,
(*continually*) **-yenjeera**   something floating
ekitengejja *n7*
flock (*of sheep or goats*) *n* **eggana** *n5*, **ekisibo** *n7*

flock of birds **ekibinja ky'ebinyonyi** *n7* (*small* **akabinja k'ebinyonyi** *n12*)

flog (*whip*) *vt* **-swanyuula**

frontier *n* **ensalo** *n9*

¹flood *n* **amataba** *n6*

²flood *vi* **-yanjaala**, *eg. Omugga gwanjadde. ('The river is flooding.'),* (*eg. due to pipe bursting*) **-yalaala.** *See* overflow

floor *n* (1) *Refer to* **wansi** (*'below'*), *eg. Wansi waliwo ekiwempe. ('The floor is covered with a carpet.');* (2) (*of a multistorey building*) **omuko** *n3,* *eg. omuko ogusooka ('first floor'),* **omwaliiro** *n3* on the floor **wansi** something spread on the floor **ekyaliiro** *n7,* **omwaliiro** *n3*

flop down (*lie down anyhow, eg. when tired*) *vi* **-gaŋŋalama**

flour *n* **obuwunga** *n14, eg. obuwunga bwa muwogo ('cassava flour'). Types of flour include:* (*maize*) **akawunga** *n12,* (*finger millet*), **akalo** *n12,* (*wheat*) **eŋŋaano** *n9.*

flourish (*of plants*) *vi* **-gimuka**

flourishing (*of plants*) *adj* **-gimu**

flow (*eg. of water*) *vi* **-kulukuta,** (*in great quantity*) **-kulugguka,** *eg. Ettaka likulugguse. ('There has been a landslide.'). See* ooze out   flow into **-kulukutira,** *eg. Amazzi gakulukutidde mu mufulejje. ('The water is flowing into the drain.')*

¹flower *n* **ekimuli** *n7*

²flower *vi* **-mulisa**

flu *n* **fulu** *n1,* (*serious*) **yegu** *n1*

flung *See* fling

flush *vt* **-sika amazzi,** *eg. Sika amazzi ng'omaze okukozesa toyireeti. ('Flush the toilet after use.')* flush out (*eg. animal in a hunt*) **-wamatula,** (*at a run*) **-fubutula,** (*with beating of bushes*) **-saggula**

flute (*musical instrument*) *n* **omulere** *n3,* **endere** *n9* flute player **omulere** *n1*

flutter (about) (*as a harassed chicken*) *vi* **-papala**

¹fly *n* **ensowera** *n9,* (*tsetse*) **ekivu** *n7,* (*black fly; Simulium*) **embwa** *n9,* (*fruit fly; Drosophila*) **akabu** *n12,* (*sand fly*) **akatugu** *n12,* (*horsefly*) **kawawa** *n1,* (*lake flies*) **esssami** *n9. See* gnat   fly whisk **emboobo** *n9*   cake made of lake flies **ekiwumi ky'essami** *n7*

²fly *vi* (*flew*) **-buuka**   fly an aeroplane **-vuga ennyonyi**   fly into a rage **-eecwacwana.** *See* upset (be easily)   fly up (*as a flock of birds*) **-buukira**

¹foam *n* (1) (*lather*) **ejjovu** *n5,* **ekyovu** *n7,* **ebyovu** *n8;* (2) (*as in a mattress*) **sipongi** *n9*

²foam (up) (*eg. of milk boiling up*) *vi* **-bimba**

foe *n* **omulabe** *n1*

foetal membranes *n* **ensungwe** *n9,* **ensundwe** *n9*

fog *n* **olufu** *n11*

foil (*prevent*) *vt* **-ziyiza**

¹fold (*eg. in cloth*) *n* **olufunyiro** *n11. See* seam

²fold (up) *vt* **-funya,** (*many times*) **-funyafunya.** *See* roll   fold one's arms **-gombaganya emikono**   fold up sleeves **-funya emikono**   fold up trousers

-funya empale   be(come) folded **-eefunya**

foliage *n* **ebikoola** *n8*

folk *n* **abantu** *n2*   folk belief/custom **akalombolombo** *n12*   folk story **olufumo** *n11*

follow *vt* (1) (*come after*) **-goberera,** *eg. Yamugoberera nga agenze ku luzzi. ('He followed her to the well.');* (2) (*go wherever someone goes*) **-londoola,** *eg. Omukessi yamulondoola okuva ku nsalo ya Kenya. ('The spy followed him from the Kenyan border.');* (3) (*conform to*) **-tuukiriza.** *See* come next; pursue   follow shortly after **-wondera,** *eg. Yalwisibwa mu kibuga n'awondera Musoke enkeera n'amusanga e Masaka.' ('She was delayed in town and followed Musoke to Masaka next day.')*

follower *n* **omugoberezi** *n1*

following *adj.* *Use* **-ddirira** (*'come after'*) *or* **-ddako** (*'come next'*) *in rel* (**7.1**), *eg.* (1) **omwezi oguddirira** (*'the following month'*); (2) **omwezi oguddako** (*'the following month'*)

folly (*foolishness*) *n* **obusiru** *n14*

fond of, be (*like*) *vt* **-yagala**

fondle *vt* **-kwatakwata**

font *n* (1) (*for baptisms*) **ebbatirizo** *n5;* (2) (*script; typeface*) **ekyapa** *n7*

fontanel *n* **akawompo** *n12*

food *n* **emmere** *n9,* (*of mixed ingredients*) **akatogo** *n12,* (*especially prepared, or for the Kabaka*) **katuuso** *n1,* (*for a long journey*) **entanda** *n9,* (*offered to a visitor*) **obugenyi** *n14,* (*without sauce*) **amaluma** *n6* (*or* **emmere ennuma**), (*cooked inwrapped in banana leaves*) **emmere ensuulemu.** *See* banana (*for words relating to eating matooke*)   be ready to eat (*of food*) **-ggya,** *eg. Emmere eyidde. ('Food is ready.')*   cooked food that has gone cold **emmere empolu**   dried sliced food (*for storage*) **mutere** *n1, eg. mutere wa mbidde ('dry sliced bananas),* (*of sweet potatoes*) **kasodde** *n1*   give food to (1) (*for a long journey*) **-sibirira entanda;** (2) (*from one's plate*) **-ddiza emmere**   go without food (1) (*during the day*) **-siiba enjala;** (2) (*during the night*) **-sula enjala**   have food ready (*to eat*) **-yiisa emmere**   left-over food **emmere efisse,** (*kept for eating later*) **amawolu** *n6* (*lump of cold matooke* **eggwolu** *n5*)   ready-to-eat food (*served from the payment*) **tonninnyira-mu-kange**   serving place for food **olujjuliro** *n11*   something to eat **ekyokulya** *n7*

food parcel (*food wrapped in banana leaves for cooking*) *n* (1) (*of solid food*) **omuwumbo** *n3, eg. omuwumbo gwa lumonde ('parcel of potatoes');* (2) (*of more liquid food*) **oluwombo** *n11, eg. oluwombo lw'ebyinyeebwa ('parcel of groundnut sauce'). See* banana (*for words relating to preparing and unwrapping food parcels*)

¹fool (*idiot*) *n* **omusiru** *n1. See* imbecile   make a fool of **-siruwaza**

²fool (*trick*) *vt* **-guumaaza.** *See* feint; outwit   be fooled **-guumaala**

foolish (*stupid*) *adj* **-siru** be(come) foolish
-siruwala

foolishness *n* **obusiru** *n14*

foot *n* (*pl.* feet) (1) (*of the body*) **ekigere** *n7*; (2)
(*measure of length*) **fuuti** *n9* foot-and-mouth
disease **kalusu** *n1* (at the) foot of the bed
emirannamiro foot rot (*athlete's foot*)
obugeregere *n14* go on foot **-tambuza ebigere,**
-kuba akagere inward-pointing feet **ebitege** *n9*

football *n* **omupiira** *n3* football coach **omutendesi**
w'omupiira *n1* football lover **omwagazi**
w'omupiira *n1* football match **empaka**
z'omupiira *n10* football pitch **ekisaawe**
ky'omupiira *n7* football player **omusambi**
w'omupiira *n1* play football **-samba** (*or*
-zannya, *or* **-kuba**) **omupiira** show fancy
footwork (*in football*) **-canga omupiira**

footpath *n* **akakubo** (k'ebigere) *n12*

footprint *n* **ekigere** *n7*

footstep *n* **ekigere** *n7*. *See* trampling light noise of
footsteps (*of unknown origin*) **enswagiro** *n10*

for (*also* on behalf of) *pre* **ku lwa**, *eg.* Yakikola ku
lw'abaana be. ('He did it for his children.'), (*with
pronoun* **N11.4**) **ku lwa-**, *eg.* ku lwaffe ('for us').
'for' is often expressed using prepositional verbs
(**N22**), *eg.* Yafumbira abaana. ('She cooked for the
children.'). for ever and ever **emirembe**
n'emirembe for example **okugeza**

forage *vi* **-saka**

forager *n* **omusasi** *n1*

forbid *vt* (forbade) (1) *Use* **-kkiriza** ('allow') *in neg*
(**N21**), *eg.* Sibakkiriza kuleekaana mu kibiina. ('I
forbid you to shout in class.'); (2) (*refuse*) **-gaana,**
eg. Maama we yamugaana okuva awaka. ('His
mother forbade him to leave the house.'); (3) (*ban*)
-wera, *eg.* Abaana baabawera okufuluma geeti.
('They forbade the children to go out of the gate.')
be forbidden *Use* **-kkirizibwa** ('be allowed') *in neg*
(**N21**), *eg.* Tekikkirizibwa kuleekaana mu kibiina.
('It is forbidden to shout in class.'). *See* taboo (be)

forbidden *adj* (1) (*banned*) **-were**; (2) (*taboo*) **-a**
omuzizo

¹**force** *n* (1) (*strength*) **amaanyi** *n6*; (2) (*compulsion*)
obuwaze *n14* apply force (to) **-kkatira**, *eg.*
Yakkatira essanduuko esobole okusiba. ('She
applied force to the case to shut it.') by force
olw'empaka, (*emphasising compulsion*)
olw'obuwaze take away by force (*someone
unwilling*) **-kaazakaaza**

²**force** *vt* **-waliriza**, *eg.* Yawaliriza abaana okugenda
mu ssomero. ('He forced the children to go to
school.'), **-kakaabiriza** force entry (*through*)
-menya, *eg.* Nnasuula ekisumuluzo ne mmenya
oluggi lw'ennyumba yange. ('I lost the key and
forced entry into my house.). *See* break into force
in (*something that does not fit easily*) **-kakaatika,**
eg. Yakakaatika engoye mu ssanduuko. ('She forced
the clothes into the case.') force into **-wagaanya,**

eg. Nnawagaanya omukono gwange mu kituli. ('I
forced my arm into the hole.') force oneself
-eewaliriza, -eekakaba. *See* nerve oneself force
oneself on (*impose oneself*) **-eepaatiika** force
oneself through (*eg. a crowd or vegetation*)
-waguza, *eg.* Abayizzi baawaguza ensiko. ('The
hunters forced their way through the bush.'),
-eeyigaanya be forced **-walirizibwa, -kakibwa**

¹**ford** *n* **awasomokerwa** *n16*, **aw'okusomokera** *n16*,
w'osomokera *n16*

²**ford** *vt* **-somoka**

forebear *n* **jjajja** *n1*

foreboding of death *n* **ekyebikiro** *n7*

¹**forecast** *n* **enteebereza** *n9* weather forecast
enteebereza y'obudde

²**forecast** *vt* **-teebereza**

forehead *n* **ekyenyi** *n7*, (*protruding*) **empumi** *n9*
person with protruding forehead **ow'empumi** *n1*

foreign *adj* **-gwira**, *eg.* emmere engwira ('foreign
food') foreign affairs **ensonga z'ebweru** *n10*

foreigner *n* **omugwira** *n1*, **munnaggwanga** *n1*

foreman *n* **nnampala** *n1*

forest *n* **ekibira** *n7*. *The title of the traditional head
forester of the Kabaka is* **Kasenge**.

forestall *vt* **-gema**

foretell *vt* **-lagula** be foretold **-lagulwa**

forewarn *vt* **-labula** be forewarned **-labuka**

¹**forge** (*metal workshop*) *n* **essasa** *n5*

²**forge** *vt* (1) (*counterfeit*) **-gingirira**; (2) (*make from
metal*) **-weesa** forge a signature **-gingirira**
omukono

forged (*counterfeit*) *adj* **-gingirire**

forgery *n* **ekigingirire** *n7*

forget *vt* **-eerabira** make forget **-eerabiza**

forgive (*also* let off) *vt* **-sonyiwa** be forgiven
-sonyiyibwa

forgo *vt* **-eerekereza**

fork (*cutlery*) *n* **ewuuma** *n9*

¹**form** *n* (1) (*shape; way something has been made*)
enkola *n9*; (2) (*shape; way something has grown*)
enkula *n9*; (3) (*class in school*) **ekibiina** *n7*. *See*
type

²**form** (*make*) *vt* **-kola** form a skin **-kwata olubibi,**
eg. Amata gakutte olubibi. ('The milk has formed a
skin.'), (*crust on left-over matooke*) **-bembeera**
form from clay **-bumba**

former *adj.* *Use verb* **-li** *or* **-ba** ('be') *according to
tense* (**N20.1**) *in rel* (**N7.1**), *eg.* Eyali omwami we
musawo. ('Her former husband was a doctor.')

formerly *adv* **edda**

fornicate *vi* **-yenda**

fornication *n* **obwenzi** *n14*

fornicator *n* **omwenzi** *n1*

fort *n* **ekigo** *n7*

forthright *adj* **-eesimbu**

fortitude *n* **obugumu** *n14*

fortunate *adj* **-a omukisa** fortunate person
ow'omukisa *n1* be fortunate **-eesiima**

fortunately *adv* **eky'omukisa** but fortunately **kasita**

fortune *n* (1) (*luck*) **omukisa** *n3*; (2) (*wealth*) **obugagga** *n14* fortune-teller **omulaguzi** *n1*. *See* prophet fortune-telling **obulaguzi** *n14* consult a fortune-teller **-eeraguza** good fortune **eggwiiso** *n5* have good fortune **-gwa mu bintu** tell someone's fortune **-lagula**

forty *num* (**amakumi**) **ana** (**N8.1**)

forward (*in front*) *adv* **mu maaso** go forward **-eeyongera mu maaso**

forwardness (*of a person*) *n* **okweyisaawo** *n15*

¹foul (*bad*) *adj* **-bi**

²foul (*eg. in football*) *n* **ekisobyo** *n7*

found *See* find

foundation *n* **omusingi** *n3*

founder *n* **omutandisi** *n1*

fountain pen *n* **ekkalaamu ya bwino** *n9*

four *num* **nnya**. *The stem is* **-na** (*with numeral concord* **N4.2**) (**N8.1**), *eg.* **ebintu bina** ('*four things*'). four hundred **bikumi bina** (**N8.1**) four thousand **enkumi nnya**

fourteen *num* **kkumi na nnya, kkumi -na** (*with numeral concord* **N4.2**) (**N8.1**), *eg.* **ebintu kkumi na bina** ('*fourteen things*')

fourth *adj/num* **-a okuna** (**N7.1**), *eg.* **olunaku olw'okuna** ('*fourth day*'). *Elision is sometimes seen, eg.* **olunaku olwokuna** ('*fourth day*').

fourthly *adv* **ekyokuna**

fowl (*chicken*) *n* **enkoko** *n9*

fracas *n* **akavuvuŋŋano** *n12*

fraction *n* **ekitundu** *n7*

¹fracture *n* **obuvune** *n14*

²fracture *vt* **-menya** be fractured **-menyeka**

fragment (*eg. broken-off piece*) *n* **ekipapajjo** *n7*, (*small*) **akapapajjo** *n12*. *See* siftings

fragrance *n* **akawoowo** *n12*

frame (*of door/window*) *n* **omwango** *n3*

framework *n* **ekitindiro** *n7*, (*of sticks over termite mound, built when catching flying ants*) **omugala** *n3*. *The following refer to the framework of a mud and wattle wall:* (1) (*framework as a whole*) **ebizizi** *n8*, **enzizi** *n10*; (2) (*single course in framework; band of reeds*) **ekizizi** *n7*, **oluzizi** *n11*. make a framework **-tindira** put framework in pot (*to support food bundle during steaming*) **-tindira entamu** put up framework for a house **-baga ennyumba**

franc *n* **ffalanga** *n5*

France *n* **Bufalansa** *n9*

francolin (*type of bird*) *n* **enkwale** *n9*

frankly *adv* **mu mazima**

frantic, be (*having much to do*) *vi* **-buguutana**

fraud *n* **obubi** *n14*

fraudster *n* **omukumpanya** *n1*, (*one who deliberately fails to repay a debt*) **omulyazaamaanyi** *n1*. *See* con man; hypocrite

fraudulent, be *vi* **-wampanya**, (*through not revealing information*) **-kuusa**

fray *vt* **-sensula** be frayed **-sensuka**

frayed *adj* **-sensufu**

¹free (*without charge*) *adj* **-a obwereere**, *eg.* **ekirabo kya bwereere** ('*free gift*') freed person (*eg. from jail*) **omute** *n1*

²free *vt* **-ta**, *eg.* **Omusibe bamutadde.** ('*They freed the prisoner.*'), (*tethered or penned animal*) **-yimbula**, *eg.* **Baayimbula embuzi.** ('*They freed the goats.*'), (*animal on rope or leash*) **-sumulula** free oneself (1) (*person from hold, or animal from trap*) **-eetakkuluza**; (2) (*from being restricted*) **-eesumattula**, *eg.* **Embuzi yeesumattudde.** ('*The goat has freed itself.*'); (3) (*from being tied*) **-kutula**, *eg.* **Embuzi ekutudde.** ('*The goat has freed itself.*') be set free (*released*) **-teebwa**

freedom *n* **eddembe** *n5*, (*to do what one likes*) **ebbeetu** *n5*

free-hand *n* **ebbeetu** *n5*, *eg.* **Abaana be yabawa ebbeetu okukola kye baagala.** ('*He has given his children a free-hand to do what they like.*')

freeze *vi* **-kwata bbalaafu/omuzira**

French (*language*) *n* **Olufalansa** *n11* French person **Omufalansa** *n1*

frequency (*of a broadcast*) *n* **omukutu** *n3*, **amayengo** *n6*

frequently *adv* **emirundi mingi**

fresh *adj* (1) (*of milk*) **-lamu**, *eg.* **amata amalamu** ('*fresh milk*'); (2) (*of news, newly brewed beer, etc.*) **-su**, *eg.* **amawulire amasu** ('*fresh news*'); (3) (*of fish or fruit*) **-lungi**

fret (*worry*) *vi* **-eeraliikirira**

friction between people *n* **akakuubagano** *n12*

Friday *n* **Olwokutaano** *n11*, **Fulayide**

fridge *n* **firiigi** *n9*

fried *adj* **-siike**, *eg.* **amagi amasiike** ('*fried eggs*')

friend *n* **ow'omukwano** *n1* friend of **mukwano** *n3* (*with pos* **N12**), *eg.* **mukwano gwange** ('*my friend*') close friend of **munywanyi** *n7* (*with pos* **N12**), *eg.* **munywanyi wange** ('*my friend*'), **wa kinywi** *n1* make friends (with) **-kwana**, *eg.* **Nnamukwana.** ('*I made friends with her.*') my friend **munnange**, your friend **munno**, *etc.* (*stem* **-nna-** **N12**) my friend *form of address* **mwana wattu**

friendship *n* **omukwano** *n3*, (*through compatability; bonded*) **ekinywi** *n7*

fright *n* **entiisa** *n9*, (*when startled*) **ekyekango** *n7* give a fright to **-kuba entiisa**, *eg.* **Omwana yatukuba entiisa bwe yagwa mu muliro.** ('*The child gave us a fright when she fell into the fire.*')

frighten *vt* **-tiisa**

frightened *adj*. *Use* **-tya** ('*fear*') *in rel* (**N7.1**), *eg.* **abantu abatidde** ('*frightened people*') be frightened **-tya**. *See* startled

frightening *adj* **-a entiisa** something frightening **ekyentiisa** *n7*

frightful (*very bad*) *adj* **-bi ennyo**

fringe (*on clothing*) *n* **akajwenge** *n12*

frisk *vt* -yaza mu mpale
frock *n* ekiteeteeyi *n7*
frog *n* ekikere *n7* tree frog olulenga *n11*
froghopper (*type of insect*) *n* entonnyeze *n9*
frogmarch *vt* -kaazakaaza
frolic *vi* -ligita, tiguka. *See* tumble about
from *pre* okuva, *eg. Yakola okuva essaawa emu okutuuka essaawa bbiri. ('He worked from seven to eight o'clock.').* 'okuva' *referring to place can be followed by either 'mu', 'ku' or (with place name) 'e', eg.:* (1) okuva mu, *Yatambula okuva mu kyalo. ('He walked from the village.');* (2) okuva ku, *eg. Ennyanja ogiraba okuva ku lusozi luno. ('You can see the lake from this hill.);* (3) okuva e, *eg. Yatambula okuva e Masaka. ('He walked from Masaka.'). Two verbs can be equivalent to 'from'* (1) -yima (*'do from elsewhere'), eg. Yayima Masaka n'atuweereza ekirabo. ('He sent us a present from Masaka.');* (2) -sinziira (*'do from a given point'), eg. Yasinziira Masaka n'atuweereza ekirabo. ('He sent us a present from Masaka.'). 'From' is incorporated in the basic meanings of certain verbs, eg.* come from -va from now on okuva kaakati from over (*on the other side of, eg. a valley*) emitala wa from time to time buli kiseera
front front (court)yard oluggya lw'emiryango *n11* front door oluggi lw'emiryango *n11* (in the) front part of the home emiryango front room (*of a house*) eddiiro ly'emiryango *n5* in front mu maaso in front of mu maaso ga, (*before pronoun* N11.4) mu maaso ga-, *eg. Yatuula mu maaso gaffe. ('He sat in front of us.')* in front of the hearth wamberi
frontier *n* ensalo *n9*
frost *n* omuzira *n3*
froth *n* ejjovu *n5*, ekyovu *n7*, ebyovu *n8*, (*unwanted, from roasted sorghum in beer making*) enkanja *n10*
frown *vi* -siba emitaafu frown line (*on forehead*) omutaafu *n3*
frozen *adj. Use* -kwata bbalaafu (*'freeze') in rel* (N7.1), *eg. enkoko enzite ekutte bbalaafu ('frozen chicken')*
frugal with, be *vt* -kekkereza, *eg. Akekkereza sukaali. ('She is frugal with the sugar.')*
¹**fruit** *n* ekibala *n7* fruit bat ekinyira *n7* fruit fly akabu *n12* fruit tree omuti ogw'ebibala *n3*
²**fruit** (*or bear fruit*) *vi* (1) (*of plants other than bananas*) -bala, *eg. Omuyembe gubaze. ('The mango tree is fruiting.');* (2) (*of banana plants*) -ssa, *eg. Ekitooke kissizza. ('The banana plant is fruiting.')*
fruitful (*useful*) *adj* -a omugaso
fruitless (*useless*) *adj* (1) *Use* obwereere (*'fruitlessly'), eg. Nnatambulidde bwereere. ('My journey was fruitless.');* (2) *Refer to* omugaso (*'benefit') with neg* N21, *eg. Okutambula kwange*

tekwabaddemu mugaso. (*'My journey was fruitless.'*)
fruitlessly (*or* uselessly) *adv* bwereere
fry *vt* -siika, -kuba ekijiiko
frying pan *n* fulampeni *n9*
fuel (*eg. petrol*) *n* amafuta *n6. See* charcoal; firewood; gas
fugitive *n* omubombi *n1*
fulfil *vt* -tuukiriza
full *adj* -jjuvu, *eg. jjaaga enzijuvu ('full jug'), (of food, of a person).*-kkufu full-grown (*adult*) *adj* -kulu full serving musera (*invariable adjective*), *eg. Mpa ekikopo kya sukaali musera. ('Give me a full cup of sugar.')* full stop akatonnyeze *n12*, akasirisa *n12* be full -jjula, *eg. Jjaaga ejjudde. ('The jug is full.'), (of food)* -kkuta, (*of heat, happiness, etc.*) -bugaana. *See* crowded; stuffed with (be)
fumble about (*struggling to do something difficult*) *vi* -kikiitana
fumes *n* omukka *n3*
fumigate *vt* -fuuyira
fun *n* ebinyuma *n8*, ebisanyusa *n8* have fun -nyumirwa
¹**function** *n* (1) (*formal event*) omukolo *n3*; (2) (*role; job*) omulimu *n3*
²**function** (*work*) *vi* -kola become functional -lamuka, *eg. Ekyuma kiramuse. ('The machine is functional.')* make functional -lamusa
fundamentals *n* ennono *n9*
funeral *n* okuziika *n15* funeral rites olumbe *n11* conclude funeral rites -yabya olumbe
fungus *n* (1) (*mould*) obukuku *n14*; (2) (*type of whitish-yellow bracket fungus, grows on dead wood; second totem of Lugave Clan*) amaleere *n6*; (3) (*white fungus inside termite mounds*) ebikanja *n8. See* mushroom stinkhorn fungus omutima gw'ettaka *n3*
funnel *n* omubinikiro *n3*, omuzindaalo *n3*, (*small*) akabinikiro *n12. See* cone funnel-like structure (*of folded leaf or paper, used eg. for catching termites*) olusoggo *n11*
funny faces, make -eeginga, -eekonga, -eemoola
furious, become *vi* -eecwacwana, (*very*) -swakira. *See* angry
furl *vt* -zinga
furnace *n* ekyokero *n7*, (*blacksmith's*) ttanuulu *n9*
furniture *n* ebintu by'omu nnyumba *n8* furniture workshop ebbajjiro *n5*
further *adv. Use* -yongera (*'continue'), eg. Tujja kwongera okukuteesako. ('We will discuss this matter further.')* further than there okusukkawo, *eg. Yagenda okusukkawo. ('He went further than there.')* go further (*in moving*) -eeyongerayo, *eg. Yeeyongerayo mu maaso ku luguudo. ('She went further along the road.')*
furtively *adv* obubba
fury *n* obusungu *n14*

fussy, be (*choosy*) *vi* -eeronda. *See* fastidious
fussing about **akajanja** *n12*   make a fuss -eereega
future, the *n* ekiseera eky'omu maaso *n7*, ebbanga
erijja mu maaso *n5*   in the future **mu maaso, gye
bujja**

G,g

gabble *vi* -sabuliza
Gabon viper *n* essalambwa *n5*
gain (*get*) *vt* -funa. *See* benefit; profit   gain from
-funamu, -ganyulwa
gait *n* entambula *n9*
gale *n* kibuyaga *n1*, (*strong enough to blow things
into the air*) **kikuŋŋunta** *n1*   blow a gale -kunta
gall bladder *n* akalulwe *n12*
gallon *n* ggalani *n9*
gallows *n* akalabba *n12*
gamble *vi* -kuba kkalata/zzaala
gambler *n* omukubi wa kkalata/zzaala *n1*
gambling *n* kkalata *n1*
game *n* omuzannyo *n3*, (*of short duration*)
akazannyo *n12*, (*type of board game*) **omweso** *n3*
(*played with seeds* **empiki** *n10*). *Games played by
children include:* (1) (*tumbling about; played by
boys with short sticks*) **embirigo** *n9*; (2) (*tag*)
kawuna *n12*; (3) (*dressing up to scare*) **ekikulejje**
n7; (4) (*someone plays dead*) **omuzannyo gwa
ssemufu**; (5) (*hopscotch*) **kkongojja** *n1*; (6)
(*sliding down a steep slope on a banana stem
'omogogo'*) **gogolo** *n1*; (7) (*with spinning tops*)
enkuyo *n10*.   game pit (*dug to trap animals*)
obuya *n14*   place where games are played
aw'okuzannyira *n16*   play games (*not being
serious*) -zannya buzannyi
gang *n* ekikuukuulu *n7*
gaol *See* jail
gap *n* omwagaanya *n3*, omuwaatwa *n3*, (*small*)
akaagaanya *n12*. *See* tooth (*for gaps relating to
teeth*)
gape (*be open-mouthed*) *vi* -yasaamirira
garage *n* eggalagi *n9*
garbage *n* ebisasiro *n8*, ebisaaniiko *n8*
garden *n* ennimiro *n9*, (*banana*) olusuku *n11*,
(*overgrown*) ekisambu *n7*, (*long overgrown*)
ekikande *n7*. *See* plot
²**garden** *vi* -lima
gardener *n* omulimi *n1*
gargle *vi* -munyunguza
garlic *n* katunguluccumu *n1*. *See* clove
garment *n* ekyambalo *n7*, ekyokwambala *n7*. *See*
cloth; wraparound   worn-out garment (*used for
hunting, etc.*) **akajumbi** *n12*. *See* rag
gas *n* (1) (*eg. oxygen*) omukka *n3*; (2) (*fuel for
cooking, etc.*) ggaasi *n1*. *See* oxygen; petrol
gash (*cut made by blade*) *n* olubale *n11*
gasp *vi* -laakiira

gate *n* geeti *n9*   main gate **wankaaki** *n1*
gatekeeper *n* omuggazi *n1*
gather (*forage*) *vt* -saka, *eg*. Yagenda okusaka
ebyokulya okuva mu kibira. ('*She went to gather
things to eat from the forest.*'). *See* assemble;
collect   gather firewood -sennya (*or* -tyaba) enku
gather in contributions -sonda, *eg*. Basonda essente
okuzimba essomero. ('*They are gathering money to
build the school.*')   gather in great numbers
-eekuluumulula, *eg*. Ebire byekuluumulula
ng'enkuba egenda okutonnya. ('*Clouds are
gathering for the rains.*')   gather together (1) *vi*
-kuŋŋaana, *eg*. Abantu bakuŋŋaana. ('*The people
are gathering together.*'); (2) *vt* -kuŋŋaanya, *eg*.
Omukadde yakuŋŋaanya baganda be bonna. ('*The
old man gathered together all his descendants.*')
gather up indisciminently -kukumba, *eg*.
Yakukumba engoye zonna ennungi n'embi
n'azitwala. ('*He gathered up all the clothes, good
and bad, and took them away.*')
gatherer (*eg. of wild food*) *n* omukuŋŋaanya *n1*
gathering (*meeting*) *n* olukuŋŋaana *n11*   enjoyable
social gathering **ekinyumu** *n7*
gave *See* give
gay (*happy*) *adj* -sanyufu   be gay -sanyuka
gaze, be in a -tangaalirira. *See* look at; stare
gear (*of vehicle*) *n* ggiya *n9*
gecko *n* ekinya *n7*
general (*rank in army*) *n* jenero *n1*
generally *adv* okutwalira awamu
generation *n* omulembe *n3*, *eg*. omulembe
gw'abaana baffe ('*our children's generation*')
generosity *n* obugabi *n14*   be generous -gaba
generous person **omugabi** *n1*
Genesis (*book of*) *n* Olubereberye *n11*
genet *n* akasimba *n12*
genie *n* ejjiini *n5*
gentle *adj* -wombeefu. *See* calm   gentle person
omuwombeefu *n1*
gentleman *n* omwami *n1*
gentleness *n* obuwombeefu *n14*
gently *adv* (1) ekimpoowooze; (2) *Use*
-eegendereza ('*be careful*'), *eg*. Yateeka omwana
wansi nga yeegendereza. ('*She put the baby down
gently.*')
genuine *adj* -a ddala, *eg*. sipeeya wa Toyota owa
ddala ('*genuine Toyota spare part*')
gerbil *n* akayozi *n12*
germ *n* akawuka (akatalabika) *n12*
German *n* (1) (*person*) Omugirimaani *n1*; (2)
(*language*) Olugirimaani *n11*
Germany *n* Bugirimaani *n9*, Girimaani *n9*
germinate *vi* -mera. *See* sprout
get *vt* (got) -funa, *eg*. Ŋŋenda okufuna ssente. ('*I am
going to get some money.*'). *See* benefit from;
bring; fetch   get away -paala, *eg*. Embuzi ekutudde
n'epaala. ('*The goat broke free and got away.*').
See escape; leave   get better (*improved in health*)

-ssuuka, *eg. Leero assuuseemu. ('She is a bit better today.'). See* cured   get for *-funira, eg. Yamufunira enku. ('He got firewood for her.')*   get from (1) (*benefit from*) **-funamu**, *eg. Mu kukola ku leediyo, yafunamu kumanyibwa. ('She got well known from working on the radio.'),* **-ganyulwa**; (2) (*take from*) **-ggya**, *eg. Nja kukiggya mu kabada. ('I will get it from the cupboard')*   get into (*enter*) **-yingira**, *eg. Bonna baayingira mu bbaasi. ('They all got into the bus.')*   get out **-vaamu**, *eg. Twagala kuvaamu mu takisi. ('We want to get out of the taxi.'),* (*at a place*) **-viiramu**, *eg. Twagala kuviiramu ku kkanisa. ('We want to get out at the church.'). See* escape   get out of the way of **-viira**, *eg. Yaviira bbaasi. ('She got out of the way of the bus.')*   get ready (*prepare oneself*) **-eetegeka**   get somewhere (*make progress with a task*) **-senvula**   get there (*arrive at a place*) **-tuukayo**   get to (*arrive*) **-tuuka**, *eg. Ebbaasi etuuse e Masaka. ('The bus has got to Masaka.')*   get together (*assemble*) (1) *vi* **-kuŋŋaana**, *eg. Twetaaga okukuŋŋaana tuteese eby'embaga. ('We need to get together to discuss wedding matters.');* (2) *vt* **-kuŋŋaanya**, *eg. Yatukuŋŋanya okuteesa eby'embaga. ('He got us together to discuss the wedding.')*   get up (1) (*stand up*) **-yimuka**; (2) (*from bed*) **-va mu buliri**. *See* wake up   get up early (*in the morning*) **-keera**   get used to (*accustomed*) **-manyiira**

ghee *n* omuzigo *n3*

ghost *n* (1) (*spirit of departed person*) omuzimu *n3*; (2) (*nature spirit*) omusambwa *n3*. *See* spirit   come back as a ghost **-luluma**, *eg. Taata yaluluma. ('Father has returned.')*   Holy Ghost Omwoyo Omutukuvu *n3*

giant *adj* **-nene ennyo**

giddiness *n* kammunguluze *n1*, kantoolooze *n1*

gift *n* ekirabo *n7*, ekitone *n7*. *See* contribution; present   gift from bridegroom to bride's parents (*on morning of wedding*) kaasuzekatya *n1*   gift of appreciation akasiimo *n12*   gifts offered to the Kabaka amakula *n6*

gigantic *adj* **-nene ennyo**

giggle *vi* **-sekaseka**

gin (*Ugandan*) *n* walagi *n1*, enguuli *n9*

gin cotton **-sunsula ppamba**

ginger (*spice*) *n* entangawuuzi *n9*

ginnery *n* ginale *n9*

giraffe *n* entugga *n9*

gird oneself (*for action*) *vr* **-fungiza**, *eg. Yafungiza alabirire abaana be yekka. ('She girded herself to look after her children single-handedly.')*

girdle (*belt of cloth, used by women for keeping money*) *n* omukandala *n3*

girl *n* omuwala *n1*, (*very pretty*) nnalulungi *n1*

girlfriend *n* muganzi *n1* (*with pos N12*), *eg. muganzi wange ('my girlfriend'),* omwagalwa *n1*   favourite girlfriend kabiite *n1*

girth *n* obunene *n14*

give *vt* (*gave*) **-wa**. *See* contribute   give a present **-tona ekirabo**   give away/out **-gaba**, (*extravagantly*) **-gabangula**   give in (*surrender*) **-eewaayo**   give items to a bride who is starting a home **-sibirira entanda**   give money in appreciation to (*eg. dancer*) **-fuuwa ssente**   give notice of visiting (to) **-laga**, *eg. Tumaze okulaga. ('We have given notice of visiting.')*   give on behalf of **-weera**, *eg. Mpeera Musoke essente ze yeetaaga. ('Give Musoke the money that he needs on my behalf.')*   give regards to **-labira**   give to **-gabira**, *eg. Agabira abaavu ssente. ('She gives money to the poor.'),* (*as a present*) **-tonera**, *eg. Yabatonera ekirabo. ('She gave them a present.')*   give to all **-bunya**, *eg. Tubunyizza emmere abantu bonna. ('We have given food to everyone.')*   give too little (to) **-kena**, *eg. Abagenyi yabakena emmere. ('She gave the visitors too little food.'). See* mean (be)   give up (1) (*stop doing something*) **-lekera awo**, *eg. Yalekedde awo okunywa sukaali mu kisiibo. ('He gave up taking sugar for Lent.');* (2) (*abandon*) **-va ku**, *eg. Yava ku kirowoozo ky'okufuuka omusawo. ('He gave up the idea of becoming a doctor.'). See* abort; abstain; disheartened (become); lose hope; surrender   give up one's seat for **-segulira**   give way (*collapse, eg. of wall or the ground*) **-yigulukuka**   be given **-weebwa**   something given ekiweebwayo *n7*

giver *n*. *Use* omuntu (*'person'*) *with* **-wa** (*'give'*) *in rel* (**N7.1**), *eg. abantu abawa ('givers'),* (*generous person*) omugabi *n1*   giver of a feast omugabuzi *n1*

gizzard *n* enkoko enkulu *n9*

glad *adj* **-sanyufu**   be glad **-sanyuka**   be glad for **-sanyukira**

gladden *vt* **-sanyusa**

gladness *n* essanyu *n9*

glance (at) *vit* **-suuliza eriiso**. *See* peep

gland *n* ensulo *n9*   swollen lymph gland ensanjabavu *n9*

glare (*by a person*) *vi* **-tunula enkaliriza**   glare at **-tunuulira enkaliriza**

glass *n* eggiraasi *n9*   glass chimney (*of lamp*) ekirawuli *n7*

glasses (*spectacles*) *n* gaalubindi *n10*

¹gleam (*of light*) *n* ekimyanso *n7*

²gleam *vi* **-myamyansa**

glean *vt* **-londalonda**

glide (*as a bird*) *vi* **-seeyeeya mu bbanga**   glide away (*as a snake*) **-eemulula**

glimmer (*as a star*) *vi* **-munyeenya**

glisten *vi* **-meremeenya**

glitter *vi* **-masamasa**

gloom (*semi-darkness*) *n* obukwafu *n14*

gloominess (*glumness*) *n* eggume *n5*

gloomy (*also* glum) *adj* **-a eggume**. *See* dark   gloomy person ow'eggume *n1*

glorify

glorify *vt* **-gulumiza**
glory *n* **ettendo** *n5*
glossy, be (*of the skin*) *vi* **-nyereketa**, **-nyerettuka**
¹**glue** *n* **ggaamu** *n1*
²**glue** *vt* **-kwasa**
glum *See* gloomy
glutton *See* eat
gnat *n* (1) (*lake fly*) **essami** *n5*; (2) (*type that buzzes around the head annoyingly*) **akazungirizi** *n12*. *See* fly
gnaw *vt* **-keketa**
go *vi* (*went*) **-genda**, *eg. Tugenda mu kyalo. ('We are going to the village.')*, (*in a certain direction*) **-dda**, *eg. Oluguudo ludda ku kkono. ('The road goes to the left.')*, (*as far as*) **-koma**, *eg. Twakoma ku kyalo ekisooka. ('We went as far as the first village.')*. *See* start   **go after** (*follow*) **-goberera**, *eg. Nja kumugoberera e Masaka. ('I will go to Masaka after her.')*   **go around** (1) (*encircle*) **-eetooloola**, *eg. Ekisenge kyetooloola olubiri. ('The wall goes around the palace.')*; (2) (*be distributed to all*) **-buna**, *eg. Emmere ebunye. ('The food went around.')*; (3) (*everywhere purposefully*) **-talaaga**, *eg. Yatalaaga amasomero okumanya obuzibu bwe galina. ('She went around the schools to find the problems they face.')*. *See* wander; (4) (*make a detour*) **-eebalama**, (*to avoid being seen*) **-eebalaamiriza**   **go astray** **-waba**   **go away for a while** **-eewungula**   **go badly** (*of affairs*) **-gootana**   **go back** **-ddayo**, *eg. Azzeeyo mu kyalo. ('He has gone back to the village.')*. *See* return   **go beyond** *See* protrude   **go down** (1) (*descend*) **-kka**, *eg. Enjuba ekka. ('The sun is going down.')*; (2) (*subside*) **-teewulukuka**, *eg. Ekizimba kiteewulukuse. ('The swelling has gone down.')*; (3) (*deteriorate*) **-ddirira**, *eg. Omutindo gw'engoye guddiridde. ('The standard of clothing has gone down.')*. *See* reduced (be)   **go down a slope** **-serengeta**   **go everywhere** (*travel all over*) **-talaaga wonna**   **go for** (*fetch*) **-kima**, **-nona**   **go from** **-va**, *eg. Yavudde mu nnyumba ku ssaawa bbiri. ('He went from the house at 8 o'clock.')*. *See* leave   **go further** **-eeyongerayo**, *eg. Nneeyongerayo ku luguudo. ('I went further along the road.')*   **go into** (*enter*) **-yingira**   **go of one's own accord** (*or go without being invited*) **-eetwala**   **go off** (1) (*of something under tension, eg. a trap*) **-masuka**, (*making a sound*) **-banduka**; (2) (*go sour*) **-kaatuuka**, *eg. Omubisi gukaatuuse. ('The juice has gone off.')*; (3) (*of milk*) **-fa**, *eg. Amata gafudde. ('The milk has gone off.')*; (4) (*of cooked food*) **-gaga**, *eg. Emmere egaze. ('The food has gone off.')*. *See* explode; leave   **go off the track** (*astray*) **-waba**   **go on and on** (*of rain*) **-fudemba**   **go oneself** **-eegenderayo**, *eg. Nsazeewo okwegenderayo ku dduuka. ('I decided to go to the shop myself.')*   **go out** (*of a light or fire*) **-zikira**, *eg. Omuliro guzikidde. ('The fire has gone out.')*

go out through **-fulumira**, *eg. Baafulumira emiryango. ('They went out through the front door.')*   **go outside** (*exit*) **-fuluma**, *eg. Bafuluma ebweru. ('They are going outside.')*   **go over a hill** **-vvuunuka**   **go past** **-yisa**, *eg. Twayisa edduuka yaabwe nga tuli mu mmotoka. ('We went past their shop while we were in the car.')*, **-yita ku**   **go personally** (*to a person*) **-tuukirira**, *eg. Nze nnamutuukirira ne mmusaba ssente. ('I went to him personally to ask for money.')*   **go to** (*arrive at*) **-dda**, *eg. Akakubo kano katuuka e Makindye? ('Does this path go to Makindye?')*   **go up** (*ascend*) **-linnya**   **go uphill** **-yambuka**   **go where not wanted** (*or allowed*) **-saalimbira**. *See* trespass   **go wherever** (*someone*) **goes** **-londoola**
goal *n* (1) (*aim*) **ekigendererwa** *n7*; (2) (*in football*) **eggoolo** *n9*
goat *n* **embuzi** *n9*, (*small/young*) **akabuzi** *n12*, (*with two-coloured coat*) **embuzi eya bitanga**, (*with three-coloured coat*) **embuzi eya katangambale**   **goat meat** **ennyama y'embuzi** *n9*   **billy goat** **sseddume w'embuzi** *n1*   **Mr Goat** **Wambuzi** *n1*
goatee (*type of beard*) *n* **akalevu** *n12*
goatherd *n* **omulunzi w'embuzi** *n1*, (*chief, of the Kabaka*) **Kawuka** *n1 title*
gobble up (*food*) *vt* (1) (*with enjoyment*) **-miringusa**; (2) (*through hunger*) **-kavvula**
god *n* (1) (*as the Creator*) **Katonda** *n1*; (2) (*Christian; Lord God*) **Mukama Katonda** *n1*; (3) (*Muslim*) **Allah** *n1*, **Mungu** *n1*; (4) (*deity in Kiganda traditional religion*) **lubaale** *n1*. *There are many lubaale, among them (and associated phenomena):* (*death and disease*) **Walumbe**, (*earthquakes*) **Musisi**, (*hunting*) **Ddungu**, (*Lake Victoria; bringer of life*) **Mukasa**, (*Lake Wamala*) **Wamala**, (*plaque*) **Kawumpuli**, (*rainbow*) **Musoke**, (*sky*) **Ggulu**, (*smallpox*) **Kawaali**, (*thunder and lightning*) **Kiwanuka**, (*war*) **Kibuuka**. *There are several names for God, referring to his perceived attributes:* **Ddunda** (*'Chief Herdsman'*), **Liisoddene** (*'Big-eyed'*), **Nnamugereka** (*'Alloter of Fate'*), **Ssewannaku** (*'Thee one with no beginning'*)   **God forbid!** **Kikafuuwe!**
godparent *n* **omuyima** *n1*   **serve as godparent to** **-eeyimirira**
goitre *n* **eddookooli** *n5*
goliath heron (*type of bird*) *n* **ekimbala** *n7*
gold *n* **zaabu** *n1*
golf *n* **goofu** *n9*
gonorrhoea *n* **enziku** *n9*, **enjoka ensajja** *n10*, **baanabagalye** *n1*   **person with gonorrhoea** **omuziku** *n1*
¹**good** *adj* **-lungi**, (*fairly*) **-lungirungi**   **good enough** **-saamusaamu**   **Good gracious!** **Kyokka bannange!**   **good person** **omulungi** *n1*   **be in good order** **-longooka**   **have a good time** **-cakala**   **in good order** *adj* **-longoofu**   **put in good order**

-longoosa

²**good** *n* obulungi *n14* be good (1) (*rather than bad*) -**beera omulungi**; (2) (*should*) -**saanira**, *eg. Osaanidde ogende ewa jjajja wo. ('It would be good if you went to your granny's.'),* -**gwanira** be good that (*advantageous*) -**lyoka** *followed by verb in narrative tense* (**N16**), *eg. Nnalyoka ne ndaba omwami. ('It was good that I saw the chief.')* become good -**longooka**, *eg. Bwe yakula, yalongooka. ('When he grew up, he became good.')* look good (*pleasing*) -**nyuma** look good on -**nyumira**, *eg. Olugoye lumunyumira. ('The dress looks good on her.')*

goodbye *interj* **weeraba** (*pl.* **mweraba**) say goodbye to -**siibula**

goodness *n* **obulungi** *n14*

goods (*things*) *n* **ebintu** *n8*

goose, spur-winged *n* **embaata kabuzi** *n7* goose pimples **olutiko** *n11* develop goose pimples -**mera olutiko**

gooseberry, cape *n* **entuntunu** *n9*

gorge (*on food*) *vi* -**eepiika emmere**

gorgeous look gorgeous -**nyuma** look gorgeous on -**nyumira**

gorilla *n* **ekisodde** *n7*

gospel *n* **enjiri** *n9*

gossip *n* (1) (*idle talk*) **olugambo** *n11*; (2) (*person*) **ow'olugambo** *n1*

got *See* get

gourd (*also* calabash) (*plant*) *n* **ekiryo** *n7*. *The following are fruit types:* (1) (*large*) **ekita** *n7*; (2) (*with neck, used for holding drinks; one variety used as a musical horn*) **endeku** *n9*; (3) (*small, edible*) **omungu** *n3*; (4) (*wild type; fruit inedible and very hard*) **akatanga** *n12*. *The following are made from gourds:* (1) (*bowl*) **empaawo** *n9*; (2) (*ladle or cup*) **akendo** *n12*; (3) (*long-necked gourd with hole cut for drinking*) **olwendo** *n11*.

govern *vt* -**fuga** be governable -**fugika** be governed -**fugibwa**

governance *n* **obufuzi** *n14*. *See* leadership way of governing **enfuga** *n9*

government *n* **gavumenti** *n9*. *The traditional units of government in Buganda are:* **essaza** *n5* ('*county*'), **eggombolola** *n9* ('*sub-county*'), **omuluka** *n3* ('*parish*'). government department **ekitongole kya gavumenti** *n7*

governor *n* **gavana** *n1*

gown *n* (1) (*traditional dress of Baganda men*) **ekkanzu** *n9*; (2) (*sign of office; also academic gown*) **egganduula** *n5*

grab *vt* -**pakula**, -**kwakkula**, *eg. Omubbi yankwakkuddeko ensawo yange n'abulira mu bantu. ('The thief grabbed my bag and disappeared into the crowd.'). See* loot; snatch

¹**grade** (*of product*) *n* **omutindo** *n3*, *eg. engoye za mutindo mulungi ('good grade clothes')* low grade **omutindo gwa wansi**

²**grade** (*put in categories*) *vt* -**gereka**

grading *n* **engereka** *n9*

gradually *adv* **empolampola**

graduate *n* **owa digiri** *n1*

grain *n* **empeke** *n9*, *eg. empeke ya kasooli ('grain of maize'),* (*small*) **akaweke** *n12* grain of doubt **akakunkuna** *n12*, *eg. Taliimu kakunkuna. ('There is not a grain of doubt.')* grain of sand **akaweke k'omusenyu**

gram (*unit of weight*) **gulaamu** *n9* green gram (*type of pulse*) **mpokya** *n1*

grammar *n* **ggulama** *n1*

gramophone *n* **ggulamufooni** *n9*

granadilla, giant (*resembles a large passion fruit*) *n* **wujju** *n1*

granary *n* **ekyagi** *n7*

grandchild *n* **omuzzukulu** *n1* grandchild of **muzzukulu** (*with pos* **N12**), *eg. muzzukulu wange ('my grandchild')* great grandchild **omuzzukulu omwana** great-great grandchild **omuzzukulu nakabirye** have a grandchild -**zzukuza**

granddaughter *n* **omuzzukulu omuwala** *n1*

grandfather *n* **jjajja omusajja** *n1*

grandmother *n* **jjajja omukazi** *n1*

grandparent *n* **jjajja** *n1*

grandson *n* **omuzzukulu omulenzi** *n1*

grant *vt* (1) (*give*) -**wa**; (2) (*agree*) -**kkiriza** grant a divorce -**gattulula obufumbo** grant asylum -**wa obubudamo** grant permission -**wa olukusa**

grape (*vine/fruit*) *n* **omuzabbibu** *n3*

grapefruit *n* **sseccungwa** *n1*

grasp (*hold*) *vt* -**kwata**. *See* understand

grass *n* (1) (*general term*) **omuddo** *n3*; (2) (*as used for thatch, fodder, in brewing or strewn on floor*) **essubi** *n5*; (3) (*piece of dry grass*) **ekisubi** *n7* (*small* **akasubi** *n12, long* **olusubi** *n11*). *Types of grass include:* (1) (*couch grass; Digitaria scalarum*) **olumbugu** *n11*; (2) (*small creeping type; Cynodon*) **kalandalugo** *n1*; (3) (*elephant grass; Pennisetum purpureum*) **ekisagazi** *n7*; (4) (*lawn grass with narrow leaves; Cynodon transvaalensis*) **jjiija** *n1*; (5) (*lemon grass; Cymbopogon citratus*) **ekisubi** *n7*; (6) (*lawn grass; paspalum*) **paasipalamu** *n1*; (7) (*with bristles on spikelets; Setaria verticillata*) **ekikwatandiga** *n7*; (8) (*spear grass; Imperata cylindrica*) **essenke** *n5* (*flowering stem* **akaseekende** *n12*); (9) (*lemon-scented, spread on floors; Cymbopogon nardus*) **etteete** *n5*; (10) (*guinea grass, used for making brooms; Panicum maximum*) **mukonzikonzi** *n1*; (11) (*Brachiara decumbens*) **kyukyu** *n1*; (12) (*grows in rocky places near lakes; used for making baskets*) **obuyanja** *n14*; (13) (*difficult weed to remove; Sporobolus africanus*) **kagiri** *n1*; (14) (*type spread on floors of shrines*) **kalenziwe** *n1*. area of grass (1) (*cut*) **awasaawe** *n16*; (2) (*of essenke*) **olusenke** *n11*. *See* lawn

grasshopper *n* (1) (*types not eaten*) **ejjanzi** *n5*; (2)

(*eaten*) **enseenene** *n9*. *Colour variants include*: (*green*) **enseenene kulumbisi,** (*brown*) **enseenene kulunkalu,** (*greenish-purple*) **enseenene mwebe.** *See* cricket type of insect resembling a grasshopper **omusontwa** *n3*

grate (*to make powder*) *vt* **-sira** grate and dissolve medicinal clay stick **-sira emmumbwa**

gratitude *n* **okusiima** *n15* be grateful for **-sima,** *eg. Nsiimye nnyo ekirabo ky'ompadde.* (*'I am very grateful for your gift.'*)

gratuity *n* **akasiimo** *n12*

grave *n* **amalaalo** *n6*, (*hole dug for human burial*) **entaana** *n9* deep in the grave **emagombe**

graveyard *n* **ekiggya** *n7*, (*royal*) **amasiro** *n6* public graveyard (*mostly used for burying foreigners*) **limbo** *n9*

gravy *n* **omucuuzi** *n3*, **ssupu** *n1*

graze *vt* (1) (*the skin*) **-nuubula;** (2) (*by animals*) **-lya** be grazed (*of the skin*) **-nuubuka,** *eg. Evviivi lyange linuubuse.* (*'My knee is grazed.'*) grazing area (*for livestock*) **ettale** *n5*, (*fresh-looking, as after a fire*) **ekiddo** *n7*

[1]grease *n* **giriisi** *n1*

[2]grease *vt* **-teekamu giriisi**

great (*important*) *adj* **-kulu.** *See* big; much

greatness (*importance*) *n* **obukulu** *n14*

Greece *n* **Buyonaani** *n9*

greed *n* **omululu** *n3*

greedy *adj* **-a omululu.** *See* insatiable greedy person **ow'omululu** *n1* be greedy **-lulunkana** be greedy for **-lulunkanira,** *eg. Alulunkanira emmere.* (*'He is greedy for food.'*) eat greedily **-liisa omululu**

Greek *n* (1) (*person*) **Omuyonaani** *n1*; (2) (*language*) **Oluyonaani** *n1*

green *adj* **-a kiragala,** *eg. olugoye olwa kiragala* (*'green garment'*), (*of wood; unseasoned*) **-bisi**

greens, edible (*green vegetables; spinach*) *n* **enva endiirwa** *n10*. *Types include*: (1) (*Amaranthus*) **doodo** *n1*, (*spiny*) **doodo w'amaggwa,** (*with red stem*) **ebbugga** *n5*, (*with small leaves, rarely eaten nowadays; cooks very quickly*) **embooge** *n9*, (*large, recently introduced*) **enkunga** *n9*; (2) (*cabbage*) **emboga** *n9*, (*Kikuyu cabbage*) **sukuma** *n1*; (3) (*Cleome*) **ejjobyo** *n5*; (4) (*Solanum aethiopicum*) **nnakati** *n1*, **nnakasugga** *n1*; (5) (*Solanum nigrum*) **ensugga** *n9*; (6) (*young pumpkin leaves*) **essunsa** *n9*. add greens to food parcel (*when cooking*) **-seruza enva**

greet *vt* **-buuza,** *eg. Yabuuzizza abagenyi.* (*'He greeted the guests.'*), **-lamusa.** *See* welcome greet for **-labira,** *eg. Obandabire.* (*'Give them my greetings.'*) pass someone without greeting **-yita ku muntu**

greeting *n* **ennamusa** *n9* send greetings to **-tumira,** *eg. Mbatumidde.* (*'Give them my greetings.'*)

grew *See* grow

grey *adj* **-a ekivuvvu** grey hair **envi** *n10* become grey-haired **-mera envi**

grief *n* **ennaku** *n9* be grief-striken **ennaku -yitirira**

grieve *vt* **-kungubaga.** *See* wail

grill *vt* **-kalirira**

grimace (*in disgust*) *vi* **-eenyinyimbwa**

grin *n* **akamwenyumwenyu** *n12*

grind *vt* (ground) (1) (*mill between stones*) **-sa;** (2) (*sharpen blade on stone*) **-wagala.** *See* crush; pound grind for/at (*mill*) **-seera** grind teeth **-luma amannyo** be ground (*milled*) **-seebwa**

grindstone (*also* millstone) *n* (1) (*lower*) **olubengo** *n11*, (*small*) **akabengo** *n12*; (2) (*upper*) **enso** *n9*

grip *vt* **-kwata**

gristle *n* **akabebenu** *n12*

gritty, be (*of food*) *vi* **-lumira,** *eg. Omuceere gulumira.* (*'The rice is gritty.'*)

groan *vi* **-sinda** groan in distress **-sindogoma** groan in pain **-sinda bulwadde**

grog (*added to clay in pottery making*) *n* **ensibo** *n9*

[1]groom (*bridegroom*) *n* **omugole omusajja** *n1*

[2]groom (*smarten someone up*) *vt* **-nyiriza** groom oneself **-eenyiriza** well-groomed *adj* **-nyirivu**

groove *n* **enjola** *n9*

grope (for) (*eg. in the dark*) *vit* **-wammanta**

[1]ground (*land*) *n* **ettaka** *n9*. *See* land ground floor **wansi** *n16* ground rent **obusuulu** *n14* grounds (*reasons*) **ensonga** *n10* on the ground **ku ttaka, ku ddongo** put on the ground **-teeka wansi**

[2]ground *v*. *See* grind

ground-bow (*one-stringed musical instrument*) *n* **ssekitulege** *n1*

groundnut *n* (1) (*peanut*) **ekinyeebwa** *n7*; (2) (*bambara*) **empande** *n9*. *See* peanut

groundsheet (*tarpaulin*) *n* **ettundubaali** *n5*

group *n* (1) (*crowd, flock, swarm, etc.*) **ekibinja** *n7*; (2) (*society; association*) **ekibiina** *n7*; (3) (*category*) **ettuluba** *n5*; (4) (*cluster; concentration*) **ekikuukuulu** *n7*. *See* type blood group **ekika ky'omusaayi** *n7*

grovel *vi* **-eekulukuunya**

grow *v* (grew) (1) (*become established, of plants*) *vi* **-mera,** *eg. Omuti gumeze mu lusuku.* (*'A tree has grown in the banana garden.'*); (2) (*increase in size*) *vi* **-kula,** *eg. Omuti gukuze bulungi.* (*'The tree has grown well.'*); (2) *vt* **-lima,** *eg. Alima lumonde.* (*'She is growing potatoes.'*) grow in amount **-yala,** *eg. Ente ziyaze.* (*'The cows are growing in numbers.'*) grow slack (1) (*deflated*) **-teewulukuka;** (2) (*loose, as a rope*) **-lebera** grow up in **-kulira,** *eg. Nnakulira London.* (*'I grew up in London.'*) grow very poorly/thin **-koozimba, -konziba,** (*of animals*) **-kundugga.** *See* stunted (be) grow well (*of plants*) **-gimuka** start growing (*of a plant*) **-loka** way of growing **enkula** *n9*

growing point (*of a plant*) *n* **omutunsi** *n3*

growl *vi* **-vuuma** growl at **-vuumira**

grown-up *adj* **-kulu** grown-up person **omukulu** *n1*

growth (*swelling*) *n* **ekizimba** *n7*

grudge *n* **ekiruyi** *n7*   bear a grudge **-beera n'ekiruyi**

grumble *vi* **-eemulugunya**, *eg. Beemulugunya ku muwendo gw'ebintu. ('They are grumbling about prices.')*, (*in dissatisfaction*) **-tolotooma**

grumpy, be (*in response to a request*) *vi* **-eekaanya**, *eg. Yeekaanya nga mmugambye okwoza ebintu. ('He was grumpy when I asked him to wash the dishes.'). See* complain

grunt (*as a pig*) *vi* **-fuguma**

guano *n* **kalimbwe** *n1*, **kasookolindo** *n1*

[1]**guarantee** *n* **omusingo** *n3*, **akakalu** *n12*   put up as a guarantee **-singayo** (*or* **-singawo**), *eg. Yasingayo ennyumba ye mu bbanka. ('He put up his house to the bank as a guarantee.')*   put up as a guarantee for (*someone*) **-singira**

[2]**guarantee** *vt* **-eeyimirira**, *eg. Musoke yeeyimirira ebbanja ya Mukasa. ('Musoke guaranteed Mukasa's loan.')*

guarantor *n* **omweyimirizi** *n1*

[1]**guard** *n* **omukuumi** *n1*, (*of palace*) **omumbowa** *n1*

[2]**guard** *vt* **-kuuma**   guard for/at, *etc.* **-kuumira**   be on one's guard **-eekuuma**. *See* prepared (be)   be guarded in speech **-eekuuma mu njogera**

guardian (*of a minor*) *n* **omukuza** (**w'omwana**) *n1*. *See* regent   Guardian of the Princes **Kasujju** *n1* title

guava *n* (1) (*tree*) **omupeera** *n3*; (2) (*fruit*) **eppeera** *n5*

guerrilla *n* **omuyeekera** *n1*   guerrilla warfare **obuyeekera** *n14*   wage guerrilla warfare **-yeekera**

[1]**guess** *n* **enteebereza** *n9*

[2]**guess** *vit* **-teeba**

guest *n* **omugenyi** *n1*, (*of honour*) **omugenyi omukulu**   be a guest **-genyiwala**   receive a guest **-kyaza**   uninvited guest **kyereeta** *n1*

[1]**guide** *n* **omukulembeze** *n1*

[2]**guide** *vt* **-kulembera**. *See* show how

guideline *n* **endagiriro** *n9*

guile *n* **olukwe** *n11*

guilt *n* **ekisobyo** *n7*   be guilty **-singa**, *eg. Gumusinze. ('He was found guilty.' – 'omusango' understood)*

guinea fowl *n* **enkofu** *n9*

guitar *n* **endongo** *n9*, **ggita** *n9*

guitarist *n* (1) (*one who strums*) **omukubi w'endongo** *n1*; (2) (*one who plucks*) **omusunyi w'endongo** *n1*; (3) (*one who sings while playing*) **kadongokamu** *n1*

gulf *n* **ekyondo** *n7*

gullet (*oesophagus*) *n* **omumiro** *n3*

gully *n* **olukonko** *n3*

gum *n* (1) (*glue*) **ggaamu** *n1*; (2) (*in the mouth*) **ekibuno** *n7*: (3) (*from a tree*) **amasanda** *n6*

gun *n* **emmundu** *n9*, (*artillery piece*) **omuzinga** *n3*   gun barrel **omudumu gw'emmundu** *n3*   gun shot **emmundu** *n9*   machine gun **emmundu ewandula**
amasasi, luwandulamasasi *n11*   pretend (*or* imitation) gun **ekibundubundu** *n7*

gunfire (*sound of*) *n* **omusinde gw'emmundu** *n3*   give a gun salute **-kuba emizinga**

gunman *n* **omutujju** *n1*

gunny bag *n* **egguniya** *n9*, **ekkutiya** *n9*

gunpowder *n* **obuganga** *n14*

gunshot *n* **ekyasi** *n7*

gush out (*squirt out*) *vi* **-tiiriisa** (*subject and object reversed compared to English*), *eg. Ettanka etiiriisa amazzi. ('Water is gushing out of the tank.')*

gust (*of wind*) *n* **kikuŋŋunta** *n1*

guts (*intestines*) *n* **ebyenda** *n8*. *See* courage

gutter *n* **olugogo** *n11*

gymnasium *n* **ekizannyiro** *n7*

H,h

habit (*behaviour*) *n* **empisa** *n9*. *See* manner   bad habit **omuze** *n3*   make a habit (of) **-eemanyiiza**

habitually *adv* **bulijjo**   do habitually *Use* **-tera** *in present tense followed by inf* (**N19**), *eg. Atera okutambula ng'amaze okulya ekyenkya. ('He habitually goes for a walk after breakfast.')*

had *See* have

hades (*underworld*) *n* **amagombe** *n6*

haggard, look *vi* **-kanduka**, **-kayuka**

haggle (*bargain*) *vi* **-lamuuliriza**. *See* argue

hail *n* **omuzira** *n3*

hair *n* (1) (*on head*) **enviiri** *n10* (*one* **oluviiri** *n11*), (*grey*) **envi** *n10* (*one* **oluvi** *n11*); (2) (*soft hair on forehead* **omuttunta** *n3*); (3) (*pubic*) **ebiza** *n8* (*one* **ekiza** *n7*); (4) (*of an animal*) **ebyoya** *n8* (*short* **obwoya** *n14*, *one* **akooya** *n12*); (5) (*long, eg. on maize cob*) **enjoya** *n10* (*one* **olwoya** *n11*); (6) (*short and stinging, eg. on grass or caterpillar*) **amajimbi** *n6* (*one* **ejjimbi** *n5*). *See* stubble; tuft

hairbrush *n* **bulaasi y'enviiri** *n9*

hairdresser *n* **omusazi w'enviiri** *n1*. *See* barber; braider

half *n* **ekitundu** *n7*, *eg. essaawa emu n'ekitundu ('half past seven')*, (*exactly*) **kimu kya kubiri**   half an hour **ekitundu ky'essaawa**

hall (*open-sided, used for meetings*) *n* **ekigango** *n7*   audience hall of the Kabaka **Masengere**

halo (*around saint's head*) *n* **omuge** *n3*   halo around the moon **embuga y'omwezi** *n9*

halt *v* (1) (*stop moving*) *vi* **-yimirira**, *eg. Baayimirira ku bitaala. ('They halted at the traffic lights.')*; (2) *vt* **-yimiriza**, *eg. Yayimiriza emmotoka ku bitaala. ('He halted the car at the traffic lights.')*. *See* abandon; stop; suspend   Halt right there! (*command*) **Lekeraawo!**

halve *vt* **-kutulamu wakati**

[1]**hammer** *n* **ennyondo** *n9*, (*short wooden type used for beating banana stems, etc.*) **enkonyo** *n7*. *See* mallet

²**hammer** *vt* **-komerera**

hammerkop *n* **nnaddibanga** *n1*. *See* nnaddibanga (*in Part 2 of dictionary*)

hammock-like structure (*in house, used for storage*) *n* **olusuubo** *n11*

hamper *vt* **-ziyiza**

¹**hand** *n* (1) (*of a person*) **omukono** *n3*; (2) (*of a clock or watch*) **akalimi** *n12*. *The plural 'hands' (of a person) is* **engalo** *n10*. <u>hand of bananas</u> **ekiwagu** *n7* <u>hand pump</u> (*for drawing water*) **nayikonto** *n9*, **essundiro ly'amazzi** *n5* <u>have one's hands full</u> **-kwatagana** <u>hold out one's hand</u> (*to catch something*) **-tega omukono** <u>left hand</u> **omukono ogwa kkono** <u>on the other hand</u> **ku ludda olulala** <u>put hands around</u> **-vumbagira** <u>right hand</u> **omokono ogwa ddyo**

²**hand (over)** *vt* **-kwasa** <u>hand in</u> (*submit*) **-waayo** <u>hand to</u> (*pass*) **-weereza**

handbag *n* **ensawo y'omu ngalo** *n9*

handcuffs (*pair of*) *n* **empingu** *n10*

handful *n* **olubatu** *n11*

handgrip (*of bike*) *n* **ekiwaawo ky'eggaali** *n7*

handicap *n* **obulemu** *n14* <u>handicapped person</u> **omulema** *n1* <u>be(come) handicapped</u> **-lemala**

handkerchief *n* **akatambaala** *n12*

¹**handle** *n* (1) (*of cup*) **omukonda** *n3*; (2) (*of tool, eg. hoe*) **omuyini** *n3*; (3) (*of door*) **omunyolo** *n3*; (4) (*of shield*) **omuwambiro** *n3*. *See* knife

²**handle** *vt* (1) (*fondle; finger*) **-kwatakwata**; (2) (*issues*) **-kolako**, *eg. Ebizibu bye abikozeeko bulungi.* (*'She has handled her problems well.'*). *See* squeeze <u>handle and squeeze</u> (*something soft, eg. knead dough in bread making*) **-nyigootola**, **-nyiganyiga**, (*and make flat, eg. when making a chapati*) **-kanda** <u>handle carefully</u> *Use* **-kwata** (*'hold'*) *with* **-eerembereza** (*'do carefully'*), *eg. Yakwata essowaani nga yeerembereza.* (*'She handled the plates carefully.'*), **-kwata empola**

handsome *adj* **-lungi** <u>handsome person</u> **omulungi** *n1* <u>be(come) handsome</u> **-lungiwa** <u>make handsome</u> **-lungiya**

handwriting *n* **omukono** *n3*

hang *vt* **-wanika**, *eg. Yawanika ensawo ku musumaali.* (*'He hung the bag on a nail.'*), (*kill someone by hanging*) **-wanika ku kalabba** <u>hang about (for)</u> (*keep waiting*) **-lindirira** <u>hang around the neck</u> **-yambika** <u>hang back</u> (*move reluctantly*) **-walira** <u>hang down</u> (*dangle*) (1) *vi* **-leebeeta**, **-lengejja**; (2) **-leebeesa**, **-lengezza** <u>hang one's head down</u> **-koteka omutwe** <u>hang oneself</u> (*kill oneself*) **-eetugga**, **-eeyimbamu muguwa** <u>hang over</u> (1) *vi* **-bunduka**, *eg. Ekitambaala kibunduse ku mmeeza.* (*'The tablecloth is hanging over the edge of the table.'*); (2) *vt* **-bundula** <u>hang up</u> (*put at a higher level*) **-wanika**, *eg. Yawanika ekifaananyi ku kisenge.* (*'He hung the picture on the wall.'*)

hanger-on (*someone who won't go away*) *n* **olukokobe** *n11*

haplochromis (*type of small fish*) *n* **enkejje** *n9*

happen *vi* (1) **-liwo** *or* **-baawo** (*'be there'*) *according to tense* (**N20.1**), *eg. Kiki ekiriwo?* (*'What is happening?'*); (2) **-beerawo**, *eg. Embaga eneebeerawo ddi?* (*'When will the wedding happen?'*); (3) **-faayo**, *eg. Nnaakubuulira ebifuddeyo.* (*'I will tell you what has happened.'*); (4) **-tuukawo**, *eg. Kiki ekyatuuseewo?* (*'What has happened?'*); (5) (*of a prophecy*) **-tuukirira**, *eg. Yagamba nti bbaasi ejja kujja ne kituukirira.* (*'She said the bus would come and it did.'*)

happening *See* event <u>a happening</u> **ekifa** *n7*

happiness *n* **essanyu** *n5*

happy *adj* **-sanyufu** <u>Happy New Year.</u> *greeting* **Kulika omwaka.** <u>happy person</u> **omusanyufu** *n1* <u>be happy</u> **-sanyuka**. *See* appreciative (be); elated (be) <u>be happy for/about</u> **-sanyukira** <u>make happy</u> **-sanyusa**

harass *vt* **-walana**, (*with persistent requests*) **-peeka**. *See* trouble; worry

harasser *n* **omuwalanyi** *n1*

harassment *n* **empalana** *n9*

harbour *n* **omwalo** *n3*

hard *adj* (1) (*physically, or difficult*) **-kalubo**; (2) (*difficult*) **-zibu**; (3) (*of cold matooke, a hide, etc.*) **-kakanyavu**. *See* stiff <u>be(come) hard</u> (1) (*physically, or difficult*) **-kaluba**; (2) (*difficult*) **-zibuwala**; (3) (*of cold matooke, a hide, etc.*) **-kakanyala** <u>give (someone) a hard time</u> (*harass*) **-walana** <u>have a hard time</u> (*in affairs*) **-gootaana** <u>make hard</u> (1) (*physically, or difficult*) **-kalubya**; (2) (*difficult*) **-zibuwaza**

hard-hearted *adj* **-a omutima omukakanyavu**, *eg. Musoke alina omutima omukakanyavu.* (*'Musoke is hard-hearted.'*)

hardness *n* **obukalubo** *n14*

hardship (*difficulties*) *n* **ebizibu** *n8*. *See* suffering <u>cause hardship to</u> (*persecute*) **-yigganya** <u>suffer hardship</u> **-laba ennaku**

hard-working *adj* **-nyiikivu** <u>hard-working person</u> **omunyiikivu** *n1* <u>be hard-working</u> **-nyiikira**

hardy *adj* **-gumu**

hare *n* **akamyu** *n12*

harelip, person with *n* **nnakimu** *n1*

¹**harm** *n* **akabi** *n12*

²**harm** *vt* **-lumya** <u>deeds done deliberately to harm</u> **ebyambyone** *n8*

harmonica *n* **akalanga** *n12*

harmonise *vi* **-tuukagana**, *eg. Amaloboozi gaatuukagana.* (*'The voices harmonised.'*) <u>cause to harmonise</u> **-tuukanya**, *eg. Omuyimbisa yagezaako okutuukanya amaloboozi g'abayimbi.* (*'The conductor tried to get the singers to harmonise.'*)

harp (*bow-harp, with strings arranged vertically to the soundbox*) *n* **ennanga** *n9* <u>play the harp</u> **-kuba ennanga**

harp on (*about something annoyingly*) *vi* **-yeeya**

harp on about to **-yeeyereza**

harpist *n* **omukubi w'ennanga** *n1*

harpoon *vt* **-swaga**

harshly *adv* **n'ebboggo**   person who speaks harshly **ow'ebboggo** *n1*   speak harshly **-boggoka**   speak harshly to **-boggolera**

harshness (*severity*) *n* **obukambwe** *n14*   harsh manner of speech **ebboggo** *n5*

hartebeest *n* **ennangaazi** *n9*

¹harvest *n* **amakungula** *n6. See* plenty (time of)

²harvest *vt* **-kungula**, (*bananas*) **-yunja**. *See* dig up; pick

harvester *n* **omukunguzi** *n1*

has *See* have

hassle *vt* **-tawaanya**. *See* persecute

hasten *v* (1) (*be quick*) *vi* **-yanguwa**; (2) (*do quickly*) *vt* **-yanguya**

hastily *adj. Use* **-papa** (*'rush'*) *in present tense as aux v* (**N19**), *eg. Yakoze apapa.* (*'He did it hastily.'*)

hat *n* **enkuufiira** *n9*, (*with wide brim*) **sseppeewo** *n9. See* cap; fez; helmet

hatch *vt* **-yalula**

hate *vt* **-kyawa**   cause to hate **-kyayisa**   someone hated **omukyawe** *n1*

hater *n* **omukyayi** *n1*

hatred *n* **obukyayi** *n14. See* bitterness

haughtiness *n* **obwewulize** *n14*   be haughty **-eewulira**

haul *vt* **-sika**. *See* drag

haunt *vt* **-lulumira**

have *vi/aux v* (had, has) **-lina** *or* **-ba na** (*according to tense* **N20.1**) **N20.2**, *eg.* (1) *Omukyala ajja kuba n'abaana basatu okulabirira.* (*'The lady will have three children to look after.'*); (2) *Musoke alina amagi.* (*'Musoke has the eggs.'*)   have to (*conveying a sense of obligation*) **-lina** *followed by inf* (**N19**), *eg. Alina okuyamba muganda we.* (*'She has to help her sister.'*)

haven (*place of safety*) *n* **obubudamo** *n14. See* refuge

¹hawk (*type of bird*) *n* **kakubampanga** *n1*

²hawk (around) (*goods for sale*) *vt* **-tembeeya**

hawker (*peddler*) *n* **omutembeeyi** *n1*

haze *n* **olufu** *n11*   hazy vision **ekifu ku maaso** *n7*

he *pro* **ye**. *The verb prefix is* **a-** (**N15**).

¹head (*chief*) *adj* **-kulu**

²head *n* (1) (*of the body*) **omutwe** *n3*; (2) (*of an organisation*) **omukulu** *n* head of a clan **omukulu w'ekika** *n1*, **ow'akasolya** *n1*   head of a family line **omukulu w'oluggya**   head of a training institution **omukulu wa ssettendekero** *n1*   head of a village **omwami w'ekyalo** *n1*   head of cattle **omugongo gw'ente** *n3*   head of palace administration **omukulu w'olubiri**   head of the house **nnyinimu** *n1*, **nnyini nnyumba** *n1*   (at the) head of the bed **emitwetwe**   back of the head **enkoona** *n9*   crown of the head **obutikkiro** *n14*, (*on which things are*

carried) **obwetikkiro** *n14*   lower one's head **-koteka omutwe**   raise one's head (*tilting the head back, eg. to look up*) **-lalama**, **-lalika omutwe**   turn head suddenly (*eg. when startled*) **-maguka**

³head (*be in charge of*) *vt* **-kulira**   head for (*aim for*) **-yolekera**, *eg. Bwe yannyuse n'ayolekera ewa ssengaawe.* (*'When he finished work he headed for his aunt's home.'*)

headache *n* **omutwe oguluma** *n3. See* migraine   have a headache **omutwe -luma** (*with personal object*), *eg. Omutwe gunnuma.* (*'I have a headache.'*)

headband *n* **omuge** *n3*

headcloth *n* **ekiremba** *n7*

headdress, bridal *n* **kadaali** *n1*

heading *n* **omutwe gw'ekiwandiiko** *n3*

headline *n* **omutwe omukulu** *n3*

headman *n* **nnampala** *n1*

headphone *n* **akazindaalo ak'oku matu** *n12*

headquarters *n* **ekitebe ekikulu** *n7*

headscarf *n* **akatambaala ak'oku mutwe** *n12*

headship *n* **obukulu** *n14*

headteacher *n* **omukulu w'essomero** *n1*

heal *vt* **-wonya**   be healed **-wona**

healer *n* **omuganga** *n1*, (*one who communicates with a spirit*) **omusawuzi** *n1. See* doctor

health *n* **obulamu** *n14*   health centre **eddwaliro** *n5*   health matters **ebyobulamu** *n8*

healthy *adj* **-lamu**   healthy person **omulamu** *n1*   be(come) healthy **-lamuka**

¹heap (*also pile*) *n* **entuumu** *n9. The following refer to types of heap:* (1) (*large, of firewood*) **omuganda entuumu** *n3*, **ekiganda entuumu** *n7*; (2) (*of things for sale, eg. fruit*) **omulengo** *n3*; (3) (*organised, eg. of counters in a game, or for division among people*) **omuteeko** *n3*; (4) (*of earth for planting sweet potatoes*) **ekikata** *n7*, **ekibibi** *n7*; (5) (*of rubbish or dung*) **envumbi** *n9*; (6) (*of rubbish, gathered by flowing rain water*) **effumbiko** *n5*; (7) (*large, of firewood*) **egganda** *n5*.

²heap *vt* **-tuuma**, *eg. Enku yazituuma bulungi.* (*'She heaped up the firewood well.'*), (*neatly*) **-panga**, *eg. Enku zipange zonna wamu.* (*'Heap all the firewood together.'*)   heap high **-tindikira**, *eg. Baatindikira emigugu ku loole.* (*'They heaped the luggage high on the lorry.'*)   heap in piles (*for sale*) **-lenga**   be heaped up (*eg. of bricks or firewood*) **-pangibwa**

hear *vt* **-wulira**   hear from **-wuliza**, *eg. Sikyabawuliza.* (*'I don't hear from them any more.'*)   be heard (*audible*) **-wulikika**

heart *n* **omutima** *n9. Figurative uses:* (1) (*spiritual centre*) **omwoyo** *n3*; (2) (*emotional core*) **emmeeme** *n9*.   Heart Clan *There are two* (**N29**): **Kika kya Mutima Muyanja** *and* **Kika kya Mutima Musaggi**. *A member of the Mutima Muyanja Clan is sometimes known as* **Omuyanja** *n1.*   be broken-hearted **-nyolwa mu mutima**   break someone's heart **-menya omutima**   lose heart -ggwaamu amaanyi

heartbeat (*pulse*) n entunnunsi *n9*

heartburn n ekikeeto *n7* cause heartburn (to) -keeta, *eg. Emmere enkeeta. ('The food is giving me heartburn.')*

hearten vt -gumya omwoyo

hearth n ekyoto *n7. See* cooking area area at back of the hearth enkoto *n9* caretaker of the royal hearth Musolooza *n1 title* in front of the hearth wamberi royal hearth (*with perpetual flame kept burning during the lifetime of the Kabaka*) ggombolola *n1*

[1]heat n ebbugumu *n5* be in heat (*sexually receptive, of an animal*) -lundugga on heat (*of a dog*) mu ggobe

[2]heat vt -bugumya heat bark of barkcloth tree (*to soften and improve the colour*) -fumba nnabugi

heated (up) adj -bugumye

heathen n omukaafiiri *n1*

heave (on) (*eg. a rope*) vt -sika heave a sigh -ssa ekikkowe heave up (*eg. a boulder*) -binula

heaven n eggulu *n9*

heavy adj -zito be heavy -zitowa be heavy for (*of load or problems*) -zitoowerera, *eg. Essanduuko ejja kumuzitoowerera. ('The suitcase will be heavy for her.')* make heavy -zitoya

hedge n olukomera *n11*

heel n (1) (*of the foot*) ekisinziiro *n7*; (2) (*of a high-heeled shoe*) akakondo *n12*

heifer n ennyana *n9*

height n obuwanvu *n14. See* elevation

heighten vt -wanvuya

heir n omusika *n1. See* beneficiary; co-heir be an heir -sika be heir to -sikira, *eg. Nnasikira ssenga wange. ('I became my aunt's heir.')* carry out ceremony to install an heir -yabya olumbe install an heir -ssaako omusika. *See* invest

held *See* hold

helicopter n ennyonyi nnamunkanga *n9*

hell n ggeyeena *n9*

hello interj (1) (*form of greeting*) Oli otya? (*pl.* Muli mutya?) (N28); (2) (*Hey, you there!*) Owange! Hello, may I come in? Kkoodi!

helmet n eremeti *n9* (*or* erementi), ekikuufiira *n7*

helmsman n omugoba *n1* seat of the helmsman (*in a canoe*) akalumba *n12*

[1]help n obuyambi *n14* appeal for help to -kubira omulanga. *See* plead come to the help of -dduukirira

[2]help vt -yamba, -beera. *See* assist help one another -yambagana, -beeragana help oneself -eeyamba

helper n omuyambi *n1*, omubeezi *n1* person who comes to help omudduukirize *n1*

helpful adj -yambi

helping (*of food*) n olubega *n11* second helping olubega olw'okubiri

helpless, act (*pretend to be incapable*) vi -kekkera

[1]hem n olukugiro *n11*, (*wider*) eddinda *n5*

[2]hem vt -kugira

hemp (*cannabis*) n enjaga *n9*, enjaaye *n9*

hen n enkoko *n9. See* chicken hen roost oluwe *n11*

hence *See* therefore

henceforth adv okuva kati

henpeck vt -sojja

[1]her pos -e (N11.4) with pronominal concord (N4.2), *eg.* (1) ekiso kye ('*her knife*'); (2) eggi lye ('*her egg*'). *The forms for the various noun classes are listed in Column 6 of Table 9.*

[2]her pro ye. *The verb prefix is* mu- (N15.1).

herald n matalisi *n1*

herb n (1) (*herbaceous plant*) omuddo *n3*; (2) (*medicinal plant*) eddagala *n5* apply herbal ointment to tummy of pregnant woman -tenga olubuto herbal mixture for bathing (1) (*for bathing babies*) ekyogero *n7*; (2) (*for adults*) ekyoogo *n7* take a herbal bath -naaba eddagala

[1]herd n eggana *n5*, ekisibo *n7*

[2]herd vt -lunda

herdsman n (1) (*of livestock generally*) omulunzi *n1*; (2) (*of cattle*) omulaalo *n1*, omuyima *n1. See* shepherd chief herdsman of the Kabaka (*cattle keeper*) Ssebalijja *n1 title*

here adv wano, (*over here*) eno, (*on here*) kuno, (*in here*) muno here and there wano na wali Here I am. Nzuuno. *Similar phrases follow the same pattern* (N9.1). be here and there (1) (*like a fly*) -zunga; (2) (*like a swift*) -tayira

hereditary adj -a ensikirano

heredity n ensikirano *n9*

heritage n ebyensikirano *n8. See* tradition

hero n omuzira *n1*

heroic adj -zira

heroism n obuzira *n14*

heron n ssekanyolya *n1*, (*goliath*) ekimbala *n7*

hers pos (*pronoun*) owuwe, ababe, etc. (N11.4), *eg. Engatto eno yange, eyo yiye. ('This shoe is mine, that is hers.'). The forms for the various noun classes are listed in Column 12 of Table 9.*

herself pro. *Reflexive verbs take prefix* -ee- (N18). by herself yekka she herself ye yennyini (*or* ye kennyini)

hesitate vi -sikattira, *eg. Yasikattira nga tannayingira mu dduuka. ('She hesitated before entering the shop.'). See* doubt; waver be hesitant (about) -tamattama, *eg. Yaddamu nga atamattama. ('She was hesitant in her reply.'). See* reluctant (be); uncertain (be)

hew vt -tema

hex n ettalo *n5. See* spell

hibiscus (*small red-leafed type, medicinal; roselle*) n musaayi *n1*

[1]hiccup(s) n kasikonda *n1*, *eg. Alina kasikonda. ('He has hiccups.')*

[2]hiccup vi -sikondoka

[1]hide (*animal skin*) n eddiba *n5. See* skin

²hide vt (hid) **-kweka**, eg. Switi yamukweka. ('He hid the sweets.'), (during transit) **-kukusa**, eg. Enjaga baagikukusa nga bagitadde mu mupiira gwa sipeeya. ('They hid the marijuana by putting it in the spare tyre.'). See avoid; suppress hide information (from) **-kisa**, eg. Yankisa. ('She hid information from me.'). See cover up; deceive hide oneself (from) **-eekweka**, eg. Yeekweka mu kabada. ('He hid himself in the cupboard.'), (from danger) **-eekukuma** come out of hiding **-eekwekula** hiding place obwekwekero n14 person who hides the truth omukuusa n1

¹high adj **-wanvu**, (of termite mound, hill, etc.) **-gulumivu**, (extremely high; sky high) **-tumbiivu**. See tall high-up person (socially) owa waggulu n1 be high **-wanvuwa**, (of a termite mound, hill, etc.) **-gulumira**

²high adv **waggulu**, eg. Ekkanisa eri waggulu ku lusozi. ('The church is high on the hill.') a little higher wagguluko be high on drugs **-tamiira** enjaga make high(er) **-wanvuya**, **-gulumiza** make higher **-yongerako obuwanvu**

highly adv **ennyo**, eg. Bamussaamu nnyo ekitiibwa. ('She is highly respected.')

highway n oluguudo n11

hill n olusozi n11 (small akasozi n12) far side of a hill enzivuunuko n9 go down a hill **-serengeta**, eg. Oluguudo luserengeta. ('The road goes down the hill.') go over a hill **-vvuunuka**, eg. Bavvuunuka olusozi okutuuka ku kyalo. ('They went over the hill to the village.')

hilly adj **-a ensozi**

him pro **ye**. The verb prefix is **mu-** (N15.1).

himself pro. Reflexive verbs take prefix **-ee-** (N18). by himself yekka he himself ye yennyini (or ye kennyini)

hinder vt **-kaluubiriza** be hindered in breathing **-ziyira**

Hindi (language) n Oluyindi n11

hindrance n ekikaluubiriza n7, ekizibuwaza n7

hinge n eppata n9

hint (to) vt (1) (through the eyes) **-temyako**; (2) (through touching lightly) **-sunyako**

hip n ekikugunyu n7 put hands on hips **-kwata mu mbinabina**

hipbone (of human) n bbunwe n1

hippopotamus n envubu n9

hire vt (1) (a person) **-pakasa**; (2) (something) **-pangisa**. See employ hired worker omupakasi n1

his pos DETERMINER **-e** (N11.4) with pronominal concord (N4.2), eg. (1) ekiso kye ('his knife'); (2) eggi lye ('his egg'). The forms for the various noun classes are listed in Column 6 of Table 9. PRONOUN owuwe, ababe, etc. (N11.4), eg. Engatto eno yange, eyo yiye. ('This shoe is mine, that is his.'). The forms for the various noun classes are listed in Column 12 of Table 9.

hiss vi **-saala** hiss at (make sucking noise expressing contempt) **-sooza**

history n ebyafaayo n8

hit vt (1) (strike) **-kuba**, (repeatedly) **-kubirira**, (person with fist) **-funtula**, **-wuttula**; (2) (knock) **-koona**, eg. Emmotoka yamukoona. ('A car hit him.'). See collide with; knock; pound; slap; spank hit a nail **-komerera omusumaali** hit at/in (a place) **-kubira**, eg. Yamukubira mu bbaala. ('He hit him in the bar.') hit one another **-kubagana** hit oneself **-eekoona**, eg. Yeekoona ekigere ku jjinja. ('He hit his foot on a stone.') hit with **-kubisa**, eg. Nnamukubisa muggo. ('I hit him with a stick.'), (forcefully) **-koonyesa**, eg. Amayinja yagakoonyesa nnyondo. ('He hit the stones with a hammer.')

hitherto adv okutuusa kaakati

hitter (person) n omukubi n1

hive (for bees) n omuzinga (gw'enjuki) n3

hives (allergic skin reaction) n ebirogologo n8

hoarse (of the voice) adj **-saakaavu** become hoarse **-saakaala**

hoarseness (of the voice) n obusaakaavu n14

hobble along vi **-sejjera**

hodgepodge n ekintabuli n7

¹hoe n enkumbi n9

²hoe vt **-lima n'enkumbi**

hog n embizzi n9

hoist vt **-linnyisa**. See lift

hold vt (held) **-kwata**, eg. Akutte ekikopo. ('She is holding a cup.'). See cling hold at an angle **-sulika**, eg. Ekikopo yakisulika. ('She held the cup at an angle.'), **-wunzika**, eg. Ekikondo kinywedde. ('The post is holding firm.') hold firmly to a point of view **-nywerera ku ndowooza** hold for **-kwatira**, eg. Yamukwatirako ekikopo. ('He held the cup for her.') hold hands **-kwatagana emikono** hold in the hand **-kwata mu ngalo** hold in the lap **-lera** hold in the mouth (without swallowing) **-batika** hold one's breath **-tuyira** hold onto **-eekwata ku**, eg. Yeekwata ku kisenge nga atambula. ('He held onto the wall while walking.') hold up (1) (delay) **-lwisa**, eg. Emmotoka zaamulwisa. ('The traffic held him up.'); (2) (physically) **-wanirira**, eg. Empagi ewanirira ettabi ly'omuti. ('The post is holding up the branch of the tree.'); (3) (clothing, eg. when walking through wet ground) **-fungiza**; (4) (at gunpoint) **-songamu emmundu**, eg. Omubbi yansongamu emmundu. ('The thief held me up at gunpoint.') be held (seized) **-kwatibwa** be held up (delayed) **-lwisibwa**, (temporarily) **-sikattira** something used for holding up (physically; prop) ekiwanirira n7

hole n ekituli n7, (in the ground; pit) ekinnya n7, (dug for human burial) entaana n9, (dug in termite mound when catching flying termites) envubo n9. See cavity; depression; hollow hole dug for pit latrine **ekinnya kya buyonjo** be(come) holed **-botoka**, *eg. Endobo ebotose. ('The bucket has become holed.),* **-wummuka** develop holes *(eg. of a road or wall)* **-womoggoka** make a hole **-botola ekituli**, *eg. Yabotola ekituli mu ndobo. ('She made a hole in the bucket.'),* **-wummula**

holed *adj* **-botofu**, *eg. endobo embotofu ('bucket with holes')*

holiday *n* **oluwummula** *n11. See* day off have a holiday **-wummula**

holiness *n* **obutukuvu** *n14*

Holland *n* **Budaaki** *n9*

¹hollow *n* **ekiwowongole** *n7. See* cavity hollow in a tree **ekiwowongole mu muti**

²hollow (out) *(scoop out, eg. wood when making a canoe or drum) vt* **-woola** be(come) hollow **-fuuka ekiwowongole**

holy *adj* **-tukuvu, -tuukirivu** Holy Bible **Ekitabo Ekitukuvu** *n7* holy communion **okusembera** *n15* Holy Ghost **Omwoyo Omutukuvu** *n3* Holy Land **Ensi Entukuvu** *n9* holy matrimony **obufumbo obutukuvu** *n14* holy water **amazzi g'omukisa** *n6* adminster holy communion to **-sembeza** be holy **-tukula** make holy **-tukuza** receive holy communion **-sembera**

homage to, pay **-wa ekitiibwa**

home *n* **amaka** *n6, eg. amaka ga Musoke ('Musoke's home'),* **awaka** *n16. See* house; residence at home **eka, awaka** at the home of **ewa** *eg. ewa Musoke ('at Musoke's home')* at my home **ewange**, at your home **ewuwo**, at her/his home **ewuwe**, *etc.* **(N11.5)** back of the home **emmanju**, *eg. Abaana bali mmanju. ('The children are at the back of the home.')* front of the home **emiryango** move home **-senguka**

homeless, be *vi* **-bungeeta**

homestead *n* **amaka** *n6. See* compound

homosexual *(person) n* **omusiyazi** *n1*

homosexuality *n* **obusiyazi** *n14*

honest *adj* **-a amazima** honest person **ow'amazima** *n1*

honestly *adv* **n'amazima**

honesty *n* **amazima** *n6*

honey *n* **omubisi gw'enjuki** *n3, (of stingless bees)* **omubisi gwa kadoma** take honey from bees **-wakula enjuki**

honeycomb *n* **ebisenge by'enjuki** *n8*

¹honour *n* **ekitiibwa** *n7*

²honour *vt* **-wa** *(or* **-ssaamu***)* **ekitiibwa** honour one's totem **-eddira**

honourable *adj* **-a ekitiibwa** honourable person **oweekitibwa** *n1* The Honourable *title* **Oweekiitibwa**, *eg. Oweekitiibwa Mukyala Mpanga ('The Honourable Mrs Mpanga')*

hood *(bonnet of vehicle) n* **boneti** *n9*

hoof *n* **ekinuulo** *n7, (of cow, cooked for eating)* **ekirenge** *n7*

¹hook *n* **eddobo** *n5*

²hook *vt* **-loba**

hooligan *n* **omuyaaye** *n1*

hoop *n* **nnamuziga** *n9*

hoot *(when driving vehicle) vi* **-fuuwa** *(or* **-kuba***)* **eŋŋombe**

hop *vi* **-kongojja**

¹hope *n* **essuubi** *n5* lose hope **-ggwaamu essuubi**

²hope *vi* **-suubira**, *(on someone's behalf; wish for)* **-yagaliza**, *eg. Mbaagaliza akabaga akalungi. ('I hope they have a good party.'). See* wish hope for the best **-kwatirira**, *eg. Tukwatiridde aleme kufa. ('We hope he doesn't die.')* be hoped **-suubirwa**

hopscotch *n* **kkongojja** *n1*

horn *n* (1) *(of an animal)* **ejjembe** *n5*; (2) *(of a vehicle; also hunting horn)* **eŋŋombe** *n9*; (3) *(musical instrument made from gourd)* **ekkondeere** *n9, (decorated with beads and played with royal drums)* **akawunde** *n12* horn player **omukondeere** *n1*

hornbill *n* **eŋŋaaŋa** *n9*

hornet *n* **kalalankoma** *n12. See* wasp

horrid *adj* **-bi ennyo**

horror *n* **ekibabu** *n7*, **ekibambulira** *n7*

horse *n* **embalaasi** *n9*

horsefly *n* **kawawa** *n1*

hose *n* **olupiira** *n11*

hospital *n* **eddwaliro** *n5*

¹host *(giver of a feast) n* **omugabuzi** *n1*

²host *vt* **-sembeza**

hostage *n* **omuwambe** *n1*

hostel *n* **ekisulo** *n7* student hostel **ekisulo ky'abayizi**

hostility *n* **empalana** *n9. See* prejudice be hostile to one another **-walaggana**, *(rub one another up the wrong way)* **-kuubagana**

hot *adj. Use* **-yokya** *('be hot') in rel* **(N7.1)**, *eg. emmere eyokya ('hot food'). See* spicy; warm hot-tempered **-a obusungu** be(come) hot (1) **-yokya**, *eg. Amazzi gookya. ('The water is hot.')*; (2) *(red hot, of metal)* **-yengerera** be too hot (for) *(of sunshine)* **-babira**, **-kaalaama**, *eg. Olwaleero omusana gukaalaamye nnyo. ('It is very hot today.'),* **-eeberengula**. *See* burn

hotchpotch *n* **omugoyo** *n3*

hotel *n* **wooteeri** *n9*

hour *n* **essaawa** *n9* lunch hour **amalya g'ebyemisana** *n6*

house *n* (1) **ennyumba** *n9*, **enju** *n9 (small* **akayumba** *n12)*; (2) *(small apartment in block)* **omuzigo** *n3*; (3) *(of more than one storey)* **kalina** *n9*, **ennyumba ya kalina, ennyumba ya ggoloofa** *n9. See* hut; shelter house broker **bbulooka w'amayumba** *n1* house owner **nnannyinimu** *n1*, **nnannyini nnyumba, nnyinimu** *n1* house rent **busuulu w'ennyumba** *n1* house servant **omukozi w'awaka** *n1* abandoned house **ekifulukwa** *n7* external edge of a house **olusebenju** *n11* rest house **omugiini** *n3* thatched house **ennyumba**

y'essubi   three-storey house **kalinaasatu** *n9*   two-storey house **kalinaabiri** *n9*

houseboy *n* **omusumaami** *n1*

household *n* **amaka** *n6*

¹how *adv* **nga**, *eg. Nga kibi! ('How bad!')*

²how *conj* **bwe** (**N26**), *eg. Simanyi bwe kikola. ('I don't know how it works.')*

³how? *interr* (1) (*referring to manner*) **-tya?** (**N13**), *eg. Olima otya? ('How do you cultivate?')*; (2) (*referring to quantity*) *Use* **-yenkana wa?** (*'be equal to where?'*), *eg. Omuggo gwenkana wa obuwanvu? ('How long is the stick?')*   How are you? *greeting* **Oli otya?** (*pl.* **Muli mutya?**) (**N28**) How big is it? **Kyenkana wa?** (*pl.* Byenkana wa?) How far did you get? (*asking where one has got to with work*) **Otuuse wa?**   how many? (*or* how much?) **-meka?** (*with numeral concord* **N4.2**) (**N8.1**), *eg. (1) amagi ameka? ('how many eggs?')*; (2) Weetaaga emiti emeka? ('How much wood do you need?')   how often? **emirundi emeka?**, *eg. Ojja wano emirundi emeka? ('How often do you come here?')*

however *conj* **naye**

howl *vi* **-woowoola**

HQ *n* **ekitebe ekikulu** *n7*

huddle up (*through shyness*) *vi* **-eekomomma**

hug *vt* **-wambaatira**, (*affectionately*) **-gwa mu kifuba**, *eg. Yagwa mutabani we mu kifuba. ('He hugged his son closely.')*

huge *adj* **-nene ennyo**

¹hum *n* **ekiwuuma** *n7*

²hum *vi* (1) (*as an engine*) **-wuuma**; (2) (*as a bumble bee*) **-vuuvuuma**   hum a tune **-muumuunya oluyimba**

human *n* **omuntu** *n1*

humane *adj* **-a obuntu**

humanity *n* **obuntu** *n14*

humble person *n* **omwetoowaze** *n1*, **ow'eggonjebwa** *n1*   humble oneself before **-eetoowaliza**   be humble **-eetoowaza**

humiliate *vt* **-swaza**

humiliation *n* **obuswavu** *n14*

humility *n* **obwetoowaze** *n14*, **eggonjebwa** *n5*

hump (*on back of person/animal*) *n* **ebbango** *n5*   road hump **ekigulumu** *n7*, (*small*) **akagulumu** *n12*

hunchback *n* **ow'ebbango** *n1*   be hunched over **-kootakoota**, *eg. Omukadde akootakoota. ('The old man is hunched over.')*

hundred *num* **kikumi** *n7* (**N8.1**)   hundred thousand **emitwalo kkumi**, **akasiriivu** *n12*

hunger *n* **enjala** *n9*   hungry person **omuyala** *n1*   be hungry (1) **enjala -luma** (*with personal object*), *eg. Enjala emuluma. ('He is hungry.')*, **-li muyala**, *eg. Ndi muyala. ('I am hungry.')*; (2) **-lumwa enjala** (*with personal subject*), *eg. Alumwa enjala. ('He is hungry.')*

¹hunt *n* **omuyiggo** *n3*

²hunt *vt* **-yigga**. *See* track down

hunter *n* **omuyizzi** *n1*, (*one who sets traps*) **kitezi** *n1*

hunting   hunting net **ekitimba ky'abayizzi** *n7*   place where an animal is cornered **ekizigo** *n7*

hurl (*eg. ball*) *vt* **-kasuka**, **-kanyuga**   hurl a stone **-vuumuula ejjinja**   hurl down *See* throw down   hurl forward (*eg. a car*) **-diimuula**

hurriedly *adv* **mu bwangu**, **embagirawo**. *See* rush (in a)

hurry *vi* (1) (*in moving*) **-yanguwa**; (2) (*in doing*) **-yanguya**, *eg. Yoza ebintu nga oyanguya. ('Hurry up with washing the dishes.')*. *See* frantic (be)

hurt *v* (1) (*of oneself*) *vi* **-luma** (*with personal object*), *eg. Erinnyo linnuma. ('My tooth is hurting.')*; (2) (*someone else*) *vt* **-lumya**, *eg. Yannumya. ('He hurt me.')*. *See* sting   hurt through knocking a wound (1) (*of oneself*) **-eekosa**; (2) (*someone else*) **-kosa**, *eg. Yankosezza mu bbwa. ('He knocked me and made my sore hurt.')*   be hurt **-lumwa**

husband *n* (1) **bba** *n1*, *eg. bba wa Sanyu ('Sanyu's husband')*. *The stem* **bba-** *is used for plurals, eg. ba bbaffe ('our husbands')*; (2) **omwami** (*with pos* **N12**), *eg. omwami wange ('my husband')*   my husband **baze**, your husband **balo** (**N12**)   husband of wife's sister **musangi** *n1* (*with pos* **N12**), *eg. musangi wange ('my wife's sister's husband')*   leave one's husband **-noba**, *eg. Yasalawo okunoba. ('She decided to leave her husband.')*

husbandry, animal *n* **obulunzi** *n14*   look after animals **-lunda**   method of animal husbandry **ennunda** *n9*   person who looks after animals **omulunzi** *n1*

hush (*quieten*) *vt* **-sirisa**   hush up (*suppress information*) **-vubiikiriza**. *See* conceal   rock a baby to sleep **-siisiitira omwana**

husk (*eg. beans*) *vt* **-susa**

husks *n* **ebisusunku** *n8*

husky (*of the voice*) *adj* **-saakaavu**   be(come) husky **-saakaala**

hut (*with thatched roof*) *n* **olusiisira** *n11*, (*small*) **akasiisira** *n12*

hyacinth, water *n* **ekiddo ku nnyanja** *n7*

hyena *n* **empisi** *n9*

hygiene *n* **ebyobuyonjo** *n8*

hymn *n* **oluyimba lw'eddiini/ekkanisa** *n11*

hypocricy *n* **obunnanfuusi** *n14*

hypocrite *n* **munnanfuusi** *n1*   praise hypocritically **-kiina**

hyrax *n* **enjoga** *n9*

I,i

I *pro* **nze**. *The verb prefix is* **n-** (**N15**). *There are many spelling variants* (**N5**; *see Table 3*).

ibis (*hadada*) *n* **mpaabaana** *n1*

ice *n* **omuzira** *n3*, (*as in fridge*) **bbalaafu** *n1*   pieces of ice (*as in a drink*) **amayinja ga bbalaafu** *n6*

Id

Id *n* **Yidi** *n9*

idea *n* **ekirowoozo** *n7*

identical (to), be *vi* **-linga**, *eg. Empandiika ye eringa eya Musoke. ('His handwriting is identical to Musoke's.')*

identify *vt* **-manya erinnya**, *eg. Omanyi erinnya ly'omuti guno? ('Can you identify this tree?')*

identity card *n* **ekitambulizo** *n7*

idiocy *n* **obusiru** *n14*

idiom *n* **ekisoko** *n7*

idiot *n* **omusirusiru** *n1. See* imbecile

idiotic *adj* **-sirusiru**

idle *(of an engine) vi* **-teetera**, *eg. Yingini eteetera. ('The engine is idling.')* idle person *(unemployed)* **omuntu atalina ky'akola** *n1* be idle *(kill time instead of working)* **-kongoola.** *See* lazy (be); loiter

[1]**if** *conj* (1) *(in conditional sentences)* **singa** *(with conditional tense N18), eg. Singa yajja, nnandimulabye. ('If he had come, I would have seen him.'), (referring to the future)* **bwe (N27)**, *eg. Bw'oba omusanzeeyo, muwe ebbaluwa eno. ('If you find him there, give him this letter.')*; (2) *(whether)* **oba (N27)**, *eg. Simanyi oba agenze. ('I don't know if he has gone.')*; (3) *(after verbs of knowing, understanding, hearing, etc.)* **nga**, *eg. Simanyi nga tunaagenda e Kampala. ('I do not know if we will go to Kampala.')*, **obanga**

ignite *vt* **-koleeza** be ignited **-koleera**

ignorance *n* **obutamanya** *n14* feign ignorance **-eewugguusa** through ignorance **olw'obutamanya**

ignorant *(uninformed) adj* **-bisi, -buguyavu** ignorant person **omuntu atamanyi** *n1*, **omubuguyavu** *n1* be ignorant *Use* **-manya** *('know') in neg* **(N21)**, *eg. Musoke tamanyi. ('Musoke is ignorant.')*

ignore *vt* (1) *Use* **-faayo ku** *('care about') in neg* **(N21)**, *eg. Tafaayo ku kye mmugamba. ('She ignores what I say to her.')*; (2) *(family member against cultural norms)* **-boola.** *See* aloof (keep); attention (pay no); neglect ignored family member *(eg. one not invited to family gatherings)* **omuboole** *n1*

ill *(sick) adj* **-lwadde** ill person **omulwadde** *n1*, *(very)* **omuyi** *n1* be(come) ill **-lwala**, *(frequently)* **-lwalalwala**, *(extremely thin, weak and sickly)* **-kenena.** *See* waste away make ill **-lwaza**

ill-disciplined *adj* **-lalu** ill-disciplined person **omulalu** *n1* be ill-disciplined **-lina** *or* **-ba na** *('have') according to tense* **(N20.1)** *followed by* **eddalu** *('bad behaviour'), eg. Abaana baabwe balina eddalu. ('Their children are ill-disciplined.')*

ill feelings *n* **ffitina** *n9*

ill-mannered *adj* **-a empisa embi**

ill-treat *vt* **-yisa obubi**

ill will *n* **ettima** *n5*

illegal, be *vi* **-menya etteeka**, *eg. Kimenya etteeka okutunda enjaga. ('It is illegal to sell cannabis.')*

illness *n* **obulwadde** *n14, (serious, near death)* **olumbe** *n11. See* disease; madness; pain illness associated with body pains and strange dreams *(mostly of women)* **ebigalanga** *n8*;

illuminate *vt* **-mulisa**

illustrate *(show how) vt* **-lagirira.** *See* draw

illustration/image *(picture) n* **ekifaananyi** *n7. See* appearance; example

imagine *vit* **-teebereza.** *See* think

imam *n* **omuwalimu** *n1*

imbecile *n* **ekigwagwa** *n7*

imbibe *(drink) vt* **-nywa**

imitate *vt* **-koppa**, *eg. Omwana we akoppa buli kintu ky'akola. ('Her child imitates everything she does.'). See* mimic

immature, be *vi. Use* **-kula** *('mature') in 'not yet' tense* **(N18)**, *eg. Emmwanyi tezinnakula. ('The coffee beans are immature.')*

immediate *(instant) adj* **-a obuliwo** with immediate effect **embagirawo**, *eg. Etteeka lino litandika mbagirawo. ('This regulation starts with immediate effect.')*

immediately *adv* **amangwago**

immerse *vt* **-bbika.** *See* dip immerse oneself **-ebbika**

immigrant *n* **omusenze** *n1*

immigrate *(settle at a new place) vi* **-senga**

imminent, be *vi* (1) *(of rain)* **-bindabinda**; (2) *(of tears)* **-tuubatuuba**

immoral *adj* **-gwagwa**, *(sexually)* **-kaba** immoral person **omugwagwa** *n1, (sexually)* **omukaba** *n1* be(come) immoral **-gwagwawala**, *(sexually)* **-kabawala**

immorality *n* **obugwagwa** *n14, (sexual)* **obukaba** *n14*

immortality *n* **obutafa** *n14*

immunise *vt* **-gema endwadde**

immutable, something *n* **ekitakyusibwa** *n7*

impatience *n* **obutagumiikiriza** *n14* be impatient *(with)* **-gumiikiriza** *('be patient') in neg* **(N21)**, *eg. Teyagumiikiriza. ('He was impatient.')*

impede *vt* **-kaluubiriza**, *eg. Ekkubo ebbi lyatukaluubiriza mu lugendo. ('The bad road impeded us on the journey.')* be impeded in breathing **-ziyira**

impediment *n* **ekikaluubiriza** *n7*, **ekizibuwaza** *n7*

imperfection *n* **akamogo** *n12*

impertinence *n* **ekyejo** *n7*

impertinent *adj* **-a ekyejo**

implore *vt* **-eegayirira**

import *vt* **-yingiza**

importance *n* **obukulu** *n14*

important *adj* **-kulu** important person **omukulu** *n1* act important **-eegulumiza** something important **ekikulu** *n7. See* matters (something that)

importation *n* **ennyingiza** *n9*

importune *vi* **-peeka**

impose *vt* **-teekawo**, *eg. Omukulu w'essomero*

yateekawo amateeka amapya. ('The head master imposed new rules.') impose one's will on (a person, taking advantage) -yiikiriza impose oneself (on person or group) -eebereka, -eepaatiika. See intrude

impossible be impossible (for) (1) Use -soboka or -yinzika ('be possible') in neg (**N21**), eg. Tekisoboka kusala luguudo. ('It is impossible to cross the road.'); (2) (too much for) -lema, eg. Omulimu gwannema. ('The job was impossible for me.') become impossible (of a person or thing) -fuukira omuteego make impossible for -lemesa, eg. Yannemesa okukola. ('He made it impossible for me to work.')

imposter n omuntu eyeefuula ky'atali n1 be an imposter -eerimbika

impotence n obunafu n14

impotent adj -nafu

impoverish vt -yavuwaza be(come) impoverished -yavuwala

impregnate vt -siiga, eg. Wasiize eddagala ku muti? ('Did you impregnate the wood with preservative?'), (make pregnant) -funyisa olubuto

impression (image) n endabika n9

imprison vt -siba mu kkomera be imprisoned -sibibwa

imprisonment n obusibe n14

improper (also inappropriate) adj. Use -saana or -gwana ('be suitable') in neg (**N21**) in rel (**N7.1**), eg. empisa ezitasaana ('improper behaviour') improper acts ebyambyone n8

improve v (1) vi -longooka, eg. Empisa ze zirongoose. ('His behaviour has improved.'); (2) vt -longoosa, eg. Alongoosezza empisa ze. ('He has improved his behaviour.'). See better (become) improve one's behaviour -eddako continue to improve -eeyongera obulungi, eg. Yeeyongera okusoma obulungi. ('She is continuing to improve in her studies.')

improved adj -longoofu

improvisation (eg. in music or speech) n ekisoko n7

improvise vt -tetenkanya

impudence n ekitigi n7

in pre mu in case conj si kulwa nga, eg. Tomuwa mmere si kulwa nga taagyagale. ('Don't give her food in case she doesn't like it.') in general (altogether) okutwalira awamu in here muno in order to (or in order that) Use subjunctive tense (**N17**), eg. Yasoma nnyo alyoke asobole okufuna omulimu omulungi. ('She studied hard in order to get a good job.') in there omwo, muli. (**N9.1**) in which (also where) mwe, eg. Eno y'ensawo mwe nnateeka ekitabo. ('This is the bag in which I put the book.'). Subject relative clauses are also used (**N7.2**).

inability n obutayinza n14, obutasobola n14

inappropriate See improper

inattentive adj -mantaavu be inattentive -mantaala. See look around

incapable, consider (a person) vt -gaya

incendiary (arsonist) n omwokerezi n1

incense n obubaani n14 incense tree (Canarium) omuwafu n3 (fruit empafu n9, seed enje n9) burn incense -nyookeza obubaani

incessantly adv obutaggwa, obutalekeraawo, obutamala, (of rain) obutakya, eg. Enkuba etonnya obutakya. ('It is raining incessantly.') talk incessantly (with nothing much to say) -yogera olumoonyere

inch n yinki n9

incident See event

incidentally adv kozzi

incite to riot vt -sasamaza

¹incline n. See slope

²incline (tilt) vt -wunzika, -sulika, eg. Yasulika omutwe ku ddyo. ('He inclined his head to the right.') be inclined (1) (tilted) -eewunzika, -eesulika; (2) (be disposed towards) -tera (**N19**), eg. Atera okwebaka nga amaze okulya. ('He is inclined to sleep after eating.')

include vt -teekamu, eg. Omuzannyi ono muteekemu mu ttiimu. ('Include this player in the team.'). See count in

including conj na/ne (**N5**), eg. Twala byonna na kino. ('Take everything including this.')

income n ennyingiza n9

incompletely, do (not do things properly) vi -galangatana

incomprehension n obutategeera n14

incontinent, be vi -eenyaga

inconvenience vt -kaluubiriza

incorrect adj. Use -tuufu ('correct') in neg (**N21**), eg. Kye yagamba si kituufu. ('What she said is incorrect.')

increase v TRANSITIVE USES -yongera, eg. Bayagala okwongera ku bungi bwa kasooli mu sitoowa. ('They want to increase the amount of maize in the store.'), (cause to increase) -yongeza, eg. Baayongezezza ebisale by'essomero ('They increased the school fees.'). See raise; turn up increase in number -yaza, eg. Ayazizza ebitooke. ('She has increased the number of her banana plants.') INTRANSITIVE USES -eeyongera, eg. Amagezi g'omwami geeyongedde. ('The wisdom of the chief has increased.') increase in number -yala, eg. Ebitooke biyaze mu lusuku. ('The banana plants have increased in number in the garden.'), -wera

increment n ennyongeza n9

incubate vt -maamira

incurable adj -a olukonvuba incurable illness obulwadde obw'olukonvuba, obulwadde obutawona n14 waste away through an incurable illness -konvuba

indecent adj -gwagwa

indecision *n* obutasalawo *n14*

indeed *adv* ddala   Yes indeed! Weewaawo!, Kye kyo!, Kye kyo kyenninyi!

indemnity *n* engassi *n9*

independence (*self-rule*) *n* okwefuga *n15*   be independent (1) (*self-ruling, of a country*) -eefuga; (2) (*self-sufficient, of a person*) -eemalirira; (3) (*being able to sustain oneself*) -eeyimirizaawo, -eebeezaawo   become independent (*of a country*) -eetwala

index (*of a book*) *n* endagiriro *n9*   index finger olunwe *n11*

India *n* Buyindi *n9*

Indian (*person*) *n* Omuyindi *n1*, (*member of a certain Hindu merchant caste*) Omunyani *n1*   Indian language Oluyindi *n11*

indicate (to) *vt* -laga, *eg.* Yandaga essowaani we ziri. (*'He indicated to me where the plates are kept.'*)

indication *n* endagiriro *n7*

indifference *n* obutafaayo *n14*   be indifferent (to) Use -faayo ku (*'care about'*) in neg (N21), *eg.* Tafaayo ku bulamu bw'abaana be. (*'He is indifferent to his children's health.'*)   express indifference -badala

indigenous *adj* -a ekinnansi, *eg.* eddagala ly'ekinnansi (*'indigenous medicine'*)   indigenous person (*original inhabitant*) nnansangwawo *n1*

indiscriminate *adj* -a omuyoolerero, *eg.* ebintu bya muyoolerero (*'indiscriminate collection of things'*)

indiscriminately *adv* lufaaya, *eg.* Abantu baabatwala lufaaya mu kkomera. (*'They took everyone to prison indiscriminately.'*)

individually (*one-by-one, of people*) *adv* kinnoomu, *eg.* Yayogera na bo kinnoomu. (*'He talked to them individually.'*)

indolence *n* obunaanya *n14*. See laziness   be indolent -naanya   indolent person omunaanya *n1*, nnalwenaanya *n1*

induct *vt* -tendeka   induct a spirit (*for spirit possession*) -tendeka lubaale

indulge (*spoil*) *vt* -ginya, *eg.* Omuwala oyo talina mpisa, nnyina yamuginya nnyo. (*'That girl has no manners, her mother indulged her.'*). See pamper; spoil

industrious *adj* -nyiikivu   be industrious -nyiikira

inebriated See drunk

ineffectively, work (*have problems in affairs*) *vi* -ziringitana, *eg.* Omulimu gwabwe guziringitanye. (*'Their efforts were ineffective.'*)

inequality *n* obutali bwenkanya *n14*

inevitable, be *vi.* Use -eewalika (*'be avoidable'*) in neg (N21), *eg.* Enjala teyeewalika. (*'Hunger is inevitable.'*)

infancy *n* obuto *n14*, (*very young*) obuwere *n12*

[1]**infant** *adj* -to

[2]**infant** *n* akaana *n12*, (*very young*) omuwere *n1*

infatuated, be *vi* -tijja, -tinkiza

infatuation *n* akatinko *n12*

infect *vt* -siiga obulwadde   be(come) infected -siigibwa, (*of a wound; septic*) -tana

infectious disease *n* obulwadde obukwata *n14*

inferior (to), be *vi* -singa obubi, *eg.* Kino kisinga kw'ekyo obubi. (*'This is inferior to that.'*)

infertile (*of a woman*) *adj* -gumba   infertile land olunnyo *n11*

infidel *n* omukaafiiri *n1*

infidelity (*sexual*) *n* obwenzi *n14*

infinity *n* obutabalika *n14*

infirm *adj* (1) (*ill*) -lwadde; (2) (*weak*) -nafu   be(come) infirm (*ill*) -lwala

infirmary *n* eddwaliro *n5*

inflammation (*of finger or toe*) *n* entunuka *n9*. See boil; swelling   become inflamed (*of a boil*) -yengerera

inflate *vt* (1) (*using a pump*) -pika omukka mu; (2) (*using the mouth*) -fuuwamu omukka mu   become unflated -nyiiga

influenza *n* fulu *n1*, (*more serious*) yegu *n1*

inform *vt* -tegeeza, *eg.* Njagala okukutegeeza nti omwana wo mulwadde. (*'I want to inform you that your child is ill.'*), -manyisa, -nyumiza. See disclose to; divulge; report; say to; tell; tip off   inform of an intention to visit -laga, *eg.* Nnamulaga okugenda okumulaba. (*'I informed him that I would go and see him.'*)   inform on -wawaabira, *eg.* Muliraanwa we yamuwawaabira ku poliisi. (*'He informed on his neighbour to the police.'*). See denounce   be informed (*told*) -buulirwa

information *n* ebyokumanya *n8*. See news   pump (*a person*) for information -kemekkereza   sources of information ebyokumanyisa *n8*   withhold information from -kisa, *eg.* Yankisa abantu abaali bajja. (*'She withheld information from me about the people who were coming.'*), -zibira

informer *n* omuloopi *n1*   person informed on omuloope *n1*

infrequently *adv* ebbalirirwe

infuriate *vt* -nyiiza (*or* -sunguwaza) ennyo   be(come) infuriated -nyiiga (*or* -sunguwala) ennyo

infuriated *adj* -nyiivu/-sunguwavu ennyo

ingenuity *n* amagezi amangi *n6*

ingratiate oneself (with) *vit* -eeguya, *eg.* Yeeguya mukama we. (*She ingratiated herself with her boss.'*)

inhabit *vt* -beeramu

inhabitant *n* omutuuze *n1*. See resident   original inhabitant (*already present at a place*) nnansangwawo *n1*, (*of the land that became Buganda*) Omulasengeye *n1*

inhale *vt* -sika omukka

inherit (*become an heir*) *vi* -sika   be an heir to -sikira   inherit the kingship -lya obwakabaka

inheritance *n* obusika *n14*

initial See first   initial stages (*of a task*) amabaga *n6* do initial stages of a task **-baga**

initiate (*start*) *vt* **-tandika**. *See* induct

initiative do/go on one's own initiative **-eetuma**
on the initiative of **ku bwa**, *eg. ku bwa Musoke ('on Musoke's initiative')*, (*with pronouns*) **ku bwa-** (**N11.4**), *eg. ku bwange ('on my initiative.')*

inject (*give an injection to a person*) *vt* **-kuba empiso**, *eg. Nnaasi yatukuba empiso. ('The nurse gave us injections.')* inject oneself **-eekuba mpiso**

injection *n* **empiso** *n9*, (*given to an animal*) **ekkato** *n5*

injure *vt* **-lumya** be injured **-lumwa** injured person **omuntu alumizibwa** *n1*

injury *n* **ekisago** *n7*. *See* wound

injustice *n* **obutalibwenkanya** *n14*

ink *n* **bwino** *n1*

in-laws *n* **abako** *n2*. *A male in-law of a male is* **omuko** *n1*, *or* **mukoddomi** *n1* (*with pos* **N12**), *eg. mukoddomi wange ('my brother in-law')*. in-laws **bakoddomi** *n2* (*with pos* **N12**), *eg. bakoddomi bange ('my in-laws')*

inn *n* **wooteeri** *n9*

innards (*internal organs*) *n* **ebyenda** *n8*

inner *adj* **-a omunda**, *eg. oluggi olw'omunda ('inner door')*. *See* tube (inner)

innocence *n* (1) (*not knowing*) **obutamanya** *n14*; (2) (*without guilt*) **obutaba na musango** *n14* be innocent (*legally*) Use **-zza omusango** ('*commit a crime*') *in neg* (**N21**), *eg. Atazzizza musango. ('He was innocent.')*

inoculate *vt* **-gema obulwadde**

inquire (about) *vt* **-buuza**. *See* ask

insane *adj* **-lalu**

insanity *n* **obulalu** *n14*

insatiable (*for food*) *adj* **-wuukuufu** be insatiable **-wuukuuka**

inscribe *vt* (1) (*write*) **-wandiika**; (2) (*make pattern, on wood or pot*) **-yola**

inscription *n* **ekiwandiiko** *n7*

insect *n* **ekiwuka** *n7* (*small* **akawuka** *n12*). *Types include*: (1) (*secretes fluid*) **entonnyeze** *n9*; (2) (*bores into barkcloth trees*) **jjegeju** *n1*; (3) (*looks like a praying mantis; lives in stems of banana plants*) **nnabangogoma** *n1*; (4) (*carries around a cocoon-like home*) **ensombabyuma** *n9*; (5) (*carries around a home like a tiny bundle of firewood*) **kasennyanku** *n1*. *See also individual types*

insecticide *n* **eddagala eritta ebiwuka** *n5*. *See* mothball

insert *vt* (1) (*put in*) **-yingiza**, *eg. Yayingiza ekisumuluzo mu kkufulu. ('She inserted the key in the lock.')*; (2) (*handle in hoe, pole in ground, bullet in gun, etc.*) **-wanga**, *eg. Yawanga enkumbi. ('She inserted the handle in the hoe.')*; (3) (*push/slip in*) **-sonseka**, *eg. Yasonseka olupapula mu kitabo. ('He inserted a piece of paper in the book.')*; (4) (*something within*) **-waayiramu**, *eg. Essaati yagiwaayiramu ekiwero okugigaziya. ('He*

inserted some material to widen the shirt.') *See* enter; stuff in insert oneself **-eeyingiza**, *eg. Yeeyingiza mu mboozi. ('She inserted herself into the conversation.')*

[1]**inside** *adv* **munda** inside out **ku bikukujju**, *eg. Essaati agyambalidde ku bikukujju. ('He is wearing the shirt inside out.')*

[2]**inside** *pre* **munda mu**

insides (*internal organs*) *n* **enda** *n9*

insist (on) *vi* **-nywerera ku**, *eg. Yanywerera ku ky'agamba. ('She insisted she was right.')* be insistent **-lemera ku kigambo**, *eg. Yalemera ku kigambo nti Musoke ye yatwala essente. ('He was insistent that Musoke took the money.')* be insistent with **-kuutira**, *eg. Nnamugamba asasule essente ne mmukuutira akikole. ('I told him to pay the money and insisted that he does it.')*

insolence *n* **ekyejo** *n7*

insolent *adj* **-a ekyejo**

insomnia *n* **obuteebaka** *n14*

inspect *vt* **-kebera**, (*on a tour*) **-lambula** inspect soldiers on parade **-lambula ennyiriri z'abaserikale**

inspector *n* **omukebezi** *n1*, (*one who tours*) **omulambuzi** *n1*

inspire *vt* **-jjumbiza** be inspired by **-labira ku**, *eg. Abaana baalabira ku ye okukola ennyo. ('The children were inspired by him to work hard.')*

instalment *n* **ekitundu** *n7* pay in instalments **-sasula mu bitundutundu**

install *vt* (1) (*eg. sink in kitchen*) **-teekamu**; (2) (*eg. new bishop*) **-teekako** install an heir **-ssaako omusika**

instance *See* event; example for instance **okugeza**

instant (*immediate*) *adj* **-a obuliwo**

instead of *pre* **mu kifo kya**

instigate *vt* **-tandika**

instruct *vt* **-lagirira**. *See* train

instruction *n* **endagiriro** *n9*

instructor *n* **omulagirizi** *n1*. *See* trainer

instrument (*tool*) *n* **ekikozesebwa** *n7* musical instrument **ekivuga** *n7*

insubordination *n* **obutawulira** *n14*

insufficient *adj.* Use **-mala** ('*be enough*') *in rel* (**N7.1**) *in neg* (**N21**), *eg. obujulizi obutamala ('insufficient evidence')* be insufficient (for) (1) (*not enough for a purpose*) Use **-mala** ('*be enough*') *in neg* (**N21**), *eg. Emmere temala bantu bonna. ('The food is insufficient for all.')*; (2) (*not all will receive some*) **-buna** ('*go around*') *in neg* (**N21**), *eg. Emmere tejja kubuna. ('The food is insufficient for all.')*

insuline *n* **ekirungo ekiyongeza sukaali mu mubiri** *n7*

[1]**insult** *n* **ekivumo** *n7*

[2]**insult** *vt* **-vuma**, (*repeatedly*) **-vumirira**, (*by refusing to take something offered*) **-ziririra**, *eg. Yamuwadde emmotoka n'agimuziririra. ('She*

offered him a car but he insulted her by refusing to accept it.'). See drive away   insult one another -**vumagana**

insurance *n* **yinsuwa** *n9*

insurgency *(rebellion) n* **obujeemu** *n14*

insurgent *n* **omujeemu** *n1*. See guerrilla

intelligence *n* **amagezi** *n6*

intelligent *adj* **-gezi**   intelligent person **omugezi** *n1*

intend *vi* **-genderera**, *eg. Ŋŋenderera kumuwasa. ('I intend to marry her.')*   intend *(to do something)* next day **-sulirira**, *eg. Asuliridde okutambula. ('She intends to travel tomorrow.')*

intensely *(very) adv* **ennyo**

intensify *vi* **-eeyongera**, *eg. Kibuyaga yeeyongera. ('The storm intensified.')*

intention *n* **ekigendererwa** *n7*   go with the intention of **-genderera**

intentionality *n* **obugenderevu** *n14*

intentionally *adv* **mu bugenderevu**

inter *vt* **-ziika**

intercede *(between) vi* **-tabaganya**, *eg. Yasalawo okubatabaganya. ('He decided to intercede in their dispute.')*

intercept *vt* **-taayiza**

intercessor *n* **omuwolereza** *n1*

intercourse, sexual *n* **okwegatta** *n15*   have sexual intercourse **-eegatta mu mukwano, -eebaka n'omuntu**

[1]interest *(monetary) n* **amagoba** *n6*   strong interest *(keenness)* **obujjumbizi** *n14*

[2]interest *vt* **-yagazisa**, *eg. Abayizi omusomesa yabaagazisa ebyafaayo. ('The teacher interested the pupils in history.')*   be interested in *(care about)* **-faayo ku**, *eg. Afaayo ku kusoma kw'abaana be. ('He is interested in the education of his children.')*   be interesting **-nyuma**

interfere *(in another's affairs) vi* **-eeyingiza**, *eg. Musoke yeeyingiza mu nsonga zange. ('Musoke is interfering in my affairs.')*. See meddle

interior *pre* **munda mu**

internal *adj* **-a munda**

internet *n* **interneti** *n9*, **omutimbagano** *n3*   internet provider **omukutu gwa interneti** *n3*

interpret *(translate) vt* **-vvuunula, -taputa**. See explain   interpret a dream for **-lootolola ekirooto**

interpretation *(meaning) n* **amakulu** *n6*. See translation

interpreter *(translator) n* **omuvvuunuzi** *n1*, **omutaputa** *n1*

interrogate *vt* **-buuliriza**. See question   be interrogated **-buuzibwa**

interrupt *vt* **-salako**, *eg. Yali ayogera n'amusalako. ('He interrupted him while he was speaking.')*

intersection *n* **amasannanzira** *n6*

intertwine *vt* **-gombeza**, *eg. Jjo nnali ŋŋombeza mmuli. ('Yesterday I was intertwining reeds.')*. See interweave; weave   become intertwined **-gombagana**. *See* tangled (become)

interval *n* **ebbanga** *n5*

interweave *vt* (interwove) (1) *(mat or basket)* **-luka**; (2) *(reeds or sticks; intertwine)* **-gombeza**. See plait; weave   interweave cane *(rattan)* **-gombeza enga**   interweave reeds **-gombeza emmuli**

intestines *n* **ebyenda** *n8*   large intestine **ebyenda ebinene**   small intestine **ebyenda ebitono**

intimidate *vt* **-tiisatiisa**

intimidated *adj* **-tiitiizi**

into *pre* **mu**

intoxicant *n* **ekitamiiza** *n7*

intoxicate *vt* **-tamiiza**   be(come) intoxicated **-tamiira**

intoxicated *adj* **-tamiivu**

intrepid *adj* **-gumu**   intrepid person **omugumu** *n1*, *(one who keeps struggling to achieve)* **omukakaalukanyi** *n1*

[1]intrigue *n* **olukwe** *n11*

[2]intrigue (against) *vt* **-lyamu olukwe**

introduce *(person or proposal) vt* **-yanjula**. See admit; announce   introduce oneself *(formally)* **-eeyanjula**

introduction *n* **ennyanjula** *n9*   ceremony of introduction *(of man to family of prospective wife)* **okwanjula** *n15*

intrude *(oneself) vi* **-eeyingiza**, *eg. Yeeyingiza mu nsonga za muliraanwa we. ('He intruded himself into his neighbour's affairs.')*. See impose

intrusiveness *n* **olunderebu** *n11*

invade *vt* **-zinda**. See attack

invader *n* **omuzinzi** *n1*. See attacker

invasion *n* **omuzindo** *n3*

invent *vt* **-yiiya**

invented *adj* **-yiiye**

invention *n* **ekiyiiye** *n7*   method of invention **enjiiya** *n9*

inventor *n.* Use **-yiiya** *('invent')* in rel (N7.1), *eg. abantu abayiiya ('inventors')*

invest *(besiege) vt* **-zingiriza**   invest an heir **-sumika omusika**, *(tying on barkcloth)* **-siba ekifundikwa**, *eg. Yasiba ekifundikwa ku lubugo okuteekako omusika. ('He tied a knot in the barkcloth to invest the heir.')*   invest money **-teeka essente**, *eg. Essente ze yaziteeka mu kugula takisi. ('He invested his money in a taxi.')*

investigate *vt* **-noonyereza**

investigator *n* **omunoonyerezi** *n1*

invite *vt* **-yita**   be invited **-yitibwa**   go without being invited **-eetwala**

invoice *n* **invoyisi** *n9*

involve *vt* **-yingiza**, *eg. Yayingiza Maliya mu kibiina. ('She involved Mary in the group.')*   involve oneself **-eetabula**, *eg. Yeetabula mu ebyobufuzi. ('She involves herself in politics.')*   become involved with **-eegatta ku**, *eg. Maliya yeegatta ku kibiina ky'abakyala. ('Mary become involved in the women's group.')*. See participate

iroko *(type of tree) n* **omuvule** *n3*

¹iron n (1) (*type of metal*) **ekyuma** n7; (2) (*for pressing clothes*) **eppaasi** n9   iron ore **amasengere** n6   iron sheet **ebbaati** n5

²iron (*clothes*) vt **-golola**

irritate vt **-nyiiza**   be irritated **-nyiiga, -nyiizibwa**, (*easily*) **-nyiiga** (*or* **-sunguwala**) **mangu**. *See* upset (be)

irritated adj **-nyiivu**

irritation n **ekinyiiza** n7

Islam n **Obusiraamu** n14

Islamic adj **-siraamu**   Islamic affairs **ebyobusiraamu** n8

island n **ekizinga** n7, (*floating island of vegetation that has broken away from a swamp*) **ekisamba** n7

isolated place (*difficult to access*) n **ensokolosokolo** n9

Israel n **Yisirayiri** n9

¹issue (*matter*) n **ensonga** n9. *See* offspring

²issue (*distribute*) vt **-gaba**   issue to **-gabira**, *eg. Ofiisa yagabira abaserikale emmundu.* (*'The officer issued guns to the soldiers.'*)

it pro. *A subject or object pronoun is expressed by a pronominal concord placed as a prefix on a verb* (**N15.1**), *the pronominal concord being in the noun class of the noun to which it refers* (**N4.2**). *The various forms are shown in Column 9 of Table 1. Examples (referring to 'ekitabo' 'book'): (1) Kiri wano. ('It is here.'); (2) Nkirina. ('I have it.'). There are also free-standing pronouns based on the stems* **-o** (*ordinary pronouns*) *or* **-e** (*pronouns of emphasis*) (**N10.1**), *eg. (1) Ente yo ejja? ('The cow, is it coming?'; (2) Eggi ly'oleese? Yee, eggi lye ndeese. ('Have you brought the egg? Yes, I have brought it.')*

Italian (*person*) n **Omuyitale** n1

Italy n **Yitale** n9

¹itch n **obuwere** n14. *See* skin condition

²itch vt **-siiwa** (*the person concerned can be indicated by an object pronoun*), *eg. Omukono gunsiiwa. ('My arm is itching.'), (of the throat)* **-kolokoota**, *eg. Obulago bunkolokoota. ('My throat is itching.')*

item n **ekintu** n7

itemise vt **-menya**

itinerant merchant n **omutembeeyi** n1

its pos DETERMINER **waagwo, waayo** (**N11.4**), *etc., eg. omukira gwayo ('its tail', eg. referring to the tail of a dog 'embwa')* PRONOUN **owaagwo, abaagwo**, *etc.* (**N11.4**)

itself pro **-nnyini** (**N11.6**) *prefixed by pronoun of emphasis* **N10.1**, *eg. (1) ekibbo kyennyini ('the basket itself'); (2) ebibbo byennyini ('the baskets themselves'). Reflexive verbs take the prefix* **-ee-** (**N18**), *eg. Embwa yeeraba. ('The dog saw itself.'), from Embwa yalaba. ('The dog saw.')*   by itself **-okka** (**N7.3**) *with pronominal concord* (**N4.2**), *eg. Embwa emu yatuula yokka. ('One dog sat by itself.')*

ivory n **essanga** n5   ivory bracelet **eggemo** n5

J,j

jabber vi **-sabuliza**

jack (*eg. to raise a car*) n **ejjeeke** n9   Jack (*the name*) **Jaaka** n1

jackal n **ekibe** n7

jacket n **ekkooti** n5

jackfruit (*tree; fruit*) n **ffene** n1, **ekifenensi** n7   segment of jackfruit **omuwula gwa ffene** n3

Jacob n **Yakobo** n1

¹jail (*also* gaol) n **ekkomera** n5, **mbuzeekogga** n1. *See* cell; prison

²jail (*also* gaol) vt **-siba mu kkomera**

jailer (*also* gaoler) n **omukuumi w'ekkomera** n1

¹jam n **jjaamu** n1   traffic jam **jjaamu w'emmotoka**

²jam v   jam in(to) **-kakaatika**, *eg. Yakaatika engoye mu dduloowa. ('She jammed the clothes into the drawer.')*   jam open **-zizika**, *eg. Yazizika oluggi. ('He jammed open the door.')*   be jammed in (*crowded to capacity*) **-fumbekera**, *eg. Ebintu bifumbekedde mu kisenge. ('The things are jammed into the room.'). See* stuck (*under* stick)   get jammed **-wagama**   get jammed in **-wagamira**, *eg. Engalo yange yawagamira mu kituli. ('My finger got jammed in the hole.')*

January n **Omwezi ogw'olubereberye** n3, **Gatonnya, Janwali**

jar n **ekikyupa** n7, **jjaaga** n9. *See* bottle; pot

jaundice n **enkaka** n9

Java plum n **jambula** n1

jaw n **oluba** n11

jawbone (*of dead person*) n **akaba** n12, (*royal*) **akaba ka Kabaka**

jealousy n (1) (*general term; also sexual as felt by a woman*) **obuggya** n14; (2) (*sexual, as felt by a man*) **ebbuba** n5; (3) (*envy; due to not having something another person has*) **ensaalwa** n9   be jealous **-kwatibwa obuggya**, (*sexual, as felt by a man*) **-kwatibwa ebbuba**. *See* wish   make jealous **-kwasa obuggya**

jeer at vt **-jerega**

jerry can n **ekidomola** n7 (*small* **akadomola** n12)

Jessica n **Jesika** n1

jest vi **-saaga**

jester n **omusaazi** n1, **kazannyirizi** n1. *See* clown

Jesus n (1) (*Prot*) **Yesu** n1; (2) (*RC*) **Yezu** n1

Jew n **Omuyudaaya** n1

jibes at, make vt **-sojja**

jigger n **envunza** n9   jigger egg **akagina** n12   place where jigger grows **ekibondo** n7, (*when small*) **akabondo** n12

job n (1) (*work*) **omulimu** n3; (2) (*set manual task*) **ekkatala** n5. *See* task

John n **Yokana** n1

join vt (1) (*group or organisation*) **-yingira**, *eg.*

Yayingira mu magye. ('He joined the army.'), (*actively involved*) **-eegatta ku**, eg. *Musoke yeegatta ku kibiina ekiwola ssente. ('Musoke joined the money lending society.')*; (2) (*end-to-end*) **-yunga**, eg. *Ayunze emiguwa ebiri. ('She has joined the two ropes.')*. See unite
joined *adj* **-gatte**
joiner (*carpenter*) *n* **omubazzi** *n1*
joint (*segment*) *n* **ennyingo** *n9*
joist *n* **olwaliiro lw'akasolya** *n11*
¹**joke** *n* **olusaago** *n11*
²**joke** *vi* **-saaga**
joker *n* **omusaazi** *n1*, **kazannyirizi** *n1*
jolly *adj* **-sanyufu**
Joseph *n* **Yozefu** *n1*
jostle one another *vi* **-sindikagana**
journalist *n* **munnamawulire** *n1*, **omuwandiisi w'amawulire** *n1*, **ow'amawulire** *n1*
¹**journey** *n* **olugendo** *n11*, (*long*) **eggendo** *n5*, (*outward*) **amagenda** *n6*, (*return*) **amadda** *n6*, (*upward*) **amambuka** *n6*, (*downward*) **amaserengeta** *n6*. See safari; travel make a very long journey **-tindigga eggendo** start a journey **-situla**, eg. *Onoositula ku ssaawa mmeka? ('What time will you start the journey?')*
²**journey** *vi* **-tambula**, (*leisurely*) **-seeyeeya**
jowls *n* **amayuuga** *n6*
joy *n* **essanyu** *n5*
joyful *adj* **-sanyufu**
jubilant, be *vi* **-jaganya**
jubilation *n* **ekijaguzo** *n7*
¹**judge** (*legal*) *n* **omulamuzi** *n1*, **omusazi w'emisango** *n1*
²**judge** *vt* (1) (*in court*) **-lamula**, (*unfairly*) **-saliriza**; (2) (*estimate*) **-gera**. See prejudiced (be)
judgement *n* (1) (*in court*) **ennamula** *n9*, **ensala y'omusango** *n9*; (2) (*opinion*) **endoowoza** *n9* pass judgement (*in court*) **-sala omusango** pass judgement on **-salira omusango**, (*unfairly*) **-saliriza omusango** place where judgement is given **eggwoolezo** *n5*
jug *n* **omudumu** *n3*, **jjaaga** *n9*
juice *n* (1) (*banana*) **omubisi** *n3*, (*concentrated*) **emberenge** *n9*; (2) (*orange*) **emicungwa** *n4*; (3) (*pineapple*) **omunaanansi** *n3*
July *n* **Omwezi ogw'omusanvu** *n3*, **Kasambula**, **Julaayi**
¹**jumble** (*of things*) *n* **ekintabuli** *n7*
²**jumble (up)** *vt* **-tabula**
jump (over) *vit* **-buuka**, eg. *Engabi yabuuka olukomera. ('The bushbuck jumped over the fence.')*. See skip jump a queue **-buuka olunyiriri** jump into/onto **-buukira**, eg. *Embwa yambuukira. ('The dog jumped up on me.')* jump start a car **-tegula emmotoka**
junction *n* **amasaŋŋanzira** *n6*
June *n* **Omwezi ogw'omukaaga** *n3*, **Ssebaaseka**, **Jjuuni**

jungle *n* (1) (*forest*) **ekibira** *n7*; (2) (*uncultivated land*) **ensiko** *n9*
Jupiter (*the planet*) *n* **nnabisaaniiko** *n1*
just *adv* (1) *Use verb prefix* **-aka-** (**N18**), eg. *Yaakalya. ('She has just eaten.')*.; (2) *Use* **-va** (*'come from'*) *as aux v* (**N19**), eg. *Nva kulya. ('I have just eaten.')*. See only just as (*in time*) **nga**, eg. *Yatuuka nga nze nvaawo. ('She arrived just as I was leaving.')* just like **nga … bwe** (**N26**), eg. *Kola nga bwe nkola. ('Do just as I do.')*
justice (*fairness*) *n* **obwenkanya** *n14* chief justice **omulamuzi omukulu** *n1* place of justice **eggwolezo** *n5*
justification (*reason*) *n*. *Use conjunction* **kwe** (*'therefore'*) *with or without* **ensonga** (*'reason'*) (**N27**), eg. (1) *Ensonga eyandeese wano kwe kukulaba. ('My justification for coming here was to see you.')*; (2) *Ekyandeese wano kwe kukulaba. ('My justification for coming here was to see you.')*
jut out (*from within*) *vi* **-kukunala**, eg. *Akasimu kaali kakukunadde mu nsawo. ('The mobile phone jutted out of his pocket.')*. See stick out make jut out **-kukunaza**
jute sack/bag *n* **ekkutiya** *n9*
jutting out *adj* **-kukunavu**

K,k

kapok tree See silk cotton tree
keel *n* **omugongo** *n3*
keen *adj* **-jjumbizi** be keen on **-jjumbira**, eg. *Ajjumbira ekibiina ky'abakyala. ('She is keen on the women's group.')*
keenness *n* **obujjumbizi** *n14*
keep *vt* (*kept*) (1) (*animals*) **-lunda**, eg. *Olunda enkoko? ('Do you keep chickens?')*; (2) (*put away; store*) **-tereka**, eg. *Njagala kutereka ssente ngule olugoye. ('I want to keep some money to buy a dress.)* keep aloof from other people **-eesuula** keep away from (*avoid*) **-eewala**, eg. *Nneewala ekyalo ekyo. ('I keep away from that village.)* keep for (1) (*safeguard*) **-kuumira**, eg. *Mmukuumira ebisumuluzo bye. ('I am keeping his keys for him.')*; (2) (*store for*) **-terekera** keep on (*persist in, despite lack of success*) **-kanda**, eg. *Nnakanda kumunnyonnyola nga takikkiriza. ('I kept on explaining to him but he did not believe it.')*. See continue keep safe (*protect*) **-kuuma**, eg. *Omwami akuuma abantu. ('The chief is keeping the people safe.')* keep to oneself **-eesamba**
keg *n* **eppipa** *n5*
Kenya *n* **Kenya** *n9*
Kenyan (*person*) *n* **Munnakenya** *n1*
kept See keep
kernel *n* **ekinyusi** *n7*
kerosine *n* **palafiini** *n9*, **amafuta g'ettaala** *n6*
kestrel *n* **magga** *n1*

kettle *n* ebbinika *n9*

key *n* (1) (*for lock*) ekisumuluzo *n7*; (2) (*of a xylophone*) eddinda *n5*

khaki cloth *n* kkakki *n1*

[1]**kick** (*in fighting*) *n* olusambaggere *n11*

[2]**kick** *vt* -samba   kick a ball hard (*in football*) -diimuula omupiira   kick legs about (*eg. as response to pain*) -sambagala. *See* thrash about   kick off (*in football*) -yanja omupiira

kid *n* (1) (*child*) omwana *n1*; (2) (*young goat*) akabuzi *n12*

kidney *n* ensigo *n9*   kidney bean ekinjanjaalo *n7*

Kiganda *adj* -a ekiganda, *eg.* empisa z'ekiganda (*'Kiganda customs'*), -ganda, *eg.* eŋŋoma eŋŋanda (*'Kiganda-type drum'*)

kill *vt* -tta   kill off a friendship -tta omukwano   kill time (*not work when one should*) -kongola   be killed -ttibwa   someone killed omutte *n1*

killer *n* omussi *n1*

killing *n* obussi *n14*

kiln *n* ekyokero *n7*, (*for baking bricks*) ttanuulu y'amatofaali *n9*. *See* furnace

kilo (*unit of weight*) *n* kiro *n9*

kilometre *n* kiromita *n9*

kin *n* ab'oluganda *n2*

[1]**kind** (*merciful*) *adj* -a ekisa   kind person ow'ekisa *n1*   be kind -beera n'ekisa

[2]**kind** (*sort; type*) *n* engeri *n9*, ekika *n7*

kindle a fire -kuma omuliro

kindness *n* ekisa *n7*   through kindness olw'ekisa

king *n* kabaka *n1*. *Titles of kings*: (1) (*of Buganda*) Kabaka *n1*, (*deceased*) Ssekabaka *n1*; (2) (*of Bunyoro or Toro*) Omukama *n1*; (3) (*of Ankole*) Omugabe *n1*; (4) (*of Busoga*) Kyabazinga *n1*. King's Lake (*near Mengo Palace*) Ekinyanja kya Kabaka

kingdom *n* obwakabaka *n14*

kingfisher *n* (1) (*pied*) magga *n1*, ssekabira *n1*; (2) (*blue types*) akasumagizi *n12*

kingship *n* obwakabaka *n14*

kinship *n* oluganda *n11*

Kinyarwanda (*language of Rwanda*) *n* Olunyarwanda *n11*

kiss *vt* -nywegera

kitchen *n* effumbiro *n5*, (*as out-house*) ekiyungu *n7*

kite (*type of bird*) *n* kamunye *n1*

kleptomaniac *n* omwetoozitoozi *n1*

knead (*dough*) *vt* -nyiganyiga, (*and make flat, eg. when making a chapati*) -kanda   knead clay -kulunga ebbumba

knee *n* evviivi *n5*

kneecap *n* enso y'evviivi *n9*

kneel (*eg. in church*) *vi* -fukamira   kneel before (*as mark of respect*) -fukaamirira, *eg.* Yafukaamirira ssengaawe. (*'She knelt before her aunt.'*)

knickers *n* empale *n9*, (*small*) akawale *n12*

[1]**knife** *n* ekiso *n7* (*small* akaso *n12*), (*curved type used for peeling plantains*) akambe *n12*. *See*

dagger; machete; slasher   knife without a handle ekiso eky'engera, akambe ak'engera   person wounded by a knife omufumite *n1*

[2]**knife** (*a person*) *vt* -fumita ekiso

knit *vt* -luka   knit with -lukisa, *eg.* Alukisa empiso. (*'She is knitting with needles.'*)

knock *vt* (1) (*hit accidentally*) -koona, *eg.* Nnakoonye ekikopo. (*'I knocked the cup.'*); (2) (*repeatedly, eg. on door*) -konkona, *eg.* Nnakonkona ku luggi. (*'I knocked on the door.'*)   knock into (*collide with*) -tomera, *eg.* Emmotoka yatomera omuti. (*'The car knocked into the tree.'*)   knock-kneed person ow'obutagali *n1*   knock oneself (*on something*) -eekoona

[1]**knot** *n* ekituttwa *n7*, *eg.* Yasiba ebituttwa mu nviiri ze. (*'She tied knots in her hair.'*), (*tied in barkcloth*) ekifundikwa *n7*

[2]**knot** *vt* -tugga. *See* invest; tie   become knotted (up) -eetugga, *eg.* Akaguwa keetuzze. (*'The string has become knotted up.'*). *See* tangled (become)

know *vt* -manya. *See* understand   know one another -manyigana   be knowable -manyika   Let us know. Otuwulire.

knowledge *n* amagezi *n6*   knowledgeable person omumanyirivu *n1*, omumanyi *n1*

known *adj* (1) (*to a person*) -manyi; (2) (*widely known*) -manyifu   be(come) known -manyibwa, *eg.* Kimanyiddwa bw'osimba ensigo zino. (*'It is known how to plant these seeds.'*)   make known to (*inform about*) -manyisa   someone known (1) (*to a person*) omumanyi *n1*; (2) (*known to many*) omumanyibwa *n1*   well-known *adj* -manyifu

knuckles   crack the knuckles -nonkola   sound of knuckles being cracked ekinonko *n7*

kob, Uganda *n* empala *n9*

Koran (*also* Qur'an) *n* Kulaani *n9*

kraal *n* ekiraalo *n7*, olugo (lw'ente) *n11*

kwashiorkor *n* kwasakko *n1*

L,l

[1]**label** *n* akapande *n12*. *See* badge; logo

[2]**label** (*mark*) *vt* -lamba

[1]**labour** (*work*) *n* omulimu *n3*, (*communal*) bulungibwansi *n14*, (*forced*) akasanvu *n12*. *See* chore; work; worker   labour pains (*in childbirth*) ebisa *n8*   be in labour (*during childbirth*) -lumwa okuzaala

[2]**labour** (*work*) *vi* -kola

labourer *n* omupakasi *n1*, (*casual*) omupakasi wa lejjalejja *n1*. *See* worker

lace *n* (1) (*of shoe or boot*) akaguwa k'engatto *n12*; (2) (*type of material*) laasi *n9*

lace up a shoe -siba engatto

lacerate *vt* -taagula. *See* fray

[1]**lack** *n* ebbula *n5*

[2]**lack** *vt* -bulwa, *eg.* Musoke abulwa ssente okutwala

abaana be mu ssomero. ('Musoke lacks money to take his children to school.') lack fixed abode -bundabunda be lacking -bula (often with combined adverbial affixes N24.2), eg. Ku mmeeza kubulako ekikopo kimu. ('One cup is lacking from the dining table.')

lad n omulenzi n1

ladder n eddaala n5, (for stripping bark from barkcloth trees) obuyungo n14, (self-standing, in form of a tripod) enkandaggo n9

¹ladle n (1) ekijiiko ekisena n7 (small akendo n12); (2) (made from gourd) olwendo n11

²ladle (out) vt -sena. See dip in

lady n omukyala n1 ladies and gentlemen (introducing a speech) abakyala n'abaami

lag (behind) vit -sigala emabega, eg. Omuddusi omu yasigala emabega. ('One of the runners lagged behind.'). See come unwillingly; last (be)

laid See lay

lake n ennyanja n9 (small akayanja n12). See fly Lake Albert **Muttanzige** lake flies essami n9 Lake Victoria **Nnalubaale** in the middle of the lake ebuziba King's Lake (near Mengo Palace) **Ennyanja ya Kabaka**

lamb n akaliga n12

lame adj -lema lame person omulema n1 become lame -lemala

lameness n obulema n14

lament vi -wooba. See cry; moan

lamentation n ekiwoobe n7

lamp n ettaala n9 (small akataala n12), ettabaaza n9 lamp post omuti gw'ettaala n3 lamp wick olutambi n11 paraffin lamp ettaala y'amafuta, (small type, with naked flame) tadooba n9

¹land n (1) (country) ensi n9; (2) (soil; ground) ettaka n9; (3) (type of landed property in Buganda) mailo n9; (4) (contrasted with water) olukalu n11. See area; plot land broker bbulooka w'ettaka n1 land rent obusuulu n14 land title ekyapa ky'ettaka n7 clan land obutaka n14 dry area of land olukoola n11 dug over land (newly dug) awalime n16, (deeply dug) awakabale n16 infertile land olunnyo n11 plot of land ekibanja n7

²land land a boat ashore -tuuka ku lukalu land an aeroplane -ssa ennyonyi ku ttaka

landing (site) (for a boat) n (1) (general area where boats are landed; harbour) omwalo n3; (2) (place where a particular boat lands) ekigobero n7

landslide n okukulugguka kw'ettaka n15

language n olulimi n11 bad (shameful) language (profanities) ebyobugwemufu n8

lantana (plant) n akayuukiyuuki n12

lantern (paraffin) n ettaala n9

¹lap (for holding a child) n omubiri n3 hold in the lap -lera

²lap (lick up) vt -komba

large adj (1) (big) -nene; (2) (wide) -gazi

larva n (1) (maggot) envunyu n9; (2) (found in maize grains) ndiwulira n1; (3) (white, of a beetle, lives in rotting vegetation) ekisokomi n7; (4) (in entula fruits) mmoggo n9; (5) (beetle larva, in sweet potatoes) kawuuzi n1; (6) (beetle larva, in banana stems) entenvu n9; (7) (of bott fly) ekimmonde n7; (8) (in dry stems of raffia palm; eaten in Ssese Islands) essiinya n5; (9) (inside a cocoon) nnamatimbo n1. See insect

¹lash (whip) n kifaalu n9, kibooko n9

²lash (whip) vt -kuba kifaalu. See beat; tie

¹last adj (1) -a enkomerero, eg. ekyekiro eky'enkomerero ('the last supper'); (2) Use -yita ('pass') in rel (N7.1), eg. omwaka oguyise ('last year'); (3) (in line, order, etc.) Use -sembayo ('be last') in rel (N7.1), eg. Guno gwe muti ogusembayo mu lunyiriri. ('This is the last tree in the row.') last-born child omuggalanda n1 last rites amasaakalamentu amavannyuma n6 be last -komererayo, -semba, eg. Omuwala ono yasembye mu kibiina. ('This girl came last in class.') put/make last -sembyayo, eg. Tujja kusembyayo okulonda omukulu mu lukuŋŋaana. ('We will make choosing the leader the last item at the meeting.')

²last (long) vi -wangaala, eg. Leediyo yo ewangadde. ('Your radio has lasted.')

lasting adj (1) -a olubeerera, eg. omukwano ogw'olubeerera ('lasting friendship'); (2) Use -ggwaawo ('be finished') in neg (N21) in rel (N7.1), eg. omukwano ogutaggwaawo ('lasting friendship'). See long-lasting

lastly adv ekyenkomerero, ekisembayo, oluvannyuma

late adv ekikeerezi, eg. Bazze kikeerezi. ('They came late.') be late -keerewa, eg. Ennyonyi ekeereye. ('The plane was late.') It's late. **Obudde buyise.** make late -keereya. See delay

late, the adj (1) (recently deceased) omugenzi (invariable adjective), eg. omugenzi Musoke ('the late Musoke'); (2) (dead for longer) nguli (invariable adjective), eg. nguli jjajjange ('my late grandfather')

later adv edda, oluvannyuma, gye bujja a little later eddako

latest adj -pya, eg. Bbenzi enkola empya ('the latest Mercedes Benz')

latex (of plant) n amasanda n6

¹lather n ejjovu n5, ekyovu n7, ebyovu n8

²lather vi -mmuka, eg. Ssabbuuni ammuse. ('The soap has lathered.')

Latin n Olulattini n11

latrine n mugwanya n9, lattuliini n9. See lavatory pit latrine kaabuyonjo n12

¹laugh n enseko n10

²laugh vi -seka laugh at -sekerera burst into laughter -tyetyemuka, (high-pitched) -tema (or -kuba) akalali, (scornful) -tema akakule make laugh -sesa

laughter *n* **enseko** *n10*, (*loud and high-pitched*) **akalali** *n12*, (*scornful*) **akakule** *n12*

laundry *n* (1) (*clothes for washing*) **engoye ez'okwoza** *n10*; (2) (*place where clothes are washed*) **ewa ddobbi** *n23*

laundryman *n* **ddobbi** *n1*

lavatory *n* (1) (*pit-latrine*) **akayu (ka buyonjo)** *n12*, **kaabuyonjo** *n12*; (2) (*public lavatory*) **kaabuyonjo k'olukale**, (*urinal*) **ekiyigo** *n7*, (*gents*) **abaami** *n2*, (*ladies*) **abakyala** *n2*; (3) (*flush toilet*) **toyireeti** *n9* lavatory paper **ekikookooma** *n7*, **ekipapula eky'okwerongoosesa** *n7* go to the lavatory **-eeyamba**. *See* defecate; urinate

law *n* **etteeka** *n5*

lawcourt *n* **ekkooti y'amateeka** *n9*

lawn (*grass*) *n* **omuddo** *n3*

lawnmover *n* **akuuma akasala omuddo** *n12*

lawyer *n* **munnamateeka** *n1*, **looya** *n1*, **puliida** *n1*. *See* advocate; pleader

lay (down) *vt* (laid) **-galamiza**, *eg. Yagalamiza ensawo ya kasooli wansi.* (*'She laid the sack of maize down.'*), (*carefully*) **-ganzika**, *eg. Yaganzika ekimuli ku ssanduuko.* (*'She laid a wreath on the coffin.'*). *See* lie down; put down lay an egg **-biika eggi** lay (*a baby*) down to sleep **-zazika**, *eg. Yamuzazise mu kitanda.* (*'She laid down the baby to sleep.'*) lay out a dead body **-golola omufu** lay out a mat **-yala omukeeka** lay out a mat for **-yaliirira omukeeka**, *eg. Yayaliirira abagenyi emikeeka.* (*'She spread out mats for the guests.'*) lay out in groups for sale **-lenga** lay the table **-tegeka emmeeza**

layer *n* **omuko** *n3*, (*lining; covering*) **omwaliiro** *n3*. *See* covering; membrane

laziness *n* **obugayaavu** *n14*. *See* indolence

lazy *adj* **-gayaavu** lazy person **omugayaavu** *n1* be lazy **-gayaala** be lazy about (*doing something*) **-gayaalira** laze about **-eegayaaza** make lazy **-gayaaza**

¹lead *n* (1) (*for dog*) **olujegere lw'embwa** *n11*; (2) (*type of metal*) **essasi** *n5*

²lead *vt* (led) (1) (*be in front of*) **-kulembera**; (2) (*be boss of*) **-kulira** lead astray **-wabya**, *eg. Kinneeraliikiriza nti amuwabya.* (*'It worries me that he is leading her astray.'*). *See* deprave; seduce lead to (1) (*go to*) **-genda**, *eg. Oluguudo luno lugenda e Kampala?* (*'Does this road lead to Kampala?'*); (2) (*result in*) **-vaamu**, *eg. Okukola ennyo kuvaamu obugagga.* (*'Hard work leads to riches.'*); (3) (*bring*) **-leeta**, *eg. Okuyamba abantu kireeta omukwano.* (*'Helping people leads to friendship.'*)

leader *n* (1) (*person at the front*) **omukulembeze** *n1*; (2) (*boss*) **omukulu** *n1*

leadership *n* **obukulembeze** *n14*. *See* seniority

leaf *n* (1) **ekikoola** *n7*; (2) (*of banana plant*) **olulagala** *n11*, (*turning yellow*) **ekireka** *n7*, (*withered and dry*) **essanja** *n5*, (*withered and dry,*

when tied in a bundle) **ekisanja** *n7*; (3) (*of a palm*) **olusansa** *n11*

leaflet (*of paper*) *n* **akapapula** *n12*

leafy (*of vegetation*) *adj* **-saakaativu** be(come) leafy **-saakaatira**

leak *vi* (1) (*with continuous flow*) **-tiiriika**, *eg. Endobo etiiriika.* (*'The bucket is leaking.'*); (2) (*dripping*) **-tonnya**

¹lean *adj* (1) (*thin*) **-tono**; (2) (*of person or animal after losing weight*) **-kovvu**; (3) (*without fat, of meat*) **-kapa**, *eg. ennyama enkapa* (*'lean meat'*) become lean (*thin, of a person or animal*) **-kogga**

²lean (on/against) *v* (lent) (1) *vi* **-eesigama**, *eg. Yeesigamye ku kisenge.* (*'He is leaning against the wall.'*); (2) *vt* **-eesigamya**, *eg. Nneesigamya enkumbi ku kisenge.* (*'I leant the hoe against the wall.'*) lean one's head backwards **-lalama**, **-lalika omutwe** lean over **-eewunzika**, *eg. Ekitooke kyewunzise.* (*'The banana plant is leaning over.'*). *See* tilt

leanness (*thinness*) *n* **obutono** *n14*, (*of person or animal after losing weight*) **obukovvu** *n14*

leap (over) *vi* **-buuka**

learn *vt* **-yiga** learn at/for **-yigira**, *eg. Yayigira mu ssomero okuwandiika.* (*'She learnt to write at school.'*) learn by heart **-kwata bukusu**

learned *adj* **-yigirize**

learner *n* **omuyizi** *n1*

learning *n* **okuyiga** *n15*. *See* education

lease *vt* **-pangisa**

leash (*for dog*) *n* **olujegere lw'embwa** *n11*

leather *n* **eddiba** *n5*

¹leave (*permission*) *n* **olukusa** *n11* take leave of (*say goodbye to*) **-siibula**

²leave *v* (left) **TRANSITIVE USES -leka**, *eg. Nnalese abaana mu ssomero* (*'I left the children at school.'*). *See* abandon leave alone **-vaako**, *eg. Muveeko.* (*'Leave him alone.'*) leave for **-lekera**, *eg. Omwana mulekerewo emmere.* (*'Leave some food for the child.'*) leave one's husband **-noba** leave out (*skip over*) **-buukawo**, *eg. Yateeka empapula mu nnyumba z'abantu ng'abuukawo emu.* (*'He distributed the leaflets leaving out every other house.'*) **INTRANSITIVE USES** (1) (*go*) **-genda**, *eg. Ŋŋenda kaakati.* (*'I am leaving now'*); (2) (*go from*) **-va**, *eg. Yavudde mu nnyumba ku ssaawa bbiri.* (*'He left the house at 8 o'clock.'*). *See* abandoned (become); potency (lose) leave home (*to live elsewhere*) **-senguka** leave in protest **-eekandula**, (*enraged, from a meeting; storm out*) **-eekandagga** Leave off (*doing something*) right there! *command* **Lekeraawo!** leave off work (1) (*at one's regular time*) **-nnyuka**, *eg. Abakozi bano bannyuka ku ssaawa kkumi.* (*'These workers leave off work at 4 o'clock.'*); (2) (*of one's own accord*) **-ennyula** leave on a journey **-situla**, *eg. Tujja kusitula ku ssaawa bbiri.* (*'We will leave at 8 o'clock.'*) leave stealthily

(*steal away*) **-ebba**, **-eemulula** <u>be left</u> (*remain*)
-sigala, *eg. Ekitabo kyasigadde mu kisenge kyange.
('The book was left in my room.'). See* lag behind
<u>be left with</u> (1) (*remain with*) **-sigaza**, *eg. Nsigazza
ebitabo bibiri. ('I am left with two books.');* (2)
(*something to do*) **-sigalira**, *eg. Wasigalidde
kuteekako nzigi. ('What is left to do is putting on
the doors.')* **IN MATHS -funa**, *eg. Ssatu ggyako
emu ofuna bbiri. ('Three take away one leaves
two.')*

leaven *vt* **-zimbulukusa** <u>be leavened</u>
-zimbulukuka

leavings *n* (1) (*of bananas and grass, from beer
making*) **ebikamulo** *n8*; (2) (*from brewing
'amalwa'*) **ebikanja** *n8*; (3) (*of tea leaves, after
brewing tea*) **ebikamulo bya caayi**

led *See* lead

leech *n* **ekinoso** *n7*

¹left (*side; direction*) *adj* **-a kkono**, *eg. omukono
ogwa kkono ('left side')* <u>left-handed</u> **-a
enkonokono** <u>left-handed person</u> **ow'enkonokono**
n1

²left (*direction*) *n* **kkono** *n1, eg. Genda ku kkono.
('Go left.')*

³left *v. See* leave

left-over (*surplus*) *adj* (1) *Use* **-lema** (*'be left over'*)
or **-sigalawo** (*'be left with'*) *in rel* (**N7.1**), *eg.
emmere eremye* (or *esigaddewo*) (*'left-over food'*)
<u>left-over cooked food</u> **emmere y'amawolu** *n9*,
amawolu *n6* (*one lump of left-over matooke*
eggwolu *n5*) <u>be left over</u> **-fikka**, *eg. Ebitabo bibiri
bifisse ('Two books are left over.')* <u>have left over</u>
-fissa, *eg. Nnafissizza ssente. ('I had some money
left over.')* <u>something left over</u> **enfissi** *n9*

leg *n* **okugulu** *n15*

legatee *n* **omulaamire** *n1*

legend *n* **olufumo** *n11. See* story

legislate *vi* **-teeka amateeka**

legislation *n* **ebyamateeka** *n8*

leisure *n* **eddembe** *n5* <u>leisure time</u> **ebiseera
eby'eddembe** *n8*

lemon *n* (1) (*tree*) **omuliimu** *n3*; (2) (*fruit*) **enniimu**
n9 <u>lemon grass</u> **ekisubi** *n7*

lend *vt* (1) (*things*) **-yazika**; (2) (*money*) **-wola**

lender *n. Use rel* (**N7.1**), *eg.* (1) (*of things*) **omuntu
ayazika** *n1*; (2) (*of money*) **omuntu awola** *n1*

length *n* **obuwanvu** *n14*

lengthen *vt* **-wanvuya**

lenient person *n* **omukubyabyayi** *n1* <u>be lenient
with</u> **ddiramu**, *eg. Yali wa kisa n'amuddiramu
n'amuleka. ('He was lenient with her and let her
go.')*

¹lent (*borrowed, of things*) *adj* **-yazike**

²Lent (*in Christian calendar*) *n* **Ekisiibo** *n7*

³lent *v. See* lean

leopard *n* **engo** *n9*

leper *n* **omugenge** *n1*, **ow'ebigenge** *n1*

leprosarium *n* **ejjanjabiro ly'ebigenge** *n5*

leprosy *n* **ebigenge** *n8* <u>contract leprosy</u> **-gengewala**

lessen (*reduce*) *vt* **-kendeeza**. *See* fewer (make);
smaller (make) <u>become less</u> (*reduced*) **-kendeera**

lesson *n* (1) (*in school*) **essomo** *n9*, **lesoni** *n9*; (2)
(*Bible reading*) **ekitundu** *n7*

lest (*in case*) *conj* **si kulwa nga**, *eg. Twala manvuuli
si kulwa nga enkuba etonnya. ('Take an umbrella
lest it rains.')*

let *vt* (1) (*allow*) **-leka** (*in subjunctive tense*) *or* **ka**
(*invariable verb*) (**N17**), *eg.* (1) *Baleke bazannye.
('Let them play.');* (2) *Ka bazannye. ('Let them
play.')*; (2) (*rent*) **-pangisa**, *eg. Tupangisa
ennyumba yaffe. ('We are letting our house.')* <u>let
alone</u> (*not even*) *conj* **wadde** <u>let down</u>
(*disappoint*) **-yiwa**, *eg. Yatuyiwa. ('He let us
down.')* <u>let go</u> (*release*) **-ta** <u>let go of one another</u>
-taŋŋana <u>let in</u> **-yingiza**, *eg. Toyingiza embwa mu
nnyumba. (Don't let the dog into the house.')*,
(*unintentionally*) **-yingiriza** <u>let</u> (*someone*) <u>in on</u>
(*confidential or private information*) **-sunirako** <u>let</u>
(*someone*) <u>off</u> (*forgive*), *eg. Omuyizi yeegayiridde
omusomesa amusonyiwe. ('The student pleaded
with the teacher to let her off.')* <u>let oneself in</u>
(*enter*) **-eeyingiza** <u>let up</u> (*reduce in intensity*)
-kendeera, *eg. Enkuba ekendedde. ('The rain is
letting up.')*

lethargic (*also* <u>listless</u>) *adj* **-yongobevu** <u>be
lethargic</u> **-yongobera**

lethargy *n* **obuyongobevu** *n14*

letter *n* (1) (*eg. for posting*) **ebbaluwa** *n9*; (2) (*of the
alphabet*) **ennyukuta** *n9* <u>letter box</u> (*for letters in
post office*) **akasanduuko k'ebbaluwa** *n12*

leukemia *n* **lukeemiya** *n9*, **kkansa w'omu musaayi**
n1

¹level (*of land*) *adj* **-seeteevu**, *eg. Wabbali
w'omugga waseeteevu. ('The land near the river is
level.')* <u>level area of land</u> **omuseetwe** *n3*

²level *n* (1) (*in an organisation*) **eddaala** *n5*; (2)
(*form in school*) *Refer to* **ekibiina** (*'class'*), *eg.
ekibiina eky'okubiri ('Level 2'). See* floor; stage;
standard <u>level of advancement</u> (*RC*) **omugigi** *n3*

³level *vt* **-seeteeza**, *eg. Baaseeteeza ettaka okusima
omusingi. ('They levelled the land to dig the
foundations.')*, **-tereeza** <u>be level</u> **-seeteera**,
-tereera

lever up *vt* **-binula** <u>be levered up</u> **-binuka**

levy *n* **endobolo** *n9. See* tribute

lewd *adj* **-gwagwa**

liaison, sexual (*secret*) *n* **enkolagana y'ekyama** *n9*

liane *n* **ekimera ekiranda** *n7*

liar *n* **omulimba** *n1*, (*habitual*) **kalimbira** *n1*

¹libel *n* **akalebule** *n12*

²libel *vt* **-lebula**. *See* accuser falsely

libelous *adj* **-a akalebule**

liberate *vt* **-nunula** <u>be liberated</u> **-nunulwa**
<u>liberated person</u> **omununule** *n1*

liberator *n* **omununuzi** *n1*

liberty *n* **eddembe** *n5. See* free-hand

library *n* etterekero ly'ebitabo *n5*, enkuluze y'ebitabo *n9*

licence *n* layisinsi *n9*

licentious person *n* omukaba *n1*

lick *vt* -komba

lid *n* ekisaanikira *n7* (*small* akasaanikira *n12*) put lid on -saanikira take lid off -saanukula

¹lie (*deceit*) *n* ekyobulimba *n7*. *See* unfounded assumptions flagrant lie obulimba obw'enkukunala *n14*

²lie (to) (*utter falsehood*) *vi* -limba, *eg. Jjo wannimba.* (*'You lied to me yesterday.'*) lie down -galamira, *eg. Yagalamira wansi.* (*'He lay down on the ground.'*), (*to rest*) -eebakamu, (*anyhow, when tired; flop down*) -gaŋŋalama. *See* lay down lie in wait (for) -teega, *eg. Ateega ababbi.* (*'He is lying in wait for the thieves.'*) lie on one's back -eegalika, *eg. Embwa yeegalise.* (*'The dog is lying on its back.'*) person who lies in wait (*to ambush*) omuteezi *n1*

life *n* obulamu *n14* eternal life obulamu obutaggwaawo

¹lift *n* give a lift to (*in a vehicle*) -twalako

²lift *vt* -situla, *eg. Yasitula ensawo n'agiteeka ku loole.* (*'He lifted the sack and put it on the lorry.'*) lift for -situlira, *eg. Yamusitulira omugugu.* (*'He lifted the load for him.'*) lift load and place on (1) (*one's own head or back*) -eetikka omugugu; (2) (*someone else's head or back*) -tikka omugugu lift out of water -nnyulula lift up one's clothing -fungula engoye, *eg. Yafungula engoye n'atulaga ekiwundu ku kugulu.* (*'She lifted up her clothing to show us the wound on her leg.'*), (*eg. when walking through a swamp*) -fungiza engoye, (*immodestly*) -eefungula, *eg. Yeefungula okulaga amagulu.* (*'She lifted up her clothing to show her legs.'*) lift up one's head (*leaning the head back*) -lalama, -lalika omutwe

ligament *n* ekinywa *n7*

¹light *adj* (1) (*in weight*) -wewufu; (2) (*not dark*) -tangaavu. *See* light-skinned light-fingered person (*pilferer*) ow'engalo *n1* be light (1) (*in weight*) -wewuka; (2) (*not dark*) -tangaala be light-fingered -eetoolatoola get light (*at dawn*) obudde -tangaala, obudde -kya, *eg. Obudde butangadde.* (*'It has become light.'*) make light (1) (*in weight or a task*) -wewusa; (2) (*in colour*) -yerusa; (3) (*of matters; not take them seriously*) -balaata

²light *n* (1) (*lamp*) ettaala *n9* (*large* ekitaala *n7*), ettabaaza *n9*; (2) (*not dark*) obutangaavu *n14* light bulb balubu *n9* electric light (*lamp*) ettaala y'amasannyalaze hand-held light ettaala y'omukono shine a light on -mulisa traffic lights ebitaala *n8*

³light (*candle or lamp*) *vt* -koleeza light a fire -kuma omuliro

lighter (*for striking a flame*) *n* ekikoleeza *n7*

lightness (*of skin colour*) *n* obweru *n14* light-skinned (*of a person*) *adj* -yeru, (*fairly*) -a akatakketakke light-skinned person omweru *n1* be(come) light-skinned -yeruka -make oneself light-skinned -eeyerusa

lightning *n* eraddu *n9*. *See* flash; strike

¹like *conj* nga (**N26**), *eg. Ayimba ng'ekinyonyi.* (*'She sings like a bird.'*). *The following are used in answers to questions based on the verb '-tya?'* (*'how?'*) (**N13**): (1) like this -ti, *eg. Ayimba bw'ati.* (*'She sings like this.'*); (2) like that -tyo, *eg. Ayimba bw'atyo.* (*'She sings like that.'*) be like (*eg. in character or appearance*) -linga, *eg. Alinga maama we.* (*'She is like her mother.'*). *See* ressemble just like nga bwe, *eg. Kola nga bwe nkola.* (*'Do just like I do.'*) look like -faanana

²like *vt* -yagala. *See* tasty (be) like one another -yagalana be liked -yagalwa

likely, be *vi* -yinza, *eg. Enkuba eyinza okutonnya.* (*'It is likely to rain.'*), -labika, *eg. Kirabika ajja kujja.* (*'It is likely she will come.'*), -linga

likeness (*appearance*) *n* enfaanana *n9* be like (*resemble*) -faanana liken oneself to -eefaanaanyiriza ne, *eg. Yeefaanaanyiriza n'omusawo.* (*'He likened himself to a doctor.'*)

likewise *adv* bwe -tyo (**N13**), *eg. Yatambula n'avaawo ne Musoke naye bw'atyo.* (*'She walked away and Musoke did likewise.'*)

liking *n* okwagala *n15*

lily lily trotter (*type of bird*) omutasalanjala *n3* canna lily (*type of plant*) eddanga *n5*

Lima bean *n* akayindiyindi *n12*

limb (*branch*) *n* ettabi *n5*. *See* arm; leg

lime *n* (1) (*tree*) omulimaawa *n3*; (2) (*fruit*) akalimaawa *n12*, ennimaawa *n9*

¹limit *n* ekkomo *n5*. *See* boundary; end

²limit *vt* -teeka ekkomo

limited *adj* -gere, *eg. Omwami ampadde ebbanga ggere okuddayo.* (*'My husband has given me a limted period of time to be here.'*)

¹limp (*slack*) *adj* -lebevu be limp -lebera

²limp (*in walking*) *vi* -wenyera

¹line *n* (1) olunyiriri *n11*, layini *n9*; (2) (*drawn*) olukoloboze *n11*, (*as a margin*) olusittale *n11*, (3) (*on hand or neck*) ekiseera *n7*; (4) (*cord; string*) akaguwa *n12*; (5) (*cable; wire*) waaya. *See* fishing line; margin; queue be out of line -soolooba, *eg. Akati kamu kasooloobyemu.* (*'One stick is out of line.'*), -yitamu

²line (*put a lining*) *vt* -yaliira line up -teeka mu lunyiriri, *eg. Eccupa yaziteeka mu lunyiriri.* (*'She lined up the bottles in a row.'*). *See* queue line with -yaliira, *eg. Yayaliira empapula mu masa.* (*'She lined the shelves with paper.'*)

lineage *n* olulyo *n11*, olubu *n11*. *See* recite

linger *vi* -eerwisa

lining *n* omwaliiro *n3*, olwaliiro *n11* lining of banana leaves (*eg. in basket*) enjaliiro *n10* put a

lining -yaliira
link *vt* -yunga
lintel *n* linto *n9*
lion *n* empologoma *n9*
lip *n* omumwa *n3*
lipstick *n* erangi y'emimwa *n9*
liquid stream of flowing liquid olukulukuse *n11*
traces left by a flowing liquid enkulukuse *n10*
liquify *vt* -saanuusa become liquified -saanuuka
lisp *n* ekirimi *n7* person with a lisp ow'ekirimi *n1*
talk with a lisp -yogera n'ekirimi
¹list *n* olukalala *n11*, *eg. olukalala lw'amannya ('list of names')*
²list *v* (1) *(of a boat)* *vi* -eekubiira; (2) *(itemise)* *vt*
-menya, *eg. Yamenya ebintu bye twali twetaaga okukola. ('She listed the things we needed to do.')*
make a *(written)* list -wandiika ebintu
listen *vi* -wulira listen to -wuliriza, *(carefully)*
-tegereza listen to one another -wuliziganya
listener *n. Use* -wulira *('listen') in rel (N7.1), eg. abantu abawuliriza ('listeners')*
listless *See* lethargic
litre *n* liita *n9*
litter *(rubbish)* *n* ebisasiro *n8*, ebisaaniiko *n8*
little *adj* -tono, *(rather little)* -tonotono a little *adv*
katono, *eg. Omwana asoma katono. ('The child reads a little.')*
¹live *adj* -lamu
²live *vi* (1) *(be living) Use* -li *or* -ba *('be') according to tense (N20.1) followed by* omulamu *('living person'), eg. Akyali mulamu. ('He is still living.')*;
(2) *(at a place)* -beera, *eg. Mbeera wano. ('I live here.')* live alone *Use* -sula *('stay') with* -okka *('alone' N7.3), eg. Asula yekka. ('He is living alone'), (of a woman)* -eeyombekera live long
-wangaala, *eg. Yawangaala. ('He had a long life.')*
lively become more lively -camuka. *eg. Abantu abali ku kabaga bacamuse. ('The people at the party have become more lively.')*
liver *n* ekibumba *n7*
livestock keeper *n* omulunzi *n1. See* husbandry
living *adj* -lamu living person omulamu *n1* living
room eddiiro *n5*
Livingstone potato *n* ennumbu *n9 (type of root vegetation, also called 'Plectranthus yam')*
lizard *n* omunya *n3, (monitor)* enswaswa *n9,
(agama, blue-headed)* ekkonkome *n5, (red and black skink)* embalasaasa *n9. See* gecko
¹load *n* omugugu *n3 (large* eggugu *n5). See* bundle;
luggage put a load on (1) *(someone's head or back)* -tikka omugugu, *eg. Yamutikka omugugu. ('He put a load on her head.')*; (2) *(on one's own head)* -eetikka omugugu
²load *vt* -pakira, *eg. Mmaze okupakira ebintu ku loole. ('I have finished loading the things onto the lorry.')*
¹loaf *(of bread)* *n* omugaati *n3*, bboofulo *n9*
²loaf (about) *vi* (1) *(loiter)* -leeya; (2) *(kill time*

when one should be working) -kongola
loan *vt* (1) *(things)* -yazika; (2) *(money)* -wola
receive a loan (1) *(of things)* -eeyazika; (2) *(of money)* -eewola
loathe *vt* -kyawa
local *adj* -a wano, *eg. edduuka lya wano ('local shop')* local person owa wano *n1*
locate *vt* -zuula
location *(place)* *n* ekifo *n7* change location *(eg. of a business)* -ejjulula
¹lock *n* ekkufulu *n9*
²lock *vt* -siba lock in -sibira be locked up
-sibibwa
locked *adj* -sibe something locked ekisibe *n7*
locust *n* enzige *n9* swarm of young locusts
lusejjera *n1*
lodge *v* (1) *(spend the night)* *vi* -sula; (2) *(put up for the night)* *vt* -suza lodge a complaint -waaba
omusango lodge a complaint against -waabira
become lodged *(stuck)* -wagama become lodged
in -wagamira, *eg. Eggumba liwagamidde mu bulago bwe. ('A bone has got lodged in his throat.')*
lofty *adj* -gulumivu. *See* high be lofty -gulumira
log *n* (1) *(piece of wood)* omuti *n3 (big* ekiti *n7)*; (2)
(for timber) endoddo *n9*; (3) *(on which barkcloth is beaten)* omukomago *n3*; (4) *(hollowed out, for making into a drum)* omulugwa *n3*; (5) *(for firewood)* ekisiki *n7*; (6) *(placed on ground as barrier, eg. to hold drying beans in place)*
omuziziko *n3* long logs placed at base of
firewood pile enjaliiro z'enku *n10*
loggerheads, at *adv* mu kalumannyweera
logic *n* ensonga *n9* argue logically -woza ensonga
logo *n* akabonero *n12*
loiter *vi* -leeya
loneliness *n* ekiwuubaalo *n7*
lonely *adj* -wuubaavu feel lonely -wuubaala
long *adj* (1) *(of size)* -wanvu, *eg. olutindo oluwanvu ('long bridge')*; (2) *(of time)* -nene, *eg. ebbanga eddene ('long time')* long ago edda ennyo long-
lived/lasting *adj* -wangaazi long-lost person *(one who is absent)* omuntu azaawuse *n1* long time
hence edda *(with verb in future tense)* be(come)
long -wanvuwa be long-suffering -gumiikiriza
be long-winded *(digress)* -landagga in the long
run oluvannyuma ennyo last/live long
-wangaala make long -wanvuya something very
long olukoloddoli *n11, eg. olukoloddoli lwa loole ('a very long lorry')* talk for too long -yogera
butamala
long for *(crave)* *vt* -yaayaanira, -yoya
longclaw, yellow-throated *(type of bird)* *n*
ennyonyi ndiisa *n9*
longevity *n* obuwangaazi *n14*
loofah *n* ekyangwe *n7*
¹look *n* take a look -labako *(or* -laba ku*), eg. Ka ndabe ku kiwundu kyo. ('Let me take a look at your*

wound.')

²look (*in a certain way*) *vi* **-tunuza**, *eg. Yatunuza obukambwe. ('He looked fierce.')* look after (1) (*supervise*) **-labirira**; (2) (*protect*) **-kuuma**; (3) (*animals*) **-lunda**; (4) (*goats or sheep*) **-sumba** look after oneself **-eerabirira, -eefaako** look alike **-faanagana**, *eg. Abaana bafaanagana. ('The children look alike.')* look alike to **-faanaganira**, *eg. Banfaanaganira. ('They look alike to me.')* look around (1) (*in a distracted way*) **-labankana**; (2) (*suddenly, eg. when surprised*) **-maguka** look around for (*searching*) **-suuliza enkessi**, *eg. Mbega wa poliisi yasuuliza enkessi n'azuula Musoke we yakweka emmundu. ('The detective looked around to find where Musoke had hidden the gun.')* look at (*see*) **-laba**, *eg. Twalinnya ku kasozi okulaba ennyanja. ('We climbed the hill to look at the lake.').* See overlook; stare look at oneself **-eeraba** look beyond (*the immediate*) **-buusa amaaso** look down in shyness **-eemoola** look down on (*despise*) **-nyooma**. See contempt look for (*seek*) **-noonya**, (*on behalf of*) **-noonyeza** look forward to **-eesunga**, *eg. Nneesunga okusaba. ('I am looking forward to going to church.')* look from side to side **-magamaga** look good (*attractive*) **-wooma**, *eg. Awoomye. ('She looks good.')* look good on **-woomera**, *eg. Olugoye lumuwoomera. ('The dress looks good on her.')* look like (*resemble*) **-faanana**, (*to someone*) **-faanaanyiriza** *See* resemble look stern **-eekaba** look up (*tilting the head back*) **-lalama** make look alike **-faananya**, *eg. Musoke yawunze ensawo ye n'afaananya eyange. ('Musoke decorated his bag and made it look like mine.')* person who looks after animals **omulunzi** *n1*

looking at *conj* **okulabira ku**, *eg. Okulabira ku kye bakola, naffe ka tukole bwe tutyo. ('Looking at how they do it, let's do it the same way.')*

looking glass (*mirror*) *n* **endabirwamu** *n9*

looks (*appearance*) *n* **enfaanana** *n9*

looper (*caterpillar*) *n* **nnabeefunye** *n1*

loose *adj* (1) (*slack*) **-lebevu**; (2) (*not attached*) **-a omwera**, *eg. amatooke ag'omwera ('loose plantains').* See wobbly be(come) loose (*slack*) **-lebera**, *eg. Omuguwa gw'engoye gulebedde. ('The washing line is loose.')* be loose-fitting (on) **-sagala**, *eg. Empale emusagala. ('His trousers are loose-fitting.')* get loose (*from being tied or held*) **-eetakkuluza**, *eg. Omusibe yeetakkuluza n'adduka. ('The prisoner got loose and ran away.')* let loose (1) (*set free*) **-ta**; (2) (*tied or penned animal*) **-yimbula**; (3) (*release from a trap*) **-tegulula** make loose (*slacken*) **-leegulula**

loosen *vt* (1) (*slacken, eg. a rope*) **-lebeza**; (2) (*eg. belt or tie*) **-takkuluza**; (3) (*release pressure*) **-teewuluza**, *eg. Nnateewuluza essaati olw'ebbugumu. ('I am loosening my shirt because of the heat.')*

looseness (*slackness*) *n* **obulebevu** *n14*

¹loot *n* **omunyago** *n3*

²loot *vt* **-nyaga**

looted *adj* **-nyage**

looter *n* **omunyazi** *n1*

looting *n* **obunyazi** *n14*

lop *vt* **-temako**

lop-sided, be (*lean to one side*) *vi* **-eekubiira**, *eg. Yaweeka ensawo ku ggaali ne yeekubiira. ('He put the sack on the bike lop-sidedly.')*

loquat (*tree*) *n* **omusaali omuzungu** *n3*

Lord God *n* **Mukama Katonda** *n1*

lorry *n* **loole** *n9*, (*long*) **lukululana** *n9*

lose *vt* (lost) **-buza**, *eg. Abuzizza essaawa yange. ('She has lost my watch.'),* (*often*) **-buzaabuza**, (*through death*) **-fiirwa**, *eg. Afiiriddwa omwana we. ('She has lost her child.'),* (*through something coming out*) **-vaamu**, *eg. Olugoye luvaamu erangi. ('The dress is losing its colour.')* lose a court case **omusango -singa** (*with personal object*), *eg. Omusango gunsinze. ('I have lost the case.')* lose a day **-yosa**, *eg. Yayosezza kubanga yabadde mulwadde. ('She lost a day because of illness.')* lose control **-lemerera**, *eg. Emmotoka yamulemerera mu kaseerezi n'ewaba. ('He lost control of the car on a slippery road.')* lose heart **-ggwaamu amaanyi** lose hope **-ggwaamu essuubi** lose one's reputation **-yonoona erinnya** lose one's sight **-ziba amaaso** lose self-control (*become wild*) **-taama, -taamuuka** lose shape (1) (*of something solid, eg. metal*) **-gooma**; (2) (*through being badly damaged*) **-gongobala**; (3) (*eg. bundle due to being squashed or losing contents*) **-soosootoka** lose strength (*of a person*) **-ggwaamu endasi, -sereba** lose supernatural power **-fuluka** lose weight (1) (*of person or animal*) **-kogga**; (2) (*through losing contents*) **-sowottoka** become lost **-bula**, *eg. Ekitabo kibuze. ('The book is lost.'). A person concerned may be indicated by an object pronoun, eg. Ekitabo kyange kibuze. ('My book is lost.'). See away (be)* be lost in/at **-bulira** person who has lost weight **omukovvu** *n1*

loss (*bereavement*) *n* **okufiirwa** *n15* be at a loss (*baffled*) **-soberwa**, *eg. Nsobeddwa eky'okukola. ('I am at a loss about what to do.'), **-bulwa**, *eg. Nnabulwa eky'okuddamu. ('I was at a loss for an answer.')* feel a loss (*eg. when a person departs*) **-wuubaala**

¹lost *adj.* Use **-bula** (*'become lost'*) in rel (**N7.1**), *eg. ekitabo ekibuze ('lost book')*

²lost *v. See* lose

lot, a *adv* **ennyo**, *eg. Akaaba nnyo. ('He cries a lot.')* lots (*a lot of*) **enkumuliitu** *n9, eg. enkumuliitu y'ebisaaniko ('lots of rubbish'). See* excessive; many be quite a lot **-wera**

lotion *n* **ebizigo** *n8*

lottery (*also* lottery ticket) *n* **akalulu** *n12* play the lottery -kuba akalulu

loud, be *vi* -woggana, *eg. Bbandi ewoggana. ('The band is loud.')* loud-mouthed person *(bumptious)* ow'akababba *n1*

loudly *adv* waggulu, *eg. Ayogerera waggulu. ('He talks loudly.')*

loudspeaker *n* omuzindaalo *n1*

louse *n* ensekere *n9*

lout *n* omuyaaye *n1*

¹love *n* okwagala *n15* love affair omukwano *n3* love of muganzi *(with pos N12), eg. muganzi wange ('my love')* loved one omwagalwa *n1, (one not seen for a long time)* kabuladda *n1*

²love *vt* -yagala love one another -yagalana be loved -yagalwa

loved *adj* -ganzi

lovely *adj* -lungi

¹low *(not high) adj* -a wansi

²low *(moo, as a cow) vi* -kaaba

¹lower *adv* wansi, *(on a slope)* emmanga, *eg. Omusiri guli mmanga. ('The field is lower down.')* lower class person owa wansi *n1* a little lower wansiko, wansinsi

²lower *vt* -ssa, *eg. Bassa ebendera olw'okukungubaga. '(They lowered the flag as a sign of mourning.'),* -yongerako wansi, *eg. Ekifaananyi yakyongerako wansi ku kisenge. ('She lowered the position of the picture on the wall.'),* -wanula lower one's gaze *(look down)* -ssa amaaso lower one's head *(eg. in shame)* -koteka omutwe. *See* bow lower one's voice *(in volume)* -kendeeza ku ddoboozi

loyalty, pledge -wera. *See* pledge

lubricate *vt* -teekamu oyiro lubricating oil oyiro *n1*

luck *(also good luck) n* omukisa *n3* bad luck omukisa omubi, ekisiraani *n7* good luck eggwiiso *n5*

luckily *adv* eky'omukisa

lucky *adj* -a omukisa lucky nut *(type of plant; Thevetia)* obusitaani *n14*, kamuseenene *n12* lucky person ow'omukisa *n1* be lucky -eesiima have a lucky escape -lula

Lucy *n* Luusi *n1*

Luganda *(language) n* Oluganda *n11*

luggage *n* emigugu *n4 (one piece* omugugu *n3, a lot* engugu *n9)*

Luke *n* Lukka *n1*

lukewarm, be *vi* -yokerera

lull *(period of quiet) n* akasiriikiriro *n12* lull *(a baby)* to sleep -siisiitira

lunatic *See* mad

lunch *n* ekyemisana *n7*

lunchhour *n* ebyemisana *n8*

lung *n* egguggwe *n5*

lungfish *n* emmamba *n9 (young* omuguya *n3). The pectoral fins are called* amabeere *n6.*

Lunyoro *(language) n* Olunyoro *n11*

Luo *(person) n* Omuluulu *n1*

lure *vt* -sendasenda

Lusoga *(language) n* Olusoga *n11*

lust after *vt* -eegomba

luxuriant *(of vegetation; thick and leafy) adj* -saakaativu be luxuriant *(of vegetation)* -saakaatira

luxuriousness *n* obwejalabi *n14*

luxury *n* ekintu eky'okwejalabya *n7* give oneself a luxury -eejalabya person having luxury omwejalabi *n1*

lying *n* obulimba *n14*

lymph gland, swollen *n* ensanjabavu *n9*

lyre *(musical instrument) n* endongo *n9*, entongooli *n7* lyre player omusunyi w'endongo *n1*

M,m

macadam *n* kkoolaasi *n1*

machete *n* ejjambiya *n5*

machine *n* ekyuma *n7*, masiini *n9* machine gun emmundu ewandula amasasi *n9*, luwandulamasasi *n9*

mad *adj* -lalu mad person *(or* lunatic*)* omulalu *n1*, *(one having a fit of madness)* omuzoole *n1* drive mad -lalusa go mad -laluka, -gwa eddalu. *See* disturbed pretend to be mad -eeralusa

Madagascar periwinkle *(plant) n* akamuli *n12*

madam *n* nnyabo *n1*

made *See* make

madness *n* eddalu *n5*, obulalu *n14*, *(fit of)* akazoole *n12*, *(of a young woman after giving birth, from breaking a taboo)* amakiro *n6* have a fit of madness -zoola

maggot *n* envunyu *n9*. *See* larva

magician *n* omufuusa *n1* perform magic -fuusa

magistrate *n* omulamuzi *n1*, omusazi w'emisango *n1* magistrate's court ekkooti ento *n9*

magnificent *adj* -a ekitalo, -a kulabako, makula *(invariable adjective), eg. Alina emmotoka makula. ('He has a magnificent car.')*

magnify *vt* -zimbulukusa be magnified -zimbulukuka

mahogany *(type of tree; Entandrophragma) n* omuyovu *n3*

maid *(house servant) n* omukozi w'awaka *n1*

mail *n* ebbaluwa *n10*

maim *vt* -lemaza be(come) maimed -lemala

main *adj* -kulu. *See* large

mainly *adv. Use* -singa *('be more'), eg. Basinze kusimba kasooli. ('They have mainly planted maize.')*

maintain *vt* (1) *(look after)* -labirira, *eg. Musoke alabirira oluggya. ('Musoke is maintaining the compound.');* (2) *(cause to continue)* -beezaawo, *eg. Ebintu bino byetaagisa olw'okubeezaawo obulamu. ('These things are needed to maintain* *life.')* maintain oneself (*or* itself) **-yimirirawo**

maize *n* (1) **kasooli** *n1* (*one cob* **omunwe gwa kasooli** *n3*); (2) (*grain, or dry cob*) **emberenge** *n9*; (3) (*core of cob after removal of grains*) **ekikongoliro** *n7*; (4) (*stalk after removal of cobs*) **ekisoolisooli** *n7* maize beer **kkwete** *n1* maize flour **obuwunga bwa kasooli** *n14*. See bbando (*in Part 2 of the dictonary*) maize meal **akawunga** *n12* maize porridge **obuugi** *n14* make maize meal **-goya akawunga** remove grains from cob **-kongola kasooli** roasted maize **kasooli omwokye**

major *adj.* Use **-singa obunene** ('*be most in size or extent*'), *eg. Ekizibu kye ekisinga obunene bwavu.* ('*His major problem is poverty.*')

[1]**make** (*brand*) *n* **enkola** *n9. See* type make-up (*nature; character*) **enkula** *n9*

[2]**make** *vt* (made) (1) (*manufacture*) **-kola**, *eg. Akola enkumbi.* ('*He makes hoes.*'); (2) (*amount to*) **-wera**, *eg. Emu gattako emu ziwera bbiri.* ('*One and one makes two.*'); (3) (*create*) **-tonda**, *eg. Katonda yatonda ensi.* ('*God made the world.*'); (4) (*compel*) **-waliriza, -kakaakiriza** make a bed **-yala obuliri**, *eg. Ayaze obuliri.* ('*He has made the bed.*') make a bed for **-yalira obuliri**, *eg. Yamwalira obuliri.* ('*He made a bed for her.*') make a copy **-kola kopi** make an effort **-fuba, -ssaamu amaanyi** make beer (*from bananas*) **-sogola omwenge** make for/at **-kolera**, *eg. Musoke akolera taata we entebe.* ('*Musoke is making a chair for his father.*') make from/into **-kolamu**, *eg. Omuweesi ayokya ekyuma asobole okukolamu enkumbi.* ('*The blacksmith is heating iron to make into a hoe.*') make oneself (*force oneself*) **-eewaliriza, -eekakaba** make up (*invent*) **-yiiya**. *See* fake; lie; reconcile make up to (1) (*a required amount*) **-weza**, *eg. Weza kiro bbiri.* ('*Make it up to two kilos.*'); (2) (*to repair a relationship*) **-gatta**, *eg. Musoke yagulira mukyala we ekiteeteeyi okumugatta.* ('*Musoke bought his wife a dress to make up to her.*') make way for (*move out of the way of*) **-segulira** make with clay **-bumba** make with wood **-bajja** be made **-kolebwa**, *eg. Eggaali eno ekolebwa mu Kyayina.* ('*This bicycle is made in China.*'), (*of a bed*) **-yala**, *eg. Obuliri bwale.* ('*The bed is made.*') be made into **-kolebwamu**, *eg. Omuti guno gujja kukolebwamu emmeeza.* ('*This wood will be made into a table.*')

malady *See* disease; illness

malaria *n* **omusujja gw'ensiri** *n3*, **maleeriya** *n9*

male *adj* **-sajja**, (*of certain animals*) **-lume**, *eg. ente ennume* ('*bull*')

maleness *n* **obusajja** *n14*

malice (*also* malevolence) *n* **ettima** *n5*

malicious (*also* malevolent) *adj* **-a ettima**

maliciously *adv* **n'ettima**

malign *See* slander

mallet (*for making barkcloth*) *n* **ensaamu** *n9. The mallets used for the stages of beating are*: (1) (*stage 1; coarsely toothed*) **ensaasi** *n9* (*also known as* **enkubi** *n9*); (2) (*stage 2; flatter toothed*) **empuuzo** *n9*; (3) (*stage 3; finely toothed*) **enzituzi** *n9. See* barkcloth

man *n* (1) (*human*) **omuntu** *n1*; (2) (*male*) **omusajja** *n1*, (*tall and thin*) **sserugooti** *n1*, (*strong*) **kirimaanyi** *n1. See* person become a man **-sajjakula** big man (*having more than one major asset, eg. children, wives, houses, money*) **ssemaka** *n1*

manage *v* (1) (*be able*) *vi* **-sobola, -yinza**; (2) (*supervise*) *vt* **-labirira**; (3) (*operate; run*) *vt* **-ddukanya** be manageable (*doable*) **-koleka**

management *n* (1) (*the way things are run*) **enzirukanya** *n9*; (2) (*the people managing*) **abaddukanya** *n2*

manager *n* **omuddukanya** *n1*, **maneja** *n1* my manager **mukama wange**, your manager **mukama wo**, *etc.* (**N12**)

manfully *adv* **amasajja**

mangabey *See* monkey

mange (*skin disease of dogs*) *n* **olukuku** *n11*

manger (*as in the Bible*) *n* **emmanvu** *n9*

mangle (*with claws*) *vt* **-taagula**

mango (*tree; fruit*) *n* **omuyembe** *n3. Varieties include* **kagoogwa, kufuta, doodo, lubeere, kanaana** (*the first two medicinal*).

mangrove tree (*freshwater*) *n* **omukusu** *n3*

mania *n* **akazoole** *n12*

maniac *n* **omulalu** *n1*

manioc *See* cassava

mankind *n* **obuntu** *n14*

manliness *n* **obusajja** *n14*

manna *n* **mmaanu** *n1*

manner (*way*) *n* **engeri** *n9. See* way

manners *n* **empisa** *n10* good manners **empisa ennungi, obuntubulamu** *n14* well-mannered person **omuntumulamu** *n1*

mannikin (*small finch-like bird found in flocks*) *n* **akasanke** *n12*

mantis, praying *n* **nkongolamabeere** *n1. The insect that lives in stems of banana plants and looks like a praying mantis is* **nnabangagoma** *n1*.

manufacture *vt* **-kola**, (*with metal*) **-weesa**

manure *n* **nnakavundira** *n1*

many *det* **-ngi**. *See* commonplace; lots

map *n* **maapu** *n9*

marabou stalk *n* **kalooli** *n9*

[1]**March** (*month*) *n* **Omwezi ogw'okusatu** *n3*, **Mugulansigo, Maaci**

[2]**march** (*as soldiers*) *vi* **-kumba**

margarine *n* **magirini** *n1*, **bulubbanda** *n1*

margin (*ruled line on page*) *n* **omusittale** *n3. See* boundary; edge

Maria *n* **Maliya** *n1*

Mariam *n* **Maliyamu** *n1*

marijuana *n* **enjaga** *n9*, **enjaaye** *n9*

¹mark *n* (1) (*spot; stain*) **ebbala** *n5* (*small* **akabala** *n12*); (2) (*symbol*) **akabonero** *n12*. *See* speck Mark (*the name*) **Makko** *n1* tribal marks on body **enjokyo** *n10* (*one* **oluyokyo** *n11*)

²mark *vt* (1) (*examine*) **-kebera**; (2) (*label*) **-lamba**; (3) (*put a mark, eg. dot*) **-tonnyeza**; (4) (*mark with a sharp point; scratch*) **-kolobola**

marker (*examiner*) *n* **omukebezi** *n1*

¹market *n* **akatale** *n12* market stall **omudaala** *n3* market supervisor **ssentala** *n1*

²market (*sell*) *vt* **-tunda**

marketing *n* **entunda** *n9*

marksman *n* **omukubi wa ssabbaawa** *n1*

marriage *n* **obufumbo** *n14* married person **omufumbo** *n1*, (*one married in church*) **omugatte** *n1* stage of married life (*for a woman*) **eddya** *n5*, *eg. Ali mu ddya ery'okusatu.* ('*She is her third marriage.*') state of being newly married **obugole** *n14*

marrow (*of bone*) *n* **obusomyo** *n14*

marry *vt* (1) (*by a man*) **-wasa**, *eg. Yokana yawasa Maliya.* ('*John married Mary.*'); (2) (*by a woman*) **-fumbirwa**, *eg. Maliya yafumbirwa Yokana.* ('*Mary married John.*'); (3) (*following Christian rites*) **-gatta**, *eg. Omwawule yabagatta jjo.* ('*The priest married them yesterday.*') marry one another **-fumbiriganwa** be joined in marriage (*in church*) **-gattibwa**

marsh *n* (1) (*wetland*) **olutobazzi** *n11*; (2) (*muddy place where one can get stuck*) **entubiro** *n9*. *See* swamp

martyr *n* **omujulizi** *n1*

¹marvel *n* **ekyewuunyisa** *n7*, **ekyamagero** *n7* marvels **amagero** *n6*

²marvel (at) *vit* **-eewuunya**

marvellous *adj* **-a amagero**

Mary *n* (1) (*mainly Prot*) **Mmeere** *n1*; (2) (*RC*) **Maliya** *n1*; (3) (*Muslim*) **Malyamu** *n1* Virgin Mary **Biikira Maliya** *n1*

masculine *adj* **-sajja**

masculinity (*also* manliness) *n* **obusajja** *n14*

¹mash (*sweet potatoes and beans*) *n* **omugoyo** *n3*

²mash *vt* (1) (*eg. potatoes*) **-sotta**, **-gotta**; (2) (*mix something thick, involving stirring*) **-goya**. *See* crush mash cooked bananas (*by squeezing omuwumbo*) **-nyiga emmere** mash maize meal **-goya akawunga**

masher (*for mashing*) *n* **ekisotta** *n7*

mask *n* **akakookolo** *n14*

mass (*religious; mainly RC*) *n* **emmisa** *n9*

massage *vt* **-siimuula**

massive *adj* **-nene ennyo**

mast *n* **omulongooti** *n3*, **omunaala** *n3* telephone mast **omulongooti gw'essimu**

master (*boss*) *n* **omukulu** *n1*. *See* teacher master of **mukama** (*with pos* **N12**), *eg. mukama wange* ('*my master*') master of ceremonies **kalabaalaba**

w'omukolo *n1*

masterbate *vi* **-eemazisa**

mastitis (*inflamed breast*) *n* **ebbanyi** *n5*

mat *n* (1) (*coarse type, made from papyrus or banana fibre*) **ekiwempe** *n7*; (2) (*coarse type, made from whole palm leaflets*) **kyaki** *n1*; (3) (*finely woven, made from split palm leaflets*) **omukeeka** *n3*; (4) (*used by itinerant labourers*) **ekirago** *n7* border strip of mat **ensandaggo** *n9* lay out a mat for (*eg. to put plates on*) **-yaliira ekiwempe** put border strip on mat **-sandagga** prayer mat (*of Muslims*) **omusaalo** *n3*

¹match (*contest*) *n* **empaka** *n10* matches (*for lighting*) **ebibiriiti** *n8* (*one* **akati k'ekibiriiti** *n12*)

²match (*harmonise with*) *vi* **-kwatagana**, *eg. Engoye ze zikwatagana.* ('*Her clothes are matching.*')

matchbox *n* **ekibiriiti** *n7*

¹mate (*close friend*) *n* **wa kinywi** *n1*. *See* companion; friend my mate form of address **mwana wattu, munnange**

²mate (*mount by male animal*) *vi* **-linnyira**

material (*fabric*) *n* **olugoye** *n11*, (*shiny*) **olugoye olumasamasa**, (*striped*) **olugoye lw'ebikuubo**

maternity *n* **mateniti** *n9* maternity home (*or* ward) **ezzaaliro** *n5*

mathematics *n* **okubala** *n15*

matrimony *n* **obufumbo** *n14* holy matrimony **obufumbo obutukuvu**

matron of honour *n* **kalabaalaba w'omugole** *n1*

¹matter *n* (1) (*affair*) **ensonga** *n9*; (2) (*substance*) **ekintu** *n7* matter of contention **kalumannywera** *n1* about the matter that *conj* **olwekyo kye**

²matter *vi. Use adjective* **-kulu** ('*important*'), *eg. Ensonga zino nkulu.* ('*This business matters.*') something that matters **eky'ensonga** *n7*

Matthew *n* **Matayo** *n1*

mattress *n* **omufaliso** *n3*

¹mature *adj* **-kulu**

²mature *vi* **-kula**

maul *vt* **-taagula**

¹May (*month*) *n* **Omwezi ogw'okutaano** *n3*, **Muzigo, Maayi**

²may *aux v* (1) **-linga**, *eg. Alinga agenze.* ('*She may have gone.*'); (2) *Use* **-yinza** ('*might*'), *eg. Ayinza okuba ng'agenze.* ('*She may have gone.*')

maybe (*also* perhaps) *adv* (1) *Use* **-linga** *as aux v in present tense* (**N19**), *eg. Alinga anajja.* ('*Maybe she will come.*'); (2) **-yinza**, *eg. Ayinza okuba nga ajja.* ('*Maybe she will come.*'); (3) **oboolyawo**, *eg. Oboolyawo anajja.* ('*Maybe she will come.*'); (4) **osanga**, *eg. Osanga anajja.* ('*Maybe he will come.*')

mayor *n* **mmeeya** *n1*

me *pro* **nze**. *The verb prefix is* **n-** (**N15**) *with many spelling variants* (**N5**).

meal *n* **emmere** *n9*, *eg. Tulya mmere.* ('*We are having a meal.*'), (*for invited guests*) **ekijjulo** *n7* finger millet meal **akalo** *n12* maize meal akawunga *n12*, **bbando** *n1* (*sometimes mixed with cassava flour*)

mealtime *n* **malya** *n6*, **kiseera kya malya** *n7*, **kiseera kya kulya**

¹**mean** (*miserly*) *adj* **-kodo** mean person **omukodo** *n1* be(come) mean **-kodowala** be mean to **-kodowalira**, *eg. Mukama wange ankodowalira.* (*'My boss is mean to me.'*). See give too little

²**mean** (*signify*) *vt* **-tegeeza**, *eg. Ekigambo kino kitegeeza ki? ('What does this word mean?')*

meaning *n* **amakulu** *n6*

meanness (*stinginess*) *n* **obukodo** *n14*

measles *n* **olukusense** *n11*, **mulangira** *n1* contract measles **-kusensa** develop a skin rash (*through measles*) **-yiwa**

¹**measure(ment)** *n* **ekipimo** *n7*, **ekigero** *n7* chest (*or bust*) measurement **ekifuba** *n7* measured amount **omugereko** *n3* unit of measure for burial cloth (*about 4 metres*) **looti** *n9*

²**measure** *vt* **-pima**, **-gera** measure out (*put in groups for sale*) **-lenga** way of measuring **empima** *n9*

measured *adj* **-gere**

meat *n* **ennyama** *n9*, (*under the hide*) **kaabuuyi** *n1* dried meat (*stored for future use*) **omukalo** *n3* piece of meat **ekifi** *n7*, (*large*) **ekiyingula** *n7*, (*boneless*) **omuwula gw'ennyama** *n3* raw meat **ennyama embisi, ennyama eteri nfumbe**

Mecca *n* **Maaka** *n7*

mechanic *n* **omufundi** *n1*, **ffundi** *n1*, **makanika** *n1*

medal/medallion *n* **omudaali** *n3*

meddle *vi* **-eeyingiza**, *eg. Yeeyingiza mu bintu byange. ('He is meddling in my affairs.').* See involve oneself meddle in **-bambira**

meddler *n* **ow'akajanja** *n1*

meddlesomeness *n* **akajanja** *n12*

mediate (between) *vi* **-tabaganya**, *eg. Atutabaganya. ('She is mediating between us.')*

mediator *n* **omutabaganya** *n1*

medicinal medicinal clay stick **emmumbwa** *n9* medicinal plant **eddagala** *n5*

medicine *n* (1) (*substance used in treatment*) **eddagala** *n5*, (*indigenous*) **eddagala ly'ekinnansi**, (*to induce pregnancy*) **eddagala ly'oluzaalo**; (2) (*as an art or profession*) **obusawo** *n14*. See herb

meditate (on) *vit* **-fumiitiriza**

¹**medium** (*average*) *adj* **-a ekigero**

²**medium** (*mouthpiece of a spirit*) *n* **omukongozi** *n1*, (*of a lubaale*) **omulubaale** *n1*, (*of a nature spirit*) **mmandwa** *n1*, (*someone who participates in a spirit possession ritual*) **omusamize** *n1*. See spirit become a medium (*of a lubaale*) **-tendeka lubaale** practice mediumship (*as a group activity*) **-samira**

meek *adj* **-wombeefu** meek person **omuwombeefu** *n1* be meek **-eewombeeka**

meekness *n* **obuwombeefu** *n14*

meet *vt* (met) **-siŋŋaana**, **-sanga**, (*by arrangement*) **-sisinkana**, *eg. Tusisinkane ku Sheraton. ('Let's*

meet at the Sheraton.')* meet unexpectedly **-sangiriza**

meeting *n* (1) (*gathering*) **olukuŋŋaana** *n11*; (2) (*formal, eg. of a committee*) **olukiiko** *n11*. See encounter meeting hall (*open-sided building*) **ekigango** *n7* meeting place **ekkuŋŋaaniro** *n5* attend a meeting **-kiika** close a meeting **-fundikira olukuŋŋaana** emergency meeting **olukiiko olw'amangu** hold a meeting **-kuba olukuŋŋaana**, (*in private or secret*) **-twekobaana**

melt *v* (1) *vi* **-saanuuka**; (2) *vt* **-saanuusa**

member (*of a group*) *n* **munnakibiina** *n1*, **memba** *n1* member of a clan **ow'ekika** *n1*

membership *n* **obwamemba** *n14*

membrane *n* **akabubi** *n12*

memorial *n* **ekijjukizo** *n7*

memorise *vt* **-kwata** passage to be memorised **ekikwate** *n7*

memory *n* **okujjukira** *n15*

menace *vt* **-tiisa**

mend *vt* **-ddaabiriza**, (*something mechanical*) **-kanika** mend one's ways **-eddako**

meningitis *n* **mulalama** *n1*

menstruate *vi* **-lwala omwezi** menstrual pains **enjoka ez'eddumi** *n10*

mental asylum *n* **ennyumba y'abalalu** *n9*

mention (to) *vt* **-yogerako**, *eg. Kyogereko na ye olabe ky'agamba. ('Mention it to him and see what he says.')*

Mercedes Benz *n* **bbenzi** *n9*

merchandise *n* **ebyokutunda** *n8*

merchant *n* **omusuubuzi** *n1*, (*itinerant*) **omutembeeyi** *n1*

merciful *adj* **-a ekisa** feel merciful towards **-kwatibwa ekisa**

mercy *n* **ekisa** *n7*

mere *adj* (1) (*only*) **-okka** (**N7.3**); (2) (*just; ordinary*) **-yereere**

merely *adv* **ekyo kyokka**. See **N23**

merit (*deserve*) *vt* **-saanira**, **-gwanira**

merry-making *n* **ebbinu** *n5*, **ekijaguzo** *n7*, **entujjo** *n5*. See celebration make merry **-jaguza**. See elated (be); romp

mess *n* **omuvuyo** *n3*, **akavuyo** *n12*. See confusion

mess up *vt* **-dobonkanya**, **-gootaanya**, **-vuluga**. See spoil; tamper with be messed up **-dobonkana**, **-gootaana** go badly (*of affairs*) **-gozoobana**

message *n* **obubaka** *n14* text message **essemwesi** *n9*

messenger *n* **omubaka** *n1*

Messiah *n* **Masiya** *n1*

messy See dirty; untidy

met See meet

metal *n* **ekyuma** metal worker **omuweesi** *n1* metal workshop **essasa** *n5* do metalwork **-weesa** metallic smell **oluwugge** *n11*

metaphor *n* **ekisoko** *n7*

method *n* **enkola** *n9*

metre *n* miita *n9*

Mexican sunflower (*Tithonia*) *n* kimala empaka kikoowa. *Name needs confirmation.*

microphone *n* akazindaalo *n3*, omwogererwa *n3*

microscope *n* ekyuma ekizimbulukusa *n7*

midday *n* essaawa mukaaga ez'emisana

[1]**middle** *adj* -a wakati, *eg.* ennyumba ya wakati (*'the middle house'*)

[2]**middle** *n* amakkati *n6*, *eg. amakkati g'ekibuga* (*'middle of the town'*) in the middle **mu makkati**, **wakati** in the middle of **mu makkati ga**, (*in the centre of a space*) **wakati mu**, *eg. Ekkanisa eri wakati mu kibuga.* (*'The church is in the middle of the town.'*), (*between items*) **wakati wa**

midnight *n* essaawa mukaaga ez'ekiro

midrib of banana leaf *n* omugoŋŋoonyo *n3*, omuziŋŋoonyo *n3* remove midrib of banana leaf -yubuluza olulagala

midway *adv* wakati

midwife *n* omuzaalisa *n1*, (*traditional*) omuzaalisa w'ekinnansi

midwifery *n* obuzaalisa *n14*

[1]**might** (*strength*) *n* amaanyi *n6*

[2]**might** (*could*) *aux v.* Use -yinza (*'be able'*), *eg. Ayinza okujja edda.* (*'He might come later.'*)

mighty (*strong*) *adj* -a amaanyi

migraine *n* omutwe omuteezi *n3*

migrate (*move home*) *vi* -senguka

mild (*moderate*) *adj* -saamusaamu. *See* meek

mildew *n* obukuku *n14* become mildewed -kukula

mile *n* mayiro *n9*, mailo *n9*

military *adj* -a amagye military engagement olutalo *n11*, olutabaalo *n11*

[1]**milk** *n* amata *n6*, (*boiled*) amata amafumbe, (*curdled*) bbongo *n1* milk pot ekyanzi *n7* cease giving milk (*of a cow*) -kamiza

[2]**milk** *vt* -kama

mill (*grind grain*) *vt* -sa mill about in confusion (*of people*) -vuvuŋŋana mill (*grain*) for -seera, *eg. Yamuseera kasooli.* (*'She milled the maize for him.'*) be milled (*of grain*) -seebwa

millet, finger *n* (*plant*) obulo *n14*, (*flour/meal*) akalo *n12*, (*porridge*) obusera *n14*, (*beer*) amalwa *n6*

million *num* akakadde *n12*, miriyoni *n9* millions (*uncountable large number*) akatabalika *n12* ten million akawumbi *n12*

millipede *n* eggongolo *n5*, (*type found in thatch*) ekiboobi *n7* millipede-like animal (*appears at a particular time of year*) kaamwaka *n1*

millstone *See* grindstone

mimic *vt* -geegeenya, (*annoyingly*) -yeeya. *See* copy

[1]**mind** *n* (1) (*thoughts*) ebirowoozo *n8*; (2) (*spirit; heart*) omutima *n3*. *See* spirit apply one's mind -teekako (*or* -ssaako) omwoyo be out of one's mind -wunga lose one's mind (*become demented*) -wutta, -wuttuka

[2]**mind** *v* (1) (*care*) *vi* -faayo ku, *eg. Afaayo ku* ndabika ye. (*'He minds about his appearance.'*); (2) (*look after*) *vt* -labirira, *eg. Ani alabirira abaana?* (*'Who is minding the children?'*). *See* guard; look after

[1]**mine** (*eg. for ore*) *n* ekirombe *n7*

[2]**mine** *pos* (*pronoun*) owange, abange, *etc.* (**N11.4**), *eg. Ekitabo ekyo kikye, kino kyange.* (*'That book is his, this is mine.'*). *The forms for the various noun classes are listed in Column 10 of Table 9.*

[3]**mine** (*eg. ore*) *vt* -sima

miner *n* omulombe *n1*

minibus taxi *n* takisi *n9*, kamunye *n9*

minister *n* (1) (*of religion*) omwawule *n1*; (2) (*of government*) minisita *n1* ministerial affairs (*governmental*) obwaminisita *n14* Prime Minister of Buganda **Katikkiro** *n1* title (*a chief minister of a clan is also called katikkiro*)

ministry *n* (1) (*religious; Prot*) obwawule *n14*; (2) (*of government*) minisitule *n9*

minuret *n* omunaala ogw'omuzigiti *n3*

minus (*subtract*) *vt* -toolako, *eg. Bbiri toolako emu wasigalawo emu.* (*'Two minus one is one.'*)

[1]**minute** (*very small*) *adj* -sirikitu

[2]**minute** (*unit of time*) *n* eddakiika *n9*

miracle *n* ekyamagero *n7*

mire (*muddy place where one can get stuck*) *n* entubiro *n9*. *See* swamp; wetland

mirror *n* endabirwamu *n9*

miscarry *vi* (1) (*by a woman*) -vaamu olubuto, *eg. Omukyala avuddemu olubuto.* (*'The lady had a miscarriage.'*), olubuto -vaamu, *eg. Olubuto luvuddemu.* (*'She miscarried.'*); (2) (*by an animal*) -sowola, *eg. Ente yasowodde.* (*'The cow miscarried.'*). *See* abort

miscellaneous *adj* -a omuyoolerero

miscellany (*large number of assorted things*) *n* kalonda *n1*, omuyoolerero *n3*, *eg. Mu kisero mulimu omuyoolerero gw'ebintu.* (*'There is a miscellany of things in the basket.'*). *See* mixture

mischief *n* ettigi *n5*, ttigimbuli. *See* naughty; unruly be mischievous -li wa ttigimbuli, *eg. Musoke yali wa ttigimbuli nga akyali muto.* (*'Musoke was mischievous when he was young.'*)

miser (*mean person*) *n* omukodo *n1*

miserable (*sad*) *adj* -nakuwavu miserable person omunakuwaavu *n1* be(come) miserable -nakuwala make miserable -nakuwaza

miserliness *n* obukodo *n14*

miserly *adj* -kodo be(come) miserly -kodowala

misery *n* ennaku *n9*, obunyiikaavu *n14*. *See* suffering experience misery -laba ennaku

misfortune *n* omukisa omubi *n3*, ekisiraani *n7* continued misfortune olutwe *n11*

misgiving *n* enkenyera *n9*, akakenyera *n12* have misgivings -kenyera

mislay/misplace *vt* -buza

mislead *vt* -buzaabuza, -kyamya, (*by confusing*) -balankanya

¹miss (*girl*) *n* **omuwala** *n1*   have a near miss (*close shave*) **-yita ku lugwanyu**

²miss *vt* (1) (*an opportunity*) **-subwa**, *eg. Nsubiddwa olugendo.* (*'I missed the trip'*), **-suba** (*with personal object*), *eg. Olugendo lunsubye.* (*'I missed the trip.'*); (2) (*a day or regular activity*) **-yosa**, *eg. Tayosa kusoma mawulire.* (*'He never misses reading the newspaper.'*)   miss the target **-kuba ebbali**   be missing (1) (*lost*) **-bula**, *eg. Embwa ebuze.* (*'The dog is missing.'*). *A concerned person can be indicated by an object pronoun, eg. Embwa yange embuze.* (*'My dog is missing.'*); (2) (*lost; not seen*) *Use* **-labika** (*'be seen'*) *in neg* (**N21**)*, eg. Essowaani bbiri tezirabika.* (*'Two plates are missing.'*); (3) (*lacking at a place*) **-bulawo**, *eg. Wabulawo essowaani bbiri mu kabada.* (*'Two plates are missing from the cupboard.'*)

mission (*religious*) *n* **minsani** *n9*

missionary *n* **omuminsani** *n1*

mist *n* **olufu** *n11*

mistake *n* **ekisobyo** *n7*   be mistaken **-sobako**   correct a mistake **-golola ekisobyo**   make a mistake **-sobya**

mister *n* **ssebo** *n1*, (*as a title*) **Mwami** (*abbrev.* **Mw.**), *eg. Mwami Musoke* (*'Mr. Musoke'*)

mistletoe (*semi-parasitic plant with orange to reddish flowers*) *n* **enzirugaze** *n9*

mistreat *vi* **-yisa obubi**. *See* overwork

mistrust *vt* **-eekeka**

misunderstanding *n* **obutategeeragana** *n14*

mite (*on chickens*) *n* **akaloolo** *n12*

mix (up) *vt* (1) (*eg. with a spoon*) **-tabula**, *eg. Atabula sukaali n'obuwunga.* (*'She is mixing sugar and flour.'*); (2) (*accidentally or carelessly*) **-tabika**, *eg. Ntabise obutambaala ne ssokisi.* (*'I have mixed up the handkerchieves and socks.'*); (3) (*something thick*) **-goya**, *eg. Agoya omugoyo.* (*'She is mixing the bean and potato mash.'*); (4) (*on a larger scale, eg. when mixing cement*) **-kologa**; (5) (*things that should not be mixed*) **-gattika**. *See* combine   mix up (1) (*someone's mind*) **-tabula omutwe**, *eg. Antabudde omutwe.* (*'He has mixed me up.'*); (2) (*physically and deliberately, eg. shuffle playing cards*) **-canga**; (3) (*by rolling something around, eg. ball of matooke in sauce*) **-vulunga**   mix up words deliberately **-cangacanga**   be mixed up **-eetabula**, *eg. Ebintu byange byetabudde ne bibyo.* (*'My things are mixed up with yours.'*), (*mentally, not knowing what to do*) **-tabulwa**

mixed *adj* **-tabule, -tabike**

mixture *n* (1) (*organised assortment*) **ekintabuli** *n7*; (2) (*unsorted collection*) **twalatugende** *n1*. *See* miscellany

moan *vi* **-sinda**. *See* complain

mobile phone *n* **akasimu** *n12*

mobilise (*people*) *vt* **-kumaakuma**, *eg. Yakumaakuma abantu be bazimbe essomero.* (*'He*

mobilised his people to build the school.'*), **-kuŋŋanya**

mock *vt* **-kiina, -duulira**

mocker *n* **omuduuzi** *n1*, **omukiinyi** *n1*

mockery *n* **obuduuze** *n14*, **okukiina** *n15*

mode (*way*) *n* **engeri** *n9*

model (*brand*) *n* **enkola** *n9*. *See* type

moderate *adj* **-saamusaamu**

moderately *adv. Use suffix* **-ko** *on adjective or adverb* (**N24.3**)*, eg. ekisenge ekineneko* (*'moderately large room'*)

moderation *n* **obusaamusaamu** *n14*

modern *adj* **-a omulembe**   modern times **ennaku zino** *n10*   be modern **-tuukira ku mulembe**

modernity *n* **omulembe gw'ennaku zino** *n3*

modesty *n* **ensonyi** *n9*   be modest *Use* **-eeraga** (*'show off'*) *in neg* (**N21**)*, eg. Musoke teyeeraga, talaga buyigirize bwe.* (*'Musoke is modest about his qualifications.'*). *See* shyness

modify *vt* **-kyusaamu**

Mohammed *n* **Muwamadi** *n1*

moisten *vt* **-bisiwaza**. *See* wet (make)   become moist (*gradually, eg. of salt in a damp atmosphere*) **-nnyuukirira**

molar tooth *n* **eggego** *n5*

mole (*on skin*) *n* **ensundo** *n9*

mole cricket (*insect*) *n* **nnamunyeenye** *n1*

mole-rat (*rodent*) **effukuzi** *n5*

molest *vt* **-lumya**

molten, become *vi* **-saanuuka**

moment *n* **akaseera** *n12*, *eg. akaseera k'eddembe* (*'moment of peace'*)   brief moment **akadde** *n12*, *eg. Bw'ofuna akadde jjangu onnyambe.* (*'When you have a moment come and help me.'*)

monarch *n* **kabaka** *n1*

Monday *n* **Olwokusooka** *n11*, **Bbalaza, Kazooba, Mmande**

money *n* **ssente** *n10*, **ensimbi** *n10*. *See* cowrie; wealth   place for keeping money **etterekero ly'essente/ensimbi** *n5*

mongoose *n* (1) (*banded*) **akakolwa** *n12*, **akatulume** *n12*; (2) (*marsh and large grey*) **eggunju** *n9*; (3) (*white-tailed*) **lunywamunte** *n11*. *It is possible that* **kaneene** *is another name for marsh mongoose.*

monitor lizard *n* **enswaswa** *n9*

monk *n* **omumonaaki** *n1*

monkey *n* (1) (*general term; also vervet*) **enkima** *n9*; (2) (*black and white colobus*) **engeye** *n9*; (3) (*red-tailed*) **nnakabugo** *n1*; (4) (*grey-cheeked mangabey*) **wagaba** *n1*, **ssewagaba** *n1*. *See* baboon

month *n* **omwezi** *n3*, **ezzooba** *n5* (*traditionally, 'ezzooba' referred to a lunar month*)   last month **omwezi oguyise, omwezi oguwedde**   next month **omwezi ogujja, omwezi oguddako**

moo (*as a cow*) *vi* **-kaaba**

mood *n* **embeera** *n9*

moon *n* **omwezi** *n3*, (*full*) **omwezi**

ogw'eggabogabo, (*new*) omwezi ogubonese. *Names given to children born at the time of the new moon*: (1) (*males*) **Kiboneka**; (2) (*females*) **Nnakiboneka** be new (*of the moon*) **-boneka**, *eg. Omwezi gubonese. ('There's a new moon.')*

mop *vt* **-siimuula**

morality/morals *n* **empisa** *n10*

more more than *conj* **okusinga**, *eg. Njagala kino okusinga ekyo. ('I like this more than that.')* be more than **-singa obungi** (*often with enclitic* **N24.2**), *eg. Nneetaaga omusenyu ogusingawo obungi ku gw'oleese. ('I need more sand than you brought.').* See exceed have more **-eeyongera** (*often with enclitic* **N24.2**), *eg. Njagala okweyongera emmere ('I want to have more food')* put more **-yongera** (*often with enclitic* **N24.2**), *eg. (1) Yayongerako amatofaali ku kisenge. ('He put more bricks on the wall.'); (2) Yayongeramu sukaali mu caayi. ('He put more sugar in the tea.')*

moringa (*type of tree*) *n* **omulinga** *n3*

morning *n* **enkya** *n9*, (*early, before about 9 am*) **amakya** *n6. See* dawn morning next day **enkeera** morning-time **obudde obw'oku makya** *n14* Good morning. *greeting* **Wasuze otyanno?** (*pl.* **Mwasuze mutyanno?**) (**N28**) in the morning **enkya** this morning **enkya ya leero**

mortar *n* (1) (*for grinding*) **ekinu** *n7* (*small* **akanu** *n12*); (2) (*used in brick laying, etc.*) **seminti** *n9*, (*of mud*) **obudongo** *n14. See* plaster

Moses *n* **Musa** *n1* Moses basket **ekibaya** *n7*

mosque *n* **omuzigiti** *n3*

mosquito *n* **ensiri** *n9* mosquito net **akatimba k'ensiri** *n12*

moss *n* **enkonge** *n9*

mostly (*also* most of) *adv.* Use **-singa** ('*be more'*), *eg. Abaana abasinga bawala. ('The children are mostly girls.')*

moth *n* **ekiwojjolo** *n7*

mothball(s) *n* **kattannyenje** *n1*

mother *n* **maama** *n1*, *eg. maama wa Musoke ('Musoke's mother'),* (*in an honorific sense*) **nnakazadde** *n1*, (*of a newborn child*) **nnakawere** *n1*, (*of twins*) **Nnaalongo** *n1* title, (*of the Kabaka*) **Nnamasole** *n1* title my mother **mmange**, her/his mother **nnyina**, *etc.* (*stem* **nnya- N12**)

mother-in-law *n* **nnyazaala** *n1*

motion (to) (*beckon*) *vt* **-wenya**

motivate *vt* **-jjumbiza**

motive *n* **ekigendererwa** *n7*

motorcar *n* **emmotoka** *n9*

motorcycle *n* **ppikipiki** *n9*, (*taxi*) **bodaboda** *n9*

motorcyclist *n* **owa ppikipiki** *n1*, **omuvuzi wa ppikipiki** *n1*, (*as taxi driver*) **owa bodaboda** *n1*

¹**mould** *n* (1) (*for making bricks*) **olutiba** *n11* (*small* **akatiba** *n12*); (2) (*fungus*) **obukuku** *n14*

²**mould** (*make with clay*) *vt* **-bumba**

mouldy (*with fungus*) *adj* **-kukuvu** mouldy cassava (*with black streaks*) **muwogo w'obulaala** *n1*

become mouldy **-kukula** make mouldy **-kukuza**

mound (*of earth*) *n* (1) (*small*) **ekifunvu** *n7* (*big* **eggulumu** *n5*, big and disorganised **ekigulumu** *n7*); (2) (*on which to plant sweet potatoes*) **ekikata** *n7*; (3) (*planted with sweet potatoes*) **ekikata kya lumonde**. *See* embankment; heap; termite mound make earth mounds (*for planting sweet potatoes*) **-tema ebikata**

mount *v* (1) (*mate, by male animal*) *vi* **-linnyira**; (2) (*climb on*) *vt* **-linnya**, *eg. Yalinnya eggaali. ('He mounted the bicycle.').* See increase mount a horse **-eebagala embalaasi**

mountain *n* **olusozi** *n11*

mourn *vi* **-kungubaga.** *See* wail mourn for **-kungubagira**, *eg. Akungubagira omwami we. ('She is mourning for her husband.')*

mourner *n* **omukungubazi** *n1*

mourning *n* **okukungubaga** *n15*

mouse *n* **emmese** *n9*, (*type found in banana gardens, probably dormouse*) **kikirikisi** *n7*

mousebird *n* **omujjonkezi** *n3*

mousetrap *n* **akamasu** *n12*

moustache *n* **obusuulubu** *n14* (*big* **amasuulabu** *n6*, pointed **obuswiriri** *n14*)

mouth *n* (1) (*external*) **omumwa** *n3*; (2) (*internal*) **akamwa** *n12* bad-mouthing (*talking badly about someone*) **akamwa akabi** *n12* be open-mouthed **-yasaamirira** hold in the mouth (*without swallowing*) **-batika** open one's mouth **-yasama** keep one's mouth shut **-bunira** make open the mouth (*eg. that of a baby, to feed*) **-yasamya**

mouthpiece (*of a spirit*) *n* **omusamize** *n1*, (*of a lubaale*) **omulubaale** *n1*, (*of a nature spirit*) **mmandwa** *n1*

move *v* TRANSITIVE USES **-kyusa**, *eg. Nnyambaako okukyusa emmeeza? ('Can you help me move the table?').* See remove move (*something*) aside (*to make room*) **-seetula**, *eg. Nnaseetudde bbookisi atuule. ('I moved the box aside so she could sit.')* move from higher to lower position **-wanula, -ssa** INTRANSITIVE USES **-vaawo**, *eg. Ekinya ekibadde ku kisenge kivuddewo. ('The gecko which was on the wall has moved.'),* (*travel*) **-tambula**, *eg. Abantu batambula ku luguudo. ('The people are moving along the road.'). The following refer to ways of moving (of a person):* (*busily, bustling about*) **-eetala, -tawuka**, (*whole body about, a response to pain*) **-sansagala**, (*repeatedly getting up and down*) **-situnkana**, (*to a rhythm*) **-digida.** *See* plod along; stalk move about (1) (*of something not fixed properly*) **-sagaasagana**; (2) (*of someone within a limited area*) **-eetalira.** *See* shaky (be); sway move about restlessly **-sattira** move aside (*of oneself, to allow someone to sit*) **-seetuka** move away from **-viira**, *eg. Yalina obusungu nze ne mmuviira. ('He was angry so I moved away from him.')* move away stealthily **-eeseebulula** move forward bit by bit

-eeseetula, *eg. Yagenda yeeseetula mu lunyiriri. ('She moved forward slowly in the queue.')* <u>move from higher to lower position</u> **-wanuka**, *eg. Ekikopo kyawanuse ku ssa ne kigwa. ('The cup fell from the shelf.')* <u>move home</u> **-senguka**, *eg. Tusenguse ne tulaga e Masaka. ('We have moved to Masaka.')* <u>move home to</u> **-sengukira**, *eg. Yasengukira London. ('She has moved to London.')* <u>move reluctantly</u> **-sikattira**, *(and physically resisting)* **-walira** <u>move slowly</u> **-sooba**, *(at snail pace)* **-soonooka ng'ekkovu** <u>move to a new location</u> *(of a business)* **-ejjulula** <u>move to and fro</u> *(not fixed properly; wobbly)* **-nyeenya**

movie *See* film

mow grass **-sala omuddo**. *See* slash <u>mown area</u> **awasaawe** *n16*

Mr. *abbrev* **Mw.**, *eg. Mw. Musoke ('Mr. Musoke')*

Mrs. *abbrev* **Muky.**, *eg. Muky. Musoke ('Mrs. Musoke')*

much *det* **-ngi**, *eg. Sirina ssente nnyingi. ('I don't have much money.')* <u>how much?</u> *(1) Use* **-yenkana wa?** *('be equal to where?'), eg. Weetaaga petulooli yenkana wa? ('How much petrol do you need?'); (2)* **-meka?** <u>very much</u> *adv* **ennyo**

mucky *(eg. of water containing sediment) adj* **-siikuufu**. *See* dirty <u>be(come) mucky</u> **-siikuuka**, **-fuukuuka**

mucus *n* **eminyira** *n4*

mud *n (1)* **ebitosi** *n8; (2) (a piece, eg. on foot or shoe)* **ekitoomi** *n7 (smaller* **ekisooto** *n7); (3) (grey wet clay in valley)* **ettosi** *n5; (4) (when used in building; mortar)* **obudongo** *n14; (5) (when used as plaster)* **olufuufu** *n11* <u>become stuck in mud</u> **-tubira** <u>layer of mud</u> *(in mud and wattle wall)* **ekizizi** *n7*

¹muddle *(mess) n* **omuvuyo** *n3. See* confusion

²muddle (up) *(mess up) vt* **-vuluga**

muddy *adj* **-a ebitosi**, *eg. ekkubo lya bitosi ('muddy road')* <u>muddy place</u> **awantu awali ebitosi** *n16, (where one could get stuck)* **entubiro** *n9*

mudfish *(type of catfish) n* **emmale** *n9*

mug *n* **eggama** *n9*

Muhima *n* **Omuyima** *n1*

mulberry *n (1) (giant yellow, an indigenous tree) (plant)* **omugunga** *n3, (fruit)* **ekigunga** *n7; (2) (type grown as food for silkworms)* **enkenene** *n9*

mulch *vt* **-bikka**

mule *n* **ennyumbu** *n9*

multiplication *n* **okubazaamu** *n15* <u>multiplication table</u> **emirundi** *n4*

multiply *v* **TRANSITIVE USES** *(1) (increase in amount or number)* **-yaza**, *eg. Ayazizza ente ze. ('He has multiplied his cows.'); (2) (in maths)* **-bazaamu**, *eg. Bbiri bazaamu bbiri ofuna nnya. ('Two multiplied by two makes four.')* **INTRANSITVE USES** *(1) (increase in amount or number)* **-yala**, *eg. Ente ziyaze. ('The cows have multiplied.'); (2) (of banana plants by suckering)* **-zaala**, *eg. Ebitooke bizadde. ('The banana plants have multiplied.')*

multi-storey building *n* **kalina** *n9*, **ekizimbe kya kalina** *n7*, **ggoloofa** *n9*

multitask *vi* **-yimbagatanya**

multitude *(of people) n* **enkuyanja** *(or* **enkumuliitu) y'abantu** *n9*

mum *(mummy) n* **maama** *n1* <u>keep mum</u> *(say nothing)* **-wumba emimwa**

mumble *vi* **-lya ebigambo**, *(in dissatisfaction)* **-tolotooma**

mummy *n* **maama** *n1*

mumps *n* **amambulugga** *n6*

mung bean *n* **mpokya** *n1*

¹murder *n* **obutemu** *n14*

²murder *vt* **-temula** <u>someone murdered</u> **omutemule** *n1*

murderer *n* **omutemu** *n1*

¹murmur *n* **oluvuuvuumo** *n11*

²murmur *vi* **-vuuvuuma**, *(in dissatisfaction)* **-tolotooma**

muscle *n* **ennyama** *n9* <u>muscle ache</u> **nnakanyama** *n1*

mushroom *n* **akatiko** *n12. Edible types include: (1) small and white; found where ennaka termites occur)* **akanakanaka** *n12; (2) (found where entunda termites occur)* **akatundatunda** *n12; (3) (small, yellow-white; found where embaala termites occur)* **akabaala** *n12*, **nnamulondo** *n1; (4) (found where ensejjere termites occur)* **akasejjeresejjere** *n12; (5) (mauve, found in mulched banana gardens and where empawu termites occur)* **kinyulwa** *n1; (6) (whitish-grey with brown gills; in banana gardens)* **akasukusuku** *n12; (7) (grows on dry leaves in banana gardens)* **akasanjasanja** *n12; (8) (white, grows on dung; second totem of Mbogo Clan)* **endeerwe** *n9; (9) (white, grows on residues from banana beer making)* **kannassogolero** *n12; (10) (large, edible; found in grassland and banana gardens, very rare)* **gudu** *n1; (11) (very large, greyish; in grassland)* **empeefu** *n9; (12) (oyster mushroom)* **akatiko akazungu**; *(13) (delicious, but leaves an itchy throat)* **lukoota** *n12; (14) (another type, traditionally harvested in groups of nine and not eaten by women)* **enkulungutanyi** *n9. See* fungus; termite

mushy, become *(eg. of a squashed fruit) vi* **-footoka**. *See* soft

music *n* **ennyimba** *n10*, **muziki** *n1*, **omumuziki** *n3* <u>musical instrument</u> **ekivuga** *n7*

musician *n (1)* **omuyimbi** *n1*, **omudongo** *n1, (in a band)* **owa bbanda** *n1; (2) (plays a blown instrument)* **omufuuyi** *n1; (3) (plays a struck instrument)* **omukubi** *n1; (4) (plays a plucked instrument)* **omusunyi** *n1*

musky smell *n (1) (of snake, goat, etc.)*

ekkalalume *n5*; (2) (*of new earthenware pot, some mushrooms, etc.*) omuga *n3*

Muslim *n* Omusiraamu *n1*, (*fundamentalist*) tabuliki *n1* become a Muslim -siramuka

must *aux v* -teekwa *followed by inf* (**N19**), *eg. Nteekwa okumuyamba. ('I must help him.')*

mustard *n* kalidaali *n1*

mutilate *vt* -temaatema

mutineer *n* omujeemu *n1*

¹**mutiny** *n* obujeemu *n14*

²**mutiny** *vi* -jeema

mutter *vi* -vuuvuuma, (*in dissatisfaction*) -tolotooma, (*to oneself*) -eewuunuunya

mutton *n* ennyama y'endiga *n9*

muzzle *n* enkoligo *n9*

my *pos (determiner)* -ange (**N11.4**) *with pronominal concord* (**N4.2**), *eg.* (1) embwa yange (*'my dog'*); (2) eggi lyange (*'my egg'*). *The forms for the various noun classes are listed in Column 4 of Table 9.* My dear! Mwana wattu!

myself *pro. Reflexive verbs take the prefix* -ee- (**N18**). by myself nzekka   I myself nze kennyini

mystery *n* ekitategeerekeka *n7*

myth *n* olufumo *n11*

N,n

nag *vt* -sojja

nagger *n* omutayirizi *n1*

¹**nail** *n* (1) (*used in construction*) omusumaali *n3*; (2) (*of finger/toe*) olwala *n11*

²**nail (down)** (*hammer*) *vt* -komerera

naïve (*uninformed*) *adj* -bisi naïve person (omuntu) ataliimu katoola

naivity *n* obubisi *n14*

naked *adv* obukunya, *eg. Abaana bali bukunya. ('The children are naked.')*, obwereere

¹**name** *n* erinnya *n5*

²**name** *vt* -tuuma, *eg. Baamutuuma amannya asatu. ('They gave her three names.')*, -wa erinnya. *See* nickname   name after (*someone*) -bbula mu, *eg. Omwana baamubbula mu jjajjaawe. ('They named the baby after his grandfather.')* be named -tuumibwa

nanny *n* yaaya *n1*

Naomi *n* Nawume *n1*

nap, take a -eebakako

napkin *n* akatambaala *n12*

nappy *n* nnappi *n9*

narrate (*story/legend*) *vt* -fuma, -gera, -nyumiza. *See* tell

narrow *adj* -funda be(come) narrow -funda, (*tapered*) -sondowala   make narrow -funza, (*taper*) -sondowaza

nasty (*bad*) *adj* -bi

nation *n* (1) (*a people; tribe*) eggwanga *n5*; (2) (*state*) ensi *n9* United Nations Amawanga

Amagatte

national *adj* -a eggwanga, (*referring to a state*) -a ensi national anthem oluyimba lw'eggwanga *n11*

¹**native** *adj* -a ekinnansi, *eg. eddagala lya kinnansi ('native medicine')* native-born enzaalwa *n9*, *eg. Mwana nzaalwa y'e London. ('She is a native [daughter] of London.')*

²**native** (*person*) *n* (1) (*locally born*) omuzaaliranwa *n1*; (2) (*person already present; indigenous person*) nnansangwawo *n1*; (3) (*citizen of a country*) munnansi *n1* native of Munna- *n1* (*with place name* **N12**), *eg. Munnabuddu ('native of Buddu')*

natural resources *n* obugagga obw'ensibo *n14*

nature *n* (1) (*make-up, of something living*) enkula *n9*; (2) (*make-up, of something inanimate*) enkola *n9*; (3) (*creation*) obutonde *n14* nature spirit emmandwa *n9* fundamental nature ennono *n9*

naughtiness *n* ekitigi *n7*

naughty *adj* -a ekitigi. *See* unrestrained; unruly

nauseate *vt* -sinduukiriza (*or* -zza) emmeeme, *eg. Emmere eno ensinduukiriza emmeeme. ('This food nauseates me.'). See* offend feel nausea emmeeme -sinduukirira (*with personal object*), *eg. Emmeeme ensinduukirira. ('I feel nauseated.')*

navel *n* ekkundi *n5*

navy *n* empingu *n9* chief of Kabaka's navy Gabunga *n1* title

¹**near** *adv* okumpi   come near (*approach*) -sembera come near to -semberera

²**near** *pre* okumpi na

nearby *adv* okumpi

nearly *adv* kata (*followed by subjunctive* **N17**), *eg. Kata ennyonyi etuleke. ('We nearly missed the plane.')*, kumpi, *eg. Ali kumpi okuweza ssente ze yeetaaga. ('He has nearly got sufficient money.'). See* about to (be)

neat (*smart*) *adj* -yonjo. *See* attractive   make neat -yonja. *See* arrange   pack neatly (*saving space*) -panga

neatness *n* obuyonjo *n14*

necessitate (*also* be necessary) *vi* -eetaagisa, *eg. Kyetaagisa okugenda e Kampala okugula engoye. ('It is necessary to go to Kampala to buy clothes.')*

necessity *n* obwetaavu *n14* of necessity olw'obuwaze

neck *n* ensingo *n9*, obulago *n14*. *See* throat back of the neck enkoto *n9* put a rope around one's neck -eeyimbamu   stiff neck olukya *n11*   turn one's neck to one side (*as a gesture of disapproval or irritation*) -kubiira ensingo

necklace *n* ekyomubulago *n7*, akakuufu *n12*, (*made from ettembe seeds*) olutembe *n11*

¹**need** *n* obwetaavu *n14*, ekyetaagisa *n7*, ekyetaago *n7*, okwetaaga *n15*

²**need** *vt* -eetaaga be needed -eetaagibwa, *eg. Abasawo beetaagibwa mu Bungereza. ('Doctors are needed in England.')*

needle *n* empiso *n9*, (*used in basket-making; awl*)

olukato *n11*

neem (*type of tree*) *n* **omuttankuyege** *n3*

neglect *vt* **-lagajjalira**, (*a personal relationship or matter in hand*) **-suulirira**

negligence *n* **obulagajjavu** *n14*

negligent *adj* **-lagajjavu** be negligent **-lagajjala**

negotiate *vi* **-teesa** negotiate with one another **-teesaganya**

negotiation *n* **enteesaganya**

neigh *vi* **-kaaba**

¹neighbour *n* **ow'omuliraano** *n1* neighbour of **muliraanwa** (*with pos* **N12**), *eg. muliraanwa wange ('my neighbour')* be neighbours **-liraanagana**

²neighbour *vt* **-liraana**

neighbourhood *n* **omuliraano** *n3*

neither *See* nor

nephew *n* (1) (*male of next generation, related by blood*) **muganda** *n1* (*with pos* **N12**), *eg. mutabani wange ('my nephew')*; (2) (*son of man's sister*) **omujjwa** *n1*. *For greater precision for a blood relative, use* **mutabani wa muganda** (*with pos* **N12**), *eg. mutabani wa muganda wange ('my nephew' – in the English sense).*

nerve *n* **akasimu** *n12* nerve oneself (*to do something*) **-eevaamu, -eekakaba** lose one's nerve **-terebuka**

nest *n* **ekisu** *n7* nesting basket (*for hen*) **ekiyonjo** *n7*

¹net *n* (1) (*long, used for hunting larger animals, eg. antelopes*) **ekitimba** *n7*; (2) (*long, used for catching smaller animals, eg. cane rats*) **olutuula** *n11*; (3) (*small*) **akatimba** *n12* net covering a cot **akatimba akabikka ku kibaya** net covering food **akatimba akabikka ku byokulya** fishing net (1) (*trawl; catches everything*) **essambo** *n5*; (2) (*fine-meshed, for catching enkejje*) **akasambo** *n12*, **ekiragala** *n7*; (3) (*cast net*) **ponyoka** *n1*; (4) (*undersize; illegal*) **mukokota** *n1* mosquito net **akatimba k'ensiri**

²net *vt* **-kwasa**

nettle *See* stinging plant

neurone *n* **akawuzi k'akasimu** *n12*

never *adv* (1) (*referring to an occasion*) *Use verb in present tense* (**N16**) *in neg* (**N21**), *eg. Nnamulinda n'atajja. ('I waited for him but he never came.')*; (2) (*referring to habitual action*) *Add suffix* **-nga** *on verb* (**N18**), *eg. Totyanga kubuuza by'otomanyi. ('Never be afraid to ask about things you do not know.')* never again **kikafuuwe** never ending **obutamala** Never mind! **Si nsonga!**

nevertheless *conj* **kyokka, wabula**

new *adj* **-ggya, -pya**. *See* recent new-born child **omuwere** *n1* be new (*of the moon*) **-boneka** make like new (*renew*) **-zza obuggya/obupya** something new **ekiggya** *n7*

newcomer *n* **omuggya** *n1*, (*newly settled in a place*) **omusenze** *n1* be a newcomer **-senga** receive a

newcover **-senza** state of being a newcomer **obusenze** *n14*

newness *n* **obuggya** *n14*, **obupya** *n14*

news *n* **amawulire** *n6* What news? **Mawulire ki?, Bigambo ki?**

newspaper *n* **olupapula lw'amawulire** *n11*, **amawulire** *n6*

newsreader *n* **omusomi w'amuwulire** *n1*

¹next *adj. Use* **-ddako** (*'do next'*) *or* **-jja** (*'come'*) *in rel* (**N7.1**), *eg. (1) omwezi oguddako ('next month'); (2) omwezi ogujja ('next month')* next day **olunaku oluddako**

²next *adv* **ekiddako, ekiddirira** be next (*in time*) **-ddako**, *eg. Ggwe onoddako okulaba omusawo. ('You will be next to see the doctor.')* be next to (*neighbour*) **-liraana** put next to **-liraanya**

NGO (*abbrev of* non-governmental organisation) *n* **ekibiina eky'obwannakyewa** *n7*

nib *n* **akafumu** *n12*

nibble *vt* **-lyako katono**

nice (*good*) *adj* **-lungi** look nice (*in appearance*) **-wooma** look nice on **-woomera**

¹nickname *n* **erinnya eppaatiike** *n5*

²nickname *vt* **-paatiikako erinnya**, *eg. Bampaatiikako erinnya lya Bbutaddene. ('They called me 'big tummy'.)* be nicknamed **-yita**

niece *n* (1) (*female of next generation, related by blood*) **muwala** (*with pos* **N12**), *eg. muwala wange ('my niece')*; (2) (*daughter of man's sister*) **omujjwa** *n1*. *For greater precision for a blood relative, use* **muwala wa muganda** (*with pos* **N12**), *eg. muwala wa muganda wange ('my niece' – in the English sense).*

night (*also* night-time) *n* **ekiro** *n7* night watchman **omukuumi w'ekiro** *n1* at night **ekiro** become night **obudde -ziba** depth of the night **ettumbi** *n5* do all night **-keesa obudde**, *eg. Amazina gaakeesezza obudde. ('The dancing went on all night.')* do until night-time **-zibya obudde** last night **ekiro kya jjo** spend the night **-sula**, (*with something in mind for next day*) **-sulirira**, *eg. Nsuliridde okulaba omusawo enkya. ('I am expecting to see the doctor tomorrow.')*

nightclub *n* **kikeesa** *n7*, **kikiri** *n7*

night-dancing (*a form of witchcraft*) *n* **obusezi** *n14* night-dancer **omusezi** *n1* practice night-dancing **-sera**

nightmare *n* **ekirooto ekibi** *n7* have a nightmare **-loota ekitiisa**

Nile *n* **Kiyira** *n3* Nile perch (*fish*) **empuuta** *n9*

nine *num* **mwenda** nine hundred **lwenda** nine thousand **kenda**

nineteen *num* **kkumi na mwenda**

ninety *num* **kyenda**

ninth *adj/num* **-a omwenda** (**N7.1**)

nipple *n* **ennywanto** *n9*

nit *n* **eggi ly'ensekere** *n5*

no *det. Use verb prefix* **te-** (*or for first person* singular **si-**) (**N21**), *eg. (1) Tetulina nkoko. ('We have no hens.'); (2) Sirina nkoko. ('I have no hens.')* **no** *interj* **nedda** no longer *Use prefix* **-kya-** *with verb in neg* (**N18**), *eg. Takyakola. ('She no longer works.')*

Noah *n* **Nuwa** *n1*

nobody *See* no-one

nod *vt* **-nyeenya omutwe** nod off *(doze off)* **-sumagira.** *See* sleep

node *n* **ennyingo** *n9*

noise *(made by many people talking loudly)* **okuwoggana** *n15. See* din light noise of footsteps *(of unknown cause)* **enswagiro** *n10* make a lot of noise (1) **-woggana, -leekaana;** (2) *(of many people talking)* **-yoogaana,** *(loudly, continuously and sounding unpleasant)* **-lasana;** (3) *(as of many children at play)* **-kuba embeekuulo.** *See* din (make a); shout sudden noise *(eg. explosion)* **ekibwatuka** *n7* unwanted noise **kkerere**

non-conformist *(person)* *n* **kyewaggula** *n1*

non-governmental organisation *See* NGO

nonsense *n* **ekitaliimu (nsa)** *n7* talk nonsense **-yogera ebitaliimu**

noon *n* **essaawa mukaaga ez'emisana**

no-one *(also* nobody*) pro* **muntu n'omu** *(with verb in neg* **N21***)*

nor *conj. Use* **wadde** *('not even'), eg. Siraba Musoke wadde Mukasa. ('I see neither Musoke nor Mukasa.')*

normal *adj. Use* **bulijjo** *('normally'), eg. Bulijjo akola bw'atyo. ('That is his normal behaviour.')*

normally *adv* **bulijjo.** *See* usually

north *n* **amambuka** *n6*

nose *n* **ennyindo** *n9, (bunged-up)* **ekibobe** *n7* be bunged up *(blocked, of the nose)* **-vumbeera, -feekera, -fumbeka, -zibikira,** *eg. Ennyindo yange ezibikidde. ('My nose is bunged up.')* be nosy *(intruding into another's affairs)* **-lingiriza** blow one's nose **-nyiza** dried particle in nose **akakakampa** *n12*

nosebleed have a nosebleed **-eerumika**

not *adv* **si,** *eg. Musoke si musawo. ('Musoke is not a doctor.'). The verb prefix is* **te-** *(or first person singular* **si-***)* (**N21**), *eg. (1) Taseka. ('She is not laughing.'); (2) Siseka. ('I am not laughing.').* not even **wadde** not even a little **n'akatono** *(after verb in neg* **N21***), eg. Temwasigaddemu bbiya n'akatono. ('There's no beer left, not even a little.')* not one **na -mu** *(after verb in neg* **N21***), eg. Tewali n'omu eyajja. ('Not one person came.')* not yet *Use verb prefix* **-nna-** *with neg* (**N18**), *eg. Sinnakikola. ('I have not yet done it.')*

¹notch *n* **eddibu** *n5*

²notch *vt* **-libula.** *See* chip be notched **-libuka,** *eg. Ekikopo kiribuse. ('The cup is notched.')*

notched *adj* **-libufu**

¹note *(written)* *n* **akabaluwa** *n12* bank note **olupapula lw'ensimbi** *n11* demand note

(requesting payment) **ebbaluwa ebanja** *n9*

²note *(pay attention to)* *vt* **-tegereza**

noted *(celebrated)* *adj* **-yatiikirivu**

nothing *pro. Use neg* (**N21**), *eg. Wano tewali kintu. ('There is nothing here.')* for *(or* with*)* nothing **obwereere, obusa**

¹notice *n* (1) *(announcement)* **ekirango** *n7,* **ekirangiriro** *n7;* (2) *(sign)* **ekipande** *n7* give notice of **-langa,** *eg. Yalanga olukuŋŋaana. ('He gave notice of the meeting.')* give notice of visiting (to) **-laga,** *eg. Nnamulaze olunaku lwe ŋŋenda okumulaba. ('I gave him notice of the day I would visit him.')*

²notice *(see)* *vt* **-laba,** *eg. Nnalaba nga muliraanwa alina emmotoka empya. ('I noticed that my neighbour had a new car.'). See* detect

notify *(inform)* *vt* **-tegeeza,** *(of an intention to visit)* **-laga.** *See* tell

notion *(idea)* *n* **ekirowoozo** *n7*

nought *n* **nooti** *n9*

noun *n* **erinnya** *n5* noun class *(in grammar)* (**N4.2, N6**) **olubu lw'amannya** *n11*

nourishment *n* **ekiriisa** *n7*

¹novel *(new)* *adj* **-ggya, -pya**

²novel *(type of book)* *n* **ekitabo ky'olugero** *n7*

novelty *n* **ekiggya** *n7*

November *n* **Omwezi ogw'ekkumi n'ogumu** *n3,* **Museenene, Noovemba**

now *adv* **kaakati, kati** up to now **okutuuka kati** now that *(meaning 'since' in the sense of enabling an action) Use* **-gidde** *in present tense* (**N16**) *followed by subjunctive* (**N17**), *eg. Ogidde ojje, gira tukole omulimu guno. ('Now that you have come, let's do this job.')* now and then *Use* **-gira** *followed by narrative tense* (**N16**), *eg. Agira n'afumba. ('He cooks now and then.'). The suffix* **-nga** *is added with the past and future tenses* (**N18**), *eg. Anaagiranga n'ajja okutulabako. ('He will come and see us now and then.')*

nowadays *adv* **ennaku zino**

nozzle *n* **omudumu** *n3*

nude *adj* **-yereere** (in the) nude *adv* **obwereere, obukunya**

nuisance be a nuisance to **-teganya**

nullify *vt* **-sazaamu**

numb, be(come) *vi* **-sannyalala**

number *n* **omuwendo** *n3,* **ennamba** *n9* number plate **ennamba y'emmotoka** *n9*

numbness *n* **obusannyalavu** *n14*

numerous *adj* **-ngi**

nun *n* **omubiikira** *n1*

¹nurse *n* (1) *(sick person's)* **omujjanjabi** *n1,* **nnaasi** *n1,* **nnansi** *n1;* (2) *(child's)* **omulezi w'omwana** *n1*

²nurse *vt* (1) *(a patient)* **-jjanjaba;** (2) *(a child)* **-lera** nurse oneself **-ejjanjaba**

nursing *(as an art or profession)* *n* **obujjanjabi** *n14* nursing home **ejjanjabiro** *n5*

nut *(for bolt)* *n* **empeta** *n9,* **nnatti** *n9* groundnut

(*peanut*) **ekinyeebwa** *n7*, (*bambara*) **empande** *n9*
nutrient *n* **ekiriisa** *n7*
nutrition *n* **ebyendiisa** *n8*

O,o

oar *n* **enkasi** *n9*
oath *n* **ekirayiro** *n7. See* pledge   take an oath
   -layira
obedience *n* **obuwulize** *n14*
obedient *adj* **-wulize**   obedient person **omuwulize**
   n1   be obedient to **-wulira**, *eg. Yamuwulira. ('He*
   was obedient to her.'), **-gondera**, *eg. Agondera*
   mukama we. ('She is obedient to her boss.')
obese *adj* **-gevvu ennyo**   obese person **omuntu**
   omugevvu (*or* **omunene**) **ennyo** *n1*   grow obese
   -gejja
obesity *n* **obugevvu** *n14*, **obunene** *n14*
obey *vt* **-wulira**   obey the law **-kwata amateeka**
¹**object** (*thing*) *n* **ekintu** *n7. See* objective
²**object (to)** *vi* **-gaana**, *eg. Yaŋŋaana okuzimba*
   ekisenge. ('He objected to me building the wall.')
   have objections **-wakana**
objective (*aim*) *n* **ekigendererwa** *n7*
obligation *n* **ekintu ky'olina okukola** *n7*   be
   obliged (*must*) **-teekwa** *followed by inf* (**N19**)
obliterate *vt* **-zikiriza**, **-saanyawo**, (*by fire*) **-sirissa**
   be obliterated **-zikirira**, **-saanawo**, (*by fire*)
   -sirikka
obscene *adj* **-gwagwa**
obscenity *n* **obugwagwa** *n14*
obsequious (to), be *vit* **-eeguya**
observe *vt* (1) (*perceive*) **-laba**; (2) (*hold to*)
   -kwata, *eg. Akwata olunaku lwa Ssabbiiti. ('He*
   observes the Sabbath.')
obsession *n* **akatinko** *n12*   be obsessed **-tinkiza**,
   -tijja   someone obsessed **ow'akatinko** *n1*
obsolete   become obsolete **-diba**   make obsolete
   -dibya
obstacle *n* (1) (*something that prevents*) **ekiziyiza**
   n7; (2) (*something that makes difficult*)
   ekizibuwaza *n7*, **ekikaluubiriza** *n7*
obstetric ward *n* **ezzaaliro** *n5*, **mateniti** *n9*
obstetrics *n* **ebyokuzaalisa** *n8*
obstinacy *n* **emputtu** *n10*
obstinate *adj* **-a emputtu**, (*and difficult;*
   unbending) **-kakanyavu**   obstinate person
   ow'emputtu *n1*, (*and difficult; unbending*)
   omukakanyavu *n1*   be obstinate **-lina** *or* **-ba na**
   (*'have'*) *according to tense* (**N20.1**) *followed by*
   emputtu (*'obstinancy'*), *eg. Alina emputtu. ('She is*
   obstinate.'), (and difficult) **-kakanyala**
obstruct *vt* **-ziba**, *eg. Abakozi bazibye ekkubo. ('The*
   workers obstructed the road.')   be obstructed
   -ziba, *eg. Ekkubo lizibye. ('The road is*
   obstructed.')   be obstructed in movement
   (*temporarily delayed*) **-sikattira**

obstruction *n* **ekizibye** *n7*, **ekisikattizza** *n7*
obtain *vt* **-funa**   obtain for/at **-funira**   obtain from
   -funamu   be obtainable **-funika**
obvious *adj* **-a enkukunala**, *eg. Amazima gaali ga*
   nkukunala. ('The truth was obvious.')   be obvious
   (1) *Use* **-eeraga** (*'show off'*) *with* **-okka** (*'alone'*
   N7.3); (2) **-eeraga bwerazi**, *eg. Kyeraga bwerazi*
   nti mubbi. ('It is obvious he is a thief.'), **-laba**
   bulabi, *eg. Tukiraba bulabi nti Mukasa mubbi. ('It*
   is obvious to us that Mukasa is a thief.'), **-labika**
   bulabisi   something obvious **ekyenkukunala** *n7*
obviously *adv* **kya nkukunala**, *eg. Ekyo kituufu kya*
   nkukunala. ('That is obviously true.')
occasion *n* (1) (*formal event*) **omukolo** *n3*; (2)
   (*occurrence*) **omulundi** *n3*, *eg. emirundi ebiri*
   (*'two occasions'*)   on the occasion of **ku**, *eg. ku*
   mazaalibwa ge ('on the occasion of his birthday')
occasionally *adv* **olumu n'olumu**, **oluusi n'oluusi**.
   See now and then   very occasionally **ebbalirirwe**,
   obw'olumu
occupant *Use* **-beera** (*'live at'*) *in rel* (**N7.1**) *with*
   mu (*'in'*), *eg. Ababeera mu nnyumba eyo bagagga.*
   (*'The occupants of that house are rich.'*)
occupation (*work*) *n* **omulimu** *n3*
occupy *vt* **-beeramu**, *eg. Musoke abeeramu mu*
   ofiisi eno. ('Musoke occupies this office.')   occupy
   too much space (1) (*of a person, or of things in a*
   room) **-zimbagala**, *eg. Emigugu mingi*
   gizimbagadde mu kisenge. ('There are many
   bundles in the room occupying too much space.');
   (2) (*of a plant*) **-zijjagala**
occur *vi* (1) (*be at*) **-beera** , *eg. Enjovu zibeera mu*
   kibira kino. ('Elephants occur in this forest.'); (2)
   (*be seen*) **-labika**, *eg. Enjovu zirabika mu kibira*
   kino. ('Elephants occur in this forest.')
occurrence (*occasion*) *n* **omulundi** *n3*
ocean *n* **oguyanja** *n20*
o'clock *Use* **essaawa** *n9* (*'time'*) (**N25.1**), *eg.*
   essaawa bbiri ('8 o'clock')
October *n* **Omwezi ogw'ekkumi** *n3*,
   Mukulukusabitungotungo, Okitobba
odd (*unusual*) *adj. Use* **-a bulijjo** (*'usual'*) *in neg*
   (**N21**), *eg. Si kya bulijjo okulaba Musoke mu*
   maduuka. ('It is odd to see Musoke shopping.')
odour *See* smell
oesophagus *n* **omumiro** *n3*
of *pre* **-a** (**N11.1**). *Takes pronominal concord* (**N4.2**),
   eg. (1) emmotoka ya Musoke ('car of Musoke'); (2)
   omuti gwa Musoke ('tree of Musoke'). The forms for
   the various noun classes are listed in Column 11 of
   Table 1.
off *pre* **ku**, *eg. Biggyeeko ku mmeeza. ('Take them off*
   the table.')
offal (*intestines*) *n* **ebyenda** *n8*
offence *n* (1) (*something that annoys*) **ekinyiiza** *n7*;
   (2) (*crime*) **omusango** *n3*   commit an offence **-zza**
   omusango
offend *vt* **-sina**, *eg. Ebigambo bye bansina. ('His*

words offended me.'). See annoy; fed up (make) person easily offended *(touchy)* **ow'entondo** *n1*

offender *(legal) n* **omuzzi w'omusango** *n1*

offer *vt* **-waayo** offer oneself *(volunteer)* **-eewaayo**

offering *(religious) n* (1) *(in church)* **ekirabo** *n7*, **ekiweebwayo** *n7*; (2) *(to a lubaale)* **ekigali** *n7* make an offering (1) *(in church)* **-waayo ekirabo**; (2) *(to a lubaale or spirit)* **-wonga**

office *n* **ofiisi** *n9*. *See* position office of an omutongole *(appointed official)* **ekitongole** *n7* assume an office *(official position)* **-lya obukulu**

officer *n* **ofiisa** *n1* prison officer **omukuumi w'ekkomera** *n1*

¹official *adj* **-tongole**

²official *(person) n* **omutongole** *n1* appoint as an official **-tongoza** become an official **-tongola** state of being an official **obutongole** *n14*

officially *adv* **mu butongole**

offload *vt* **-tikkula**. *See* unload

offside, be *(in football) vi* **-teega** person who is offside **omuteezi** *n1*

offspring *n* **ezzadde** *n5*

often *adv* (1) Use **-tera** *('do habitually')* in present tense *(N16)* followed by inf *(N19)*, eg. *Atera okujja wano. ('He often comes here.')*; (2) *(many times)* **emirundi mingi** how often? **emirundi emeka?** not too often **ebbalirirwe**

oh *interj (in entreaties)* **ayi**, eg. *Ayi Katonda tuyambe! ('Oh God help us!')*

¹oil *n* **amafuta** *n6*, eg. *amafuta g'entungo ('sesame oil'),* *(for cooking)* **obutto** *n14*, *(lubricating)* **oyiro** *n1* oil palm **omunazi** *n3 (fruit* **ekinazi** *n7)* oil well **ekirombe ky'amafuta** *n7* be oily *(of the skin)* **-nyereketa, -nyerettuka**

²oil *(lubricate) vt* **-teekamu oyiro**

ointment *n* **ebizigo** *n8*

OK *interj* **kale**

old *adj* **-kadde**, eg. *entebe enkadde ('old chair'),* *(in the past)* **-a edda**, eg. *amawulire ag'edda ('old news').* *See* worn-out old age **obukadde** *n14* old person **omukadde** *n1*, **omuzeeyi** *n1*. *See* elder become old **-kaddiwa** begin to look old **-kayuka, -kanduka** make old **-kaddiya**

oleander, yellow *(type of small tree) n* **obusitaani** *n14*, **kamuseenene** *n12*

olive *(as in the Bible) n* (1) *(tree)* **omuzeyituuni** *n3*; (2) *(fruit)* **enzeyituuni** *n9*

omen, bad *n* **ekyebikiro** *n7*

omit *vt.* Use verb in neg *(N21)*, eg. *Saamugambye. ('I omitted to tell him.')*. *See* forget

omitting *pre.* Use **-buukawo** *('jump over')*, eg. *Gaba ebitabo nga obuukawo omuntu omu. ('Give out the books omitting every other person.')*

on *pre* (1) *(referring to place or a day)* **ku**, eg. *Ku Mmande yaleka ekitabo ku mmeeza. ('She left the book on the table on Monday.')*; (2) *(with date)* **nga**, eg. *nga Jjuuni bbiri ('on June 2nd ')*; (3) *(meaning 'when' and followed by present*

participle) **bwe**, eg. *Bwe yandaba n'adduka. ('On seeing me, he ran away.')*. *See* as soon as on account of *(because of)* **olwa** on arrival *(as soon as arriving)* **olutuuka** on behalf of **ku lwa, ku lwa-** *(N11.4)*. *See* for on here **kuno** on purpose **mu bugenderevu** on the other hand **ku ludda olulala** on the side of *(beside)* **ku mabbali ga** on-the-spot **-a obuliwo**, eg. *omutango gwa buliwo ('on-the-spot fine')* on there **okwo, kuli.** *(N9.1)* on top *(on the surface)* **kungulu.** *See* above on top of *(on the surface of)* **kungulu ku** on which *(where)* **kwe**, eg. *Eno y'emmeeza kwe nnateeka ekitabo. ('Here is the table on which I put the book.')*. *Subject relative clauses are also used (N7.2).*

¹once *(one time) adv* **omulundi gumu** once upon a time **awo olwatuuka, lwali lumu** at once *(immediately)* **amangwago, kaakati** do once in a while **-gira**, eg. *Agira n'agenda e Kampala. ('He goes to Kampala once in a while.')*

²once *(when) conj* **bwe**, eg. *Bwe tubayita, bateekwa okujja. ('Once we call them, they must come.')*

one *num* **emu**. The stem is **-mu** *(with numeral concord N4.2)* *(N8.1)*, eg. *ekintu kimu ('one thing').* *See* single one after another **kumukumu** one-by-one **-mu -mu** *(N8.1)*. *Takes numeral concord (N4.2)*, eg. *Mpeereza kimu kimu. ('Give me the things one-by-one.'),* *(of people)* **kinnoomu**, eg. *Abantu bajja kinnoomu. ('The people are coming one-by-one.')* one day **lumu** one of us **omu ku ffe**, one of you **omo ku mmwe**, etc. not even one *(person)* **n'omu** with neg *(N21)*, eg. *Tewali muntu n'omu eyakkirizza. ('Not even one person agreed.')*

oneness *n* **obumu** *n14*

oneself *pro.* Reflexive verbs take prefix **-ee** *(N18)*, eg. *Endabirwamu esobozesa okweraba. ('A mirrow allows one to see oneself.')* by oneself *(alone)* **bw'omu**

onion *n* **akatungulu** *n12*

only *adj/adv* **-okka** *(N7.3)*. Takes pronominal concord *(N4.2)*, eg. *(1) ekintu kimu kyokka ('only one thing'); (2) omuti gumu gwokka ('only one tree').*

onto *pre* **ku**

onwards *adv* **mu maaso**

ooze (out) *vi* **-kenenuka**

¹open *adj* **-ggule**

²open *vt* (1) *(door, shop, etc.)* **-ggula** *(usually with enclitic* **-wo** *N24.2)*, eg. *Ggulawo oluggi. ('Open the door.')*; (2) *(something wrapped, fastened, etc.)* **-sumulula**, eg. *Yasumulula ekitereke. ('She opened the parcel.')*; (3) *(partially)* **-wenjula**, eg. *Yawenjula olutimbe okulaba ebweru. ('She opened the curtain a little to look outside.')* open a book **-bikkula ekitabo** open one's eyes **-zibula amaaso**, *(wide)* **-kanula amaaso** open one's hand (1) *(to receive something)* **-teekawo omukono**; (2)

(*to catch something*) **-tega omukono** open the mouth (1) (*of oneself*) **-yasama**, *eg. Omulwadde yayasama okumuliisa. ('The patient opened her mouth to be fed.')*; (2) (*of someone else*) **-yasamya omumwa** open up (*unblock*) **-zibukula** come open (1) (*eg. of a door*) **-gguka**, *eg. Oluggi lugguse. ('The door has come open.')*; (2) (*uncovered*) **-bikkuka**, *eg. Ekitabo kibikkuse. ('The book has come open.')*; (3) (*of something wrapped, fastened, etc.*) **-sumulukuka**, *eg. Ekitereke kisumulukuse. ('The parcel has come open.')*; (4) (*partially*) **-wenjuka**, *eg. Olutimbe luwenjuse. ('The curtain has come open.')* be open with (*someone mentally*) **-eeyabiza** be wide open (*of the eyes, eg. due to fright*) **-kanuka**

opener *n* **ekisumulula** *n7*

opening (*gap*) *n* **omwagaanya** *n3* (*small* **akaagaanya** *n12*), **omuwaatwa** *n3*

openly (*publicly*) *adv* **mu lwatu**, *eg. Yayogera mu lwatu. ('He spoke openly.')*

open-mouthed, be *vi* **-yasaamiirira**

operate *vt* (1) (*manage*) **-ddukanya**; (2) (*use, eg. machinery*) **-kozesa** operate on (*a patient, medically*) **-longoosa**, *eg. Baamulongoosa okugulu. ('They operated on his leg.')*

operation *n* (1) (*work*) **omulimu** *n3*; (2) (*surgical*) **okulongoosa** *n15*

opinion *n* **endowooza** *n9*

opponent (*rival*) *n* **omuvuganyi** *n1*

opportunity *n* (1) (*luck; chance*) **omukisa** *n3*; (2) (*space; room to act*) **ebbanga** *n5*

oppose *vt* **-gaana**, *eg. Musoke yagaana oluguudo okuyita mu ttaka lye. ('Musoke opposed the road going through his land.')*. See compete with

opposite (*facing*) *pre* **mu maaso ga**

opposition (*in parliament*) *n* **oludda oluvuganya gavumenti** *n11*

oppress *vt* **-nyigiriza**

or *conj* **oba**, *eg. Oyagala mucungwa oba lyenvu? ('Do you want an orange or banana?')*

oracle (*diviner*) *n* **omulaguzi** *n1*

orange *n* (*tree; fruit*) **omucungwa** *n3* orange juice **emicungwa** *n4*, (*concentrated*) **emicungwa emika**

ordain *vt* **-yawula** be ordained **-yawulwa** ordained person **omwawule** *n1*

ordeal (*suffering*) *n* **ekibonoobono** *n7* administer trial by ordeal **-nywesa amaduudu**

¹**order** (*command*) *n* **ekiragiro** *n7* be out of order (*of machinery*) **-fa** be put in good order (*tidied up*) **-longooka** in good order *adj* **-longoofu** in order to (1) Use subjunctive tense (**N17**), *eg. Yagalamira asobole okwebaka. ('She lay down in order to sleep.')*; (2) Use inf (**N18**), *eg. Nneetaaga omuliro okufumba. ('I need a fire in order to cook.')*. See so that put in good order **-longoosa**

²**order** (*command*) *vt* **-lagira**, (*in army or police*) **-duumira**, (*in an unpleasant way*) **-junga** order (*something*) from a distance **-lagiriza** be ordered **-lagirwa**

ordinary *adj* **-a bulijjo**

ore, iron *n* **amasengere** *n6*

organ (*musical instrument*) *n* **ennanga** *n9* play the organ **-kuba ennanga**

organisation *n* **ekibiina** *n7*

organise *vt* **-tegeka**, *eg. Ali mu kutegeka emizannyo. ('He is organising the games.')*

organiser *n* (1) **omutegesi** *n1*; (2) Use **-tegeka** (*'organise'*) in rel (**N7.1**), *eg. (abantu) abategeka ('organisers')*

organist *n* **omukubi w'ennanga** *n1*

oribi (*type of antelope*) *n* **akasirabo** *n12*

origin *n* (1) (*source*) **ensibuko** *n9*; (2) (*beginning*) **entandikwa** *n9*

original See first original inhabitant (*one already present at a place*) **nnansangwawo** *n1*

originate *v* (1) (*arise*) *vi* **-sibuka**, *eg. Omugga gusibuka awo. ('The river originates there.')*; (2) (*invent*) *vt* **-yiiya**

originator *n* (1) (*inventor*) **omuyiiya** *n1*; (2) (*founder*) **omutandisi** *n1*

ornament (*embellish*) *vt* **-wunda**. See decorate

orphan *n* (1) (*lost one parent*) **mulekwa** *n1*; (2) (*lost both parents*) **enfuuzi** *n9* (*pl.* **abaana enfuuzi**)

orphanage *n* **amaka ga ba mulekwa** *n6*

orphaned *adj* **-fuuzi**

Orthodox christian *n* **omusoddookisi** *n1*

Orthodox Church *n* **Ekkanisa y'Abasoddookisi** *n9*

orthography *n* **empandiika** *n9*

ostrich *n* **mmaaya** *n9*

other *adj* **-lala**, *eg. omuti omulala ('the other tree')* on the other hand **ku ludda olulala** the other day **jjuuzi**

otherwise *adv* **oba si ekyo**

otter *n* **ennonge** *n9*

ought *aux v* (1) (*must*) **-teekwa** *followed by inf* (**N19**), *eg. Oteekwa okukyogerako ne mukamaawo. ('You ought to discuss it with your boss.')*; (2) (*would be best*) **-saanira**, *eg. Kisaanidde otwale omulimu guno. ('You ought to take this job.')*, **-gwanira**

ounce *n* **awunzi** *n9*

our *pos* (*determiner*) **-ffe** (**N11.4**) *with pronominal concord* (**N4.2**), *eg. (1) embwa yaffe ('our dog'); (2) ekiso kyaffe ('our knife.'). The forms for the various noun classes are listed in Column 7 on Table 9.*

ours *pos* (*pronoun*) **owaffe, abaffe**, *etc.* (**N11.4**), *eg. Ebitabo ebyo byammwe, bino byaffe. ('Those books are yours, these are ours.')*

ourselves *pro. Reflexive verbs take the prefix* **-ee-** (**N18**). by ourselves **ffekka** we ourselves **ffe ffennyini**

oust *vt* **-goba**

out (*outside*) *adv* **wabweru, ebweru** out of **okuva ku**, *eg. Yagaggawala okuva mu kukola ennyo.*

('*She got rich out of working hard.*') out-of-shape
See deformed be out-of-order (*of machinery*) -fa
take out -ggyamu, *eg. Yakiggyamu mu nsawo.* ('*He
took it out of the bag.*')

outcrop (*of rock*) *n* olwazi *n11*, ekyaziyazi *n7*

outcry, make an -laajana, *eg. Abantu baalaajana
ng'etteeka liyise.* ('*There was an outcry when the
law was passed.*')

outer *adj* -a ebweru, *eg. oluggi olw'ebweru* ('*outer
door*')

outline (*draft*) *n* ebbago *n5*

[1]outside *adv* wabweru, ebweru

[2]outside *pre* wabweru (*or* ebweru) wa

outskirts *n* obusammambiro *n14*

outstanding *adj* (1) (*distinguished*) -yatiikirivu; (2)
(*sticking out*) -kukunavu be outstanding
(*distinguished*) -yatiikirira, *eg. Yayatiikirira mu
kuzannya goofu.* ('*He was outstanding at golf.*'),
(*and confident*) -eekansa, *eg. Musoke yeekansa mu
kuzannya omupiira.* ('*Musoke is outstanding at
football.*')

outward journey *n* amagenda *n6*

outwit *vt* -sinza amagezi

oven *n* oveni *n9*

over *pre. Meaning can be incorporated in the verb,
eg. Yabuuse olukomera.* ('*He jumped over the
fence.*') from over (*from across*) emitala wa, *eg.
Yava emitala w'ekisenyi.* ('*He came from over the
swamp.*') over there wali

overburden (*with load or problems*) *vt*
-zitoowerera. *See* burden; overload be
overburdened (by) -zitoowererwa

overcast weather *n* obudde bw'ekikome *n14*

overcharge *vt* -seera person who overcharges
omuseezi *n1*

overcharging *n* obuseezi *n14*, okuseera *n15*

overcoat (*long heavy type*) *n* kabuuti *n9*

overcome *vt* -vvuunuka, *eg. Ebizibu yabivvuunuse.*
('*He overcame his difficulties.*'), -wangula. *See*
win

overcooked, be (*of sweet potatoes*) *vi* -wolottala

overeat *vi* -eepiika emmere

overfamiliarity *n* olummanyimmanyi *n11. See*
intrusiveness be overfamiliar with -eemanyiiza
nnyo, -manyiira nnyo

overfeed *vt* -piika emmere, *eg. Omwana amupiise
emmere.* ('*She has overfed the child.*')

overflow *vi* -yiika, *eg. Amazzi gayiika okuva mu
bbenseni.* ('*The water is overflowing from the
basin.*'), (*of a river*) -wagulula, *eg. Omugga
guwaguludde.* ('*The river is overflowing.*')

overgarment *n* ekikubiro *n7*

overgrown (*of plants*) *adj* -zijjagavu overgrown
land (1) (*weedy, after the harvest*) ekisambu *n7*;
(2) (*longer abandoned*) ekikande *n7. See* jungle;
scrub; thicket allow to become overgrown -zisa
be(come) overgrown (1) (*of agricultural land*)
-zika; (2) (*of tracks, etc., by plants*) -zijjagala, *eg.*

Ekibira kizijjagadde. ('*The forest is impassable.*' –
because the tracks have become overgrown)

overhang *See* hang over

overhaul an engine -siba yingini

overindulge (on) *vt. Use adv* funduukululu ('*to
the ultimate*'), *eg. Twalidde funduukululu.* ('*We
overindulged on food.*')

overjoyed, be *vi* -tijja

overload *vt* -binika, -tikka nnyo, -tikka akabindo

overlook *vt* -tunuulira, *eg. Ennyumba etunuulidde
ennyanja.* ('*The house overlooks the lake.*'). *See*
forget overlook a fault -tta ku liiso. *See* cover up

overpower *vt* -sinza amaanyi

overpraise *vt* -saakiriza

overripe (*of fruit*) *adj* -bolerevu become overripe
-bolerera

overseas *adv* emitala w'amayanja go overseas to
work (*implying illegally*) -genda ku kyeyo

oversee (*supervise*) *vt* -labirira

overstretched, be (*to bursting point*) *vi* -pinduuka

overtake (*pass*) *vt* -yisa

overtax *vt* -liika omusolo, *eg. Baamuliika omusolo.*
('*She was overtaxed.*')

overthrow a government -suula gavumenti

overturn *vt* -vuunika. *See* knock over be
overturned -eevuunika

overwhelm *vt* -yitirirako, *eg. Emirimu
gyamuyitirirako.* ('*The work overwhelmed her.*').
See conquer be overwhelmed by (*an emotion*)
-faako, *eg. Yafaako ensonyi.* ('*He was
overwhelmed by shame.*') be overwhelmed by
grief ennaku -yitiriirako

overwork *v* (1) *vi* -kola okukamala; (2) *vt*
-tuntuza, *eg. Omukulu atuntuza abakozi.* ('*The
boss overworks the workers.*')

owe *vt* -banja (*subject and object reversed
compared to English*), *eg. Musoke mmubanja
ssente.* ('*Musoke owes me money.*')

owing to *conj* olwa, *eg. Olw'enkuba okutonnya
amakubo gaseerera.* ('*Owing to the rain, the roads
are slippery.*')

owl *n* ekiwuugulu *n7*

own (*possess*) *vt. Use* -lina *or* -ba na ('*have*')
according to tense (**N20.1-20.2**), *eg.* (1) *Nnali
nnina emmotoka.* ('*I used to own a car.*'); (2) *Nja
kuba n'emmotoka mu bbanga ttono.* ('*I shall soon
own a car.*') my own, your own, *etc. Use
possessive determiner* (**N11.4**), *eg. Kino kitabo
kyange.* ('*This is my own book.*')

owner *n* nnannyini *or* nnyini *n1* (*followed by item
owned* **N11.6**), *eg. nnannyini kitabo* ('*owner of the
book*'). *A pronoun referring to the possessor can be
given as a suffix* (**N11.6**), *eg. nnannyinikyo* ('*its
owner*' – *referring to a book*). house owner
nnyinimu *n1*, nnannyinimu *n1*, nnyini nnyumba
n1

ownership *n* obwannannyini *n14*

ox *n* ente endaawo *n9*

oxygen *n* omukka gw'obulamu *n3*, okisigyeni *n9*
oyster mushroom *n* akatiko akazungu *n12*
oysternut (*large climber with edible seeds*) *n*
ekinyeebwa ekizungu *n7*

P,p

pacify *vt* (1) (*calm someone down*) -kkakkanya; (2)
(*from being annoyed*) -nyiigulula. *See* soothe be
pacified (1) (*calmed down*) -kkakkana; (2) (*from
being annoyed*) -nyiigulukuka
¹pack (*carried on back*) *n* makinoola *n9*
²pack *vt* -pakira, *eg. Ensawo za ppamba tuzipakidde
mu sitoowa. ('We have packed the bags of cotton in
the store.')* pack food for a journey -siba entanda,
(*for someone*) -sibirira entanda pack neatly
(*saving space*) -komeka, -panga pack tightly
-ggumiza, *eg. Njagala okuggumiza emmere mu
sseffuliya. ('I want to pack the food tightly in the
pan.')*, (*with pressing down*) -kkatira, *eg.
Twakkatira ppamba mu nsawo. ('We packed the
cotton tightly in the sack.')* be tightly packed
-ggumira, *eg. Saaniika emmere eggumire ('Pack
the food bundle tightly.' – 'in the pot' understood).
See* crowded tightly packed *adj* -ggumivu, *eg.
Essanduuko nzigumivu. ('The suitcase is tightly
packed.')*
package/packet *n* pakiti *n9*, ekipakiti *n7*, (*made
from banana fibre*) ettu *n5*. *See* parcel packet of
flying ants (1) (*eg. offered for sale*) ettu ly'enswa
n5; (2) (*as formerly part of brideprice*) omtwalo
gw'enswa *n3*
pact, blood *n* omukago *n3*
pad (*on head for load*) *n* enkata *n9*
¹paddle *n* enkasi *n9*
²paddle *vt* -kuba enkasi
paddler (*of canoe*) *n* omuvuzi w'eryato *n1*,
(*occupying rear seat*) omulumba *n1*
¹padlock *n* ekkufulu *n9*
²padlock *vt* -siba ekkufulu
pagan *n* omukaafiiri *n1*
paganism *n* obukaafiiri *n14*
page *n* (1) (*eg. of book*) olupapula *n11*, omwaliiro
gw'olupapula *n3*; (2) (*young person in the service
of the Kabaka*) omusiige *n1* front page (*eg. of
newspaper*) omuko ogusooka *n3*
paid *See* pay
pail (*bucket*) *n* endobo *n9* (*small* akalobo *n12*),
baketi *n9* milk pail ekyanzi *n7*
pain *n* obulumi *n14*. *Types of pain include*: (1) *in
abdomen*) enjoka *n10*, (*recurring*) enjoka
ensaanuusi, (2) (*menstrual*) enjoka ez'eddumi;
(3) (*after childbirth*) kawammansi *n1*; (4)
(*stinging, eg. caused by cut*) obubalagaze *n14*; (5)
(*sudden, in side or shoulder*) kinsimbye *n1*; (6)
(*general body pain*) ekimenyoomenyo *n7*; (7)
(*slight pain where a bone has been broken,*

fractured or dislocated) obuvune *n14*. *See* illness
be in pain -lumwa, *eg. Nnumwa. ('I am in pain.'),
(in a particular place*) -lina obulumi, *eg. Nnina
obulumi mu mugongo. ('I have back pain.')* be
pained (*emotionally*) -nyolwa, *eg. Yanyoleddwa
nnyo okufiirwa kw'omwana we. ('He was pained by
the death of his child.')* cause pain to -lumya
have a shooting pain -myansa, *eg. Bwe yalinnya
wansi ekigere ne kimumyansa. ('When he stepped
down, he felt a shooting pain in his foot.')* take
pains (*take trouble*) -tegana, *eg. Yategana
okulongoosa ekisenge. ('She took pains to clean the
room properly.')*
¹paint *n* erangi *n9*
²paint *vt* -siiga erangi
paintbrush *n* bulaasi esiiga langi *n9*
painted *adj* -a erangi
painter *n* omusiizi *n1*, (*artist*) omusiizi
w'ebifaananyi painter of nails omusiizi w'enjala
painting *n* ekifaananyi ekisiige *n7*
pair *n* omugogo *n3*, *eg. omugogo gw'engatto ('pair
of shoes')*
palace (*also* palace compound) *n* olubiri *n11*
palace guard omumbowa *n1* head of palace
admistration omukulu w'olubiri *n1* Mengo
Palace olubiri lw'e Mengo person who serves in
the palace omugalagala *n1*
palatable smell (*of food*) *n* eggwoowo *n5*
palate (*roof of mouth*) *n* akabuno *n12*, ekisasi mu
kamwa *n7*
pale, grow (*in colour*) *vi* -tukuulirira
palisade *n* olukomera *n11*
¹palm (*of hand*) *n* ekibatu *n7*
²palm (*type of tree*) *n*. *General terms*: (*palm tree*)
omunazi *n3*, (*leaf*) olusansa *n11*, (*fruit*) ekinazi
n7. *The following refer to types of palms*: (1) (*wild
date palm; Phoenix*) (*plant*) olukindukindu *n11*,
olukindu *n11*, (*pole*) olukoma *n11*, (*fruit*)
empirivuma *n9*; (2) (*raffia*) (*plant and midrib of
leaf*) ekibo *n7*, (*fruit*) embo *n9*, (*fibre*) obuso *n14*;
(3) (*fan palm; Borassus*) akatuugo *n12*, entunku
n9; (4) (*coconut*) (*plant*) omunazi *n3*, (*fruit*)
ekinazi *n7*, (*oil*) ennazi *n9*. *See* rattan palm skirt
(*worn by dancers*) ekisenso *n7* Palm Sunday
Olunaku lw'Amatabi *n11*, Olunaku lw'Ensansa
palpitate *vi* -pakuka, *eg. Omutima gwange
gupakuka. ('My heart is palpitating.')*
pamper *vt* -biibiita. *See* indulge; spoil
pan *n* sseffuliya *n9*, sseppiki *n9*
pancake *n* kabalagala *n1*
pancreas *n* ennuuni *n9*
pang of pain *n* obulumi *n14*
panga (*machete*) *n* ejjambiya *n5*
pangolin *n* olugave *n11*
panic (*cause panic to*) *vt* -gugumula. *See* shock
make off in panic -gugumuka run away in panic
-dduka muwawa. *See* shocked (be)
pant *vi* -wejjawejja

pants/panties *n* akawale *n12*, **empale** *n9*. *See* trousers; underpants

papacy *n* obwappaapa *n14*

paper *n* olupapula *n11*　newspaper olupapula lw'amawulire *n11*, amawulire *n6*　toilet paper *See* lavatory paper　wrapping paper olupapula olusabika

papyrus *n* ekitoogo *n7*, (*young tufts*) obugala *n14*

parable *n* olugero *n11*

parade *n* paleedi *n9*

paradise *n* eggulu *n5*

paraffin *n* palafiini *n9*, amafuta g'ettaala *n6*

paralysed, be(come) *vi* -sannyalala. *See* lame (become)

parasite (*person; pest who won't go away*) *n* olokokobe *n11*

parcel *n* (1) (*eg. for posting*) ekitereke *n7*; (2) (*made of banana fibre*) ettu *n5*. *See* banana (*for vocabulary relating to preparation and serving of food from food parcels*)

parched, become *vi* -kala

pardon *vt* -sonyiwa

parent *n* omukadde *n1*, omuzadde *n1*　parent of mukadde (*with pos* **N12**), *eg.* mukadde wange ('*my parent*')

parentage *n* obuzadde *n14*

parish *n* (1) (*ecclesiastical*) obusumba *n14*; (2) (*governmental*) omuluka *n3*　parish chief owoomuluka *n1*

¹park *n* ppaaka *n9*

²park (*a vehicle*) *vt* -simba

parking *n* ensimba *n9*

Parkinson's disease *n* obulwadde bw'obuko *n14*

parliament *n* olukiiko lw'eggwanga *n11*, palamenti *n9*　Buganda parliament olukiiko lwa Buganda　parliamentary building of Buganda Bulange *n9*

parrot *n* enkusu *n9*　like a parrot obukusu

parson *n* omwawule *n1*, omusumba *n1*

¹part *n* ekitundu *n7*, *eg.* Akozeeko ekitundu ky'ebibuuzo. ('*She has done part of the examination.*'), (*role in play*) ekitundu ky'omuzannyo. *See* portion; share, spare　for my part ku lwange, for your part ku lulwo, *etc.* (**N11.4**)

²part　part company (*go different ways*) -yawukana　part curtains -bikkula entimbe

partially cooked (*of food*) *adj* -a kakoolakoola

partner *See* companion　fail to get a partner -diba

participant (*in a competition*) *n* omuvvunkanyi *n1*

participate *vi* -eetaba, *eg.* Yeetaba mu paleedi. ('*He participated in the parade.*')

particularly *adv* naddala, *eg.* Njagala nnyo ebibala naddala emicungwa. ('*I like fruit especially oranges.*')　be particular (*choosy*) -eeronda

partition *n* ekyawulamu *n7*, (*curtain as partition in room*) eggigi *n5*　barkcloth partition (*as room divider*) eggigi ly'embugo

partridge (*francolin*) *n* enkwale *n9*

part-time *adj* -a ekiseera, *eg.* omulimu gw'ekiseera ('*part-time job*')

party (*social gathering*) *n* embaga *n9* (*small akabaga n12*), (*for bride or groom before wedding*) kasiki *n12*. *See* celebration　change one's political party -sala eddiiro　drinking party ekinywi *n7*　political party ekibiina ky'obufuzi *n7*　wedding party embaga y'obugole

paspalum (*type of grass*) *n* paasipalamu *n1*

¹pass (*eg. on mountain track*) *n* omuwaatwa *n3*

²pass *v* (1) (*go past, in time or space*) *vi* -yita ku, *eg.* Tujja kuyita ku kkanisa okutuuka ewa Musoke. ('*We will pass the church to get to Musoke's.*'); (2) (*cause to pass*) *vt* -yisa, *eg.* Baayisa ekiteeso mu lukiiko. ('*They passed the proposal at the meeting.*'); (3) (*hand to*) *vt* -weereza, *eg.* Mpeereza omunnyo. ('*Pass me the salt.*')　pass an examination -yita ebibuuzo　pass by (*make a detour around*) -eebalama, (*to avoid being seen*) -eebalaamiriza　pass one another (*moving in opposite directions*) -yisiŋŋanya, *eg.* Tujja kuyisiŋŋanya ku luguudo. ('*We will pass one another on the road.*')　pass one's leg over (*a seated person, a gesture of disrespect formerly done by children*) -yisa okugulu mu nju, -yisaamu olugaayu　pass out (*faint*) -zirika　pass sentence -sala omusango　pass sentence on -salira omusango, (*unfairly*) -saliriza omusango　pass someone without greeting -yita ku muntu　pass the day -siiba, *eg.* Yasiibye akola. ('*He passed the day working.*')　pass the night -sula, *eg.* Nnasula mu wooteeri. ('*I passed the night in a hotel.*')　pass (*something*) through (*eg. thread through eye of needle*) -yisaamu (*or* -yisa mu)　pass time (*a period of time*) Use -mala ('*finish*') , *eg.* Olunaku twalumala mu bbaala. ('*We passed the day in the bar.*')　pass wind (*fart*) -kuba ddoti

passage *n* (1) (*corridor*) olukuubo *n11*; (2) (*between buildings in a town*) ekikuubo *n7*　passage to be memorised ekikwate *7*

passenger *n* omusaabaze *n1*　passenger seat (*on bike*) ekkaliya *n9*

passer-by *n* omuyise *n1*

passion *n* obwagazi *n14*. *See* craving; love　passion fruit (*plant; fruit*) akatunda *n12*　be passionate about (*zealous*) -jjumbira

Passover *n* Okuyitako *n15*

passport *n* paasipooti *n9*

¹past *adj.* Use -yita ('*pass*') in rel (**N7.1**), *eg.* Tetwamulabako omwaka oguyise. ('*We did not see her during the past year.*')　go past -yita ku, *eg.* Yayita ku nnyumba yaffe n'atatukyalira. ('*He went past our house without visiting us.*')　in the past edda

²past *pre* okuyita ku, *eg.* Twavuga okuyita ku nnyumba. ('*We drove past the house.*')

paste *vt* -kwasa

pastor *n* omusumba *n1*

pasture *n* ettale *n5*, (*fresh and rampant, eg. as grown up after a fire*) ekiddo *n7*

pat *vt* -kubako

[1]**patch** (*eg. on clothing or tyre*) *n* ekiraka *n7*   patch of crops omusiri *n3*   patch of different coloured skin ekibambya *n7*   patch of open land ekibangirizi *n7*   put on a patch -kuba (*or* -teekako) ekiraka

[2]**patch** *vt* -paapira, *eg. Mpaapira empale eyulise. ('I am patching the torn trousers.')*

path *n* ekkubo *n5* (*small* akakubo *n12*), (*made through vegetation*) oluwenda *n11*. See trail   make a path (1) (*by walking or pushing through vegetation*) -kuba oluwenda; (2) (*by cutting*) -tema oluwenda

patience *n* obugumiikiriza *n14*

patient (*ill person*) *n* omulwadde *n1*   be patient (with) (1) (*tolerate*) -gumiikiriza, *eg. Gumiikiriza mmale okukola emirimu gino. ('Be patient while I finish these tasks.')*; (2) (*wait a while*) -kwatirirako, *eg. Nkwatiriddeko ekimala. ('I have been patient enough.')*

[1]**patrol** *n* potolo *n9*. See scouting

[2]**patrol** *vi* -lawuna. See tour

patron *n* omuyima *n1*

patterned *adj* -a ebibomboola, *eg. olugoye olw'ebibomboola ('patterned dress')*. See checked; decorated   make pattern on (1) (*by carving, eg. on pot or wood*) -yola; (2) (*by painting*) -tona

Paul *n* Paulo *n1*

pauper *n* omwavu *n1*, (*very poor*) lunkupe *n1*

pause *vt* -yimirizaamu, *eg. Yayimirizaamu firimu. ('He paused the film.')*   pause and reconsider (*what one is saying*) -eekomako

paw *n* ekigere *n7*

pawpaw *n* (1) (*tree*) omupaapaali *n3*; (2) (*fruit*) eppaapaali *n5*   male pawpaw fruit (*small and inedible, medicinal*) eppaappaali essajja

[1]**pay** *n* omusaala *n3*, empeera *n9*

[2]**pay** *vt* (*paid*) -sasula   pay a formal call on the Kabaka -lanya   pay attention -teekako (*or* -ssaako) omwoyo, *eg. Teekako omwoyo ng'ovuga emmotoka. ('Pay attention when you drive.')*   pay damages -wa engassi, -liwa   pay fees for -weerera, *eg. Aweerera omwana wa Musoke. ('He is paying for the education of Musoke's child.')*   pay for/at -sasulira   pay in instalments -sasula mu bitundutundu   make pay -sasuza. See revenge

payment *n* ekisasulibwa *n7*. See fee   down payment akakalu *n12*, omusingo *n3*   make down payment (*first instalment on sum owed*) -sibako ssente   on-the-spot payment essente za buliwo *n10*

pea(s) *n* kawo *n1*. See pigeon pea

peace *n* emirembe *n4*   make peace between (*reconcile*) -tabaganya

peaceful *adj* -a emirembe. See calm; settled

peaceful and settled (*of a person*) -tebenkevu   be(come) peaceful and settled -tebenkera

peacock *n* muzinge *n1*

peak *n* entikko *n9*

peanut (*also* groundnut) *n* ekinyeebwa *n7*. See groundnut   peanut sauce enva z'ebinyeebwa *n10*   peanuts in their shells ebinyeebwa by'ebikuta   roasted peanuts ebinyeebwa ebisiike

pear *n* peya *n9*

pearl *n* eddulu *n5*

peasant *n* omukopi *n1*   peasant-like *adj* -kopi

pebble *n* akayinja *n12*

peck *vt* -bojja, -sojja   peck one another -bojjagana, -sojjagana

peculiar, something (*unusual*) *n* ekintu ekitali kya bulijjo *n7*

[1]**pedal** *n* ekigere *n7*   bicycle pedal ekigere ky'eggaali

[2]**pedal** (*a bicycle*) *vt* -sotta. See ride

peddle (*goods*) *vt* (1) -tembeeya okutunda; (2) *Use* -tambuza (*cause to travel*), *eg. Batambuza amazzi ag'okutunda. ('They are peddling water for sale.')*

peddler (*itinerant trader*) *n* omutembeeyi *n1*

pedestal *n* ekituuti *n7*

pedestrian *n* ow'ebigere *n1*

pedigree *n* olulyo *n11*

pee (*urinate*) *vi* -fuka, -fuuyisa

[1]**peel** See peeling

[2]**peel (off)** *v* TRANSITIVE USES (1) (*something stuck down*) -bambula, *eg. Mmambudde akapande. ('I have peeled off the label.')*, -gagambula; (2) (*outer cover of fruit or vegetable*) (*with a knife*) -waata, (*by hand*) -susa. See strip   peel off bark from (*a tree*) -susumbula   peel off bark from a barkcloth tree -subula omutuba   peel yams after cooking -sosola endaggu   INTRANSITIVE USES (1) (*of something stuck down*) -bambulukuka, *eg. Erangi ebambulukuse. ('The paint is peeling off.')*, -gagambuka; (2) (*of the skin*) (*eg. due to allergic reaction*) -yubuka, *eg. Njubuse mu maaso. ('My face is peeling.')*, (*when scalded by boiling water*) -bambuka; (3) (*of bark from a tree*) -susumbuka, *eg. Ekikuta kya kalittunsi kisusumbuse. ('The eucalyptus bark is peeling off.')*

peeler (*person*) *n* omususi *n1*

peeling (*also* peel) *n* ekikuta *n7*, *eg. ekikuta kya lumonde ('potato peeling')*   peeling place (*for bananas*) eggwaatiro *n5*   plantain peels ebiwata *n8*

peep (at) *vi* -lingiza. See glance   keep peeping at -lingiriza

[1]**peg** *n* enkondo *n9* (*small, eg. for tent* akakondo *n12*), (*for stretching skins*) olubambo *n11*   plant used for making pegs (*for stretching skins*) kabambamaliba *n1*

[2]**peg (out)** (*eg. skin to dry*) *vt* -bamba   person who pegs out skins omubambamaliba *n1*

pen *n* (1) (*for writing*) **peeni** *n9*, (*biro*) **bayiro** *n9*, (*fountain pen*) **ekkalaamu ya bwino** *n9*; (2) (*enclosure for animals*) **ekisibo** *n7*, (*for cattle*) **ekiraalo** *n7*, **olugo** *n11*

penalty (*in football*) *n* **peneti** *n9*. *See* fine

pencil *n* **ekkalaamu**   coloured pencil **ekkalaamu ya langi**

pendant *n* **omudaali** *n3*

penetrate *vt* **-yingira**

penholder *n* **ekijugo** *n7*

penis *n* **obusajja** *n14*, **akasolo** *n12*, **embolo** *n9* (*impolite*)

penitent, be *vi* **-bonerera**

Pentecost *n* **Pentekoti** *n9*

people *See* person

pepper (*chilli*) *n* **kaamulali** *n1*, **ppiripiri** *n1*

pepperbark tree (*Warburgia*) *n* **abasi** *n1*, **omukuzannume** *n3*

perceive *vt* (1) (*see*) **-laba**; (2) (*with other senses*) **-wulira**. *See* understand

perch (*hen roost*) *n* **oluwe** *n11*   Nile perch (*type of fish*) **empuuta** *n9*

perfect *adj* **-tuukirivu**   be perfect **-tuukirira**   make perfect (*give a good finish*) **-yooyoota**

perforate *vt* **-botola**, **-wummula**   be(come) perforated **-botoka**, **-wummuka**

perforated *adj* **-botofu**

perform *vt* (1) (*act*) **-zannya**; (2) (*do*) **-kola**

performance (*play*) *n* **omuzannyo** *n3*, **katemba** *n1*

performer (*actor; player*) *n* **omuzannyi** *n1*

perfume *n* **akawoowo** *n12*, **kalifuwa** *n1*

perhaps *See* maybe

peril *n* **akabi** *n12*

period *n* (1) (*of time*) **ekiseera** *n7* (*short* **akaseera** *n12*); (2) (*school lesson*) **lesoni** *n9*. *See* era; menstruate

perish *vi* **-zikirira**, **-saanawo**, (*in a fire*) **-sirikka**. *See* die

periwinkle, rosy (*type of plant*) *n* **akamuli** *n12*

perk up the ears (*to listen*) **-tega amatu**

permanent *adj* **-a olubeerera**   permanent job **omulimu gw'olubeerera** *n3*

permission *n* **olukusa** *n11*

¹**permit** *n* (1) (*permission*) **olukusa** *n11*; (2) (*licence*, *eg. to drive*) **pamiti** *n9*

²**permit** *vt* **-kkiriza**, *eg. Omuserikale yanzikiriza okuyingira.* ('The policeman permitted me to enter.'), (*make possible for*) **-ganya** (*verb usually used in neg*), *eg. Omwana teyamuganya kwebaka.* ('The child did not permit her to sleep.')   be permitted **-kkirizibwa**

perplex *vt* **-sobera**   be perplexed **-soberwa**, *eg. Asobeddwa ekyokukola.* ('She is perplexed about what to do.')

persecute *vt* **-yigganya**. *See* torment

persecution *n* **obuyigganyi** *n14*   religious persecution **obuyigganyi bw'eddiini**, **empalana y'eddiini** *n9*

persecutor *n* **omuyigganyi** *n1*

perseverance *n* **obunyiikivu** *n14*

persevere (at) *vi* **-nyiikira**, *eg. Anyiikidde okusoma.* ('She has persevered at her studies.')

persevering *adj* **-nyiikivu**

persist *vi* **-mala ebbanga ddene**, *eg. Amaze ebbanga ddene nga anoonya omulimu.* ('She persisted in trying to get a job.')   persist in (*despite lack of success*) **-kanda** (*followed by inf*), *eg. Nnakanda kumugamba tugende nga tayagala.* ('I persisted in asking him to go, but he didn't want to.')   persist in one's demands (*on someone*) **-eesiba ku**, *eg. Yeesibye ku Musoke amuwe ssente.* ('He persisted in asking Musoke for money.')

persistence (*of a person*) *n* **obunyiikivu** *n14*

persistent *adj* (1) (*of a person*) **-nyiikivu**; (2) (*of rain, etc.*) **-nyiinyiitivu**   be persistent (1) (*of a person*) **-nyiikira**; (2) (*of rain, etc.*) **-nyiinyiitira**, **-kanyiza**, *eg. Enkuba ekanyizza okutonnya.* ('The rain is persistent.'). *See* intensify

person *n* (*pl.* people) **omuntu** *n1*, (*witty and clever*) **omukalabakalaba** *n1*, (*big and tall*) **empaladdume** *n9*, (*tall and well built*) **omuwagguufu** *n1*, (*tall and handsome*) **omusoobolokofu** *n1*, (*outspoken and aggressive*) **nnalukalala** *n1*   person of **munna-** (*with name of place* **N12**), *eg. Munnakampala* ('Kampala person')   person who does things on her/his own **ssekinnoomu** *n1*   a person like me **gamba nga nze**   beloved person long absent **kabuladda** *n1*

perspiration *n* **entuuyo** *n10*

perspire *vi* **-tuuyana**

persuade *vt* **-sendasenda**, **-sikiriza**. *See* tempt

perturb (*disturb*) *vt* **-fuukuula**, **-siikuula**, **-tabula**. *See* worry   be perturbed **-fuukuuka**, **-siikuuka**, **-tabuka**

peruse (*look closely at*) *vt* **-eekaliriza**

pervert *vt* **-kyamya**. *See* lead astray

perverted *adj* **-kyamu**

pester *vt* **-tayirira**, (*making demands*) **-peeka**

pesterer (*also* pest) *n* **omutayirizi** *n1*. *See* hanger-on

pesticide *n* **eddagala eritta ebiwuka** *n5*

pestle *n* (1) (*large, eg. for pounding groundnuts*) **omusekuzo** *n3*; (2) (*small, eg. for mashing cooked food*) **ekisotta** *n7*

Peter *n* **Petero** *n1*

petrol *n* **amafuta g'emmotoka** *n6*, **petulooli** *n1*   petrol pump **pampu y'amafuta** *n9*   petrol station **sitenseni y'amafuta** *n9*, **essundiro ly'amafuta** *n5*

Pharisee *n* **Omufalisaayo** *n1*

phase (*of a process; stage*) *n* **omutendera** *n3*, *eg. emitendera gy'okuzimba ennyumba* ('phases of building a house')

phlegm *n* **ekikolondolwa** *n7*. *See* spit   bring up phlegm **-kolondola**, *eg. Yagogola omumiro n'akolondola.* ('He cleared his throat and spat out phlegm.')

phone *See* telephone

¹photograph *n* ekifaananyi *n7* have one's photograph taken (*by someone else*) -eekubisa ekifaananyi

²photograph *vt* -kubisa ekifaananyi

photographer *n* omukubi w'ebifaananyi *n1*

physician (*doctor*) *n* omusawo *n1*

piano *n* piyano *n9*

pick *vt* (1) (*harvest peas, fruit, etc.*) -noga; (2) (*choose*) -londa   pick a fight -wakula olutalo   pick a quarrel with -sosonkereza, -kyokooza   pick on (*impose one's will on*) -yiikiriza. *See* bully   pick one's nose -eesokoola mu nnyindo   pick one's teeth -eesokoola mu mannyo   pick out (1) (*from a selection*) -londamu, *eg. Yalondamu ebibala ebisinga obulungi. ('She picked out the best fruit.')*; (2) (*unwanted things*) -sosola, *eg. Yasosola amagumba mu kyennyanja. ('He picked out the bones from the fish.')*; (3) (*from within*) -sokoola, *eg. Yasokoola omunwe gwa kasooli mu nsawo. ('She picked out a maize cob from the sack.')*; (4) (*extract with an implement, eg. needle*) -tundula, *eg. Yatundula eriggwa mu ngalo ye. ('He picked out the thorn from her finger.')*. *See* remove; take out   pick out as an example -nokolayo   pick out for oneself (*be choosy*) -eerondera, *eg. Yeeronderamu olugoye olusinga obulungi. ('She picked out the best of the dresses.')*, (*selecting the best*) -eeroboza   pick out one's share -lobola   pick up (1) (*one-by-one*) -londalonda; (2) (*indiscriminently, eg. rubbish with a spade*) -yoola   pick up and eat flying ants -bojjerera enswa   be picked (*eg. of fruit*) -nogebwa   keep on picking up (*or* pick up several things) -londerera

pickaxe *n* ensuuluulu *n9*

¹pickpocket *n* omusazi w'ensawo *n1*

²pickpocket *vi* -sala ensawo

picky, be (*choosy*) *vi* -eeronda

picture *n* ekifaananyi *n7*

piece *n* (1) (*something removed, of wood, pottery, cassava, etc.*) olubajjo *n11*; (2) (*fragment*) ekipapajjo *n7* (*small akapapajjo n12*); (3) (*of something divisible, eg. segment*) omuwula *n3*. *See* part; portion; slice; strip   piece of meat ekifi *n7*

pierce *vt* (1) (*make a hole*) -wummula, *eg. Omuwala yawummula amatu ge. ('The girl pierced her ears.')*, -botola; (2) (*with a blade*) -fumita   be pierced (*by a person*) -wummuka, *eg. Endobo ewummuse. ('The bucket is pierced.')*, -botoka

piercing (*in lower lip for stud*) *n* empami *n9*

pig *n* embizzi *n9*, (*wild*) embizzi ey'omu nsiko

pigeon *n* enjiibwa *n9*, (*green*) entawunzi *n9*

pigeon pea *n* enkoolimbo *n9*, entinnamuti *n9*

pigment *n* erangi *n9*

pigmy (*person*) *n* omumbuti *n1*

¹pile *n* entuumu *n9*. *See* heap (*for types of pile*)

²pile *vt* -tuuma. *See* heap   pile up (*heap neatly*) -panga

pilfer *vi* -eetoolatoola

pilferer *n* omwetoozitoozi *n1*

pilgrim *n* omulamazi *n1*   make a pilgrimage -lamaga

pill *n* akakerenda *n12*. *See* capsule

pillage *vt* -nyaga

pillaged *adj* -nyage

pillager *n* omunyazi *n1*

pillar *n* empagi *n9*, (*central, of a round house*) eggwagi *n5*

pillion *n* ekkaliya *n9*

pillow *n* omutto *n3*

pillowcase *n* pirokesi *n9*

¹pilot (*of an aeroplane*) *n* omuvuzi (*or* omugoba) w'ennyonyi *n1*

²pilot (*an aeroplane*) *vt* -vuga

pimple *n* embalabe *n9*, (*infected*) akatulututtu *n12*. *See* skin condition; wart   goose pimples olutiko *n11*

¹pin *n* eppini *n9*, (*safety*) ekikwanso *n7*, ekikwaso *n7*   pins and needles amasannyalaze *n6*   have pins and needles -sannyalala

²pin *vt* -siba n'eppini

pincers *n* magalo *n9*

pinch (*with fingers*) *vt* -suna. *See* steal

pinch of salt *n* otunnyo *n13*

pine (*type of tree*) *n* payini *n1*

pineapple *n* ennaanansi *n9*   pineapple beer (*or juice*) omunaanansi *n3*

pint *n* payinti *n9*

pip (*on shoulder pad*) *n* ennyota *n9*

pipe *n* (1) (*eg. for water*) omudumu *n3*, (*underground* omudumu ogw'omu ttaka); (2) (*for smoking tobacco*) emmindi *n9*; (3) (*musical instrument*) omulere *n3*, endere *n9*   pipe player (*musician*) omulere *n1*   exhaust pipe ekizoosi *n9*   water pipe omudumu gw'amazzi

pirate *n* omunyazi *n1*

pistol *n* basitoola *n9*

pit *n* (1) (*hole*) ekinnya *n7*; (2) (*dug for human burial*) entaana *n9*; (3) (*game pit for trapping animals*) obuya *n14*; (4) (*bottomless abyss*) ennyanga *n9*. *See* mine; quarry   pit latrine kaabuyonjo *n12*

pitch (*for games*) *n* ekisaawe *n7*

pitch a tent -simba eweema

pitcher (*for water*) *See* pot

pitfall trap *n* obuya *n14*

pith (*inside inflorescence stalk of banana plant*) *n* omututumba *n3*

¹pity *n* obusaasizi *n14*

²pity *vt* -saasira   pity oneself -eesaasira

placard *n* ekipande *n7*

¹place *n* ekifo *n7*, (*some place*) awantu *n16*, *eg. awantu awali ettosi ('muddy place')*   place of awa, *eg. awa Musoke ('Musoke's place')*   place of the dead amagombe *n6*   at my place ewange, at your place ewuwo, *etc.* (**N11.5**)   at the place of ewa, *eg.*

place

ewa Musoke ('at Musoke's place') in many places **wangi** in my place **omwange**, in your place **omumwo**, *etc.* (**N11.5**) in one place **awamu** my place **awange**, your place **awawo**, *etc.* (**N11.5**) What's-it-called? (*referring to a place whose name is not remembered*) **gindi**, *eg. Twagenda e gindi.* ('*We went to what's-it-called.*')

²**place** *vt* (1) (*put*) **-teeka** (*often with enclitic* **N24.2**), *eg. Ŋŋenda kuteeka entebe kumpi n'oluggi.* ('*I am going to place a chair near the door.*'); (2) (*place down*) **-ssa** (*often with enclitic* **N24.2**), *eg. Yassa ebitabo ku mmeeza.* ('*He placed the books on the table.*'). *See* put   place across **-kiika**, *eg. Baakiika omuti mu luguudo.* ('*They placed a log across the road.*')   place for (*someone*) **-teekera**   place oneself across **-eekiika**, *eg. Yeekiika mu mulyango gw'edduuka.* ('*He placed himself across the entrance to the shop.*')   place under (*to prop up*) **-zizika**, *eg. Omulwadde yamuzizika omutto.* ('*She placed a pillow under the patient's head.*')   place upright (*eg. a post*) **-simba**   be placed **-teekebwa**   be placed down **-ssibwa**

placenta *n* **ekitanyi** *n7*, **omwana ow'emabega** *n1*   cover a placenta with banana leaves (*part of traditional birth rites*) **-fugika**

plague *n* (1) (*bubonic*) **kawumpuli** *n1*; (2) (*cattle*) **nsotoka** *n1*

plain (*level area of land*) *n* **omuseetwe** *n3*

plaintiff *n* **omuwaabi** *n1*

plait *vt* (1) (*rope*) **-langa**; (2) (*mat or basket*) **-luka**; (3) (*stiff materials, eg. reeds*) **-gomba**. *See* interweave; weave

plaited (*of hair*) *adj* **-sibe**

plaiter (*of hair*) *n* **omusibi w'enviiri** *n1*

¹**plan** *n* **enteekateeka** *n9*, **entegeka** *n9*, **pulaani** *n9*

²**plan** *vt* **-teekateeka**, **-tegeka**   plan to do next day **-sulirira**   make a plan **-sala amagezi**

¹**plane** (*for carpentry*) *n* **eranda** *n9*. *See* aeroplane

²**plane** (*wood*) *vt* **-landa**   person who planes wood **omulanzi** *n1*, **omuwazi** *n1*

plank *n* **olubaawo** *n11*

¹**plant** *n* **ekimera** *n7*, (*cultivated*) **ekirime** *n7*, (*planted*) **ekisimbe** *n7*, (*self-sown*) **ekimererezi** *n7*, (*medicinal*) **ekimera ky'eddagala** *n5*, (*creeping or climbing*) **ekimera ekiranda**

²**plant** (*a plant, post, etc.*) *vt* **-simba**. *See* sow   plant oneself (*take up position*) **-eesimba**   plant sweet potatoes **-byala amalagala**

plantain *n* (1) (*type of banana*) **gonja** *n1* (*single fruit* **omugonja** *n3*); (2) (*type of small herb; Plantago*) **bukumbu** *n1*   plantain-eater (*type of bird*) **ekkookootezi** *n5*

plantation, banana *n* **olusuku** *n11*

planting *n* **ensimba** *n9*   planting season **amasimba** *n6*

¹**plaster** *n* **pulasita** *n9*, (*mud used as plaster*) **olufuufu** *n11*

²**plaster** (*eg. a wall*) *vt* **-kuba pulasita (ku)**, (*with*

mud) **-siiga olufuufu**   plaster on dung (*on earth floor, to hold down dust and give a smooth finish*) **-maala obusa**   plaster on too much (*cream, plaster, etc.*) **-metta**, (*on oneself*) **-eemetta**

plastic *n* **pulaasitiika** *n9*   plastic bag **akaveera** *n12*

plate *n* **essowaani** *n9*, (*used as scoop to serve matooke from an omuwumbo*) **akabezo** *n12*

plateau *n* **omuseetwe** *n3*

platform (*eg. used for delivering speeches*) *n* **akadaala** *n12*. *See* verandah

¹**play** *n* (1) (*general word*) **omuzannyo** *n3*; (2) (*as in the threatre*) **katemba** *n1*

²**play** *vit* **-zannya**. *See* enjoy oneself; romp. *The following verbs are used for playing musical instruments:* (1) (*wind instruments, eg. flute*) **-fuuwa**; (2) (*bowed instruments, eg. fiddle*) **-kuuta**; (3) (*struck instruments, eg. drum or guitar*) **-kuba**, (*pound a drum*) **-sekebbula**; (4) (*plucked instruments, eg. guitar*) **-suna**.   play a return match **-ddiŋŋana**   play around with (*in a teasing or joking way*) **-zannyiikiriza**   play cards **-kuba** (*or* **-zannya**) **caanisi**   play football **-samba** (*or* **-zannya**, *or* **-kuba**) **omupiira**   play games (*not being serious*) **-zannya buzannyi**   play omweso **-yesa**   play the clown **-eeginga**, **-eemonkoola**, **-eemoola**   play the game of embirigo **-kuba embirigo**   play the lottery **-kuba akalulu**   play the organ **-kuba ennanga**   play with **-zannyisa**, *eg. Azannyisa omupiira.* ('*She is playing with a ball.*')   something to play with **ekyokuzannyisa** *n7*

player *n* **omuzannyi** *n1*. *See* musician

playful person *n* **kazannyirizi** *n1*   be playful **-zannyirira**

playground *n* **ekizannyiro** *n7*, **aw'okuzannyira** *n16*, **w'ozannyira** *n16*

playing cards *n* **caanisi** *n1*

playing field *n* **ekisaawe ky'emizannyo** *n7*,

plea (*of a defendant*) *n* **empoza** *n9*

plead (*argue a case*) *vi* **-woza**. *See* appeal; cry out   plead for **-wolereza**, *eg. Looya yamuwolereza.* ('*The lawyer pleaded for him.*'). *See* represent   plead for oneself **-eewolereza**   plead to/with **-eegayirira**   make a plea to **-eegayirira**, *eg. Yeegayirira okumusonyiwa.* ('*He pleaded to him for foregiveness.*')

pleader *n* **owuwolereza** *n1*, **puliida** *n1*. *See* advocate; lawyer

pleasant *adj* **-lungi**   pleasant taste (*or* smell) of food **ensa** *n9*

please *vt* **-sanyusa**. '*Please*' in requests is sometimes expressed by adding **ku** (*or enclitic* **-ko** (**N24.3**), *eg.* (1) *Mpa ku kambe ako.* ('*Please pass me that knife.*'); (2) *Ndeeteraayo ku mazzi.* ('*Bring me some water please.*')

pleased *adj* **-sanyufu**   be pleased **-sanyuka**. *See* appreciate   be pleased by/with **-sanyukira**. *See* enjoy

pleasing be pleasing **-nyuma**, *eg. Oluyimba*

lunyuma. ('The song is pleasing.'), (in taste or appearance) **-wooma** be pleasing to **-nyumira**, *eg. Oluyimba lumunyumira. ('He finds the music pleasing.'), (in taste or appearance)* **-woomera** make pleasing **-nyumisa**, *(in taste or appearance)* **-woomesa**

pleasure *n* **essanyu** *n5* something that causes pleasure **ekisanyusa** *n7*

pleat *n* **evvuunya** *n5* pleated skirt **sikaati y'amavuunya** *n9*

Plectranthus yam *(type of root crop) n* **ennumbu** *n9*

[1]**pledge** *(oath; vow) n* **obweyamo** *n14. See* surety

[2]**pledge** *vt* **-eeyama**, *eg. Beeyama okuyamba okuzimba essomero. ('They pledged to help build the school.'), (particular item or amount)* **-eetema**, *eg. Beetema essiringi emitwalo kkumi okuyamba okuzimba essomero. ('They pledged a hundred thousand shillings to help build the school.')* pledge loyalty **-wera**, *eg. Yawera mu maaso ga Kabaka. ('He pledged loyalty to the king.')* pledge loyalty to **-werera** pledge revenge **-wera enkolokooto**

plentiful *adj* **-a jjenjeero**, *eg. Sukaali wa jjenjeero ennaku zino. ('Sugar is plentiful these days.'). See* abundant be(come) plentiful **-yala**, *eg. Kasooli ayaze mu katale. ('There is plenty of maize in the market.')* make plentiful **-yaza**

plenty *adj* **-ngi**, *eg. emmere nnyingi ('plenty of food')* time of plenty *(of food, especially matooke)* **ekyengera** *n7*

pliability *n* **obugonvu** *n14*

pliable *adj* **-gonvu** be pliable **-gonda**

pliers *n* **magalo** *n9*

plod (along) *vi* **-senvula**

[1]**plot** *n* (1) *(of land)* **ekibanja** *n7*, **puloti** *n9*; (2) *(of land after removal of crops)* **ekisambu** *n7*, *(longer abandoned)* **ekikande** *n7*; (3) *(conspiracy)* **olukwe** *n11. See* field plot of crops **omusiri** *n3* dug-over plot *(of land)* **awalime** *n16*, *(deeply)* **awakabale** *n16*

[2]**plot (against)** *vit* **-lyamu olukwe**, *eg. Omukozi we yamulyamu olukwe. ('His employee plotted against him.'). See* collude

plough *vi* (1) *(with a tractor)* **-lima ne tulakita**; (2) *(with oxen)* **-lima n'ente**

pluck *vt* (1) *(a fruit)* **-noga**; (2) *(a bird)* **-maanya**, *eg. Nnamaanya enkoko. ('I plucked the chicken.')*; (3) *(a stringed instrument)* **-suna**. *See* detach pluck a maize cob *(from the plant)* **-nuula kasooli** pluck grains from a maize cob **-kongola kasooli**

[1]**plug** *n* (1) *(stopper; obstruction)* **ekizibikira** *n7*; (2) *(electrical)* **pulaaga** *n9*

[2]**plug** *vt* **-zibikira**

plumage *n* **ebyoya by'ekinnyonyi** *n8*

plumber *n* **ow'amazzi** *n1*, **omuntu akola ku mazzi** *n1*

plump *(of person or animal) adj* **-nene, -gevvu**

plumpness *n* **obunene** *n14*, **obugevvu** *n14*

[1]**plunder** *n* **omunyago** *n3*

[2]**plunder** *vt* **-nyaga**

plundered *adj* **-nyage** victim of plunder **omunyage** *n1*

plunderer *n* **omunyazi** *n1*

plunge *(into liquid) vt* **-bbika**. *See* dive

pneumonia *n* **lubyamira** *n1*

poach animals **-bbirira ensolo**

poacher *n* **omuntu abbirira okutta ensolo** *n1*

pocket *n* **ensawo** *n9*

pod *n* **ekikuta** *n7, eg. ekikuta ky'ebinjanjaalo ('bean pod')*

[1]**point** *n* (1) *(dot)* **akatonnyeze** *n12*; (2) *(score in a game)* **akagoba** *n12*; (3) *(reason)* **ensonga** *n9* point of view **endowooza** *n9* be on the point of *(doing something)* **-tera** *in near future tense* **(N16)** *followed by inf* **(N19)** go off the point *(digress)* **-landagga** stick to one's point *(eg. in a debate)* **-lemera ku nsonga**

[2]**point** *(sharpen) vt* **-songola** point at **-songa ku**, *eg. Yasonga ku kiwuka. ('He pointed at the insect.'). See* aim at point out one's preference *(out of options)* **-eesooka** point out to *(show)* **-laga**, *eg. Twamulaga ennyumba mwe twabeeranga. ('We pointed out to him the house where we used to live.')* point with the finger **-songa olunwe** point with the lips **-songamu omumwa**, *(in annoyance; pout)* **-songoza emimwa**

pointed *(sharp) adj* **-songovu**

pointer *n* (1) *(eg. used on blackboard)* **akasonga** *n12*; (2) *(on computer screen)* **akalazi** *n12*

pointless *(in vain) adj. Refer to* **omugaso** *('benefit')* *with neg* **(N21)**. *See* fruitless

pointlessly *adv* **obwereere, obusa**

[1]**poison** *n* **obutwa** *n14*, *(from Datura)* **amaduudu** *n6. See* venom

[2]**poison** *vt* **-wa obutwa**

poisonous *adj* **-a obutwa**

poke *vt* **-sokotta** poke one's nose into another's affairs **-lingiriza**

pole *n* **omuti** *n3*, *(of wild date palm)* **olukoma** *n11*, *(for punting a canoe)* **omwoko** *n3*, *(supporting a hunting net)* **olugwanyu** *n11*, *(sloping, of round house, from top to ground)* **omukomba** *n3. See* post electricity pole **omuti gw'amasannyalaze** *n3* pruning pole **olusolobyo** *n11* telephone pole **omuti gw'essimu**

police *n* **poliisi** *n9* police man/woman **owa poliisi** *n1*, **omupoliisi** *n1*, **omuserikale wa poliisi** *n1* police station **poliisi** *n9*

policy *n* **enkola** *n9*

polio *n* **pooliyo** *n9*

[1]**polish** *n* **polisi** *n9*, *(for shoes)* **eddagala ly'engatto** *n5*

[2]**polish** *vt* (1) *(eg. shoes)* **-nyiriza, -kuba eddagala**; (2) *(floor, furniture, etc.)* **-kuba polisi**; (3) *(metal)* **-zigula** be polished **-nyirira**

polished

polished *adj* **-nyirivu**   state of being polished
obunyirivu *n14*

polite (*well-mannered*) *adj* **-a empisa nnungi**   polite
person (*courteous*) **omuntumulamu** *n1*

politeness *n* (1) (*good manners*) **empisa ennungi**
n9; (2) (*courtesy; good breeding*) **obuntubulamu**
n14

political party *n* **ekibiina ky'obufuzi** *n7*   change
one's political party **-sala eddiiro**

politician *n* **munnabyabufuzi** *n1*

politics *n* **ebyobufuzi** *n8*

pollinate vanilla **-tundula ebimuli bya vanira**

pollution *n* **obukyafu** *n14*

polythene sheet/bag *n* **akaveera** *n12*

pomegranate *n* (1) (*plant*) **omukomamawanga** *n3*;
(2) (*fruit*) **enkomamawanga** *n9*

pomposity *n* **obwepansi** *n14*

pompous, be *vi* **-eepanka**   pompous person
omwepansi *n14*

pond *n* **ekidiba** *n7*, (*big*) **ettaba** *n5*

ponder *vt* **-fumiitiriza**. *See* think about

pool *n* (1) (*pond*) **ekidiba** *n7* (*big* **ettaba** *n5*); (2)
(*puddle*) **ekitaba** *n7*   swimming pool **ekidiba**
ekiwugirwamu

pool up (*puddle*) *vi* **-legama**

poor *adj* **-yavu**, **-naku**   poor person **omwavu** *n1*,
(*very*) **lunkupe** *n1*   Poor thing! **Bambi!**   be(come)
poor **-yavuwala**   make poor **-yavuwaza**

poorly (*badly*) *adv* **obubi**

pop *vi* **-tulika**

popcorn *n* **emberenge** *n10*

pope *n* **ppaapa** *n1*

popular, be *vi* **-yagalibwa**, *eg. Musoke ayagalibwa*
mu bakozi banne. ('*Musoke is popular among his*
workmates.')

population (*of people*) *n* **abantu** *n2*

porch (*of grass hut*) *n* **ekisasi** *n7*

porcupine *n* **nnamunnungu** *n1*

pork *n* **ennyama y'embizzi** *n9*

porridge *n* (1) (*of maize*) **obuugi** *n14*; (2) (*of finger*
millet) **obusera** *n14*

port *n* **omwalo** *n3*

portal *n* **omukutu** *n3*

portent, evil *n* **ekyebikiro** *n7*

porter *n* **omwetissi** *n1*

portion *n* (1) (*of food, soap, etc.*) **ekitole** *n7*; (2)
(*part, eg. slice of cassava*) **ekiwayi** *n7* (*smaller or*
longer **oluwayi** *n11*). *See* allocation; part; piece;
share

posho (*maize meal*) *n* **akawunga** *n12*

¹**position** *n* (1) (*place*) **ekifo** *n7*; (2) (*level in*
organisation) **eddaala** *n5*   high position (*seniority*)
obukulu *n14*   receive a high position unexpectedly
-koonola ekifo   take up position (*physically, of*
oneself; plant oneself) **-eesimba**

²**position** (*place; put*) *vt* **-teeka**

possess *vt*. Use **-lina** or **-ba na** ('*have*') according
to tense (**N20.1**) (**N20.2**), *eg. (1) Alina ennyumba*

nnyingi. ('*He possesses many houses.*'); (2) *Ettaka*
lino lyonna lijja kuba lyaffe. ('*We will soon possess*
all this land.')   be possessed (*by a spirit*) (1)
-linnyibwako empewo, *eg. Alinnyiddwako*
empewo. ('*She has been possessed by a spirit.*'); (2)
(*by the spirit of a deceased kabaka*) **-linnya ku**
jjoba; (3) (*mainly referring to night-dancers*) **-liko**
ekitambo; (4) (*by the Holy Spirit*) Use **-jjula** ('*be*
filled with'), *eg. Abayigirizwa ba Yesu bajjula*
Omwoyo Omutukuvu ne batanula okwogera ennimi
endala. ('*The Holy Spirit came down to the*
disciples who started to speak in strange tongues.').
See communicate with a spirit; spirit possession

possessions (*belongings*) *n* **ebintu** *n8*

possible   be possible *aux v* **-soboka**, *eg. Kisoboka*
okugendayo. ('*It is possible to go there.*')   make
possible for (1) **-sobozesa**, *eg. Yansobozesezza*
okugula emmere. ('*She made it possible for me to*
buy food.'); (2) (*by not getting in the way*) **-ganya**
(*a verb often used in the negative*)

possibly *adv*. Use **-soboka** or **-yinzika** ('*be*
possible'), *eg. Kisoboka okuba nga kituufu.* ('*It is*
possibly correct.')

¹**post** *n* (1) (*of a building*) **empagi** *n9* (*central, of a*
round house **eggwagi** *n5*); (2) (*as used for fencing*)
ekikondo *n7*; (3) (*short, eg. for tying up an animal*)
enkondo *n9*; (4) (*of wild date palm*) **olukoma** *n11*.
See pole   lamp post **omuti gw'ettaala** *n3*

²**post** (*mail*) *n* **ebbaluwa** *n10*

post a letter **-twala ebbaluwa mu ppoosita**

post office *n* **ppoosita** *n9*   post office box
akasanduuko k'ebbaluwa *n12*

poster *n* **ekipande** *n7*

postpone *vt* **-yongezaayo**, *eg. Olunaku*
olw'okuwummula balwongezaayo. ('*The date of the*
holiday was postponed.'). *See* delay; procrastinate

pot *n* (1) (*for water; pitcher*) **ensuwa** *n9*, (*long-*
necked) **ensumbi** *n9* (*small* **akasumbi** *n12*); (2)
(*large*) **ettogero** *n5*; (3) (*for cooking*) **entamu** *n9*,
ensaka *n9* (*small* **akasaka** *n12*); (3) (*of metal*)
sseppiki *n9*, **sseffuliya** *n9*; (4) (*big caste iron*
cooking pot) **ddongobulaaya** *n9*   pot with broken
lip **ensuwa ya kimogo**   milk pot **ekyanzi** *n7*
prepare water pot for use (*by smoking it internally*)
-nyookeza ensuwa   water pot with two spouts
ensumbi y'emimwa ebiri

potato *n* (1) (*sweet*) **lumonde** *n1*; (2) (*Irish*)
akammonde akazungu *n12*; (3) (*Livingstone*)
ennumbu *n9*   potato and bean mash **omugoyo** *n3*
air potato (*bud yam*) **ekkobe** *n5*   cuttings of sweet
potatoes **amalagala** *n6* (*one* **omuko gw'amalagala**
n3)   disease of sweet potatoes (*beetle larva attacks*
tubers) **kawuuzi** *n1*   dried sliced potatoes (*for*
storage) **kasodde** *n1*, **mutere wa lumonde** *n1*
roasted potatoes **lumonde omwokye**   time for
digging up potatoes **amasoggola** *n6*   trailing shoot
of sweet potato plant **omulanda** *n3*   unpalatable
old potato **lumonde omuwutta, lumonde**

omuwuttaavu <u>way of planting sweet potatoes</u> **embyala** *n9*

potency *n* **amaanyi** *n6*, *(sexual, of a man)* **amaanyi ag'ekisajja** <u>lose potency</u> (1) *(sexual, of a man)* **-ggwaamu amaanyi ag'ekisajja**; (2) *(spiritual)* **-fuluka**, *eg. Omusawo omuganda yafuluka. ('The traditional doctor has lost his power.'). See* impotent

pothole *(in road) n* **ekikonko** *n7*, **ekinnya mu luguudo** *n7. See* bump; ruts

potsherd *(curved fragment of pot, used for mixing herbs, etc.)* **oluggyo** *n11*

potter *n* **omubumbi** *n1*, *(in the service of the Kabaka)* **omujoona** *n1* <u>potter's wheel</u> **olubumbiro** *n11*

pottery *n* (1) *(workshop)* **ebbumbiro** *n5*; (2) *(items of pottery)* **ebibumbe** *n8. See* potsherd <u>ground-up pieces of broken pottery</u> *(grog, used in making pots)* **ensibo** *n9* <u>make pottery</u> **-bumba**

potty *(for relieving oneself) n* **ekidoli** *n7*

poultry *n* **enkoko** *n10*

¹**pound** *n* (1) *(weight)* **eraatiri** *n9*; (2) *(currency)* **pawunda** *n9*

²**pound** *vt* (1) *(in large mortar)* **-sekula**; (2) *(in small mortar)* **-sotta**, **-gotta**. *See* crush; grind; pulverise; punch <u>pound a drum</u> *(beat very hard)* **-sekebbula eŋŋoma** <u>be pounded</u> *(of a drum)* **-sekebbuka**

pounded *(crushed) adj* **-sekule**

pour *v* TRANSITIVE USES **-yiwa**, *eg. Ayiwa amazzi mu sseffuliya. ('She is pouring water into the pan.')*, **-fuka**, *eg. Afuka amazzi mu sseffuliya. ('She is pouring water into the pan.'). See* decant; drain out <u>pour for</u> **-fukira**, *eg. Yamufukira ekyokunywa. ('She poured out a drink for him.')* <u>pour out</u> *(solids)* **-fukumula**, *(a liquid in large quantity)* **-bunduggula** <u>keep pouring water for</u> **-fukirira**, *eg. Omuwala afukirira omukyala anaabe mu ngalo. ('The girl is pouring water for the lady to wash her hands.')* INTRANSITIVE USES **-yiika**, *eg. Amazzi gayiika mu kituli. (Water is pouring out of the hole.')* <u>pour out</u> *(of solids)* **-fukumuka** <u>pour with rain</u> **enkuba -tonnya**, *eg. Enkuba etonnya. ('It is pouring with rain.')*

pout *vi* **-songoza omumwa**. *See* upset

poverty *n* **obwavu** *n14*

powder *n* **pawuda** *n1* <u>edible green powder</u> (1) *(made from leaves of ejjuuni)* **ettimpa** *n5*; (2) *(made from leaves of empindi)* **eggobe** *n5*

power *n* **amaanyi** *n6. See* ability; potency

powerful *adj* **-a amaanyi**

¹**practice** *n* (1) *(repetitive exercising)* **pulakitisi** *n9*; (2) *(method)* **enkola** *n9*

²**practice** *vi* **-eegezaamu**, *eg. Yeeyezaamu mu piyano buli lunaku. ('She practices the piano every day.')* <u>practice religion</u> **-soma eddiini**

practicing *n* **okwegezaamu** *n15*, *eg. Okwegezaamu ennyo kyamuyamba okubeera omukugu mu kukuba ennanga. ('Frequent practicing helped him to*

become an expert at playing the organ.')

¹**praise** *n* **ettendo** *n5. See* exalt

²**praise** *vt* **-tenda**, **-waana**, *(hypocritically)* **-kiina**

praiseworthy *adj* **-a ettendo**

prattle *(on and on) vi* **-legejja**, **-legesa**

pray *vi* **-saba**, **-wonga**, *(of Muslims)* **-saala** <u>pray for/at</u> **-sabira**

prayer *n* **okusaba** *n15*, **essaala** *n9* <u>prayer beads</u> (1) *(RC)* **ssapule** *n9*; (2) *(of Muslims)* **kalaadi** *n9* <u>prayer book</u> *(of Anglicans)* **enjatula** *n9* <u>prayer mat</u> *(of Muslims)* **omusaalo** *n3* <u>prayers of the rosary</u> *(RC)* **olubu lwa ssapule** *n11* <u>call to prayers</u> *(of Muslims)* **-yaziina**

praying *n* **okusaba** *n15* <u>praying mantis</u> **nkongolamabeere** *n1* <u>praying place</u> *(in traditional religion; shrine)* **essabo** *n5*

preach *vt* **-buulira**

preacher *n* **omubuulizi** *n1*

preaching *n* **okubuulira** *n15*

preamble *n* **ennyanjula** *n9*

precede *vt* **-sookayo**, *eg. Muganda we ye yamusookayo mu ssomero. ('His sister preceded him at school.')*

precise *See* exact

precisely *See* exactly

predict *(think) vi* **-lowooza**. *See* guess; prophecy

pre-empt *vt* **-soona**, *eg. Yansoona okugula ettaka. ('He pre-empted me in buying the land.'). See* want

prefer *vt* (1) *Use* **-yagala okusinga** *('like more than')*, *eg. Njagala omucungwa okusinga eryenvu. ('I prefer an orange to a banana.')*; (2) **-singira** *(with reversed subject and object compared with English)*, *eg. Kino kye kimusingira obulungi. ('He prefers this one.')*

preferably *conj* **waakiri**, *eg. Waakiri mpa ekyo. ('Preferably I'll have that one.')* <u>be preferable</u> *(indicating personal preference)* **-kira**, *eg. Ekitabo kino kikira ekyo obulungi. ('This book is preferable to that.')*

pregnancy *n* (1) *(of a woman)* **olubuto** *n11*; (2) *(of an animal)* **eggwako** *n5* <u>pregnant woman</u> **ow'olubuto** *n1* <u>be pregnant</u> **-li olubuto**, *eg. Ali lubuto. ('She is pregnant.')*, *(of the queen)* **-lina ettu lya Mugema**, *eg. Alina ettu lya Mugema. ('The queen is pregnant.')* <u>be(come) pregnant</u> (1) *(of a woman)* **-funa olubuto**; (2) *(of an animal)* **-funa eggwako**, **-waka** <u>make pregnant</u> **-funyisa olubuto** <u>medicine to induce pregnancy</u> **eddagala ly'oluzaalo** *n5*

prejudice *n* **kyekubiira** *n7* <u>be prejudiced</u> **-eekubiira**. *See* judge unfairly

prematurely <u>wean prematurely</u> *(a child)* **-yosera**

premonition of death *n* **ekyebikiro** *n7*

preoccupied, be *(having lots of things to do) vi* **-kulungutana**, *eg. Omusawo akulungutana n'emirimu. ('The doctor is preoccupied with his work.'). See* busy (be)

preparation *n* **entegeka** *n9*, **enteekateeka** *n9*

prepare

prepare *vt* -tegeka, -teekateeka   prepare for -tegekera, *eg. Njagala kutegekera omwami engoye z'anaayambala. ('I want to prepare the clothes which he will wear.')*   prepare oneself -eetegeka, -eeteekateeka   prepare oneself for -eetegekera, *eg. Beetegekera embaga. ('They are preparing themselves for the wedding.')*   prepare oneself for action (*gird oneself*) -eefungiza   be prepared -eerinda, *eg. Eggye lyerinda okulumbibwa. ('The army is prepared for the invasion.')*

prepared (*ready*) *adj* -eetegefu

preparedness *n* obwetegefu *n14*

preposition (*part of speech*) *n* nnakalazi *n1*

[1]**present** *adj* -a leero, *eg. olunako lwa leero ('the present day')*   at present (*now*) **kaakati**   be present (1) **liwo** *or* **-baawo** (*'be there'*) *according to tense* (**N20.1**), *eg. (1) Nnaliwo mu kuziika. ('I was present at the funeral.'); (2) Nja kubaawo mu kuziika. ('I will be present at the funeral.'); (2) (in the future and emphasising place)* **-beerawo**, *eg. Nja kubeerawo mu lukuŋŋaana. ('I will be present at the meeting.')*

[2]**present** (*gift*) *n* ekirabo *n7*, ekitone *n7*. *See* contribution; gift   give a present **-wa ekirabo, -tona**   give a present to **-tonera**

[3]**present** *vt* (1) (*give*) **-wa**; (2) (*hand in; submit*) **-waayo**   present a case (*eg. at a meeting*) **-yanjula ensonga**

presentation (*of man to family of prospective wife*) *n* okwanjula *n15*

presented (*of a gift or prize*) *adj* -tone

presenter (*announcer*) *n* omwanjuzi *n1*

preserve (*spare for future use*) *vt* -taliza. *See* safeguard   preserve meat (*by drying over a fire*) **-kalirira ennyama**   be preserved (*spared from disaster*) **-wona**

preside over (*a meeting*) *vt* -kubiriza

president *n* pulezidenti *n1*, (*of the country*) omukulembeze w'eggwanga *n1*, (*of a meeting*) omukubiriza *n1*

[1]**press** *n* (1) (*newspapers*) empapula z'amawulire *n10*; (2) (*journalists*) ab'amawulire *n2*; (3) (*printing press*) ekyapa *n7*   press conference olukiiko olw'abamawulire *n11*

[2]**press** (*squeeze*) *vt* -nyiga. *See* handle; squeeze   press clothes (*iron*) **-golola engoye**   press down/into **-kkatira**, *eg. Yakkatira engoye mu ssanduuko. ('She pressed the clothes into the case.')*

pressing   pressing place for bananas (*to extract juice*) essogolero *n9*   time of pressing bananas amasogola *n6*

pressure   high blood pressure puleesa *n1*   take pressure off (*give relief*) -teewuluza

pressurise *vt* -nyigiriza, *eg. Maama we yamunyigiriza okufuna omulimu. ('His mother pressurised him into getting a job.'), (someone verbally)* -pika ebigambo

prestige *n* ekitiibwa *n7*

presume (*think*) *vi* -lowooza

presumption *n* endowooza *n9*   be presumptuous -eetulinkiriza

pretend *vt* -eefuula, *eg. Yeefudde atategeera. (She pretended not to understand.')*   pretend not to know -eewugguusa   pretend not to like something (*when one does*) -eegira   pretend to be asleep -eebasabasa, (*by snoring*) -eefuluusa   pretend to be clever -eegeziwaza   pretend to be dead -eefiisa   pretend to be ill -eerwaza   pretend to be mad -eeralusa   pretend to be unable to work -kekkera, *eg. Omukazi oyo akekkera nnyo. Tasobola kulima. ('That woman pretends to be unable to work. She won't garden.')*

pretty *adj* -lungi

prevent *vt* (1) -ziyiza, *eg. Baamuziyiza okuyingira. ('They prevented him from entering.'); (2) Use* -ganya (*'allow to do'*) *in neg* (**N21**), *eg. Omwana teyamuganya kukola mirimu. ('The baby prevented her from working.'). See* limit; prop up   prevent illness -gema obulwadde   prevent rain -gema enkuba

previous *adj. Use* -yita (*'pass'*) *in rel* (**N7.1**), *eg. wiiki eyise ('the previous week')*

prey *n* omuyiggo *n3*

price *n* omuwendo *n3*, ebbeeyi *n9*   ask the price of -lamuza   set a price -lamula omuwendo

prick *vt* -fumita

prickle *n* eriggwa *n5*

pride *n* amalala *n6*

priest *n* (1) (*Prot*) omwawule *n1*; (2) (*RC*) omusossodooti *n1*; (3) (*of any religion*) kabona *n1*

primary (school) *n* pulayimale *n9*

prime minister *n* (1) (*of Buganda*) Katikkiro *n1 title*; (2) (*of a country*) ssaabaminisita *n1*   prime ministerial affairs (*relating to the Katikkiro*) obwakatikkiro *n14*   residence of the prime minister of Buganda Butikkiro *n9*

prince *n* omulangira *n1*, (*eldest son of the Kabaka*) Kiweewa *n1 title*   head of the princes Ssaabalangira *n1 title* (*also called* **Lumaama**)

princess *n* omumbejja *n1*

[1]**principal** (*chief*) *adj* -kulu

[2]**principal** (*eg. of a school*) *n* omukulu *n1*

[1]**print** *n* ekyapa *n7*   in print mu kyapa

[2]**print** *vt* (1) (*with a printer*) -kuba mu kyapa; (2) (*write with capital letters*) -wandiika mu kyapa

printer *n* (1) (*person*) omukubi w'ekyapa *n1*; (2) (*machine*) ekyuma ekikuba mu kyapa *n7*

printing press *n* ekyapa *n7*

prison *n* ekkomera *n5*, mbuzeekogga *n1*. *See* cell   prison officer omuserikale w'ekkomera *n1*

prisoner *n* omusibe *n1*   prisoner-of-war omuwambe *n1*   escaped prisoner omubombi *n1*   take prisoner -wamba

private *adj* -a ekyama   private parts (1) (*of a woman*) obukazi *n14*, ebiko *n8*; (2) (*of a man*) obusajja *n14*   in private contemplation **mu lusirika**

privately *adv* (1) **mu kyama**; (2) *Use* **-okka** (*'alone'*) (**N7.3**), *eg. Njagala okwogera naawe nga oli wekka. ('I want to talk to you privately.')*   in private session **mu kafubo**

prize *n* **ekirabo** *n7*

probably *adv* **oboolyawo**, *eg. Oboolyawo agenze. ('She has probably gone.'). See* maybe

probation to, give (*try out on a job*) *vt* **-gezesaako**

probe *vt* **-sokotta**   probe into (*investigate*) **-noonyereza**

problem *n* (1) (*trouble; difficulty*) **omutawaana** *n3*; (2) (*personal*) **ennyiike** *n9, eg. Nnina ennyiike, okugulu kinnuma. ('I have a problem, my leg hurts.'). See* obstacle; stumbling block   be a problem to **-tawaanya**, (*burdensome, of a person*) **-zimbirira**   become problematic (*of a person or thing*) **-fuukira omuteego**   have problems (*in affairs*) **-ziringitana, -gootaana**   sort out problems **-golola ensonga**   unresolved problems between people **kalumannyweera** *n1*

procedure *n* **enkola** *n9*

proceed *vi* **-eeyongerayo**, *eg. Beeyongerayo okukola. ('They proceeded with the work.')*

¹**process** *n* **enkola** *n9*

²**process** *vt* **-kola**

proclaim *vt* **-langirira**   proclaim war **-langirira olutalo**

proclamation *n* **ekirangiriro** *n7*

procrastinate *vi* **-lagaalaganya**

procure *vt* **-funa**

prod *vt* **-sokotta**

¹**produce** (*things for sale*) *n* **ebyokutunda** *n8*

²**produce** *vt* (1) (*make*) **-kola**, *eg. Ekkolero lino likola engoye. ('This factory produces clothes.')*; (2) (*result in*) **-vaamu**, *eg. Okulya emmere nnyingi kuvaamu okugejja. ('Eating a lot of food produces obesity.')*; (3) (*bring*) **-leeta**, *eg. Aleese ebikopo bye ebisinga obulungi. ('She produced her best cups.'). See* cause; reproduce   produce fruit (*of a plant*) **-bala ebibala**   produce in abundance (*farm produce*) **-yaza**, *eg. Ayazizza emmere. ('She has produced a lot of food.')*   produce shoots (*sucker, of a plant*) **-sibuka**, (*of a banana plant*) **-zaala**, *eg. Ebitooke bizadde. ('The banana plants have produced shoots.')*, (*of a recently planted banana plant*) **-kkulira**. *See* bud; sprout   produce spreading (*or* climbing) shoots **-landa**

product *n* **ekikole** *n7*

productive (*fertile, of land*) *adj* **-gimu**

profanities *n* **ebyobugwemufu** *n8*   use profane language **-wemula**

proficiency (*expertise*) *n* **obukugu** *n14*   be proficient **-kuguka**, *eg. Yakuguka mu kubajja. ('He is proficient at carpentry.')*

proficient (*expert*) *adj* **-kugu**

¹**profit** *n* (1) (*financial*) **amagoba** *n6*; (2) (*use*)

omugaso *n3*   make a profit **-funamu amagoba**, *eg. Baatunda ennyumba ne bafunamu amagoba. ('They sold the house and made a profit.')*, **-gobolola**

²**profit (from)** *vt* **-ganyulwa**, *eg. Mu kulima aganyuddwaamu ssente. ('He has profited from farming.')*, **-funamu**

profitable *adj* (1) (*financially*) **-a amagoba**; (2) (*beneficial*) **-a omugaso**   be profitable (1) (*financally*) **-ganyula**; (2) (*beneficial*) **-gasa**, *eg. Okusoma kigasa. ('It is profitable to study.')*

progeny *n* **ezzadde** *n5*

programme *n* (1) (*arrangement*) **entegeka** *n9*, **enteekateeka** *n9*; (2) (*on TV or radio*) **pulogulaamu** *n9*

¹**progress** (*development*) *n* **enkulaakulana** *n9*   fail to make progress (*eg. of a project*) **-ziŋŋama**   make progress **-senvula**, *eg. Kati tusenvudde. ('Now we are making progress.')*

²**progress** (*develop*) *v* (1) *vi* **-kulaakulana**; (2) *vt* **-kulaakulanya**. *See* advance

prohibit *vt* **-wera**

prohibited *adj* **-were**, (*on ritual grounds*) **-a omuzizo**   be prohibited (*taboo*) **-zira**

prohibition (*taboo*) *n* **omuzizo** *n1*

¹**project** (*task*) *n* **pulojekiti** *n9*

²**project** (*stick out*) *vi* **-yitamu**, *eg. Akati kamu kayitamu mu muganda. ('One stick is projecting out of the bundle.')*, **-kukunala**   project above *Use* **-singako obuwanvu** (*'exceed in height'*), *eg. Omuti ogumu gusingako emirala obuwanvu. ('One tree projects above the others.')*

projecting (*jutting out*) *adj* **-kukunavu, -a enkukunala**

prolapse   have a prolapse (*of the rectum*) **emmeeme -gwa**

prolonged (*eg. of rain*) *adj* **-nyiinyiitivu**   be prolonged **-nyiinyiitira, -kanyiza**

prominent *adj* (1) (*important*) **-kulu**; (2) (*well-known*) **-manyifu**; (3) (*jutting out*) **-kulumbavu**. *See* famous

promiscuity *n* **obutambuze** *n14*. *See* adultery   promiscuous person **omutambuze** *n1*

¹**promise** *n* **ekisuubizo** *n7*

²**promise** *vt* **-suubiza**

promote *vt* (1) (*in rank*) **-kuza**; (2) (*a product; advertise*) **-langa**   promote oneself **-eekuza**   be promoted (*in an organisation*) **-linnya eddaala**

pronoun *n* **nnakasigirwa** *n1*

pronounce (*say*) *vi* **-yogera**

pronunciation *n* **enjogera** *n9*   way of pronounciation **enjatula** *n9*

proof *n* **obukakafu** *n14*

¹**prop** *n* (1) (*something used for holding up; support*) **ekiwanirira** *n7*; (2) (*as used in a play*) **ekyokuzannyisa** *n7*

²**prop (up)** *vt* (1) (*hold up; support*) **-wanirira**, *eg. Yateekawo empagi okuwanirira omuti. ('He placed

a post to prop up the tree.'), (in a temporary sort of way) -**yigika**; (2) *(place under, to prevent movement)* -**zizika**, *eg. Yateekawo ejjinja okuzizika sseffuliya ereme kugwa. ('She has propped up the saucepan with a stone to prevent it from falling.)* prop oneself up (with) -**eezizika**, *eg. Nneezizise omutto. ('I propped myself up with a pillow.')*

propaganda *n* **pokopoko** *n1*

propeller *n* **ekiwujjo** *n7*

proper *(correct) adj* -**tuufu**

properly *(well) adv* **bulungi**   not do things properly -**galangatana**

property *(things) n* **ebintu** *n8. See* wealth

prophecy *n* (1) *(fortune-telling; divination)* **obulaguzi** *n14*; (2) *(as in the Bible)* **obunnabbi** *n14*

prophesy *vt* -**lagula**   be prophesied -**lagulwa**

prophet *(as in the Bible or Koran) n* **nnabbi** *n1. See* fortune-teller

proposal *n* **ekiteeso** *n7*

propose *vt* -**leeta ekiteeso**

proprietor *(owner) n* **nnannyini** *n1. See* owner

prosecute *vt* -**waabira**, *eg. Bamuwaabira nga bamulanga obubbi. ('They are prosecuting her for theft.')* take a case to court -**waaba omusango**. *eg. Yawaaba omusango mu kkooti. ('He took the case to court.')*

prosecutor *n* **omuwaabi** *n1*   state prosecutor **omuwaabi wa gavumenti**

prospect (for) *vt* -**noonyereza**. *See* search for

prostitute *n* **malaaya** *n1*   prostitute oneself -**laaya**

prostitution *n* **obwamalaaya** *n14*

prostrate oneself *(in obeisance) vr* -**eeyala**, *eg. Abaami beeyama ne bawera mu maaso ga Kabaka. ('The chiefs prostrated themselves and pledged loyalty before the Kabaka.')*

protect *vt* (1) *(watch over; guard)* -**kuuma**, (2) *(from misfortune)* -**gema**, *eg. Baagema abaana obulwadde bwa pooliyo. ('They innoculated the children to protect them from polio.'). See* prevent; rescue   protect oneself (1) *(safeguard)* -**eekuuma**; (2) *(from misfortune)* -**eegema**

protector *(person) n* **omukuumi** *n1*

protectorate *n* **eggwanga erikuumibwa** *n5*

¹**protest** *(demonstration) n* **okwekalakaasa** *n15*   hold a protest *(demonstrate)* -**eekalakaasa**   leave in protest *(eg. a meeting)* -**eekandula**, *(storm out)* -**eekandagga**

²**protest** *(refuse) vi* -**gaana**, *eg. Yaŋŋamba okugenda ne ŋŋaana. ('He told me to go but I protested.'). See* argue; dispute; grumpy (be)   protest about -**wakanya**, *eg. Baawakanya eky'okuzimba oluguudo. ('They protested about the building of the road.')*   protest angrily -**eereega**

Protestant *n* **Omupolotesitante** *n1*, **Omupoto** *n1*

protestor *n* **omuwakanyi** *n1. See* demonstrator

protrude *v* (1) *(stick out from within)* vi -**yitamu**, vt -**yisaamu**; (2) *(bulge out because of something*

inside) vi -**kukunala**, vt -**kukunaza**

protruding *(sticking out) adj* -**kukunavu**

proud *adj* -**a amalala**. *See* arrogant   feel proud of achievements -**eenyumiririza**, *eg. Yeenyumiririza mu buwanguzi bwa mutabani we. ('He is proud of his son's achievements.')*

prove *vt* -**kakasa**   be proved -**kakasibwa**

proven *adj* -**kakafu**

proverb *n* **olugero** *n11*

provide *vt* -**leeta**, *eg. Oyinza okuleeta emmere ku mbaga? ('Can you provide food for the wedding?'). See* procure   provide food for -**gabula**, *eg. Yagabula abagenyi mu Sheraton. ('He provided food for the guests at the Sheraton.')*   provide for -**funira**, *eg. Yafunira abaana be emmere. ('He provided food for his children.')*   provided that *(if)* **bwe**, *eg. Tujja kugenda bwe wanaabaawo emmotoka. ('We shall go provided there is transport.')*

provisional *adj* -**a ekiseera**, *eg. gavumenti ey'ekiseera ('provisional government')*

provisions *(for a journey) n* **entanda** *n9*

provoke *vt* -**sosonkereza**   provoke one another *(exchanging angry words)* -**nonoogana**

prow *(of a canoe) n* **ekiyinda** *n7*

prowl (about) *vi* -**baalabaala**

prune *(banana plant) vt* -**salira**. *See* cut   pruning pole **olusolobyo** *n11*

psalm *n* **zabbuli** *n9*

pseudostem of banana plant *('trunk') n* **omugogo** *n3*

psychiatrist *n* **omusawo w'obwongo** *n1*

puberty *n* **obuvubuka** *n14*

pubic region *n* (1) *(of a man)* **nkuunokuuno** *n9*; (2) *(of a woman)* **ekinnyi** *n7*   pubic hair **ebiza** *n8* *(one* **ekiza** *n7)*

public *adj* -**a olukale**   public telephone **essimu ey'olukale** *n9*   public toilet **kaabuyonjo** *(or* **akayu**) **k'olukale** *n12*   public ward *(in hospital)* **waada y'olukale** *n9*   public welfare **ebyembeera by'abantu** *n8*   be(come) public *(known)* -**manyibwa**   in public **mu lwatu, mu lujjudde**   make public (1) *(announce)* -**yatula**; (2) *(a previously private matter)* -**yasanguza**

publicise *vt* -**langa**, -**langirira**

publicity *n* **ekirango** *n7*, **ekirangiriro** *n7*

publicly *adv* **mu lwatu**, *eg. Yayogera mu lwatu. ('He said it publicly.')*

¹**puddle** *n* **ekitaba** *n7*

²**puddle (up)** *vi* -**legama**, *eg. Amazzi galegamye mu mufulejje. ('The water is puddled up in the drain.')*

puff adder *n* **essalambwa** *n5*

pugnacity *(disposition to fight) n* **olugono** *n11*   pugnacious person **ow'olugono** *n1*

pull *vt* -**sika**, *eg. Yasika omuguwa. ('He pulled the rope.')*   pull along the ground *(drag)* -**kulula**, -**walula**   pull down (1) *(a construction)* -**menya**; (2) *(a climbing plant)* -**landulula**   pull grains off a

maize cob -**kongola kasooli**   pull off (*something
stuck down*) -**bambulako**, *eg. Yabambulako
akapande ku ssanduuko. ('She pulled the label off
the case.')*   pull off pieces from -**kuunyuula**, *eg.
Akuunyuula omugaati. ('She is pulling off pieces of
bread.')*   pull on (*something in dressing, eg. shoe*)
-**naanika**   pull oneself along (*as a cripple*)
-**eewalula**, -**eekulula**   pull oneself away (*from
being held; escape*) -**eesikambula**   pull out (1) (*eg.
nail*) -**sikamu**; (2) (*uproot; extract*) -**kuula**, *eg.
Akuula omuddo. ('He is pulling out weeds.')*; (3)
(*item from within*) -**sowola**, *eg. Yasowolamu
olumuli. ('She pulled out a reed.', eg. from a
bundle)*   pull up (*clothing, eg. trousers when
walking through water*) -**fungiza**

pullet (*young hen*) *n* **enkoko enseera** *n9*

pulpit *n* **ekituuti** *n7*

pulsate *vi* -**tujja**. *See* throb

pulse *n* **entunnunsi** *n9*

pulverise (*eg. a tablet*) *vt* -**merengula**. *See* crush;
pound   be pulverised -**merenguka**

pulverised *adj* -**merengule**

[1]**pump** *n* **ebbomba** *n9*, (*for petrol*) **pampu** *n9*
bicycle pump **ebbomba y'eggaali**   hand pump (*for
drawing water*) **nayikonto** *n9*

[2]**pump (up)** (*eg. tyre*) *vt* (1) (*using the mouth*)
-**fuuwa omukka mu**; (2) (*using a pump*) -**pika
omukka mu**   pump water (*using a hand pump*)
-**sunda amazzi**   pumping place **essundiro** *n5*

pumpkin *n* (1) (*plant*) **ekiryo** *n7*; (2) (*flower*)
akatundwe *n12*; (3) (*fruit*) **ensujju** *n9*; (4) (*young
leaves, eaten as vegetable*) **essunsa** *n5*   remove
unwanted parts of pumpkin leaves (*before cooking*)
-**sunsula essunsa**

punch (*hit*) *vt* -**kuba**. *See* thump   punch a hole
-**kubamu ekituli**

punctual, be *vi* -**kwata obudde/essaawa**

punctuate (*put in punctuation marks*) *vt* -**teekamu
obubonero**   punctuation mark **akabonero** *n12*

[1]**puncture** *n* **akatuli** *n12*   have a puncture **omupiira**
-**yabika**, *eg. Omupiira gwabise. ('The tyre is
punctured.')*

[2]**puncture** (*pierce*) *vt* -**fumita**

punish *vt* -**bonereza**. *See* discipline

punishment *n* **ekibonerezo** *n7*

pupil *n* (1) (*learner*) **omuyizi** *n1*; (2) (*of eye*)
emmunye *n9*

puppy *n* **akabwa** *n12*

purchase *vt* -**gula**

purchaser *n* **omuguzi** *n1*

pure *adj* -**tuufu**

purgative *n* **eddagala ery'okweyabya** *n5*

purified *adj* -**longoose**

purify *vt* -**longoosa**. *See* decant

purity *n* **obulongoofu** *n14*. *See* righteousness

purple *adj* -**a kakobe**

purpose *n* **ekigendererwa** *n7*   on purpose **mu
bugenderevu**   for no purpose **obwereere, obusa**

purposefully *adv* **mu bugenderevu**   do
purposefully -**genderera**

purse *n* **ensawo** *n9*, **omufuko** *n3*

pursue *vt* -**goba**, *eg. Baagoba abanyazi okubasuuza
ebintu byabwe. ('The pursued the looters to recover
their goods.')*, (*follow shortly after*) -**wondera**, *eg.
Poliisi yawondera ababbi ne basuuza omunyago.
('The police pursued the theives and recovered the
loot.')*

pus *n* **amasira** *n6*

push *vt* -**sindika**, *eg. Yasindika oluggi okuluggula.
('He pushed the door to open it.'). See* force   push
back (1) (*eg. earth to level it*) -**senda**; (2) (*in a
continuing way*) -**sindiikiriza**, *eg. Poliisi
yasindiikiriza abayizi ne bafuluma ekizimbe. ('The
police pushed the students out of the building.')*
push hard (*in labour*) -**sindika omwana**   push in
(*something compressible*) -**kkatira**, *eg. Yakkatira
engoye mu nsawo. ('She pushed the clothes into the
sack.')*   push into (*insert*) -**sonseka**, *eg. Yasonseka
akati mu kiganda. ('He pushed the stick into the
bundle.'). See* cram into; force into; jam in   push
one another -**sindikagana**   push oneself forward
(*seeking advantage*) -**eeyisaawo**   push sticks into a
fire (*to stoke it*) -**seesa omuliro**   push through (*a
narrow space*) -**wagaanya**, *eg. Yawagaanyizza
n'atuuka mu maaso. ('He pushed his way to the
front.')*, -**eeyigaanya**   push (*someone*) to do
something (1) (*urge; egg on*) -**pikiriza**; (2)
(*disrupting his/her plans*) -**kulungutanya**

pushiness *n* **okweyisaawo** *n15*

puss *See* cat

put *vt* -**teeka** (*often with enclitic N24.2*), *eg. Teeka
entebe mu lunyiriri. ('Put the chairs in a line.'). See*
place   put a limit -**teekako ekkomo**   put across
-**kiika**, *eg. Bakiise omuti mu kkubo. ('They put a
log across the road.')*   put around -**eetoolooza**, *eg.
Olukomera baalwetoolooza ennyumba. ('They put
a fence around the house.')*   put around the neck
(1) (*of person or animal*) -**yambika**; (2) (*of oneself*)
-**eeyambika**   put aside (1) (*store for future use*)
-**tereka**; (2) (*place on one side*) -**ssa wabbali**   put
at an angle (*slant; tilt*) -**wunzika**, -**sulika**   put back
-**zza** (*often with enclitic N24.2*), *eg. Yabizzaamu mu
kabada. ('She put them back in the cupboard.')*
put cover/lid on -**saanikira**   put down (1)
(*physically*) -**ssa** (*often with enclitic N24.2*), *eg.
Kisse ku mmeeza. ('Put it down on the table.')*,
-**teeka wansi**; (2) (*be dismissive of*) -**dibaga**. *See*
kill   put for (*someone*) -**teekera**   put in(to) (1)
-**teekamu**, *eg. Teekamu amazzi mu kikopo. ('Put
some water in the cup.')*; (2) (*insert*) -**yingiza**, *eg.
Yayingiza ekisumuluzo mu kkufulu. ('She put the
key into the padlock.')*   put in/on (*eg. handle on
hoe, or bullet in gun*) -**wanga**   put in charge -**sigira**
put last -**sembyayo**   put in compact form
-**komeka**, -**panga**   put more (*increase*) -**yongera
ku**, *eg. Yayongera amafuta mu mmotoka ye. ('She*

put more petrol in her car.') put off *(postpone)* **-eeyongerayo.** *See* avoid; lazy about (be); procrastinate put on *(place on)* **-teekako, -ssaako.** *See* apply; dress; stick on put on an electric light **-teekako ettaala** put on plaster *(eg. on wall during building)* **-siiga olufuufu** put on the body *(something tight, eg. shoe or ring)* **-naanika** put *(load)* on head of (1) *(someone else)* **-tikka;** (2) *(oneself)* **-eetikka** put on too much *(eg. ointment)* **-metta** put on top *(superimpose)* **-bereka** put out (1) *(outside)* **-fulumya;** (2) *(fire/light)* **-zikiza,** *(with water; douse)* **-vubiriza** put out to dry **-yanika,** *(on a line)* **-yanika ku kaguwa,** *(on the ground)* **-yanika ku ttaka** put right *(straighten out)* **-tereeza** put sideways **-kiika** put to the side **-zza ebbali** put together (1) *(in one place)* **-teeka awamu,** *eg. Yateeka emirengo ebiri awamu. ('She put the two piles together.');* (2) *(combine)* **-gatta,** *eg. Nnagasse ebikopo by'omupunga byombi. ('I put the two cups of rice together.');* (3) *(things of different types; mix up)* **-gattika,** *eg. Yagattika ebijanjaalo eby'engeri bbiri mu nsawo. ('She put two types of beans together in the sack.').* See assemble put under hot ashes **-vumbika** put under house arrest **-sibira** *(or* **-sibirira mu nnyumba)** put up *(raise from a lower* level) **-wanika,** *eg. Yawanika ekifaananyi ku kisenge. ('He put up the picture on the wall.')* put up as a guarantee **-singawo,** *eg. Nsinzeewo ettaka lyange. ('I am putting up my land as a guarantee.')* put up for the night *(accommodate)* **-suza** put up one's hand **-golola omukono.** *See* surrender put up with *(be long-suffering)* **-gumiikiriza,** *eg. Yagumiikiriza mukama we okumuyisa obubi. ('He put up with bad treatment from his boss.')* put up with difficulties **-gumira ebizibu** put upright *(eg. a post)* **-simba** put water on a fire *(to quench it)* **-vubiriza omuliro** put words into someone's mouth **-kookera ebigambo** be put *(placed)* **-teekebwa**

putrid *adj* **-vundu**

putrify *v* (1) *vi* **-vunda;** *vt* **-vunza**

puzzle *(riddle)* *n* **ekikokyo** *n7* crossword puzzle **akakunizo** *n12*

puzzled, be *vi* **-soberwa,** *eg. Nnasoberwa eky'okukola. ('I was puzzled about what to do.')*

pygmy *n* **omumbuti** *n1. See* dwarf

python *n* **ttimba** *n1*

Q, q

quagmire *n* **entubiro** *n9,* **akateebe** *n12*

[1]**quake** *(earthquake)* *n* **musisi** *n1*

[2]**quake** *(shake)* *vi* **-kankana**

qualification *n* **ekisaanyizo** *n7. See* competence; education

quality *(standard)* *n* **omutindo** *n3, eg. omutindo gwa waggulu ('high quality')*

quantity *n* **obungi** *n14, eg. Njagala okumanya obungi bwa kasooli. ('I want to know the quantity of maize.'),* *(in a question)* Use **-yenkana wa?** *('be equal to what?'),* *eg. Weetaaga kasooli yenkana wa? ('What quantity of maize do you want?')* great quantity **enkumuliitu** *n9, eg. enkumuliitu ya kasooli ('great quantity of maize')*

[1]**quarrel** *n* **oluyombo** *n11. See* feud pick a quarrel with **-sosonkereza,** *(looking for a fight)* **-kyokooza**

[2]**quarrel** *vi* **-yomba,** *eg. Nnayomba na ye. ('I quarrelled with him.')* quarrel in/at **-yombera,** *eg. Baayombedde mu katale. ('They quarrelled in the market.')* quarrel with **-yombesa,** *eg. Nnamuyombesa. ('I quarrelled with him.')* quarrel with one another **-yombagana.** *See* bicker

quarrelsome *adj* **-yombi** quarrelsome person **omuyombi** *n1,* **kayombera** *n1*

quarry *n* (1) *(for obtaining stone, etc.)* **ekirombe** *n7,* **kkwale** *n9;* (2) *(prey)* **omuyiggo** *n3*

quarter *n* **kimu kya kuna** *n7, eg. Njagala kimu kya kuna ekya kiro. ('I want a quarter of a kilo.')*

queen *n* (1) *(eg. of England)* **kkwini** *n1;* (2) *(of Buganda)* **Nnaabagereka** *n1 title* Queen-mother *(of Buganda)* **Nnamasole** *n1 title* Queen-sister *(of Buganda)* **Nnaalinnya** *n1 title*

quench quench a fire **-zikiza omuliro,** *(by putting on water)* **-vubiriza omuliro** quench one's thirst **-wonya ennyonta** be quenched *(of a fire)* **-zikira**

[1]**question** *n* **ekibuuzo** *n7* question mark **akabuuza** *n12*

[2]**question** *vt* **-buuza,** *(intensively for information; interrogate)* **-kemekkereza**

questioner *n* **omubuuza** *n1*

[1]**queue** *n* **olunyiriri** *n11,* **olukalala** *n11*

[2]**queue** *vi* **-simba olunyiriri**

quick *(fast)* *adj* **-yangu.** *See* adroit quick-witted **-kalabakalaba, -gezigezi.** *See* clever be quick **-yanguwa,** *eg. Yanguwa ogende e Kampala. ('Be quick and go to Kampala.')*

quickly *adv* **amangu.** *See* rapidly do quickly **-yanguya,** *eg. Yanguya okukola. ('Do the work quickly.')* run quickly **-dduka embiro**

quickness *n* **obwangu** *n14,* *(of the mind)* **obukalabakalaba** *n14*

[1]**quiet** *(of a person)* *adj* (1) *(at a particular time)* **-sirifu;** (2) *(by nature)* **-sirise.** *See* calm quiet person *(by nature)* **omusirise** *n1*

[2]**quiet(ness)** *n* (1) *(of a person)* **obusirise** *n14;* (2) *(period of quiet; lull)* **akasiriikiriro** *n12. See* peace be/keep quiet **-sirika,** *eg. Nnasaba abantu okusirika tuwulire amawulire. ('I asked the people to be quiet so that we could listen to the news.')* keep quiet about **-sirikira,** *eg. Amawulire yagasirikira. ('He kept quiet about the news.')* period of quietness **olusirika** *n11*

quieten (down) *v* (1) *(calmed down, of a body of water, weather, situation, etc.)* *vi* **-teeka,** *eg. Ennyanja eteese. ('The lake has quietened down.');*

(2) (*a person*) vt -**sirisa**, *eg. Yalera omwana amusirise. ('She put the child in her lap to quieten her.')* rock a baby to sleep -**siisiitira omwana**

quietly *adv* **kasirise** talk quietly -**yogera mpolampola** walk quietly -**tambuza buggereggere**

quit *vt* -**vaako**, *eg. Omulimu aguvuddeko. ('She has quit her job.').* See leave

quite (*fairly*) *adv. Add suffix* -**ko** *or* -**mu** (N24.3), *eg.* **bulungiko** ('*quite well*') Quite so! **Weewawo!, Kyekyo!** be quite a lot -**wera**, *eg. Enkuba eweze. ('There has been quite a lot of rain.')*

Qur'an See Koran

[1]**quiver** (*for arrows*) *n* **omufuko** *n3*

[2]**quiver** (*shake*) *vi* -**kankana**

quote *vt* (1) (*cite; refer to*) -**juliza**; (2) (*pick out as an example*) -**nokolayo** quote a price (*by seller*) -**lamula omuwendo**

R,r

rabbit *n* **akamyu** *n12*

rabies *n* **lebiizi** *n1*

race (*competition*) *n* **empaka** *n10* cycle race **empaka z'okuvuga eggaali** running race **empaka z'okudduka** *n10*, **embiro z'empaka** *n10* sack race **empaka z'okuddukira mu kkutiya** short-distance race **empaka z'akafubutuko** *n10*

rack *n* (1) *for drying utensils*) **akatandaalo** *n12*; (2) (*suspended in kitchen for storage or for smoking food*) **ekibanyi** *n7*

racket *n* (1) (*din*) **oluyoogaano** *n11*; (2) (*for a game, eg. tennis*) **ekiwujjo** *n7*. See din; noise make a racket (*of many people talking*) -**yoogaana**

radio *n* **leediyo** *n9* radio mast **omulongooti gwa leediyo** *n3*

raffia (*also* raphia) (*palm*) *n* (1) (*tree and midrib of leaf*) **ekibo** *n7*; (2) (*fibre*) **obuso** *n14* (*one piece* **akaso** *n12*); (3) (*fruit*) **embo** *n9*

rafter *n* **omukomba** *n3*

rag *n* **akaziina** *n12*, **oluziina** *n11*. See duster

[1]**rage** (*temper*) *n* **obusungu** *n14* fly into a rage -**eecwacwana** storm out in a rage -**eekandagga**

[2]**rage** (*of a fire*) *vi* -**tuntumuka**

ragged (*frayed*) *adj* -**sensufu** be ragged -**sensuka** make ragged -**sensula**

[1]**raid** *n* **omuzindo** *n3*. See attack

[2]**raid** *vt* -**zinda**. See attack raid house to house (*by police*) -**kuba potolo**

raider *n* **omuzinzi** *n1*. See attacker

railway *n* **leerwe** *n9* railway carriage **ekigaali** *n7* railway line **oluguudo lw'eggaali y'omukka** *n11* go off the rails (*start behaving badly*) -**eeyinula**

[1]**rain** *n* **enkuba** *n9*. See drizzle receptacle for catching rain water **ennembeko** *n9*

[2]**rain** *vi* **enkuba** -**tonnya**, *eg. Enkuba etonnya. ('It is raining.').* See drizzle. *Ways of raining include*: (1)

(*persistently, over a period of days to months*) **enkuba** -**kanyiza kutonnya**, *eg. Enkuba ekanyizza okutonnya. ('It has been raining all the time.')*; (2) (*on and on*) **enkuba** -**fudemba**, *eg. Enkuba yafudemba. ('It rained on and on.').* be about to rain **enkuba** -**bindabinda**, *eg. Enkuba ebindabinda. ('It is about to rain.')* ease up (*of rain*) **enkuba** -**sammuka, enkuba** -**kankamuka** prevent rain -**gema enkuba** stop raining **enkuba** -**kya**, *eg. Enkuba ekedde. ('The rain has stopped.')*

rainbow *n* **musoke** *n1*

raincoat *n* **omupiira gw'enkuba** *n3*

rainy rainy season See season rainy weather **obudde obw'enkuba** *n14*

raise *vt* (1) -**yimusa**, *eg. Omusomesa yayimusizza omutindo gw'ekibiina. ('The teacher raised the standard of the class.')*; (2) (*physically; put at a higher level*) -**wanika**, *eg. Twawanika bendera. ('We raised the flag.')*; (3) (*increase the level of flame, price, etc.*) -**yongeza**, *eg. Yayongeza eddoboozi lya leediyo. ('He raised the volume of the radio.')*; (4) (*weapon to strike*) -**galula**. See turn up; uplift raise a child -**kuza** (*or* -**lera**) **omwana** raise one's eyes -**yimusa amaaso** raise one's hand -**yimusa omukono** raise one's hands (*in surrender*) -**wanika emikono** raise one's voice (1) (*in volume*) -**yimusa eddoboozi**; (2) (*in anger*) -**kaalaamya eddoboozi** raise the alarm (*through ululation*) -**kuba enduulu** raise the price -**linnyisa ebbeeyi/omuwendo** be raised up (*physically*) -**wanikibwa**

rake (up) *vt* -**leekinga**, *eg. Genda oleekinge ebikoola. ('Go and rake up the leaves.')*

[1]**ram** (*male sheep*) *n* **endiga ennume** *n9*, **sseddume w'endiga** *n1*

[2]**ram** *vt* -**sindika**, *eg. Yasindika ejjinja wansi mu mupiira. ('He rammed a stone under the wheel.')* ram down (*earth, post, etc.*) -**komerera** ram into -**tomera**, *eg. Yatomera ekisenge. ('He rammed [the vehicle] into the wall.')*

Ramadhan *n9* **Alamanzaani**

ramble *vi* (1) (*in walking*) -**tambulatambulako**; (2) (*in speaking; be long-winded*) -**landagga**

rampage *vt* -**goma**

ran See run

ranch *n* **eddundiro** *n5*

rancour *n* **ffitina** *n9*

rank (*eg. in army*) *n* **eddaala** *n5* rank (*or* line) of soldiers **olunyiriri lw'abaserikale** *n11* high rank **obukulu** *n14*

ransack *vt* -**taganjula**, -**tankuula**, -**tinkuula**

[1]**ransom** *n* **ekinunulo** *n7*

[2]**ransom** *vt* -**nunula**

rant at (*someone*) *vi* -**wowogganira**

rap (*eg. on door*) *vt* -**konkona**

rape *vt* -**kwata** rape a girl -**sobya ku muwala**

raphia See raffia

rapid *adj* -**a kafubutuko**. See fast

rapidly *adv* **kafubatuko**. *See* quickly

rapids *(on a river)* *n* **ebiyiriro** *n8*

rare *adj* (1) **-a ebbula**, *eg. ekinyonyi kya bbula ('rare bird')*; (2) *Use* **-labikalabika** *('be seen frequently')* *in neg* **(N21)**, *eg. Guno omuti tegulabikalabika. ('This is a rare type of tree.')*; (3) *(not normal)* **si -a bulijjo**, *eg. Ekyo si kya bulijjo. ('That was a rare event.')*

rarely *adv* (1) **ebbalirirwe**, *eg. Wano ajjawo bbalirirwe. ('He rarely comes here.')*; (2) *Use* **-tera** *('do habitually')* *in neg* **(N21)** *followed by inf* **(N19)**, *eg. Tatera kujja wano. ('He rarely comes here.')*

¹rash *(foolish)* *adj* **-siru** act rashly *(in a foolhardy way)* *Use* **-lowooza** *('think')* *in neg* **(N21)**, *eg. Yakola nga talowoozezza. ('He acted rashly.')*. *See* recklessly (do)

²rash *(on the skin)* *n*. *See* skin condition

raspberry *n* **enkenene** *n9*

rastafarian *n* **omulaasi** *n1*

rat *n* **emmese** *n9*, *(giant pouched)* **ensombabyuma** *n9*. *See* cane rat; gerbil; mole-rat; mouse   rat trap **akamasu** *n12*

rather *adv* (1) *(fairly)* *Use enclitic* **-ko** *or* **-mu** **(N24.3)**, *eg. Lumonde ono agula ssente nnyingiko. ('These potatoes are rather expensive.')*; (2) *(preferably)* **waakiri**, *eg. Waakiri nfumba emmere okusinga okulongoosa ennyumba. ('I would rather cook than clean the house.')*   rather have *(of two poor choices)* **-funda ne**, *eg. Nfunda ne Musoke. ('I'd rather have Musoke.', eg. to win an election)*. *See* prefer

rattan *n* **oluga** *n11*

¹rattle *n* (1) *(musical instrument; reedbox type)* **ensaasi** *n9*; (2) *(for babies)* **akasaasi** *n12*. *See* shaker

²rattle *v* (1) *vi* **-kubagana**, *eg. Ekizoosi ekubagana. ('The exhaust pipe is rattling.')*; (2) *vt* **-nyeenya**, *eg. Kibuyaga anyeenya amadirisa. ('The storm is rattling the windows.')*   rattle about *(in a container)* **-wulunguta**, *eg. Mu ŋŋoma mulimu akawulunguta. ('There is something rattling about inside the drum.')*

rave rave against **-yogerera amafuukuule**, *eg. Bwe yatamiira n'atandika okwogerera gavumenti amafuukuule. ('When he got drunk he started to rave against the government.')*

ravine *n* **olukonko** *n11*

raw *adj*. *Use* **-fumbe** *('cooked')* *in neg* **(N21)**, *eg. ennyama etali nfumbe ('raw meat')*

razor *n* **akamwa ebirevu** *n12*, **akamweso** *n12*   razor blade **wembe** *n9*, **akawembe** *n12*, **eggirita** *n9*, **akagirita** *n12*

reach *vt* (1) *(arrive at)* **-tuuka**, *eg. Tutuuse eka. ('We have reached home.')*; (2) *(a number or amount)* **-weza**, *eg. Awezezza emyaka kkumi. ('He has reached ten years old.')*. *See* amount to   reach everywhere **-buna**, *eg. Amawulire g'akabenje gabunye. ('The news of the accident has reached everywhere.')*   reach for **-kununkiriza**, *eg. Yakununkiriza omunnyo. ('She reached for the salt.')*

react suddenly *(start up)* *vi* **-baguka**, *eg. Yabaguka nga awulidde emmundu. ('He reacted suddenly when he heard the gun shot.')*

read *vt* **-soma**. *See* peruse   read for/to **-somera**, *eg. Yamusomera ekitabo. ('She read the book to him.')*

reader *n* **omusomi** *n1*

readily *(willingly)* *adv*. *Use* **-yagala** *('like')* *as aux v* **(N19)**, *eg. Yagenda ayagala. ('He went readily.')*

readiness *(preparedness)* *n* **obwetegefu** *n14*

reading *n* **okusoma** *n15*, *(Bible lesson)* **ekitundu** *n7*

ready *(prepared)* *adj* **-eetegefu**   ready-made clothes **engoye entunge** *n9*   ready-to-eat food *(served from the pavement)* **tonninnyira-mu-kange**   be ready *(of cooked food)* **-ggya**, *eg. Emmere eyidde. ('The food is ready.')*   be ready for action *(on one's guard)* **-eerinda**   get ready *(of oneself)* **-eetegeka**, *eg. Yeetegese okugenda. ('He is ready to go.')*, **-eeteekateeka**   make ready *(prepare)* **-tegeka**, *eg. Ategeka ekisenge omunaabeera akabaga. ('She is making the room ready for the party.')*, **-teekateeka**

real *(authentic)* *adj* **-a ddala**

realise *vi* (1) *(understand)* **-tegeera**, *eg. Bwe nnalaba engugu ne ntegeera nti agenda kusenguka. ('When I saw the amount of luggage I realised he was moving home.')*; (2) *(know)* **-manya**, *eg. Olwo lwe nnamanya nti mubbi. ('That is the day I realised that he was a thief.')*

really *adv* **ddala**, *eg. Oli musajja ddala! ('You really are a man!')*

reap *(harvest)* *vt* **-kungula**

reappear *vi* (1) *Use* **-ddamu** *('resume')* *with* **-labika** *('be seen')*, *eg. Musoke yaddamu n'alabika oluvannyuma lwa ssabbiiti bbiri. ('Musoke reappeared after two weeks away.')*; (2) *(of a long-lost person)* **-zaawuka**, *eg. Daudi yazaawuka oluvannyuma lw'emyaka mingi nga taliiwo. ('David has reappeared after many years away.')*

¹rear *(rear end of a person or animal; bottom)* *n* **ennyuma** *n9*. *See* stern   be at the rear *(be last)* **-semba**, *eg. Daudi ye yasemba ku lunyiriri. ('David was at the rear of the queue.')*   to the rear **emabega**, *eg. Yagenda emabega. ('He went to the rear.')*, *(of the home)* **emmanju**   to the rear of **emabega wa**

²rear *(bring up child or animal)* *vt* **-kuza**

reason *n* **ensonga** *n9*   bring out reasons **-nokola ensonga**   by reason of **ku lwa**   for what reason? *(why?)* **lwa nsonga ki?**   that is the reason why **y'ensonga lwaki**. *See* that's why   without reason **nga tewali nsonga**

reassure *vt* **-gumya**

¹rebel *n* (1) *(insurgent)* **omujeemu** *n1*; (2) *(non-conformist)* **kyewaggula** *n1*

²rebel *vi* **-jeema**, *(against social conformity)*

-eewaggula

rebellion (*insurgency*) *n* **obujeemu** *n14*   end a rebellion **-jeemulukuka**

rebellious *adj* **-jeemu**

rebuke *vt* **-nenya**

recall *vt* **-jjukira**

receipt *n* **lisiiti** *n9*

receive *vt* (1) (*get*) **-funa**, *eg. Yafuna ekitereke ku Mmande. ('She received the parcel on Monday.');* (2) (*a newcomer to a place*) **-senza**   receive a high position unexpectedly **-koonola ekifo**   receive a visitor **-kyaza omugenyi**

recent (*eg. of news*) *adj* **-su**. *See* new

recently *adv* **jjuuzi**

receptacle (*for catching rainwater*) **ennembeko** *n9*

recess *n* **ekiwummulo** *n7*   have a recess **-wummula**

recipe *n* **enfumba** *n9*

recite one's lineage (*before the Kabaka*) **-lanya**

recklessly, do *vi* **-babaalukana**. *See* rash

reckon (*think*) *vi* **-lowooza**

recline (*lie down*) *vi* **-galamira**. *See* sit

recognise *vt* **-tegeera**, (*officially*) **-tongoza**, *eg. Musoke baamutongoza nga omukulu w'essomero. ('Musoke became officially recognised as the head of the school.')*

recommend *vt* **-semba**

recommendation *n* **obusembi** *n14*, **ekyasembebwa** *n7*

[1]**recompense** (*reward; pay*) *n* **empeera** *n9*

[2]**recompense** *vt* (1) (*reward; pay*) **-weera**; (2) (*compensate*) **-liwa**

reconcile *vt* **-tabaganya**   be reconciled **-tabagana**

reconnaissance (*secret*) *n* **ekikwekweto** *n7*

reconnoitre *vt* (1) (*spy out*) **-ketta**; (2) (*scout out*) **-ziga**

reconsider *vt* **-eddamu**, (*mend one's ways*) **-eddako**   pause and reconsider (*when speaking*) **-eekomako**

[1]**record** *n* (1) (*in sports*) **likoda** *n9*; (2) (*written*) **ekiwandiiko** *n7*; (3) (*musical disc*) **ejjinja lya gulamufooni** *n5*

[2]**record** (*write down*) *vt* **-wandiika**

recorder (*machine for recording*) *n* **akuuma akakwata amaloboozi** *n12*

recount (*a story*) *vt* **-gera**, **-fuma**. *See* tell

recover *vt* **-eddiza**, *eg. Yeddiza ebintu byonna bye baali babbye. ('She recovered everything that was stolen.')*   recover from near death experience **-komayo**. *See* better (get)   recover one's strength **-ddamu amaanyi**

recruit (*eg. workers*) *vt* **-wandiisa**

rectify *vt* **-longoosa**

recur *vi* **-ttuka**, *eg. Obulwadde buttuse. ('The disease has recurred.')*

recurrence *n* **obuddiro** *n14*

recurrent *adj* **-a olutentezi**, *eg. omusujja ogw'olutentezi ('recurrent fever')*

red *adj* **-myufu**, (*sorghum-coloured; reddish-brown*) **-a akawembawemba**, (*colour of red subsoil*) **-a ekikuusikuusi**   be(come) red **-myuka**, (*red-hot, of metal*) **-yengerera**, (*of the rising or setting sun, or eyes*) **-twakaala**   make red **-myusa**

reddish *adj* **-myufumyufu**, **-myukirivu**

redeem *vt* **-nunula**

redeemer *n* **omununuzi** *n1*

reduce *vt* **-kendeeza**, *eg. Akendeezezza ente ze. ('She has reduced the number of her cows.')*. *See* abbreviate; loosen   reduce the price (*through bargaining*) **-sala ku muwendo**   become reduced **-kendeera**, *eg. Omuwendo gukendedde. ('The price has been reduced.')*. *See* diminish; go down; subside

redundant   become redundant **-diba**   make redundant **-dibya**

reed *n* (1) (*cane of elephant grass*) **olumuli** *n11*; (2) (*cane from ekiyulu plant*) **enjulu** *n9*. *See* fence

reedbuck *n* **enjaza** *n9*

reel about *vi* **-zunga**, **-tagala**

refer to (*cite; quote*) *vt* **-juliza**

[1]**referee** *n* (1) (*in football*) **ddiifiri** *n1*, **omusazi w'omupiira** *n1*; (2) (*for an applicant for a job*) **omujulirwa** *n1*

[2]**referee**   referee a football match **-sala omupiira**, (*unfairly*) **-saliriza omupiira**   be a referee for (*an applicant*) **-eeyimirira**

reflect (*throw back light*) *vt* **-kuba ekimyanso**, *eg. Endabirwamu ekuba ekimyanso ku kisenge. ('The mirror is reflecting the light onto the wall.')*   reflect on (*think about*) **-lowoozaako** (*or* **-lowooza ku**). *See* ponder

reflection *n* (1) (*in a mirror*) **ekifaananyi ky'olaba mu ndabirwamu**; (2) (*thought*) **ekirowoozo** *n7*

reform *vt* **-longoosa**

refrain (from) *vt* **-eewala**, *eg. Yeewala okunywa omwenge nga mulwadde. ('He refrained from drinking alcohol when he was ill.')*   refrain from eating (*one's totem*) **-eddira**, *eg. Yeddira enseenene. ('He refrains from eating grasshoppers.' – being a member of the Grasshopper Clan)*

refreshed, be *vi* **-dda obupya**

refrigerator *n* **firiigi** *n9*

refuge *n* (1) (*sanctuary*) **obubudamo** *n14*; (2) (*place of safety*) **obukkukiro** *n14*   give refuge to **-wa obubudamo**   take refuge **-budama**. *See* shelter (take)

refugee *n* **omunoonyi w'obubudamu** *n1*

refund money **-ddiza essente**

refusal *n* **okugaana** *n15*

refuse *vit* **-gaana**, *eg. Nnamusabye okumpa ekitabo n'agaana. ('I asked him to give me the book but he refused.'),* (*flatly*) **-eerema**, *eg. Abakozi beeremye okuddayo okukola. ('The workers flatly refused to return to work.')*. *See* disobey; reject; resist; unresponsive (be)   refuse to comply with (*be*

regain

defiant) **-eekobogooza** refuse to give **-mma**, *eg. Nnakimumma. ('I refused to give it to her.')* refuse to move **-lemera**, *eg. Yalemera mu nnyumba. ('She refused to move from the house.')* refuse to part with **-gaanira**, *eg. Yagaanira ekitabo kyange. ('She refused to part with my book.')* refuse to take *(something offered)* **-zirira**, *(in a deliberately insulting way)* **-ziririra** refuse to take the blame - **eekazaakaza**

regain *vt* **-eddiza**, *eg. Yeddiza essente ze. ('She regained her money.')* regain good condition **-lamuka** regain one's hearing **-zibuka amatu** regain one's sight **-zibuka amaaso** regain one's strength **-ddamu amaanyi**, *(after illness)* **-ddamu endasi**, *eg. Azzeemu endasi. ('She is regaining her strength.')*

regard *vt* (1) *(think)* **-lowooza**, *eg. Yalowooza nti empisa ze si nnungi. ('He regarded her behaviour as not good.')*; (2) *(take)* **-twala**, *eg. Nkitwala nti kikulu. ('I regard it as serious.')*. See look at; see give regards to *(greetings)* **-labira**, *eg. Mundabire. ('Give him my regards.')*

regarding *pre* **ku**, *eg. Eriyo amawulire agafa ku mulimu? (Is there news about the job?')*

regent *n* **liijenti** *n1*, **omukuza wa kabaka** *n1*

region *(of a country)* *n* **ekitundu** *n7*

register *(eg. someone on a course)* *vt* **-wandiika** register oneself **-eewandiisa**

regress *vi* **-ddirira**, *eg. Omwana addiridde mu kusoma. ('The child has regressed in his studies.')*

[1]**regret** *n* **obwennyamivu** *n14*

[2]**regret** *vt* (1) *(disappointed)* **-saalirwa**, *eg. Nsaalirwa obutamulaba. ('I regret not seeing her.')*, **-ejjuukiriza**; (2) *(feeling remorse)* **-ejjusa**, *eg. Nnejjusa obutawuliriza kye yagamba. ('I regretted not listening to what she said.')*. See envy cause regret *(cause someone to wish to have something)* **-saaliza**

regular *adj* **-a bulijjo**, *eg. emmere yange eya bulijjo ('my regular diet')*

regularly *adv* **bulijjo**

regulate *vt* **fuga**

regulation *n* **etteeka** *n5*

regurgitate *vt* **-booga**

rehearsal *n* **okwegezaamu** *n15*

rehearse *vt* **-eegezaamu**

[1]**reign** *n* **okufuga** *n15*, *eg. okufuga kwa Ssekabaka Chwa ('the reign of King Chwa')*

[2]**reign (over)** *vit* **-fuga**

reimburse *vt* **-liwa**, *eg. Nja kukuliwa. ('I shall reimburse you.')*

reject *(something offered)* *vt* **-zira**, *eg. Yazira olugoye lwe nnamuwa. ('She rejected the dress that I gave her.')*, **-zirira**, *eg. Yanzirira emmere gye nnamuwa. ('He rejected the food I gave him.')*, *(in a deliberately insulting way)* **-ziririra** reject feeding at the breast *(of a baby)* **-zira amabeere**

rejoice *vi* **-jaguza**, *(shown through rhythmic*

movement) **-digida**

rejoicing *(also* time of rejoicing*)* *n* **ekijaguzo** *n7*

rejoin *vt* **-komawo mu**, *eg. Yakomawo mu kkanisa yaffe. ('He has rejoined our church.')*

relate *(tell)* *vt* **-buulira**, *(in detail)* **-ttottola** relate to *(of affairs)* **-kwatagana na/ne**, *eg. Ensonga eno ekwatagana n'eyo. ('This matter relates to that.')* be related to *(through kinship)* Refer to **oluganda** *('kinship')*, *eg. Si wa luganda lwaffe. ('He is not related to us.')* relating *(concerning)* Use **-kwata ku** *('hold to')* in *rel* (**N7.1**), *eg. ebintu ebikwata ku Musoke ('matters relating to Musoke')*

relationship *n* (1) *(through blood)* **oluganda** *n11*; (2) *(through marriage)* **obuko** *n14*

relative *(by blood)* *n* **ow'oluganda** *n1*, *(of the same lineage)* **ow'olulyo** *n1* relatives (1) *(by blood)* **ab'oluganda** *n2*; (2) *(through marriage)* **abako** *n2* relative of **muganda** *(with pos* **N12**), *eg. muganda wange ('my relative')*

relax *vi* **-wummula**. See calm down; relieved (be)

release *vt* (1) *(free person or animal)* **-ta**; (2) *(set off trap or spring)* **-masula**, *eg. Emmese yamasula akamasu. ('The mouse has released the trap.')*; (3) *(tied or penned animal)* **-yimbula**. See unclasp; unfasten be released (1) *(of a captive)* **-teebwa**; (2) *(of trap or spring)* **-masuka**, *eg. Akamasu kamasuse. ('The trap was released.')* released person *(eg. from jail)* **omute** *n1*

reliability *n* **obwesigwa** *n14*

reliable *adj* **-eesigwa** reliable person **omwesigwa** *n1*

relieve *vt* (1) *(take pressure off)* **-teewulula**; (2) *(someone on duty)* **-nnyula**, *eg. Omukuumi ow'ekiro yannyudde ow'emisana. ('The night watchman relieved the day guard.')*; (3) *(on rotation)* **-liivula**, *eg. Eggye lya Bungereza lyaliivudde ery'Amerika. ('The British army relieved the American one.')* relieve oneself **-eeteewuluza** be(come) releaved (1) *(in pressure, tension, etc.)* **-teewulukuka**; (2) *(of pain)* **-kkakkana**, *eg. Obulumi bukkakkanye. ('The pain is relieved.')*; (3) *(of worries)* **-weera**

religion *n* **eddiini** *n9* traditional religion **eddiini ey'obuwangwa**

religious religious believer **omukkiriza** *n1* religious offering **ekiweebwayo** *n7*. See sacrifice member of a religious order **munnaddiini** *n1*

religiousness *n* **obusomi** *n14*

relinguish *vt* **-va ku**, *eg. Yasalawo okuva ku bukulu bw'essomero. ('She decided to relinguish the headship.')*

[1]**relish** *(side dish, served with the main dish 'emmere')* *n* **enva** *n10*. See greens food without relish **amaluma** *n6*, *eg. Nnalidde maluma. ('I ate food without relish.')*

[2]**relish** *(like)* *vt* **-yagala** relish food **-woomerwa emmere**, *eg. Abagenyi baawoomeddwa emmere. ('The guests relished the food.')*

relocate (*move home*) *vi* **-senguka**. *See* move
reluctance (*misgiving*) *n* **enkenyera** *n9*,
 akakenyera *n12* be reluctant **-kenyera**, *eg.*
 Abadde akenyera mu kugenda mu kibuga. (*'He was
 reluctant to go to the town.'*) be reluctant to move
 (1) (*hesitant*) **-sikattira**, *eg. Embuzi nnagitwala
 ng'esikattira.* (*'I took the goat, but it was reluctant
 to go.'*); (2) (*physically resisting*) **-walira** be
 reluctant to work (*holding the work demeaning*)
 -eeginika express reluctance (*in response to a
 request*) **-limu enkenyera, -eekaanya**
rely on *vt* (1) (*trust*) **-eesiga**; (2) (*depend on*)
 -beezaawo (*with personal object*), *eg. Omusaala
 gwe gwe gumubeezaawo.* (*'He is relying on his
 salary.'*)
remain *vi* (1) (*surplus to requirements*) **-fikka**, *eg.
 Emmere efisse.* (*'Some food has remained.'*); (2)
 (*stay behind*) **-sigala**, *eg. Asigadde n'abaana.* (*'He
 has remained with the children.'*)
remainder (*also* remains) *n* **ebisigadde** *n8*,
 ebisigaddewo *n8*, (*surplus*) **enfissi** *n9*
remaining *adj.* Use **-sigalawo** (*'remain there'*) in rel
 (**N7.1**), *eg. abantu abasigaddewo* (*'the remaining
 people'*) have remaining (*left-over*) **-fissa**, *eg.
 Nfissizza ssente.* (*'I have some money remaining.'*)
¹remark *n* **ebigambo** *n8*
²remark (*say*) *vi* **-gamba**
remarkable *adj.* **-a ekitalo**
¹remedy (*cure*) *n* **ekiwonya** *n7*
²remedy *vt* (1) (*cure*) **-wonya**; (2) (*correct*)
 -longoosa
remember *vt* **-jjukira**
remind *vt* **-jjukiza**, (*unpleasantly*) **-langira** remind
 one another **-jjukanya** remind oneself **-ejjukiza**
reminder *n* **ekijjukizo** *n7*
remorse, feel *vi* **-ejjusa**
remote *adj.* Refer to **ewala** (*'far away'*), *eg. Abeera
 mu nsi y'ewala.* (*'He lives in a remote country.'*)
 remote from **wala okuva**, *eg. Ekibira kiri wala
 okuva wano.* (*'The forest is remote from here.'*)
 remote place (*difficult to access*) **ensokolosokolo**
 n9
remove *vt* (1) (*take away*) **-ggya** (*often with enclitic
 N24.2*), *eg. Njagala okuggya ebintu mu nnyumba.*
 (*'I want to remove the things from the house.'*); (2)
 (*extract with an implement, eg. needle*) **-tundula**,
 eg. Yatundula eriggwa okuva mu kigere kye. (*'She
 removed the thorn from his foot.'*); (3) (*wanted
 from unwanted*) **-sunsula**, *eg. Yasunsula
 emmwanyi.* (*'He removed the coffee beans from the
 husks.'*); (4) (*something stuck down*) **-bambula**, *eg.
 Baabambula tayiro okuva ku kisenge.* (*'They
 removed the tiles from the wall.'*). *See* move; strip;
 take off remove all (*eg. sediment in a well; clean
 out*) **-kokota** remove crust from left-over matooke
 (*that has been stored in hot ashes*) **-bembula**
 emmembe ku matooke remove from danger
 (*save*) **-taasa** remove from drying in the sun (*eg.*

laundry) **-yanula** remove from within **-sokoola**,
 eg. Yasokoola ensigo mu ndeku. (*'She removed the
 seeds from the gourd.'*) remove grains from a
 maize cob **-kongola kasooli** remove midrib of
 banana leaf **-yubuluza olulagala** remove outer
 covering of (*fruit or vegetable; shell, husk, etc.*)
 -susa remove roof (*or* thatch) from **-sereekulula**
 remove scales (*from a fish*) **-ggyako
 amagalagamba** remove vegetation (*in
 preparation for planting*) **-sambula ensiko** be
 removed from **-vaamu ebbala** (*subject and object
 reversed compared to English*), *eg. Essaati
 evuddemu amabala.* (*'The stains have been
 removed from the shirt.'*)
remunerate *vt* **-sasula**
remuneration *n* **omusaala** *n3*, **empeera** *n9*
rend (*tear*) *vt* (rent) **-yuza**
render useless *vt* **-ttattanya** be rendered useless
 -ttattana
renew (*do again*) *vt* **-ddamu**, *eg. Baddamu
 okulayira ewa Kabaka.* (*'They renewed their
 loyalty to the king.'*)
renounce *vt* **-leka**, *eg. Yaleka ebibi bye n'asaba
 okusonyiyibwa.* (*'She renounced her sins and asked
 for foregiveness.'*)
renovate *vt* **-zza obuggya/obupya**
renown (*fame*) *n* **ettutumu** *n5*
renowned *adj.* (1) (*famous*) **-tutumufu**; (2) (*for
 good or ill*) **lukulwe** *invariable adjective*
 renowned person **ow'ettutumu** *n1*, *eg. Musoke wa
 ttutumu mu bayimbi ab'e Kampala.* (*'Musoke is
 renowned as a singer in Kampala.'*)
¹rent (*payment to landlord*) *n* **obusuulu** *n14*, **envujjo**
 *n9. Traditionally, 'obusuulu' is labour and
 'envujjo' is produce in kind (beer, barkcloth, etc.),
 in either case given to a landowner or chief. See
 tear house/room rent **busuulu w'ennyumba** *n1*
²rent (*hire*) *vt* **-pangisa**. *See* rend
repair *vt* **-ddaabiriza**, (*something mechanical*)
 -kanika, (*make functional*) **-lamusa** be repaired
 -lamuka, *eg. Emmotoka eramuse.* (*'The car is
 repaired.'*)
repay money owed *vt* **-sasula ssente**, (*in part*)
 -sasulako ssente deliberately fail to repay a debt
 -lyazaamaanya
repeal *vt* **-ggyawo**
repeat *vt* **-ddamu**, (*again and again*) **-ddiŋŋana**,
 (*again and again annoyingly*) **-yeeya** repeat to
 -ddiramu, *eg. Yatuddiramu ebigambo
 by'ayogedde.* (*'He repeated to us what she had
 said.'*) be repeated **-ddibwamu** something
 repeated **ekiddibwamu** *n7*
repeatedly *adv* **emirundi mingi** go repeatedly (*to
 the same place*) **-eewuuba** tell repeatedly (*be
 insistent*) **-kuutira**
repel (*also* repulse) *vt* **-goba**. *See* defeat be repelled
 (*by*) **-eewala**, *eg. Nneewala empisa ze.* (*'I was
 repelled by his behaviour.'*)

repent

repent *vi* -eenenya
replace *vt* -zzaawo, -dda mu kifo kya
repletion *n* obukkufu *n14*, omukkuto *n3*
¹reply *n* okuddamu *n15*
²reply (to) *vit* -ddamu. *See* respond
¹report *n* lipoota *n9* school report lipoota
y'essomero
²report (*tell*) *vt* -buulira report a wrong-doing
-waaba, -loopa. *See* inform on person who is
reported on omuloope *n1* person who reports a
wrong-doing omuloopi *n1*
reporter (*eg. for newspaper*) *n* omukuŋŋaanya (*or*
omusasi) w'amawulire *n1*
represent *vt* -kiikirira. *See* plead for
representative *n* omukiise *n1*
repress *vt* -nyigiriza
reproach (*also* reprimand) *vt* -nenya. *See* discipline;
punish; upbraid reproach oneself -eenenya be
reprimanded -nenyezebwa
reproduce (*of animals or plants*) *vi* -zaala. *See* copy
repudiate *vt* -eesammula
repulse (*drive back*) *vt* -goba. *See* defeat feel
repulsion -eenyinyimbwa, -eenyinyala, *eg.*
Empisa ze nzeenyinyala. (*'Her behaviour repulses
me.'*). *See* disgust something repulsive
ekyenyinyalwa *n7*
reputation *n. Use* -manyibwa (*'be known'*), *eg.*
Amanyiddwa nga bw'ayamba abantu. (*'He has a
reputation for helping people.'*) damage a
reputation -siiga enziro lose one's reputation
-yonoona erinnya
request *vt* -saba
require *vt* -eetaaga be required -eetaagisa
requirement *n* ekyetaagisa *n7*
rescue *vt* -nunula, *eg.* Eryato lyabwe lyabbira naye
eryato eddala ne libanunula. (*'Their boat sank but
another boat rescued them.'*). *See* salvage go to
the rescue of -taasa, *eg.* Yagenda okutaasa ebintu
bye nga omuliro gwaka. (*'He went to rescue his
property from the fire.'*)
rescuer *n* omununuzi *n1*
research *vt* -noonyereza
researcher *n* omunoonyerezi *n1*
resemblance *n* enfaanana *n9*
resemble *vt* -faanana, (*according to another
person*) -faananya, *eg.* Musoke yanfaananyizza
muganda wange. (*'Musoke thinks I resemble my
brother.'*)
resentment *n* ffitina *n1*
¹reserve (*eg. of food*) *n* ensibo *n9*
²reserve (*eg. room in hotel*) *vt* -eekwata
reserved person (*in character*) *n* ow'eggume *n1*
reside (at/in) *vt* -beera, *eg.* Mbeera Tooro. (*'I
reside in Tooro.'*)
residence *n* obutuuze *n14*, (*of the Kabaka*)
Twekobe *n9*, (*of the Katikkiro*) Butikkiro *n9*. *See*
home
resident *n* omutuuze *n1*, (*long-term resident of the

land*) omutaka *n1*, (*long-term resident of the
land, less closely connected to the Kabaka; more in
touch with the ancestral spirits of the place*)
omutakansi *n1*
residue *See* dregs; leavings; froth
resign *vt* -lekulira
resin (*also* rosin) (*for bow*) *n* obubaani *n14*
resist (*physically*) *vt* -walira, *eg.* Baamutwala ku
poliisi nga awalira. (*'He resisted being taken to the
police station.'*). *See* refuse
resolute (*determined*) *adj* -nyiikivu, -malirivu be
resolute -nyiikira, -malirira
¹resolve (*determination*) *n* obunyiikivu *n14*,
obumalirivu *n14*
²resolve (*nerve oneself to do something*) *vi*
-eevaamu. *See* decide resolve a dispute -ggyawo
enkaayana, *eg.* Yabayamba okuggyawo
enkaayana. (*'He helped them resolve their
dispute'*) be resolved (*determined*) -malirira, *eg.*
Yamalirira okukola obulungi emirimu gye. (*'She
resolved to do well at her work.'*). *See* gird oneself
resonate (*also* resound) *vi* -waawaala
resource *n* ekyokukozesa *n7* natural resources
obugagga obw'ensibo *n14*
resourceful person (*who finds a way to do things*)
n omugerengetanya *n1* be resourceful
-gerengetanya
¹respect *n* ekitiibwa *n7* respected person
ow'ekitiibwa *n1*
²respect *vt* -wa (*or* -ssaamu) ekitiibwa
respiration (*breathing*) *n* okussa *n15*
respire (*breathe*) *vi* -ssa omukka
resplendent, be *vi* -nekaanekana
respond *vi* (1) (*reply*) -ddamu; (2) (*answer back*)
-yanukula, *eg.* Nnamuyita naye teyannyanukula.
(*'I called her but she did not respond.'*); (3) (*with a
sound rather than speech*) -wuuna; (4) (*by
answering 'wangi' when called*) -yitaba, *eg.*
Musoke yamuyita naye teyamuyitaba. (*'Musoke
called him, but he did not respond.'*)
response *n* okuddamu *n15* give a response (to)
-nyega (*a verb often used in the negative*), *eg.*
Nnamubuuza wa omwami we gy'agenze naye
teyanyega. (*'I asked where her husband had gone
but she did not respond.'*)
responsibility *n* obuvunaanyizibwa *n14*
responsible position ekifo eky'obuvunaanyizibwa
n7 be held responsible -vunaanyizibwa be
responsible for (*eg. an organisation*) -kulira hold
responsible (*accuse*) -vunaana
¹rest (*period of rest*) *n* okuwummula *n15*, (*during
the day; siesta*) eggandaalo *n5* rest house
omugiini *n3* the rest of (*remainder*) *Use*
-sigalawo (*'remain'*) *in rel* (**N7.1**), *eg.* emmere
esigaddewo (*'the rest of the food'*)
²rest *vi* (1) (*take a nap*) -eebakako; (2) (*take a
siesta*) -gandaala. *See* calm down; holiday (have a)
nine-day period of rest (*for the Kabaka, after

enthronement) **obwerende** *n14*   rest on (1) *vi*
-eesigama, *eg. Eddaala lyesigamye ekisenge. ('The
ladder is resting against the wall.')*; (2) *vt*
-eesigamya, *eg. Nneesigamya eddaala ku kisenge.
('I rested the ladder on the wall.')*

restaurant *n* **wooteeri** *n9*, **ekirabo** *n7*

restlessness *n* **obutatereera** *n14*, (*of a crowd
moving about*) **akasattiro** *n12*   be restless *Use*
-tereera ('*be settled*') *in neg* (**N21**), *eg. Abantu
baali tebateredde. ('The people were restless.')*, (*of
a sick person*) **-boyaana**   move about restlessly (*of
a person*) **-sattira**

restore (*renew*) *vt* **-zza obuggya/obupya**   restore
eyesight **-zibula amaaso**   restore health **-wonya**
restore hearing **-zibula amatu**   restore (*someone
something borrowed*) **to** (*someone*) **-ddiza**   be
restored (1) (*in health*) **-wona**; (2) (*in sight*)
-zibuka amaaso; (3) (*in hearing*) **-zibuka amatu**

restrain *vt* **-komako**, *eg. Yabakomako ne batalwana.
('He restrained them from fighting.')*. *See* prevent
restrain oneself **-eekomako**. *See* give up

restrict (*narrow*) *vt* **-funza**. *See* forbid; prevent
restrict children (*to prevent them wandering off*)
-kugira abaana

restriction *n* **ekiziyiza** *n7*

result *n* **ekivaamu** *n7*. *The tense of the noun can
vary according to the timing* (**N6**), *eg.* (*past*)
ekyavaamu, (*near future*) **ekinaavaamu**, (*far
future*) **ekirivaamu**.   result in **-vaamu**, *eg.
Okutema emiti kuvaamu obutafuna nkuba. ('Cutting
trees results in loss of rain.')*   as a result of
ekivuddeko, ekivuddemu

resume *vt* (1) (*after some time*) **-ddira**, *eg. Bwe
yakomawo okuva e Bungereza yaddira omulimu
gwe mu bbanka. ('When he returned from England,
he resumed his work at the bank.')*; (2) (*more
immediately*) **-dda ku**, *eg. Bwe yagenda ne nzira ku
mulimu gwange. ('When she left I resumed my
work.')*

resurrection *n* **amazuukira** *n6*   be resurrected
-zuukira

retail *adj* **-a lejjalejja**, *eg. edduuka lya lejjalejja
('retail shop')*   at retail **lejjalejja**

retailer *n* **omusubuuzi ow'edduuka** *n1*

retain *vt* **-sigazaawo**, *eg. Yasigazaawo ensigo
ez'okusimba oluvannyuma. ('She retained some
seeds to plant later.')*. *See* keep; spare

retaliate *vi* **-eesasuza**   retaliate against **-woolera
eggwanga**

retarded, be physically *vi* **-kona**, (*of children*)
-ziŋŋama, (*of animals*) **-konziba**

retch *vi* **-eegoga**

retire (*from work*) *v* (1) *of oneself*) *vi* **-mala
omulimu**, **-wummula**, **-nnyuka**; (2) (*someone
else*) **-wummuza ku mulimu**

retirement *n* **okuwummula** *n15*

retract *vt* (1) (*statement, law, etc.*) **-menyawo**; (2)
(*withdraw*) **-ggyayo**, *eg. Yaggyayo omukono mu*

ddirisa. ('She retracted her arm from the window.')
retract into (*return to*) **-dda mu**, *eg. Ekkovu lyadda
mu ssonko. ('The snail retracted into its shell.')*

[1]**retreat** (*religious*) *n* **olusirika** *n11*, *eg. Babadde mu
lusirika. ('They have been on a retreat.')*. *See*
refuge

[2]**retreat** (*go back*) *vi* **-dda ennyuma/emabega**

retrogression *n* **akaddannyuma** *n12*

[1]**return** (*recurrence*) *n* **obuddiro** *n14*   return journey
amadda *n6*

[2]**return** *v* (1) *vi* **-dda** (*commonly used with enclitic*
N24.2), *eg. Onodda ddi eka? ('When will you
return home?')*, **-komawo**, *eg. Nnagenda e Masaka
ne nkomawo enkeera. ('I went to Masaka and
returned the next day.')*, (*of a long-absent person*)
-zaawuka, *eg. Yazaawuka. ('He has returned at
last.')*; (2) *vt* **-zza** (*commonly used with enclitic*
N24.2), *eg. Ekitabo kyange yakizzizza. ('She has
returned my book.')*   return to (1) (*a previous
activity*) **-ddira**, *eg. Saagala kuddira mulimu ogwo.
('I don't want to return to that job.')*; (2) (*someone
something borrowed*) **-ddiza**, *eg. Nnakimuddiza ('I
returned it to her.')*

rev (up) (*an engine*) *vt* **-linnya omuliro**

reveal *vt* (1) (*something hidden*) **-kwekula**; (2) (*a
secret*) **-yatula**. *See* disclose; divulge; uncover   be
revealed (*made public*) **-yatuka**, *eg. Ekyama
kyayatuka. ('The secret was revealed.')*

revelation *n* **okubikkulirwa** *n15*   (Book of)
Revelations (**Ekitabo ky'**) **Okubikkulirwa**

revenge   take revenge (*retaliate*) **-eesasuza**   take
revenge on **-woolera eggwanga**

revenue (*income*) *n* **ennyingiza** *n9*. *See* tax

reverberate (*resonate*) *vi* **-waawaala**

reverend *n* **omwawule** *n1*, *eg. Omwawule Musoke
('the Reverend Musoke')*

[1]**reverse (side)** *n* **oludda olulala** *n11*. *See* inside
out

[2]**reverse** *vit* **-dda emabega**, *eg. Nnatomera
emmotoka ye nga nzira emabega. ('I knocked his
car while reversing.')*

revile *vt* **-vuma**   revile oneself **-eevuma**

revise (*modify*) *vt* **-kyusaamu**

revive *vt* **-zza obuggya/obupya**

revoke *vt* **-ggyawo**

[1]**revolt** (*rebellion*) *n* **obujeemu** *n14*   end a revolt
-jeemulukuka

[2]**revolt** (*rebel*) *vi* **-jeema**, (*against social conformity*)
-eewaggula

revolted by, be (*disgusted*) *vi* **-eetamwa**, *eg.
Yawulira nga yeetamiddwa enneeyisa y'omwana
we. ('He felt revolted by the behaviour of his son.')*
something revolting **ekyenyinyalwa** *n7*

revolution (*social or political*) *n* **enkyukakyuka** *n9*

revolutionary *adj. Use* **-kyusa embeera** ('*change
the situation*'), *eg. Emmotoka yakyusa embeera
y'abantu. ('The car was a revolutionary
invention.')*

revolve *vt* -eetoolooza, *eg. Yeetoolooza omupiira.* *('He revolved the wheel.')* revolve around -eetooloola, *eg. Ensi yeetooloola enjuba.* *('The earth revolves around the sun.')*

revolver *n* basitoola *n9*

reward *n* (1) *(recompense)* empeera *n9*; (2) *(present)* ekirabo *n7*

reward *vt* (1) *(recompense)* -weera; (2) *(give a prize to)* -wa ekirabo

rheumatism *n* ekimenyoomenyo *n7*

rhinitis *(bunged-up nose)* *n* ekibobe *n7*

rhinoceros *n* enkula *n9*

rhythmic movement *(eg. in time to music)* *n* omudigido *n9* move to a rhythm -digida way of moving to a rhythm endigida *n9*

rib *n* olubiriizi *n11*

rice *n* omupunga *n3*, omuceere *n3*

rich *adj* -gagga rich person omugagga *n1*, *(very)* nnaggagga *n1* be(come) rich -gaggawala make rich -gaggawaza

riches *n* ebyobugagga *n8*

rid get rid of (1) *(eliminate)* -malawo, *eg. Twagala kumalawo omusujja gw'ensiri mu nsi.* *('We want to get rid of malaria in the country.')*; (2) *(remove)* -ggyawo, *eg. Yaggyawo ekitanda ekikadde.* *('She got rid of the old bed.')*

riddle *n* ekikokyo *n7* speak in riddles -kokya, *eg. Musoke akokya.* *('Musoke speaks in riddles.')*

ride *vt* (1) *(an animal)* -eebagala; (2) *(bicycle or motorcycle)* -vuga. See pedal give a ride to *(in a vehicle)* -twalako

ridge *n* omugongo *n3*

ridgepole *(of roof)* *n* omulabba *n3*

ridicule *vt* -jerega. See taunt

rifle *n* emmundu *n9*

¹right *adj* (1) *(correct)* -tuufu; (2) *(direction)* -a ddyo, *eg. omukono ogwa ddyo ('the right side')* be right *(correct)* -li *or* -ba *('be') according to tense* (**20.1**) *followed by* -tuufu, *eg. (1) Yali mutuufu.* *('He was right.')*; *(2) Ajja kuba mutuufu.* *('He will be right.')* put right (1) *(correct)* -tereeza; (2) *(show someone the right way to do things)* -wabula. See repair right-handed person omuntu akozesa omukono ogwa ddyo something right ekituufu *n7* That's right! Kyekyo kyennyini!, Kituufu!

²right *(direction)* *n* ddyo *n1*, *eg. Genda ku ddyo.* *('Go right.')*

³right *(turn right way up)* *vt* -vuunula

righteous *adj* -tuukirivu

righteousness *n* obutuukirivu *n14*

rightness *n* obutuufu *n14*

rigid *adj* -kakanyavu be(come) rigid -kakanyala

rim *n* (1) *(of basket, pot, etc.)* omugo *n3*; (2) *(of cup)* omumwa *n3*; (3) *(of wheel)* olupanka *n11*

rind *(of fruit)* *n* ekikuta *n7*

rinderpest *n* nsotoka *n1*

¹ring *n* (1) *(jewellery)* empeta *n9*; (2) *(pad of grass on head for load)* enkata *n9* ring of reeds *(in roof of thatched house)* ekizizi *n7* engagement ring empeta nkusibiddaawo *n9*

²ring *v* (1) *(of bell or telephone)* *vi* -vuga, *eg. Essimu evuga.* *('The telephone is ringing.')*; (2) *(make a telephone call to)* *vt* -kubira, *eg. Yamukubira.* *('He rang her.')* ring a bell -kuba ekide

ringworm *n* (1) *(on the head)* ebiguuna *n8* *(single patch ekiguuna n7)*; (2) *(on the body)* oluwumu *n11*

rinse *vt* -munyunguza

¹riot *n* akeegugungo *n12*

²riot *vi* -eegugunga incite to riot -sasamaza

riotous *adv* -sasamavu be riotous -sasamala, *eg. Abantu bonna basasamadde.* *('Everyone is ready to riot.')*, -jagalala

riotousness *n* akasasamalo *n12*

rip *(with claws or nails)* *vt* -taagula. See tear be ripped *(by claws or nails)* -taaguka

ripe *adj* -yengevu

ripen *vi* -yengera start to ripen -yengerera

ripped *(by claws or nails)* *adj* -taagufu. See torn

rise *vi* (rose) (1) *(originate, of a river)* -sibuka, *eg. Omugga gusibuka mu nsozi.* *('The river rises in the mountains.')*; (2) *(of the sun or moon)* -vaayo, *eg. Enjuba evuddeyo.* *('The sun has risen.')*. See stand up rise early -keera, *eg. Abaana bakeera.* *('The children rise early.')* rise from the dead -zuukira rise to a great height *(eg. of a mountain or aeroplane)* -tumbiira rise up (1) *(of milk boiling up)* -bimba, *eg. Amata gaabimba ne gayiika.* *('The milk rose up and spilt over.')*; (2) *(of bread dough)* -zimbulukuka

rites carry out rites (1) *(birth rites for twins)* -yalula *(or* -zina) abalongo; (2) *(conclude funeral rites)* -yabya olumbe last rites amasaakalamentu amavannyuma *n6*

rival *n* omuvuganyi *n1*

river *n* omugga *n3* *(small akagga n12)* River Nile Kiyira *n1* across the river emitala w'omugga at the river *(as a source of water)* emugga

road *n* ekkubo *n5* *(narrow akabubo n12, in poor condition ekikubo n7)*, oluguudo *n11* road barrier *(broken branch on road)* omusanvu mu kkubo *n3* road hump ekigulumu *n7* *(small akagulumu n12)* road junction amasannanzira *n6*, sitenseni *n9* road sign ekipande ky'oluguudo *n7*

roadblock *n* loodibulooka *n9*, *(one mounted by police)* ekiddo *n7*

roam (about) *vi* -leereeta, *(without restrictions)* -taayaaya, *(like a swallow)* -tayira, *(aimlessly)* -yenjeera

roar *vi* (1) *(as a lion)* -wuluguma; (2) *(as a waterfall or torrential rain)* -yira

¹roast *adj* -yokye, *eg. ennyama enjokye ('roast meat')*, *(of peanuts or maize grains)* -siike, *eg. ebinyeebwa ebisiike ('roast peanuts')* roasted coffee beans emmwanyi enfumbe *n10* roasted maize **kasooli omwokye** *n1*   roasted potatoes **lumonde omwokye** *n1*

²**roast** *vt* **-yokya**, *(peanuts or maize)* **-siika**

rob *vt* **-bba.** *See* loot   person who has been robbed **omunyage** *n1*

robber *n* **omubbi** *n1*, *(violent)* **kkondo** *n1*. *See* looter; thief

robbery *n* **obubbi** *n14*. *See* looting

robe *(type worn as sign of office)* *n* **egganduula** *n5*. *See* tunic

robin chat *(type of bird)* *n* **ennyonza** *n9*

¹**rock** *n* **ejjinja** *n5*. *See* stone   rock outcrop **olwazi** *n11*, **ekyaziyazi** *n7*   rock salt **omunnyo ogw'ekisula** *n3*

²**rock** *(move back and forth)* *vt* **-suuba**   rock oneself **-eesuuba**   rock *(a baby)* to sleep **-siisiitira**

role *n* (1) *(job)* **omulimu** *n15*; (2) *(in a play)* **ekitundu ky'omuzannyo** *n7*

¹**roll** *n* **omuzingo** *n3*   roll of cloth **ejjoola** *n9*   bread roll **bbanzi** *n9*, **akagaati** *n12*   piece of material cut from roll **olupande** *n11*

²**roll** *v* TRANSITIVE USES roll (along) (1) **-yiringisa**, *eg. Ayiringisa omupiira gwa mmotoka. ('He is rolling the car tyre along.')*; (2) *(to make round or oval)* **-kulunga**, *eg. Omubumbi akulunga ebbumba. ('The potter is rolling the clay into a cylinder.')*. *See* fold   roll around *(in something, causing mixing)* **-vulunga**, *eg. Avulunga ennyama mu buwunga. ('She is rolling around the meat in flour.')*   roll around ball of matooke in sauce **-vulunga ettooke**   roll lump of matooke into a ball **-kulunga ettooke**   roll one's eyes **-mulungula amaaso**, *(in contempt)* **-ziimuula**, *eg. Yanziimuula. ('He rolled his eyes at me in contempt.')*, *(in madness)* **-zoola amaaso**   roll up **-zinga**, *eg. Azinga omukeeka. ('He is rolling up the mat.')*, *(sleeves or trousers)* **-funya**, *eg. Funye empale oyite mu mugga. ('Roll up your trousers and cross the river.')* INTRANSITIVE USES **-eevulunga**, *eg. Embizzi yeevulunga mu bitosi. ('The pig is rolling in the mud.')*   roll about *(eg. of an object in a container)* **-wulunguta**   roll down **-yiringita**, *eg. Omupiira guyiringita. ('The ball is rolling down.' – a slope understood)*

Roman Catholic *See* Catholic

Rome *n* **Roma** *n7*

romp *vi* **-ligita**, **-tiguka**, **-binuka**

¹**roof** *n* **akasolya** *n12*. *See* timber *(for structural elements of roof)*   edge of roof *(extending beyond wall)* **ekisasi** *n7*, **akabuno** *n12*   remove roof from **-sereekulula**

²**roof** *vt* **-sereka**. *See* thatch   roof with **-seresa**, *eg. Nseresa mabaati. ('I am roofing with iron sheets.')*

roof-rack *(of vehicle)* *n* **akatanda** *n12*

roofer *n* **omuseresi** *n1*

room *n* (1) *(in a building)* **ekisenge** *n7*; (2) *(space; opportunity)* **ebbanga** *n5*   room rent **ssente z'ennyumba** *n10*   living *(or* dining*)* room **eddiiro**

n5, *(at the front of the house)* **eddiiro ery'emiryango**, *(at the back of the house)* **eddiiro ery'emmanju**   make room for *(by giving up one's seat)* **-segulira**   make room for someone to sit *(by shifting aside)* **-seetuka**, *eg. Nnaseetuse ye atuule. ('I made room for her to sit.')*   take up room *See* occupy

roost *(hen perch)* *n* **oluwe** *n11*

root *n* **omulandira** *n3*   root crop **emmere ey'omu ttaka** *n9*   take root *(of a cutting)* **-loka**

rootlet *n* **akalandira** *n12*

rope *n* **omuguwa** *n3* *(small* **akaguwa** *n12)*, *(made from strip of bark from Triumfetta)* **ekinsambwe** *n7*

rosary *n* **ssapule** *n9*. *Can be made of 'ettembe' seeds.*

rose *v*. *See* rise

roselle *(red-flushed hibiscus)* *n* **musaayi** *n1*

rosin *(also* resin*)* *(for bow)* *n* **obubaani** *n14*

rosy periwinkle *(type of plant)* *n* **akamuli** *n12*

¹**rot** *n* **obuvundu** *n14*   dry rot **empumbu** *n9*

²**rot** *v* (1) *vi* **-vunda**; (2) *vt* **-vunza**. *See* bad (go)

rotate *v* (1) *vi* **-eetooloola**; (2) *vt* **-eetoolooza**   work in rotation *(shifts)* **-kola mu mpalo**

rotten *adj* **-vundu**   something rotten **ekivunze** *n7*

rough *(to the touch)* *adj* **-kuubuufu**   rough skin on foot *(especially heel)* **enkyakya** *n10*   be(come) rough (1) *(to the touch)* **-kuubuuka**; (2) *(of water)* **-siikuuka**, *eg. Ennyanja esiikuuse. ('The lake has become rough.')*   make rough (1) *(to the touch)* **-kuubuula**; (2) *(water)* **-siikuula**, *eg. Kibuyaga asiikudde ennyanja. ('The wind has made the lake rough.')*   speak roughly *(harshly)* **-yogera n'ebboggo**

round *adj* **-eetooloovu**, *eg. ennyumba enneetooloovu ('round houses')*   round worm *(Ascaris)* **enfaana** *n9*   make one's rounds *(as a doctor)* **-lawuna**   make round *(eg. lump of matooke or piece of clay)* **-kulunga**

round up *(eg. goats)* *vt* **-kuŋŋaanya**

roundabout *n* **enkulungo** *n9*

rouse *vt* **-golokosa**. *See* wake up

rout *vt* **-goba**

route *n* **ekkubo** *n5*   take a longer route **-eekooloobya**

¹**row** *n* (1) *(quarrel)* **oluyombo** *n11*; (2) *(line)* **olunyiriri** *n11*, *(eg. of beads or teeth)* **olubu** *n11*

²**row** *(quarrel)* *vi* **-yomba**, *eg. Nnayomba ne Musoke. ('I rowed with Musoke.')*, *(with one another)* **-yombagana**

rowdiness *n* **effujjo** *n5*

royal   royal family **olulyo olulangira** *n11*, **abaana b'eŋŋoma** *n2*, **abaana ba mujaguzo**   royal tombs **amasiro** *n6*

rub *vt* **-kuuta**. *See* grate; stroke   rub against **-kuuba**, *eg. Emmotoka yagikuuba ku kisenge. ('He rubbed the car against the wall.')*. *See* scrape   rub in dirt **-kulukuunya**   rub in ointment **-siimuula omuzigo**, *(for medicinal purposes)* **-siimuula eddagala**   rub one another up the wrong way **-kuubagana**, *eg. Musoke ne Mukasa bakuubagana. ('Musoke and Mukasa rub one another up the wrong way.')* rub oneself **-eekuuta**, *eg. Yeekuuta n'ekyangwe. ('He rubbed himself with a loofah.')* rub out *(erase)* **-sangula** rub smooth *(sand)* **-wawula** rub together *(clothes in washing)* **-kunya** be rubbed out *(erased)* **-sanguka**

rubber *n* (1) *(for erasing)* **labba** *n9*; (2) *(of valve)* **akawago** *n12* rubber tree (1) *(Hevea)* **pala** *n1*; (2) *(Funtumia africana) (name when used medicinally)* **nnamukago** *n1*, *(name when used for timber)* **enkago** *n9* something made of rubber **omupiira** *n3*

rubbing rubbing one another up the wrong way **embojjanyi** *n9* way of rubbing *(clothes together in washing)* **enkunya** *n9*

rubbish *(also* trash*) n* **ebisasiro** *n8*, **ebisaaniiko** *n8* rubbish dump **awayiibwa ebisaaniiko** *n16* heap of rubbish *(collected by flowing rain water)* **effumbiko** *n5*

rude *adj.* Use **-yogera obubi** *('speak rudely'), eg. omuntu ayogera bubi ('rude person')* rude manner of speech **ebboggo** *n5*

rudely *(in speech) adv* **n'ebboggo** talk rudely **-koboggoka**

rug *n* **ekiwempe** *n7*

ruin *vt* **-yonoona**. *See* damage; wreck be(come) ruined **-yonooneka**

ruined *adj* **-yonoonefu**

¹rule *n* (1) *(governance)* **obufuzi** *n14*; (2) *(regulation)* **etteeka** *n5*

²rule *(govern) vt* **-fuga** rule a margin *(on a page)* **-saza omusittale**

ruled *(governed) adj* **-fuge** ruled line **olukoloboze** *n11*, *(drawn as a margin)* **omusittale** *n3* be ruled **-fugibwa** person who is ruled **omufuge** *n1*

ruler *n* (1) *(person)* **omufuzi** *n1*; (2) *(for measuring)* **luula** *n9*, **fuuti** *n9*

ruling *(judgement) n* **ennamula** *n9*, *(in court case)* **ensala y'omusango** *n9* make a ruling *(in court case)* **-sala omusango** way of ruling *(governing)* **enfuga** *n9*

¹rumble *n* **ekiwuuma** *n7*

²rumble *vi* (1) *(of thunder)* **-duduma**, *eg. Eggulu liduduma. ('The thunder is rumbling.')*; (2) *(of the stomach)* **-gulumba**, *eg. Olubuto lwamugulumbye ekiro kyonna. ('His stomach rumbled all night.')*

rummage (through) *vt* **-fuukuula**, *eg. Omubbi yafuukudde ebintu mu kabada ng'anoonya ssente. ('The thief rummaged through the things in the cupboard looking for money.'),* **-tankuula**, *eg. Ababbi baatankuula ebintu bye. ('The thieves rummaged through her things.'). See* disorganise; disturb; ransack

rumour *n* **olugambo** *n11* rumour-monger **omusaasaanyi w'olugambo** *n1* spread a rumour **-saasaanya** *(or* **-bungeesa***)* **olugambo**

rumple (up) *(eg. sheets) vt* **-vungavunga**

¹run *v* (ran) (1) *(way of moving fast) vi* **-dduka**, *eg. Musoke adduka. ('Musoke is running.'), (very fast)* **-dduka kafubutuko**; (2) *(operate; manage) vt* **-ddukanya**, *eg. Ani addukanya ofiisi? ('Who is running the office?'). See* dash; flow; rush out run about all over the place **-tigoma** run away (1) *(from captivity)* **-bomba, -toloka**; (2) *(of a wife or servant)* **-ebbako** run into (1) *(collide with)* **-tomera**; (2) *(meet by chance)* **-siŋŋaana**, *eg. Nnamusiŋŋaanye mu kibuga. ('I ran into him in town.')* run on/to **-ddukira**, *eg. Musoke addukira ku luguudo. ('Musoke is running on the road.')* run out (1) *(become used up)* **-ggwaawo**, *eg. Omunnyo guweddewo. ('The salt has run out.'), (dwindle, as a bar of soap)* **-ggweerera**; (2) *(rush out)* **-fubutuka**, *eg. Engabi yafubutuka mu kisaka. ('The bushbuck ran out of the thicket.')* run poorly *(of a motor)* **-pipira** run to the help of **-dduukirira** cause to run about in panic **-tigomya**

run-away *(fugitive) n* **omubombi** *n1*

runner *n* (1) *(person)* **omuddusi** *n1*; (2) *(of a plant)* **ekiranda** *n7*

running *n* **okudduka** *n15*. *See* race running race **embiro z'empaka** *n10* running stomach *See* diarrhoea be running *(of an engine)* **-tokota**, *eg. Yingini etokota. ('The engine is running.')*

ruse *n* **akakodyo** *n12*

rush *v* (1) *vi* **-papa**, *eg. Nnakola mpapa okumala emirimu. ('I rushed to finish the work.'), (be frantic)* **-buguutana**; (2) *(hurry someone) vt* **-papya, -buguutanya** rush about wildly (1) *(as a chicken being chased)* **-paala, paaluuka**; (2) *(as a thief being chased)* **-bama** rush into *(eg. of an animal into bush)* **-eefubitika** rush out **-wamatuka**, *eg. Yawamatuka mu nnyumba. ('She rushed out of the house.'), (at a run)* **-fubutuka** rush to/for **-yanguyira**, *eg. Baayanguyira okumuyamba. ('They rushed to help him.')* in a rush **pakupaku**

¹rust *n* **obutalagge** *n14*

²rust *vi* **-talagga**

rustle *(make sound like trampling on dry leaves) vi* **-kwakwaya**, *eg. Ebikoola bikwakwaya. ('The leaves are rustling.')* rustling sound **ekikwakwaya**, *eg. Mpulidde ekikwakwaya. ('I hear a rustling sound.')*

rusty *adj* **-talavvu**

rut *(of a dog) vi* **-lundugga**

ruts *(on a road) n* **ebisirikko** *n8*, *eg. oluguudo lwa bisirikko ('rutted road') (small* **obusirikko** *n14)*

Ruth *n* **Luusi** *n1*

ruthless *adj* **-kambwe**

Rwanda *n* **Rwanda** *n9* language of Rwanda *(Kinyarwanda)* **Olunyarwanda** *n11* person of Rwanda **Omunyarwanda** *n1*

Rwenzori *(Mountains) n* **Gambalagala**

S,s

Sabbath *n* **Ssabbiiti** *n9*
sabotage *vt* **-kotoggera**
¹sack *n* (1) (*bag*) **ensawo**; (2) (*gunny bag*) **ekkutiya** *n9*, **egguniya** *n9*
²sack (*dismiss worker*) *vt* **-goba**
sacrament *n* **essaakalamentu** *n5*   sacrament of mass (*RC*) **ekitambiro ky'emmisa** *n7*
sacred *adj* **-tukuvu**
¹sacrifice (*also* sacrificial animal) *n* **ssaddaaka** *n9*   place of sacrifice **ettambiro** *n5*
²sacrifice *vt* (1) (*an animal, to a god or spirit*) **-saddaaka**; (2) (*give as an offering*) **-waayo**, *eg. Yesu yawaayo obulamu bwe ku lwaffe. ('Jesus sacrificed his life for us.').* See dedicate   sacrifice to (*lubaale or spirit*) **-wongera**   person who sacrifices **omutambizi** *n1*
sacrificial *adj* **-wonge**
sad *adj* **-nakuwavu**. *See* regretful; unhappy   sad person **omunakuwavu** *n1*   be(come) sad **-nakuwala, -beera n'ennaku**   make sad **-nakuwaza**
sadness *n* **obunakuwavu** *n14*, **ennaku** *n9*
safari *n* **ssafaali** *n9*. *See* journey   safari ant **ensanafu** *n9*
safe (*for valuables*) *n* **eggwanika** *n5*, **sseefu** *n9*   be safe Use **-funa akabi** (*'be in danger'*) in neg (**N21**), *eg. Tajja kufuna kabi nga ali mu nnyumba yange. ('She will not be in danger in my house.')*
safeguard *vt* **-kuuma**
safely *adv* **obulungi**, *eg. Atuuse bulungi. ('He has arrived safely.')*
safety *See* refuge; sanctuary   safety pin **ekikwanso** *n7*, **ekikwaso** *n7*
sag *vi* **-lagaya**, *eg. Waaya y'amasannyalaze eragaya. ('The electricity cable is sagging.')*
¹sail *n* **ettanga** *n5*
²sail *vt* **-seeyeeya**
sailing ship *n* **ekyombo** *n7*
sailor *n* **omulunnyanja** *n1*
saint *n* **omutuukirivu** *n1*
saintly *adj* **-tuukirivu**
salary *n* **omusaala** *n3*, **empeera** *n9*
sale (*time of lowered prices*) *n* **layisi** *n1*
salesperson *n* **omutunzi** *n1*, (*itinerant*) **omutembeeyi** *n1*
saliva *n* **amalusu** *n6*, (*dried dribble*) **engeregeze** *n10*. *See* slime
salt *n* **omunnyo** *n3*   pinch of salt **otunnyo** *n13*   rock salt **omunnyo ogw'ekisula**
¹salute *n* **saluti** *n9*   give a gun salute **-kuba emizinga**
²salute (*as in the army*) *vt* **-kuba saluti**
salvage *vt* **-taakiriza**, *eg. Yataakiriza ebintu ebimu okuva mu nnyumba ng'ekutte omuliro. ('He salvaged some of his belongings from the burning house.')*

salvation (*religious*) *n* **obulokozi** *n14*
same *adj* **-e -mu** (*'e' with pronominal concord and '-mu' with numeral concord* **N4.2**), *eg. Erangi zino ze zimu. ('These colours are the same.')*   at the same time **ku kiseera kye kimu**   be the same **-yenkana**, *eg. Abaana benkana obuwanvu. ('The children are the same height.')*   in the same way **mu ngeri y'emu**   make the same (*equal*) **-yenkanya**, *eg. Yeenkanyizza emmere gy'agabye. ('He is making the amounts of food to give out the same.')*   the same **ky'ekimu** *n7*, *eg. Musoke yagambye ky'ekimu. ('Musoke said the same.')*   the same as (1) (*'the same' used as an adjective*) **-e -mu ne**, *eg. Obubaka buno bwe bumu n'obwo. ('This message is the same as that.');* (2) (*'the same' used as a noun*) **kye kimu ne**, *eg. Emmotoka eno kye kimu n'eyo. ('This car is the same as that.')*
samosa *n* **ssumbuusa** *n9*
sample *n* **sampulo** *n9*
sanctify *vt* **-tukuza**
sanctuary *n* **obubudamo** *n14*. *See* refuge   grant sanctuary **-wa obubudamo**   take sanctuary **-budama**
¹sand *n* **omusenyu** *n3*   lake sand (*coarse-grained, used for brick-laying*) **omusenyu gw'ennyanja**   river sand (*fine-grained, used for plastering*) **omusenyu gw'omugga**   sandy area (*of land*) **olusenyi** *n11*
²sand (*also* sandpaper) (*rub smooth*) *vt* **-wawula**
sandal (*shoe*) *n* **engatto** *n9*. *See* clog; slipper
sandpaper *n* **oluwawu** *n11*   sandpaper tree (*Ficus exasperata*) **omuwawu** *n3*, (*leaf*) **oluwawu** *n11*
sandstone *n* **ebisibosibo** *n8*
sanitation *n* **ebyobuyonjo** *n8*
sap *n* **amasanda** *n6*, *eg. amasanda ga matooke ('sap from cooking bananas')*
Sarah *n* **Saala** *n1*
sarcasm *n* **obuduuze** *n14*   sarcastic person **omuduuze** *n1*   be sarcastic **-duula**   be sarcastic to **-duulira**
sari *n* **ssaali** *n9*
sat *See* sit
Satan *n* **Sitaani** *n1*
satchel *n* **ensawo** *n9*
satisfaction *n* **obumativu** *n14*, (*through eating*) **obukkufu** *n14*
satisfied *adj* **-mativu**, (*through eating*) **-kkufu**   satisfied person (*through eating*) **omukkufu** *n1*   be satisfied **-matira**, (*through eating*) **-kkuta**, *eg. Nzikuse. ('I feel satisfied.' − by the food)*
satisfy *vt* **-matiza**, (*with food*) **-kkusa**
Saturday *n* **Olwomukaaga** *n11*, **Wammunyeenye, Ssatade, Olunaku olw'Obwerende** (*for Seventh-Day Adventists*)
sauce (*relish eaten with the main food 'emmere'*) *n* **enva** *n10*, **ssupu** *n1*. *See* gravy   food without sauce **amaluma** *n6*, *eg. Twalidde maluma. ('We ate food*

without sauce.') groundnut sauce **enva z'ebinyeebwa** thick sauce made from pounded termites and groundnuts **ekipooli** *n7*

saucepan *n* **sseffuliya** *n9*, **sseppiki** *n9*

saucer *n* **essoosi** *n9*

sausage tree (*Kigelia*) *n* **omussa** *n3*

savage *adj* **-kambwe**

savannah *n* **olukoola** *n11*

save *vt* (1) (*cure*) **-wonya**; (2) (*through religion*) **-lokola**; (3) (*from danger*) **-taasa**. *See* rescue; spare; store save money (*through economising*) **-kekkereza ssente** be saved **-lokoka**. *See* escape; survive

saved (*through religion*) *adj* **-lokole**. *See* born-again someone saved **omulokole** *n1*

savings (*financial*) *n* **ssente entereke** *n10*

saviour *n* **omununuzi** *n1*, **omulokozi** *n1*

[1]saw *n* **omusumeeno** *n3*

[2]saw (*cut*) *vt* **-sala**

[3]saw (*perceived*) *See* see

sawdust *n* **empumbu y'embaawo** *n9*

saxophone *n* **omulere** *n3*

say (to) *vit* **-gamba** say farewell to **siibula** that is to say **kwe kugamba nti**

saying *n* **enjogera** *n9*, (*common utterance; expression*) **eŋŋombo** *n9*, (*proverb*) **olugero** *n11*, (*with a hidden meaning*) **ekisoko** *n7*

scab (*on wound*) *n* **ekigalagamba** *n7*, **ekikakampa** *n7*

scabbard *n* **ekiraato** *n7*

scabies *n* **wayirindi** *n1*

scaffold *n* **akalabba** *n12*

scaffolding *n* **amadaala** *n6*

scald (*burn*) *vt* **-yokya**

scale (*of fish*) *n* **ekigalagamba** *n7* (*big* **eggalagamba** *n5*) remove scales (*from a fish*) **-ggyako amagalagamba** scrape a fish (*to remove scales*) **-kalakata ekyenyanja**

scales (*fror weighing*) *n* **minzaani** *n9*

scapegoat *n* **ow'olutwe** *n1*, (*animal to which an evil spirit is transferred*) **ekyonziira** *n7*

scar *n* **enkovu** *n9*, (*on head, from fighting*) **olubale** *n11*, (*from surgery*) **olukindo** *n11* tribal scars on body (*made by burning*) **enjokyo** *n10* (*one* **oluyokyo** *n11*)

scarce *adj* **-a ebbula** be(come) scarce **-bula**

scarcity *n* **ebbula** *n5*

[1]scare *n* **entiisa** *n9*

[2]scare *vt* **-tiisa**. *See* shock be scared **-tya**

scarecrow *n* **akakookolo** *n12*

scarf *n* **akatambaala ak'oku mutwe** *n12*

scarify (*by burning*) *vt* **-yokya**

scatter *v* (1) (*become scattered*) *vi* **-saasaana**, *eg. Abantu baasaasaana nga emmundu zitandise okuvuga.* (*'The people scattered when the shooting started.'*); (2) (*cause to scatter*) *vt* **-saasaanya**, *eg. Baasaasaanya ebisaaniiko mu luggya lwange.* (*'They scattered rubbish in my yard.'*); (3) (*drop things here and there*) *vt* **-suulasuula**. *See* discard scatter grass on floor **-sasira essubi**, *eg. Yasasira essubi wansi mu nnyumba.* (*'She scattered grass on the floor of the house.'*)

[1]scent *n* **akawoowo** *n12*. *See* smell get the scent of **-konga**

[2]scent *vt* **-wunyirwa**

scepticism *n* **okubuusabuusa** *n15* be sceptical **-buusabuusa**

sceptre (*of the Katikkiro*) *n* **ddamula** *n9*

scheme (*plan*) *n* **entegeka** *n9*, **enteekateeka** *n9*

scheme against *vt* **-kola olukwe**

scholar *n* **omusomi** *n1*

scholarship (*grant for studying*) *n* **sikaala** *n9*

[1]school *n* **essomero** *n5*, (*boarding*) **essomero ly'ekisulo**, (*co-educational*) **essomero ery'ekintabuli**, (*primary*) **pulayimale** *n9*, (*secondary*) **siiniya** *n9*, **sekendule** *n9*

[2]school (*teach*) *vt* **-yigiriza**

schoolteacher *n* **omusomesa** *n1*

science *n* **ssaayansi** *n1*

scientist *n* **munnassaayansi** *n1*

scissors *n* **makansi** *n9*

scoff at *vt* **-nyooma**. *See* contempt

scoffer *n* **omunyoomi** *n1*

scold *vt* **-nenya**

[1]scoop *n* **ekijiiko ekisena** *n7*, (*made from a gourd*) **olwendo** *n11* (*small* **akendo** *n12*), (*made from banana leaf and used as a spoon; or of metal and used to dish out paraffin, etc.*) **akawujjo** *n12*, (*plate or piece of banana leaf, used to serve cooked matooke from omuwumbo*) **akabezo** *n12*

[2]scoop (out) *vt* (1) (*excavate; dig deeply, eg. when laying a pipe*) **-yiikuula**, **-wuukuula**; (2) (*wood, eg. when making a drum*) **-woola** scoop up (*eg. rubbish*) **-yoola**

scoopful (*of cooking oil, etc.*) *n* (1) (*cupful*) **ekikopo** *n7*; (2) (*spoonful*) **ekijiiko** *n7*

scorch *vt* **-yokya**, (*accidentally, eg. burn food when cooking*) **-siriiza**. *See* burn; singe

scorched *adj* **-yokye**. *See* singed be scorched **-siriira**, *eg. Sseffuliya esiridde.* (*'The pan is scorched.'*), (*on the point of burning, eg. of something too close to a fire*) **-babirira**

score (*in a game*) *n* **akagoba** *n12* score a goal **-kuba eggoolo** be scored (*of a goal*) **ggoolo -nywa**, *eg. Ggoolo enywedde.* (*'It's a goal.'*)

[1]scorn *n* **obuduuze** *n14*

[2]scorn *vt* **-duulira** be scornful **-duula**

scorner *n* **omuduuze** *n1*

scorpion *n* **enjaba y'obusagwa** *n9*

scour (*scrub*) *vt* **-kuuta**. *See* scrape

[1]scout *n* (1) (*person who spies out*) **omukessi** *n1*; (2) (*as in boy scouts*) **omusikaawutu** *n1*

[2]scout (out) (*reconnoitre*) *vt* **-ziga**, (*secretly*) **-kwekweta** scout for (*look for on someone's behalf*) **-suuliza enkessi**

scouting *n* **obusikaawutu** *n14* secret scouting

patrol **ekikwekweto** *n7*

scrap (*of food*) *n* **akakunkumuka** *n12*

scrape *vt* (1) (*using a cutting motion*) **-kalakata**, *eg. Akalakata ekyennyanja. ('She's scrapping the fish.' – to remove scales*); (2) (*shave off, eg. weeds with a hoe*) **-walakata**; (3) (*vigourously, eg. pan to remove burnt food*) **-kolokota**, *eg. Akolokota esseffuliya eyasiridde. ('She is scraping the burnt pan.')* scrape a hide **-baaga ensolo** scrape against **-kulubula**, *eg. Emmotoka yo ekulubudde emmotoka yange. ('Your car has scraped against mine.')* See graze; rub; scratch scrape oneself **-eekulubula**, *eg. Omwana yeekulubudde ku muti. ('The child scraped herself on the tree.')* scrape with a hoe **-wala**, *eg. Awala. ('She is scraping the ground with a hoe.')* be scraped (*eg. of the skin*) **-kulubuka**

scraped (*eg. of the skin*) *adj* **-kulubufu** scraped area of land (*from using a hoe*) **awawalakate** *n16*

scraper *n* (1) (*person who scrapes*) **omuwazi** *n1*, *eg. omuwazi w'amaliba ('scraper of hides')*; (2) (*implement used for scraping*) **ekiwalakata** *n7*

[1]**scratch** *n* (1) (*made by sharp point*) **olukoloboze** *n11*; (2) (*made by nails or claws*) **olukwagulo** *n11*

[2]**scratch** *vt* **-takula**, *eg. Yamutakula mu mugongo. ('He scratched her back for her.')*, (*more forcefully*) **-yagula**, (*with claws or nails*) **-taagula**, *eg. Ppusi yantaagudde. ('The cat scratched me.')*, (*using a sharp point*) **-kulubula** scratch oneself (*eg. due to an itch*) **-eetakula**, (*forcefully*) **-eeyagula** be scratched **-kulubuka**, *eg. Emmeeza ekulubuse. ('The table is scratched.')*, (*by claws*) **-taaguka**

scratched *adj* **-kulubufu**, (*by claws or nails*) **-taagufu**

scratcher (*for hair*) *n* **akakulula** *n12*

scream *vi* **-leekana**

screen (*eg. used as divider in room*) *n* **olutimbe** *n11*. See partition screen of banana leaves (*in doorway*) **ebisanja by'oluggi** *n8* TV screen **olutimbe lwa ttivvi**

[1]**screw** *n* **omusumaali gw'enjola** *n3*

[2]**screw** *vt* **-nyoola**

screwdriver *n* **sukuluduleeva** *n9*

scribble *v* **-wandiika vvulugu**

scribe *n* **omuwandiisi** *n1*

script (*something written*) *n* **ekiwandiiko** *n7*. See font

scripture *n* **ebyawandiikibwa ebitukuvu** *n8*

[1]**scrub** (*bushy place*) *n* **ekisiko** *n7*. See savannah; thicket

[2]**scrub** (*rub*) *vt* **-kuuta** scrub oneself **-eekuuta**

scrutinise *vt* **-eetegereza**, **-eekaliriza**, **-ekkaanya**, (*very carefully*) **-tunuulira enkaliriza**. See examine; inspect

scuffle *n* **akavuvuŋŋano** *n12*

scum *n* (1) (*from roasted sorghum in beer-making*) **enkanja** *n10*; (2) (*on gravy or heated milk; skin*)

olububi *n11. See* sediment

sea *n* **ennyanja** *n9* (*big* **amayanja** *n6*)

[1]**seal** (*mark*) *n* **akabonero** *n12*, (*of red wax*) **envumbo** *n9* put one's seal (*stamp*) **-ssaako** (*or* **-koonako**) **sitampu**

[2]**seal** (*eg. an envelope*) *vt* **-siba** keep one's lips sealed (*keep quiet*) **-wumba emimwa**

seam (*fold*) *n* **olufunyiro** *n11. See* hem put a seam on **-teekako eggemo**

seaman *n* **omulunnyanja** *n1*

seamstress *n* **omutunzi** *n1*

search *vt* **-noonya**, (*in cluttered, bushy or crowded places*) **-wenja**, (*looking for illicit goods*) **-yaza**, *eg. Abapoliisi baayaza ennyumba ye. ('The police searched his house.')*, (*a person or property*) **-fuuza**. See prospect search for (*on someone's behalf*) **-noonyeza**, *eg. Nnali mmunoonyeza engatto e Kampala. ('I was searching for shoes for her in Kampala.')* person who searches **omufuuzi** *n1*

[1]**season** (*period of the year*) *n* **ekiseera** *n7* dry season **ekyeya** *n7* rainy season **ekiseera ky'enkuba**, (*long rains – March-May*) **ttoggo** *n1*, (*short rains – September-November*) **ddumbi** *n1* season of grasshoppers (*November*) **Museenene** *n3* season of plenty (*of food, especially matooke*) **ekyengera** *n7*

[2]**season** (*food with salt, spice, etc.*) *vt* **-lunga** season (*food*) sufficiently with **-noza**, *eg. Nnanozezza omunnyo. ('I have seasoned the food.')* season (*food or drink*) with **-siwa** be seasoned enough (*of food*) **-noga**, *eg. Omunnyo gunoze. ('The food is seasoned enough with salt.')*

seasoning (*flavouring*) *n* **ekirungo** *n7*

[1]**seat** (*chair*) *n* **entebe** *n9*, (*small* **akatebe** *n12*, *large, or worn-out* **ekitebe** *n7*) seat in a canoe **olubanga** *n11* (*pl.* **emmanga**), (*for the helmsman*) **akalumba** *n12* seat of government **ekitebe kya gavumenti** seat of the emotions (*of a person*) **emmeeme** *n9* passenger seat on bike **ekkaliya** *n9* seating area **w'otuula** *n16*, **awatuulwa** *n16*, **awatuulibwa** *n16* take a seat and settle down (*eg. to work*) **-kkalira**

[2]**seat** *vt* **-tuuza** person responsible for the seating of the Kabaka **Mutuuza** *n1 title*

seatbelt *n* **omusipi ogw'oku ntebe** *n3*

[1]**second** *adj/num* **-a okubiri** (N7.1), *eg. ekintu eky'okubiri ('second thing'). Elision is sometimes seen, eg. ekintu ekyokubiri ('second thing').* second-in-command **omumyuka** *n1* be second-in-command (*to*) **-myuka**

[2]**second** (*unit of time*) *n* **akatikitiki** *n12*

[3]**second** (*eg. person in election*) *vt* **-semba**

secondary school *n* **sekendule** *n9*, **siiniya** *n9*

secondly *adv* **ekyokubiri**

secrecy *n* **enkiso** *n9. See* secretiveness

[1]**secret** *adj* **-a ekyama** secret dealings **enkolagana y'ekyama** *n9*

[2]**secret** *n* **ekyama** *n7* keep secret (*from*) **-kuusa**,

eg. Yakimukuusa. ('He kept it secret from her.').
See conceal   tell a secret to -sunirako

secretary n omuwandiisi n1, sekulitale n1

secretion n (1) (eg. enzyme from cell) ekirungo n7;
(2) (from eye) obujonjo n14

secretive adj -a amankwetu

secretiveness n amankwetu n6. See secrecy
move about secretively -kwekweta

secretly adv mu kyama   do secretly -kukuta

sect (eg. of a religion) n akabiina n12, ekibiina n7,
ekiwayi n7

section n (1) (part) ekitundu n7 ; (2) (of an
organisation) ekitongole n7. See segment

secure vt (1) (make firm) -nyweza; (2) (obtain)
-funa   be secure (firm) -nywera, eg. Asibyewo
oluggi lunywedde. ('He has locked the door so it is
secure.')

security n (1) (guarantee) omusingo n3, akakalu
n12; (2) (defence affairs) ebyokwerinda n8
security guard omukuumi n1   put up security for
(stand bail) -eeyimirira

sediment (dregs) n obukudumu n14, ebikudumu
n8, (from roasted sorghum in beer making)
enkanja n10

seduce vt -sigula. See entice; tempt

seducer n omusiguze n1. See tempter

see vt (saw) -laba, eg. Nkulaba. ('I see you.'), (at a
distance) -lengera, eg. Nnagenze ku lusozi
okulengera ekibuga. ('I went on the hill to see the
town.'). See visible (be); visit   see for (greet for)
-labira, eg. Oyinza okumundabira? ('Can you see
her for me?')   see off (a visitor, through
accompanying a short distance on the way)
-werekera   see one another -labagana   see
oneself -eeraba   see what will happen -labira
awo, eg. Nnaalabira awo. ('I shall see what will
happen.')   be seen -labika, eg. Yalabise mu kibuga
leero. ('She was seen in town today.'), (frequently)
-labikalabika   person who sees omulabi n1, (who
sees all, not missing a trick) kaliisoliiso n1

seed n ensigo n9, (type used as a counter in game of
omweso) empiki n9

seedbed n bbeedi n9

seedling n endokwa n9, ensibuka n9

seek vt (sought) -noonya

seeker n omunoonyi n1

seem (look likely) vi -labika, eg. Kirabika
ng'enkuba egenda okutonnya. ('It seems that it's
going to rain.')   seem like (look like) -faanana, eg.
Ekinyonyi kino kifaanana ekyo. ('This bird seems
like that one.')

seer n omulaguzi n1

segment n (1) (section) ennyingo n9; (2) (of
something divisible) omuwula n3. See part
segment of an orange omuwula gw'omucungwa
segment of sugar cane ennyingo y'ekikajjo

seize vt -kwata, (by force; pillage) -nyaga. See
appropriate; loot; snatch   be seized -kwatibwa

select vt (1) (choose) -londa, eg. Twagala okulonda
omuntu anaakola omulimu guno. ('We want to
select a person for the work.'); (2) (pick out)
-londamu, eg. Londamu omuyembe ogusinga
obunene. ('Select the biggest mango.')   select for
oneself -eerondera

¹-self pro (1) (as part of pronoun of emphasis N11.6)
-nnyini, eg. Kabaka ye yennyini ajja. ('The king
himself is coming.'); (2) (as part of reflexive
pronoun N18) Use prefix -ee, eg. Nneesiiga
ebizigo. ('I am smearing myself with ointment.')

²self-   self-doubt obuteekakasa n14   self-important
person omwepansi n1   self-sown plant
ekimererezi n7   be self-confident -eekakasa   be
self-controlled -eefuga   be self-employed
-eekozesa   be self-reliant (or self-sufficient)
-eemalirira, -eebeezaawo   have self-pity
-eesaasira   lack of self-discipline obuteekomako
n14   lose self-control (go wild) -taama, -taaluuka
person lacking self-discipline omuntu ateekomako
n1

selfish, be vi -eefaako (or -eerowoozaako) -okka,
eg. Beerowoozaako bokka. ('They are selfish.')

sell vt -tunda

seller n omutunzi n1

selling n okutunda n15, (from the pavement)
okutundira ku lubalaza   place of selling
ettundiro n9   way of selling entunda n9

semen n amazzi g'obusajja n6

semester n olusoma n11

semi-darkness n ekibululu n7

seminary n sseminaariyo n9

send vt (sent) (1) (a person) -tuma, eg. Nnamutuma
okuleeta amagi. ('I sent him for eggs.'), (for a task)
-sindika, eg. Nnasindika Musoke okugenda
okulima. ('I sent Musoke to go and dig.'); (2) (a
thing) -weereza, eg. Yamuweereza ebimuli. ('She
sent him flowers.')   send away (dismiss) -goba
send back -zzaayo, eg. Yazzaayo emmotoka gye
yeeyazika. ('She sent back the car she had
borrowed.')   send for -tumya, eg. Nnatumizza
amagi. ('I sent for eggs'), (summon a person) -yita
send greetings to (through someone) -tumira, eg.
Antumidde. ('He has sent me greetings.')   send off
(a visitor, through accompanying a short distance
on the way) -werekera   send to (a person) (1)
(with a message) -tumira, eg. Katonda yatutumira
Musa eyali nnabbi. ('God sent the prophet Moses to
us.'); (2) (for a task) -sindikira, eg.
Nnamusindikira Musoke okulima. ('I sent Musoke
to him to dig.'). See return to   send (usually a
child) to serve (1) (to the Kabaka) -siiga mu lubiri;
(2) (to a chief) -siiga mu kisaakaate   be sent (of a
person) -tumibwa   person sent omutume n1

senile adj -wunguutufu, -buguyavu   senile person
omuwuttufu n1, omuwuttaavu n1, omuwutta n1
be(come) senile -wunguutuka, -wutta, -buguyala

senior adj -kulu   senior school (secondary) siiniya

n9, **sekendule** *n9*

seniority *n* **obukulu** *n14*

¹sense (*meaning*) *n* **amakulu** *n6*

²sense (*through any sense except sight*) *vt* **-wulira**

sensitive plant *n* **akafansonyi** *n12*, **weewumbeko omuko wuuyo ajja**. *These names appear to apply to any plant whose leaves or leaflets that fold up when touched. These include* Aeschynomen sensitivua, Biophytum *spp. and* Mimosa pudica.

sent *See* send

sentence *n* (1) (*written*) **sentensi** *n9*; (2) (*punishment*) **ekibonerezo** *n7*   pass sentence (*in court*) **-sala omusango**   pass sentence on **-salira omusango**, (*unfairly*) **-saliriza omusango**

sentry *n* **omukuumi** *n1*

separate *v* (1) *vi* **-yawuka**, *eg. Nze nnayawuka ne Musoke nga mmaze okwogera naye. ('I separated from Musoke after speaking with him.')*; (2) *vt* **-yawula**, *eg. Yayawula emiyembe n'amenvu. ('She separated the mangoes from the bananas.'). See* divorce   separate from one another **-yawukana**, *eg. Bwe baamala okwogera ne bayawukana. ('When they finished talking they separated from one another.')*   separate from one's husband **-noba**   separate oneself (*from a person or group; dissociate oneself*) **-eeyawula**, *eg. Yeeyawudde ku banne. ('He has separated himself from his companions.')*   separate people (*or* animals) fighting **-taasa**, *eg. Yagezaako okutaasa abalwana. ('He tried to separate the fighters.'),* (*when locked together*) **-takkuluza**   be separated **-yawulwa**. *See* divorce (get)   cause to separate **-yawukanya**, *eg. Mukasa y'eyayawukanya Musoke ku banne. ('Mukasa caused Musoke to separate from his group.')*

separation *n* **enjawukana** *n9*

separator (*eg. divider*) *n* **ekyawulamu** *n7*

September *n* **Omwezi ogw'omwenda** *n3*, **Mutunda**, **Ssebutemba**

septic, grow (*infected*) *vi* **-tana**

serene *adj* **-teefu**   be(come) serene **-teeka**, (*and peaceful, of a person*) **-tebenkera**

serious (*committed*) *adj* **-nyiikivu**   be serious **-nyiikira**, *eg. Anyiikidde okusoma. ('He is serious about studying.')*   look serious and stern **-eekaba**   not be serious *Use* **-faayo ku** (*'care about'*) *in neg* (**N21**), *eg. Tafaayo ku kusoma. ('She is not serious about her studies.'). See* indolent (be); lazy (be)   something serious (*important*) **ekikulu** *n7*

sermon *n* **okubuulira** *n15*

serpent *n* (1) (*snake generally*) **omusota** *n3*, (2) (*poisonous snake*) **omusota gw'obutwa**

serval cat *n* **emmondo** *n9*

servant *n* **omukozi** *n1*, (*one working in a home*) **omukozi w'awaka** *n1*   person who serves **omuweereza**, (*in a palace*) **omugalagala** *n1*. *See* waiter; waitress

serve *vt* **-weereza**   serve food **-bega emmere**. *See* banana (*for words relating to serving food from food parcels*)

server (*of food*) *n* **omubega w'emmere** *n1*, (*at a feast*) **omugabuzi** *n1*

service *n* (1) (*in church*) **okusaba** *n15*, **okusinza** *n15*, (*morning service*) **okusaba kw'enkya**, (*evening service*) **okusaba kw'akawungeezi**; (2) (*by a waiter*) **empeereza** *n9*; (3) (*eg. to the community*) **obuweereza** *n14*

serving (*helping of food*) *n* **olubega** *n11*   serving place (*for food*) **olujjuliro** *n11*   serving plate/leaf (*for dishing out matooke*) **akabezo** *n12*   full serving (*of food or drink*) **omusera** *n3*

sesame (*also* simsim) *n* **entungo** *n9*   sesame oil **amafuta g'entungo** *n6*   wild sesame **olutungotungo** *n11*, **ebitungotungo** *n8*

session (*eg. sitting*) *n* **olutuula** *n11*   in a work session **mu kafubo**

set *v* (1) (*of the sun*) *vi* **-gwa**, *eg. Enjuba egudde. ('The sun has set.')*; (2) (*put; place*) *vt* **-teeka**, *eg. Yakiteeka ku mmeeza. ('He set it on the table.')*; (3) (*a bone*) *vt* **-yunga**, *eg. Omuyunzi ayunze omukono. ('The bonesetter has set the arm.')*   set a dog on **-weerera** (*or* **-sindikira**) **embwa**   set a trap **-tega omutego**   set an examination **-tegeka ebibuuzo**   set down (*place down*) **-ssa wansi**   set fire to a house (*as arson*) **-yokerera**   set free (1) (*release*) **-ta**; (2) (*tethered or penned animal*) **-yimbula**   set money aside (*over a period of time, little by little*) **-sonda ssente**   set off (1) (*trap or spring*) **-masula**; (2) (*on a journey*) **-simbula**, *eg. Twasimbudde mu mmotoka. ('We set off in the car.')*   set off from (*on a journey*) **-simbuka**, *eg. Yasimbuka Kampala okugenda e Masaka. ('She set off from Kampala to go to Masaka.')*   set off on a journey **-situla**, *eg. Yasitula okugenda e Masaka ku makya. ('He set off to Masaka at dawn.'),* (*of a vehicle*) **-simbula**, *eg. Ebbaasi esimbula ku ssaawa ssatu. ('The bus sets off at 9 o'clock.')*   set right (*correct*) **-tereeza**   set (*someone*) straight (*show someone the right way to do things*) **-wabula**   set upright (*eg. post*) **-simba**   be set free (*released*) **-teebwa**   be set off (*of trap or spring*) **-masuka**

settle (*in a new place*) *vi* **-senga**, *eg. Yasenga ku kyalo. ('He has settled in the village.')*   settle a dispute between **-tabaganya**, *eg. Yagezaako okubatabaganya. ('He tried to settle their dispute.')*   settle affairs (*sort out problems*) **-tereeza** (*or* **-golola**) **ensonga**   settle down **-tereera**, *eg. Embeera mu Kampala eteredde. ('The situation in Kampala has settled down.')*   settle in a place for a long time **-siisira mu kifo**   be(come) settled (1) (*longer term; and peaceful, of a situation*) **-tebenkera**; (2) (*more immediate*) **-tereera**, *eg. Mutereere bulungi mu bifo byammwe tusimbule. ('Settle in your seats so we can set off.')*; (3) (*of a dispute*) **-weera**

settled *adj* (1) (*of a situation*) **-tebenkevu**; (2) (*of* the weather) **-kkakkamu**. See calm be(come) peaceful and settled (*of a person*) **-tebenkera** newly settled person (*at a place*) **omusenze** *n1* state of being newly settled **obusenze** *n14*

seven *num* **musanvu** seven hundred **lusanvu** seven thousand **kasanvu**

seventeen *num* **kkumi na musanvu**

seventh *adj* **-a omusanvu** (**N7.1**) Seventh-Day Adventist **Omuseveniside** *n1*, **Omwadiventi** *n1*

seventy *num* **ensanvu**

several *det*. Use **-weraako** ('*be quite a few*') in rel (**N7.1**), *eg*. Nnalaba bbaasi eziweraako. ('*I saw several buses.'*). See many; some

severe *adj*. Use adverb **ennyo** ('*very*'), *eg*. Omutwe gunnuma nnyo. ('*I have a severe headache.*')

severity (*harshness*) *n* **obukambwe** *n14*

sew *vt* **-tunga**. See stitch sew backstitch **-tunga kaddannyuma** sew for **-tungira**, *eg*. Yamutungira empale. ('*She sewed the trousers for him.*')

sewage *n* **kazambi** *n1*

sewer *n* (1) (*for waste*) **omufulejje gwa kazambi** *n3*; (2) (*person who sews clothes*) **omutunzi** *n1*

sewing machine *n* **ekyalaani** *n7*

sex be sexually unfaithful **-baliga** period of sexual abstinence (*for a man*) **ekiseera kya bwerende**. *Traditionally practiced when making barkcloth, beer or pottery, or when thatching.* sexual depravity **obukaba** *n14* sexual intercourse **okwegatta** *n15* sexual organs See private parts sexually depraved *adj* **-kaba**

¹**shade** (*also* shadow) *n* **ekisiikirize** *n7*

²**shade** *vt* **-siikiriza**

shaft (*of spear*) *n* **olunyago** *n11*

shake *v* (shook) **TRANSITIVE AND REFLEXIVE USES -nyeenya**, *eg*. Yanyeenya amatabi okufuna emiyembe. ('*He shook the branches to get the mangoes.*'), (*vigourously*) **-sinsimula**, (*make tremble, eg. caused by explosion*) **-jugumiza**, *eg*. Musisi yajugumiza ennyumba. ('*The earthquake shook the house.*'), (*forcefully, with swaying motion*) **-yuuguumya**, *eg*. Kibuyaga yayuuguumiza emiti egimu ne gigwa. ('*The gale shook the trees and caused some to fall.*'). See churn shake about **-suukunda**, *eg*. Emmotoka etusuukunze mu bisirikko. ('*The car shook us about on the rough road.*') shake from side to side (*as a tree in a gale*) **-yuuza** shake hands **-kwata mu ngalo** shake off **-kunkumula**, *eg*. Empewo ekunkumudde ebikoola okuva ku muti. ('*The wind is shaking leaves off the tree.*'), (*a liquid, sand, etc.*) **-sammula**, *eg*. Yasammula omusenyu okuva mu ngalo ze. ('*He shook the sand off his hands.*') shake off from oneself **-eekunkumulako**, *eg*. Embwa yeekunkumulako amazzi. ('*The dog is shaking off water.*') shake oneself **-eekunkumula** shake out wet clothes (*when putting them out to dry*) **-sinsimula engoye**

shake palm leaves (*on Palm Sunday*) **-nyeenya amatabi** shake water off one's hands **-eesammula amazzi** **INTRANSITIVE USES -jugumira**, *eg*. Ennyumba yajugumira nga musisi ayita. ('*The house shook in the earthquake.*'), (*with to and fro movement*) **-yuuguuma**. See quiver; shaky (be); shiver; sway; tremble; vibrate shake from side to side (*as a tree in a gale*) **-yuuga** shake with fear **-tiribira** be shaken about **-eesuukunda**, *eg*. Emmotoka yeesuukunda mu bisirikko. ('*The car was shaken about on the rough road.*') be shaken off (*of things*) **-kunkumuka**, *eg*. Ebikoola bikunkumuse ku muti. ('*The leaves are being shaken off the tree.*')

²**shaken** (*churned*) *adj* **-sunde**

shaker (*musical instrument; gourd containing seeds or stones*) *n* **ensaasi** *n9*. See rattle

shaking shaking disease (*Parkinson's disease*) **obulwadde bw'obuko** *n14*

shaky (*wobbly*) *adj* **yegeyege** (*invariable adjective*), *eg*. Ekikondo kiri yegeyege. ('*That post is shaky.*') be shaky **-nyeenya**, *eg*. Emmeeza enyeenya. ('*The table is shaky.*'), **-yuuga**, *eg*. Ekikondo kiyuuga. ('*The post is shaky.*'). See unstable

shall See will

sham *n* **ekikwangala** *n7*

¹**shame** *n* **ensonyi** *n9*. See disgrace feel shame **-kwatibwa ensonyi**, **-swala**

²**shame** *vt* **-kwasa ensonyi**, **-swaza**, *eg*. Musoke yamuggyamu essaati n'amuswaza mu bantu. ('*He removed Musoke's shirt and shamed him before the people.*'). See disgrace

shameful *adj* **-swavu**, **-a obuswavu**, *eg*. Kye yakola kya buswavu. ('*What he did is shameful.*'). See depraved; disgraceful shameful language (*profanities*) **ebyobugwemufu** *n8*

shape *n* (1) (*way something has been made*) **enkola** *n9*; (2) (*way something has grown*) **enkula** *n9*

shard (*curved fragment of pottery*) *n* **oluggyo** *n3*

¹**share** *n* **omugabo** *n3*, **omutemwa** *n3*, (*measured amount*) **omugereko** *n3*, (*for a chief; produce, or income from produce*) **endobolo** *n9*. See part; tythe shares (*in a company*) **emigabo** *n4*

²**share (with)** *vt* **-gabana**, *eg*. Njagala tugabane ekirabo kyange. ('*I want you to share my prize with me.*') share one's food with (1) (*a person, as a gesture of friendship or favour*) **-ddiza emmere**; (2) (*a little, especially with a child*) **-sunirako** share out (*distribute among*) **-gabanya**, *eg*. Yagabanya ssente n'azibawa. ('*He shared out the money and gave it to them.*') be shared by all (*everyone receives some*) **-buna**, *eg*. Emmere ebunye. ('*All got a share of the food.*')

sharp *adj* (1) (*of blade*) **-yogi**, *eg*. ekiso ekyogi ('*sharp knife*'); (2) (*of point*) **-songovu**. See clever

sharpen *vt* (1) (*blade*) **-wagala**; (2) (*point*) **-songola**

sharpened *adj*. Use **-sala** ('*cut*') in rel (**N7.1**), *eg*. enkumbi esala ('*sharpened hoe*')

sharpener *n* ekiwagala *n7*
sharpness *n* (1) (*of blade*) obwogi *n14*; (2) (*of point*) obusongovu *n14*
shatter *vt* -yasa, (*into many pieces*) -yasaayasa. *See* break; crumble   shatter with -yasisa, *eg. Ensuwa yagiyasisa jjinja. ('She shattered the pot with a stone.')*   be shattered (*into many pieces*) -yatikayatika
shattered *adj* -yatifu
shave *vt* -mwa, (*oneself*) -eemwa   shave off wood -walakata omuti   shave the head -walakata omutwe   have a close shave (*near miss*) -yita ku lugwanyu
shaving (*of wood, etc.*) *n* olubajjo *n11* (*small* akabajjo *n12*)
shawl *n* leesu *n9*
she *pro* ye. *The verb prefix is* a- (N15).
sheath (*eg. for dagger*) *n* ekiraato *n7*   sheath of banana leaf ekigogo *n7*, (*when used as a gutter*) olugogo *n11*
¹shed *n* (1) (*small building*) akayumba *n12*; (2) (*temporary construction*) ekidaala *n7*
²shed (*lose*) *vt* -suula, *eg. Omuti gusudde ebikoola. ('The tree is shedding leaves.')*   shed leaves (*of a tree*) -kunkumula ebikoola   shed tears -kulukusa amaziga   shed the skin (*of a snake*) -eeyubula
sheep *n* endiga *n9*
sheet *n* (1) (*for bed*) essuuka *n9*; (2) (*of paper*) olupapula *n11*   iron sheet ebbaati *n5*
shelf *n* essa *n5*. *See* rack
¹shell *n* (1) (*of egg*) ekisosonkole *n7*; (2) (*of pod or groundnut*) ekikuta *n7*; (3) (*of tortoise*) ekiwaawo *n7*; (4) (*of cowrie*) ensimbi *n9*   shell-shaped *adj* -a ekiwaawo   snail shell essonko *n5*
²shell (*eg. peas*) *vt* -susa
¹shelter *n* (1) (*of grass, branches, etc., eg. for an overnight when travelling*) ekikaabugo *n7*; (2) (*temporary construction*) ekisaakaate *n7*; (3) (*temporary construction, eg. made for an event*) ekidaala *n7*; (4) (*for barkcloth making*) ekkomagiro *n5*. *See* refuge; sanctuary
²shelter *vi* (1) (*from rain*) -eggama, *eg. Beggama enkuba wansi w'omuti. ('They sheltered from the rain under a tree.')*; (2) (*from sun or rain*) -eewogoma. *See* avoid; dodge
shepherd *n* omusumba *n1*
¹shield *n* engabo *n9*
²shield *vt* (1) (*someone from danger*) -taasa; (2) (*someone from blame*) -zibira, -bikkirira   shield oneself (*eg. from a spear thrust*) -eewoma
¹shift (*in a work schedule*) *n* oluwalo *n11*. *See* turn
²shift *v* (1) *vi* -seeseetuka, *eg. Omugugu guseeseetuse ku katanda. ('The luggage has shifted on the roof-rack.')*; (2) *vt* -seeseetula, *eg. Aseeseetula omugugu ku katanda. ('He is shifting the position of the luggage on the roof-rack.')*. *See* move   shift aside (*to make room*) (1) (*of oneself*) *vi* -seetuka, *eg. Yaseetuse omwana atuule. ('He*

shifted aside to let the child sit.')*; (2) (*move someone or something*) *vt* -seetula, *eg. Yaseetula emigugu okufuna ebbanga. ('He shifted the luggage to make space.')*
shilling *n* essiringi *n9. The following are slang*: one thousand shillings olwasa *n11*, ten thousand shillings omuda *n3*, two hundred shilling coin ekido *n7*, engege *n9*.
shine *v* (shone) **TRANSITIVE USES** (1) (*polish*) -nyiriza; (2) (*metal, eg. silver*) -zigula   shine a torch -kuba (*or* -mulisa) ttooci   shine shoes -kuba ku ngatto eddagala   **INTRANSITIVE USES** (1) (*of a light or the sun*) -yaka, *eg. Omusana gwaka. ('The sun is shining.')*; (2) (*very hotly, of the sun*) -eeberengula; (3) (*on and off, as a firefly*) -munyeenya. *See* glisten; sparkle
shininess *n* obunyirivu *n14*
²shiny *adj* -nyirivu   shiny material olugoye olumasamasa *n11*   be shiny (1) (*polished*) -nyirira, *eg. Engatto zinyiridde. ('The shoes are shined.')*; (2) (*sparkly*) -masamasa, -tangalijja; (3) (*glossy*) -nyereketa, -nyerettuka
¹ship *n* emmeeri *n9*, (*types with sails; dhow*) ekyombo *n7*. *See* boat; canoe; ferry
²ship (*goods*) *vt* -tambuza
shirt *n* essaati *n9*   T-shirt ekijoozi *n7*, omujoozi *n3*
¹shit (*impolite*) *n* amazi *n6* (*impolite*). *See* droppings; excrement
²shit (*impolite*) *vi* -nya (*impolite*). *See* lavatory (go to the)
shiver *vi* (1) (*uncontrollably, eg. from cold or illness*) -tintima, *eg. Yali atintima olw'obunnyoguvu. ('He was shivering from the cold.')*; (2) (*potentially can be controlled*) -kankana, -tiribira. *See* shake; tremble
¹shock *n* ensisi *n9. See* fright   go into shock -funa (*or* -gwamu) ensisi, (*with the heart racing*) emmeeme -tyemuka, *eg. Emmeeme yantyemuse. ('I went into shock.')*
²shock *vt* -eesisiwaza, -kutula omutima, *eg. Kyankutula omutima. ('It shocked me.')*, (*causing the heart to race*) -tyemula emmeeme. *See* dumbfound; panic; repulse; startle   be shocked (*startled; taken aback*) -eesisiwala, *eg. Nneesisiwala okulaba ebiwundu bye. ('I was shocked to see his injuries.')*, (*with the heart racing*) omutima -tyemuka   shocking event ekikangabwa *n7*
shoe *n* engatto *n9*, (*canvas*) engatto ya lusejjera, (*high-heeled*) engatto y'akakondo, (*type of wooden shoe; clog*) omukalabanda *n3*, (*slipper*) essapatu *n9*   shoe brush bulaasi y'engatto *n9*   shoe lace akaguwa k'engatto *n12*   shoe polish eddagala ly'engatto *n5*   shoe repairer omukozi w'engatto *n1*, (*one who sews*) omutunzi w'engatto *n1*
shoebill (*type of bird*) *n* bbuulwe *n9*
shoelace *n* akaguwa k'engatto *n12*

shoeshiner

shoeshiner *n* **omukubi w'engatto** *n1*
shone *See* shine
shoo away *vt* **-siiya**
shook *See* shake
¹**shoot** (*of a plant*) *n* (1) **endokwa** *n9*, **ensibuka** *n9*;
(2) (*of banana plant*) **endukusa** *n9*, **ensukusa** *n9*,
(*of very young beer banana plant*)
akasukwasukwa *n12*. *See* bud side-shoot
akawakatirwa *n12* trailing shoot (*especially of
sweet potato*) **omulanda** *n3*
²**shoot** (*eg. a gun*) **-lasa**. *See* hurl; produce shoots;
sling shoot a gun **-lasa** (*or* **-kuba**, *or* **-teeba**)
emmundu shoot an arrow **-lasa** (*or* **-sindika**)
akasaale shoot at (*someone running away, with a
gun*) **-wereekereza amasasi** shoot at goal **-teeba
eggoolo**
shooter *n* **omuteebi** *n1*
shooting (*sound of*) *n* **omusinde gw'emmundu** *n3*
shooting star **kibonoomu** *n1*
¹**shop** *n* **edduuka** *n5*, (*on the pavement*) **edduuka
ery'oku lubalaza**
²**shop (for)** *vit* **-gula**, *eg. Yagenze okugula engatto
leero. ('He went shopping for shoes today.')*
shopkeeper *n* **ow'edduuka** *n1*
shopping *n* **okugula** *n15* shopping bag (*large
woven type*) **ekikapu** *n7*
shore *n* **olubalama** *n11*
short *adj* **-mpi** be(come) short **-yimpawala** in
short (*in brief*) **mu bumpimpi, mu bufunze**
shortage *n* **ebbula** *n5* be short of (*lacking*)
-bulawo, *eg. Wabulawo entebe bbiri. ('We are
short of too chairs.')*, **-buzaayo**, *eg. Tubuzaayo
entebe bbiri. ('We are short of two chairs.')*
shorten *vt* **-yimpawaza, -kendeeza obuwanvu**
shortly (*soon*) *adv* **mangu**
shorts (*trousers*) *n* **empale ennyimpi** *n9*
shot (*from a gun*) *n* **emmundu** *n9*
should *aux v* **-saana**, *eg. Tusaana okugenda
okumulaba. ('We should go and see her.')*, **-gwana**
shoulder *n* **ekibegabega** *n7* shoulder blade (*of
cow*) **enkwakwa** *n9* carry on the shoulders (*a
person*) **-kongojja** throw over the shoulder (*a
garment*) **-eesuulira**
¹**shout (of approval)** *n* **omuzira** *n3*
²**shout** *vi* **-woggana, -leekaana**. *See* din (make a);
noise (make)
shouting *n* **okuwoggana** *n15*, **okuleekaana** *n15*.
See din
shove (*push*) *vt* **-sindika** shove in (*cram into*)
-kkatira
¹**shovel** *n* **ekitiiyo** *n7*
²**shovel (up)** *vt* **-yoola**
¹**show** *n* (1) (*exhibition*) **omwoleso** *n3*; (2) (*festival;
performance*) **ekivvulu** *n7*
²**show** *vt* **-laga**, *eg. Yandaga ennimiro ye. ('She
showed me her garden.')*. *See* exhibit show
disrespect towards **-yisa amaaso** show from a
distance **-lengeza** show how **-lagirira**, *eg.*

*Yandagirira okufumba. ('He showed me how to
cook.')* show off **-eeraga**, (*wanting to be praised*)
-kola bampaane show (*someone*) the right way to
do things **-wabula** showing-off **ekikolwa ekya
bampaane**
shower (*rain*) *n* **enkuba** *n9*
shred *vt* **-yuzaayuza**, *eg. Empewo eyuzizzayuzizza
ebendera. ('The wind has shredded the flag.')*. *See*
fray be shredded **-yulikayulika**
shrewd *adj* **-kalabakalaba, -gezigezi** shrewd
person **omukalabakalaba** *n1*
shrewdness *n* **obukalabakalaba** *n14*
shrine (*of a lubaale; temple*) *n* **ekiggwa** *n7*, **essabo**
n5 personal shrine **essabo ly'ssekinnoomu**
shrink *vi* **-eetugga**
shrivel (*of a plant*) *vi* **-wotoka**
shrivelled (*of a plant*) *adj* **-wotofu**
shroud (*burial cloth*) *n* **looti** *n9*
shrug the shoulders **-wanika ebibegabega**
shudder with shock *vi* **-eesisiwala**
shuffle cards **-canga caanisi**
shun *vt* **-eewala**, (*a family member*) **-boola**. *See*
distance oneself
¹**shut** *adj* **-ggale**
²**shut** (*door, shop, etc.*) *vt* **-ggala** (*often with enclitic*
-wo *N24.2*) shut in (*eg. dog in kennel*) **-ggalira**
shut one's mouth **-buniza emimwa** shut oneself
in **-eggalira** be shut in (*confined*) **-sibwa**
shutter release (*of camera*) *n* **emmanduso** *n9*
shy *adj* **-a ensonyi** feel shy **-kwatibwa ensonyi**.
See avoid look shy **-sonyiwala**, (*coy*) **-loola**
shyness *n* **ensonyi** *n10* huddle up through shyness
-eekomomma
sick *adj* **-lwadde**. *See* ill; sickly sick person
omulwadde *n1*, (*very*) **omuyi** *n1* be sick (1) (*ill*)
-lwala; (2) (*vomit*) **-sesema**. *See* emaciated; retch
be sick of **-eetamwa**, *Nneetamiddwa okulya
lumonde buli lunaku. ('I am sick of eating potatoes
every day.')* cause to be sick (*make vomit*)
-sesemya feel sick (*nauseous*) **emmeeme**
-sinduukirira (*with personal object*), *eg. Bwe
ntambulira mu bbaasi emmeeme ensinduukirira.
('When I travel by bus I feel sick.')*, **emmeeme**
-siikuuka make feel sick **-sinduukiriza**
emmeeme, *eg. Emmere yatusinduukiriza
emmeeme. ('The food made us feel sick.')*
sicken *vt* **-tama**, *eg. Okulya lumonde buli lunaku
kuntamye. ('Eating potatoes every day sickens
me.')*
sickle *n* **nnajjolo** *n9*. *See* slasher sickle cell disease
siiko-seero *n9*
sickly (*weak and lethargic*) *adj* **-yongobevu**. *See* ill
sickly person **omuyongobevu** *n1* be sickly
-yongobera become sickly and thin (*emaciated*)
-nyaaluka
sickness *n* **obulwadde** *n14*
side *n* **oludda** *n11*, *eg. oludda lw'ennyumba ('side of
the house')*, **oluuyi** *n11*, (*left or right, contrasted*

now she is silent.')

silently *adv* **kasirise**

silk *n* **liiri** *n9*   silk cotton tree *(kapok tree; Ceiba)* **kifampa** *n1*, **kifamba** *n1*, **omufampa** *n3*, **omuti gwa ppamba** *n3*. *The fibre from this tree is called* **ffampa** *n1* (*or* **ppamba** *n1*).

silkworm *n* **akasaanyi (akakola engoye)** *n12*

silly *(of a person) adj* **-siru**. *See* stupid

silver *n* **ffeeza** *n9*

similarity *(likeness) n* **enfaanana** *n9*   be similar to **-faanana**, *eg. Ebendera eno efaanana eyo. ('This flag is similar to that.'). See* like (be); match

simple *adj* **-yangu**

simpleton *n* **omubuyabuya** *n1*

simsim *See* sesame

simulium *(type of biting fly) n* **embwa** *n9*

¹sin *n* **ekibi** *n7*

²sin *vi* **-yonoona**

since *conj* REFERRING TO REASON **nga ... bwe (N27)**, *eg. Nga omuti bwe guli ogumu tetugutema. ('Since there is only one tree, let's not fell it.'), (in the sense of allowing something to be done)* **-gidde ... gira** *(both '-gidde' and 'gira' being followed by verbs in the subjunctive N17), eg. Ogidde ojje gira twale obuliri ffembi. ('Since you have come, we can make the bed together.')* REFERRING TO TIME (1) **kasookedde**, *eg. Kasookedde nzija wano simulabanga. ('Since I came here, I have not seen him.'); (2) (referring to a particular day; ever since)* **okuva lwe**, *eg. Okuva lwe yatuuka, abadde mulwadde. ('Since he arrived here he has been ill.'); (3) (referring to a particular time)* **okuva ku**, *eg. Okuva ku Mmande enkuba ebadde etonnya. ('It has been raining since Monday.')*

sinfulness *n* **obwonoonyi** *n14*

sing *vt* **-yimba**, *(in a traditional way; clearly and pleasantly)* **-yimba n'eggono**, *(in a loud clear voice)* **-kooka**, *(vibrato)* **-yimba n'eddoboozi eritiribira obulungi**

singe *(eg. banana leaves to soften them) vt* **-babula**. *See* scorch   be singed **-babuka**

singed *adj* **-babule**. *See* scorched

singer *n* **omuyimbi** *n1*

singing *n* **okuyimba** *n15*

single. *See* one   a single *adj* (1) *Use* **-mu -okka** *('one only') (with numeral and pronominal concords respectively N4.2), eg. ente emu yokka ('a single cow'); (2) (of certain consumables, eg. food, cigarettes) Use* **omunwe** *n3 ('unit'), eg. omunwe gwa muwogo ('a single tuber of cassava')*

singly *(one-by-one, of people) adv* **kinnoomu**

¹sink *(basin) n* **sinki** *n9*

²sink *(become submerged) vi* **-bbira**

sinner *n* **omwonoonyi** *n1*

sip *vt* **-wuuta**. *See* drink

sir *n* **ssebo** *n1*. *See* honourable

sisal *n* (1) *(plant)* **ekigoogwa** *n7*; (2) *(fibre)*

---

with front or back) **obukiika** *n14*, *eg. obukiika bwa kkono ('left side')*   side dish *(served with the main food 'emmere')* **enva** *n10*, *(greens)* **enva endiirwa**   side of house *(outer edge)* **olusebenju** *n11*   side-shoot *(of plant)* **akawakatirwa** *n12*   at/to the side **wabbali**, *eg. Ebintu biteeke wabbali. ('Put the things to the side.'),* **ebbali, emabbali**. *See* beside   at/to the side of **wabbali wa, ebbali wa**, *eg. ebbali w'oluguudo ('at the side of the road'),* **ku mabbali ga**   go to the side **-dda ebbali**   left side **omukono ogwa ddyo**   on both sides **erudda n'erudda, eruuyi n'eruuyi**   on the other side of **ku ludda olulala lwa**, *(at a distance, eg. over a valley or swamp)* **emitala wa**, *eg. Ennyumba ye eri mitala wa kisenyi. ('His house is on the other side of the swamp.')*   other side of a hill **enzivuunuko** *n9*   right side **omukono ogwa kkono**   to the side **erudda**

side with *(support) vt* **-wagira**, *eg. Mu kulonda nnawagira Musoke. ('I sided with Musoke in the election.')*

sideline *(a family member) vt* **-boola**

sideways *adv* **obukiika**   place sideways **-kiika**   place oneself sideways **-eekiika**, *eg. Yatudde yeekiise. ('He is sitting sideways.')*

siege to, lay *vt* **-zingiza**

siesta *n* **eggandaalo** *n5*   take a siesta **-eebakako emisana**

¹sieve *n* **ekikuŋŋunta** *n7* *(small* **akakuŋŋunta** *n12)*. *See* filter

²sieve *(also* sift*) vt* **-kuŋŋunta**. *See* filter

siftings *(larger pieces of groundnuts, etc., remaining after pounding or sieving) n* **empulunguse** *n10*. *See* shell

¹sigh *n* **ekikkowe** *n7*

²sigh *vi* **-ssa ekikkowe**

sight *n* **okulaba** *n15*   grow dim *(of sight)* **amaaso -yimbaala**   lose one's sight **-ziba amaaso**   poor sight *(misted eyes)* **ekifu ku maaso** *n7*   regain one's sight **-zibuka amaaso**   restore sight to **-zibula amaaso**

¹sign *(notice; poster) n* **ekipande** *n7* *(small* **akapande** *n12)*. *See* logo; signal   road sign **akapande k'oluguudo**

²sign *(write one's name) vt* **-ssaako** *(or* **-teekako**) **omukono**. *See* signal

¹signal *n* **akabonero** *n12*

²signal (to) *(beckon) vt* **-wenya**. *See* touch; wink

significance *(meaning) n* **amakulu** *n6*

signify *(mean) vt* **-tegeeza**. *See* mean

Sikh *n* **Omusingasinga** *n1*

¹silence *(period of) n* **akasiriikiriro** *n12*. *See* quiet   absolutely silent   be cce, *eg. Abaana babadde basirise be cce. ('The children were absolutely silent.')*

²silence *vt* **-sirisa**

silent *adj* **-sirifu**   be(come) silent **-sirika**, *eg. Yali ayogera naye kati asirise. ('She was talking but*

obugoogwa *n14*

sister *n* (1) (*female blood relative in general*)
ow'oluganda *n1*, (*having the same mother*)
ow'enda emu *n1*; (2) (*religious*) omubiikira *n1*.
Sisters of females are **muganda** (*with pos* **N12**), *eg.*
muganda wange ('*my sister'*). *Sisters of males*
(*having the same mother*) *are*: my sister
mwannyinaze, your sister **mwannyoko**, his sister
mwannyina, *etc.* (*stem* **mwannyi- N12**).

sister-in-law (*of a man*) *n* mulamu *n1* (*with pos*
N12), *eg.* mulamu wange ('*my sister-in-law'*)

sit *vi* (sat) -tuula, (*with legs apart*) -tuula -eebamba,
(*on the edge of a chair*) -tuula ku kapapajjo, (*with*
legs crossed above the knee) -tuula -salako, *eg.*
Ntudde nsazeeko. ('*I am sitting with legs crossed.'*),
(*upright*) -tuula -tereera. *The following refer to*
sitting positions on the ground: (*reclining on one*
elbow) -simba olukokola, (*supported on one arm*)
-simba olukono, (*with legs extended*) -tuula
-lannama, *eg. Atudde alannamye.* ('*He is sitting*
with legs extended.'), (*with legs spread widely*
apart) -tuula -leeguula, *eg. Yatudde ng'aleegudde*
amagulu ge. ('*He sat with legs spread widely*
apart.'), (*with crossed legs, or in yoga position*)
-gombeza amagulu. sit an examination -tuula
ebibuuzo sit at one's ease (*settled down*) -kkalira
be sat on -tuulwako

sitatunga *n* enjobe *n9*

site (*place*) *n* ekifo *n7*. See landing site

sitting (*session*) *n* olutuula *n11*. See sit sitting
room eddiiro *n5*

situate *vi.* Use -li *or* -ba ('*be'*) according to tense
(**N20.1**), *eg. (1) Ennyumba eri ku lusozi.* ('*The*
house is situated on the hill.'); *(2) Emmeeza ejja*
kuba bweru. ('*The table will be situated outside.'*).
See place; put

situation *n* embeera *n9* difficult (*or* tight) situation
akanyigo *n12*

six *num* mukaaga six hundred lukaaga six
thousand kakaaga

sixteen *num* kkumi na mukaaga

sixth *adj/num* -a omukaaga (**N7.1**)

sixty *num* enkaaga *n9*

size (*bigness*) *n* obunene *n14*, *eg. Twagala*
okumanya obunene bw'ennyumba. ('*We want to*
know the size of the house.'). *For questions, use*
-yenkana wa? ('*be equal to what?'*), *eg.*
Ennyumba yenkana wa? ('*What size is the*
house?').

sizzle *vi* -saala

skeleton (*bones*) *n* amagumba *n6*

¹sketch (*drawing*) *n* ekifaananyi *n7*

²sketch (*draw*) *vt* -kuba ekifaananyi

skewer *n* omusito *n3*, oluti *n11*

skid *vi* -seerera

skilful *adj* (1) (*gained through experience*)
-manyirivu; (2) (*adroit*) -jagujagu; (3) (*expert*)
-kugu

skill *n* (1) (*gained through experience*)
obumanyirivu *n14*; (2) (*expertise*) obukugu *n14*

skim off (*eg. cream*) *vt* -ggyako

¹skin *n* (1) (*of the body*) (*of a person*) olususu *n11*,
(*of an animal*) eddiba *n5*, (*thick and fatty, eg. of a*
pig) ekigodo *n7*; (2) (*of a fruit*) ekikuta *n7*; (3)
(*formed on gravy, milk, etc.*) olububi *n11* (*thin, eg.*
membrane) akabubi *n12*). See crust. *An animal*
skin, as formerly used as clothing, is known as: (1)
(*stiff type, worn by the common people*) koppe *n1*;
(2) (*soft, prepared by careful scraping*) eddiba
ekkunye *n5*. *Types of skin condition include*:
(*moist and healthy*) olususu olunyirivu, (*dry*)
olususu olusiiwuufu, (*greasy*) olususu
olunyerettufu. cast-off skin of snake ekiyubwe
n7 form a skin (1) (*on gravy, milk, etc.*) -kwata
olububi; (2) (*on left-over matooke*) -bembeera
loose skin at base of finger nail akatakkuluze *n12*
patch of different coloured skin ekibambya *n7*
peeling skin (*of a person*) olukuta *n11*

²skin (*an animal*) *vt* -baaga

skin condition (*also* skin disease) *n*. *Types include*:
(1) (*rash with small swellings*) obutulututtu *n14*
(*one patch akatulututtu n12*); (2) (*with spaced-out*
itchy swellings, as with chickenpox) obutuulituuli
n14, (*with larger sized swellings*) ebituulituuli *n8*;
(3) (*with small, closely spaced swellings*) olusolo
n11; (4) (*circular rash with discoloured skin,*
caused by fungal infection) ebiyobyo *n8*; (5)
(*urticaria; caused by allergic reaction*)
ebirogologo *n8*; (6) (*ringworm of the head*)
ebiguuna *n8* (*one patch ekiguuna n7*); (7)
(*ringworm of the body, contagious*) oluwumu *n11*;
(8) (*cracked sole of the foot*) enkyakya *n10*; (9)
(*roughness and irritation of skin, caused by*
shaving) ebisukko *n8*; (10) (*painful cut, especially*
between fingers or toes) ensalika *n9*; (11)
(*athlete's foot*) obugeregere *n14*; (12) (*dry flaky*
place on skin) ebikakampa *n8*; (13) (*itchy patches*
on skin; also 'mange' of dogs) olukuku *n11*; (14)
(*causes severe scratching*) ekyeyago *n7*. See acne;
blister; boil; dandruff; eczema; itch; measles;
pimple; wart develop a skin rash butuka, (*with*
measles) -yiwa

skink (*red and black type*) *n* embalasaasa *n9*

skip *v* (1) (*with a rope*) *vi* -buuka omuguwa; (2)
(*jump over*) *vt* -buukawo, *eg. Omusomesa yagenda*
agaba ekkalaamu mu kibiina nga abuukawo
omwana omu. ('*The teacher gave out pencils to the*
class, skipping every other child.') skip a day (*or*
regular activity) -yosa, *eg. Ku lwokubiri yayosa*
teyajja kukola. ('*He skipped a day and did not*
come to work on Tuesday.')

skirt *n* sikaati *n9*, (*of palm fibre, worn by dancers*)
ekisenso *n7* mini-skirt akateeteeyi ak'enkuggu
n12

skull *n* ekiwanga *n7*, (*of a dead person*) oluwanga
n11

sky *n* eggulu *n5*. *See* space

slack (*loose*) *adj* -lebevu. *See* lazy   be(come) slack -lebera, *eg. Omuguwa gulebedde. ('The rope is slack.'),* (*loose-fitting, eg. of cloths*) -sagala. *See* deflated (become)

slacken *vt* -lebeza, *eg. Alebezezza omuguwa. ('She has slackened the rope.'),* -legulula. *See* loosen; pressure off (take)

slackness (*looseness*) *n* obulevevu *n14*

slag (*waste from iron smelting*) *n* amatale *n6*

¹slander *n* akalebule *n12*

²slander (*also* malign) *vt* -lebula. *See* accuse falsely

slanderer *n* ow'akalebule *n1*

slanderous *adj* -a akalebule

slant *v* (1) *vi* -eewunzika, *eg. Eddaala lyewunzise. ('The ladder is slanting.'),* -eesulika; (2) *vt* -wunzika, *eg. Awunzika omutwe. ('He is slanting his head.'),* -sulika

¹slap *n* oluyi *n11*

²slap *vt* -kuba oluyi, (*hard*) -bambika oluyi

slapdash way, do in a *vt* -jabula

slash (*vegetation*) *vt* -saawa   area of slashed vegetation awasaawe *n16*

slasher (*for cutting vegetation*) *n* oluso olusaawa *n11*. *See* sickle

slat (*on roof, for attaching tiles or iron sheets*) *n* eŋŋanzikiro *n9*

slate (*for writing on*) *n* ejjinja *n5*

slaughter (*an animal*) *vt* -baaga. *See* kill   slaughtering place ebbaagiro *n5*. *See* abattoir

slaughterer (*of animals*) *n* omubaazi *n1*

slave *n* omuddu *n1*   slave trader omusuubuzi w'abantu *n1*

slavery *n* obuddu *n14*   slaving expedition ekiwendo ky'abasuubuzi b'abantu *n7*

slay *vt* -tta

¹sleep *n* otulo *n13*   illness marked by tendency to sleepiness akasumagizi *n12*

²sleep *vi* -eebaka, *eg. Yeebase. ('She is sleeping.'),* (*briefly; nap*) -eebakako. *See* doze off   be sleepy -bongoota, -wulira otulo   be unable to sleep -bulwa otulo   put to sleep -eebasa, *eg. Nneebasizza omwana. ('I have put the baby to sleep.')*   rock a baby to sleep -siisiitira omwana

sleeping sickness *n* mmongoota *n1*

sleepy *adj* -eebafu

sleeve *n* omukono *n3*, *eg. omukono gw'essaati ('shirt sleeve')*

slender *adj* -tono

¹slice *n* ekiwayi *n7*, (*smaller or longer*) oluwayi *n11*   slices of dried food (*of root crops, for storage*) endere *n10*, *eg. endere za lumonde ('dried sliced potatoes')*

²slice *vt* -salaasala

slide *vi* -seerera, *eg. Emmotoka yaseerera ku luguudo. ('The car slid on the road.')*   slide along (*to make room*) (1) (*of oneself*) -seetuka; (2) (*someone or something*) -seetula

sliding (*down a steep slope on a banana stem 'omugogo', a game played by children*) *n* gogola *n1*

slightly *adv* katono

slim *adj* -tono   grow slim -toniwa. *See* weight (lose)

slime *n* ennaanu *n10*   be slimy -naanuuka

¹sling *n* (1) (*for slinging stones*) envuumuulo *n9*; (2) (*for carrying bundle on shoulder*) olwambalizo *n11*

²sling *vt* -vuumuula, *eg. Yavuumuula ejjinja ne likuba embwa. ('He slung the stone and hit a dog.'). See* hurl; throw   sling with a catapult -lasa butida

¹slip (*cutting of a plant*) *n* endokwa *n9*   slips of sweet potatoes (*for planting*) amalagala *n6* (*one omuko gw'amalagala n3*)

²slip (*on the ground*) *vi* -seerera   slip aside *See* shift   slip away (*sneak off*) -ebba, (*as a snake*) -eemulula   slip from one's grasp (*eg. of a dog*) -sumattuka   slip into (1) (*sneak into*) -sensera, *eg. Ekibe kyasensera mu kisaka. ('The jackal slipped into the bush.');* (2) (*push into; insert*) -sonseka; (3) (*of oneself, eg. of a snake into a hole*) -eesonseka. *See* enter   slip on(to) the body (*shoe, bracelet, etc.*) -naanika   slip oneself free eesumattula, *eg. Embwa yeesumattudde ku lujegere. ('The dog has slipped its leash.')*   slip out (*eg. item from bundle*) *vi* -sowoka. *See* pull out; reveal   slip over (*make a false step while walking, the foot slipping to one side*) -neguka

slipper (*flip-flop*) *n* ssapatu *n9*

slipperiness *n* obuseerezi *n14*

slippery *adj* -seerevu   slippery place akaseerezi *n12*   be slippery -seerera   make slippery -seereza

slit *vt* -sala

slither along (*as a snake*) *vi* -eewalula

¹slobber *n* engeregeze *n10*

²slobber *vi* -geregeza

slogan *n* eŋŋombo *n9*

slope (*also* incline) *n* (1) (*downward*) akaserengeto *n12*; (2) (*upward*) akasozi *n12*   go down a slope -serengeta   go up a slope -yambuka

sloth (*laziness*) *n* obugayaavu *n14*

slothful (*lazy*) *adj* -gayaavu

slough the skin -eeyubula, *eg. Omusota gweyubudde. ('A snake has sloughed its skin.')*

¹slow *adj*. *Use* empola ('*slowly*'), *eg. omuntu ayiga empola ('a slow learner')*   person slow at doing things ow'olulembe *n1*, ow'olukobo *n1*

²slow (down) (*eg. a vehicle*) *vt* -kendeeza sipiidi

slowly *adv* (1) empola, *eg. Azimba ennyumba ye mpola. ('He is building his house slowly.');* (2) (*in doing things*) n'olusoobo, *eg. Akola n'olusoobo. ('He works slowly.');* (3) *Use* -sooba ('*move slowly*') *as aux v* (**N19**), *eg. Akola asooba. ('She works slowly.'). See* endlessly

slowness (*in doing things*) *n* olulembe *n11*, olusoobo *n11*, olukobo *n11*, *eg. Alina olukobo. ('She is slow in doing things.')*   be deliberate and slow in one's actions **-eerembereza**

slug *n* **ekkovu** *n5*   be sluggish *(in one's movements)* **-sooba**

slumber *(sleep)* *vi* **-eebaka**

slurp *(eat or drink noisily)* *vt* **-solobeza**

sly *adj* **-kalabakalaba**, **-gezigezi**

smack *vt* **-kuba**, *eg. Yamukuba ku ttama. ('She smacked him on the cheek.')*

small *adj* **-tono**, *(very)* **-sirikitu**   become smaller **-toniwa**   make smaller **-toniya**   rather small **-tonotono**   something very small **akasirikitu** *n12*

smallness *n* **obutono** *n14*

smallpox *n* **kawaali** *n1*

¹smart *adj* (1) *(attractive)* **-nyirivu**; (2) *(clever)* **-gezi**   look smart **-nyirira**   smarten (up) **-nyiriza**   smarten oneself up **-eenyiriza**

²smart *(sting)* *vi* **-balagala**. *A person concerned can be indicated by an object pronoun, eg. Amaaso gambalagala. ('My eyes are smarting.').* make smart **-balagala**, *eg. Ssabbuuni ambalagala mu maaso. ('The soap is making my eyes smart.')*

smarting *(stinging)* *adj* **-balagavu**

smartness *(attractiveness)* *n* **obunyirivu** *n14*

smash *vt* (1) *(shatter)* **-yasa**, *eg. Ayasizza ensuwa. ('He has smashed the pot.')*; (2) *(eg. car in an accident)* **-sesebbula**. *See* break; crumple up   be(come) smashed (1) *(shattered, eg. of a pot)* **-yatika**; (2) *(eg. of a car in an accident)* **-sesebbuka**

smashed *adj* (1) *(shattered, eg. of a pot)* **-yatifu**; (2) *(eg. of a car in an accident)* **-sesebbufu**. *See* crumpled up

smear *vt* **-siiga**, *(oil or butter on body)* **-saaba**. *See* cover   smear cow dung *(on earth floor)* **-maala obusa**   smear on too much **-metta**, *(on oneself)* **-eemetta**   smear oneself (with) *(eg. ointment)* **-eesiiga**   be(come) smeared **-siigibwa**

¹smell *(also odour)* *n* (1) *(as produced)* **ekiwunya** *n7*; (2) *(the way something smells)* **empunya** *n9*. *The following are types of smell:* (1) *(pleasant, eg. perfume)* **akawoowo** *n12*, **akaloosa** *n12*; (2) *(pleasant, of food, especially of sauce 'enva')* **eggwoowo** *n5*; (3) *(bad body odour)* **olusu** *n11*; (4) *(stink, eg. of rot or drain)* **ekivundu** *n7*; (5) *(of burning from metal saucepan)* **ebbabe** *n5*; (6) *(of burning flesh or fur)* **evvumbe** *n5*; (7) *(musky, eg. of python or male goat)* **ekkalalume** *n5*; (8) *(of water pot 'ensuwa' that has been prepared for keeping water; also palatable smell of food, especially of sauce 'enva' containing mushrooms)* **omuga** *n3*; (9) *(of metal saucepan not washed properly)* **oluwugge** *n11*.   omit an offensive smell **-cuuma**, *eg. Omudumu gwa kazambi ogwabise gucuuma. ('The burst sewage pipe is omitting an offensive smell.')*

²smell *v* (1) *(have a smell)* *vi* **-wunya**, *eg. Ente ziwunya. ('The cows smell.')*; (2) *(act of smelling)* *vt* **-wunyirwa**, *eg. Mpunyirwa ente. ('I smell*

cows.'). *See* sniff   smell to **-wunyira**, *eg. Embwa empunyira bubi. ('The dog smells bad to me.')*

smelt *(ore, to obtain metal)* *vt* **-saanuusa**

¹smile *n* **akamwenyumwenyu** *n12*

²smile *vi* **-mwenya**, *(often)* **-mwenyamwenya**

smith *(blacksmith)* *n* **omuweesi** *n1*

¹smoke *n* **omukka** *n3*

²smoke *v* TRANSITIVE USES **-koomera**, *(meat or fish)* **-kalirira**, *(tobacco)* **-fuuwa**, **-nywa**, **-fuuweeta**   smoke a pipe **-fuuweeta emmindi**   smoke barkcloth *(to give it a good smell)* **-koomera** *(or* **-nyookeza***)* **embugo**, *(with omugavu wood)* **-koomera embugo n'omugavu**   smoke new water pot *(to prepare it for use)* **-nyookeza ensuwa**   smoke out a pit latrine *(to drive away smells)* **-nyookeza akayu**   smoke out bees **-nyookeza enjuki**   INTRANSITIVE USES *(of a fire)* **-nyooka**   be smoked **-komerwa**, *eg. Embugo tezoozebwa naye zikoomerwa okwongeramu akawoowo. ('Barkcloth is not washed but smoked.' – imparts a good odour)*

smoker *n* (1) *(of tobacco)* **omunywi wa taaba** *n1*; (2) *(of cigarettes)* **omufuuyi wa ssigala** *n1*; (3) *(of cannabis)* **omuyaga** *n1*, **omuyaaye** *n1*

smooth *(to the touch)* *adj* **-weeevu**   be smooth **-weeera**   make smooth **-weeeza**. *See* sandpaper

smoothness *n* **obuweweevu** *n14*

smoulder *vi* **-nyooka**

SMS *n* **eseemwesi** *n9*

smuggle *vt* **-kukusa**

snack(s) *n* **obumpwankipwaki** *n14*

snail *n* **ekkovu** *n9*   snail shell **essonko** *n5*

snake *n* **omusota** *n3*, *(poisoness)* **omusota gw'obutwa**. *Types include:* (1) *(small green type)* **nnawandagala** *n1*; (2) *(puff adder; Gabon viper)* **essalambwa** *n9*; (3) *(python)* **ttimba** *n1*; (4) *(cobra)* **enswera** *n9*; (5) *(long poisonous type, rare; possibly mamba)* **olubirango** *n11*; (6) *(blind)* **nnamugoya** *n1*; (7) *(small poisonous type)* **empiri** *n9*.

snap (off) *v* TRANSITIVE USES **-wogola**, *eg. Bwe yanoga omuyembe yawogola ettabi. ('When he picked the mango, he snapped off the branch.')*. *See* break; detach   snap off cob *(from maize stalk)* **-nuula kasooli**   snap off maize grains *(from cob)* **-kongola kasooli**   snap open noisily **-bandula**   snap the fingers **-kuba entoli**   INTRANSITIVE USES (1) *(of a branch)* **-wogoka**, *eg. Ettabi liwogose. (The branch has snapped.')*; (2) *(of a rope)* **-kutuka**, *eg. Omuguwa gwakutuse. (The rope has snapped.')*   snap open *(of something under tension)* **-pasuka**, *(noisily)* **-banduka**. *See* go off; set off

¹snare *(for catching animals)* *n* **omutego** *n3*

²snare *(trap)* *vt* **-tega**

snatch *vt* **-nyakula**, **-pakula**, **-kwakkula**. *See* grab; pull; seize   person who snatches *(type of thief)* **omunyakuzi** *n1*

sneak sneak into (*eg. animal into bush*) **-sensera** sneak off **-ebba, -eemulula**

sneer at *vt* **-nyooma**. *See* contempt

¹**sneeze** *n* **omwasi** *n3*

²**sneeze** *vi* **-yasimula**

sniff (at) *vit* **-wunyiriza**, *eg. Embwa ewunyiriza emmere. ('The dog is sniffing at the food.')*

snob *n* **ow'olunkulu** *n1*

snobbery *n* **olunkulu** *n11*

snore *vi* **-fuluuta** pretend to be asleep (*by faking snoring*) **-eefuluusa**

snort *vi* (1) (*by pig*) **-fuguma**; (2) (*by person*) **-feesa**

snot *n* **eminyira** *n4*

snow *n* **omuzira** *n3*

snuffle (*of a person*) *vi* **-feesa**

¹**so** *adv.* Use **ennyo** ('*very*'), *eg. Nnabadde nkooye nnyo ne seebaka. ('I felt so tired that I could not sleep.')*. *See* so-so

²**so** (*therefore*) *conj.* Use narrative tense (**N16**), *eg. Enjala yabadde ennuma ne nfumba emmere. ('I felt hungry so I cooked some food.')*. *See* therefore so-and-so (*referring to a person whose name is not remembered*) **gundi** so far Use tense infix **-aka-** (**N18**), *eg. Nnaakawaata eminwe gya lumonde ebiri. ('I have so far peeled two potatoes.')* so long as **bwe**, *eg. Nja kukuyamba bw'onookola ennyo. ('I will help you so long as you work hard.')* so that Use subjunctive with **-lyoka** (*which is also in the subjunctive*) (**N17**), *eg. Nneeyambudde ndyoke nnaabe. ('I undressed so that I could wash.')*

soak *vt* **-nnyika**. *See* wet be(come) soaked (1) (*purposefully, eg. of clothes being washed*) **-nnyikira**, *eg. Engoye zinnyikidde bulungi mu mazzi. ('The clothes have been well soaked in water.')*; (2) (*in the rain*) **-toba**, *eg. Nnatoba nnyo mu nkuba. ('I got completely soaked in the rain.')*. *See* absorb

soaked *adj* **-nnyike**. *See* damp; sodden

soap *n* **ssabbuuni** *n1* bar of soap **omuti gwa ssabbuuni** *n3* tablet of soap **ekitole kya ssabbuuni** *n7*

sob *vi* **-kaaba**

sober up *vi* **-tamiirukuka**

social event *See* event

socialism *n* **nnaakalyakaani** *n1*

society (*organisation*) *n* **ekibiina** *n7*, *eg. Ekibiina ky'Olulimi Oluganda ('Luganda Language Society')* member of a society **munnakibiina** *n1* voluntary society **ekibiina eky'obwannakyewa**

sock(s) *n* **ssokisi** *n9*

socket (*electrical*) *n* **soketi** *n9* come out of a socket **-nuuka** take out of a socket **-nuula**

sodden (*too watery, of food*) *adj* **-serebevu**, (*of cooked matooke*) **-biririvu**. *See* soaked; soggy be sodden **-serebera**, (*of cooked matooke*) **-biririra**

sodomy *n* **obuseegu** *n14*

soft *adj* (1) (*pliable; tender*) **-gonvu**; (2) (*smooth to the touch*) **-weweevu** be(come) soft (1) (*pliable; tender*) **-gonda**; (2) (*smooth to the touch*) **-weweera** soft-hearted person (*lenient*) **omukyabyayi** *n1* be too soft (*as an overripe fruit*) **-bootaboota**. *See* mushy too soft (*as an overripe fruit*) *adj* **-booteevu**

soften *vt* (1) (*make pliable; tenderise*) **-gonza**; (2) (*make smooth to the touch*) **-weweeza**; (3) (*with water or saliva*) **-vubiriza** soften young banana leaf (*by singeing briefly over a fire*) **-babula oluwombo**

softly (*of sound; quietly*) *adv* **mpolampola** walk softly **-tambuza buggereggere**

softness (*pliability*) *n* **obugonvu** *n14*

¹**soil** *n* **ettaka** *n5* soil erosion **okukulukuta kw'ettaka** *n15* black soil **ettaka eriddugavu** infertile soil **ettaka ly'olunnyo** red soil **ettaka erimyufu** subsoil **olukuusi** *n11*

²**soil** (*make dirty*) *vt* **-ddugaza**, (*permanently discolour*) **-gubya** soil oneself (*through defecation*) **-eegendera** be(come) soiled **-ddugala**, (*permanently discoloured*) **-guba**, *eg. Essaati ye egubye. ('His shirt is soiled.')*, (*on parts of clothing, eg. armpits*) **-gubaasira**

soiled *adj* (1) (*permanently discoloured*) **-gubu**; (2) (*on parts of clothing, eg. armpits*) **-gubaasivu**

solder *v* **essasi** *n5*

soldier *n* **omujaasi** *n1*, **omuserikale** *n1*

sole (*of shoe*) *n* **soole** *n9*

solicit (*ask*) *vt* **-saba**. *See* prostitute oneself

solicitor *See* lawyer

solid *adj* (1) (*firm; fixed*) **-nywevu**; (2) (*hard*) **-gumu** go solid (*eg. of water turned to ice*) **-kwata**

solve a problem (*find a solution*) **-sala amagezi**. *See* sort out

Somali (*person*) *n* **Omusomali** *n1*

some *det* (1) **-mu** (**N8.1**). *Takes numeral concord* (**N4.2**), *eg. ebintu ebimu ('some things')*; (2) (*a portion of*) Use suffix **-ko** on verb and/or preposition **ku**, *eg. Nywako ku mazzi. ('Drink some water.') – this can be a polite way of making a request* (**N24.3**).

someone *pro.* Use **omuntu** ('*person*'), *eg. Ndeetera omuntu amanyi okusoma. ('Bring me someone who can read.')* someone else **omulala** *n1*

sometimes *adv* **oluusi, emirundi egimu**

somewhere *adv* **awantu**

son *n* **mutabani** *n1* (*with pos* **N12**), *eg. mutabani wa Musoke ('Musoke's son')* son of a princess **ssaava** *n1*, **ssewava** *n1* eldest son of the Kabaka **Kiweewa** *n1* title

son-in-law *n* **omuko** *n1*, **mukoddomi** *n1* (*with pos* **N12**), *eg. mukoddomi wange ('my son-in-law')*

song *n* **oluyimba** *n11*

soon *adv* (1) **mangu**, *eg. Ajja mangu. ('He is coming soon.')*; (2) **kumpi**, *eg. Ali kumpi kutuuka? ('Is he coming soon?')*; (3) Use **-tera** ('*be about to*') in near future tense (**N16**) followed by inf (**N19**), eg. Anaatera okutuuka? ('Is he coming soon?'). See as soon as

soot n enziro n9

soothe vt (1) (speak softly to) -**wooyawooya**; (2) (using the hand, eg. to soothe an insect bite) -**siisiriza**. See calm down; hush soothe the throat -**weweeza obulago**, -**weweeza omumiro**

soothsayer n omulaguzi n1

sorcerer n omulogo n1

sorcery n obulogo n14

sore n ebbwa n5, (cold sore) ekisuyu n7. See pimple; skin condition be sore (hurt) -**luma** (with personal object), eg. Ekiwundu kinnuma. ('My wound is sore.')

sorghum n omuwemba n3 sorghum added to banana juice (in beer-making) emberenge n9 sorghum-coloured (reddish-brown) adj -**a kawembawemba** add roasted sorghum (in beer making) -**siwa muwemba**

sorrel (type of plant; Oxalis) n (1) (small, yellow-flowered) kajjampuni n1; (2) (larger, purple-flowered; a weed) kanyeebwa n1

sorrow n ennaku n9

sorry feel sorry for (pity) -**saasira** feel sorry for oneself -**eesaasira**. See disappointed I'm so sorry for you! **Ng'olabye!** (pl. **Nga mulabye!**) I'm sorry. **Nsonyiwa.** say sorry Use -**sonyiwa** ('forgive') with -**genderera** ('do deliberately') in neg (**N16**). eg. Nsonyiwa sigenderedde kukuyiira caayi. ('I'm sorry to have spilt tea on you.') say sorry to -**eetondera**, eg. Nnamwetondedde. ('I said sorry to her.') So sorry. **Nga kitalo.**, **Manti.**

[1]**sort** (type) n ekika n7, engeri n9. See way

[2]**sort (out)** (organise) vt -**tegeka**, eg. Oyinza okunnyamba okutegeka engoye zino? ('Can you help me sort these clothes?'). See separate sort out affairs -**tereza** (or -**gonjoola**) ensonga

so-so adv bwe -**tyo** bwe -**tyo** (**N13**), eg. Nnamubuuzizza bw'ali n'agamba nti ali bw'atyo bw'atyo. ('I asked her how she is and she said so-so.')

sought See seek

soul n omwoyo n3. See emotional core

[1]**sound** (in good condition) adj -**lamu**

[2]**sound** n ekintu ekivuga n7, (of the human voice) eddoboozi n5. Types of sound include: (1) (cracking of the knuckles) ekinonko n7; (2) (hum, rumble, etc.) okuwuuma n15; (3) (trampling) omusinde n3; (4) (of a gun shot) emmundu n9. make deep rumbling sound (like distant drums) -**sindogoma** something that makes a sound ekivuga n7

[3]**sound** vi -**vuga**, eg. Ekide kivuga. ('The bell is sounding.'), (deep heavy sound; rumble) -**duduma**, (as a kettle heating or engine idling) -**tokota**, (of drums) -**lawa**, eg. Eŋŋoma zirawa. ('The drums are sounding.'), (crackle, as an untuned radio) -**kwakwaya**, (make sudden loud noice, as an

explosion) -**bwatuka** sound an alarm call -**kuba enduulu**, (against someone) -**kubira enduulu** sound drums (as a warning) -**laya eŋŋoma**

soup n omucuuzi n3, ssupu n1

sour (of juice) adj -**kaatuufu** be(come) sour (1) (of juice) -**kaatuuka**; (2) (of milk) -**fa**. See tart person of sour disposition (glum) ow'eggume n1

source n ensibuko n9, eg. Eno ye nsibuko y'omugga. ('This is the source of the river.'). See beginning at the water source emugga water source ensulo n9

sourness (bitterness) n obukaayi n14

south n amaserengeta n6, obukiika bwa ddyo n14

souvenir n ekijjukizo n7

sovereign n (1) (king) kabaka n1; (2) (queen) kkwini n1. See ruler

[1]**sow** (female pig) n embizzi enkazi n9

[2]**sow** (seeds) vt -**siga**. See plant

sow-thistle (type of plant; Sonchus) n kakovu n1

sower (of seeds) n omusizi n1

sowing time n amasiga n6

soya (bean) n ssoya n1

space n ebbanga n5, eg. Waliwo ebbanga mu kabada. ('There is space in the cupboard.'), (space within, eg. eye of a needle) eŋŋango n9. See gap; hollow; vacancy spaces between the fingers empataanya z'engalo n10 deepest space obwengula bw'ebbanga n14 open space (of definite size, eg. house plot or clearing in the jungle) ekibangirizi n7 take up too much space (1) (of a person, items in a store, etc.) -**zimbagala**; (2) (of a plant) -**zijjagala**

spaced-out adv entalaga, eg. amannyo ag'entalaga ('spaced-out teeth')

spade n ekitiiyo n7. See spear (digging)

span n (1) (distance from end of thumb to end of middle finger, stretched apart) oluta n11; (2) (from fingertip to fingertip of outstretched arms) ekifuba n7

spank vt -**kuba**

[1]**spare** adj -**a sipeeya**, eg. omupiira gwa sipeeya ('spare tyre'). See surplus

[2]**spare (part)** n sipeeya n1

[3]**spare** vt (1) (put aside) -**tereka**, eg. Yatereka sukaali ow'okukozesa oluvannyuma. ('He spared some sugar to use later.'); (2) (preserve) -**taliza**, eg. Nnataliza omuti omuto nga nkoola omuddo. ('I spared the young tree when I was weeding.'). See retain; save be spared (survive misfortune) -**lama**, eg. Omukyala yali mulwadde nnyo, naye n'alama. ('The lady was near death, but was spared.'). See surplus (be) have to spare (left-over) -**fissa**, eg. Tufissizza ssente. ('We have some money to spare.')

sparingly, use (economically) vt -**kekkereza**, eg. Yakozesa ssabbuuni ng'amukekkereza. ('He used the soap sparingly.')

spark n ensasi n9

sparkle *vi* -masamasa, -temagana

sparrow *n* enkazaluggya *n9*

speak *vi* (spoke; spoken) -yogera, *eg. Nnayogedde naye jjo. ('I spoke with him yesterday.'). Ways of speaking include*: (1) (*for too long*) -yogera olukobo; (2) (*harshly*) -boggoka, -boggola; (3) (*in a clear pleasant voice*) -yogera n'eggono; (4) (*in a deep low voice*) -doodooma; (5) (*in a light-hearted joky way*) -bereega; (6) (*in riddles*) -gereesa; (7) (*loudly*) -yogerera waggulu, -yogerera -woggana, -yogerera -leekaana, *eg. Yayogera aleekaana. ('She spoke loudly.')*; (8) (*loudly in anger*) -kaalaamuka; (9) (*with dignity*) -yogeza ssimbo; (10) (*with kindness*) -yogeza kisa; (11) (*without thinking*) -sumattula (*or* -wamatula) ebigambo; (12) (*badly or rudely*) -yogera bubi. *See* chatter; gabble; jabber; talk   speak a language fluently -fuuweeta olulimi   speak badly about (*someone*) -vumirira   speak for/in -yogerera, *eg. Ayogerera mu kkanisa. ('He spoke in church.')*   speak harshly to -boggolera   speak to at a distance -lagiriza ebigambo   way of speaking enjogera *n9*

speaker *n* omwogezi *n1*, (*of parliament*) sipiika *n1*, (*loudspeaker*) omuzindaalo *n3*

[1]**spear** (*also* spearhead) *n* effumu *n5*   spear grass (*Themeda*) essenke *n5*, (*flowering stem*) akaseekende *n12*, (*patch of spear grass*) olusenke *n11*   digging spear ekifumu *n7*   person wounded by spear omufumite *n1*

[2]**spear** *vt* -fumita effumu. *See* harpoon

spearsman *n* omufumisi *n1*

special *adj* -a enjawulo   special hire (*taxi*) sipesulo *n9*

specialist *n* omukugu *n1*

speck *n* akatolobojjo *n12*

specimen (*something to look at*) *n* ekyokulabako *n7*

spectacles *n* gaalubindi *n10*

spectator *n* omulabi *n1*

speculate (*imagine*) *vt* -teebereza

speech *n* okwogera *n15*   part of speech (*in grammar*) olubu lw'ebigambo *n11*

speechless, be (*dumbfounded*) *vi* -wuniikirira

[1]**speed** *n* sipiidi *n9*   speed hump ekigulumu *n7*

[2]**speed** *v*   speed in a car (*of a driver*) -diimuula (*or* -vuumuula) emmotoka   speed up (*accelerate*) -yongeza omuliro, -yongeza sipiidi

speedily *adv* (1) (*in doing things*) mu bwangu, mangu; (2) (*in running*) embiro, *eg. Yadduka embiro. ('She ran speedily.')*, emisinde

[1]**spell** *n* (1) (*hex*) ettalo *n5*; (2) (*evil spell*) eddogo *n5*, (*affecting a whole family or neighbourhood*) omuteego *n3*   cast an evil spell (on) -loga, *eg. Aloze taata wange. (He has cast a spell on my father.')*   remove an evil spell -ggyako (*or* -vumula) eddogo   remove an evil spell from (*on the part of the original curser*) -vumulula

[2]**spell** *vt* (spelt) -wandiika, *eg. Ekigambo kino*

okiwandiika otya? ('How do you spell this word?')

spelling *n* empandiika *n9*

spend *vt* (spent)   spend money -kozesa ssente, *eg. Akozesezza ssente ze zonna. ('She spent all her money.')*   spend the day -siiba, *eg. Yasiiba waka. ('She spent the day at home.')*   spend the night -sula, *eg. Yasula waka. ('She spent the night at home.'),* -lya ekisula, (*in preparation*) -sulirira   spend time -mala ekiseera, -mala obudde, -mala ebbanga, *eg. Jjo yamala ebbanga mu nnimiro. ('Yesterday she spent time in her garden.'),* (*a long time at a place*) -malayo ebbanga eddene, *eg. E Masaka nnamalayo ebbanga ddene. ('I spent a long time in Masaka.')*

spherical *adj* -eekulungirivu   make spherical -kulunga

spice (*for flavouring food*) *n* ekirungo *n7*

spicule *n* ejjimbi *n5*

spicy (*of food*) *adj* -baalaavu   be spicy -baalaala

spider (*also* spider web) *n* nnabbubi *n1*

spike *n* (1) (*spur*) ejjindu *n5*; (2) (*of metal, at end of pole or spear*) omuwunda *n3*

spill *vt* (spilt) -yiwa, *eg. Yayiwa amazzi. ('She spilt the water.')*   spill on -yiira, *eg. Yayiira entebe amata. ('She spilt milk on the chair.')*   be spilt -yiika, *eg. Amazzi gayiise. ('The water is spilt.')*

spin *v* (1) *vi* -eebonga; (2) *vt* -bonga

spinach *See* greens

spinal cord *n* enkizi *n9*

spine *n* (1) (*backbone*) (*of a person*) olugongogongo *n11*, (*of an animal*) ekigongo *n7*; (2) (*thorn*) eriggwa *n5*

spinning top *n* (1) (*carved of wood*) enkuyo *n9*; (2) (*omuwafu seed*) enje *n9*

spinster *n* nnakyeyombekedde *n1*

spire *n* ekitikkiro *n7*

[1]**spirit** (*of a person, or supernatural*) *n* (1) (*of a person; the soul*) omwoyo *n3*; (2) (*of a person; heart*) omutima *n3*; (3) (*of a departed person; ghost*) omuzimu *n3*; (4) (*whirlwind, associated with departed person*) akazimu *n12*; (5) (*deity in Kiganda traditional religion*) lubaale *n1*; (6) (*nature spirit, associated with place, tree, etc.*) emmandwa *n9*; (7) (*manifestation of a nature spirit, often appearing in the form of a woman*) omusambwa *n3*; (8) (*associated with a fettish*) ejjembe *n5*; (9) (*evil spirit controlled by a living person*) ekyokoola *n7*. *See* genie; god   spirit possession (*associated with night-dancing*) ekitambo *n7*. *See* communicate with a spirit; medium; possessed (be)   be in high spirits (*elated*) -sagambiza   bearer of a spirit omukongozzi *n1*   Holy Spirit Omwoyo Omutukuvu   person possessed by a spirit (1) (*by an emmandwa*) mmandwa *n1*; (2) (*by a lubaale*) omulubaale *n1*   person who takes part in a spirit possession ritual omusamize *n1*

[2]**spirit** (*alcoholic*) *n* omwenge *n3*. *See* gin

spirituality

spirituality *n* **obusomi** *n14*

[1]**spit** *n* **amalusu** *n6*. *See* phlegm

[2]**spit** *vi* **-wanda amalusu**, *eg. Yawanda amalusu wansi.* (*'He spat on the ground.'*)   spit out food **-wanda emmere**

spite *n* **ettima** *n5*

spiteful *adj* **-a ettima**   spiteful person **ow'ettima** *n1*

spitefully *adv* **n'ettima**

spittle *n* **amalusu** *n6*

spittlebug (*type of insect*) *n* **entonnyeze** *n9*

splash *v* (1) *vi* **-sammuka**, *eg. Amazzi gasammuse wansi.* (*'The water splashed on the ground'.*); (2) *vt* **-sammula**, *eg. Yasammudde amazzi ku kisenge.* (*'She splashed water on the wall.'*)   splash on **-sammuliza**, *eg. Yansammuliza amazzi.* (*'She splashed water on me.'*)

splayfootedness *n* **embaliga** *n10*   be splayfooted **-baliga**   splayfooted person **ow'embaliga** *n1*

spleen *n* **akataago** *n12*, (*enlarged*) **akabengo** *n12*

splendid *adj* **-a ekitalo, makula** (*invariable adjective*), *eg. Yazimba ennyumba makula.* (*'He built a splendid house.'*)

splendour *n* **ekitalo** *n7*

splice *vt* **-luka**

[1]**splinter** (*of wood*) *n* **akapapajjo** *n12* (*big* **ekipapajjo** *n7*)

[2]**splinter** *vi* **-bajjuka**, *eg. Ekiti kyabajjuka bwe yakikoona.* (*'The log splintered when he hit it.'*)

[1]**split** *adj* (1) (*of a bag*) **-yabifu**; (2) (*in two, eg. of a rope*) **-kutufu**

[2]**split** (*narrow break; gap*) *n* **olwatika** *n11*

[3]**split** *v* TRANSITIVE USES **-yabiza**, *eg. Ayabizza ensawo.* (*'He has split the bag.'*), (*by chopping*) **-yasa**, *eg. Yayasa ekisiki n'embazzi.* (*'He has split the log with an axe'*)   split off (*relating to wood*) **-bajjula**, *eg. Abajjula ekisiki.* (*'He is splitting off a piece of the log.'*)   split open (*eg. a sack*) **-lyebula**   split and detach (*layers of a cut down banana stem*) **-gogombola omugogo**   INTRANSITIVE USES **-yabika**, *eg. Ensawo eyabise.* (*'The bag is split.'*)   split off (*relating to wood*) **-bajjuka**, *eg. Ekiti kibajjuse.* (*'A piece of wood has split off.'*)   split open (*eg. of a sack*) **-lyebuka**   split up (*separate*) **-yawukana**, *eg. Musoke ne mukyala we baayawukanye.* (*'Musoke and his wife have split up.'*)

splutter along (*as a defective engine*) *vi* **-pipira**

[1]**spoil** (*loot*) *n* **omunyago** *n3*

[2]**spoil** *v* (spoilt) TRANSITIVE USES (1) (*damage; waste*) **-yonoona**, *eg. Enneeyisa ye eyonoonye akabaga.* (*'His behaviour spoiled the party.'*); (2) (*through crushing or squashing*) **-sogonyola**; (3) (*pamper a person*) **-biibiita, -gira ekyejo**. *See* bungle; indulge; mess up; pamper   INTRANSITIVE USES (1) (*through being crushed or squashed*) **-sogonyoka**; (2) (*of root crops left too long in the ground*) **-wutta**   be(come) spoilt **-yonooneka**, *eg. Ebbinika*

eyonoonese. (*'The kettle is spoilt.'*). *See* bad (go)

spoilt *adj* **-yonoonefu**, *eg. omwana omwonoonefu* (*'spoilt child'*)   spoilt behaviour **obwonoonefu** *n14*, **ekyejo** *n7*   spoilt person **omwonoonefu** *n1*

spoke (*also* spoken) *See* speak

spokesperson *n* **omwogezi** *n1*

sponge *n* **siponji** *n9*, (*made from pith in banana stem*) **ekinyirikisi** *n7*, (*loofah*) **ekyangwe** *n7*

sponger (*parasitic type of person*) *n* **olukokobe** *n1*

[1]**sponsor** *n* **omuyima** *n1*

[2]**sponsor** *vt* (1) (*stand up for*) **-eeyimirira**, *eg. Yamweyimirira ng'ayingira mu kibiina.* (*'She sponsored his membership of the committee.'*); (2) (*through paying fees*) **-weerera**, *eg. Yaweerera omwana mu ssomero.* (*'He sponsored the child at school.'*)

spool *n* **ekidondi** *n7* (*small* **akadondi** *n12*)

spoon *n* **ekijiiko** *n7* (*small* (*small; teaspoon*) **akajiiko** *n12*, serving **ekijiiko ekisena**), (*made from banana leaf*) **akawujjo** *n12*, (*large flat wooden cooking implement*) **omulawo** *n3*

sport (*game*) *n* **omuzannyo** *n3*   sports day **olunaku lw'emizannyo** *n11*

sportsground *n* **ekisaawe ky'emizannyo** *n7*

[1]**spot** *n* (1) (*dot*) **akatonnyeze** *n12*; (2) (*eg. small stain*) **akabala** *n12*; (3) (*place*) **ekifo** *n7*. *See* speck   on-the-spot *adj* **-a buliwo**, *eg. omutango ogwa buliwo* (*'on-the-spot fine'*)

[2]**spot** (*see*) *vt* **-laba**

spotted *adj* (1) (*eg. with stains*) **-a ebibalabala**; (2) (*patterned*) **-a ebibomboola**

spout (*eg. of teapot*) *n* **omumwa** *n3*

sprat (*small fish*) *n* (1) (*haplochromis*) **enkejje** *n9*; (2) (*smaller, silvery*) **mukene** *n1*

sprawl oneself out (*lie down anyhow; flop down*) *vi* **-gaŋŋalama**   fall sprawling on the ground **-galanjuka**

[1]**spray** (*liquid and fragments given off by bark when beaten*) *n* **obuleebo** *n14*

[2]**spray** *vt* **-fuuyira**. *See* water

spread *v* TRANSITIVE USES **-saasaanya**, *eg. Baasaasaanya obupapula obulanga olukuŋŋaana.* (*'They spread leaflets announcing the meeting.'*), (*confidential or secret information*) **-laalaasa, -bungeesa**   spread a rumour **-saasaanya** (*or* **-bungeesa**) **olugambo**   spread butter **-siiga bbata**   spread evenly **-ttaanya**, *eg. Yattaanya obusa mu lusuku lwonna.* (*'She spread the dung all over the banana garden.'*)   spread everywhere **-bunya**, *eg. Yabunya amawulire wonna.* (*'He spread the news everywhere.'*)   spread grass on floor **-sasira essubi**, *eg. Asasidde essubi.* (*'She has spread grass on the floor.'*)   spread on with the hand **-siisiriza**, (*on oneself*) **-eesiisiriza**, *eg. Omukyala yeesiisiriza vasiriini ng'amaze okunaaba.* (*'The lady is spreading vaseline on her body after bathing.'*)   spread out (1) (*beans, weeds, etc.*) **-yanjala**, *eg. Tuyanjala ebijanjaalo bikale.* (*'We are spreading*

out the beans to dry.'); (2) (*mat, cloth, skin, etc.*)
-yala, *eg. Yayala omukeeka wansi.* ('She has spread
out a mat on the floor.'); (3) (*with a purpose in
mind*) **-yaliira**. See flatten spread out for
-yaliirira, *eg. Yayaliirira abagenyi omukeeka.*
('She spread out a mat for the guests.') someone
who spreads (*litter, rumour, etc.*) **omusaasaanyi** *n1*
something spread out (*for a purpose*) **omwaliiro** *n3*
INTRANSITIVE USES (1) (*of a disease, water,
people, etc.*) **-saasaana**, *eg. Amazzi gasaasaana.*
('The water is spreading.'); (2) (*of a plant or a fire*)
-landa spread everywhere **-buna wonna**, *eg.
Amawulire gabunye wonna.* ('The news has spread
everywhere.') be spread everywhere (1) (*of
rumours or a fire*) **-bungeesebwa**; (2) (*of a fire*)
-landa be spread out (*broad*) **-yagaagala**, *eg.
Omugugu guyagaagadde.* ('The bundle is spread
out'). See flattened (be)
spread out (*broad*) *adj* **-yagaagavu**, *eg, Omugugu
mwagaagavu.* ('The bundle is spread out.')
[1]**spring** (*water source*) *n* **ensulo** *n9* at the spring
emugga
[2]**spring** *vt* (sprung) **-masula**, *eg. Emmese emasudde
akamasu.* ('The mouse has sprung the trap.')
spring out **-fubutuka**, *eg. Omuyizzi yafubutuka mu
kifo kye yali yeekweseemu.* ('The hunter sprang out
of his hiding place') be sprung **-masuka**, *eg.
Akamasu kamasuse.* ('The trap has been sprung.')
sprinkle (on) *vt* **-mansira**, *eg. Yamansira amazzi ku
ssaati nga agenda okugigolola.* ('She sprinkled
water on the shirt when she was going to iron it.'),
(*a solid*) **-mamirirako**, *eg. Yamamirirako
omunnyo.* ('She sprinkled on salt.') sprinkle water
on **-fukirira**, *eg. Afukirira ebimera.* ('She is
sprinking water on the plants.')
[1]**sprint** *n* **embiro z'akafubatuko** *n10*
[2]**sprint** *vi* **-dduka embiro**, *eg. Yadduka embiro mu
kakubo.* ('He sprinted down the track.')
[1]**sprout** (*of a plant*) *n* **endokwa** *n9*
[2]**sprout** *vi* (1) (*of shoot or cutting*) **-loka**, *eg.
Endokwa zirose.* ('The cuttings have sprouted.');
(2) (*of sweet potatoes or beans*) **-leeta emitunsi**,
eg. Ebinjaalo bireese emitunsi. ('The beans have
sprouted.'); (3) (*of a recently planted banana plant*)
-kkulira, *eg. Ekitooke kikkulidde.* ('The banana
plant has sprouted.'). See germinate; produce
shoots
sprung See spring
spur (*on cock's foot*) *n* **ejjindu** *n5*
sputum *n* **ekikolondolwa** *n7*
[1]**spy** *n* **omukessi** *n1*, **mbega** *n1*
[2]**spy (on)** *vt* (1) **-ketta**, *eg. Ababaka b'Amerika
baketta aba Russia.* ('Members of the American
embassy are spying on the Russians.'), **-bega**; (2)
(*peep at secretly*) **-lingiriza**, *eg. Yabalingiriza mu
kituli ky'ekisumuluzo.* ('He spied on them through
the keyhole.')
spying *n* **obukessi** *n14*

[1]**squabble** *n* **oluyombo** *n11*
[2]**squabble** *vi* **-yombagana**
squall *n* **kikuŋŋunta** *n1*
squalor *n* **obujama** *n14*
squander *vt* (1) (*waste*) **-yonoona**; (2) (*use
extravagantly*) **-diibuuda** squander money
-wemmenta ssente
[1]**squash** (*type of vegetable*) *n* **ensujju** *n9*
[2]**squash** *vt* **-betenta**, *eg. Yalinnye ettooke
n'alibetenta.* ('She trod on the banana and
squashed it.'), (*something very soft*) **-footola**, *eg.
Yalinnye ekisaanyi n'akifootola.* ('He stepped on
the caterpillar and squashed it.'). See flatten;
squeeze get squashed (1) (*as a soft fruit*)
-betenteka, *eg. Yasudde eppaapaali ne libetenteka.*
('He dropped the pawpaw and it got squashed.');
(2) (*of something very soft*) **-footoka**, *eg.
Eppaapaali lyabadde lyengedde nnyo. Bwe
lyagudde ne lifootoka.* ('The pawpaw was so ripe
that when it fell it got completely squashed.'); (3)
(*stuck onto*) **-kwatira**, *eg. Ebiwuka bingi
byakwatidde ku ndabirwamu y'emmotoka.* ('Many
insects got squashed on the windscreen.')
squashed (*of something very soft*) *adj* **-footose**
squat *vi* **-sitama**
[1]**squeeze** *n* **akanyigo** *n12*
[2]**squeeze** *vt* **-nyiga**, **-nyigiriza**, (*many times, eg.
dough in bread making*) **-nyiganyiga**. See handle;
knead squeeze and dissolve (*herbs in water*)
-yenga squeeze through (*eg. a crowd*) **-wagaanya**
squeeze to extract liquid **-kamula**, *eg. Yakamula
emicungwa.* ('She squeezed the oranges.')
squint *n* **endali** *n9* person with a squint **ow'endali**
n1
squirrel *n* (1) (*ground*) **kaamuje** *n1*; (2) (*tree*)
enkerebwe *n9*
squirt (out) *v* (1) *vi* **-tiiriika**; (2) *vt* **-tiiriisa**
Ssese Islands, person of *n* **Omusese** *n1*
language of Ssesse Islands **Olusese** *n11*
stab *vt* **-fumita**
stabilised, be *vi* **-tereera**
stack *vt* **-komeka**, **-sengeka**, **-panga**
staff *n* (1) (*stick*) **omuggo** *n3*; (2) (*ceremonial, of the
Katikkiro*) **ddamula** *n1*. See worker
stage *n* **siteegi** *n9*, (*in a career*) **eddaala** *n5*, (*in a
process, eg. building a house*) **omutendera** *n3*, (*of
advancement in Catholicism*) **omugigi** *n3*. See level
early stages of a task **amabaga** *n6*
stagger *vi* **-tagala**, *eg. Yatamiira naye n'asobola
okutuuka eka ng'atagala.* ('He got drunk, but
managed to stagger home.'), **-tambula -zunga**
(**N19**), *eg. Atambula azunga.* ('He is staggering.')
[1]**stain** *n* **ebbala** *n5*, (*large*) **ekibambya** *n7*
[2]**stain** *vt* **-teeka ebbala**, *eg. Bwino atadde ebbala ku
ssaati ye.* ('The ink has stained his shirt.'),
(*permanently discolour*) **-gubya** be(come) stained
(1) **-jjamu** (*or* **-beeramu**) **amabala**, *eg. Essaati
ezzeemu amabala.* ('The shirt has got stained.'); (2)

(*on parts of clothing, eg. collar*) -**gubaasira**; (3) (*permanently*) -**guba**. *See* dirty (become)

stained (*leaving marks*) *adj* -**a ebibalabala**

staircase (*also* stairs) *n* **amadaala** *n6*

stake (*eg. for tying up an animal*) *n* **enkondo** *n9*

stalemate, come to a *vi* -**lemagana**

staleness (*of food*) *n* **obulaala** *n14*   stale cassava (*with black spots*) **muwogo wa bulaala** *n1*

stalk *n* (1) (*type of bird; maribou stalk*) **kalooli** *n1*; (2) (*stalk of banana inflorescence*) (*hard, outside the leaf sheaves*) **ekikolokombo** *n7*, (*soft, inside the leaf sheaves*) **omututumba** *n3*

stalk (*eg. an animal*) *vt* -**sooberera**

¹stall (*eg. in market*) *n* **omudaala** *n3*

²stall *vi* -**zikira**, *eg. Emmotoka yazikidde ng'eri ku bitaala. ('The car stalled at the traffic lights.')*   stall for time -**palappalanya**, *eg. Bwe nnamusaba okunsasula, n'apalappalanya. ('When I asked him to repay me, he stalled for time.')*

stammer *vi* -**naanaagira**

stammerer *n* **omunaanaagize** *n1*

¹stamp (*for postage*) *n* **sitampu** *n9*. *See* seal   put one's stamp (*seal*) -**ssaako** (*or* -**koonako**) **sitampu**

²stamp   stamp a letter -**teekako sitampu ku bbaluwa**   stamp one's foot -**koona ekigere**, *eg. Yakoona ekigere kye wansi. ('He stamped his foot on the ground.')*

¹stampede *n* **akagugumuko** *n12*

²stampede *v* (1) *vi* -**gugumuka**; (2) *vt* -**gugumula**

stanch *See* staunch

stand *v* (stood) **TRANSITIVE USES** -**yimiriza**, *eg. Essanduuko yagiyimiriza mu nsonda. ('She stood the suitcase in the corner.')*   stand in the way of (*blocking the way*) -**eekiika mu kkubo lya**   stand up for (*as guarantor*) -**eeyimirira**. *See* vouch for   stand up to (*eg. a bully or someone overcharging*) -**kaliramu**, *eg. Yamukaliramu. ('He stood up to him.')*, (*more aggressively*) -**tambaala**   **INTRANSITIVE USES** -**yimirira**, *eg. Ayimiridde okumpi n'omuti. ('She is standing near the tree.')*. *The following refer to ways of standing* (*posture*): (1) (*at attention*) -**yimirira busimbalaala**; (2) (*on tiptoe*) -**kangalala**; (3) (*still*) -**yimirira butengerera**; (3) (*upright*) -**yimirira busimba**; (4) (*with one hip higher than the other*) -**yiguliza**; (5) (*without supporting oneself, as a child learning to walk*) -**eetengerera**, *eg. Omwana yeetengerera. ('The child is standing up on his own.')*   stand apart -**eesuula**, *eg. Ennyumba emu yeesudde okuva ku ndala. ('One house stands apart from the others.')*   stand in an election -**eesimbawo**   stand on one's own two feet (*be independent*) -**eemalirira**   stand out *See* outstanding (be); protrude   stand steady (*well fixed*) -**nywera**, *eg. Enkondo enywedde. ('The post stood steady.')*   stand still -**yimirirawo**   stand up (1) (*rise*) -**yimuka**, *eg. Yayimuka ng'amaze okulya. ('She stood up after eating.')*, -**situka**; (2) (*in church, to*

sing a hymn or say the creed) -**golokoka**; (3) (*of hair*) -**sunsumala**; (4) (*with difficulty; struggle to one's feet*) -**eekakamula**   keep standing up to do things -**situnkana**

standard (*level of achievement*) *n* **omutindo** *n3*, *eg. Essomero lino lya mutindo gwa waggulu. ('This school has a high standard.')*. *See* flag; level; stage

stank *See* stink

star *n* **emmunyeenye** *n9*   morning star (*Venus*) **nnabaliwo** *n1*   shooting star **kibonoomu** *n1*

¹stare (*also* with a fixed stare) *n* **enkaliriza** *n9*

²stare *vi* -**tunuula**, *eg. Yayimirira n'atunuula. ('She stood and stared.')*. *See* gaze; glare; transfixed (be)   stare at -**tunuulira enkaliriza**, *eg. Musoke yatunuulira omusota enkaliriza. ('Musoke stared at the snake.')*   stare vacantly and idiotically -**lozoolera**, -**lolobala**

starling *n* (1) (*blue*) **nnamugala** *n1*; (2) (*glossy*) **enkwenge** *n9*

¹start *n* **entandikwa** *n9*

²start (*eg. an engine*) *vt* -**tandika**   start a journey -**simbula**, *eg. Tujja kusimbula essaawa bbiri. ('We will start the journey at 8 o'clock.')*, -**situla**, (*from a certain place*) -**simbuka**, *eg. Tujja kusimbuka Lubaga. ('We will start from Rubaga.')*   start at/with -**sookera**, *eg. Yasookera ku kulongoosa eddiiro ery'emmanju. ('She started with cleaning the back room.')*   start up (*react suddenly*) -**baguka**, (*from sleep*) -**wawamuka mu tulo**

starter (*also* starting button) (*of engine*) *n* **emmanduso** *n9*

startle *vt* -**kanga**. *See* shock   be startled (by) -**eekanga**, *eg. Omwana yeekanga embwa. ('The child was startled by the dog.')*

starvation *n* **enjala** *n9*   starving person **omuyala** *n1*

¹state *n* (1) (*situation*) **embeera** *n9*; (2) (*country*) **ensi** *n9*. *See* nation

²state (*say*) *vt* -**gamba**

statement *n* (1) (*verbal*) **ebigambo** *n8*; (2) (*written*) **ekiwandiiko** *n7*

station *n* **sitenseni** *n9*   petrol station **sitenseni y'amafuta, essundiro ly'amafuta** *n5*   train station **sitenseni (y'eggaali y'omukka)**

stature *n* **obuwanvu** *n14*

status   person of high social status **owa waggulu** *n1*

¹staunch (*steadfast*) *adj* -**gumu**

²staunch (*also* stanch) (*eg. flow of blood*) *vt* -**ziyiza**

stay *vi* (1) (*be at*) -**beera**, *eg. Beera wano nga nkola. ('Stay here while I work.')*; (2) (*during the night*) -**sula**, *eg. Nnasuze mu nnyumba eno ekiro kya jjo. ('I stayed in this house last night.')*; (3) (*remain*) -**sigala**, *eg. Yasigala alabirire abaana. ('He stayed to look after the children.')*   let stay (*for the night*) -**suza**   place of stay (*for the night*) **ekisulo** *n7*

steadfast (*staunch*) *adj* -**gumu**. *See* fixed   be steadfast -**guma**. *See* firm (stand)

steady (*not moving*) *adj* -**nywevu**. *See* strong   make steady -**nyweza**

steal vt (stolen) **-bba**, (one-by-one) **-somola**. See embezzle; loot; pilfer   steal away stealthily **-ebba**, **-ebbirira**, eg. Yebbirira n'agenda okugula ekirabo. ('He stole out to buy a present.'), **-eeseebulula**   steal for **-bbira**, eg. Abaana be yababbira emmere. ('He stole food for his children.')   steal money **-bba** (or **-lya**) ssente

stealing n okubba n15

stealthily, do vt **-bbirira**

steam n omukka n3

steamer (ship) n emmeeri n9

steep adj **-wanvu**

steeple n omunaala gw'ekkanisa n3

steer vt **-goba**

steering (wheel) n siteeringi n9

steersman n omugoba n1

¹stem n (1) (of a plant) **enduli** n9; (2) (of a smoker's pipe) **oluseke** n11; (3) (of a word in grammar) **ekikolo** n7. See stalk; trunk

²stem v (1) (come from) vi **-va**, eg. Empisa ennungi ziva mu maka. ('Good manners stem from the home.'); (2) (prevent) vt **-ziyiza**, eg. Bbandeegi eziyizza omusaayi okujja. ('The bandage has stemmed the flow of blood.')

¹step n (1) (of a staircase) **eddaala** n5; (2) (footstep) **ekigere** n7. See gait

²step (on) vi **-linnya**, eg. Balinnya ku muddo. ('They are stepping on the grass.')   step aside (when walking, eg. to avoid a collision) **-dda ebbali**   step down (1) (descend) **-kka wansi**, eg. Yakka wansi okuva ku ddaala. ('He stepped down from the ladder.'); (2) (give up a position) **-va mu kifo**, eg. Yava ku bukulu bw'essomero. ('He stepped down from the headship of the school.')   be stepped on **-linnyibwako**

stern (of a canoe) n **ekirumba** n7   at the stern (of a canoe) **ebulumba**

sternness (dourness) n **ekkabyo** n5. See fierce   look stern **-eekaba**, **-tunuza ekkabyo**

stethoscope n ekiwuliriza n7

¹stick n (1) (general term) **omuggo** n3, (small) **akaggo** n12, (long) **oluti** n11, (very small) **akati** n12; (2) (short, for beating cores of banana stems to make sponges) **enkonyo** n9; (3) (used in game of embirigo) **embirigo** n9, (4) (for administering punishment) **akaswanyu** n12, **kibooko** n9. See broomstick; club; hammer; pole; staff   stick for digging up sweet potatoes **omuggo ogusima lumonde, ensobyo** n9   medicinal clay stick **emmumbwa** n9   small stick used for measuring **akati akapima**   throwing stick (for felling fruit) **enkonyogo** n9   tooth-cleaning stick **omuswaki** n3

²stick v (stuck) **TRANSITIVE USES -kwasa**, eg. Yakwasa akapande ku ssanduuko. ('He stuck the label on the case.')   stick at (persevere) **-nyiikira**, eg. Yanyiikira okusoma. ('She has stuck at her studies.')   stick out (1) (extend beyond) **-yisaamu** (or **-yisa mu**), eg. Yayisa omukono mu ddirisa.

('He stuck his arm out of the window.'), **-sooloobya**. See jut out, (make); protrude   stick to one's point (eg. in an argument) **-lemera ku nsonga**   stick upright (eg. a post) **-simba**   **INTRANSITIVE USES** be stuck down (adhere) **-kwata**, eg. Akapande kakutte. ('The label is stuck down.')   stick out (1) (out from within) **-yitamu**, eg. Akati akamu kayiseemu mu muganda. ('One stick is sticking out of the bundle.'), **-soolooba**; (2) (cause to bulge out, due to something inside) **-kukunala**. See bulge out; extend beyond; jut out; protrude   stick to (or be stuck on) **-kwatira**, eg. Ekipande kikwatidde ku kisenge. ('The poster is stuck on the wall.')   stick up (of hair) **-sunsumala**   get stuck **-laalira**, eg. Eggumba limulaalidde mu mumiro gwe. ('A bone has got stuck in his throat.'), (delayed) **-lwisibwa**, (jammed) **-wagama**   get stuck in **-wagamira**, eg. Emmere ewagamidde mu mumiro gwange. ('The food is stuck in my throat.')   get stuck in mud **-tubira**, eg. Loole yatubidde mu ttosi. ('The lorry got stuck in the mud.')   something stuck in the throat **empagama** n9

sticking out (jutting out) adj **-kukunavu, -a enkukunala**

sticky, be vi **-kwatira**, eg. Ekipande kikwatira. ('The label is sticky.')

stiff adj **-kakanyavu**   stiff neck **olukya** n11   be(come) stiff **-kakanyala**

stiffen vt **-kakanyaza**

stiffness (of materials) n obukakanyavu n14. See muscle ache   lose stiffness (of materials) **-lebera**

¹still (calm; serene) adj **-teefu**

²still adv. Use verb prefix **-kya-** (**N18**), eg. Akyafumba. ('She is still cooking.')

³still (make calm) vt **-sirisa**, eg. Yesu yasirisa amayengo. ('Jesus stilled the waves.')   be(come) still (serene) **-teeka**

sting vt (stung) (1) (by bee) **-luma**, eg. Enjuki emulumye. ('A bee has stung him.'); (2) (by plant or caterpillar) **-yokya**, eg. Ekisaanyi kinjokezza. ('The caterpillar has stung me.'); (3) (through contact with certain substances) **-balagala**, eg. Omunnyo gumbalagala mu kiwundu. ('The salt is making my wound sting.')

stinginess (meanness) n obukodo n14

stinging (smarting) adj **-balagavu**   stinging pain **obubalagaze** n14   stinging plant Types include: (1) (stinging nettles) **kibugga** n1, **omwennyango** n3; (2) (type of climbing herb) **kamyu** n1.

stingy (mean) adj **-kodo**   stingy person **omukodo** n1   be(come) stingy **-kodowala**

¹stink n (1) (of rot or drain) **ekivundu** n7; (2) (bad body smell) **olusu** n11. See smell

²stink vi (stank) **-wunya obubi, -cuuma**

stinkhorn fungus n omutima gw'ettaka n3

stir vt **-tabula**, eg. Tabula sukaali mu caayi. ('Stir sugar into the tea.'), (on a bigger scale, eg. when making porridge) **-kologa**, eg. Kologa mu buugi *tebukwatira ku ntobo. ('Stir the porridge so it does not get stuck to the pot.')* stir and dissolve (*eg. herbs in water*) **-yenga** stir up (1) (*ants, bees, people emotionally, etc.*) **-saanuula**; (2) (*sediment or people*) **-tabangula**, *eg. Abaana batabangudde amazzi mu luzzi. ('The children have stirred up sediment in the well.').* See agitate stir up trouble for oneself **-eesiikuulira enkukunyi** be stirred (*eg. of tea*) **-tabuka** be(come) stirred up (1) (*of ants, bees, etc.*) **-saanuuka**, *eg. Enjuki zasaanuuse. (The bees were stirred up.')*; (2) (*of sediment*) **-tabanguka**

¹stitch (*pain in one's side*) *n* **kamenya** *n1*

²stitch (*sew*) *vt* **-tunga**, (*using backstitch*) **-tunga kaddannyuma** stitch together a mat (*from woven strips*) **-sona omukeeka**

stockade (*for cows*) *n* **ekiraalo** *n7*, **olugo** *n11* military stockade **enkambi** *n9*

stockings (*for a man*) *n* **enkampa** *n10*

stoke a fire (*by pushing in firewood*) **-seesa omuliro**

¹stolen *adj* **-bbe**. See looted something stolen **ekibbe** *n7*

²stolen *v*. See steal

stomach *n* (1) (*tummy*) **olubuto** *n11*; (2) (*the digestive organ*) **ssebusa** *n1*, (*of non-ruminant animal, eg. pig – when inflated, used as a fishing float*) **eggomo** *n5* stomach ulcers **amabwa mu ssebusa** *n6* have a running stomach See diarrhoea stomach pain **enjoka** *n10* swollen stomach disease **entumbi** *n9*

stomp out (*of a meeting*) *vi* **-eekandagga**

stone *n* **ejjinja** *n5*, (*crumbly sandstone, used in pottery*) **ebisibosibo** *n8*, (*hard stone, used in pottery*) **embaalebaale** *n10*. See grindstone cooking stone **essiga** *n5*

stood See stand

stool (*small seat*) *n* **akatebe** *n9*. See faeces

¹stoop (*rounded shoulders*) *n* **entumba** *n9* stooped-over person **ow'entumba** *n1*

²stoop *vi* **-kutama**, *eg. Yakutama okuyingira ennyumba. ('He stooped to enter the house.')* be stooped over **-kootakoota**, *eg. Omukadde akootakoota. ('The old person is stooped over.')*

¹stop (*for bus or taxi*) *n* **siteegi** *n9* full stop (*punctuation mark*) **akatonnyeze** *n12*, **akasirisa** *n12*

²stop *v* TRANSITIVE USES (1) (*something moving*) **-yimiriza**, *eg. Yayimiriza emmotoka ku bitaala. ('He stopped the car at the traffic lights.')*; (2) (*put a stop to*) **-komya**, *eg. Abantu baakomya okuleka abaana bokka awaka. ('The people stopped leaving their children alone at home.')*; (3) (*doing an activity*) **-lekera awo** (*followed by inf* **N19**), *eg. Yalekera awo okuzimba nga ssente ziweddewo. ('He stopped building due to a shortage of money.')*; (4) (*indicating that the amount that has been done is sufficient*) **-malira**.

See prevent; suspend stop dealing with (*give up with a person*) **-vaako**, *eg. Nnamuvaako. ('I have stopped dealing with him.')* Stop there! *as on order* **Lekeraawo!** stop up (*block*) **-ziba**, *eg. Nziba ekituli. ('She is stopping up the hole.')*. See block; clog cause to stop work **-nnyula** INTRANSITIVE USES (1) (*of person or thing moving*) **-yimirira**, *eg. Emmotoka yayimirira ku bitaala. ('The car stopped at the traffic lights.')*; (2) (*cease, related to a limit*) **-koma**, *eg. Poliisi yagambye abantu bakomye okuleka abaana bokka awaka. ('The police told the people to stop leaving their children alone at home.')* stop raining **enkuba -kya**, *eg. Enkuba ekedde. ('The rain has stopped.')* stop work (1) (*at one's regular time*) **-nnyuka**; (2) (*of one's own accord*) **-ennyula**

stoppage *n* **ekiziyiza** *n7*

stopper *n* **ekizibikira** *n7*. See cork

¹store *n* **eggwanika** *n5*, **sitoowa** *n9*, (*place for storage*) **etterekero** *n5*

²store *vt* **-tereka** store for **-terekera**, *eg. Yamuterekera enku. ('He stored the firewood for her.')*

storey (*of a building*) *n* **omwaliiro gw'ekizimbe** *n3* multistorey building **kalina** *n9* three-storey building **kalinaasatu** two-storey building **kalinaabiri**

stork (*bird*) *n* (1) (*maribou*) **kalooli** *n9*; (2) (*open-billed*) **enkoonamasonko** *n9*

storm *n* **kibuyaga** *n1* become stormy **obudde -fuukuuka**, *eg. Obudde bufuukuuse. ('The weather has become stormy.')*

storm out (*of a meeting*) *vi* **-eekandagga**

story *n* **olugero** *n11* folk story **olufumo** *n11* make up a story **-yiiya olugero** tell a story to **-nyumiza**

story-telling *n* **okufuma** *n15*

stout *adj* (1) (*fat*) **-gevvu**; (2) (*durable*) **-gumu** be stout (1) (*fat*) **-gejja**; (2) (*durable*) **-guma**

stove *n* **sitoovu** *n9*, (*charcoal*) **essigiri** *n9*

¹straight *adj* (1) (*eg. of a line*) **-tereevu**, *eg. oluguudo olutereevu ('straight road')*; (2) (*of an object*) **-golokofu**, *eg. omuti omugolokofu ('straight tree')*

²straight *adv* **obutereevu** straight up (*upright*) *adv* **obwesimbu** be straight **-tereera** get straight to the point **-tuukira ku nsonga** Go straight on. (*in giving directions*) **Genda butereevu., Genda busimba., Leega buleezi.** set (*someone*) straight (*show the right way to do things*) **-wabya**

straighten (out) *vt* (1) (*put right*) **-tereeza**, *eg. Yannyamba okutereeza ekiwempe. ('He helped me straighten the mat.')*; (2) (*stretch out*) **-golola**. See sort out

straightforward *adj* **-a enkukunala**, *eg. obujulizi obw'enkukunala ('straightforward evidence')* straightforward person **omwesimbu** *n1* not be straightforward with (*someone*) **-balankanya**

straightforwardness *n* **obwesimbu** *n14*

strain (*filter*) *vt* **-sengejja**, (*ashes to get salt*) **-genekera**. See drain; effort (make an) be strained (*filtered*) **-sengejjebwa**, (*of salt solution from ashes*) **-geneka** place for straining (*when making beer*) **essengejjero** *n5*

strainer *n* **akasengejja** *n12*, (*large, of sticks and grass, used in beer making*) **ekitaliri** *n7*

strand of cowrie shells *n* **olukalala lw'ensimbi** *n11*

stranger *n* **omugwira** *n1*

strangle *vt* **-tuga**

strap (*eg. for tying goods on bike*) *n* **olukoba** *n11* (*small* **akakoba** *n12*)

straw (*as used for drinking*) *n* **oluseke** *n11*

stray *vi* **-va ku**, *eg. Embuzi bbiri zaava ku zinnaazo.* (*'Two goats have strayed away from the others.'*). See lost (be) stray dog **embwa etaayaaya**

stream *n* **akagga** *n12*

street *n* **oluguudo** *n11*

strength *n* **amaanyi** *n6*, (*of a person*) **endasi** *n9*. See toughness give strength to (*a person*) **-zzaamu endasi**. See encourage regain strength **-ddamu amaanyi**, (*of person or animal after illness*) **-ddamu endasi**

strengthen *vt* **-gumya**. See encourage

[1]**stress** *n* (1) (*emphasis*) **essira** *n5*; (2) (*worry*) **obweraliikirivu** *n14*

[2]**stress** (*emphasise*) *vt* **-ggumiza**, (*repeatedly*) **-kubiriza** be stressed (*worried*) **-eeraliikirira**

stretch (*something elastic or sticky*) *vt* **-naanuula**. See spread; straighten; tighten; widen stretch a drum (*to tune it*) **-leega eŋŋoma** stretch legs apart **-leeguula amagulu** stretch one's leg **-leega okugulu** stretch oneself **-eegolola** stretch out **-golola**, *eg. Yagolola omukono gwe.* (*'She stretched out her arm.'*) stretch out a skin to dry **-bamba eddiba** stretch the neck **-nuula ensingo** be stretched (*of something elastic or sticky*) **-naanuuka** person who stretches (*eg. hides*) **omuleezi** *n1* sit with legs stretched out (*while seated on the ground*) **-tuula -lannama**

stretcher *n* (1) (*for carrying a sick person*) **olunnyo** *n11*; (2) (*for carrying a dead person*) **akannyo** *n12*

strew *vt* **-sasira**, *eg. Baasasidde etteete mu ssabo.* (*'They have strewn grass in the shrine.'*)

strict *adj* **-kambwe**

strife *n* **empaka** *n10*

[1]**strike** (*by workers*) *n* **akeediimo** *n12* go on strike **-eediima**

[2]**strike** *v* (1) *vi* (*of lightning*) **-gwa**, *eg. Eggulu ligwa.* (*'Lightning is striking.'*); (2) *vt* (*hit*) **-kuba** strike a tent (*take down*) **-simbulawo eweema** strike at goal (*in football*) **-teeba eggoolo** strike off (*person from official list, eg. errant doctor*) **-wanduukulula** strike root (*of a cutting*) **-loka**

striker *n* (1) (*person who refuses to work*) **omuntu eyeediimye** *n1*; (2) (*in football*) **omuteebi** *n1*

striking (*conspicuous, especially of clothes*) *adj* **matankane** (*invariable adjective*)

[1]**string** *n* **akaguwa** *n12*, (*of a musical instrument*) **olukoba** *n1*. See cord; fibre string of banana fibre (*used to lift off leaves covering food bundle after cooking*) **omugondoli** *n3* string of beads (*worn by young girls*) **ebiti** *n8*

[2]**string** (*eg. beads*) *vt* **-teeka ku kaguwa**

[1]**strip** *n*. See border strip cut from midrib of banana leaf (*used in basket-making*) **akakeedo** *n12* strip of bark (*from shrub Triumfetta, used as cord*) **ekinsambwe** *n7* strip of barkcloth (*used as clothing*) (1) (*used by men*) **ekikunta** *n3*; (2) (*used by women*) **omutanda** *n3* decorative strip on busuuti **omudalizo** *n3* put decorate strip on busuuti **-daliza omudalizo**

[2]**strip (off)** *vt* (1) (*something stuck down*) **-bambula**, *eg. Kibuyaga yabambuddeko amabaati ku nnyumba.* (*'The wind stripped the sheets from the roof.'*); (2) (*carefully*) **-bambulula**, *eg. Yabambulula amabaati ku nnyumba.* (*'He stripped the sheets off the house.'*); (3) (*eg. beads from string or leaves from twig*) **-wulula**, *eg. Yawulula embira ku kaguwa.* (*'She stripped the beads off the string.'*). See peel (*for words relating to stripping bark from a tree*) strip grains from maize cob **-kongola kasooli** strip midrib from banana leaf **-yubuluza olulagala** strip off clothes (*undress*) **-eeyambula** strip roof from **-sereekulula**, *eg. Abaseresi basereekulula ennyumba.* (*'The roofers are stripping the roof from the house.'*) be(come) stripped off (*eg. of roof sheets by wind*) **-bambulukuka**

stripe *n* **ekikuubo** *n7* (*thin* **akakuubo** *n12*)

striped *adj* **-a ebikuubo**, *eg. essaati y'ebikuubo* (*'striped shirt'*)

strive *vi* **-fuba**. See aspire; persevere

[1]**stroke** (*illness*) *n* **situlooka** *n9*

[2]**stroke** (*with the hand*) *vt* **-weeweeta**. See rub

stroll (about) *vi* **-tambulatambulako**

strong *adj* **-gumu**, *eg. olutindo olugumu* (*'strong bridge'*), (*of person or animal*) **-a amaanyi**, *eg. omusajja w'amaanyi* (*'strong man'*), (*of drink or tobacco*) **-ka**, *eg. omwenge omuka* (*'strong beer'*) be strong **-guma**, (*of person or animal*) **-beera n'amaanyi** be strong in spirit **-guma mu mwoyo**

strop *n* **ekibalangulo** *n7*

[1]**struggle** (*big effort*) *n* **ensiitaano** *n9*. See fight

[2]**struggle** *vi* (1) (*work hard*) **-siitaana**, *eg. Baasiitaana okuggya emmotoka mu lukonko.* (*'They struggled to get the car out of the ditch.'*); (2) (*eg. with carrying a heavy burden*) **-walabana**, *eg. Agenda awalabana n'omugugu.* (*'She is struggling with a heavy load.'*); (3) (*involve oneself with a difficult task*) **-kakaalukana**, *eg. Akakaalukana asobole okwezimbira ennyumba.* (*'She is struggling hard to build her house.'*). See fight; toil away; try hard; work hard struggle to do things (*especially when sick or old*) **-kekejjana**, *eg.*

Omukadde akekejjana okuyimuka. ('The old person is struggling to stand up.') struggle very hard against -**ttunka ne**, *eg. Attunka n'omusango ogw'okutta omuntu. ('She is struggling to defend herself in the murder case.')* struggle with many things to do -**tegana n'emirimu** struggle with something difficult to do -**kikiitana**

strut about *vi* (1) (*in a proud and pompous way*) -**tambula -kemba**; (2) (*showing one's importance*) -**kaalakaala**

stubble (*on face*) *n* enviiri z'oluwe *n10*

stubborn *adj* -**kakanyavu, -a emputtu**. *See* argumentative stubborn person **omukakanyavu** *n1*, **ow'emputtu** *n1* be stubborn (1) -**kakanyala**; (2) -**lina** *or* -**ba na** ('*have*') *according to tense* (**N20.1**) *followed by* **emputtu** ('*stubbornness*'), *eg. Omusajja omukadde alina emputtu. ('The old man is strubborn.')*

stubbornness *n* obukakanyavu *n14*, **emputtu** *n10*

stuck *See* stick

student *n* omuyizi *n1*

studio *n* situdiyo *n9*

studies *n* okusoma *n15* course of studies **omusomo** *n3*

study *vit* -**soma**, *eg. Asoma Olufalansa. ('He is studying French.')* study at/in -**somera**, *eg. Nsomera Gayaza. ('I am studying at Gayaza.')*

¹**stuff** (*things*) *n* ebintu *n8*

²**stuff (in)** (*force in*) *vt* -**kakaatika**, *eg. Yakakaatika ebitabo mu kabada. ('She stuffed the books into the cupboard.')*, (*in a disorderly way*) -**fuutiika** stuff food in mouth -**vuubiika emmere** stuff oneself with food -**eepiika emmere** be stuffed up (*of the nose*) *See* nose be stuffed with (*crowded*) -**fumbekera**, *eg. Ekkanisa yali efumbekedde abantu. ('The church was stuffed with people.')*. *See* crowded

stumble *vi* -**eesittala**

stumbling block *n* ekyesittazo *n7*. *See* obstacle

stump *n* (1) (*of tree*) enkonge *n9* (big **ekikonge** *n7*); (2) (*of banana plant*) enkolo *n9* basal part of tree or shrub (*above and below ground*) **ekikolo** *n7*

stung *See* sting

stunted, be *vi* -**kona**, *eg. Enkoko zaakona. ('The chickens are stunted.')*, (*of a child; fail to grow*) -**ziŋŋama**. *See* deformed

stupid *adj* -**siru** stupid person **omusiru** *n1*, (*lacking intelligence or ignorant*) **omubuguyavu** *n1* be(come) stupid -**siruwala** make stupid -**siruwaza**

stupidity (*foolishness*) *n* obusiru *n14*

stupified, be *vi* -**wuniikirira, -tangaalirira**

stutter *vi* -**naanaagira**

stutterer *n* omunaanaagize *n1*

sty (*in eye*) *n* akasekere *n12*

style (*fashion*) *n* omusono *n3*. *See* manner

stylish *adj* -**a omulembe**

sub-clan *n* essiga *n5* head of sub-clan **ow'essiga** *n1*

sub-county *n* eggombolola *n9* sub-county chief **ow'eggombolola** *n1*

subdue *vt* -**wangula**

¹**subject** *n* (1) (*someone ruled*) omufuge *n1*; (2) (*of a sentence in grammar*) omukozi *n1*; (3) (*something for discussion*) omulamwa *n3*

²**subject** (*force*) *vt* -**waliriza**, *eg. Yawaliriza bakole ky'ayagala. ('He subjected them to his will.')* be subjected -**walirizibwa**

subjection *n* obufuge *n14*

subjugate *vt* -**wangula**

submarine *n* lubbira *n9*

submerge *vt* -**bbika**. *See* dip in submerge oneself -**eebbika** be(come) submerged -**bbira**

submissive *adj* -**gonvu** submissive person **omugonvu** *n1* be(come) submissive -**gonda** be submissive towards -**gondera**

submit (*hand in*) *vi* -**waayo**, *eg. Awaddeyo lipoota. ('He has submitted the report.')*. *See* surrender submit a proposal -**yanjula ensonga, -waayo ekirowoozo**

subscription *n* ekisale *n7*

subsequently *adv* ekiddako, ekiddirira, eky'oluvannyuma

subservient *adj* -**wombeefu** be subservient -**eewombeeka**

subside (*of inflammation, anger, etc.*) *vi* -**kkakkana**. *See* deflate

subsoil *n* olukuusi *n1*

substance *n* (1) (*thing*) ekintu *n7*, *eg. ebintu by'obutwa ('poisonous substances')*; (2) (*truth; evidence*) *Refer to* **amakulu** ('*meaning*') *in neg* (**N21**), *eg. Tekiriimu makulu. ('There is no substance in it.')*. *See* flavouring

substantiate (*prove*) *vt* -**kakasa**

substitute (for) *vt* -**teeka mu kifo (kya)**

subtract *vt* -**toolako**, *eg. Bbiri toolako emu ofuna emu. ('Two subtract one makes one.')*, -**ggyako, -yawulako** subtract a part (*of produce, or income from produce – to present to a chief*) -**lobolako**

subvert (*lead astray*) *vt* -**wabya**

succeed *v* (1) (*manage; be able*) *vi* -**sobola**, *eg. Yasobola okufuna omulimu. ('She succeeded in getting a job.')*; (2) (*in a position*) *vt* -**dda mu**, *eg. Y'eyadda mu bwami nga taata we abuvuddemu. ('He succeeded his father as chief.')*. *See* heir (become an) succeed at -**tuukiriza**, *eg. Yagezaako okutuukiriza omulimu. ('She tried to succeed at her job.')*

success (*achievement*) *n* obuwanguzi *n14*

successor (*heir*) *n* omusika *n1*

such as (*for example*) *conj* okugeza a person such as me gamba nga nze

suck (*eg. a sweet*) *vt* -**nuuna**, (*through a straw*) -**nyuunyunta** suck noisily (on) (*in eating or drinking*) -**solobeza**

sucker (*of a plant*) *vi* -**sibuka**, (*of a banana plant*) -**zaala** begin to produce suckers (*of a recently*

planted banana plant) **-kkulira**
suckle *v* (1) *vi* **-yonka**; (2) *vt* **-yonsa**
Sudan *n* Sudaani *n9*
Sudanese (*person*) *n* Omusudaani *n1*
sudden *adj* **-a embagirawo**
suddenly *adv* embagirawo, *eg. Ekintu kyabadde
kya mbagirawo. ('It happened suddenly.')* die
suddenly **-fa kibwatukira**, *eg. Yafudde
kibwatukira. ('He died suddenly.')* react suddenly
(*through shock; start up*) **-baguka**
suds *n* ejjovu *n5*, ekyovu *n7*, ebyovu *n8* produce
suds **-mmuka**
suffer *vi* **-bonaabona**, *eg. Yesu yabonaabona ku
lwaffe. ('Jesus suffered for us.')* suffer from shock
-gwamu (*or* **-funa**) **ensisi**, (*with the heart racing*)
emmeeme -tyemuka suffer greatly **-dooba**
suffer hardship **-laba ennaku**
suffering *n* ekibonoobono *n7* cause suffering to
-bonyaabonya
sufficient, be *vi* (1) (*enough*) **-mala**, *eg. Emmere
emaze. ('The food is sufficient.') – meaning
'everyone will be satisfied';* (2) (*to go around*)
-buna, *eg. Emmere ebunye. ('The food is
sufficient.') – meaning 'all will get some')*
sufficiently *adv* ekimala
suffocate *vi* **-ziyira**, *eg. Nziyira. ('I am
suffocating.')*
suffocation ekiziyiro *n7*
sugar *n* sukaali *n1* sugar cane ekikajjo *n7*, (*stick*)
empango y'ekikajjo *n9*, (*segment*) **ennyingo
y'ekikajjo** *n9*, (*type of sugar cane with thin stem*)
ekirumbirumbi *n7*
suggest *vt* **-leeta ekirowoozo**
suicide suicide bomber omutujju *n1* commit
suicide **-etta**. *See* hang oneself
[1]**suit** (*of clothes*) *n* essuuti *n9*
[2]**suit** *vi* (1) (*be suitable for*) **-saanira**, *eg. Omulimu
guno gukusaanira. ('This work suits you.');* (2)
(*look good on*) **-nyumira**, *eg. Olugoye olwo
lukunyumira. ('That dress suits you.')* suit one
another **-tuukagana**
suitability *n* ekisaanyizo *n7*
suitable be suitable **-saana**, **-gwana** be suitable
for **-saanira**, *eg. Yafunye olugoye olusaanira
omukolo. ('He got clothing suitable for the
occasion.'),* **-gwanira** consider suitable for
-saanyiza
suitcase *n* essanduuko *n9*, ekkeesi *n9*
sulk *vi* **-eenyiizanyiiza**
sullen *adj* **-a ekkabyo**
sum (*total*) *n* omugatte *n3*
summarise *vt* **-funza**, **-ssa mu bumpi**
summit *n* entikko *n9*
summon *vt* **-yita**
sun *n* enjuba *n9*
sunbird *n* akanuunansubi *n12*
Sunday *n* Ssande *n9*, Ssabbiiti *n9*, Wanga *n1*
sunflower, Mexican (*Tithonia*) *n* kimala empaka

kikoowa. *Name needs confirmation.*
sunglasses *n* gaalubindi z'omusana *n10*
sunlight *n* omusana *n3*
sunshine *n* omusana *n3*, akasana *n12*
superb *adj* **-lungi ennyo**
superfluous, be *vi* **-sukkirira**. *See* excessive
something superfluous (*not needed*) **ekitetaagisa**
n7
superimpose *vt* **-bereka**
superintendence *n* endabirira *n9*
superintendent *n* omukulu *n1*
superior (to), be *vi* **-singa obulungi**, *eg. Kaawa
ono yasinga obulungi. ('This coffee is superior.'),
(indicating personal preference or advantage)*
-kira, *eg. Kaawa ono akira oyo. ('This coffee is
superior to that one.' – 'in someone's opinion')*
supernatural power *n* amagezi g'omusawuzi *n6*
lose supernatural power **-fuluka**
supervise *vt* **-labirira**
supervision *n* okulabirira *n15*
supervisor *n* (1) (*boss*) omukulu *n1*; (2) (*foreman*)
nnampala *n1*
supper *n* ekyeggulo *n7*, ekyekiro *n7*
supplant *vt* **-dda mu kifo kya**
[1]**supplement** *n* akawaayiro *n12*
[2]**supplement** *vt* **-eegatta ku**, *eg. Abaserikale bano
bajja kwegatta ku baserikale abaliwo. ('These
troops will supplement those already there.'). See*
add
supply *vt* **-leetera**, *eg. Oyinza okutuleetera
amatofaali? ('Can you supply us bricks?')*
[1]**support** *n* (1) (*prop*) ekiwanirira *n7*; (2) (*backing*)
obuwagizi *n14*
[2]**support** *vt* (1) (*prop up*) **-wanirira**, *eg. Empagi
ewaniridde akasolya. ('The pole is supporting the
roof.'),* **-yigika**; (2) (*back; encourage*) **-wagira**, *eg.
Mmuwagira mu kulonda. ('I am supporting him in
the election.'). See* second support oneself on (*or*
against) (*by leaning on*) **-eesigama**, *eg. Yeesigamye
ekisenge. ('She is supporting herself against the
wall.'). See* hold up be supported (*eg. in election*)
-wagirwa
supporter (*person*) *n* omuwagizi *n1*
suppose *vi* **-lowooza**
supposedly *adv* mbu
suppress *vt* (1) (*repress*) **-nyigiriza**, *eg. Gavumenti
enyigiriza ab'oludda oluvuganya. ('The government
is suppressing the opposition.');* (2) (*an emotion*)
-bikkako ku, *eg. Yabikkako ku nnaku nga
awulidde amawulire. ('She suppressed her sadness
when she heard the news.'). See* conceal; hide
suppress news **-vubiikiriza amawulire** suppress
pain (*with water or saliva*) **-vubiriza**, *eg. Yanywa
amazzi okuvubiriza okubalagala kwa kamulali.
('She drank water to suppress the burning from the
hot pepper.')*
sure (*certain*) *adj* **-kakafu** be sure **-kakata** make
sure **-kakasa**

surety (*collateral*) *n* **omusingo** *n3*, **akakalu** *n12*
<u>put up as surety</u> **-singawo**, *eg. Yasingawo ettaka lye.* (*'He put up his land as surety.'*) <u>put up surety for</u> **-eeyimirira**, *eg. Musoke yawaayo obukadde okweyimirira mukoddomi we.* (*'Musoke put up ten million shillings as surety for his brother-in-law.'*)

surface (*come to the surface in a liquid*) *vi* **-bbulukuka** <u>on the surface</u> (*on top*) **kungulu** <u>on the surface of</u> **kungulu ku**

surgery *n* (1) (*operation*) **okulongoosa** *n15*; (2) (*clinic*) **kiriniki** *n9*. *See* hospital

surly, be (*in response to a request*) *vi* **-eekaanya**

surmount *vt* **-vvuunuka**, *eg. Yasobola okuvvuunuka ebizibu bye.* (*'He managed to surmount his difficulties.'*)

surpass (in) *vt* **-yisa**, *eg. Amuyisizza obuwanvu.* (*'She has surpassed him in height.'*), **-singa**, *eg. Yabadde amusinga obuwanvu.* (*'She has surpassed him in height.'*) <u>make surpass</u> **-sinza**

¹**surplus** (*left-over*) *adj*. *Use* **-fikka** (*'be surplus'*) *in rel* (**N7.1**), *eg. emmere efisse* (*'surplus food'*)

²**surplus** *n* **enfissi** *n9*. *See* balance <u>be surplus</u> **-fikka**, *eg. Eccupa zino zifisse.* (*'These bottles are surplus.'* – *to requirements*)

¹**surprise** *n* **ekyewuunyisa** *n7* <u>make a surprise attack</u> **-zinduukiriza**, *eg. Abalabe baatuzinduukiriza nga twebase.* (*'The enemy made a surprise attack on us when we were sleeping.'*)

²**surprise** (*astonish*) *vt* **-eewuunyisa**, *eg. Ekisa kye kyatwewuunyisizza.* (*'His kindness surprised us.'*) <u>be surprised</u> **-eewuunya**, *eg. Nneewuunya okumusanga awo.* (*'I was surprised to meet her there.'*)

surrender *vi* **-eewaayo**, *eg. Abayeekera beewaayo eri amagye ga gavumenti.* (*'The guerillas surrendered to the government army.'*) <u>raise one's hands in surrender</u> **-wanika emikono**

surround *vt* (1) (*general word*) **-eetoolola**; (2) (*in a military sense*) **-eebungulula**, *eg. Abaserikale beebungulula abalabe.* (*'The soldiers surrounded the enemy.'*) <u>surround with</u> **-eetoolooza**, *eg. Ennyumba baagyetoolooza olukomera.* (*'They surrounded the house with a hedge.'*) <u>be surrounded (by)</u> **-eetooloolwa**, *eg. Ennyumba yeetooloddwa emiti.* (*'The house is surrounded by trees.'*), (*militarily*) **-eebungululwa**, *eg. Ekifo kyebunguluddwa abaserikale.* (*'The place is surrounded by soldiers.'*)

¹**survey** *n* <u>do a survey</u> (*by asking around*) **-buuliriza**, *eg. Baabuuliriza mu bantu okumanya essomero erisinga obulungi.* (*'They did a survey to find the best school.'*)

²**survey** *vt* **-noonyereza**. *See* investigate; look for; study <u>survey land</u> **-kuba ettaka**

surveyer (*of land*) *n* **omupunta** *n1*

survive (*calamity*) *vi* **-lama**, *eg. Mu kabenje abantu babiri be balamye.* (*'Two people survived the accident.'*)

survivor *n*. *Use* **-lama** (*'survive'*) *in rel* (**N7.1**), *eg. abantu abalamye* (*'survivors'*)

suspect *vt* **-lowoolereza**, *eg. Nnamulowoolereza okuba nti ye yabba essente.* (*'I suspected that he stole the money.'*), **-suubiriza**. *See* suspicious <u>be suspected</u> **-lowoozebwa**, *eg. Alowoozebwa nti ye yazza omusango.* (*'He is suspected of the crime.'*)

suspend *vt* (1) (*an activity*) **-yimiriza**, *eg. Baayimiriza okuzannya omupiira mu kibiina.* (*'They have suspended playing football at the club.'*); (2) (*person from organisation*) **-wummuza**, *eg. Abaana bange baabawummuza mu ssomero.* (*'They have suspended my children from school.'*); (3) (*hang up*) **-wanika**. *See* cease; dangle; stop <u>be suspended</u> (1) (*of an activity*) **-yimirizibwa**; (2) (*hung up*) **-wanikibwa** <u>in suspense</u> **mu lusuubo**

suspicious of, be (*suspect*) *vt* **-suubiriza**, (*and watchful*) **-eekengera**, *eg. Alabye omusajja n'amwekengera ng'alowooza nti mubbi.* (*'He watched the man carefully because he suspected he was a thief.'*). *See* suspect

sustain *vt* **-beezaawo**, *eg. Eyo emmere ejja kubabeezaawo.* (*'That food will sustain them.'*) <u>sustain oneself</u> (*be independent*) **-eebeezaawo**, **-eeyimirizaawo**

Swahili (*language*) *n* **Oluswayiri** *n11*

¹**swallow** (*type of bird*) *n* **akataayi** *n12*

²**swallow** (*eg. food*) *vt* **-mira**

swamp *n* **ekisenyi** *n7*. *See* island; wetland

¹**swarm** *n* **ekibinja**, *eg. ekibinja ky'enjuki* (*'swarm of bees'*) (*small* **akabinja** *n12*) <u>swarm of young locusts</u> **lusejjera** *n1*

²**swarm** (*of bees*) *vi* **-zunga**, *eg. Enjuki zaazunze.* (*'The bees have swarmed.'*) <u>swarm around</u> (*in the air, as flies above meat*) **-zungirira** <u>swarm over</u> (*as flies on meat*) **-bemberera**

swarming time *n* **omugano** *n3*, (*of flying termites*) **omugano gw'enswa**, (*of grasshoppers*) **omugano gw'enseenene**

sway *v* (1) *vi* **-yuuga**, *eg. Ettabi liyuuga.* (*'The branch is swaying.'*); (2) (*cause to sway*) *vt* **-yuuza**, *eg. Kibuyaga ayuuza emiti.* (*'The wind is swaying the trees.'*), (*more violently*) **-yuuganya**

swear *vi* (*swore*) (1) (*be determined*) **-malirira**, *eg. Poliisi emaliridde okukwata eyasse omuntu.* (*'The police swore they would catch the murderer.'*); (2) (*in court*) **-layira**, *eg. Omujulizi yalayira okwogera amazima.* (*'The witness swore to tell the truth.'*); (3) (*that one will do something*) **-eerayirira**; (4) (*use bad language*) **-wemula**. *See* curse <u>swear allegiance</u> **-wera**, *eg. Baawera mu maaso ga Kabaka.* (*'They swore allegance to the Kabaka.'*) <u>swear in</u> (*office holder or witness*) **-layiza**, *eg. Baamulayiza ng'agenda okuwa obujulizi.* (*'They swore him in as a witness.'*) <u>swear words</u> (*bad language*) **ebyobuwemu** *n8*

¹**sweat** *n* **entuuyo** *n10*

²**sweat** *vi* **-tuuyana**

sweep *vt* -yera

sweeper *n* omwezi *n1*

[1]**sweet** *adj* -woomerevu   sweet potato **lumonde** *n1*. *See* potato   something sweet **ekiwoomerera** *n7*   taste sweet (to) **-woomerera**, *eg. Sukaali awoomerera. ('Sugar is sweet.')*

[2]**sweet(s)** *n* switi *n1* (*or* ka switi, *pl.* bu switi)

sweetheart *n* kabiite *n1*

sweetness *n* obuwoomerevu *n14*

sweet-talk *vt* -kuba akalimi. *See* woo

swell *vi* (swollen) -zimba, *eg. Omukono gwe guzimbye. ('Her arm is swollen.'), (of the stomach or of milk boiling up)* -tumbiira, *eg. Olubuto lwe lutumbidde. ('His stomach is swollen.'). See* bloated (be); bulge out; leavened (be); turn up

swelling *n* ekizimba *n7*   swollen lymph gland **ensanjabavu** *n9*

swerve *vt* -weta, *eg. Yaweta emmotoka okwewala okutomera embwa. ('She swerved the car to avoid knocking the dog.')*

[1]**swift** (*fast*) *adj* -yangu   be swift **-yanguwa**

[2]**swift** (*type of bird*) *n* akataayi

swiftly *adv* amangu, (*in running*) **embiro**

swim *vi* -wuga

swimmer *n* omuwuzi *n1*

swimming pool *n* ekidiba (ekiwugirwamu) *n7*

swindle *vt* (1) (*overcharge*) -seera; (2) (*deliberately fail to repay a debt to*) **-lyazaamannya**. *See* cheat

swindler *n* (1) (*one who overcharges*) omuseezi *n1*; (2) (*one who deliberately fails to repay a debt*) **omulyazaamaanyi** *n1*

[1]**swing** *n* olusuubo *n11*

[2]**swing** *vt* -suuba, *eg. Asuuba omwana ku lusuubo. ('She is swinging the child on a swing.')*   swing one's arms **-wuuba emikono**   swing oneself **-eesuuba**

[1]**switch** *n* emmanduso *n9*, **swiki** *n9*

[2]**switch** (*change; transfer*) *vt* -kyusa   switch off a light **-zikiza ettaala**   switch off electricity **-ggyako amasannyalaze**   switch on (*something electrical*) **-teekako, -ssaako**   switch on car engine **-teekamu omuliro mu mmotoka, -tandika emmotoka**   switch one's political party **-sala eddiiro**

[1]**swollen** *adj* (1) *Use* -zimba ('*swell*') *in rel* (**N7.1**), *eg. olubuto oluzimbye ('swollen stomach'); (2) (to excess)* -tumbiivu, *eg. olubuto olutumbiivu ('swollen stomach')*

[2]**swollen** *v. See* swell

sword *n* ekitala *n7*

swore *See* swear

syllable *n* ennyingo y'ekigambo *n9*   break a word into syllables **-gattulula ekigambo mu nnyingo**   complete a syllable with a vowel **-weerera ennyukuta**

symbol *n* akabonero *n12*

sympathetic (*kind*) *adj* -a ekisa   sympathetic person **omusaasizi** *n1*

sympathise (with) *vt* -saasira, *eg. Twamusaasira.*

('We sympathised with her.'), (feeling someone's pain) **-lumirirwako**. *See* console

sympathy *n* obusaasizi *n14*. *See* consolation

syphilis *n* kabootongo *n1*   contract syphilis **-bootonga**   person with syphilis **owa kabootongo** *n1*   syphilitic chancre (*condition caused by syphilis*) **embaluka** *n9*

syringe *n* (1) (*used on people*) empiso *n9*; (2) (*big, used on animals*) **ekkato** *n5*

system *n* enkola *n9*

T,t

table *n* emmeeza *n9*. *See* rack

tablecloth *n* ekitambaala ky'emmeeza *n7*

tablet *n* (1) (*pill*) akakerenda *n12*; (2) (*blue, formerly used when rinsing washing*) **bbululu** *n1*   tablet of soap **ekitole kya ssabbuuni** *n7*

[1]**taboo** *adj* -a omuzizo

[2]**taboo** *n* omuzizo *n3*   be taboo **-zira**, *eg. Kizira omukazi okusula mu nnyumba y'omuko. ('It is taboo for a woman to stay in her son-in-law's house.')*   something taboo **ekyomuzizo** *n7*

tack (*in sewing*) *vt* -kwasa

tackle hard (*in football*) *vt* -kuba endobo

tadpole *n* akakulwe *n12*

tag (*game*) *n* kawuna *n12*   call used in tag **nkusibiddaawo** ('*I have tied you there*')

tail *n* omukira *n3* (*long* olukira *n11*), (*of snake or lizard*) **akawuuwo** *n12*. *See* backside   end of a tail (*eg. of cow – the part used to whisk away flies*) **emboobo** *n9*

tailor *n* (1) (*sewer*) omutunzi *n1*; (2) (*cutter of cloth*) **omukomozi** *n1*

take *v* (took) (1) (*have the capacity of*) *vi* -jjula, *eg. Ebbinika eyo ejjula ebikopo kkumi. ('That kettle takes ten cups.'); (2) vt* -twala, *eg. Yatwala ekirabo ewa ssengaawe. ('He took a present to his aunt's.'), (cause to arrive)* -tuusa, *eg. Ebbaasi yantuusiza eka. ('The bus took me home.'), (as prisoner; capture)* -wamba   take a long time (*to do something*) **-twalira ebbanga**, (*through delaying*) **-lwawo**, *eg. Yalwawo okujja. ('He took a long time to come.')*   take a look **-labako**   take a photograph **-kubisa ekifaananyi**. *See* photograph   take advantage of (*someone, in an exploitative way*) **-yiikiriza**   take all **-twala -onna**, (*accommodate within*) **-ggweera**, *eg. Sukaali aggweera mu nsawo. ('The bag can take all the sugar.')*   take an examination **-tuula ebibuuzo**   take apart (1) (*things joined together*) **-gattulula**; (2) (*things sewn or woven*) **-sattulula**; (3) (*disassemble, eg. machinery*) **-pangulula**, *eg. Yapangulula yingini. ('He took apart the engine.'); (4) (something tied)* **-sumulula**. *See* undo   take away (from) **-ggya** (*often with enclitic* **N24.2**), *eg. Ggya essowaani ku mmeeza. ('Take away the plates from the table.'),* (*everything*) **-malawo**, *eg. Malawo ebintu ebiri ku mmeeza.* ('Take away everything from the table.'). See subtract take back (*return*) **-zzaayo**, *eg. Yazzaayo enkumbi ewa muliraanwa we.* ('He took the hoe back to his neighbour's.') take by force (*plunder; loot*) **-nyaga** take care of (1) (*protect*) **-kuuma**; (2) (*look after*) **-labirira**; (3) (*oneself*) **-eekuuma** take cover See avoid; take shelter take cover off **-bikkula** take down (*lower physically*) **-wanula**, *eg. Yawanula ekifaananyi.* ('He took down the picture.'), **-ssa** take from **-ggyamu**, *eg. Yaggyamu ekikopo mu kabada.* ('She took a cup from the cupboard.') take (*items*) here and there (*in the hope of selling them*) **-tambuza** take in from drying (*eg. washing*) **-yanula** Take it! *order* **Kwako!** take leave of (*say goodbye to*) **-siibula** take lid off **-saanukula**, *eg. Yasaanukula sseffuliya.* ('She took the cover off the pan.') take off (1) (*of a plane*) *vi* **-situla**; (2) *vt* **-ggyako**, *eg. Bagenda okuggyako amabaati ku nnyumba.* ('They are going to take the iron sheets off the house.'), (*a load*) **-tikkula**, *eg. Atikkula embaawo ku loole.* ('He is taking the planks from the lorry.'), (*a load from oneself*) **-eetikkula**, (*something stuck down*) **-gagambula**, *eg. Yagagambudde pulasita.* ('She has taken off the plaster.'). See undress take off bedding **-yalula** take off part (*of produce, or income from produce, for a chief*) **-lobolako** take off pieces from **-somola**, *eg. Yasomola omugaati.* ('She took off pieces of bread bit-by-bit.') take oneself (*to a place*) **-eetwala** take out (1) **-ggyamu**, *eg. Ggyamu engoye mu ssanduuko.* ('Take the clothes out of the suitcase.'); (2) (*from inside*) **-fulumya**, *eg. Yafulumya emmere.* ('He took the food outside.'), **-twala ebweru**, (*something inserted, eg. handle*) **-wangula**; (3) (*something from the body with an implement*) **-tundula**, *eg. Yatundula envunza okuva mu kigere kye.* ('She took out the jigger from her foot.'). See extract; pull out take out of a hiding place **-kwekula** take out of the sun (*something drying*) **-yanula** take out of water **-nnyulula**, *eg. Yannyulula engoye.* ('She took the clothes out of water.') take part in (*participate*) **-eetaba** take place **-baawo** or **-liwo** ('be there') *according to tense* (N20.1), *eg. (1) Olukuŋŋaana lwaliwo jjo.* ('The meeting took place yesterday.'); *(2) Olukuŋŋaana lujja kubaawo enkya.* ('The meeting will take place tomorrow.') take shelter from (*eg. from rain*) **-eggama** take some **-toola** (*often with enclitic* N24.2), *eg. Yatoolako ebinyeebwa n'abirya.* ('She took some peanuts and ate them.') take time (*to do something*) **-twala ekiseera**, **-twala ebbanga**, *eg. Yatwala ekiseera okusalawo.* ('He took time to decide.') take to **-twalira**, *eg. Yamutwalira emmere.* ('He took food to her.') take up room (1) (*of a person, items in store, etc.*) **-zimbagala**; (2) (*of a plant*) **-zijjagala** take

vengeance **-woolera eggwanga** be taken aback (1) (*dumbfounded*) **-wuniikirira**; (2) (*showing visible shock*) **-eesisiwala**

tale (*story*) *n* **olugero** *n11* folk tale **olufumo** *n11*
talent *n* **ekitone** *n7*
talk (*speech; lecture*) *n* **okwogera** *n15*. See conservation; gossip be all talk and no action **-kuba amatama, -kuba kkerere**
talk *vi* **-yogera**, *eg. Sirika, Musoke ayogera.* ('Be quiet, Musoke is talking.'). See chat; chatter; drawl; speak; stammer. *Ways of talking include:* (1) (*incessantly; prattle on*) **-jegera**; (2) (*loudly*) **-yogerera waggulu**; (3) (*harshly*) **-yogera -boggoka**; (4) (*rapidly and unclearly; jabber*) **-sabuliza**; (5) (*for too long*) **-yogera butamala, -yogera olulondakambe**, (*with nothing much to say*) **-yogera olumoonyere**. talk about **-yogerako** (or **-yogera ku**), *eg. Baali batwogerako.* ('They were talking about us.') talk badly about **-vumirira** talk behind the back of **-geya** talk nonsense **-yogera ebitaliimu** talk with/to **-yogera ne**, *eg. Ayogera n'omusomesa.* ('He is talking with the teacher.')
tall *adj* **-wanvu** tall person (1) (*and big*) **empaladdume** *n9*; (2) (*and well-built*) **omuwaggufu** *n1*; (3) (*and strong*) **omulangaatira** *n1*
tallness *n* **obugulumivu** *n14*
talon *n* **olwala** *n11*
tamarind *n* (1) (*tree*) **omukooge** *n3*; (2) (*fruit*) **enkooge** *n9*
tame *adj* **-fuge**. See domesticated
tame *vt* **-fuga** be tamed **-fugibwa**
tamper with *vt* **-tigiinya**
tangerine *n* **mangada** *n1*
tangle (up) *vt* **-tugga**, *eg. Atuzze emiguwa* ('He has tangled up the ropes.'). See intertwine be(come) tangled **-eetugga**
tank *n* **ttanka** *n9* water tank **ttanka y'amazzi**
tanner *n* **omuwazi** *n1*, (*chief, of the Kabaka*) **Kiyini** *n1 title*
tannia (*type of yam, plant similar in appearance to taro*) *n* **ejjuuni (erikaluba)** *n5*. The edible cormlets are called **obukopa** *n14*.
tantalise (*by pretending to offer*) *vt* **-kookoonya**
Tanzania *n* **Tanzaniya** *n9*
Tanzanian (*person*) *n* **Omutanzaniya** *n1*
tap (*eg. on water pipe*) *n* **taapu** *n9*
tap (*knock*) *vt* **-konkona**, *eg. Yakonkona ku luggi.* ('She tapped on the door.')
tape *n* **olutambi** *n11* tape measure **olukoba olupima** *n11*
taper (*of barkcloth, for carrying fire*) *n* **enfuuzi** *n9*
taper (*narrow*) *v* (1) *vi* **-sondowala**; (2) *vt* **-sondowaza**
tapeworm *n* **enjoka zi nnamumwa** *n10*
target *n* **ssabbaawa** *n9*
target (*aim at*) *vt* **-yolekeza**

tarmac *n* kkoolaasi *n1*

tarnish (*spoil*) *vt* -yonoona, (*a reputation*) -siiga enziro become tarnished (*loose shine, of metal*) -zigama

taro (*also* cocoyam) *n* ejjuuni (erigonda) *n5*

tarpaulin *n* ettundubaali *n5*

tart have a tart taste (*as an unripe fruit*) *vi* -kambagga

task *n* (1) (*set manual task*) ekkatala *n5*; (2) (*something to do*) ekyokukola *n7*. See job task master nnampala *n1* do initial stages of a task -baga

tassel *n* omujunga *n3*

[1]**taste** (*pleasant, of food*) *n* ensa *n9*

[2]**taste** *vt* -kombako, lozaako, (*referring to alcohol*) -lega. *Types of taste include*: (1) (*bitter or sour*) -kaayirira; (2) (*tart, as an unripe fruit*) -kambagga (*and causing tingling in the cheeks*) -nywanywagala; (3) (*as an unripe raspberry*) -tuŋŋununa. taste good to -woomera, *eg. Emmere empoomera. ('The food tastes good to me.')* What does the food taste like? **Emmere ewooma etya?**

taster (*of beer*) *n* omulezi *n1*

tasty be tasty -wooma, *eg. Emmere ewooma. ('The food is tasty.')*. See delicious be tasty to -woomera make tasty -woomesa, *eg. Omufumbi awoomesezza emmere. ('The cook made the food tasty.')*

taunt *vt* (1) (*by pretending to offer*) -kookoonya; (2) (*by repeating something annoyingly; harping on*) -yeeya

taut *adj*. See tight become taut -eereega, *eg. Omuguwa gwereeze. ('The rope is taut.')* draw taut -leega, *eg. Yaleega omuguwa. ('He drew the rope taut.')*

tavern (*bar*) *n* ebbaala *n5*

[1]**tax** *n* empooza *n9*, omusolo *n3*, (*paid in kind to chief or landowner*) envujjo *n9* tax assessor omugeresi w'omusolo *n1* tax collector omuwooza *n1* tax payer omuwi w'omusolo *n1* place where taxes are collected eggwoolezo *n5* way of taxing empooza *n9*

[2]**tax** *vt* -wooza

taxi *n* takisi *n9*, (*14-seater communal*) kamunye *n1*, (*single hire*) sipesulo *n9*, (*motorbike*) bodaboda *n9* taxi driver owa takisi *n1*, (*motorcyclist*) owa bodaboda *n1* taxi park ppaaka ya takisi *n9* taxi stop siteegi *n9*

TB *n* akafuba *n12*

tea *n* caayi *n1* (*or* chai) tea leaves amajaani *n6*, (*used*) ebikamulo bya caayi *n8*

teach *vt* -yigiriza, -somesa. See train

teacher *n* omuyigiriza *n1*, omusomesa *n1* headteacher omukulu w'essomero *n1*

teaching *n* okuyigiriza *n15*, okusomesa *n15* way of teaching enjigiriza *n9*, ensomesa *n9*

team *n* ettiimu *n9*

teapot *n* ettipoota *n9*, bbuli *n9*

[1]**tear** *n* (1) (*from eye*) ezziga *n5*; (2) (*eg. in cloth*) awayulifu *n16* tear gas omukka ogubalagala *n3* tears in the eye (*about to cry*) ebiyengeyenge *n8* be on the verge of tears (*of a baby*) -tuubatuuba

[2]**tear** *vt* (tore; torn) -yuza, *eg. Eriggwa lyayuza olugoye lwe. ('The thorn tore her dress.')*, (*into shreds*) -sensula, (*with nails or claws*) -taagula. See rip tear down (*climbing plant*) -landulula tear off (*something stuck down*) -bambula, *eg. Yabambulako akapande. ('She tore off the label.')* tear off a piece of -kooza tear open (*something sealed*) -yabuluza be torn -yulika, (*to pieces*) -sensuka, (*by claws or nails*) -taaguka

tease (*in a playful way*) *vt* -zannyiikiriza. See taunt; torment

teaspoon *n* akajiiko *n12*

teat *n* ennywanto *n9*

technique *n* enkola *n9*

technology *n* tekinologiya *n9*

teem on (*eg. flies on dung*) *vi* -bemberera. See whirl about

teenager *n* omutiini *n1*

teeth See tooth

telecommunications *n* ebyempulizaganya *n8*

[1]**telephone**(*also* phone) *n* essimu *n9*, (*mobile*) akasimu *n12*, (*public*) essimu y'olukale telephone call essimu *n5* telephone mast omulongooti (*or* omunaala) gw'essimu *n3*

[2]**telephone** (*also* phone) *v* (1) *vi* -kuba essimu; (2) *vt* -kubira, *eg. Nja kumukubira. ('I shall telephone her.')*

television *n* ttivvi *n9*

tell *vt* (told) -buulira, *eg. Yambuulira ky'alowooza. ('She told me her thoughts.')*. See disclose; divulge; inform; say tell a dream to -lootolola tell a story -gera (*or* -fuma) olugero, *eg. Afuma olugero lwa Baganda. ('He is telling the story of the Baganda.')* tell a story to -nyumiza olugero, *eg. Yanyumiza abaana olugero. ('She told a story to the children.')* tell off (*reprimand*) -nenya tell on (*denounce*) -loopa tell untruths -sala ebigambo

temper bad temper obusungu *n14*

temperament *n* enkula *n9*

temperature *n* ebbugumu *n5*

temple (*Jewish*) *n* yeekaalu *n9*. See shrine

temporary *adj* -a ekiseera, *eg. abakozi b'ekiseera ('temporary employees')* temporary construction ekisaakaate *n7*, (*eg. made for an event*) ekidaala *n7*, (*shelter, eg. to pass the night when travelling*) ekibaabugo *n7* temporary work omulimu gw'ekiseera *n3* temporary worker omukozi wa lejjalejja *n1*

tempt *vt* -kema be tempted -kemebwa

temptation *n* ekikemo *n7*

tempter *n* omukemi *n1*

ten *num* kkumi *n5* ten thousand omutwalo *n3*

tenant *n* omupangisa *n1*

tend (*look after*) *vt* -**labirira**

tender (*eg. of meat*) *adj* -**gonvu** be(come) tender -**gonda**, *eg. Fumba ennyama egonde.* (*'Cook the meat so that it becomes tender.'*)

tenderise (*eg. meat*) *vt* -**gonza**

tendon *n* **ekinywa** *n7*, (*Achilles*) **oluteega** *n11*, (*at back of knee*) **olutegetege** *n11*, (*of the back*) **omuziisa** *n3* tendons of the neck **ebikya** *n8*

tennis (*also* tennis ball) *n* **ttena** *n9* tennis racket **ekiwujjo** *n7*

tent *n* **eweema** *n9*

tenterhooks, on *adv* **ku bwerende**

tenth *adj/num* -**a ekkumi** (**N7.1**)

term (*in school*) *n* **olusoma** *n11*

terminate *v* (1) (*split up; separate*) *vi* -**yawukana**, *eg. Baayawukana bulungi.* (*'They terminated their relationship amicably.'*; (2) (*someone's employment*) *vt* -**goba**, *eg. Mukama we amugobye.* (*'The boss has terminated her employment.'*). See end terminate at -**koma**, *eg. Leerwe ekoma Kampala.* (*'The railway terminates at Kampala.'*)

terminus *n* **ekigobero** *n7*

termite (*also* white ant) *n* (*worker; soldier*) **enkuyege** *n9*, (*flying*) **enswa** *n9*, (*queen*) **nnamunswa** *n1. Types of termites include*: (1) (*small edible type*) **ennaka** *n9*; (2) (*other edible types*) **empawu** *n9*, **entunda** *n9*, **ensejjere** *n9*, **embaala** *n9*, **embobya** *n9*; (3) (*small inedible types*) **obuggalamatu** *n14*, **obumpoowooko** *n14*. See ant termite mound **ekiswa** *n7*, (*small, dark coloured type, very hard*) **enkulukuku** *n9*, (*abandoned*) **ekiswa ekifulufu**, (*type made by embaala termites*) **ekibaala** *n7. Termite mounds made by other types of termites are named following this pattern*: (*made by 'ennaka' termites*) **ekiswa ky'ennaka**, (*made by ''empawu' termites*) **ekiswa ky'empawu**, *etc.* pick up and eat flying termites -**bojjerera enswa** swarming of flying termites **omugano gw'enswa** *n3*

terrestrial animals ebisolo by'oku lukalo *n8*

terrible *adj* -**bi nnyo**

terrify *vt* -**tiisa** be terrified -**tya ennyo**

terror *n* **ekyentiisa** *n7* terrifying event **ekikangabwa** *n7*

terrorism *n* **obuzigu** *n14*

terrorist *n* **omutujju** *n1*, **omukanzi** *n1*

¹test *n* **ekigezo** *n7. See* examination

²test *vt* -**gezesa**

testament last testament **ekiraamo** *n7* New Testament (*of Bible*) **Endagaano Empya** *n9* Old Testament **Endagaano Enkadde**

testicles *n* **ebibeere** *n8*, **ebinege** *n8* (*impolite*)

testify *vi* -**wa obujulizi**

testimony *n* **obujulizi** *n14*

tetanus *n* **tetanaasi** *n1*

¹tether (*rope*) *n* **omuguwa** *n3*

²tether (*tie*) *vt* -**siba**

tethered *adj* -**sibe**

text *n* (1) (*something written*) **ekiwandiiko** *n7*; (2) (*SMS*) **eseemwesi** *n9* send a text (*SMS*) -**wereeza eseemwesi**

thank *vt* -**eebaza**, *eg. Luusi yanneebaza.* (*'Lucy thanked me.'*), (*more formally*) -**eeyanza**, *eg. Nneeyanzizza nnyabo.* (*'Thank you madam.'*) Thank her/him. **Mwebaze.** Thank them. **Beebaze.** Thank you. **Weebale.** (*pl.* **Mwebale.**), (*to a cook for the food*) **Ofumbye nnyo nnyabo.**, (*to a host*) **Ogabudde.** Thank you for your work. **Gyebale emirimu.** Thank you very much. **Nneeyanzizza nneyanzeege.**

¹that (*introducing reported speech*) *conj* **nti**, *eg. Yagamba nti enjala yali ebaluma.* (*'He said that they were hungry.'*), (*conveying uncertainty*) **mbu**, *eg. Yagamba mbu bagenze.* (*'He said that they had gone.' – but maybe they had not*) that is to say **kwe kugamba nti** That's right! (*or* That's so!) *interj* **Otyo!** that's why (*or* that is the reason why) (1) *Use* **kye…-va** (**N10.2**), *eg. Nnawulidde nti oli wano kyenvudde nzija.* (*'I hears that you were here, that's why I came.'*); (2) (*for positive statements*) *Use* **kwe** (**N27**) *followed by inf* (**N18**), *eg. Nnawulidde ng'oli wano, kwe kujja.* (*'I heard you were here, that's why I came.'*); (3) (*for negative statements*) *Use* **bwe** (**N27**) *followed by neg inf* (**N18**), *eg. Nnawulidde ng'oli wano, bwe butajja.* (*'I heard you were here, that's why I did not come.'*)

²that *dem* (*pl. those*) -**li** (**N9.1**), (*demonstrative of reference*) -**o** (**N9.1**). *Both stems take the pronominal concord* (**N4.2**), *eg. (1) ente eri* (*'that cow'*); (2) *ente eyo* (*'that cow'*). *The forms for the various noun classes are listed in Columns 4 and 5 of Table 8.*

³that (*also* which) *rel* (*or conj*). *The* **SUBJECT RELATIVE** *is formed by adding the initial vowel* (**N3**) *appropriate to the noun of reference to the verb* (**N7.1**), *eg. Ente ezo ezirya omuddo zange.* (*'Those cows that are grazing are mine.'*). *The* **OBJECT RELATIVE** *is* -**e** (**N10.1**) *with pronominal concord* (**N4.2**), *eg. Ente z'olaba zange.* (*'The cows that you see are mine.'*).

thatch *vt* -**sereka n'essubi**, *eg. Aserese ennyumba n'essubi.* (*'He has thatched the house.'*) thatch tightly -**ggumiza essubi** thatch with -**seresa**, *eg. Ennyumba yagiseresa ssubi.* (*'He thatched the house with grass.'*)

thatched thatched house (1) (*thatched with grass*) **ennyumba y'essubi** *n9*; (2) (*thatched with banana fibre*) **ennyumba y'essanja** thatched hut (*round type*) **olusiisira** *n11* (*small*) **akasiisira** *n12*

thatcher *n* **omuseresi** *n1*, (*chief, of the Kabaka*) **Wabulaakayole** *n1* title

the *det. Not directly translated in Luganda.*

theft *n* **obubbi** *n14*

their *pos* (*determiner*) -**abwe** (**N11.4**) *with pronominal concord* (**N4.2**), *eg. (1) embwa yaabwe* (*'their dog'*); (2) *ebiso byabwe* (*'their knives'*). *The* forms for the various noun classes are listed in Column 9 of Table 9.

theirs *pos (pronoun)* **owaabwe, abaabwe,** *etc.* (**N11.4**), *eg. Engatto zino zaffe, ezo zaabwe. ('These shoes are ours, those are yours.')*

them *pro. An object pronoun is expressed by a pronominal concord* (**N4.2**) *placed as a prefix on a verb* (**N15.1**), *eg. Oziraba? ('Do you see them?', eg. referring to 'ente' 'cows'). The personal form is* **ba-,** *eg. Obalaba? ('Do you see them?', eg. referring to 'abakozi' 'workers'). The impersonal forms are listed in Column 9 of Table 1. There are also free-standing pronouns based on the stems -o and -e (the last for pronouns of emphasis* **N10.1**), *eg. (1) Ente, zo zijja. ('The cows, they are coming.'); (2) Ente zino ze zange. ('It is these cows that are mine.').*

theme *n* **omulamwa** *n3*

themselves *pro* **-nnyini** (**N11.6**). *The prefix is the pronoun of emphasis* (**N10.1**), *eg. (1) ebintu byennyini ('the things themselves.'); (2) abantu bennyini ('the people themselves'). Reflexive verbs take the prefix* **-ee-** (**N18**), *eg. Nneeraba. ('I saw myself.'), from Nnalaba. ('I saw.')* by themselves (1) *(referring to people)* **bokka;** (2) *(referring to things)* **-okka** (**N7.3**) *with pronominal concord* **N4.2**)

then *conj* (1) *(indicating a desirable outcome) Use* **-lyoka** *as aux v, both verbs being in the subjunctive* (**N17**), *eg. Soma nnyo olyoke ofune omulimu. ('Study hard, then you will get work.'),* **lwe;** (2) *(referring to a statement made)* **awo,** *eg. Awo olowoozaawo otya? ('Then, what do you think?')* and then **ate**

theory *(thought) n* **endowooza** *n9*

there *adv* **-li** (**N9.2**). *The four forms are:* **wali,** *(over there)* **eri,** *(on there)* **kuli,** *(in there)* **muli.** *There are also adverbs of reference based on the stem* **-o** (**N9.2**), *the four forms being:* **awo,** *(over there)* **eyo,** *(on there)* **okwo,** *(in there)* **omwo.** *'There' can also be expressed by an enclitic* (**N24.2**), *eg. Ekitabo okirabyeeyo? ('Do you see the books over there?').* There they are. *(referring to people)* **Baabali.** *Similar phrases follow the same pattern* (**N9.1**). there is **waliwo,** *eg. Waliwo sukaali. ('There is the sugar.'). Similar phrases follow the same pattern* (**N20.4**).

therefore *(also* so, hence, thus*) conj* (1) **kwe** (**N27**). *Followed by inf* (**N18**), *eg. Yalwadde ekifuba, kwe kujja okulaba omusawo. ('He had a cough, therefore he came to see the doctor.');* (2) **kye-...-va** (**N10.2**), *eg. Yampise kyennavudde nzija. ('He called me, therefore I came.')* therefore ... not **bwe** (**N27**) *Followed by neg inf* (**N18**)

thermometer *n* **memeta** *n9*

these *See* this

they *pro. A subject pronoun is expressed by a pronominal concord* (**N4.2**) *placed as a prefix on a*

verb (**N15.1**), *eg. (1) Biri wano. (They are here.', eg. referring to 'ebitabo' books'); (2) Ziri wano. ('They are here.', eg. referring to 'ente' 'cows'). The personal form is* **ba-,** *eg. Bali wano. ('They are here.', eg. referring to 'abasawo' 'doctors'). Free-standing pronouns* (**N10.1**) *are occasionally used, eg. (1) Byo biri wano. ('They are here.', eg. referring to 'ebitabo' books'); (2) Bo bali wano. ('They are here.', eg. referring to 'abaana' 'children').*

thick *adj* (1) *(wide)* **-gazi;** (2) *(dense, of vegetation, porridge, etc.)* **-kwafu.** *See* stupid

thicket *n* **ekisaka** *n7*

thickness *(width) n* **obugazi** *n14*

thief *n* **omubbi** *n1,* *(expert)* **kabbira** *n1,* *(petty; pilferer)* **omwetoozitoozi** *n1,* *(murderous)* **omuzigu** *n1. See* looter

thieve *vt* **-bba**

thigh *n* **ekisambi** *n7*

[1]thin *adj* **-tono,** *(very, not used of people)* **-a oluwewere,** *eg. olupapula lwa luwewere ('thin piece of paper'), (of person or animal after losing weight)* **-kovvu,** *(worn thin, of cloth or garment)* **-yabirivu.** *See* worn be(come) thin **-toniwa,** *(lose weight, of person or animal)* **-kogga,** *(and sickly)* **-nyaaluka** grow very thin **-konziba, -koozimba,** *(because of incurable illness)* **-konvuba** make thin **-toniya,** *(person or animal)* **-kozza** person who has become thin **omukovvu** *n1*

[2]thin *(seedlings) vt* **-ggiza**

thing *n* **ekintu** *n7*

think *vi* *(thought)* **-lowooza** think about *(reflect on)* **-lowoozaako** *(or* **-lowooza ku**), *eg. Alowooza ku mulimu gwe buli lunako. ('She thinks about her work every day.'), (carefully)* **-fumiitiriza,** *(give thought to a person)* **-suulira omwoyo,** *eg. Yatusuulira omwoyo n'ajja atulabako. ('He thought about us and came to see us.')* think about oneself **-eerowoozaako** think alike **-ssa ekimu** think highly of oneself **-eemanya** think things over **-eerowooza** keep on thinking **-lowoolereza**

thinking *n* **okulowooza** *n15* way of thinking **endowooza** *n9*

thinness *n* **obutono** *n14,* *(of person or animal, after losing weight)* **obukovvu** *n14*

third *adj/num* **-a okusatu** (**N7.1**), *eg. ekintu eky'okusatu ('third thing'). Elision is sometimes seen, eg. ekintu ekyokusatu ('third thing').* one-third **kimu kya kusatu**

thirdly *adv* **ekyokusatu**

thirst *n* **ennyonta** *n9,* *(extreme)* **enkalamata** *n9* be thirsty (1) **ennyonta -luma** *(with personal object), eg. Ennyonta ennuma. ('I am thirsty.');* (2) **-lumwa ennyonta** *(with personal subject), eg. Nnumwa ennyonta. ('I am thirsty.')*

thirteen *num* **kkumi na ssatu, kkumi na -satu** *(with numeral concord* **N4.2**) (**N8.1**), *eg. ebintu kkumi na bisatu ('thirteen things')*

thirty *num* (**amakumi**) **asatu** (**N8.1**)

this *dem* (*pl.* these) **-no** (**N9.1**) *with pronominal concord* (**N4.2**), *eg.* (1) *ente eno* ('*this cow*'); (2) *ente zino* ('*these cows*'). *The forms for the various noun classes are listed in Column 3 of Table 8.*

thorn *n* **erigwa** *n5*

thorn-apple (*type of plant*) *n* **amaduudu** *n6*

thoroughly *adv* **ddala**

those *See* that

though (*also* even though) *conj* **newankubadde**, **wadde**, *eg. Wadde mwavu naye musanyufu.* ('*Poor though she is, she is happy.*') as though *Use* **-linga** ('*look like*'), *eg. Alinga alabye omuzimu.* ('*She looks like she has seen a ghost.*')

¹thought *n* **ekirowoozo** *n7*

²thought *v. See* think

thoughtfulness *n* **okulowooza** *n15*

thoughtlessness *n* **obutalowooza** *n14*

thousand *num* **lukumi** *n11* (*pl.* **enkumi**) (**N8.1**)

thrash about (*as response to pain*) *vi* **-sansagala**. *See* kick

thread *n* (1) (*eg. of cotton*) **ewuzi** *n9* (*thin* **akawuzi** *n12*); (2) (*of screw*) **enjola** *n10*

threaten *vt* **-tiisatiisa** threaten to rain **enkuba -bindabinda** be threatening (*of the weather*) **obudde -zijjagala**

three *num* **ssatu**. *The stem is* **-satu** (*with numeral concord* **N4.2**) (**N8.1**), *eg. ebintu bisatu* ('*three things*'). three-by-three **-satu -satu** (**N8.1**), *eg. Bajja basatu basatu.* ('*They came three-by-three.*') three hundred **bikumi bisatu** (**N8.1**) three thousand **enkumi ssatu** all three of **-onsatule** (**N7.3**) *with pronominal concord* (**N4.2**), *eg. ebintu byonsatule* ('*all three things*')

threw *See* throw

throat *n* **obulago** *n14*, (*oesophagus*) **omumiro** *n3*. *See* neck something stuck in the throat **empagama** *n9*

throb *vi* (1) (*palpitate, of the heart*) **-pakuka**; (2) (*of the head, with a headache*) **-bobba**, *eg. Omutwe gumbobba.* ('*My head is throbbing.*'); (3) (*of the body, with severe pain*) **-tujja** cause to throb **-tuzza**

throne *n* **nnamulondo** *n9*

¹throttle (*accelerator*) *n* **ekyomuliro** *n7*

²throttle (*strangle*) *vt* **-tuga**

¹through (*because of*) *conj* **olwa**, *eg. Twabuze olw'obutamanya makubo.* ('*We got lost through not knowing the roads.*')

²through *pre* (1) *Use* **-yita** ('*pass*') *in rel* (**N7.1**), *eg. akakubo akayita mu kibira* ('*path through the forest*'); (2) **mu**, *eg. akakubo mu kibira* ('*path through the forest*'); (3) *Use* **-a omu** ('*of in*') (**N24.1**), *eg. akakubo k'omu kibira* ('*path through the forest*')

¹throw (*in wrestling*) *n* **ekigwo** *n7*

²throw (*eg. ball*) *vt* (threw) **-kasuka**, **-kanyuga** throw away (*discard*) **-suula**, (*anywhere*)

-suulasuula throw down (1) (*eg. load*) **-ggunda**, *eg. Baggunda emigugu wansi.* ('*They threw the loads to the ground.*'), **-lindiggula**; (2) (*heavily, an opponent in wrestling*) **-megga** (*or* **-ligga**, *or* **-biriga**) **ekigwo**, *eg. Yamumegga ekigwo.* ('*He threw him to the ground.*') throw down anyhow **-suulasuula** throw into confusion **-tabulatabula** throw out (*eject*) **-fulumya** throw out shoots (*of a plant*) **-landa** throw over the shoulder **-eesuulira**, *eg. Yeesuulira leesu.* ('*She threw the shawl over her shoulder.*'), **-suula ku kibegabega** throw up earth (*by burrowing animal*) **-fukula ettaka**, *eg. Nnamulimi afukula ettaka.* ('*The ant bear is throwing up earth.*') be thrown about **-eesunda**, *eg. Twesunda mu bbaasi ng'eyise ku kigulumu.* ('*We were thrown about in the bus when it passed over a bump.*') be thrown down **-eggunda**, *eg. Tweggunda mu bbaasi ng'eyita ku kagulumu.* ('*We were thrown down in the bus when it hit a bump.*'), (*heavily*) **-eerindiggula** be thrown into confusion **-tabulwatabulwa**

thrush, African (*type of bird*) *n* **bbuukamugogo** *n1*

thrust (*push*) *vt* **-sindika**

thug *n* **omutujju** *n1*

thumb *n* **engalo ensajja** *n9*, *eg. engalo yange ensajja* ('*my thumb*') thumb piano (*musical instrument*) **akadongo** *n12*

thumbprint *n* **ekinkumu** *n7* put one's thumbprint **-ssaako ekinkumu**

thump (*hit hard with the fist*) *vt* **-funtula**, **-wuttula** with a thump be ddu, *eg. Yasuula emigugu wansi be ddu.* ('*He threw the load down with a thump.*')

thunder *vi* (1) (*with a thunderclap*) **eggulu -bwatuka**, *eg. Eggulu libwatuka.* ('*It is thundering.*'); (2) (*distant rumbling*) **eggulu -duduma**

thunderbolt (*lightning*) *n* **eraddu** *n9*

Thursday *n* **Olwokuna** *n11*

thus *See* therefore

tibia *n* **olulundulirunduli** *n11*

tick (*parasite*) *n* **enkwa** *n9*

tick over (*of an engine*) *vi* **-teetera**

ticket *n* **ttikiti** *n9*

¹tickle *n* **obunyonyoogeze** *n14*

²tickle *vt* **-nyonyoogera**

tidings (*news*) *n* **ebifaayo** *n8*

¹tidy *adj* **-longoofu**

²tidy (up) *vt* **-longoosa** be tidied **-longooka**

¹tie (*worn around neck*) *n* **ettaayi** *n9*

²tie *v* (tied) (1) (*have equal scores in game*) *vi* **-sibagana**; (2) (*tie up; fasten*) *vt* **-siba**. *See* draw taut; knot tie a knot in barkcloth **-siba ekifundikwa** tie up a food parcel (*before cooking*) **-siba emmere** tie with **-sibya**, **-sibisa**, *eg. Nnakisibisa kaguwa.* ('*I tied it with string.*') be tied (up) **-sibibwa**, *eg. Omuwumbo gusibiddwa.* ('*The food parcel is tied up.*') person who ties **omusibi** *n1* something tied **ekisibe** *n7*

tied *adj* -sibe

tight (*firm*) *adj* -nywevu   tight-fitting **kamiimo** (*invariable adjective*), *eg. empale kamiimo ('tight-fitting trousers')*   tight situation (*crowding; or difficult situation*) **akanyigo** *n12*   be (too) tight on -**miima**, *eg. Olugoye lukumiimye. ('The dress is tight on you.')*

tighten *vt* (1) (*eg. knot*) -**nyweza**; (2) (*eg. belt*) -**myumyula**; (3) (*draw taut; stretch*) -**leega**   become tightened (*taut*) -**eereega**

tilapia *n* engege *n9*

tile *n* (1) (*on roof*) ettegula *n5*; (2) (*on floor or wall*) tayiro *n9*

till (*cultivate*) *vt* -**lima**, (*deeply*) -**kabala**   tilled land awalime *n16*, (*deeply*) awakabale *n16*

tilt *vt* -**wunzika**, *eg. eg. Yawunzika eggiraasi n'ayiwa amazzi. ('He tilted the glass and spilt the water.')*, -**sulika**   tilt one's head back (*eg. to look upwards*) -**lalika** omutwe   be tilted -**eewunzika**, *eg. Eggiraasi yeewunzise. ('The glass is tilted.')*, -**eesulika**

timber (*planks, etc.*) *n* embaawo *n10*   timbers in roof: (1) (*joist*) olwaliiro lw'akasolya *n11*; (2) (*rafter*) omukomba *n3*; (3) (*ridgepole*) omulabba *n3*; (4) (*slat*) ennanzikiro *n9*

time *n* (1) (*of day*) essaawa *n9*, *eg. Essaawa mmeka? ('What is the time?')*; (2) (*part of the day*) obudde *n14*, *eg. obudde obw'oku makya ('morning time')*, (*short*) akadde *n12*, *eg. Bw'ofuna akadde leero, ojja ne nkubuulira. ('When you get time today, come and I shall tell you.')*; (3) (*a particular time, or period of time*) ekiseera *n7*, *eg. ekiseera kino mu mwaka ('this time of the year')*, (*short*) akaseera *n12*; (4) (*opportunity; space*) ebbanga *n5*, *eg. Tunaafuna ebbanga okwogera. ('We shall find a time to talk.')*, (*brief*) akabanga *n12*; (5) (*occasion*) omulundi *n3*, *eg. omulundi gumu ('one time')*. For more on time, see **N25**. *The following refer to the times of certain activities*: (1) (*digging up sweet potatoes*) amasoggola *n6*; (2) (*eating*) amalya; (3) (*harvesting*) amakungula *n6*; (4) (*planting*) amasimba *n6*; (5) (*sowing*) amasiga *n6*; (6) (*weeding*) amakoola *n6*.   time of plenty (*of food, especially matooke*) ekyengera *n7*   have time (*for an activity*) -**ba**/-**li** according to tense (**N20.1**) with **n'ekiseera**, *eg. Onooba n'ekiseera okundaba enkya? ('Will you have time to see me tomorrow?')*   take a long time for -**twalira** ebbanga, *eg. Kyantwalira ebbanga okumala omulimu. ('It took me time to finish the job.')*   at the same time **kumu**   at the same time as **ku** kiseera kye kimu ne   be for some time -**mala** ekiseera, *eg. Amaze ekiseera nga mulwadde. ('She has been ill for some time.')*   destined time entuuko *n9*   spend time -**mala** obudde, *eg. Obudde bwe abumala ng'asoma. ('She passes her time reading.')*, -**mala** ekiseera, -**mala** ebbanga   take a long time (*to do something*) -**twalira**

ebbanga   take time (*delay*) -**lwawo**, *eg. Nnaluddewo okwebaka. ('I took time to go to sleep.')*   in time (*or* while there is still time) **bukyali**   very bad time **kiseera kya kazigizigi**   waste time -**mala** obudde, -**mala** ebiseera

timepiece *n* omulenganjuba *n3*

times *n* (1) (*era; period*) omulembe *n3*, ebiro *n8*, *eg. mu biro bya Mwanga ('in Mwanga's times')*; (2) (*referring to quantity*) emirundi *n4*, *eg. Yambuuza emirundi ena. ('He asked me four times.')*   in former times **edda**

timid *adj* -tiitiizi   timid person omutiitiizi *n1*   be timid -**tiitiira**

timidity *n* obutiitiizi *n14*

tin *n* (1) (*can, eg. of food*) omukebe *n3*; (2) (*four gallon tin*) eddebe *n5*. See jerry can   tin opener ekisumulula emikebe *n7*

tingle (*of the cheeks*) *vi* -**nywanywagala**, *eg. Amatama gannywanywagala. ('My cheeks are tingling.')*

tingling *n* (1) (*in the cheeks*) obunyanywagavu *n14*; (2) (*in the limbs; pins and needles*) amasannyalaze *n6*

tiny *adj* -sirikitu, -tini   something tiny akasirikitu *n12*

[1]**tip** *n* (1) (*gratuity*) akasiimo *n12*; (2) (*pointed end*) akasongezo *n12*   person who tips (*gives gratuity*) omufuuyi wa ssente *n1*

[2]**tip** (*give a gratuity*) *vi* -**wa** akasiimo   tip off (1) (*a liquid*) -**bundula**; (2) (*leak information*) -**bbirako**   be tipped off (*of a liquid*) -**bunduka**

tipsy *adj* -tamiivu. See drunk

tiptoe   on tiptoe obunkenke, *eg. Atambuza bunkenke. ('She is walking on tiptoe.')*   stand on tiptoe -**kangalala**

tire *vt* -**kooya**   become tired -**koowa**, *eg. Akooye. ('She is tired.')*   become tired of (*fed up with*) -**tama**, *eg. Okukola kuntamye. ('I am tired of working.')*, -**nyiwa**

tired *adj* -koowu   tired person omukoowu *n1*

tiredness *n* obukoowu *n14*

title (*of a land holding*) *n* ekyapa ky'ettaka *n7*

to *pre* (1) **ku**, *eg. Genda ku nnyumba. ('Go to the house.')*; (2) (*into*) **mu**, *eg. Genda mu kisenge kyo. ('Go to your room.')*; (3) (*with place names*) **e**, *eg. Agenda e Bungereza. ('She is going to England.')*; (4) (*with certain nouns*) **e-**, *eg. Agenze emugga. ('She has gone to get water.')*; (5) (*to where someone is*) Use subject relative clause (**N7.2**), *eg. Genda eri Paulo. ('Go to Paul.')*. See as far as   to the place (*or* home) of **ewa**, *eg. Yagenda ewa ssengaawe. ('He went to his aunt's house.')*

toad *n* ekikere *n7*

toast *n* omugaati omwokye *n3*

tobacco *n* taaba *n1*   false tobacco (*plant used as tobacco substitute*) ssetaaba *n1*

today *adv* leero, olwaleero

toddler *n* ebbuje *n5*

toe *n* akagere *n12*, (*big*) ekigere ekisajja *n7*, (*little*) akagere ka nnasswi

together *adv* wamu, *eg. Twakolera wamu.* (*'We worked together.'*) together with **ne**, *eg. Agenze wamu n'omuwala we.* (*'He went together with his daughter.'*), (*with pronoun*) **na-**, *eg. Agenze naye.* (*'He went together with her.'*)

togetherness *n* obumu *n14*

toil (away) *vi* -faabiina, -kuluusana. *See* struggle; work

toilet *See* latrine; lavatory flush toilet toyireeti *n9*

token of thanks *n* akasiimo *n12*

told *See* tell

tolerate *vt* –gumiikiriza

toll a bell -kuba ekide

tomato *n* (1) (*plant*) omunyaanya *n3*; (2) (*fruit*) ennyaanya *n9* tree tomato (*Cyphomandra*) ekinyaanya *n7*

tomb *n* amalaalo *n6* royal tombs amasiro *n6*

tomorrow *adv* enkya tomorrow morning enkya ku makya day after tomorrow okwosa enkya, *eg. Nja kumulaba okwosa enkya.* (*'I will see her the day after tomorrow.'*)

ton *n* ttani *n9*

tongue *n* olulimi *n11*

tonic herbs *n* (1) (*for bathing babies*) ekyogero *n7*; (2) (*for bathing adults*) ekyoogo *n7*

tonight *adv* ekiro kya leero, ekiro kino

too *adv* ne (*or prefix* **na- N10.1**), *eg. (1) Ne Musoke mmwagala.* (*'I like Musoke too.'*); *(2) Naye mmwagala.* (*'I like him too.'*) too close (together) (*crowded together, mostly used of crops*) **mu kifuko**, *eg. Kasooli baamusimba kifuko.* (*'They have planted the maize too close.'*) too much ennyo, *eg. Anywa nnyo.* (*'He drinks too much.'*), (*with reference mainly to salt or sugar*) -ka, *eg. omunnyo omuka* (*'too much salt'*), (*indicating extremeness*) okukamala, *eg. Akola okukamala.* (*'She works too much.'*) ask for too much money -liika ssente be too big (for) (*especially of clothes*) -sagala, *eg. Empale ensagala.* (*'The trousers are too big for me.'*) be too much (for) (*excessive*) -yitirira, *eg. Sukaali yayitiridde mu caayi.* (*'There is too much sugar in the tea.'*) drink too much -nywa funduukululu. *See* drunk (get) eat too much -lya funduukululu. *See* stuff oneself give too little (to) -kena, *eg. Abaana baabakena emmere.* (*'They gave the children too little food.'*) give too much money to -piika ssente, *eg. Yamupiise ssente.* (*'He gave him too much money.'*) have too many things to do (*or hold*) -byangatana occupy too much space (1) (*of a person, things in a store, etc.*) -zimbagala; (2) (*of a plant*) -zijjagala speak for too long -yogera olukobo

took *See* take

tool *n* ekikozesebwa *n7*, (*one used for cultivation*) ekyokulimisa *n7*

tooth *n* (*pl.* teeth) erinnyo *n5*, (*canine*) essongezo *n5*, (*molar*) eggego *n5*. *The following refer to gaps between teeth*: (1) (*gap between teeth caused by tooth loss*) eddibu *n5*, *eg. Alina amalibu.* (*'He has teeth missing.'*); (2) (*having naturally spaced out teeth*) -a entalaga, *eg. Alina amannyo ag'entalaga.* (*'He has spaced-out teeth.'*); (3) (*natural gap between incisor teeth*) omuzigo *n3*. *A person who has lost a tooth is* ow'eddibu *n1*. *To have overlapping teeth is* -gerekera, *eg. Amannyo ge gaagerekera.* (*'His teeth are overlapping.'*). overlapping teeth amannyo ag'engereka row of teeth olubu lw'amaanyo *n11*

toothache have toothache erinnyo -luma (*with personal object*), *eg. Erinnyo limuluma.* (*'He has toothache.'*)

toothbrush *n* akasenya *n12*, omuswaki *n3*

toothless *adj* -a ekibungu toothless person ow'ekibungu *n1*

toothpaste *n* eddagala ly'amannyo *n5*, kologeeti *n9*

toothpick *n* akati akasokoola amannyo *n12*

toothstick *n* omuswaki *n3*

top *n* (1) (*summit*) entikko *n9*; (2) (*spinning top*))made from omuwafu seed) enje *n9*, (*carved from wood*) enkuyo *n9* on top (*on the surface*) kungulu. *See* above on top of kungulu ku put on top of (*superimpose*) -bereka

top up (*fill*) *vt* -jjuuliriza

topple (over) *v* (1) *vi* -sinduka; (2) *vt* -sindula topple a government -suula gavumenti

¹torch *n* ttooki *n9*, (*made of reeds*) omumuli *n3*, (*of grass, wood, etc.*) ekitawuliro *n7*, (*of barkcloth*) enfuuzi *n9*

²torch (*ignite*) *vt* -koleeza

tore *See* tear

torment *vt* (1) (*vex; harass*) -walana; (2) (*persecute*) -yigganya

tormentor *n* (1) (*one who harasses*) omuwalanyi *n1*; (2) (*one who persecutes*) omuyigganyi *n1*

¹torn *adj* -yulifu, (*to shreds*) -sensufu, (*by claws or nails*) -taagufu

²torn *v. See* tear

tortoise *n* enfudu *n9*

¹torture *n* ekibonyoobonyo *n7*

²torture *vt* -bonyaabonya

toss (*eg. a coin*) *vt* -kasuka toss about restlessly (*of a sick person*) -boyaana toss up a child -buusabuusa omwana be tossed about (*as in a car on a rough road*) -eesunda

¹total (*of summed figures*) *n* omugatte *n3*

²total (*amount to*) *vt* -wera, *eg. Ssente ziweze ssiringi kikumi.* '*The money totals 100 shillings.*')

totem *n* omuziro *n3*, (*second totem of clan*) akabbiro *n12* honour one's totem -eddira, *eg. Nneddira nseenene.* (*'The grasshopper is my totem.'*)

totter along (*as child or old person*) *vi* -sejjera

touch vt -**kwata ku**, eg. Yakwata ku mmeeza. ('She touched the table.'), (someone as a signal; to caution) -**sunyako**   touch one another -**kwatagana**, eg. Teeka entebe mu lunyiriri zikwatagane. ('Put the chairs in a line so that they are touching.')

touchiness n **entondo** n10   touchy person (easily offended) **ow'entondo** n1

tough (durable) adj -**gumu**   tough person **omugumu** n1   be tough (of meat) -**kaluba**, eg. Ennyama ekaluba. ('The meat is tough.')

toughness (durability) n **obugumu** n14

tour vt -**lambula**

tourism n **obulambuzi** n14

tourist n **omulambuzi** n1

tow vt -**sika**

towards pre. Use -**yolekera** ('point towards'), eg. Yatambula ng'ayolekedde ekyalo. ('He walked towards the village.')   look towards -**tunuulira**

towel n **ettawulo** n9. See **enkumbi** (in Part 2 of the dictionary)

tower n **omunaala** n3

town n **ekibuga** n7   town clerk **omukulu w'ekibuga** n1   town dweller **munnakibuga** n1

toy n **ekyokuzannyisa ky'omwana** n7

toy with (triffle with) vt -**zannyisa**

traces (left by a flowing liquid) n **enkulukuse** n10. See track; trail

trachea n **omumiro** n3

[1]**track** (path) n **akakubo** n12, (rough road; road in poor condition) **ekikubo** n7, (made by a passing animal) **ekisinde** n7, (made by walking or cutting through vegetation) **oluwenda** n11, (continuous track) **omukululo** n3   tyre tracks **emikululo gy'emmotoka**

[2]**track (down)** (eg. animal in hunt) vt -**ziga**

tractor n **tulakita** n9

[1]**trade** n **obusuubuzi** n14   trade association **ekibiina ky'abasuubuzi** n7   trade mark **akabonero k'obusuubuzi** n12   trade union **ekibiina ky'abakozi** n7

[2]**trade (in)** vit -**suubula**, eg. Asuubula ssabbuuni. ('She trades in soap.'), (all sorts of things) -**suubulasuubula**   trade at -**suubulira**, eg. Asuubulira Mengo. ('She trades at Mengo.')

trader n **omusuubuzi** n1, (itinerant) **omutembeeyi** n1

tradition n **akalombolombo** n12, (associated with place of birth) **ekyobuzaaliranwa** n7, (associated with tribe or nation) **ekyobuwangwa** n7

traditional adj -**a ekinnansi**, eg. ennyimba ez'ekinnansi ('traditional songs')   traditional culture **ebyobuwangwa** n8   traditional medicine **eddagala ly'ekinnansi** n5   traditional religion **eddiini ey'obuwangwa** n9

traffic n **tulafiki** n9   traffic jam **akalippagano k'emmotoka** n12, **jjaamu** n1   traffic lights **ebitaala** n8

tragedy n **ekitalo** n7   How tragic! **Nga kitalo!**

[1]**trail** (small path) n **akakubo** n12. See track   trail of safari ants **omugendo gw'ensanafu** n3

[2]**trail (behind)** vt -**goberera**, eg. Abaana bagoberera kitaabwe nga bakooye. ('The tired children are trailing along behind their father.'). See follow

trailer (of vehicle) n **ekyana** n7

[1]**train** n **eggaali y'omukka** n9

[2]**train** vt -**tendeka**

trained adj -**tendeke**

trainer n **omutendesi** n1

training institute n **ettendekero** n5, (high level) **ssettendekero** n1

traitor n **ow'enkwe** n1

trample (on) vt -**linnyirira**, eg. Abantu balinnyirira ennimiro yange. ('The people are trampling on my garden.')   trample on bananas (to extract juice) -**sogola omubisi**   trample on mud (to use in building) -**samba obudongo**

trampling (sound of) n **omusinde** n3

tranquil (serene) adj -**teefu**   be(come) tranquil -**teeka**

tranquility n **obuteefu** n14

transfer vt. Use -**kyusa** ('cause to change') and -**twala** ('take'), eg. Kkampuni yamukyusa okuva e Kampala n'emutwala e Masaka. ('The company transferred her from Kampala to Masaka.')

transfixed, be vi -**tangaalirira**

transform vt (1) (alter) -**kyusa**, eg. Essomero lyakyusa empisa ze. ('The school transformed his behaviour.'); (2) (make into) -**kolamu**, eg. Konteyina osobola okugikolamu akaduuka. ('You can transform a container into a little shop.'); (3) (change the nature of) -**fuusa**, eg. Amagye gaamufuula omuntu mulamu. ('The army transformed him into a decent person.')

transgress (do wrong) vt -**sobya**. See exceed

transgression (wrong-doing) n **ekisobyo** n7

transgressor (wrong-doer) n **omusobya** n1

transient adj -**a ekiseera**

translate vt -**vvuunula**, -**kyusa mu lulimi**

translation n **enzivuunula** n9, **entaputa** n9

translator n **omuvvuunuzi** n1, **omutaputa** n1

transmit vt -**weereza**

transparency n **obutangaavu** n14

transparent adj **tangaavu**   be transparent -**tangaala**

transplant vt -**simbuliza**

transport vt -**tambuza**

transportation n **entambula** n9

[1]**trap** n **omutego** n3, (for catching mice and rats) **akamasu** n12   basket trap (1) (for catching fish) (for catching 'enkejje') **omuya** n3, (with hole at base) **eggala** n5, (made from reeds) **akabigo** n12, (made from sticks of ejjerengesa) **omugomo** n3; (2) (for catching lake flies) **olutente** n11   pitfall trap **obuya** n14   set a trap -**tega omutego**, eg. Abayizzi

baatega omutego mu kibira. ('The hunters set a trap in the forest.') small cramped enclosure (in which movement is difficult) **akakunizo** n12

²**trap** vt -**kwata** trap with -**teza** get trapped (of a liquid puddling up) -**legama**

trash See rubbish

¹**travel** n **obutambuze** n14, **okutambula** n15 way of travelling **entambula** n9

²**travel** vi -**tambula**, (in a leisurely way) -**seeyeeya**, (in a means of transport) -**saabala**, eg. Nnasaabadde mu takisi. ('I travelled by taxi.') travel across water -**somoka** travel all over (purposefully, eg. on an inspection tour) -**talaaga**. See roam; wander travel by -**tambulira**, eg. Nnatambulidde mu bbaasi. ('I travelled by bus.') travel by foot -**tambuza bigere**

traveller n **omutambuze** n1

trawl n **essambo** n5

tray n **ettule** n9, (for winnowing) **olugali** n11

treacherous adj -**a olukwe**

treachery n **olukwe** n11

¹**tread** (of tyre) n **enjola** n10

²**tread (on)** vt -**linnya**, eg. Balinnya ku kiwempe kyange. ('They are treading on my carpet.'). See crush tread on bananas in beer making -**sogoza bigere** tread on bananas to make beer -**sogola omwenge**

treason n **olukwe** n11

treasure n **obugagga** n14

treasurer n **omuwanika** n1 residence of the Royal Treasurer (of Buganda) **Buwanika** n9

treasury n **eggwanika** n5, (royal treasury of Buganda) **enkuluze** n9

¹**treat** (luxury) n **ekintu eky'okwejalabya** n7. See luxury give oneself a treat -**eejalabya**

²**treat** vt (1) (behave towards) -**yisa**, eg. Akuyisa atya? ('How does he treat you?'); (2) (an ill person) -**jjanjaba**, eg. Omusawo ajjanjaba omulwadde. ('The doctor is treating the patient.') treat (someone) as of no value -**dibaga** treat lightly (make light of matters) -**balaata**. See lazy treat oneself (as a patient) -**ejjanjaba** treat with contempt -**linnyirira**, eg. Baamulinnyiridde. ('They treated her with contempt.')

treatment centre (where medical help is available) n **ejjanjabiro** n5

treaty n **endagaano** n9

tred on vt (trod) -**linnya**

tree n **omuti** n3 (small **akati** n12), (planted near house to ward off evil spirits) **omuwambo** n3 tree stump **enkonge** n9

tremble vi -**kankana**, eg. Omuzinga gwavuze ennyumba n'ekankana. ('The cannon sounded and the house trembled.'), (due to earthquake, etc.) -**jugumira**, eg. Ettaka lyajugumidde olwa musisi. ('The ground trembled from the earthquake.'). See shake; shiver; shudder make tremble -**kankanya**

trembling n **ekikankano** n7

trench n **olunnya** n11, (dug as boundary) **olusalosalo** n11

trespass vi -**saalimba**

trial (legal) n **omusango** n3. See test

tribal adj -**a eggwanga** tribal marks on body (made by burning) **enjokyo** n10 (one **oluyokyo** n11)

tribe n **eggwanga** n5

tribunal n **eggwolezo** n5

tribute (given to chief or landlord) n **envujjo** n9. See levy deliver tribute -**vujjirira envujjo**

¹**trick** n **akakodyo** n12, **akazannyo** n12 dirty trick **akakwe** n12

²**trick** (fool) vt -**guumaaza**. See deceive; feint; outwit be tricked -**guumaala**

trickle vi -**ttulukuka**. See flow

tried See try

triffle with (toy with) vt -**zannyisa**

trigger n **emmanduso** n9

trim vt -**komola**

¹**trip** (journey) n **olugendo** n11

²**trip (up)** v (1) (of oneself) vi -**eesittala**, eg. Nneesittala ku jjinja. ('I tripped up on a stone.'); (2) (someone else) vt -**tega**, eg. Nnatega Musoke. ('I tripped up Musoke.'), (in wrestling) -**siba enkalu**, (in football) -**kuba endobo**

¹**triumph** n **obuwanguzi** n14

²**triumph (over)** vit -**wangula**

trod see tred

trombone n **eggwaala** n5

troops (army) n **eggye** n5. See soldier

¹**trouble** n **omutawaana** n3, **akatyabaga** n12, (serious) **leenya** n1, (in affairs) **engozoobano** n9. See difficulties experience trouble (in affairs) -**goozobana** fall into trouble -**gwa ku mutawaana**, (in a serious way) -**gwa mu leenya** take trouble (make an effort) -**tegana** take trouble with -**teganira**, -**tawaanira**

²**trouble** (give trouble to) vt -**tawaanya**, eg. Emboozi yamutawaanya. ('The conversation troubled him.'). See harass; worry be troubled (about) (worried) -**eeraliikirira** be troubled by a child (eg. because of bad behaviour) -**taabuukana n'omwana** be troubled by work -**taabuukana n'emirimu**

trough (hollowed-out tree trunk used for brewing) n **eryato ery'omwenge** n5. See beer boat

trousers n **empale** n9, (long) **empale empanvu**, (drain-pipe) **empale ya kamiimo**. See shorts

trowel (for brick-laying) n **omwiko** n3

truce n **akasiriikiriro mu kulwana** n12

truck n **loole** n9, (long) **lukululana** n9

trudge along vi -**tambula -bebbera** (N19)

true adj (1) (right) -**tuufu**; (2) (genuine) -**a ddala**

truly adv **ddala**, eg. Mulungi ddala. ('She is truly good.')

trumpet n **tulampeti** n9, **omulere** n3. See horn

trumpeter n **omufuuyi wa tulampeti** n1

trunk n (1) (of tree) **enduli** n9); (2) (of banana plant – actually pseudostem) **omugogo** n3; (3) (of an *elephant*) **omukono** *n3*; (4) (*box; suitcase*) **essanduuko** *n9*

¹trust *n* **obwesige** *n14*

²trust *vt* **-eesiga**

trustworthiness *n* **obwesigwa** *n14*

trustworthy *adj* **-eesigwa**   trustworthy person **omwesigwa** *n1*

truth *n* **amazima** *n6*   the truth **ekyamazima** *n7*   dig out the truth from (*persuade to reveal*) **-kemekkereza**   person who hides the truth **omukuusa** *n1*

truthfully *adv* **mu mazima**

try *v* (*tried*) **-gezaako**   try hard (1) (*strive*) **-fuba**; (2) (*in a long-term committed way*) **-kazana**, *eg. Baakazana okulaba ng'abaana baabwe basoma.* (*'They tried hard to educate their children.'*). *See* toil away   try on (*of oneself*) **-eegezaamu**, *eg. Yeegezaamu olugoye.* (*'She tried on the dress.'*)   try out (1) (*test*) **-gezesa**, *eg. Agezesa mmotoka.* (*'He is trying out the car.'*); (2) (*someone for a job*) **-gezesaako**. *See* taste

tsetse fly *n* **ekivu** *n7*

tub (*barrel; drum*) *n* **eppipa** *n5*

tube *n* **oluseke** *n11*   tube fiddle (*musical instrument*) **endingidi** *n9*   inner tube (1) (*of ball or tyre*) **oluwago** *n11*, **akawago** *n12*; (2) (*of car tyre*) **omupiira gw'omunda** *n3*

tuberculosis *n* **akafuba** *n12*, **ttibbi** *n1*

¹tuck (*hem*) *n* **olukugiro** *n11*

²tuck (*hem*) *vt* **-kugira**   tuck in bedding **-fundikira obuliri**   tuck in shirt **-fungiza essaati**, **-kuba ekikalu**

Tuesday *n* **Olwokubiri** *n11*

tuft (*of hair on shaven head*) *n* **ejjoba** *n5*

tug (along) *vt* **-walula**   have a tug of war **-sika omuguwa**

tulip tree (*Spathodea*) *n* **ekifabakazi** *n7*

tumble (down) (*fall*) *vi* **-gwa**, *eg. Ekisenge kyagwa nga musisi ayise.* (*'The wall tumbled down when the earthquake struck.'*)   tumble about (*eg. of children playing*) **-eebiriga**

tumbler (*drinking glass*) *n* **eggiraasi** *n9*

tummy *n* **olubuto** *n11*   tummy pain **enjoka** *n10*

tumour *n* **ekizimba** *n7*

¹tune *n* **oluyimba** *n11*

²tune (*a strung musical instrument*) *vt* **-leega**

tunic (*worn by men*) *n* **ekkanzu** *n9*

turaco *n* **effulungu** *n5*

turban *n* **ekiremba** *n7*

turbulent   become turbulent **-fuukuuka**, *eg. Obudde bufuukuuse.* (*'The weather has become turbulent.'*)   make turbulent **-fuukuula**

turkey *n* **ssekkokko** *n9*

turmoil (*state of social unrest*) *n* **akayuuguumo** *n12*. *See* commotion; confusion

¹turn (*shift*) *n* **oluwalo** *n11*, (*in a polygamous marriage*) **ekisanja** *n9*   take turns **-kola mu mpalo**   turn-ups (*on trousers*) **amagemo** *n6*

²turn *v* **TRANSITIVE USES** **-kyusa**, *eg. Yakyusa emmotoka n'etunula ku nnyanja.* (*'He turned the car to face the lake.'*). *See* swerve   turn a door handle **-nyoola omunyolo**   turn down (1) (*reduce in quantity, eg. level of sound*) **-kendeeza**; (2) (*refuse*) **-gaana**   turn inside out **-fuula ku bikukujju**, *eg. Yafuula vesiti ye edde ku bikukujju.* (*'He turned his vest inside out.'*)   turn off a car engine **-zikiza emmotoka**   turn off a light **-zikiza ettaala**   turn off electricity **-ggyako amasannyalaze**   turn off water **-siba amazzi**   turn on (*electricity, radio, etc.*) **-teekako**, **-ssaako**   turn one's back on **-kuba amabega**, *eg. Yankuba amabega.* (*'He turned his back on me.'*)   turn over (*upside down*) **-vuunika**, *eg. Yavuunika ebbenseni.* (*'She turned over the basin.'*)   turn over a page **-bikkula olupapula**   turn over in one's mind (*ponder*) **-fumiitiriza**. *See* think   turn over on the back **-galika**   turn right way up **-vuunula**   turn the head suddenly (*eg. when startled*) **-maguka**   turn up (*level of sound, etc.*) **-tumbula**, *eg. Atumbudde omuliro.* (*'She has turned up the heat.'*) **INTRANSITIVE USES** **-kyuka**, *eg. Yakyuka atunuulire ennyanja.* (*'He turned to look at the lake.'*)   turn back **-weta**, *eg. Baaweta ne baddayo.* (*'They turned back to where they came from.'*)   turn left **-dda ku kkono**   turn off **-kyama**, *eg. Emmotoka yakyama ku kkono.* (*'The car turned off to the left.'*)   turn off at **-kyamira ku**, *eg. Okyamira ku mayiro ttaano n'odda ku kkono.* (*'Turn off left at mile five.'*), **-wetera**   turn off from **-va ku**, *eg. Yava ku luguudo olunene.* (*'He turned off from the main road.'*)   turn right **-dda ku ddyo**   turn sour (1) (*of milk*) **-fa**; (2) (*of juice; sour*) **-kaatuuka**   turn up (*appear*) **-labika**, *eg. Empeta yange eyali ebuze yalabise.* (*'My lost ring has turned up.'*)   be turned up (*of flame, sound, etc.*) **-tumbuka**

turnboy *n* **ttanibboyi** *n1*

turning place *n* (1) (*for turning around*) **aw'okukyukira** *n16*, **w'okyukira** *n16*; (2) (*for turning off*) **aw'okukyamira** *n16*, **w'okyamira** *n16*

turtle *n* **enfudu** *n9*

tusk *n* **essanga** *n5*

TV *n* **ttivvi** *n9*

twelve *num* **kkumi na bbiri**, **kkumi na -biri** (*with numeral concord N4.2*) (**N8.1**), *eg. ebintu kkumi na bibiri* (*'twelve things'*)

twenty *num* (**amakumi**) **abiri** (**N8.1**)

twice *adv* **emirundi ebiri**

twig *n* **akatabi** *n12*, (*for cleaning teeth*) **omuswaki** *n3*, (*on road, to block traffic*) **omusanvu** *n3*

¹twin *adj* **-longo**

²twin *n* **omulongo** *n1*. The titles of twins are: (1) (*for males*) (*elder*) **Wasswa**, (*younger*) **Kato**; (2) (*for females*) (*elder*) **Babirye**, (*younger*) **Nnakato**. *The child born before twins is* **Kigongo** *and the child born after twins is* **Kizza** (*regardless of gender*). *A* child after 'Kizza' is: (1) (male) **Kaggwa**; (2) (female) **Nakaggwa**; then the next child is: (1) (male) **Kityo**; (2) (female) **Nakityo**; then the next child is: (1) (male) either **Kitooke** or **Kiteerera**; (2) (female) **Nnansukusa**. father of twins **Ssaalongo** mother of twins **Nnaalongo** perform birth rights for twins **-yalula** (or **-zina**) **abalongo**

¹twine (string) n **akaguwa** n12, (made from Triumfetta) **ekinsambwe** n7. See fibre

²twine vt **-langa**

twinkle vi **-munyeenya**

twist vt **-nyoola**   twist the truth **-gombeza ensonga**   be twisted **-nyoolwa**

twitching of the eye n **ekisulo** n7

two num **bbiri**. The stem is **-biri** (with numeral concord **N4.2**) (**N8.1**), eg. ebintu bibiri ('two things').   two-by-two **-biri -biri** (**N8.1**), eg. Ebisolo byayingira mu lyato lya Nuwa bibiri bibiri. ('The animals went into the ark two-by-two.')   two hundred **bikumi bibiri** (**N8.1**)   two hundred shilling coin **ekido** n7 or **engege** n9 (both slang)   two thousand **enkumi bbiri**

¹type n (1) (kind; sort) **ekika** n7, **engeri** n9 ; (2) (typeface) **tayipu** n9. See way

²type (on keyboard) vt **-kuba tayipu**

typeface See font

typewriter n **tayipu** n9

typhoid n **tayifooyidi** n9

tyranny n **enfuga eya nnaakyemalira** n9, **obwannaakyemalira** n14

tyrant n **nnaakyemalira** n1

tyre n **omupiira** n3   tyre tracks **emikululo gy'emmotoka** n4

tythe (given to the church; tenth of income) n **endobolo ekimu eky'ekkumi** n9

U,u

udder n **ekibeere** n7

Uganda n **Uganda** n9   Uganda kob **empala** n9

Ugandan (person) n **Munnayuganda** n1

ugly adj **-bi**   ugly person **omubi** n1   be(come) ugly **-bijja**

ulcer n **ebbwa** n5   stomach ulcers **amabwa mu ssebusa**

ululate vi **-kuba enduulu**, (requesting people to come and help) **-dduukirira enduulu**

ululation n **enduulu** n10 1

um (make sound used when pausing in speech) **-muumuunya**

umbilical cord n **ekirira** n7, (dried) **akalira**, (of the Kabaka) **omulongo** n1

umbrella n **manvuuli** n9, **tamusiya** n9   umbrella tree (Musanga) **kaliba** n1

umpire (in football) n **omusazi w'omupiira** n1   umpire a football match **-sala omupiira**

unable, be vi (1) (unable to manage) Use **-sobola** ('be able') in neg (**N21**), eg. Saasobola kukola kubanga nnali mulwadde. ('I was unable to work because I was ill.'); (2) (unable to find) **-bulwa**, eg. Nnabulwa omulimu. ('I was unable to get work.'); (3) (fail) **-lemwa**, eg. Nnalemeddwa okufuna ssente. ('I was unable to obtain the money.')

unannounced, arrive vi **-gwa bugwi**

unappreciative, be vi (1) Use **-siima** ('appreciate') in neg (**N21**), eg. Ekirabo kyaffe teyakisiima. ('She was unappreciative of our gift.'); (2) (express dissatisfaction with what one has been given) **-toma**. See dissatisfied (be); grumble; reject

unassertive adj **-wombeefu**   unassertive person **omuwombeefu** n1   be unassertive **-wombeeka**

unavailable, make oneself vi **-eebuzaabuza**

unavoidable, be vi. Use **-eewalika** ('be avoidable') in neg (**N21**), eg. Okumusinkana tekyewalika. ('Meeting him is unavoidable.')

unaware, be vi. Use **-manya** ('know') in neg (**N21**), eg. Nnali simanyi nti ajja. ('I was unaware that she was coming.')

unbending (of person/material) adj **-kakanyavu**   be unbending **-kakanyala**

unblock vt **-zibukula**   be(come) unblocked **-zibukuka**

unbridled See unrestrained

uncertain adj **-a mbu**   be uncertain (about) Use **-manya** ('know') in neg (**N21**), eg. Simanyi kya kukola. ('I am uncertain about what to do.'). See hesitant (be)

unclasp vt **-takkuluza**

uncle n (1) (maternal) **kojja** n1, eg. kojja wo ('your uncle'); (2) (paternal) **taata omuto** n1   my (maternal) uncle **kojjange**, your uncle **kojjaawo**, etc. (stem **kojja- N12**)   eldest brother of the Queen mother (uncle of the Kabaka) **Ssaabaganzi** n1 title

unclean, be (dirty) vi **-ddugala**

uncleanliness n **obuligo** n14

unclog vt **-zibukula**   be(come) unclogged **-zibukuka**

uncoil vt **-zingulula**   be(come) uncoiled **-zingulukuka**

uncomfortable, feel vi **-wulira obubi**

uncommon adj **si -a bulijjo**, eg. Engeri y'omuti guno si ya bulijjo. ('This type of tree is uncommon.')

unconcerned, be vi. Use **-faayo** ('care about') in neg (**N21**), eg. Tafaayo kuva mu mulimu. ('She is unconcerned about losing her job.'). See attention (pay no)

unconsciousness n **obutategeera** n14   state of unconsciousness (coma) **okuzirika** n15

uncontrollable (wild in behaviour) adj **-taamaavu**

uncontrolled (in behaviour) adj **-bambaavu**   uncontrolled behaviour (1) (wildness) **obutaamaavu** n14; (2) (lacking self-discipline) **obuteekomako** n14   be uncontrolled in behaviour (in a socially unacceptable way) **-bambaala**

unconvinced, be *vi* **-sigalamu enkenyera**, *eg. eg. Yannyonyodde naye nnasigaddemu enkenyera. ('She explained but I remained unconvinced.'),* **-sigalamu akakunkuna** failure to be convinced **enkenyera** *n9*

uncooked *(eg. of meat) adj* **-bisi**

uncork *vt* **-sumulula** be(come) uncorked **-sumulukuka**

uncover *vt* **-bikkula,** *(partially)* **-wenjula,** *(by removing a lid)* **-saanukula** uncover oneself *(eg. by removing bedding)* **-eebikkula** be(come) uncovered **-bikkuka,** *(partially)* **-wenjuka,** *(through removing a lid)* **-saanukuka**

uncultivated land *n* **ensiko** *n9*

uncultured person *n* **omukopi** *n1*

undaunted *adj* **-gumu**

undecided, be *vi. Use* **-salawo** *('decide') in neg* **(N21)**, *eg. Yali tasazeewo kya kukola. ('He was undecided what to do.')*

[1]**under** *(also* underneath*) adv* **wansi**

[2]**under** *(also* underneath*) pre* **wansi wa**

undercooked, be *vi* **-kona.** *See* cook lightly

underestimate *vt* **-gaya,** *eg. Nnabadde ngaya Musoke, naye omulimu yagukoze bulungi. ('I underestimated Musoke, but he did the job well.')* underestimate oneself **-eegaya**

undergarment *(worn under busuuti) n* **ekikooyi** *n7. See* bra; knickers; underpants; vest

undermine *(sabotage) vt* **-kotoggera,** *eg. Mukama we yamukotoggera. ('His boss undermined him.')*

underneath *See* under

underpants *n* **akawale ak'omunda** *n12, (boxer type)* **pajama** *n9*

understand *vt* **-tegeera** understand one another **-tegeeragana** be understandable **-tegeerekeka** become understood *(clear; explained)* **-nnyonnyoka**

understanding *adj* **-tegeevu** understanding person **omutegeevu** *n1* come to an understanding **-tegeeragana** mutual understanding **entegeeragana** *n9*

undertake *vi* **-eetema,** *eg. Yeetema okuwa ssente ez'okugula ebyokunywa. ('He undertook to give money for the drinks.')*

underworld *n* **amagombe** *n6, (place to which Walumbe descended)* **ettanda** *n9* in the underworld **emagombe**

undo *vt* **-jjulula,** *(something tied, wrapped, locked, etc.)* **-sumulula,** *eg. Yasumulula ekitereke. ('She undid the parcel.'), (something sewn or stitched)* **-sattulula.** *See* disentangle; take apart; unplait; unravel become undone **-jjulukuka,** *(of something locked, wrapped, etc.)* **-sumulukuka,** *eg. Ekitereke kisumulukuse. ('The parcel has become undone.'), (of something sewn or stitched)* **-sattulukuka,** *eg. Omukeeka gusattulukuse. ('The mat has become undone.')*

undress *v* (1) *(oneself) vr* **-eeyambula;** (2)

(someone else) vt **-yambula**

undue familiarity *n* **olummanyimmanyi** *n11*

uneasy *(of a crowd; riotous) adj* **-sasamavu** become uneasy **-sasamala**

unemployed person **omuntu atalina ky'akola** *n1*

unexpected, be *vi* **-gwako bugwi,** *eg. Nnamuguddeko bugwi mu katale. ('I encountered her unexpectedly in the market.'),* **-labira awo,** *eg. Nnalabidde awo ng'azze. ('I was not expecting her to come.')* die unexpectedly **-fa ekibwatukira, -fa ekikutuko** receive a high position unexpectedly **-koonola,** *eg. Yakoonodde obwami. ('He unexpectedly became chief.')*

unfairly, judge *vt* **-saliriza**

unfaithful, be sexually *vi* **-baliga**

unfasten *vt* **-sumulula** become unfastened **-sumulukuka**

unfold *vt* **-yanjuluza** become unfolded **-yanjulukuka**

unforthcoming, be *(unresponsive) vi* **-eesisiggiriza**

unfortunate *See* unlucky

unfortunately *See* unluckily

unfounded assertion(s) **ebya njwanjwa** *n8*

unhappy *adj. Use* **-sanyufu** *('happy') in neg* **(N21),** *eg. Si musanyufu. ('He is unhappy.'). See* regretful; sad

unify *vt* **-gatta,** *eg. Kabaka yagatta ensi. ('The king unified the country.')*

uninformed *adj* **-bisi**

uninvited guest *n* **kyereeta** *n1*

unison, in *adv* **lufaaya**

unit *(a single) n* **omunwe** *n3*

unite *v* (1) *vi* **-eegatta,** *eg. Ensi bbiri zeegatta okulwanyisa omulabe. ('The two countries united to fight the enemy.');* (2) *vt* **-gatta,** *eg. Kabaka yagatta amawanga abiri. ('The king united the two tribes.'). See* join

united *adj* **-gatte** United Kingdom **Bungereza** *n9* United Nations **Amawanga Amagatte** *n6*

universal *adj* **-a buli wantu**

university *n* **ssettendekero** *n1*, **yunivasite** *n9*

unjustly, judge *vt* **-saliriza**

unknown *adj. Use* **-manyibwa** *('be known') in neg* **(N21)** *in rel* **(N7.1),** *eg. abantu abatamanyiddwa ('unknown people')*

unless *conj. Use* **bwe** *('if') with neg* **(N21),** *eg. Bwe tutagenda kaakati, bbaasi ejja kutuleka. ('Unless we go now, the bus will leave us behind.')*

unload *vt* **-tikkula,** *eg. Yatikkula emigugu okuva mu bbaasi. ('He unloaded the luggage from the bus.'), (item by item, eg. boxes from a lorry)* **-pakulula** unload oneself **-eetikkula,** *eg. Yeetikkula omugugu. ('She unloaded the bundle.' – from her head)*

unlock *vt* **-sumulula** become unlocked **-sumulukuka**

unluckily *(also* unfortunately*) adv* **eky'omukisa omubi, eby'embi**

unlucky, be *(also* unfortunate*) vi . Use* **omukisa**

351

('*luck*') *with neg* (**N21**), *eg. Teyali wa mukisa okufuna omulimu.* ('*She was unlucky not to get the job.*') be serially unlucky **-lina olutwe**, *eg. Musoke alina olutwe. Buli lw'afuna omulimu nga bamugoba.* ('*Musoke is an unlucky person. Whenever he gets a job, he gets fired.*')

unmarried unmarried man **omuwuulu** *n1* unmarried state (*for a man*) **obuwuulu** *n14* become unmarriageable (*especially of a woman*) **-dibira**. *See* **-dibira** (*in Part 2 of the dictionary*)

unnecessary, be *vi. Use* **-eetaagisa** ('*be required*') *in neg* (**N21**), *eg. Amateeka gano tegeetaagisa.* ('*These laws are unnecessary.*')

unpack *vt* **-ggyamu**, *eg. Yaggyamu ebintu mu ssanduuko ye.* ('*She unpacked her suitcase.*')

unpaid *adj* **-a obwereere**, *eg. omulimu gw'obwereere* ('*unpaid work*')

unpeg (*a hide*) *vt* **-bambula**

unpick (*stitches*) *vt* **-tungulula**

unplait (*also* unravel) *vt* **-langulula** become unplaited **-langulukuka**

unresolved, be (*deadlocked*) *vi* **-lemagana** unresolved problems between people **kalumannyweera** *n1*

unresponsive, remain (*unforthcoming*) *vi* **-eesisiggiriza**

unrest (state of) (*of people*) *n* **akasasamalo** *n12*, (*involving commotion*) **akayuuguumo** *n12* be in a state of unrest (*of a crowd*) **-sasamala**, **-jagalala**

unrestrained (*in behaviour*) (*also* unbridled) *adj* **-bambaavu**. *See* naughtiness unrestrained behaviour **obubambaavu** *n14* be unrestrained **-bambaala**. *See* unruly

unripe *adj* **-bisi**

unroll *vt* **-zingulula** become unrolled **-zingulukuka**

unruly *adj* **-lalu**. *See* mischievous unruly behaviour **eddalu** *n5*, **obulalu** *n14* unruly person **omulalu** *n1* be(come) unruly **-laluka**, **-eeralusa**

unsatisfactory, something *n* **enkenyera** *n9*, *eg. Nnina nkenyera mu bintu bye yaŋŋambye.* ('*I am not satified with what he told me.*'). *See* dissatisfied

unscrew *vt* **-sumulula**

unseasoned (*of wood*) *adj* **-bisi**

unsettled, be (*of the weather*) *vi* **-tabanguka**

unstable *adj* **-yuuganyi**. *See* wobbly unstable person (*fickle*) **omuyuuganyi** *n1* be unstable **-yuugana**, *eg. Enkondo eyuugana.* ('*The post is unstable.*') make unstable **-yuuganya**

unstack *vt* **-teekulula**

unstick *vt* (*unstuck*) **-gagambula** become unstuck **-gagambuka**

unstitch *vt* **-tungulula** become unstitched **-tungulukuka**

unstring (*eg. beads*) *vt* **-wulula**

unsure about, be (*relunctant; have misgivings*) *vi* **-kenyera**. *See* hesitate

untangle *vt* **-taggulula**. *See* disentangle become untangled **-taggulukuka**

untidy *adj. Use* **-longoofu** ('*tidy*') *in neg* (**N21**), *eg. Ekisenge si kirongoofu.* ('*The room is untidy.*')

untie *vt* **-sumulula** become untied **-sumulukuka**

[1]until *conj* **okutuusa bwe**, *eg. Twayogera okutuusa bwe twebaka.* ('*We talked until we went to sleep.*'), **okutuusa lwe**

[2]until *pre* **okutuusa**, *eg. Sijja kumanya okutuusa enkya.* ('*I will not know until tomorrow.*') until now **okutuusa kaakati**

untrained *adj. Use* **-tendekebwa** ('*be trained*') *in neg* (**N21**) *in rel* (**N7.1**), *eg. omusomesa atatendekebwa* ('*untrained teacher*')

untrap *vt* **-tegula**

untwist *vt* **-langulula** become untwisted **-langulukuka**

unusual *adj* **si -a bulijjo**, *eg. Embeera y'obudde si ya bulijjo.* ('*The weather is unusual.*') something very unusual **ekikulejje** *n7*

unwell (*ill*) *adj* **-lwadde** be(come) unwell **-lwala** feel unwell **-wulira bubi**

unwilling, be *vi. Use* **-yagala** ('*want*') *in neg* (**N21**), *eg. Yali tayagala kugenda.* ('*He was unwilling to go.*') come unwillingly (*causing delay*) **-sikattira**, *eg. Embuzi ezze esikattira.* ('*The goat came unwillingly.*'), (*physically resisting*) **-walira** express unwillingness (*in response to a request*) **-eekaanya**

unwind *vt* **-zingulula** become unwound **-zingulukuka**

unwrap *vt* **-sabuukulula**. *See* banana (*for vocabulary relating to serving up food from food parcels*) become unwrapped (*eg. of a parcel*) **-sabuukulukuka**

unyielding person *n* **omukakanyavu** *n1* be unyielding (*in denying something one has done*) **-eekangabiriza**

[1]up (*above*) *adv* **waggulu**

[2]up (*above*) *pre* **waggulu wa** up the hill **waggulu** (*or* **engulu**) **ku lusozi**, *eg. Ekkanisa eri waggulu ku lusozi.* ('*The church is up the hill.*') up to (*as far as*) **okutuuka ku**, *eg. Lima okutuuka ku muti.* ('*Dig up to the tree.*'), (*with place names*) **okutuuka e**, *eg. Yatambula okutuuka e Kampala.* ('*She journeyed up to Kampala.*'), (*in time*) **okutuusa ku**, *eg. Yayogera okutuusa ku ssaawa ttaano.* ('*He spoke up to 11 o'clock.*'). *See* until up to here **okutuuka wano**

upbraid *vt* **-yogerera amafuukuule**. *See* reproach

uphill *adv* **emambuka, engulu**, *eg. Bagenze engulu.* ('*They have gone uphill.*') uphill journey **amambuka** *n6* go uphill **-yambuka**, *eg. Baayambuka okugenda ku kyalo.* ('*They went uphill to the village.*')

uplift *vt* **-linnyisa**, *eg. Omukulu omupya yalinnyisa omutindo gw'essomero.* ('*The new head uplifted the standard of the school.*')

upon *pre* **ku**

upper *adj* **-a waggulu**, *eg. Kiteeke ku ssa erya*

waggulu. *('Put it on the upper shelf.')*

¹upright *adj* (1) *(of things)* Use **-eesimba** *('be upright')* in rel (**N7.1**), *eg. ekikondo ekyesimbye ('upright post')*; (2) *(of people)* **-eesimbu** upright person *(honest and straightforward)* **omwesimbu** *n1*

²upright *(vertical) adv* **obusimba** be upright **-eesimba** place upright **-simba**, *eg. Yasimba enkondo mu ttaka. ('He placed the post upright in the ground.')* sit upright **-tuula -tereera** stand upright **-yimirira busimba**

uprightness *(in character) n* **obwesimbu** *n14*, **obugolokofu** *n14*, **obusimbalaala** *n14*

uprising *n* **akajagalalo** *n12*

uproar *(din) n* **oluyoogaano** *n11* make an uproar *(of people)* **-yoogaana**

uproot *vt* **-simbula**, *(using a tool)* **-sigula**, *(by hand, eg. pull out weed or tooth)* **-kuula**, *(something firmly embedded, eg. tree)* **-siguukulula** be uprooted (1) *(eg. of a tree in a gale)* **-siguka**; (2) *(from a socket)* **-kuuka**

upset *vt* (1) *(make sad or annoyed)* **-nyiiza**; (2) *(knock over)* **-samba**. *See* confuse; disorganise; distress; disturb; harass be upset *(sad; annoyed)* **-nyiiga**, *(easily)* **-sunguwala mangu** show that one is upset *(extending over a period of time)* **-eesunguusula**

upside down, be *vi* **-eevuunika**, *eg. Eryato lyevuunise. ('The boat is upside down.')* turn upside down **-vuunika**, *eg. Baavuunika eryato. ('They turned the boat upside down.')*

upstairs *adv* **waggulu mu kalina**, *eg. Asula waggulu mu kalina. ('He lives upstairs.')*, **mu ggoloofa**

upstanding person **omwesimbu** *n1*

upward upward journey **amambuka** *n6* upward slope **akasozi** *n12*

urbanite *n* **munnakibuga** *n1*

urge *vt* (1) *(exhort; stress repeatedly)* **-kubiriza**; (2) *(keep pushing someone to do something; egg on)* **-pikiriza**. *See* encourage; insist urge on with shouting *(in hunting)* **-yamira**, *eg. Yayamira embwa mu muyiggo. ('He urged on the dogs in the hunt.')*

urinal *n* **ekiyigo** *n7*

urinate *vi* **-fuka, -fuuyisa**, *(by males)* **-kunkumula omusulo** urinate on oneself *(of males)* **-eefukira, -eekunkumulira**

urine *n* **omusulo** *n3*, **susu** *n1*, **enkali** *n9*

urticaria *n* **ebirogologo** *n8*

us *pro* **ffe**. *The verb prefix is* **tu-** (**N15**).

¹use *n* **omugaso** *n3* way of using **enkozesa** *n9*

²use *vt* (1) **-kozesa**, *eg. Nnyinza okukozesa ku nkumbi yo? ('Can I use your hoe?')*; (2) *(make use of)* **-eeyambisa**, *eg. Yeeyambisa muggo okutambula. ('He uses a stick to help him walk.')* use extravagantly *(wastefully)* **-diibuula** use sparingly *(economically)* **-kekkereza** use up

-malawo, *eg. Tumazeewo amatooke. ('We have used up the plantains.')*, *(something that gets worn down, eg. tablet of soap)* **-ggweereza** be(come) used up **-ggwaawo**, *eg. Amatooke gaweddewo. ('The plantains are used up.')*, *(of something that gets worn down)* **-ggweerera**, *eg. Ssabbuuni aggweeredde. ('The soap is becoming used up.')*

used to *(referring to the past) aux v.* Use far past tense (**N16**) *and suffix* **-nga** (**N18**), *eg. Yakolanga wano. ('She used to work here.')* be(come) used to *(accustomed)* **-manyiira**, *eg. Bamanyidde okukola ennyo. ('They have become used to hard work.')*

useful *adj* **-a omugaso** be useful (to) **-gasa**, *eg. Ensawo ejja kugasa okutereka ebintu. ('The bag will be useful for storing things.')*

usefulness *n* **omugaso** *n3*

uselessly *See* fruitlessly

usual *adj* **-a bulijjo**, *eg. ekyokunywa kyange ekya bulijjo ('my usual drink')*

usually *adv* **bulijjo**, *eg. Bulijjo agenda ku ssaawa bbiri. ('He usually goes at 8 o'clock.')* be/do usually **-tera** in present tense (**N16**) *followed by inf* (**N19**), *eg. Ntera okulya lumonde. ('I usually eat potatoes.')*

usurp *vt* **-eetulinkiriza**

uterus *n* **nnabaana** *n1*

utilise *vt* **-kozesa**

utter *(speak) vt* **-yogerako**

utterly *(completely) adv* **ddala**

V,v

vacancy *(for work) n* **ekifo** *n7*, *eg. Waliwo ekifo. ('There is a vacancy.')*

vacant *adj* **-yereere**, *eg. ennyumba enjereere ('vacant house')*. *See* abandoned

vacate *vt* **-va mu** *(or* **-vaamu**), *eg. Baava mu bisenge byabwe. ('They vacated their rooms.')*

vacation *n* **oluwummula** *n11* take a vacation **-wummula**

vaccinate (against) *vt* **-gema**, *eg. Nnansi agemye abaana akafuba. ('The nurse has vaccinated the children against TB.')*

vacillate *vi* **-yuugayuuga**

vagabond *n* **kireereese** *n1*, **omubungeesi** *n1* be a vagabond **-leereeta, -bungeeta bubungeesi**

vagina *n* **obukazi** *n14*, **emmana** *n9* *(vulgar)*

vain, be *(conceited) vi* **-eemanya** in vain *(without benefit)* **obwereere, obusa**

valiant *adj* **-zira**

valley *n* **ekiwonvu** *n7* *(long* **oluwonvu** *n11)*, **ekikko** *n7*. *See* depression

valour *n* **obuzira** *n14*

valuable *adj* (1) *(monetary)* **-a omuwendo**; (2) *(useful)* **-a omugaso**

value *n* (1) *(monetary)* **omuwendo** *n3*; (2) *(use)* **omugaso** *n3*

valve *n* akatima *n12*

vanilla *n* vanira *n1*

vanish *vi* -bula

vanity *n* okwewulira *n15*, obwewulize *n14*, okwemanya *n15*

vanquish *vt* -wangula

vapour *n* omukka *n3* give a vapour bath to -yoteza take a vapour bath -eeyoteza

variation (*on a theme*) *n* ekisoko *n7*

variegated *adj* -tobeke make variegated (*of varied colours, shapes, etc.*) -tobeka

variety (*type; sort*) *n* ekika *n7*, engeri *n9*

various *det.* Use -ngi (*'many'*), *eg. Waliwo amakubo mangi agagenda ku ffaamu.* (*'There are various ways to go to the farm.'*)

vary *vt* -kyusaako

vaseline *n* vasiriini *n9*

vast *adj* -nene ennyo

vat (*hollowed-out tree trunk used for brewing*) *n* eryato ery'omwenge *n5*, (*smaller*) emmanvu *n5*

vault (over) *vt* -buuka

veer *vi* -dda, *eg. Yadda ku kkono.* (*'He veered to the left.'*). *See* swerve

vegetable(s) *n* enva *n10* green vegetables (*served with the main food 'emmere'*) enva endiirwa. *See* greens

vegetation *n* ebimera *n8*

vehicle *n* ekidduka *n7*

veil *n* akakaaya *n12*

vein *n* omusuwa *n3*

vendetta *n* ekiruyi *n7*

vendor *n* omutunzi *n1*

venerate *vt* -ssaamu ekitiibwa, *eg. Abantu bassaamu omwawule waabwe ekitiibwa.* (*'The people venerated their reverend minister.'*). *See* worship

venereal disease *n* endwadde y'obukaba *n9*

vengeance, take -woolera eggwanga, *eg. Baawoolera eggwanga ku balabe baabwe.* (*'They took vengeance on their enemies.'*)

venom *n* obusagwa *n14*

venomous *adj* -a obusagwa

ventilator *n* akamooli *n12*

Venus (*planet*) *n* nnabaliwo *n1*

verandah *n* olubalaza *n11*, (*on platform, raised above ground level*) ekifugi *n7*

verb *n* ekikolwa *n7*

verdict (*in court case*) *n* ensala y'omusango give a verdict -sala omusango

verify *vt* -kakasa

verse (*of the Bible*) *n* olunyiriri *n11*

vertical *adj* -a obusimba

verticality *n* obwesimbu *n14*

vertically *adv* obusimba

vertigo *n* kammunguluze *n1*, kantoolooze *n1*

vervet monkey *n* enkima *n9*

very *adv* ennyo

vessel *n* (1) (*ship*) emmeeri *n9*, (*with sails*)

ekyombo *n7*; (2) (*receptable for catching rain water*) ennembeko *n9*; (3) (*for milk*) ekyanzi *n7*. *See* boat; canoe pot blood vessel omusuwa *n3*

vest *n* effulaano *n9*, vesiti *n9*

vet(erinarian) *n* omusawo w'ebisolo *n1*

vex *vt* (1) (*annoy*) -nyiiza; (2) (*confuse; worry*) -eeraliikiriza be vexed (1) (*annoyed*) -nyiiga; (2) (*worried*) -eeraliikirira

vibrate *vi* -kankana

vibrato *n* eggono *n5* (*this refers to the traditional Kiganda way of singing – clearly and pleasantly*) sing vibrato -yimba n'eddoboozi eritiribira obulungi

vicar *n* omusumba *n1*

¹vice *n* (1) (*bad habit*) omuze *n3*; (2) (*carpenter's*) ejjiribwa *n5*

²vice- (*second-in-charge*) omubeezi *n1*, *eg. omubeezi wa ssettendekero* (*'vice-chancellor'*)

vicinity *n* omuliraano *n3*

vicious *adj* -kambwe

victim (*of robbery or plunder*) *n* omunyage *n1*. *See* injured person

victor *n* omuwanguzi *n1*

victory *n* obuwanguzi *n14* be victorious (over) -wangula

video *n* vidiyo *n9*

¹view (*opinion*) *n* endowooza *n9*

²view (*see*) *vt* -laba, (*from afar*) -lengera, *eg. Wano walengera nnyo.* (*'There is a good view from here.'*) block the view of (*in sight line*) -siikiriza

viewer *n* omulabi *n1*

vigilant about, be (*care*) *vi* -faayo nnyo ku, *eg. Abazadde baafaayo nnyo ku kuyiga kw'abaana.* (*'The parents were vigilant about their children's education.'*)

vigorous *adj* -a amaanyi

vigour *n* amaanyi *n6*

village *n* ekyalo *n7*, (*traditional village area; extending from stream to hilltop*) omutala *n3* village head nnannyini kyalo *n1*

villager *n* ow'ekyalo *n1*, munnakyalo *n1*

vine *n* (1) (*grapevine*) omuzabbibu *n3*; (2) (*climbing plant in general*) ekiranda *n7*

violate *vt* -sobya. *See* rape

violence *n* ebikolwa eby'obukambwe *n8*

violent *adj* -kambwe

viper, Gabon *n* essalambwa *n9*

virgin (*girl*) *n* embeerera *n9* Virgin Mary Biikira Maliya *n1*

virginity *n* obubeererevu *n14*

virile *adj* -a amaanyi

virility *n* amaanyi *n6*

virtuous *adj* -lungi virtuous person omulungi *n1*

viscera *n* ebyenda *n8*

visible, be *vi* (1) -labika, *eg. Kirabika okuva wano.* (*'It is visible from here.'*); (2) (*from afar*) -lengerekeka, *eg. Ekibuga kirengerekeka okuva ku lusozi olwo.* (*'The town is visible from that hill.'*), (*of the new moon*) **-boneka**. *See* see

vision *n* (1) (*sight*) **okulaba** *n15*; (2) (*miraculous sighting*) **okulabikirwa** *n15* blurred vision **ekifu ku maaso** *n7* have a vision (*miraculous sighting*) **-yolesebwa**

¹visit *n* **olukyala** *n11* be/go on a visit **-genyiwala** make a visit **-kyala**, *eg. Twagenda okukyala ewa Musoke. ('We went to visit Musoke.')* on a visit **ku bugenyi** receive on a visit **-genyiwaza**

²visit *vt* (1) (*a place*) **-kyala**, *eg. Twakyala e Masaka. ('We visited Masaka.')*; (2) (*a person*) **-kyalira**, *eg. Twakyalira Musoke. ('We visited Musoke.')* visit a place frequently **-eewuuba**, *eg. Yeewuuba wano. ('He frequently visits here.')*

visiting *adj* **-genyi** give notice of visiting **-laga**, *eg. Twalaga nga tujja kugendayo enkya. ('We gave notice that we would visit tomorrow.')*

visitor *n* **omugenyi** *n1* food (*or* drink) offered to a visitor **obugenyi** *n14* receive a visitor **-kyaza** see off a visitor (*by escorting a short distance on the way*) **-werekera omugenyi**

vitality *n* **amaanyi** *n6*

vitamin *n* **vitamiini** *n9*

vocation (*calling*) *n* **okuyitibwa** *n15*

¹voice *n* **eddoboozi** *n5*

²voice (*say*) *vt* **-gamba**

volcano *n* **olusozi oluwandula omuliro** *n11*

volume (*of sound*) *n* **eddoboozi** *n9*

voluntarily *adv* **kyeyagalire**

voluntarism *n* **obwannakyewa** *n14* voluntary society **ekibiina kya ba nnakyewa** *n7*

voluntary *adj* **-a nnakyewa**

¹volunteer *n* **nnakyewa** *n1*

²volunteer *vi* **-eewaayo**, *eg. Yeewaayo okuyamba essomero. ('She volunteered to help the school.')*

¹vomit *n* **ebisesemye** *n8*

²vomit *vi* **-sesema** cause to vomit **-sesemya**

voom (*make noice like a revving car*) *vi* **-vuuma**

¹vote *n* **akalulu** *n12*

²vote *vi* **-kuba akalulu**

voter *n* **omulonzi** *n1*

vouch for *vt* **-teekerako akabega**

¹vow *n* **obweyamo** *n14*, (*oath*) **ekirayiro** *n7*

²vow *vi* **-eeyama**, (*take an oath*) **-layira** vow allegiance **-wera** vow revenge **-wera enkolokooto**

vowel *n* (**ennyukuta**) **enjatuza** *n9*, (**ennyukuta**) **empeerezi** *n9*

¹voyage *n* **olugendo** *n11*. *See* journey

²voyage *vi* **-tambula**

vulgarity (*bad manners*) *n* **empisa embi** *n10*

vulture *n* **ensega** *n9*

W,w

waddle *vi* **-baatabaata, -baatira**

wag *vt* **-wuuba, -tenga**

wage (*pay*) *n* **omusaala** *n3*, **empeera** *n9* wages **emisaala** *n4*

wage war (on) **-tabaala**

wagtail, pied (*type of bird*) *n* **nnamunye** *n1*

¹wail (*of distress*) *n* **ekiwoobe** *n7*. *See* cry

²wail *vi* **-kuba ekiwoobe**, (*in grief*) **-yaziirana**, *eg. Yayaziirana nga maama we afudde. ('She wailed when her mother died.')*. *See* cry out

waist *n* **ekiwato** *n7*, (*thin*) **olukende** *n11* be thin-waisted **-kenduka**

waistband *n* (1) *worn for comfort after losing someone*) **ekimyu** *n7*; (2) (*of beads, worn by very young girls, formerly made with sticks*) **ebiti** *n8*; (3) (*of beads, worn by women as a love charm*) **olutiiti** *n14*; (4) (*worn as a charm, for good luck or protection*) **ensiriba** *n9*

wait (for) *vit* **-linda**, *eg. Nnakulinda. ('I waited for you.')*, (*keep waiting*) **-lindirira**, *eg. Nnakulindirira ku siteegi ya bbaasi. ('I kept waiting for you at the bus stop.')* wait a while **-lindako** wait upon (*serve*) **-weereza** lie in wait (for) (*to ambush*) **-teega**

waiter/waitress *n* **omuweereza** *n1*

wake (up) *v* (woke) (1) (*of oneself*) *vi* **-zuukuka**, (*suddenly from deep sleep*) **-sisimuka**; (2) (*someone else*) *vt* **-zuukusa**, (*suddenly from deep sleep*) **-sisimula**. *See* get up wake and get up (*of oneself*) **-golokoka** start up from sleep **-wawamuka mu tulo**

¹walk(ing) *n* **okutambula** *n15* take a walk **-tambulako** take for a walk **-tambuza**, *eg. Yatwala abaana okubatambuza. ('He took his children for a walk.')* way of walking **entambula** *n9*

²walk *vi* **-tambula**. *The following describe ways of walking* (*using aux verbs* (**N19**): (*fast*) **-tambula -yanguwa**, (*with a wiggle*) **-tambula -bigula**, (*slowly*) **-tambula -sooba**, (*trudge along*) **-tambula -bebbera**, (*with a swaying motion*) **-tambula -yuuga**. *Ways of walking are also expressed by*: (*backwards*) **-tambula kaddannyuma**, (*in a leisurely way*) **-tambulatambulako, -lembalemba**, (*on tiptoe*) **-tambuza bunkenke**, (*slowly*) **-tambula kasoobo**, (*very slowly, like a snail*) **-soonooka**, (*softly or stealthily*) **-tambuza buggereggere**, (*with inward-pointing feet*) **-tambuza bitege**, (*with outward-pointing feet*) **-tambuza mbaliga**. *See* strut; waddle walk out in disagreement (*eg. from a meeting*) **-eekandula**

walker *n* **ow'ebigere** *n1*

walking *n* **okutambula** *n15* walking stick **omuggo** *n3* way of walking **entambula** *n9*

wall *n* **ekisenge** *n7*, (*as boundary to a property*) **ekikomera** *n7*

wallow *vi* **-eekulukuunya**

wander (about) aimlessly *vi* **-leereeta, -yenjeera, -bungeeta**

wanderer *n* kireereesi *n1*

[1]**want** (*need*) *n* ekyetaago *n7*

[2]**want** *vt* (1) (*wish to do*) **-yagala**, *eg. Njagala okugenda e Kampala enkya. ('I want to go to Kampala tomorrow.')*; (2) (*crave; lust after*) **-eegomba**, *eg. Neegomba nnyo okulaba enjovu. ('I very much want to see elephants.')* be wanted (*desired*) **-eegombebwa** cause to want (*covet*) **-eegombesa**, *eg. Emmotoka ye yeegombesa buli agiraba. ('Everyone who sees his car wants it.')* want to have (*an item, before others can get it; preempt*) **-eesooka**, *eg. Nze nneesoose olugoye luno. ('I want to have this dress.' – when clothes are being distributed)*

war *n* olutalo *n11*, olutabaalo *n11*, (*major; world war*) ssematalo *n1* wage war (on) **-tabaala**

waragi *n* walagi *n1*, enguuli *n9*

ward (*in hospital*) *n* waada *n9* maternity ward mateniti *n9* public ward waada y'olukale

ward off (*disease, misfortune, etc.*) *vt* **-gema**, (*from oneself*) **-eegema**

warden *n* omukuumi *n1* church warden omuweereza *n1* prison warden omuserikale w'ekkomera *n1*

warehouse (*store*) *n* sitoowa *n9*

wares (*things to sell*) *n* ebyokutunda *n8*

warfare *n* ebyolutalo *n8*

[1]**warm** *adj.* Use **-buguma** (*'be warm'*) in rel (**N7.1**), *eg. amazzi agabuguma ('warm water')*

[2]**warm** *vt* **-bugumya**, *eg. Abugumya amazzi. ('She is warming the water.')* warm oneself (by) **-yota**, *eg. Bayota omuliro. ('They are warming themselves by the fire.')* be(come) warm **-buguma**, *eg. Amazzi gabuguma. ('The water is warm.')*

warmed *adj* **-bugumye**

warmth *n* olubugumu *n11*

warn *vt* **-labula**, *eg. Yandabula nti omusajja mubbi. ('He warned me that the man is a thief.'). See* caution be warned (*forewarned*) **-labuka**

warp *vt* **-goomya** be(come) warped **-gooma**

warped *adj* **-goomu**

warrior *n* omutabaazi *n1. See* fighter

wart *n* ensundo *n9*

warthog *n* engiri *n9*

was *See* be

wash *v* (1) (*oneself*) *vi* **-naaba**, *eg. Nja kunaaba engalo. ('I will wash my hands.')*; (2) (*someone else*) *vt* **-naaza**; (3) (*things*) *vt* **-yoza** wash in/at (1) (*oneself*) **-naabira**, *eg. Nja kunaabira engalo zange mu bbenseni. ('I will wash my hands in the basin.')*; (2) (*someone else*) **-naaliza**, *eg. Abaana nnabanaaliza ebweru. ('I washed the children outside.')*; (3) (*things*) **-yoleza**, *eg. Yoleza ebintu ebweru. ('Wash the things outside.')* wash with (1) (*relating to people*) **-naabisa**, *eg. Abaana baanaabisa ssabbuuni. ('The children washed with soap.')*; (2) (*relating to things*) **-yozesa**

washbasin *n* ebbenseni *n9. See* sink

washerman *n* ddobbi *n1*

washing (*laundry*) *n* engoye ez'okwoza *n10* washing place (1) (*for people*) ekinaabiro *n7*, (*place within which one washes*) omw'okunaabira *n18*; (2) (*for things*) aw'okwoleza *n16* washing powder (*for clothes*) omo *n9* something used for washing (*referring to a person, eg. a bucket*) ekinaabirwamu *n7*

wasp *n* ennumba *n9*, (*large black and yellow mason wasp; makes pot-like nest on ceilings*) bbumbuzzi *n1*, (*black mason wasp; makes pot-like nests on ceilings*) muyizzitasubwa *n1. See* hornet

[1]**waste** *n* (1) (*rubbish*) ebisasiro *n8*, ebisaaniiko *n8*; (2) (*of grass and bananas after extracting banana juice*) ebikamulo *n8*; (3) (*of banana leaves after cooking a food parcel*) essaaniiko *n5*; (4) (*from straining or squeezing, especially when brewing 'amalwa'*) ebikanja *n8*; (5) (*filth; sewage*) kazambi *n1*; (6) (*from smelting iron ore*) amatale *n6* waste pipe omufulejje gwa kazambi *n3*

[2]**waste** *vt* **-yonoona**, *eg. Yayonoona essente ze nga anywa omwenge. ('He wasted his money on alcohol.')*, (*use extravagantly*) **-diibuula**, *eg. Adiibuula amazzi. ('She is wasting water.')* waste away **-koozimba**, **-konziba**, (*through an incurable illness*) **-konvuba**. *See* thin (become) waste time **-yonoona ebiseera**, **-mala obudde**, **-mala ebiseera**

wasteful *adj* **-diibuuzi** use wastefully **-diibuuda**

[1]**watch** (*timepiece*) *n* essaawa *n9* watch of the night ekisisimuka *n7* wrist watch essaawa y'oku mukono

[2]**watch** *vt* **-laba**, *eg. Tugenda kulaba mupiira. ('We are going to watch the football.')* watch over (1) (*guard*) **-kuuma**; (2) (*look after*) **-labirira** be watchful of (*someone, having suspicions*) **-eekengera**, *eg. Bwe yawulira enjogera yaabwe n'abeekengera. ('When he heard the way they talked, he watched them carefully.')*

watcher *n* omulabi *n1. See* night watchman

watchfulness *n* obwerende *n14*

[1]**water** *n* amazzi *n6*, (*very little*) otuzzi *n13*, (*from the porch or roof*) amazzi g'ekisasi, (*rainwater*) amazzi g'enkuba, (*flowing on the ground during or after rain*) mukoka *n1* water channel (*eg. in swamp*) omwala *n3* water hyacinth ekiddo ku nnyanja *n7* water lettuce kitengejja *n1* water pipe omudumu gw'amazzi *n3* water pot *See* pot water pump (*hand type*) nayikonto *n9* water source (*spring, river or well*) ensulo *n9* water weed (*green and slimy*) enkonge *n9* at the water source emugga boiled water amazzi amafumbe boiling water amazzi ageesera cold water amazzi agannyogoga go under water **-bbira mu mazzi** hot water amazzi agookya place for crossing water *See* cross put water on a fire (*to douse it*) **-vubiriza omuliro** travel across water **-somoka** warm water amazzi agabuguma

[2]**water** *vt* (1) (*animals*) **-wa amazzi**; (2) (*plants*)

-fukirira <u>water down</u> (*dilute*) -saabulula,
-jungulula <u>be watered down</u> -saabulukuka
<u>watered-down</u> *adj* -a lujjulungu, -a jjuule
waterbuck *n* ensama *n9*
waterfall *n* ekiyiriro *n7*
watering place (*for livestock*) *n* ekyesero *n7*
watery (*of food*) *adj* -serebevu, (*of matooke*)
-biririvu <u>watery eyes</u> (*about to cry*)
ebiyengeyenge *n8* <u>be too watery</u> (*of food*)
-serebera, *eg. Omuceere guserebedde. ('The rice is
watery.'),* (*of matooke*) -biririra, *eg. Emmere
ebiriridde. ('The matooke is watery.')* <u>make too
watery</u> (*food*) -serebeza
wattle framework (*of mud and wattle wall*) *n*
ebizizi *n8*
¹**wave** (*on water*) *n* ejjengo *n5*
²**wave** *vt* -wuuba <u>wave down</u> (*eg. taxi*) -kuba
omukono, -yimiriza <u>wave to/for</u> -wuubira, *eg.
Atuwuubira. ('She is waving to us.'). See* beckon
wavelength (*of a broadcast*) *n* omukutu *n3*,
amayengo *n6*
waver (*vacillate*) *vi* -yuugayuuga. *See* doubt
wax *n* envumbo *n9*
waxbill (*type of small bird*) *n* akagugumusi *n12*
way *n* (1) (*manner*) engeri *n9*; (2) (*route*) ekkubo
n5; (3) (*custom; habit*) empisa *n9. The following
are ways of doing things (all in noun class n9):*
(*building*) enzimba, (*cultivating; digging; farming*)
ennima, (*deep digging*) enkabala, (*doing*) enkola,
(*growing*) enkula, (*looking after*) endabirira,
(*measuring*) empima, (*planting sweet potatoes*)
embyala, (*playing*) enzannya, (*ruling*) enfuga,
(*seeing*) endaba, (*speaking*) enjogera, (*story-
telling*) enfumo, (*taxing*) empooza, (*teaching*)
enjigiriza, (*thinking*) endowooza, (*travelling;
walking*) entambula, (*using*) enkozesa, (*working
together*) enkolagana, (*writing*) empandiika. <u>by
the way</u> kozzi <u>in the same way</u> mu ngeri y'emu
<u>make a way</u> (*eg. introduction to someone
influential*) -tema oluwenda. *See* path (make a)
<u>make way for</u> (1) (*get out of the way of*) -viira, *eg.
Baaviiridde emmotoka ya pulezidenti. ('They made
way for the president's car.');* (2) (*shift over when
seated*) -segulira, *eg. Segulira omukyala atuule.
('Make way so that the lady can sit.')*
we *pro* ffe. *The verb prefix is* tu- (N15).
weak *adj* -nafu, (*from illness*) -gonvu. *See* lethargic
<u>weak person</u> omunafu *n1*, (*from illness*)
omugonvu *n1* <u>be(come) weak</u> -nafuwa, *eg.
Olutindo lunafuye. ('The bridge has become
weak.'),* (*of a sick person*) -gonda
weaken *vt* -nafuya, *eg. Obutalagge bunafuyizza
olutindo. ('The rust has weakened the bridge.')*
weakness *n* obunafu *n14*
wealth *n* obugagga *n14*, emmaali *n9*
wealthy *adj* -gagga <u>wealthy person</u> omugagga *n1*,
(*very*) nnaggagga *n1* <u>be(come) wealthy</u>
-gaggawala <u>make wealthy</u> -gaggawaza

wean *vt* -ggyako ku mabeere, *eg. Omwana
amuggyako ku mabeere. ('She is weaning the
baby.')* <u>wean too soon</u> -yosera. *See* child <u>be
weaned</u> -va ku mabeere, *eg. Omwana avudde ku
mabeere. ('The baby has been weaned.')*
<u>nutritional deficiency</u> (*of a child, caused by
premature weaning*) obwosi *n14*
weapon *n* ekyokulwanyisa *n7*
wear (*clothes*) *vt* -yambala <u>wear out</u> (1) (*tyre,
pencil, etc.*) -ggweereza; (2) (*clothing*) -yabirira
<u>something to wear</u> ekyokwambala *n7*
weariness *n* obukoowu *n14*
weary *adj* -koowu <u>be(come) weary</u> -koowa, *eg.
Akooye okukola. ('She is weary of working.')*
<u>make weary</u> -kooya
weather *n* embeera y'obudde *n9. See* obudde (*in
Part 2 of the dictionary*) <u>weather forecast</u>
enteebereza y'obudde *n9*
weave *vt* (wove, woven) (1) (*mat or basket*) -luka;
(2) (*reeds or cane; intertwine*) -gombeza, *eg.
Tuzimba ekisaakate nga tugombeza emmuli. ('We
are building the fence interweaving reeds.')*
<u>weave with</u> (*mat or basked*) -lukisa, *eg. Alukisa
nsansa. ('She is weaving with palm leaves.')*
weaver *n* omulusi *n1* <u>weaver bird</u> endegeya *n9*
web (*of spider*) *n* nnabbubi *n1*
wed *vt* (1) (*woman by a man*) -wasa; (2) (*man by a
woman*) -fumbirwa <u>be wed</u> (*of a couple*)
-fumbiriganwa, (*in church*) -gattibwa <u>newly
weds</u> abagole *n2* <u>state of being newly wed</u>
obugole *n14*
wedding *n* embaga *n9*
¹**wedge** *n* empano *n9*
²**wedge (in)** *vt* -wagika, *eg. Yawagika ekiti wansi
w'emmeeza. ('He wedged a piece of wood under
the table.')*
Wednesday *n* Olwokusatu *n11*
¹**weed(s)** *n* omuddo *n3* <u>slimy water weed</u> enkonge
n9
²**weed** *vt* (1) (*by hand*) -koola; (2) (*by hoeing*) -wala
omuddo <u>be(come) weedy</u> -zika, *eg. Omusiri
guzise. ('The plot is weedy.')* <u>time for weeding</u>
amakoola *n6*
week *n* essabbiiti *n9*, wiiki *n9*, dimansi *n9* <u>last
week</u> wiiki eyise <u>next week</u> wiiki ejja
weekend *n* wiikendi *n9*
weekly *adv* buli wiiki
weep *vi* -kaaba, (*with freely flowing tears*)
-kulukusa amaziga
weevil (*on banana plants*) *n* kayovu *n1*
weigh *vt* -gera, -pima <u>weigh up</u> (*evaluate*)
-geraageranya
weight *n* obuzito *n14* <u>gain weight</u> (*of person or
animal*) -gejja <u>lose weight</u> (1) (*of person or
animal*) -kogga, (*become extremely thin and
unhealthy*) -kenena; (2) (*through losing contents,
eg. of a sack*) -sowottoka <u>person who has gained
weight</u> omugevvu *n1* <u>person who has lost weight</u>

omukovvu *n1*

welcome *vt* **-yaniriza**, *eg. Genda oyanirize abagenyi.* (*'Go and welcome the guests.'*). *See* greet Welcome back. **Kulikayo.** (*pl.* **Mukulikeeyo.**)

welfare *n* **ebyembeera** *n8* public welfare **ebyembeera by'abantu**

[1]**well** (*good*) *adv* **obulungi** Well done. **Kulika.** (*pl.* **Mukulike.**), **Yogaayoga.** feel well **-eewulira bulungi** get well **-wona**

[2]**well** (*water source*) *n* **oluzzi** *n11* at the well **emugga** keeper of the royal well **Kalindaluzzi** *n1* *title*

well-behaved *adj* **-a empisa nnungi**

well-being *n* **embeera y'obulamu** *n9*

well-groomed *adj* **-nyirivu** be well-groomed **-nyirira** state of being well-groomed **obunyirivu** *n14*

well-known *adj* **-manyifu**. *See* distinguished; famous well-known person **omumanyifu** *n1*, **omumanyibwa** *n1*

well-mannered *adj* **-a empisa nnungi**. *See* cultured well-mannered person **ow'empisa** *n1*, **omuntumulamu** *n1*

well up (*of an emotion*) *vi* **-tumbuka** (*with personal subject*), *eg. Yatumbuse n'aseka.* (*'Laughter welled up within her.'*)

wellington boot *n* **magetisi** *n9*

went *See* go

were *See* be

west *n* **obugwanjuba** *n23* to/at the west **ebugwanjuba**

wet *adj* (1) *Use* **-toba** (*'get wet'*) *in rel* (**N7.1**), *eg. engatto etobye* (*'wet shoes'*); (2) (*of clothes, etc.*) **-bisi** wet one's bed **-fuka ku buliri** get wet **-toba**, *eg. Engoye zange zaatobye mu nkuba.* (*'My clothes got wet in the rain.'*), **-bisiwala**, (*slightly*) **-toberera**, (*completely*) **-totobala**, (*dripping*) **-tonnyolokoka** make wet **-tobya**, *eg. Enkuba yatobezza engoye zange.* (*'The rain made my clothes wet.'*), **-bisiwaza**

wetland *n* **olutobazzi** *n11*. *See* swamp

wetness *n* **obubisi** *n14*

[1]**what?** *interr* **ki?** (**N13**), *eg. Ayogera ki?* (*'What is he saying?'*), (*referring to a quantity*) *Use* **-yenkana wa?** (*'be equal to what?'*), *eg. Ennyumba yenkana wa obunene?* (*'What size is the house?'*) what ... called? (*used when a name is not remembered*) (1) (*of a person*) **gundi**, *eg. Genda obuulire gundi.* (*'Go and tell what's-she-called.'*); (2) (*of a place*) **gindi**; (3) (*of a thing*) **nnankani** what for? **-aki?**, *eg. Ebyuma bino byaki?* (*'What are these tools for?*), **ki?** (*with prepositional verb* **N22**) (**N13**), *eg. Yakigulira ki?* (*'What did he buy it for?'*) what is it? **kiki?** (**N13**), *eg. Kiki ky'akoze?* (*'What is it that she's done?'*) what ... like? **-tya?** (*verb used only in present tense* **N13**), *eg. Omwana yali atya?* (*'What was the child like?'*) what sort of? **-a engeri ki?**, *eg. Ogwo muti gwa ngeri ki?* (*'What sort of tree is that?'*) What time is it? **Essaawa mmeka?**

[2]**what** *rel* (*object relative pronoun, or conjunction*) (1) **kye** (**N10.1**), *eg. Oyinza okumbuulira ky'omanyi.* (*'Can you tell me what you know?'*); (2) **kya** (*followed by infinitive*), *eg. Simanyi kya kukola.* (*'I do not know what to do.'*)

whatever *pro* **kyonna**, *eg. Oyinza okufuna kyonna ky'oyagala.* (*'You can have whatever you want.'*)

wheat *n* **eŋŋaano** *n9*

wheel *n* **nnamuziga** *n9* potter's wheel **olubumbiro** *n11* steering wheel **siteeringi** *n9*

wheelbarrow *n* **ekigaali** *n7*

wheelchair *n* **akagaali k'abalema** *n12*

[1]**wheeze** *n* **ekiyiriitiro** *n7*

[2]**wheeze** *vi* **-yiriitira**

[1]**when** *conj* **bwe, lwe, we.** (**N10.2**), *eg. Bwe nnaamala okugula ebintu nja kugenda eka.* (*'When I finish shopping I will go home.'*), (*while*) **nga** (**N25.3**), *eg. Tovuga ng'okooye.* (*'Don't drive when you are tired.'*). *See* after; as soon as; if

[2]**when?** *interr* **ddi?** (**N13**)

whenever *conj* **buli lwe**, *eg. Nja kugenda buli lwe nsobola.* (*'I will go whenever I can.'*)

where *conj/rel* (1) **we** (**N10.2**), *eg. Oyinza okumbuulira omugga we guli?* (*'Can you tell me where the river is?'*); (2) *Use subject relative clause* (**N7.2**), *eg.* (1) *Genda awali emiti.* (*'Go where the trees are.'*); (2) *Genda mu kisenge omuli abantu.* (*'Go into the room where there are people.'*). *Examples of the use of subject relative clauses in negative sentences:* (1) *Genda awatali miti.* (*'Go where there are no trees.'*); (2) *Genda mu kisenge omutali bantu.* (*'Go into the room where there are no people.'*). *See* in which; on which over there where **gye**, *eg. Genda Musoke gy'ali.* (*'Go over there where Musoke is.'*)

where? *interr* **wa?**, *eg. Ogenda wa?* (*'Where are you going?'*), **ludda wa?**, *eg. Ekiso kye kiri ludda wa?* (*'Where is his knife?'*). (**N13.1**)

whereas *conj* **so nga**

wherever *conj* **buli we**, *eg. Buli we tutambula, tulaba abantu.* (*'Wherever we walk, we see people.'*)

whether *conj* **oba, nga.** *See* if

whetstone *n* **ekibalangulo** *n7*

[1]**which?** *interr* **ki?** (**N13**), *eg. Oyagala kiso ki?* (*'Which knife do you want.'*), **-luwa?** (**N13**), *eg. Ekiso kye kye kiruwa?* (*'Which is his knife?'*)

[2]**which** (*also* that) *rel* (*also conj*) *The* **SUBJECT RELATIVE** *is formed by adding the initial vowel of the noun of reference to the verb* (**N7.1**), *eg. Emmotoka eyazze ya mu muganda wange.* (*'The car which arrived is my brother's.'*). **OBJECT RELATIVE -e** (**N10.1**). *Takes pronominal concord* (**N4.2**), *eg. Ente ze baagula ziri awo.* (*'The cows which they bought are there.'*) in which

mwe, <u>on which</u> **kwe. (N10.2)**

while *conj* **nga**, *eg. Nnamulaba ng'alima. ('I saw her while she was digging.')*, **nga bwe**, *eg. Yayogera nga bw'alya. ('He spoke while eating.')*. **(N25.3)**

whine and protest *(in response to a request) vi* **-eekaanya**

¹**whip** *n* **kifaalu** *n9*, **kibooko** *n9*. *See* cane

²**whip** *(flog) vt* **-swanyuula**. *See* cane

whirl (about) *(in the air) vt* **-zunga**, *eg. Ensowera zizunga. ('The flies are whirling about.')*, *(annoyingly)* **-eetayirira**, *eg. Ensowera zimwetayiridde ku mutwe. ('Flies are whirling around his head.')*

whirlwind *n* **akazimu** *n12*

whisk, (fly) *n* **emboobo** *n9*

whiskers *n* **obuswiriri** *n14*

¹**whisper** *n* **akaama** *n12*

²**whisper** *vi* **-yogera mu kaama** <u>whisper to</u> **-kuba akaama**, *eg. Yankuba akaama n'aŋŋamba nti afunye ssente nnyingi. ('He whispered to me that he had received a lot of money.')*

¹**whistle** *n* (1) *(through the lips)* **oluwa** *n11*; (2) *(as blown by referee)* **effirimbi** *n9* <u>blow a whistle</u> *(by referee)* **-fuuwa effirimbi**

²**whistle** *vi* (1) *(using the lips)* **-fuuwa oluwa**; (2) *(as the wind)* **-wuuma**

white *adj* **-yeru**. *See* light-skinned <u>white ant</u> *See* termite <u>white person</u> **omuzungu** *n1* <u>white person's</u> *adj* **-zungu** <u>white person's language</u> **oluzungu** *n11* <u>make white</u> **-yerusa**

whither? *interr* **wa?**

¹**who?** *(or* <u>whom?</u>*) interr* **ani? (N13)**

²**who** *rel pro.* The **SUBJECT RELATIVE** *is formed by adding the initial vowel of the noun class of the subject to the verb* **(N7.1)**, *eg. Abo abalaba muwanike emikono. ('Those who can see raise your hands.')* **OBJECT RELATIVE gwe** *(pl.* **be***)* **(N10.1)**, *eg. Simanyi gwe bayinza okulaba. ('I do not know who they can see.')*

whoever *pro* **buli**, *eg. Buli anaalya emmere, ajje wano. ('Whoever will eat, let him come here.')*

whole *adj* (1) *(all)* **-onna (N7.3)**. *Takes pronominal concord* **(N4.2)**, *eg. ekibiina kyonna ('the whole class')*; (2) *(entire; undivided)* **-lamba**, *eg. Yalidde omucungwa mulamba. ('He ate the whole orange.')*

wholesale *adj* **-a kolijja**, *eg. edduuka lya kolijja ('wholesale shop')*

wholesaler *n* **omusubuuzi omunene** *n1*

¹**whom?** *interr* **ani? (N13)**

²**whom** *rel pro.* See who *(object relative)*

whooping cough *n* **ekifuba ekiraakiira** *n7*

whore *n* **malaaya** *n1*

whose? *interr* **-a ani? (N13)**, *eg. Ennyumba eno y'ani? ('Whose house is this?')*

¹**why** *conj* **lwaki**, *eg. Simanyi lwaki azze. ('I don't know why she has come.')*. <u>that's why</u> **kye...-va** **(N10.2)**, *eg. Nnabadde sirina mmere kyenvudde ŋŋenda mu katale. ('I had no food, that's why I*

went to the market.')

²**why?** *interr* **lwaki? (N13)**, *eg. Lwaki ajja? ('Why is she coming?')*. *See* reason

whydah, pin-tailed *(bird) n* **kkunguvvu** *n1*

wick *(for lamp) n* **olutambi lw'ettaala** *n11*

wicked *adj* **-bi**

wickedness *n* **obubi** *n14*

wide *adj* **-gazi**. *See* spread out <u>be(come) wide</u> **-gaziwa**

widen *vt* **-gaziya**. *See* stretch apart

widespread, become *(reach everywhere) vi* **-buna**, *eg. Obwavu bubunye wonna. ('Poverty has become widespread.')*. *See* commonplace

widow *n* **nnamwandu** *n1*

widowhood *n* **obwannamwandu** *n14*

width *n* **obugazi** *n14*

wife *n* **mukyala** *n1 (with pos* **N12***)*, *eg. mukyala wa Musoke ('Musoke's wife')*, **muka** *n1 (followed by name of husband)*, *eg. muka Musoke ('Musoke's wife')*, *(of a prince)* **omuzaana** *n1. Formerly, the wives of the Kabaka and major chiefs were called:* *(principal)* **Kaddulubaale** *n1*, *(second)* **Kabejja** *n1*, *(third)* **Nnassaza** *n1*. <u>fellow wife</u> **muggya** *(with pos* **N12***)*, *eg. muggya wange ('my fellow wife')* <u>official wife</u> *(married in church)* **omukyala w'empeta**

wig *n* **ekiviiri ekigule** *n7*, **wiigi** *n9*

wiggle, walk with a *vi* **-tambula -bigula**

wild *adj* **-a omu nsiko**, *eg. ebimera by'omu nsiko ('wild plants')*, *(in behaviour)* **-taamaavu**. *See* unrestrained <u>be(come) wild</u> *(in behaviour, eg. of a deranged person or enraged animal)* **-taaluuka** <u>drive wild</u> *(in behaviour)* **-taaluula**, *eg. Yataaludde enjuki ne ziruma abantu. ('He drove the bees wild and they started to sting people.')*, *(and angry; deranged)* **-taamuula** <u>run wild</u> (1) *(of overgrown land)* **-zika**, *eg. Ettaka lizise. ('The land has run wild.')*; (2) *(of a person in behaviour)* **-laluka**, *eg. Abaana be balaluse. ('Their children have run wild.')*

wilderness *(also* <u>wild</u>*) n* **eddungu** *n5* <u>wild area</u> *(uncultivated land; bush)* **ensiko** *n9*

wildness *(in behaviour) n* **obutaamaavu**

¹**will** *(also* <u>shall</u>*) aux v. Indicates future tense* **(N16, N19)**, *eg. (1) Nnamulaba. ('I shall see him.')*; (2) *Nja kumulaba. ('I will see him.')*

²**will** *n* (1) *(last testament)* **ekiraamo** *n7*, *(of the Kabaka)* **eddaame** *n5*; (2) *(determination)* **obumalirivu** *n14* <u>will to</u> *(bequeath to)* **-laamira** <u>make a will</u> **-laama**, *eg. Omugenzi Musoke teyalaama. ('The late Musoke did not make a will.')*

willingly *adv* (1) *Use* **-yagala** *('want') as aux v* **(N19)**, *eg. (1) Yagenda ayagala. ('He went willingly.')*; (2) *Use* **-eesiimira** *('do through one's own choosing')*, *eg. Yeesiimidde. ('He went willingly.')*

wilt *vi* **-wotoka**, *eg. Kasooli awotose. ('The maize has wilted.')* <u>begin to wilt</u> **-wotookerera**

wilted

wilted *adj* -wotofu

win *v* (won) (1) (*in sports*) *vi* -**goba**, *eg. Ttiimu yaffe y'eyagobye. ('Our team has won.');* (2) (*be best*) *vi* -**singa**, *eg. Yasinze empaka. ('He won the competition.');* (3) (*victorious*) *vt* -**wangula**, *eg. Bawangudde olutalo. ('They won the war')* <u>win a court case</u> -**singa omusango** <u>win at omweso</u> -**malamu omweso** <u>win over</u> (*in religion*) -**kyusa**, *eg. Yabakyusizza ne bafuuka Abakatoliiki. ('He won them over for Catholicism.')*

wince *vi* -**eesisiwala**

¹wind *n* (1) (*in the air*) **empewo** *n9*, (*strong*) **kibuyaga** *n1*, (*gust; squall*) **kikuŋŋunta** *n1*, (*on-shore wind from Lake Victoria*) **enkoma** *n9*; (2) (*colic, of babies*) **obwandu** *n14*, **obwoka** *n14* <u>pass wind</u> (*fart*) -**kuba ddoti** <u>smelly wind</u> (*brought up through the mouth*) **empiiyi** *n9*

²wind (*coil*) *vt* -**zinga** <u>wind up</u> -**nyoola**, *eg. Essaawa nginyodde. ('I have wound up the clock.')* <u>wind around</u> -**zingirira** <u>wind up a conversation</u> -**wumbawumba emboozi** <u>wind up a speech</u> -**wumbawumba** (*or* -**wunzika**) **okwogera** <u>be long-winded</u> (*in speech; ramble*) -**landagga**

window *n* **eddirisa** *n5* <u>window frame</u> **omwango gw'eddirisa** *n3*

windpipe *n* **omumiro** *n3*

windscreen *n* **endabirwamu y'emmotoka** *n3*

wine *n* **envinnyo** *n9*, (*made from empirivuma fruits*) **obugeme** *n14*

wing *n* **ekiwaawaatiro** *n7*, (*of a termite*) **ekyoya** *n7*

wink at *vi* -**temyako**, *eg. Yamutemyako. ('He winked at her.')*

winner *n* **omuwanguzi** *n1*

winnow *vt* -**wewa**

winnowing tray *n* **olugali** *n11* <u>something used for winnowing</u> **ekiwewa** *n7*

wipe *vt* -**siimuula** <u>wipe off</u> (*erase*) -**sangula** <u>wipe oneself</u> -**eesangula** <u>wipe out</u> (*destroy*) -**zikiriza**, -**saanyawo** <u>wipe with</u> -**siimuuza**, *eg. Asiimuuza kawero ku lubaawo. ('She is wiping the board with a duster.')* <u>be wiped off</u> (*erased*) -**sanguka** <u>be wiped out</u> (*destroyed*) -**zikirira**

wire *n* **oluuma** *n11*, **waaya** *n9* <u>barbed wire</u> **sseŋŋenge** *n1*

wireless *n* **leediyo** *n9*

wisdom *n* **amagezi** *n6*

wise *adj* -**gezi** <u>wise person</u> **omugezi** *n1* <u>grow wise</u> -**geziwala**

wish (*would like to have*) *vi.* Use -**yagala** (*'like'*) *with prefix* -**andi**- (**N18**), *eg. Nnandiyagadde emmotoka. ('I wish I had a car.').* See hope <u>wish on someone's behalf</u> -**yagaliza**, *eg, Musoke mmwagaliza okufuna emmotoka. ('I wish Musoke gets a car.').* See suitable for (consider) <u>cause (someone) to wish to have</u> -**saaliza**

witch *n* **omulogo** *n1*

witchcraft *n* **obulogo** *n14.* See night-dancing <u>practice witchcraft</u> -**loga**

with *pre* **ne** (**N5**), *eg. Nnagenda ne Musoke e Masaka. ('I went with Musoke to Masaka.'). The word stem* **na**- *is used with pronouns* (**N10.1**), *eg. nabyo ('with them', eg. referring to 'ekitabo' 'books'). Causative verbs can incorporate 'with' into their inherent meanings* (**N23**), *eg. Ennyumba yagizimbya matofaali. ('He built the house with bricks.')* <u>with me</u> **nange**, <u>with you</u> **nnaawe**, <u>with her/him</u> **naye**, *etc.* (**N10.1**)

withdraw (*take away*) *vt* -**ggyayo**, *eg. Yaggyayo ssente mu bbanka. ('He withdrew money from the bank.')* <u>withdraw from</u> -**vaamu**, *eg. Yavaamu mu mpaka. ('She withdrew from the competition.')*

wither (*of a plant*) *vi* -**wotoka** <u>begin to wither</u> -**wotookerera**

withered *adj* -**wotofu**

withhold (from) *vt* -**mma**, *eg. Nnasaba Musoke ekitabo naye yakinnyima. ('I asked Musoke for the book but he withheld it from me.')* <u>withhold information (from)</u> -**zibira**, *eg. Yazibira ekituufu. ('He withheld the truth.'),* -**kisa**

¹within *adv* **munda**

²within *pre* **munda mu**

without *pre* (1) Use subject relative clause in neg (**N7.2**), *eg. Awatali ssente obulamu buba buzibu. ('Without money life is difficult.'),* (*on something*) **okutali**, *eg. Tulya mugaati okutali bbata. ('We eat bread without butter.'),* (*in something*) **omutali**, *eg. Njagala caayi omutali sukaali. ('I want tea without sugar.');* (2) **nga** with verb in neg (**N21**), *eg. Toyinza kuvuga nga tolina mafuta. ('You cannot drive without petrol.')* <u>without delay</u> **obutalwawo**

witness *n* **omujulirwa** *n1*, (*in court*) **omujulizi** *n1* <u>be a witness for</u> -**julira**, *eg. Nnamujulira. ('I was a witness for him.')*

wits (*intelligence*) *n* **amagezi** *n6* <u>be at one's wits' end</u> (*not knowing what to do*) -**butaabutana**. See baffled (be)

wizard *n* **omulogo** *n1*

wobbly *adj* **yegeyege** (*invariable adjective*) <u>be wobbly</u> (*not firmly fixed*) -**nyeenya**, *eg. Emmeeza enyeenya. ('The table is wobbly.')*

woke See wake

wolf *n* **omusege** *n3*

woman *n* **omukazi** *n1*, (*living alone, without a husband*) **nnakyeyombekedde** *n1*, (*very pretty*) **nnalulungi** *n1*, (*tall and thin*) **nnalugooti** *n1*, (*who has given birth once*) **ow'oluzaala olumu** *n1*, (*who has given birth twice*) **ow'enzaala ebbiri** *n1*. See person <u>become a woman</u> -**kaziwala**

womb *n* **nnabaana** *n1*, **enda** *n9*

won See win

¹wonder *n* **ekyewuunyisa** *n7* <u>wonders</u> **amagero** *n6*

²wonder (at) *vit* -**eewuunya**, *eg. Nnali nneewuunya lwaki tojja kundaba. ('I was wondering why you do not come to see me.')*

wonderful *adj* -**a amagero**, *eg. Embaga yabadde y'amagero. ('The party was wonderful.'),* -**a**

makula (*invariable adjective*), *eg. Embaga yabadde makula.* (*'The party was wonderful.'*)

woo *vt* **-yogereza**

[1]**wood** *n* (1) (*the material*) **omuti** *n3*; (2) (*piece of*) **ekiti** *n7* (*small* **akati** *n12*); (3) (*piece of wood deliberately removed from another, eg. for carpentry*) **ekibajjo** *n7*; (4) (*partially burnt*) **ekisiki** *n7*; (5) (*shaped, eg. plank*) **olubaawo** *n11*. *See* firewood; forest; plank; timber do woodwork **-bajja**, *eg. Abajja entebe.* (*'He is making a chair.' – from wood*) something made of wood **ekibajje** *n7* unseasoned wood **omuti omubisi**

wooden *adj* **-a omuti**, *eg. entebe y'omuti* (*'wooden chair'*)

woodpecker *n* **enkonkonamuti** *n9*

wool *n* **wuulu** *n9*

word *n* **ekigambo** *n7*

[1]**work** *n* (1) (*task; job*) **omulimu** *n3*; (2) (*work in general*) **emirimu** *n4*; (3) (*casual work*) **omulimu gwa lejjalejja**; (4) (*something to do*) **ekyokukola** *n7*; (5) (*chore; assignment*) **ekkatala** *n5* agree on a work arrangement **-patana** communal work **bulungibwansi** *n14* hard-working **-nyiikivu** hard-working person **omunyiikivu** *n1* in a work session **mu kafubo**, *eg. Bali mu kafubo ka kulongoosa nnyumba.* (*'They are in a work session cleaning the house.'*) initial work (*on a task*) **amabaga** *n6* leave off work *See* stop work my workmate **mukozi munnange**, your workmate **mukozi munno**, *etc.* (**N12**) not do one's share of the work **-kongola** unpaid work **omulimu gw'obwereere** voluntary work **omulimu gwa nnakyewa**

[2]**work** *vi* **-kola**, (*hard*) **-fuba**, (*for money*) **-pakasa**, (*be functional, of machinery*) **-lamuka**, *eg. Emmotoka eramuse kaakati.* (*'The car is now working.'*). *See* persevere; struggle; toil away work abroad (*usually implying illegality*) **-kuba ekyeyo** work at **-kolera**, *eg. Akolera Mengo.* (*'She works at Mengo.'*) work for (1) (*a person*) **-kolera**, *eg. Nkolera Mwami Musoke.* (*'I am working for Mr Musoke.'*); (2) (*a purpose*) **-kolerera**, *eg. Nkolerera ssente.* (*'I am working for money.'*) work for oneself **-eekozesa**, *eg. Kati yeekozesa.* (*'He now works for himself.'*) work in turns **-kola mu mpalo** work metal **-weesa** work oneself up (*emotionally*) **-eetabula** work out (*how to do something*) **-sala amagezi** work together **-kolagana** work too much **-kola okukamala** work wood **-bajja** be hard-working **-nyiikira** become worked up (*emotionally*) **-tabuka**, *eg. Abantu batabuse olw'emisolo.* (*'The people are worked up because of the taxes.'*), **-eecanga**

worker *n* **omukozi** *n1*, (*skilled*) **omufundi** *n1* (*or* **ffundi** *n1*) , (*hired*) **omupakasi** *n1*, (*casual*) **omupakasi wa lejjalejja**

working (*of machinery*) *adj* **-lamu** working day **olunaku olw'okukola** *n11* be hard-working (*of a*

person) **-nyiikira** hard-working *adj* **-nyiikivu** way of working **enkola** *n9*

workplace *n* **aw'okukolera** *n16*, **w'okolera** *n16*

workshop *n* **ekkolero** *n5*, (*for woodwork*) **ebbajjiro** *n5*, (*for metalwork*) **essasa** *n5*

world *n* **ensi** *n9*

worm (*earthworm*) *n* **olusiriŋŋanyi** *n11* intestinal worms **ebiwuka by'omu lubuto** *n8*, **enjoka** *n10* roundworm (*Ascaris*) **enfaana** *n9* tapeworm **enjoka zi nnamumwa**

worm-eaten, be(come) *vi* **-wumba**, *eg. Entebe ewumbye.* (*'The chair is worm-eaten.'*)

worn worn-out clothing (*rags*) **enziina** *n10*, **obuziina** *n14* worn thin (*of cloth or garment*) *adj* **-yabirivu** be worn thin (*of cloth or garment*) **-yabirira** become worn down (*of something that has dwindled, eg. tablet of soap*) **-ggweerera**. *See* crumble; disintegrate look worn out (*of a person*) **-kanduka**

worn-out *adj* **-kooye**. *See* old

worried *adj* **-eeraliikirivu**

[1]**worry** *n* (1) (*in general*) **obweraliikivu** *n14*; (2) (*a specific worry*) **ekyeraliikiriza** *n7*

[2]**worry** *vt* **-eeraliikiriza**, *eg. Omulimu gumweraliikiriza.* (*'The job worries him.'*). *See* harass; trouble be worried (about) **-eeraliikirira**, *eg. Yeeraliikirira omulimu gwe.* (*'He is worried about his job.'*), (*feeling someone's pain*) **-lumirirwa**, *eg. Omukyala alumirirwa abaana be abatalina mmere.* (*'The woman is worried that her children have no food.'*) Don't worry. **Tofaayo.** (*pl.* **Temufaayo.**)

orse be worse than **-singa obubi**, *eg. Kino kisinga kiri obubi.* (*'This is worse than that.'*) become worse **-eeyongera obubi**, *eg. Obudde bweyongedde okuba obubi.* (*'The weather has got worse.'*), (*of a sore*) **-sajjuka**, *eg. Ebbwa lisajjuse.* (*'The sore has got worse.'*)

[1]**worship** *n* **ensinza** *n9* place of worship **essinzizo** *n5*

[2]**worship** *vt* **-sinza**. *See* venerate

worst, be *vi*. *Use* **-singa** (*'be more than'*) *with neg* (**N21**), *eg. Omwana ono y'asinga obutamanya kusoma.* (*'This is the worst child at reading.'*)

worth, be *vi* (1) (*useful*) **-gasa**, *eg. Kigasa okumukozesa.* (*'He is worth employing.'*); (2) (*financially*) **-gula**, *eg. Ennyumba eno egula ssente mmeka?* (*'What is this house worth?'*) something worth seeing **ekintu ekisaana okulabako** *n7* treat (*someone*) as of no worth **-dibaga**

would *aux v. Use verb prefix* **-andi-** (**N18**), *eg. Nnandiyagadde okumanya ekituufu.* (*'I would like to know the truth.'*) would have *Use verb prefix* **-andi-** *with* **singa** (*'if'*) (**N18**), *eg. Singa nnamanya nnandibadde ŋŋenze okumulaba.* (*'If I had known I would have gone to see him.'*)

wound *n* **ekiwundu** *n7*, (*open*) **ebbwa** *n5*, (*made by blade*) **olubale** *n11*. *See* injury

wove (*also* woven) *v. See* weave

woven *adj* **-luke** something woven **ekiruke** *n7*

¹wrangle *n* **akanyonyoogano** *n12*

²wrangle *vi* **-nyonyoogana**, (*with shouting, not listening to one another*) **-yasiikana**. *See* bicker

wrap (up) *vt* **-sabika**, *eg. Nsabise ekitereke.* (*'I have wrapped the parcel.'*), (*involving wrapping around*) **-zinga**, *eg. Bazinze omulambo mu lubugo.* (*'They have wrapped the corpse in barkcloth.'*) wrap around **-zingirira**, *eg. Omukono gwe yaguzingirira ne bbandeegi.* (*'He wrapped the bandage around his arm.'*). *See* cover completely wrap for (*someone*) **-sabikira** wrap oneself (up) **-eesabika**, *eg. Yeesabise mu bulangiti.* (*'He wrapped himself up in a blanket.'*), **-eezingirira** wrap up a food parcel (*for cooking*) **-siba emmere** wrap up one's arguments **-wunzika ensonga** be wrapped **-sabikibwa**, *eg. Ekitereke kisabikiddwa.* (*'The parcel is wrapped up.'*), (*wound round*) **-zingibwa**, *eg. Omulambo guzingiddwa.* (*'The corpse is being wrapped up.'*)

wraparound (*garment*) *n* **omunagiro** *n3*

wrapping paper *n* **olupapula olusabika** *n11*

wrath *n* **obusungu** *n14*

wreck *vt* **-faafaaganya**, *eg. Afaafaaganyizza emmotoka.* (*'He has wrecked the car.'*), **-ttattanya** be wrecked **-faafaagana**, *eg. Emmotoka efaafaaganye.* (*'The car is wrecked.'*), **-ttattana**

wrestle *vi* **-meggana**, *eg. Bameggana.* (*'They are wrestling.'*), **-kwata ekigwo** wrestle with one another **-eeriga**

wrestler *n* **omumegganyi** *n1*

wrestling *n* **ekigwo** *n7*

wriggle *vi* **-eetigoonyola**

wring (out) (*eg. wet clothes*) *vt* **-kamula**

wrinkle (*on skin*) *n* **olukanyanya** *n11*. *See* frown line

wrist *n* **ekiseke** *n7*

wristwatch *n* **essaawa y'oku mukono** *n9*

write *vt* (*wrote*) **-wandiika** write to/for **-wandiikira**, *eg. Mpandiikira poliisi.* (*'I am writing to the police.'*) write with **-wandiisa**, *eg. Yawandiisa kkalaamu.* (*'She wrote with a pencil.'*)

writer *n* **omuwandiisi** *n1*

writhe *vi* **-eetigoonyola**

writing *n* **empandiika** *n9* handwriting **omukono** *n3* in writing **mu buwandiike** something written **ekiwandiiko** *n7*, **ekiwandiike** *n7*

¹wrong *adj* **-sobu**, *eg. Yakonkona ku luggi olusobu.* (*'He knocked on the wrong door.'*); (2) (*incorrect*) Use **si ntuufu** (*'not right'*), *eg. Endagiriro ye si ntuufu.* (*'His instructions are wrong.'*)

²wrong *n* **ekisobu** *n7*, wrong-doing) **ekisobyo** *n7* be/go wrong (1) (*err*) **-soba**, *eg. Ebintu bisobye.* (*'Things have gone wrong.'*); (2) (*spoiled*) **-yonooneka**, *eg. Okusoma kw'omwana we kwayonooneka bwe yagenda mu ssomero eryo.* (*'Her son's studies went wrong when he went to that school.'*). *See* badly (go); bungled (be) do wrong **-sobyako**, *eg. Yamusobyako.* (*'He has wronged her.'*). *See* sin go wrong for **-sobako**, *eg. Ebintu binsobyeko.* (*'Things have gone wrong for me.'*) something gone wrong **ekisobye** *n7*

wrong-doer *n* **omusobya** *n1*. *See* sinner

wrong-doing *n* (1) (*sin*) **ekibi** *n7*; (2) (*deeds done deliberately to annoy or harm*) **ebyambyone** *n8*. *See* mistake report a wrong-doing **-loopa**, **-waaba** reporter of a wrong-doing **omuloopi** *n1*, **omuwaabi** *n1*

wrongly *adv* **mu nsobi**

wrote *See* write

X,x

xylophone *n* (1) (*with 12 keys*) **amadinda** *n6*, **entaala** *n9*; (2) (*with 22 keys*) **akadinda** *n12* key of a xylophone **eddinda** *n5*

Y,y

yam (*Dioscorea*) *n. Types include:* (*fist-sized, bristly*) **endaggu** *n9*, (*long, yellow-fleshed*) **balugu** *n1*, (*white*) **kyetutumula** *n1*, (*with large soft pink tuber*) **ekisebe** *n7*, (*with dark-coloured flesh*) **kaama** *n1*, (*with hard flesh, keeps for long after cooking*) **ekikongo** *n7*, (*bud yam*) **ekkobe** *n5*, (*another type*) **nnandigoya** *n1*. *See* cassava; cocoyam; Livingstone potato; tannia

yard *n* (1) (*measure of length*) **yaadi** *n9*; (2) (*courtyard*) **oluggya** *n11*. *See* courtyard

yarn (*thread*) *n* **ewuzi** *n9*. *See* story

¹yawn *n* **ekyayuuyo** *n7*

²yawn *vi* **-yayuuya**

year *n* **omwaka** *n3*, (*year level in school*) **omugigi** *n3*, *eg. omugigi ogw'okuna* (*'year 4'*) last year **omwaka oguyise** next year **omwaka ogujja**

yearly *adv* **buli mwaka**

yearn *vi* **-yaayaana**, *eg. Ayaayaana okufumbirwa.* (*'She is yearning to get married.'*) yearn for **-yaayaanira**, *eg. Ayaayaanira omulimu omulungi.* (*She is yearning for a good job.'*), **-yoya**

yearning *n* **ekyoyo** *n7*, **ekyoyooyo** *n7*, (*especially for food*) **amaddu** *n6*. *See* greed

yeast *n* **ekizimbulukusa** *n7*

yell *vi* **-leekaana**

yellow *adj* **-a ekyenvu**, *eg. omupiira gwa kyenvu* (*'yellow ball'*)

yes *interj* **yee**, (*reply to being called*) **wangi**

yesterday *adv* **jjo** yesterday afternoon **jjo olweggulo, eggulo lya jjo** yesterday morning **jjo ku makya** day before yesterday **okwosa jjo**

yet not yet Use verb infix **-nna** (**N18**) *with neg* (**N21**), *eg. Tannajja.* (*'He has not yet come.'*)

yield *vi* (1) (*of a crop*) **-bala**, *eg. Ebinjanjaalo bibaze nnyo. ('The beans have yielded well.');* (2) (*of bananas*) **-ssa**, *eg. Amatooke gassizza nnyo. ('The bananas have yielded well.');* (3) (*surrender*) **-eewaayo**, *eg. Abalabe beewaddeyo eri amagye gaffe. ('The enemy yielded to our army.')*

yoghurt *n* **yogati** *n1*, **bbongo** *n1*

yoke *n* **ekikoligo** *n7*. *See* burden

yolk *n* **enjuba y'eggi** *n9*

you *pro* SINGULAR **ggwe**. *The verb prefixes are:* (*subject*) **o-**, (*object*) **ku-** (**N15**). PLURAL **mmwe**. *The verb prefixes are:* (*subject*) **mu-**, (*object*) **ba-** (**N15**).

young *adj* **-to** young person **omuto** *n1*

your *pos (determiner)* SINGULAR **-o** (**N.11.4**) *with pronominal concord* (**N4.2**), *eg.* (*1*) **embwa yo** (*'your dog'*); (*2*) **ekiso kyo** (*'your knife'*). *The forms for the various noun classes are listed in Column 5 of Table 9.* PLURAL **-ammwe** (**N11.4**) *with pronominal concord* (**N4.2**), *eg.* (*1*) **embwa yammwe** (*'your dog'*); (*2*) **ekiso kyammwe** (*'your knife'*). *The forms for the various noun classes are listed in Column 8 of Table 9.*

yours *pos (pronoun)* SINGULAR **owuwo, ababo,** *etc.* (**N11.4**), *eg. Ekitabo ekyo kikye, kino kikyo. ('That book is hers, this one is yours.'). The forms for the various noun classes are listed in Column 11 of Table 9.* PLURAL **owammwe, abammwe,** *etc.* (**N11.4**), *eg. Ebitabo ebyo byabwe, bino byammwe. ('Those books are theirs, these ones are yours.')*

yourself *pro. Reflexive verbs take the prefix* **-ee-** (**N18**). by yourself **wekka** by yourselves **mwekka** you yourself **ggwe wennyini** (*or* **ggwe kennyini**) you yourselves **mmwe mwennyini**

youth *n* (1) (*person*) **omuvubuka** *n1*; (2) (*stage in life*) **obuvubuka** *n14*. *See* childhood become a youth **-vubuka**

Z,z

zeal *n* **obujjumbizi** *n14*

zealot *n* **omujjumbizi** *n1*

zealous *adj* **-jjumbizi** be zealous about **-jjumbira**

zebra *n* **entulege** *n9*

zero *num* **zzeero** *n9*

PART 4

NOTES

References to notes (Part 4) are marked N1, N2, *etc*.

The main points are given in larger type

Relatively minor points are given in smaller type

Table 1. The twenty-one noun classes, grouped into ten genders and the four adverbial noun classes used for place, showing aspects of the concordial system. See **N4.2** for further explanation.

1	2	3	4	5	6	7	8	9	10	11	12	13
						Concords				Short words based on pronominal concord		
Gender	Noun class	Used for adv nc	Examples of nouns	English	IV	nom con	num con	pro con	Variants	Stem -a	Stem -e	Stem -o
NOUN CLASSES USED FOR ORDINARY NOUNS (some also used for adverbial noun classes of cause and reason, manner or time)												
mu/ba	1		omuntu	person	o-	mu-	o-	gu-		See Table 5		
	2		abantu	people	a-	ba-	ba-	ba-				
mu/mi	3		omuti	tree	o-	mu-	gu-	gu-	gw-	gwa	gwe	gwo
	4		emiti	trees	e-	mi-	e-	gi-	gy-	gya	gye	gyo
li/ma	5		erinnya	name	e-	li-	li-	li-	ly-,ri-,ry-	lya	lye	lyo
	6	m	amannya	names	a-	ma-	a-	ga-		ga	ge	go
ki/bi	7	cm	ekintu	thing	e-	ki-	ki-	ki-	ky-	kya	kye	kyo
	8		ebintu	things	e-	bi-	bi-	bi-	by-	bya	bye	byo
n/n	9		ente	cow	e-	n-	e-	e-,gi-	y-,gy-	ya	ye,gye	yo
	10		ente	cows	e-	n-	-	zi-	zi	za	ze	zo
lu/n	11	cmt	olugalo	finger	o-	lu-	lu-	lu-	lw-	lwa	lwe	lwo
	10		engalo	fingers	e-	n-	-	zi-		za	ze	zo
ka/bu	12	mt	akatale	market	a-	ka-	ka-	ka-		ka	ke	ko
	14	cmt	obutale	markets	o-	bu-	bu-	bu-	bw-	bwa	bwe	bwo
ku/ma	15	c	okutu	ear	o-	ku-	ku-	ku-	kw-	kwa	kwe	kwo
	6	m	amatu	ears	a-	ma-	a-	ga-		ga	ge	go
gu/ga	20		oguyanja	ocean	o-	gu-	gu-	gu-	gw-	gwa	gwe	gwo
	22		agayanja	oceans	a-	ga-	ga-	ga-		ga	ge	go
tu/-	13		otulo	sleep	o-	tu-	tu-	tu-	tw-	twa	twe	two
ADVERBIAL NOUN CLASSES USED FOR PLACE (some also used for time)												
	16	pt	wansi	below	a-	wa-	wa-	wa-,-wo	w-	wa	we	wo
	23	p	eka	at home	e-			e-,yo	y-,-gy-	wa	ye,gye	yo
	17	pt	ku muti	on the tree	o-	ku-	ku-	ku-,-ku	kw-	kwa	kwe	kwo
	18	pt	mu kyalo	in the village	o-	mu-	mu-	mu-,-mu	mw-	mwa	mwe	mwo

Abbreviations:
COLUMN 3: *adv nc* = adverbial noun classes, c = cause and reason, m = manner, p = place, t = time.
COLUMN 6: *IV* = initial vowel (**N3**).
COLUMNS 7-9: *nom con* = nominal concord, *num con* = numeral concord, *pro con* = pronominal concord.

N1. THE ALPHABET, SPELLING RULES AND PRONUNCIATION

The Luganda alphabet is similar to the English, though lacking the letters **q** and **x** and with the extra letter **ŋ** (sometimes written **ng'** or **n̲**). **h** is rare. The Luganda vowels are **a**, **e**, **i**, **o** and **u**, with **w** and **y** being semi-vowels (having some of the properties of vowels). Some combinations of letters (known as compounds) are pronounced as single sounds, notably: (1) consonants followed by **w** or **y** (*eg.* **bw**, **by**); and (2) **m**, **n** or **ŋ** followed by another consonant (*eg.* **mb**, **ng**, **ŋŋ**).

m, n or ŋ followed by another consonant are known as **NASAL** compounds, *eg.* **mb**, **ng**, **ŋŋ**. A word or stem (N2) is said to be **NASALIZED** if a nasal compound follows immediately after the first vowel, *eg.* **-yimba** ('sing'), **ssenga** ('aunt'), **-gannalama** ('lie down anyhow'). There are also some other nasalized stems beginning **g** or **l**, *eg.* **-gaana** ('refuse'), **-lima** ('cultivate') (note that the second vowels are either **m** or **n**).

Letters are sometimes written double, *eg.* **aa**, **bb**. A double consonant indicates either that extra emphasis is given to the letter or that there is a slight delay on the consonant while it is being said. Thus, **dd** is pronounced as in 'ma<u>d d</u>og'. A double vowel is pronounced long. In speech, the initial vowel of one word can become incorporated in sound into the last vowel of the preceding word, which can cause confusion as to how the words should be spelt.

There are rules governing the use of double letters, most importantly: (1) a double vowel is never written at the beginning or end of a word, except in interjections such as **yee** ('yes'); (2) a double vowel is never written <u>before</u> a double consonant (the vowel is pronounced <u>short</u> in this case); (3) a double vowel is never written <u>before</u> a nasal compound (but the vowel is pronounced <u>long</u>); (4) a double vowel is rarely written <u>after</u> a compound ending in **w** or **y**, except sometimes in the case of **ny** (which, along with its emphasised form **nny**, is regarded by linguists as a single consonant). Rules regarding the doubling of the final vowels of verbs on addition of the adverbial suffixes **-wo**, **-yo**, **-ko** and **-mu** are given in **N24.2**.

Letters are pronounced much as in English, though noting these points:

a as in 'f<u>a</u>ther'.
c as in '<u>ch</u>urch' (not hard as in '<u>c</u>up').
e as in 'b<u>e</u>rry'.
g is hard as in 'good', except when followed by **i** or **y**, when it is softer and closer to **g** as in 'gene'.
gy and **j** are pronounced very similarly.
i as in 'm<u>ea</u>t'.
k is hard as in 'kid', except when followed by **i** or **y**, when it is softer and closer to **ch** as in 'church'.
l and **r** are pronounced in similar ways. The spelling convention is that **l** (rather than **r**) is used, except when the preceding letter is **e** or **i**. Thus, the word **eryato** ('boat') becomes **lyato** if the initial **e** is dropped.
ny as in 'fi<u>n</u>ger'.
ŋ as in 'si<u>ng</u>ing'.
o as in 'd<u>o</u>llar'.
u as in 't<u>o</u>'.
w and **y** are pronounced softly, with little emphasis.

N2. STEMS AND AFFIXES

Many words in Luganda are compound, being composed of stems with one or more attachments (affixes) added. Stems give the basic meanings of words, *eg.* **-kazi** ('woman'), **-laba** ('see'), **-a** ('of'), **-no** ('this'). Affixes fall either before or after the stem and are known as **PREFIXES** or **SUFFIXES** accordingly. More than one prefix or suffix may be present, those lying <u>within</u> words (rather than at their ends) being also known as **INFIXES**.

1	2	3	4	5	6	7	8	9	10	11	12	13	14	15	16
	pers	Subject prefixes and their English equivalents		Object prefixes and equivalent English pronouns		Relative pronouns		Ordinary free-standing pronouns	'I myself', 'you yourself', *etc.*	'I only', *etc.* stem -okka	'of' Stem -a	*pro of em* Stem -e	*dem of ref* Stem -o	*pro suf*	'and me', *etc.*
						subj	*obj*								
si. 1ˢᵗ		n-¹	I	n-¹	me	a-⁴	gwe	nze	nze kennyini	nzekka	(o)wa	ye, gwe⁶	oyo	-nge	nange
2ⁿᵈ		o-²	you	ku-³	you			ggwe	ggwe wennyini⁵	wekka				-o⁷	naawe
3ʳᵈ		a-²	he, she	mu-³	her, him			ye	ye yennyini⁵	yekka				-e⁷	naye
pl. 1ˢᵗ		tu²	we	tu-³	us	aba-⁴	be	ffe	ffe ffennyini	ffekka	(a)ba	be	abo	-ffe	naffe
2ⁿᵈ		mu²	you	ba-	you			mmwe	mmwe mwennyini	mwekka				-mmwe	nammwe
3ʳᵈ		ba-	they	ba-	them			bo	bo bennyini	bokka				-bwe	nabo

Table 2. Aspects of the concordial system for the personal cases (*mu/ba* gender). See **N4.3** for further explanation.

1. **n-** has many spelling variants, *eg.* **m-**, **nzi-** (**N5**). See Table 3.
2. These are replaced before a vowel by **w-** (for **o-**), **y-** (for **a-**), **tw-** (for **tu-**) and **mw-** (for **mu-**).
3. These are replaced before a vowel by **kw-** (for **ku-**), **mw-** (for **mu-**) and **tw-** (for **tu-**).
4. These are replaced before a vowel by **y** and with reflexive verbs (**N18**) by **e-** (for **a-**) and **abe-** (for **aba-**).
5. **kennyini** can be used instead of **wennyini** or **yennyini** (**N11.6**).
6. **ye** is used to emphasise the subject of a verb and **gwe** the object.
7. The possessive pronouns are irregular. They are **owuwo** ('yours'), **owuwe** ('hers', 'his') (**N11.4**).

Abbreviations:
COLUMN 1: *si.* = singular, *pl.* = plural.
COLUMN 2: *pers* = person.
COLUMN 7: *subj* = subject.
COLUMN 8: *obj* = object.
COLUMN 13 *pro of em* = pronoun of emphasis.
COLUMN 14 *dem of ref* = demonstrative of reference.
COLUMN 15 *pro suf* = pronominal suffix.

As a demonstration of a stem with affixes, the word **akyabiggyako** ('He is still taking them off.', *eg.* things from a table) can be broken down into **a-** + **-kya-** + **bi-** + **-ggya** + **-ko**, consisting of a subject pronoun prefix **a-** ('he'), tense prefix **-kya-** ('still'), object pronoun prefix **bi-** ('them'), verb stem **-ggya** ('take away') and adverbial suffix **-ko** ('off'). **-kya-** and **bi-** are infixes, as well as prefixes.

The same stem (or variants on it) is commonly found in several parts of speech, *eg.* **essanyu** (noun 'happiness'), **-sanyufu** (adjective 'happy'), **-sanyusa** (verb 'make happy'). There are some general rules governing how words are transformed between parts of speech, among them:

- Nouns are often derived from verbs by substituting **i** for the final **a** (or **e** in the case of the modified stem form **N14**), *eg.* (1) **omulimi** ('farmer'), from **-lima** ('cultivate'); (2) **omuguzi** ('buyer'), from **-guze** (modified stem form of **-gula** 'buy').

- Many adjectives are derived from verbs by substituting **u** or **e** for the final **a**, or else are based on the modified stem form. For instance: (1) **amenvu amavundu** ('rotten bananas'), where the adjective **-vundu** ('rotten') is derived from the verb **-vunda** ('be rotten'); (2) **amata amafumbe** ('boiled milk'), where the adjective **-fumbe** ('boiled') is derived from the verb **-fumba** ('cook'); (3) **omulenzi omulwadde** ('sick boy'), where the adjective **-lwadde** ('sick') is the modified stem form of the verb **-lwala** ('be ill').

- The addition of the suffixes **-wala** or **-wa** to adjectives or nouns can give verbs expressing 'become', *eg.* (1) **-yavuwala** ('become poor'), from **-yavu** ('poor'); (2) **-kaddiwa** ('become old'), from **-kadde** ('old').

- The addition of the suffix **-iro** to verbs can give nouns showing the places where activities are performed, *eg.* (1) **ennimiro** ('garden'), from **-lima** ('cultivate'); (2) **effumbiro** ('kitchen'), from **-fumba** ('cook'). Note that, in the case of **ennimiro**, the **l** of **-lima** is changed to **n** through sound and spelling change (**N5**).

NOTE ON INFLECTION IN LUGANDA AND ENGLISH COMPARED. Inflection is a term used in linguistics to refer to the property of words whereby grammatical functions are indicated by changes <u>within</u> words, rather than (for instance) through the use of additional words or changes in their order. Luganda is a highly inflected language, with its many noun classes and concordial agreements (**N4**), the use of affixes on verbs to convey tense and sense (**N16, N18**), the addition of enclitics to give adverbial and prepositional meanings (**N22, N24**), and others. English does have some inflexions, but, in general, it is a much less inflected language than Luganda. Examples of inflection in English are found in the formation of derived verbs (*eg.* 'undo', from 'do' – as mentioned under 'verbs' in Part 1 of this book) and the common addition of the letter **s** to form the plurals of nouns. Modern European languages differ in their degrees of inflection, for instance German being a much more inflected language than English. This example is significant in terms of the evolution of English, because English is a Germanic language first spoken in England at about 500 AD, being introduced by Germanic invaders. Interestingly, the first type of English spoken in England (known as Old English) was a much more inflected language than English later became. The complicated word endings found in Old English had started to disappear by 800 AD and prepositions came in as separate words. [Information from Melvyn Bragg (2003) *The adventure of English*, Hodder and Stoughton, London]

N3. THE INITIAL VOWEL

The initial vowel (*IV*) is a vowel (**a, e** or **o**) beginning many nouns or words in concordance with them (see **N4** for an explanation of concordance). The *IV* is sometimes referred to as a pre-prefix, since it precedes the concord prefix (**N4**). Words commonly starting with *IVs* may sometimes lack them and, conversely, *IVs* may sometimes be present on words from which they are normally absent. The inclusion or omission of the *IV* can be a nuanced matter, adding subtlety to the language.

A general rule governing the use or non-use of the *IV* with nouns and numbers is that its presence indicates greater particularity or precision and its absence greater generalisation or indefinitiveness, as shown by these pairs of examples (relevant *IVs* underlined): (1) **Nfumbe** <u>e</u>**mmere?** ('Shall I cook the food?' – *ie.* right now); (2) **Nfumbe mmere?** ('Shall I cook food?' – or do something else?); (3) **abantu** <u>a</u>**babiri** ('the two people'); (4) **abantu babiri** ('two people').

Some further general rules governing the presence or absence of *IVs* are (relevant *IVs* underlined):

- NOUNS generally take an *IV*, *eg.* **Ndaba** <u>o</u>**muntu.** ('I see a person.'), but there are exceptions, including: (1) when the noun is the object of a negative verb, *eg.* **Siraba muntu.** ('I do not see a person.'); (2) often with nouns used for close personal relationships, *eg.* **mukyala wange** ('my wife') (**N12**); (3) after **ku** ('on'), **mu** ('in') or **buli** ('each'), *eg.* **buli muntu** ('each person'); (4) before **ki?** ('what?') (**N13**), *eg.* **Kintu ki?** ('What thing?'); (5) usually after a causative verb indicating 'with', *eg.* **Aliisa wuuma.** ('He is eating with a fork.') (**N22**).

- COMPOUND NOUNS (composed of the preposition **-a** 'of' and a following noun **N11.2**) generally either take *IVs* on both parts of the word, *eg.* <u>e</u>**ky**<u>e</u>**nnyanja** ('fish') or lack them on both, *eg.* **kyannyanja** ('fish'). In this example, the word **ekyennyanja** is derived from **ekintu** ('thing' – understood) + **eky'** (= **ekya** 'of') + **ennyanja** ('lake'). See **N11.2** for more information.

- **ADJECTIVES** generally follow the *IV* patterns of their nouns, *eg.* (1) **Ndaba omuntu omulungi.** ('I see a good person.'); (2) **Silaba muntu mulungi.** ('I do not see a good person.'). Adjectives retain an *IV* in phrases starting with **ku** ('on') or **mu** ('in'), *eg.* **mu nnyumba ennene** ('in the big house'). The adjective **-ngi** ('many', 'much') normally lacks an *IV*, *eg.* **ennyumba nnyingi** ('many houses').

- The **PREPOSITION -a** ('of') normally lacks an *IV*, *eg.* **ennyumba za Daudi** ('houses of David'). See **N11.1** for more information.

- **POSSESSIVE DETERMINERS** lack an *IV*, *eg.* **ennyumba zange** ('my houses') (**N11.4-11.5**).

- **POSSESSIVE PRONOUNS** normally take an *IV*, *eg.* **ezange** ('mine', *eg.* referring to houses) (**N11.4-11.5**).

- **ADVERBS** generally lack an *IV*, *eg.* **bulungi** ('well'), but this is a weakly defined rule.

- *IVs* are omitted from nouns, adjectives, the preposition **-a** ('of') and possessive pronouns in statements of condition when the verb **-li** ('be') is understood but omitted (**N20.1**), *eg.* (1) **Ono musawo.** ('This person is a doctor.') (note that there is no **o** on the noun **omusawo**); (2) **Ye muwanvu.** ('He is tall.') (**o** is lacking from the adjective **omuwanvu**); (3) **Ennyumba eno ye musawo.** ('This house is the doctor's.') (**e** is lacking from the preposition **eya** 'of' and the noun **musawo**); (4) **Ennyumba zino zange.** ('These houses are mine.') (**e** is lacking from the possessive pronoun **ezange**).

N4. CONCORDANCE

N4.1. THE POWER OF THE NOUN

The noun dominates the sentence, causing modifications to words referring to it. This influence is expressed through its effect on the affixes of other words, which are brought into **CONCORDANCE** (agreement) with it according to its noun class. The influence of the noun class of a dominant noun can be illustrated by comparing two similar sentences headed by nouns of different noun classes: (1) **Abawala abasatu abatono bali b'olaba balya emmere yaabwe.** ('Those three small girls whom you see are eating their food.'); (2) **Embwa ssatu entono ziri z'olaba zirya emmere yaazo.** ('Those three small dogs which you see are eating their food.'). The dominant noun in the first case is **abawala** ('girls') and in the second **embwa** ('dogs'), belonging to different noun classes.

Many parts of speech are subject to concordance. In the first example above, the noun **abawala** ('girls') has influenced **CONCORDS** on a number **abasatu** ('three'), an adjective **abatono** ('small'), a demonstrative **bali** ('those'), an object relative **b'** (abbreviated from **be** 'who'), a subject prefix on a verb **balya** ('they are eating') and a possessive **yaabwe** ('their'). In this case, concordance is achieved through the use of similar sounding forms throughout, always including the letter **b**, *ie.* **aba**, **ba**, **b'** and **bw**. These forms resonate with the prefix (**aba-**) of the dominant noun (**abawala**). In contrast, the second example shows the introduction of a quite different set of forms based on the letter **z**, *ie.* **zi**, **z'** and **z**. There is no obvious connection with the spelling or sound of the prefix (**em-**) of the dominant noun **embwa** ('dogs'). Only the prefix (**en-**) of the adjective (**entono** 'small') has a measure of phonetic resonance with **embwa**.

Nouns are assigned to twenty-one **NOUN CLASSES**, seventeen of which are used for 'ordinary' nouns (**N6**) and four for 'adverbial nouns' associated with 'place' (**N24**) (Table 1). Some of these 21 noun classes are further used for other types of adverbial nouns, associated with 'time' (**N25**), 'manner' (**N26**), and 'cause and reason' (**N27**) (see Column 3 of Table 1).

Ordinary nouns are similar to nouns in an English sense, *eg.* 'David', 'house', 'honesty'. Different noun classes are typically used for the singulars and plurals of ordinary nouns, generally in a predictable way. Thus, nouns in noun class one (*n1*) are typically the singulars of nouns having plurals in noun class 2 (*n2*), nouns in noun class 12 (*n12*) are typically the singulars of nouns having plurals in noun class 14 (*n14*), and so on. These pairs of typically linked singular and plural noun classes are referred to as **GENDERS**, ten of which are recognised. The numbering system used here for the noun classes (*n1, n2, etc.*) and the classificatory system used for the genders (*mu/ba, mu/mi, etc.*) follow *Luganda-English Dictionary* by Murphy.

N4.2. THE CONCORDIAL SYSTEM

Table 1 illustrates aspects of the concordial system. *mu/ba* (the personal gender) contains a series of concords absent from the other genders, associated with the personal cases ('I', 'you', *etc.*) (Table 2). Concords in the *mu/ba* gender tend to be irregular, especially in the singular cases.

COLUMNS 1 AND 2 of Table 1 show the 10 genders and 21 noun classes, the latter consisting of 17 noun classes used for ordinary nouns and 4 adverbial noun classes used for place. All genders except *tu/-* have two noun classes, these being typically used for singulars and plurals respectively. Note that there are 23 rows for noun classes on the table, though actually there are only 21 noun classes. This is because two of the noun classes are listed twice (*n6* and *n10*), each providing the plurals of two singular noun classes (*n5/n15* and *n9/n11* respectively).

COLUMN 3 shows the noun classes used for adverbial nouns of place (**N24**), time (**N25**), manner (**N26**), and cause and reason (**N27**).

COLUMNS 4 AND 5 list typical nouns of each noun class. Note that the adverbs **wansi** ('below') and **eka** ('at home') can sometimes act as nouns, as can two-word phrases such as **ku muti** ('on the tree') and **mu kyalo** ('in the village').

COLUMN 6 shows the initial vowels (*IV*) (**N3**) associated with the noun classes.

COLUMNS 7-10. CONCORDS. There are three types: (1) **NOMINAL CONCORDS**, used for nouns and adjectives (**N6, N7**); (2) **NUMERAL CONCORDS**, used for the cardinal numbers 1-5 and **-meka** ('how many?') (**N8**); and (3) **PRONOMINAL CONCORDS**, used for pronouns and associated words (see **N10** and various other notes).

COLUMN 8. The numerals 2-5 in noun class *n10* typically lack initial vowels, the first consonants of the stems being doubled, *eg.* **ente bbiri** ('two cows', stem = **-biri** 'two') (**N8.1**).

COLUMN 9. In the case of noun class *n9*, the prefix **e-** is used for <u>subject</u> pronouns and **gi-** for <u>object</u> pronouns. In the case of the adverbial noun classes of place, the prefixes **wa-, e-, ku-** and **mu-** are used for <u>subject</u> pronouns and the suffixes **-wo, -yo, -ko** and **-mu** for <u>object</u> pronouns (**N24.2**).

COLUMN 10. These are spelling variants of the concords caused by sound change (**N5**). The most common spelling changes are replacement of **u** by **w** and **i** by **y** before vowels, and **l** by **r** after **e** or **i**. Noun class *n5* is particularly liable to spelling change (see details in **N5**). Nouns with singulars in *n9* usually have plurals (in *n10*) spelt in the same way, *eg.* **ente** (*n9* 'cow'), **ente** (*n10* 'cows'). However, for some words in *n9* of foreign origin, the plural concord **zi** is used, generally as a separate word, *eg.* **loole** (*n9* 'lorry'), **zi loole** (*n10* 'lorries').

COLUMN 11. The stem **-a** is the **PARTICLE OF POSSESSION** (see under 'Prepositions' in Part 1 of the dictionary). These words mean 'of' (**N11**). There is sometimes an initial vowel.

COLUMN 12. The stem **-e** is the **PARTICLE OF EMPHASIS** (see under 'Pronouns' in Part 1 of the dictionary). These words are equivalent to various parts of speech in English, *eg.* pronouns of emphasis, object relative pronouns (*eg.* 'who', 'whom', 'which') and conjunctions (*eg.* 'where', 'when') (**N10**). There is no initial vowel.

COLUMN 13. The stem **-o** is the **PARTICLE OF REFERENCE** (see under 'Pronouns' in Part 1 of the dictionary). These words are used to direct attention to something close in sight or mind. Words in ordinary noun classes in this column are demonstratives ('that', 'those', *etc.*) **N9**) and ordinary free-standing pronouns ('it', 'them', *etc.*) (**N10**). An initial vowel is included with demonstratives, but not with free-standing pronouns. Words in the adverbial noun classes of place are adverbs, *eg,* **awo** ('there').

Next letter(s) after n [1]	Stem	Spelling change [2]	Examples		
EXAMPLES BASED ON ADDITION OF n- ('I') TO VERB STEMS (PRESENT TENSE)					
			Stem	1st person *si.*	English
b	*nas*	nb→mm	-bumba	mmumba	I potter
	non-nas	n→m	-bala	mbala	I count
bb		nb→nzi	-bba	nziba	I steal
dd		ndd→nzir	-dduka	nziruka	I run
ee		n→nn	-eetaaga	nneetaaga	I need
g	*nas*	ng→ŋŋ	-genda	ŋŋenda	I go
gg		ng→nzi	-ggala	nzigala	I shut
jj		nj→nzi	-jja	nzija	I come
kk		nk→nzi	-kka	nzika	I descend
l	*nas*	nl→nn	-linda	nninda	I wait
	non-nas	nl→nd	-leeta	ndeeta	I bring
m		n→m	-mala	mmala	I finish
mm		nm→nnyi	-mma	nnyima	I refuse to give
nn		nn→nnyi	-nnyika	nnyinyika	I soak
ŋ		nŋ→ŋŋ	-ŋoola	ŋŋoola	I sneer at
p		n→m	-pima	mpima	I measure
ss		ns→nzi	-ssa	nzisa	I set down
tt		nt→nzi	-tta	nzita	I kill
vv		nv→nzi	-vvuunula	nzivuunula	I translate
w		nw→mp	-wulira	mpulira	I hear
y	*nas*	n→nn [3]	-yambala	nnyambala	I dress
	non-nas	ny→nj [3]	-yagala	njagala	I like
zz		nz→nzi	-zza	nziza	I send back
OTHER EXAMPLES OF SPELLING CHANGE ON ADDITION OF n-					
a [4]		n→nn	-kola	nnakola	I worked
ggy [5]		ngg→mp	-ggya	empya [6]	new
mp [7]		n→nnyi	-mpi	ennyimpi [6]	short
ng [7]		n→nnyi	-ngi	nnyingi [6]	many

Table 3. Spelling change on the addition of the prefix n-. The upper rows show the effect of adding the subject prefix n- ('I') to verb stems starting in various ways. The bottom five rows provide other examples of spelling change caused by the addition of n-.

1. Letters are single (*eg.* b) unless given double (*eg.* bb).
2. The letter(s) shown before the arrow are the added n plus any following letters subject to spelling change. The letter(s) after the arrows are the replacements.
3. There are exceptions. The first person singular of -yita ('call', 'pass') is **mpita**. The first person singular of -yenkana ('be equal') is **nnenkana**. Derived verbs based on -yita and -yenkana follow the same pattern.
4. An a is found after an added n with the far past tense (as in this example) and some other tenses (**N16**; **N18**).
5. A similar type of spelling change is seen in the plural (**empya** *n10*) of the noun **oluggya** (*n11* 'courtyard').
6. Forms of adjectives for noun class *n10*.
7. A similar type of spelling change is seen in the plural (**ennyimbe** *n10*) of the noun **olumbe** (*n11* 'serious illness').

Abbreviations:
nas = nasalized (**N1**).
non-nas = non-nasalized (**N1**).

N4.3. PERSONAL CASES

Table 2 illustrates aspects of the concordial system for the personal cases, *ie.* noun classes *n1* and *n2* (the *mu/ba* gender).

COLUMNS 1 AND 2 show the rows used for the 1st, 2nd and 3rd persons singular and plural.

COLUMNS 3-6 show the subject and object prefixes of verbs (**N15**) and equivalent English pronouns.

COLUMNS 7 AND 8 are relative pronouns. The <u>subject</u> relative pronoun is a prefix on the verb (**N7.1**), while the <u>object</u> relative pronoun is free-standing (**N10.1**).

COLUMN 9 shows the ordinary free-standing pronouns (**N10.1**).

COLUMN 10. These words mean 'I myself', 'you yourself', *etc.* (**N11.6**).

COLUMN 11. These words (meaning 'I only', 'you only', *etc.*) are formed by prefixing the ordinary free-standing pronoun to the stem **-okka** (exception **wekka**). The same pattern is found with the stems **-onna** ('any', 'all'), **-ombi** and **-ombiriri** ('both'), and **-onsatule** ('all three') (**N7.3**). These stems can also be used with the impersonal noun classes, *eg.* **ekintu kyokka** (*n7* 'the thing only').

COLUMN 12. These words mean 'of' (**N11.1**).

COLUMN 13. These words are pronouns of emphasis (**N10.1**). With the singular cases, **ye** is used to emphasise the subject of a verb and **gwe** the object.

COLUMN 14. Demonstratives of reference (**N9.1**).

COLUMN 15. These pronominal suffixes are found with possessive determiners and possessive pronouns (**N11.4**), possessive nouns (**N12**), and words used for phrases such as 'and me', 'you also', *etc.* (**N10.1**).

COLUMN 16 shows the words for 'and me', 'you also', *etc.* (**N10.1**). Similar constructions can also be used with the impersonal noun classes, *eg.* **nakyo** (*n7* 'and it').

N5. SOUND AND SPELLING CHANGE

Sound change is common in spoken Luganda. The purpose is simple – it makes speaking easier. Sound change occurs partly <u>within</u> words, related to interactions between stems and their affixes or between adjoining affixes. Many of these sound changes are reflected in the spellings of the written words. Sound change also occurs <u>between</u> words, but this is largely ignored in how the words are spelt.

Sound change between words arises because people do not typically speak words as independent units, but rather tend to run them one into another without pause. Thus (an example from *A Luganda Grammar* by Ashton *et al.*), the sentence **Yita omuntu oyo.** ('Call that person.') is actually heard as **Yitoomuntwoyo.** Here the influence of neighbouring words on one another has resulted in the loss (in sound) of the last **a** of **yita**, the lengthening of the vowel **o** of **omuntu** and the appearance of a new sound (signified by **w**) caused by interaction between the **u** at the end of **omuntu** and the **o** at the beginning of **oyo**.

Some notable instances of spelling change:

r replaces l after **e** or **i**, *eg.* **ekintu ekirungi** ('good thing'). Compare this with **abantu abalungi** ('good people'). The stem is **-lungi** ('good'). Exceptions are made for the names of certain countries, people, and languages, *eg.* **Olunyarwanda** ('language of Rwanda').

w replaces o or u before a vowel, *eg.* the word for 'of' in noun class *n3* is **gwa**, composed of **gu-** (pronominal concord) + **-a** ('of').

w replaces uy with many stems beginning **ya, ye** or **yo**, *eg.* **okwagala** ('to love'), composed of **o-** (*IV*) + **ku-** (infinitive prefix 'to') + **-yagala** ('love'). However, many verbs beginning **ya, ye** or **yo** have two forms of the infinitive, contracted and uncontracted, *eg.* both **okuyogera** and **okwogera** ('to speak') can be used for the infinitive of **-yogera** ('speak').

y replaces a, e or **i** before a vowel, *eg:* (1) **yakola** ('he worked'), composed of **a-** ('he') + **-a-** (far past tense) + **-kola** ('work'); (2) **ente yalya** ('the cow ate'), where **yalya** is composed of **e-** (*n9* 'it') + **-a-** (far past tense) + **-lya** ('eat'); (3) **gya** (*n4* 'of'), composed of **gi-** (pronominal concord) + **-a** ('of').

When 2 or more different vowels become neighbours, then the first vowel(s) is lost or changed to the second, *eg.* **beesiga** ('they trust'), composed of **ba-** ('they') + **-eesiga** ('trust'). **Stems beginning with ya, ye or yo** are liable to similar contraction with loss of the **y**, *eg.* (1) **baagala** ('they like'), composed of **ba-** (*n2* 'they') + **-yagala** ('like') (the uncontracted form **bayagala** is also found); (2) **Ennaanansi zengedde.** ('The pineapples are ripe.'), where **zengedde** is composed of **zi-** (*n10* 'they') + **-yengedde** ('are ripe'); (3) **Engoye zino zooze!** ('Wash these clothes!'), where **zooze** is composed of **zi-** (*n10* 'them') + **-yoze** ('wash'). **mailo** ('mile') is an exception.

The singulars of nouns in n5 and concordant adjectives are frequently irregular. The regular noun prefix is **eri-**, seen, for example, in **erinnya** ('name'). More usually, the singular form is contracted from the plural by doubling the first (single) consonant of the stem, *eg.* (1) the singular of **amagi** ('eggs') is **eggi** ('egg'); (2) the singular of **amatabi** ('branches') is **ettabi** ('branch'). The following exceptions should be noted:

- Plural stems starting with **l** or **n** (non-nasalized) begin **dd** in the singular, *eg.* **amalwaliro amanene** ('the big hospitals') becomes **eddwaliro eddene** ('the big hospital') in the singular.

- Plural stems starting with a vowel or **y** begin **jj** in the singular, *eg.* **amayinja** ('stones') becomes **ejjinja** ('stone').

- Plural stems starting with **w** begin **ggw** in the singular, *eg.* **amawanika** ('stores') becomes **eggwanika** ('store').

THE n- PREFIX is particularly liable to modification, sometimes also involving one or more following letters (Table 3). The **n-** prefix is encountered with the personal subject pronoun 'I', the personal object pronoun 'me' and nominal concords in noun classes *n9* and *n10*, as well as other instances. Nasalized and non-nasalized stems (**N1**) differ in the ways that they are modified, as shown on Table 3.

MISCELLANEOUS NOTES ON SPELLINGS

1. A principal case when sound change <u>between</u> words is recognised in the written language is when apostrophes are substituted for vowels in certain short words ending in **a** or **e**, *eg.* **amaaso n'amatu** ('eyes and ears'). Here **n'** is short for **ne** ('and').
2. The way that some compound words are given (with or without apostrophes, or elided) varies between authors. This is particularly common with words beginning with **-a** ('of') (**N11.2**), *eg.* (1) (separate words with an apostrophe) **ow'ekyalo** ('villager', *lit.* '[person understood] of the village'); (2) (single word) **owoomuluka** ('parish chief'), *lit.* '[chief understood] of the parish').
3. It would be useful to codify the rules governing the use of **na** rather than **ne** ('and', 'with').
4. Combinations such as 'and/with us', 'and/with it', *etc.* are usually given as single words, *eg.* **naffe** ('and us'), **nakyo** ('and it'), but as separate words in some circumstances, *ie.* **na ffe, na kyo**.
5. **n'omu** and **n'emu** ('and one') can sometimes be seen as **noomu** and **neemu**, as in **abantu kkumi noomu** ('eleven people') and **ente kkumi neemu** ('eleven cows'), instead of **abantu kkumi n'omu** and **ente kkumi n'emu**.
6. Some ordinal numbers can sometimes be seen in elided form (**N7.1**), *eg.* **omuntu owookubiri**, instead of **omuntu ow'okubiri** ('second person').
7. 'of on/at' and 'of in' (**N24.1**) can sometimes be seen in elided form, *eg.* **ebisolo byoku lukalu** instead of **ebisolo by'oku lukalu** ('terrestrial animals', *lit.* 'animals of on dry land').
8. **eddwaliro** ('hospital') and **eddwaniro** ('battlefield') are spelt with only one **a**, despite this **a** being pronounced long. Contrast this with **eggwaatiro** ('peeling place'), in which the **a** is also pronounced long, but the accepted spelling has two **a**'s. One explanation given is the more forceful pronounciation of **d** compared with **g**.
9. Enclitic forms of **-gwa** ('fall') and **-gya** ('fit'), such as **-gwamu** and **-gyamu**, have only single **a**'s, even though the **a** is pronounced long.
10. The proclitics **we, gye, kwe** and **mwe** (**N24.2**) should be given as separate words according to the all-Buganda Conference of 1947, which established the standard orthography used for Luganda. However, Ashton et al. in *A Luganda Grammar*, as well as some other grammarians, hold that the enclitics should be prefixes to the following verbs that follow, *eg.* (1) (spelling according to the spelling rules) **Ekitabo we kiri? Yee, we kiri.**; (2) (what the spelling should be, according to some grammarians) **Ekitabo we kiri? Yee, weekiri.** (both meaning 'Is the book there? Yes, it is.')

N6. ORDINARY NOUNS

A noun in Luganda is a word that induces concordance (**N4**). There are two types of nouns. **ORDINARY NOUNS** are more or less equivalent to English nouns, while **ADVERBIAL NOUNS** have no parallel in English. Adverbial nouns and adverbial noun classes are dealt with in other notes. They refer to aspects of place (**N24**), time (**N25**), manner (**N26**), and cause and reason (**N27**).

Ordinary nouns consist of a stem, a prefix (nominal concord **N4**) and often an initial vowel (**N3**). Thus, the noun **omuntu** ('person') consists of the stem **-ntu**, the prefix **mu-** and the initial vowel **o-**.

Most words that qualify nouns are placed after (rather than before) them, *eg*. **engatto zange zino essatu ennene** ('these three big shoes of mine'). This phrase consists of a noun **engatto** ('shoes') and the following qualifying words: **zange** ('mine'), **zino** ('these'), **essatu** ('three') and **ennene** ('big'). Possessives (such as **zange** in this case) always come first in the sequence, immediately after the noun. Adjectives usually come last (**ennene** in this case). The word **buli** ('each', 'every') is exceptional in that it precedes rather than follows the noun, *eg*. **buli ngatto** ('each shoe'). There are no Luganda words equivalent to the articles 'a', 'an' or 'the', although the inclusion or exclusion of an initial vowel can indicate greater precision or indefinitiveness respectively (**N3**).

Ordinary nouns are assigned to 17 noun classes, further grouped into 10 genders (**N4**). The ways that noun classes (numbered *n1, n2, etc*.) are assigned to genders (*mu/ba, mu/mi, etc.*) are shown on Table 1. Most genders contain two noun classes, normally used for the singulars and plurals of nouns respectively. Each noun class is associated with particular concords (**N4**).

Certain types of item or concepts tend to be associated with particular genders and noun classes, though often fairly loosely. Many noun stems are found in more than one gender, conveying different aspects of a root idea, *eg*. **omuganda** (*n1* 'a member of the Baganda people'), **Buganda** (*n9* 'Buganda' – the country), **ekiganda** (*n7* 'something pertaining to Buganda'), **oluganda** (*n11* 'the Luganda language').

mu/ba GENDER (*n1* and *n2*). This gender is typically used for people, *eg*. **omusajja** ('man'). There is a group of nouns in this gender that lack initial vowels (*IVs*). They are sometimes placed in special noun sub-classes, for instance in sub-classes *n1a* (for singulars) and *n2a* (for plurals) in *Luganda-English Dictionary* by Murphy. Some of these words begin in the singular (*n1a*) with the normal prefix **mu-**, *eg*. **muganda** ('brother of'), while others begin in other ways, *eg*. **lumonde** ('potato'). Some have prefixes that carry special meanings, *eg*. the prefixes **ssaa-** (masculine) and **nnaa-** (usually feminine) convey the idea of high prestige, *eg*. (1) **Ssaabasajja** ('first among men', a title of the Kabaka); (2) **nnaalongo** ('mother of twins'). **ssema-** indicates enormous size, importance, *etc*., *eg*. **ssematalo** ('world war'), from **olutalo** ('war'). Personalised animals or scary mythological beings can carry the prefix **wa-**, *eg*. (1) **Wanjovu** ('Mr. Elephant'); (2) **Walumbe** ('god of death and disease'). Some nouns in the *n1a* noun sub-class lack plural forms (as does **lumonde**), while others take the prefix **ba** (lacking an *IV* and written as a separate word), *eg*. **ba kabaka** ('kings'), from **kabaka** ('king'). Some nouns with singulars in *n1a* have plurals in other noun classes (but with detached prefixes), *eg*. the plural of **nnamunswa** ('queen termite') is **bi nnamunswa** ('queen termites'), which is a noun in noun class *n8*.

Proper nouns, such as the names of towns (*eg*. **Kampala**), rivers (*eg*. **Mayanja**), counties (*eg*. **Buddu**) and hills (*eg*. **Makindye**) are placed in noun class *n1*. They can also be used preceded by worlds indicating the categories to which they belong, *eg*. **Ekibuga Masaka** *n7* ('Masaka Town'), **Omugga Mayanja** *n3* ('River Mayanja'), **Akasozi Makindye** *n12* ('Makindye Hill'). Counties are designed as follows: **Essaza ly'e Buddu** ('Buddu County').

mu/mi GENDER (*n3* and *n4*). Many trees are placed in this gender, *eg*. **omupeera** ('guava tree'). **omukwano**, a noun in this gender, means 'friendship' (singular) or 'friends' (plural), *eg*. **omukwano gwaffe** ('our friendship'), **emikwano gyaffe** ('our friends'). It can also be used in the singular, without an initial vowel and followed by a possessive, to mean 'friend', *eg*. **mukwano gwaffe** ('our friend') (**N12**). For this use only, **mukwano** is exceptional among Luganda nouns in simultaneously causing concordance in two different noun classes. The possessive (*ie*. **gwaffe** in the example above) is in *n3*, but all other parts of speech are in *n1*. This is illustrated in the following example from *The Essentials of Luganda* by Chesswas: **Mukwano gwange omu yekka gwe njagala wuuno azze.** ('Here is my only friend that I like, he has arrived.'). **omukwano** also occurs preceded by the possesive **-a** ('of' **N11.1**) to give a noun meaning 'friend', *ie*. **ow'omukwano** (in noun class *n1*).

-bbe stolen	**-kyamu** crooked	**-seerevu** slippery
-bisi raw	**-lala** other	**-sekule** pounded
-bongofu chipped	**-lalu** mad	**-siike** roasted
-botofu holed	**-lamba** entire	**-siru** foolish
-ddugavu black	**-lamu** live	**-songovu** pointed
-fu dead	**-lema** lame	**-suffu** excessive
-funda narrow	**-lokole** saved	**-taagufu** scratched
-gagga rich	**-londe** chosen	**-tabule** mixed
-ganzi favourite	**-longo** twin	**-ti** fearful
-genyi visiting	**-longoofu** in good order	**-to** young
-ggale shut	**-longoose** purified	**-tone** decorated
-ggule open	**-lunde** domesticated	**-tono** small
-gonvu soft	**-lungi** good	**-tumbiivu** swollen
-ggya new	**-luusi** female	**-tutumufu** famous
-goomu deformed	**-manyi** known	**-wombeefu** gentle
-gumu strong	**-manyifu** well known	**-wotofu** withered
-gwagwa depraved	**-megufu** broken off	**-wulize** obedient
-jama filthy	**-mpi** short	**-yabise** burst
-jeemu rebellious	**-myufu** red	**-yangu** fast
-jjumbizi zealous	**-nafu** weak	**-yawufu** different
-ka strong	**-naku** poor	**-yereere** empty
-kaatuufu sour	**-nene** big	**-yeru** white
-kadde old	**-ngi** many	**-yogi** sharp
-kakafu certain	**-nyiikivu** hard-working	**-yulifu** torn
-kalu dry	**-nyiivu** annoyed	**-zibu** difficult
-kalubo hard	**-pya** new	**-zira** brave
-kambwe fierce	**-sa** empty	**-zito** heavy
-kulu mature	**-saamavu** riotous	
-kyafu dirty		

Table 4. Common adjectives

Noun class	'first'	'second'	'third'	'fourth'
n1	asooka	ow'okubiri	ow'okusatu	ow'okuna
n3	ogusooka	ogw'okubiri	ogw'okusatu	ogw'okuna
n5	erisooka	ery'okubiri	ery'okusatu	ery'okuna
n7	ekisooka	eky'okubiri	eky'okusatu	eky'okuna
n9	esooka	ey'okubiri	ey'okusatu	ey'okuna
n11	olusooka	olw'okubiri	olw'okusatu	olw'okuna
n12	akasooka	ak'okubiri	ak'okusatu	ak'okuna
	'fifth'	'sixth'	'tenth'	'twentieth'
n1	ow'okutaano	ow'omukaaga	ow'ekkumi	aw'abiri
n3	ogw'okutaano	ogw'omukaaga	ogw'ekkumi	ogw'abiri
n5	ery'okutaano	ery'omukaaga	ery'ekkumi	ery'abiri
n7	eky'okutaano	eky'omukaaga	eky'ekkumi	eky'abiri
n9	ey'okutaano	ey'omukaaga	ey'ekkumi	ey'abiri
n11	olw'okutaano	olw'omukaaga	olw'ekkumi	olw'abiri
n12	ak'okutaano	ak'omukaaga	ak'ekkumi	ak'abiri

Table 5. Selected ordinal numbers.

Some grammarians use elided forms for numbers greater than one. For example, the elided forms for noun class *n1* are: **owookubiri** ('second'), **owookusatu** ('third'), **owookuna** ('fourth'), **owookutaano** ('fifth'), **owoomukaaga** ('sixth'), **owekkumi** ('tenth') and **awaabiri** ('twentieth').

li/ma GENDER (*n5* and *n6*). This gender is sometimes used to indicate large size or strength, *eg.* **essajja** (*n5* 'very big man'), from **omusajja** (*n1* 'man'). *n6* is further used for liquids, *eg.* **amata** ('milk'), and times of activities, *eg.* **amakoola** ('time of weeding').

ki/bi GENDER (*n7* and *n8*). Many inanimate objects fall into this gender, *eg.* **ekintu** ('thing'), which is further used for 'things' in general, for instance when nouns of different genders are added together, *eg.* **Amagi ne lumonde biri mu kisenge.** ('The eggs and the potatoes are in the room.'). In this example, **amagi** ('eggs') and **lumonde** ('potatoes') belong to different noun classes (*n6* and *n1* respectively), but the sum total of the two is placed in *n8*, the plural noun class within the *ki/bi* gender (this is shown by the use of the subject prefix **bi-** in 'biri' 'they are'). Compared to the *mu/mi* and *n/n* genders, the *ki/bi* gender can imply greater definitiveness, *eg.* (1) **ekisolo** (*n7* 'the animal', *ie.* the one there), compared with **ensolo** (*n9* 'an animal' – more general); (2) **ekiti** (*n7* 'piece of wood'), compared with **omuti** (*n3* 'wood' – the material). The *ki/bi* gender can also imply large size or poor condition, *eg.* (1) **ekinnyaanya** (*n7* 'tree tomato plant'), compared with **omunnyaanya** (*n3* 'tomato plant'); (2) **ekisawo** (*n7* 'big bag' or 'bag in poor condition'), compared with **ensawo** (*n9* 'bag').

n/n GENDER (*n9* and *n10*). Many common objects are placed in this gender, *eg.* **emmeeza** ('table'), also animals, *eg.* **embwa** ('dog') and 'ways of doing', *eg.* **enzimba** ('way of building'). Many words of foreign origin, lacking the usual *n9* prefix **en-**, are placed in this gender, *eg.* **wiiki** ('week'). The names of countries, such as Bufalansa ('France'), are placed in *n9*, even if they start with the prefix **Bu-** (normally associated with noun class *n14*).

lu/n GENDER (*n11* and *n10*). Many long things are placed in this gender, *eg.* **oluviiri** ('hair').

ka/bu GENDER (*n12* and *n14*). This gender is sometimes used to show smallness, *eg.* **akantu** (*n12* 'small thing'), from **ekintu** (*n7* 'thing'). *n14* has several other uses in addition to forming the plurals of nouns with singulars in *n12* (*eg.* **obuntu** 'small things'), for instance: (1) it is used for many abstract nouns (that lack singular equivalents), *eg.* **obuyinza** ('authority'); (2) it is found in many adverbs, some of which double as nouns, *eg.* **obulungi** ('well', 'goodness'); (3) it is found in the negative infinitive (**N18**) giving words that can sometimes double as nouns, *eg.* **obutayinza** ('not to be able', 'inability').

ku/ma GENDER (*n15* and *n6*). The ku- noun class includes infinitives when acting as nouns, *eg.* **Okukula kudda buto.** ('To grow old is a return to childhood.') (a Luganda proverb). Such nouns do not have plurals. Otherwise, this gender contains only two nouns, **okugulu** ('leg') and **okutu** ('ear').

gu/ga GENDER (*n20* and *n22*). This gender is used for enlarged or grotesque forms, *eg.* **ogusajja** ('big hunk of a man'). The subject prefix **ga-** on a main verb after the auxiliary verb **-mala** ('finish') can be equivalent to the adverb 'anyhow', *eg.* **Yamala gayogera gye ndi.** ('He talked to me anyhow.'). There are no nouns exclusive to this gender, which is little used.

tu/- GENDER (*n13*): This gender contains only one noun class (*n13*) without an associated plural. *n13* can be used to convey the idea of 'a little bit of', *eg.* **otuzzi** (*n13* 'a little drop of water'), from **amazzi** (*n6* 'water'). Otherwise, the only noun in this gender is **otulo** ('sleep').

Some nouns in Luganda are constructed from simpler parts. There are some words that start with the possessive **-a** (**N11.2**), *eg.* **ekyenkya** ('breakfast'), and others formed from subject relative clauses (**N7.1**), *eg.* **eyeesimbyewo** (*pl.* **abeesimbyawo**) ('candidate'). The use of subject relatives to form nouns can result in subtle distinctions compared with the English translations, as with the following words, all of which can be translated as 'obstacle', but with different understandings: (1) **ekiziyiza** ('obstacle', *lit.* 'something that prevents'); (2) **ekizibuwaza** ('obstacle', *lit.* 'something that makes difficult'); (3) **ekiremesa** ('obstacle', *lit.* 'something that makes impossible'). The verbs used in these nouns are **-ziyiza** ('impede'), **-zibuwala** ('become difficult') and **-lemesa** ('make impossible'). A further subtlety with some compound nouns is that they can be placed in different tenses according to the time of reference. For examples, the addition of the prefix **eki-** (*pl.* **ebi-**) to the verb **-vaamu** ('come out from') gives the following nouns, all meaning 'result': **ekivaamu** ('result' – in the present), **ekyavaamu** ('result' – in the past), **ekirivaamu** ('result' – in the future).

N7. ADJECTIVES AND RELATED PARTS OF SPEECH

N7.1. ORDINARY NOUN CLASSES

An **ADJECTIVE** follows the noun and takes the **NOMINAL CONCORD (N4)**. The nominal concord is underlined in the following examples: (1) **omuti o<u>mu</u>nene** ('big tree'); (2) **ekibira e<u>ki</u>nene** ('big forest'). The noun is sometimes absent but understood, in which case the adjective represents both the noun and the adjective. In this case, the meaning varies according to the noun class, *eg.* **o<u>mu</u>bi** (*n1* 'bad person'), **e<u>ki</u>bi** (*n7* 'bad thing'). Some common adjectives are listed in Table 4. See **N3** on the use of initial vowels with adjectives.

Gender	Noun class	-mu	-biri	-satu	-na	-taano	(kkumi na) -mu	(abiri na) -mu	-meka?
Stem:		'one'[1]	'two'	'three'	'four'	'five'	'eleven'	'twenty-one'	'how many?'
mu/ba	1	omu					kkumi n'omu[2]	abiri mu omu	
	2	abamu	ababiri	abasatu	abana	abataano			bameka?
mu/mi	3	ogumu					kkumi na gumu	abiri mu gumu	
	4	egimu	ebiri	esatu	ena	etaano			emeka?
li/ma	5	limu[3]					kkumi na limu	abiri mu limu	
	6	agamu	abiri	asatu	ana	ataano			ameka?
ki/bi	7	ekimu					kkumi na kimu	abiri mu kimu	
	8	ebimu	ebibiri	ebisatu	ebina	ebitaano			bimeka?
n/n	9	emu					kkumi n'emu[4]	abiri mu emu	
	10	ezimu	ebbiri	essatu	ennya	ettaano			mmeka?
lu/n	11	olumu					kkumi na lumu	abiri mu lumu	
	10	ezimu	ebbiri	essatu	ennya	ettaano			mmeka?
ka/bu	12	akamu					kkumi na kamu	abiri mu kamu	
	14	obumu	obubiri	obusatu	obuna	obutaano			bumeka?
ku/ma	15	okumu					kkumi na kumu	abiri mu kumu	
	6	agamu	abiri	asatu	ana	ataano			ameka?

Table 6. Cardinal numbers 1-5, 11 and 21, and '-meka?' in the main noun classes.

IVs given in bold type are always used; *IVs* in weak italic type are optional according to context.

1. The plural forms mean 'some'.
2. The elided form **kkumi noomu** is sometimes seen.
3. **erimu** with an initial vowel.
4. The elided form **kkumi neemu** is sometimes seen.

378

Another way of expressing an adjectival concept is through a **POSSESSIVE PHRASE**, consisting of the preposition **-a** ('of') (**N11.1**) followed by a noun, *eg.* **entebe y'omuti** ('wooden chair', *lit.* 'chair of wood') (**y'** = **ya**).

SUBJECT RELATIVES are formed by adding the initial vowel (*IV*) of the noun of reference to the verb, *eg.* **ekiso ekibuze** ('the knife which is lost'). In this example, the word **ekibuze** can be broken down into **e-** (*IV*) + **ki-** (*n7* pronominal concord) + **-buze** ('is lost'). Subject relatives in Luganda are sometimes equivalent to English nouns (see **N6**) or adjectives (for example, **ekiso ekibuze** can also be translated as 'lost knife').

See **N10.1** on the use of subject relative clauses following a pronoun of emphasis and **N21** on the formation of negative subject relatives.

Adjectives based on subject relatives sometimes vary in tense according to the time of reference, adding subtlety lost in the English translation. Thus, the English phrase 'the following day' would be translated differently in Luganda according to when an event occurred, *eg.* by **olunaku olwaddako** if the day of reference was in the past, **olunaku oluddako** if the day is today and **olunaku oluliddako** if the day is in the future.

Some details of the way in which subject relatives are formed should be noted. With *n9*, only one **e** is given and therefore **ente erya** means both 'the cow eats' and 'the cow which is eating'. The prefix in *n1* is **a-** for all singular cases and **aba-** for all plural cases, *eg.* **Ffe abayimbye tugenda kaakati okulya.** ('We who were singing are now going to eat.'), though these are replaced before **y** and with reflexive verbs by **e-** and **abe-**, *eg.* **Ffe abeetisse emigugu tugenda okuwummula.** ('We who are carrying the luggage are going to rest.'). There is a spelling change in the near future tense (**N16**) if the noun of reference is in *n9*, *eg.* **ente eneegenda** ('the cow which will go'), the normal tense infix **-naa-** being replaced by **-nee-**.

ORDINAL NUMBERS. 'First' can be translated by a subject relative clause, *eg.* **omuti ogusooka** ('the first tree'), in which **ogusooka** can be broken down into **o-** (*IV*) + **gu-** (*n3* pronominal concord) + **-sooka** ('be first') (Table 5). Possessive phrases based on the preposition **-a** ('of') are used for all higher numbers, *eg.* **omuti ogw'abiri mu gumu** ('the twenty-first tree'), the numbers 2-5 taking the prefix **oku-**, *eg.* **omuti ogw'okubiri** ('the second tree').

Some grammarians recommend elision for ordinal numbers above one (Table 5), *eg.* **omuti ogwabiri mu gumu** ('the twenty-first tree'), **omuti ogwokubiri** ('the second tree'). Elided forms are always used for days of the week (the word **olunaku** being understood) (**N11.2**), *eg.* **Olwokubiri** ('Tuesday', *lit.* ['day' – understood] 'of second).

A COMPARISON can be conveyed by use of the verb **-singa** ('be more than'), *eg.* **Omuti guno munene okusinga ogwo.** ('This tree is bigger than that one.'). Superlatives are sometimes indicated thus: **Ku miti gino omumpi gwe guluwa?** ('Which is the smallest of these trees?').

N7.2. ADVERBIAL NOUN CLASSES

The pronominal concords (**N4**) of the four adverbial noun classes of place (**N24**) occur in **SUBJECT RELATIVE CLAUSES**, literally meaning 'where there is', 'on where there is not', *etc.*, but more simply equivalent to **CONJUNCTIONS** or **PREPOSITIONS** such as 'where', 'on there', 'in there', 'to', 'on' or (in the negative) 'without'. The following illustrate the use of these subject relatives for each of the four place noun classes:

(*n16*): **Awali omukka tewabula omuliro.** ('Where there is smoke, there is fire.'). Here, **awali** (*lit.* 'where there is') can be broken down into **a-** (*IV*) + **wa-** (*n16* pronominal concord) + **-li** ('is').
(*n23*): **Genda eri Paulo.** ('Go to Paul.'). Here, **eri** (*lit.* 'over there where is') can be broken down into **e-** (*IV*) + **e-** (*n23* pronominal concord) + **-li** ('is'). Only one **e** is written (**N1**) and **l** changes to **r** after **e** (**N5**).
(*n17*): **Kiteeke ku mmeeza okutali kitambaala.** ('Put it on the table without a cloth.'). Here, **okutali** (*lit.* 'on where there is not') can be broken down into **o-** (*IV*) + **ku-** (*n17* pronominal concord) + **-ta-** ('not' **N21**) + **-li** ('is').
(*n18*): **Omwo omufumbira emmere mulimu omukka.** ('Where there's cooking, there's smoke.'). **omufumbira** can be broken down into **o-** (*IV*) + **mu-** (*n18* pronominal concord) + **-fumbira** ('cook at').

The pronominal concord (**lu-**) associated with the *n11* **ADVERBIAL NOUN CLASS OF TIME** (**N25.2**) is found in subject relative clauses, being equivalent to **CONJUNCTIONS** of time, such as 'as soon as', 'when', 'on' and 'directly', *eg.* **Olulaba Kabaka ne balekeraawo okukola.** ('As soon as they see the king, they stop working.'). These subject relative clauses can be placed in different tenses according to the time of an event, *eg.* (1) (past tense) **Olwamala okukola ne ŋŋenda eka.** ('When I finished work I went home.'); (2) (present tense) **Olumala okukola genda eka.** ('When you finish work go home.'); (3) (near future tense) **Olunaamala okukola tujja kugenda eka.** ('When we finish work we will go home.'). The tense infixes used in these examples are **-a-** (past tense) and **-naa-** (near future) (**N16**).

N7.3. -onna, -okka, -ombi(riri) and -onsatule

The following stems take the pronominal concord (**N4**): **-onna** ('any', 'all'), **-okka** ('alone', 'only'), **-ombi** and **-ombiriri** ('both of') and **-onsatule** ('all three of'). Spelling change (**N5**) often occurs, *eg.* **ebintu byonna** ('all the things'), where **byonna** is derived from **bi-** (pronominal concord *n7*) + **-onna** ('all') (**bi-** changes to **by-** before a vowel **N5**). The personal cases are exceptional in that the prefix is the ordinary free-standing pronoun (**N10.1**), *eg.* **ffenna** ('all of us'). The **o** of **-onna** is dropped in this case because there is a preceding vowel (**N5**). Examples of the personal cases are given in Column 11 of Table 2.

1	**emu** [1] *or* **-mu** [2]	3000	**enkumi ssatu**
2	**bbiri** [1] *or* **-biri** [2]	4000	**enkumi nnya**
3	**ssatu** [1] *or* **-satu** [2]	5000	**enkumi ttaano**
4	**nnya** [1] *or* **-na** [2]	6000	**akakaaga**
5	**ttaano** [1] *or* **-taano** [2]	7000	**akasanvu**
6	**omukaaga**	8000	**akanaana**
7	**omusanvu**	9000	**akenda**
8	**omunaana**	10,000	**omutwalo** *or* **omutwalo gumu**
9	**omwenda**	20,000	**emitwalo ebiri**
10	**ekkumi**	30,000	**emitwalo esatu**
20	**abiri** *or* **amakumi abiri** [3]	40,000	**emitwalo ena**
30	**asatu** *or* **amakumi asatu** [3]	50,000	**emitwalo etaano**
40	**ana** *or* **amakumi ana** [3]	60,000	**emitwalo mukaaga**
50	**ataano** *or* **amakumi ataano** [3]	70,000	**emitwalo musanvu**
60	**enkaaga**	80,000	**emitwalo munaana**
70	**ensanvu**	90,000	**emitwalo mwenda**
80	**ekinaana**	100,000	**emitwalo kkumi** *or* **akasiriivu**
90	**ekyenda**	200,000	**emitwalo abiri** *or* **obusiriivu bubiri**
100	**ekikumi**	300,000	**emitwalo asatu** *or* **obusiriivu busatu**
200	**bibiri** *or* **ebikumi bibiri** [4]	400,000	**emitwalo ana** *or* **obusiriivu buna**
300	**bisatu** *or* **ebikumi bisatu** [4]	500,000	**emitwalo ataano** *or* **obusiriivu butaano**
400	**bina** *or* **ebikumi bina** [4]	600,000	**emitwalo nkaaga** *or* **obusiriivu mukaaga**
500	**bitaano** *or* **ebikumi bitaano** [4]	700,000	**emitwalo nsanvu** *or* **obusiriivu musanvu**
600	**olukaaga**	800,000	**emitwalo kinaana** *or* **obusiriivu munaana**
700	**olusanvu**	900,000	**emitwalo kyenda** *or* **obusiriivu mwenda**
800	**olunaana**	1,000,000	**akakadde**
900	**olwenda**	2,000,000	**obukadde bubiri**
1000	**olukumi**	10,000,000	**akawumbi** *or* **obukadde kkumi**
2000	**enkumi bbiri**	'infinity'	**obutaggwa** [5]

Table 7. Cardinal numbers. The initial vowels in bold type are generally used, while those in weak italic type are optional according to context.

1. Form used when there is no connection with a specific noun.
2. Numeral concords are added according to the noun class (Table 5).
3. The longer forms must be used when referring to nouns in noun class *n6*.
4. The longer forms must be used when referring to nouns in noun class *n8*.
5. obutaggwa means 'never ending'.

N8. CARDINAL NUMBERS

N8.1. ORDINARY NOUN CLASSES

NUMBERS 1-5 are adjectives taking the **NUMERAL CONCORD (N4)**, as too does the interrogative **-meka?** ('how many?', 'how much') (Table 6). There is usually no *IV*, *eg.* **ebintu bibiri** ('two things'). The addition of an *IV* gives greater particularity, *eg.* **ebintu ebibiri** means 'the two things' or 'two of the things'. The plurals of **-mu** ('one') mean 'some' or 'certain', *eg.* **ebintu ebimu** ('some things') – an *IV* is included in this case. Free-standing numbers used without reference to any particular noun are placed in the *n/n* gender (without *IVs* for numbers two to five), *ie.* **emu, bbiri, ssatu, nnya, ttaano** ('1,2,3,4,5').

NUMBERS ABOVE 5 are nouns (Table 7). As with 1-5, the *IV* is often omitted, *eg.* **abantu kkumi** ('10 people'), though included to give greater particularity, for instance **abantu ekkumi** can mean 'the ten people' or 'ten of the people'.

The nouns **amakumi** ('tens') and **ebikumi** ('hundreds') are usually omitted with the numbers 20-50 and 200-500 respectively, though they must be included if there is a possibility of confusion with other numbers. In particular, the full forms must be used for: (1) 20-50 when referring to nouns in noun class *n6*, *eg.* **amagi amakumi ana** ('forty eggs'); and (2) 200-500 when referring to nouns in noun class *n8*, *eg.* **ebintu bikumi bina** ('four hundred things'). **lukumi** ('1000'), **enkumi** ('1000s'), **omutwalo** ('10,000') and **emitwalo** ('10,000s') are often omitted in ordinary speech when referring to 'thousands' or 'tens of thousands', *eg.* **ssatu** can mean '3000' and **ebiri** can mean '20,000'.

Intermediate numbers are constructed by adding together the numbers shown on Table 7 using the conjunctions **na** or **mu**. **na** is used when a number is joined to **kkumi** ('ten'), *eg.* **kkumi na mukaaga** ('16'), and **mu** in all other cases, *eg.* **abiri mu mukaaga** ('26'). As a further illustration, the number 4,444,414 is **obukadde buna mu mitwalo ana mu nnya mu nkumi nnya mu bina mu kkumi na nnya**. If the number refers to a noun, then the digits 1-5 take the numeral concord (**N4**), *eg.* (1) **emiti kkumi na gumu** ('11 trees'); (2) **ebintu kkumi na kimu** ('11 things').

DISTRIBUTIVE NUMERALS can be given by duplicating the numeral, *eg.* **Ebisolo byayingira bibiri bibiri.** ('The animals entered two-by-two.'). Alternatively, the word **kinna...-mu** can be used, with **-mu** in the singular and placed in the appropriate noun class, *eg.* (1) **Baabala ebiwuka kinnakimu.** ('They counted the insects one-by-one.'); (2) **Baabala obutungulu kinnakamu.** ('They counted the onions one-by-one.'). The words **kinnoomu** and **kinneemu** are used for noun classes *n1* and *n9* respectively, *eg.* **Abantu baayingidde kinnoomu.** ('The people came one-by-one.').

8.2. ADVERBIAL NOUN CLASSES

The numeral **-mu** ('one') is found in various adverbial noun classes, *eg.* (1) (*n16* – place) **awamu** ('together'); (2) (*n14* – manner) **obwomu** ('alone'), *eg.* **Ali bwomu mu kisenge.** ('She is alone in the room.'); (3) (*n7* – *manner*) **kye kimu** ('the same'), *eg.* **Eno kye kimu n'eri.** ('This is the same as that.'). As an example of the construction of these words, the word **awamu** can be broken down into **a-** (*IV*) + **wa-** (*n16* pronominal concord) + **-mu** ('one').

N9. DEMONSTRATIVES

N9.1. ORDINARY NOUN CLASSES

There are three kinds of demonstrative in Luganda (Table 8), rather than the two of English ('this', 'that'). Their stems are **-no** ('this'), **-li** ('that') and **-o** (usually translated 'that'). All take the pronominal concord (**N4**), *eg.* **ekintu kino** ('this thing'), **ekintu kiri** ('that thing'), **ekintu ekyo** ('that thing'). Note that, with **-li**, **l** changes to **r** after **i** (**N5**). **-no** and **-li** do not take initial vowels, but **-o** always does. The same words are used for both demonstrative determiners and demonstrative pronouns (see under 'Adjectives and determiners' and 'Pronouns' in Part 1 of the dictionary for explanations of these parts of speech).

The additional category of demonstratives (lacking from English) is the one based on the stem **-o**. These demonstratives (known as demonstratives of reference) imply 'closeness', that is visually close to the speaker or person addressed, or referred to previously (*ie.* mentally close), *eg.* **Njagala ekintu ekyo.** ('I want that thing.', *ie.* that one right there).

Demonstrative clauses such as 'he is here' and 'there it is' are expressed in Luganda by single words varying according to noun class (Table 8, Columns 6-8), *eg.* **Ekikopo kiikino.** ('Here is the cup.'). 'Here I am.' is **Nzuuno.**, 'Here (s)he is.' is **Wuuno.** and 'Here we are.' is **Tuutuno.**

1	2	3	4	5	6	7	8
		Demonstratives			Demonstrative clauses		
Stem:		-no	-li	-o [1]	-no	-li	-o [1]
Gender	Noun class	'this'	'that'	'that' *or* 'this'	'he is here', 'there it is', *etc.*		
ORDINARY NOUN CLASSES							
mu/ba	1	ono	oli	oyo	wuuno	wuuli	wuuyo
	2	bano	bali	abo	baabano	baabali	baabo
mu/mi	3	guno	guli	ogwo	guuguno	guuguli	guugwo
	4	gino	giri	egyo	giigino	giigiri	giigyo
li/ma	5	lino	liri	eryo	liirino	liiriri	liiryo
	6	gano	gali	ago	gaagano	gaagali	gaago
ki/bi	7	kino	kiri	ekyo	kiikino	kiikiri	kiikyo
	8	bino	biri	ebyo	biibino	biibiri	biibyo
n/n	9	eno	eri	eyo	yiino	yiiri	yiiyo
	10	zino	ziri	ezo	ziizino	ziiziri	ziizo
lu/n	11	luno	luli	olwo	luuluno	luululi	luulwo
	10	zino	ziri	ezo	ziizino	ziiziri	ziizo
ka/bu	12	kano	kali	ako	kaakano	kaakali	kaako
	14	buno	buli	obwo	buubuno	buubuli	buubwo
ku/ma	15	kuno	kuli	okwo	kuukuno	kuukuli	kuukwo
	6	gano	gali	ago	gaagano	gaagali	gaago
gu/ga	20	guno	guli	ogwo	guuguno	guuguli	guugwo
	22	gano	gali	ago	gaagano	gaagali	gaago
tu/-	13	tuno	tuli	otwo	tuutuno	tuutuli	tuutwo
ADVERBIAL NOUN CLASSES OF PLACE							
		'here'	'there'	'there'	'here is the place', *etc.*		
	16	wano	wali	awo	waawano	waawali	waawo
	23	eno	eri	eyo	eyeeno	eyeeri	eyeeyo
	17	kuno	kuli	okwo	kuukuno	kuukuli	kuukwo
	18	muno	muli	omwo	muumuno	muumuli	muumwo

Table 8. Demonstratives.

1. Demonstratives of reference.

N9.2. ADVERBIAL NOUN CLASSES

The pronominal concords of place **wa-**, **e-**, **ku-** and **mu-** (**N24.1**) can be added to the demonstrative stems to make demonstrative adverbs, such as **wano** ('here'), **eno** ('over here'), **kuli** ('on there') and **omwo** ('in there') (Table 8). Examples of the use of demonstrative stems with adverbial prefixes of time (**N25.2**) are **luli** (*n11* 'the other day') and **awo** (*n16* 'then').

Demonstrative clauses such as 'the place is here' and 'it is on there' are expressed in Luganda by single words varying according to adverbial noun class (Table 8, Columns 6-8, bottom 4 rows). An example of their use is **We twateeka ebintu waawano.** ('Here is the place where we put the things.', *lit.* 'The place we put the things, the place is here.').

N10. FREE-STANDING PRONOUNS AND RELATED WORDS

N10.1. ORDINARY NOUN CLASSES

There are three types of **FREE-STANDING PRONOUNS** in Luganda: (1) ordinary pronouns, based on the stem **-o**; (2) pronouns of emphasis; (3) object relative pronouns, the last two based on the stem **-e**. All take the **PRONOMINAL CONCORD (N4)**. There is no initial vowel. Both ordinary pronouns and pronouns of emphasis can sometimes form parts of longer words (despite their designation as 'free-standing').

ORDINARY PRONOUNS are listed in Column 13 of Table 1 and Column 9 of Table 2. Most ordinary <u>personal</u> pronouns are irregular. Ordinary pronouns are used in contexts such as (pronouns underlined): (1) **Ente, <u>zo</u> zijja.** ('The cows, they are coming.'); (2) **Kino kifaanana nga <u>kyo</u>.** ('This one looks like it.'); (3) **<u>Mmwe</u> bazimbi? Nedda, <u>ffe</u> tuli babazzi.** ('Are you the builders? No, we are the carpenters.'). Ordinary free-standing pronouns are used relatively infrequently in Luganda, partly because the commonest uses of such pronouns in English (as the subject and object pronouns of verbs) are usually expressed through pronominal concords prefixed to verbs (**N15.1**). Ordinary pronouns prefixed by **na-** mean 'and/with her', 'and/with it', *etc.*, *eg.* **naffe** ('and us'), **nakyo** (*n7* 'and it'). Note that 'and/with me' is **nange** and 'and/with you *si.*' is **naawe** (see Column 16 of Table 2). In some circumstances, combinations such as **naffe** and **nakwyo** are given as two separate words, *eg.* **na ffe**, **na kyo**.

PRONOUNS OF EMPHASIS are listed in Column 12 of Table 1 and Column 13 of Table 2. Identically spelt words are used as **OBJECT RELATIVES PRONOUNS**. Noun classes *n1* and *n9* are exceptional in having two forms of pronouns of emphasis (**ye** and **gwe** in *n1*; **ye** and **gye** in *n9*). The **ye** forms are used relatively rarely, being found only when it is the <u>subject</u> of the sentence that is being emphasised. See **N21** on formation of <u>negative</u> object relatives.

-e STEM PRONOUNS (a term that encompasses both pronouns of emphasis and object relative pronouns) refer to nouns or pronouns already mentioned or understood (either in the same sentence or earlier), linking them to nouns, verbs or other parts of speech that follow. These pronouns can be equivalent to various parts of speech in English, including pronouns (*eg.* 'I', 'it', 'they'), object relatives ('who', 'whom', 'which') or short clauses (*eg.* 'it is they that'). This is a case where the grammars of Luganda and English can diverge with no straightforward equivalence. Examples of the use of **-e** stem pronouns are as follows (**-e** stem pronouns underlined):

- **enjovu <u>ze</u> twalaba** ('the elephants which we saw'). This is an example of the use of an **-e** stem pronoun as an object relative.
- **<u>Y'</u>eyasemba mu kibiina.** ('He was bottom of the class.'). '**eyasemba mu kibiina**' is a subject relative clause (**N7.1**) following the pronoun of emphasis **y'** (= **ye**). The literal translation is '**It is he who was bottom of the class.**'
- **Ani yasemba mu kibiina? Musoke <u>ye</u> yasemba.** ('Who was bottom of the class? Musoke, it was he that was bottom.').

THE SAME is translated by a pronoun of emphasis followed by **-mu** ('one'), both words being concordant with the noun, *eg.* **omuti gwe gumu** ('the same tree', *lit.* 'the tree it is one'). **THE SAME AS** is identical, but with **na/ne** ('with') added, *eg.* **Omuti guno gwe gumu na guli.** ('This tree is the same as that.'). The negative of the last example is **Omuti guno si gwe gumu na guli.** ('This tree is not the same as that.').

N10.2. ADVERBAL NOUN CLASSES

The stem **-o** is found with pronominal concords of place (**N24.1**) to give adverbs of reference (underlined in the examples below). These adverbs are used relatively infrequently.

(*n16*) **Awo <u>wo</u> waliwo ki?** ('What is there in that place?').
(*n23*) **Eyo <u>yo</u> walabyeyo ki?** ('What did you see over there?').
(*n17*) **Ku mmeeza okwo <u>kwo</u> kuliko ki?** ('What is on that table?').
(*n18*) **Mu nsawo omwo <u>mwo</u> mulimo ki?** ('What is in that bag?').

Words formed from the stem **-e** prefixed by a pronominal concord are found in various adverbial noun classes. Similarly to **-e** stem pronouns in the ordinary noun classes (**N10.1**), these words refer to nouns or pronouns already mentioned or understood, linking them to nouns, verbs or other parts of speech that follow. These words can be equivalent to various parts of speech in English.

The following illustrate the use of these words (underlined) as **PROCLITICS** – see Part 1 of the dictionary for an explanation of this grammatical term):

- **Ekitabo we kiri? Yee, <u>we</u> kiri.** ('Is the book there? Yes it is.')
- **Ekitabo gye kiri? Yee, <u>gye</u> kiri.** ('Is the book over there? Yes it is.')
- **Ekitabo kwe kiri? Yee, <u>kwe</u> kiri.** ('Is the book on there? Yes it is.')
- **Ekitabo mwe kiri? Yee, <u>mwe</u> kiri.** ('Is the book in there? Yes it is.')

The use of **-e** stem words in the adverbial noun classes as **CONJUNCTIONS** or **RELATIVE PRONOUNS** is illustrated by the following examples:

PLACE (see also **N24.1**)

- (*n16*) **Wano abaana si <u>we</u> basula.** ('This is not where the children spend the night.').
- (*n23*) **Genda eri <u>gye</u> bali.** ('Go over there where they are.').
- (*n17*) **Ku mmeeza eyo <u>kwe</u> nnateeka essowaani.** ('That is the table on which I put the plates.
- (*n18*) **Tojja mu kisenge <u>mwe</u> twogerera.** ('Don't come into the room in which we are talking.').

TIME (see also **N25.3**)

- (*n11*) **<u>Lwe</u> bajja wano, nnali siriiwo.** ('When they came here, I was away.'). The understood noun of reference for **lwe** is **olunaku** ('day').
- (*n14*) **<u>Bwe</u> nnagenda okumulaba, yasanyuka.** ('When I went to see him, he was happy.'). If the suffix **-nga** is placed on the verb, the conjunction **bwe** means 'whenever', *eg.* **Bwe nnagendanga okumulaba yasanyuka.** ('Whenever I went to see him, he was happy.'). The understood noun of reference for **bwe** may be **obudde** ('time of the day').
- (*n16*) **<u>We</u> yagendera, nnali sinnajja.** ('When he left, I had not yet come.').

MANNER (see also **N26**)

- (*n14*) **Ensimbi <u>bwe</u> zigenda si <u>bwe</u> zidda.** ('How money goes is not how it returns.').

CAUSE AND REASON (see also **N27**)

- (*n7*) **Kitange mulwadde, <u>kyenvudde</u> sigenda kulima leero.** ('My father is ill therefore I am not digging today.'). This conjunction (**kye...-va**), meaning 'that is the reason' or 'therefore', consists of two parts **kye** and **-va**. The verb **-va** ('come from') acts here as an auxiliary verb (**N19**), declinable by case and tense. The main verb that follows (**-genda** 'go' in this case) is always placed in the present tense. The following are further examples of the use of this construction: (1) **Kitange yali mulwadde jjo, <u>kyetwava</u> tutalima.** ('My father was ill yesterday, therefore we did not work.'); (2) **Nnina okusoma ku Mmande, kyennaava sisobola kulima.** ('I will be studying on Monday, therefore I will not be able to dig.').

- (*n14*) **Kitange yali mulwadde jjo, bwe butalima.** ('My father was ill yesterday, therefore there was no digging.'). The conjunction **bwe** ('therefore', 'that's why') in this construction is followed by the negative infinitive (**N18**).

- (*n15*) **Alwadde ekifuba, kwe kujja okulaba omusawo.** ('He has a cough therefore he has come to see the doctor.'). The adverb **kwe** ('therefore', 'that's why') is followed by the (positive) infinitive (**N18**).

N11. POSSESSIVES AND POSSESSION

N11.1. a- ('of') IN ORDINARY NOUN CLASSES

The preposition 'of' is translated by the stem **-a** taking the pronominal concord (**N4**; Table 1, Column 11), *eg.* **engatto za Daudi** ('the shoes of David'). In possessive phrases of this type, the first noun (*ie.* **engatto** 'shoes' in this case) is known as the possessed noun and the second noun (**Daudi** 'David') as the possessor. The letter **a** is omitted from the 'of' word if the possessor starts with a vowel, *eg.* **enguudo z'ekibuga** ('the streets of the town') (**z'** = **za**). **Engatto za Daudi** can also mean 'The shoes belong to David.', though the pronunciation is different (more stress is placed on **za**).

The way that possessive phrases are spoken can be misleading as regards their spelling. This is because the initial vowels of possessor nouns (*eg.* the **e** of **ekibuga** in the example above) can be heard as if attached to the 'of' word, with a pause heard before continuation of the rest of the noun, *ie.* the phrase in the paragraph above is heard as **enguudo** [pause] **ze** [pause] **kibuga**.

An initial vowel (*IV* **N3**) is not normally added to the preposition **-a**, except when other words intervene between the two nouns, *eg.* **ebikoola ebinene eby'omuti** ('the big leaves of the tree') (**eby'** = **ebya**) (relevant *IV* underlined). An *IV* is also used if the preceding noun is absent but understood, *eg.* **ab'eno** ('people of this place'). The understood noun here is **abantu** ('people'). However, in such cases, the *IV* is omitted: (1) with a negative, *eg.* **Toyita ba Mukasa.** ('Don't call Mukasa's people.'); or (2) where the verb 'be' or 'belong to' is understood, *eg.* **Omwana ono wa Mukasa.** ('This child is Mukasa's.').

Phrases starting with **-a** (**POSSESSIVE PHRASES**) can be equivalent to various parts of speech in English (relevant parts of speech underlined in these examples):

- nouns, *eg.* **ow'ebigere** ('walker') (**omuntu** 'person' understood). Some of these nouns can be seen written in either elided or non-elided form, *eg.* **owaakasolya** or **ow'akasolya** ('head of a clan').
- adjectives, *eg.* **emmeeza y'omuti** ('wooden table', *lit.* 'table of wood').
- ordinal numbers, *eg.* **omuntu ow'okuna** ('fourth person').
- prepositions, *eg.* **abayizi b'e Makerere** ('students of Makerere', *lit.* 'students of at the place Makerere'). This construction is sometimes seen with the apostrophe missing, *eg.* **abayizi be Makerere** ('students of Makerere'). An initial vowel can be added to the preposition **-a** when a distinction is drawn between items, *eg.* **Abayizi ab'e Makerere bambala bulungi okusinga ab'e Kyambogo.** ('Makerere students dress better than those of Kyambogo.')
- adverbs, *eg.* **lwa kisa** ('though kindness').
- interrogatives, *eg.* **Engoye ezo z'ani?** ('Whose clothes are these?').
- conjunctions, *eg.* **Nnazze olw'okuba yampise.** ('I came because she called me.').

Adverbial nouns sometimes act as possessors (underlined in the examples that follow with their noun classes indicated in italics). Some of these nouns consist of two words. (1) (*n16*) **oluggi olw'emmanju** ('back door', *lit.* 'door of at the back part of the home'); (2) (*n17*) **ensolo ez'oku nsozi** ('mountain animals', *lit.* 'the animals of on mountains') – note that an *IV* (**o-**) is included on **ku** ('on'); (3) (*n18*) **amakubo ag'omu kibuga** ('the town's roads', *lit.* 'the roads of in the town') – an *IV* is included on **mu** ('in').

| | | | Personal possessive determiners | | | | | | Personal possessive pronouns | | | imp pos determiners and pronouns | |
| | | | | | | | | | | | | 'its/their(s)' See N11.4 | |
Gender	Noun class	IV	-nge 'my'	-o 'your' *si.*	-e 'her/his'	-ffe 'our'	-mmwe 'your' *pl.*	-bwe 'their'	-nge 'mine'	'yours' *si.*	'hers/his'	'its/their(s)'	
			NOUN CLASSES USED FOR ORDINARY NOUNS										
mu/ba	1	o	wange	wo	we	waffe	wammwe	waabwe	owange	owuwo	owuwe	waa-	
	2	a	bange	bo	be	baffe	bammwe	baabwe	abange	ababo	ababe	baa-	
mu/mi	3	o	gwange	gwo	gwe	gwaffe	gwammwe	gwabwe	ogwange	ogugwo	ogugwe	gwa-	-gwo
	4	e	gyange	gyo	gye	gyaffe	gyammwe	gyabwe	egyange	egigyo	egigye	gya-	-gyo
li/ma	5	e	lyange	lyo	lye	lyaffe	lyammwe	lyabwe	eryange	eriryo	erirye	lya-¹	-lyo
	6	a	gange	go	ge	gaffe	gammwe	gaabwe	agange	agago	agage	gaa-	-go
ki/bi	7	e	kyange	kyo	kye	kyaffe	kyammwe	kyabwe	ekyange	ekikyo	ekikye	kya-	-kyo
	8	e	byange	byo	bye	byaffe	byammwe	byabwe	ebyange	ebibyo	ebibye	bya-	-byo
n/n	9	e	yange	yo	ye	yaffe	yammwe	yaabwe	eyange	eyiyo	eyiye	yaa-	-yo
	10	e	zange	zo	ze	zaffe	zammwe	zaabwe	ezange	ezizo	ezize	zaa-	-zo
lu/n	11	o	lwange	lwo	lwe	lwaffe	lwammwe	lwabwe	olwange	olulwo	olulwe	lwa-	-lwo
	10	e	zange	zo	ze	zaffe	zammwe	zaabwe	ezange	ezizo	ezize	zaa-	-zo
ka/bu	12	a	kange	ko	ke	kaffe	kammwe	kaabwe	akange	akako	akake	kaa-	-ko
	14	o	bwange	bwo	bwe	bwaffe	bwammwe	bwabwe	obwange	obubwo	obubwe	bwa-	-bwo
ku/ma	15	o	kwange	kwo	kwe	kwaffe	kwammwe	kwabwe	okwange	okukwo	okukwe	kwa-	-kwo
	6	a	gange	go	ge	gaffe	gammwe	gaabwe	agange	agago	agage	gaa-	-go
gu/ga	20	o	gwange	gwo	gwe	gwaffe	gwammwe	gwabwe	ogwange	ogugwo	ogugwe	gwa-	-gwo
	22	a	gange	go	ge	gaffe	gammwe	gaabwe	agange	agago	agage	gaa-	-go
tu/-	13	o	twange	two	twe	twaffe	twammwe	twabwe	otwange	otutwo	otutwe	twa-	-two
			ADVERBIAL NOUN CLASSES USED FOR PLACE										
	16	a	wange	wo	we	waffe	wammwe	waabwe	awange	awawo	awawe	wa-	-wo
	23	e	wange	wo		waffe	wammwe	waabwe	ewange	ewuwo	ewuwe	wa-	-yo
	17	o	kwange			kwaffe	kwammwe	kwabwe	ekwange	okukwo	okukwe	kwa-	-kwo
	18	o	mwange			mwaffe	mwammwe	mwabwe	omwange	omumwo	omumwe	mwa-	-mwo

Table 9. Possessive determiners and pronouns.

¹ **erya-** with pronouns.

ABBREVIATIONS:
COLUMN 3: *IV* initial vowel.
COLUMNS 5 and 11: *si.* singular.
COLUMNS 8: *pl.* plural.
COLUMNS 13 and 14: *imp pos* impersonal possessives.

11.2. a- IN ORDINARY NOUN CLASSES
(COMPOUND WORDS)

By convention, some combinations of -a and a following possessor are written as single words, eg: (1) the interrogative **lwaki?** ('why?'), which can be broken down into ['cause' – understood] + **lwa** (n11 'of') + **ki?** ('what?'); (2) **ebyokukozesa** ('equipment'), which can be broken down into **ebintu** ('things' – understood) + **eby'** (= **ebya** n8 'of') + **okukozesa** ('to use'). Some of these combined words can sometimes be seen written in either elided or non-elided form, for instance with some ordinal numbers (Table 5).

If an *IV* is lacking in a compound word, then this is typically so for both parts of its parts, eg. (1) **ebyokulya** ('food') becomes **byakulya** without the two *IV*s; (2) **Olwokusatu** ('Wednesday') becomes **Lwakusatu**. However, if such words are preceded by **ku** or **mu**, then this change does not occur, eg. **Ku Lwokusatu tuddayo eka.** ('On Thursday we are going home.'). Compare with **Olunaku leero Lwakusatu.** ('Today is Thursday.')

Compound words starting with -a are particularly common in the following noun classes:

- *n1* and *n2*. The understood noun is often **omuntu** (*pl.* **abantu**) ('person'). An example is **oweekitiibwa** (*pl.* **abeekitiibwa**) ('honorable person'), where **oweekitiibwa** can be broken down into **omuntu** ('person' – understood) + **ow'**- (= **owa** n1 'of') + **ekitiibwa** ('honour'). Note that the **a** of **owa** is lost through spelling change (**N5**). **omukulu** ('head') is the understood noun in words such as **owessaza** ('county chief').

- *n7* and *n8*. The understood noun is **ekintu** (*pl.* **ebintu**) ('thing'). An example is **ebyokunywa** ('drinks'), which can be broken down into **ebintu** ('things' – understood) + **eby'** (= **ebya** n7 'of') + **okunywa** ('to drink').

- *n11*. A commonly understood noun is **olunaku** ('day'), as in the days of the week, eg. **Olwokuna** ('Thursday'), which may be broken down into **Olunaku** ('day' – understood) + **olw'** (= **olwa** n11 'of') + **okuna** ('to be four').

- *n14*. An example is **obwakabaka** ('kingdom'), which may be broken down into '['matters' – understood] + **obwa** (n14 'of') + **kabaka** ('the king').

N11.3. -a IN ADVERBIAL NOUN CLASSES

Some **PREPOSITIONS OF PLACE** consist of two words, the first an adverbial noun in a place noun class (**N24**) and the second -a in concordial agreement (**N4**). Prepositions are underlined in these examples:

- (*n16*) <u>wansi w'</u>omuti ('below the tree') (**w'** = **wa**).
- (*n23*) <u>emabega w'</u>omuti ('behind the tree') (**w'** = **wa**).

N11.4. POSSESSIVE DETERMINERS AND PRONOUNS
(ORDINARY NOUN CLASSES)

PERSONAL POSSESSIVE DETERMINERS (*eg.* 'our' in 'our house') are constructed from -a ('of') with a pronominal concord (**N4**) followed by an ordinary free-standing pronoun (**N10.1**). For example, **yaffe** ('our') in **ennyumba yaffe** ('our house') can be broken down into **ya**- (n9 'of', concordant with **ennyumba**) + **-ffe** ('us'). There is no initial vowel (*IV*). A full list of personal possessive determiners is given in Table 9.

PERSONAL POSSESSIVE PRONOUNS (*eg.* 'ours') are constructed as personal possessive determiners, but with an *IV* added, eg. **eyaffe** ('ours') in **Ennyumba yaabwe nnene; eyaffe ntono.** ('Their house is big; ours is small.'). The various words meaning 'mine' are listed in Column 10 of Table 9 to illustrate. Other personal cases follow the same pattern except for the 2nd and 3rd persons singular ('yours', 'hers/his'), which are irregular (listed in Columns 11 and 12 of Table 9). The *IV* is omitted when the verb 'be' is understood, eg. **Ennyumba ntono yaffe.** ('The small house is ours.').

ku followed by a personal possessive pronoun in noun class *n11* means 'on behalf of' or 'for', eg. (1) **ku lwange** ('for me'); (2) **ku lulwe** ('for her/him'). **ku** followed by a personal possessive pronoun in noun class *n14* means 'on the initiative of', eg. (1) **ku bwange** ('on my initiative'); (2) **ku bubwe** ('on her/his initiative'). There is no *IV* on the pronoun. **ku bwa** and **ku lwa** are also used before nouns, eg. (1) **ku lwa Musoke** ('for Musoke'); (2) **ku bwa Musoke** ('on Musoke's initiative'). In this case **ku** is sometime seen joined to **lwa** or **lwa**, eg. **kulwa Musoke** ('for Musoke').

IMPERSONAL POSSESSIVE DETERMINERS ('its' or 'their') are constructed as personal possessive determiners, but with numerous variants depending on the noun classes of the two nouns of reference. Readers can construct all possible forms of these determiners by combining one item from each of the last two columns of Table 9 with one another, selected according to the relevant noun classes. For example, the possessive determiner appropriate for 'its', referring to the leaves (**ebikoola** *n8*) of a tree (**omuti** *n3*), is **byagwo**, which can be broken down into **bya-** (*n8* 'of', concordant with **ebikoola**) + **-gwo** (*n3* 'it', concordant with **omuti**).

IMPERSONAL POSSESSIVE PRONOUNS ('its' or 'ttheirs') are constructed as impersonal possessive determiners but with an *IV* added, *eg.* **ebyagwo** is the pronoun used for 'its' when referring to the leaves of a tree.

N11.5. POSSESSIVE DETERMINERS AND PRONOUNS (PLACE NOUN CLASSES)

The reference to an adverbial noun class can be through either the first or second part of the determiner or pronoun. The following is an example of a determiner in which the <u>possessor</u> (the second part of the word) is in an adverbial noun class: **omuntu waawo** ('a local person', *lit.* 'a person of a place'), where **waawo** can be broken down into **wa-** (*n1* 'of', concordant with **omuntu**) + **awo** ('there'). The pronominal equivalent of **waawo** has an initial vowel, *ie.* **owaawo** ('her' or 'him', referring to a person of a place).

If the adverbial concord is found on the <u>possessed</u> (first) part of a pronoun, then the resulting word is translated by a possessive phrase in English referring to 'home' or 'place', *eg:* **awaffe** ('our home'), **omwaffe** ('in our place'). These words always take an initial vowel.

Stem:	kita-	nnya-	bba-	jjajja-	kojja-
	'father of'	'mother of'	'husband of'	'grandparent of'	'uncle of' (mother's brother)
SINGULARS					
my	kitange	mmange	baze	jjajjange	kojjange
your *si.*	kitaawo	nnyoko [1]	balo	jjajjaawo	kojjaawo
her/his	kitaawe	nnyina	(bbaawe) [2]	jjajjaawe	kojjaawe
our	kitaffe	nnyaffe	bbaffe	jjajjaffe	kojjaffe
your *pl.*	kitammwe	nnyammwe	bbammwe	jjajjammwe	kojjammwe
their	kitaabwe	nnyaabwe	bbaabwe	jjajjaabwe	kojjaabwe
EXAMPLES OF PLURALS (3rd person plural)					
their	ba kitaabwe	ba nnyaabwe	ba bbaabwe	ba jjajjaabwe	ba kojjaabwe

Stem:	ssenga-	mwannyina-	munna-	mukama-
	'aunt of' (father's sister)	'brother/sister of' [3]	'friend of' or 'companion of'	'boss of'
SINGULARS				
my	ssennange	mwannyinaze	munnange	mukama wange
your *si.*	ssengaawo	mwannyoko	munno	mukamaawo
her/his	ssengaawe	mwannyina	munne	mukamaawe
our	ssengaffe	mwannyinaffe	munnaffe	mukama waffe
your *pl.*	ssengammwe	mwannyinammwe	munnammwe	mukama wammwe
their	ssengaabwe	mwannyinaabwe	munnaabwe	mukama waabwe
EXAMPLES OF PLURALS (3rd person plural)				
their	ba ssengaabwe	ba nnyinaabwe	ba nnaabwe	bakama waabwe

Table 10. Possessive nouns used for relationships.

1. Impolite; better to use **maama wo** ('your mother').
2. **bbaawe** not used.
3. Referring to the opposite sex, *ie.* a female's brother or a male's sister.

N11.6. nnyini and nnannyini

nnyini or **nnannyini** followed by a noun means 'owner of', *eg.* **nnyini nnyumba** ('owner of the house'). There is no initial vowel on the noun. **nnyini** and **nnannyini** can be prefixes to ordinary pronouns (**N10.1**), *eg.* **nnyiniyo** ('its owner', referring to a house). Both **nnyinimu** and **nnannyinimu** mean 'owner of the house'.

-nnyini can also be found as a suffix to a pronoun of emphasis (**N10.1**), giving words translatable by '-self' or 'the actual', *eg.* **ente yennyini** ('the cow itself'), **omwami yennyini** ('the actual chief'). An ordinary free-standing pronoun (**N10.1**) can be added for emphasis, *eg.* **ente zo zennyini** ('the cows themselves'). Omission of the noun results in a pronominal meaning, *eg.* **zo zennyini** ('they themselves', *eg.* referring to cows). The personal forms ('I myself', you yourself, *etc.*) are given in Column 10 of Table 2.

N12. RELATIONSHIPS

Many relationships can be written as two-word phrases consisting of a noun and a possessive determiner (**N11.4**). Examples: **maama wo** ('your mother'), **muganda wo** ('your brother' or 'your sister'), **mukama wo** ('your boss'), **mukoddomi wo** ('your brother-in-law'), **mukwano gwo** ('your friend'), **mukyala wo** ('your wife'), **muwala wo** ('your daughter'), **muzzukulu wo** ('your grandchild'). An initial vowel is typically not included, though sometimes can be. In some cases there are single-word alternatives (**POSSESSIVE NOUNS**) to these two-word phrases, *eg.* **nnyina** ('her/his mother') (Table 10).

Notes. (1) Some terms for relationships can have wider meaningw than expressed by typical English translations. For example, **muganda gwo**, which is typically translated as 'your brother' or 'your sister' in English, can refer to more distant blood relations in Luganda. (2) The noun **mukwano** is unusual in that the possessive is in noun class *n3* (rather than noun class *n1*) (**N6**), which is is why 'your' in 'your friend' above is given as **gwo** (not **wo**) (**N6**).

-nna- ('with') is a stem signifying 'attachment', 'belonging' or 'ownership', with affixes added at both ends. The prefix is the pronominal concord (**N4**) and the suffix an ordinary free-standing pronoun (**N10.1**). The resulting words in the personal gender (*mu/ba*) mean 'friend(s)', 'fellow(s)' or 'companion(s)', *eg.* **bannaffe** ('our friends'). **bannaffe** can be broken down into **ba-** ('they') + **-nna-** ('with') + **-ffe** ('us'). An example of the use of this stem for an impersonal gender is **ginnaayo** ('its companion'), which would (for instance) be the appropriate form to use for a cow which is the companion of another cow (both the prefix **gi-** and the suffix **-yo** are in noun class *n9* - see Columns 9 and 13 on Table 1). **-nna-** can be used in noun classes *n1* and *n2* to give nouns indicating belonging to a place or profession, *eg.* **Munnabuddu** ('person of Buddu), **munnamateeka** ('lawyer').

N13. INTERROGATIVES

Ordinary sentences can be made interrogative by a change in tone, *eg.* **Òsòmà kìtàbò?** ('Are you reading a book?'), from **Òsómá kítábó.** ('You are reading a book.').

Some interrogatives are invariable:

- **ddi?** ('when?'), *eg.* **Ogenda ddi?** ('When are you going?'). This interrogative always comes directly after the verb.
- **ki?** ('what?', 'which?', 'what sort of?'), *eg.* (1) **Oyagala ki?** ('What do you want?'); (2) **Muti ki?** ('Which tree?' or 'What sort of tree is it?'). When used with a prepositional verb (**N22**), **ki?** may be translated 'what for' or 'why?', *eg.* **Ogendera ki?** ('Why are you going?').
- **wa?** ('where?'), *eg.* **Ekiso kiri wa?** ('Where is the knife?'). The noun **ludda** ('side') is sometimes added before **wa?**, *eg.* **Ekiso kiri ludda wa?** ('Where is the knife?').

389

Table 11. Formation of modified stem forms (*msf*) of verbs (N14), and of causative verbs (N22).

Conditions of use		Examples of verbs		Modified stem form (*msf*)		First causative		Second causative	
Last consonant of normal stem form	Other conditions	Normal stem form	English	Final letter(s) of *msf*	Examples		Examples	Stem ends	Examples
k,t[1]		-leka	leave	se	-lese	e→a[2]	-lesa		-lekesa
d,g,j[1]		-genda	go	ze	-genze	e→a[2]	-genza		-gendesa
l,r	Stem under 5 letters	-kola	work	ze	-koze		-koza		-kozesa
	Stem over 4 letters	-yingira	enter	dde	-yingidde	dda→za[2]	-yingiza		
b,m,n,p		-soma	see	ye	-somye	e→a[2]	-somya		-somesa
		-fumba	cook		-fumbye		-fumbya		-fumbisa
w	Non-passive verbs	-fuuwa	blow		-fuuye		-fuuya		-fuuyisa
	Passive verbs	-leetebwa	be brought	eddwa[3,5]	-leeteddwa			esa[3,7]	
		-salwa	be cut	iddwa[4,6]	-saliddwa			isa[4,7]	
y	Non-causative verbs	-zannya	play	e	-zannye				-zannyisa
y	Causative verbs (mostly)	-somya	cause to read	ezza[3]	-somezza				-somesa[8]
		-limya	cause to cultivate	izza[4]	-limizza				-limisa[8]
s		-sesa	make laugh		-sesezza				-sesesa
		-kisa	hide		-kisizza				-kisisa
z		-lowooza	think	zza[9]	-lowoozezza				-lowoozesa
		-buuza	ask		-buuzizza				-buuzisa
	rare form	-kkiriza	believe		-kkirizza				-kkirizisa

Some monosyllabic verbs are exceptions to the rules shown here, as are a few common verbs. Modified verb forms (*msf*) are irregular in: -kwata (-kutte), -manya (-manyi), -teeka (-teeka) and -twala (-tutte). The verb -teeka is exceptional in having two forms of *msf* (-takke, -teese).

1. If these letters are doubled (*eg.* kk, dd), then the s or z in the *msf* is also doubled, *eg.* the modified verb form of -yigga is -yizze.
2. The substitutions shown refer to the *msf*, not the normal stem form.
3. If the penultimate vowel is e or o.
4. If the penultimate vowel is a, i or u.
5. Occasionally ebbwa.
6. Occasionally ibbwa.
7. The second causative is formed by substituting esa or isa for the final a (of, variously, the normal stem form or the first causative).
8. The y's are lost through spelling change (N5).
9. Used for stems over two syllables and with short penultimate vowels.

The following interrogatives have plural forms or otherwise take concords:

- **kiki?** (*pl.* **biki?**) ('what is it?'), *eg.* **Kiki ekigudde?** ('What is it that's fallen?'). **baki?** means 'what sort of people are they?'.
- **ani?** (*pl.* **baani?**) ('who?', 'whom?'), *eg.* (1) **Omusawo y'ani?** ('Who is the doctor?'); (2) **Bo be baani?** ('Who are they?'). The words **y'** (= **ye**) and **be** in these examples are copulas (see under 'Pronouns' in Part 1 of the dictionary for an explanation of this term).
- (with numeral concord) **-meka?** ('how many?', 'how much?') (Table 6), *eg.* **emiti emeka?** ('how many trees?'). When **-meka?** qualifies **emirundi** ('times'), the meaning is 'how often?', *eg.* **Owuga emirundi emeka buli wiiki?** ('How often do you swim each week?').

The following interrogatives take concords prefixed to the possessive **-a** ('of') (**N11.1**):

- **-a ani?** ('whose?'), *eg.* **Ekitabo ky'ani?** ('Whose is the book?', *lit.* 'The book [is] of whom?').
- **-a wa?** ('from where?'), *eg.* **Abantu bano ba wa?** ('Where are these people from?').
- **-aki?** ('what for?'), *eg.* **Ennyumba eno yaaki?** ('What is this house for?'). Note that in this case the two parts of the construction (**-a** 'of' + **ki** 'what?') are combined into a single word. This interrogative can be found in adverbial as well as ordinary noun classes, *eg.* **Wano waaki?** ('What is this place for?'). **-aki?** in the *n11* adverbial noun class of cause means 'why?', *eg.* **Lwaki ozze?** ('Why have you come?'). **lwa nsonga ki?** also means 'why?' (or 'for what reason?'), *eg.* **Ozze lwa nsonga ki?** ('Why have you come?').

-tya? ('how?', 'what ... like?') is an interrogative verb found only in the present tense, *eg.* (1) **Akola atya?** ('How does he work?'); (2) **Ennyumba yali etya?** ('What was the house like?'). Responses to such questions are often based on the verbs **-ti** ('be this') or **-tyo** ('be that') often preceded by the conjunction **bwe** ('like') (**N26**), *eg.* (1) **Akola bw'ati.** ('He works like this.'); (2) **Akola bw'atyo.** ('He works like that.'). As with **-tya?**, **-ti** and **-tyo** are verbs found only in the present tense. **bwe -tyo** can sometimes alternatively be translated by the adverb 'likewise', *eg.* **Nnagenda e Kampala okulaba John ne Musoke by'atyo bwe yakola.** ('I went to Kampala to see John and Musoke did likewise.'). **bwe -tyo bwe -tyo** means 'so-so', *eg.* **Omulimu gwe gugenda gutya? Bwe gutyo bwe gutyo.** ('How is her work? So-so.'). **-tyanno** is an expanded version of **-tya?** only seen in greetings (**N28**), *eg.* **Osibye otyanno?** ('Good evening?', *lit.* 'How have you spent the day?').

The verb **-luwa?** (**-ruwa?** after **e** or **i** N5) means 'where is?', *eg.* **Embwa eruwa?** ('Where is the dog?'). **-luwa** can be broken down into **-li** ('be') + **wa?** ('where?'), with **u** replacing **i**.

The verb **-yenkana** ('be equal to') is frequently used in questions or answers concerning quantity, *eg.* **Emmotoka ye yenkana wa?** ('What size is his car?').

N14. VERBS: STEMS AND AFFIX ORDER

Verbs in Luganda are stems, normally with one or more affixes added. With few exceptions (*eg.* **-li**, **-linga**, **-tya**, **-ti**, **-tyo**), each verb has two forms of stem, a **NORMAL STEM FORM** and a **MODIFIED STEM FORM** (*msf*). Thus, the normal stem form of **okukola** ('to do') is **-kola** and the *msf* is **-koze**. Rules governing the formation of *msf* are given in Table 11. There are a few exceptions to these rules, especially in the case of monosyllabic verbs. Luganda verbs given as headwords in Part 2 of the dictionary have their *msf's* shown in brackets (see Figure 3), except where their constructions are obvious from neighbouring entries.

Tense/sense/form	Condition of verb	Affix[1]	Examples (mostly based on -kola 'work')		Comments
			THE SIX SIMPLE TENSES (N16)		
Present[2]	Normal stem form	none	nkola	I work	Habitual or always true
Perfect	Modified stem form	none	nkoze	I have worked	Just done or continuing state
Near past	Modified stem form	-a-	nnakoze	I worked	Within last 24 hours
Far past	Normal stem form	-a-	nnakola	I worked	Over 24 hours ago
Near future	normal stem form	-naa-	nnaakola	I shall work	Within next 24 hours
Far future	normal stem form	-li-	ndikola	I shall work	Over 24 hours in the future
			SUBJUNCTIVE AND IMPERATIVE (N17)		
Subjective	Present tense	-e	nkole	let me work	For more on uses, see N17
Imperative	Present tense	none	kola!	work!	Subjunctive used for plurals
			INFINITIVES (N18)		
Positive infinitive	Normal stem form	oku-	okukola	to work	Can act as a noun in n15 (N6)
Negative infinitive	Normal stem form	obuta-	obutakola	not to work	Can act as a noun in n14 (N6)
			FURTHER VERB TENSES, SENSES AND FORMS (N18)		
'just'	Normal stem form	-aka-	nnaakakola	I have just worked	See N20.3 for the use of these affixes in compound tenses
'would/should'	Modified stem form	-andi-	nnandikoze	I would work[3]	
'still'	Normal stem form	-kya-	nkyakola	I am still working	
'no longer'	Negative verb	-kya-	sikyakola	I no longer work	
'not yet'	Negative verb	-nna-	sinnakola	I have not yet worked	
'before'	Negative verb, after nga	-nna-	nga sinnakola	before I work	
Reflexive		-ee-	nneekoona	I knocked myself	

Table 12. Verb tenses, senses and forms.

1. All the affixes are prefixes to the verb, except for -e (subjunctive), which is a suffix.
2. Also used for the narrative tense, preceded by ne ('and') (N16).
3. Also means 'I would have worked'.

The order for placing affixes on verbs is as follows:

IV[1] - **negative**[2] - **subject**[2] - **tense** - **object**[3,4] - **verb stem**[5] - **sense**[6] - **place**[4]

1. An initial vowel is found with the subject relative (**N7.1**).
2. The subject comes before the negative with a subject relative (**N21**).
3. Some verbs can have two objects (**N15.1**).
4. 'Place' can be a subject, object or both in Luganda (**N24.2**). Place objects differ from normal objects in being suffixes rather than prefixes.
5. Normal or modified stem form.
6. Here, 'sense' refers to the suffixes associated with derived verbs (**N22**). The reflexive affix **-ee-** is exceptional in being a prefix rather than a suffix. It comes immediately before the verb stem (**N18**).

N15. SUBJECT AND OBJECT PRONOUNS AS AFFIXES ON VERBS

N15.1. PRONOMINAL PREFIXES
(ORDINARY NOUN CLASSES)

Pronominal concords (**N4**) provide the **SUBJECT AND OBJECT PRONOUNS** of verbs. They are listed by noun class in Column 9 of Table 1 and, for the personal cases ('I', 'me', *etc.*), in Columns 3 and 5 of Table 2. Sound and spelling change often occur (**N5**). The following examples illustrate the use of these prefixes:

- **Nkola.** ('I do.') = **n-** ('I') + **-kola** ('do').
- **Nkulaba.** ('I see you.') = **n-** ('I') + **ku-** ('you') + **-laba** ('see').
- **Mmulaba.** ('I see her.') = **n-** ('I', **n** becomes **m** before **m N5**) + **mu** ('you') + **-laba** ('see'),
- **Enjala ennuma.** ('I am hungry.'). Here the subject is **enjala** ('hunger'). **ennuma** can be broken down into **e-** (*n9* 'it', referring to **enjala**) + **n-** ('me') + **-luma** ('hurt'). The **l** of **-luma** is changed to **n** following the addition of the **n** (**N5**). **-luma** is an example of a verb in which the subject and object are interchanged compared to the English translation (such verbs are relatively few); in such cases the object in Luganda can be equivalent to an English possessive, *eg.* **Erinnyo linnuma**. ('My tooth is aching.').
- **Omusawo alaba ennyumba.** ('The doctor sees a house.') = **omusawo** ('doctor'), **a-** ('he'/'she', referring to the doctor) + **-laba** ('see') + **ennyumba** ('a house'). In this example, the object (**ennyumba**) follows the verb (**-laba**) and there is no object prefix on the verb.
- **Emmere agifumba.** ('She is cooking food.') = **emmere** ('food'), **a-** ('she') + **gi-** (*n9* 'it', concordant with **emmere**) + **-fumba** ('cook'). In this example, the object (**emmere**) precedes the verb (**-laba**) to provide emphasis. An object prefix (**gi-**) is placed on the verb in this case.
- **Kimuwe.** ('Give him it.') = **ki-** (*n7* 'it') + **mu-** ('him') + **-we** (imperative of **-wa** 'give' **N17**). This example has two objects, the second being an indirect object in English (*ie.* meaning 'to him'). In cases where there are two object prefixes, as here, then the personal concord is placed immediately before the verb. See under 'Verbs' in part 1 of the dictionary for an explanation of the difference between direct and indirect objects.

The subject prefix **ki-** (*n7*) is used for the impersonal 'it', *eg.* (1) **Kisoboka wano okutambulawo.** ('It is possible to walk here.'); (2) **Kyali kizibu okulowooza.** ('It was difficult to think.'). In the second example, **kyali** = **ki** ('it') + **-a-** (far past tense **N16**) + **-li** ('is'). The **i** on **ki-** is changed to **y** following the addition of **a** (**N5**).

Tense:	(Prefix)	Present	Perfect	Near past	Far past	Near future	Far future
TI:		None	None	-a-	-a-	-naa-[1]	-li-[2]
ST:		Normal	msf	msf	Normal	Normal	Normal

Example 1: -kola ('do') – a regular verb

I	n-	nkola	nkoze	nnakoze[3]	nnakola[3]	nnaakola[3]	ndikola[4]
You	o-	okola	okoze	wakoze	wakola	onookola[5]	olikola
(S)he	a-	akola	akoze	yakoze	yakola	anaakola	alikola
We	tu-	tukola	tukoze	twakoze	twakola	tunaakola	tulikola
You	mu-	mukola	mukoze	mwakoze	mwakola	munaakola	mulikola
They	ba-	bakola	bakoze	baakoze	baakola	banaakola	balikola

Example 2: -eekuba ('hit oneself') – an -e stem verb

I	n-	nneekuba[3]	nneekubye[3]	nneekubye[3]	nneekuba[3]	nneekuba[3,6]	ndyekuba[4]
You	o-	weekuba	weekubye	weekubye	weekuba	oneekuba	olyekuba
(S)he	a-	yeekuba	yeekubye	yeekubye	yeekuba	aneekuba	alyekuba
We	tu-	twekuba	twekubye	twekubye	twekuba	tuneekuba	tulyekuba
You	mu-	mwekuba	mwekubye	mwekubye	mwekuba	muneekuba	mulyekuba
They	ba-	beekuba	beekubye	beekubye	beekuba	baneekuba	balyekuba

Example 3: -yera ('sweep') – a -y stem verb liable to contraction

I	n-	njera	njeze[7]	nnayeze[3]	nnayera[3]	nnaayera[3]	ndyera[4]
You	o-	oyera	oyeze	wayeze	wayera	onooyera[5]	olyera
(S)he	a-	ayera	ayeze	yayeze	yayera	anaayera	alyera
We	tu-	twera	tweze	twayeze	twayera	tunaayera	tulyera
You	mu-	mwera	mweze	mwayeze	mwayera	munaayera	mulyera
They	ba-	beera	bayeze	baayeze	baayera	banaayera	balyera

Table 13. The six simple tenses, declined for the personal cases (**N16**).

[1] **-nee-** replaces **-naa-** when the subject is in noun class *n9*, *eg.* ente eneegenda ('the cow will go').
[2] **y** replaces **i** before a vowel (**N5**).   [3] **n** is doubled before **a** or **ee** (**N5**).   [4] **d** replaces **l** after **n** (**N5**).
[5] **-noo-** replaces **-naa-** following **o-**.   [6] Better to use nja kwekuba (**N19**), which avoids ambiguity about the tense.
[7] **j** replaces **y** after **n** (**N5**).

Abbreviations:
COLUMN 1: TI tense infix (**N16**). ST stem type (**N14**).
COLUMNS 4 and 5: *msf* modified stem form (**N14**).

N15.2. OBJECTS AND PREPOSITIONAL COMPLEMENTS

The following examples illustrate points of similarity and divergence between Luganda and English in the use of objects and prepositional complements. See under 'Verbs' in Part 1 of the dictionary for an explanation of 'prepositional complement'.

- **Nnima ennimiro n'enkumbi.** ('I am digging the garden with a hoe.'). In this case the grammar in Luganda and English is identical. The verbs in both languages have direct objects (**ennimiro**, 'garden'). Prepositional complements (**n'enkumbi**, 'with a hoe') are used in the same way.
- **Yakiwa Paulo.** ('He gave it to Paul.'). Here a direct object in Luganda (the noun **Paulo**) is replaced by a prepositional complement in English ('to Paul').
- **Yattibwa laddu.** ('He was killed by lightning.'). The verb here is passive (**-ttibwa**, 'be killed'). Passive verbs in English are often followed by prepositional complements headed by the preposition 'by', as here. There is no object. In contrast, passive verbs in Luganda can incorporate the preposition 'by' into their inherent meanings and are sometimes followed by direct objects. Passive verbs in Luganda form a category of derived verbs (**N22**), many of which incorporate prepositions into their inherent meanings.
- **Yamukaabira.** ('He cried for her.'). **-kaabira** ('cry for') is an example of a prepositional verb, another type of derived verb found in Luganda (**N22**). Note the replacement of the prepositional complement 'for her' in English by the object prefix **mu-** ('her') in Luganda.

N15.3. PRONOMINAL AFFIXES OF PLACE

The four subject prefixes of place are **wa-**, **e-**, **ku-** and **mu-** and the four object prefixes of place are the enclitics **-wo**, **-yo**, **-ku** and **-mu**. See **N20.4** for the use of these concords with the verb **-ba/-li** ('be'), **N24.2** for their use with other verbs and **N7.2** for their use in subject relatives. The following examples illustrate how these affixes can be equivalent to subject and object pronouns:

- (**wa-** as subject pronoun) **Nja kugenda ku dduuka nga waggule.** ('I will go the shop if it [*lit.* the place] is open.')
- (**-wo** as object pronoun) **Ndabyewo.** ('I have seen it there.')

N16. THE SIX SIMPLE TENSES AND THE NARRATIVE TENSE

There are six simple tenses, based variously on either the normal or modified stem forms of the verb (**N14**) (Table 12). Most tenses have distinctive tense prefixes (infixes). Table 13 shows examples of these tenses, declined for the personal cases. The examples given include a regular verb (**-kola**), an **-e** stem verb (**-eekuba**) and a **-y** stem verb liable to contraction (**-yera**). Verbs with stems beginning **e** or **y** show spelling change on the addition of certain prefixes (**N5**). The six simple tenses are:

- **PRESENT TENSE**, *eg.* **Nkola.** ('I work.'). The present is used for things that are habitual or always true. It is sometimes used for near future events, *eg.* **Okomawo ddi?** ('When are you coming back?').
- **PERFECT TENSE**, *eg.* **Nkoze.** ('I have worked.'). This is used when an action has just taken place or has caused a state of affairs that is continuing. It is sometimes used when the present tense would be used in English, *eg.* (1) **Mmanyi.** ('I know.'); (2) **Ndwadde.** ('I am ill.'); (3) **Ntudde.** ('I am sitting,', in the sense of 'I am seated.'). For comparison, note that **Ntuula.** (in the present tense) is also translatable as 'I am sitting.', but in the sense of 'I am in the process of sitting down.'). The perfect tense is sometimes used to express a complement, *eg.* **Otuyambye!** ('You have helped us!').
- **NEAR PAST TENSE**, *eg.* **Nnakoze.** ('I worked.') – referring to a time within about the last 24 hours.
- **FAR PAST TENSE**, *eg.* **Nnakola.** ('I worked.') – referring to a time more than about 24 hours ago.
- **NEAR FUTURE TENSE**, *eg.* **Nnaakola.** ('I shall work.') – referring to a time within about the next 24 hours.
- **FAR FUTURE TENSE**, *eg.* **Ndikola** ('I shall work.') – referring to a time more than about 24 hours into the future.

Spelling note: Verbs whose stems begin with double consonants cause exceptional spellings in some cases. This is because a double vowel is never written before a double consonant (**N1**). For example, with the verb **-ggula** ('open'), **baggula** means both 'they open' (present tense) and 'they opened' (far past tense), while **Nnaggulawo oluggi.** means both 'I opened the door.' (far past tense) and 'I will open the door.' (near future tense).

NARRATIVE TENSE.

NARRATIVE TENSE. This is used to describe a sequence of events often (but not necessarily) in the past. The first verb in the sequence is placed in the tense of the events and the rest in the narrative. The narrative tense is spelt in the same way as the present tense, the verbs in the sequence being connected to one another by the conjunction **ne** ('and'), *eg.* **Nnagenda eka ne nfumba ne ndya.** ('I went home, cooked and ate.'). For the negative narrative, see **N21**. The verb **-lyoka** is sometimes found as an auxiliary (**N19**) following the final **ne**. It carries the meaning 'and then', *eg.* **Nnagenda eka ne ndya ne ndyoka nneebaka.** ('I went home, ate and then slept.').

The use of the narrative tense sometimes conveys special meanings, for example:

- **-gira** followed by the narrative means 'now and then', *eg.* **Musoke agira n'ajja wano.** ('Musoke comes here now and then.').
- **-lyoka** followed by the narrative means 'be good that' or 'be advantageous that', *eg.* **Yalyoka n'ayogera.** ('It was a good that he spoke.').
- **-mala** followed by the narrative (with the verb in the positive), means 'do eventually' or 'decide to anyway', *eg.* (1) **Amaze n'atuuka.** ('He eventually arrived.'); (2) **Amaze n'agenda.** ('He decided to go anyway.').
- **-mala** followed by the narrative (with the verb in the negative) means 'in fact' or 'changed one's mind', *eg.* (1) **Amaze n'atagenda ku mbaga.** ('In fact he did not go to the wedding.'); (2) **Mmaze ne sigenda.** ('I have changed my mind and am not going.').

N17. SUBJUNCTIVE AND IMPERATIVE

There is only one **SUBJUNCTIVE TENSE**, based on the present tense but with the final **a** changed to **e**, *eg.* **Nkole.** ('Let me work.'), from **nkola** ('I work'). The singular **IMPERATIVE** is the normal verb stem, *eg.* **Kola!** ('Work!'), from the stem **-kola**. The final **a** changes to **e** if there is an object, *eg.* **Kikole!** ('Do it!'), unless the object is the 1st person singular, *eg.* **Mbuulira!** ('Tell me!'). For the negative subjunctive, see **N21**.

The subjunctive is used to convey an imperative: (1) with all plurals, *eg.* **Mukole!** ('Work!'); (2) with **-e** stem verbs, *eg.* **Weebake!** ('Go to sleep!'); (3) when a command refers to someone or something else (the subject is omitted in this case), *eg.* (1) **Mugambe!** ('Tell him!'); (2) **Kifune** ('Get it!').

The subjunctive is used for the second of two linked verbs: (1) to express purpose or reason, *eg.* **Nnafumba emmere mulye.** ('I cooked the food so that you can eat.'); (2) when there are two linked commands, *eg.* **Genda ofumbe.** ('Go and cook.'); (3) after verbs of telling, commanding or allowing, *eg.* **Ndeka nsome.** ('Please, leave me to study.'); (4) with the verbs **-saana** or **-gwana** ('be suitable'), to convey a sense of obligation, *eg.* **Osaana oyambe ku mirimu.** ('It would be good if you helped with the work.'); (5) with the verb **-sooka** ('be first'), to tell someone what to do first, *eg.* **Sooka olime.** ('First do the digging.'). The auxiliary verb **-lyoka** is sometimes included as an additional verb in the subjunctive to indicate a desired outcome, *eg.* **Yajja alyoke ayogere.** ('He came so that he could talk.').

The subjunctive is used for both of two linked verbs: (1) when suggesting what to do, *eg.* **Tugende tukole.** ('Let's go and work.'); (2) when a second command refers to someone else, *eg.* **Mugambe afumbe.** ('Tell him to cook.'); (3) with the verb with the verb **-sooka**, to describe a task that will be done first, *eg.* **Nsooke nnime.** ('First, I'll do the digging.').

The following words followed by the subjunctive have special meanings: (1) **gira** (*pl.* **mugire**), to convey a sense of needing to get on with something, *eg.* **Gira tugende.** ('Come on, let's go.'); (2) **ka**, to indicate the intention of doing something in the near future, *eg.* **Ka nsome.** ('I am going to read.' or 'Let me read.'); (3) **kata** (or **katono**), to indicate 'almost' or 'nearly', *eg.* **Kata nkisuule.** ('I almost dropped it.') (the English translation is usually in the past tense). The verb **-gidde** (used only in the present tense) means 'since', in the sense of enabling a person to get on with something, *eg.* **Agidde ajje, gira ka twogere ku ky'okugula ettaka.** ('Since he has come, let's talk about buying the land.').

N18. FURTHER VERB TENSES, SENSES AND FORMS

There are various other verb tenses, senses and forms, additional to the six simple tenses and the narrative tense (**N16**), and the subjunctive and imperative (**N17**). Table 12 provides a summary.

The (positive) **INFINITIVE** prefix is **ku-**, *eg.* **okukola** ('to work'), and the **NEGATIVE INFINITIVE** prefix is **buta-**, *eg.* **obutakola** ('not to work'). These examples are shown with initial vowels (**o-** in both cases). Infinitives can sometimes act as nouns, as shown by their abilities to induce concordance (**N4**). Their noun classes are *n15* and *n14* respectively.

The following tenses have their own prefixes (infixes), placed immediately after the subject prefix. See **N20.1** and **N20.3** for additional information on these tenses. The tense infixes are underlined in the following examples:

1. The **'JUST'** or **'SO FAR' TENSE** has the infix **-aka-**, *eg.* (1) **Yaakatuuka.** ('He has just arrived.'); (2) **Nnaakalongoosa ebisenge bibiri.** ('I have so far cleaned two rooms.').

2. The **'WOULD'**, **'SHOULD'** or **CONDITIONAL TENSE** has the infix **-andi-** and uses the modified stem form, *eg.* **Nnandiyagadde okumulaba.**, which means both (1) 'I would like to see him.' (*ie.* in the future) and (2) 'I would have liked to see him.' (*ie.* in the past). **-andi-** can occur in either or both parts of a conditional sentence, the word 'if' being translated by **singa**, *eg.* **Singa yalima ennimiro ye, yandifunye emmere.** ('If he had cultivated his garden, he would have got food.').

3. The **'STILL' TENSE** has the infix **-kya-**, *eg.* **Akyasoma.** ('He is still studying.'). **-kya** with a negative verb (**N21**) means 'no longer', *eg.* **Takyasoma.** ('He no longer studies.').

4. The **'NOT YET' TENSE** has the infix **-nna-**, the verb being in the negative (**N21**), *eg.* **Tannasoma ekitabo kino.** ('He has not yet read this book.'). If **nga** is present before the verb, then the conjunction 'before' or 'until' is indicated, *eg.* (1) **Tojja nga sinnakugamba.** ('Don't come before I tell you.'); (2) **Omuntu nga tannafuna maka, takula.** ('Until a man has acquired his own home, he is not fully grown up.')

The **REFLEXIVE** is marked by the infix **-ee-** placed immediately before the verb, *eg.* **Yeekuba.** ('He hit himself.'), where **yeekuba** can be broken down into **a-** ('he') + **-ee-** (reflexive) + **-kuba** ('hit') (note that **a** changes to **y** before a vowel **N5**). Table 13 shows the declination of a reflexive verb (**-eekuba** 'hit oneself') for the personal cases. Note that the verb stem is contracted with one **e** being lost after a double consonant ending in **w** or **y** (**N1**); for example, **Twekuba.** ('We are hitting ourselves.'), which can be broken down into **tu-** ('we') + **-ee-** (reflexive) + **-kuba** ('hit') (**tu-** becomes **tw-** before a vowel **N5**). While most **-e** stem verbs are derived from simpler verbs, there are some that exist only in the reflexive, lacking known simpler non-reflexive verbs from which they have been derived, *eg.* **-eebaka** ('sleep'). Some of these verbs lack obviously reflexive meanings from the perspective of the English language. There are some verbs where the use of the reflexive changes the meaning from transitive to intransitive, *eg.* **-tugga** ('knot'), **-eetugga** ('become knotted').

THE ADDITION OF THE SUFFIX -NGA to a verb gives tenses or senses that can indicate habitual or repetitive action. The following provide examples (verb used = **-kola** 'work'): (1) **Kolanga nnyo.** ('Always work hard.'); (2) **Sikolanga.** ('I never worked.'); (3) **Nnakolanga.** ('I used to work.'); (4) **Nnaakolanga.** ('I shall always work.'). See also **-linga** in **N20.1**.

Present[1]	Perfect[1]	Near past[1]	Far past[1]	Near future[1]	Far future[1]
SUBJECT IN ORDINARY NOUN CLASS[2]					
-ba/-li AS A SIMPLE VERB					
ali	abadde	yabadde	yali	anaaba	aliba
'he is'[3]	'he has been'	'he was'		'he will be'	
tali	tabadde	teyabadde	teyali	taabe	taliba
'he is not'	'he has not been'	'he was not'		'he will not be'	
-ba/-li IN COMPOUND TENSES					
aba ali[4]	abadde ali	yabadde ali	yabanga ali	anaaba ali	aliba ali
'he is'	'he has been'	'he was'		'he will be'	
aba akola[5]	abadde akola	yabadde akola	yali akola	anaaba akola	aliba akola
'he is working'	'he has been working'	'he was working'		'he will be working'	
SUBJECT IN PLACE NOUN CLASS[6]					
-ba/-li AS A SIMPLE VERB					
waliwo	wabaddewo	waabaddewo	waaliwo	wanaabaawo	walibaawo[7]
'there is/are'	'there has/have been'	'there was/were'		'there will be'	
tewali(wo)[7]	tewabadde(ewo)[7]	tewaabadde(wo)[7]	tewaali(wo)[7]	tewaabe(ewo)[7]	tewaliba(awo)[7]
'there is/are not'	'there has/have not been'	'there was/were not'		'there will not be'	
RELATIVE CLAUSES					
awali	awabadde	awaabadde	awaali	awanaaba	awaliba
'where there is/are'	'where there has/have been'	'where there was/were'		'where there will be'	
awatali	awatabadde	awataabadde	awataali	awataabe	awataliba
'where there is/are not'	'where there has/have not been'	'where there was/were not'		'where there will not be'	
-ba/-li IN COMPOUND TENSES					
wali waliwo	wabadde waliwo	waabadde waliwo	waali waliwo	wanaaba waliwo	waliba waliwo
'there is/are'	'there has/have been'	'there was/were'		'there will be'	

Table 14. Examples of the use of the verb -ba/-li ('be') (N20).

1. Indicates tense of auxiliary verb in the case of compound verbs.
2. The example taken is the third person singular personal case ('he/she').
3. For 'he', read 'he or she' throughout.
4. This combination of two present tenses can mean 'happens to be', eg **Bw'aba akola, mugambe ayimirize.** ('If he happens to be working, tell him to stop.')
5. Indicates a sense of apology or doubt as to how the statement will be received, ie 'He has been working.' – but maybe he should not have been.
6. **wa** adverbial noun class used in these examples.
7. The suffixes in brackets are added with certain uses.

398

N19. AUXILIARY VERBS

An auxiliary verb is one associated with a main verb, giving a new or modified meaning. See **N20.3** for the use of **-ba/-li** ('be') as an auxiliary verb.

There are many verbs that can act as auxiliaries coming <u>before</u> main verbs in the infinitive, among them:

- **-lina** to convey a sense of obligation ('have to'), *eg.* **Mulina okuva mu kisenge essaawa nnya.** ('You have to vacate the room by ten o' clock'.).

- **-genda**, meaning 'going to be' or 'be about to' in the immediate future, *eg.* **Ŋenda okufumba.** ('I am about to cook.').

- **-jja**, meaning 'going to' or 'will' in the near future (within about 24 hours), *eg.* **Ajja kukola olweggulo.** ('She will work in the afternoon.'). When **-jja** is used as an auxiliary verb, its first person singular in the present tense is **nja** (not **nzija** as otherwise).

- **-lekera awo** (or **-lekeraawo**) meaning 'stop doing' or 'discontinue', *eg.* **Yalekera awo okuyimba mu kwaya.** ('She has stopped singing in the choir.').

- **-mala**, to convey the idea of an action completed, or equivalent to the adverb 'already' or (if preceded by **nga**) the conjunction 'after', *eg.* (1) **Mmaze okulya.** ('I have already eaten.'); (2) **Nga mmaze okulya, nja kugenda.** ('After eating, I will leave.').

- **-sooka**, meaning 'first' or 'do first', *eg.* **Twasooka kulya ne tugenda okukola.** ('First we ate and then we went to work.').

- **-teekwa**, meaning 'must', *eg.* **Oteekwa okugenda okuyamba.** ('You must go and help.').

- **-tera**, meaning (1) (in present tense) 'do usually' or 'do habitually', *eg.* **Ntera okufumba.** ('I usually cook.'); (2) (in near future tense) 'be about to', *eg.* **Nnaatera okwogera.** ('I am about to speak.'), or equivalent to the adverbs 'usually', 'almost', 'nearly' or 'soon', *eg.* **Nnaatera okumala.** ('I have almost finished.').

- **-va**, to denote an action just performed, *eg.* **Nva kukola.** ('I have just been working.'). See **N10.2** for the use of **-va** as an auxiliary verb attached to **kye** (**kye...-va**) meaning 'therefore'.

- **-yagala** means 'be about to', or 'be likely to', *eg.* **Enkuba eyagala kutonnya.** ('It is about to rain.').

-mala followed by a main verb with the prefix **ga-** conveys the idea of (1) inevitability or obligation, *eg.* **Nnamala galya.** ('I ate.' – even though I had no interest in doing so); or (2) acting carelessly, *eg.* **Yamala gayogera.** ('He spoke without thinking.').

There is a category of auxiliary verbs that come <u>after</u> main verbs, modifying their meanings. The main verb can be in any tense, but the auxiliary is always in the present. These auxiliary verbs are sometimes equivalent to English adverbs. Examples: (1) **Atambula azunga.** ('He is staggering.'); (2) **Baatambula basooba.** ('They walked very slowly.'); (3) **Yagenda ayagala.** ('He went willingly.'); (4) **Twakoze tupapa.** ('We worked hastily.'); (5) **Yayogera awoggana.** ('She spoke loudly.').

N20. THE VERBS 'BE' AND 'HAVE'

N20.1. -ba/-li AS A SIMPLE VERB
(SUBJECT IN AN ORDINARY NOUN CLASS)

The verb 'be' has two stems, **-ba** and **-li** (becoming **-ri** after **e** or **i** N5) (Table 14). Only **-ba** has a modified stem form (**-badde**). **-ba** has a prepositional form (**N22**) **-beera**, meaning 'be/live at', *eg.* **Mbeera Makindye.** ('I live at Makindye.'), and some other derived forms, *eg.* **-beerera**, **-beeza**).

-li is the verb usually used for the present and far past tenses and also occurs in the 'still' tense (**N18**), *eg.* (1) (present tense) **Ali wano.** ('She is here.'); (2) (far past tense) **Yali wano.** ('She was here.'); (3) ('still' tense) **Akyali wano.** ('She is still here.'). **-li** with suffix **-nga** means 'seem', 'be likely', 'maybe' or 'probably' *eg.* **Alinga alwadde.** ('She seems ill.'). **-li** can be used to describe a condition, *eg.* **Ali lubuto.** ('She is pregnant.'), though the verb is sometimes omitted, *eg.* (1) **Omusawo mulungi.** ('The doctor is good.', *lit.* 'The doctor [is – understood] good.'); (2) **Olugoye lwa kiragala.** ('The dress is green.', *lit.* 'The dress [is – understood] of green.'). Initial vowels are omitted from the words immediately following 'be' if the verb is omitted (that is, from **mulungi** and **lwa** in the last examples).

-ba is found in all six simple tenses (**N16**) and in the special tenses 'just', 'would' and 'not yet' (**N18**).

The use of **-ba** rather than **-li** in the present and far past tenses is exceptional. It implies that something is usually done or is habitual, *eg.* **Abagenyi bwe baba wano, tubawa ebyokunywa.** ('When guests are here, we give them drinks.'). **-ba** in the far past tense requires the suffix **-nga**, *eg.* **Yabanga mu dduuka.** ('He was usually in the shop.').

N20.2. 'HAVE'

The addition of the suffix **-na** ('with') to **-li** gives a verb meaning 'have' in the sense of ownership or long-term association, *eg.* **Alina abaana babiri.** ('She has two children.'. *ie.* referring to the number that she has given birth to). **na** is also found with **-ba**, but as a separate word, *eg.* **Yabadde n'abaana babiri.** ('She had two children.'). If **na** is used as a separate word with **-li**, then the reference is to a situation at a particular time, *eg.* **Ani ali n'abaana?** ('Who has the children?' – meaning 'Who is with the children at this time?').

The addition of the enclitics **-ko** ('on there') or **-mu** ('in there') (**N24.2**) to **-li** gives verbs meaning 'have' in the sense of 'have on top' (**-ko**) or 'contain' (**-mu**), *eg.* (1) **Entebe eriko omutto.** ('The chair has a cushion.'); (2) **Ekikopo kirimu amazzi.** ('The cup has water.'). If **ku** or **mu** are used, but not attached to **-li**, then the meaning is different, *eg.* **Ekikopo kiri mu mazzi.** ('The cup is in the water.'). See **N20.4** for more on the use of **-ba/-li** with **-ko** and **-mu**.

N20.3. -ba/-li AS AN AUXILIARY VERB
(SUBJECT IN AN ORDINARY NOUN CLASS)

-ba/-li can act as an auxiliary verb (**N19**), forming a range of **COMPOUND TENSES** (Table 14). The subject prefix is present on both verbs. Generally, **-ba** is the stem used, except with the far past tense when it is **-li**. **-ba** is further found as an auxiliary in the 'not yet' and 'would' tenses (**N18**).

The main verb is only found in the present and perfect tenses or in the special tenses 'just', 'still' and 'not yet' (**N18**). **-li** (but not **-ba**) can be used as a main verb, but only in the present tense.

The general principle regarding **CHOICE OF TENSE** with compound tenses is that the tense of the auxiliary shows the time of an event or situation and that of the main verb what was happening at that time.

The following are examples of the use of **-ba/-li** as an auxiliary verb:

- **Leero abadde akola.** ('He has been working today.').
- **Ku ssaawa bbiri yabadde akola mu nnyumba.** ('He was working in the house at 8 o' clock.').
- **Jjo yali akola mu nnyumba.** ('He was working in the house yesterday.').
- **Enkya anaaba akola mu nnyumba.** ('Tomorrow he will be working in the house.').

HABITUAL ACTIONS

- **Ku ssaawa ettaano aba ali mu katale.** ('He is in the market at 11 o' clock.').
- **Ku ssaawa ettaano aba agenda mu katale.** ('He goes to the market at 11 o' clock.').
- **Ku ssaawa ettaano yabanga ali mu katale.** ('He used to be in the market at 11 o' clock.').
- **Ku ssaawa ettaano yabanga agenda mu katale.** ('He used to go to the market at 11 o' clock.').

- **Abadde yaakakola omulimu ogwo.** ('He has just done that job.'). ('just' tense)
- **Ku ssaawa emu yali akyakola.** ('He was still working at 7 o' clock.'). ('still' tense)
- **Yali tannasoma kitabo kino.** ('He had not yet read this book.'). ('not yet' tense)
- **Singa mbadde mmanyi, nnandigenze okumulaba.** ('If I had known, I would have gone to see her.'). ('would' tense)

N20.4. -ba/-li WITH PRONOMINAL AFFIXES OF PLACE

The four subject affixes of place are the prefixes **wa-**, **e-**, **ku-** and **mu-** and the four object affixes of place (**ENCLITICS**) are the suffixes **-wo**, **-yo**, **-ko** and **-mu**. More information on these affixes is given elsewhere, especially in **N24.2**, **N7.2** (subject relatives) and **N20.2** ('have').

When the pronominal affixes of place are used in combination with **-ba/-li**, the resulting words are equivalent in English to phrases such as 'there are', 'there will be', *etc.*, for example:

- **Waaliwo abantu bangi mu kkanisa.** ('There were many people in church.'). An alternative way of saying the same thing, using **-li** as both auxiliary and main verb is **Waali waliwo abantu bangi mu kkanisa.** ('There were many people in church.').
- **Leero e Kampala eriyo abantu bangi.** ('There are many people in Kampala today.').
- **Ku mmeeza kwaliko galubindi zange.** ('My glasses were on the table.') (**ku = kw** before a vowel **N5**).
- **Mu kisenge mulimu entebe nnyingi.** ('There are many chairs in the room.').

The **NEGATIVE EQUIVALENTS** of expressions such as 'there are', 'there will be', *etc.* take the prefix **te-** (**N21**) and lack place objects. For instance, the negatives of the four examples above are as follows (note that the initial vowels of the nouns that follow are dropped **N3**):

- **Tewaali bantu bangi mu kkanisa.** ('There were not many people in church.').
- **Leero e Kampala teri bantu bangi.** ('There are not many people in Kampala today.').
- **Ku mmeeza tekwali galubindi zange.** ('My glasses were not on the table.').
- **Mu kisenge temuli ntebe nnyingi.** ('There are not many chairs in the room.').

-beera (rather than **-ba/-li**) is used with paired enclitics when referring to something habitual, *eg.*:

- **Bulijjo wabeerawo omuntu akuuma ennyumba.** ('Usually there is someone guarding the house.')
- (negative) **Ku Ssande tewabeerawo muntu akuuma nnyumba.** ('On Sundays there is no-one guarding the house.')

A **QUESTION** such as **Engoye ziri wano?** ('Are the clothes here?') can be answered affirmatively by **Ziri wano.** ('Yes.', *lit.* 'They are here.') and negatively by **Teziriiwo.** ('No.', *lit.* 'They are not here.'). A place object (**-wo**) is used in the latter case and the vowel of the verb **-li** is doubled. Greater prominence can be given to place in an affirmative response by adding an adverb of emphasis (**N10.2**), *eg.* **We ziri.** ('Yes.', *lit.* 'It is here that they are.'). Grammatically, the adverb of emphasis (**we** in this case) is a proclitic (see under 'Adverbs' in Part 1 of the dictionary for an explanation of this term).

The addition of the enclitic **-wo** to **-ba/-li**, together with the prefix **eki-** (*pl.* **ebi-**), gives nouns meaning 'a happening' or 'event'. This is an example of a noun that can be placed in different tenses according to the time of the event (**N6**), *eg.* **ekiriwo** ('event' – happening now), **ekibaddewo** ('event' – near past), **ekyaliwo** ('event' – far past), **ekinaabaawo** ('event' – near future) and **ekiribaawo** ('event' – far future).

Table 15. The negatives of the six simple verb tenses, declined for the personal cases (N21).

TI:		None	None	-a-		none	-li-
ST:		Normal	msf	msf	Normal	Normal	Normal
		Example 1: -kola ('do') – a regular verb					
I	si-	sikola	sikoze	saakoze	saakola	siikole	sirikola
You	to-	tokola	tokoze	tewakoze	tewakola	tookole	tolikola
(S)he	ta-	takola	takoze	teyakoze	teyakola	taakole	talikola
We	tetu-	tetukola	tetukoze	tetwakoze	tetwakola	tetuukole	tetulikola
You	temu-	temukola	temukoze	temwakoze	temwakola	temuukole	temulikola
They	teba-	tebakola	tebakoze	tebaakoze	tebaakola	tebaakole	tebalikola
		Example 2: -eekuba ('hit oneself') – an -e stem verb					
I	si-	seekuba	seekubye	seekubye	seekuba	seekube	siyekuba
You	to-	teweekuba	teweekubye	teweekubye	teweekuba	teweekube	tolyekuba
(S)he	ta-	teyeekuba	teyeekubye	teyeekubye	teyeekuba	teyeekube	talyekuba
We	tetu-	tetwekuba	tetwekubye	tetwekubye	tetwekuba	tetwekube	tetulyekuba
You	temu-	temwekuba	temwekubye	temwekubye	temwekuba	temwekube	temulyekuba
They	teba-	tebeekuba	tebeekubye	tebeekubye	tebeekuba	tebeekube	tebalyekuba
		Example 3: -yera ('sweep') – a -y stem verb liable to contraction					
I	si-	siyera	siyeze	saayeze	saayera	siiyere	siriyera[1]
You	to-	toyera	toyeze	tewayeze	tewayera	tooyere	toliyera[1]
(S)he	ta-	tayera	tayeze	teyayeze	teyayera	taayere	taliyera[1]
We	tetu-	tetuyera	tetuyeze	tetwayeze	tetwayera	tetwayere	tetuliyera[1]
You	temu-	temuyera	temuyeze	temwayeze	temwayera	temwayere	temuliyera[1]
They	teba-	tebayera	tebayeze	tebaayeze	tebaayera	tebaayere	tebaliyera[1]

1. **Siryera, tolyera, talyera, tetulyera, temulyera and tebalyera** are also used.

Abbreviations:
COLUMN 1: TI tense infix (N16), ST stem type (N14).
COLUMNS 4 and 5: *msf* modified stem form (N14).

402

N21. NEGATIVES

The negative is usually formed by adding the prefix **te-** to the verb, *eg.* (1) **Tetukola.** ('We are not working.'); (2) **Ebitabo tebiri ku mmeeza.** ('The books are not on the table.'); (3) **Mu kyalo temuli bantu bangi.** ('There are not many people in the village.'). The verbs in these examples can be broken down into (1) **te-** ('not') + **tu-** ('we') + **-kola** ('work'); (2) **te-** ('not') + **bi-** ('they', concordant with **ebitabo**) + **-li** ('are') (= **-ri** after **i N5**); (3) **te-** ('not') + **mu-** (place subject **N24.2**) + **-li** ('is').

The prefix for the first person singular is **si-**, *eg.* **Sikola.** ('I am not working.'). **si**, as a freestanding word, is used for the negative copula, *eg.* **Si nsonga.** ('It is not a problem.') (see under 'Pronouns' in Part 1 of the dictionary for an explanation of the term 'copula'). In the case of compound tenses (**N20.3**), the negative prefix is placed on the main (not auxiliary) verb, *eg.* **Twali tetukola.** ('We were not working.').

SOUND AND SPELLING CHANGE often occurs (**N5**), *eg.* (1) **Takola.** ('He is not working.'), from **te-** ('not') + **a-** ('he') + **-kola** ('work'); (2) **Saakola.** ('I did not work.'), from **si-** ('I not') + **-a-** (past tense) + **-kola** ('work'); (3) **Saagala.** ('I do not like.'), from **si-** ('I not') + **-yagala** ('like'). See Table 14 for examples of negatives with the verb **-ba/-li**. Note that, when an enclitic is added, the vowel before the enclitic is usually doubled, *eg.* **tewaliimu** ('there is/are not') – not **tewalimu**.

Table 15 shows examples of the six simple tenses declined in the negative for the personal cases. The examples given include a regular verb (**-kola**), an **-e** stem verb (**-eekuba**) and a **-y** stem verb liable to contraction (**-yera**). Note that the present and far past tense of **-e** stem verbs are spelt identically, as are the perfect and near past.

The **NEGATIVE OF THE NEAR FUTURE TENSE** is exceptional. There is no tense infix. Instead, the negative present tense is used, the vowel of the subject prefix being doubled and the final **a** of the stem being replaced by **e**, *eg.* **Tekiikole.** ('It will not work.'). The same construction forms the **NEGATIVE SUBJUNCTIVE** when used to ask a question, *eg.* **Tetuusome?** ('Shall we not read?'). Otherwise, the negative subjunctive is expressed through using **-lema** ('fail') as an auxiliary verb in the (positive) subjunctive (**N17**) followed by a main verb in the infinitive, *eg.* **Kwata omuggo oleme kugwa.** ('Hold the stick so that you do not fall.').

The **PREFIX -ta-** forms the negative in several contexts:

- To form the negatives of subject relatives (**N7.1**), *eg.* **omuntu atakola** ('a person who does not work'). Subject relative clauses in the negative can sometimes be equivalent to English adjectives, *eg.* **abantu abatamanyiddwa** ('unknown people', *lit.* 'people who are not known'). The negatives of subject relative clauses in the place noun classes can mean 'without' (**N7.2**), *eg.* **Njagala caayi omutali sukaali.** ('I want tea without sugar.').
- To form the negatives of object relatives (**N10.1**), **engoye z'atayambala** ('the clothes which she is not wearing'). The first person singular is exceptional in using the prefix **si-**, *eg.* **omulimu gwe sikola** ('the job which I am not doing').
- To form the negative of the narrative tense (**N16**), **Baababuuza ne bataddamu.** ('They questioned them, but they did not answer.').
- To form the negative infinitive (**N18**), *eg.* **obutayinza** ('not to be able'). These words are sometimes equivalent to English abstract nouns, *eg.* 'inability' in this case.

Table 16. Formation of commoner types of derived verbs (N20) based on suffixes. For causative verbs, see Table 11.

Type of derived verb	Second last vowel of simple verb[2]	Simple verb	English	Suffix of derived verb[1]	Derived verb	English
DERIVED VERBS BASED ON SIMPLER VERBS						
Associative		-kuba	hit	-agana, -ana, -aŋŋana[3]	-kubagana	hit one another
		-yagala	love		-yagalana	love one another
		-tta	kill		-ttaŋŋana	kill one another
Causative				See Table 11		
Conversive		-simba	plant	-ola, -ula, -olokoka, etc.	-simbula	uproot
		-ggala	close		-ggula	open
		-vuunula	turn right way up		-vuunika	turn upside down
		-sumulula	open		-sumulukuka	become opened
Intensive	e, o	-wa	give	-ereza	-weereza	serve
	a, i, u	-mala	finish	-iriza	-maliriza	finish completely
Passive	e, o	-loga	bewitch	-ebwa[4]	-logebwa	be bewitched
	a, i, u	-kuba	hit	-ibwa[4]	-kubibwa	be hit
		-buulira	tell	-wa[4]	-buulirwa	be told
Prepositional	e, o	-kola	work	-era	-kolera	work for
	a, i, u	-laba	see	-ira	-labira	see for
Double prepositional	e, o	-genda	go	-erera	-genderera	intend
	a, i, u	-laga	show	-irira	-lagirira	instruct
Stative	e, o	-kola	do	-eka	-koleka	be doable
	a, i, u	-zimba	build	-ika	-zimbika	be buildable
DERIVED VERBS BASED ON ADJECTIVES		Adjective	English			English
Inceptive		-yavu	poor	-wala	-yavuwala	become poor
		-tono	small	-wa	-toniwa	diminish

1. The suffixes shown replace the final vowel of the verb, *eg.* the **a** of **-kuba**.
2. For example, this vowel is **u** in the case of **-kuba**.
3. **-aŋŋana** replaces **-agana** when the last consonant of the simple verb is **g** or the verb is monosyllabic.
4. **-ebwa** and **-ibwa** are the usual suffixes used for the passive. **-wa** is less common.

- In negative phrases following the conjunction **bwe** meaning 'if' or 'since', *eg.* **Ebbaasi bw'etazze, tugendere mu takisi.** ('Since the bus did not come, let us go by taxi.').

N22. DERIVED VERBS

Derived verbs are new verbs derived from simpler verbs through the addition or substitution of letters. They usually carry meanings related to those of the simpler verbs. See under 'Verbs' in Part 1 of the dictionary for information on derived verbs in English. Apart from reflexive verbs (**N18**) and reduplicative verbs (**N23**), derived verbs in Luganda involve modification to the ends of simpler verbs, *eg.* the simple verb **-manya** ('know') is the starting point for the derived verbs **-manyisa** ('make known' or 'inform') and **-manyika** ('be knowable') (Figure 1). **-isa** and **-ika** are suffixes (**N2**) added to a simple verb in these examples. Several suffixes have alternative spellings depending on whether the last but one vowel of the simple verb is **a**, **i** or **u** (*eg.* -l<u>a</u>ba) or **e** or **o** (*eg.* -s<u>o</u>ma) (see Table 16). More than one suffix can be present, *eg.* **-labirira** ('look after') (= **-laba** + **-ira** + **-ira**). There is an order to the addition of suffixes. For instance, the causative suffix is always added after the prepositional, not the other way round. Some further rules governing the formation of derived verbs are given on Tables 16 and 11 (for causative verbs).

The following are commoner types of derived verbs based on suffixes:

ASSOCIATIVE VERBS denote reciprocity (*eg.* **-yagalana** 'love one another') or some other aspect of association. **-yagalana** is formed from the simple verb **-yagala** ('love') plus the associative suffix **-ana**. Associative verbs can be derived from prepositional or causative verbs, *eg.* **-liisagana** ('feed one another'), which is formed from the causative verb **-liisa** ('feed') with the associative suffix **-agana**. **-liisa** is derived from the simple verb **-lya** ('eat').

CAUSATIVE VERBS. There are two types of causative verbs, known as first and second causatives, the former being generally formed by replacing the final **e** of the modified stem form by **a** and the latter by replacing the final **a** of the first causative or of the simple verb by **-esa** or **-isa** (Table 11). Depending on the verb, the causative can mean either or both of 'cause to do' or 'do with', *eg.* (1) **Aliisa omwana.** ('She is feeding the baby.'); (2) **Aliisa kijiiko.** ('She is eating with a spoon.'). The simple verb in both these cases is **-lya** ('eat'). The initial vowel is usually dropped on a noun following a causative meaning 'do with'.

CONVERSIVE VERBS have changed but related meanings compared with those of the simpler verbs from which they are derived, *eg.* **-lagula** ('prophesy'), from **-laga** ('show'). There are several types of reversive suffixes, all including the vowels **o** or **u** (**-ola**, **-olokoka**, **-ula**, **-ulukuka**, *etc.*) In some cases, the addition of a conversive suffix results in a reversal of meaning, *eg.* (1) **-simbula** ('uproot'), from **-simba** ('plant'); (2) **-ggula** ('open'), from **-ggala** ('close'). Some conversive verbs exist in pairs, with those ending in **-oka** or **-uka** being intransitive and those ending **-ola** or **-ula** being transitive, *eg.* **-vumbuka** ('be discovered'), **-vumbula** ('discover'). See under 'Verbs' in Part 1 of the dictionary for definitions of the terms 'transitive' and 'intransitive'. The double conversive suffixes **-okoka** and **-ukuka** indicate a final state as a result of an action. For example, the intransitive verb **-langulukuka** ('become unplaited') is conversive with **-langulula** ('unplait'). The simple verb is **-langa** ('plait').

INCEPTIVE VERBS are unusual among derived verbs in being based on adjectives or nouns, rather than verbs. Inceptive verbs mean 'become', *eg.* (1) **-gaggawala** ('become rich'), from **-gagga** ('rich'); (2) **-toniwa** ('become small'), from **-tono** ('small').

INTENSIVE VERBS carry the meaning of doing something continually or repeatedly, combined with endeavour, *eg.* **-weereza** ('serve'), from **-wa** ('give').

PASSIVE VERBS. The passive is used when the subject of the sentence is the recipient of an action, *eg.* **Yakubibwa Musoke.** ('He was hit by Musoke.') (simple verb = **-kuba** 'hit'). The passive is sometimes avoided by using an active (*ie.* non-passive) verb with the impersonal 'they' as subject, *eg.* **Engatto bazitunze.** ('They have sold the shoes.'), instead of **Engatto zatundibwa.** ('The shoes are sold.').

PREPOSITIONAL VERBS are used: (1) where a preposition such as 'for', 'to' or 'at' would be used in English, *eg.* **Yakolera Musoke.** ('He worked for Musoke.') (simple verb = **-kola** 'work'); (2) with **ddala** to convey the idea of doing something completely or thoroughly, *eg.* **Kolera ddala.** ('Work as well as you can.'); (3) with **bwereere** to convey the idea of an action taken for no purpose or without pay, *eg.* **Bakolera bwereere.** ('They are wasting their time.'). The prepositional suffix (**-era** or **-ira**) is repeated in **DOUBLE PREPOSITIONAL VERBS**, *eg.* the double prepositional verb **-genderera** ('do deliberately') is derived from the prepositional verb **-gendera** ('go for'), itself derived from the simple verb **-genda** ('go'). Double prepositional verb are used when two prepositional meanings are combined or to convey the idea of intensive, continuing or repeated action, *eg.* **-lindirira** ('keep waiting'), from **-linda** ('wait').

STATIVE (or **NEUTER**) **VERBS** express a state of affairs, or the possibility or capability of reaching such a state, *eg.* (1) **Omukono gwange gumenyese.** ('My arm is broken.'); (2) **Omulimu guno tegukoleka.** ('This work is difficult to do.'). The simple verbs in these examples are **-menya** ('break') and **-kola** ('do'). Some stative verbs are also conversive.

N23. REDUPLICATION

A syllable, stem or word is sometimes repeated, generally resulting in a new or modified meaning, *eg:* (1) (example of a verb) **-tambulatambula** ('walk from place to place continuously'), from **-tambula** ('walk'); (2) (example of a noun) **akaduukaduuka** ('just a poor little shop'), from **edduuka** ('shop'); (3) (example of an adjective) **-tonotono** ('fairly small'), from **-tono** ('small'); (4) (example of an adverb) **mpolampola** ('slowly and carefully'), from **mpola** ('slowly'). Reduplication can indicate repeated or concerted action, *eg.* **-teekateeka** ('prepare'), from **-teeka** ('put'). Reduplication of a number makes a distributive numeral, *eg.* **Ebisolo byayingira bibiri bibiri.** ('The animals entered two-by-two.'), from **bibiri** ('two').

Both parts of reduplicative verbs are modified in the case of modified stem forms, *eg.* **-teeseteese** from **-teekateeka**.

A verb preceded by the same verb in the infinitive emphasises that something really is true, *eg.* **Okubba abba.** ('He really does steal.').

A verb followed by the same verb, but with the prefix **bu-** and the last **a** changed to **i**, can indicate either that an activity occupies all of a person's time or that an activity is being undertaken in a way that is not serious. For example, **Asoma busomi.** can mean either that a person is studying and doing nothing else or that a person is studying ineffectively. Other variants of this type of reduplication mean 'mere' or 'merely' *eg.* (1) **omuntu obuntu** ('a mere person'); (2) **twala butwazi** ('just take it'); (3) **leeta buleesi** ('merely bring').

N24. PLACE

N24.1. THE FOUR ASPECTS OF PLACE

There are four aspects of place in Luganda, each associated with a particular noun class and affixes (Table 1). Their prefixes are:

- **wa-**, which indicates a particular place or place generally.
- **e-**, which indicates place away from the speaker ('over there').
- **ku-**, which indicates place above ('on') or place as direction ('to', 'at').
- **mu-**, which indicates place within ('in').

wa occurs as a free-standing word in the **INTERROGATIVE wa?** 'where?' **N13**), *eg.* **Ente eri wa?** ('Where is the cow?'). **e**, **ku** and **mu** are all free-standing **PREPOSITIONS**, *eg.* **ku lusozi** ('on the hill'), **mu nnyumba** ('in the house'), **e** only being used before the names of places, *eg.* **e Makerere** ('at Makerere'). Nouns following **ku** or **mu** lack initial vowels (**N3**). Phrases such as the foregoing can form parts of **POSSESSIVE PHRASES** when combined with the possessive **-a** ('of'), *eg.* **ennyumba z'e Kampala** ('houses of Kampala') (**z'** = **za** 'of'). The prepositions **ku** and **mu** are given initial vowels in such cases, *eg.* (1) **abalimi ab'oku lusozi** ('hill farmers'); (2) **ebintu by'omu nnyumba** ('house things', *ie.* 'furniture'). See **N11.1** for more information.

Some **ADVERBS** of place are single words or short phrases headed by the prefixes or words **wa-**, **e-**, **ku(-)** or **mu(-)**, *eg.* **wansi** ('below'), **emabega** ('behind'), **kumpi** ('close'), **mu maaso** ('in front'). Some such adverbs can be followed by **-a** ('of') or **na** ('with') to give **PREPOSITIONS**, *eg.* **wansi w'ennyumba** ('below the house'), **emabega w'ennyumba** ('behind the house'), **kumpi n'ennyumba** ('near the house'), **mu maaso g'ennyumba** ('in front of the house'). The **CONJUNCTIONS** 'where', 'over there where', 'on which' and 'in which' are translated by **we**, **gye**, **kwe** and **mwe** respectively, which are formed by attaching the prefixes **wa-**, **gi-**, **ku-** or **mu-** to the stem **-e** (**N10.2**).

An example of an **ADVERBIAL NOUN OF PLACE** is **awasomokerwa** ('place for crossing water' or 'ford'). **CONCORDANCE** induced by an adverbial noun of place is illustrated by the following: (1) **Awantu we mutadde emmeeza si walungi.** ('The place where you put the table is not a good one.'); (2) **Awafulumirwa awaali.** ('The exit is over there.'). The following illustrates the use of a place noun class in possessives: (1) **Awange we wano; awawe we wali.** ('My place is here; his is over there.'). See also **N11.5**.

The following examples illustrate how the meaning of a sentence changes depending on whether an adverbial noun of place or an ordinary noun (**N6**) dominates the sentence: (1) (place noun) **Mu nnyumba temuli bantu.** ('There are no people in this house.'); (2) (ordinary noun) **Ennyumba eno teriimu bantu.** ('There are no people in this house.'). In the first example, the prefix **mu-**, seen on **-no** ('this') and **-li** ('be'), is concordant with the two-word place noun **mu nnyumba** ('in the house'). In the second example, the prefix **e-**, seen on **-no** ('this') and **-ri** 'be', **-li** = **-ri** after **e N5**), is concordant with the ordinary noun **ennyumba** ('house'), which is in noun class *n9*. Although both sentences can be translated in the same way, they carry different implications. The implication with (1) is that the people are not within the house (but they are expected to be there later), while the implication with (2) this house is not being occupied by people.

N24.2. PLACE AFFIXES ON VERBS

The four subject affixes of place are the prefixes **wa-**, **e-**, **ku-** and **mu-** and the four object affixes of place are the suffixes **-wo**, **-yo**, **-ko** and **-mu** (the latter are known as **ENCLITICS** – see under 'Adverbs' in Part 1 of the dictionary). See **N15.3** for examples illustrating the use of these affixes as pronouns and **N20.4** for the use of these affixes with the verb **-ba/-li** ('be').

SUBJECT AND OBJECT PRONOUNS OF PLACE IN COMBINATION are found on some verbs to make general statements or ask general questions (place pronouns underlined in the following examples), *eg.* (1) <u>Wasigaddewo</u> **eccupa bbiri.** ('There remain two bottles.'), in which **wasigaddewo** can be broken down into **wa-** (place subject) + **-sigadde** (modified stem form of **-sigala** 'remain') + **-wo** (place object); (2) **Mu kkolero eryo** <u>mukolamu</u> **ani?** ('Who works in that workshop?').

PLACE OBJECTS ON VERBS WITHOUT MATCHING PLACE SUBJECTS can be equivalent to the English adverbs 'there', 'over there', 'on (there)' and '(with)in'. Examples (place suffixes underlined): (1) **Ggula<u>wo</u> oluggi.** ('Open the door [there].'); (2) **Agenzee<u>yo</u>.** ('He has gone over there.'); (3) **Biteeke<u>ko</u>.** ('Put them on.'); (4) **Yingira<u>mu</u>.** ('Go in.').

References to place in connection with verbs are sometimes rendered by free-standing pronouns alone, by the use of enclitics alone, or by a combination of the two, *eg.* (1) **Ebiso biri ku mmeeza.** ('The knives are on the table.'); (2) **Emmeeza eriko enfuufu.** ('The table is dusty.'); (3) **Tulowooza ku Musoke.** ('We are thinking about Musoke.'); (4)

Musoke tumulowoozaako. ('We are thinking about Musoke.'). The use of the enclitic implies that place has already been mentioned, or at least is in the minds of those concerned.

The general rule governing the **LENGTH OF THE FINAL VOWEL** of the verb before a place object is that normally it is single (as in **ggulawo** and **biteekeko** seen in examples earlier), but is doubled: (1) in the case of verbs having **s** or **z** as their final consonants (*eg.* **agenzeeyo**); (2) with some monosyllabic verbs, *eg.* **vaayo** ('come from over there'). With **-ba/-li**, the final vowel is single in the positive (*eg.* **waliwo** 'there is'), but doubled in the negative (*eg.* **tewaliiwo** 'there is not'), except for the far past (*eg.* **tewaaliwo** 'there was not') (Table 14).

Questions such as **Mu nnyumba eno musulamu abaana?** ('Do the children sleep in this house?') can be answered affirmatively by **Basulamu.** ('Yes.', *lit.* 'They sleep in there.') or negatively by **Tebasulamu.** ('No.', *lit.* 'They do not sleep in there.'). The place aspect of the response can be given greater prominence: (1) (for an affirmative response) by using an adverb of emphasis (N10.2), *eg.* **Mwe basula.** (*lit.* 'In there they sleep.'); or (2) (for a negative response) through the use of coupled subject and object pronouns of place, *eg.* **Temusulamu.** The relevant noun (*ie.* **baana** 'children' in this case) can be added as a second object, *ie.* **Temusulamu baana. mwe** in the first example is a **PROCLITIC** (see under 'Adverbs' in Part 1 of the dictionary for an explanation of this term).

Some common verbs are very frequently found with place objects, among them:

- **-dda** ('return'): **-ddawo** ('be next'), **-ddayo** ('go back'), **-ddako** ('come next' or 'be altered'), **-ddamu** ('reply').
- **-ggya** ('take away'): **-ggyawo** ('take away from there'), **-ggyayo** ('take away from over there'), **-ggyako** ('take off'), **-ggyamu** ('take out').
- **-va** ('come from'): **-vaawo** ('come from there'), **-vaayo** ('come from over there'), **vaako** ('come off'), **-vaamu** ('come out').

N24.3. OTHER USES OF ADVERBIAL SUFFIXES

There are other uses of adverbial suffixes on verbs, apart from being indicators of place. Their addition to verbs can lessen the forcefulness of the verbs, or indicate partialness or a temporary state of affairs. They can also be used for politeness. Examples (suffixes underlined): (1) **Fumbawo amatooke.** ('Cook some plantains.'); (2) **Yozaayo engoye.** ('Clean some of the clothes.'); (3) **Aliko obusungu.** ('He is angry.' – at this moment); (4) **Yalyako ku mmeere.** ('He ate some of the food.'); (5) **Mpaako ku binyeebwa byo ndeeko.** ('Please give me some peanuts to eat.' – this is a polite way of making a request). (6) **Nkulowoozaako.** ('I am thinking about you.'); (7) **Amufaanana? Afaananamu katono.** ('Does she look like her? She does a little.'). The third example above can be compared with **Alina obusungu.** ('He is angry.' – by temperment, *lit.* 'He has anger.').

-ko and **-mu** can also be found as diminutives on adjectives and adverbs, *eg.* **Omuwala we mulungi? Mulungiko.** ('Is her daughter good? Yes, fairly.').

Verbs can have more than one adverbial suffix, *eg.* **Teekamuko sukaali mu caayi.** ('Put a little sugar in the tea.'). Here the suffix **-mu** on **-teeka** is an indicator of place ('in') and **-ko** is a diminutive ('a little').

N25. TIME

N25.1. TIME OF THE DAY

The word for hour is **essaawa**. 'What is the time?' is **Essaawa mmeka?**. The time of day is counted from 6 a.m. or 6 p.m., *eg.* **essaawa bbiri** is '8 o'clock', not '2 o'clock'. Morning, night-time, *etc.* can be distinguished through the use of appropriate phrases, *eg.* (1) **essaawa bbiri ez'enkya** ('8 a.m.', *lit.* 'hour two of the morning'; (2) **essaawa mukaaga ez'ekiro** ('midnight', *lit.* 'hour six of the night'). Minutes past the hour are given as follows, *eg.* **essaawa kkumi n'eddakiika kkumi na ttaano** ('4.15', *lit.* 'hour ten and minutes ten and five') or using constructions such as **ku ssaawa kkumi kuyiseeko eddakiika kkumi na ttaano** ('4.15', *lit.* 'on hour ten there has passed minutes ten and five'). Half past is **ekitundu** ('part'), *eg.* **essaawa kkumi n'ekitundu** ('4.30'). Minutes before the hour can be expressed either by adding minutes to the hour (as above) or through subtracting them from the next hour using the verbs **-sigala** ('remain') or **-bula** ('be lacking') together with **-wera** ('reach'), *eg.* **Esigadde** (or **Ebula**) **eddakiika kkumi okuwera essaawa omunaana** ('1.50', *lit.* 'There remain (or are lacking) minutes ten to reach hour eight.'). 'At' with time is **ku**, *eg.* **ku ssaawa emu** ('at 7 o'clock'). 'About' (approximately) with time is **nga**, *eg.* **essaawa nga bbiri** ('about 8 o'clock').

N25.2. NOUN CLASSES OF TIME

Similarly to 'place' (**N24**), 'time' can act as a noun in Luganda, as shown by its ability to influence concords. There are **SIX NOUN CLASSES OF TIME**, three otherwise also used for ordinary nouns (*n11, n12, n14*) and three otherwise used for 'place' (*n16, n17, n18*) (see Column 3 of Table 1). The ideas associated with the noun classes of time are as follows:

- (*n11*). The concord **lu-** refers to the understood noun **olunaku** ('day'). Example of its use are **awo olwatuuka** and **lwali lumu**, both meaning 'once upon a time'.

- (*n12*). The concord **ka-** refers to the understood noun **akaseera** ('short period of time'). An example of its use is the adverb **kaakano** ('now'), based on the demonstrative stem **-no** ('this') (**N9**). In this case, the concord is reduplicated (**N23**).

- (*n14*). The concord **bu-** possibly refers to the understood noun **obudde** ('occasion'). An example of its use is the conjunction **bwe** ('when') (**N10.2**), based on the stem **-e** (**bu-** = **bw-** before a vowel **N5**).

- (*n16*). The concord **wa-** refers to a particular occasion. An example of its use is the adverb **awo** ('then'), based on the demonstrative stem **-o** (**N9**) (the **a** of the concord **wa-** is lost before a vowel **N5**).

- (*n17*). The concord **ku-** (or word **ku** in an adverbial phrase) refers to a particular time within a period, *eg.* **Yatuuka jjo ku makya.** ('He arrived yesterday morning.').

- (*n18*). The concord **mu-** (or word **mu** in an adverbial phrase) refers to a span of time within a period, *eg.* **Alituuka mu wiiki ejja.** ('He will arrive sometime next week.').

N25.3. CONJUNCTIONS OF TIME

There are three **-e** stem conjunctions meaning 'when' – **lwe**, **bwe** and **we** (see **N10.2** for examples). See **N7.2** for information on the use of the pronominal concord **lu-** in subject relative clauses to convey a meaning equivalent to the English conjunction 'as soon as'.

The **CONJUNCTION nga**, sometimes followed by **bwe**, is used with 'time', 'manner' (**N26**) and 'cause and reason' (**N27**). According to context, it can mean 'when', 'while', 'as, 'after', 'like', 'if', and others. The following examples illustrate its use with time:

- **Musoke nnamulaba nga ntambula.** ('I saw Musoke while I was walking.' or 'While walking, I saw Musoke.'). When **nga** introduces a subordinate clause in which the verb is in the present tense (as in this and the next example), then the events or states mentioned in the main and subordinate clauses refer to the same time. **nga** can be translated as 'while', 'when' or 'as'.

- **Twayogera nga bwe tutambula.** ('We talked as we walked.'). The replacement of **nga** by **nga bwe** implies that the two events or states mentioned are of equal significance.

- **Tunaalya nga tutuuse e Masaka.** ('We will eat when we arrive at Masaka.'). This use of these particular tenses means that the events or states mentioned in the main and subordinate clauses are in the near future and sequential in time. **nga** can be translated by 'on' or 'after'.

- **Nnalaba Musoke nga sinnavaayo.** ('I saw Musoke before I left.'). In this case, the verb in the subordinate clause (**-vaayo** 'leave') is in the 'not yet' tense and **nga** means 'before'. See further examples in **N18**.

- **Nja kugenda e Masaka nga mmaze okulya.** ('After I have eaten, I will go to Masaka.'). Here, **nga** is followed by the auxiliary verb **-mala** ('finish') and then a main verb (**-lya** 'eat') in the infinitive. The meaning of **nga** is 'after' or 'as soon as'.

The **SUFFIX -nga** on verbs can indicate a repetitive or habitual action, *eg.* **Nnafumbanga buli lunaku.** ('I used to cook every day.') (**N18**). See **N20.1** for the use of **-linga**.

N26. MANNER

There are five **NOUN CLASSES OF MANNER**, all otherwise used for ordinary noun classes (see Column 3 of Table 1). Each is typically associated with a particular aspect of manner. The following are the concords associated with these noun classes, illustrated by examples of **ADVERBS**:

- **ma-** (*n6*) indicates manner as a process, *eg.* **mangu** ('quickly').
- **ki-** (*n7*) expresses 'in a manner like', *eg.* **ekizungu** ('in a white person's way').
- **lu-** (*n11*) expresses the manner in which an action is done, *eg.* **olumoonyere** ('incessantly').
- **ka-** (*n12*) expresses degree, measure or extent of an action, *eg.* **kasirise** ('quietly').
- **bu-** (*n14*) expresses state, *eg.* **bulungi** ('well').

Many adverbs of manner are based on adjectival stems, such as **-zungu** ('white person's') and **-lungi** ('good') in the examples above. Some adverbs of manner begin with the possessive **-a** ('of') (**N11.1**), *eg.* (1) **bwomu** ('alone'); (2) **lwa kisa** ('through kindness'). **bwomu** can be broken down into **bu-** (concord, *n14* adverbial noun class of manner) + **-a** ('of') + **o-** (initial vowel) + **-mu** ('one'). **kinnoomu** ('one-by-one') is a distributive numeral (**N8.1**) consisting of **ki-** (concord, *n7* adverbial noun class of manner) + **na** ('and') + **o-** (initial vowel) + **-mu** ('one'). In both **bwomu** and **kinnoomu**, the **-a** of the 'of' or 'and' component is lost because it is followed by a different vowel (**N5**).

The prefix **bu-** is found in the **CONJUNCTION bwe** ('how', 'like', 'as' **N10.2**) *eg.* **Simanyi bw'akikola.** ('I do not know how she does it.'). **bwe** means 'like' when used with the verbs **-ti** or **-tyo** in answers to questions using the **INTERROGATIVE VERB -tya?** ('how?', 'what like?') (**N13**), *eg.* **Akola atya? Akola bw'ati.** ('How does she work? She works like this.').

The **CONJUNCTION nga** followed by a noun or pronoun means 'as' or 'like', *eg.* **Ayimba ng'ennyonza.** ('She sings like a bird.'). **nga ... bwe** can mean 'just like', *eg.* Yatandika okwambala nga nze bwe nyambala. ('She started to dress just like me.'). **nga** in **EXCLAMATIONS** can mean 'what!' or 'how!', *eg.* **Ng'oyambadde!** ('How well you are dressed!'). The **VERB -linga** means 'look like', *eg.* **Alinga omulwadde.** ('It looks like she is ill.').

N27. CAUSE AND REASON

The **CONCORD lu-** with the possessive **-a** ('of') is found in various parts of speech expressing cause or reason. Examples are **lwa buwaze** ('by force' – adverb) and **lwaki?** ('why?' – interrogative **N13**). **ku(-)** ('on') can be present as an initial preposition, *eg.* **ku lwange** ('for me') (**N10.3**).

The **CONJUNCTION olwa** followed by a positive or negative infinitive (**N18**) means 'because of' or 'through'. **olwa** followed by **okuba** or **okubanga** (or **kuba** or **kubanga** without **olwa**) means 'because'. The use of these and similar conjunctions is illustrated below (conjunctions underlined):

- <u>Olw'</u>okusinga banne mu kibiina, Musoke kyavudde afuna ekirabo. ('Because of coming top in class, Musoke received a prize.').
- <u>Olw'</u>obutamanya kkubo kyenvudde mbula. ('Through not knowing the road, I got lost.').
- <u>Olw'</u>okubaawo ekiwunya, twaggadde eddirisa. ('Because of the smell, we closed the window.').
- Twaggadde eddirisa <u>olw'okuba</u> nga waliwo ekiwunya. ('We closed the window because of the smell.').
- Saagenda <u>olw'okubanga</u> nnali sirina ssente. ('I did not go because I had no money.').
- Gezaako okwebaka <u>kuba</u> (or <u>kubanga</u>) oli mukoowu. ('Try to sleep because you are tired.')
- Mu katale waaliwo abantu bangi, n'<u>olw'ekyo</u> kyali kizibu okumulaba. ('There were many people in the market, therefore it was difficult to see her.').

The **CONJUNCTION kye...-va** seen in the first two examples above introduces clauses explaining the consequences of events or situations for people. It can often be translated as 'that is the reason' or 'therefore'. See under 'Cause and reason' in **N10.2** for more on this conjunction.

The following examples demonstrate the use of various other conjunctions of conditionality, explanation or uncertainty, including the **CONJUNCTIONS nga, bwe and nga ... bwe** (conjunctions underlined):

- **Simanyi ng'anajja.** ('I do not know whether he is coming.').
- **Enkuba bw'etonnya, ebirime bikula bulungi.** ('If it rains, the crops grow well.'). **bwe** is alternatively translated by 'when' in this case.
- **Enkuba bw'etatonnya, abantu babeera bayala.** ('If it does not rain, the people go hungry.') This is the negative equivalent of the above, using the prefix **-ta-** (see **N21**).
- **Nga bwe bazze, tutandike akakiiko.** ('Since they have come, let's start the meeting.').
- **Ng'enkuba bw'etonnya, ayinza obutajja.** ('Since it is raining, she could not come.').
- **Ne bw'anaagaana okunziramu nja kugendayo.** ('Even if he refuses to answer me, I will go there.').
- **Singa tetwaguze mugaati, tetwandibadde na kyakulya.** ('If we had not bought bread, we would not have food.'). The conjunction **singa** ('if') is used here with the conditional tense (marked by the verb infix **-andi- N18**).
- **Newankubadde mulwadde akyakola.** ('Although she is ill, she is still working.').

The **CONJUNCTIONS kwe and bwe**, followed respectively by the positive or negative infinitive, give sentences translatable in English by sentences that include the conjunctions 'because', 'therefore' or 'that's why' (see also under 'Cause and reason' in **N10.2**):

- **Ekimulwazizza kwe kukola ennyo.** ('She is ill because of overwork.').
- **Ekimubeezezza obulungi bwe butakola nnyo.** ('She is well because she is not overworking.').

Grammatically, the above constructions can be analysed as consisting of subject relative clauses (**ekimulwazizza** and **ekimubeezezza N7.1**) followed by pronouns of emphasis (**kwe** and **bwe N10.1**) concordant with the noun classes of the positive and negative infinitives (*n15* and *n14* **N18**). The subject prefix in the relative clauses (**ki-**) refers to the understood noun **ekintu** ('thing' **N15.1**).

N28. GREETINGS

A short greeting is **Oli otya?** (*pl.* **Muli mutya?**) ('How are you?'). The response is **Bulungi.** ('Well.'). Another option is **Gy'oli?** (*lit.* 'How are you?') – response **Gye ndi.** ('OK.').

More formal greetings are: (1) (in the morning) **Wasuze otyanno?** (*pl.* **Mwasuze mutyanno?**) ('Good morning., *lit.* 'How did you spend the night?'); (2) (after midday) **Osiibye otyanno?** (*pl.* **Musiibye mutyanno?**) ('Good afternoon/evening.', *lit.* "How did you spend the day?'). The response in both cases is usually **Bulungi.** ('Well.').

Greeting exchanges are antiphonal with the two parties alternating in their questions, statements and responses. Exchanges are often liberally punctuated by non-verbal exclamations using sounds such as **eee!** and **mmm!**. It is essential to maintain the rhythm of the exchange – for example, after a greeting such as **Wasuze otyanno?** and the response **Bulungi.**, then the first party must make a further utterance (for example **mmm!**) before the second party can enquire in turn **Wasuze otyanno?**.

Greetings can be extensive and may include the following (among others):

- **Agafaayo?** ('What is happening where you come from?'), or **Agafuddeyo** ('What has been happening?'). The response is **Ekyali.** or **Nnungi.** The prefix **ga-** seen here is concordant with the understood noun **amawulire** ('news').

- **Eradde.** The response is **Eradde.**, **Mirembe.** ('peace') or **Maamu.**

- **Nsanyuse okukulaba.** (*pl.* **Nsanyuse okubalaba.**) ('I am pleased to see you.'). The response is **Nange.** (*pl.* **Naffe.**) ('And I.'), or **Kale ssebo.** ('And I too sir.') or **Kale nnyabo.** ('And I too madam.').

- **Kulikayo.** (*pl.* **Mukulikeeyo.**) ('Welcome back.', after completion of a journey). The response is **Nvuddeyo.** (*pl.* **Tuvuddeyo.**) ('I have come from there.') or **Nkomawo.** (*pl.* **Tukomyewo.**) ('I have returned.').

- **Ndaba ku ki?** ('Whom do I see?') – an expression of pleasure on meeting someone who has been absent for some time. The response is **Ku nze.** ('It's me.').

The etiquette on entering a host's home is to sit down after exchanging initial pleasantries. Then the host and family will move around the visitors welcoming each in turn. If the hosts are eating at the time of arrival, the visitors will be invited to sit down and share the meal. Only when this has ended will formal greetings begin.

N29. SOCIETY

The King of Buganda is the **Kabaka** and a deceased king **Ssekabaka**. The royal lineage can be traced back many generations to **Kintu**, the first king in the present dynasty (Table 17). He is estimated to have reigned at about 1200-1230 AD (Nuwagaba 2014). The Queen is **Nnaabagereka**, the Queen-sister **Nnaalinya** and the Queen-mother **Nnamasole**. The Queen-sister, who is the co-heir (**lubuga**) of the Kabaka (see below), traditionally ran a parallel court to that of the Kabaka and is sometimes herself addressed as 'Kabaka'.

The country is traditionally divided into an hierarchy of administrative areas, the largest being the **Ssaza** ('county'), then the **Ggombolola** ('sub-county') and finally the **Muluka** ('parish'). The respective office holders are **Owessaza**, **Oweggombolola** and **Owoomuluka**. Each village and place has its respected leaders – **abakulu b'ekyalo** ('village elders') and **abakulu b'abataka** ('elders of the place'). Table 18 lists the names of the traditional counties and the titles of their chiefs, while Figure 4 shows their geography. There is a traditional parliament (**Lukiiko**) and Prime Minister (**Katikkiro**), who is responsible for the day-to-day affairs of the kingdom. There are many traditional office holders, including **Kawuula** (in charge of the King's drums), **Gabunga** (responsible for the King's canoes), **Kawuka** ('Chief goatherd'), **Kawuuta** ('Chief cook'), **Ssebalijja** ('Chief herdsman') and **Sseruti** ('Chief brewer').

1. Kintu	13. Kimbugwe	25. Kyabaggu
2. Chwa I Nabakka	14. Kateregga	26. Jjunju
3. Kimera	15. Mutebi I	27. Ssemakookiro
4. Ttembo	16. Jjuuko	28. Kamaanya
5. Kiggala	17. Kayemba	29. Ssuuna II
6. Kiyimba	18. Tebandeke	30. Muteesa I (Mukaabya)[1]
7. Kayima	19. Ndawula	31. Mwanga II
8. Nnakibinge	20. Kagulu (Tebuucwereke)[1]	32. Kiweewa
9. Mulondo	21. Kikulwe	33. Kalema
10. Jjemba	22. Mawanda	34. Daudi Chwa II
11. Ssuuna I	23. Mwanga I	35. Edward Muteesa II
12. Ssekamaanya	24. Namugala	36. Ronald Mutebi II

Table 17. Kings of Buganda.

1. Nicknames given by their subjects.

COUNTY	TITLE OF COUNTY CHIEF	COUNTY	TITLE OF COUNTY CHIEF
Buddu (Bugangazzi) [1]	Pookino Kiyimba	**(Buyaga)** [1]	Kyambalango
Bugerere	Mugerere	Gomba	Kitunzi
Bulemeezi	Kkangaawo	Kabula	Lumaama
Buluuli	Kimbugwe	Kkooki	Kaamuswaga
Busiro	Ssebwaana	Kyaddondo	Kaggo
Busujju	Kasujju	Kyaggwe	Ssekiboobo
Butambala	Katambala	Mawogola	Muteesa
Buvuma	Mbuubi	Mawokota	Kayima
Buweekula	Luweekula	Ssese	Kkweeba
		Ssingo	Mukwenda

Table 18. Counties (**amasaza**) of Buganda and titles of their chiefs.

1. Known as the 'lost counties', these countries were transferred to Bunyoro following a referendum in 1964.

The identities of the Baganda are strongly linked traditionally to their membership of lineages (**embu**), descent being reckoned along the male line (except in the case of the Kabaka, who takes his mother's clan). The major social units, which are nested, are the clan (**ekika**), sub-clan (**essiga**), branch (**omutuba**), lineage (**olunyiriri**), courtyard (**oluggya**) and house (**enju**) (Table 19). There are said to be 52 clans in all. Several clans were already in Buganda at the time of arrival of Kintu, while others came with him or later with Ssekabaka Kimera (estimated reign 1275-1330 AD), when he came to Buganda from Bunyoro. Kimera was a grandchild of the second king of Buganda (Ssekabaka Chwa II), but had been born in Bunyoro following the sending away of his father (Kalemeera) from Buganda. Each clan has a head (**Owaakasolya**) and a prime minister (**Katakkiro**), and, except for the royal clans of **Abalangira n'Abambejja** ('Princes and princesses') and **Ababiito be'Kkooki** ('Princes of Kkooki), a totem (**omuziro**). Each clan has a secondary totem (**akabbiro**). The eating of totems is taboo to clan members.

One theory for the origin of the name 'Buganda' is that it comes from **obuganda** ('small bundles'), the Baganda being seen as a collection of disparate peoples, who have come together over the passage of time to live in one land under the leadership of the Kabaka. The Baganda people are said to have historically welcomed and assimulated others. There is also a legend that traces the name Buganda to a king of that name ruling at a time of peace. He was a member of a pre-Kintu dynasty, his reign being estimated at *ca. 1120-1140 AD* (Nuwagaba 2014).

Marriages can only occur between members of different lines. This allows a distinction to be made between relatives by blood (**ab'oluganda**) and relatives by marriage (**abako**). Wives retain membership of the clans of their birth, but children belong to the clan of the father. Inheritence of a social position is through nomination of an heir (**omusika**), who must be of the same clan and gender. A male heir is provided with a consort (**lubuga**), who must be a close female relative, such as a sister.

Ceremonies (**emikolo**) traditionally mark the passage through life of the Baganda, among them **okwanjula** (introduction of a prospective groom to the clan), **embaga** (wedding) and **olumbe** (death rites, including installation of an heir). Children are given names unique to their clans and, these days, commonly Christian or Islamic forenames additionally. Surnames in the English style are more rarely used. Twins hold special status, their birth being marked by a ceremony (**okwalula abalongo**). The party held for a bride or groom before a wedding is called **kasiki**.

Some aspects of Kiganda culture have changed greatly over recent years, paralleling major changes in societies and cultures found all over the world. The introduced religions of Christianity and Islam have proved major influences, the first Protestant and Catholic missionaries arriving in 1877 and 1879 respectively, and Islam coming earlier (about 1848). Alexander McKay (1849-1890) was an early Protestant missionary, whose accomplishments including translating parts of the New Testament into Luganda, establishing a printing press and starting a school. The inscription on McKay's tombstone

NAME OF CLAN (also totem, except for clans marked * which have no totem)   **SECONDARY TOTEM** (Akabbiro)

1. CLANS THAT PREDATE KINTU

Ffumbe (Civet)	Kikere (Frog)
Lugave (Pangolin)	Maleere (Bracket fungus)
Ngeye (Colobus monkey)	Kkunguvvu (Pin-tailed whydah)
Nnyange (Cattle egret)	Kkunguvvu (Pin-tailed whydah)
Njaza (Reedbuck)	Ngujulu (unidentified animal)

2. CLANS THAT CAME WITH KINTU

*Abalangira n'Abambejja (Princes and Princesses)	Eŋŋoma (Drum)
Ngo (Leopard)	Kasimba (Genet)
Nvuma (fruit of Water Chestnut) [1]	Katinvuma (type of plant) [2]
Ŋŋonge (Otter)	Kaneene (possibly Marsh Mongoose) [a]
Njovu (Elephant)	Nvubu (Hippopotamus)
Nvubu (Hippopotamus)	Njovu (Elephant)
Mpindi (Cowpea) [3]	Kiyindiru (wild relative of Cowpea) [4]
Kkobe (Bud yam) [5, b]	Kaama (wild yam) [6]
Mmamba (Lungfish) [c]	Muguya (Young lungfish)
Ntalaganya (Blue duiker)	Kiyindiru (wild relative of Cowpea) [4]
Mbwa (Dog)	Kide kya Mbwa (Dog bell)
Nkima (Monkey)	Kaamukuukulu (Laughing dove)
Mpeewo (Bush duiker)	Kayozi (Gerbil)
Mpologoma (Lion)	Ngo (Leopard)
Nnamuŋŋoona (Pied crow)	Mutima (Heart)
Nkejje (Haplochromis fish)	Kiyemba (type of Haplochromis)

3. CLANS THAT ARRIVED WITH KIMERA

Nseenene (Edible grasshopper)	Nnabangogoma (Stick grasshopper)
Mbogo (Buffalo)	Ndeerwe (type of mushroom)
Nkerebwe (Tree squirrel)	Kikirikisi (probably Dormouse) [a]
Kibe (Jackal)	Mpiri (type of poisonous snake) [a]
Musu (Cane rat)	Kayozi (Gerbil)
Ngabi (Bushbuck) [d]	Jjerengesa (type of shrub) [7]
Butiko (Mushroom)	Nnamulondo (type of small mushroom)
Nsuma (Elephant snout fish)	Kasulubbana (Elephant snout fish)
Kasimba (Genet)	Ngo (Leopard)
Kayozi (Gerbil)	Nsombabyuma (Giant pouched rat)

4. CLANS THAT CAME ON THEIR OWN

Ndiga (Sheep)	Mpologoma (Lion)
Mutima Muyanja (Heart) [e]	Mawuggwe (Lungs)
Nte (Cow)	Ŋŋaali (Crested crane)
Kinyomo (Drop-tail ant)	Mutima (Heart)
*Ababiito b'e Kkooki (Royal family of Kkooki) [f]	Mazzi g'Ekisasi (Water from the Eaves)
Nswaswa (Monitor lizard)	Goonya (Crocodile)
Lukato (Awl)	Kabbo kasa (Empty basket)
Kiwere (type of plant) [8]	Sekafu (Yellow wagtail) [g]
Nkula (Rhinoceros)	Bunnassogolero (type of mushroom)
Nnyonyi Ndiisa (Yellow-throated longclaw)	Sekafu (Yellow wagtail) [g]
Nnyonyi Nnakinsige (Firefinch) [g]	Kkunguvvu (Pin-tailed whydah)
Njobe (Sitatunga)	Bugala (young tufts of papyrus)

5. OTHER CLAN

Mutima Musaggi (Heart of the Earth) [e]	Muzibiro (Blood clotted in the heart)

Table 19. Clans of the Baganda.

This list should not be taken as authoritative. It is incomplete and some of the information given is disputed. Please consult the Buganda Kingdom Website and *Totems of Uganda: Buganda edition* by Nuwagaba (2014) (see reference list). People especially interested should consult the Kingdom of Buganda and the heads of clans. **NOTES** a. The following identifications are given in Nuwagaba: **Kaneene** Cannibal fish, **Kikirikisi** Dephua mouse, **Mpiri** Puff adder. b. The bud yam **Nkobe** is a plant that originated in Asia. Its use as a totem indicates that it has long been in Uganda, a testament to ancient contact between Africa and Asia. c. Two **Mmamba** clans are sometimes recognised, but there is only one according to the Katikkiro of the clan, who was consulted for the present dictionary. According to Nuwagaba, one **Mmamba** Clan predates Kintu and the other came with him. d. There are two sections in the **Ngabi** clan, **Ngabi Ennyunga** and **Ngabi Nsamba**. e. There are two Mutima clans. The totem of **Mutima Muyanga** Clan is a heart from an animal and that of the **Mutima Musaggi** Clan the stinkhorn fungus **Mutima gw'ettaka**. f. Members of **Ababiito b'e Kkooki** are also known as **Ababoobi**. g. The identifications of **Sekafu** as Yellow Wagtail and **Nnyonyi Nnakinsige** as Firefinch would benefit from confirmation. **SCIENTIFIC NAMES OF PLANTS**: 1. *Trapa natans*, 2. *Rhynchosia hirta*, 3. *Vigna unguiculata* (cultivated type), 4. *Vigna unguiculata* (wild type), 5. *Dioscorea bulbifera*, 6. *Dioscorea abyssinica* and *D. odoratissima* (both called **kaama**), 7. *Acalypha bipartita*, 8. *Rumex usambarensis*.

at Namirembe Cathedral reads 'Founder of Education in Uganda' – an epitaph that would have been more accurate if the words 'formal European' or, even more precisely, 'formal Protestant British' had been included. The epitaph is misleading in that education did, of course, exist in Uganda prior to the coming of European missionaries and teachers, or Muslim Imams. Much was transmitted (and continues to be transmitted) through family and community culture, including the behaviour expected of individuals according to their social positions, how to raise children and how to interact with the natural world. There was also a traditional system of higher education in Buganda prior to the arrival of outsiders, with promising youngsters from all levels of society being taken into the courts of the Kabaka and major chiefs (**mu lubiri** and **mu kisaakate** respectively) to be taught the art of governance and how leaders should behave.

Reference cited: Nuwagaba, Taga F. (2014). *Totems of Uganda*. Published by Taga Nuwagaba and Nathan Kiwere.

N30. A BRIEF HISTORY OF LUGANDA

Luganda has a common origin at about 3000 BC with 250-500 other modern languages belonging to the Bantu group of the Niger-Congo language family (the number of languages is debatable, depending on the criteria used for distinguishing between a language and a dialect). All Bantu languages, which today are distributed widely across central, eastern and southern Africa, are descended from an extinct common language, known as Proto-Bantu, once spoken in a restricted area close to the present-day border between Cameroon and Nigeria. Comparative studies of Bantu languages have demonstrated that many Luganda words can be traced back to root words in Proto-Bantu, in doing so revealing something of the culture. Examples include **-bumba** ('make pottery'), **embuzi** ('goat'), **eŋŋoma** ('drum'), **eryato** ('boat') and **eddobu** ('fish-hook'). The Proto-Bantu speakers were agriculturalists growing crops possibly in small clearings that they made in rainforest, otherwise obtaining food by gathering wild plants, hunting and fishing. Their crops included yams (*Dioscorea*), a legume (probably cowpea), bambara groundnut, castor bean and gourds. Over the generations, the descendants of the speakers of Proto-Bantu spread out far to the east and south in Africa and, as they did so, so their languages diverged. Comparative studies of Bantu languages present exceptional opportunities to study the evolution of language and culture.

Linguistic research has demonstrated that the same noun classes can be identified across all Bantu languages (though modified by evolution). This discovery has allowed the application of a common way of numbering the noun classes for all Bantu languages (followed in the present dictionary). The number of noun classes found in total in all modern Bantu languages is 23 and the total number reconstructed for Proto-Bantu about 24. A major feature of linguistic evolution within Bantu languages has been the loss of noun classes, the number surviving in modern Bantu languages being very variable. Luganda has the highest number of noun classes known for any Bantu language (21) and in this respect is regarded as exceptionally conservative, close to the Proto-Bantu original.

The linguistic ancestors of the Baganda moved from the Cameroon/Nigeria borderland southwards through the Congo rainforest, possibly using a savanna corridor that opened up when the climate became drier at about 2000 BC. Their arrival in southwest Uganda probably dates to the first few centuries BC. Knowledge of several new technologies was acquired over the following centuries from speakers of the Nilo-Saharan language family (already present in the interlacustrine area), including the growing of the cereals finger millet and sorghum, the keeping of cows and sheep, and how to work iron. Modern words in Luganda acquired from root words in Nilo-Saharan languages include **obulo** ('finger millet'), **obusera** ('finger millet porridge'), **ente** ('cow'), **enkumbi** ('hoe'), **ekinu** ('mortar'), **ennyondo** ('hammer') and **ennumbu** ('*Plectranthus* yam'). There was also some contact with speakers of Southern Cushitic languages (which belong to the Afro-Asiatic language family). The modern Luganda words **endogoyi** ('donkey') and **ekirira** ('umbilical cord') are derived from roots in this source.

A substantial number of words have entered Luganda from Swahili and, before that, often from Arabic. Examples include **ekitabo** ('book', from Swahili **kitabu** and Arabic **kitab**), **Bulaaya** ('Europe'), **eddiini** ('religion'), **edduuka** ('shop') and **malayika** ('angel'). The first direct contact between Luganda and Swahili speakers may have been during the early 19th Century AD, but indirect cultural contact between Buganda and the East African coast, and lands beyond, was much earlier. This is shown, for instance, by

415

the early arrival of domestic animals and crops in Uganda. Goats and sheep (originally domesticated in the Middle East) and cattle (possibly originally domesticated in north-east Africa) were in Uganda during the first millennium BC. The banana, a crop that originated in New Guinea and south-east Asia, probably came to Uganda during the first millennium AD, following earlier carriage across the Indian Ocean, likely by people speaking an Indonesia language, and then its transport inland from the coast. The invention of the perennially productive banana garden (**lusuku**) and, in western Uganda, of large-scale cattle-keeping may have been instrumental in achieving a surplus of economic production and the development of more hierarchical societies, such as the kingdoms of Buganda and Bunyoro-Kitara. It is known that there was a wave of major reduction of forest in Uganda at about 1000 AD, which could be related to this major socio-economic change.

A further wave of agricultural change was triggered much later by the arrival of a number of major crops of American origin. One of the first to arrive was tobacco (**taaba**), present in the Ugandan area by 1700 AD, followed, at about 1800 AD, by maize (**kasoli**), American beans (**ebinjanjaalo**), peanuts (**ebinyeebwa**) and sweet potatoes (**lumonde**). Cassava (**muwogo**) was a later arrival, possibly not present until colonial times. One result of this influx of American crops, as well as others introduced earlier from Asia (such as bananas, sugar cane and cocoyam), seems to have been the substantial displacement of certain crops that had been common earlier. Thus, it seems that peanuts (**ebinyeebya**) have largely displaced the bambara groundnut (**empande**), American beans (**ebijanjaalo**) the cowpea (**empindi**) and bananas (**ebitooke**) certain yams (**kaama**, *etc.*). Bananas may also have displaced the indigenous banana-like plant ensete (**ekitembe**). Ensete does not have edible fruits (like the banana), but other parts of the plant can be eaten, as has been recorded in Uganda at times of famine. Ensete is a major food crop in parts of Ethiopia to this day.

English has contributed many words to Luganda, such as **bulangiti** ('blanket'), **emmotoka** ('car') and **leerwe** ('railway'), and continues to do so apace. The extent to which words recently introduced from English or other foreign languages should be considered as 'proper' Luganda is a matter of on-going debate. Some trade names have entered the language and become generalised in meaning, for example **eggirita** ('razor blade', from 'Gillette' a brand name). There are cases where Luganda words have been applied to introduced items considered to be similar, for instance the application of the name of an indigenous tree **omuwoloola** (*Entada africana*) to the introduced flame tree *Delonix regia*. Loquat (*Eriobotrya japonica*), which is a fruit tree introduced to Uganda, is called **omusaali omuzungu** ('the white man's omusaali'), adapted from **omusaali** (*Garcinia buchananii*), an indigenous fruit tree. English names taken into Luganda can be modified to fit into the Luganda noun class system, as with **omusikaawutu** ('scout', with the personal prefix **omu-**) and **obusikaawutu** ('scouting', with the abstract prefix **obu-**). The word **ekyuma kalimagezi** ('computer') is a composite invention, based on **ekyuma** ('machine'), **akali** ('which is' with the diminutive prefix **ka-** meaning that the machine is small) and **amagezi** ('cleverness'). The word **akatafofaali** ('cell', as of the human body) and, even more so, the further refinements of **akatafaali akamyufu** ('red blood cell') and **akatafaali akeeru** ('white blood cell') appear to be deliberate inventions, founded on a diminutive of **ettafaali** ('brick'). Time will tell whether such words and terms become part of everyday speech.

The arrival of Islam and Christiantity in Uganda in the 19th century resulted in the introduction of new religious terms, in some cases modifications of existing concepts, such as **Omwoyo Omutukuvu** ('the Holy Spirit'), from **omwoyo** ('spirit', 'soul'). Differences between Catholicism and Anglicism, compounded by early conflict between Catholic and Protestant missionaries, has left its mark on the modern language, with these two branches of Christiantity using different words for a number of central aspects of the religion, including for 'Jesus' (**Yezu** for Catholics, **Yesu** for Protestants) and 'Christianity' (**Omukirisitu** for Catholics, **Omukulisitaayo** for Protestants). Some standardised spellings have been suggested, for instance **Omukirisito** ('Christianity').

Sources:

Ehret, C. (1998). An *African Classical Age: Eastern and Southern Africa in World History: 1000 BC to 400 AD*. Oxford: James Currey.
Ehret, C. (2011). *History and testimony of language*. Berkeley: University of California Press.
Hamilton, A.C., Karamura, D. and Kakudidi, E. (2006). History and conservation of wild and cultivated plant diversity in Uganda: forest species and bananas as case studies. *Plant Diversity* 38, 23-44.
Lejju, B.J., Taylor, D., Robertshaw, P. (2005). Late-Holocene environmental variability at Munsa archaeological site, Uganda: a multicore, multiproxy approach. *The Holocene* 15, 1044-1061.
Robertshaw, P., Kamuhangire, E.R., Reid, A., Young, R., Childs, S.T. and Pearson, N. (1997). Archaeological research in Bunyoro-Kitara: preliminary results. *Nyame Akuma* 48, 70-77.

Schoenbrun, D.L. (1994). *A green place, a good place: agrarian change, gender and social identify in the Great Lakes Region to the 15th Century*. Portsmouth: Heinemann.

Snoxall, R.A. (1938). Word importation into Bantu language with particular reference to Ganda. *Uganda Journal* 5, 267-283.

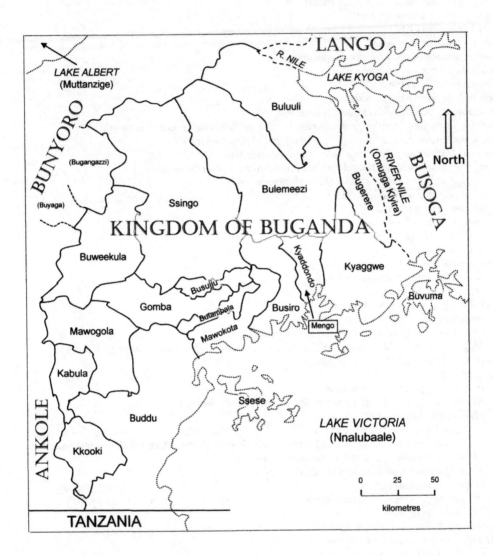

Figure 4. Traditional counties of Buganda, as of 1965. Bugangazzi and Buyaga, known as the 'lost counties', passed from Buganda to Bunyoro in 1964 following referenda. The historic heartland of Buganda may be considered to be Busiro, where there are many royal tombs (**amasiro**). Ankole, Bunyoro and Busoga are the traditional areas of other nations (kingdoms or tribes), as of 1965.

(edited and augmented by Dr Christine Kabuye)

Abrus precatorius **olusiiti** *n11* (*seed* **ensiiti** *n9*)

Acacia gerrardii **omunyinya** *n3*

A. hockii **akasaana** *n12*

A. mildbraedii **omukinga** *n3*

A. sieberiana **omuwaawa** *n3*, **mweramannyo** *n1*

Acalyphya bipartita **ejjerengesa** *n5*

Acanthus pubescens **ettovu** *n5*

Achyranthes aspera **akakubansimu** *n12*

Aeschynomene elaphroxylon (ambatch) **omulindi** *n3*

A. sensitiva (sensitive jointvetch) **akafansonyi** *n12*, **weewumbeko omuko wuuyo ajja**

Afrocarpus falcatus (syn. *Podocarpus falcatus*) (podo) **omuseenene** *n3*

A. gracilior (syn. *Podocarpus gracilior*) (podo) **omuseenene** *n3*

Afromomum mildbraedii **ekitungulu** *n7*, **kafumitattaka** *n1* (*fruit* **ettungulu** *n5*)

Agave sisalana (sisal) **ekigoogwa** *n7* (*fibre* **obugoogwa** *n14*)

Ageratum conyzoides **nnamirembe** *n1*

Albizia coriaria **omugavu** *n3*

A. glaberrima **ennongo** *n9*

A. grandibracteata **ennongo** *n9*

A. zygia **ennongo** *n9*

Alchornea cordifolia **oluzibaziba** *n11*

Aleurites moluccana **kabakanjagala** *n1*

Aloe spp. (aloe) **ekigagi** *n7*

Alstonia boonei **omubajjangalabi** *n3*

Amaranthus dubius (spinach) **doodo** *n1*

A. graecizans supsp. *sylvestris* (spinach) **embooge entono** *n9*

A. lividus (red spinach) **ebbugga** *n5*; (*with small leaves*) subsp. *polygonoides* **embooge entono** *n9*

A. spinosus (spiny spinach) **doodo w'amaggwa** *n1*

A. sp. (large spinach) **enkunga** *n9*

Ananas comosus (pineapple) **ennaanansi** *n9*

Annona reticulata (custard apple) **omusitaferi** *n3* (*fruit* **ekisitaferi** *n7*)

Antiaris toxicaria **kirundu** *n1*

Arachis hypogaea (peanut) **ekinyeebwa** *n7*

Aristolochia elegans (Dutchman's-pipe) **kasero** *n1*, **ensawo y'enkima** *n9*, **emmindi y'omukadde**

Artocarpus heterophyllus (jackfruit) **ekifenensi** *n7*, **ffene** *n1*

Asparagus africanus (wild asparagus) **kadaali** *n1*

Aspilia africana **makaayi** *n1*

Azadirachta indica (neem) **omuttankuyege** *n3*

Basella alba **enderema** *n9*

Bauhinia spp. (camel-foot tree) **ekigali** *n7*

Beilschmiedia ugandensis **omwasa** *n3*

Bidens pilosa (black jack) **ssere** *n1*

Biophytum petersianum **akafansonyi** *n12*, **weewumbeko omuko wuuyo ajja**

B. sensitivum **akafansonyi** *n12*, **weewumbeko omuko wuuyo ajja**

Blighia unijugata **omukuzannyana** *n3*

Borassus aethiopum (fan palm) **akatuugo** *n12*, **entunku** *n9*

Bothriocline longipes (syn. *Erlangea tomentosa*) **ettwatwa** *n5*

Brachiaria decumbens **kyukyu** *n1*

Bridelia micrantha **katazzamiti** *n1*

Brugmansia suaveolens (angel's trumpet) **amaduudu** *n6*

Cajanus cajan (pigeon pea) **enkoolimbo** *n9*, **entinnamuti** *n9*

Calamus deeratus (rattan) **oluga** *n11*

Canarium schweinfurthii (incense tree) **omuwafu** *n3* (*fruit* **empafu** *n9*, *seed* **enje** *n9*, *resin* **obubaane** *n14*)

Canavalia ensiformis (jack bean) **mukomota** *n1*

Canna bidentata (canna lily) **eddanga** *n5*

Cannabis sativa (hemp, marijuana) **enjaga** *n9*, **enjaaye** *n9*

Capsicum annuum (chilli pepper) **kaamulali** *n1*, **ppiripiri** *n1*

C. frutescens (chilli pepper) **kaamulali** *n1*, **ppiripiri** *n1*

Cardiospermum grandiflorum **olunyereketo** *n11*

C. halicacabum **olunyereketo** *n11*

Carica papaya (pawpaw) **omupaapaali** *n3*, (*fruit* **eppaapaali** *n5*, *male tree* **ppappaali essajja**)

Casuarina equisitifolia **falaawo** *n1*

Catharanthus roseus (Madagascar periwinkle; rosy periwinkle) **ssekajja** *n1*

Ceiba pentandra (kapok tree) **kifampa** *n1*, **kifamba** *n1*, **omuti gwa ppamba** *n3* (*fibre* **ffampa** *n1*, **ppamba** *n1*)

Centella asiatica **embutamu** *n9*

Chenopodium ambrosioides **kattaddogo** *n1*

C. opulifolium **omwetango** *n3*

Chrysophyllum albidum **omululu** *n3*

Cinnamomum zeylanicum (cinnamon) (*plant*) **omudalasiini** *n3* (*spice* **budalasiini** *n14*)

Cissampelos mucronata **akavamagombe** *n12*

Citrus aurantifolia (lime) **omulimaawa** *n3* (*fruit* **akalimaawa** *n12*)

C. limon (lemon) **omuliimu** *n3* (*fruit* **enniimu** *n9*)

C. reticulata (tangerine) **mangada** *n1*

C. sinensis (orange) **omucungwa** *n3* (*juice* **emicungwa** *n4*)

Cleome gynandra (spinach) **ejjobyo** *n5*

Clerodendron capitatum **ekisekeseke** *n7*

C. myricoides **kikonge** *n1*

Cocos nucifera (coconut palm) **omunazi** *n3* (*fruit* **ekinazi** *n7*, *oil* **ennazi** *n9*)

Coffea (several species) (coffee) **omumwanyi** *n3*, (*berry, bean* **emmwanyi** *n9*)

Colocasia esculenta (taro, cocoyam) **ejjuuni erigonda** *n5* (*leaf; also, powder from leaf* **ettimpa** *n5*)

Combretum molle **endagi** *n9*

Commelina benghalensis **ennanda** *n9*

Conyza bonariensis **kafumbe omusajja** *n1*

Cordia africana **omukebu** *n3*

Crassocephalum vitellinum **kitonto** *n1*

Crotalaria spp. **akasambandege** *n12*

Cucurbita pepo (pumpkin) (*plant*) **ekiryo** *n7*, (*leaf* **essunsa** *n5*, *flower* **akatundwe** *n12*, *fruit* **ensujju** *n9*).
   Variety with small round edible fruits **omungu** *n3*

Cymbopogon citratus (lemon grass) **ekisubi** *n7*

C. nardus **etteete** *n5* (*flowering stem* **akaseekende** *n12*)

Cynodon transvaalensis **jiija** *n1*

Cynodon (several species) **kalandalugo** *n1*

Cyperus papyrus (papyrus) **ekitoogo** *n7* (*young tuft of inflorescence* **obugala** *n14*)

Cyphomandra betacea (tree tomato) **ekinyaanya** *n7*

Cyphostemma adenocaule **akabombo** *n12*

C. sp. **ekibombo** *n7*

Datura stramonium (thorn-apple) **amaduudu** *n6* (*poison and intoxicant* **amaduudu** *n6*)

Delonix regia (flame tree) **omwoloola** *n3*

Desmodium ascendens **mutasukkakkubo** *n1*

Dichrostachys cinerea **omuwanika** *n3*

Digitaria scalarum (couch grass) **olumbugu** *n11*

Dioscorea abyssinica-rotundata (cultivated yams). Types recognised include: (*fist-sized, with bristles*)
   endaggu *n9*, (*long and yellow*) **balugu** *n1*, **kyetutumula** *n1*.

D. abyssinica **kaama** *n1*

D. alata **ekisebe** *n7*, **nnandigoya** *n1*

D. bulbifera (bud yam, air potato) **ekkobe** *n5*

D. minutiflora **ekikongo** *n7*

D. odoratissima **kaama** *n1*

Dovyalis macrocalyx **omutunku** *n3* (*fruit* **akatunku** *n12*)

Dracaena fragrans **oluwaanyi** *n11*, **omulamula** *n3*

D. steudneri **ekkajjolyenjovu** *n5*

Eichhornea crassipes (water hyacinth) **ekiddo ku nnyanja** *n7*

419

Ehretia cymosa **omusuga** *n3*
Eleusine coracana (finger millet) **obulo** *n14* (*meal* **akalo** *n12, porridge* **obusera** *n14*)
Ensete ventricosum (wild banana) **ekitembe** *n7* (*seed* **ettembe** *n9, necklace made from seeds* **olutemben***11*)
Entada abyssinica **omwoloola** *n3*
Entandrophragma spp. (mahogany) **omuyovu** *n3*
Eragrostis olivacea **akayanja** *n12*
Eriobotrya japonica (loquot) **omusaali omuzungu** *n3*
Erythrina abyssinica (coral tree) **eggirikiti** *n5,* **omuyirikiti** *n3*
E. excelsa **omubajjangabo** *n2*
Eucalyptus spp. (eucalyptus) **kalittunsi** *n1*
Euphorbia candelabrum (candelabra tree) **enkuukuulu** *n9*
Euphorbia hirta **kasandasanda** *n1*
E. tirucalli (pipe euphorbia) **enkoni** *n9*
Ficus carica (Mediterranean fig) **omutiini** *n3*
F. exasperata (sandpaper tree) **omuwawu** *n3* (*leaf* **oluwawu** *n11*)
F. mucuso **mukunyu** *n1*
F. natalensis (barkcloth tree) **omutuba** *n3* (*stripped of bark* **nnasabula** *n1*)
F. ovata **omukookoowe** *n3*
F. saussureana **omuwo** *n3*
F. sur **kabalira** *n12,* **omukunyu** *n3*
F. sycomorus **omukunyu** *n1*
Flueggea virosa **olukandwa** *n11*
Funtumia africana (African rubber tree) (*name when used medicinally*) **nnamukago** *n1, (name when used for timber*) **enkago** *n9*
Galinsoga parviflora (gallant soldier) **kafumbe omukazi** *n1*
Garcinia buchananii **omusaali omuganda** *n3* (*fruit* **ensaali** *n9*)
Gloriosa superba **emmere ya nnamunye** *n9,* **ffukutu** *n1*
Glycine wightii **ekibowabowa** *n7*
Gomphocarpus physocarpus **akafumbo** *n12* (*fibre* **ppamba** *n1,* **ffampa** *n1*)
Grewia mollis **omukomakoma** *n3*
Guizotia scabra **ekimyula** *n7*
Hallea rubrostipulata **enzingu** *n9,* **omuzingu** *n3*
H. stipulosa **enzingu** *n9,* **omuzingu** *n3*
Harungana madagascariensis **omulirira** *n3,* **omukaabiransiko** *n3*
Hewittia sublobata **musotataluma** *n1*
Hevea braziliensis (rubber tree) **pala** *n1*
Hibiscus subdariffa (roselle, red hibiscus) **musaayi** *n1*
H. surattensis **nnantayitwakomusota** *n1*
Hoslundia opposita **kamunye** *n1*
Hydnora abyssinica (*possibly* **omutima gw'ettaka** *n3*)
Hypoestes aristata **muzuukizi** *n1*
Imperata cylindrica (spear grass) **essenke** *n5* (*fibre from inflorescence* **obufumbo** *n14, flowering stem* **akaseekende** *n12,* **obwanyo** *n14*)
Ipomoea batatas (sweet potato) **lumonde** *n1*
I. tenuirostris **akabowabowa** *n12*
Jatropha multifida **ekiroowa** *n7*
Justicia betonica **nnaalongo** *n1*
J. exigua **kazunzanjuki** *n1*
Kalanchoe densiflora **ekiyondo ekyeru** *n7*
K. lanceolata **ekiyondo ekiddugavu** *n7*
Kigelia africana (sausage tree) **omussa** *n3*
Lactuca capensis **oluwoomerambuzi** *n11*
Lagenaria siceraria (gourd, squash) (*plant* **ekiryo** n7, *large fruit* **ekita** *n7, small fruit* **endeku** *n9*)
L. sphaerica (wild inedible gourd) **akatanga** *n12*
Laggera alata (false tobacco) **ssetaaba** *n1*
Lantana camara (lantana) **akayuukiyuuki** *n12*
L. trifolia **akayuukiyuuki** *n12*
Laportea ovalifolia (nettle) **kibugga** *n1*

Leonotis nepetifolia **ekifumufumu** *n7*

Loranthaceae (mistletoe, types with orange or reddish flowers) **enzirugaze** *n9*

Lovoa brownii **enkoba** *n9*

Luffa cylindrica (loofah) **ekyangwe** *n7*

Lycopersicon esculentum (tomato) **omunnyaanya** (*fruit* **ennyaanya** *n9*)

Macaranga schweinfurthii **omweganza** *n3*

Maesa lanceolata **ekiwondowondo** *n7*

Maesopsis eminii **omusizi** *n3*

Mangifera indica (mango) **omuyembe** *n3*

Manihot esculenta (cassava) **muwogo** *n1*

Marantochloa leucantha **amawulugungu** *n6*

M. purpurea **ekiyulu** *n7* (*fibre* **enjulu** *n9*)

Markhamia lutea (*larger trees*) **omusambya** *n3*, (*smaller plants*) **oluasambya** *n11*

Microglossa pyrifolia **kafugankande** *n1*

Milicia excelsa (iroko) **omuvule** *n3*

Mimosa pudica (sensitive plant) **akafansonyi** *n12*, **weewumbeko muko wuuyo ajja** *n1*

Mimusops bagshawei **omusandasanda** *n3*

Momordica foetida **ebbombo** *n5*, **lujjula** *n1*

Mondia whytei **omulondo** *n3*

Moringa oleifera (moringa) **omulinga** *n3*

Morus alba (mulberry, silkworm plant) **enkenene** *n9*

Musa (bananas). *Bananas are classified scientifically into genome groups, based on the contributions of genes from two wild species of bananas (found in East and Southeast Asia to Western Melanesia). There are two genome groups of bananas that have been in Uganda for a long time (probably since the early centuries AD). They are the East African Highland genome group (matooke and beer bananas) and the Plantain genome group (types collectively known in Buganda as 'gonja'). All other types of bananas have been introduced into Uganda since 1900 AD. See* banana (*in Part 3 of the dictionary for more on Luganda banana vocabulary*)

Musanga cecropioides (umbrella tree) **kaliba** *n1*

Myrianthus holstii (giant yellow mulberry) **omugunga** *n3* (*fruit* **ekigunga** *n7*)

Newtonia buchananii **empewere** *n9*

Nicotiana tabacum (tobacco) **taaba** *n1*

Ocimum basilicum (basil) **kakubansiri** *n1*

O. gratissimum **omujaaja** *n3*

Olea capensis subsp. *welwitschii* (Elgon olive) **omusugga** *n3*

O. europea (Mediterranean olive) **omuzeyituuni** *n3* (*fruit* **enzeyituuni** *n9*)

Opuntia ficus-indica (cactus) **engabo ya Kabaka** *n9*

Oxalis corniculata (sorrel) **kajjampuni** *n1*

O. latifolia (sorrel) **kanyeebwa** *n1*

Oxyanthus speciosus. Possibly **akamwanyimwanyi** *n12. See Psydrax parviflora*

Oxygonum sinuatum **kafumitabagenda** *n1*

Panicum maximum **mukonzikonzi** *n1*

Paspalum (type of lawn grass) **paasipalamu** *n1*, **paasikalamu** *n1*

Passiflora edulis (passion fruit) **akatunda** *n6*

P. quadrangularis (giant granadilla) **wujju** *n1*

Pennisetum purpureum (elephant grass) **ekisagazi** *n7* (*cane* **olumuli** *n11*)

Persea americana (avocado) **ovakkedo** *n1*, **vvakkedo** *n1*, **ova** *n1*

Peucadenum grantii **ekisekeseke** *n7*

Phaseolus aureus (mung bean, green gram) **mpokya** *n1*

Phaseolus lunatus (Lima bean) (*with large flat seeds*; butter bean) **ekigaaga** *n7*, (*with smaller seeds*) **akayindiyindi** *n12*

Phaseolus vulgaris (kidney bean) **ekijanjaalo** *n7*, (*type with white seeds with black stripes*) **ekijanjaalo ekya nnamunye**, (*with red seeds resembling peanuts*) **kanyeebwa** *n1*

Phoenix reclinata (wild date palm) **olukindukindu** *n11*, **olukindu** *n11* (pole from trunk **olukoma** *n11*, *leaf* **olusansa** *n11*, *fruit* **empirivuma** *n9*, *wine made from fruit* **obugeme** *n14*)

Phyllanthus ovalifolius **mutulika** *n1*

Phytolacca dodecandra **oluwoko** *n11*

Physalis minima **akatuntunu akatono** *n12*

P. peruviana (cape gooseberry) **entuntunu** *n9*
Piliostigma thonningii (camel-foot tree) **ekigali** *n7*
Piptadeniastrum africanum **empewere** *n9*
Pistia stratiotes (water lettuce) **kitengejja** *n1*
Pisum sativum (pea) **kawo** *n1*
Plantago palmata (plantain) **bukumbu** *n1*
Plectranthus punctatus subsp. *edulis* (Livingstone potato, Plectranthus yam) **ennumbu** *n9*
Podocarpus (podo) *See Afrocarpus.*
Polyscias fulva **ssettaala** *n1*
Portulaca oleracea **ssezzira** *n1*
Portulaca quadrifida **obwanda** *n14*
Prunus africana **entaseesa** *n9*
Pseudarthria hookeri **ekikakala** *n7*
Pseudospondias microcarpa **omuziru** *n3* (*fruit* **enziru** *n9*)
Psidium guajava (guava) **omupeera** *n3* (*fruit* **eppeera** *n5*)
Psorospermum febrifugum **akanzironziro** *n12*
Psydrax parviflora. Possibly **akamwanyimwanyi** *n12*. See *Oxythanus speciosus*
Punica granatum (pomegranate) **omukomamawanga** *n3* (*fruit* **enkomamawanga** *n9*)
Pycnanthus angolensis (African false nutmeg) **olunaba** *n11*
Pycreus nitidus **eggugu** *n5*
Raphia farinifera (raffia palm) **ekibo** *n7* (*leaf midrib* **ekibo** *n7, fruit* **embo** *n9, fibre* **obuso** *n14*)
Rhus natalensis **akakwansokwanso** *n12*
R. vulgaris **akakwansokwanso** *n12*
Rhynchosia hirta **katinvuma** *n12*
Ricinus communis (castor-oil plant) **omusogasoga** *n3* (*fruit* **ensogasoga** *n9*)
Rubus spp. (wild raspberry) **enkenene** *n9*
Rumex abyssinicus **ekiwere** *n7*
Saccharum officinarum (sugar cane) **ekikajjo** *n7*, (*stick* **empango y' ekikajjo** *n9, segment* **ennyingo y' ekikajjo** *n9*)
Sapindus saponaria **omuyiki** *n3* (seed **empiki** *n9*)
Sapium ellipticum. See Shirakiopsis
Sechium edule **ensusuuti** *n9*
Senna didymobotrya **omukyula** *n3*
S. hirsuta **omuttanjoka** *n3*
S. occidentalis **omuttanjoka** *n3*
S. ramosissimum **omuttanjoka** *n3*
Sesamum calycinum (wild sesame) **olutungotungo** *n11*
S. indicum (sesame, simsim) **entungo** *n9*
Sesbania bispinosa **omuzimbandegeya** *n3*
Setaria verticillata **ekikwatandiga** *n7*
Shirakiopsis elliptica (syn. *Sapium ellipticum*) **omusasa** *n3*, **omuzzaŋŋanda** *n3*, **omuzzanvuma** *n3*
Sida tenuicarpa **akakumirizi** *n12*, **keeyeeyo** *n12*
Smilax anceps **olukolokolo** *n11*
Solanum aculeastrum **ettengo** *n5* (*fruit also* **ettengo**). *The Luganda names of Solanum aculeastrum and similar looking species need to be confirmed.*
S. aethiopicum (spinach) **nnakati** *n1*, **nnakasugga** *n1*
S. anguivii **katunkuma** *n1*
S. campylacanthus **entengotengo** *n9*
S. gilo **omutula** *n3* (*fruit* **entula** *n9*)
S. incanum **akatengotengo** *n12* (*fruit* **entengo** *n9*)
S. macrocarpon **nnume y'ekyalo** *n1*
S. melongena (egg plant, aubergine) **bbiriŋŋanya** *n1*
S. nigrum (spinach) **ensugga** *n9*
S. tuberosum (Irish potato) **akammonde akazungu** *n12*
Sonchus oleraceus (sow-thistle) **kakovu** *n1*
Sorghum bicolor (sorghum) **omuwemba** *n3*
Spathodea campanulata (tulip tree) **ekifabakazi** *n7*
Spondianthus preusii **emmimbiri** *n9*, **obutwa** *n14*

Sporobolus africanus **kagiri** *n1*
Steganotaenia araliacea **omuwanula** *n3*
Symphonia globulifera **omuyanja** *n3*
Syzygium cumini (Java plum, jambolan) **jambula** *n1*
Syzygium guineense **akalunginsanvu** *n12*
Tabernaemontana pachysiphon **ebbeere ery'enkima** *n5*
Tamarindus indica (tamarind) **omukooge** *n3* (*fruit* **enkooge** *n9*)
Teclea nobilis **enzo** *n9*
Telfairia pedata (oysternut) **ekinyeebwa ekizungu**
Tephrosia nana **muluku omutono** *n1*
Tetradenia riparia **kyewamala** *n1*
Tetradenia urticifolia **ekibwanukulata** *n7*
Thevetia peruviana (lucky nut, yellow oleander) **obusitaani** *n14*, **kamuseenene** *n12*
Thunbergia alata **akasaamusaamu** *n12*, **ntuddebuleku** *n1*
Tithonia diversifolia (Mexican sunflower) **kimala empaka kikoowa**. *Name needs to be confirmed.*
Toddalia asiatica **kawule** *n1*
Tragia benthami **kamyu** *n1*
Trapa natans (*seed* **envuma** *n9*)
Treculia africana (African breadfruit) **omuzinda** *n3*
Trema orientalis **kasiisa** *n1*
Trilepsium madagascariense **omugwi** *n3*
Tristemma mauritianum **nnantooke** *n1*
Triumfetta macrophylla **ekinsambwe** *n7*
T. rhomboidea **akawugula** *n12*
Uapaca guineensis (freshwater mangrove) **omukusu** *n3*
Urtica massaica **omwennyango** *n3*
Vangueria apiculata **omutugunda** *n3* (*fruit* **ettugunda** *n5*)
Vernonia amygdalina **omululuuza** *n3*
V. auriculifera **ekikookooma** *n7*
V. cinerea **kayaayaana** *n1*
Vitis vinifera (grape vine) **omuzabbibu** *n3*
Vigna subterranea (bambara groundnut) **empande** *n9*
V. unguiculata. There are two types: (1) (cowpea) **empindi** *n9* (*edible powder made from leaves* **eggobe** *n7*);
    (2) (*wild type*) **ekiyindiru** *n7*.
Warbugia ugandensis (pepperbark tree) **abasi** *n1*, **omukuzannume** *n3*
Xanthosoma sagittifolium (tannia) **ejjuuni erikaluba** *n5* (*leaf, also powder from leaf* **ettimpa** *n5*; *edible
    cormlets* **obukopa** *n14*)
Zanthoxylum chalybeum **entale y'eddungu** *n9*
Zanthoxylum gilletii **omunyenye** *n3*
Z. rubescens **omunyenye** *n3*
Zea mays (maize) **kasooli** *n1* (*styles* **oluyange** *n11*)

N32. THE DICTIONARY TEAM

Alan Hamilton is a botanist who has undertaken research on the environmental history of East Africa and written a field guide to the forest trees of Uganda. He has lectured in Botany at Makerere University in Uganda and Environmental Science at the University of Ulster (UK). Subsequently, he worked for the conservation groups WWF and Plantlife International, concentrating on community involvement in conservation and sustainable development. He is a Doctor of Science of the University of Cambridge (UK) and an Honorary Professor of Kunming Institute of Botany, Chinese Academy of Sciences.

Naomi Namisango Hamilton (née Masembe) of the Nseenene (Grasshopper) Clan, was educated at Gayaza High School and King's College Budo, graduating from Makerere College (University of East Africa) in 1970 with a BSc in Botany and Zoology. She has worked as a school teacher and university administrator. She and Alan married in 1971 and have two children, Susan and Patrick.

Phoebe Nakibuule Mukasa of the Mpologoma (Lion) Clan is an authority on the Luganda language and Kiganda culture. Known as Ssenga Nakibuule, she has presented numerous programmes on the Luganda language on the radio and TV and is the author of several books in Luganda. She helped found the *Ekibiina ky'Olulimi Oluganda* (Luganda Language Society) in 1958 and establish the annual *Engule* competition in 2003, which awards a prize to the person who can best demonstrate knowledge of the Luganda language and Kiganda culture. She was Minister of Culture in the Buganda Government between 2002 and 2008.

David Ssewanyana Masembe was educated at Makerere College, later receiving a Higher Diploma in Electrical Engineering from Uganda Technical College, Kyambogo (1979). He has worked in various retail businesses in Kampala and has kept cows, pigs and chickens, as well as growing oyster mushrooms, on his small urban farm.

Cephas S.N.K. Ssentoogo is a retired professional teacher, who worked for seventeen years as headmaster of primary schools. His interest in Kiganda cultural norms started at an early age, becoming an enthusiast for Kiganda music and later obtaining a Diploma in Cultural Studies and English. He has worked as an editor for Wavah Books Ltd, especially of Luganda books, presented numerous educational programmes on Luganda on CBS Radio, and others on WBS TV, and written a number of educational articles on Luganda for BUKEDDE, a Luganda language newspaper. He was Secretary of the Luganda Language Society for nine years. His work on promoting Kiganda culture and Luganda was recognised in 2011 through receipt of an Honorary Doctorate in Humanities from Fairland University.

Christine Sophie Kabuye is a plant taxonomist and an ethnobotanist. A graduate of Makerere University, she went on to head the East African Herbarium in Nairobi, Kenya (1971-1994). Besides being a specialist in grasses, she is particularly interested in food and medicinal plants. Over the years she has been involved in biodiversity conservation and local community issues. She was president of the International Society of Ethnobiology from 1994 to 1996, and, in 2016, was instrumental in the hosting of its 15th Congress in Uganda. Since 2004 she has been a volunteer lecturer in Botany and Ethnobotany at Makerere University.

Cover photo: Part of an **ekibbo** basket, photographed from beneath. It is made from dried **obukeedo** strips taken from the midribs of banana leaves, bound into bundles with **enjulu** fibre.